A CHARACTERISTIC STREET IN NAZARETH

STREET SCENE IN BETHLEHEM

Irwin's
BIBLE COMMENTARY

With an Introduction to Each Book of The Bible and 25,000 Text References with Explanations

Edited by

C. H. IRWIN, M. A., D. D.

With a Foreword on

THE STUDY OF THE BIBLE

Universal Book and Bible House

PHILADELPHIA, PA.

Irwin's Bible Commentary was registered for copyright under the title The International Bible Commentary

IBC

PRINTED IN THE U. S. A.

CONTENTS

NEW TESTAMENT

BIBLE STUDY

The Bible has served as a source of comfort and inspiration to mankind for twenty-five centuries or more; and is recognized as the inspired record of God's unfolding revelation of His character and purposes. We do not come close to the best in the Bible unless we appreciate that it comes to us from God. We are wilfully careless if we lose what the Bible has to give us by thinking of it only as a mystical and perhaps magical book, and forgetting that it was set down for us by human folks like ourselves as they were moved by the Holy Spirit for human needs, and to satisfy human longings.

Some people seem to suppose that because the Bible is a divinely inspired book, they can get its full riches without the use of intelligence or scholarship. It is true that the sublimest truths are simple truths, and that devout and earnest souls have for centuries been constantly refreshed and strengthened, by coming face to face with the Book just as it is written. Nevertheless, nobody can successfully deny that unaided study of this sort is study of the surface, and that to persist in such a use of the Bible only is like working a gold mine with a pan instead of with the rock crusher and the hydraulic washer. In the following pages the great problems of religion and theology are discussed comprehensively and without prejudice, and the Scriptures are also followed line upon line, with minuter comments that explain each doubtful point.

The following are seven essentials for intelligent and fruitful Bible study, for which assistance is given in this one-volume Commentary.

1. **Explanation of Historical References.** Few of us have read deeply enough in the world's history to appreciate the changing situations in the near East which have come during the more than four thousand years represented in the Bible story. The rise and fall or disappearance of empires and peoples, the changes of geographical names and boundaries, the religious faiths that have come and gone, the great men who were contemporaneous with the Bible heroes, the thoughts and theories out of which were born the longings and convictions of the prophets, the

psalmists, and the teachers of both Testaments, are matters little understood by the average lover of the Bible. One cannot understand even Jesus, the greatest of Prophets and Teachers, without knowing something at least of what was commonly felt and thought and believed by the men and women who were his forefathers and his neighbors.

The word "Hittite" means no more to most of us than the words "Amalekite" or "Hivite," and yet is it not worth while for us to know that the Hittites were one of the greatest races of early history? When we read, among the list of the kings who fought in the Valley of Siddim, or the Salt Sea, along with the kings of the neighborhood of Sodom the name of Amraphel, is it not of interest to know the possibility of his identity with Hammurabi, whose code of laws has come to us as one of the most important historical documents of the past? Do all of us know where the Queen of Sheba came from, which of the Pharaohs was the Pharaoh of Joseph and which the Pharaoh of the Oppression, or which was the Herod of the massacre of the innocents and which the Herod of the trial of Jesus? Such things we need a commentary to tell us, if we are to stand on solid ground historically, appreciate the men of antiquity, and connect our secular knowledge with our Biblical knowledge.

2. Citation of Related Passages in Other Parts of the Bible. There are four gospels and two or more accounts of the rise and fall of Israel. We have only a partial knowledge of the acts and words of Jesus if we read of them in only one gospel. We get a very different impression of Jewish history from the Books of the Kings and the Books of the Chronicles, yet not many of us know how to find things in one gospel that are related in another, or how to hunt down the parallel stories of the downfall of Israel. Do we all know that Jonah is mentioned in a book other than the one that bears his name, or that certain psalms and prophecies are found in more than one place? These are but a few illustrations of the fact that these sixty-six separate books are related by intertwining lines of thought as well as by parallels of description and history.

3. Descriptions of Ancient Customs. The details of the Jewish festivals and other ceremonials, the significance of removing the shoe in a certain legal transaction, how certain old traditions and customs have survived even to this day, are all items of interest, not only in making vivid but even in explaining the orientalism of the Bible. A collection that goes so far back, and is so far away in space and frame of thought as well as in time, needs constant interpretation if we are to have any clear conception of the religious ideas and ideals of the men of old.

4. Explanation of Terms and Phrases Unfamiliar to Modern Readers. It is impossible to read so familiar a lyric as the Shepherd Psalm (the Twenty-third) and get its full import without help. The "rod" and the "staff" do not mean what they do today. "The valley of the shadow" and the "table in the wilderness" are full of concealed significance. Even its spiritual meaning is deepened when we know what such allusions meant in the country and among the men from whom they had their origin.

5. Mention of Contrasting Interpretations. Perhaps the most successful of the achievements of Irwin's Bible Commentary is its giving fairly the views of sincere scholars, where they differ, without prejudice or rancor, and letting the reader choose between them. Ordinarily one who wishes to know about a difficult book, like Jonah or Daniel, will find a single viewpoint explained in the authority to which he turns, but will not be permitted to know that any other view exists. While this commentary is moderately conservative, yet in its pages conscientious scholars of different schools have been permitted to present their various interpretations.

6. Analysis of a Progressive Chain of Thought. Although we read the Bible too much by verses and proof texts, we are never just to its content when we stop with a mere citation. Each chapter or passage has its purpose, and every book has its carefully worked-out train of thought. Too many commentaries are satisfied with fragmentary explanations. This edition is particularly valuable to the preacher who seeks something more from the Bible than a text, and to the teacher who is not content with the mere extract, that has been cut up for mastication and digestion in Sunday schools.

7. Clearer Renditions of the Original Text. Many persons still prefer the ancient translations of the Scriptures for public reading, but surely no one is willing, in his private reading and personal study, to stop with a rendering, no matter how beautiful, that is ambiguous or incorrect. Irwin's Bible Commentary does not offer continuously fresh translations of the Bible, but wherever a new rendering takes advantage of some recently discovered manuscript that is valuable, or a modern translation corrects a mistaken impression, such help to the real interpretation of the word is freely given.

The reader is advised that a brief general instruction has been provided for each of the books of the Bible. It would be well, whenever taking up the study of any book, to glance over the appropriate introduction, until its contents are familiar, so as to be able to turn back to it whenever necessary, and then, when engaged in regular study, to refer, page by page, to the line-by-line comments on the passage that he has before him.

It remains only to urge that such a useful work as this does not become the real property of its owner unless, through thorough reading, its contents enter his mind, his thinking, and his practice in everyday life.

IRWIN'S BIBLE COMMENTARY

GENESIS

The Book of Beginnings

INTRODUCTION

The true name of this Book in modern English is "In the Beginning." So the Jews called it, from its very first word in Hebrew (*Bereshith*). The word Genesis ("Origin") was the name given by the ancient Greek translators in the version known as the Septuagint.

This Book records the origin of the world and of its inhabitants, especially of man, his state of innocence, his fall, the hope of pardon and restoration, and the separation of a family from which should spring the chosen people and man's Redeemer.

The Book of Genesis is thus a grand introduction to the History of Redemption. It reveals God in His creative power and wisdom, in His holiness, shown in the punishment of sin, in His mercy also, forgiving the penitent, and in His faithfulness to His promises. The method of access to God by sacrifice is clearly displayed.

The names by which the Divine Being is known also indicate His character. He is spoken of as *El* "God" or *Elohim* (the plural form), *Adonai* "Lord," and *El-Shaddai* "Almighty God." He is also described as *Jehovah* or *Jahveh*. This word really means "He who was and is and shall be," and is best translated as the French version renders it (*l'Eternel*) and as Dr. James Moffatt has recently done in his translation—The Eternal.

So far as the human authorship is concerned, Moses no doubt reduced to order and embodied in his work earlier oral and written narratives. "We may safely recognise in the Pentateuch a pre-Mosaic, a Mosaic, and a post-Mosaic element, the second of these being supreme" (*The Bible Handbook*, by Angus and Green, R.T.S.). But it appears rather rash to dogmatise as to these several documents, as Professor Sayce has well pointed out in his reference to the composite novels of Besant and Rice and, in French, of Erckmann and Chatrian (Sayce: *Monument Facts and Higher Critical Fancies*, 1910, p. 18).

The Book may be divided into three parts: (1) From the Creation to the Deluge; (2) from the Deluge to the Call of Abraham; (3) from the Call of Abraham to the Death of Joseph.

There are many things in the Book which attest its truthfulness. Among these may be mentioned its simplicity of style, its absence of exaggeration, its marked contrast with the childishness of heathen legends, even while they bear witness to the same events, and its historical references to other nations, their manners and customs, references which the discoveries of archæology, especially in Egypt, increasingly confirm.

We have always to bear in mind that its language was adapted to a primitive people, in the infancy of human thought. Figurative language may have often been used, but the essential facts are there.

As to the moral difficulties which sometimes present themselves, they are in themselves a confirmation of the truthfulness of the narrative. The Scripture writers "do not stop to explain, to qualify, or to extenuate the errors and evils that they record." They show us men as they lived. If they had given us the story of absolutely blameless lives, it would have been reasonably objected that such persons never lived. By the sins even of God's servants we are warned to avoid the same faults; by their punishments we are taught God's justice and holiness; and by their forgiveness and restoration we learn that God's mercy is infinite and that there is hope for the most unworthy.

CHAPTER I

1 In the beginning God created. This declaration assumes the being of God, distinguishes the Creator from His creation, denies the eternity of matter, and, by attributing both the heaven and the earth to the same Maker, contradicts the notion of two eternal opposing principles. For poetical versions of the narrative of the creation see Job xxxviii. 4–11; Psa. civ.; cxxxvi. 5–9; Prov. viii. 24–30. Lord Balfour in his Gifford Lectures (1923), speaking of the three great values, all vital to the highest life of mankind—Love, Beauty, Truth—said that we could not maintain those values permanently at their highest level if we banish from the world the idea of design, of creation, of a God who is Himself the author and sustainer of these high values.

2 without form and void. Or, "desolation ('waste,' R.V.) and emptiness"; terms used (as in Isa. xxxiv. 11; Jer. iv. 23) to describe a devastated region.

moved. Or, "was brooding over" (see Deut. xxxii. 11); a metaphor referring to the life and beauty which the power of the Spirit would produce. The form of the word denotes *continuousness.*

3 light. That is, upon the earth, which was previously dark. The first thing called forth by the Divine word is "light," as distinguished from the "lights" or rather luminaries or light-bearers; as the sun, moon, and stars are called (ver. 14). Light is the fundamental condition of all organic life in the world. This statement of the existence of light, before the mention of the sun, moon, and stars, was a favourite objection with sceptics of the 18th century, who asked, "How could light exist before the Sun?" But the progress of science, and especially the "nebular theory," disposed of that. The great geologist Dana used this very statement "as a proof of the divine origin of the document, on the ground that no one would have guessed what must have seemed so unlikely then" (Monro Gibson: *The Ages before Moses*). Lord Kelvin, too, on scientific grounds concluded that the earth was in existence long before the sun.

5 the evening and the morning, etc. Literally, "There was evening and there was morning, one day" (so R.V.). The Hebrews begin the day with the evening. If the "days," as many think, were creative epochs of unknown length, "evening" and "morning" would be a natural figure for the commencement and the close of each period.

6 firmament. Or, "expanse"; the space occupied by the atmosphere.

7 under the firmament. The waters "under the firmament" are the waters of the globe itself; those "above" are the waters floating in the atmosphere, which accumulate in clouds.

8 Heaven. The word Heaven signifies in some places the air; in others, the regions in which are the sun, moon, and stars; and in others again, the unseen dwelling-place of God, which is therefore called the "third heaven" (2 Cor. xii. 2).

11 the herb. Rather, as in ver. 12, simply "herb"; a word embracing all plants between grasses and trees. This botanical classification is popular, not scientific.

in itself. So as to perpetuate its species.

14 lights. Rather, "Let there be luminaries" (a different word from that in ver. 3) "in the expanse of heaven to divide," etc.

16 and God made. (Or, perhaps, "appointed," as in 1 Sam. xii. 6, R.V.; 2 Chron. xiii. 9; Job xiv. 5; Psa. civ. 19.)

two great lights. Rather, "the two great luminaries." Not necessarily then first created; it may mean that they were then made to appear, or that they were then appointed to their uses. The moon is obviously termed a "great light" in comparison with the stars, because of its appearance and use to us. The last clause of the verse is simply "and the stars."

20 abundantly. Rather, "Let the waters swarm with swarms of living creatures, and let fowl fly above the earth."

21 great whales. "The great sea-monsters" (R.V.). This probably includes both fish and the great water-saurians.

26 Let Us. Or, "We will make,"—a solemn announcement of the Divine purpose.

27 His own image. With a spiritual personality, and those intellectual and moral qualities which fitted him, as God's representative on earth, to govern the lower creatures; and to know, love, and commune with his Creator. (See Eph. iv. 24; Col. iii. 10.) God's last and noblest work was man. In this narrative He appears first as

creating things only *material*, the heavens and the earth. He then endows matter with *vegetable* life; then with *animal* life. Now the material and the animal are united with the *spiritual.*

28 upon the earth. This Divine gift to man of dominion over these creatures emphatically condemned all those systems of idolatry which consisted in the worship of them.

30 meat. *i.e.,* "food."

31 very good. The separate works are "good"; the whole is "very good."

CHAPTER II

1 host. In their vast numbers and diversity; marshalled and moving together like an army.

2 rested. This Divine repose implies neither fatigue nor inactivity (Isa. xl. 28). God ceased to create because He had completed His plan to His own satisfaction; see Exod. xxxi. 17.

3 and sanctified it. God set it apart for special religious use by man (Mark ii. 27). The existence of the Sabbath from the beginning of the world is indicated by the artificial division of time into weeks, which prevailed in the earliest ages (Gen. viii. 10, 12; xxix. 27, 28), and by the peculiar provision of food for the Sabbath, and directions respecting it (Exod. xvi. 23), before the law was given at Sinai. It has, however, since been subjected to various regulations, first in its temporary adaptation to the Mosaic economy (Exod. xx. 8–11; xxxi. 13, 14), and now as a memorial of the great fact of the Saviour's resurrection, and as set apart for the spiritual worship and services of His disciples (Acts xx. 7; 1 Cor. xvi. 2; Rev. i. 10). If the "days" of ch. i. are to be understood as creative epochs (see note, verse 5), the Sabbatic rest of the Creator may be taken as extending through the whole period of man's history. This view is confirmed by the fact that no "evening and morning" are specified with regard to the "seventh day." See also John v. 17.

4 These are the generations. Rather, "This is the history," or "account." Such a phrase commonly indicates the commencement of a new narrative (see ch. v. 1; vi. 9; xi. 10; Matt. i. 1); and frequently a *family history.*

the day. To be taken generally, of an era, including the successive epochs of creation. Cp. Exod. vi. 28; Numb. iii. 1; Isa. xi. 16.

Lord God. Literally, "JEHOVAH God (*Elohim*)." This name occurs here for the first time. The word LORD, wherever printed in the English Bible in capital letters, stands for the Hebrew JAHVEH or JEHOVAH; see Introduction and Exod. vi. 3. This Name (implying self-existence, and therefore unchangeableness and eternity) is applied to "the Living God," in His personal covenant-relation to His people. "Lord," where not printed in capital letters, represents the Hebrew *Adonai,* "lord" or "master": and "the Lord GOD," a combination frequent in Ezekiel, stands for *Adonai Jehovah.*

5 and every plant of the field, etc. Or, "and no plant of the field was yet in the earth, and no herb of the field had yet sprung up. For the LORD God," etc. "And there went up a mist," etc. (R.V.). This is probably another description of the state referred to ch. i. 2, 6, 7.

7 living soul. Or, as the words are rendered in ch. i. 21, "living creature."

8 garden. The Greek version has "paradise"; a form of the Oriental word used here, as well as in Eccl. ii. 5; Song of Songs iv. 12. Its application to the garden of Eden seems to have led to its use in Luke xxiii. 43 (see note); 2 Cor. xii. 4; Rev. ii. 7.

eastward. *i.e.,* as one comes from the East.

Eden. "Eden" means pleasantness or delight. The cuneiform inscriptions have cleared up its position. The Sumerian name of the plain of Babylonia was Edin. Its Assyrian equivalent was *Zeru,* the name still applied to the depression between the Tigris and Euphrates (see Sayce, article "Eden" in *Peloubet's Dict. of Bible*).

9 good and evil. These two trees were so named from the uses to which God applied them; appointing the one to be the means of preserving man's life, the other to be the test of his intelligent obedience.

11 Pison, etc. It seems to be most probable that "Pison" is the Arakhtu, or canal on which Babylon was built, and "Gihon" the Kerkha; and that "Havilah" is the desert of North Arabia. "Hiddekel" is the Tigris (see Dan. x. 4). The Euphrates (Heb. *Phrat*) is the well-known "great river."

12 bdellium. Probably either pearl or some precious stone. The true "bdellium" is a gum.

13 Ethiopia. Heb., "Cush."

14 toward the east of Assyria. Or, "in front of Assyria" (R.V.); *i.e.,* between the land of Assyria and the country of the narrator.

15 man. Or, "Adam." In the A.V. these two renderings are used indifferently. The R.V. distinguishes between the word with the article in the original ("the man") and the proper name Adam without the article.

to dress it. "To cultivate it." Paradise was not a place of exemption from work.

17 shalt surely die. This is the proper English rendering of the emphatic Hebrew idiom, "dying thou shalt die." As Adam lived long after the fall, in what sense are these words to be taken? Possibly as the loss of *all* the life that Adam had; and as the moral union of his soul with God, resemblance to Him, and the enjoyment of His presence and favour, was his *life* in its highest sense, the loss of these would be the most awful penalty to which he could be subjected. The terms *life* and *death* are frequently used in Scripture with these meanings; see John iii. 36; v. 40; Rom. vi. 23; viii. 6, etc. Or, the transgression implies the ending of man's first estate and the beginning of that in which death reigned. Cp. Rom. vi. 23; Jas. i. 15.

18 meet for him. Rather, "a help corresponding to him"; his counterpart, brought into the world for him (1 Cor. xi. 9).

23 shall be called, etc. In the Hebrew: "shall be called *Isshah,* because she was taken out of *Ish.*"

24 one flesh. This passage forbids both divorce and polygamy. See Matt. xix. 4–6; Mark x. 8; Rom. vii. 2; 1 Cor. vi. 16; Eph. v. 31.

CHAPTER III

1 serpent. Cp. Rev. xii. 9; xx. 2; and for an application by St. Paul, 2 Cor. xi. 3.—**Yea.** Or, "indeed!" as if surprised; awakening doubt.—**every,** *i.e.,* "any" (R.V.).

5 as gods. Or, "as God" (R.V.). A bold affirmation now displacing suggestion (cp. John viii. 44). The tempter showed his subtlety by attacking the *woman,* when she was *alone,* and by expressing doubt as to the restriction, which he seems to exaggerate, before he asserts that its defiance would bring not harm, but good. Satan still thus tempts, by suggesting dishonourable thoughts of God, and encouraging false hopes of advantage from sin. The woman's answer minimises the permission, exaggerates the prohibition, and seems to throw doubt on the threatening.

6 good for food, " the lust of the flesh " ; *pleasant* (R.V., " a delight ") *to the eyes,* " the lust of the eyes " ; " *to be desired to make one wise,*" " the pride of life " : 1 John ii. 16 ; and cp. Jas. i. 14, 15.

7 Their eyes. Innocence was gone. The fallen nature now found itself amidst new conditions.—**sewed.** Or, " tied."—**aprons.** Rather, " girdles."

8 hid themselves. Shame and terror came into the world with sin. The folly of seeking to hide from God is often noted (Psa. cxxxix. 7 ; Job xxxiv. 21, 22 : cp. Heb. iv. 12, 13).

11 shouldest not eat. God requires confession of sin ; not that He may be informed, but that the sinner may be humbled.

12 The man said. Note the endeavour to transfer blame : " The man said, The woman . . ." ; " The woman said, The serpent . . ." (ver. 13) ; a futile expedient (Gal. vi. 7).

14 life. The blow is aimed at the tempter, whose utter defeat and degradation are predicted. Cp. Psa. lxxii. 9 ; Isa. lxv. 25 ; Micah vii. 17.

15 it shall, etc. " They shall strike at thy head, and thou shalt strike at their heel " (*Moffatt*). This promise is the beginning of prophecy. Our Lord seems to refer to it in John xii. 31 and Luke x. 18. It applies to the whole arrangement of Divine mercy, and foretells struggle and suffering, leading to final victory, in man's conflict with evil : see Rom. xvi. 20. But its primary fulfilment is seen in the Second Adam, who " was born of woman " that, by His humiliation and death, He might triumph over Satan : see Rom. v. 8, 10, 21 ; Gal. iv 5 ; Heb. ii. 14–16 ; 1 John iii. 8.

16 rule over thee. For the bearing of the Gospel upon this, see 1 Tim. ii. 15, and note.

20 Eve. That is, Life (*Zoë,* LXX). Thus Adam not only recognises her as the progenitor of all persons who should possess life ; but especially regards the sentence in ver. 15 as implying a promise of that living Seed by whom the great enemy was to be subdued, and the life forfeited restored to man.

22 one of Us. Like God in moral discernment.

24 Cherubim. Rather, " the Cherubim " (R.V.). The Cherubim were symbols of Jehovah's presence. They support His throne (Rev. iv. 6-9), or bear His chariot (Ezek. i. 4-25), representing the subordination of all beings and agencies to His control. They appear in connexion with displays of His mercy or power (Exod. xxv. 18, 22 ; Psa. lxxx. 1 ; xcix. 1 ; Isa. vi. 2) (" the burning ones," an epithet of the Cherubim), and are generally accompanied with a sword-like flame or a bright cloud (Ezek. i. 4, 13). They here appear as guardians of a covenant *destroyed,* they are seen next as guardians of a covenant *concluded* (Exod. xxv. 18–22).

CHAPTER IV

1 Cain, or, " possession " ; **from the Lord,** or, " a man with Jehovah " (" with the help of," R.V.) ; or, " I have gotten a man, Jehovah."

2 Abel, or " vanity." The name of the firstborn child expressed the mother's hope, that of the second her disappointment. Before the birth of Abel, Eve had learned that the deliverance of the race was not to be expected in Cain.—**of sheep.** Heb., " of a flock " ; either sheep or goats.

3 Of the fruit. There was no care, no selection on Cain's part. He just took what came to hand.

4 Firstlings. Cp. Exod. xiii. 2 ; Numb. xviii. 17.—**the fat.** Heb., " fatnesses " ; either meaning the *best* and *finest* (as in Numb. xviii. 12, 29 ; Psa. lxxxi. 16 ; cxlvii. 14) ; or so called because the fat parts were selected for sacrifice (Lev. iii. 16 ; ix. 24).

respect unto Abel. The acceptance of the offering was the result both of the offering (" the firstfruits " and " the fat ") and of the man who offered it. In Heb. xi. 4 it is attributed to Abel's faith. Cain offered a *meat,* or rather *food offering* alone ; presenting himself and his property to God as if he had not been a sinner needing an atoning sacrifice. Abel offered a *sin offering* (accompanied perhaps with the other : see Exod. xxix. 38–41) ; thus confessing his guilt as a sinner, and declaring his faith in God's promised salvation.

7 If thou doest, etc. Literally, " If thou doest right is there not a lifting up (*i.e.,* either of thine own ' fallen ' countenance, or of God's upon thee) ? and if thou doest not well, sin coucheth at the door (like a wild animal ready to spring upon thee)." The law of Divine retribution is here powerfully stated. Moffatt's interpretation is somewhat different : " If your heart is honest, you would surely look bright. If you are sullen, sin is lying in wait for you, eager to be at you—but you ought to master it."

8 talked. Literally, " said unto " (R.V. " told "). The Septuagint, the Samaritan, and other versions have, " Cain said to Abel his brother, Let us go into the field."—**slew him.** Our Lord names Abel as the first martyr (Matt. xxiii. 35).

9 keeper. Cain's words combine falsehood, cruelty, and contempt of Divine authority.

10 Thy brother's blood. Cp. the old and new covenants contrasted in Heb. xii. 24.

14 slay me. Adam and Eve had probably other children, to whose vengeance the murderer would feel himself exposed.

15 set a mark upon. Rather, " gave a token to " (R.V. " appointed a sign for "). For the anguish of the wanderer, cp. Job xv. 20–24.

22 an instructor, etc. Or, " forger of every tool."—" Brass," rather copper ; so in general.

23 my hurt. Or, " I have killed a man who wounded me, a young man who gave me a stroke."

24 sevenfold. The poem is obscure from its brevity. It may refer to a transaction in which Lamech (perhaps in self-defence) had killed a young man, and claims protection for himself. There may be an allusion to the inventions of Tubal-cain. He now has weapons with which he means to defend himself ; and vaunts these as far more effectual than the threatening of God.

CHAPTER V

3 likeness. That is, in Adam's own sinful likeness ; evidently contrasted with the " likeness of God " (ver. 1), in which he himself had been created.

Seth. Through Seth the line of Adam lives on. Seth becomes, as it were, the spiritual firstborn.

5 and he died. The repetition of the words is striking and is said to have awakened men to repentance.

22 walked with God. Denoting close intimacy ; so Noah (Gen. vi. 9). Cp. the phrase " walk before" God (Gen. xvii. 1; Psa. cxvi. 9 and reff.). With these cp. also Amos iii. 3; 1 John i. 6, 7.

24 was not. That is, was no longer on earth, as explained in Heb. xi. 5: "Enoch was translated that he should not see death."

CHAPTER VI

2 sons of God. Possibly descendants of Seth who worshipped Jehovah: see ch. iv. 26, and cp. Exod. iv. 22; Deut. xxxii. 5; Psa. lxxiii. 15. Other interpretations offered are (1) young men of rank; (2) angels; (3) descendants of Cain.

daughters of men. Daughters of the other race, the Cainites.

took them wives. Cp. 1 Kings i. 1–3; 2 Cor. vi. 14.

3 My spirit, etc. Or, "My spirit shall not strive (or, 'dwell,' as in the Septuagint version) in man for ever, in his errors he is flesh." Moffatt renders: "Human creatures are but flesh; my spirit is not to be immortal in them; they shall not live more than a hundred and twenty years."

4 giants (Heb., "the Nephilim"). These men may have been great in stature and strength; but the word seems to refer chiefly to the lawless and tyrannical use of brute force.

6 it repented. This is spoken after the manner of men, as "remembered" (viii. 1), "look" (ix. 16), and "came down to see" (xi. 5, 7, etc.). Representations of God's character and doings are adapted to the understanding of man. Hence His abhorrence of sin and His determination to punish it are spoken of as if they affected Him as they would affect us (cp. Numb. xxiii. 19; Mal. iii. 6; James i. 17); whilst His forbearance and forgiveness are represented under the guise of repentance and putting away of wrath (1 Sam. xv. 11; 2 Sam. xxiv. 16).

8 Noah found grace. Cp. Moses (Exod. xxxiii. 13, 17).

14 an ark. Noah's ark was, taking the cubit as eighteen inches, 450 feet long, 75 broad, and 45 high.—**gopher.** Probably *cypress*.

16 window. "A light," R.V.—**finish it.** The meaning seems to be that the roof of the ark was to be brought up to a ridge of a cubit wide.

18 covenant. The word "covenant," in Scripture, frequently signifies a solemnly declared purpose or promise of God, relating sometimes to the earth and the lower animals (see Gen. ix. 10), but generally to man, in which case it infers corresponding obligations on his part.

22 so did Noah. The exactitude and completeness of Noah's obedience are recorded with emphatic repetition (vii. 5), and referred to with approbation (Heb. xi. 7; and cp. 1 Pet. iii. 20).

CHAPTER VII

1 Thee have I seen righteous. The security of the faithful is frequently stated in the O.T. For the safety of Noah contrasted with the destruction of other men, cp. Psa. xci. 7, 8; Prov. xiv. 26.

2 clean. That is, such as were appointed to be offered in sacrifice or used for food (Lev. xi.).—**by two.** Of these only one pair was to be taken, as being generally less serviceable to man.

11 second. Probably the second of the civil Hebrew year, afterwards called Marchesvan; which would fix the day of entering the ark about November 7. This time of the year was well adapted for collecting the requisite stores of food. For our Lord's reference to the event, see Matt. xxiv. 37–39.

16 God. Elohim. **The Lord.** Jehovah, The Eternal, The Covenant God.—**shut him in.** Or, as the Chaldee reads, "protected him."

17 Forty days. The period of full development of the Deluge. In ver. 24, *one hundred and fifty days* may imply period of the flood at its height, at the end of which it abated (viii. 3). Almost all peoples have traditions of a deluge; even the isolated tribes of the Amazon region in S. America.

19 whole heaven. The words, sometimes used in a restricted sense (Deut. ii. 25), are supposed by many to be so employed here, the deluge and its destructive effects being local. But see ver. 23.

CHAPTER VIII

1 remembered. See note on vi. 6, and cp. Gen. xix. 29.

3 abated. Or, "began to abate."

4 Ararat. Ararat is the name, not of a mountain, but of a region in Armenia. Containing the sources of important rivers which flow in all directions, it was well adapted to be the nucleus of a new population.

11 plucked off. Not a floating leaf, but broken off by the dove from a tree now above the waters.

14 second. The same month in which he had entered it; having been in the ark one year and ten days, according to the Hebrew text; or exactly one year, according to the Septuagint.

21 a sweet savour. Literally, "a savour of rest," or satisfaction; an expression often used (Lev. xxvi. 31) to signify that the offering was acceptable to God (cp. Eph. v. 2).—**any more for.** See Isa. lvii. 16. Were God still to deal with men simply and strictly according to their deserts, they could expect nothing but judgement upon judgement. Instead of this, He mercifully spares them, and encourages them to seek Him in hope and obedience (Psa. cxxx. 4), "though the bent of man's mind is indeed towards evil" (*Moffatt*).—**for the imagination.** Rather, "for that the imagination" (R.V.); the reason for the *curse*, not for the *remission*.

CHAPTER IX

2 all that moveth upon the earth. Literally, "all wherewith the ground teemeth," *or*, "creepeth," R.V.

4 the blood. Lev. xvii. 10, 11, 12, shows that this prohibition was intended to give a peculiar sacredness to *life*, especially in connexion with the idea of atonement. Even the blood of beasts, being appointed as an expiatory substitute for man's forfeited life, was not to be treated as common.

5 life of man. God having spared man's forfeited life, that he may have time to repent, sacredly guards it against injury (Exod. xxi. 12, 28).

6 blood be shed. This may be simply an announcement that God in His providence will requite blood with blood; cp. Matt. xxvi. 52. Or it may refer to legal retribution. Some suppose that it warrants the punishment of death for murder only. But there is no such restriction in the Mosaic laws.

13 my bow. It is not said here that God first formed the rainbow after the flood: the words may be translated, "I do *appoint* My bow in the cloud to be a token (or, testimony) of the covenant," etc. The rainbow is the chosen symbol of grace returning after wrath (Ezek. i. 27, 28; Rev. iv. 3; x. 1).

25 Canaan. Canaan is the only one of Ham's children here mentioned, perhaps because he had instigated or shared in his father's misconduct; or perhaps with reference to the subsequent history which records the sins of his descendants, and their expulsion from the land destined for the Israelites; so in vers. 18, 27.—**brethren.** That is, his descendants should be slaves of the lowest class to the posterity of Shem and Japheth.

26 Shem. This benediction on Shem includes the peculiar religious distinction of the family of Shem, and especially the promised Messiah. The covenant name JAHVEH is here used in connexion with Shem, but not with Japheth.

27 he. The word "he" may refer to God or to Japheth. "Let him (Japheth) dwell in the tents of Shem," R.V., or "may he be welcome" (*Moffatt*).—**servant.** The future family of mankind is, in this prophecy concerning the three sons of Noah, viewed as distributed into three great divisions; and the curse laid on *Canaan*, the blessing associated with *Shem*, and the power and enlargement assigned to *Japheth*, have all been realised in the history of the world.

CHAPTER X

1 were sons. Many of the names in this genealogical table are plurals; and several have the formal termination used to designate a tribe. Hence it has been thought that the greater part of them are names of nations; which may, however, have been so called from their founders. These nations were early and frequently intermixed; but it is probable that the descendants of *Japheth* occupied Armenia, the Caucasus, and Asia Minor, spreading thence through Europe and the northern parts of Asia and India, and perhaps also through America; that the nations descending from *Shem* settled in the central parts of Asia, extending their colonies into India on the east, and the north of Arabia on the west; and that *Ham's* family took possession of the south of Mesopotamia and Arabia, whence they passed on to Palestine and Africa. The brief notes on the succeeding verses chiefly point out the supposed perpetuation of the ancient names in modern forms. "Gomer," the Cimbri, Cymry, whence the Celtic races. On "Magog," see Ezek. xxxviii. 2, 3, note. "Madai" are the Medes; "Javan" may be the Ionian Greeks; "Meshech" the Moschi; "Tiras," the inhabitants of Mount Taurus; "Elishah," Elis, Hellas; "Tarshish," the Tyrrheni or Etruscans; "Kittim" was the name of the inhabitants of Cyprus, of which Kitium was one of the most ancient cities; "Cush," see note on ch. ii. 13; "Mizraim" was a well-known appellation of Egypt; the dual form including Upper and Lower Egypt.

9 hunter. From the *chase* he went on to *war.* "Before the Lord," implying his great power; the hunters of the ancient world naturally became its heroes.

11 went forth Asshur. Rather, "he (Nimrod) went forth into Assyria." So R.V. This was an aggression upon the heritage of Shem. See ver. 22.

the city Rehoboth. Rather, "Rehoboth- Ir" (R.V.), meaning "Streets of the city" or "its suburbs" (*Moffatt*). It is not unlikely that this place, with Calah and Resen, ultimately formed part of the "great city" Nineveh. See Jonah i. 2; iii. 2, 3; Nahum ii. 4.

13 begat. That is, the following nations were of the Mizraite or Egyptian race: these names denoting peoples, not individuals, as in ch. xxv. 3, etc.

14 Philistines. Rather, "the Philistines"; who, coming from Egypt, established themselves along the coast of Canaan, and gave their name (*Palestine*) to the whole country.

21 Eber. The ancestor of the Hebrew race, and therefore prominently mentioned here. The words may read, "the elder brother of Japheth" (so R.V.).

22 Elam. Often used in Scripture for Persia. (Cp. "Elymais.") Arphaxad was the ancestor of the Casdim or Chaldeans. Lud, according to Josephus, was the ancestor of the Lydians. Aram is Syria, as Asshur is Assyria.

CHAPTER XI

2 from the east. Or, "in the east." Probably descending the Eastern mountains to "Shinar," Babylonia.

3 brick. There is no stone in this district; and the ancient bricks and pottery found here are fine and well burned.

slime. Bitumen, or asphalt; a natural production of the district, of a peculiarly adhesive nature.

4 heaven. An idiomatic expression, meaning a very great height. See Deut. i. 28; Dan. iv. 11.

5 came down. See note on vi. 6.

9 Babel. The name, probably, conferred by the builders. The word in Hebrew means *confusion.* The miracle of Pentecost reverses that of Babel, and suggests the gathering together in Christ of those whom the dispersion scattered abroad. See John xi. 52.

12 Salah. The genealogy given by St. Luke introduces "Cainan" between Arphaxad and Salah; and the present readings of the Septuagint agree with it.

26 seventy. As in ch. v. 32, this is the date of the birth of the eldest. Comparing xi. 32 with xii. 4, we infer that Terah was one hundred and thirty years old at the birth of Abram. Probably, then, Haran, although mentioned last (cp. v. 32), was the eldest; and if, as the Jews affirm, Sarai was the same as Iscah, his daughter (ver. 29), it will follow, from xx. 12, that Haran and Abraham were sons of two different wives of Terah.—**Haran.** The preceding verses (10–26), with ch. v. and Matt. i. 1–16, form together a complete genealogy of Christ.

28 Ur. The Babylonian Uru, now Mugheir or Mukkeyah on the W. bank of the Euphrates. Since the Great War (1914–1918), the British Museum and the University of Pennsylvania have had a Joint Expedition excavating in Mesopotamia. In 1922 its workers commenced at Ur. Here and there on the burnt bricks, the newest of which date from 550 B.C. and the oldest of which have outlived 4000 years, "one can read the names of Nebuchadrezzar or of that King Ur-Engur whose buildings were of a respectable antiquity when Abraham was born" (Mr. C. L. Woolley in *The Times*, Nov. 24, 1924). In March 1925, the expedition found a limestone slab with the portrait of the builder, and his own record of its conception. Sir Frederic Kenyon of the British Museum said it was the most important early monument of Babylonia that has yet been found.—**Chaldees.** The Chaldees appear to have been originally a tribe of warriors from the north-east of Mesopotamia, probably the mountains of Kourdistan

(See Isa. xxiii. 13; Habak. i. 6–11.) They afterwards overran the south, which from them took the name of Chaldæa, and where they formed the caste of priests and soldiers.

31 went forth. See xv. 7; Acts vii. 3.

Haran. Properly "Charran," as in Acts vii. 4; a different word from the name of Abram's brother. It is generally identified with Charræ, near Edessa. In Isa. xxxvii. 12, it appears as subject to the Assyrians, and in Ezek. xxvii. 23 as a Tyrian mart.

CHAPTER XII

1 the Lord had said. Rather, "the Lord said" (R.V.). Repeating the command which summoned Abram from his former home, and was as yet only partially obeyed.—**father's house.** Abram's father and other near relatives had accompanied him from Chaldæa as far as Charran, and had settled there (see xxvii. 43); but he was to proceed farther, and to be completely separated from them (cp. Luke xiv. 26).

3 blessed. The special blessing which had been promised to our first parents, and then to the line of Shem (ch. ix. 26), is here distinctly limited to one branch of that family. This promise to Abram is repeated (xviii. 18; xxii. 18, and cp. Acts iii. 25, 26; Gal. iii. 8). Henceforward Abram and his descendants are almost the only subjects of the sacred history.

4 So Abram departed. In faith (Heb. xi. 8–10).

6 Sichem. Or, "Shechem," or "Sychar," now Nablûs, lying between Mount Gerizim and Mount Ebal. This is one of the richest and loveliest parts of Palestine.—**the plain.** Rather, "oak," or "terebinth" (R.V.). So ch. xiii. 18; meaning a grove of these trees. And so in subsequent passages.

7 appeared. In what way we are not told. God sometimes appeared in human form (xviii.); at other times in visions or dreams (xv. 1). In Stephen's address before the Jewish council (Acts vii. 2), the first call to Abraham is stated to have been given by the "God of glory"; implying such a display of the Divine Majesty as left no room for hesitation.—**Unto thy seed.** See Gal. iii. 16.

altar. In token of his faith in the promise, and as a pledge of the maintenance of the worship of Jehovah in his family. See ch. xviii. 19.

8 a mountain. Rather, "the mountain" (R.V.), *i.e.* the mountain region.

9 the South. "The Negeb," the southern tract of Judæa. Abram made no settlement in Canaan; and the only land he ever acquired there was a grave. See Acts vii. 5; Heb. xi. 8–10.

10 Egypt. Already the abode of a powerful nation, with kingly government and court.

11 to look upon. The seclusion of women was less strict in Egypt than in other Oriental countries. In contrast to the dark complexions of the natives, the fairness of the Mesopotamian race would be attractive.

12 shall see. Veils were probably not then used; or, at least, they were not so large as since in the East. See xx. 16.

13 sister. For the danger, cp. Gen. xx. 11; xxvi. 7; and, for the true policy, see Prov. xxix. 25; Jer. xvii. 7 and reff.

my soul. "My life."

15 Pharaoh. "Pharaoh" was the title of most of the Egyptian kings down to the Babylonian conquest. Akin to Heb. *Pireha,* "prince" or "leader."—**Pharaoh's house.** To undergo the purification preparatory to becoming one of his wives.

20 sent him away. In an honourable way; probably with an escort.

CHAPTER XIII

1 South. "Abram went up" to the "Negeb," the southern highlands of Canaan.

2 very rich. His servant dwells on the source of Abram's wealth (Gen. xxiv. 35).

3 on his journeys. "By stages."—**Beth-el.** The place known by this name to the *narrator,* but not to Abram himself.

4 the place of the altar. At Shechem (xii. 6, 7).

7 in the land. The Canaanites (xii. 6) inhabited the cities and maritime districts, the Perizzites occupied the open country. There was therefore less room for these pastoral chiefs with their large flocks, and the more need to preserve peace among their dependants.

9 to the left. Abram waived his right for peace' sake; carrying out principles afterwards clearly stated in the New Testament (Rom. xii. 10, 18).

10 all the plain. Rather, "circuit," the land lying round the Jordan, probably where it falls into the Dead Sea. This, "as far as Zoar," appeared abundantly watered and as fertile as Egypt, which they had lately left. The great salt lake had not yet burst forth.

11 Jordan. Lot disregarded the character of the people, who, abusing the fertility of their country, lived in pride, idleness, and debauchery (see Ezek. xvi. 49; 2 Pet. ii. 7, 8). He soon paid dearly for his unwise choice; whilst Abram's disinterestedness was rewarded by a renewal of God's promise (vers. 14–17).

18 in the plain. Rather, "the oaks," or "terebinths" (R.V.); see note on xii. 6. Mamre was the name of an Amorite, probably the chieftain of the district.—**Hebron.** Hebron, one of the most ancient cities in the world (Numb. xiii. 22), formerly called Kirjath-Arba (xxiii. 2, note; Josh. xiv. 15), is now named El Khalîl, "the friend," in reverent remembrance of "the friend of God."

CHAPTER XIV

1 Amraphel. The name is probably identical with that of Hammurabi, King of Babylon, about 2100 or 1958 B.C., whose Code of Laws was discovered at Susa in 1902.—**king.** This word is applied to the sovereign of a nation, the ruler of a single town, or the chieftain of a tribe. "Shinar" is Southern Babylonia; "Ellasar" the capital of a kingdom owing allegiance to Elam. It has been identified with the Chaldæan town Larsa, now Senkereh.—**Chedorlaomer.** Identified with Kudin-Lagamar, whose name has in recent years been found in Babylonian inscriptions. "Elam" was in Lower Mesopotamia, at the head of the Persian Gulf. "Nations," or, as in R.V., a proper name, Goim or Guti, a people in Asia Minor.

2 Zoar. The five cities here mentioned, often called the Pentapolis, were in the lower part of the plain of Jordan; they seem to have maintained a federal union (see next verse).

5 Rephaim, Zuzim, Emim. These nations, whose origin is unknown, occupied the country east of Jordan and the land of Seir, and part of Palestine, before the Amorites, Edomites, and Canaanites took possession of it. Many among them were of extraordinary stature. See Deut. ii.; iii. 11.

6 Horites. "Cave-men." Cave-dwellings are still found in the sandstone cliffs of Edom. "Seir," like "Trossachs," means "bristling," and describes a region abounding in woods and thickets.—**the wilderness.** This expedition was on a large scale. The invaders ravaged the highlands along the east of the Jordan, to the Elanitic Gulf. They then turned westward across the north of the peninsula of Sinai, nearly to the borders of Egypt, and thus descended upon the vale of Siddim, through the mountain passes. "The royal names here given, the political situation presupposed by the narrative, the possibility of campaigns in the distant west on the part of the Chaldæan monarchs, all alike find support and verification in ancient cuneiform texts."—*Sayce.*

7 Hazezon-tamar. Afterwards *Engedi,* now *Ain-Jidi.*

10 slimepits. "Petroleum wells" (*Moffatt*). The lake which now covers the lowest part of the Jordan valley occasionally throws up great quantities of bitumen.—**the mountain.** That is, to the mountainous district around the valley.

13 Hebrew. The first occurrence of the word. Whether he was so called from his ancestor Eber (Gen. x. 21; xi. 14–29), or because he was a foreigner (as the name "Eber" signifies), it is not easy to determine. The Septuagint reads, "he who was from beyond," *i.e.,* the Euphrates. Luther translates it "the foreigner." In the Old Testament, "Hebrew" is the name applied to the chosen people by foreigners; "Israelite" is their own title of privilege. In the New Testament, "Hebrews" seems to denote the Jews who retained the ancient language, in distinction from "Grecians," or Greek-speaking Jews. "Jew" properly belongs to the tribe of Judah; and is not used of the entire nation until after the dispersion of the ten tribes.

14 armed. Rather, "led forth" (R.V.).—**Dan.** "Dan" is probably Laish. See Judges xviii. 29. The use of a later name ("Dan"), here and elsewhere, shows that the words of Moses were modernised by a later hand.

17 Shaveh. *i.e.,* "plain," different from Shaveh in ver. 5.

18 Melchizedek. Melchizedek, "King of Righteousness" (as his name signifies) and "of Peace" (as the name of his city indicates), is the *first* person in the Bible called a "priest," the *only* person beyond the family of Aaron recognised as priest of the true God; and the *only* individual who was permitted to unite the priestly and kingly offices until Christ came. Of his race, parentage, time of birth, appointment, and death, nothing is recorded. A tablet of Amenophis, discovered in Egypt, 1889, confirms the existence (about 1400 B.C.) on Mount Moriah of "the city of the god Unas, whose name (there) is Salim." For the application to our Lord, see Psa. cx. 4; Heb. v., vi., vii.—**Salem.** Some identify this place with the Shalem of ch. xxxiii. 18, and the Salim of John iii. 23. It is, however, most probable (see Psa. lxxvi. 2) that Salem was the earliest name of Jerusalem; which lay on Abram's homeward route, and was the most likely place for the king of Sodom to reach from the Vale of Siddim. The Jebusites afterwards changed its name for a while. See Judges xix. 10; 1 Chron. xi. 4.

20 And he. "He," Abram: "him," Melchizedek. See Heb. vii. 2, 4.

CHAPTER XV

1 shield. Cp. Psa. iii. 3.—**reward.** Or, "and exceeding great is thy reward"; a declaration which accounts for Abram's question in the next verse.

2 Lord God. "Adonai Jehovah," names here first found combined. See note, ii. 4.—**I go.** Either, "I continue" or "pass away," *i.e.,* "die."—**steward.** Rather, "my heir." (Heb., "son of possession.")

3 in my house. Probably either Eliezer or his son, according to the custom of the country.

6 righteousness. This faith was, in its principle, its object, and its operation, one with that of Christian believers (Rom. iv.; Gal. iii. 6; Heb. xi.).

8 Whereby shall I know? Cp. Judg. vi. 17; Luke i. 18.

12 sleep. For sleep or trance, experienced by others to whom Divine revelations were given, see Numb. xxiv. 4; 1 Sam. xix. 24; Job iv. 13, 14; xxxiii. 14, 15; Dan. x. 8, 9; Acts x. 10; 2 Cor. xii. 1–4.

13 four hundred years. On the difficulties attending this computation of time, see Exod. xii. 40.

16 in the fourth generation. That is, from the going down of Jacob and his family into Egypt. Moses and Caleb belonged to the fourth generation from Levi and Judah.—**Amorites.** The Amorites being the principal nation among the Canaanites, their name is here used for the whole.

17 smoking furnace. The word rendered "smoking furnace" sometimes means a portable oven used for baking bread, and often represents the punishment of God's enemies (see Psa. xxi. 9; Mal. iv. 1); whilst "a burning lamp" (or "torch," R.V.) is the symbol of deliverance. See Isa. lxii. 1.

18 the river . . . the great river. The Nile and Euphrates represent (as in Isa. xxvii. 12; Jer. ii. 18) the two great kingdoms which were to be the opposite limits of the territories of Israel. The dominions of David and Solomon appear to have extended thus far (2 Chron. ix. 26).

19 Kadmonites. "The Easterns." Cp. "children of the East" (Beni-Kedem), Judg. vi. 3. For the "Kenites," see Numb. xxiv. 21.

CHAPTER XVI

1 no children. A calamity; sometimes a punishment. See xxv. 21; Lev. xx. 20; Jer. xxii. 30; and cp. Psa. cxxvii. 3, 4.

7 angel. Messenger. Any Divine agent or messenger, whether a providential dispensation, a man, a being of a higher order, or, as here, when called "the angel [of] Jehovah," the WORD of God, revealing Him in human form (Exod. xxiii. 20, 21; see also ch. xlviii. 16; Exod. iii. 2; xiv. 19; Isa. lxiii. 9; Josh. v. 13; Judg. ii. 1; vi. 11; xiii. 3): in all which passages the angel is spoken of in language, and his appearance attended by circumstances, which betoken actual, personal Deity). Fulfilled in the history of the various tribes of Arabs, many of whom are descended from Ishmael; and who have even to the present day remained a fierce, hardy, and distinct race. For many years they subsisted largely by plunder.

13 Thou. Perhaps the best translation is, "Thou art the God of vision" (*i.e.,* "that revealest Thyself"); "God Seen" (*Moffatt*). The last clause means, "Lo, I live, after seeing God?"

14 Beer-lahai-roi. "Well of life and vision," *i.e.,* of life after a vision of God.

CHAPTER XVII

1 Almighty God. EL-SHADDAI; a Divine title now first used, referring to the exercise of God's power now about to be shown in the birth of Isaac. It is frequent in the Book of Job; it is used by Balaam (Numb. xxiv. 4, 16); and is united with Jehovah (Jahveh), the peculiar designation of God as the God of Israel, in Ruth i. 20, 21; Exod. vi. 2.

4 nations. Abram was the *natural* progenitor not only of the Israelites, but also of the Ishmaelites and Edomites, as well as of many Arabian tribes. But the promise seems to refer to him chiefly as the *spiritual* father of all believers (Rom. iv. 11, 17; Gal. iii. 29).

5 made thee. "Abram" signifies "high father"; a title such as might be borne by any ordinary sheikh. "Abraham" is "father of a multitude."

10 circumcised. Circumcision was practised by other ancient nations, especially by the Egyptians; so that at the time of the Exodus, to be uncircumcised was "the reproach of Egypt" (Josh. v. 9). The descendants of Ishmael observe the rite to this day as punctiliously as do the Jews.

14 cut off. That is, from all their peculiar privileges; in some cases accompanied by further punishment (cp. Lev. xviii. 29 with xx. 10-16).

15 Sarai. Probably "contentious" (fr. Heb. verb *sara*, "to strive"). *Sarah* means "princess."

17 laughed. The act of reverence that accompanied this laughter and the absence of reproof (contrast Sarah's case, xviii. 13), shows that this cannot have been the laughter of scornful incredulity. Cp. John viii. 56.

18 live. A word often including all good. See 2 Pet. i. 3. Whilst Abraham gratefully accepts the promise, he prays that Ishmael may not be excluded from the blessing.

19 Isaac. Laughter. Or "he sports."

25 thirteen years old. This is the age at which the children of many Arabian tribes are now circumcised.

CHAPTER XVIII

1 in the plains. Rather, "by the oaks," or "terebinths" (R.V.).

2 three men. Two of whom were angels in human form, and the third Jehovah. See note on xvi. 7. The patriarch, however, was not at first aware of their celestial nature (Heb. xiii. 2): so that he was performing only an ordinary act of hospitality, such as the Arabs still practise.

3 My Lord. Abraham addressed one of the three, distinguished from the other two by some mark of superiority.

4 wash your feet. This is the first attention required where people travel barefooted, or with open sandals.

8 butter. Curdled milk.

10 according to the time of life. Rather, "when the season cometh round" (R.V.); "this time next year."—**in.** Rather, "*within* the tent door."

12 laughed. See on xvii. 17. Sarah forgot or disbelieved the promise and the covenant, of which she must have heard.

17 I do. This narrative illustrates the high privilege of the believer in his relation to God (Amos iii. 7). We see, on the one hand, God's testimony to Abraham's piety (ver. 19); the gracious revelation of His purposes (vers. 17, 18); and His readiness to answer His servant's prayers (ver. 26, etc.): on the other, Abraham's humble boldness (ver. 23, etc.) and perseverance in pleading not only for the righteous, but even for the reprobates in Sodom.

19 know him. Literally, "I have known him" (*i.e.*, "have chosen him"), "in order that he may command," etc. Abraham was admitted to this intimate communion with God partly that through him his children might be taught to obey God.

32 ten's sake. Abraham's plea rests on the principle that many sinners should escape rather than that a few righteous should be involved in their doom. And this principle God, as "the Judge of all the earth," sanctions and acts upon. So it is still, the ungodly world is spared and blessed for the elect's sake. Cp. Jer. v. 1.

CHAPTER XIX

1 two angels. Literally, "the two angels," resuming the narrative from xviii. 22.—**the gate.** This term, which is often used, means an open place at the entrance of the town, which was then, as it still is in some parts of the East, the public resort for business or amusement, and the place where the king or the judges sat to administer justice (Deut. xvii. 5; xxv. 7; Ruth iv. 1-12; 2 Sam. xv. 2; 2 Kings vii. 1; Job xxix. 7).

8 my roof. Lot's proposal proved his abhorrence of the wickedness of the Sodomites, and his anxiety to preserve the rights of hospitality, then and now, in Asiatic countries, a most sacred obligation (see Lev. xix. 33, 34; Judges xix., xx.; and cp. Rom. xii. 13; Heb. xiii. 2; 1 Pet. iv. 9). Lot's error was in supposing "that a man may commit a smaller sin lest others should commit a greater."

11 Blindness. Cp. Elisha's prayer (2 Kings vi. 18), and the punishment of Elymas (Acts xiii. 11).

15 iniquity. Or, "punishment" (R.V. marg.).

20 a little one. Zoar, being so small, would contain but few sinners, and therefore Lot hopes it might be spared.

22 come thither. Abraham's intercession, so far as regards Lot, is answered (ver. 29); though not in Abraham's own way.

24 out of heaven. Probably a volcanic eruption, in which the ignited sulphur descending kindled the bituminous soil. Bitumen, sulphur, and salt, with volcanic products, still abound in the neighbourhood. This judgement is often referred to (Deut. xxix. 23; Isa. iii. 9; xiii. 19; Jer. xlix. 18; Amos iv. 11; Zeph. ii. 9); and is used as a warning to the ungodly (Matt. x. 15; Rom. ix. 29; 2 Pet. ii. 6; Jude 7).

26 salt. Lot's wife was guilty of both disobedience and worldliness; see Luke xvii. 32, 33, and note. She was probably suddenly struck dead, and her form became incrusted with salt (or bituminous ash).

37 Moab. Moabites and Ammonites were in after ages neighbours, and often enemies, of Israel. *Moab*, "from [my] father": *Ben-ammi*, "son of my people." From the Moabite race, so disgraced in its origin, came an ancestress of the Messiah (Ruth i., iv.).

CHAPTER XX

2 Abimelech. "Father king." Abimelech probably was not a personal, but a regal name, like *Pharaoh* in Egypt.—**My Sister.** See note on xii. 13.

16 he is to thee, etc. Or, "It (*i.e.*, the silver) is for a covering of the eyes (*i.e.* a propitiating gift, amends) for all who are with thee (either thy attendants, or all who may fall in with thee); and in all respects thou art thus righted (*i.e.* for all that has happened)." The last clause may mean "thou art directed," so as to guard in future against danger

CHAPTER XXI

1 as He had said. See xvii. 19. and for comment on the faith of Sarah, Heb. xi. 11.

6 will laugh. An allusion to Isaac's name: literally, "God hath prepared laughter for me" (R.V. marg.). Abraham's surprise (xvii. 17) and Sarah's incredulity (xviii. 12) give place to the laughter of satisfaction and sympathy, interrupted by the "mocking laugh" of the youthful scoffer (ver. 9), who probably counted on being able by his superior age and strength to regain the pre-eminence which he had now lost.

14 bottle. Formed of a kid-skin, the legs of which met over the shoulder of the bearer.

and the child. *i.e.*, Abraham "gave" the lad to Hagar. The word here rendered "child" is translated "young man" in iv. 23; xviii. 7; and is applied in xxxvii. 30 to Joseph when seventeen years of age.

15 cast the child. Rather, "placed the lad." Ishmael was now nearly seventeen years old, but was probably less able than his mother to bear the heat. This shrub, the *retem*, still abounds in this desert (1 Kings xix. 5).

19 opened. Directed attention to that which in her anxiety she had overlooked. Where wells are valuable they are often carefully concealed. God was showing Hagar and Ishmael, both by their suffering and their deliverance, that they were still under His watchful care, and that whilst He would chasten them for their faults, He would preserve them for Abraham's sake. Friendly relations were still maintained between the families (xxv. 9; xxviii. 8, 9).

21 Paran. A district of table-land between Egypt and Edom, extending from Beersheba nearly to Sinai, still inhabited by Arabs, who boast their descent from Ishmael, and retain the customs of the patriarchs.

22 the chief captain of his host. The presence of this personage shows that this was not a private but a public transaction. Phichol, "the mouth of all," like Abimelech, was probably an official name.

25 well. The possession of wells of good water is a matter of great importance in such a country. (Cp. xiii. 7; xxvi. 15.)

29 seven. For other uses of seven, see Gen. ii. 3; Exod. xii. 15; Lev. xxv. 8; Numb. xxiii. 1; Prov. ix. 1; Acts vi. 3; Rev. i. 4; viii. 2. Herodotus (iii. 8) says that the Arabs ratify a treaty by putting blood on *seven* stones.

33 grove. Literally, a "tamarisk" (R.V.); probably a memorial of Abraham's residence and worship there.

CHAPTER XXII

1 did tempt. That is, proved his faith and obedience. Abraham's faith was supported by the conviction that God could raise up Isaac from the dead (Heb. xi. 19). His obedience was rewarded by fresh promises (vers. 15-18). Dr. Marcus Dods (*Expositor's Bible*) on the whole narrative says: "So far from introducing into Abraham's mind erroneous ideas about sacrifice, this incident finally dispelled from his mind such ideas and permanently fixed in his mind the conviction that the sacrifice God seeks is the devotion of the living soul not the consumption of a dead body."

2 Moriah. *i.e.*, the land *afterwards* called Moriah. It was the site of the Temple (2 Chron. iii. 1).

4 third. The distance is nearly fifty miles, and takes more than twenty hours with camels. The length, giving time for reflection, proved that the conduct of Abraham was deliberate.

8 provide. Heb. "see"; perhaps, "choose." See ver. 14.

11 angel of the Lord. See on xvi. 7.

12 Now I know. For comment on Abraham's action see Heb. xi. 17-19; Jas. ii. 21-24.

14 Jehovah-jireh. Repeating his word, ver. 8 (*Elohim jireh*, "God will provide").—**shall be seen.** *i.e.*, "shall be provided."

16 sworn. The oath of God adds nothing to the validity of His promise; but it does to the consolation of the believer, showing God's condescension to the weakness of our faith; see Heb. vi. 17-19.

17 gate. Places of concourse for official and judicial proceedings, business and gossip (Gen. xix. 1; Deut. xvii. 5; Ruth iv. 1-12; 2 Sam. xv. 2; etc.).

18 seed. Or, "through thy seed." This, as explained in Gal. iii. 16, intimates that the Messiah should be of the posterity of Abraham. And cf. Gal. iii. 8, 9.

CHAPTER XXIII

1 old. Sarah is the only woman whose complete age is mentioned in the Scriptures. At her death Isaac was thirty-seven years old.

2 Kirjath-arba. Abraham had therefore emigrated northward again. Hebron (El Khalil) is still a place of importance.

3 sons of Heth. Elsewhere called the *Hittites.*

6 bury thy dead. This was probably only a form of Oriental politeness; for the tribes of Palestine jealously restricted the use of their burying-places to their own people.

18 for a possession. These transactions between Abraham and the Hittites find a parallel in the manners of the people to this day. They negotiate through a third party (ver. 8), they make offers which it is understood will not be accepted (ver. 11), they settle their bargains at the gates, the place of public resort (ver. 10), they ask a price in a most courteous form (ver. 13). They secure witnesses, whose testimony is sufficient even if there be no written deeds (ver. 18), and in their purchases they are most explicit in matters of detail (ver. 17).

CHAPTER XXIV

1 old. One hundred and forty years of age: Isaac being, at this time, forty. See xxv. 20.

2 his eldest servant. Probably Eliezer of Damascus (xv. 2).

thigh. A solemn form of attestation found also in xlvii. 29. The commission to the chief servant; his anxiety for a providential sign; the present of the nose-jewel and armlets, of no little weight; the invitation of Laban, and the part which, as Rebekah's brother, he takes in the transaction; the refusal of the servant to partake of hospitality till the business was settled; the decision of the question without reference to Rebekah's inclinations; her sudden separation from her parents and country, and her mode of presenting herself to her destined husband; with the important assurance that "he loved her" who thus became his wife—are all vivid pictures of Eastern life. See Thomson, *The Land and the Book*, sec. 38, pp. 403-406.

4 my country. Not to Ur, but to Haran (Charran), where Abraham's brother had remained. See xi. 31; xii. 1-5.

10 hand. Or, "having all goodly things of his master in his hand" (R.V.).—**Mesopotamia.** Literally, "Aram [the lowland] of the two rivers"; *i.e.*, of the Tigris and Euphrates.—**the city of Nahor.** *i.e.*, Haran. See xi. 31; xxvii. 43.

14 thereby. Heb., "by her."

15 shoulder. "The Egyptian and the negro carry on the head; the Syrian, on the shoulder or the hip."—*Thomson.*

16 went down. In the East many wells are enclosed, and reached by a long flight of steps, as the well of Siloam at Jerusalem.

20 camels. An uncommon act of zealous kindness. It was no light labour to go up and down the steps several times, carrying the water which the camels needed. The sign which the servant had asked was thus clearly granted.

21 to wit. That is, "to know." The very success of his plan bewildered him. He knew not yet, moreover, whether the damsel was of his master's family.

22 earring. Heb., simply "a ring"; which might be, as in xxxv. 4, an earring; or, as in Isa. iii. 21; Ezek. xvi. 12, a "nose-ring"; an ornament common in the East.

31 thou blessed of the Lord. The language of the Arabs, to the present day, often expresses a piety and generosity to which, like Laban, they are really strangers. The sight of the jewels may have helped to dispose him the more to hospitality See ver. 30.

32 he. That is, Laban, either personally or by his servants.

34 He said. The first speech recorded in the Bible.

49 that I may turn, etc. *i.e.*, that I may seek out some other branch of the family of Terah, and so discharge my vow.

50 bad or good. "We can have no voice in the matter."

53 jewels . . . precious things. A dowry to Rebekah; a purchase-gift to her relatives.

55 [**a few**], etc. Literally, "days, or ten," *i.e.*, about ten days. The business brooked no delay.

59 nurse. A personal attendant exempt from the husband's control, always of great importance in an Eastern family. The name of Rebekah's servant was Deborah (xxxv. 8).

65 vail. By dismounting and veiling herself she showed the customary respect to Isaac as a chief and her future husband.

67 death. Which had happened three years before.

CHAPTER XXV

1 again. Heb., "and Abraham added and took a wife," *i.e.*, took another wife beside Sarah and Hagar. *When* he did this is not said. The age which Abraham's sons by Keturah had attained at his death makes it likely that Keturah was a secondary wife (called in Scripture a concubine: see 1 Chr. i. 32) during the latter part of Sarah's life.

4 children of Keturah. Keturah="frankincense." A tribe *Katûrâ*, living near Mecca, is mentioned by later Arab writers. *Zimran*, perhaps the *Zabram* of Ptolemy, also near Mecca and the Red Sea. *Jokshan* has not been identified. *Medan* is probably the same as *Madan*, worshipped by an Arab tribe at Yemen. *Midian* is the best known of all, down to the time of 1 Kings xi. 18. *Ishbak* has been identified with Jasbuk of the cuneiform inscriptions as a tribe whose king fought against Shalmaneser II. *Shuah* is perhaps *Suchu*, a tribe south of Carchemish on the Euphrates. Cp. Bildad the Shuhite. (See, for all these, *Peloubet's Bible Dictionary.*) This part of Abraham's family had no promise or special privilege to keep them distinct. See ver. 6.

8 gathered to his people. Fulfilling the promise, xv. 15. *Full* ("of years" not in orig.); *i.e.*, "satisfied." Compare the expression "full of days," xxxv. 29.

12 Ishmael. This account of Ishmael is here added to close the history of Abraham, and to show that God's promise respecting him (xvii. 20) was fulfilled. Some of the names in the following list cannot now be identified.

13 Nebaioth. Esau married Nebaioth's sister (xxviii. 9; xxxvi. 3), and thus the Edomites were connected with this tribe of Ishmael (2 Kings xiv. 7); and other tribes eventually were merged in this powerful clan.

Kedar. The Assyrian inscriptions of Esarhaddon and Assurbanipal make it clear that this was a powerful Arab tribe, the Kidraei. Cp. Psa. cxx. 5; Isa. lx. 7; Jer. ii. 10 · xlix. 29; Ezek. xxvii. 21.

16 castles. The fortified encampments, more or less permanent, which nomad tribes resort to, in the intervals of their wanderings.

18 died. "Settled" (A.V.). Heb., "fell"; most probably meaning, **had his portion** (referring to xvi. 12). The Ishmaelites had their portion "before," *i.e.*, on the east, or more probably "in the presence of" all their brethren. They intermixed themselves with the Arab tribes (see x. 26-29); and it is now reckoned more honourable to be descended from Ishmael than to be of pure Arab blood.

19. generations. Isaac is now the head of the chosen family, and heir of the great promise.

20 the Syrian of Padan-aram. Or, "the Aramæan of the lowlands of Syria." So "Aramæan" in xxviii. 5 is rendered "Syrian."

21 barren. This long childlessness of Rebekah as well as of Sarah might be designed to make it felt that the heirs of the promise were God's special gifts.

22 If it be so. Or, "is it so" [usually]? The Divine answer (in the metrical form of prophecy) predicts the future history, not of her sons, but of their descendants; and is used by Paul (Rom. ix. 12) to show God's sovereignty in the choice of the Jews to be His nation.

26 Jacob. "Supplanter." Esau means "**hairy.**" Their birth was fifteen years before the death of their grandfather Abraham, though that event is mentioned in a previous verse, to complete his biography.

30 red. Heb., "with that red, that red"; the repetition denoting intense eagerness. Lentils, boiled with oil and garlic, make a dark red pottage, still used among the Arabs. In the name *Edom* there was a reference not only to this exclamation, but to the complexion of Esau. See ver. 25.

31 thy birthright. So far as this birthright consisted of the temporal advantage of the chieftainship, with a double share in the family property,

Jacob does not appear ever to have received it. But the more important religious distinction of inheriting the Divine promise, which Esau despised (Heb. xii. 16), was conferred upon Jacob; first by his father's blessing (xxviii. 4), and then by Divine communication (xxviii. 13–15, etc.). This transaction with Esau could not *convey* the birthright, but only secure the elder brother's consent to its transference.

CHAPTER XXVI

1 The first famine. See xii. 10.—**Abimelech.** See xx. 2. This transaction was eighty years afterwards. It is unlikely that the same Abimelech and Phichol (ver. 26) were still in office.

2 Egypt. The hundredfold harvest (ver. 12) would confirm Isaac's attachment to the land, and his faith in the Divine promises.

10. lightly. Easily.

12 sowed. This change in Isaac's habits seems to have alarmed the Philistines, as showing a design on his part to settle in their land.

19 water. Literally, "living water," an expression frequently used in Scripture for *flowing*, in distinction from *still* or *stagnant* water. See John iv. 10.

23 Beer-sheba. Although the strife about the wells had ceased, Isaac withdrew, probably to ensure peace, to the place where his father had made a treaty with the chief of Gerar for the possession of the wells (xxi. 23–34); and his movement seems to have been appreciated by Abimelech, who came to him there to renew the treaty.

24 sake. Isaac had been made to feel that though bidden to stay in the land, he was to be a stranger in it; now, lest his faith should fail, he is assured of the certainty of the promise.

26 Phichol. See xxi. 32.

33 unto this day. The old well may have been stopped, as others had been (ver. 18); and this was probably opened close by. The name now again given to the well, *Beersheba*, differs slightly from that in xxi., referring more expressly to the *oath* of the treaty: see xxi. 32. In Wady-es-Seba, which answers to this locality, two large wells, besides other small ones, have been found near the ruins of an ancient town. The British troops in the Great War drew water from these wells.

34 Hittite. These women were Canaanites; and Esau's marriage with them was a further proof that he disregarded the traditions of his family.

CHAPTER XXVII

1 old. The ages of Isaac and his son are inferred from a comparison of the following passages: xxx. 25; xxxi. 38, 41; xli. 46, 53, 54; xlv. 6. Supposing Jacob to have been twenty years in Charran, he will be now seventy-seven, and his father one hundred and thirty-seven (the age of Ishmael at his death). But if we allow forty years for Jacob's residence in Charran (as seems almost necessary), he will be now only fifty-seven, and Isaac one hundred and seventeen; and Isaac in that case must have lived more than fifty years after these transactions. These computations, however, are difficult and uncertain.

16 skins. The hair of the young of the Syrian goat is peculiarly soft and silky. It was used in later days by the Romans as an artificial substitute for human hair.

17 Jacob. All the parties were to be blamed: Isaac, for seeking to set aside the Divine oracle (xxv. 23) to indulge personal partiality; Esau, for wishing to deprive his brother of the blessing he had relinquished; Rebekah and Jacob, for attempting to secure it by fraudulent means. Jacob suffered for his deception in his separation from his mother for the rest of her life, for they seem never to have met again (see on xxxv. 8); as well as by fear of his brother and in the endurance of many years of toil and hardship.

27 raiment. The sportsman's rough dress would long retain the smell of the aromatic herbs with which Palestine abounds.

28 God give thee. In the blessing here pronounced, the spiritual promises are much less explicit than usual. A fertile country, extended power, and superiority in his own family, are the most prominent. The value of the dew in a land which was often without rain for months together is often noticed in Scripture, as well as in other books.

33 where. Or, "Who then is he"? (R.V.).—**shall be blessed.** Isaac saw that God had been over-ruling his own weakness, and the deceitfulness of Jacob, for the accomplishment of the promise; and though he "trembled," he acquiesced.

39 the fatness, etc. Or, "Away from the fertile part of the earth, and from the dew of heaven from above; for in thy desert thou shalt live: and thou shalt serve thy brother; but the time shall come when thou shalt wander freely; for thou shalt break his yoke from off thy neck."

45 both. Of one by murder, and of the other by the "avenger of blood."

46 Rebekah said. To contrive a pretext for sending Jacob to Haran, which Rebekah managed with characteristic duplicity.

CHAPTER XXVIII

1 blessed him. Not, as before, unwittingly, but designedly, fully; making over to him the chief promise (see ver. 4), the spiritual blessings, before almost left out of sight.

9 his wife. There was a similarity of condition, as well as of taste and habits, between Ishmael and his son-in-law. A certain kindliness seems to have prompted the step which Esau took. He wished to do as much as he could to gratify his father.

10 Haran. This was a journey of about four hundred miles; undertaken ostensibly for the same purpose as that of Abraham's servant to the same place, many years before; but in circumstances so different (see xxiv. 10, 32), as might well make Jacob feel that he was already under the chastening hand of God, on account of his sin.

12 a ladder, etc. A symbol of God's providence, carried on partly through "ministering spirits," while God Himself is above all to guide and control their movements. The dream, with subsequent Divine promise, would cheer the loneliness of Jacob's journey, and keep him from seeking a home in the land of his exile. Our Lord refers to this vision, John i. 51.

16 knew it not. "I feared, when I left my father's house, that I had left the Lord behind; but lo! He is here!"

17 heaven. Hitherto Jacob had aspired, with a blind ambition, to the results of Divine favour. He now has a deep sense of the presence of God; "an important turning-point in his spiritual history—the first step from *Jacob* to ISRAEL."

18 pillar. See also xxxi. 45, 51, 52; xxxv. 14; Exod. xxiv. 4. Jacob carried *oil* as an essential part of an Eastern traveller's provision. For its use in setting apart the stone as consecrated, cp. Exod. xxx. 26-30.

CHAPTER XXIX

1 people. Literally, "sons of the East," along the waters of the Euphrates. Judges vi. 3, 33; vii. 12; viii. 10.

2 well's mouth. To protect it from waste, and from drifting sand.

5 son. Or descendant—Laban, son of Bethuel (xxiv. 15, 29), was Nahor's grandson.

9 kept them. A laborious employment in which women of rank were, and still are, often occupied. Exod. ii. 16.

12 father's brother. Jacob was Laban's sister's son, *i.e.*, his nephew: the term "brother" is often used for a near kinsman.

17 tender-eyed. That is, weak-eyed; a physical defect.

18 serve thee. A wife is generally purchased in the East; and if her husband has not money, he obtains her by service to her father.

21 my days. The days here spoken of may be days of *service;* meaning that Jacob's seven years of service had expired: or they may be days of *betrothal,* or of marriage festivity. This latter supposition assumes that the marriages took place at the commencement of the seven years of servitude; and taking it thus, it would extend the period before Jacob's departure into Egypt to a length which seems to be required by the number of his grandchildren. In this case, ver. 20 is to be considered as a parenthesis.

23 Leah. The bride being wholly concealed by a large veil, this deception was easily practised. Jacob, who cheated Esau, is in turn cheated by Laban (Matt. vii. 2).

26 younger. A similar prejudice still prevails in the East, and has led to similar impositions. The sting of the reply lay in the reference to the right of the first-born. Recall Gen. xxvii. 35, 36.

27 week. That is, her week or marriage festivity. Laban probably practised this deception in order to secure Jacob's valuable services for a longer time. It seems, however, that Jacob married Rachel immediately after Leah's nuptial feast, and that the second (if not the first) seven years of servitude were subsequent to the double marriage. See on ver. 21.

29 maid. See on xxiv. 59.

32 affliction. The word Reuben means "Behold a son." But it seems to be a case of paronomasia by no means infrequent in the Hebrew Scriptures, and to refer to the phrase "hath looked upon my affliction."

love me. Knowing the importance attached to a son, especially in Abraham's family.

CHAPTER XXX

1 I die. She who said this afterwards died in childbirth: see xxxv. 16-19; and cp. Job v. 2.

3 knees. That is, adopt as my own.

6 judged me. That is, "hath taken cognizance of my cause." There is a contrast between the names given by Leah, and those by Rachel. The former express deep conjugal affection and thankfulness to God; the latter chiefly successful rivalry. Mark the importance of the laws afterwards given, Lev. xviii. 18; Deut. xxi. 15-17.

8 great wrestlings. Heb., "wrestlings of God"; perhaps she had prayed for children, and now regarded this as an answer.

11 A troop. Heb., "In luck." *Gad* means luck or fortune.

14 mandrakes. This, though probable, is only a conjectural rendering. The fruit of the mandrake (*atropa mandragora*) is round and yellow, like a small orange, fragrant and luscious; still believed in the East to promote fecundity.

22 Remembered. Marking a turning-point (cp. viii. 1).

24 Joseph. "He gives increase."

25 Send me away. His term of service for his wives being finished.

30 since my coming. Heb., "at my foot"; *i.e.,* "whithersoever I turned" (R.V.). The French version has "dès mon arrivée."

32 spotted. Parti-coloured sheep and goats are rare in the East, the sheep being generally white, and the goats dark.

my hire. Not those already speckled, but those which shall be born so, after these have been removed from the flock. Laban took all the speckled sheep and goats to a distance, and put them under the care of his own sons (ver. 35), probably thinking that the advantage was all on his side. Not finding it so, he repeatedly changed the terms of his agreement; sometimes allowing Jacob only the spotted, and sometimes only the streaked. See xxxi. 8.

33 righteousness. That is, "my *honesty* in not taking what is yours by agreement will be seen."

37 hazel and chesnut. More likely, "almond" and "plane" (R.V.). "Pilled" is now spelt *peeled*, and "strakes," *streaks.*

40 lambs. Jacob set aside those which by their colour fell to him.

42 he put them not in. This device was the crowning point in Jacob's artifice. Had his plans been applied to all the sheep and goats, Laban would have detected a stratagem; xxxi. 7, 8, show that even as it was he suspected some unfairness.

CHAPTER XXXI

3 Return. See xxviii. 15.

10 dream. Jacob had used craft to increase his flocks; and had been met by Laban with almost equal cunning; but in this dream he is reminded that, without such devices, the case may be left in God's hands. All his crafty policy is thus implicitly rebuked.

12 rams. Rather, "he-goats" (A.V. marg., R.V.).

15 our money. Rather, "price"; for Jacob had paid for his wives by labour. Laban, however, had received all the benefit of this labour, had the payment been made in the regular way, part of it would have come to them as their dowry.

18 carried away. The inhabitants of the Syrian deserts have few household goods; so that a large body can break up their encampment and remove everything in a few hours.

19 images. Heb. "teraphim." Perhaps images with a human head, and as oracles (Judges xvii. 5; Ezek. xxi. 21; Zech. x. 2); used as *family idols.*

21 the river. *i.e.*, the Euphrates.

23 Gilead. On that part of the great Gilead mountain-chain which lies north of the Jabbok. It was probably more than 200 miles from Haran

Jacob, having nearly three days' start of Laban (ver. 22), and being already three days' journey from him, might travel this distance without much exceeding the ordinary rate. Laban's was a forced march of about 35 miles a day for seven days.

34 furniture. The hard frame of the saddle is often covered with cushions and shawls, which are removed when a caravan halts, and are used to lie or sit upon.

35 rise up. As a son or daughter is expected to do in the presence of a father. And see Lev. xix. 32.

36 What is my trespass? Laban's search being unsuccessful, and his charge apparently groundless, Jacob finds opportunity to use the language of indignant virtue.

39 unto thee. See the subsequent law in Exod. xxii. 10–13; alluded to in Amos iii. 12.

40 by night. In the high open plains of Syria the night is often bitterly cold, though the day may be intensely hot.

42 Fear. The object of Isaac's reverence. See ver. 53.

43 what can I do? That is either, "What can I do to show my love for them now at parting?" or "What harm can it be thought that I should do them?"

53 the God of Nahor. Rather, "the gods of Nahor." Laban wished to hallow the contract by the sanction of his own gods, as well as of Jahveh. Jacob swore only by the latter.

CHAPTER XXXII

1 angels. In visible appearance, in great numbers. Possibly referred to in Psa. xxxiv. 7. As at his departure from Canaan, so now at his return, God gives him assurance and evidence of Divine watchfulness.

2 Mahanaim. That is, "two camps" or "hosts"; probably his own company and the host of angels. General Gordon in one of his messages from Khartoum wrote, "The hosts are with us: Mahanaim."

9 O God. This prayer contains four pleas, derived from (1) God's Covenant, pledged also by His Name Jahveh (xxviii. 13); (2) His command to Jacob to return to Canaan (xxxi. 3, 13); (3) His past mercies (cp. xxiv. 27); (4) His promises (xxviii. 13–15).

10 over this Jordan. From the highland of Gilead the whole course of the Jordan is visible.

13 which came to his hand. This probably means "that which was in his possession." The largeness of the present, the care shown in its selection, and the separation of the droves, so as to make Esau feel the value of the gift, and the directions to the servants—all show anxiety to appease his brother. But so far there is no expression of regret or penitence for the wrong that he had done.

22 the ford Jabbok. Or, "the ford *of* Jabbok," is a rapid but narrow stream flowing into the Jordan from the east.

24 a man. Or, The Eternal Himself in a human form (ver. 30). It was He who wrestled with Jacob. A contest partly corporeal (ver. 25); partly spiritual (Hos. xii. 3, 4). Jacob had previously aimed to obtain the fulfilment of God's promises by cunning. God now teaches him to put aside such means, and to throw himself dependently upon His care. Jacob succeeds when, ceasing to wrestle, ne betakes himself to prayer. Then *Jacob* becomes *Israel;* the Supplanter becomes the Prince.

28 prevailed. Some ancient versions render the last clause, "thou hast power with God, and with men thou shalt prevail"; making Jacob's successful importunity with God a pledge of his success with Esau.

30 preserved. It was a prevailing belief that no one could see *any* manifestation of the Deity, and live. Cp. Exod. xxxiii. 20.

31 halted. He limped; carrying with him a token of what had occurred, and a memento of the weakness which had necessitated the conflict, possibly, like Paul's thorn in the flesh, to keep him from being unduly lifted up (2 Cor. xii. 7). *Penuel* and *Peniel* are the same.

32 eat not. A traditional custom, not enforced by any law.

CHAPTER XXXIII

3 seven times. An act of submission to his elder brother.

10 the face of God. The unexpected kindness shown by Esau is taken as a pledge of God's favour and protection. Cp. Job xxxiii. 26.

11 urged. The acceptance of a present, called here a "blessing," is deemed of peculiar importance in the East, as a ratification of friendship (2 Kings vi. 15).

13 tender. Besides Joseph there were probably some young children belonging to Jacob's servants.

14 unto Seir. For other reasons it was better that they should journey and dwell apart. Jacob, however, who was now on his way towards Shechem, proposes to visit his brother at Mount Seir, where as a guest the laws of hospitality would protect him. There is no record that the visit was paid.

15 Let me find grace. That is, "Pardon me for declining the offer." An armed guard ("some of the folk") with Jacob might lead to mischief. And he is conscious of a higher Protector.

17 Succoth. "Booths" were wanted for the rainy season and winter. Jacob meant to stay here for a considerable time.

18 to Shalem. Rather, "And Jacob came safely," or "in peace, to the city of Shechem" (R.V.). See xxviii. 21; xxxii. 9.

19 pieces of money. Heb., *kesita*="weighed out"; a weight. In the other two places where this Hebrew word *kesita* occurs (Josh. xxiv. 32; Job xlii. 11), as well as here, the word is rendered "lambs" in some of the ancient versions. It has been thought to mean either lambs given in barter; or weights made in the form of lambs, like the lion weights of Assyria and the antelope weights of Egypt; or else coins bearing the image of a lamb, as in later times in Phœnicia.

20 El-elohe-Israel. "God, the God of Israel." Jacob here claims his new and honourable name (xxxii. 28), and associates it first with the worship of God. It does not seem to have been commonly employed until his residence in Egypt: while "Jacob" continues to be his usual name.

CHAPTER XXXIV

1 went out. A friendly visit, but culpable, for Jacob's family was to be separate from the Canaanites.

2 defiled. Literally, "humbled" (R.V.). The Hebrew word commonly implies force.

7 Folly in Israel. The sacred writer here uses

a phrase of later times to express the brothers' sense of the dishonour done to the chosen race. Cp. Josh. vii. 15; Judges xx. 6.

12 to wife. In the ardour of his passion, Shechem adds to his father's proposals far more liberal offers of his own. His frank confession of the wrong contrasts strongly with the deceitful dealings of Jacob's sons: see ver. 19.

13 the sons of Jacob. Especially Simeon and Levi, xlix. 5.

19 honourable. *i.e.*, in public estimation; which may partly account for the general submission of the people to the rite.

25 Simeon and Levi. These two were the leaders; probably accompanied by their servants, and possibly by some of their brothers.—**boldly.** Or, "unawares" (R.V.).

29 in the house. Thus one sin leads to another. Dinah's laxity leads to seduction, or violence: this to wrath; wrath thirsts for revenge; and revenge works itself out in treachery, murder, and lawless depredation. For the Christian duty see Rom. xii. 19; 1 Thess. v. 15. The horror with which Jacob himself regarded the transaction appears in his dying adjurations, xlix. 5, 6.

CHAPTER XXXV

1 thy brother. Jacob seems to have forgotten his vow (ch. xxviii. 22), or at least to have too long delayed its performance.

2 strange gods. Probably such objects of idolatrous worship as the teraphim (xxxi. 19, 34); Rachel's household deities.—**be clean.** Personal cleanliness has always been regarded as a natural symbol of moral purity. Cp. Heb. x. 22.

4 earrings. Ornaments representing objects of idolatrous worship were, and still are, common among the heathen, and are used as charms. Cp. xxxv. 4; Hos. ii. 13.—**oak.** It seems not unlikely that Gen. xii. 6; Josh. xxiv. 26; Judges ix. 6, 37, all refer to this tree.

5 the terror of God. *i.e.*, "a great terror" (R.V.).

8 Rebekah's nurse. From this it seems likely that Rebekah's mother was dead, and that her nurse had returned to Padan-aram, attaching herself to the household of Jacob and his wives.

9 And God appeared. This second appearance is fulfilment of the promise made in the former; and the second pillar (ver. 14) is a testimony that the faith and hope indicated by the former (xxviii. 18, etc.) had been justified by the event.

11 God Almighty. "El-Shaddai." This is the name by which God revealed Himself to Abraham (xvii. 1), and gave him the promise now so far fulfilled: see also xxviii. 3.

15 Bethel. Renewing the name with a fuller meaning.

16 Ephrath. Or, "Ephratah": see Micah v. 2.

18 Benjamin. "Son of the right hand," or "son of good fortune," as contrasted with "Benoni," "Son of my sorrow."

19 buried. A building called the Tomb of Rachel, now covered with a Turkish mosque, is shown between Jerusalem and Bethlehem. But see 1 Sam. x. 2.

22 heard it. That is, with displeasure, as he afterwards showed by taking away the birthright. See xlix. 4.

26 in Padan-aram. All but Benjamin, who was born in Canaan (vers. 16–19).

27 the city of Arbah. Rather, "Kirjath-Arba," or Hebron (see Josh. xiv. 13).

29 died. This is mentioned by anticipation. Jacob was a hundred and twenty years old when his father died (xxv. 26; xxxv. 28); but he was a hundred and thirty when he went into Egypt (xlvii. 9); and Joseph had preceded him at least twenty years (cp. xxxvii. 2; xli. 46, 53, 57). So that Isaac's death occurred at least ten years after the former, and ten years before the latter of those events.

CHAPTER XXXVI

1 Esau. Here (as in ch. xxv. 12–18, with respect to Ishmael) the history of Isaac's family is closed with a brief notice of Esau's descendants, who were afterwards intimately connected with the Israelites, either as enemies, or allies, or subjects. Many of the names differ from those found in other passages; but it was common to have several names, and to have a name varied into different forms, retaining the same meaning. The same name, also, was common to many persons; such as Amalek, Eliphaz, Teman, Aholibamah. The "dukes" were apparently heads of tribes, now called sheikhs; and over the whole were kings. The kingdom was probably, at first, elective; and afterwards hereditary. The Horites of Seir are introduced, as Esau's family intermarried with them; though they afterwards destroyed or expelled them.

2 wives. On the difficulties which have arisen in comparing this list of Esau's wives with xxvi. 34; xxviii. 9, see note on ver. 1.—**daughter of Zibeon.** *i.e.*, the daughter of Anah [and so the grand-] daughter of Zibeon. In the second clause the Samaritan, Septuagint, and Syriac, read Anah "son of Zibeon."

6 country. That is, the country of Seir. Esau had dwelt there before, but returned to Canaan at Isaac's death; now, however, he finally leaves Canaan, and takes his share of the property with him.

11 Teman. The Temanites were renowned for valour and wisdom. Eliphaz the Temanite was one of the chief friends of Job, whom some identify with Jobab (ver. 33).

24 the mules. The Hebrew word occurs nowhere else. It should be translated "hot springs" (R.V.). So the Vulgate.

28 Uz. See on xxii. 21.

31 Israel. God's promise to Jacob, "kings shall come out of thy loins," is here alluded to as yet waiting its fulfilment. Or the clause may have been added later. The words mark the contrast between the early development of the power and polity of the Edomites, and the longer wanderings of the chosen people.

37 river. Cp. Gen. x. 11.

39 Hadar. Or, "Hadad." See 1 Chron. i. 50. As his death is not recorded, it is supposed that he was contemporary with Moses, and is the king mentioned in Numb. xx. 14. The name was common, in later times, in the royal families of Edom and Syria.

CHAPTER XXXVII

2 the generations of Jacob. Or, "the family history of Jacob," now the head of the chosen race.—**Joseph.** The history of Joseph may be viewed (1) historically, in relation to the Israelitish nation; (2) personally, as a type of providential disposition, by which the elect are guided from humiliation to triumph, from sorrow to joy;

(3) prophetically, as offering analogies to the life of our Lord; and (4) morally, as showing how God may bring good out of evil.

3 colours. Some render this "a dress of [many] pieces," or, "a long garment with sleeves" (R.V. marg.). It was probably a dress reaching to the wrists and ankles, suitable for persons exempt from labour.

5 a dream. Significant dreams sent by God; hastening their own fulfilment by the malice they excited. For other dreams with significance, see xx. 3–7; xxxi. 24; Matt. i. 20, ii. 12, xxvii. 19.

10 to the earth. The first dream relates to Joseph's brethren, and seems to imply greater *wealth;* the second includes his parents, and points to higher *dignity.*

14 brethren. The remembrance of the massacre at Shechem by the sons of Jacob may have made their father anxious.—**Shechem.** About fifty miles from Hebron. Dothan was probably about twelve or fifteen miles farther.

20 pit. These water holes were generally in part natural, but were often further excavated, so as to be wide at the bottom, though narrow at the mouth. Empty cisterns were often used as prisons: see Jer. xxxviii. 6; xl. 15.

25 Ishmeelites. In ver. 28, "Midianites" are mentioned; and these two nations are found united against Israel (Judges viii. 22, 24). Both were descendants of Abraham, the one people by Hagar, the other by Keturah.—**myrrh.** See the presents to Joseph (xliii. 11). Although this event occurred more than 3,500 years ago, we have all the features of a caravan crossing the desert at the present day.

26 Judah. Reuben and Judah, though otherwise very faulty, here contrast favourably with their brothers Simeon and Levi. In the massacre of the Shechemites the latter stood alone, or at least took the lead, although the former were as closely related to Dinah. See on xliii. 3.

28 twenty pieces of silver. Probably shekels, and if so, equivalent to about $15 in our money. This, however, does not decide the money value. The same sum is specified in Lev. xxvii. 5, as the redemption price of a youth between five and twenty years of age.

29 rent his clothes. A frequent sign of mourning in the East; the outer or inner garment, or both, being torn down the front, from the neck to the girdle (cp. Job i. 20).

32 the blood. This was not the *first* time in Jacob's experience when a "kid of the goats" had been killed in order to deceive (xxvii. 9). By such coincidences God sometimes fixes attention on His law of retribution.

34 sackcloth. Another token of grief, used also by persons professing disregard for bodily comfort (Isa. xx. 2).

35 the grave. Rather, "Sheol," (Greek, "Hades"): the place of the departed; the first occurrence of the word in Scripture.

36 Egypt. Familiar even to modern times as a mart for slaves.—**officer.** Heb., "eunuch"; but the word signifies also chamberlain, courtier, or officer.—**guard.** Heb., "chief of the slaughtermen," or "executioners"; "governor of the prison" (*Moffatt*).

CHAPTER XXXVIII

1 at that time, *i.e.,* during this period, though before the later events of the previous chapter. This narrative is necessary to complete the genealogy of our Lord. It contrasts the purity of Joseph with the licentiousness of Judah; illustrates the Oriental institution of marriage with a brother's widow; and, in the pollution originated by Judah's marriage and friendship with heathens, shows how the neglect of religious privileges and the violation of religious restrictions may lead to the grossest crimes.—**down.** To the lowlands in the southwest. Adullam was a royal city of the Canaanites. Near it was David's retreat, 1 Sam. xxii. 1.

5 Cherib. Otherwise called Achzib; part of the possession of the tribe of Judah, Josh. xv. 44; Micah i. 14.

8 marry her. The firstborn of such a marriage being reckoned the child of the deceased brother. This custom was restricted by the law of Moses (Deut. xxv. 5–10).

11 grown. This was probably only a pretext. Judah may have thought that Tamar had caused the death of his two sons by magical practices.

13 sheep. Sheep-shearing was an occasion of festivity.

14 in an open place. Rather, "at the gate of Enaim" (R.V.), a little village on the way to Timnath; called Enam in Josh. xv. 34 (so ver. 21).

15 harlot. Or, "a dedicated woman," *i.e.,* devoted to the licentious worship of Astoreth, to whom "a kid of goats" was the appropriate offering.—**covered.** Or, "muffled"; so that he did not recognise her.

18 signet. A seal-ring, worn on the right hand, or suspended from the neck.—**bracelets.** Or, "cord" (R.V.), or "chain," by which the sealring was suspended. (So ver. 25.)

23 to her. That is, "Let her keep my pledges herself; I have fulfilled my part of the agreement in sending the kid, and have nothing more to do with the matter."

24 burnt. Judah, as head of the family, pronounces sentence; and treats Tamar rigorously as an adulteress, as she was legally Shelah's wife. Later, under the Mosaic law, this was the punishment of unchastity in a priest's daughter (Lev. xxi. 9).

29 How hast thou, etc. Rather, "Wherefore hast thou made a breach for thyself?" (R.V.).

CHAPTER XXXIX

1 Egyptian. Potiphar is three times specially called an "Egyptian"; from which it has been inferred by some that he was serving a foreign king, perhaps one of the Shepherd dynasty, and by others that at this time there were many Canaanites in Pharaoh's service. But the intention may be to mark this as the beginning of the servitude of Abraham's descendants to the Egyptians.

2 house. A situation better than that of a field-slave.

3 saw that the Lord was with him. Acknowledging Jahveh simply as the God of Joseph.

5 for Joseph's sake. Cp. Laban's admission, xxx. 27.

6 save the bread. A proverbial expression signifying the full confidence which Potiphar put in Joseph, though a slave; or the words may mean that as the food of Egyptians was prepared differently from that of foreigners (see xliii. 32), Joseph had no concern with his master's table.—**well favoured.** That is, handsome in *form* and *face.*

9 against God. And not only against *Potiphar.* The contrast between Judah falling into Tamar's snare, and Joseph resisting entreaties, shows the influence of true godliness, and proves that "the

Eternal was with Joseph" in temptation, as well as in business and in suffering (1 Cor. x. 13).

12 garment. The hyke, or upper garment, was a large robe rather loosely fastened.

14 she called. Sinful love may change into hatred (2 Sam. xiii. 15) and the tempter become the accuser.

20 bound. "Prison," literally "roundhouse." This was probably attached to Potiphar's own house (see xl. 3, where "the captain of the guard" is most likely to be understood of Potiphar himself). State prisoners were here confined, and Joseph is placed among them as a slave. His captivity, rigorous at first (Psa. cv. 18), did not long continue so. It is not improbable that Potiphar heard his wife's story with some suspicion, which was afterwards strengthened; although, to save appearances, Joseph was left in prison.

CHAPTER XL

2 chief, etc. That is, the principal cup-bearer, and the chief cook: both officers of high rank at the Egyptian court. Rabshakeh, Sennacherib's general (see 2 Kings xviii. 17, and note), was, as his name imports, "chief cup-bearer" in the Assyrian court; and cp. Nehemiah (Neh. i. 11).

8 no interpreter. "Being in prison we cannot have recourse to a diviner." The Egyptian sages prided themselves upon their interpretation of dreams.

9 before me. It has been objected to this, on the authority of Herodotus (ii. 77) and Plutarch (Isis and Osiris, vi.), that the vine was not cultivated, nor wine drunk, in Egypt. Monuments of the oldest dynasties, however, abundantly prove the objection to be groundless.

15 dungeon. Or, "pit," the word used in xxxvii. 16. This accounts for the expression "lift up," in vers. 13, 19.

16 white baskets. Or, "baskets of white bread."

17 head. A scene illustrated by many Egyptian monuments. The dishes were carried in baskets on the heads of the cooks from the kitchen to the dining-room, across a wide open court, open to birds.

19 from off thee. The addition of these last words to those used in ver. 13 marks the difference between the two. The chief cook was probably beheaded, and the corpse gibbeted to be devoured by birds.

CHAPTER XLI

1 two full years. Probably from the release of the chief cup-bearer.—**Pharaoh.** Some scholars think that this monarch belonged to one of the dynasties of "Shepherd kings," a race alien in blood and habits from Egyptians, and hated by them. This would account for his favour to Jacob hereafter. And see on xlvi. 34.

2 the river. "The Nile." The cattle in Egypt are fond of immersing themselves in water, except the head, in the heat of the day.—**in a meadow.** Rather, "among the sedge, a favourite food of cattle in Egypt, both when green and when dried": and so ver. 18. See Job viii. 11.

5 stalk. The wheat grown in Egypt (*triticum compositum*) has several ears clustered on one stalk. The symbolism of these dreams is very striking. Cows were the emblems of the Egyptian goddess of the earth and of its fertility. This depended upon the river Nile, from which they appear to come up.

6 east wind. Coming over the hot and sandy deserts of the Sinaitic peninsula.

13 restored. That is, "foretold my restoration." So Jeremiah is said to "pull down" and "destroy" those nations whose downfall and destruction he foretold (Jer. i. 10).

14 shaved. The Egyptians (*Herodotus*, ii. 36) allowed the hair and beard to grow as a sign of mourning. Joseph shaved on liberation.

34 fifth. In ordinary times Egypt exports great quantities of corn, and a fifth part of the produce would suffice to provide for the years of famine.

40 according unto thy word, etc. Literally, "on thy mouth every one of my people shall kiss": perhaps alluding to the custom of kissing the written mandates of a superior.

42 ring. Documents being at that time only *sealed*, and not signed, the bestowment of a signet-ring involved the control of the property or kingdom of him who gave it (Esth. iii. 10).—**fine linen.** Or, "cotton" (R.V. marg.); a description of fine muslin which formed the robe of honour.

43 knee. In the original, "Abrek," an Egyptian word, "Bow down"; hence, "good luck! hail!"

45 Zaphnath-paaneah. Some take this as a compound Hebrew word, and signifying "a revealer of secrets"; or, "the man to whom secrets are revealed." Most likely the name is Egyptian, and is rendered by some, "saviour of the world." Brugsch translates it "prince of the life of the world." Pharaoh naturalises Joseph by giving him an Egyptian name and an Egyptian wife.—**priest.** The priests being the highest caste of nobility and of state-officers in Egypt, it was natural that Pharaoh should connect Joseph with them. Probably, "Poti-pherah" means "he who belongs to (*i.e.*, the priest of)" the *Sun*. The city "On" was called by the Greeks *Heliopolis*, or, "the City of the Sun," and by the Hebrews afterwards *Beth-shemesh*, with the same meaning; Jer. xliii. 13. It was at Heliopolis that "Cleopatra's Needle," now on the Thames Embankment, once stood, and its twin obelisk is still to be seen at Heliopolis.

48 all the food. That is, every *kind* of food: ver. 34 showing that only the fifth part was to be actually taken.

51 Manasseh. "Causing forgetfulness."

52 Ephraim. "Fruitfulness."

CHAPTER XLII

4 mischief. Jacob may have suspected that Joseph had had foul play at his brothers' hands, and feared their jealousy of Rachel's remaining son. Benjamin was probably now from twenty-two to twenty-five years old.

6 earth. According to Joseph's dream of the sheaves bowing down (xxxvii. 7). See ver. 9.

7 unto them. Possibly to bring his brethren to repentance, and to learn the real state of his father's family.

8 knew not him. It was full twenty years since they had sold him; and his rank and dress added to his disguise.

9 Spies. No uncommon danger in the times. Cp. Numb. xxi. 32; Josh. ii. 1.

14 That is it, etc. A Hebrew form of speech conveying a strong assertion, to be found, with slight variations, in many parts of the Bible. See Matt. xxvii. 11.

15 By the life of Pharaoh. It is still common in the East to protest " by the head," or the life " of the king "; and the king himself does the same, as did Pharaoh (xli. 44). In the New Testament the commandment is, " Swear not at all " (Matt. v. 34).

18 I fear God. Meaning, " My religion will lead me to deal justly with you." A declaration likely to awaken their consciences, and to make them regard their present sufferings as a Divine retribution: see ver. 21.

24 Simeon. The instigator of the massacre at Shechem (xxxiv. 25) is likely to have been the harshest in the scene at Dothan (xxxvii. 20).

25 their sacks. Rather, " their vessels " (R.V.). Beside the large sacks, they had smaller bags containing food for their journey.

27 in the inn. Eastern inns, called *khans,* are merely large open courts, surrounded with piazzas: no food is provided; but the travellers attend to their own wants.

28 failed them. An uneasy conscience is soon alarmed. It appears from ver. 35 that only one sack had been opened on the way home; when they found the money in the rest, their apprehensions were renewed.

36 bereaved. Upon *me* falls the bereavement; against *me* are all these things.

38 to the grave. Cp. his lamentation over Joseph (xxxvii. 35) and see 1 Kings ii. 6.

CHAPTER XLIII

3 Judah. The strong and dominating character of Judah makes itself felt at this crisis. Cp. his action as shown in xxxvii. 26, 27, and see xlix. 8–10 and 1 Chr. v. 2.

8 the lad. So called as the youngest, though he was married, and had sons.

11 best fruits. Heb., " song of the land," *i.e.,* its most famous produce.

12 double money. The money for the last supply of corn, as well as " other money " (ver. 22) for that which was now to be procured.

16 noon. Indications of ancient Egyptian usages,—the dining at noon, the rigid attention to precedence at table, and the careful separation between Egyptians and those of a different nation. Their use of animal food is proved by the testimony of Herodotus (bk. ii. c. 37, 77), and by the evidence of existing monuments.

32 by themselves. Not difficult according to Eastern custom, as there is a separate tray for every two or three guests, who form a group round it. And it is a mark of honour to a person to put as many dishes as possible upon the tray set before him. See ver. 34.

Egyptians. Egyptians were as careful of ceremonial purity as Pharisees. The dislike of native Egyptians to shepherds is shown on their monuments. Cp. xlvi. 34.

33 according to his birthright . . . another. It is not said that Joseph thus placed them. They may have taken their seats in their natural order, and " marvelled " at the strangeness of the circumstances in which they found themselves.

CHAPTER XLIV

5 he divineth. Probably a popular mode of expressing Joseph's superhuman wisdom; or perhaps a phrase intended to increase their alarm. Ancient writers say that the Egyptians divined by cups, observing the light of the ripples on the surface, or of gold jewels and other things thrown in, as well as the way in which such articles arranged themselves. But Joseph had a better guide (xli. 16). Cp. ver. 15.

7 these words. " Such words as these " (R.V.); a respectful phrase.

18 and said. The simple earnestness of truth made Judah's pleading eloquent, and well fitted to affect Joseph's heart.

28 the one. Joseph thus learns his own story from the unconscious speaker.

33 a bondman. It was Judah who proposed selling Joseph as a slave (xxxvii. 27); now he offers himself to undergo the same lot.

CHAPTER XLV

5 grieved. Cp. 2 Cor. ii. 6, 7.

6 earing. An old English word signifying *ploughing.* It occurs in A.V.: Exod. xxxiv. 21; Deut. xxi. 4; 1 Sam. viii. 12; Isa. xxx. 4.

8 God. Literally, " the God," *i.e.,* the God of our family. Joseph's thoughts are fixed on the workings of Divine providence.—**father.** That is, " counsellor," or " guardian "; as in Judges xvii. 10.

10 Goshen. Near the north-east frontier of Egypt, which they might protect from irruption: whilst they would have room for the pasture of their numerous cattle and sheep near to Canaan, the destined home of the chosen race.—**near unto me.** Zoan, a royal residence, was near Goshen.

19 do ye. Pharaoh empowers Joseph to invite his family to settle in Egypt with the royal sanction, which made their subsequent oppression the more inexcusable.

20 stuff. Such property as they could not conveniently carry away.

24 fall not out. He may have feared that mutual reproaches might produce a quarrel.

CHAPTER XLVI

1 Beer-sheba. Jacob did not pass the place where he and his fathers had worshipped, nor cross the boundary of Canaan, without obtaining the sanction of God. For the fulfilment of this promise in ver. 3, see Deut. x. 22.

4 put his hand upon thine eyes. To close them in death.

7 his daughters. Including sons' wives and grand-daughters.

10 a Canaanitish woman. Implying, apparently, that marriage with a Canaanite was an exception to the rule in Jacob's family.

13 Job. Called " Jashub," Numb. xxvi. 24; 1 Chron. xxiv. 11.

15 thirty and three. In this number, Er and Onan are of course omitted.

26 threescore and six. That is, besides Jacob himself; when he is added, with Joseph and his two sons, the number is seventy. See next verse.

27 threescore and ten. This is not a list of persons who actually travelled with Jacob to Egypt (cp. in ch. xxxv., vers. 16–18, with vers. 24–26); but a genealogical table of founders of families in the several tribes about the period of Jacob's migration. This account cannot be harmonised with Numb. xxvi., 1 Chron. iv., etc., in default of information as to the changes in the family relations of the Israelites, first between the settlement in Egypt and the exodus, and secondly between the entrance upon Canaan and the establishment of the kingdom. If all the missing facts were known, the harmony would doubtless be clear.

34 land of Goshen. Thus, while enjoying a fertile settlement, they would be kept distinct from the Egyptians and preserved from the contamination of their idolatry and vices.

every shepherd, etc. This language of Joseph appears to imply that what was an abomination to the Egyptians would be a recommendation to Pharaoh; and some think that this apparent anomaly, together with the king's heartiness in receiving the family of Israel, and his readiness to give them charge of his own cattle, favours the opinion that the king belonged to the hated shepherd race, the Hyksos, at one time dominant in Egypt. These invaders were a wandering pastoral people from the north-east, akin in habits of life, though not in religion, to the family of Jacob. The antipathy of the true Egyptian race to all shepherds is illustrated in many ways by ancient monuments (cp. xli. 1).

CHAPTER XLVII

2 men. Rather, "he took from among his brethren five men" (R.V.).

6 men of activity. Or, as in Exod. xviii. 25, "able men."

9 pilgrimage. What Pharaoh calls "life" Jacob designates a "pilgrimage"; not only in reference to his wanderings in Canaan and Mesopotamia, and now to Egypt; but because he had learned to regard himself as a stranger and pilgrim on earth. See Heb. xi. 13; xiii. 14; 1 Pet. ii. 11. —**Few and evil.** Oriental depreciation such as would still be used in the East.

11 Rameses. Or, "Raamses" (Exod. i. 11). This was a city, perhaps with a district of the same name, in the land of Goshen. From this place, at the exodus, the people reached the Red Sea in two days; Exod. xii. 36; Numb. xxxiii. 6.

18 second. Rather, "the next year"; for it was probably the last of the seven; whence the request for "seed," ver. 19. The Egyptians trusted the prediction of Joseph that the famine was now about to cease, and were therefore anxious to sow their fields again.

19 servants. The monarchy became consolidated by the purchase of the land, which was to be rented of the crown (see vers. 24, 26); by the provision made for a regular revenue, derived from a moderate taxation, and by the formation of cities as centres both of authority and of wealth. *Servants* in ver. 25, may be understood as *tenants,* somewhat in the feudal sense.

22 priests. The caste of nobles. As the learned and ruling class was maintained in part by allowances of food and wine from the royal stores, they were not under the necessity of disposing of their lands. See *Herod.*, bk. ii. c. 37.

26 the fifth part. Joseph thus provided a revenue sufficient for all state purposes, yet not oppressive to the people. Joseph's rate of twenty per cent. is a moderate rental when compared with taxes at times levied on the fellahs of Egypt.

29 in Egypt. This would remind Joseph, and all his family, that Canaan, not Egypt, was to be their country.

31 bed's head. The Greek translators, differing only in a vowel point, render the word "staff." The idea, however, is the same; as the spear of the warrior and the staff of the chief were set at the bed's head. The patriarch turned himself in a posture of devotion. See Heb. xi. 21.

CHAPTER XLVIII

1 Manasseh and Ephraim. These sons of Joseph were born during the years of plenty. Jacob had come to Egypt in the second year of the famine, and had now been there seventeen years. Manasseh and Ephraim had therefore arrived at manhood.

5 are mine. Ephraim and Manasseh thus became heads of tribes; and Joseph, Rachel's firstborn, inherited the double portion of the birthright which Reuben had forfeited. See ver. 22; 1 Chron. v. 1, 2; Deut. xxi. 17. "By faith" (Heb. xi. 21) "Jacob blessed" these two young men, who were already in the eye of the world much greater as sons of the viceroy of Egypt than they could be as children of the aged shepherd from Palestine.

6 after the name of their brethren. That is, they shall be regarded as belonging to one or other of the tribes called by their elder brothers' names. Hence no other sons of Joseph appear in the genealogies. See xlvi. 20.

14 wittingly. That is, purposely; "crossing his hands," as the Septuagint freely renders it.

15 fed me. "Has been my Shepherd," as in Psa. xxiii. 1. See ch. xlix. 24.

16 Angel. See on xvi. 7; xviii. 2; xxxii. 24. The word "redeemed" is probably alluded to in Isa. xliv. 23; xlix. 7.

19 This prophecy was fulfilled by the relative numbers of the two tribes at the time of taking the census in the wilderness, and by the precedence always accorded to Ephraim when both are mentioned. Numb. i. 33, 35; ii. 19, 21; Deut. xxxiii. 17.—**greater.** Though Manasseh had more land in the apportionment of Canaan, Ephraim was always the more powerful tribe, ranking next to Judah. The ten tribes, after their separation, were called collectively by the name of *Ephraim* (Hosea viii., ix.).

20 bless. That is, shall use thy name (the names of thy two sons) as a benediction.

22 I took. Possibly references to an event otherwise unnoticed in Jacob's life, when he had to regain by force the land he had purchased near Shechem. Others think that the acquisition, as well as the gift, is future, and that Jacob speaks of the conquest and distribution of the land by Joshua. "Shechem," the word here rendered "portion" (literally, "shoulder," or "mountain-slope," R.V. marg.), fell to the lot of Ephraim.

CHAPTER XLIX

1 last days. Or, "hereafter." Prophecies of the future destinies and characters of the twelve tribes, as well as references to their founders. Cp. with Deut. xxxiii.; and with the allotments of the different tribes, as in Josh. xiii.–xix. The six sons of Leah are first mentioned, then the four sons of Bilhah and Zilpah, last of all the sons of Rachel.

4 Unstable. Or, "boiling up." See other forms of the same word rendered "light" in Judges ix. 4; Zeph. iii. 4; and "lightness" in Jer. xxiii. 32. The preceding verse vividly describes the privileges of the firstborn; this as solemnly declares them to be forfeited. No judge, prophet, prince, or person of renown is found of this tribe; nor was the tribe itself ever distinguished for anything good. See Judges v. 15, 16.

5 habitations. Or, "their swords are weapons of violence" (R.V.); but perhaps it is better to read, with the Septuagint and Samaritan, "They perpetrated wickedness by their devices."

6 a wall. Rather, "they houghed an ox" or "oxen" (R.V., A.V. marg.); a metaphorical phrase, denoting their treachery (xxxiv.).

7 I will. Jacob is said to *do* that which he predicts. Similar phraseology is common in the prophetical writings. The fulfilment of this prophecy was strikingly diverse in the two cases. The tribe of Simeon was divided through very feebleness and inability to maintain their position in any one place. Cp. Numb. i. 22, 23; xxvi. 12–14; 1 Chron. iv. 38. Long before the captivity, it was entirely absorbed in the tribe of Judah. See Josh. xix. 1, 9; Judges i. 3, 17. Cp. 1 Kings xii. 23. In the blessing of Moses (Deut. xxxiii.), Simeon is entirely passed over. Levi, with similar numerical weakness (Numb. iii. 39), was also dispersed, but for the highest and holiest purposes. See Deut. x. 9. The heroic zeal displayed by this tribe for Jahveh (Exod. xxxii. 26–28) could not repeal the curse, but changed it into a blessing—the tribe of Levi being scattered through the land as the religious guides and instructors of the people.

8 enemies. Over all thine enemies thou shalt be victorious. The supremacy among the tribes and the promise of Messiah are separated from the rest of the birthright, and given to Judah. See 1 Chron. v. 2, and note on ch. xlviii. 5.

9 old lion. Rather, "lioness." These figures, rising in a beautiful climax, indicate the warlike character and power of the tribe. First, it is compared to a *lion's whelp;* then to a full-grown *lion;* then to a *lioness*, which, when roused in defence of her cubs, exceeds all in fierceness. This progressive imagery prepares for the crowning prediction of "the Lion of the tribe of Judah." See Rev. v. 5.

10 Shiloh. "The peaceful one." Having announced the sovereignty of Judah, the patriarch goes on to declare that it should have no end, until One should come bearing the name of "Shiloh," whose sway both Israel and all mankind should acknowledge. The subsequent history presents the fulfilment of this prediction. In the journeyings of the Israelites through the wilderness, and under the theocracy in the promised land, the tribe of Judah took the precedence; after the return of the people from Babylon it absorbed the others, and gave its name to the whole nation; and even under the dominion of the Romans it retained a measure of authority. But, on the appearance of Christ, all this quickly passed away, to make room for the spiritual and ultimately universal reign of the Prince of peace.—**people.** Literally, peoples (R.V.). In Genesis the great prophecy is developed from the announcement of a Deliverer belonging to the *human race*, so far as to specify the particular tribe from which He should spring. Abraham among the descendants of Noah (xii. 3); Isaac of the children of Abraham (xxi. 12); Jacob of the offspring of Isaac; and now Judah, of Jacob's children, are successively pointed out as the depositaries of the blessing.

12 milk. The appearance of the people would indicate their happy lot. Vers. 11, 12 describe, in poetical terms, the peace and plenty which in the best times of the nation would be the lot of the tribe; and they seem to point onwards to the blessings of the Messiah's reign.

13 Zidon. Probably not the *city*, which lay far to the north, but the *territory* of the Zidonians: the word "haven" referring either to the Zidonian ports, or, more probably, to the coast of Zebulun on the Sea of Galilee. Tiberias was within this tribe. See Josh. xix. 10–16, and map of Canaan.

14 burdens. Or, "two stalls." "Sheepfolds" (R.V.). Within the portion of this tribe lay the rich plain of Jezreel, bordered by the range of Carmel and the hills of Galilee. The men of Issachar occasionally displayed both valour and wisdom. See Judges v. 15; 1 Chron. xii. 32.

16 judge. So the name "Dan" signifies. The stealthy character of their warfare (resembling that of the Bedouin) is illustrated in Judges xviii.; and it is aptly represented by the attack of the *cerastes*, or horned viper, which lies unperceived in the sand.

19 troop. The words "troop" and "overcome" are allusions to the name *Gad*, whose tribe was much exposed to predatory incursions from the Syrian and Arabian deserts. "At last" (lit. "upon the heel") may be rendered "in the rear," or "in return." In marching to the conquest of Canaan, the tribe of Gad was part of the advanced guard of the whole army. See Josh. i. 12–15.

21 Naphtali, etc. "A slender oak is Naphtali with lovely boughs" (*Moffatt*). The "goodly words" of Deborah's song (Judges v.) celebrated the deeds of this tribe, Barak being "of Kedesh-Naphtali."

24 strong. Strength of character distinguished Joseph—he resisted the bad influence of his brothers' sins and the temptation to youthful lust; he endured slavery and imprisonment; he sustained the heaviest burdens and greatest dignities of government, and kept his faith in God's promises unimpaired by worldly prosperity. This blessing on Joseph, which was fulfilled in the portions of Ephraim and Manasseh, is the fullest and most elaborate of all. "Heaven above," with its rains and dews—"the deep," the western sea, the Lake of Tiberias, and the Jordan through much of its course—and "the everlasting hills," Mount Ephraim and Mount Gilead—promoted the increase of their families and of their possessions, and made Joseph as a "fruitful bough by a well." See Deut. xxxiii. 13–17.

26 everlasting hills. Or, "The blessings of thy father exceed the blessings of the eternal mountains, the desirable things of the everlasting hills." Cp. Deut. xxxiii. 15.

27 spoil. In the first times of Israel, the Benjamites were noted for their fierce military spirit and success in war. From them sprang Ehud, the second judge, and Saul, the first king. They were afterwards united with Judah, shared in its privileges, and returned in large numbers from Babylon.

29 said to them. The charge formerly given to Joseph is now given to all his sons; who, though once estranged from one another, were to unite at their father's grave, like Isaac and Ishmael at the burial of Abraham (xxv. 9), and Jacob and Esau at that of Isaac (xxxv. 29).

CHAPTER L

2 physicians. Persons of high rank in Egypt had a number of family physicians, each devoting himself to one class of diseases. In later times, the embalmers formed a distinct class. This art was carried to such perfection by the Egyptians that their mummies remain to the present day.

3 and ten days. That is, a month of mourning (see Numb. xx. 29; Deut. xxxiv. 8) besides the forty days of embalming.

4 house of Pharaoh. Joseph could not leave his master's country without permission, which he could not solicit in person because as a mourner, being unshaven (see Herodotus, bk. ii., c. 36), he could not appear before the king. See xli. 14.

17 father. Not only children of the same father, but worshippers of the same God.

22 a hundred and ten. Until the seventy-first year after his family came to Egypt, and the fifty-fourth after his father's death. Cp. ch. xli. 46, 47 with ch. xlv. 11.

24 visit you. Neither his own alliance and prosperity in Egypt, nor the length of time which had elapsed since the promise was given, had impaired his faith.

25 took an oath. For the fulfilment of this command see refs. in next note. As Joseph remained, by position and office, an Egyptian until the day of his death, the expression of his faith and hope was so much the more striking.

26 Egypt. That his remains might be ready for removal at the proper time. This would serve to keep up among the Israelites the expectation of a return to Canaan. See Exod. xiii. 19; Josh. xxiv. 32.

EXODUS

The Book of Deliverance

INTRODUCTION

The title Exodus, "going out," was given to this book by the Greek translators, because it records the departure of the Israelites from Egypt. The Hebrew title is *Shemoth*, "Names," from the opening words. It is the story of those who came into Egypt and of those who were brought out of it.

Moses is the great figure of the book. His discovery by Pharaoh's daughter leads to his being taken to the royal palace and being trained in all the learning of the Egyptians (ii. 5, 10; cp. Acts vii. 22; Heb. xi. 24–26). Then follows his sympathy with his brethren in their slavery, his flight into Midian, and his further training there in the solitudes of the desert by communion with God, and by the hardships of the desert life, for his high office as the leader of God's people and their great Lawgiver (ii. 11–iv. 20). His faith and courage are shown in his confronting Pharaoh (v.–x.).

The institution of the Passover is the solemn closing scene of the bondage in Egypt, an institution cherished by the Jews to this day, honoured and continued by the Lord Jesus Christ Himself, and prefiguring the heavenly feast of completed redemption through the Lamb that was slain (xii.; cp. Matt. xxvi. 17–29; Mark xiv. 12–22; Luke xxii. 7–20; John i. 29; Rev. v. 6, 12; vii. 14).

The flight from Egypt, the crossing of the Red Sea, and the desert journeyings of the Israelites, are told in simple but thrilling language (xii. 31, 37–42, 51; xiii. 17–xix. 2). And then there is the giving of the Law at Mount Sinai (xix. 3–xxxi. 18), with the rebellion of the people and the touching and self-effacing intercession of Moses on their behalf (xxxii.) and the subsequent enactment of the ceremonial laws. The closing chapters (xxxv. xl.) describe the building of the Tabernacle, and the Divine presence manifested in and upon it, the light and protection of the people in their journeyings.

CHAPTER I

7 the land was filled. According to the promise (Gen. xlvi. 3). See xii. 37. The people were not, it appears, confined to the district of Goshen.

8 knew not. This Pharaoh is now generally understood to have been Ramses II., called "the Pharaoh of the Oppression" (so Sayce, Brugsch, Ebers). His mummy was found in 1881 at Deir el-Bahari. Two colossal statues of him are to be seen amid the ruins of Memphis, near Bedrashen, 20 miles from Cairo, and some of his hieroglyphics may be seen on Cleopatra's Needle, now on the Thames Embankment. "The Pharaoh of the Exodus" was his son, Merenptah. See on Gen. xlvi. 34. The prophecy of Gen. xv. 13, is to be fulfilled.

11 Pithom and Raamses. Both these cities were

in the district of Heliopolis (" On," which name the Septuagint adds to the other two), near the canal which joined the Nile and the Red Sea. " Pithom " (" House of Tum," the Sun-god worshipped at Heliopolis) was identified by Naville, in 1883, as Tel-el-Maskhutu, about 20 miles from Tel-el-Kebir, and the ruins of the treasure-houses have been found, constructed of two kinds of brick, one ordinary, the other without straw. Raamses, now Tel-el-Retabeh, 10 miles west of Pithom.

15 Hebrew midwives. Probably the *chief* among them, responsible for all the rest. Their names are Egyptian.

21 made them houses. That is, He " increased and prospered their families."

CHAPTER II

1 a man. Amram, the son of Kohath, and grandson of Levi. His wife's name was Jochebed.

2 a son. Jochebed's two other children, Miriam and Aaron, were born, probably, before the last edict of Pharaoh.—**a goodly child.** Heb., " fair to God " (Acts vii. 20); *i.e.*, in God's sight. Cp. Heb. xi. 23.

3 bulrushes. The papyrus (*cyperus papyrus*), of which boats were often made. The " flags " were another kind of *cyperus*, from which the Red Sea took its Hebrew name.—**slime.** The river mud, *pitch*, bitumen, rendering the vessel water-tight.

4 sister. Probably Miriam.—**to wit,** to know (cp. Gen. xxiv. 21; 2 Cor. viii. 1).

5 to wash herself. " To bathe " (R.V.). Contrary to modern custom, but apparently permitted in ancient Egypt as monuments show.

10 became her son, by adoption; and thus received the training that fitted him for his special work. Josephus says that Moses was engaged in a campaign against the Ethiopians. Cp. Acts vii. 22.—**Moses.** An Egyptian word, meaning " drawn forth."

11 unto his brethren. According to Acts vii. 23, Moses was now forty. It is plain, from Heb. xi. 24-27, that Moses now boldly espoused the cause of God's people, renouncing the advantages of his rank among the Egyptians.

14 Who made thee, etc. " The reproach of the Christ," Heb. xi. 26.

15 Midian. The Midianites were partly settled and partly nomadic; they were associated with the Ishmaelites (Gen. xxxvii. 25, 28), the Amalekites (Numb. xxiv. 20; Judg. vii. 12), and the Moabites (Numb. xxii. 7). They frequented the deserts south-east of Palestine. The tribe with which Moses was allied was called **Kenites.**

by a well. Cp. Gen. xxix. 10.

18 Reuel, or " Raguel," Numb. x. 29. Perhaps the same as Jethro (ch. iii. 1); or, more likely, Jethro's father, and their grandfather.

24 God heard. This means that God now interposed to deliver them. See on Gen. vi. 6. Observe the climax: " heard "; " remembered "; " looked upon "; " had respect unto " them (" took knowledge of them," R.V.). Comp. Ps. cv. 42; cvi. 44, 45.

CHAPTER III

1 the mountain of God. So called by anticipation: see xix. " Horeb " (meaning *dried*, or *waste*) was probably the name of the group; " Sinai " (meaning " jagged," or " pierced with fissures ") of a single mountain. See xvii. 6; xix. 11.

2 the angel. The Divine Mediator, who is called the " Messenger of the covenant " (Mal. iii. 1). The fire which did not injure the bush is a symbol of God's omnipotence; which, even when put forth for destruction, can preserve those whom He designs to deliver.

5 put off thy shoes. As is still done in the East in the presence of superiors, or on entering a sacred place. Cp. Josh. v. 15.

6 I am the God. For our Lord's use of the incident, see Matt. xxii. 32; Mark xii. 26; Luke xx. 37.

8 a good land. Canaan was large compared with Goshen, and was very fruitful (Deut. viii. 7). The fulfilment of this promise is often referred to, *e.g.* Numb. xiii. 27; Deut. xxvi. 9; Ezek. xx. 6.

10 unto Pharaoh. Not the Pharaoh of chap. i., 80 years previously, but his son Merenptah, a man of similar disposition.

11 Who am I? Moses had now learned that self-distrust which prepared him in his future work to rely wholly upon God's strength. Cp. Jer. i. 4-7.

14 I AM. JAHVEH, frequently written JEHOVAH, by an adoption of vowels from the word (*Adonai*) for " Lord," substituted by the Jews to avoid the pronunciation of the " ineffable Name." The name expresses God's self-existence, faithfulness, and unchangeableness. See on vi. 3.

15 The Lord God of your fathers. More exactly, " The Eternal, the God of your fathers "; *God of Abraham*, etc., reminding the Israelites of the covenant into which He had entered with their ancestors, and His promises. Cp. Gen. l. 24.

18 three days' journey. God designed the complete deliverance of Israel from Egypt; but this limitation of the demand in the first instance made Pharaoh's refusal the more inexcusable.

19 a mighty hand. He will even resist the miraculous display of Almighty power.

22 borrow. The words " borrow " and " lend " in this and the parallel verses, may be better translated " ask " and " grant," as in the early English versions and R.V. The Hebrew word here rendered " borrow " is in Psa. cxxii. 6 translated " pray for "; and the word rendered " lend " is used in 1 Sam. i. 28, where there is evidently no thought of reclaiming the gift. The demand was legitimate, as recompense for asking labour in the days of slavery.

CHAPTER IV

5 That they may believe. Cp. John iii. 2.

10 Slow of speech. Cp. Jeremiah's plea and the answer (Jer. i. 6, 7), and the witness of Acts vii. 22, " Moses was . . . mighty in words. . . ." See also Luke xii. 11, 12.

16 instead of God. The meaning is, " He shall be the organ of thy communications to the people, as thou shalt be of Jehovah's."

21 I will harden. The controlling agency of God does not interfere with the liberty of Pharaoh, nor oblige him to sin; but places him in circumstances which would influence aright a well-disposed mind, while they led a man of his character to the course of resistance and hardihood which he pursued. " As the heat of the sun moistens the wax and dries the clay, softening the one and hardening the other; so, through the long-suffering of God, some receive good and others evil, some are softened and others hardened " (Theodoret, *Quæst.* 12 *in Ex.*). For similar cases see Deut ii. 30; Josh. xi. 20; and cp. John xii. 37-40.

22 My firstborn. These terms are often used afterwards to express the love which God cherishes towards His people. The word "firstborn" especially points to the peculiar prerogative of Israel as the chosen people of God; cp. Hosea xi. 1. The threat which follows was literally fulfilled (xii. 29).

24 kill him. We learn nothing of the way in which Moses' life was threatened (some have conjectured a sudden and serious illness), but he who would serve God and His people must himself keep Divine commands. Moses seems to have neglected, in the case of his own son, the law of Gen. xvii. 10–14. Possibly his wife Zipporah had opposed the circumcision.

25 sharp stone. Sharpened flints were anciently used instead of knives, especially in religious rites.

CHAPTER V

2 Who is the Lord? That is, "I acknowledge Him not as my God." He regarded Jehovah only as the national God of the Hebrews, powerless in comparison with the gods of Egypt.

4 let. An old English word, meaning "hinder." Cp. Rom. i. 13.

7 straw. The bricks commonly used in Egypt were not burnt, but dried in the sun, and mixed with chopped straw to make them more durable.

12 instead of straw. Heb., "*for straw,*" *i.e.*, to serve as straw (so R.V.). The stubble was gathered from the reaped fields; the straw, more plentifully and easily, from the threshing-floors.

CHAPTER VI

1 with a strong hand. Probably, with eagerness and determination; as resolute in dismissing as he had been in retaining them.

3 Jehovah. See iii. 14. This name (JAHVEH) seems to have been used by the patriarchs with other names expressing the revealed perfections of God. See Gen. xiv. 22; xv. 2, 8; xxii. 14; xxiv. 7, 12; xxvii. 20; xxviii. 16; xxxii. 9; xlix. 18, etc. But the full significance of the name, as representing the Divine *self-existence* and *unchangeableness,* and especially God's *unfailing faithfulness,* had never been made known to them as it was now about to be revealed to their descendants. Under the title of "EL-SHADDAI," *God Almighty,* He had entered into covenant with Abraham and his posterity (Gen. xvii. 1). Now when He is about to fulfil one great promise of that covenant, He selects the title JEHOVAH ("The Eternal") as the covenant-name of the God of Israel. So our Lord speaks of His "new name" (Rev. iii. 12).

7 take you to Me. By the renewal of the covenant about to take place on Sinai. See xix. 5.

9 they hearkened not. Mistrust made them deaf to the words of comfort. Their hopefulness when the message first reached them (iv. 31) is in striking contrast with this despair.

12 uncircumcised. Applied to that which is displeasing or unfit for use. "Hearts" (Lev. xxvi. 41); "ear" (Jer. vi. 10). Moses assumes some moral hindrance on his own part.

14 their fathers' houses. This extract (vers. 14–27) from the genealogy of Jacob's family (see Gen. xlvi. 8–10) exhibits the relation of the leaders of Israel to those whom they delivered, and shows that God brought the people out of Egypt in the *fourth* generation, as He had promised (Gen. xv. 16).

20 father's sister. This word may include many female relatives. The Septuagint and Syriac versions render it "cousin."

CHAPTER VII

1 a god to Pharaoh. Moses was a god to Aaron as the revealer of the Divine will (iv. 16); and to Pharaoh as the executor of that will.—**thy prophet.** The meaning of the word "prophet" as not only a *fore*-teller, but a *forth*-teller of the Divine word, is well illustrated here.

11 wise men. The names of two of them, Jannes and Jambres, are given in 2 Tim. iii. 8. It has been a question whether these magicians performed real miracles by Satanic power, or whether they only practised feats of jugglery, such as the Egyptians still perform. Their failure in the case of the lice or gnats (viii. 18) renders the latter supposition the more probable. The *wise men* were, in general, professors of magic arts; the *sorcerers* were mutterers of magic formulæ: the *magicians* were perhaps custodians of the sacred or hieroglyphic books.

15 he goeth out unto the water. It was the time of year (about the middle of June) when the rise of the Nile was officially noted and registered, under the personal superintendence of the king.

17 the river. The Nile was an object of reverence This, and most of the subsequent plagues, resembled in some outward respects natural phenomena not uncommon in Egypt; but here, their miraculous character was demonstrated by the fact that they were precisely foretold; that they occurred with unwonted violence and in rapid succession; that they came and ceased immediately at Moses' word; that the sorcerers could only increase, not remove, the visitation, and at length were forced to retire baffled and powerless; and, above all, by the last and decisive plague.

18 fish. Fish were worshipped by many, and constituted the principal food of a large portion of the people. The ordinary redness of the Nile in summer, occasioned either by ochreous earth brought down from the upper country, or by minute insects, has no injurious effect upon the fish, and does not render the water unfit for use.

19 upon their streams, etc. The tributaries of the Nile, and the canals, trenches, and ponds connected with it.

21 and there was blood. Rather, "and the blood was."

25 seven days. The usual discoloration of the water lasts about three weeks.

the Lord had smitten. As the first miracle, which was merely demonstrative, had been disregarded, the others which followed were to be acts of judgement. Of these, the first nine were preparatory to the tenth, the great act of judgement which, as previously announced (iv. 22, 23), was to carry with it the complete prostration of the adversary, and the deliverance of Israel. They manifested the absolute sovereignty of Jehovah over all creation, especially over the favourite objects of Egyptian idolatry, and whatever the people deemed most valuable. There is also discernible in them a gradual ascent from the lower to the higher departments of nature. They probably succeeded each other very rapidly, and were all comprised between January and April.

CHAPTER VIII

2 frogs. These the Egyptians reverenced.

3 come into thine house. The Nile and the neighbouring marshes are commonly full of frogs, as the narrative itself implies (9, 11), but they are generally kept under by serpents, crocodiles, and storks, so as to occasion no serious annoyance. Some have supposed that there was a natural connexion between this and the foregoing plague, as the corrupt state of the Nile would contribute to the increase of these creatures; but, whatever natural agencies might be employed, the plague would still be miraculous." See on ch. vii. 17.

9 Glory over me. "You may have the honour of saying when" (*Moffatt*).

10 that thou mayest know. The sudden removal of the plague on the "morrow" would be as strong a proof of God's power as its infliction.

16 lice. A common annoyance of the country, intensely aggravated on this occasion. The Greek translators, who lived in Egypt, supposed *mosquitoes* to be meant.

26 the abomination. This may mean, the killing of their sacred animals and the use of the flesh in a sacrificial feast will be "an abomination to the Egyptians."

CHAPTER IX

3 the camels. Cp. Gen. xii. 16. Camels do not appear to have been used in the interior of Egypt, but on the frontier.

6 all the cattle of Egypt died. That is, there was death among all the cattle of Egypt; no kind was spared.

7 not one of the cattle, etc. This exemption showed clearly that the plague was from Jehovah, the God of Israel. But Pharaoh, in his hardness of heart, probably attributed it to the Hebrews' superior skill in the treatment of cattle.

9 dust. The irritation produced by dust and heat occasions many purulent diseases in Egypt, especially ophthalmia.

11 the magicians. The preceding divine judgements had been principally directed against the objects of idolatrous worship. This plague affected the chief supporters of this idolatry, who now retire, and do not appear again in the history.

15 I will stretch out. Rather, "I *might* stretch out," etc.; "and thou *shouldest* be cut off from the earth. But in very deed for this cause I have made thee stand"; meaning either, "I have preserved thee through all" (as the Septuagint understood the passage), or "I have raised thee up" (as it is rendered in Rom. ix. 17), "in order to make thee see My power," etc. Pharaoh was not destroyed at once, that God might make the more signal and varied displays of His power.

18 hail. Violent hailstorms are rare in Lower Egypt.

20 He that feared, etc. This shows that on some of the Egyptians the plagues were beginning to exert a salutary effect.

23 fire ran along upon the ground. Or, "ran to the earth" (so R.V.), *i.e.*, the lightning struck into the ground.

31 bolled. "Bolled" means *come into blossom*, which was the case about the end of February. In the case of the barley and the flax, the stalk, being stiff, was broken by the hail. The wheat and rye (rather *spelt*) had not risen to a stalk; and the blade would yield, and so escape serious injury.

CHAPTER X

4 coast. The word "coast" in old English means *district*, or *border* (so R.V.), without any reference to the sea and land. See Josh. i. 4.

6 neither thy fathers, etc. This visitation (as the terms of the threatening imply) was well known in Egypt as a terrible scourge; but now surpassed any that had gone before. The fearful nature of this plague may be learned from Joel i. 11.

7 this [man]. The word "man" is not in the Hebrew. Some render it, "How long shall this *course of conduct* be a snare to us?" referring to Pharaoh's obstinate opposition.

10 look to it. Or, "See, that evil is before you"; *i.e.*, "Your purposes are evil."

13 the east wind brought the locusts. *i.e.*, over from Arabia.

15 was darkened. As is the case even with ordinary swarms of locusts. These, however, were unusual in size and number.

19 west wind. The west or "sea-wind" in Egypt, blowing from north-west, would carry the locusts to the "Sea of Suph," or "weeds"; *i.e.*, the Red Sea.

21 darkness. This visitation is connected by many with the Egyptian sirocco or chamsin—a hot, scorching wind from the desert of Sahara, sometimes accompanied with dense darkness, owing to the atmosphere being filled with fine sand.

22 thick darkness. The sun was one of the chief objects of Egyptian worship.

23 light in their dwellings. The sirocco did not extend to the district of Goshen, being miraculously withheld or turned aside.

CHAPTER XI

1 And the Lord said, etc. Vers. 1–3 are to be taken as a parenthesis; either repeating what God *had* said to Moses before his last interview with Pharaoh, or recording a secret revelation made to him while in the monarch's presence, which, after a short silence, he begins to utter (ver. 4) before he withdrew.

4 will I go out. This, which was the last and decisive plague, was also the one most plainly inflicted by direct Divine interposition, not only bearing no resemblance to any natural phenomenon, but occurring without intervention of any known agency.

5 all the firstborn. According to the original threatening to Pharaoh in ch. iv. 23.

behind the mill. The lowest slaves in the household ground the corn for the family in a hand-mill made of two stones.

beasts. So that even the childless would be smitten in the loss of the sacred animals.

6 a great cry. Egyptians are loud and vehement in uttering their grief.

CHAPTER XII

1 And the Lord spake, etc. The final plague is introduced by the institution and first celebration of the Passover. The Israelites were now to reckon the months of the year from the first month of their release (Deut. xvi. 1).

4 according to the number. The Jewish practice was, that not fewer than ten persons, nor more than twenty, should partake of one lamb.

5 without blemish. An emblem of Him who was "holy, harmless, undefiled," and is hence denominated "a Lamb without blemish and without spot" (1 Pet. i. 19; Heb. ix. 14).—**or from the goats.** Kids were taken as well as lambs as late as the great Passover in King Josiah's reign (2 Chron. xxxv. 7). In later times lambs were chiefly used.

6 evening. The time was between the ninth

hour (about 3 p.m.) and sunset, when the fifteenth day began.

7 take of the blood. Thus it became a ceremonial expiation to all who partook of the lamb within the house. For the "blood of sprinkling," see Heb. ix. 22; xii. 24; 1 Pet. i. 2.

8 unleavened bread. As symbolical of inward purity; the fermentation produced by leaven implying a process of corruption, emblematical of depravity (1 Cor. v. 8). There is also here a memorial of their *haste* in departing (Deut. xvi. 3).—**bitter [herbs].** This has been supposed to represent the bitter bondage of the Hebrews in Egypt, also to set forth the necessity of godly sorrow for sin.

9 the purtenance. "The inwards" (R.V.).

11 your loins girded, etc. That is, as travellers; for in the house the robe was usually left loose, and the sandals taken off. The attitude was that of *faith*, expecting immediate deliverance. This part of the institution does not appear to have been permanent.

11 passover. This word represents the meaning of the Hebrew "Pesach," or Chaldee "Pascha"; which, however, includes the idea of *protection*: the "passing" being as of a bird with outstretched wings. See ver. 27. This passing *over* (in mercy) is expressed by a different word from the passing *through* (in judgement), ver. 12.

12 gods. This may mean either *princes* (see Isa. xix. 1), or the objects of idolatrous worship; but perhaps it rather signifies *powers* in general, referring to whatever constituted the chief objects of their dependence.

14 a memorial. The Passover was both a memorial of Israel's preservation and deliverance, and a remarkable type of the great Sacrifice by which a greater deliverance was to be accomplished. Cp. Luke xxii. 19.

15 unleavened bread. Hence it is frequently called "the feast of unleavened bread." Lev. xxiii. 6; Luke xxii. 1; and cp. Acts xii. 3; xx. 6.

26 What mean ye by this service? The Jews have formalised this command by requiring the son in the family, at a set time during the celebration of the paschal supper, to ask his father, "What meaneth this?" To which the father answers, "We eat this Passover because the Lord passed over the houses of our fathers in Egypt. We eat these bitter herbs because the Egyptians made the lives of our fathers bitter in Egypt," etc. And cp. Josh. iv. 6.

29 the firstborn. If this was occasioned by pestilence, as some have suggested, still the miraculous nature of the visitation is sufficiently apparent in the facts; that it broke out precisely at the time predicted by Moses; that it destroyed all the firstborn in one night; that it extended to cattle as well as human beings; and that the Israelites were exempt from the scourge.

32 and bless me also. Showing his abject terror of what might yet follow: "Let us part friends."

33 We be all dead men. They seem to have feared a still more terrible plague, which might destroy them all.

35 jewels. Or, "vessels." On the "borrowing" and "lending," see on iii. 22.

36 such things as they required. This phrase is not in the original, which means simply, "let them have what they asked" (R.V.). Thus God took care that the Israelites should obtain their hard-earned wages from their oppressors.

37 Succoth. Or, "booths." This was their first station.

Six hundred thousand. If the word *Eleph* (fr. *Alaph*), here translated "thousand," be understood in its other meaning of "family," one of the great difficulties as to the numbers of the people is removed. If there were 600,000 men, the total number of the Israelites would be between two and three millions. (See Flinders Petrie: *Researches in Sinai.*)

38 mixed multitude. The "mixed multitude" were probably in part Egyptians, and children of mixed marriages (Lev. xxiv. 10, 11).

40 four hundred and thirty years. From the first calling of Abraham (Gen. xii.) to this time, exactly 430 years elapsed.

47 neither shall ye break a bone. This command was added probably because the Passover was intended to be typical as well as commemorative. See John xix. 33, 36.

49 that sojourneth. This shows that dedication to God, rather than descent from Abraham, entitled the Israelites to their privileges. Others could become "children of Abraham" by *adoption.* See Matt. iii. 9.

CHAPTER XIII

2 firstborn. This applied only, as afterwards explained (vers. 12, 15), when the first child was a son.

9 eyes. This figurative command is derived from the Egyptian custom of wearing jewels upon the hand and forehead. The Jews, however, of later times, interpreted it literally, wearing passages of the Law written on parchment, called *phylacteries*, the Greek form of the Heb. for "frontlets." Exod. xiii. 1-16; Deut. vi. 8.

13 ass. The ass is probably put for all domestic animals (of which it was the chief) not fit for sacrifice. Hence the law is afterwards extended to the "firstling of unclean beasts" generally. See Numb. xviii. 15.

18 harnessed. Either "in an orderly manner," or "equipped"; *i.e.*, prepared for their march; "armed" (R.V.).

21 a pillar of a cloud. This symbol of the Divine presence, called the Shekinah, seems to have had the appearance of a lofty column.

CHAPTER XIV

2 turn. That is, to the right, southwards. The Red Sea, as late as the Roman time, extended through the Bitter Lakes to near Ismailia (now on the Suez Canal). Here it was very shallow and therefore the most likely place for the "strong east wind" (ver. 21) to blow the waters back and leave a dry crossing. See Flinders Petrie: *Researches in Sinai*, and Sir J. W. Dawson: *Egypt and Syria* (R.T.S.).

Pi-hahiroth. This word, if, as is likely, it be Egyptian or Coptic, means, "a place where grass grows."

5 turned against. Or, "changed towards" (R.V.).

7 chariots. The ancient monuments of Egypt represent its military force as consisting entirely of war-chariots and infantry.

8 with a high hand. As conquerors rather than as fugitives.

14 hold your peace. That is, "leave it to Him." The frequent murmurings and rebellions of the Israelites are pathetically commemorated in Psa. cvi.; and in Psa. lxxviii. forcibly contrasted with God's mercies.

21 a strong east wind. The use of natural agencies may be observed in many miracles, both of the Old and New Testaments.

23 went in. Pharaoh and his host, hurrying onward in their pursuit with blind impetuosity, probably did not perceive the danger of their position, amid the twofold darkness of the night and of the cloud, till it was too late to return.

25 took off. Some ancient versions read "bound," or "clogged."

28 there remained. This event was known to the surrounding nations and aided the subsequent conquests of the Israelites. See xv. 16; Josh. ii. 9–11.

31 that great work. Literally, "the great hand"; *i.e.*, the great power.

CHAPTER XV

1 Then sang Moses. When books were almost unknown, national histories were preserved in songs. God, on this as on other occasions (see Deut. xxxii.), directed Moses to use this mode of perpetuating the remembrance of His mercies; cp. 2 Sam. i. 18.

triumphed gloriously. Or, "He is highly exalted" (R.V. marg.).

2 will prepare Him a habitation. Rather, "will glorify Him." So it is rendered in the old English versions, in accordance with the Greek, Syriac, Latin, etc., and with the parallelism of the passage ("will praise Him," R.V.).

11 fearful in praises. *i.e.*, to be praised with solemn awe.

14 Palestina. "Philistia" (R.V.). The Philistines were among the most warlike of the enemies of Israel. See xiii. 17; 1 Sam. iv., etc.

16 still as a stone. *i.e.*, remain quiet, so as to offer no opposition. The delay of the forty years' wandering lessened but did not destroy this dread on the part of the Canaanites. See Numb. xx. 18; xxii.; Josh. ii. 10; ix. 10.

17 the mountain of Thine inheritance. The whole of Canaan was hilly; but this seems prophetically to designate the site of the future temple.

20 Miriam. Or, "Mary"; it being the same name; a "prophetess," as speaking under Divine direction.—**with dances.** A dance of triumph, as in Judges xi. 34. Cp. Psa. cxlix. 3; cl. 4.

22 Shur. Surrounding the head of the Gulf of Suez, and called Etham (Numb. xxxiii. 8), from the town of that name on its edge (xiii. 20).

23 bitter. The brackish water found in the wells of the desert would be very distasteful after the water of the Nile. Arabs regard the water of Marah as the worst in the desert. These trials would teach trust in God's providence.

24 the people murmured. Praises proceeding from gratified self-love will soon be changed into murmurs when our circumstances alter. See Psa. cvi. 12–14.

25 a tree. In some countries water is purified naturally by similar means; but neither Moses, who was well acquainted with this part of the desert, nor its present Arab inhabitants, to whom such a remedy would be invaluable, appear to know anything of it. Some have supposed that the tree was the *ghurkud*, which is found near the bitter springs of Arabia, and bears a refreshing berry, which might make water palatable. But these berries are not ripe at the time of year when the Israelites were at Marah.

27 Elim. Probably Wady Ghurundel—a fertile valley, where, according to travellers, fountains, and trees, especially tamarisks and palm-trees, are still found. It has been noted that the wells equal the number of the tribes, and the trees the number of the Elders (xxiv. 9).

encamped. The places in the subsequent narrative were probably the head-quarters of Moses and the priests; the people spreading themselves over the neighbourhood. Numb. xxxiii. has a list of encampments, those only, apparently, being mentioned which were distinguished by prolonged stay, or by some remarkable event.

CHAPTER XVI

Would to God. Rather, "Would that" (so R.V.).

we did eat bread to the full. Having wandered a whole month through deserts, they had not only consumed the provisions they brought from Egypt, but had probably lost or killed many of their cattle. And the people, as yet weak in faith, reverted discontentedly to the past, and looked despondingly to the future; cp. Numb. xi. 4, 5.

5 sixth day. An indication that the Sabbath was known among the Hebrews before the Law was given at Sinai.

13 quails came up. One of those vast flocks which in spring migrate northwards from Africa and Arabia was brought by God over this spot. See Numb. xi. 31, 32.

15 It is manna. Rather, "they said one to another, What is this?" Others translate: "It is a portion" or "It is a gift" (of God). This provision began just when other food failed, it accompanied the Hebrews in all their forty years' wanderings, and it ceased on the day after they began to eat the corn of Canaan. It was doubled and preserved every sixth day, and withheld every Sabbath. See Numb. xi. 7, 8. For our Lord's reference to the event, see John vi. 31, 32.

16 omer. "Omer" is probably the name of a bowl or vessel in common use (vers. 18, 33). As a *measure*, it occurs only in this chapter; and must be distinguished from the homer.

22 told Moses; *i.e.*, of the double quantity that was found; an expression of astonishment. The Sabbath had, in all probability, been practically disregarded during the years of bondage.

34 Testimony. That is, the Ark of the testimony (see xxv. 16), which was soon afterwards made. This book being written after the ark was made, the fact is anticipated in the history.

CHAPTER XVII

6 I will stand. Probably manifesting Himself in the pillar of *cloud*.

9 Amalek. The tribes of the Amalekites appear to have wandered through the Desert of Paran (now called Et-Tih), which occupied the tableland between Horeb and Palestine. Deut. xxv. 17, 18, shows that this attack was marked by peculiar craftiness and cruelty. Their hostility was lasting (Judges iii. 13; vi. 33; vii. 12; 1 Sam. xv.; xxx.).

9 the rod of God. Moses, as commander of the host of Israel, not only watches the fight, but lifts up the wonder-working rod in sight of the people, bringing down help from on high (Psa. cxli. 2), and assuring them of victory, as fighting under the banner of Jehovah. See ver. 15.

CHAPTER XVIII

2 after. Probably after the occurrence in iv. 25.

11 for, etc. Or, "yea: [He is so] in the [very] thing that they [the Egyptians] acted haughtily against them" [the Israelites]; meaning that the wickedness of the Egyptians towards the Israelites became an occasion for God to display His almighty power and supremacy.

12 to eat bread. A thanksgiving feast. Cp. Deut. xii. 7; 1 Chron. xxix. 22.

21 able men. Jethro's judicious proposal, which he piously made subject to the command of God (ver. 23), accorded with a subsequent Divine arrangement (Numb. xi. 16, 17); and probably laid the foundation of the municipal polity of the Hebrews. The Saxon institutions of Alfred resembled this plan.

22 priests. Probably the chiefs of families, who, in patriarchal times, discharged the duties of priests.

CHAPTER XIX

2 the desert of Sinai. Probably either Wady esh Sheikh, or Wady Feiran. Here the Israelites remained nearly a year.

3 the Lord called. The beginning of those transactions between God and the chosen nation, called the Covenant of Sinai; by which God became their King, establishing a theocracy, typical of the spiritual dominion of the future Messiah. On God's part, it began with a reference to the recent deliverance (ver. 4), and with promises of future blessings, as reasons for their obedience (ver. 5); which they, on their part, promised (ver. 8). Upon this, a solemn assembly was called (ver. 10); a summary of the Law was given, first orally (xx.), then through Moses (xx. 22-xxiii. 33); and the covenant was ratified, first with blood (xxiv. 6), and then by a Divine vision, and a sacred feast (vers. 9-11). After this, Moses twice ascended the mountain to meet God; and went often into "the tabernacle of the congregation" (the Tent of Meeting) to receive His instructions.

4 I bare you on eagles' wings. Alluding to the eagle's care for her young. Cp. Deut. xxxii. 11. The words "I bare you on eagles' wings and brought you unto myself" are inscribed on the monument on the Thames Embankment to the officers and men of the Royal Air Force who fell in the War of 1914-1918.

5 My covenant. The Jews, as a nation, broke this covenant; and God afterwards promised to make with them a new and better covenant: see Jer. xxxi. 33; xxxii. 40; Heb. viii. 7-10. This *national* covenant must be distinguished from that covenant of grace, the blessings of which are *personal*, and limited to true believers.—**all the earth is Mine.** This assertion of Jehovah's sovereignty over the whole earth would guard the Israelites against the heathen notion that He was merely a national deity, whose dominion is confined to His own peculiar people and their land.

6 kingdom of priests. A sacred kingdom, all the subjects of which are "priests," separated from all pollution, for the service of Jehovah, their invisible King. See 1 Pet. ii. 9; Rev. i. 6.

12 up into the mount. Rather, as in ver. 13, "up to the mountain." The people were not to approach the mountain during their three days of preparation; but as soon as the trumpet gave the signal they were to go up to the foot of the mountain (ver. 17); but even then not to pass the bounds (ver. 21).

19 Moses spake. Saying, "I exceedingly fear and quake" (Heb. xii. 21). The allusion to this awfully august scene in Heb. xii. 18-24 shows how far the sublimest material display of the power of Jehovah is surpassed by the spiritual glory of the gospel. Its effect upon the minds of the people is described in Deut. v. 24-28; xviii. 16.

CHAPTER XX

1 God spake. In these commandments a natural order is observable. They present (1) JEHOVAH as the *sole object* of worship; (2) the *mode* of worship, accordant with His *spiritual* nature; (3) the *intelligent reverence;* and (4) the *constant regularity* required in worship. They then provide rules for social life; beginning with (5) its foundation in family relations; and forbidding any actions injurious to (6) the *life,* (7) the *personal purity,* (8) the *property,* and (9) the *reputation* of others; as well as (10) all selfish and irregular desires. It is further to be noticed, that though most of these laws specify *actions,* the ninth refers to *words,* and the tenth extends to the *thoughts* and *desires* of the heart.

The Ten Commandments are summed up and enforced by our Lord (Matt. xxii. 36-40) and in part by St. Paul (Rom. xiii. 9, 10).

2 thy God. The peculiar claims of Jehovah here mentioned are (1) His covenant-relation to His people: "thy God"; (2) His marvellous deliverance of them: "out of Egypt."

3 before Me. Rather, "besides Me." Jehovah *alone* is God; cp. 1 Cor. viii. 5, 6.

4 likeness. *i.e.,* for worship, as the Egyptians did of the sun, the bull, the crocodile, etc. See Deut. iv. 15-19.

5 visiting the iniquity. This is not spoken of eternal condemnation, but of the temporal consequences of sin; and is to be understood as modified by the repentance of either parents or children. See Ezek. xviii.

6 unto thousands. That is, unto thousands *of generations;* or, in other words, *for ever.* See Psa. cxxxvi.

7 in vain. Referring, in the first instance, to profanity and false swearing (lit. "Thou shalt not lift up the name of Jehovah thy God for vanity," or "for falsehood"), and hence to irreverence in any form.

8 Remember. Implying that the Sabbath was an ancient, though perhaps it had become a neglected and almost forgotten, institution; and the command required constant attention. The variations in the language of this command on the various occasions on which it was given (see ch. xxxi. 13; Lev. xix. 3, 30) indicate that there is no necessary connection between the *seventh* day and the *rest* day, and that therefore, quite consistently with the spirit and design of the law, the day of the week might be changed in a new dispensation. The Sabbath among the Jews had ceremonial regulations of temporary duration; but these are clearly distinguishable from the original law, which was regarded and enforced by our Lord.

12 that thy days may be long. See Eph. vi. 2, 3; which, as addressed to Gentiles (ii., iii. 1), shows that this promise (Eph. vi. 2), though primarily made to the Jews, was not limited to them as part of their national covenant, but has an extensive meaning and application.

19 lest we die. The people, overwhelmed with terror at this Divine manifestation, abandon the privilege which God had given to them of direct communion with Himself, and choose in preference the mediatorship of Moses. For particulars see Deut. v., xviii. Cp. Gal. iii. 19, 20.

20 God is come to prove you. By making you to feel your own sinfulness and His majesty, thus inducing a becoming reverence towards Him, and dread of sin.

23 Ye shall not make, etc. These laws disclose a superiority to all the known maxims and practices of the ancient world, and a preparation for the still higher principles of Christianity. In the repetition of the Law at the end of the forty years in the wilderness, some of these laws appear in an enlarged and more spiritual form (see Deuteronomy throughout); whilst in the prophetical writings in subsequent ages, we find a still nearer approximation to the development of morality and holiness in the Gospel. Note the distinction between the *moral* law, which requires spiritual and perfect obedience, and the punishments and rewards of which God Himself inflicts; and the *political* law, which had reference to the outward conduct, and the violation of which was punishable by the civil magistrate. The latter, by restrictive enactments, aimed to diminish the frequency and to remedy the mischiefs of existing evil practices, afterwards emphatically condemned in the New Test. See Matt. xix. 8, 9.

25 thy tool. Possibly to prevent the idolatrous sculpture and licentious practices of the Egyptians and other heathen nations being introduced into the worship of Jehovah; cp. Josh. viii. 30, 31.

CHAPTER XXI

2 a Hebrew servant. Selling himself through poverty, or being sold for theft. Slavery was at that time almost universal in the world; but the Jewish law was, for the slave, a law of mercy. (See also Deut. v. 14; xii. 18; xvi. 11, and compare with the condition of the slave in ancient and modern heathen lands.) Many social usages were permitted for a time to the Hebrews, through "the hardness of their heart" (Matt. xix. 8), *i.e.*, because they were not prepared for a nobler and more liberal code.

4 a wife. That is, one of the master's own slaves.

6 judges. Or rather, "unto God" (Elohim), who was supposed to preside at the tribunal. "Unto the local sanctuary" (*Moffatt*). See Psa. lxxxii. 6; John x. 34, 35.—**awl.** The boring of the ear, in sign of servitude, which was customary in Syria and other countries, denoted the strict and close obedience which such a servant was to render to his master. See on Psa. xl. 6.

11 without money. By giving new rights to the *slave-wife,* this law both protected her and restricted the practice of polygamy.

12 He that smiteth a man. Evidently, *designedly.*

13 deliver. "If it was accidental" (*Moffatt*).—**appoint.** As was afterwards done. See Numb. xxxv.; Josh. xx.

15 smiteth his father. God, as the Divine Father, requires that parents be regarded as peculiarly sacred. Any injury or dishonour done to them (ver. 17) is to be treated as an insult offered to Him.

21 his money. In the death of his slave he is mulcted to the extent of the slave's value. The homicide of a slave was now for the first time recognised as culpable. The way was thus opened for a legislation still more humane. Cp. vers. 26, 27, where a personal injury to a slave was made a ground for compulsory emancipation. The "continuing for a day or two" was to be taken as presumptive proof that the fatal result was not *intended.*

23 life for life. As a principle of *civil jurisprudence* this is equitable, and is found in the laws of other nations; but its perversion by *personal* revenge led to abuses condemned by our Lord: see Matt. v. 38, 39.

27 his tooth's sake. These injuries to the "eye" and to the "tooth" seem to be mentioned in this law as the *greatest* and the *least,* including by implication all other personal injuries.

28 the ox shall be surely stoned. To keep before the people the sacredness of human life, even the irrational animal is treated as a murderer.

CHAPTER XXII

1 a sheep. The larger amount of restitution required in this case than in that in ver. 4 seems to arise from the persistency in crime shown by the man proceeding to sell or kill; also from the increased difficulty, and perhaps expense, of proving the theft.

2 breaking up. Or, "breaking *in*" (R.V.), which is commonly done in Eastern countries by digging through the mud wall: see Matt. xxiv. 43.

3 for he should. "For" to be omitted. If a thief steals in the day, and is not killed, then "he shall make full restitution: and if he cannot, he shall be sold."

13 let him bring it for witness. That is, some part of the animal, as the horns, hoofs, etc., which the man must bring as a proof of his innocence.

15 if it be a hired thing, etc. "If it be hired it goes in the hire"; *i.e.,* the hire is supposed to cover common wear and damage. Of course, wilful and careless mischief would be excepted.

17 the dowry of virgins. This law is placed here partly because the daughter was regarded as the property of the father, and was paid for by the bridegroom, either in money or by service. See Gen. xxix. 15–18, etc.

18 a witch. All pretensions to witchcraft involved the guilt of doing homage to supernatural powers other than God; cp. Lev. xix. 26, 31.

27 sleep. In the East the *hyke*, or cloak, is often the poor man's only bed and covering at night.

28 the gods. *Elohim,* meaning, perhaps, God, the King of Israel (so R.V.); referring to murmuring against His laws or officers. See on xxi. 6.

29 liquors. Heb. "tear"; *i.e.,* the oil or wine pressed from fruit; and perhaps the valuable gums frankincense and myrrh. See Matt. ii. 11.

CHAPTER XXIII

2, 3 Thou shalt not follow, etc. "Nor must you bear witness in court so as to side with an unjust majority; neither must you be partial to a poor man's plea" (*Moffatt*).

5 and wouldest forbear, etc. Perhaps, "thou shalt forbear to leave (it) him (alone); thou shalt surely loosen (it)." Though the grammatical construction of this sentence is difficult, the sense is plain.

6 Thou shalt not. Vers. 6–9 are addressed to *judges.*

19 mother's milk. "Probably to inculcate a tender appreciation of the natural order and of the relation between a mother and her offspring. It was against nature to make the mother an accomplice in the death of her child." (F. B. Meyer: *Devotional Commentary: Exodus.* R.T.S.)

20 angel. See Exod. xiv. 19, 20; and cp. Isa. lxiii, 9.

21 My name is in him. That is, "My attributes are his."

31 the sea of the Philistines. The Mediterranean Sea; also called the "hinder sea" (Deut. xi. 24); the "western sea" (Deut. xxxiv. 2, R.V. marg.; Joel ii. 20).—**the river.** From the Desert of Shur or Paran, on the south of Judea, to the river Euphrates; actually possessed only under David and Solomon. See on Gen. xv. 18; and 1 Kings iv. 21.

CHAPTER XXIV

4 Twelve. Cp. the twelve stones of Josh. iv. 3, 8, 9.

8 sprinkled it on the people. On this ratification of the covenant with blood, see the comment in Heb. ix. 18–22.

10 the God of Israel. That is, the bright symbol of His presence; rendered by the Chaldee version, "the glory of the God of Israel"; by the Greek, "the place where the God of Israel stood."—**a paved work,** etc. Or rather, "a work of brilliant sapphire, even like the very heaven (R.V.) for brightness."

11 laid not His hand. That is, not to destroy them. Part of the sacrifices was eaten by the elders of Israel, in token of friendship with God, in conformity with a very ancient custom. See Gen. xxvi. 30; xxxi. 54.

CHAPTER XXV

3 gold. The people had probably acquired considerable wealth in gold and silver from the gifts of the Egyptians (xii. 35, 36) and from the spoil of those found "dead upon the seashore" (xiv. 30) at the Red Sea.

brass. Rather, "copper"; as also in xxxi. 4.

4 and blue, etc. That is, some materials dyed with those colours, which were very costly.

5 badgers. Possibly a species of *seal* or *sea-cow,* which abounded on the shores of the Sinaitic peninsula, and supplied skins for tents and sandals. ("Seal-skins," R.V., "*or,* porpoise-skins," marg.)—**shittim.** This was probably the *acacia vera,* still called "shunt" by the Arabs, which produces gum-arabic ("acacia wood," R.V.).

7 ephod. "apron," see xxvii. 4, 6.

10 ark. Rather, "chest," or "box." It was about four feet long, by about two and a half feet broad and deep.

11 crown. Or, "rim"; and at ver. 24.

16 Testimony. That is, the tables of the Decalogue; which was called the *Testimony,* because it bore witness to God's covenant with Israel, and to the nature of His requirements.

17 mercy seat. Heb., "a lid" or "cover," hence the seat or the throne of mercy, or a propitiation. The "seat" was a rectangular plate of gold. It was the "throne of grace" (Heb. iv. 16), where God's sovereign mercy was displayed in the bright cloud which rested upon it (ver. 22). The Greek name of the mercy seat, literally "the propitiatory," is applied to Christ in Rom. iii. 25.

18 cherubim. This is the plural form. The word "cherubims," as read in most editions of the A.V. is a mistake. This was probably a symbolical representation of the Divine presence, with special reference to the manifestation of mercy. See Psa. lxxx. 1; and on Gen. iii. 24.

19 even of the mercy seat. Rather, "out of the mercy-seat," so that they formed a component part of it.

22 between the two cherubim. Hence God is frequently spoken of, and addressed in prayer, as dwelling "between the cherubim" (2 Kings xix. 15; Psa. lxxx. 1).

27 over against. That is, on the top of the legs, which came up to the rim of the table.

29 dishes, etc. Probably to put the bread in. The other articles are spoons or cups for the frankincense (Lev. xxiv. 7); and bowls for wine for the drink offerings, as well as to hold the blood of the sacrifices, which was to be sprinkled within the sanctuary.

30 shewbread. Heb., "bread of faces," or "of presence"; from its being placed in the *presence* of the Lord; the "continual bread" (Numb. iv. 7). The shewbread was the offering of the Israelites to their Divine King (Lev. xxxiv. 8); the *twelve* loaves having reference to the number of the tribes.

31 candlestick. Rather, "lamp," or "candelabrum." A representation of the lampstand in the second temple is found on the Arch of Titus at Rome. The word rendered "bowl" may designate the cup of a flower. The Jews say that the "knops" resembled pomegranates, and the "flowers" lilies. For the symbolical meaning of the candlestick, see Zech. iv. 2, 3, 12–14; Rev. i. 12, 20; iv. 5; xi. 4.

38 tongs. Or, "snuffers," or "lamp-scissors."

CHAPTER XXVI

1 the tabernacle. This word means, "dwelling-place" (*i.e.,* of God); and designates the interior structure of wood covered by embroidered curtains; over which was the *tent*—a triple covering, first one of woven goats' hair, and two above of skins. It contained two compartments—the holy place, and the most holy—separated by the great vail. It was formed of forty-eight boards of shittim (or acacia) wood, about seventeen feet long and two and a half broad; covered with gold, and resting on bases of silver; and bound together by five transverse bars or beams of the same wood, likewise plated with gold; so that it had the appearance inside of a wall of gold. The length was about fifty-two or fifty-four feet, the breadth sixteen or eighteen, and the height about eighteen. It was so constructed, as to be easily taken apart and carried from place to place. For its symbolical reference see Heb. ix. 14, 24. The ark of God had no more substantial dwelling-place till the building of the temple. It was the seat and symbol of the Divine kingdom upon earth. With evident reference to the ancient temple, it is written, "The Word was made flesh, and dwelt [tabernacled] among us" (John i. 14). See also John ii. 19; 2 Cor. vi. 16; Eph. ii. 22; Col. i. 19; ii. 9; Heb. viii. 2; ix. 11, 24.

6 taches. A Celtic word, the same as "tack," found also in the derived word "attach," and meaning buckles or clasps.

7 goats' [hair]. A coarse sort of cloth made from goats' hair is still used in the East for covering tents. The Asiatic goat has longer and finer hair than the European. "*a covering,*" *i.e.,* "a tent over the tabernacle" (R.V.).

10 which coupleth the second. *i.e.,* to correspond with the first or "outmost" curtain.

17 tenons. "pegs."

31 vail. The vail of separation between the holy place, where the priests ministered daily, and the most holy, into which the high priest *alone* entered once a year, seems to represent the concealment of God's brightest glory from the view of man, as well as to intimate that, except through the future atonement, the infinitely holy majesty of God must be inaccessible to sinful man. When a further revelation of the Divine character was made, and the plan of redemption was completed by the death of Christ, the vail was rent from top to bottom (Matt. xxvii. 51). See also Heb. x. 19, 20.

CHAPTER XXVII

1 an altar. This was a hollow wooden chest plated with copper, about nine feet square, and five feet in height, with a grating inside, upon which the sacrifices and the fuel were laid, with an ash-pan underneath. Upon the horns of the altar the blood of the victim was put with the priest's finger (Lev. iv. 25, 30); and sometimes sacrifices were bound to them (Psa. cxviii. 27). For an example of taking sanctuary at the altar, see 1 Kings i. 50, 51.

9 twined. Or, "netted." It appears to have been open work except at the entrance. The court was about 175 feet in length, and 87 in breath. It was entirely uncovered. The entrance was on the east side, and was 35 feet broad. As the people at large were not permitted to enter the tabernacle, on account of its peculiar sacredness, this court was constructed in connexion with it, that the worshippers might here personally appear before God, and hold communion with Him as present among them.

10 fillets. Rather, "cross-bars," to connect the capitals of the pillars, and sustain the curtains.

17 filleted. Rather, "joined with rods."

burn always. The words "always" here, and "continually" in Lev. xxiv. 2, mean *every night*, as explained in ver. 21, and in xxx. 7, 8, where the *dressing* the lamps in the morning is distinguished from the *lighting* them in the evening. See also 1 Sam. iii. 3. It is probable that during the day the outer vail of the tabernacle was lifted up, as in ordinary tents, so as to give sufficient light for the ministrations of the sanctuary.

21 tabernacle of the congregation. Or, "tent of meeting" (R.V.); *i.e.*, at which the priests, and on certain occasions, the people, gathered before Jehovah. Observe that the "meeting" was with *Him.* This expression is here applied to the sanctuary for the first time, but is often used afterwards.

CHAPTER XXVIII

1 thy brother. This is the first express appointment of Aaron and his sons to the priesthood, though the Divine intention had been intimated before. In patriarchal times the head of the family, or of the community, generally offered sacrifices on their behalf; and occasionally individuals, on account of eminence of character, or other circumstances, acted as priests beyond the circle of their own family or tribe. See xx. 24; xxiv. 5; Gen. xiv. 18–20.

2 beauty. The richness and beauty of the high priest's dress befitted the splendid ceremonial which shadowed forth the spiritual glories of the Redeemer and of the Gospel.

6 ephod. A priestly garment of this kind is represented in ancient Egyptian paintings. It was a close vest, reaching from under the shoulders nearly to the knees, fastened around with a girdle (ver. 8), and above with straps (ver. 7), chained and clasped with two engraved onyx stones set in gold.

11 ouches. Settings or sockets. The word also appeared as "nouche" and "owche."

12 a memorial. Thus Aaron appeared before Jehovah as the representative of the people whose name he bore.

15 breastplate of judgement. So called because worn when the high priest obtained from God oracular decisions. See ver. 30.

17 stones. It is hardly possible to ascertain what some of these gems were. The "ligure" (ver. 19) is probably "jacinth" (R.V.), or perhaps opal.

30 the Urim and the Thummim. "The Lights and the Perfections"; some means (now unknown) of ascertaining the Divine will by lot (Numb. xxvii. 27).

32 a hole. Rather, "and there shall be an opening for the head" (R.V.); probably for the priest's head.—**habergeon.** A piece of armour defending the neck and breast.

33 pomegranates. The form of the pomegranate rendered it particularly suitable for imitation in carved work.

36 Holiness to the Lord. This was evidently symbolical of the holiness necessary to him who mediates between man and God; Lev. x. 4; Heb. vii. 26.

37 mitre. Or, "turban": so "bonnet" in ver. 40.

41 consecrate. The Hebrew word here translated "consecrate," literally means "fill the hand." Then "to give a charge or office over to any one." Cp. the word *mandate* (Lat. *mandare*).

CHAPTER XXIX

10 shall put their hands. To imply that they needed "remission of sins." See, for the contrast, Heb. vii. 26–28.

22 rump. The fat tail (R.V.) of the Arabian sheep.

24 shalt wave. A mode of presenting the offering to God. So "heave," or "lift up," ver. 27. These ceremonies of the altar service are now first mentioned.

25 for a burnt-offering. Rather, "upon the burnt-offering" (R.V.). This consecration-offering is also a thank-offering.

40. deal. A share, division, or part. A "tenth deal" means a tenth part of an *ephah. Hin*, about $1\frac{1}{2}$ gallons.—**beaten oil.** Olive berries, if beaten or sqeezed while green, yield the best oil.

43 the tabernacle. Rather, "and it [*i.e.*, the place] shall be," etc.

CHAPTER XXX

2 the height thereof. About 42 inches high, and 20 square.

7 Aaron. This was apparently not a duty belonging exclusively to the high priest, though regarded as a priestly function. See Luke i. 9, 10; from which it also appears that it became the practice of the people to pray in the outer court of the temple at the time of offering incense, and that when the priest came out he blessed the people.

10 an atonement. By sprinkling the blood of the sacrifice upon the corner of the altar. This direction shows that sacrifice is required in order to give efficacy to intercession.

12 a ransom. All the people were to pay equally to the maintenance of the service, that they might feel that all of every rank equally needed and equally benefited by the atonement and offerings. The amount was small, being little more than twenty-five cents. (See Matt. xvii. 24, for Christ's compliance with this law.)

18 brass (copper). As the sacrifices represented the atonement of Christ, so the *laver* with its rites represented the "washing of regeneration and renewing of the Holy Ghost." No one is permitted to approach God without undergoing the double purification of the altar and the laver—the blood and the Spirit of Jesus. There were two washings of the priests—the one general and entire, performed once for all on their consecration and admission to the sanctuary (xxix. 4); the other partial, and repeated daily within the court of the tabernacle. See Heb. x. 19–22.

19 their hands . . . their feet. The hands being in constant use, and the feet exposed to dust, particularly required frequent cleansing (Matt. xv. 2; John xiii. 10).

25 oil. This seems to represent the communications of the Holy Spirit, both enlightening (1 John ii. 20) and cheering (Psa. xlv. 7, 8), as well as qualifying for official work (Isa. lxi. 1–3). Hence anointing oil was used to inaugurate priests (ver. 30), kings (1 Kings i. 39), and prophets (1 Kings xix. 16).

32 Upon man's flesh. That is, not upon other men's; as perfumes were commonly used as a welcome to guests and for personal comfort. That which is peculiarly consecrated to the service of God must not be used as a common thing.

34 stacte. Probably the gum called *opobalsamum.*

35 a perfume, etc. Rather, "incense, a perfume after the art of the perfumer" (R.V.). The word *apothecary* is now obsolete in this sense.

CHAPTER XXXI

2 called by name. That is, "specially appointed." See Isa. xlv. 3.

3 the spirit of God. This expression sometimes denotes any extraordinary endowment, without necessarily implying personal piety. See ver. 6; 1 Sam. x. 6, 10, and cp. James i. 17.

10 cloths of service. Rather, "garments of office." Some render "finely wrought garments" (R.V.).

13 My Sabbaths ye shall keep. The observance of the Sabbath is here strongly enjoined on the Israelites as a perpetual "sign" that they were "sanctified," or separated from all other people, to serve the true God, the Creator of all things (ver. 17).

17 was refreshed. Heb., "took breath."

CHAPTER XXXII

1 delayed. Moses had been absent from the camp for more than a month. This long delay was probably intended to test the people's fidelity to Jehovah; and the result shows how deeply they had become tainted with Egyptian idolatry.

gods. Rather, "a god." So vers. 4, 8.

2 earrings. Some suppose that Aaron, wishing to keep the people from forsaking Jehovah, hoped by this proposal to divert them from their purpose; presuming that they would naturally be loth to part with such costly ornaments. If so, his temporising policy met with deserved failure.

4 a molten calf. There was probably a roughly-made centre of wood, upon which the gold, molten into plates, was fastened; the image of the calf being then finished by hand. It could therefore be burned and ground to powder (see ver. 20). Apis, one of the principal Egyptian deities, was represented by a calf, which was used as an image of Jehovah (see ver. 5), in direct violation of the second command in the Decalogue.

6 rose up to play. They gave themselves up to the wanton licentiousness which accompanied heathen festivals.

9 it is a stiffnecked people. A frequent image, taken from a refractory beast, which will not bend its neck to the yoke: here obviously meaning a self-willed, obstinate people.

17 Joshua. Joshua had accompanied Moses as his attendant (xxiv. 13), and was probably awaiting his return at a lower part of the mountain.

20 drink of it. As they had no other water to drink. They were thus made to loathe the object of their idolatrous worship.

25 naked. The word rather means *disorderly, reckless,* or *licentious.* "Aaron had let them loose, for a derision (whispering) among their enemies" (R.V.). See ver. 6; 1 Cor. x. 7, 8. Moses felt deeply how much the people had disgraced themselves in the eyes of their heathen enemies.

26 all the sons of Levi. There were probably many *individuals* belonging to the other tribes who answered to this appeal; but the Levites as a tribe ranged themselves on the side of Jehovah and His servant.

29 Consecrate. Heb., "Fill your hand." That is, "Show yourselves devoted to God's service by this act of holy indignation."

32 if Thou wilt forgive their sin. The unfinished sentence shows the strength of emotion.—**blot me,** etc *i.e.,* "take me from among the living,"—apparently offering to bear the people's sin himself as their substitute. But no one, except the Divine Redeemer, who "gave Himself for us," is able to expiate sin. See Rom. ix. 3.—**thy book.** Cp. Dan. xii. 1; Rev. iii. 5; xx. 12, 15; xxii. 19.

34 Mine Angel. In opposition to "Myself." See xxxiii. 3.

CHAPTER XXXIII

5 I will come up. Rather, "If I go up into the midst of thee for one moment, I shall consume thee" (R.V.).

6 by the mount Horeb. Rather, "from mount Horeb onward" (R.V.); *i.e.,* at Horeb they ceased to wear them.

7 the Tabernacle. This, which is mentioned before the construction of the tabernacle according to the directions given at Sinai, was probably the tent in which Moses transacted the duties of his office, and where he held intercourse with God; hence called "the tent of meeting." See xxvii. 21. Its removal outside the camp intimated the withdrawal of God's special presence.

11 face to face. Not that Moses actually saw God, for "no man hath seen God at any time" (see John i. 18); but this expression signifies freedom and familiarity of intercourse.

12 I know thee by name. That is, "I have particular regard for thee."

14 My presence. The privilege which has been taken away (ver. 3) is restored, in answer to Moses' prayer. Cp. Josh. xxi. 44.

23 thou shalt see, etc. "Face," "hand," and "back," are figurative expressions in this, as in many other passages of Scripture. See on Gen. vi. 6. The passage evidently means that God would reveal to Moses so much of His glory, and chiefly of His moral perfections, as he could endure. Cp. John i. 18.

CHAPTER XXXIV

1 two tables. Preparatory to the renewal of the covenant with Israel, of which the laws contained on the two tables formed the basis.

5 proclaimed the name. That is, He declared His perfections. This was by the words uttered in vers. 6, 7.

7 keeping mercy for thousands, etc. Or, perhaps, "keeping mercy to a thousand generations; forgiving iniquity, transgression, and sin; and acquitting even him who is not innocent; visiting the iniquity of the fathers upon the children to the third or to the fourth generation only." The *thousand* generations to which mercy is extended (xx. 6, note) are put in contrast with the *third* and *fourth* generation upon which iniquity is visited.

9 stiffnecked. Jehovah had given this as His reason for not going with them (xxxiii. 3); but Moses inverts the argument; alleging that such a people peculiarly needed a leader so merciful and forgiving as God had just declared Himself to be.

13 images. Rather, "pillars" (R.V.).

groves. Heb., "Asherim"; *i.e.*, statues, or symbols, of Ashtoreth. See Judges ii. 13; iii. 7.

15 whoring. This figure is often used to represent unfaithfulness to Jehovah as the God of Israel (Deut. xxxi. 16; Judges ii. 17; etc.).

24 thrice in the year. At the Passover, at Pentecost and at the Feast of Tabernacles (Deut. xvi. 16).

29 shone. Literally, "shot out rays." This was, no doubt, intended to inspire the people with deeper reverence for Moses.

33 And [till]. The old versions supply "when," instead of "till"; intimating that when delivering the Divine message Moses was unveiled.

CHAPTER XXXV

5 an offering unto the Lord. There was room for almost every person to testify his zeal by some offering; for while the wealthy could bring gold and precious stones, the poorer class might furnish the skins and the hair of goats; and the women spun the goats' hair for the tent coverings (ver. 26); as is done to this day by the females among the Bedouins (cp. 2 Cor. ix. 7).

18 pins. Pegs to fasten the cords to the ground.

22 earrings. Or, "nose jewels." *Rings,* or "signets." *Tablets,* or "balls," or perhaps "necklaces."—**every man that offered.** "And every man who offered an offering of gold for the Lord [came]."

CHAPTER XXXVI

The remainder of the Book contains a minute description of the construction of the several parts of the tabernacle, the sacred utensils, and the priests' garments; also an account of the amount of gold, silver and brass consumed; the erection and consecration of the tabernacle; and the consecration of Aaron and his sons (xxxvi. 8–xxxix. 32). On the completion of all the required arrangements, the "cloud," the symbol of Jehovah's presence, descends upon the tabernacle; and it henceforth directs the movements of the Israelites through all their journeyings (xl. 33–38).

8 made he them. On the subjects mentioned in this and the three following chapters see notes on xxv.–xxvii.

CHAPTER XXXVIII

8 looking glasses. Brasen (or copper) or other metallic mirrors were a common female ornament among the Egyptians and Israelites.—**the women assembling.** Perhaps "of the serving" or ministering women, who served at the gate of the tabernacle of the congregation. The same Hebrew word is used with reference to the *services* of the priests: see Numb. iv. 23, 35, 39, etc.; viii. 25. A Jewish commentator, Aben Ezra, says, "They came daily to the tabernacle to pray, and to hear the words of the law." See 1 Sam. ii. 22; Luke ii. 37.

25 the silver, etc. The talent being three thousand shekels, this exactly agrees with ver. 26. The value of the gold and silver was about £200,000; towards which the parting gifts of the Egyptians no doubt contributed largely.

CHAPTER XL

2 tabernacle. The interior wooden structure; see ver. 19.

3 cover. Or, "hide." The ark was behind the vail.

15 an everlasting priesthood. To last as long as the Mosaic dispensation did.

17 the second year. The second year of the Israelites' deliverance.

19 tent. Probably the *under* covering.

20 the Testimony. That is, the tables of the covenant. See xxxi. 18; and cp. Heb. ix. 4, note.

34 a cloud. The visible sign of Jehovah's special presence, called the *Shekinah,* a Hebrew word signifying "dwelling."

LEVITICUS

God's Call to Worship

INTRODUCTION

The Hebrew title of this Book is *Vayyikra,* from its first word "And He called." *Leviticus* was the name given to it by the Greek translators, the Levites being responsible for carrying out the laws of tabernacle worship.

The Book may conveniently be divided into three sections.

1. **Laws relating to public worship** (i.–xvi.). This includes directions as to the various kinds of sacrifices, provision for the priests, the consecration of

Aaron and his sons, the punishment of Nadab and Abihu, and the Great Day of Atonement.

2. **Laws relating to personal and social life** (xvii.–xxv.). These include the life of the family, the relations of the sexes, the treatment of the workers by their employers, and the provision for the poor.

3. **The blessings promised for obedience, the punishment for disobedience, and the conditions of voluntary vows** (xxvi., xxvii.).

Both the ceremonial and moral enactments are bound together by the one great sanction or claim: "I am the Lord thy God" (xviii. 30; xix. 3, 4, 5, 10, 31, 34, 37, etc.). And surely this is the only foundation on which law can be based. There must be a supreme authority, higher than all human law-givers. There must be a Divine power which can enforce the observance of law by nations as well as by individuals. The ceremonial observances taught the Jewish people the holiness of God; the moral and social regulations were the practical outcome of it. Those who imagine that this Book is one of old-world or ritual interest only would do well to study such passages as xix. 9–18, and xxv. They would find, perhaps, a solution of some of our modern social problems.

The Christian, at any rate, will note that Christ more than once appealed to this Book as an authority (Matt. viii. 4, cp. Lev. xiv. 3–10; Matt. xii. 4, cp. Lev. xxiv. 9; John vii. 32, cp. Lev. xii. 3). As Dr. S. H. Kellogg has well pointed out in his Introduction to Leviticus (*Expositor's Bible*), "Not only did our Lord use language which implied the truth of the Jewish belief regarding the origin and authority of the Mosaic law, but He formally teaches it; and—what is of still more moment—He rests the obligation of certain duties upon the fact that this law of Leviticus was a revelation from God to Moses for the children of Israel."

And, finally, the Christian will find in Hebrews ix. the connexion, as one of type and shadow with the reality, between the ceremonies and sacrifices of Leviticus and the perfect sacrifice and mediation of our great High Priest.

CHAPTER I

1 the tabernacle of the congregation. *i.e.*, "the tent of meeting" (R.V.). The law of sacrifice, as a remedial institute, was promulgated, not from the mountain top like the moral law, but from the mercy-seat. See Exod. xxv. 22.

2 If any man of you bring. It is taken for granted that sacrificial offerings would be made, as they always had been in religious worship; but they are now to be more minutely regulated, to present the great truths as to the sinner's reconciliation to God, and to afford expression to the wants and feelings of the worshippers.

3 If his offering. This was evidently a voluntary offering, like those in ii., iii.; but it was to be wholly consumed. As distinguished from the sin and trespass offerings (iv., v.), it appears to have been intended to express special and entire devotion to God, as well as a deep sense of general sinfulness. It was always connected with a meal offering and a drink offering (Numb. xv. 3, etc.).—**a burnt sacrifice of the herd.** The three classes of victims here mentioned, viz., bullocks (ver. 3), sheep or goats (ver. 10), and fowls (ver. 14), were suited to the means of different classes of persons. See 2 Cor. viii. 12.

4 he shall put his hand upon the head. Thus in effect confessing his sin, and symbolically transferring his guilt to the substituted victim.—**to make atonement.** Heb., "to cover." The phrase is generally understood to mean that the expiation covers the sinner from the Divine wrath, so that he is treated as a righteous person.

5 And he shall kill. That is, the offerer took some ostensible part in what was chiefly done by the practised Levites.—**sprinkle the blood.** By this act the life of the victim was considered as presented to God, and accepted by Him, in the stead of the offerer. Cp. Heb. xii. 24; 1 Pet. i. 2.

9 shall burn all. The victim having been slain and its blood sprinkled on the altar, as an expiatory sacrifice, it was then to be wholly burnt upon the altar, in token of the offerer's entire consecration to the Divine service. Cp. Rom. vi. 13; xii. 1, 2.

15 wring off his (its) head. Probably without dividing it from the body. Cp. ver. 17 and ch. v. 8.

CHAPTER II

1 meat offering. Rather, *meal*, or *wheaten* offering. The word *meat* never refers to *flesh*, in the Levitical offerings; nor was the meal offering properly a sacrifice. The greater part of it was to be used for food, not to be burned. It consisted principally of flour, or flour made into cakes; to which was added a suitable quantity of wine for a drink offering. See Exod. xxix. 40, 41; Lev. xxiii. 13; Numb. xv. 5, 10, etc. When presented alone, it appears to have been an expression of gratitude for ordinary providential blessings; while its reception through the intervention of the priest, and the oblation of part of it by fire, keep in view the mediation of Christ as the only acceptable way of offering praise. See Heb. xiii. 15, 16. The various forms in which it was allowed to be made (vers. 2, 4, 5, 7) were suited to the diversified circumstances of the people.

2 memorial of it. That is, a part as representing the whole.

5 in a pan. Rather, "on a plate," or "slice." The Arabs of the desert use a plate of iron, or a gridiron, for cooking their cakes, which are often very thin.

6 shalt part. Rather, "shalt break." Bread was not cut, but broken (Lev. viii. 7; Matt. xiv. 19; xxvi. 26; Acts xx. 11).

11 leaven. The leaven used by the Hebrews was not the *cause*, but rather the *effect* of fermentation. It consisted of the acid lees of wine, or dough, kept till sour. In this corruption had already begun. Hence it naturally became an emblem of moral corruption, insincerity, and hypocrisy; from which the symbolical offerings, representing the holy lives of the worshippers, must be kept separate (see Luke xii. 1; 1 Cor. v. 8). "Honey" includes all that is sweet, and may have been forbidden because it turns sour. Or, as leaven signifies corruption, so honey may suggest the cloying sweetness of worldly enjoyment. Salt, on the contrary (ver. 13), as a preservative of animal substances from decay, was an emblem of purity, perfection, and perpetuity (see Matt. v. 13; Mark ix. 49, 50; Col. iv. 6); and for this reason, as well as from being eaten with every meal, it was a symbol of friendship.

14 full ears. Or, "the fresh ear" (R.V.); *i.e.*, not flour, as in ver. 12, but fresh grain of the new barley, or wheat; the first food which the new harvest afforded.

CHAPTER III

1 peace offering. The peace offering is often mentioned with the burnt offering, which it invariably follows, as intimating that reconciliation was made, and the offerer restored to Divine favour. It was the only sacrifice of which the people were permitted to eat the flesh. God was supposed Himself to partake of the feast with the offerer and his friends: thus giving a religious character to social festivities, and indicating the completeness of the Divine reconciliation. It therefore might include the expression of gratitude and of devoted consecration (see vii. 12–16; Psa. xxii. 25, 26; Heb. xiii. 15). The need of an atoning sacrifice, in order to acceptance, is kept prominently in view in these offerings (see ver. 2). The feelings of a true worshipper in presenting the sacrifices and offerings prescribed in this and the two preceding chapters are set forth in Psa. lxvi. 13–20.—**of the herd.** Here we see the same gradation in the offerings, adapted to the means of different classes of persons, as in the burnt offering, and the meal offering: viz., the bullock or heifer (ver. 1), the lamb (ver. 6), and the goat (ver. 12).

4 with the kidneys. Rather, "upon the kidneys"; *i.e.*, the fat which covers the kidneys.

5 upon the burnt sacrifice. A burnt sacrifice was offered every morning (vi. 12): so that all the following sacrifices of the same day were laid *upon* it.

9 the whole rump. Rather, "the fat tail," as R.V. The tail of many Eastern sheep is broad and fat, and is reckoned the finest part of the animal.

17 neither fat nor blood. That is, neither the fat nor suet within (vers. 14, 15), nor the blood of the larger vessels. These were to be wholly separated from common use, and reserved for sacrificial purposes; the "fat" being presented to the Lord as the best part of the victim, and the "blood" offered as an atonement, in substitution for the offerer's life (see xvii. 11). The heathen sometimes drank the blood of their sacrifices. See Psa. xvi. 4.

CHAPTER IV

2 through ignorance. Or, "unwittingly" (R.V.). As distinguished from sins of presumption (Numb. xv. 22, 28), that is, deliberately and wilfully committed. The phrase allows us to include sins of thoughtlessness, and urgent or plausible temptation, as well as of absolute ignorance. The penalty was proportioned to the position of the offender. It fell most heavily upon the high priest, whose victim was to be as costly as that of the whole congregation; and was, like that, to be offered with the peculiar solemnity of the sevenfold sprinkling, and to be wholly consumed outside the camp, as if he required a new consecration

3 according to the sin of the people. Rather, "to the guilt of the people," for sin committed by the priest in his office, as their representative, brought guilt on them.

6 seven times. Seven, regarded as a perfect number, was used to express a perfect and complete action.

12 shall he carry forth. Or, "one shall carry forth." The thought is that the sacrifice, having sin transferred to it, has become abominable in God's sight, and is therefore removed beyond the sacred precincts (cp. Heb. xiii. 11).

13 are guilty. Or, "are suffering the penalty"; and so in ver. 22. In Psa. xxxiv. 22, and Isa. xxiv. 6, the same word is rendered "are desolate."

28 a female. As being less costly than a ruler's sin-offering (ver. 23).

CHAPTER V

1 do not utter it. That is, if a person hear the judge utter an oath of adjuration requiring witnesses to come forward, and he be able to give testimony, and shall refuse or neglect to do so, he shall be guilty. Cp. Prov. xxix. 24.

3 hid from him. That is, hidden from him *at the time*, though it afterwards come to his knowledge.

4 if a soul swear. This law would tend to prevent inconsiderate oaths. A person might find that what he had sworn to do was either impossible or wrong. In such cases he would be guilty only of rashness in making an inconsiderate oath; which, however, as implying a vow made to God, required expiation. *Pronouncing* should rather be "speaking idly." "If a soul swear rashly" (R.V.).

11 the tenth part of an ephah. About $3\frac{3}{5}$ pints. The expense was so small that poverty would not be a bar to any man's pardon.

15 a trespass. The word "trespass," as distinguished from "sin" (iv. 2), is probably intended to imply some fraud or positive injury, either in withholding what ought to have been offered to God, through carelessness (ver. 15) or through ignorance (ver. 17); or in defrauding a neighbour (vi. 1–7). Hence, full compensation and proportionate fine were required (ver. 16), as well as atonement. And the lesson was taught for all ages, that he who seeks a free forgiveness through Christ, must not neglect such restitution or reparation of his offences against God and man as may ever be within his power. See Matt. v. 23, 24; Luke xix. 8.—**in the holy things.** *i.e.*, in withholding any of the appointed dues or offerings. See Mal. iii. 8.

CHAPTER VI

2 to keep. A proved offence of this kind, without confession, was punished by manifold restitution (Exod. xxii. 7, 15). This law appears to be designed to encourage confession and restitution when the offence could not be proved by the evidence of others.

3 in any of all these, etc. This includes a failure to restore anything borrowed; or the false denial of having received anything belonging to another; or the appropriation of it to oneself.

9 It is the burnt offering, etc. Rather, "the burnt offering shall be upon the hearth of the altar all night." The remains of the evening burnt offering were to be left upon the altar all night; and the fire was to be kept alive.—**burning in it.** Or, "with it." So, too, in ver. 12.

14 meat offering. This refers to the flour-offering of the daily oblation; not that mentioned in ii. 1, 2.

16 Aaron and his sons. By this and other offerings, part of which belonged to the priests, those who gave attendance in turn at the tabernacle were maintained during their absence from their own cities.—**with unleavened bread shall it be eaten.** Rather, "unleavened shall it be eaten"; the words "with" and "bread" not being in the Hebrew.

28 the earthen vessel . . . shall be broken. Being porous, it was capable of the same cleansing as a copper vessel. Sacred things were thus kept distinct.

CHAPTER VII

8 the skin. Valuable for rugs or mattresses. Compare the record of what is probably the *first* sacrifice (Gen. iii. 21).

13 leavened bread. That is, ordinary bread; this being regarded as a friendly feast. See on iii. 1.

15 eaten the same day. This would tend both to promote hospitality and liberality to the poor, and to prevent the superstitious use of consecrated food.

19 shall eat. Or, "may eat"; *i.e.*, the flesh of these offerings, with the exception of that here mentioned as having touched something unclean, may be eaten by clean persons.

20 cut off from his people. *i.e.*, "excommunicated."

23 Ye shall eat, etc. Rather, "Ye shall not eat any fat of ox," etc.; viz., not of the animals particularly mentioned: see on iii. 17. But the use of blood is in *every case* forbidden (Lev. iii. 17; xvii. 10, etc.).

CHAPTER VIII

3 gather thou all the congregation. That all might see that Aaron did not take the office upon himself. See Heb. v. 4.

7 the girdle. The girdle is an important part of dress in countries where long loose robes are worn.

8 the Urim and the Thummim. See on Exod. xxviii. 30.

23 ear . . . hand . . . foot. A token that all the bodily senses and active powers were consecrated to God's service. See further on xiv. 14.

33 door of the tabernacle. That is, of the tabernacle court; for they were not allowed to live in the holy place.

CHAPTER IX

4 peace offerings, etc. On this solemn occasion all the different kinds of offerings were presented, except the trespass offering, which would not be needed, as being provided for cases of injury. See ch. v. and notes.

13 with the pieces thereof. Rather, "piece by piece," as R.V.

15 And he brought, etc. Aaron is now deemed fit to minister for the people.—**for sin.** The sin was laid upon the victim, or imputed to it: hence the expression in 2 Cor. v. 21.

23 the glory. Probably in the cloudy pillar, the symbol of the Divine presence.

24 and consumed, etc. God thus testified His acceptance of the offerings presented to Him, as He did again at the dedication of Solomon's temple (2 Chron. vii. 1; and cp. 1 Kings xviii. 38).

CHAPTER X

1 strange fire. Not the holy fire from the altar, but common fire. No express prohibition is recorded, but after the command to keep the sacred fire on the altar continually burning (Lev. vi. 12, 13), the use of any other was an act of presumption.

2 devoured. Rather, "slew," for the bodies and garments were unconsumed (see ver. 5). A wilful deviation from a divinely-prescribed ritual demanded punishment: cp. Numb. xvi. 35. The same fire at whose appearing the people had so lately rejoiced (ix. 24) destroyed those who despised it. So the ministry which is to some a "savour of life" becomes to others a "savour of death" (2 Cor. ii. 16).

6 Uncover not, etc. These were ordinary tokens of mourning. Perhaps the special reason for this command was that the priests bore a public character; and they who acted for God at the altar should be foremost in testifying to the righteousness of His judgements.

9 Do not drink wine. This command, introduced in connexion with the death of Aaron's sons, may suggest that they had acted under the excitement of wine.

16 he was angry. This deviation from the law alarmed Moses, but the affliction of the family was allowed as an excuse for it. This event, so painful to Aaron, would be, both to the priests and to the people, a lesson on the necessity of obedience to the Divine law. See Heb. xii. 29.

CHAPTER XI

2 These are the beasts, etc. Rather, "These are the living creatures which ye may eat among all (large) beasts (or cattle) that are on the earth." The distinction was designed to strengthen the barriers between the Israelites and other nations (see Lev. xi. 43–49; xx. 24–26; and cp. Peter's vision, Acts x. 12). The preparatory nature of such restrictions is shown in Heb. ix. 9, 10. See also Rom. xiv. 14, 17; 1 Cor. viii. 8.

3 parteth . . . clovenfooted . . . cheweth. A clean animal must have *all* these marks. The division of the hoof must not be into more than two parts; nor must it, like the camel's, be incomplete.

4 the camel. Both the flesh and the milk of the camel are used by the Arabs.

5 coney. *Shaphan,* "the hider," a small animal, about the size of a rabbit (the *hyrax Syriacus,* or rock-badger, R.V. marg.), living in the clefts of the rocks. It is not, any more than the hare, strictly speaking, a ruminant animal; but it works the jaws as if re-chewing its food. The object of the law was to furnish outward marks easily discernible.

7 swine. Swine appear not to have been eaten by Orientals generally; and particularly not by the Egyptians, who, however, offered them to some idols: see Herodotus, ii. 47. The use of swine's flesh for food in hot countries is said to produce cutaneous diseases.

13 among the fowls. Instead of a general rule being given here, the exceptions are specified; probably including in each all birds of similar kind. Many of these cannot now be ascertained; but most likely they were all carnivorous.

16 owl. Rather, "ostrich" (R.V.).

18 swan. The purple water-hen. The same Hebrew word occurs in ver. 30, among the lizards, and is rendered "mole"; but is most likely the chameleon.

20 fowls. Rather, "flying creatures." *All* flying creatures having more than two feet, except the locust tribe, were unclean.

22 the locust, etc. These four kinds are all of the same genus. Locusts are much used as food by the poor in some countries (Matt. iii. 4).

29 weasel. Some suppose this to be the mole, the word translated "mole" meaning probably the chameleon (see on ver. 18). Those translated "tortoise" and "ferret," probably denote species of lizards.

36 toucheth their carcase. In attempting to draw it out. The pit or fountain, receiving fresh supplies of water, was clean.

38 water. Probably to soften it for food, not for sowing.

39 any beast—die. *i.e.,* of itself. See xvii. 13, 15.

40 he that eateth. *i.e.,* unwittingly; for he who did this knowingly would be cut off from the people as a presumptuous transgressor. See Numb. xv. 30.

42 creeping things. Including such species as the caterpillar, the worm, the centipede, and especially serpents.

45 ye shall therefore be holy. This ceremonial holiness represents that purity of spirit and conduct which God requires in His people (see 1 Pet. i. 16). Indeed, the careful observance of these precepts, upon the principles here enjoined, would tend to promote real holiness, by exercising and strengthening the spirit of obedience, while it would keep the Israelites from mingling with surrounding heathen. For the dangers of ceremonialism, see Matt. xxiii. 23–26.

CHAPTER XII

1 The Lord spake. These various purifications, restrictions, and sacrifices were, no doubt, of physical value. Further, they remind us that all the processes of our life are subject to the control of God, and are more or less affected by conditions of our fallen nature.

8 if she be not able. As the mother of Jesus was able to bring only this offering (Luke ii. 24), she was evidently of the poorer class.

CHAPTER XIII

2 leprosy. The name "leprosy" was given to a wide class of diseases of the skin very prevalent in Egypt and in Asia. It was sometimes inflicted as a special judgement for sin, and is hence called a *plague,* or *stroke:* see Numb. xii. 10; 2 Kings v. 27; 2 Chron. xxvi. 20. Leprosy is an apt symbol of sin and its effects; to which there are many striking references in the process of cleansing: see xiv., xv. Its symptoms and treatment are here described, not so much medically as ceremonially.

5 the priest shall look on him. Three varieties are mentioned, only two of which are malignant; and of these, one is not at first sight distinguishable from a harmless eruption. Hence the need of repeated inspection.

6 be somewhat dark. *i.e.,* "be dim" (R.V.), or "faded." So in subsequent verses.

13 if the leprosy, etc. In this case the whole matter of the disease came out into a dead white scurf, which soon fell off. Vers. 16 and 17 refer to a similar case of a speedy cure by the total eruption of the poison from the body, when the reddish raw flesh turns white.

23 a burning boil. Rather, "the burning (*i.e.,* 'the scar,' R.V.) of the boil," which falls off when the cure is complete.

28 it is a rising of the burning. Or, "it is (only) the scar of the burn" (R.V.).

46 his clothes shall be rent, etc. Tokens of grief and humiliation; leprosy being regarded as a Divine infliction. See on ver. 1.

46 he shall dwell alone. Lest he should infect others. There are still, in some countries of the East, separate houses, and even villages, for lepers. So strictly was this regulation enforced, that even Miriam, the sister of Moses, was not exempted from it (Numb. xii. 15); nor, at a later period, was king Uzziah (2 Chron. xxvi. 19–21). See also 2 Kings vii. 3; Luke xvii. 12. Naaman remained in office; so that his case must have been of the milder order (2 Kings v. 1).

CHAPTER XIV

2 cleansing. Leprosy being regarded as an expressive token of sin, its removal was to be accompanied with purifying ceremonies and offerings, uniting confessions of guilt and pollution with grateful acknowledgment of God's mercy.

14 ear . . . hand . . . foot. (Cp. viii. 23.) Intimating that the *whole man* was cleansed; as afterwards the application of the oil to these same parts (vers. 17, 18) intimated that the whole man, with all his powers, was consecrated to God his Saviour. The combination of these ceremonies (vers. 13–18) reminds us that whenever the blood of Christ is applied to the sinner for justification, the anointing of the Spirit is granted for sanctification. These two are inseparable; and both are necessary to our acceptance with God. See Heb. x. 22; 1 John ii. 20.

CHAPTER XV

The laws in this chapter were designed and fitted to secure personal chastity, and were physically advantageous.

CHAPTER XVI

1 the two sons of Aaron. The death of Aaron's sons (x. 1, 2) gave occasion to the promulgation of this law; which, on the one hand, jealously guarded the most holy place; "signifying that the way into the holiest was not yet made manifest," until Christ, "by His own blood, entered in once for all into the holy place, having obtained eternal redemption for us" (Heb. ix. 8, 12); and on the other hand it would tend to allay Aaron's fear of approach to God, and to encourage him, amidst the conscious imperfections of the daily services, by a yearly expiation for himself and his family.

5 two kids. Two were necessary, to represent *forgiveness* by putting away sin.

8 for the scapegoat. Heb., "for Azazel" (so R.V.). The word may be rendered, "a complete sending away," hence an averting or expiation. By many expositors Azazel is regarded as a proper name—of a demon, or of Satan himself. The treatment of the second victim, which was not killed, but sent away by an instructed person (ver. 21) into the desert, implied that the sins confessed and atoned for were laid on him" (Isa. liii. 6), and thus "removed" from the people (Psa. ciii. 12), and for ever "put away" (Heb. ix. 26).

9 offer. Rather, "present." The goat was not yet to be *offered*.

10 atonement with him. Rather, "*for* him"; as was to done afterwards in the case of the holy of holies (ver. 16), the "tent of meeting" (ib.), and the brazen altar (ver. 18). Atonement had to be made for all these, to remove whatever of ceremonial uncleanness was regarded as attaching to them from contact with the people.

12 bring it within the vail. This annual entrance of the high priest, enveloped in a cloud of incense, within the vail, carrying in his hand the blood of the sacrifice, was an image of the Redeemer's entrance into heaven, to present before the Father His atoning blood and effectual intercession. And the resumption of the gorgeous dress by the high priest before he came out of the holy place, to complete the services of the day (ver. 24), aptly represented the passing away of the Saviour's temporary humiliation, and the glory in which He is to appear at His second coming (Heb. ix. 28).

13 the mercy seat. Signifying that his only hope of safety was in the revealed mercy of God, through the great propitiation.

17 no man. Not even any of the priests who ordinarily ministered within the sanctuary. This injunction makes the typical character of the high priest very conspicuous, as representing Him who performed *alone* the whole work of our atonement. Cp. Isa. lxiii. 3; Heb. ix. 12–14.

29 afflict. Heb., "humble," by fasting and confession. The sense of sin in the minds of the people was to be deepened by every available means, and to be brought out in becoming forms of penitential grief.

CHAPTER XVII

3 killeth an ox. This law refers to animals killed both for sacrifice and for food. It could only be carried out in the camp, and was modified at the entrance of the people into Canaan (Deut. xii. 4–28). Before this law was given, the slaughtering of animals in the open field had often given occasion to idolatrous sacrifices (ver. 7).

7 devils. The word translated "devils" means "rough or hairy ones," and signifies "goats" (R.V.) or "satyrs" (R.V. marg.), in which form the false gods of the heathen were often represented. The Egyptians of Mendes, a district not far from Goshen, worshipped a living goat, with the most horrible abominations.

10 eateth blood. The prohibition given before (vii. 26, 27) is here repeated, with the important reason for it (ver. 11).

11 that maketh an atonement for the soul. Rather, that maketh an atonement *by* the soul; *i.e.*, by the victim's life (R.V.).

13 cover it with dust. Probably that it might not be profaned by any other animal eating of it.

14 it is for the life thereof. Heb., "for as to the life of all flesh, it is its blood in its life."

15 eateth. That is, of course, in ignorance; for when this was done knowingly, it was punished by cutting off.

CHAPTER XVIII

2 Say unto them, etc. The repetition of the declaration, "I am Jehovah your God," all through this chapter and the next, gives an emphatic sanction to the series of commands by which Israel, or the "peculiar people" of The Eternal, was separated from the nations around.

3 Egypt. The Egyptians appear, from the testimony of ancient writers (see *Herodotus*, ii. 46), to have gone beyond most other nations in allowing and encouraging the unions condemned in this chapter.

6 to uncover, etc. This phrase denotes especially the marriage union, but extends to any kind of sexual intercourse.

16 thy brother's wife. Supposing that the brother had not died childless. See Gen. xxxviii. 8; Deut. xxv. 5.

18 to vex her. Or, as in R.V., "to be a rival *to her*."

21 to Molech. Molech (now first mentioned), also called "Milcom," "Moloch," and "Malcham," was the "king" or fire-god of the Ammonites, and, like the "Baal" of the Phœnicians, originally stood for the sun. Children were consecrated to this idol by passing through the fire, and were often burnt alive. See xx. 2–5 and 2 Kings xxiii. 10. Mr. R. A. S. Macalister in his excavations at Gezer for the Palestine Exploration Fund in 1902 found in the ruins of the ancient temple of the Amorites a series of jars each of which contained the skelton of a very young infant. "The marks of fire on two of these made it abundantly clear that these children were the victims of sacrifices."

25 vomiteth out her inhabitants. Not only do these sins provoke special judgement by their heinous wickedness, but they naturally tend to produce physical deterioration and the decrease of population.

CHAPTER XIX

5 at your own will. Rather, "for your acceptance"; *i.e.*, that ye may be accepted (R.V.); taking care therefore to do it in accordance with Divine regulations.

14 fear thy God. That is, "though thou dost not fear the deaf and the blind, who cannot help themselves, yet remember that God both hears and sees.—**the poor . . . the mighty.** The perversion of justice may arise from two opposite causes; undue sympathy with the weak, and undue deference to the strong.

16 shalt thou stand. Referring to the *rising up* in court of accusers and witnesses.

17 not suffer sin upon him. Rather, "not bear sin because of him" (R.V.). He who suffers sin to pass unreproved becomes partaker of it, and does unkindness to his brother.

18 thou shalt love thy neighbour as thyself. The second great commandment of the law (Matt. xxii. 39).

23 uncircumcised. As if unclean, unfit for food. The precept was adapted to secure the growth and full value of fruit-bearing trees. The planter was not to enjoy the fruit as his own until the *fifth* year, the fruit of the fourth being brought into the house of Jehovah as a thank-offering (Deut. xxvi. 2–11).

28 print any marks upon you. This was done by the Egyptians, and still prevails among the Arabs and Hindoos. Cp. Jer. xvi. 6; xlviii. 37.

29 thy daughter. Such sins were committed in connexion with idolatrous worship (Numb. xxv. 1), and still exist to-day in the East.

31 Regard not. *i.e.*, "turn ye not unto" (as R.V.).

36 ephah. The standard of dry measure; *hin*, of liquid measure. The hin (about 3 quarts) equalled one-sixth of the ephah.

CHAPTER XX

2 Unto Molech. See xviii. 21.

14 burnt with fire. Probably after being put to death by stoning, as in Josh. vii. 25; or by strangulation. So also in xxi. 9.

CHAPTER XXI

1 defiled for the dead. "defile himself" (R.V.). Even by attending the funeral. For the ordinary priest this rule did not apply to certain near relationships, but for the high priest it was absolute: see verses 11, 12.

4 [being] a chief man. Literally, "as a husband." The priest was a public character, sustaining important relations to the people in sacred things.

5 neither shall they shave. Herodotus says (6, iii. 36) that priests in other countries allowed the hair to grow, but among the Egyptians they shaved. See Isa. xv. 2; Jer. vii. 29.

7 profane. *i.e.*, according to Jewish writers, "of illegitimate birth."

8 Thou. *i.e.*, the Jewish community.

12 Neither shall he go out of the sanctuary. Not leaving the service of God for any claims of earthly relationship.

22 the most holy. The sin and trespass offerings, and the meal offering (ii. 3).—**the holy.** The remaining offerings, as peace offerings, tithes, first-fruits, and sacrificial gifts generally.

CHAPTER XXII

2 separate themselves. That is, in the following cases, ver. 3 and following.

10 stranger. A person not of the priestly race; and so in ver. 12.

11 they shall eat of his meat. This law shows, in a remarkable manner, the unity which belongs to a household; the servants, as well as the children, being treated as a part of it.

19 at your own will. Rather, "for your acceptance"; *i.e.*, "in order that you may be accepted, it must be a male," etc. See R.V., and cp. xix. 5.

22 ye shall not offer these. Only the best and most perfect offerings could be worthy of Divine acceptance; fitting representatives of the Divine anti-type, "who, through the Eternal Spirit, offered Himself without spot unto God" (Heb. ix. 14).

25 stranger's hand. That is, the same offering shall apply to a foreigner's offering, as to that of an Israelite.

29 at your own will. See on ver. 19.

CHAPTER XXIII

2 feasts. Or, "appointed times" (for one of them was a fast), or "assemblies"; so called as being the occasions on which assemblies were to be held for religious purposes.

7 servile. That is, nothing that belonged to a man's worldly business. Other necessary work, such as the preparing of food, was not forbidden on this day.

8 seven days. The paschal feast has already been fully described in Exod. xii. The offerings to be made during the eight days' feast are given at length in Numb. xxviii. 16–25.

11 the priest shall wave it. This was to be done on the first day after the Passover Sabbath. A sheaf of barley was usually presented, as that was the first grain reaped. After this the produce might be used, the whole offering having been consecrated to God by the offering of the first-fruits. See Rom. xi. 16. It was on the morning of the same day upon which the high priest waved before the Lord the first ripe sheaf that the great Head of the Church arose from the dead, the "*first-fruits* of them that slept" (1 Cor. xv. 20).

16 fifty days. Hence called in Greek the feast of "Pentecost" (*fiftieth*), held at the distance of seven weeks (and therefore called the "feast of *weeks*") from the second day of the passover when the first ripe barley-sheaf was presented. In Exod. xxiii. 16 it is called the "feast of harvest," and the "feast of first-fruits" (see Numb. xxviii. 26; Deut. xxvi.); because on that occasion the first-fruits of the wheat harvest were presented to God. These were offered in the form, not of *ears* of corn, but of baked *loaves*. The form of confession and thanksgiving prescribed in Deut. xxvi. was commonly used on these occasions. The feast is commonly regarded by Christians as having prefigured the outpouring of the Holy Ghost, fifty days after Christ, our Passover, had been sacrificed for us. It was largely attended in the later times of Jewish history. See Acts ii. 1, 9–11, etc.; and Josephus.

17 leaven. As representing the people's ordinary food.

24 the seventh month. The "blowing of trumpets" served as a signal to give notice of the beginning of the great festival month, the seventh of the sacred year, completing the whole series, as the seventh-day Sabbath completed the week. It marked also the beginning of the *civil* year; according to which all civil contracts and transactions were regulated.

27 day of atonement. See on ch. xvi.

35 feast of tabernacles. The feasts of Israel had a threefold reference: to the seasons of the natural year, to the history of the people, and to the coming blessings of the Gospel. The feast of Tabernacles was so named from the booths (tents or arbours, see vers. 40–43) which the Hebrews made to dwell in during its continuance. It is also called the "feast of ingathering" (Exod. xxiii. 16; xxxiv. 22; Deut. xvi. 13): for it was held after the labours, not only of the harvest, but also of the vintage and the fruit season generally. It naturally became a most joyous festival, both as observed shortly after the day of expiation, when the great Atonement, with its attendant blessings, had been exhibited; and as commemorating the Israelites' life in the wilderness, followed by their happy settlement in a fruitful land, the ingathering of whose rich produce it also celebrated. More victims were offered at this feast than at any other: see Numb. xxix 12-38. In later ages, it was the custom to pour profusely upon the temple courts water drawn from the pool of Siloam, amidst great rejoicings and the singing of Psa. cxiii.-cxviii.; and, in the evening, to illuminate the court of the women, whilst Psa. cxx.-cxxxiv. were sung. Many suppose that these ceremonies are alluded to in Isa. xii. 3; John vii. 37-39; viii. 12. The festival thus had reference to the times when the "fulness of the Gentiles" shall be brought into the Church (Zech. xiv. 16).

CHAPTER XXIV

10 an Egyptian. There were many such persons among the Hebrews, and they occasioned no little mischief. The notice of this man's parentage shows the bad consequences which commonly follow such mixed marriages. Children are apt, in such cases, to take after the worse side.

11 blasphemed. Spoke reproachfully of Jahveh. This sin was treason under the theocracy, and was punished by death, ver. 23. See Exod. xx. 7; Lev. xix. 12; and Heb. x. 28.

CHAPTER XXV

2 a sabbath. It is doubtful whether the sabbatic year began with the civil or the sacred year; whether the three years mentioned in ver. 21 were three full years, or parts of three consecutive years; and whether the jubilee was the forty-ninth or the fiftieth year—or, rather, whether it was part of each of those years, as beginning with Tisri, which was the first month of the civil and the seventh of the sacred year, while the sabbatic year began with Abib, the first month of the sacred year.

4 sabbath of rest. In later times this law seems not to have been regularly observed; for at the beginning of the Babylonian captivity it was announced that the country was to lie waste for seventy years, to make up for the neglected Sabbatic years. See 2 Chron. xxxvi. 21. See also Lev. xxvi. 34, 35, 43.

5 of thy vine undressed. Lit., "of thy Nazirite," or "separation."

6 shall be meat for you. *i.e.*, food for *all* of you, without distinction. The produce of the uncultivated fields during the "year of rest" was to be shared by all in common.

9 jubile. or, jubilee. Heb., "joyful sound," connected with the proper name *Jubal;* Gen. iv. 21.

27 restore the overplus. That is, he shall pay a sum equal to the value of the income for the years still remaining until the jubilee: but if he be unable to pay this, still his family inheritance shall be restored to him in the year of jubilee (ver. 28).

39 sold unto thee. Slavery already existed among the Hebrews in a modified form; and, although not at once absolutely forbidden, it was put by these laws under great restraints, with a view to its ultimate extinction. See also Exod. xx. 10; xxi. 20; xxvi. 27; Deut. v. 14; xii. 18; etc. In the case of the Israelite, the condition here spoken of was not properly one of slavery, but a voluntary service ending in the year of jubilee.

50 shall it be with him. Rather, "shall *he* be with him" (R.V.); *i.e.*, he shall be considered as having been with him as a servant during that time. Israelites were never to be considered as slaves, bought once for all; but their time of service was like that of day-labourers, engaged from year to year.

CHAPTER XXVI

1 image of stone. Rather, "a figured stone" covered with hieroglyphics.

10 because of the new. Literally, "*from before* the new" (R.V.); the old stock will not be exhausted when the new comes in, and must be brought out of the storehouse to make room for it.

12 I will walk among you. Cp. Matt. i. 23 and 2 Cor. vi. 16.

16 do this unto you. The judgements here threatened rise one above the other in intensity, in four separate degrees (vers. 18-20; 21, 22; 23-26; 27-33), if the people would not yield to the first chastisements, but still persevered in their iniquity.

26 in one oven. The supply of food would be so scanty that instead of every family having an oven for itself (as is usual in the East), the bread of several families would be baked in one oven; when each would take care not to lose the smallest portion of their share. Cp. Ezek. iv. 16.

29 ye shall eat, etc. See 2 Kings vi. 28, 29; Lam. iv. 10; Ezek. v. 10; and Josephus's account of the siege and capture of Jerusalem by the Romans.

35 did not rest in your sabbaths. As it had been tilled in the Sabbatical years, contrary to the Divine command, it should now remain uncultivated. See xxv. 4.

44 I will not cast them away, etc. Intimating that, notwithstanding the inflictions of judgement, and the dispersion of the nation, it should still continue in existence, as we see at this day. See Rom. xi. 1, 2.

CHAPTER XXVII

2 When a man shall make a singular vow. Literally, "when a man sets apart a vow," making a special offering over and above the prescribed sacrifices; such as the solemn dedication of his person, or child, or any part of his property, to the service of God. See Gen. xxviii. 20, 22; Judges xi. 30, 31; 1 Sam. i. 11, 28. This law is generally understood as providing a redemption price, which might be *substituted* for the person or property so consecrated. Some, however, suppose that this amount of money was to be paid in *addition* to the offering of the person, as a visible declaration that he had devoted himself to God.

16 the seed. "the sowing" (R.V.)—**a homer of barley-seed.** "The sowing of a homer" (R.V.); *i.e.*, the land requiring so much (ten ephahs, Ezek. xlv. 11) to sow it with. A homer was about 11 bushels, and 50 shekels=seven pounds.

26 no man shall sanctify it. As firstlings were to be offered in sacrifice (Exod. xiii. 15), it would have been a mere mockery to make them the subject of a vow.

29 devoted of men. This means not devoted *by* men, but devoted *from among* men; such as the Canaanitish nations (see Numb. xxi. 2, and note; Deut. vii. 2, 24), the city of Jericho (Josh. vi. 17), the Amalekites (Deut. xxv. 19; 1 Sam. xv. 3), and other evil-doers and enemies of Jehovah.

NUMBERS

THE BOOK OF THE WILDERNESS

INTRODUCTION

AGAIN, for this fourth book of the Pentateuch, the original Hebrew title *Bemidhbar* ("In the Wilderness") is at once more poetical and more appropriate than the title "Numbers," given by the Greek translators.

The Book records the two numberings of Israel, the one in the second year of their journeyings (i.–iv.), the other on the borders of Canaan, 38 years afterwards (xxvi.). The intervening chapters record various laws and observances (v.–x.); the appointment of seventy elders; the expedition of the spies (xiii., xiv.); the rebellion of Korah and regulations of the priesthood (xvi.–xix.); the smiting of the Rock, the Brazen Serpent, and the story of Balaam (xx.–xxiv.). The closing chapters record the conquest of Midian (xxxi.), the partition of the territory east of Jordan (xxxii.), the boundaries of the Promised Land (xxxiv.), and enactments about the Cities of Refuge (xxxv.).

This Book of the Wilderness is full of lessons for the Christian and of encouragements for life's pilgrim path.

CHAPTER I

1 the tabernacle of the congregation. *i.e.*, "the tent of meeting" (R.V.), as elsewhere.

3 shall number. Or, "shall muster." So throughout.

by their armies. *i.e.*, in their several divisions or corps; "by their hosts" (R.V.).

5 stand with you. *i.e.*, "assist you in numbering the people." The order of the tribes is: first, the sons of Leah (omitting Levi, ver. 47); then the sons of Rachel; lastly, those of the handmaids.

16 the renowned. Rather, "those called" (R.V.); *i.e.*, the chief men in their respective tribes, who were hence "called," or summoned, to form a sort of national council out of "the congregation" for this purpose, Exod. xviii. 21.

21 five hundred. As all the sums are *hundreds*, except one fifty, it is probable that numbers less than fifty were omitted.

46 all they that were numbered (mustered), etc. See note on Exod. xii. 37. The Hebrew word *Eleph*, which may mean either "thousand" or "family," is used here also.

48 had spoken. Rather, "spake" (R.V.).

50 over the tabernacle. Not to officiate in the tabernacle, but to take charge of it.—**Testimony.** Rather, "the Testimony" (R.V), *i.e.*, the Tables of the Law. Cf. Ex. xxv. 16.

51 stranger. One who is not a Levite. See iii. 10, 38; 1 Sam. vi. 19; 2 Sam. vi. 6, 7.

53 that there be no wrath. *i.e.*, lest the wrath of God should be incurred by those who were not Levites venturing to "come nigh" and profane the sanctuary.

CHAPTER II

2 far off about the tabernacle of the congregation. "Over against the tent of meeting," R.V. It is the Oriental usage to place the monarch and his chief officers in the centre of the camp.

3 captain. The chiefs appointed to preside over the mustering (see i. 5-14) were commanders of the several tribes.

9 camp of Judah. Judah, Issachar, and Zebulun, who formed the first camp, were all descendants of the same mother; and so were Ephraim, Manasseh, and Benjamin, who made the third. The "camp of Judah," which formed the van, and that of Dan, in the rear, were the most numerous of the four grand divisions.—**throughout their armies.** Rather, "according to" (R.V.), or "by their hosts."—**These shall first set forth.** Or rather, "These shall be the first to strike camp"; literally, "pull up" (the tent pegs). And so in vers. 16, 24, 31.

14 Reuel. Called in i. 14, "Deuel," the similar Hebrew letters *D* and *R* (ד and ר) being exchanged, probably by mistake. So in several other cases.

CHAPTER III

4 in the sight of Aaron. *i.e.*, in his presence; during his life. See also 1 Chron. xxiv. 19.

10 the stranger. That is, any one besides the priests, though even of the tribe of Levi; and so in ver. 38.

25 tabernacle. That is, the coverings of the tabernacle; for the Merarites had charge of the boards (ver. 36).

27 Kohathites. It is worthy of note that in the Kohathites were included the sons of Moses, who had no higher employment than that of taking care of the sacred vessels, and carrying burdens in connexion with this service. See also iv. 24-28.

39 twenty and two thousand. See note on ch. i. 46 and Exod. xii. 37.

41 the cattle of the Levites. The cattle of the Levites were not to be taken from them, or to be offered in sacrifice; but both they and their cattle were to be presented before the Lord, that *they* might be set apart for God's service and their cattle for their use and support as God's ministers.

46 Six hundred thousand. See note on ver. 39.

47 five shekels apiece. This was the amount levied on the firstborn in after times, as a perpetual revenue to the priesthood (see xviii. 16). How it was raised in the present instance we are not told.

49 the redemption money. This law suggests the contrast stated in 1 Pet. i. 18.

CHAPTER IV

3 thirty years old. This is reconciled with viii. 24 by supposing that for the first five years of their service the Levites were learning their duties, and occupied only in inferior departments. Under the new arrangements which David afterwards made, their service began at the age of twenty. See 1 Chron. xxiii. 24-32.—**fifty years.** After which, though in attendance, they were relieved from the heavier duties.—**the host.** Or " warfare," *i.e.*, service, as vers. 35, 39, 43.

7 covers. Rather, " bowls." See Exod. xxv. 29.

10 a (the) **bar.** Probably a sort of frame (R.V.), or " bier," carried between two persons. The same word, in xiii. 23, is rendered " staff."

15 shall come. The prohibition against the Levites entering the most holy place only applied while the cloud rested upon it. The sacred utensils were to be covered by the priests, the sons of Aaron, before they were taken by the Kohathites: see vers. 17-20. These coverings were designed to insure security and respect, signifying the reverence due to sacred things.—**the burden.** That is, " that which shall be borne " by them, viz., on their shoulders, and not on the waggons, see vii. 9.

18 Cut ye not off. That is, " Do not occasion the cutting off " ; be careful lest your negligence tempt their curiosity, and lead them to destruction.

20 covered. The word here rendered " covered " means " swallowed."

24 and for burdens. *i.e.*, to attend to the curtains, etc., of the tabernacle while it is standing, and to carry them when it is removed.

26 that is made for them. Rather, " that is to be done with them " (R.V.).

33 the service, etc. While the Israelites were journeying the Kohathites were to carry the *sacred things* of the tabernacle—including the brazen altar, the ark, the vessels of the sanctuary, etc. The Gershonites were charged with all the *drapery* of the tabernacle—the curtains, hangings, etc. And the duty of the Merarites was to convey the more *bulky* and *heavy* materials—the boards, bars, pillars, etc., which were delivered to them by name. Each class had to carry upon their journey the things which they had under their care in their ordinary service (ver. 31). The large number of persons employed would enable the tabernacle to be put up and taken down in a very short time.

CHAPTER V

2 out of the camp. That is, beyond its precincts. See Lev. xiii. 46.

7 with the principal thereof. Rather, " shall restore his trespass in its sum " ; *i.e.*, all that he has wrongfully taken ; adding a fifth as a fine. The penalty was lighter than it would have been in case of his conviction by legal evidence, and not by his own confession. See Exod. xxii. 1.

8 the ram, etc. Presupposing an acquaintance with the law in Lev. vi. 6, 7 ; vii. 7.

12 If any man's wife, etc. The legal punishment of adultery, when proved, was death by stoning (John viii. 5) ; but sometimes the crime might be *suspected* on the part of the husband, and a feeling of " jealousy " awakened within him, with or without cause. Hence the present enactment.

13 with the manner. Rather, " in the act " (R.V.).

15 he shall bring her offering. *i.e.*, he must provide it for her out of his own property.—**no oil,** etc. The absence of oil and frankincense in this offering probably implied the baseness of the crime ; and showed that it was not an oblation, but an " offering of memorial " to the Lord, calling upon Him to punish the accused, if guilty.

16 before the Lord. God here directs a solemn appeal to be made to Himself, to bring to light hidden crime, or to vindicate suspected innocence. None of the actions here prescribed had any natural tendency to produce these effects on the woman, *even when guilty ;* and they could only do so by special Divine interposition. They, therefore, totally differ from the ordeals by fire, boiling water, etc., which have been devised by human superstition, in which it was scarcely possible for the *innocent* to escape uninjured.

19 instead of thy husband. Heb., " under thy husband " ; or, " being in the power of thy husband." (See R.V. and marg.)

21 make thee a curse and an oath. *i.e.*, an example of the fulfilment of the imprecated curse.

23 a book. Or, " scroll " ; or, " writing."

CHAPTER VI

2 Nazarite (spelled more correctly, *Nazirite,* as R.V.) means " separated." Such vows had been previously named (Lev. xxvii.) ; but regulations are here prescribed, partly to prevent superstitious practices, and partly to insure faithfulness in keeping them. They might be made either for a limited period or for life. They were undertaken by some —as by Samson and John the Baptist—in obedience to Divine appointment before their birth ; and by others—as the family of the Rechabites—through several ages, in compliance with the injunctions of their ancestor (Jer. xxxv. 2-19). But generally the Nazirites' vow was a voluntary one, which any person might make, of peculiar separation from the world, and devotedness to the exercises of religion. The abstinence from wine, and other observances of an external kind, did not form their whole peculiarity ; but many of the Nazirites rendered to God a *spiritual* as well as an outward service, and were distinguished for real piety. It appears to have been regarded as a public blessing when God prompted many to consecrate themselves in this way to Him. See Amos ii. 11.

7 the consecration of his God. Rather, " his separation unto God."

11 sinned. *i.e.*, broke (although involuntarily) the rules of his separation, and therefore needed expiation.

12 shall consecrate, etc. *i.e.*, he shall begin a new term of self-consecration, or separation, to continue for the same length of time as he had originally vowed.

14 a sin offering. When the period of his separation had been fulfilled, he still needed a sin offering.

24 The Lord bless thee, etc. This comprehensive benediction is supposed to have been used at various times ; and especially when the priest who had offered incense returned from the sanctuary to the people. (See Luke i. 22.) Here, as other cases, we gain by rendering "Jahveh" (the Lord) as the Hebrews understood and understand it: "THE ETERNAL." His is an eternal, abiding presence—benediction, light and peace. The triple form of the blessing has led many to infer a reference to the Trinity.

CHAPTER VII

8 unto the sons of Merari. Double the number was given to the Merarites, because their charge consisted of the bulkier and heavier parts of the tabernacle. See on iv. 33.

10 for dedicating of the altar. Rather, "the dedication-gift of the altar" (R.V.); *i.e.*, a gift for its consecration.

11 each prince on his day. Hebrew, "one prince a day, one prince a day"; an expressive repetition.

13 a hundred and thirty [shekels]. About five pounds.—**shekel of the sanctuary.** The shekel used as a standard of weight in respect of all holy things.

16 sin offering. It is observable that these offerings were accompanied by all the ordinary kinds of sacrifices, including a sin offering.

89 when Moses was gone. This seems to be a general statement, not referring to any particular time; "when Moses went" (R.V.).

CHAPTER VIII

2 When thou lightest. This, the Jews say, was done by fire from the altar; the middle lamp being first lighted, and the rest from that.—**over against the candlestick.** That is, to the part of the tabernacle in front of the candlestick, which stood on the south side, and which was the only means of lighting the interior when the curtains in front were let down.

9 the whole assembly. Probably by their representatives; either the elders or some of the firstborn, in whose place the Levites were consecrated. The whole assembly was gathered because all the people were interested in the transaction. The same was the case at the consecration of the priests (Lev. viii. 3, 4).

11 Aaron shall offer, etc. Heb., "wave the Levites for a wave offering," *i.e.*, dedicate them. See Exod. xxix. 24. This was probably done by some significant gestures or movements, similar to those used with the ordinary wave offering. Cp. Rom. xii. 1.

CHAPTER IX

1 In the first month. This direction was evidently given before the transactions already recorded (cp. i. 1, 2); and it is mentioned here to introduce what follows in vers. 6–14.

10 yet he shall keep the passover. This arrangement is a clear instance of the subordination of non-essentials to the *spirit* of a religious institution. See 2 Chron. xxx. 2.

14 a stranger. *i.e.*, one who had received circumcision according to the law in Exod. xii. 48, 49. This provision seems to have foreshadowed the admission of Gentiles into the Church, although the Jews in later ages misapprehended its spirit. See Acts xv.; Gal. ii. 3, etc.

22 they journeyed. Hebrew literature witnesses to the impression this guidance left on the mind of the nation. See, *e.g.*, Psa. lxxvii. 20; lxxviii. 14.

CHAPTER X

1 Make thee two trumpets. One for each of Aaron's sons. Others were afterwards added, in Solomon's time, to the number of 120; see 2 Chron. v. 12. As a different word (connected in Josh. vi. 6 with the mention of horns) is always applied to the jubilee trumpets, it has been supposed that these were not used then. The sound of the trumpet became to the Hebrews a symbol of religious joy (see Psa. lxxxix. 15), and it aptly represents the message of the Gospel. The form of these trumpets, which were straight, is seen on the Arch of Titus at Rome.

9 shall be remembered. As this blowing of the trumpets was appointed by God, it was to be regarded by the Israelites as a token of Divine remembrance and deliverance. Cp. xxxi. 6; 2 Chron. xiii. 12, 14.

11 the second year. The period since the erection of the tabernacle on the first day of the first month in the second year after the departure from Egypt is thus calculated: Seven days were spent in the consecration of the tabernacle and its furniture. On the eighth, Moses began the consecration of Aaron and his sons, which lasted seven days. On the fourteenth began the Passover, which lasted till the twenty-second. The rest of the month may have been occupied in receiving and delivering the laws contained in Leviticus. On the first day of the second month, Moses began to number the people, which might occupy three days. On the fourth, the Levites were numbered. On the fifth, they were presented to God, and given to the priests. On the sixth, they were consecrated. On the seventh, their several charges were given to them. After this, the princes began their offerings, which lasted from the eighth to the nineteenth; and on the twentieth day of the second month in the second year the people removed from Sinai.

12 Paran. The name "Paran" seems to be applied to the sandy desert now called er-Ramleh, as well as the great central desert of the peninsula named et-Tih. See xii. 16; xiii. 3. The Israelites probably crossed its eastern side, where the route is always dreary, and often harassing.

17 the tabernacle was taken down. *i.e.*, the curtains and boards were removed by the Gershonites and Merarites, who followed immediately after Judah's division, so that, on reaching the place of encampment, they might set up the tabernacle before the arrival of the Kohathites (ver. 21).

21 the sanctuary. Meaning here the hallowed utensils (see xviii. 29) which the Kohathites were appointed to carry. See on iv. 33.

29 Hobab. Hobab had probably remained behind with Moses, when his father Jethro left the camp. As the Israelites were now removing from Sinai, and going to a distance from his own country, he wished to return home. His answer to Moses' request is not recorded; but, from Judges i. 16; iv. 11, and 1 Sam. xv. 6, it appears probable that Hobab complied.

31 instead of eyes. Though the pillar of cloud would mark the direction and length of their daily journeys, the people would still need information as to the nature of the ground, the situation and qualities of the springs and the pasturages, the collection of fuel, and many other particulars. Hobab's presence would also facilitate any intercourse they might need to hold with neighbouring tribes.

33 went before them. Separated from the rest of the "hallowed things" (ver. 21), and carried by the priests in front of the whole procession, as the leader and guide of the route. Cp. Josh. iii. 3–6.

CHAPTER XI

1 the people complained, etc. Either, "the people were complaining wickedly in the ears of the Lord"; or, "were complaining of evil." The cause of their complaining was probably the fatigues and trials of their march in the desert. But the daily journeys were short, the supply of food constant and certain, and the Divine guidance and protection evident. The murmurings and rebellions of the people were peculiarly sinful and displeasing to God, after the proofs they had received of His care and bounty, and the revelations He had given to them at Sinai of Himself and His covenant relation to them.

2 Moses prayed. Cp. 1 Sam. vii. 9; Jas. v. 16.

5 melons. Perhaps the *water-melon,* which now grows abundantly in Egypt, and is highly valued throughout the East for its refreshing qualities.—**leeks.** Perhaps, rather, the *lotus.*—**onions.** Onions are a staple article of diet for the poor in Egypt. Herodotus mentions onions and garlic among the food of the workmen at the Pyramids.

7 as coriander seed. That is, like *in shape,* being round. On "bdellium," see Gen. ii. 12.

9 fresh oil. Or, "cakes baked with oil" (R.V., marg.). In Exod. xvi. 31 it is said to have had the taste of "wafers with honey." Both descriptions imply that it was alike pleasant and wholesome. The variety of cooking and the pleasantness of taste are adduced as proofs of the unreasonableness of the people's complaint.

9 fell upon it. Or, "fell with it," R.V., marg.

15 out of hand. That is, "outright," or at once.—**my wretchedness.** Cp. 1 Kings xix. 4; Jonah iv. 3. Great as was the provocation, Moses spoke unbecomingly; undervaluing the honour conferred upon him as the minister of Divine power; losing sight of the obligation he was under by the Divine commission; magnifying his own doings, and forgetting that God did, in effect, bear the burden, and that His grace could make His servant equal to still greater requirements.

17 will come down. *i.e.,* in the cloudy pillar. See ver. 25.

the spirit. As a flame is not diminished by others being kindled from it, so God does not diminish the wisdom, energy, and courage which distinguished Moses, by endowing the seventy with them. Cp. Acts vi. 1–6.

25 prophesied. See on Gen. xx. 7.—**did not cease.** "Did so no more" (R.V.); Heb., "did not add." Their *permanent* function was not to prophesy.

28 forbid them. Cp. Luke ix. 49, 50; John iii. 26.

31 brought quails. Vast flocks of these migratory birds still frequent Egypt and the neighbouring countries. In this, as in many other miracles, God did not dispense with the operation of secondary causes. Cp. the account in Psa. lxxviii. 26–28.

let them fall. More literally, "sent them forth (or dispersed them) over the camp."—**upon.** Or, "above" (R.V.). Wearied with their long flight over the sea, they flew within easy reach of the people.

32 ten homers. If literally so, it is more than a hundred bushels; and it can hardly be supposed that he gathered only for his own use. The word is rendered "heaps" in Exod. viii. 14.—**spread them all abroad.** In order to dry them; having learned to cure them, probably, from the Egyptians: see *Herodotus,* ii. 77.

CHAPTER XII

1 the Ethiopian woman. Possibly Zipporah, as the Midianites (to whom, as a Kenite, she belonged) settled in the Arabian Cush, and connected themselves with the Amalekites, most of whom were Cushites (cp. Habak. iii. 7). Her return to Moses at Sinai, and the influence of her brother Hobab, might awaken the jealousy of Miriam and Aaron. But would a union which had subsisted for forty years give umbrage to Miriam and Aaron? It may therefore be that Moses had lately married another wife, perhaps having lost Zipporah by death. There was no legal objection to such a marriage, as the woman was not a Canaanite.

3 Moses was very meek. This clause was probably inserted when the Pentateuch was finished, after the death of Moses. The character of Moses aggravates the crime of Miriam and Aaron; and shows why God took up the matter, though Moses did not.

7 My servant Moses, etc. Rather, "Not so My servant Moses (who is faithful in all My house); with him will I speak," etc. The distinguished honour here given by God to His *servant* Moses is appropriately used in Heb. iii. 3–6, to enhance the honour of the *Son* of God.

14 If her father, etc. That is, "If her father had thus signified his displeasure against her, would she not be so troubled and concerned at it as to shut herself up for some time, being ashamed of her folly?" Spitting in a person's presence was a mark of extreme displeasure.

15 seven days. The time prescribed for the exclusion of the leper; see Lev. xiii. 4, 5.

CHAPTER XIII

3 by the commandment. The proposal to search the land, according to Deut. i. 22–25, originated with the people, and "pleased" Moses also, as in itself natural and reasonable. As, however, the issue too plainly showed, there was a latent feeling of unbelief, making them unfit for so arduous a task as the conquest of Canaan, which could be successful only when undertaken in cheerful faith. This desire of the people was sanctioned by Jehovah, both as a concession to their weakness and to show the power and danger of unbelief. They were now at Kadesh-barnea, at the southern border of the promised land, between the deserts of Paran (et-Tih) and Zin (el-Arabah), on the borders of Edom, a little north-west of Mount Hor. It was afterwards the south-eastern point of the portion of Judah.

16 called. Or, "had called," at the time of his victory over Amalek (Exod. xvii. 9–13). *Hoshea* means "salvation"; *Jehoshua,* "the salvation of Jehovah."

17 southward. Not southward from the place where they were now encamped, but into the southern part of Canaan (the Negeb).

21 Zin. On the south-east of Palestine. It is a part of the long desert valley stretching from the Elanitic Gulf, at Elath, or Ezion-geber, to the Dead Sea, now called el-Ghor and el-Arabah. Kadesh lies on its border.—**Rehob.** Rehob was on the north of Palestine; a city and chieftaincy of Syria, near Mount Hermon. Hamath was a large city on the river Orontes, lying still farther north.

22 Anak. The Anakim were descended from Arba, who gave his name to Kirjath-arba, or Hebron. The date of the foundation of Hebron indicates the time when the Anakim had taken possession of the district; probably extending their settlements to Zoan (or Tanis) in Lower Egypt, called also Avaris ("place of departure," *i.e.*, of caravans leaving Egypt), between the Tanitic and Pelusiac mouths of the Nile. They seem to have been numerous at this period; but in the time of David only a few individuals remained.

23 brook. Rather, valley (R.V.), now called a *wady*. The water of these valleys is soon exhausted in the dry season.—**upon a staff.** Lest the berries should be injured. The grapes of Palestine are still very large, and bunches have been known to weigh twelve pounds each.

30 Caleb. And Joshua with him: see xiv. 30.

32 an evil report. There were two reports—the minority report of Caleb and Joshua and the majority report of the other spies. Cp. Josh. xiv. 8, 9.

CHAPTER XIV

2 in this wilderness. Their wish was granted: see vers. 28–35.

9 they are bread for us. This probably means, "we shall consume them easily and completely": cp. xxiv. 8; Psa. xiv. 4.—**their defence.** Their gods.

11 provoke. Or, "despise" (R.V.).

21 all the earth, etc. "As truly as I live, and as all the earth shall be filled with My glory, because," etc. (R.V.).

22 tempted Me. By doubting My power and faithfulness.—**ten times.** That is, many—a definite for an indefinite number.

25 dwelt. Rather, "are dwelling"; *i.e.*, are awaiting you in the valley. They were also on the hill: see ver. 45.

29 twenty years old and upward. Those who had reached this age had been witnesses of all God's wonders in Egypt and the desert; so that their unbelief was altogether inexcusable. Cp. xxxii. 11, 12; Deut. i. 35, 36.

33 forty years. This includes the whole time of "wandering," from the departure out of Egypt to the entrance into Canaan.—**whoredoms.** This term is frequently used to express unfaithfulness to the Divine covenant, especially by idolatry. See Ex. xxxiv. 15; Judges ii. 17 and Ezek. xxiii. 35; and cp. Rev. xvii. 1.

34 each day for a year. The correspondence in number between the years of wandering and the days spent in searching the promised land was well fitted to affect the Israelites, whose minds were still in a rude and infantile condition. It set vividly before them the connection between sin and its punishment; while every successive year in this term of penal discipline brought with it a new and solemn call to repentance, by reminding them of the original cause of their rejection.—**My breach of promise.** Or, "ye shall know My forsaking" ("alienation," R.V.). This generation, having forsaken God, shall now know what it is to be forsaken by Him.

45 Hormah. Its later name (see also Josh. xv. 30). It appears from Judges i. 17, that its former name was Zephath.

CHAPTER XV

1 And the Lord spake. The events recorded in xv.–xix. occurred before the end of the thirty-seven years of wanderings in the desert; but the dates are not stated.

3 an offering. This precept was an addition to the previous laws of sacrifices. The wheat offering was to be proportioned to the victim, and so to the means of the offerer.

22 if ye have erred. Undesigned transgressions of the *ceremonial* law, into which, through the negligence of ungodly priests and rulers, "the whole congregation" (ver. 24) might fall. Other sins of thoughtlessness had been already provided for: see Lev. iv.

27 any soul. "A single person," in distinction from the former case (ver. 22), in which the whole congregation was implicated.

30 presumptuously. This also probably refers to *positive institutions*, such as the Sabbath (see vers. 32–36). In knowingly disobeying them, a man directly "despised" the authority of the God of Israel.

cut off. The principle of this punishment was not peculiar to the Mosaic economy, but reappears in Christianity in a still more awful form: see Matt. xii. 31, 32; Acts v. 1–10; Heb. vi. 4–8; 1 John v. 16. Under both dispensations there is excision for those who obstinately reject and "despise the word of the Lord."

38 fringes. Or, "tassels." In the Hebrew Book of *Daily Prayers* (see note on Deut. vi. 4) there is one "When putting on the Taleth," praying that the wearer may be wrapped in the Divine precepts.—**borders.** Perhaps "corners" (R.V., marg.).—**ribband.** Or, "line"; or, "lace," as in Exod. xxviii. 28, 37. These were of the same colour as the high priest wore on his breastplate and mitre; and it is supposed that they were designed to indicate that the Hebrews were, as priests, consecrated to God, and to prevent their sinning through forgetfulness: see Exod. xix. 6; 1 Pet. ii. 5, 9.

CHAPTER XVI

1 Korah. Korah was cousin to Moses and Aaron: see Exod. vi. 18, 20, 21. The Kohathites and the Reubenites, having their camps near to each other (ii. 10; iii. 29), could the more easily conspire together; and the princes of Reuben, as descendants of Jacob's eldest son, might be displeased at losing the precedence usually connected with the birthright. On is not mentioned afterwards; perhaps he withdrew from the conspiracy.

2 famous in the congregation. Rather, "called to the assembly" (R.V.); see i. 16.

4 fell upon his face. Under an overwhelming sense of the evil of this matter: see xiv. 5; Numb. xvi. 4, 22; xx. 6.

5 to-morrow. This delay gave time for reflection and repentance. The words, "The LORD will show who are His," are quoted from the Septuagint, in 2 Tim. ii. 19.

6 Take you censers. Assume the office which you claim, that we may see whom the Lord will choose.

7 too much. Retorting their charge against himself (ver. 3); as Elijah threw back Ahab's: see 1 Kings xviii. 17, 18.

11 what is Aaron? *i.e.*, your rebellion is not so much against Aaron as God, who gave him the office to which you aspire. Cp. Exod. xvi. 8.

13 a land that floweth, etc. Applying to Egypt the Divine description of the promised land: see Exod. iii. 8; Lev. xx. 24.

14 wilt thou put out the eyes, etc.? *i.e.*, "dost thou think to blind us to thy treachery?"

15 I have not taken one ass. As many rulers would. Cp. 1 Sam. xii. 3; Acts xx. 33.

19 gathered all the congregation. Probably not absolutely *all* the people. But the whole narrative shows that many were inclined to side with the conspirators; from whom, however, they separated themselves when the danger became imminent. See vers. 27, 41.

30 quick. Here and elsewhere in Scripture in its old English sense, meaning *alive.* Cp. Psa. lv. 15; cxxiv. 3, etc.

32 that appertained unto. Or, "took part with." Some, at least, of his family, who probably remained in his tent in the Kohathites' quarters, were not involved in his doom; for the prophet Samuel, and the singers his descendants, were of this family. See xxvi. 11, and cp. 1 Sam. i. 1 with 1 Chron. vi. 33-38. See also title of Psa. lxxxiv.

35 a fire from the Lord. As Nadab and Abihu had been destroyed (Lev. x. 2).

38 souls. Or, "lives" (R.V.).

a sign, etc. To keep the people in mind of the fate of the conspirators, and tend to prevent rebellion.

39 wherewith they. Rather, "which they" (R.V.).

48 the plague was stayed. The efficacy of Aaron's interposition was a further attestation of his Divine commission. He is here a type of Christ; who, by His atonement and intercession, has averted from all who live by Him the penalty which their sins have deserved (Heb. vii. 22-26).

CHAPTER XVII

2 rods. These "rods," or staves, were, no doubt, carried by the "princes" as symbols of authority; and as they were always made of well-seasoned and durable wood, this miracle would be the more striking. The budding of such a staff is used by ancient poets to represent an absolute impossibility.

4 I will meet. Rather, "I meet" *customarily,* as R.V.

9 every man his rod. Every one evidently recognised his own.

10 before the Testimony. *i.e.,* in the ark, in front of the Tables of the Law (Heb. ix. 4). The rod was lost before the building of the Temple (1 Kings viii. 9).

13 cometh anything near. Heb., "cometh near, cometh near," *i.e.,* in any degree maketh the least approach.

CHAPTER XVIII

1 bear the iniquity. *i.e.,* the *punishment* of the iniquity. The priests were to be answerable for any irregularities in discharging the duties of the sanctuary. These commands were given with renewed strictness, that the priests and Levites might be on the watch to prevent future danger; as well as to remind both them and the people that the honour of their ministry was attended with corresponding responsibility.

2 tabernacle of witness. *i.e.,* "tent of the Testimony" (R.V.).

8 hallowed things. The priests had no share at all of the land, and the Levites had little besides their cities; an arrangement obviously intended to keep up their peculiar position in the community. The Levites, however, had a tithe of the produce, out of which they set apart one-tenth for the priests. The priests had also reserves from the various offerings; some being shared among them all, and some appropriated to those who were actually on service.—**by reason of the anointing.** Rather (as R.V. marg.), "for a portion of the anointing," *i.e.,* of the priesthood.

11 every one that is clean. These offerings, like the tithes (ver. 31), were thus distinguished from the "*most* holy" things belonging to the priests, which might only be eaten by the priests themselves in the most holy place (ver. 10).

19 salt. A "covenant of salt" signifies an everlasting covenant (see 2 Chron. xiii. 5); probably in reference to the preserving quality of salt. (Matt. v. 13; Mark ix. 50; Col. iv. 6. Every meat offering was seasoned with salt (Lev. ii. 13).)

CHAPTER XIX

1 The Lord spake. The judgements which had lately fallen on the camp of Israel having, probably, caused defilement to many of the survivors by bringing them into contact with the dead, directions are given as to the method of preparing and using a general means of purification.

2 the ordinance of the law. *i.e.,* what is ordained by the law.—**without spot.** Heb., "perfect."

3 give her unto Eleazar. It must not be done by the high priest, as he was to avoid all pollutions.

7 unclean. As the priest who took the heifer's blood on his finger, and the man who burnt her, and the man who gathered her ashes, all contracted uncleanness by so doing, it was hereby signified that sin had been laid upon the animal.

9 water of separation. The "water of separation," or of purification, was formed by mixing in spring water the ashes of the heifer, together with other ingredients (ver. 6), which were also used in the cleansing of lepers (Lev. xiv. 6, 7). The sprinkling of the blood, and of the water containing the ashes, was a type of the work of Christ; probably representing the combined justification and sanctification of the believer: see Heb. ix. 13, 14.—**a purification for sin.** *i.e.,* "a sin offering" (R.V.).

11 the dead body. This enactment tended to prevent unnecessary or superstitious practices with regard to the dead, and to insure speedy burial; it also served to keep before the people the connexion between sin and death.

12 He shall purify, etc. Or, "He that shall purify himself with it on the third day and on the seventh day, he shall not be clean": see R.V. marg.

13 shall be cut off from Israel. Though the pollution contracted was only ceremonial, yet the neglect of the purification prescribed would make the ceremonially unclean man *morally* guilty.

CHAPTER XX

1 Kadesh. In thus bringing the Israelites back to Kadesh, the scene of their fathers' rebellion and exclusion from Canaan (Numb. xiv.), God was giving the younger generation an impressive warning, lest they too should "fall after the same example of unbelief."

8 the rod. Called in ver. 11 "*his* rod," with which he had wrought former miracles (Exod. xvii. 1-6). It appears from the next verse to have been laid up, like the rod of Aaron (xvii. 10), "before Jehovah" in the sanctuary.

12 believed Me not. In both the actions and the language of Moses and Aaron on this occasion, there are indications of a petulance inconsistent with that calm faith in God which they commonly display. (See Exod. xvii. 1-6; and Psa. cvi. 33.) In detail, too, they departed from the instructions given. Moses smote the rock twice; which, at this time, he does not seem to have been directed to do at all. By seeming, also, to claim for *themselves* the power of fetching water from the rock, he withheld from Jehovah His due honour.—**sanctify Me.** That is, "to treat Me as the Holy One of Israel."

14 unto the king of Edom. A similar request seems to have been sent to the Moabites (Judges xi. 17).—**thy brother Israel.** Descended from a common ancestor, Isaac.

19 I will pay for it. Water is scarce and valuable in that district, and the permission to use it often has to be purchased.

21 Israel turned away from him. As the Israelites had refused to enter Canaan from the south, and were not now to be allowed to do so, the nearest route from Kadesh to the point at which to invade the land was eastward through Idumea. But the passes through the mountains of Seir were few and difficult, mere ravines, easily defended. Had the Israelites, as they desired, marched through one of these, they would quickly have reached the edge of the Great Desert on the eastern side of Idumea. But the refusal of Edom compelled them to travel along the western border of Idumea to Ezion-geber (see xxi. 4); and then, crossing the mountain-ridge at a depression in the range (probably the pass of Wady el-Ithm), to go along its eastern side to the land of Moab.

22 Hor. On the east of the desert of Zin (el-Arabah), and west of Petra; now called, from the event here related, Djebel Nebi Harun; or, "the mount of the prophet Aaron."

28 Eleazar his son. The investiture of Eleazar before the death of Aaron seems to indicate the perpetuity of the priestly office; and may remind us of Him who, because He continueth ever, hath an unchangeable priesthood (Heb. vii. 24).

CHAPTER XXI

1 king Arad the Canaanite. Rather, "the Canaanite king of Arad" (R.V.). Arad was a city in the south of Palestine (Josh. xii. 14). This conflict probably occurred while the Israelites were at Kadesh, awaiting the return of messengers from Edom.—**the spies.** The Heb. word, "Atharim," here rendered "the spies," is better read as a proper name: "by the way of Atharim." So R.V.

2 destroy. Or, "devote to destruction"; and so in ver. 3. The conquest now begun was soon pushed further by Joshua (Josh. x. 41; xi. 14), and completed by the tribes of Judah and Simeon (Judg. i. 17). The fulfilment of the vow was probably inserted here, like similar passages elsewhere, to complete the narrative of Moses. "He called," etc., should rather be rendered "one called," or, "it was called."

4 the way of the Red Sea. That is, to Ezion-geber, at the head of the eastern gulf. This road along the Arabah is peculiarly rough and wearisome, lying through a dreary desert, described in Deut. viii. 15 as "that great and terrible wilderness." Cp. Psa. cvii. 4–7.

6 fiery serpents. Or, rather, "*the* fiery serpents"; pointing plainly to some well known in the neighbourhood; perhaps the *hydra*, or water-snake, described as "fiery" on account of the burning pain and inflammation attending its bite. Possibly the "serpent" was a parasitic worm (*Filaria Medinensis*). See Sir Risdon Bennett's *Diseases of the Bible*, Appendix, p. 133.

7 We have sinned. Cp. 1 Sam. xii. 19; Acts viii. 24.

9 a serpent of brass. This owed its efficacy to the Divine appointment, faith in which was expressed by the act of looking at the serpent for deliverance. It is used by our Lord to represent His crucifixion, and illustrates the freeness and accessibleness of the gospel remedy for sin, as well as the simplicity of its application by faith in Christ (John iii. 14, 15). For superstitious use afterwards made of this serpent, and its destruction by Hezekiah, see 2 Kings xviii. 4.

13 the coasts (borders) **of the Amorites.** The Amorites or "highlanders," in the time of Abraham, dwelt on the west of the Jordan (Gen. xiv. 7); but afterwards appear to have passed across the river, and to have wrested from the Moabites all that portion of their country which lay north of the Arnon.

14 The book of the wars of the Lord. The passage (14–20) is obscure. If the book is rightly named, it might be a collection of poems celebrating God's deliverances of Israel from their Egyptian and other enemies, resembling Deut. xxxii. and Psa. lxxviii., cv.; and intended to be learned and sung by the people.

What He did, etc. Rather (taking the first word as a proper name):

"Vaheb in Suphah (did He conquer),
And the valleys of Arnon,
And the slope of the valleys," etc.

(See R.V.)

18 By the direction of the law-giver, etc. Rather, "with the sceptre and with the staves" (R.V.). In the fertile districts on the east of the Jordan, on the edge of the desert, water may be found, on turning up the sand, at the depth of a few inches.

20 Jeshimon. Or, the "wilderness," probably the dreary tract on the north-east of the Dead Sea.

26 the Amorites. This is mentioned to show the right of the Israelites to Heshbon (the Amorites being descendants of Canaan), though they were not allowed by God to take any of the cities then possessed by the Moabites, who were descendants of Lot. See Deut. ii. 18, 19. Respecting the importance of this, see Judges xi. 13–27.

27 proverbs. Heb., "poems."

29 Chemosh. Chemosh was the idol worshipped by the Moabites and Ammonites. This is quoted in Jer. xlviii. 45, 46.—**He hath given**, etc. Rather, "He makes his sons fugitives, and his daughters captives," etc. (see R.V.).

CHAPTER XXII

1 on this side. That is, on the eastern side; over against Jericho.

5 Pethor. Pethor has been identified with the Pitru of the cuneiform inscriptions. It was on the west bank of the Euphrates, a few miles south of Carchemish. (See Sayce: *The Higher Criticism and the Monuments*, p. 274.)—**the land**, etc. Either Balaam's native land, or the land of the people of Balak, who, as a Moabite, was a descendant of Terah.

6 I wot (know). Under the delusion that the gods could be influenced by charms, magical incantations, etc., Balak, regarding Jehovah as merely the national god of the Israelites, hoped that His favour and protection might be turned from them by means of Balaam's malediction.

8 the Lord. "One of the main lessons in Balaam's history," says F. W. Robertson, "must ever be, to trace how it is that men who would appear respectable, conscientious, honourable, gifted, religious, may be in the sight of God accursed and heirs of perdition." He regards Balaam's case as a perversion of great gifts and a perversion of conscience. Balaam wanted to please himself without displeasing God.

19 what the Lord will say to me more. Balaam tampers with temptation against the convictions of conscience; professing deference for Divine authority, yet hankering after the "wages of unrighteousness"; an example of the danger and uselessness of attempting to compromise the claims of God and Mammon. What could be more offensive to God than to desire *permission* to disobey God's command?

20 If the men come, etc. Rather, "*Since* the men are come"; implying that such was actually the case.—**go with them.** The prohibition of the journey in the first instance had respect to its avowed and sole object, the *cursing of Israel* (see vers. 6, 11, 12). Here, while Balaam is permitted to go, the design of the journey is again expressly forbidden; though he doubtless hoped that, having got leave to go, he should in some way gain his own ends.

22 the angel. Some have taken this to be a vision presented to Balaam's mind, in a "trance," like that described in xxiv. 3, 4, 15, 16. Others have supposed that the cries of the ass (sensitive to the angel's presence) shaped themselves to the prophet's consciousness into articulate sounds. But "the point of greatest importance is to believe that God dealt with this man, opposed his perverse will by gracious influences and unexpected protests" (R. A. Watson: *Expositor's Bible*).

24 a path of the vineyards. The roads in Palestine and many Eastern countries are unenclosed, except when they pass between the fences of gardens or vineyards.

35 Go with the men. Balaam was evidently going with the secret hope that he might succeed in cursing Israel, and so gratify Balak, and obtain his rewards. As, however, God designed that Balaam not only should not curse, but should *bless*, he is commanded to proceed on his journey.

38 that shall I speak. Implying probably that he *must* do so if God requires it; and so in xxiv. 13. Accordingly the future tense is translated by "must" in xxiii. 12, 26.

40 offered. Or, "killed"; making a great feast.

41 it came to pass on the morrow, etc. Balaam on the morrow addresses himself to his task; in the hope of attaining his wishes, he is conducted by Balak from one height to another, commanding views of the camp of Israel, and has recourse to sacrifices and the customary rites of superstition. But, prompted by a Divine prophetic inspiration, he is constrained three several times, and with increasing emphasis, in spite of Balak's remonstrances, to pronounce a *blessing*, instead of a *curse*, upon the favoured people (xxii. 41; xxiii.; xxiv. 1–9). Balak gives vent to his rage in word and gesture (10, 11); but Balaam concludes his prophecy by announcing the signal triumphs awaiting Israel, and the complete destruction of their heathen foes (12–25).

Baal. This was the name of the chief Syrian and Phœnician deity, which represented the sun and the vivifying powers of nature. It bore among the Moabites the name *Baal-Peor,* and its worship here, as at Babylon, was exceedingly obscene. Balaam's expectation that sacrifices offered at such a place could propitiate Jehovah shows how much superstition may be mixed with some knowledge of the true God.

CHAPTER XXIII

1 seven. A sacred number.

7 parable. Or, "poetic prophecy." The poetical structure of the first clause appears more clearly in the Hebrew, which stands nearly thus:

"From Aram, Balak hath brought me,
The king of Moab, from the mountains of the east."

Aram. *i.e.,* Aram-Naharaim, or Aram of the two rivers (viz., *Tigris* and *Euphrates*), called in Greek *Mesopotamia,* or region between the rivers.

9 From the top of the rocks I see him. To Balaam, gazing on Israel from the height, the spirit of revelation and prophecy unfolded the future destinies of the chosen people. The description which follows of the blessedness of ancient Israel is still more applicable to the true spiritual Israel of which it was the representative. The Israelites are pronounced blessed (1) in their separation by God's choicest covenant from other nations; (2) in their multiplied numbers; and (3) in their hopes for the future. The *death* of God's people was cheered by the enjoyment of His favour, by satisfaction in reviewing the past, and by bright anticipation of the future destinies of their race, whilst their "last end" was believed to be supremely happy. But Balaam's desire for this was vain, regarding only the *end,* without any care for the *way* of attaining it.

the people shall dwell alone. "It is a people that dwelleth alone" (R.V.). In other passages (see Deut. xxxiii. 28; Jer. xlix. 31) this expression is used in connexion with "in safety."

10 The death of the righteous. Of course every one wishes this, says Robertson. "But it is one thing to wish to be saved, another to wish God's right to triumph; one thing to wish to die safe, another to wish to live holily."

the righteous. Israel is here so called as being separated from all other nations to be a "holy people unto the Lord."

13 Come, I pray thee. This proposal (like that in ver. 27) was no doubt suggested by the superstitious notion that one place was more favourable to magical rites than another.

14 field of Zophim. Rather, "to the field of the watchmen," an elevated position used for watching against the approach of enemies.

21 He hath not beheld. The Samaritan, Syriac, and all the Targums read this, "I have not beheld." The Targums, with the Septuagint and Vulgate, make the "iniquity" and "perverseness" to refer specifically to idolatry. Some scholars translate the words thus: "He will not see (*i.e.,* permit) injury to Jacob, nor allow a plot against Israel."

the shout of a king. "A shout of joy caused by the fact that The Eternal Himself was King in Israel"; "joy at the perpetual presence of this great King among the people."

22 unicorn. Probably the urus, or wild ox. See the description of its indomitable strength and fierceness in Job xxxix 9–12; and allusions to it, Psa. xxii. 21; Isa. xxxiv. 7.

23 according to this time, etc. The most probable rendering of the verse seems to be, "For there is no soothsaying in Jacob, and no divination in Israel; [but] at the [proper] time it is told to Jacob and to Israel what God doeth"; Israel had no need to resort to the arts which Balak was employing in order to ascertain the Divine will, since at the proper time God's purposes would be clearly made known.

28 top of Peor. A mountain, probably, like the "heights of Baal" (xxii. 41), where the Moabites sacrificed to Baal-Peor. The summit selected was one looking towards the wilderness, whence the Israelites had come (xxi. 20).

CHAPTER XXIV

3 whose eyes are open. Rather, "with the eyes closed"; *i.e.*, the outward sense being superseded by the inward vision.

4 falling into a trance. Rather, "falling, and with opened eyes." The power of the inspiration made him fall down (see 1 Sam. xix. 24; Dan. x. 8, 9), whilst it opened the inward sight.

7 lign aloes. Probably the *excoecaria agallocha*, a highly fragrant plant: see Psa. xlv. 8; John xix. 39.—**which the Lord hath planted.** *i.e.*, indigenous natural productions, not planted by the hand of man: see Psa. civ. 16.

7 higher than Agag. Agag seems to have been the common title of the kings of Amalek: see 1 Sam. xv. 9; Esth. iii. 1, 10; viii. 3.—**his kingdom.** Though Balaam, in uttering these predictions, may have thought only of the ancient kingdom of Israel, the Holy Spirit doubtless intended them to have a further reference to our Lord, in whom the kingdom of Israel attains its ideal glory.

9 Blessed, etc. These very words had been addressed by Isaac to Jacob (Gen. xxvii. 29), and had previously been spoken to Abraham by God Himself (Gen. xii. 3).

10 smote his hands together. In horror or rage: see Job xxvii. 23, and Lam. ii. 15.

14 advertise. Or, "inform"; or, "advise."

the latter days. That is, in the distant future, as in Gen. xlix. 1.

17 corners. Rather, "both sides," *i.e.* the whole of.

children of Sheth. Or, "sons of tumult" (R.V.). This line is quoted, with slight variations, in Jer. xlviii. 45; and the word "sheth" seems not to be a proper name, but to signify *violence* or *tumult*.

18 Edom. The people. *Seir*, the country.

19 him that remaineth. Probably meaning all that are found surviving in every city of Edom: see 1 Kings xi. 15, 16.

20 first. Rather, "chief," as in 1 Sam. xv. 21: see ver. 7.—**perish.** Amalek had been devoted to extermination: see refs.

21 Kenites. See note on xii. 1. The Kenites, except those who, with Hobab, connected themselves with Israel, gradually disappear, being mentioned only in 1 Sam. xv. 6. The Assyrians overran all these countries about the beginning of the Hebrew captivities: see 2 Kings xv. 29.—**thy nest.** In this word there is a play upon the name *Kenite*, *ken* being the Hebrew word for "nest."

23 who shall live. This prophecy probably contemplated the frequent and desolating wars of the Macedonian, Græco-Egyptian, and Græco-Syrian kings, which prepared the way for the Roman conquests.

24 And. Or, "For." "Chittim," which properly designates the Phœnician settlers in Cyprus, and thence is applied to the whole island, here seems to be a general name for the maritime nations of Southern Europe.—**Eber.** "Eber" means, probably, not the Hebrews alone, but all the nations who traced their descent to Eber (Gen. x. 25).

And he also. That is, probably, this last conqueror from the West shall perish. In this prophetic sketch of the destinies of the country through many ages, the subjugation of Moab and Edom, the extermination of Amalek, the disappearance of the Kenites, the overthrow of the Assyrian and Syrian powers, and, finally, the extirpation of the Western invaders, are depicted with wonderful accuracy; while the prediction respecting Israel indicates the glory and perpetuity of its Divine kingdom.

25 returned to his place. Balaam seems to have set out on his return home. It appears, however, from what follows, that he did not reach Mesopotamia, but that after leaving Balak he went to the Midianites, who had united with the Moabites in bringing him from his own country (see xxii. 4, 7), and was slain with them (xxxi. 8), leaving a name which has become a byword in the world.

CHAPTER XXV

1 whoredom. This narrative shows the close connexion between idolatry and licentiousness, and thus illustrates the propriety of the bold figures of some of the prophets (as in Ezek. xvi., etc.), and of the frequent use of the same word to designate both sins. We learn from xxxi. 16, and Rev. ii. 14, that Balaam suggested to Balak the use of these temptations in order to weaken the Israelites.

3 the anger of the Lord, etc. Israel's sin did that which all Balaam's enchantments could not do—it brought God's anger upon them.

4 hang them up. This means the idolators. Moses was to "take all the heads," or chiefs, that they might execute the sentence (5).—**against** (before) **the sun.** That is, during the day. The bodies of criminals were to be taken down at sunset (Deut. xxi. 23).

11 he was zealous. "If any private person," says Calvin, "should in his preposterous zeal take upon himself to punish a similar crime, in vain will he boast of being an imitator of Phinehas, unless he shall be thoroughly assured of the command of God. In order that our zeal may be approved of God, it must be tempered by spiritual prudence, and directed by His authority."

12 My covenant of peace. This promise was remarkably fulfilled; for the high priesthood continued in his family down to the time of Christ, with the exception of a short period when Eli and his family held the office, probably in consequence of some personal disqualification of the right heir: see 1 Sam. i.; 1 Kings ii. 27; and 1 Chron. vi. 4-8, compared with xxiv. 3, 6.

CHAPTER XXVI

2 Take the sum, etc. From this second census it appears that the nation, which, forty years before, was increasing rapidly, had now been considerably diminished. The change from a settled to a wandering life would not have effected this without those remarkable plagues by which God punished their repeated sins. This decrease, however, was confined to five of the tribes; and in some of them (*e.g.*, Reuben and Simeon) it appears to have been connected with recorded facts in their history.

51 These were the numbered. See note on Exod. xxxviii. 26.

55 by lot. Whilst the foregoing law apportioned the *extent* of territory, God now directs that the locality of each family should be decided by an appeal to Him by the lot.

57 the Levites. Some suppose that the tribe of Levi (which was not numbered with the rest at Mount Sinai, but by itself) did not come under the sentence that none of that generation should enter Canaan. Eleazar and Ithamar, and perhaps some others of the Levites, are supposed to have been of that generation, and yet to have entered Canaan: see Josh. xvii. 4; xxiv. 33.

CHAPTER XXVII

1 Then came, etc. By the custom of the nations with which the Hebrews were connected, daughters appear to have been deprived of all share in the paternal inheritance; which, when there was no son, went to the nearest kinsman (vers. 9–11) in the male line. The case of Zelophehad's daughters gave occasion for an improvement, by the enactment of a law which divided the inheritance among daughters if there were no sons, making their children the genealogical representatives of their father's house. Subsequently, in xxxvi., such heiresses are required to marry only into their own tribe, to prevent the alienation of any of its territory.

3 his own sin. Having been guilty of no offence which attainted his family, but having died like the rest of his generation. It is remarkable that failure of sons should have been so rare as to be mentioned only in this instance.

12 Abarim. "Abarim" was the name of the mountain-ridge on the east of the Jordan and the Dead Sea: see Deut. xxxiv. 1, and note.

15 Moses spake. It appears from Deut. iii. 23–28, that Moses petitioned again to be permitted to go over the Jordan; and, when his request was refused, meekly "set his house in order." His conduct in this instance is eminently worthy of his noble and unselfish character.

18 the spirit. That is, a special communication of His Divine influences.

20 thine honour. The ruling power delegated by God to Moses.

21 Urim. See Exod. xxviii. 30. Urim and Thummim signify light and truth.

CHAPTER XXVIII

2 Command, etc. The feasts and offerings to which the following directions relate had been enjoined before; but it is almost certain that their observance had been interrupted, or at least partially neglected, in the desert: see Amos v. 25; Acts vii. 42. Besides, these directions were given to a new generation, who were children when the former laws were given.

My bread, etc. Or, "My food for sacrifices made by fire." So called as being solemnly dedicated to God; so ver. 24.

7 strong wine. That is, of the best quality. We are to serve God with the best we have.

9 two lambs. Probably two *in addition* to the daily offerings specified immediately before. The regular observance of these rites on the Sabbath would keep this day in constant remembrance: see Ezek. xlvi. 4, 5.

26 after your weeks be out. The seven weeks from the Passover to the Pentecost.

CHAPTER XXIX

1 a holy convocation. The "trumpets" heralded the month in which fell the Day of Atonement and the Feast of Tabernacles. The days of holy convocation (see also the preceding chapter) would concur with the weekly Sabbath in promoting the knowledge of God and attention to His services.

11 a sin offering. This was besides the great annual sin offering of atonement (Lev. xvi.); signifying the imperfection of the sacrifices under the law, and their insufficiency to take away sin.

CHAPTER XXX

The laws in this chapter respecting vows are supplementary to those in Lev. xxvii., and refer to special circumstances. A "vow" is a promise to *do* something; a "bond," in the Heb. here means a vow of abstinence.

9 Evidently a parenthesis, or a verse transposed in copying.

15 he hath heard them. And not objected; he will then be dealt with as having himself broken the vow.

CHAPTER XXXI

2 Midianites. As the Midianites were not a Canaanitish nation, they would not have been molested if they had not seduced the Israelites into sin (chap. xxv. 17, 18).

5 delivered. Or, "separated."

6 Phinehas. The presence of Phinehas, the son of the high priest, was highly significant, as it was he whose holy zeal had stayed the plague: see xxv. 11.—**the holy instruments and the trumpets.** R.V. has, "the vessels of the sanctuary and the trumpets." Cp. 1 Sam. iv. 4.

7 all the males. *i.e.*, of the tribes in that neighbourhood; as the Midianites are afterwards mentioned as a powerful nation (Judges vi.).

8 Balaam. He who had instigated the sin most justly shared the punishment. See on ver. 17.

9 took the spoil, etc. Rather, "took as spoil all their," etc.

10 castles. Or, fortified encampments: see Gen. xxv. 16.

11 all the prey. A distinction appears to be made between the *spoil* and the *prey*: the former (which was perhaps taken from the persons of the slain) being retained by the soldiers; the latter being divided into halves, of which the soldiers had one, and the rest of the people the other; and a five-hundredth part being offered from the soldiers' portion, and a fiftieth from the people's, to the Lord. Thus, those who had the toil and danger justly received the larger share; though, since they acted only as representatives of the whole congregation, it was but right that the people generally should receive a portion of the booty.

17 kill every woman. This unusual severity was an act of retributive justice upon those who had occasioned the sin of Israel and the ruin of their own nation (xxv. 17, 18). To put to death all the male children would exterminate the tribes implicated, the females spared being merged in the conquering people.

28 one soul of five hundred. One out of every 500.

35 thirty and two thousand. The total population of these tribes of Midianites must have been about two hundred thousand.

49 there lacketh not one. This may be explained in part by the skill and suddenness of the attack.

50 tablets. "Necklaces" (see R.V.).

52 shekels. Amounting to about $175,000 of our money.

53 every man for himself. *i.e.*, all the common soldiers kept their spoil for themselves.

CHAPTER XXXII

1 Jazer. Now *el-Belka*, reaching from the river Arnon nearly to the Jabbok.

Gilead. Now *Jebel Ajlun*, extending from Jazer to Bashan; the south of this, with the north of Jazer, was given to the tribe of Gad. These districts are still remarkable for beauty of scenery, fine climate, and great fertility.

5 for a possession. This proposal appears selfish and unbelieving, and the reply of Moses was most just and fair.

20 before the Lord. *i.e.*, before the ark, the symbol of the Divine presence, according to the prescribed arrangement.

23 your sin will find you out. *i.e.*, it will not escape merited punishment.

33 Manasseh. This tribe was numerous, and the country east of Jordan was disproportionately large for two tribes. Hence half Manasseh, some of whose leaders had taken cities in Gilead (ver. 39), was included in the arrangement. These tribes on the east side of Jordan, which were first settled, were among the first to be displaced and carried into exile by the Assyrians.

34 built. That is, "rebuilt," or "fortified."

38 their names being changed. As bearing the names of idols, Nebo and Baal. See Exod. xxiii. 13.

41 Jair. By his great-grandfather's side Jair belonged to Judah; but his grandmother was a daughter of Machir, the son of Manasseh, and he passed into her family; Manasseh probably adopting his father, Segub.

CHAPTER XXXIII

As the people had now ended their wanderings in the desert, a list is given of their principal halting-places on the march from Egypt to the plains of the Jordan (xxxiii. 1–49).

1 journeys. Or, "stages." All the stations are not given here, as is clear from ver. 16, where Taberah is omitted. Dr. Flinders Petrie (*Researches in Sinai*, p. 205), referring to the routes mentioned in Exod. xiv. and xv. says: "It seems clear that the writer of these itineraries knew the road to the present Sinai well. The description exactly fits that road, and it will not fit any other."

4 buried. "Were burying," as the Egyptians were thus occupied, the Israelites had ample opportunity to depart unmolested.

18 Rithmah. Probably the station, not before named, in the desert of Paran, whence the spies were sent (xiii.). Its name is derived from the "retem." In March, 1905, Flinders Petrie saw the retem bushes in full flower, covered with small white blossoms; the plant is a white broom and very bitter (*Researches in Sinai*, p. 29).

40 king Arad. See note on xxi. 1.

52 ye shall drive out, etc. The Canaanites were excepted from the ordinary laws of war, and were to be utterly exterminated. (See note at the end of Joshua.) The commands which follow teach the important lesson that all temptations and incitements to sin must be resolutely kept at the furthest possible distance from us. The danger of neglecting this is illustrated by the sad defections of the Israelites.

pictures. Or, "figures"; other representations than those of idols, but having unhallowed associations.

56 shall do unto you. *i.e.*, drive you out, and destroy you; a threatening executed in the subsequent captivities and final dispersion of Israel.

CHAPTER XXXIV

In anticipation of the approaching conquest and acquisition of Canaan, the boundaries of the land are described (1–15); Joshua and Eleazar, with the co-operation of chief men chosen from the several tribes, are appointed to superintend the distribution of it (16–29); and forty-eight cities are ordered to be allotted to the Levites, including six cities of refuge (xxxv. 1–15), with precise directions as to the persons for whom they shall be available (16–34).

3 quarter. Or, "frontier."—**the outmost coast,** etc. Rather, "from the end of the Salt Sea eastward" (R.V.). The line was first S.E., then W.

4 from the south, etc. Rather, "southward of the ascent" (R.V.).

8 Hor. This mountain was on the north of Canaan, and is of course to be distinguished from the southern Mount Hor, near Edom, where Aaron died. This was probably a peak of Lebanon.

15 near Jericho eastward. *i.e.*, opposite, or over against it; and so in xxxv. 1.

CHAPTER XXXV

2 cities to dwell in. For these forty-eight cities see Josh. xxi. By the Levites being distributed over the land, the whole country would have the benefit of their religious instructions.—**suburbs.** Space for pasture lands, etc., around the towns.

8 according to his inheritance. The cities were not to be distributed equally among the tribes, but a greater number was to be taken from the richer and larger ones.

34 wherein I dwell. Thus the reason of all these laws is traced up to their Divine Author, who could not dwell in a defiled and dishonoured land.

CHAPTER XXXVI

It being represented to Moses that the enactment (xxvii. 1–11) authorising the succession of daughters to an inheritance might lead to the transference of estates to a different tribe, it is ordained that females so inheriting shall be permitted to marry only in their own tribe (1–9); and this arrangement is acted upon in the instance of the daughters of Zelophehad, which had been brought forward as a test case (10–12). So ends the legislation in the plains of Moab (13).

4 the jubilee. *i.e.*, "although the jubilee will come which is to re-establish the equality of landed property, still we have no prospect of recovering the property of our family."

13 These are the commandments, etc. Thus the laws given in the land of Moab had the same authority as those before given in the desert of Sinai. See Lev. xxvii. 34.

DEUTERONOMY

THE BOOK OF GOD'S LAW

INTRODUCTION

THE usual Hebrew title of this Book was *Hadebharim,* "the words," or, more fully, *Elleh Hadebharim,* "these words." It was taken from the first words of the Book. It embraces narrative, commands, exhortations. The title given in the English version is taken from the Greek *Deuteronomion,* "the second law." This, however, does not necessarily mean a new legislation, but in this case is obviously a repetition or enforcement of laws already given.

There are few books of the Bible about which more controversy has arisen as to date and authorship. For the purpose of this Commentary it would be profitless to enter upon the discussion here. The questions raised are chiefly of historical, literary and antiquarian interest. And in the discussion of them the great spiritual value of the Book has too often been overlooked.

Its spiritual value was experienced and attested by our Lord Himself in the hour of His great temptation. Three times He meets the tempter with the words, "It is written" (Matt. iv. 4, 7, 10), in each case a quotation from Deuteronomy (viii. 3; vi. 16; vi. 13). And on other occasions He refers to the Book as the work of Moses (cp. Matt. xix. 8 with Deut. xxiv. 1, and John v. 46 with Deut. xviii. 15, 18). The Apostles, too, more than once appealed to its authority (see Acts iii. 22; Rom. xii. 19; Gal. iii. 10; and the words of Stephen, Acts vii. 37).

In the Jewish Church, too, its words are highly prized and in constant use. One of its great messages, the "Shĕmâ" (or "Hear, O Israel" of Deut. vi. 4–9), may still be found inscribed on the door-posts and lintels of many a Jewish home. Devout Jews still carry about with them, in its little case or box, the strip of parchment containing these words, with the exhortation to love the Lord their God with all the heart.

Family religion is strongly and tenderly commended in this Book, as for instance in vi. 7, 20; xi. 18, 19; xxxi. 12, 13. Special attention is also given to the poor and the stranger (x. 18, 19; xv. 7–11; xxiv. 14–22). Many other practical commands are given, which have their message for the individual and for the nation to-day. There are few finer passages in literature than the 33rd chapter, with its blessings on the tribes; and the closing chapter, recording the death of Moses, is most touching in its simple grandeur.

CHAPTER I

As this book is chiefly a recapitulation of the history and laws before recorded (see the references given in the margin of the Bible), the following notes are confined to subjects not previously noticed. Some of these appear to be adaptations of the law to the improved character of the people, who were better prepared to submit to its spiritual precepts than their fathers had been; whilst others were probably explanations, arising out of particular events which had occurred.

1 on this side Jordan. Rather, "beyond Jordan" (R.V.). Literally, the phrase is, "at the crossing of Jordan," the context deciding which side of the river is meant.

the Red Sea. The word "*Sea*" is not in the original, which has only the word "Suph" ("weed"). Vers. 1 and 2 should be read thus:—"These are the words which Moses spake unto all Israel at the crossing of the Jordan, in the wilderness along the Arabah in front of Suph (the deep valley running north and south of the Dead Sea: R.V., marg.), between Paran (on the west), and between Tophel (on the east), and Laban (Libnah: Numb. xxxiii. 20), and Hazeroth and Di-zahab."

Tophel. Probably *et-Tafileh,* still a large village in a fertile wady running into the Dead Sea on the south-east.

2 Mount Seir. There is another route, not along the plain of the Arabah and by Mount Seir, but over the high ground to the west.

3 the eleventh month. Of the sacred year—about February.

9 I spake unto you. Referring to the appointment of judges by the advice of Jethro: see Exod. xviii. 13–27.

16 A man and his brother. "One man and another."

17 the judgement is God's. Those who act for God, as His vicegerents upon earth, must act justly, like Him.

31 bare. Including constant care and support of every kind.

36 Caleb. See Numb. xiii., xiv.; Josh. xiv. 6–14.

37 for your sakes. The unbelief of Moses and Aaron, to which this sentence is ascribed in Numb. xx. 12, was occasioned by the perverseness of the people, and so might fairly be laid to their account.

39 which in that day, etc. These, being the words of God at the time of the rebellion, ought rather to be rendered, "who at *this* day *have* no knowledge," etc.

41 ye were ready. Heb. "ye deemed it a light thing to go up" (R.V., marg.). "Went up heedlessly" (Driver).

44 the Amorites. In Numb. xiv. 45, they are described with greater precision as "the Amalekites and Canaanites"; here mention is made only of the Amorites ("highlanders"), as being the most numerous and powerful of the Canaanite tribes.

CHAPTER II

1 many days. From this it seems probable that most of the thirty-seven or thirty-eight years of wandering were spent in this neighbourhood, and not, as some have supposed, in the western desert.

4 afraid of you. When the Israelites had asked permission to pass through the land of Edom by the steep and easily-defensible passes of the mountains, they had been boldly refused (Numb. xx. 14–21). But when, after going round the southern end of the mountains [of Seir], they reached the table-land on the eastern side of Edom (see Numb. xxi. 10), it was natural that the Edomites should be afraid. It is to this latter march that the text refers.

6 buy meat (food). As the great pilgrim caravan is still supplied on its yearly march along this route from Damascus to Mecca.

7 hath blessed thee. The Israelites were not inactive in the wilderness; they kept some cattle, and probably carried on some kind of commerce with the neighbouring tribes.

8 the plain. Rather, as in the Heb. and Sept., "the Arabah"; see note on i. 1; and on Gen. xiv. 5. *Elath* and *Ezion-gaber* were a fortress and a port at the head of the eastern arm of the Red Sea, near the modern Akabah.

9 I have given, etc. The Moabites and Ammonites had conquered these lands by favour of God's special Providence, and therefore were only to be attacked if they attempted to murder or injure the Israelites.—**Ar.** The capital of Moab (see Isa. xv. 1); called also "Rabbath-Moab."

10 Emim. *i.e.,* "terrible ones." Vers. 10–12, and 20–23, are historical notices, added after this book was written; perhaps designed to show that the extermination of the Canaanites by the Hebrews was not an unprecedented act. The "Emim" and the other tribes here mentioned were the aborigines of the land, who had been conquered and nearly extirpated by the Moabites, Ammonites, etc.; see note on Gen. xiv. 5.

13 "said I." These words are not in the Hebrew. The previous verses being read as a parenthesis, the first sentence of this verse is part of what God said to Moses, in continuance of ver. 9.

29 the children of Esau. Though the Edomites refused the Hebrew host a passage through the heart of their country by those defiles which have always been jealously guarded by their possessors, they did not obstruct it in its journey round the borders. Sihon and Og, however, refused it a passage along their confines.

34 destroyed. Heb., "devoted" or "put under a ban."

37 Jabbok. This refers to the upper waters of the Jabbok (or *Zerka*), which in the higher part of its course flowed through the land of the Ammonites.

CHAPTER III

4 all his cities. That is, all his *walled* towns. Modern travellers have discovered substantial remains of numerous solidly-built deserted cities through the region here called "Argob," and in the New Testament "Trachonitis," a volcanic region, once very productive and fully peopled.

8 Hermon. This was the southern part of the eastern range of mountains parallel with Lebanon, and called afterwards Anti-Libanus (now *Djebel-esh-Sheikh*). It seems at that time to have divided the territories of the Amorites from those of the Zidonians. See ver. 9; Josh. xix. 28.

11 giants. Moffatt translates "Titans." Heb., "Rephaim" (R.V.); and so in ver. 13; one of the aboriginal races, many of whom were of large stature; see Numb. xiii. 33.—**Bedstead.** Heb., "sarcophagus." "Iron" is probably the black basalt of the country.—**the cubit of a man.** Eighteen inches. This verse, with the last clause of ver. 14, is supposed to have been added after the death of Moses.

14 Jair. See note on Numb. xxxii. 41.

the coasts. "Border" (R.V.). Geshur and Maachah are further mentioned in Josh. xiii. 13.—**Geshuri and Maachathi.** "The Geshurites and the Maachathites" (R.V.). See 2 Sam. iii. 3; x. 6; xiii. 37.—**Bashan-havoth-jair.** Perhaps, "Bashan (*i.e.*, he called) Havoth-jair."

16 from Gilead, etc. Rather, "from Gilead unto the Arnon valley, the middle of the valley and its boundary," etc. The deep and precipitous ravine or "wady" through which the Arnon flows being in some parts two miles wide, the middle of it, or where the stream runs, is specified as the boundary.

17 Ashdoth-pisgah. "The slopes of Pisgah" (R.V.).

22 The Lord. Again note the force of "The Eternal," as in the original. So also in ch. iv., where "The Eternal" is contrasted with the heathen gods (iv. 7, 15, 23, 28, 29).

24 in heaven or in earth. These words refer to the general belief among the heathen as to gods in heaven and on earth. Cp. Psa. lxxxvi. 8.

25 that goodly mountain. This may refer to the general appearance of the land of Canaan, beautifully diversified by its ranges of mountains.

CHAPTER IV

4 are alive. This circumstance (not mentioned in Numb. xiv., xxvi.) was well adapted to deter the people from idolatry; but it could have had no force unless they personally knew it to be a fact.

9 Teach them thy sons. "Deut. lays stress on the duty of training children" (*Peake*). Cp. vi. 7, 20; xi. 19, etc.

16 similitude. In vers. 16–19 we have an exact description of the two principal forms of false worship—1, the worship of *idols*, the vulgar supersitition of Egypt (vers. 16–18); and, 2, the worship of the *heavenly bodies*, the more plausible, but equally dangerous, device of the Chaldeans and Persians (ver. 19). These two kinds of idolatry were already united; and, in after ages, they were both established in the kingdom of Israel by Jeroboam's golden calf and Ahab's worship of Baal, which brought upon the nation the plagues here threatened (vers. 26–28).

19 hath divided. *i.e.*, apportioned for their use.

20 the iron furnace. A striking emblem of severe affliction.

a people of inheritance. Hence the Israelites were called a "purchased or acquired people"—a title applied in a higher sense to Christians, as being the partakers of a far greater and more glorious salvation (1 Pet. ii. 9, etc.).

34 temptations. "Trials" or "tests"; *i.e.*, the great events in Egypt and the Red Sea, by which their faith was tested.

37 in His sight. "With His presence" (R.V.).

40 for ever. Heb., "all the days"; *i.e.*, as long as ever it shall last. A promise conditioned by obedience.

43 Bezer. The exact situation of Bezer and Golan is not known. Ramoth-Gilead is supposed to be the place now called *Es-Salt.*

44 And this is the law, etc. After a short introduction (iv. 44–49), the next section of this book (v.–xxvi.) begins with a repetition of the laws given at Sinai, reciting, with slight verbal changes, the Ten Commandments, as forming the basis of the covenant between Jehovah and Israel (v. 1–21). Moses then urges the people afresh to observe diligently all the Divine commands, as summed up in love to God (vi. 1–9); warns them against forgetting their Heavenly Benefactor, as they had formerly done (10–19); and enjoins them to instruct their children in His claims and laws (20–25).

CHAPTER V

2 a covenant. The Divine condescension turned the command into a covenant, that the people might be the more strongly bound to obedience by their own solemn consent, and the more encouraged to it by God's promise, both of which are implied in the "covenant."

3 not . . . with our fathers. That is, not with them alone.

5 ye were afraid. In this brief narrative Moses mentions only one of the reasons why the people did not go up. See Exod. xix. 16, xx. 18, xxiv. 2.

6 I am the Lord, etc. "I am the Eternal, your God." There are several variations in this recital of the Decalogue as compared with Exod. xx.; but they are all of that natural description which serve to confirm the truth of the narrative.

15 And remember. In reciting the fourth commandment, Moses omits the words referring to the original institution of the Sabbath, as being well known; and he comments upon the beneficent provision for a rest to the servant as well as the master. It was important, as the people were soon about to be masters of Canaan, to keep them in mind of their former hard servitude, and of their duties to their dependants.

31 commandments . . . statutes . . . judgements. These three words appear generally to include the whole moral, ritual, and civil Law.

CHAPTER VI

In ch. vi. Moses first announces the sum and substance of all the commandments, love to God, and the obedience inseparably connected with it; and then enlarges on the contents of the first and second commandments, all relating to the true worship of God. He does this first negatively, by cautioning against worldly-mindedness (vi. 10–25), false toleration (vii.), and self-righteousness (ix., x., xi.); and then positively, by dwelling on its two great parts—fear and love.

4 The Lord our God, etc. That is, "There is no God but one, the Eternal; to whom, therefore, our entire love is due." The vers. 4–9 are called the *Shema*, from the first word of ver. 4, "Hear." They are still recited in the synagogues, and when written on small parchment scrolls are called in Hebrew *Mezuzah*, and in the Greek form *phylacteries.* They may be seen on the door-posts of Jewish houses. In the Hebrew Book of Daily Prayers, *Tephiloth Israel* (London, 1874), the Shema occurs in the "Morning Service" and in the "Morning Prayers for Children" (see Introduction above).

13 Thou shalt fear. "Thou shalt reverence."

25 to do all. This requirement of universal obedience for justification by the Law, shows that God's favour to His people does not at all relax His claims upon them; and it suggests the necessity of another "righteousness" in order to man's acceptance with Him. See Gal. iii. 19, 22, 24.

CHAPTER VII

1 the Hittites, etc. This list of nations differs from that in Gen. xv. 19–21, as some of the tribes there named had probably been merged in others, whilst some situated on the east of the Jordan had been already conquered. The Perizzites (as their name, meaning *peasants*, indicates) appear to have been dispersed over the mountains afterwards occupied by the tribes of Ephraim and Judah, and not to have dwelt in fortified cities.

2 utterly destroy. Literally, "devote" (R.V., margin). See note on ii. 34.

3 neither shalt thou make marriages. So in the New Testament, Christians are enjoined to marry only "in the Lord" (1 Cor. vii. 39); and the general rule respecting all voluntary affinities is clearly laid down in 2 Cor. vi. 14. In marriages in which this Divine rule is violated, it is presumptuous to expect a happy result.

5 images. "Obelisks."

groves. Heb., "Asherim" (R.V.). Wooden images of the goddess Ashera (Astarte, Venus).

7 fewest. *i.e.*, at the time when the promise was first made.

15 diseases of Egypt. Egypt is peculiarly subject to dysentery, ophthalmia and elephantiasis.

19 temptations. See note on iv. 34.

20 the hornet. In an agricultural community insect plagues are among the most dreaded.

23 until they be destroyed. The destruction of the Canaanites was designed by God to be gradual; but it was further delayed by the unbelief of the people. See Judges i., ii., etc.

26 a cursed thing. Solemnly devoted (R.V.) to destruction.

CHAPTER VIII

The preceding chapter contains especial warnings against *idolatry;* this chapter against *self-sufficiency.*

3 by every word. That is to say, by any means, either with or without food, which God may be pleased to appoint. So this passage is used by our Lord, Matt. iv. 4. It is the great lesson of the manna—daily dependence upon God.

4 raiment waxed not old. Some commentators refer to Isa. xlviii. 21 (where it is said "they thirsted not," *i.e.*, were not left to thirst), as a proof that such a statement is not necessarily to be taken absolutely. And it is certainly true that the garments of the common people, being almost entirely woollen, might have been furnished, in great measure, by their own flocks. They were always well clad, to remember that the ordinary conduct of God's providence affords as real, and often as striking, evidences of His power and care as miracles do.

7 a good land. Sir George Adam Smith (*Historical Geography of the Holy Land*) says that Palestine, if not a land of forests, is a land of orchards. All the fruit-trees of the temperate zone flourish in Syria—the apricot, the fig, orange, citron, pomegranate, mulberry, pistachio, almond, and especially the olive and the vine. Some of its wheat-fields are famed throughout the East. Garden vegetables thrive richly wherever there is summer irrigation.

9 brass. *i.e.*, copper.

16 at thy latter end. The design of all God's dealings with all His people is their *final* good. The immediate reference is to the great future which lay before the people in the Land of Promise. But this also was typical of eternal blessings.

CHAPTER IX

1 this day. *i.e.*, your wanderings are now at an end, and nothing remains for you but to "pass over" the Jordan, and take possession of the land.

8 Also. Rather, "even"; *i.e.*, when you had just received His commands in the most solemn manner. The land of Canaan was a gift of pure grace to the Hebrews, and not in any sense a reward of any righteousness of their own.

18 as at the first. Or, "as formerly." Much of this time, it appears from this, was spent in supplication. See Exod. xxxiv. 28, cp. with xxxii. 30.

20 I prayed for Aaron. This circumstance, which is not mentioned in the original narrative, shows that Aaron's official character as high-priest would not have screened him from the merited punishment.

CHAPTER X

6 Beeroth. "The fountains" (*e.g.*, the fountains of Bene-Jaakan, R.V.). This and the next three verses form a parenthetical fragment, which seems introduced to illustrate the *completeness* of the Divine pardon. After Aaron's sin, he had been permitted to administer the priesthood up to his death; and not only so, but when Aaron, in consequence of new transgressions (Numb. xx. 12), died in the wilderness, the high priesthood was continued in his son. Mosera was probably the place of encampment, at the base of Hor, from which Aaron ascended the mountain to die (Numb. xx. 22-29).

19 ye were strangers. The remembrance of past sufferings from the hand of man, instead of exciting revenge or misanthropy, ought to produce a tender sympathy with all the distressed. Even the "Christian" nations of to-day are slow to learn this lesson.

CHAPTER XI

2 which have not seen. Some of them (as Joshua and Caleb, with those who had entered on the journey under the age of 20) had been eye-witnesses of *all* these wonders, including those in Egypt; the rest, of those in the desert.

10 wateredst it with thy foot. By runnels or channels, which conveyed water from reservoirs through the gardens, and which were opened or closed by moving the earth with the foot. Egypt is dependent upon artificial irrigation, in connexion with the periodical overflowing of the Nile, an irrigation now made more general and effective by the Assouan Dam.

11 drinketh water, etc. This is an argument for obedience. The need of God's constant care for water and fruitfulness is more apparent in Canaan than in Egypt, where the regular supply from the Nile has to be applied by the skill and labour of man.

14 the rain of your land. The rainy season in Palestine begins in autumn, when the land is prepared for sowing; and it ends about March, when the grain is swelling before it ripens. There is rarely any rain during the summer. Upon the regular recurrence of these rains the fertility of the country depends. Whatever be the second causes of prosperity, all are alike dependent upon the blessing of God, and subject to His control. See Gen. xli. 28-30; 1 Kings xvii. 1, etc.

21 as the days of heaven upon the earth. The R.V. reads, more literally, "as the days of the heavens above the earth."

24 From the wilderness. Should be "from the wilderness to Lebanon, and from the great River [Euphrates] to the western sea [Mediterranean]."

29 mount Gerizim. Gerizim lay on the south, and Ebal on the north, of the narrow valley in which Shechem (now *Nablous*) is built. Both are precipitous hills, rising direct from the valley, about 150 yards apart; Gerizim being rather less rocky and more productive than Ebal. See ch. xxvii. 11-13.

30 champaign. Heb., "the Arabah": (so R.V.) see Numb. xxii. 1, etc., and notes.—**beside the plains.** Should be "beside the terebinth of the diviner." The oak or terebinth was, as among the ancient Druids, a sacred tree.

CHAPTER XII

1 in the land. Some of these precepts are connected with the conquest of the land, and the extirpation of all relics of former superstition; others are adaptations of previous laws to the state of the people when settled in Canaan.

2 all the places, etc. The absence of all reference in the subsequent history to idolatous *temples,* down to the time of Samson, or perhaps of Eli, leads to the inference that in Canaan, and possibly in Egypt, there had been no *building* of any kind erected as the supposed dwelling-place of God. The idolatry of Canaan was originally that "nature-worship" which at a very early period superseded the service of the God of nature.

3 groves. Heb., "Asherim" (R.V.). See note ch. vii. 5.—**the names.** These names were associated with heathen customs, and might, therefore, tend to lead the people to idolatry.

5 the place, etc. When the people were settled in Canaan, the tabernacle appears to have been erected first at Shiloh, and afterwards at Gibeon; but the ark was ultimately fixed at Jerusalem. The observance of this law would prevent the introduction of corrupt customs into their worship, and preserve the union of the tribes.

8 the things that we do here. Many of the prescribed regulations of worship were not observed in the wilderness.

13 Take heed, etc. See note on Lev. xvii. 3.

15 of the roebuck. "The gazelle" (R.V.). These animals, tame and wild, were allowed for eating, but not for sacrifice.

17 the tithe. This seems to refer to the (so-called) second tithe, of which the offerer partook as a sacrificial meal, or to some voluntary offering in fulfilment of a vow, beside what was required for the Levites.

31 they have burnt. See note on Lev. xviii. 21.

CHAPTER XIII

1 a prophet. All pretensions to a Divine commission must be tested by the revelation already given.

2 come to pass. Which might arise from contrivance, or the artful use of superior scientific knowledge.

6 If thy brother, the son of thy mother. Should read, "If thy brother or thy half-brother," *the son of thy mother.*

9 thou shalt surely kill. That is, after legal trial; the accuser and witnesses being expected to cast the first stone. As the government of Israel was a theocracy (God Himself being their King), idolatry was high treason.

13 children of Belial. "Sons of worthlessness" (R.V.), *i.e.*, good-for-nothing men; a frequent designation of the wicked and profligate.

15 destroying. Lit. "devoting." The doom of the Canaanites was to come upon such a city.

CHAPTER XIV

1 cut yourselves, etc. These barbarous and superstitious customs are still practised among many heathen nations.

4 ye shall eat. This list of clean and unclean animals differs from that in Lev. xi., where general rules are laid down, illustrated by a few examples; whereas, in this passage, the object was to enumerate the principal animals to be eaten or avoided. These precepts concerning food plainly belonged only to the Jews, and were not intended to be of perpetual and universal obligation: see Acts x. 15; 1 Tim. iv. 4.

5 pygarg. Heb., "dishon." The ibex.

15 the owl, etc. Rather, "the ostrich, and the night-hawk, and the sea-mew" (R.V.).

16 the swan. Rather, "the horned owl" (R.V.). Moffatt translates "the water-hen."

18 the lapwing. "The bittern."

21 thou shalt give it unto the stranger. Uncircumcised strangers, who merely resided among the Israelites, while required to conform to certain general regulations, were exempt from others purposely to make a distinction between them and the covenant-people.

27 not forsake him. But invite him to your feast. See xii. 18.

28 all the tithe. For two years out of three the tithe-produce might be sold, and the money spent on offerings purchased at the sanctuary and consumed there; but in the third year the produce must be preserved for the use of the Levites, and the needy at home. This provided for the wants of the non-producing classes.

CHAPTER XV

2 shall release [it]. It is now generally agreed that this precept relates only to the enforcement of such claims *during the Sabbatic year,* and not to the total remission of them. The harsh custom of selling the debtor and his family into slavery was in part prevented; whilst, by subsequent laws (12), its hardships were mitigated.

it is called the Lord's release. "For there has been proclaimed a release to the Eternal."

4 there shall be no poor. See ver. 11. The tendency of the law was to prevent pauperism; but these Divine commands could only be expected to accomplish their ends in case of the perfect obedience of the people. The presence of poor might remind them how far they fell short. But the Jews are notable for their care of their poor.

9 Beware, etc. The ill-disposed may evade the best social regulations, especially such as aim at the higher kinds of good. The observance of these, therefore, God takes under His own cognisance, enforcing them by special warnings and commands, and promising a peculiar blessing to those who conscientiously regard them.

12 thou shalt let him go free. This would apply to those who sold themselves for servants, or had been sold, either by their parents through extreme poverty, or as a punishment for some offence against the law.

18 It shall not seem hard unto thee. These laws and regulations respecting slaves are a contrast to those of the Spartans, Romans, and other ancient nations; amongst whom neither the person nor the life of the slave had any protection.

CHAPTER XVI

3 bread of affliction. Eaten in remembrance of the bitter bondage out of which they had been delivered.

15 Thou mayest not sacrifice, etc. One effect of this law was to prevent superstitious additions to the appointed rites; whilst it secured honour to the sanctuary, and unity of worship.

7 Roast. Heb., "boil."

18 Judges, etc. The next section of this discourse (xvi. 18–xxi. 9), has chiefly to do with public officers and civil polity.

21 Grove of trees. See note on ch. vii. 5.

CHAPTER XVII

6 two witnesses. If this made crime more difficult of proof, it also gave the innocent a better safeguard against false witness; and this, too, would be the tendency of the next requirement, that the witnesses should themselves execute the sentence.

14 a king. It is observable that whilst the *principles* of government are carefully and strictly settled, its outward *form* is regarded as unimportant, and left to the decision of the people. It is provided that any king of Israel shall be only a viceroy of Jehovah; and, as such, shall study His Divine law, and solemnly bind himself duly to administer it: thus establishing the supremacy of law over the monarch.

16 shall not multiply horses. At this period, horses were commonly used only in war; and it was God's design that the Israelites should not become a military people, but should depend on Him for protection. Besides, the use of horses would necessarily lead to intercourse with Egypt, whence, at that period, they were mostly procured; and thus would expose the Hebrews to the contamination of idolatry, to which they were peculiarly prone. Solomon's violation of this and the succeeding command (ver. 17) were the first steps in that course of apostasy which led to the division of the nation, the establishment of the Egyptian calf-worship, and, at last, to the entire overthrow of the kingdom (1 Kings iv. 26, etc.).

18 shall write. *i.e.*, shall have written for him.

20 that his heart be not lifted up. The monarchy was to be democratic as well as theocratic.—**and his children.** If the king obeyed the Divine law, the monarchy was to be hereditary, as it became in David's family.

CHAPTER XVIII

3 the priest's due. After repeating from Numb. xviii. 20, 23, 24 the law that the priests and Levites should "have no inheritance in Israel," Moses makes further provision for their support. In Lev. xvii. 3, 4, it was ordained that animals for food were to be slaughtered only at the entrance of the tabernacle "of meeting"; the priest receiving certain perquisites (Lev. vii. 30–34). This would be impossible after the settlement of the people in Canaan, and the priest's due from the sacrifices was therefore increased. They had in fact two portions, one from "Jehovah's inheritance," and the other "from the people."

4 shalt thou give him. The first-fruits of these things were consecrated to God; and He appropriated them to the maintenance of the priests.

8 beside that which cometh, etc. Though the Levites did not share in the division of the country, yet they might have houses and land in the suburbs of their cities. A Levite who devoted himself to constant service at the tabernacle was to retain this property, or its proceeds, if it were sold, in addition to his portion of the offerings.

10 through the fire. See note on Lev. xviii. 21.—**that useth divination.** However futile such pretensions might be, they were mischievous, both because they deluded the people, and because they were closely connected with superstition, and particularly with demon-worship.

13 perfect. *i.e.*, rendering to God a complete, not a divided allegiance.

15 a Prophet. Whilst discountenancing these false pretensions, God would, as occasion required, continue the prophetic gift among His people. Moses predicts the coming of the great Prophet, who, like himself, should be the accepted Mediator between Jehovah and His people (see v. 23–28), acting as their Legislator, Governor, and Teacher; and, in this capacity, should introduce a new dispensation—a fact which of itself shows the superiority of this Prophet, as the greater supersedes the less. See Acts iii. 22, vii. 37; Heb. iii. 1–6, xii. 18–29.

18 he shall speak. The Israelites being filled with terror at the awful majesty in which God appeared at Sinai, received the promise of a different display of His glory, which was completely fulfilled when "the Word was made flesh and dwelt among us, full of grace and truth" (John i. 14).

CHAPTER XIX

2 three cities. Three cities of refuge had been appointed for the country already conquered on the east of the Jordan (iv. 41–43). These three on the west of the Jordan made the number six. See Numb. xxxv. 6.

14 land-mark. Hedges and walls being used only to enclose gardens, the boundaries of landed property in general were marked by stones; and as these might easily be removed, special laws are made against such dishonest practices.

15 shall not rise up. That is, "shall not be accepted." The same Hebrew word is rendered "established" at the end of the verse.

21 eye for eye, etc. That is, he shall suffer the punishment which his false testimony might have brought upon the man whom he had accused. This law was maintained by the courts in spirit rather than in letter. See Matt. v. 38, 39.

CHAPTER XX

1 When thou goest out to battle. The wisdom and mercy of the Hebrew laws of war will be best seen by contrasting them with those of other nations, which were, and in many cases still are, extremely barbarous. What would the Hebrew Lawgiver have said about poison gas and other methods of "civilised" warfare? Vers. 2–9 seem designed to forbid the general levies of men so common in Asiatic warfare, and to promote the best of all courage, a firm reliance upon Jehovah. Vers. 10, 11 discountenance indiscriminate slaughter, as well as pillage and slavery. The exception of the Canaanites from this rule (16, 17) was an act of Divine retribution for gross corruption. A moral plague-spot had to be removed.

6 hath not yet eaten of it. Heb., "not made it common," *i.e.*, taken it into common use. See Lev. xix. 23–25.

19 man's life. Heb., "is the tree of the field man, that it should be besieged?" The produce of the date-palm is the principal food of several Arabian and African tribes, who have been exposed to famine by the cruelty of invaders in cutting down those trees.

CHAPTER XXI

4 a rough valley. This rather means a "wady," a ravine which had a stream running through it.

6 wash their hands. By this act the elders declare their innocence of the guilt presumptively attaching to their city, whilst the sacrifice provides for its removal.

10 When thou goest forth. Ch. xxi 10—xxv. contains laws chiefly regulating *domestic* life, and *personal* and *social* habits.

13 she shall be thy wife. This is evidently a restriction adapted gradually to suppress a wicked practice already existing. Its importance is proved by the terrible outrages to which even modern warfare often subjects the families of the conquered.

14 but thou shalt not sell her. This command intimates how binding the laws of justice and honour are, particularly in such matters.

15 the hated. "Slighted" or "less loved." This is another restrictive law, showing the mischievousness of the then prevalent custom of polygamy. The case supposed had actually occurred in the family of Jacob (Gen. xxix. 30).

18 a stubborn and rebellious son. The power of parents over their children appears originally, in most nations, to have been absolute. This law, whilst it takes from the father the power of inflicting death, adds to the punishment of filial disobedience the disgrace of a public condemnation. The Bible everywhere places duties to parents next to duties to God. The *political* and *social*, as well as *religious* importance of filial respect and obedience can hardly be overrated.

22 hang him. Or, " impale." That is, after he is dead. The Egyptians and Canaanites used to leave bodies of criminals gibbeted.

CHAPTER XXII

4 thou shalt surely help him. This law of kind and brotherly care for the property of others is one exhibition of that tenderness which is not only characteristic of Christian morality, but frequently appears in the Jewish code.

5 shall not wear, etc. The practices here prohibited had occasioned revolting licentiousness. This regulation would tend to promote a respectful delicacy between the sexes.

6 let the dam go. This law, whilst it teaches a spirit of mercy, would also tend to prevent the extirpation of any species of birds, which, in a country producing many snakes and insects, might cause serious injury. Dr. Samuel Cox (*The Bird's Nest and other Sermons*) says that this command (1) set a limit to the natural greed of men ; (2) brought the law of God into the little things of life ; (3) taught the sacredness of love.

8 a battlement. Or, " parapet." The flat roofs of the houses in Eastern countries are much used for walking and sleeping, and would therefore be dangerous without a fence. It is an interesting example of the manner in which religion protects the temporal interests of men. The principles of the Bible might be applied to the " housing question " of to-day.

12 fringes. " Tassels."

24 thou shalt put away (the) **evil.** These laws, enforced by such solemn penalties, show how hateful unchastity is to God. Those which follow (25–29) protect the victim, whilst punishing the aggressor.

CHAPTER XXIII

3 Ammonite or Moabite. A solemn intimation of the fatal consequences of attempting to injure, and especially to lead astray, the people of God. See Numb. xxv. 16–18.

6 Peace. Heb. " completeness " or welfare.

7 an Edomite. At a later period the peculiar malignity of the Edomites brought upon them special execrations ; see Psa. cxxxvii. 7 ; Isa. lxiii. 1–6, and notes.

an Egyptian. This shows that the preceding laws were not to be taken as allowing a vindictive spirit towards enemies and oppressors, for the Israelites are here taught to requite good for evil.

14 holy. The term " holy " is here used as denoting the removal of that which is offensive even in material things.

15 master. That is, *foreign* master. The land of Israel was to be (as our own country now is) an asylum for the oppressed of all nations. Cp. *Uncle Tom's Cabin*, especially chs. ix.–xiii.

24 the grapes. This used to be, and perhaps still is, the custom in Germany, where the pedestrian might pluck grapes or cherries by the roadside, enough to quench his thirst.

CHAPTER XXIV

1 a bill of divorcement. This law was intended to restrain bad practices which had gone far to annul the original law of marriage, and which still prevail among the Arabs, who not only allow a man by a word to dissolve the marriage tie, but also require that the divorced woman shall have been married to another man before her husband can take her back. Vers. 1–4 should read as one sentence, thus : " When a man, etc., let him write her, etc. (1) ; and she depart, etc., and go and become another man's, etc. (2) ; and the latter, etc. (3) ; then her former," etc. To correct the then prevailing custom, Moses allows a wife to be divorced only by a legal document, and forbids her husband to take her back after she had been married to another. For the law of Christ on this subject, see Matt. v. 31, 32 ; xix. 7–9.

6 a man's life. It was necessary, in order to grind the corn for his family. The ancient common law of England provides that no man shall be distrained of the utensils or instruments of his trade or profession—as the axe of a carpenter, or the books of a scholar, or beasts used for the plough, as long as there are other things upon which distress can be made.

7 stealing. See notes on Exod. xxi. 1–6.

10 thou shalt not go into his house. The sacredness thus given to the poor man's home strikingly illustrates the humane spirit of these laws.

13 righteousness. A good and righteous deed in the sight of God.

15 At his day, etc. Probably it is to this merciful command that we should trace the present practice in Palestine and the neighbouring countries of ending work at sunset, and paying wages daily. Luther translates, " Thou shalt give him his day's pay."

16 The fathers, etc. This would tend to prevent wholesale massacres and hereditary blood-feuds.

18 thou shalt remember, etc. The spirit of this and the following precepts is beautifully expressed by our Lord : " All things whatsoever ye would that men should do to you, do ye even so to them " (Matt. vii. 12).

CHAPTER XXV

3 Forty stripes. The Jews, in practice, allowed only thirty-nine to be given, lest the number should be inadvertently exceeded : see 2 Cor. xi. 24.

4 Thou shalt not muzzle the ox. Threshing in Palestine was performed by oxen, who were driven over the corn spread out upon a level floor, open to the air. This command enjoins a kind consideration for the beasts.

5 no child. Lit., " no son," R.V.

9 Then shall, etc. This appears to have been a concessive command, which enabled a man, by submitting to a small indignity, to escape compliance with a prevalent custom.

loose his shoe. See note on Ruth iv. 7.

13 divers weights. Lit., " stone and stone."

19 blot out the remembrance of Amalek. Some centuries later, Saul was ordered to put this sentence into execution (1 Sam. xv., see notes) ; and he incurred Divine displeasure because he did not do it effectually. The Amalekites who remained were afterwards smitten by David (1 Sam. xxx.), and subsequently by the Simeonites in Hezekiah's time (1 Chron. iv. 43).

CHAPTER XXVI

3 I profess, etc. That is, "I testify by this offering that I owe all I have to the bounty of Jehovah, who has faithfully kept all His promises."

5 answer, "speak" or testify.—**A Syrian,** etc. This seems to be a summary of Jacob's history, referring to his hasty and unprovided flight from home, and the poverty in which he came from Syria. These verses were recited at the passover; and on the next day the first sheaf was presented.

14 nor given aught thereof for the dead. Meaning either that no part of these offerings had been used in superstitious funeral ceremonies, like those of the heathen, or more probably that they had not even been taken to the house of mourning, which would have made them ceremonially unclean.

CHAPTER XXVII

The republication of the law being concluded, the Israelites are commanded, on their arrival in Canaan, to set up a memorial of it; Moses then, in a prophetic address, enlarges on the blessings attaching to obedience (xxviii. 1-14); and the curses attendant on transgression (15-68). He calls upon the people to enter anew into covenant engagement with the Eternal (xxix. 1-15), and concludes his appeal by pressing solemnly upon them the plain requirements of practical godliness, and setting before them the great alternatives, "life and death" (xxx. 11-20).

2 great stones. Books being scarce, these public monuments were of great importance. It seems likely, as the *plastering* is mentioned before the *writing*, that the uneven surface of the stones was covered with a smooth plaster, which was capable of resisting the action of the air in a dry climate, and was then engraved or painted. Such plaster inscriptions are found among the antiquities of Egypt.

4 in mount Ebal. This public and permanent record of the law was to stand on the mountain from which the curses were to be pronounced (ver. 13).

7 offer . . . and rejoice. It was only in virtue of what the altar with its burnt offerings and peace offerings represented that they could *rejoice* before God. Had the law stood there alone, it would have reminded them only of sin and condemnation; but, the altar of expiation being also there, they could worship God with joy as well as fear. Yet the altar did not annul the law, the words of which were written plainly upon the pillar.

12 Simeon, etc. All the tribes chosen to pronounce the blessings were descended from Leah and Rachel, Jacob's proper wives. The descendants of Reuben (the first-born after the flesh, but degraded from his place by his sin), and Zebulun, the youngest son of Leah, joined with the descendants of the handmaids, were to utter the curses.

15 Cursed be. Rather, "Cursed is." The sins here declared accursed are supposed to be committed in secret, and such as God only can avenge. To many of them the penalty of death was attached upon discovery and conviction.

26 all the words. R.V. omits *all.*

CHAPTER XXVIII

15 these curses. Perhaps there is nowhere to be found an enumeration of Divine punishments so awful as this; yet all of them are strikingly exemplified in the history of the Jews; especially in the repeated sieges and destruction of their cities; the desolation of their country; their captivities; their oppressed condition through many centuries; and their present dispersion over the world.

5 Store. Heb. "kneading-trough."

18. thou shalt be above. "You shall be always rising, never falling" (*Moffatt*).

21 the pestilence. The plague, on account of its ravages and its frequency, is the most dreaded scourge of Syria and Egypt.

22 a consumption. Literally, "wasting."

23 brass. No rain shall fall.

24 dust. The winds raise the hot, fine sand of the desert, and scatter it over the neighbouring regions, so as sometimes altogether to destroy their fertility.

27 botch. Rather, "boil" (R.V.). "Emerods" are "tumours."

38 (see also 42). **locust.** Cp. Joel i. 4, etc.

49 a nation. This description applies well to several oppressors of the Jews, but particularly to the Romans.

53 eat the fruit of thine own body. See 2 Kings vi. 28, 29; Jer. xix. 9, and the history of the siege of Jerusalem, as related by Josephus.

63 the Lord will rejoice. This highly figurative representation must be taken as implying that God's threatenings will be surely and thoroughly fulfilled, as His promises are.

68 ships; the slave-galleys of the Phœnicians. Cp. Joel iii. 6.—**and no man shall buy you.** Heb., "and no buyer." As their freedom from Egypt's slavery was a proof of His favour, so their return to a similar bondage would show His anger. This threatening was literally fulfilled by the Sidonians and the Romans, the latter of whom sold Hebrew captives till no man would buy them.

CHAPTER XXIX

1 The covenant. This verse, in the Hebrew Bible, is the last verse (69) of ch. xxviii.

2 Ye have seen. Strictly speaking, this was only true of Caleb and Joshua; but the people of the different generations are regarded and spoken of as forming one unbroken community. See xi. 2, and note.

3 temptations. See iv. 34, and note.

4 the Lord hath not given you. As this is spoken reproachfully, it is evident that the withholding of God's grace is attributed to the people's neglect (see v. 29).

11 the hewer, etc. These were the lowest and most laborious services, which were generally performed by slaves (Josh. ix. 21-27).

15 him that is not here. The people of future generations.

18 lest. "Beware lest."—**a root.** That is, an unperceived cause. *Gall* is "poison."

19 drunkenness to thirst. Heb., "to carry off the watered with the dry," or thirsty; a proverbial expression meaning "all." The reference is to herbage or plants (*Driver*).

29 revealed. All that is necessary for our conduct God has clearly revealed. Moses concludes his prophecy of the Jews' rejection in much the same manner as the Apostle Paul concludes his discourse on the same subject (Rom. xi. 33).

CHAPTER XXX

3 will turn thy captivity. In these gracious encouragements to repentance and promises of restoration we behold the spirit of the Gospel, though in the forms of the older dispensation. They furnished Nehemiah with a powerful plea in prayer (Neh. i. 9).

11 neither is it far off. *i.e.*, "is not beyond thy power." The Septuagint has "it is not too hard for thee." (So R.V.) That which God requires of us is neither obscure nor impracticable, but is clearly revealed, and, with God's help, easy of performance. For the application of vers. 12–14 to the Gospel, see Rom. x. 5–8. Cp. Luke xvii. 21.

16 to love the Lord thy God. This impressive close of the final publication of the law, summing up all the Divine requirements in *love*, which "is the fulfilling of the law," shows that the principle of obedience is the same under every dispensation of religion.

CHAPTER XXXI

The remaining section of this book is occupied with the closing acts of Moses' life.

2 this day. That is, "already."

3 and Joshua. It is significantly promised that both "the Lord" and "Joshua" should "go over before" them; since in Joshua's Divine appointment to his office, as well as in the very name he bore (see Numb. xiii. 16, and note), a pledge was given that The Eternal Himself would become the Leader of His people.

9 this law. The Book of the Law was entrusted to the priests both for safe custody and for public use as specified in vers. 10–13. Cp. Neh. viii. 18.

10 the year of release. As in that year the land rested from cultivation, all classes of the people could then better find time to attend this service.

12 women and children. This festival, at which the Law was read, was the only one at which women and children were required to attend.

19 this song. While the original Book of the Law was to be preserved by the side of the ark, and copied, at least in part, upon the stones set up in the centre of the land (xxvii. 2–4), it was to be impressed upon the minds of all by a national song, which has always been found a powerful method of affecting a people. The value set upon this song is shown by the numerous allusions made to it by the prophets, and by the quotations from it in the New Testament. See especially Heb. x. 30, etc.

26 in the side. Rather, "by the side" (R.V.). The "Testimony"—*i.e.*, the tables of the law—were in the ark: the "book" probably in a chest beside it. Cp. 2 Kings xxii. 8.

CHAPTER XXXII

4 the Rock. Suggesting *unchangeableness* and security.

6 bought, made, established. Heb., "produced," "made," "established" or "confirmed." The Author and Preserver of their national life.

8 to the nations. In all God's arrangements for developing and settling the nations, He kept in view the wants and interests of His chosen people.

10 apple. *i.e.*, "pupil"; an often-recurring metaphor, expressing constant and tender care.

11 As an eagle stirreth up her nest, etc. This figure finely illustrates both the training of the Hebrews in the desert, and the methods by which God prepares His people for their heavenly inheritance. The eagle arouses her brood, inciting and teaching them to fly, and afterwards guarding the weak from harm. The R.V. reads the latter part of the verse, "He spread abroad His wings, took them," etc., omitting the italicised *So* at the beginning of ver. 12.

13 honey . . . oil. In the holes of the rocks the bees build their combs, whilst the olive-tree strikes its roots into the crevices.

14 kidneys of wheat. This expression is used for fine, plump, full grains.

15 Jeshurun. A poetical name for Israel as "the upright" or "holy" nation (see Numb. xxiii. 21, and note), here represented under the figure of a high-fed mettlesome animal, a graphic description of the degeneracy of the chosen people, when led away by prosperity into pride and apostasy from God.

17 devils. Rather, "idols."

came newly up. Heb., "new [gods] which came from near."

20 froward. "Perverse."—**in whom is no faith.** That is, in whom no confidence can be placed.

21 a foolish nation. That is, a people whom they despise. This passage is quoted in Rom. x. 19, to show that the Jews might have known that, if they forsook God, He would transfer their privileges to the despised Gentiles, and that the Gentile nations should be the instruments of their punishment.

22 hell. Heb., "Sheol," *i.e.*, the under-world, the grave (from verb meaning "to be quiet," "to be at rest"). The Greek equivalent is "Hades," the unseen world.

24 burnt. Rather, "wasted" (R.V.). *Burning heat* means a burning *fever*.

27 Lest their adversaries, etc. Or, "Lest their adversaries should boast, lest they should say, Our high hand, and not Jehovah, hath done this." In this punishment of His rebellious people God will take care to cut off all occasion of boasting from the heathen instruments of His displeasure.

28 they. *i.e.*, God's rebellious people (ver. 20).

31 their rock. *i.e.*, the idols of the heathen. See vers. 4, 37.

33 dragons. "Serpents."

34 sealed up. That is, this wickedness shall not be forgotten.

35 Their foot shall slide in due time. Or, "at the time when their foot shall slide" (R.V.).

that shall come upon them. Rather, "that are ready for them"; so that their punishment is both certain and near.

36 judge. In Heb. x. 30, this is quoted as meaning, "The Lord will chastise His people." The verse should therefore be rendered, "For (or, when) the Lord will chastise His people, but (or, then) He will repent Himself," etc. God here shows that His tender mercy may be exercised in connexion with His sharpest discipline. It is to be observed that when the Apostle Paul quotes from this song, he uses the Septuagint version.

shut up, or left. A frequent proverbial expression for the bond and free, and including all classes of men.

42 And that. These italicised words are better omitted, as obscuring the sense. (So R.V.)

the beginning of revenges, etc. "From the head of the leaders of the enemy": see Judges v. 2.

43 Rejoice, etc. These words are quoted by the Apostle Paul (Rom. xv. 10) as pointing to the grand consummation of all God's dealings with Israel, whether in the way of mercy or of judgement—the final incorporation of Jews and Gentiles in one happy Christian community.

CHAPTER XXXIII

1 the man of God. A frequent name for a Divine messenger. See Judges xiii. 6, 8; 1 Sam. ix. 6–8, etc.

2 with ten thousands of saints. Heb., "from His holy myriads,"

a fiery law. Heb., "rays of fire." Cp. Hab. iii. 3, 4.

5 And He. "And He (*i.e.*, God) became king in Jeshurun (*i.e.*, righteous Israel)."

king. A prince, or chief ruler: see Judges xix. 1.

6 let [not] his men be few. The word *not* is not in the original. The R.V. reads, "yet let his men be few." The name "Simeon" is omitted in the list.

8 with Thy holy one. Heb., "with Thy godly man," etc. This is a prayer that the high priesthood may remain in the family of Aaron, "the saint of the Lord," though he had failed in the trial at Meribah, since they and their tribe had, in zealous defence of God's honour, faithfully executed justice, without any respect of persons, even though the guilty parties might be their nearest kinsmen. See Exod. xxxii. 26–29; Numb. xxv. 7, 8.

12 in safety by Him. Heb., "shall dwell safely on Him," as the rock on which he is built.

13 Blessed, etc. See note on ch. viii. 7. In this beautiful description we have all the richness of the large and valuable portions of Ephraim and Manasseh set before us.

14 by the moon. Heb., "moons," or months. The R.V. renders "the growth of the moons."

16 And for the good-will, etc. Rather, "let the good will of Him that dwelt in the bush come upon the head," etc. See Ex. iii. 2–4. This appellation calls to mind God's faithfulness and watchfulness, as well as His delivering power.

separated from his brethren. Heb., "consecrated among his brethren." The R.V. marg. has "prince among his brethren."

17 unicorns. Or, "urus"; "wild ox" (R.V.); see note on Numb. xxiii. 22. All the tribes were strong like oxen; Ephraim had "the majesty of a first-born bull, and his horns are the horns of a urus," or wild buffalo. Ephraim was always a very powerful tribe, and at the disruption, after Solomon's death, became head of the kingdom of the ten tribes. *People* should be "peoples."

18 Rejoice, Zebulun, etc. The tribes of Zebulun and Issachar were the commercial and trading tribes. They occupied the country between the Mediterranean Sea and the Sea of Galilee, including the fertile plain of Jezreel, which belonged to Issachar.

19 They shall call the people (peoples). Because God has prospered them, they are to offer to Him the sacrifices of gratitude and righteousness of life.

20 enlargeth Gad. That is, "gives him a broad territory" in the beautiful land of Gilead.

lion; should be "lioness." Gad is here represented as the leader of the Eastern tribes. This passage, which, from its brevity, is difficult, may be rendered, "He dwells as a lioness; and tears the arm, yea, the crown of the head; and he looks out the chief part for himself, for there the portion of the ruler is reserved. And he comes," etc. Gad boldly chose a district which, because it was conquered first, and was really valuable, though exposed to enemies, was, in fact, due to the principal tribe; but he was faithful to the chiefs of Israel and to Jehovah in going on to the wars.

22 He shall leap. Literally, "that leapeth forth" (R.V.), *i.e.*, the lion, which was found in large numbers in Bashan.

23 the west. Rather, "the sea" (R.V. marg.), *i.e.*, the Sea of Galilee; the same word signifying *west* and *sea* in Hebrew, because the Great or Mediterranean Sea lay to the west of Canaan. A "south land" is used, in Josh. xv. 19, for a warm, sunny country. The tribe of Naphtali, although in the north-west of Canaan, was located on the *southern* slopes of Lebanon and Hermon.

24 his foot in oil. Let his land be fertile with olives.

25 shoes. Rather, *bars* (R.V.).

iron and brass. "Thy bars shall be strong." Security and rest are promised to this tribe. Such an assurance would be peculiarly precious to a tribe situated on the north-western frontier, and therefore exposed to the incursions of the powerful nations in that quarter.

26 There is none, etc. Or, "There is none like unto God, O Jeshurun, who rideth through the heavens to thy help, and in His majesty through the clouds." (See R.V.)

27 The eternal God, etc. This glowing description of Israel's safety, triumph, and happiness should encourage the Church of God in all ages to look for protection, support, and supply of all good, and final victory over all enemies, to her faithful and Almighty Head.

28 Israel, etc. Heb., "and Israel dwells securely: alone (*i.e.*, carefully separated) is the fountain of Jacob: in a land of corn and wine."

drop down dew. The land not needing perpetual irrigation, like Egypt.

29 thy excellency. Or, "thy majesty," as in ver. 26.

found liars. That is, "will feign unto thee" through fear, professing a regard they do not feel (R.V., "shall submit themselves unto thee"); for thou wilt take possession and "tread down their fastnesses."

CHAPTER XXXIV

1 Nebo. See note on Numb. xxvii. 12. Of the chain of mountains called "Abarim," one was called *Pisgah*, and its peak, fronting the valley, *Nebo*. The heights here are very considerable, affording a wide prospect, especially towards the west.

unto Dan. As this name was not given till the time of Judg. xviii. 1, 27–29, it is evident that this account of the death of Moses is a later addition; and vers. 10–12 seem to indicate that it was made at the period when the Old Testament Scriptures were arranged, probably by Ezra.

6 no man knoweth. The burial-place of Moses was probably concealed that his tomb might not become the occasion of idolatry or superstition.

10 there arose not a prophet. This appendix to the narrative shows how the expectation of the pious Israelite was kept alive by the promise of his great Lawgiver (xviii. 15, 18): and confessedly that promise has not been fulfilled, nor can we see how it can now be accomplished, unless Jesus of Nazareth, "a Prophet mighty in word and deed before God and all the people," be the person "of whom Moses and all the prophets have spoken."

THE BOOK OF JOSHUA

INTRODUCTION

THIS is a book of action, a story of war and conquest, a record of faith and courage. It centres round the later life of Joshua after the death of Moses.

The name Joshua, or Jehoshua, is in itself an inspiration and a message. It means "The Eternal is Salvation"; and the Greek form of it is the word we know as "Jesus," the name applied to Joshua by Stephen (Acts vii. 45), and in the Epistle to the Hebrews (iv. 8).

The previous history of Joshua shows us what manner of man he was, and how he was prepared for the great leadership which was entrusted to him. He was the helper or servant of Moses (Ex. xxiv. 13) and was with him on Sinai (Ex. xxxii. 17). He and Caleb were among the "spies" sent by Moses to explore the land of Canaan, who brought in the "minority report" (Num. xiii. 30; xiv. 6–9) and encouraged the people to go up and possess the land (cp. Josh. xiv. 6, 14).

This book shows that his faith stood the test. He acts promptly upon the command of God (i. 11). Not to himself, but to God, he gives the glory (iii. 5; iv. 21–24). In time of defeat and disappointment he turns to God in humiliation and prayer (vii. 6–9). He is loyal to God's commandments and seeks to win the people to similar loyalty (viii. 32–35). The closing words of his life are an earnest appeal to the people, urging trust in God and fidelity to Him (xxiii. 6, 8; xxiv. 14, 15, 23), recalling God's help in the past (xxiii. 3, 9, 14), and promising, with absolute confidence, the continuance of that help in the future (xxiii. 10).

CHAPTER I

2 now therefore arise. Whilst Moses was living, Joshua had been designated to this work (see Numb. xxvii. 18; Deut. i. 38; iii. 28; xxxi. 23); he now receives his public commission.

this Jordan. The people were now encamped at Shittim (ii. 1), on "the plains of Moab" (Deut. xxxiv. 1), near the Jordan.

4 the wilderness. The desert which covers a large part of the Arabian peninsula formed the southern boundary of Canaan.

this Lebanon. Or, "yonder"; Lebanon being in the extreme distance on the north. It was visible from the Israelitish camp: see note on Gen. xv. 18.

the Hittites. The "Hittites," who inhabited the south of Canaan from Beersheba to Hebron, and who had been described by the spies as the most formidable of the people of the land, seem to be here put for all the nations of Canaan.

the Great Sea. That is, the Mediterranean; the largest sea known to the Israelites.

5 I will not fail thee. Formidable as the enterprise was, God's presence would be an all-sufficient help. This promise is aptly quoted in Heb. xiii. 5 to calm the anxieties of believers.

8 This book of the law. Not only "the law," but a "book" was already known to Israel in the days of Joshua.

11 victuals. Food for a march of some days.

within three days. Or, "and yet three days." Within the three days they were to move down to the Jordan, so as to cross as soon as the command was given (iii.). Probably they were to wait three whole days after the command was given: see iii. 2.

14 all the mighty men of valour. Not necessarily all the warriors of these tribes, but all that were required, and these doubtless picked men.

CHAPTER II

1 even Jericho. Or, "and Jericho" (R.V.). Jericho was about seven or eight miles from the river Jordan.

a harlot's house. It is a striking instance of the condescending grace of God, that He should implant faith in the heart of such a person, leading her to take part with His people, and to hazard her life in protecting them; and should make her the mother (see Matt. i. 5) of a son so distinguished for virtue as Boaz, and so an ancestress of the Messiah. "Many a lost one has by this word been encouraged to hope for mercy."

and lodged there. The spies may have been led to this house, partly because its situation on the town wall (ver 15) would afford an easy exit, and partly because their entrance into such a house would be least likely to awaken suspicion. But they were doubtless directed by God to one whom He had prepared to carry out His purposes.

3 which are entered into thine house. The proximity of the Hebrew camp caused unusual vigilance on the part of the king.

5 the men went out. It must be remembered that Rahab lived under the deepest moral darkness: and therefore God approved her faith, though its practical exhibition was connected with so much that was faulty: see 2 Cor. viii. 12.

6 to the roof of the house. The roofs of Eastern houses, being flat, with a parapet, were very suitable for such a purpose.

stalks of flax. The flax had doubtless just been brought in from the field and laid out to be dried: for it was the time of flax as well as of barley harvest; both being ripe about the time of the passover: see iii. 15, and note, compared with Exod. ix. 31, and note. The seasons in the Jordan valley are very similar to those of Egypt.

7 unto the fords. The men probably stopped at the river, for it was now full, and the Israelites were near the other bank.

8 they were laid down. *i.e.*, to sleep on the housetop, as is common in Palestine.

12 a true token. Heb., "a sign, or pledge of truth." This is given in ver. 14, where the spies pledge their lives.

19 his blood shall be upon his head. *i.e.*, the guilt of his death shall fall upon himself.

CHAPTER III

1 in the morning. *i.e.*, probably on the morning of the day after the order was issued to prepare for passing the river. In this verse the writer appears to resume the narrative in i. 10, 11, which was broken off by the parenthetical account given in ii. of the despatch and return of the spies: see i. 11, and note.

3 go after it. This was different from the usual order of march. The ark, probably with the bright cloud which indicated the presence of Jehovah, went first to divide the waters; and remained in the bed of the stream on the upper side, as a protection to the passing multitude.

4 two thousand cubits. About 1000 yards.

7 And the Lord said. It is probable that God made this communication to Joshua, and through him to the people, when they were all in order of march, and waiting for the command to start.

to magnify thee. As the passage of the Red Sea had demonstrated the Divine commission of Moses, so the division of the Jordan was to prove that God was now beginning to fulfil His promise, to be with Joshua as He had been with Moses.

10 Hereby ye shall know, etc. This miracle afforded encouragement to Israel, as well as discouragement to their enemies, who probably regarded the Jordan, in its then swollen state, as an impassable barrier, at least for some weeks, to the host of the Hebrews.

11 the Lord of all the earth. Who, therefore, has all nature under His control. The word for "Lord" here is *Adon*, not *Jahveh*.

12 take you twelve men. The purpose of this selection is more fully detailed in iv. 1–3.

13 the waters of Jordan shall be cut off, etc. Rather, "the waters of the Jordan shall be cut off, *even* the waters which come down from above, and they shall stand in one heap" (R.V.). *Jordan* means descending, *i.e.*, a rushing current. See Psa. cxiv. 3. To early Israel the crossing of the Jordan was as great a crisis as the crossing of the Red Sea (Sir G. A. Smith's *Historical Geography of the Holy Land*, p. 486).

15 overfloweth all his banks. The Jordan is usually easily forded; but it has a broad bed with steep banks, which it occasionally fills. This occurs during the months of March and April (the time of the barley harvest in those countries), when the snow of the mountains being melted, a large body of water comes down in a turbid, rapid current. This was just the time when the Israelites crossed; and on this account the miracle was the more impressive.

16 very far from the city Adam, etc. Or, rather, "very far off (viz., from the spot at which they crossed) near Adam, the city that is beside Zaretan": see R.V. If this be the place mentioned in 1 Kings iv. 12, it was about thirty miles above the crossing, and near the great rapids, where the accumulation of water would probably be stopped.

failed, and were cut off. Rather, "were wholly cut off" (R.V.); *i.e.*, as no more water came down from above, all flowed into the Dead Sea, leaving the channel perfectly dry.

CHAPTER IV

2 Take you twelve men. The choice was made by the tribes, and approved by Joshua (see ver. 4). On this representation of every tribe, cp. Numb. xiii. 1; 1 Kings xviii. 31.

9 in the midst of Jordan. This verse seems to indicate that two heaps of stones were made. So the LXX. reads, "twelve other stones." The priests, standing *in* Jordan "on the brink," *i.e.*, in the shallow overflow water (iii. 15), are said to be "in the midst" (ver. 17); *i.e.*, the water then entirely surrounded the place where they stood. On the subsidence of the water these stones would be left high and dry; so that they would not be carried away by the torrent.

11 in the presence of the people. As in iii. 6 11, 14; *i.e.*, they crossed and went forward till they came again in front of the people, who had halted to allow the ark to head their march.

13 forty thousand. These were not all the males of those tribes capable of service; but probably only a fair proportion of the able warriors.

19 Gilgal. The place afterwards so called (see v. 9). The Jordan was crossed on the anniversary of the day on which, forty years before, the people began to prepare for leaving Egypt by selecting the paschal lamb (Exod. xii. 3).

CHAPTER V

The miraculous entry of the Israelites into the promised land, while it filled with dismay the people of Canaan (1), gave opportunity to the new generation to undergo the rite of circumcision, as a token of their covenant-relation with Jehovah (2–9), and then to celebrate the passover (10), and the feast of unleavened bread (11); the people being now supplied with the produce of the land, in the place of the manna, which is no longer given (12).

1 until we were passed over. According to the text, this narrative must have been written by one who had passed over. But as the Hebrew marginal reading must be rendered "they," it is not safe to found anything on this passage.

2 sharp knives. Rather, "knives of flint" (R.V.). Such being used in the earliest times for this purpose (see Exod. iv. 25); a practice which is still retained among some nations.

the second time. *i.e.*, as they used to be circumcised formerly, renewing the observance of a suspended rite. Ver. 7 shows that this was not a repetition of the rite in the case of those who had been already circumcised, but the application of it, as aforetime, to those, under forty years of age, who had not yet received it.

3 at the hill of the foreskins. Or, "at the hill (Gibeah) ha-Araloth" (R.V. marg.); so named from the rite performed there.

9 the reproach of Egypt. The meaning of this phrase is doubtful; but it probably refers to the effacement of the last stain of the "house of bondage."

10 kept the passover. This celebration of the passover appears to have been the second after the Israelites left Egypt. The first was at Sinai, in the second year of their journey (Numb. ix. 1). In the same year they were rejected by God on account of their rebellion at Kadesh-Barnea; and from that time the celebration of the covenant-festival was of necessity suspended, inasmuch as the covenant itself was broken. Now, however, that the people had been "a second time" received into the covenant of Jehovah by circumcision, the passover could be observed again.

11 the old corn. Or "the produce" (R.V. marg.). After the passover, they were to keep the feast of unleavened bread; which they could not do according to the appointment as long as they had nothing but manna to live upon. They now had the means of obeying the command in Lev. xxiii. 10.

12 the manna ceased. The manna was now unnecessary; as corn began to be available.

13 there stood a man over against him. As God had manifested Himself to Moses before he entered upon his great enterprise, so He now (vi. 2) appears to Joshua, assuming a form and a name which would remind His servant of His own supremacy in the command of Israel, and of His promised guidance and protection in the anticipated conflict.

CHAPTER VI

1 was straitly shut up. Heb., "did shut up, and was shut up"; perhaps referring both to the besiegers and besieged.

4 rams' horns. Heb., "trumpets of jubilee," used on joyful occasions.

17 accursed. Rather, "devoted" (R.V.), *i.e.*, to utter destruction. For any person to appropriate anything thus devoted was sacrilege, by which he would become similarly devoted. This curse, called in Hebrew *cherem* (Gr. *anathema*), was irrevocable (see ver. 26; 1 Kings xvi. 34).

18 ye, in any wise, etc. A rather free rendering is better: "And do ye only beware of the devoted thing; lest when ye have devoted it, ye take of it, and so make the camp of Israel devoted" (R.V. marg.). As the event proved, when any of the things devoted to destruction were brought into the camp the curse was brought with them.

19 consecrated. Like the rest, "devoted"; but in another way.

20 the wall fell down flat. The word "flat" is not in the Hebrew, which means "fell down in its place," or simply "fell down." The wall collapsed. There was clearly nothing in what the people did which had any natural connexion with the result. It would, however, serve to confirm in themselves, and to exhibit to their enemies, an unhesitating obedience to the Divine commands, and a perfect reliance upon the promised aid of Divine power. See Heb. xi. 30.

21 utterly destroyed, etc. Lit., "devoted," as in preceding verses.

23 without the camp. As unfit, without purification, for admission to the community of Israel. Ver. 25 seems to intimate that Rahab was afterwards so admitted.

26 Cursed be the man, etc. The foundation would be laid at the birth of his firstborn, and if he persevered in the building, his youngest son would die at its completion. See 1 Kings xvi. 34.

CHAPTER VII

1 the children of Israel committed, etc. Achan was evidently the only offender in this matter among all the thousands of Israel—a wonderful instance of religious discipline and obedience. Yet the whole nation became implicated in the consequences of his transgression, in accordance with that principle of the Divine government that whole communities often profit by the virtues, and suffer from the vices, of a single individual. "Accursed," *i.e.*, "devoted." See vi. 17 note.

2 Ai. The same as Hai, mentioned in Gen. xii. 8.

6 rent his clothes, etc. The customary indications of violent grief and humiliation among the Orientals.

9 what wilt Thou do unto Thy great name? Joshua was even more concerned for God's glory than for Israel's safety: but his prayer shows also a mixture of despondency and unbelief.

10 Get thee up. The time which is required for vigorous reformation is not to be spent in empty grief.

14 the tribe which the Lord taketh. Intimating that the decision of the lot would be ordered by a special providence (Prov. xvi. 33).

16 by their tribes. Each tribe being probably represented by one of its chiefs.

17 the family of Judah. Read "families," and afterwards as follows: "and he brought the family of the Zarhites by households, and [*the household of*] Zabdi was taken," etc.

19 give . . . glory to the Lord. *i.e.*, honour God by a public confession of the sin which His omniscience has detected, and submission to the punishment which His justice requires.

21 a goodly Babylonish garment. Literally, "mantle of Shinar." Shinar was the ancient name of the territory of Babylon (see Gen. x. 10). The confession, *I saw, I coveted, and took*, is simply natural, and quite in accordance with the record of the first temptation, see Gen. iii. 6. But confession is too late when it is not made till the time of judgement.

24 all Israel. Acting through their chiefs, as representatives.

CHAPTER VIII

3 Joshua arose. The difficulties of this narrative will be lessened if we take vers. 3–9 as a *general outline* of the whole proceeding, and vers. 10–12 as a more *minute detail* of the arrangement adopted.

10 numbered. Rather, "mustered," or arrayed for march.

12 five thousand men. Some suppose these to have formed a second detachment, perhaps keeping open communication between the ambush (ver. 3) and the main army. Others remark that part of vers. 12, 13 is wanting in the best MSS. of the Septuagint, and ascribe the variation in the numbers given in vers. 3–12 to a transcriber's error in one place or the other. A valuable "Note on the variations in numbers mentioned in the Historical Books" will be found in the *Annotated Paragraph Bible* published by the R.T.S.

14 all his people. *i.e.*, all the survivors. When Joshua and his troops began to flee, all the rest of the men in the city came out, leaving it entirely defenceless.

18 Stretch out the spear. A preconcerted signal, apparently appointed by God.

30 As in the LXX vers. 30–35 follow ver. 2 of ch. ix., many have thought that this paragraph refers to a later period, when more of the country was conquered, and the camp at Gilgal was broken up. We must otherwise suppose a journey from the camp to Shechem (thirty miles) and back again, through an enemy's country. Many critics place the paragraph after the end of ch. xi. But the word *Then* may mean "in commemoration of this event"—not "immediately" after the destruction of Ai.

CHAPTER IX

1 in the hills, and in the valleys, etc. Both in the mountain districts, the (western) lowlands, and even the sea-coast towards Lebanon. This takes in all the rest of the country.

heard thereof. That is, of the destruction of Jericho and Ai (cp. ver. 3).

3 Gibeon. Gibeon was a large city, with villages dependent on it, about five miles north-west of Jerusalem. It is now called *El-jib.* Though the artifice of the Gibeonites was justly punished by their degradation, yet God inflicted a special plague on account of Saul's violation of the treaty made with them. See 2 Sam. xxi. 1, 2. From this we gather that, had others of the Canaanites submitted, and renounced their idolatries and crimes, they might have been spared. See 1 Tim. i. 13–17.

4 went and made. Rather, according to another reading, "went and prepared food," or "took provisions." See R.V. marg.

wine bottles. Wine-skins, which are apt to crack with heat, and sometimes mended by being tied up.

5 shoes. Rather, "sandals." "Clouted" means "patched."

14 asked not counsel. In this they were culpably negligent, as they had the means of obtaining Divine direction through the high priest.

18 all the congregation murmured. Perhaps they feared they might displease God by sparing these Canaanites.

19 We have sworn. The question of conscience whether to obey God by destroying these Canaanites, or to respect the oath taken in His name to spare them, was rightly decided by "the princes." The *reason* for "devoting" the Canaanites was that Israel might not be seduced into idolatry. In the case of these men of Gibeon the reason existed no longer, and the spirit of the command was respected by their being devoted in another way. See ver. 23.

21 hewers of wood and drawers of water. The Gibeonites were given to the Levites as servants to perform the most menial and laborious work of the tabernacle, and they were probably afterwards classed with the Nethinim. See Ezra viii. 20. Thus the curse was ultimately turned into a blessing, while their servitude to the Israelites was a permanent memorial of the Divine interposition on behalf of the latter, and helped to attest the authenticity of their early history.

23 cursed. *i.e.*, "devoted," not, like the rest of the Canaanites, to destruction, but to perpetual service in the sanctuary.

27 for the altar. This expression shows that they were not to be employed for private purposes, but for the public service in the tabernacle.

CHAPTER X

1 Jerusalem. "*City*" (or abode) "*of peace*"; perhaps given in allusion to the natural strength of its position. The meaning of the name was in some doubt until the discovery of the Tel-el-Amarna tablets in 1887. *Adoni-zedek* means "Lord of righteousness." Melchizedek, "King of righteousness," Gen. xiv., reigned also in Jerusalem.

were among them. *i.e.*, on terms of peace and friendly intercourse.

3 Hebron, etc. All these places lay within a circuit of a few miles.

5 the Amorites. This name is here, as elsewhere, used as a generic term. The people of Jerusalem were Jebusites, and those of Hebron, Hittites.

7 ascended from Gilgal. About fifteen miles.

10 up to Beth-horon. From Gibeon the road ascends to the Upper Beth-horon, and then it descends to the lower village, by a rocky and rugged pass, down which Joshua drove the foe, in the face of a fearful hailstorm, to Azekah and Makkedah. The two Beth-horons, Upper and Lower, still exist, both bearing the name of *Beitur.* Cp. xvi. 3, 5. Sir Charles Warren identified Makkedak as *el-Mughar*, south of Ekron.

12 Then spake Joshua. As Joshua *spake to the Lord,* his command was evidently given in connexion with prayer. Cp. James v. 16–18, with 1 Kings xvii. 1, for a similar miraculous answer, and the encouragement to prayer to be derived from it.

Sun, stand thou still. The language employed is general and popular, so as to discourage curious speculations upon the question, in what way or for what length of time the daylight was prolonged. This renewed intervention of Jehovah would show still more clearly to all parties that the battle was the Lord's, and that the interests of Israel were His.

upon Gibeon, etc. Gibeon was eastward of the place occupied by Joshua, and Ajalon towards the west. Mr. E. W. Maunder, F.R.A.S., of the Royal Observatory, Greenwich, thinks that the time was noon. In two articles on "Joshua's Long Day," in the *Sunday at Home* for 1904, he says that whether the sun appeared to stand still through the temporary arrest of earth's rotation or through some exaltation of the physical powers of the Israelites, it seems clear that both the prose account and the poem were written by eye-witnesses, who recorded what they themselves had seen and heard whilst every detail was fresh in their memory.

13 the book of Jasher. The "book of Jasher," or "the upright," was a collection of poetical narratives.

a whole day. Or, "when the day was complete."

15 And Joshua returned, etc. This verse is not in the Greek version; it interrupts the narrative, and is the same, word for word, as the last verse of the chapter. Probably it was misplaced here, by the error of some ancient transcriber. It is very improbable that Joshua should have gone so far away at that critical period. It is supposed by some to be a part of the quotation from the "book of Jasher."

16 in a cave. The caves of Palestine, which are large and numerous, have often served for retreats in time of danger. See Judges vi. 2; 1 Sam. xxiv. 3; 1 Kings xviii. 3, 4.

19 smite the hindmost. *i.e.*, attack them in the rear.

24 put your feet upon the necks. An ancient symbol of absolute subjection, often seen in the paintings on Egyptian tombs.

29 Makkedah. See v. 10, note.—**Libnah.** An important place in the southern hill country of Judah; now *Arak el Menshiyeh.* See xv. 42; xxi. 13.

36 Hebron. The city of Hebron seems to have lain principally in the valley, and was occupied by the Hittites; but its fortress probably remained in the hands of the Anakim till Caleb expelled them (Judges i. 20). The same was the case with Debir.

38 Debir. Debir is called Kiriath-sannah (xv. 49), the meaning of which is uncertain, and also Kiriath-sepher (xv. 15), which means "City of books"; the Targum calls it "City of archives." The latest investigations seem to place it at *Dhâheriyah,* about an hour and a quarter to the west of Hebron.

40 the South. "The Negeb," comprising most of the portions allotted to Benjamin, Judah, Simeon, and Dan. Joshua could now turn northwards without danger of being attacked in the rear.

of the vale, and of the springs. Perhaps "the lowland country (the Shephelah) and the slopes," *i.e.*, where the mountain district of Judah sinks gradually into the western plains. (So R.V.)

41 all the country of Goshen. This district (mentioned also in xi. 16), with a town of the same name spoken of in xv. 51, probably lay at the extreme south of Palestine. It has not been identified; but it must of course be distinguished from the Egyptian "Goshen."

42 at one time. *i.e.*, in one campaign.

CHAPTER XI

1 Jabin. The royal name of the chief of Hazor (see Judges iv. 2), which was a powerful city. Its site is not certainly known.

2 on the north of the mountains, etc. A more literal translation shows accurately the extent of this formidable confederacy: "on the north in the mountain (*i.e.*, Lebanon and Hermon), and in the Arabah south of Chinneroth (*i.e.*, the higher part of the Jordan valley), and in the plain (*i.e.*, of Esdraelon and towards the Mediterranean), and in the heights of Dor (or perhaps Naphoth-dor), on the west."

Chinneroth. Chinneroth is considered by some scholars to be Gennesaret, but Sir G. A. Smith thinks this improbable. It was evidently at the southern part of the Sea of Galilee.

Dor on the west. Or, by the sea. Dor, probably now *Tantura,* lay on the seashore, a few miles south of Mount Carmel, whose outlying roots may be "the heights (R.V. for 'borders') of Dor."

5 the waters of Merom. This is generally supposed to be the upper lake of the Jordan, now called *Bahr-el-Huleh.*

8 Misrephoth-maim. "Burnings of waters." Referring, perhaps, to the famous Phœnician glass manufacture, or to salt-works by the seashore, or to a hot spring.

9 houghed their horses. Or, 'hamstrung," disabling them for war.

11 he burnt Hazor with fire. Hazor was, however, rebuilt, and it became the capital of another Jabin. It is evident that in the north as well as the south the Canaanites, though subdued for the time, were not yet completely crushed. In various places they rose again to power, as the Hebrews relaxed their efforts to exterminate them. Cp. xxiii. 5–13; Judges i. 2.

13 that stood still in their strength. Heb., "standing on their hills" (or "mounds").

16 Joshua took all that land. The land was now generally in the power of the Israelites, though several fortresses were not yet reduced, and others were, probably, afterwards rebuilt and fortified by the Canaanites.

18 made war a long time. As Caleb said (xiv. 7–10) that he was forty years old when he entered the land before, and was eighty-five at the time of the division of the country, and as thirty-eight years were spent in wandering, it follows that this war must have occupied nearly seven years.

20 it was of the Lord to harden their hearts. That is, they were left to the hardness of their hearts, so as to disregard all the wonders of Divine Providence in behalf of the Israelites; and, by this obstinacy, they incurred the punishment of their crimes, which, by submission, they might have escaped.

21 from the mountains. This expression is probably meant to include all the mountainous country of Palestine, the principal parts of which are immediately specified as (the district of) Hebron, Debir, and Anab, and all the mountains of Judah and Israel, the "mountains of Judah" forming the southern, and the "mountains of Israel" the northern part of the great range running through Palestine.

23 took the whole land. *i.e.*, he gained such complete possession of the territory as to be able to portion out the "whole land" to the Israelites, in such a way, however, as perfectly corresponded with God's promise to Moses that the entire expulsion of the Canaanites should not take place "in one year, lest the land should become desolate," etc. See Exod. xxiii. 28–30; Deut. vii. 22.

CHAPTER XII

1 these are the kings, etc. It is evident that these "kings" were merely chiefs (see Judges i. 7), or, as the heads of small tribes are now called, *sheikhs.*

2 the river. Or, "valley"; now called by the Arabs a *wady,* the bed of a stream.

3 and from the plain, etc. Rather, "and the Arabah (the Jordan valley) to the sea of Chinneroth on the east side"; *i.e.*, the eastern side of the Jordan valley, between the two seas.

the Sea of the Plain, even the Salt Sea. *i.e.*, the Dead Sea, now called by the Arabs *Bahr Lût,* or the Sea of Lot.

8 the Hittites, etc.

23 the nations of Gilgal. Some, following the Greek version, suppose these to be tribes of Galilee. Moffatt translates, "the pagans in Galilee."

CHAPTER XIII

1 there remaineth yet, etc. The Canaanites were now so far subdued that the complete conquest of the land ought to have been easily effected by the Israelites; but the settlement of the boundaries of the several tribes required the influence of some person of supreme and unquestioned authority. Joshua, therefore, must apportion the land at once.

2 the borders of the Philistines. The territory of the Philistines included all the south-western coast, from Ekron to the eastern arm of the Nile, which was counted to the Canaanite, though now possessed by the Philistines. "Geshuri" lay south-west of their possessions (see 1 Sam. xxvii. 8), and must not be confounded with "Geshur" in ver. 13.

3 Sihor. Shihor. Literally, "black [river]," a name elsewhere given to the Nile, from its muddy waters. See Isa. xxiii. "Before Egypt" (*i.e.*, east of Egypt).

6 All the inhabitants . . . will I drive out, etc. After all Joshua's victories, the extreme north and south of Canaan appear to have been only hastily overrun, and the sea-coast and the richest plains, with their cities, were still unsubdued. But the panic which had seized the enemy, the slaughter of their kings and warriors, and the capture of their chief fortresses, all contributed to render the completion of the work comparatively easy.

only divide thou it by lot. Although many parts of the land still remained unconquered, the partition of the whole might be regarded as a pledge that the Lord would certainly perform His promise in driving out the remaining Canaanites, while it furnished an occasion for faith in God. "Hence," says Calvin, "the command is given; only do your duty in distributing the land, and do not even exempt from the lot that which is still held by the enemy; for I will take care to fulfil what I have promised." An expressive type of the Christian life.

8 with whom, etc. That is, with Manasseh. Here the writer resumes his narrative, explaining why Manasseh is to have only half a share on the west of Jordan—because he had already a part of his portion with Reuben and Gad on the east.

13 Nevertheless, etc. This is the first intimation of that want of faith and perseverance which occasioned the sins and sufferings enumerated in the Books of Judges and 1 Samuel.

14 the sacrifices. With the meal, wine, and oil belonging to them.

21 dukes. Tributary chiefs.

CHAPTER XIV

3 For Moses had given. Rather, "And Moses," etc. Vers. 3, 4 explain how it was that nine tribes and a half were to be provided for. Levi was to have no portion, but Joseph was to have two—a portion as of the firstborn.

6 Caleb. Before the land was divided, Caleb's special claim was satisfied. Note the simple trust in God that breathes in his address (vers. 10, 12), and the heroism that takes up the difficult task (ver. 12: "Give me this mountain").

14 because that he wholly followed the Lord. God endorsed Caleb's testimony regarding himself, "My servant Caleb hath followed Me fully" (Numb. xiv. 24).

CHAPTER XV

1 This then was the lot, etc. "The lot . . . was at the border of Edom at the desert of Zin, towards the south, from the extreme south"; *i.e.*, this was the southern extremity of the whole land.

8 the border went up, etc. So that the greater part of the city of Jerusalem, including the temple when it was built, lay just within the portion of the Benjamites; but the fortress of Zion probably belonged to Judah; see ver. 63.

the valley of the giants. Or, of Rephaim (R.V.), on the south-west of Jerusalem. It was famed for its fertility (Isa. xvii. 5), and for a victory over the Philistines gained by David, who lay in wait behind its mulberry-trees (1 Sam. v. 22–25).

14 Caleb drove thence. His expectation and God's promise were thus fulfilled.

16 will I give Achsah my daughter. Thus encouraging the valour of others, who might afterwards maintain and extend the Israelites' power. Othniel, the hero of this exploit, was the first deliverer and judge of the nation after the time of Joshua (Judges iii. 9).

17 the brother of Caleb. Kenaz being apparently the name of a common ancestor, it must be Othniel who is called Caleb's younger brother (Judges i. 13), by which word a cousin or nephew may be meant.

32 twenty and nine. The total is thirty-eight; but either there is some corruption of the text, or only twenty-nine remained in the possession of Judah, the rest being given to Simeon.

59 six cities with their villages. After this, the LXX inserts eleven other cities and villages, including Bethlehem Ephratah, some of which have been identified by travellers and scholars. The "villages" of cities are their *suburbs* or cultivated districts.

CHAPTER XVI

1 the lot of the children of Joseph. The descendants of Joseph drew one lot, in order, it would seem, that the half tribe of Manasseh and the tribe of Ephraim might not be separated.

the water of Jericho. This is the brook which takes its rise at the fountain *Ain es Sultan*, north-west of *Riha*, and flows into the Jordan. It is probably the "spring" which was healed by Elisha: see 2 Kings ii. 21.

2 Archi. Rather, "the Archites" (R.V.).

9 the separate cities. Ver. 9 should be connected with ver. 8, as it completes the description of Ephraim's inheritance, thus: "And (in addition) the cities which were separated for the children of Ephraim from the midst of the inheritance of the children of Manasseh." See xvii. 9, and note.

CHAPTER XVII

1 to wit. Rather (beginning a new sentence), as R.V.: "To Machir was [given] Gilead," etc.

a man of war. Machir and Gilead seem to be used as tribal names for their descendants in Joshua's time.

7 Asher. This "Asher" was a town on the east of Shechem, and must not be confounded with the territory of the tribes of Asher, which lay far to the north.

9 these cities of Ephraim, etc. Rather, these cities [belonged] to Ephraim among," etc., *i.e.*, the cities south of the river Kanah.

15 If thou be a great people, etc. This incident illustrates the impartiality of Joshua, who was himself an Ephraimite.

18 the outgoings. "You shall hold and clear it to its full extent" (*Moffatt*).

CHAPTER XVIII

1 Shiloh. Shiloh was situated in the very heart of the land, about twenty miles north of Jerusalem, and was therefore well adapted for the site of the Tabernacle, which remained there more than four hundred years (1 Sam. iv. 1–11); but was afterwards placed at Gibeon (1 Chron. xxi. 29).

the tabernacle of the congregation. "Tent of meeting" (R.V.). This appears to have been done as soon as the Ephraimites, in the midst of whom it was placed, had received their inheritance.

3 How long are ye slack? The wealth they had acquired from the conquered Canaanites, and the strength of the remainder, probably combined to hinder their settlement.

4 I will send them. It is probable that some survey had been made previously to the allotment of the portions to the before-mentioned tribes; but it had not been sufficiently exact. The persons now employed were therefore to make a complete measurement of the country, in order that the land might be divided into seven parts, for the tribes which were yet unprovided for. After this survey, it appeared that Judah's part was disproportionately large; therefore a portion for another tribe was taken out of it, which, on being put anew to the lot, fell to Simeon (xix. 1–9), and another portion, which fell to Dan (xix. 40–46).

5 on the north. That is, north of Shiloh.

6 before the Lord our God. *i.e.*, before the tabernacle in which Jehovah manifested His presence to the people. The lot, when thus cast in the presence of the Lord, acquired, of course, an indisputable validity. Moses had already indicated the position of the tribes (Deut. xxxiii.), and the "lot" cast by Joshua confirms the appointment.

9 by cities. *i.e.*, the cities with their cultivated districts.

CHAPTER XIX

2 and Sheba. Rather, "even Sheba."

28 Zidon. Within the boundaries of Asher were included the Phœnician cities of Accho, Tyre, and Sidon; but the Asherites were never able to expel their inhabitants: see Judges i. 31.

34 Judah upon Jordan. "and to the Jordan." Judah cannot be here meant, as it was considerably to the southward.

47 went out too little for them. The words "too little" are not in the Hebrew; "for them" should be "from," or "beyond them" (R.V.).

50 Timnath-serah. See note on xxiv. 30.

CHAPTER XX

As soon as the land was allotted among the several tribes, six cities of refuge were selected, as commanded by Moses (see Numb. xxxv.), three on each side of the Jordan, so situated as to be easily reached from any part of the country (xx.); and then forty-two additional cities are chosen out of the different tribes, for the residence of the priests and the other Levitical families (xxi. 1–43).

CHAPTER XXI

3 gave unto the Levites. Thus all the tribes had persons residing among them whose special duty it was to instruct the people in the law: see Numb. xxxv. 2–8.

41 forty and eight cities. The exact number which Moses had prescribed. It is to be observed that the Levites did not inhabit these cities to the exclusion of their brethren, who sometimes formed the larger part of the population.

43 The Divine promises to Israel being now completely fulfilled in the peaceable and undisturbed possession of the land, Joshua calls together the auxiliaries from the eastern tribes; and after praising their past conduct, and urging on them a faithful adherence to Jehovah, dismisses them to their homes, enriched with spoil (xxii. 1–9). On their way back, they erect an altar on the banks of the Jordan (10), a proceeding which awakens universal alarm, and leads the other tribes to remonstrate solemnly against this supposed act of rebellion (11–20). They repel the charge with the strongest attestations of innocence, alleging that the altar was not intended for worship, but only as a memorial to posterity of their equal share in the covenanted rights and privileges of Israel. This explanation is accepted by the people with devout joy and praise.

CHAPTER XXII

The transactions in this chapter place the character of this generation of Hebrews in a very favourable light. The faithfulness and courage of the warriors from the eastern tribes, their anxiety not to be separated from the religious privileges of Israel, the jealousy of their brethren over their supposed apostasy; and the readiness of both parties to give and receive explanation, indicate an influence of religion on the nation greater than is to be found in any other period of their history.

9 Gilead. Used here for the whole territory of the Israelites on the east of Jordan.

10 the borders of Jordan. This altar was plainly on the western side of the river. The trans-Jordanic tribes wished to retain some hold upon the religious privileges enjoyed to the full "in the land of Canaan." They were not content, therefore, with an altar on their own side of Jordan. For "over against the land of Canaan," etc., ver. 11, read, with R.V., "in the forefront of the land of Canaan, in the region about Jordan, on the side that pertaineth unto the children of Israel."

12 the whole congregation. That is, as represented by their heads of tribes and other officers: see xxiii. 2.

19 if the land of your possession be unclean. For "unclean," *Moffatt* reads, "defiled by pagans." The land apportioned to them might seem to them "unclean" or unholy, because Jehovah had not fixed His abode there, but "in the land of Canaan" (9), which He had thus characterised as His own "possession." In this case Phinehas exhorts them to cross over and receive a share with their brethren on this side of Jordan.

22 The Lord God of gods. See R.V. marg., God is invoked, by twice mentioning His three names, "El, Elohim, Jahveh." This appeal to the Almighty and Eternal was peculiarly appropriate, as they were accused of forsaking Him.

31 This day we perceive, etc. Their integrity in this instance is ascribed, directly and solely, to the preserving grace of God. "We persevere in piety only in so far as God is present to sustain us by His hand and confirm us by the agency of His Spirit" (*Calvin*).

34 a witness. A witness of their concurrence with the rest of the tribes in the same common faith.

CHAPTER XXIII

1 a long time. Joshua's administration lasted probably about twenty-six or twenty-seven years, so that this might be about fifteen years after the last division of the land.

2 for all Israel, etc. Rather, "for all Israel [viz.], for," etc.; *i.e.*, for all Israel as represented by their elders, etc.

and said. The veteran chieftain, like the aged lawgiver of Israel, closes his administration by a solemn renewal of God's covenant with His people. The subsequent history shows that the care he took to maintain the adherence of the

Israelites to their religion was by no means needless; nor is it less necessary that Christians should be often admonished to be faithful to their Divine Lord. See 2 Pet. i. 12–15.

3 the Lord your God hath done. The remembrance of God's mercies and promises should bind us to faithfulness in His service.

7 that ye come not among these nations. *i.e.*, by intermarriage and friendship with them (ver. 12). Their adherence to the law was to be maintained and shown by their abstinence from all fellowship with the Canaanites and from the worship of their gods.

CHAPTER XXIV

1 Shechem. Shechem had already been the scene of religious transactions in the history of their forefathers from the earliest times. Here Abraham, on his arrival in Canaan, was honoured with the first appearance of Jehovah, and erected his first altar in the land (Gen. xii. 7); here Jacob built an altar on his return from Mesopotamia (Gen. xxxiii. 18–20), and afterwards sanctified his house in a like manner to that now enjoined by Joshua (Gen. xxxv. 2–4). Moses selected this spot for the solemn promulgation of the law, the blessings and curses of which the people had heard and responded to from Mounts Ebal and Gerizim (viii. 30–35).

2 the flood. Rather, "river" (R.V.), *i.e.*, the Euphrates.

13 for which. The Genevan version and others read "whereon." (So R.V.).

19 Ye cannot serve the Lord. By this strong expression, Joshua sets before the people the difficulty of maintaining fidelity to Jehovah, in order to lay a deeper and surer foundation for sincerity and watchfulness. Such cautions must not discourage zeal or excuse backsliding; but should excite to watchfulness and determined effort, and to humble reliance on Divine help. For warnings somewhat similar, see Luke xiv. 25–33; Heb. xii. 25–29.

23 the strange gods. Faithful as the mass of the people were, Joshua feared that there were some idolaters among them. The purest religious community on earth cannot be supposed to be altogether unmixed. See John vi. 70.

26 under an oak, etc. Or, "under the oak which *was* in the holy place"; perhaps where Abraham's and Jacob's altars had stood.

30 Timnath-serah. Called Judges ii. 9, "Timnath heres," *i.e.*, "the portion of the sun." It has been located at Kefr Hâris, nine miles south of Shechem (Smith: *Historical Geography of the Holy Land*, p. 351 n.).

31 the elders that overlived Joshua. These had been born, or had grown up, during the journeyings in the wilderness, and consequently belonged to the generation which succeeded that of Joshua.

32 a hundred pieces of silver. See note on Gen. xxxiii. 19.

JUDGES

INTRODUCTION

THIS Book marks a transition period in the history and government of Israel. The Israelites had entered into Canaan, but the native inhabitants had not yet been driven out. Among these the Israelites settled, intermarried, initiated their idolatrous practices, and became degenerate. They were thus an easy prey to the attacks of other nations and tribes.

It was to meet these attacks that the "judges" were successively raised up. They were in the first instance deliverers, and then in quieter times governors and judges. As Dean Stanley, in his *Jewish Church*, has pointed out, the Hebrew word "shophet" (judge) is of Phœnician origin, as the Phœnicians called their judges *suffetes*. It is thus "the first trace of the influence of Syrian usage upon the fortunes of the Chosen People." "The government may be described as a republican confederacy, the elders and princes having authority in their respective tribes" (*Bible Handbook*, § 268).

The Book of Judges, like that of Joshua, is a story of heroic and triumphant faith. It is perpetuated for Christian readers in the glowing words of the Epistle to the Hebrews. There the names of Gideon and Barak, Samson and Jephthah, are enshrined among those "who by faith subdued kingdoms . . . out of weakness were made strong" (cp. Heb. xi. 32, 33, with Judges iv.; vi.–viii.; xi., xii.; xiv.–xvi.).

"Other portions of Scripture have been more profitable for doctrine, for correction, for reproof, for instruction in righteousness; but for merely human interest—for the lively touches of ancient manners, for the succession of romantic incidents, for the consciousness that we are living with the persons described, for the tragical pathos of events and character—there is nothing like the history of the Judges from Othniel to Eli" (Stanley, *The Jewish Church*, p. 252).

Exact dates are not given and cannot be supplied. "The most that can be said is that the close [of the period of the Judges] may be assigned with probability to 1000 B.C." (Prof. König in *Hastings' Dict. of the Bible*, art. "Judges").

CHAPTER I

3 Judah, Simeon. The name used for the tribes.

my lot. "My allotted territory."

7 kings. That is, petty chiefs.

8 had fought . . . had taken. "fought . . . took" (R.V.). As Jerusalem was already in the hands of Judah, it had probably been taken by Joshua. The strong fort of Zion was, however, held by the Jebusites till the time of David; and most, if not all, of the city was regained and inhabited by them: see ver. 21 and 2 Sam. v. 6–9. Vers. 8–16 appear to be a parenthetical recital of previous events, some of which had been recorded in the Book of Joshua.

9 the valley. Or, the lowland (R.V.), the *Shephelah*, extending west from the mountains of Judah to the Mediterranean, and from Joppa in the north to Gaza in the south. Vers. 10, 11 refer to 18, to the "valley."

16 the children of the Kenite. That is, the descendants of Jethro (see Numb. x. 32).

the city of palm trees. *i.e.*, Jericho: see Deut. xxxiv. 3; 2 Chron. xxviii. 15.

18 Judah took Gaza. The Septuagint has, "Though Judah did *not* take possession of Gaza, nor the borders thereof, nor of Askelon," etc. But this may have been an alteration made by the Greek translators to get rid of a difficulty, as we find these cities shortly afterwards in the hands of the Philistines, who probably soon reconquered them.

19 but could not, etc. Rather, "for he could not" (R.V.). They possessed only the mountain district.

chariots of iron. Wooden chariots, studded with iron.

20 Sons of Anak. *i.e.*, the Anakim, "the giants."

24 the entrance into the city. Not the principal gate, but some unguarded point where they might enter unresisted.

26 the land of the Hittites. We find Hittites in different parts of Palestine, but their chief settlement at this time was probably on the north-east near the borders of Syria.

27 Beth-shean, etc. All the places mentioned in this verse lay near the valley of Jezreel.—**Taanach,** now Ta-annek, has been recently explored (see Driver, *Schweich Lectures*, 1909, pp. 80–96).

28 to tribute. Or, "to task work." This course appeared more easy and more profitable; but it was opposed to the Divine command, and it soon brought its own punishment, causing the Israelites great disquiet and suffering. See 1 Kings ix. 15–17.

29 Gezer. Explored by Professor Macalister in 1902. See note on Lev. xviii. 21.

31 Accho. An ancient Phœnician city near Mount Carmel, afterwards named Ptolemais (Acts xxi. 7), and now called *Akka* by the natives.

34 into the mountain. That is, into the mountainous parts, which were the smallest portion of their lot. The same slothfulness, cowardice, and unbelief, which had kept their fathers forty years out of Canaan, now deprived them of its full possession.

35 the house of Joseph. Ephraim's portion lying close to Dan, the Ephraimites aided the Danites.

36 the going up to Akrabbim. *i.e.*, "The ascent of scorpions," so called from the great numbers of these animals which infest the country south of the Dead Sea, where the ground rises into a range of cliffs crossing the Arabah.

from the rock. "To Sela."

CHAPTER II

1 an angel. "The angel."

5 Bochim. "Weepers."

6 And when Joshua, etc. Vers. 6–9 are repeated with slight variations from Josh. xxiv. 28–31.

11 did evil. This phrase (which seems like the key-note of the whole narrative) is applied to each of the seven great apostasies of the people; and it recurs in the later history of the kings of Judah and Israel, always with reference to idolatry.

Baalim. The word "Baalim" (*lords*), being plural, intimates that the Israelites worshipped no one false god in particular, but the idols of the several tribes of Canaanites among them, who were regarded by their worshippers as tutelary deities of particular districts, from which, or from some other peculiarities, they derived their varied names; as Baal-*zephon*, Baal-*peor*, Baal-*zebub*, etc.

13 Ashtaroth. "Ashtoreth," Astarte, Venus.

14 spoilers. The predatory inroads of the Midianites and others.

16 judges. The "judges," here first named, were extraordinary officers, having temporary and sometimes only local authority, acting under Divine impulse, and often expressly called by God, in some manifest and signal way, to their office and work.

18 it repented the Lord. "The Lord was grieved."

CHAPTER III

3 five lords. This appellation (Heb. *seranim*) is used exclusively of the Philistine governors. The five "lordships" were Gath, Ashdod, Gaza, Ashkelon, and Ekron.

7 groves. The Hebrew word *Asherim*, here and elsewhere rendered "groves," means upright pillars made of trunks of trees, and used in connexion with the worship of Ashtoreth.

8 Chushan-rishathaim. Nothing more is known of this invader. Professor Strahan translates his name "Nubian of double-dyed wickedness" (*Peake's Commentary*).

9 cried unto the Lord. Those who in prosperity had cried to Baalim and Ashtoreth, now when they are in trouble cry to the Eternal. But though they were driven to God by adversity, He did not reject their prayers.

11 Othniel the son of Kenaz died. It was probably somewhere about this period that the idolatry of the Danites occurred, as well as the war with the Benjamites, related in xvii.–xxi.; also the events recorded in the Book of Ruth.

12 Relapsing into sin, the Israelites are subjected to the king of Moab for eighteen years (12–14), but are delivered by Ehud (15–29), so that for eighty years they enjoy peace (30). Shamgar, on the other hand, frees them from the Philistines (31).

13 the city of palm trees. *i.e.*, Jericho: see i. 16. Some houses had probably been rebuilt, but not the walls.

15 sent a present. Probably the tribute which Eglon had imposed.

16 cubit. About 18 inches.

19 quarries. The Hebrew word here used means ' graven images."

Keep silence. Addressed to the servants, commanding them to withdraw.

20 a summer parlour. A cool, shaded apartment, now called a *kiosk;* probably separate from the rest of the house.

21 And Ehud, etc. From this whole narrative, especially ver. 15, it may be inferred that Ehud, in performing this deed, was acting under a special commission from God, who saw fit thus to punish the oppressor of His people, after having first made use of him for their correction.

30 the land had rest fourscore years. Some suppose that this applies chiefly to the land east of Jordan, which had been oppressed by the Moabites. It seems, from ver. 31, that the south-western part of Canaan was at that time much infested by the Philistines.

31 with an ox goad. A weapon well suited for the purpose in the hands of a strong man, being six to eight feet long, and armed with a spike of iron.

CHAPTER IV

2 Hazor. *i.e.*, Canaanite king of Hazor (Josh. xi. 1–10), which city had been rebuilt, and had regained its former power.

3 twenty years. This oppression was both longer and heavier than either of the former—the repetition of the sin aggravating the offence, and increasing the chastisement.

4 a prophetess. See note on Exod. xv. 20.

6 toward mount Tabor. From vers. 6, 10, 14, taken together, it appears that Barak was first to collect his warriors on the heights of Kedesh, and then to march (perhaps for the most part in single file, so as to be less observed) along the hills to Mount Tabor, at the foot of which, in the plain of Jezreel, or Megiddo, the battle was fought.

Naphtali . . . Zebulun. These two tribes (see ch. v. 14–23) had been the principal sufferers under the oppression of Jabin; and Barak himself was of the tribe of Naphtali.

11 plain. Should be "oak," or "terebinth." See Gen. xii. 6.

15 discomfited. The Heb. word means *utterly routed.* Ch. v. 20, 21 make it highly probable that a sudden storm during the battle deluged the plain, making part of it a morass, which impeded the movements of the chariots, and filling the Kishon, which in such a case soon becomes an irresistible torrent.

fled away on his feet. A more secret, and, in a hilly country, a more speedy way of flight than in a chariot.

19 a (the) **bottle.** A skin or leather bag.

20 thou shalt say, No. Jael had brought Sisera into the inner part of the tent, into which no one would think of intruding, as it was appropriated to the women. Sisera gives Jael a lesson in falsehood: he was doomed to be repaid by treachery. Neither is defensible.

21 a nail of the tent. "A tent-pin," R.V. One of the long sharp spikes used to fasten the tent-cords to the ground.

CHAPTER V

1 Then sang Deborah. The song is in ten unequal strophes, or stanzas, as shown above. It is described by R. H. Hutton of *The Spectator* as "the greatest war-song of any age or nation." Moffatt's translation brings out in a fresh way the meaning and force of the original.

2 for the avenging of Israel, etc. Should be "for the leading of the leaders in Israel, for the people's willingness in offering themselves." See R.V.

5 The mountains melted. Rather, "were shaken" (see R.V. marg.); and so in Isa. lxiv. 1, 3. Vers. 4 and 5, which greatly resemble those referred to in the margin, portray in poetic imagery the Divine manifestations on behalf of Israel. Cp. Psa. xviii.; lxviii.; xcvii. 5.

6 In the days of Shamgar . . . of Jael. From this it would appear that the two were contemporaneous, though some scholars regard the words, "in the days of Jael" as a gloss.

10 that ride on white asses. The ass has always been much used in Palestine and Egypt for riding about the towns. It is a larger animal than our British ass.

11 They that are delivered, etc. Should read, "Far from the noise of the archers in the places of drawing water." Robbers frequently lurk about watering-places in the East, that they may fall upon travellers and others who resort thither.

13 Then He made, etc. Rather, "Then came down the residue of the nobles; the people of Jahveh came down to me with the mighty." See R.V.

14 Out of Ephraim, etc. Here begins the enumeration of the tribes who had fought under Barak.

Out of Machir came down governors. Machir was the son of Manasseh, and the father of Gilead. The meaning is, "Out of Manasseh came military leaders."

the pen of the writer. "The rod of the numberer," referring to the mustering of the troops under Barak. See R.V. marg. The rendering preferred by many (and R.V.) is, "the marshal's staff." Moffatt translates "adjutants."

15 For the divisions of Reuben. The passage is rendered in R.V., "Among the watercourses of Reuben"; intimating that the Reubenites remained at home amidst their possessions and comforts, and had many deliberations ("resolves of heart," R.V.), but without any practically useful result. The Hebrew, however, may mean either "divisions" or "watercourses" (the former taken from the dividing of streams)

17 Gilead abode beyond Jordon. That is, the Gadites, who possessed part of Gilead (see Josh. xiii. 24, 25), and perhaps also part of the half-tribe of Manasseh.

why did Dan, etc. ? That is, "Why was Dan so

intent upon his ships and merchandise?" The port of Joppa belonged to Dan.

breaches. "Creeks," or "havens."

18 Zebulun, etc. Rather, "Zebulun was a people that despised their lives unto death; and Naphtali upon the open field."

19 no gain of money. They obtained no spoil or booty; they gained nothing by it.

21 thou hast trodden down strength. Rather, as an imperative, "March on with strength" (R.V.).

22 Then were the horsehoofs broken. "Then the horse-hoofs smote *the ground*, because of the rushings, the rushings of their mighty ones," *i.e.*, in their hasty flight.

23 Curse ye Meroz. When God requires our services against His foes, it is at our peril to be neutral. Of Meroz nothing more is known.

24 Blessed above women. Jael is commended for the *patriotism* of her deed. The commendation by Deborah simply expresses the public opinion of those days.

25 Butter. Should be "sour milk" or "thick milk," a favourite and refreshing dish, not only among the Arabs still, but in many European countries, *e.g.*, Poland, Bulgaria, and in Ireland.

26 smote off, etc. Rather, as R.V., "smote through." "She violently smote his head, and she pierced and struck through his temples," *i.e.*, with the tent-pin. See iv. 21.

31 Thine enemies. Sisera and his army were the enemies of Jehovah as well as of Israel, and therefore Deborah triumphs in their destruction.

CHAPTER VI

3 the Midianites came up. These Midianites were principally wandering herdmen of the Eastern deserts, like the Bedouin Arabs of the present day. Many of them were probably descended from Abraham and Keturah (Gen. xxv. 2; 1 Chron. i. 32); but they seem to have been intermixed with Ishmaelites (Gen. xxxvii. 25, 28) and Amalekites (3).

4 unto Gaza. Across the whole breadth of the land.

5 Grasshoppers. "Locusts."

11 Ophrah. Ophrah is thought by Conder and Sir G. A. Smith to be the modern Ferata, a little to the S.W. of Shechem (Nablous).

threshed wheat. The Hebrew denotes "threshed wheat *with a flail.*" This would require less room than the ordinary treading out by cattle, and be more likely to escape notice.

12 The Lord is with thee. Once more note the force of the original, "The Eternal is with thee."

15 my family is poor. Literally, "poorest."

22 O Lord God. "Adonai Jahveh" (My Lord the Eternal).

25 the second bullock of seven years old. Perhaps this was the youngest above the age of three years (the proper age for sacrifice) left by the invaders. But some render the passage, "Take a bullock, the steer which is thy father's, and a bullock, the second of seven years, and destroy," etc. Thus there would be two bullocks used in removing the materials of the altar and the Asherah-idol, the second of which was sacrificed (26, 28).

cut down the grove. See note on iii. 7.

26 in the ordered place. Or, "in the orderly manner" (R.V.); *i.e.*, doing all in the method prescribed for sacrifice.

30 that he may die. Treating as a capital offence an effort to suppress practices which their own Divine law had made punishable with death.

32 he called him. Rather, "he was called."—**Jerubbaal.** "Let Baal fight" or "Baal fights."

34 Abi-ezer was gathered after him. Gideon's bold defiance of the heathen gods seems to have encouraged the people to trust to his leadership: see next verse.

36 Gideon said, etc. Gideon was prudent as well as bold. He fully trusted God's promise; but desired to be certain that the promise had been *really given.*

38 a bowl full. The sign was not in the quantity of dew, which was not extraordinary, but in its partial distribution. This was the more remarkable in the second case (ver. 40), as the fleece would, in the ordinary course of things, have retained the dew more than the ground.

CHAPTER VII

1 beside the well of Harod. Now 'Ain Jalûd, near Mount Gilboa.

2 too many. Man is so prone to self-sufficiency that he often needs to be taught his dependence upon Divine power.

3 proclaim, etc. According to the law in Deut. xx. 8, which is mentioned in 1 Maccab. iii. 56, as being strictly observed by Judas Maccabæus.

mount Gilead. Probably a copyist's error for "Gilboa."

5 as a dog lappeth. Not kneeling down to drink in a leisurely manner, but raising the water to the mouth in the hollow of the hand, and lapping as a dog does with his tongue. This showed a readiness for action which peculiarly fitted them for this enterpise.

8 So the people took, etc. According to the LXX and Chaldee, "And they took the victuals of the people (*i.e.*, of those who were dismissed) in their hands, and their (the dismissed one's) trumpets." This remark explains how it was that the three hundred men came suddenly into possession of so many pitchers and trumpets.

11 the armed men. See Exod. xiii. 18; Josh. i. 14; iv. 12. The Midianite warriors were encamped in order, and separate from the multitude of camp followers.

13 barley bread. The food of the poor, so representing something despised.

16 three companies. Thus the enemy's camp was completely surrounded; and the sudden blast of three hundred trumpets, the crash of as many pitchers, and the blaze of as many torches (not "lamps"), would lead the hastily-awakened Midianites to imagine that they were encompassed by a large army.

18 The sword of the Lord and of Gideon. Rather, "For the Lord, and for Gideon" (R.V.). The people themselves added the mention of "the sword," ver. 20.

19 the middle watch. There were three watches, of four hours each; the beginning of the middle watch would be about 10 p.m., when the men were in their first sleep.

21 stood every man in his place, etc. So that the Midianites might think they were surrounded by a great host. The little band had both hands engaged with the torches and the trumpets.

22 Beth-shittah. "House of the acacia," probably the modern Shutta. "Zererath," or "Zeredath." See 1 Kings xi. 26; 2 Chron. iv. 17. "Abel-meholah" was in the Jordan valley. See 1 Kings xix. 16.

15 Oreb and Zeeb. The death of these marauding chieftains (characteristically named the Raven and the Wolf) was accompanied by a fearful slaughter of the invaders, celebrated in after times among the most signal victories of Israel (Psa. lxxxiii. 9, 11, and "the day of Midian," Isa. ix. 4).

CHAPTER VIII

1 they did chide with him sharply. The conduct of the Ephraimites, on this and on other occasions (see xii. 1–7), seems to show that they claimed the leadership of the tribes. Hence their rivalry with Judah, so conspicuous in later times, referred to in Isa. vii. 5, 6; ix. 21; xi. 13. Had their arrogance not been met with the tact which Gideon shows in his courteous answer, the deliverance of Israel might not have been completed.

2 Is not the gleaning, etc. A proverbial mode of commending the smallest action (the gleaning) of one, as superior to the greatest (the vintage) of another. On the spirit of Gideon's answer compare Prov. xv. 1.

6 the princes of Succoth said, etc. Seeing that two kings of Midian with many thousand men had escaped, the princes of Succoth may have thought that Gideon's little band would after all be unequal to the contest, and that they, lying east of the Jordan, would be exposed to the vengeance of the Midianites. Still, their unbelieving and inhuman refusals of supplies, with bitter taunts, to those who were acting under the direction of Heaven was treason against their country and their Divine King; and, as such, it deserved exemplary punishment.

11 by the way of them that dwelt in tents. "By the caravan route" (*Moffatt*).

13 before the sun was up. Or, "from the ascent of Heres" (R.V.).

16 he taught. Heb., "lacerated" or "threshed."

18 whom ye slew at Tabor. This refers probably to some barbarous massacres which had been committed by the Midianite chiefs during the oppressions related in vi. 2.

resembled the children of a king. An Oriental expression, denoting extraordinary comeliness.

27 Gideon made an ephod. Gideon appears to have aimed to form a sacerdotal establishment at Ophrah. The ephod was the part of the high priest's dress worn when he inquired of God by the Urim and Thummim. Perhaps here it was an image with the representation of the priestly ephod. The great purpose, no doubt, of Gideon was to prevent resort to Shiloh, in the tribe of Ephraim. Though intended for the service of Jahveh, it was unauthorised and improper, and opened the way to superstition.

CHAPTER IX

2 Shechem. Now Nablous. Shechem belonged to the Ephraimites, in whom Abimelech aimed to rouse that well-known party spirit (see viii. 1) which, in the present instance, led to such destructive consequences both to himself and to them. It seems also to have contained a considerable remnant of the Canaanites, among whom was probably the mother of Abimelech; see vers. 18, 24, 28.

4 vain and light. "Worthless and reckless."

6 house of Millo. Should be Beth-Millo, a proper name.

made Abimelech king. This is the first time that the title of "king" was conferred in Israel.

7 Gerizim. The precipices of Mount Gerizim seem, in some parts, almost to overhang the town of Shechem. That Jotham could easily be heard in that position appears from Deut. xxvii. 12, 13; and Josh. viii. 33.

14 the bramble. Probably the buckthorn or *rhamnus*, which has very strong and sharp thorns. The same Hebrew word is used in Psa. lviii. 9. Abimelech was the bramble-king. He aspired to a position for which he had no fitness.

15 If in truth, etc. That is, as explained in the next verse, "truly and sincerely"; or, in justice and good faith towards your former ruler. By "the cedars of Lebanon" are meant the most eminent persons of the land, particularly those of Shechem.

28 who is Shechem? That is, *the Shechemites.* The meaning seems to be, "Did not Jerubbaal's son (Abimelech) and Zebul his officer serve the family of Hamor the father of Shechem? Why then should we serve him?"

31 they fortify the city. Rather, "they constrain the city to take part" against thee (R.V.).

37 by the plain of Meonenim. Rather, "on the way to the Oak of Enchanters."

45 sowed it with salt. A token of perpetual desolation.

53 all-to. Old English for *entirely.*

54 that men say not. How little Abimelech's device availed him is shown by 2 Sam. xi. 21.

CHAPTER X

1 to defend. Rather, "to save" (R.V.).

8 that year. The Septuagint has, "at that time," taking the word "year" indefinitely.

12 Maonites. Ancient versions read *Midianites.*

17 Mizpeh. "The watch-tower." In Gilead; the place where Jacob and Laban made their covenant (Gen. xxxi. 49).

CHAPTER XI

1 Gilead. A proper name used for a family appellation—"a Gileadite."

11 all his words. That is, all the words pertaining to his solemn compact with the elders.

15 Thus saith Jephthah, etc. To prove the futility of the enemy's claims, Jephthah recapitulates the leading circumstances of the conquest of this territory by Israel, showing that at that time it was not in the possession either of the Ammonites or of the Moabites, but of the Amorites. Jephthah shows his familiarity with the narrative in Numbers (xx. 14–21) and Deuteronomy (ii.).

24 Chemosh thy god giveth thee. Jephthah argues with these idolators upon their own principles. Jahveh's supremacy is plainly implied in ver. 27, "the Eternal one God."

25 Balak, king of Moab. He never thought of disputing the right of Israel to what they took from the Amorites, though it had formerly been in the possession of Moab.

29 the Spirit of the Lord came upon Jephthah. Endowing him in an extraordinary manner for the work to which he was called.

31 Whatsoever. Should read "whosoever."

38 bewailed her virginity. This expression, as well as the concluding clause of ver. 39, is adduced by some as favouring the supposition that her father's vow was fulfilled by devoting her to a life of celibacy. There is no evidence of the existence of such a practice amongst the Hebrews, or the nations with which they were connected.

39 did with her according to his vow. The

phrase has been regarded as but a veiled and delicate way of intimating the performance of the horrible sacrifice. But it may perhaps suggest that the vow was performed in reality, but not literally. The history of Abraham and Isaac would be well known by Jephthah, and its lesson would be remembered. Even if Jephthah did offer up his daughter, "it is one of the marks of rude erring man that he does take upon himself such burdens of pain in the service of the invisible Lord. . . . Jephthah and his daughter were ignorant, but not so ignorant as those who make no great offering to God. . . . We are shocked by the expenditure of fine feeling and heroism in upholding a false idea of God and obligation to Him; but are we outraged and distressed by the constant effort to escape from God which characterises our age?" (R. A. Watson in *Expositor's Bible*).

CHAPTER XII

1 And the men of Ephraim, etc. See note on viii. 1. Jephthah's position, the Ammonites being already "subdued" (cp. viii. 28), differed from that of Gideon, as well as his character.

6 Shibboleth. "Shibboleth" means *stream* and also "ear of corn," from a Heb. verb that means to *shoot forth* or *spring forth.* In many languages and dialects the sound of *sh* is not found; and it is very difficult to those who have not been early accustomed to pronounce it. The use of *s,* instead of *sh,* was evidently a well-known provincialism of the Ephraimites.

7 one of the cities. Should be rendered *his city, i.e.,* Mizpah.

9 from abroad. From other families.

14 nephews. Heb., "sons' sons"; grandsons.

CHAPTER XIII

2 Zorah. Now Sura'a. A border town in the lowlands between Judah and Dan, assigned at first to the former tribe (Josh. xv. 33), but transferred to Dan (Josh. xix. 41) and having a mixed population of both. Cp. 1 Chron. ii. 50–54.

5 Nazarite. "Nazirite" or "consecrated."

he shall begin to deliver. This intimated that the oppression of Israel by the Philistines, which had commenced before the birth of this child, would be of long duration; for the deliverance was not to *begin* till he should grow up to years of maturity. Their yoke was not fully shaken off till the time of David; and when the Hebrew kingdom was afterwards weakened by division, they again became dangerous enemies.

6 his countenance. Or, "appearance."

12 Now let thy words come to pass, etc. Or, "Now when thy words *shall come* to pass, what shall be the right manner of [training] the boy, and his work?" (R.V. marg.).

18 secret. Or, "wonderful" (R.V.); from the same Heb. root as in Isa. ix. 6.

24 Samson. "Sunny."

25 began to move him. Stirring him up to bold exploits, and inspiring him with zeal for the deliverance of his country.

the camp of Dan. Or, *Mahaneh-dan* (R.V.), as in xviii. 12.

CHAPTER XIV

2 Timnath. Now *Tibneh,* below Zoran, about three miles south-west.

4 he sought an occasion against the Philistines. It pleased God to leave Samson to follow his own inclinations; and to overrule his conduct for good to Israel. The special purpose of God in raising up Samson seems to have been to baffle the power of the whole Philistine nation by the prowess of a single individual; thereby literally fulfilling His promise (Deut. xxxii. 30). Samson was not, like most of the other judges, appointed to lead an army, but rather to be an army himself; and the whole force of the Philistines was concentrated against his person.

5 a young lion. The Hebrew word does not mean a young whelp, but a young *full-grown* lion.

8 after a time. Among the Jews, some months generally elapsed between betrothal and marriage. In this interval, a swarm of bees had established themselves in the carcase of the lion, which consisted only of the bones covered with the parched skin; the flesh and all the soft parts having either been dried up by the sun or picked out by insects and ravenous birds, so as to leave the carcase clean.

11 thirty companions. These companions, although brought with a show of respect, according to the custom in those times (see Matt. ix. 15; John iii. 29), seem to have been designed to be spies upon Samson.

12 I will now put forth a riddle. This is a favourite amusement in the East with persons of all ages and classes.

12 sheets. Rather, "linen garments" (R.V.). The thirty "changes of garments" were probably the upper vestments common in the East, usually called *caftans.*

14 Out of the eater, etc. Or, "Out of the devourer came food; and out of the strong, sweetness."

19 went up to his father's house. Showing his anger by leaving his bride.

20 his friend. Best man or groomsman.

CHAPTER XV

3 more blameless than. Rather, "blameless in regard of," etc. (R.V.).

4 foxes. "Jackals" (R.V. marg.).

firebrands. Rather, "torches" (R.V. marg.).

tail to tail. To prevent their retreat to their holes, and to keep the torches from dragging on the ground.

6 burnt her and her father. Thus her own people inflicted upon her the very doom the threat of which had induced her to betray her husband's secret: see xiv. 15, 20.

8 hip and thigh. Or, "leg on thigh." Evidently a proverbial expression, perhaps meaning "so that the limbs of the slain lay heaped one on another."

in the top. Rather, "in the cleft" (R.V.): see Isa. lvii. 5.

11 the Philistines are rulers over us. This shows strikingly the state of cowardice and degradation into which the Israelites had fallen.

14 Lehi. The writer uses the name afterwards borne by the place in honour of Samson's exploit.

16 heaps upon heaps. Heb., "a heap, two heaps." The Septuagint regards the word as a verb, "I have thoroughly destroyed them."

17 Ramath-lehi. That is, "the lifting up of the jaw-bone"; or, perhaps, "the hill of the jaw-bone."

19 in the jaw. Rather, "in Lehi": see vers. 9–14.

he called the name thereof. In this place,

called "Lehi" from the circumstance just mentioned, God, at the prayer of Samson, opened a fountain, which was called "the fountain of him that called upon God."

CHAPTER XVI

3 and took, etc. Rather, "and he laid hold of the doors of the city gates and pulled them up, with the bar," etc.: see R.V.

5 wherein his great strength lieth. Rather, "whereby his strength is great"; and so in ver. 6.

7 withs. Fresh bowstrings.

13 the seven locks. As *seven* is frequently used as a perfect number, this may be equivalent to "all my locks."

the web. Probably referring to a warp in a handloom which Delilah, like other Oriental women, was in the habit of working: see Numb. vi. 5.

21 fetters of brass. Or, "copper"; or, "with two copper" [shackles]; probably fastened to hands as well as feet, so as to secure him whilst at work.

he did grind. To Samson this would be the deepest degradation; for grinding was the work of *women*, and those the lowest slaves.

23 Dagon. The fish-god, the national deity of the Philistines: cp. 1 Sam. v. 4.

29 and on which it was borne up. Rather, "and he leaned himself upon them" (R.V.). Samson, having probably been paraded in the area, within view of the assembled multitude, requested leave to rest himself against the wooden pillars of the portico. Using his restored strength to pull down these, he destroyed the flat roof above; whilst the shock and strain, together with the weight of the crowd upon the roof, might easily bring down the rest of the edifice. This catastrophe was at once a most characteristic termination of Samson's career, and a signal vindication of the supremacy of the true God: see ver. 24.

"Nothing is here for tears, nothing to wail
Or knock the breast; no weakness, no contempt,
Dispraise, or blame; nothing but well and fair,
And what may quiet us in a death so noble."

Thus Milton, in *Samson Agonistes*, represents Manoah as speaking after Samson's death. Milton's own blindness and his domestic troubles doubtless led him to take a sympathetic view of Samson's life. And who shall judge too harshly the hero of Gaza? His was one of the complex characters that baffle criticism. A Nazirite, dedicated to God from his birth; the Spirit of the Eternal coming upon him; yet with strong passions, to which he too readily gave way, till God departed from him. But surely we may hope that there was penitence in that last prayer, "O Lord, remember me, I pray Thee, and strengthen me."

31 twenty years. It appears that Samson, as had been foretold (xiii. 5), only *began* to deliver Israel from the oppression of the Philistines, and that their power was still unbroken at the time of his death. In the First Book of Samuel (iv.) we find the Philistines again at war with the Israelites, and the distress of the latter extreme.

CHAPTER XVII

2 thou cursedst. Pronouncing an imprecation upon the thief.

3 a graven image and a molten image. Micah and his mother may have intended to honour the true God; but their proceedings were contrary to His law, and exposed them to the punishment of death. They set up a small religious establishment, apparently designed to resemble that at Shiloh.

5 a house of gods. Rather, "a house of God," a sanctuary.

teraphim. See note, Gen. xxxi. 19.

12 And Micah consecrated the Levite. This act was wholly unlawful on the part both of Micah and of the Levite, who had no right to assume the priestly office, as he was not of the family of Aaron. See xviii. 30.

13 Now know I, etc. Micah's delusion is not unusual. But no priest can ever be a substitute for the religion of heart and life.

CHAPTER XVIII

1 the tribe of the Danites. Not the whole, but a part of this tribe: see vers. 16, 21. The foregoing narrative having shown how idolatry crept into the family of Micah, this chapter relates how it was then extended into a part of the tribe of Dan, and became established in a city of note.

their inheritance. The inheritance of the Danites had been assigned to them; but up to this time they had not obtained possession of it, in consequence of their own disobedience and remissness. See Josh. xix. 40, 47; Judges i. 34, 35.

3 what makest thou? Rather, "what *doest* thou?" (R.V.).

7 that might put them to shame in anything. Describing Laish as undefended, the verse really means, "It dwelt in confidence after the manner of Zidonians (Phœnicians), quiet and confiding, and no lack of anything in the land."

Laish. Or, "Leshem" (Josh. xix. 47), may be the place now called *Tell-el-Kadi*, near the source of the Jordan. (Sir G. A. Smith, however thinks it was the modern Banias.) It appears to have been one of the most inland settlements of the Phœnicians, situated far from the coast, in the extreme north-east of Palestine, at the base of Mount Hermon. Its inhabitants, possessing considerable agricultural wealth, were not much engaged in external commerce or in war.

12 pitched in Kirjath-jearim. Not in the city itself, but in its immediate vicinity; as appears from the words that follow. This was probably the rendezvous of the emigrants, who remained here till all were ready for the march. Hence the name Mahaneh-dan (camp of Dan) was long retained: see xiii. 25.

behind Kirjath-jearim. That is, *westward* of Kirjath-jearim; for, in speaking of the points of the compass, the sacred writers begin from the east, as in Deut. xi. 24, etc. Kirjath-jearim (town of woods) is sometimes called Baal-Judah, or Kirjath-Baal; now called *Kuriat-el-Enab* (town of grapes), a village about twelve miles west of Jerusalem on the road to Joppa.

21 the carriage. Rather, "the valuables" or "goods" (R.V.).

28 they built a city. Rather, "the city" (R.V.), which they had destroyed.

29 Dan. To be a witness for them that they were Danites by birth, though removed to so great a distance from their brethren. This city is often mentioned afterwards as the northern extremity of the country (1 Sam. iii. 20, etc.).

30 Manasseh. The original reading appears to be *Moses* (so R.V.), a name which in Hebrew differs from *Manasseh* by only one letter; משה and מנשה.

This letter, נ, is in the Hebrew MSS. of this passage written in a smaller character above the line, as if interpolated to change the name, so as to save the credit of the family of their great lawgiver. The alteration is not sanctioned by any ancient authority, except the Vulgate.

until the day of the captivity of the land. This may refer either to the subjugation of the Israelites by Jabin, or to some other servitude in the time of the Judges. At Dan, in later times, Jeroboam set up one of his golden calves; probably induced to do so in part by the previous idolatrous habits of the people.

CHAPTER XIX

1 there was a certain Levite, etc. This narrative appears to have been added in order to show what disorders and crimes arise from the neglect of the will and worship of God; and to record the exemplary punishment by which one of the tribes of Israel was reduced to comparative insignificance. It thus presents an instructive parallel to the history of the tribe of Simeon.

concubine. Or, "secondary wife." See note on Gen. xxv. 1.

12 the city of a stranger. See i. 21. The Jebusites evidently had almost entire possession of the city.

13 Come. Rather, "Go on." Ramah was about six miles north of Jerusalem, and Gibeah lay about a mile and a half east of Ramah.

15 there was no man, etc. This extraordinary want of hospitality, especially towards a Levite, accords with the remarkably debased and abandoned character of the citizens of Gibeah. The only person who would receive the travellers was but a sojourner (16).

19 no want of any thing. Travellers in the East expect to obtain little more than houseroom at their resting-places, and therefore carry their provisions with them, even when they are journeying through an inhabited country.

22 sons of Belial. "Worthless fellows."

24 Behold, here is my daughter. The conduct of the Levite and his host, in this transaction, shows how much the Israelites had become contaminated with the vices of the Canaanites. See note on Gen. xix. 8. It was evidently their duty to resist the aggressors to the utmost, throwing themselves upon the protection of Providence, and not to yield in any way to the demands of brutal and desperately wicked men.

29 and divided her, etc. Barbarous as this proceeding may appear to us, it was doubtless in accordance with the notions and practices of the times (see 1 Sam. xi. 7); and, as there was no supreme magistrate over all the tribes of Israel to whom to appeal for redress, it was probably chosen as the most effectual method of rousing the people to take up the Levite's cause as one that concerned them all. The whole nation evidently regarded it as a stern adjuration solemnly requiring them to punish this outrage.

CHAPTER XX

2 all the tribes. This great national movement of the Israelites speaks favourably for the general state of feeling amongst them. Although it was begun with far too much haste, yet, when this was corrected, the manner in which it was concluded showed that mercy was not quite forgotten in the execution of justice upon their guilty brethren.

13 would not hearken. The whole tribe of Benjamin became participators in the guilt of the men of Gibeah, by taking the criminals under their protection. It is probable that an undue spirit of clanship had a large share in prompting this resistance. This affair of Gibeah is twice referred to by the prophet Hosea as the beginning of the corruption of Israel, and of all the evil that followed (Hos. ix. 9; x. 9).

15 were numbered. These numbers show a diminution of the people since the entrance into Canaan. Cp., for Benjamin, Numb. xxvi. 41; for all Israel, Numb. xxvi. 51.

18 to the house of God. The Hebrew here and in vers. 26, 31, and xxi. 2, is "Bethel," and no doubt means the town of that name. (So R.V.)

Judah shall go up first. The Israelites appear not to have consulted God respecting the war till after they had pledged themselves to it; and they then obtained a reply which gave no promise of success, but led them into a position in which their presumption and haste received a severe check. The selection of Judah to bear the brunt of this disastrous battle suggests the fear that this powerful tribe may have had some sinister design concealed beneath the guise of zeal for justice and morality.

26 and fasted. This is the first occasion in which a voluntary *fast* is mentioned in the Bible. The people ought to have *begun* with repentance, reformation, and earnest supplications for the guidance and help of Jehovah in the whole affair, instead of trusting, as they seem to have done, to the goodness of their cause and the superiority of their numbers. Upon this third occasion the direction to go up against Gibeah, given in answer to these humble and penitent prayers, was accompanied with a promise of victory.

28 stood before it (the ark). That is, he ministered as high priest.

29 Israel set liers in wait. It is worthy of notice that this third trial, made under the influence of better religious feelings than the two former, and with the encouragement of a positive assurance of success, was at the same time conducted with greater caution and more skilful generalship.

33 the meadows. Or, "the uplands." R.V. adopts the Hebrew name, "Maareh-geba" ("west of Gibeah").

35 destroyed of the Benjamites, etc. In this verse the result of the battle is briefly stated in general terms. The narrative is then resumed in vers. 36–46, giving a detailed account of the conflict and its consequences.

37 drew themselves along. Marching quietly in single file, so as to be unobserved.

45 they gleaned. They cut off all the stragglers as clean as when a field is gleaned after the harvest.

48 smote them, etc. Inflicting the punishment of the Canaanites upon those who perpetrated or abetted similar crimes.

CHAPTER XXI

2 wept sore. Now that their vow was executed they felt that the punishment had been very severe.

8 Jabesh-Gilead. Jabesh was one of the chief cities on the east of the Jordan. For other incidents in its history, see 1 Sam. xi.; xxxi. 11–13; 2 Sam. ii. 5–7; xxi. 12.

10 Go and smite, etc. This cruel determination, like the vow whose ill consequences it was meant to obviate, was certainly made without asking counsel of God.

21 if the daughters of Shiloh come out to dance. This plot might be easily executed, as, in the East, festivals are often held in the fields or gardens, and the men rarely participate in the women's amusements.

22 Be favourable, etc. Or, as R.V., "Grant them graciously unto us: because we took not for each man," etc. The meaning is, "The case is so pressing, that it behoves all parties quietly to submit. By not giving your daughters or sisters voluntarily, you have avoided the guilt of violating your solemn vow." See ver. 18. Although they escaped the *literal* breach of their vow, this expedient was in fact an *actual* evasion of it; whilst at the same time it tended to give license to fraud and violence.

THE BOOK OF RUTH

INTRODUCTION

THOUGH this Book is placed in our English version among the historical books, its true position would appear to be that which it occupies in the Hebrew Bible, where it forms part of the *Hagiographa*. It was the second of the five Megilloth or Festal Rolls, one of which was publicly read at each festival. Ruth was read at the Feast of Pentecost.

Yet it has its place in the history of Israel, as showing the ancestry of David, and in the history of the Christian Church, as giving one important link in the genealogy of the Saviour (cp. Matt. i. 5). The fact that Ruth was a Gentile, a Moabitess, was a lesson against Jewish exclusiveness, and to the Christian it is a reminder that both Jew and Gentile have their place in the kingdom of God and in the progress of humanity.

Naomi is surely a historic figure. Leaving the land of Canaan with her husband, on account of famine, she is soon left a widow with her two sons. But, though among a heathen population, she does not forget the God of her fathers, and her life influences for good both Orpah and Ruth. She is an example of the power of consistent faithfulness.

Orpah illustrates the sadness of a lost ideal. When Naomi indicates her intention of returning to Canaan, Orpah as well as Ruth desires to go with her. But she only went part of the way. She returned "to her people and to her gods," back to the degradation of Moabitish idolatry.

Ruth's is the glory of a heavenly choice. Hers was no self-seeking decision. She was going among strangers. It was a life of poverty and toil that she had to face—gleaning in the fields after the reapers. But her faith in God is shown in the words, "Thy people shall be my people, and thy God my God," and again where Boaz says to her (ii. 12), "the God of Israel, under whose wings thou art come to trust."

The whole Book is an idyll of womanhood, of family affection, of faith rewarded. "The place of Ruth in Holy Writ needs no other vindication than this—that, in her, love grew to heroism. But if it did, an ample vindication might be found in the facts that this Book shows us that every pure and unselfish affection leads to God, and is acceptable to Him; that it reveals Him to us as no less pleased by the goodness of a heathen than by that of a Hebrew; and that it also shows us that, in their better moods, the very Jews knew that there was no respect of persons with Him" (Dr. Samuel Cox: *Ruth*, in *Devotional Commentary*).

CHAPTER I

1 Beth-lehem-judah. The small town so well known in Scripture history, about six miles south of Jerusalem, originally called Ephratah, both names referring to the "fruitfulness" of the soil around this "House of Bread." It is here called Beth-lehem-judah, perhaps in distinction from Beth-lehem in Zebulun (Josh. xix. 15).

went to sojourn, etc. Indicating that the famine did not extend beyond the land of Israel.

4 took them wives of the women of Moab.

Though this was not an infraction of the letter of the law in Deut. vii. 3, which specifies only *Canaanitish* women, it was a violation of its spirit, the law being designed to prevent all admixture with idolatrous nations. The Moabites were under a special ban. See Deut. xxiii. 3. Mahlon, the elder brother, married Ruth (iv. 10).

13 would ye tarry. Alluding to the custom mentioned in Gen. xxxviii. 8; Deut. xxv. 5.

15 return thou. Some have regarded this advice as showing a want of enlightened piety in Naomi. It must, however, be remembered that she had commended both Orpah and Ruth to the care of the Eternal (8).

16 thy God my God. It is clear that Ruth was determined to adopt the religion as well as the people of her mother-in-law. Her constancy evidently touched the hearts of the people of Bethlehem (see ver. 22; ii. 6, 11), and so opened the way for the reward which God designed for her.

19 they said. The feminine form is used in the Hebrew, "the women said."

20 Naomi. "My sweet one."

Mara. "Bitter."

22 barley harvest. That is, about April.

CHAPTER II

3 gleaned. The privilege of the widow (see Deut. xxiv. 19 ff.).

14 vinegar. A weak acid wine, much used by labourers in vine-growing countries, and both cheap and refreshing. Here it is used for the sharp sauce in which the food was dipped. See John xiii. 26.

parched corn. "The grains of wheat not yet fully dry and hard, roasted in a pan or on an iron plate, and eaten with the bread, or instead of it."—*Robinson.*

and left. *i.e.*, "and left *thereof*." R.V.

17 an ephah. Nearly a bushel.

20 one of our next kinsmen. Or, "one that hath a right to redeem" the goël. See Lev. xxv. 25.

21 by my young men. To whom he had given strict orders about Ruth.

23 wheat harvest. About the end of May or beginning of June.

CHAPTER III

1 Shall I not seek rest for thee? *Rest,* lit. "resting-place"; a home. In estimating the conduct of Naomi and Ruth, we must remember that, by the custom of the Hebrews and the surrounding nations, Ruth was already virtually the wife of her late husband's nearest kinsman, and that no further marriage ceremony was needed to perfect her claim to conjugal rights (Deut. xxv. 5). Naomi seems not to have been aware that Boaz was not the nearest kinsman, whilst his character for justice, and his previous kindness to Ruth, led her to expect that he would fulfil the requirements of the customary law.

2 winnoweth. After the corn had been threshed by oxen on the open floor (see note on Deut. xxv. 4), it was winnowed by throwing it up with forks or shovels against the evening breeze, which blew away the chaff, whilst the heavier grain fell on the ground in a heap.

3 Wash thyself, etc. These were nuptial preparations. The use of oil after bathing is very important in hot climates.

7 his heart was merry. That this implies no undue mirth appears from Eccles. viii. 15, where the same phrase is used.

9 spread . . . thy skirt. Or, "thy wing": a symbol of matrimonial protection. The custom was to extend a corner of the scarf, or *tallith* (which was wound round the wearer in folds), and place it over the betrothed maiden.

10 Blessed be thou. It is evident from this that Boaz regarded Ruth's conduct (on the supposition that he was the next of kin) as not only justifiable, but praiseworthy, indicating the constancy of her attachment ("kindness") to her deceased husband, whose name and family she desired to perpetuate.

15 the vail. Rather, "the shawl," or "cloak." It is large enough to envelope the whole person; and that worn by the poorer classes is coarse and very strong.

CHAPTER IV

1 went Boaz up to the gate, etc. This presents a vivid picture of the legal proceedings of the Hebrews, used to make a transaction valid and public. Cp. Deut. xxv. 7.

5 thou must buy it also of Ruth. The Hebrew is: "Thou art also buying Ruth the Moabitess," etc.

to raise up the name of the dead. The eldest son of such a marriage was reckoned to the deceased, though he did not always bear his name.

6 lest I mar mine own inheritance. Had he had but one son by Ruth, and no other by another wife, his own name and inheritance would have been merged altogether in that of Elimelech. This narrative shows clearly the beneficial operation of the law of Deut. xxv. 7, which allowed a man, by incurring a small penalty, to decline such a marriage when it was either disagreeable or inconvenient.

7 plucked off his shoe. In Eastern countries, among unlettered people, the shoe was, and indeed still is, the pledge of a bargain, and thus the symbol of possession (see Psa. lx. 8); hence a man gave his shoe to the person to whom he transferred a property or right; and, according to the law in Deut. xxv. 9, a man who would not redeem his kinsman's right had his shoe plucked off by the widow. It is to the first-named, not the latter practice, that the text here refers.

10 to be my wife. It has been suggested that Boaz, as himself the descendant of Rahab, a "stranger" (see Matt. i. 5), would be the more willing to marry a Moabitess.

14 kinsman. Heb., goël, "kinsman and redeemer" (see note on ch. ii. 20).

17 the father of Jesse. The word "father" is probably here used, as it is often elsewhere, in the general sense of *ancestor.*

the father of David. Thus God rewarded Ruth's conjugal constancy, filial affection, and pious preference of the God and people of Israel, as well as the generosity and honour of Boaz—making them ancestors of a royal house, and, according to his human nature, of Him who is "King of kings, and Lord of lords." This is the first mention of David in our English Bible. (In the Hebrew Bible the book of Ruth follows the Song of Songs.)

1 SAMUEL

INTRODUCTION

THIS Book marks the beginning of a new era in the history of Israel. It records the lives of the two last of the judges, Eli and Samuel, and the beginning of the monarchy under Saul.

With 2 Samuel it originally formed one book, called "Samuel" in the Hebrew Canon. In the Septuagint Version, followed by the Vulgate and by many modern European versions, it is divided into two, under the title of 1 and 2 Kings, while the books entitled "1 and 2 Kings" in our English versions, are described as "3 and 4 Kings."

The closing years of Eli, recorded in the early chapters, are full of pathos, darkened as they were by the wickedness of his sons. With the birth and growth of Samuel a new hope dawns for Israel (i.–iv.). But it is hope deferred. The ark is taken and the Philistines are victorious (iv.). Then follow God's judgement on the enemy (v.–vi.), the return of the ark (vii. 1), Samuel's exhortation to Israel to repent (vii. 3), and the putting away of the heathen gods (vii. 4). Again, however, the shadow falls. Samuel's old age is darkened, as Eli's was, by the misconduct of his sons (viii. 3). The result is the people's desire for a king, that they might be like the nations round about them, a desire in which they persisted, in spite of Samuel's remonstrance and warning (viii. 11–22). This is followed by the choice and anointing of Saul (ix., x.). Very touching is the address of Samuel as he lays down his office (xii.). Saul's disobedience is punished by his rejection and God's choice of David as his successor (xv., xvi.). The remaining chapters deal with the wars with the Philistines, Saul's jealousy of David, the love of David and Jonathan, and the deaths of Saul and Jonathan on Mount Gilboa.

The story of Samuel's life is an example and inspiration for all religious teachers and leaders, and his fidelity to God may well be imitated by every Christian.

CHAPTER I

1 Ramathaim-zophim. Or "of Ramah," a Zuphite. Ramah has been identified with Beit-Rima, thirteen miles north-west of Lydda (G. A. Smith), and about the same distance from Shiloh.

Elkanah. Elkanah was a Levite of the line of Kohath and of the family of Korah (1 Chron. vi. 33–38); and his descendants, the singers, are therefore called "sons of Korah." "Ephrathite," an inhabitant of Mount Ephraim (as 1 Kings xi. 26).

3 the Lord of hosts. This name which occurs here for the first time, "JAHVEH, *the God* of hosts" (Heb., "Sabaoth"), appears to denote the supremacy of Jehovah over all orders of beings: cp. Gen. ii. 1; xxxii. 2; Psa. ciii. 21. It is frequently used afterwards, especially in the Psalms, and by the prophets Isaiah and Jeremiah, but only occurs once in the new Testament—James v. 4.

4 portions. The parts of the peace-offerings which belonged to the offerer, and on which he feasted with his family.

5 a worthy portion. The LXX (R.V. marg.) reads, "a single portion, because she had no child: howbeit Elkanah," etc.

6 her adversary. The Hebrew word here translated "adversary" occurs frequently in Scripture, but nowhere else does it denote a *person.* R.V. renders "her rival."

11 there shall no razor come upon his head. As a Levite, Samuel would have been employed, in the ordinary course of things, about the service of the tabernacle from the age of twenty-five to fifty; but, by his mother's vow, he was devoted to it from childhood, besides being subjected to the discipline of a Nazirite. This vow must have had the concurrence of her husband: see Numb. xxx. 8.

16 a daughter of Belial. Belial is not a proper name, but a Hebrew word for *worthlessness.* A "son," or "daughter," of Belial is, therefore, "a worthless person:" see Deut. xiii. 13, and note.

20 Samuel. "*Heard by God.*" Hannah's words in this verse are an explanation, not a translation of the name.

24 three bullocks. Better, "a three-year-old bullock" (see next verse).

the child was young. "The child was with her."

28 he worshipped. Some ancient versions have "*they* worshipped;" *i.e.*, Elkanah and his family.

CHAPTER II

1 horn. Horns are an Oriental symbol of power and rank, and as such are used as an ornament for the head.

5 ceased. *i.e.*, were hungry no longer. Others understand the meaning to be " have rest " (R.V. marg.), *i.e.*, have no need to work any more for bread. With this and ver. 8, cp. the words of the Magnificat (Luke i. 52, 53).

6 the grave. Heb., " Sheol," the unseen world.

8 the pillars of the earth. Both in prose and in poetry the sacred writers speak on subjects of natural science in the ordinary language of their own age and country.

10 His anointed. This prophecy refers to that kingdom which God afterwards established in the family of David, as preparatory to the kingdom of the Messiah.

12 sons of Belial. See note on i. 16.

13 the priest's custom. The only portions of the peace-offering to which the officiating priest was entitled by law were the shoulder and breast, and the cheeks and maw (see Lev. vii. 34 ; Deut. xviii. 3). Eli's sons not only defrauded the people, but they robbed God of His portion of the offering, which was essential to its acceptance : see Lev. iii. 3–5.

17 men abhorred the offering. Or, " *the* men (*i.e.*, Eli's sons) *caused* the Lord's offering to be abhorred : " see R.V. marg.

19 a little coat. Or, " robe," as in Exod. xxviii. 4, 31. It was a dress of distinction, and marked a *special* priestly dedication.

20 the loan. Or, " for the petition which she asked of Jehovah " (R.V. marg.).

21 And. Heb., " For," *i.e.*, they went home with the blessing which Eli had asked for them (20) ; " for the Lord," etc.

25 the Lord would slay them. The Heb. means, " It pleased Jehovah to slay them."

27 in Pharaoh's house. Or, as R.V., " in *bondage to* Pharaoh's house."

29 kick ye. " Trample on " or " spurn."

31 thine arm. That is, " thy power."

32 thou shalt see an enemy, etc. " Then in your straits you shall look enviously on all the prosperity I award to Israel " (*Moffatt*).

33 to grieve thine heart. Eli is addressed here as the representative of his family.

35 I will raise Me up a faithful priest. This sentence was fulfilled at the beginning of Solomon's reign, by the appointment of Zadok, of the family of Eleazar, as high priest, and in this line the priesthood of the order of Aaron remained as long as it existed.

CHAPTER III

1 The child Samuel. Better, " the boy Samuel." **—there was no other vision.** Rather, " vision was not frequent."

3 and ere the lamp, etc. Rather, as R.V., " and the lamp of God was not yet gone out, and Samuel was laid down to *sleep* in the temple of the Lord, where the ark of God was."

13 he restrained them not. How impressively does this history teach the importance of parental control and discipline ! Eli had reproved his sons (ii. 23–25), but he had not done all in his power to restrain them. Had he been unable, as a father, to check them, he ought, as high priest, to have deposed them. In both capacities, through his want of moral courage, though a good man, he sadly failed in his duty ; and his weak administration not only involved his family in ruin, but brought the affairs of the nation to the lowest ebb.

14 shall not be purged, etc. An appropriate punishment to those who had " caused the Lord's offering to be abhorred."

21 The Lord appeared again. That is, perhaps, the Eternal manifested His glory by the oracular voice in the sanctuary from between the cherubim. The following sentence, " And the word of Samuel came to all Israel," is the end of the paragraph, not, as in A.V., the beginning of a new chapter.

CHAPTER IV

1 Israel went out against the Philistines. This connects the subsequent history with that in Judges xvi. Samson was now living.

Eben-ezer. " Stone of help." The name Ebenezer was given to this place twenty years later, but before this history was written. " Aphek," or, *fortress*, the same as in Josh. xv. 53 : but not as in xxix. 1. These places lay a few miles north or north-west of Jerusalem, but have not been absolutely identified.

5 the ark of the covenant. The exultation of the Israelites and the alarm of the Philistines, when the ark was brought into the camp, indicate gross and unworthy conceptions of the Divine Being in the minds of both nations. They superstitiously imagined that the *outward symbol* insured the *actual presence* and help of the Almighty. See, in contrast with this, David's intelligent faith, 2 Sam. xv. 25, 26.

8 with all the plagues. Or, " with every kind of plague and pestilence." " In the wilderness " is an error in translation.

11 the ark of God was taken. The capture of the Ark now, and the destruction of the Temple in after times, would tend to give the Hebrews more correct views of the spirituality of God whose presence and power they were too prone to limit.

13 his heart trembled. Eli evidently distrusted the result of this superstitious expedient, which, however, he was too feeble-minded to forbid. The effect of the capture of the Ark on his aged frame, affecting him even more than his heavy family disasters, proves that, with all his weakness, there was true religious feeling.

CHAPTER V

2 Dagon. The tutelary deity of the Philistines ; having its upper part resembling the human form, and the lower like a fish. See Judges xvi. 23. The Philistines brought the Ark into his temple, in supposed triumph of their gods over the God of Israel.

4 upon the threshold. In the East, on coming into the presence of a superior, a person prostrates himself upon the threshold. Thus the idol had fallen into the most humbling position.

only the stump of Dagon. Literally, " only Dagon (*i.e.*, the fish form) was left to him." The idol derived its name from its lower part.

6 emerods. A corrupted form of the word *hæmorrhoids*. See Deut. xxviii. 27. R.V., " tumours."

CHAPTER VI

1 in the country. Here the LXX adds, " their land swarmed with mice." The Ark, having been sent away in terror from the cities, is supposed to have been left in the open country, which was then wasted by a large increase of mice.

4 five golden mice. The ancient heathen used

to consecrate to their gods memorials of their deliverance representing the evils from which they were freed.

12 turned not aside. That two kine, which had never before been under the yoke, should draw quietly and keep the road without a driver, neither halting nor turning aside; and that while lowing for their calves, to which natural instinct would have led them to return, they should be nevertheless urged forward by a stronger impulse to the very place mentioned by the Philistines, and should there stop, was clearly miraculous, and would tend the more deeply to impress upon the minds of the Philistines the lessons taught them by the plagues.

14 a great stone. Suitable to be used as an altar, and pointed out for this purpose by the halting of the kine.

15 And the Levites took down. Or, "For the Levites had taken down." Beth-shemesh was one of the priests' towns (Josh. xxi. 16).

18 of country villages. As the fields had suffered severely from the mice, they contributed their share to the trespass-offering.

Abel. For the word "Abel," some Hebrew manuscripts, with the Septuagint and Chaldee, read "Aben," signifying *a stone.* (So R.V.) This agrees with vers. 14, 15; and renders the insertion of the words "stone of" unnecessary. Then, putting a full stop after "villages," the rest may be read, "And the great stone on which they set the Ark of Jehovah still stands," etc.

19 they had looked into the ark of the Lord. This was to gratify an irreverent curiosity respecting things which God had thought fit to conceal. The Septuagint reads, "The sons of Jeconiah did not rejoice along with the men of Beth-shemesh when they saw the ark of the Lord, and he smote of them seventy men."

fifty thousand and threescore and ten. "Fifty thousand" is clearly a copyist's error. "Probably the threescore and ten is all that was originally in the text" (W. G. Blaikie in *Expositor's Bible*). Bethshemesh was but a small town or village.

CHAPTER VII

2 while the ark abode in Kirjath-jearim. The meaning of this verse may be paraphrased thus: "Now, from the time that the Ark rested at Kirjath-jearim, a long period (as much as twenty years) elapsed before all the house of Israel lamented after the Lord." These "twenty years" have been thought to synchronise with the latter twenty of the forty years' oppression by the Philistines, mentioned in Judges xiii. 1.

4 Baalim. See notes on Judges ii. 12, 13.

6 they . . . drew water. A symbolical action, which, according to accompanying circumstances and rites, might have different meanings. It was practised in after ages among the Jews, at the Feast of Tabernacles, as a sign of rejoicing, Isa. xii. 3; John vii. 37, 38. As on this occasion it was united with confession of sin, some (with the Chaldee Paraphrast) regard it as representing penitence and humiliation.

9 and offered it for a burnt offering. Samuel's prophetical commission appears to have included the temporary exercise of priestly functions. See ver. 17; ix. 13; xvi. 2, 5; and cp. 1 Kings xviii. 18–38.

heard. Rather, "answered": cp. Exod. xix. 19; Psa. xcix. 6, 8.

12 Shen. That is, "the tooth": the name of a rock.

13 all the days of Samuel. That is, of his government. When this was afterwards transferred to Saul, the Philistines soon began to regain the mastery. See xiii., xvii., xxiii. 27, 28.

15 Samuel judged, etc. Samuel's judgeship is to be dated probably from the assembly of the Israelites at Mizpeh (3–5). He was then about forty years old. While the earlier judges were generally distinguished by their warlike qualities, which they employed for the deliverance of the Israelites from external oppression, Samuel is remarkable for his attention to their social order and religious improvement. His "judgeship," *i.e.,* his religious authority, continued even when Saul was king.

16 Beth-el, and Gilgal, and Mizpeh. As these three places were near to one another, in the tribe of Benjamin, or its neighbourhood, it seems that Samuel's regular judicial authority was exercised chiefly among the central and southern tribes.

CHAPTER VIII

1 he made his sons, etc. This was done apparently without Divine direction and approval.

3 perverted judgement. A direct violation of the law in Deut. xvi. 19, the words of which are here repeated.

5 make us a king. The original constitution of the Jewish state did not require, though it would admit of, a succession of generals or judges, or a race of kings. As the appointment of the former arose from the frequent relapses of the people into idolatry, and their consequent subjugation by their enemies, so the regal institution originated in their culpable desire to resemble the nations around them (see ver. 20). A kingly government was by no means evil in itself, and indeed it had been provided for in Deut. xvii. 14. But for the nation to be immediately under the command of God, and to be, by His special interposition, in answer to fervent prayer, rescued from peril and trouble, was far better. Instead, however, of seeking the restoration of their national prosperity by sincere repentance, the Israelites chose to give up the peculiar privileges of the theocracy, and to resort to the principles and policy of other nations. So naturally does man prefer his own resources to dependence upon God's help.

6 the thing displeased Samuel. There was everything to distress him. That, after the solemn lesson taught him long ago in Eli's family, his own sons should have gone astray, must have been deeply humiliating. He must at the same time have keenly felt the disregard shown him by the people, after long years spent in their service. But still, in his displeasure he betook himself to God.

11 This will be the manner of the king. The following is a description not of what the king would have a right to do (for it is quite contrary to the law of Moses, Deut. xvii. 14–20), but of the practice of kings of the surrounding nations; and it agrees exactly with Eastern despotism where it exists still.

12 to ear. That is, "plough": see note on Gen. xlv. 6.

13 confectionaries. "Perfumers."

20 judge us, in time of peace; **go out before us,** in time of war.

CHAPTER IX

2 higher than any of the people. Suitable to the wishes of the people who, however, had to learn how incorrect were their notions of kingly qualities. Saul was a man "after *the people's* own heart."

4 Shalim, Shaalim, a name quite different from Shalem or Salem.

6 this city. That is, Ramah, where Samuel resided (ver. 5; i. 1).

7 a present. Presents are considered essential to civil and friendly intercourse in the East, particularly when an inferior approaches a superior. Articles of food are the most usual presents from the rural population: see xvi. 20. Money, however, even in small sums, is perfectly suitable. Saul, having no provision left, determined to offer Samuel a small coin, worth about 9*d*.

10 in the high place. Heights were the natural altars of the ancient world; and during the unsettled times of the Judges, especially after the sanctuary at Shiloh was destroyed, the worship of the people would be offered at the most accessible place. The centralisation of this worship enjoined in the law (Deut. xii. 11–14) was brought about gradually.

17 This verse follows ver. 14, vers. 15, 16 being parenthetic.

20 on whom is all the desire of Israel? Or, "For whom is all that is desirable in Israel? is it not for thee and for," etc. (R.V.). For the word cp. Hag. ii. 7.

24 the shoulder. Or, "the thigh" (R.V.).

that which is left. Rather, "reserved," as commanded, ver. 23.

25 upon the top of the house. On the flat roof.

CHAPTER X

1 poured it upon his head. This private anointing of Saul by Samuel, as in the case of David (xvi.), was only a prophetic intimation of the Divine purpose that Saul should eventually be elected king, and would serve to teach him that, though chosen by the people, he owed his authority to God.

3 plain. Rather, "oak."

Beth-el. Going, probably, to sacrifice at Jacob's altar (see Gen. xxxv. 6, 7; Judges xx. 18), as the regular observances of the tabernacle were interrupted.

5 the hill of God. Heb., "Gibeah of God."

a company of prophets. This is the first allusion to the so-called "schools of the prophets," of which Samuel is supposed to have been the founder. In these schools a number of men were trained to discharge the duty of public teachers. A "prophet," in the Scripture sense of the word, is not only a "*fore*-teller," but a "*forth*-teller," or expounder of the truth. By the means of the Israelite prophets the law of God became more generally known, and a marked improvement in the spirit and practice of the people was the result. Besides a knowledge of the law, they were instructed in sacred psalmody, also accompanied by "prophesying"—that is, in the art of composing and singing sacred hymns, often with instrumental music.

8 See note on xiii. 8.

12 it became a proverb. This was used as a proverbial saying when any one was seen to be mingling with persons to whom he had before been a stranger, and for whose society and pursuits his previous education and habits had not prepared him.

17 Mizpeh. Cp. Judges xx. 1; 1 Sam. vii. 5.

22 if the man should yet come thither. Probably, "Has there yet come hither a man?" *i.e.,* "some one besides those we have seen."

Stuff. "Baggage."

26 a band. Rather "the host" (R.V.). The main body of the people accompanied him from the assembly.

27 brought him no presents. A strong mark of disrespect (see note on ix. 7) and disloyalty to God, the nation, and Saul, for which they narrowly escaped death: see xi. 12, 13.

CHAPTER XI

1 Nahash the Ammonite came up. This invasion seems to have been previously threatened: see 1 Sam. xii. 12.

7 he took, etc. A symbolical action, like that recorded in Judges xix. 29.

8 Bezek. Probably Khirbet-Ibzik, north-east of Shechem, on the road to Bethshan.

three hundred thousand . . . thirty thousand. This was evidently a collection of all the men immediately available.

11 in three companies. Like Gideon, Judges vii. 16.

were scattered. How gracefully the men of Jabesh-gilead remembered this deliverance is seen in xxxi. 11–13.

13 There shall not a man be put to death. Saul's conduct upon this occasion would serve to increase his popularity; of which Samuel wisely took advantage, in order to obtain a solemn recognition of his royal dignity at Gilgal. Samuel's whole course in these transactions towards both the king and the people forms a noble close to his own political life, as well as to the patriotic actions of that succession of Divinely-appointed judges of whom he was the last.

CHAPTER XII

11 Bedan. No judge of this name is mentioned elsewhere. The Septuagint, Syriac and Arabic versions have "Barak": see also Heb. xi. 32. "Bedan" and "Barak" are much alike in Hebrew (ברק בדן).

Samuel. The Syriac and Arabic versions have "Samson," which in the Hebrew is somewhat similar to "Samuel." This, also, is favoured by Heb. xi. 32.

17 Is it not wheat harvest? Rain is almost unknown in Palestine during wheat harvest, which occupies the latter part of May and June: cp. Prov. xxvi. 1. In predicting rain at such a time, Samuel was giving proof that he spoke by Divine authority.

21 for then should ye go, etc. The Septuagint omits *for,* and the verse reads (omitting the words in italics), "and turn ye not aside after the vain things," etc.: see R.V. marg.

25 both ye and your king. Samuel, in his address presents the king in his right position, as placed *over* Israel, but *under* Jehovah, the only true Sovereign of Israel.

CHAPTER XIII

1 Saul reigned one year, etc. The former part of this verse is either wanting or altered, in the ancient versions. The words in the Hebrew form the peculiar phrase always used to denote the *age* of a king at his accession, and the *length* of his reign; only, as the margin of the Hebrew Bible suggests, some of the numbers are lost. If rendered here as elsewhere, the passage would read, "Saul was . . . years old when he began to reign, and he reigned . . . two years over Israel": see 2

Sam. ii. 10; v. 4, etc. In Acts xiii. 21, a round number, forty years, is given as the length of Saul's reign. The second verse begins a new portion of the narrative, some years after Saul's accession. Of the earlier years (ten or fifteen) of Saul's reign, we have no account.

5 thirty thousand chariots, etc. There is doubtless an error in the number here, and in 1 Chron. xix. 7. The small nation of the Philistines is here said to have many more chariots than are elsewhere found belonging to the most powerful monarchs. Thus Pharaoh pursued the Israelites with six hundred chariots, even "*all* the chariots of Egypt"; and Solomon, in the height of his glory, had not more than fourteen hundred chariots. Some versions, with the margin of the Hebrew Bible, read "three thousand"; but this number seems still too large.

8 the set time. See x. 8. Samuel came *within* the time appointed (10), though not at its commencement. He may have delayed his coming in order to test Saul's obedience.

12 and offered a burnt offering. Saul would not venture to engage the enemy without offering a sacrifice; and yet he presumed to offer sacrifice himself, though he was neither priest nor prophet.

14 thy kingdom shall not continue. The perpetuity of the kingdom is forfeited now; personal rejection does not follow until after fresh disobedience; xv. 10–23.

a man after His own heart. See Acts xiii. 22. Saul was a man "after *the people's* own heart" (ix. 2), their ideal king. But the Divine ideal is different.

15 Gibeah. The Hebrew here (as well as in ver. 16, and in xiv. 5) is "Geba"; the same place from which the Philistine garrison had been expelled (3).

six hundred men. So that, by hastening the sacrifice, he had not kept the people together (11).

19 no smith. A similar policy was pursued by the Chaldeans (2 Kings xxiv. 14; Jer. xxiv. 1; xxix. 2); and Porsenna bound the Roman people to use no iron, except in tilling their fields (Pliny, *Nat. Hist.*, 34, 14).

22 there was neither sword nor spear. They had, however, slings, and probably bows and arrows as well as the ox-goads.

23 Michmash. This seems to have been a narrow defile north of Gibeah, still called *Mukhmas,* in which were the lofty rocks mentioned in xiv. 4, 5; forming a kind of military key to the surrounding country: see Isa. x. 28, 29.

CHAPTER XIV

4 Bozez (shining) . . . **Seneh** (thorny).

10 a sign. Rather, "the sign," as R.V. If the Philistines said, "Stand where you are," it would show that they were on their guard and wanted to gain time. If, on the other hand, they said "Come up!" it would show that they did not realise their danger.

14 a yoke of oxen. The R.V. reads "half a furrow's length in an acre of land."

18 Bring hither the Ark of God. The Sept. has, "Bring hither the ephod: for on that day he wore the ephod before Israel": see ver. 3; xxiii. 9; xxx. 7. It is not probable that the Ark had been brought hither from Kirjath-jearim. The words of Uriah, in 2 Sam. xi. 11, seem to intimate that the Ark was on a later occasion with the army.

24 for Saul, etc. Rather, "and Saul adjured." The people were "distressed" by fatigue and hunger, and, seeing this, the king exacted this vow, lest their distress should lead them to halt in the pursuit.

adjured. "Caused the people to swear," probably by saying "amen" to his vow. This shows the recklessness of Saul's character. As formerly, by *rashly sacrificing,* he incurred the displeasure of God, so now, by a *rash vow,* he excites the anger of the people. His order was as unwise as it was severe; for, if time was saved, strength for the pursuit was lost.

26 behold, the honey dropped. Rather, as R.V. marg., "behold, a stream of honey." In many countries wild bees form their combs in the hollow trunks, and between or among the branches of trees, so that the honey often drops on the ground.

27 his eyes were enlightened. That is, he was refreshed.

28 And the people were faint. Rather, "are faint"—words of the speaker, not of the historian.

31 Aijalon. See Josh. x. 12. Aijalon was nearly twenty miles west of Michmash, on the way to the Philistines' own cities.

36 Then said the priest. Ahijah evidently doubted the propriety of Saul's conduct, and sought to check his self-sufficiency and haste.

39 he shall surely die. Another instance of Saul's precipitancy. It was not yet known what the crime was, or whether, if it really deserved death, it might not be expiated by a sin offering.

41 Give a perfect lot. Rather, "Show the truth": see R.V.

47 So Saul took the kingdom. This victory over the Philistines established Saul's kingdom, and enabled him to prosecute other wars. The Ammonite war has already been related in xi.; the Amalekite war (48) follows in xv.

49 the sons of Saul. These were not all of Saul's sons: see 1 Chron. viii. 33. Ishui may have died young, and Abinadab and Ishbosheth were probably younger.

51 And Kish, etc. Some copies read, "Kish . . . and Ner . . . were sons of Abiel."

CHAPTER XV

1 The Lord sent me, etc. God did not finally reject Saul till He had given him another opportunity of recovering His favour, by fully carrying out His commands. But Saul's repeated disobedience sealed his doom.

2 Amalek. The Amalekites had always been implacable enemies to Israel. Their unprovoked cruelty, related in Exod. xvii. 8–16, had called forth a Divine decree against them (Deut. xxv. 17–19). They had been parties to many of the confederacies formed against Israel (see Numb. xiv. 45; Judges iii. 13; vi. 3; Psa. lxxxiii. 7), and they had recently spoiled the land (xiv. 48). Thus, like the nations of Canaan, they had long experienced Divine forbearance; but had only gone on to fill up the measure of their sins.

3 utterly destroy. In Saul's time, and long afterwards, the customs of war were so thoroughly barbarous that when lives were spared it was not from motives of humanity, but from avarice or lust. This command, therefore, to Saul and the Israelites was not only a judicial sentence, but a test of their self-denial, in giving up the slaves, the female captives, and the rest of the booty, and acting as men who fought for God only, and not for themselves. In direct disobedience to this command, Saul spared the best of the sheep and oxen for the purpose of having a great sacrificial feast; and he spared Agag in order to have the glory of exhibiting a captive king eating bread under his table. He certainly could not plead humanity as his motive, inasmuch as the women and children had been destroyed.

6 the Kenites. Connected with Israel by Jethro, father-in-law to Moses (Judges i. 16). Jael was also a Kenite: and the Rechabites, mentioned in the later history, belonged to the same tribe.

7 Havilah. See Gen. xxv. 18. "Havilah" appears to be the name of the whole desert south-east of Palestine as far as Chaldæa. "Shur" was the part of the desert bordering on Egypt.

8 all the people. That is, the great mass of the people. A portion escaped: see xxvii. 8; xxx. 18.

11 it grieved Samuel. Rather, "displeased"; "Samuel was wroth" (R.V.).

12 set him up a place. A memorial of his victory. This "Carmel" was in the south-east of Judah: see xxv. 2, 5; Josh. xv. 55. It lay on his way from the south.

16 Stay. Or, "Leave off"; "silence."

22 to obey is better than sacrifice. "In sacrifices man offers forcibly the strange flesh of irrational animals; in obedience he offers his own will, which is rational spiritual worship." The language of Samuel anticipates that of the later prophets, and especially that of the New Testament.

23 as the sin of witchcraft. Witchcraft was a sin against which Saul zealously enforced the law: see xxviii. 3. This was, therefore, a most cutting rebuke.

24 I feared the people. While confessing his fault, he excused it; than which nothing is more common. His chief anxiety was to save his credit with the people: see ver. 30.

32 delicately. "With tottering steps" (*Moffatt*).

33 Samuel hewed Agag in pieces. As God's legate inflicting upon Agag the Divine curse, which he justifies by referring to the chief's own cruelties. It was not uncommon for distinguished criminals to be executed by the hands of eminent rulers.

CHAPTER XVI

There are some difficulties as to the chronological order of the events narrated in the central portion of this book, and they become most striking in xvii. 1–xviii. 9. David is spoken of in xvi. 18 as "a mighty valiant man, and a man of war," and as Saul's beloved minstrel and armour-bearer, though in xvii. 33, 42, 55, 56, he is called a "youth" and a "stripling." He, moreover, appears to be unknown to Saul, and ignorant of the use and weight of his armour. Some critics, following the Vatican manuscript of the Septuagint version, omit xvii. 12–31, 55–58; xviii. 1–5, 9–11, 17–19, besides a few short clauses; but this omission leaves the main difficulties. Others, with rather better success as to the object in view, but without any authority, transpose xvi. 14–23, placing it after xviii. 9. It appears best to suppose that as Samuel's narrative was now drawing to a close, only such things were mentioned by him as seemed necessary to complete it, and that the prophet who afterwards continued David's history inserted in the latter portion of Samuel's narrative the account of David's great exploit against Goliath (xvii. 1–xviii. 9), together with short notices of some preceding and succeeding events, which were in part contemporaneous with occurrences recorded by Samuel in xvi. and xviii.

2 say, I am come to sacrifice. It seems likely that whilst the worship at the Tabernacle was in abeyance, Samuel, as the chief of God's prophets, frequently offered sacrifice when he made his visits to inspect the local administration of justice, so as to keep up Divine worship. He is directed to avail himself of such a service in this case.

4 the elders of the town trembled. Probably fearing that he was come to correct some irregularities.

10 Jesse made seven, etc. Meaning seven *altogether;* David, the eighth, not being included, as he had not yet been introduced; see xvii. 12. As in 1 Chron. ii. 13–15, only seven sons of Jesse are named, *inclusive* of David, it is supposed that one died before David came to the throne.

11 he keepeth the sheep. David appears to have been but little thought of in his family, for he was left in the field, though all were invited to the sacrifice and feast. He was now probably a little less than twenty years old.

12 of a beautiful countenance. Heb., "with beautiful eyes."

14 an evil spirit. The denunciations of Samuel produced a deep melancholy in Saul's mind.

20 An ass [laden] with bread. The Sept. reads, "Jesse took a homer of bread," containing ten loaves.

21 David came to Saul. Thus David was placed in circumstances in which he might learn something of war and of government, and enlarge his knowledge of human character.

23 took a (the) harp. The harp of the Hebrews was very different from the instrument which bears that name among us. It was a light, portable stringed instrument, more like a lyre.

CHAPTER XVII

2 Elah. The part of the valley where the conflict took place is about six miles to the west of Jerusalem. "Shochoh" is now *Shuweikehs;* and the valley of Elah is now *Wady-es-Sunt;* so called from the acacia trees in it. "The narrow pass goes right up to the interior of the land near Bethlehem; so that the shepherd-boy . . . would have almost twelve miles to cover between his father's house and the camp" (*G. A. Smith*).

4 Goliath, of Gath. Goliath was descended from the race of Anakim, who had been almost exterminated by Joshua, but of whom a few had still remained in Gaza, *Gath,* and Askelon. See Numb. xiii. 32, 33; Josh. xi. 21, 22.

six cubits and a span. Reckoning the cubit at eighteen inches, Goliath's height would be nine feet nine inches. There are instances on record, both in ancient and modern times, of persons who have attained this stature.

5 a coat of mail. Composed of plates of metal, overlapping each other like the scales of a fish.

five thousand shekels. About 200 lbs. The weight of his spear's head was about 24 lbs.

6 greaves. The "greaves" were coverings for the leg, reaching from the ankle to the top of the knee, and made of hide, sometimes covered with copper.

target. This more probably means, as in Josh. viii. 18, a "spear," or light lance slung over the shoulders.

18 take their pledge. Either an assurance that they were well, or an acknowledgement of their father's present.

19 Now Saul, etc. Read either *were* or *are*. In the former case the words are the historian's (A.V., R.V.), in the latter they are part of Jesse's direction to David (R.V. marg.).

21 For Israel . . . had put. Rather (as R.V.), "And Israel . . . put."

25 free in Israel. That is, free from tribute and service: see viii. 11–17.

29 Is there not a cause? David, animated by a truly pious patriotism, saw in the gigantic Philistine only an insolent enemy of Jehovah, who would surely enable any one relying on His aid to overcome him. This narrative admirably illustrates (1) the manner in which true faith in God views, assails, and conquers enemies and obstacles at which mere human courage quails, and (2) the importance of using the *best* methods, in reliance upon Divine strength. David employed his own weapons, not Saul's.

34 a lion and a bear. Not both at once, for they do not hunt together; but on two different occasions. R.V., "When there came a lion, or a bear," etc.

38 his armour. Rather, "his apparel" (R.V.), the clothes worn under the coat of mail.

40 staff . . . scrip . . . sling. The shepherds in the East carry a bag for victuals, and a staff, which they hold in the middle, to beat the low brushwood into which the sheep stray. They are to this day particularly expert in the use of the sling. Captain Conder found the bed of the stream that runs through this valley "strewn with rounded and water-worn pebbles, which would have been well fitted for David's sling."

51 cut off his head. This was a customary token of victory in these countries, and still is so: see xxxi. 9.

52 to the valley. The Sept. reads, "to Gath."

54 to Jerusalem. Jerusalem was on David's way home, and part of it was in the hands of the Hebrews (Josh. xv. 63).

55 And when Saul, etc. See note at the beginning of xvi.

CHAPTER XVIII

1 Jonathan loved him. Jonathan's friendship for David began with admiration of his faith and courage in this great exploit, and evidently resulted from that spirit of patriotic piety which they both strikingly displayed.

4 And Jonathan stripped himself, etc. Ancient poets represent their heroes as exchanging armour, in token of friendship; and, in Eastern countries, a prince can scarcely bestow a greater mark of his favour than by the gift of some article of his dress, especially if he has already worn it.

10 prophesied. This word signifies being in a highly excited state, or frenzy: "raved" (R.V. marg.).

21 in [the one of] the twain. Or, "a second time" (R.V.): see Job xxxiii. 14. The first engagement, connected with the slaying of Goliath, had not taken effect; Saul makes a second, on the condition mentioned in ver. 25.

26 the days were not expired. Within which David was to fulfil the condition.

CHAPTER XIX

2 until the morning. Rather, "in the morning" (R.V.): see ver. 11 and note.

11 Saul also sent, etc. Psa. lix. was probably composed by David on this occasion.

to slay him in the morning. When he should come out of his wife's apartments, which were held sacred from intrusion. But even this rule Saul disregarded at last: see ver. 15.

13 an image. Rather, "the Teraphim" (R.V.). See note on Gen. xxxi. 19. The women appear to have been addicted to the use of such superstitious objects. Michal probably, like Rachel, kept this unknown to her husband.

15 in the bed. The Eastern beds consist merely of two thick cotton quilts, and in these the sick are carried when it is necessary to remove them.

18 Naioth. Probably "the dwellings," or "college" of the prophets whom Samuel had collected in Ramah. They may have hoped to be secure here from Saul's violence.

22 a (the) **great well.** Rather, "pit," or "cistern" (R.V. marg.). The Sept. has "the well of the threshing-floor."

24 and prophesied. "And he also prophesied" (R.V.). The messengers whom Saul sent were constrained, by a Divine impulse, to join in the exercises of the holy men whom they found at Ramah; and even Saul himself, throwing off his outer robes (which is all that the word "naked" means), retaining only his inner vesture and his girdle, lay as it were in a trance, during which it is probable that David made his escape from Ramah.

Wherefore they say, etc. This revived the use of the proverb which originated on another occasion: see x. 11.

CHAPTER XX

5 the new moon. A sacrifice and feast took place every new moon (see Numb. x. 10; xxviii. 11), and on such occasions David was accustomed to join the king's family.

10 Who shall tell me, etc.? Rather, "Who shall tell me if perchance thy father," etc.? (R.V.).

12 O Lord God of Israel. Rather, "The Eternal the God of Israel, *be witness*. When I have," etc. (see R.V.). The sentence, broken by the violence of Jonathan's feelings, requires the inserted words.

16 Let the Lord even require it, etc. This seems to mean, "I pray God to deal with David's enemies as with my own."

19 when thou hast, etc. Rather, "on the third day thou shalt come down quickly." Another spy like Doeg (xxi. 7), might be on the watch.

20 I will shoot, etc. These signals were agreed upon in case they should be unable to have a private interview.

26 he is not clean. Supposing that his absence from the sacrificial feast was caused by some ceremonial defilement.

30 Thou son, etc. It is a common practice among Eastern nations to express resentment against a person by abusing his parents, especially his mother, though without any personal ill-feeling towards them.

40 his artillery. Rather, as in xxi. 8, "his weapons" (R.V.).

42 Jonathan went into the city. The friends appear never to have met after this, except once by stealth in a wood (xxiii. 16).

CHAPTER XXI

1 Nob. Nob is supposed to have been in the immediate vicinity of Jerusalem, near the northern end of the Mount of Olives: see Isa. x. 32.

2 The king hath commanded, etc. David's conduct at Nob, and some other of his actions about this period, indicate a low state of religious feeling, and a want of that confidence in God which at other times so much distinguished him. He evidently needed all the discipline of subsequent years, with much of the influence of the Spirit of God.

5 and [the bread is] in a manner common. The A.V. marg. reads: "the shewbread for which I ask may be regarded as common, as there is now a fresh supply of hallowed bread in the vessel."

6 the shewbread. The shewbread taken from the table was appropriated exclusively to the priests and their families; but Moses distinctly taught that ritual observances ought to give place to moral duties. Our Lord alludes to this in Mark ii. 25. Ahimelech seems to have yielded out of respect to the pretended royal command. The day was the Sabbath, for the old bread had just been removed from the table: see Lev. xxiv. 8.

7 detained before the Lord. Doeg may possibly have been detained on his way to Gibeah by some vow or purification, or by the occurrence of the Sabbath.

11 Is not this David the king? David was widely known to be the destined king of Israel.

13 feigned himself mad. A stratagem which cannot be justified. David's motive may have been twofold; the reverence with which the insane are regarded in the East, and the security which would result from his being considered harmless. He may also have calculated on being dismissed from Gath, as actually happened.

in their hands. That is, when taken by them. See the superscription of Psa. lvi., which is supposed to have been written upon this occasion. See also the title of Psa. xxxiv., where the royal name Abimelech is used for the personal name Achish.

scrabbled. "Scrawled."

CHAPTER XXII

1 the cave Adullam. ("The cave of Adullam," R.V.) The French scholar and explorer, Clermont Ganneau identified this with 'Aid-el-ma, a view which is supported by Sir G. A. Smith. It is about 12 miles from Bethlehem and looks down the Wady-es-Sunt (see note on ch. xvii. 2).

2 four hundred men. Some of these afterwards rose to eminent stations in David's service (see 1 Chron. xi. 15, etc.). They were victims of oppression rather than lawless banditti. Many think that David wrote Psa. cxlii. about this time.

3 Mizpeh of Moab. It is not stated why David particularly selected Moab as a place of shelter for his aged parents; but as Ruth, one of his ancestors, had been a Moabitess (see Ruth i. 22), some of his kindred might still exist in that country.

5 in the hold. One of the natural fortresses either in the land of Moab or in the south-east of Judah. The position and the name suggest the possibility that this may have been the site of the celebrated fort of Masada, the last in Judæa which yielded to the Romans.

6 under a tree in Ramah. Or, "under the tamarisk tree on the height," where Saul had collected his immediate attendants.

8 all of you have conspired, etc. The consciousness of his own injustice had made Saul suspicious.

9 set over the servants. Or, "stood by the servants" (R.V.).

14 goeth at thy bidding. "Is taken into thy council" (R.V.).

15 Did I then begin, etc.? The meaning appears to be that this was no new thing, as he had inquired for others before, without ever being informed that it was wrong, or displeasing to the king.

17 footmen. Rather, "runners," or "guard" (R.V.); persons who were accustomed to run before the king when he rode or drove. They formed a kind of guard of the palace (see 2 Chron. xii. 10), and were also employed, on extraordinary occasions, as couriers or "posts": see viii. 11.

19 Nob, the city of the priests, smote he. This is a remarkable instance of the worst devices of the wicked being turned by God to the fulfilment of His own purposes. By Saul's unparalleled cruelty, the Divine denunciation against Eli (ii. 31) was fulfilled. The fifty-second Psalm is supposed to refer to this event.

CHAPTER XXIII

1 Keilah. A town in Judah, near the lowlands and the borders of the Philistines.

2 inquired of the Lord. Probably by means of Abiathar: see ver. 6.

4 inquired of the Lord yet again. Not from unbelief on his own part, but to satisfy his followers, and to inspire them with confidence.

14 Ziph. The wilderness of Ziph was part of the hilly country south-east of Hebron, in which were Maon and Carmel.

16 strengthened his hand in God. This interview with David (which proved to be the last) was probably sought by Jonathan, at some risk to himself, in order to discharge one of the most important offices of friendship; for David at this time peculiarly required that encouragement.

19 Jeshimon. Rather, "on the right hand (the south) of the desert" (R.V.); for "Jeshimon" is not a proper name: see Deut. xxxii. 10; Isa. xliii. 19; Psa. lxviii. 7. The fifty-fourth Psalm is supposed to refer to this event, or to that mentioned in xxvi. 1.

24 in the plain. Perhaps "in the Arabah on the right hand (the south) of the wilderness" (R.V.). The long desert valley or "wady" running southward from the Dead Sea is still called "the Arabah."

25 rock. Or, "he went down to Sela, and abode in the wilderness of Maon." Sela ("a rock" called by the Greeks Petra) was but a few miles east of Maon, which gave its name to the surrounding district.

28 Sela-hammahlekoth. That is, "rock of the slippings," or "escapes." Hastings (*Dict. of the Bible*) and Peake render it "rock of the divisions."

29 Engedi. Engedi ("kid's fountain" or "well of the wild goat"), still called *Ainjidy*, is situated on a very precipitous pass on the western edge of the Dead Sea. Its ancient name was Hazezon-tamar (Gen. xiv. 7): showing that the palm tree flourished in this well-watered and luxuriant spot, which was made almost inaccessible by lofty and deeply caverned cliffs. The sixty-third Psalm has reference to David's wanderings in the wilderness of Engedi.

CHAPTER XXIV

3 a cave. The large caves which abound in this neighbourhood are often used for sheltering cattle and sheep.

4 the men of David said, etc. Their words were plausible, but not true. David had a promise of the kingdom, but no command to slay the king. His answer shows the happy influence of a patient faith.

5 David's heart smote him. Though he appealed to the fact that he had contented himself with cutting off a portion of Saul's robe, as a proof of his freedom from evil intentions (11); yet, with a delicacy natural to a generous mind, he felt self-reproach for an act which might be considered as an insult.

12 the Lord avenge me of thee. The meaning of this expression seems to be shown in ver. 15.

21 thou wilt not cut off my seed. Referring to the custom, long prevalent in the East, of putting to death the children and relatives of the preceding monarch, if he belonged to another dynasty.

CHAPTER XXV

1 buried him in his house. It was usual to bury persons on their own property, sometimes in a garden or court attached to a house; and this is probably meant here, and in 1 Kings ii. 34: see 2 Kings xxi. 8.

Paran. Samuel having died, David goes farther south, into the northern part of the desert.

2 Carmel. See Josh. xv. 54, 55, and note on xxiii. 14.

6 to him that liveth. Or, "to life." The words "in prosperity" are not in the original. A salutation equivalent to "Long life to you!" like the Arabic, "May God command thee to live!"

7 we hurt them not. The words "neither was there aught missing unto them," taken in connexion with ver. 16, imply that he had protected Nabal's flocks against the incursions of hostile tribes in the wild border country; for which service it was but just that he should receive some recompense.

13 Gird ye on every man his sword. David afterwards implies (32, 33) that the vengeance which he now contemplated was unjustifiable.

17 son of Belial. See note on Deut. xiii. 13.

18 bottles. "Skins" (R.V.).

20 the covert of the hill. Probably a ravine, which she was descending on one side, as David and his men came down the other.

22 any, etc. "Any male person": "one man child" (R.V.).

26 the Lord hath withholden thee. This address is distinguished throughout by admirable tact and elegance, and rises almost to a prophetic strain in reference to David's future destiny. Abigail assumes that David would see the hand of God preventing the execution of his severe purposes, and that, with his characteristic generosity, he would rejoice in it.

29 shall be bound in the bundle of life. That is, "God will hold thy soul in life." As men bind up things which they wish to preserve, so God's people form the bundle of the living that He holds in life (Psa. lxvi. 9): whereas what is put into a sling is intended to be thrown away.

30 ruler over Israel. Abigail had doubtless heard of the Divine appointment of David as future king, and expresses her full faith in it: see xxiv. 20.

33 thy advice. Rather, "thy wisdom" (R.V.).

37 his heart died. The effect, perhaps, partly of fear; but still more of mortification ending in apoplexy.

43 Jezreel. Now Zerin.

they were also both of them his wives. David herein followed a bad practice of those times, which occasioned many disorders in his family.

CHAPTER XXVI

5 in the trench. "The place of the wagons" (R.V.).

6 Abishai. Abishai, Joab, and Asahel were sons of Zeruiah, David's sister.

7 his spear, etc. The "spear stuck in the ground" still marks the resting-place of an Arab chief. The spears are spiked at the lower end. "His bolster," literally "his head" (R.V.).

10 the Lord shall smite him. In other words, It is for God, not for me, to inflict the deserved punishment: see Rom. xii. 19.

14 David cried to the people. From ver. 17 it appears that Saul recognised David's voice, though in the faint light he could not distinguish the person.

19 let Him accept an offering. That is, let Him accept an offering *from us both;* let us join in seeking His forgiveness by sacrifice.

saying. That is, "by their actions—by driving me abroad." Some suppose that one, perhaps the chief, of the treacherous enemies to whom David alluded was Cush the Benjamite, mentioned in the title to Psa. vii.; and that this psalm expresses the feelings which animated David upon this occasion.

20 a flea. The Sept. reads, "my life."

25 shalt still prevail. This interview shows that Saul was not without better feelings, though they had become powerless through the course of sin which he had pursued. He and David never met again; but he seems not to have given up his persecution of his son-in-law.

CHAPTER XXVII

1 I shall now perish one day. David seems to have forgotten that, by the Divine command, he had been appointed to be king; and that, though Saul was faithless, God's promises could not fail. Consulting his own fears only, and not the ephod or the prophet, he took a wrong course. His position, and that of his followers, among the Philistines, who were idolaters, and enemies of his people, must have been most embarrassing.

6 Ziklag. This town had been allotted to the tribe of Simeon, but it seems to have remained in the hands of the Philistines till made over to David by Achish.

8 the Geshurites. In this proceeding David seems to have had in view his future advancement to the kingdom; clearing all the southern district of remaining hostile tribes.

10 a road. This word was used by old English writers in the sense of *inroad,* and was synonymous with the Scottish term *raid* (R.V.).

11 to bring tidings. Or, "to bring *them,*" *i.e.,* as captives (R.V.).

CHAPTER XXVIII

1 And Achish said, etc. David's false step in going to Achish now brought him into serious difficulty; so that if God had not interfered on his behalf, he must either have fought against his own sovereign and people, or have made an ungrateful return to the Philistine king, who placed implicit confidence in him, offering to make him commander of his body-guard.

3 Saul had put away, etc. This had probably been done in Saul's better days, under the guidance of Samuel; according to the Divine command in Lev. xx. 27, and Deut. xviii. 10, 11. It seems to be mentioned here as showing Saul's wickedness and desperation in having recourse to such a person (7).

4 Shunem. Probably the place now called *Solam.* The Philistines encamped on the hill called, in later times, "Little Hermon," on the north side of the deep valley which runs down from the plain of Jezreel (Esdraelon) to Beth-shan and the Jordan; whilst Saul's army occupied the hills of Gilboa, on the south of the valley. In an address by Kitchener (afterwards Lord Kitchener of Khartoum) to the British Association in 1878, he said: "Looking down upon the broad plain of Esdraelon stretched out from our feet, it is impossible not to remember that it is the greatest battle-field of the world, from the days of Joshua, and the defeat of the mighty host of Sisera, till, almost in our own days, Napoleon the Great fought the battle of Mount Tabor, and here also is the ancient Megiddo, where the last great battle of Armageddon is to be fought."

6 by Urim. See Exod. xxviii. 30, and note.

7 a woman that hath a familiar spirit. It is evident, from this narrative, that such persons pretended to have intercourse with the dead.

En-dor. There is still a village named *Endor*, about four miles south of Mount Tabor, and not far from Shunem and Nain.

13 I saw gods. "A god" (R.V.).

14 Samuel. Heb., "Samuel he," or "himself." Whatever form the vision or apparition took, it is clear that the woman had no power to "bring up" Samuel. She was astonished and frightened at his appearance. Nor is there any proof that substantiates the claims of the Spiritist media of to-day. The reader may be recommended to study Isa. viii. 19, Browning's *Sludge the Medium*, the Report of the Seybert Commission, Coulson Kernahan's *Black Objects*, and Dr. R. C. Gillie's booklet on *Spiritualism*.

16 is become thine enemy. "Is become thine adversary" (R.V.). The LXX has, "and is with thy neighbour," or "rival." This agrees with ver. 17, and with xv. 28, but is not necessary.

17 hath done to him. Or, "hath done to you" (*Moffatt*).

19 with me.

CHAPTER XXIX

1 Aphek. Not the Aphek in Judah, but in Issachar, in or near the plain of Jezreel.

by a fountain. Rather, "by the fountain"; now called *Ain Jalût*, a very large fountain near Mount Gilboa: see Robinson, *Biblical Res.*, vol. iii. pp. 167, etc.

6 Achish called David. The generous confidence of this noble-minded king, and especially his appeal to the Eternal, are worthy of particular notice.

9 the princes of the Philistines. That is, the chiefs of the other Philistine cities; for Achish was lord of Gath only, though he seems to have been commander-in-chief of the army.

10 depart. Thus, by God's merciful providence, David was not only kept from either fighting against his country or being false to his trust, but returned opportunely to rescue his wives and children, and those of his followers.

CHAPTER XXX

1 Ziklag. David's force received an important increase at this time; and a greater number soon afterwards joined him: see 1 Chron. xii. 20–22.

the south. The strength of the country having been drawn towards Jezreel, the Amalekites took the opportunity of invading the defenceless south or *Negeb*.

2 slew not any. They spared them, not from considerations of humanity, but as slaves. All the males capable of bearing arms were absent.

6 grieved. Or, "embittered," "exasperated."

encouraged ("strengthened," R.V.) **himself in the Lord his God.** He called to mind the providence and the promises of God. The "encouragements" of David are expressed in such Psalms as the third, sixth, thirteenth, seventeenth, etc.

14 Cherethites. A tribe in the extreme south-west of Palestine, closely allied to the Philistines. David afterwards had some of them as his guards (see 2 Sam. viii. 18).

16 eating and drinking and dancing. Supposing David and his men to be far away with the Philistine army.

20 all the flocks, etc. Not only recovering their own cattle, but taking possession of the booty of the marauders, which David reserved for the purpose mentioned in vers. 26, 31.

25 an ordinance. This law was different from that in Numb. xxxi. 27: that related to the *whole people*, this to the *soldiers* only.

CHAPTER XXXI

6 all his men. In 1 Chron. x. 6, it is "all his house"; probably meaning all his personal attendants then with him. Ish-bosheth, the fourth son of Saul, appears to have been absent.

7 on the other side. This seems to show that the narrator of this event was one of those who escaped to the east side of the Jordan; so that Beth-shan would be to him on "the other side" of the river.

9 they cut off his head. In 1 Chron. x. 10, it is said that "they fastened his head in the temple of Dagon."

10 house of Ashtaroth. Such a dedication was common among the ancients. This was the temple of Astarte, the Syrian Venus; cp. 2 Sam. i. 20: and Herodotus, b. i., c. 105.

10 Beth-shan. Afterwards called Scythopolis.

12 burnt them there. Probably to preserve them from further insults. This brave act of the men of Jabesh was a grateful return for Saul's deliverance of them: see xi.

---

2 SAMUEL

INTRODUCTION

DAVID as king is the central figure of this book, which covers his whole reign of forty years. After seven years in Hebron, he transferred the seat of government to Jerusalem (v. 5–9), whither he brought the ark (vi. 1–15). Then came years of war (viii.–x.), and David's great sin, with his subsequent repentance and Divine forgiveness (xi.–xii. 13). The revolt of Absalom is a sad record of a son's ingratitude, disobedience, vanity and dishonour (xiv.–xix.). There are further wars with the Philistines (xxi.), and the Book closes with David's Psalm of Thanksgiving and "last words" (xxii., xxiii.), the deeds of his heroes, and the incident of the census, which may belong to an earlier period in his life.

The Book has many noble passages, such as David's lament over Saul and Jonathan (i.), the intercession of the wise woman of Tekoah on behalf of Absalom (xiv.), David's sorrow for the death of his ungrateful son (xviii. 33), his songs of praise (xxii.) and faith (xxiii. 1–5), and the story of the "three mighty men" at the well of Bethlehem (xxiii. 15, 16).

CHAPTER I

6 And the young man that told him said. This Amalekite probably followed the camp in order to plunder the slain after the battle (1 Sam. xxxi. 8); and finding Saul's body and crown, was induced, by the hope of winning David's favour, to declare falsely that he had given the fatal wound.

9 anguish. More probably, "giddiness," resulting from his wound.

10 the crown. It is most likely that this "crown" was a cap surrounded with a broad fillet of gold, intended to serve also as a helmet.

the bracelet. Or armlet, part of the royal insignia.

18 [the use of] the bow. The words "the use of" are not in the original; and "The Bow" appears from the context, to be the *title* of the following elegy, derived, perhaps, either from the occurrence of the word "bow" in ver. 22, or from the facts related in 1 Sam. xxxi. 3. The R.V. has "*the song of* the bow."

the book of Jasher. See note on Josh. x. 13.

19 The beauty of Israel. R.V., "Thy beauty, O Israel."

thy high places. Gilboa.

20 the daughters of the Philistines. Alluding to the triumphal songs which were sung by the women: see 1 Sam. xviii. 7.

21 not fields of offerings. *i.e.*, let not yours be the fields which yield the first-fruit offerings. Cp. Joel i. 9.

the shield of the mighty, etc. These words may also be rendered, "the shield of the mighty ones is polluted (*i.e.*, with dust and blood), the shield of Saul is not anointed with oil" (cp. R.V.): see Isa. xxi. 5.

24 Who clothed you in scarlet. Literally, "with delights" or "jewels"; "Who clothed you in scarlet delicately," R.V.

CHAPTER II

1 David inquired of the Lord. David does not take a single step towards the attainment of the promised kingdom without Divine direction, inquiring first whether he should await an invitation to fill the vacant throne, and then how far he should go in attracting to himself the notice of the people. Hebron, whither God directed him to proceed, was peculiarly fitted for his purpose, on account of its patriarchal associations, its Levitical sacredness, its central position, and its influence over other cities (3) in the tribe of Judah.

4 they anointed David. The second time. The anointing by Samuel had been private, 1 Sam. xvi. 13.

Jabesh-gilead. Jabesh-gilead was one of the largest towns on the east of the Jordan, and its people had shown themselves loyal and brave.

6 requite. Rather, "show you this goodness."

8 Abner. First cousin to Saul (1 Sam. xiv. 50).

Ish-bosheth. His name was *Esh-baal* (1 Chron. viii. 33; ix. 39), *esh* or *ish* meaning *man*. *Baal* is "lord," *bosheth* shame; and the change of the former appellation to the latter was a way of marking the abhorrence of idolatry. So "Merib-baal" became "Mephibosheth," iv. 4 cp. with 1 Chron. viii. 34.

9 Ashurites. Read "Asherites," as in Judges i. 32. The verse shows the extension of Ish-bosheth's kingdom from Gilead through the north-western tribes, until all except Judah were included in it.

10 forty years old. Ish-bosheth was probably about thirty-five years of age at his father's death.

13 Joab. This distinguished commander of David's forces was son of David's sister Zeruiah. Hence he and his brothers, Abishai and Asahel, are designated by their mother's rather than their father's name.

met together by the pool. The men on both sides were probably unwilling to fight, feeling that they were fellow-countrymen; and David's men had, it is likely, received instructions to act entirely on the defensive, in accordance with his wise policy: see ver. 27.

14 Let the young men now arise, etc. A combat of picked men on each side was proposed to decide the question, and avoid the horrors of civil war. ("Play" is a euphemism for "fight.") But the plan was ineffectual, as neither side had the advantage, and a battle ensued.

16 Helkath-hazzurim. Perhaps, "the field of the sharp blades."

18 there were three, etc. R.V., "the three sons of Zeruiah were there."

21 take thee his armour. *i.e.*, "slay *him*, rather than attack a warrior like myself."

23 the hinder end of the spear. The lower end was pointed in order to fix the spear in the ground (1 Sam. xxvi. 7).

under the fifth rib. "In the abdomen." Asahel's swiftness, upon which he presumed so much, hastened his death.

27 unless thou hadst spoken. Joab throws the blame of the battle on Abner, whose proposal (see vers. 13, 14) had led to the slaughter. For "gone up from following," read, with R.V., "gone away nor followed."

29 through the plain. *i.e.*, the Arabah, or low Jordan valley. What is meant by "all Bithron" (or "the cutting") is not known.

32 they came to Hebron. About twenty-six miles from Gibeon.

CHAPTER III

3 Chileab. Named "Daniel" in 1 Chron. iii. 1.

Geshur. Geshur was in the north-west of Bashan, and on the borders of the tribe of Manasseh: see Deut. iii. 14; Josh. xiii. 11.

7 a concubine. According to the usages of the East, the wives and concubines of a deceased sovereign became the property of his successor.

8 Am I a dog's head, etc.? R.V., "Am I a dog's head that belongeth to Judah? This day do I show kindness," etc.

13 Michal, Saul's daughter. Michal had not been legally divorced, but forcibly separated from her husband, as Phaltiel might have known.

16 Bahurim. See xvi. 5; xvii. 18. Bahurim was a few miles from Jerusalem, on the road to the Jordan, and probably the last town in Ish-bosheth's dominions.

19 Benjamin. Saul having been of this tribe, the Benjamites were specially devoted to his family, and required, therefore, more persuasion than the rest.

22 from [pursuing] a troop. R.V., "from a foray."

27 smote him. Joab took advantage of the custom of blood-revenge to cover his jealousy and treachery. His sin was long afterwards remembered and punished (see 1 Kings ii. 5, 28–34). At the same time the justice of God appears in the death of Abner, who had, from personal and ambitious motives, knowingly opposed His declared will (see ver. 9), and had at last deserted Ish-bosheth only through pique or revenge.

33 as a fool dieth. "As an ungodly man." Cp. Psa. xiv. 1. "So ignoble an end to befall so brave a man!"

34 Thy hands were not bound. The hands and feet of malefactors were bound. By these expressions David meant that Abner had not been condemned in the regular course of justice, but treacherously murdered.

39 Zeruiah. See note on ii. 13, 18.

CHAPTER IV

2 Beeroth. Beeroth originally belonged to the Gibeonites, and they had been allowed to remain there after this district, at the general partition of the country, was allotted to the tribe of Benjamin: see Josh. ix. 17, 18; xviii. 25.

4 lame of his feet. Which, according to Eastern notions, would exclude Mephibosheth from succeeding to the throne.

6 wheat. The Greek version of this obscure passage is: "And, behold! the doorkeeper of his house was cleaning wheat; and she was drowsy and fell asleep. And Rechab and Baanah, the brothers, escaped notice, and went into the house," etc.

under the fifth rib. See note on ii. 23.

7 the plain. "The Arabah" (R.V.): see note on ii. 29.

10 who thought that I would have given him, etc. "Which was the reward that I gave him" (R.V.).

CHAPTER V

1 Then came all the tribes, etc. The following narratives should be compared throughout with those in 1 Chron. from ch. xi. A list of the tribes is given in 1 Chron. xii. 23–40.

3 a league. Or, "covenant" (R.V.). The kings of Israel were not absolute monarchs (see 1 Sam. x. 25; 1 Kings xii.); but whilst subject to the Divine laws, they were also bound by conditions agreed upon between them and the people.

they anointed David. For the third time: see on ii. 4. This anointing confirmed him as king of Israel as well as of Judah.

6 Except thou take away the blind and the lame. The whole passage (6–8) is very difficult, perhaps due to errors in copying. The words of the Jebusites appear to be a contemptuous boast that the most disabled part of the inhabitants were sufficient to repel David's assault on the fortress. The lower city had been early captured, though probably not long retained (see Judges i. 8, 21; xix. 10); for the fort of Zion, which was the highest part, had defied all the power of Israel, and was reckoned almost impregnable.

9 (the) **Millo.** See Judges ix. 6. Millo was "the citadel," or "keep," built where the fortress most needed to be strengthened: cp. 1 Kings xi. 27 ("the stronghold," R.V.).

11 And Hiram king of Tyre, etc. The Israelites appear to have made little progress, up to this time, in the constructive arts; but their Tyrian neighbours greatly excelled in all branches of commercial and manufacturing industry; and to them a friendly intercourse with the interior was at all times of great importance: see Acts xii. 20. Tyre was a great commercial city on the sea-coast north of Palestine, about one hundred miles from Jerusalem. Its inhabitants were not of the "devoted" nations, nor at enmity with the Israelites.

13 sons and daughters. David had in all nineteen sons; his daughters are not named (except Tamar), as they were not concerned in state affairs, nor were their names entered in the national records.

16 Eliada. Or, "Beeliada" (1 Chron. xiv. 7).

18 Rephaim. See note on Josh. xv. 8.

19 Shall I go up to the Philistines? David's frequent inquiries of the Lord present a striking contrast to the conduct of his predecessor.

20 hath broken forth upon mine enemies. "Hath broken mine enemies" (R.V.).

21 they left their images. The small tutelary gods which the soldiers carried with them as protectors in battle.

burned. Heb., "took them away" (R.V.).

23 mulberry trees. A species of balsam or of pear. Heb., *bâkâ*.

25 Gazer. Elsewhere spelt "Gezer."

CHAPTER VI

2 Baale. Read "to" instead of "from," in accordance with 1 Chron. xiii. 6; xiii. 1–6 speaks of David's going to Kirjath-jearim, with which Baale has been identified, and where the ark had been left (1 Sam. vii. 1).

3 Gibeah. "On the hill" (R.V.), as in 1 Sam. vii. 1, and so in ver. 4.

5 played. Including the idea of dancing to the music.

fir. Rather, "cypress." The Septuagint, instead of "instruments made of fir wood," has, "with all their might and with songs." This agrees with 1 Chron. xiii. 8. "*Cornets,*" "castanets" (R.V.).

11 the Lord blessed Obed-edom. Evidently with some outward and immediate tokens of Divine favour (see ver. 12), which were perpetuated to his children: see 1 Chron. xxvi. 5–8 (where we learn that Obed-edom was a Levite, of the Kohathites, through Korah: a "Gittite," or native of Gath-rimmon, a Kohathite town, Joshua xxi. 24, 25). The ark is a guest by which none who welcome it shall lose.

14 David danced. In the simpler states of society men are accustomed to give more vigorous expression to their feelings than we commonly do.

17 tabernacle. The sixty-eighth Psalm is supposed to have been composed for this occasion. The tabernacle made in the wilderness, with the altar, was now at Gibeon (1 Chron. xxi. 29); but David prepared another tent, probably similar to that of Moses, near his own residence on Mount Zion, for the reception of the ark. See Psalm lxxviii. 67, 68. After the building of the Temple, both tabernacles were superseded.

19 a good piece [of flesh]. The word used here and in the parallel passage in 1 Chron. xvi. 3 is found nowhere else, and its meaning can only be conjectured.

a flagon [of wine]. The word here rendered "flagon" means a kind of cake, prepared from dried grapes, or made with honey; "a cake of raisins" (R.V.).

20 uncovered himself. David had only divested himself of his *royal* robes, still wearing his dress of fine linen and an ephod.

21 therefore will I play. "Therefore have I made merry," etc.

CHAPTER VII

2 within curtains. That is, in a movable tent, as if it were not settled.

6 Whereas. Rather, "For" (R.V.).

7 the tribes. The change of a single letter in the Hebrew gives the word "judges"; which agrees with ver. 11, and with 1 Chron. xvii. 6.

11 will make thee a house. Thou shalt not build a house for Me, but I will build a house for thee. Thus God prepares David to regard the establishment of his family and kingdom as a token of gracious acceptance of the purpose which he was not permitted to carry out.

13 I will stablish, etc. See xxiii. 3–5; Isa. lv. 3; Jer. xxxiii. 15, 26; Acts ii. 30; xiii. 34; Heb. i. 5.

18 sat. *Sitting* (on the heels) is still a posture of reverence in the East.

19 [is] this the manner of man? The text here is obscure. According to 1 Chron. xvii. 17, the words of David were, "Thou hast regarded me according to the estate of a man of high degree": see that verse.

23 for you. Read, "for them."

CHAPTER VIII

1 Metheg-ammah. This may be translated (as R.V.), "the bridle of the mother-city"; explained by the words in 1 Chron. xviii. 1, "Gath and her towns" (lit., her daughters). Whoever, at that time, possessed Gath the chief city, held the bridle of the whole district.

2 casting them down to the ground. Rather, as R.V., "making them to lie down on the ground"; dividing them into three parts by a measuring-line, for life or for death. It is uncertain whether one-third only or, as the Septuagint and Vulgate render, one-half were saved: see Josephus, *Antiq.* vii. 5.

3 Zobah. Zobah was that part of Syria which stretches from Damascus to the Euphrates.

to recover his border. Or, "to establish his frontier": see 1 Sam. xiv. 47.

4 a thousand [chariots], and seven hundred horsemen. The word "chariots" is supplied from 1 Chron. xviii. 4, which gives the number of horsemen as "seven thousand." This is probably correct.

4 houghed. According to the special command to Joshua (Josh. xi. 6). Horses appear not to have been used by the Hebrews in agriculture, and were not to be kept for purposes of war: see Deut. xvii. 16.

9 Hamath. A large city on the Orontes under the Greeks named Epiphania, and now called el-'Aṣi. For its importance, see Isa. x. 9; Zech. ix. 2.

13 the Syrians. Heb., "Aramites." By a very slight change in the Hebrew (ד for ר), some read "Edomites" (R.V. marg.). But the Syrians appear to have been allied, as they were afterwards under Rezin (2 Kings xvi. 6), with the Edomites, mentioned in the next verse, and in 1 Chron. xviii. 12. Psalm lx. is assigned by its title to this part of David's wars: see note there.

the valley of salt. The northern part of the *Wady-el-Arabah,* south of the Dead Sea.

16 recorder. The "recorder" or "remembrancer" kept the chronicles of events and he prepared and registered the royal decrees, no doubt often acting as the king's adviser or chancellor. The "scribe," or *secretary* (18), was probably engaged in the correspondence and daily business of the government.

17 Ahimelech the son of Abiathar. These names are obviously transposed: this text and the parallel passages ought to be read, "Abiathar, the son of Ahimelech." It is probable that Zadok had been appointed high priest when the family of Ahimelech were slain, and Abiathar had fled; and that Abiathar, having attended David and been consulted by him during his wanderings, was allowed to share the office with Zadok, whose name always stands first.

18 Benaiah. See xxiii. 20.

the Cherethites and the Pelethites. (See 1 Sam. xxx. 14.) These two bands formed David's body-guard; but whether these terms are proper names or appellatives is uncertain. The Targum has "archers and slingers." Gesenius thinks that they denote "headsmen and couriers." It is likely that they were foreign mercenaries, or hired troops, like the "Swiss guards" in Rome. The Pelethites are supposed to have been "Philistines"; perhaps also the Cherethites, from Cherith, near Ascalon.

chief rulers. Heb., "Cohanim," usually rendered "priests" (so R.V.).

CHAPTER IX

3 Is there yet any, etc.? It is not surprising that David knew nothing of Mephibosheth, who was born after he had been driven from Saul's court (see iv. 4), and was brought up in obscurity on the east of Jordan (see ver. 4).

11 said the king. These words are not in the original, which reads, "and Mephibosheth eateth at my table" (see R.V. marg.).

CHAPTER X

5 the men were greatly ashamed. The Orientals have always attached great importance to the beard; and deem it a mark of extreme disgrace to be deprived of it. Hence David considerately instructed his ambassadors to remain for a time at the first town they reached on the west of Jordan.

6 they stank. A Hebraism, meaning that they had made themselves odious. We say "were in bad odour."

the children of Ammon sent and hired, etc. This is the first certain example on record of that mercenary warfare of which we afterwards find so much in history.

king Maacah. Rather, "king of Maacah," which lay on the north-east frontier of Israel. On the numbers here given, see 1 Chron. xix. 18.

Ish-tob. Rather, "the men of Tob" (see Judges xi. 3).

8 at the entering in of the gate. The gate of Rabbah, the Ammonite capital. We learn from Chronicles that the Syrian confederates were in the open country near Medeba, a distance of nearly twenty miles to the south, so that whichever army Joab attacked, he would have the other in his rear: see 1 Chron. xix. 7.

16 Hadarezer. The same as "Hadadezer." Another instance of the interchange of *r* and *d*: see on viii. 13.

the river. Euphrates.

they came to Helam. Helam was probably between Damascus and Hamath (*Hastings' Dict. of the Bible*).

18 the men of seven hundred chariots. In 1 Chron. xix. 18 the reading (A.V.) is, "seven thousand *men which fought in* chariots."

forty thousand horsemen. The reading of 1 Chron. is "footmen"; and this is probably correct.

CHAPTER XI

1 the time when kings go forth. That is, the spring.

David tarried still at Jerusalem. The king was now at the height of his glory. Worldly success and the luxuries with which wealth had surrounded him fostered the growth of selfishness and sensuality. The following narrative, and others of a similar nature (Gen. xii. 12–20; Numb. xii.; Matt. xxvi. 69–75), recording the sins of God's servants, show the veracity of the sacred historians.

2 eveningtide, "afternoon"; **arose from off his bed.** In warm climates it is customary to rise early, and repose during the heat of the day.

3 Eliam. Or, as in 1 Chron. iii. 5, "Ammiel," the two component parts of the name being reversed: see note on xv. 12.

11 The ark. See note on 1 Sam. xiv. 18.

15 Set ye Uriah, etc. "He who in the days of his persecution would not resort to plausible means of defence, is now not ashamed to resort to the greatest crimes to hide his sin."

16 observed. R.V., "kept watch upon." Moffatt translates "beleaguering."

17 went out. So as to entice the attacking force within bowshot (ver. 20).

21 Jerubbesheth. Or, "Jerubbosheth," the same as Jerubbaal (Judges vi. 32), "bosheth," *i.e.*, shame, contemptuously put for the idol Baal, like Ish-bosheth for Ish-baal: see on ii. 8.

27 displeased the Lord. This prepares the way for the reproof and retribution in the following chapter.

CHAPTER XII

1 the Lord sent Nathan, etc. Thus far David's crime seemed successful. Every obstacle was removed; and if conscience was not silenced, its voice was proudly disregarded; see Psa. xxxii. 3, 4. But now the Divine Judge appears to condemn and sentence. Henceforward his history is clouded with sorrow. The seeds of lust, treachery, and murder, which he had sown, spring up in his own household; and he must reap the fatal harvest. From this time, he appears to feel himself a humbled man, his influence and authority weakened, the buoyancy of his spirit gone, and his very trust in God less assured and gladsome than before.

10 the sword shall never depart from thine house. During his lifetime, two of his sons were slain, and Adonijah soon after his decease.

11 unto thy neighbour. Or, "to another man."

13 I have sinned against the Lord. The fifty-first Psalm expresses David's feelings upon this occasion, and shows that, while deeply affected by his own awful guilt, and by the righteous displeasure of God, he did not sink into despair, but still looked to the Divine mercy, which we find in Psa. xxxii. happily restoring him to peace, and animating him to renewed efforts after holiness. See Carlyle: *Heroes and Hero-Worship.*

hath put away thy sin. Heb., "hath made thy sin pass by," that is, hath forgiven thy sin—"thou shalt not die"; though, according to the Divine laws in Gen. ix. 6 and Lev. xx. 10, he had doubly deserved death. "Many," says Augustine, "are disposed to fall like David; but not, like David, to rise again. The fall of David has been recorded, that those who have not fallen may be kept from falling; and that those who have fallen may rise again." Note that confession precedes pardon.

24 the Lord loved him. *i.e.*, Solomon.

25 He (the Lord) **sent by the hand of Nathan,** etc. *i.e.*, commissioned Nathan to give the child the name *Jedidiah*, "beloved of the Eternal." The name *Solomon* (*i.e.*, "the peaceful"), however, continued to be used.

30 a talent of gold. Over 100 lbs.; far too heavy for any man to wear. Some, however, think that *value*, not *weight*, is intended. But it is not unlikely that the numbers both here and in xiv. 26 are corrupted.

31 under saws, etc. "To saws," *i.e.*, to the severest labours of slaves.

CHAPTER XIII

13 speak unto the king. Tamar's wish probably was to gain time. Such a marriage would have been unlawful, Lev. xviii. 9.

18 a garment of divers colours. This phrase occurs only here and in Gen. xxxvii. 3.

20 in her brother Absalom's house. Absalom was Tamar's full-brother, their mother being Maacah, daughter of the king of Geshur. In the East the ties of brotherhood are little felt, except by the children of the same mother, and a woman would look more to her full-brother than even to her father as her natural protector and avenger.

21 he was very wroth. The Septuagint adds, "But he did not grieve the soul of Amnon his son, because he loved him, because he was his first-born": see Gen. xxxiv. 25.

25 chargeable. "Burdensome" (R.V.).

37 Absalom fled. Absalom, having committed *wilful* murder, could not avail himself of one of the cities of refuge. Talmai was his mother's father: see iii. 3.

39 longed to go forth unto Absalom. The words *the soul of* are not in the original.

CHAPTER XIV

11 let the king remember the Lord. The woman would not be satisfied until she had obtained an oath as well as a promise.

13 against the people of God. The whole nation being interested in the king's conduct towards his son.

as one which is faulty. It is faulty to judge one way and act another. She implies that the king's oath to spare her son bound him to forgive Absalom.

14 neither doth God respect any person. Rather, "and God doth not take life away, but He deviseth plans," etc.: see R.V.

15 the people have made me afraid. The woman's words refer to those of her own family who, according to her story, had threatened her son's life; but they are so framed as, when the king shall have seen her real object, to apply to the people at large, among whom she professes to apprehend insurrection if Absalom were not recalled.

17 an angel. Rather, "the Angel": cp. ver. 20; xix. 27.

20 to fetch about this form of speech. "To change the face of the matter" (R.V.); *i.e.*, to bring about new relations with Absalom.

21 I have done this thing. David stands by his oath, with or against his own secret desire.

24 and let him not see my face. It was not a full and free forgiveness, and this probably led to the fatal sequel.

26 polled his head. It was the custom, in David's time, for men to wear the hair long. To "poll" is to "cut" the hair.

two hundred shekels after the king's weight. Perhaps under 4 lbs. There is probably an error in the number.

27 three sons. They seem to have died in infancy: see xviii. 18. Hence no names are given.

29 he would not come. The courtiers of David, as well as himself, were avoiding the presence of Absalom.

CHAPTER XV

1 chariots. "A chariot" (R.V.).

2 rose up early. Eastern kings and their officers rise early, and, after their devotions, proceed at once to public business.

7 after forty years. The word "forty" is a transcriber's error. With Josephus, and the Syriac and Arabic versions, we should read *four* years; *i.e.*, from the time of Absalom's apparent reconciliation with David.

12 Ahithophel. Absalom seems to have presumed that Ahithophel would be well affected to his cause. Dryden's famous political satire, *Absalom and Achitophel*, is based on this story:

"Of these the false Achitophel was first,
A name to all succeeding ages curst."

17 in a place that was far off. R.V., "in Beth-meshak," or, "the Far House," probably the last house at the foot of the hill, between the town and the Kidron.

18 the Pelethites, etc. See note on viii. 18. These "Gittites" were probably a body-guard so named as representing the band of 600 who were with David in Gath (see 1 Sam. xxvii. 2), now comprising some Philistines like Ittai (19), who had become attached to David's service, and perhaps proselytes to the true religion.

19 abide with the king. A nobly generous permission to the Gittite to accept service under any monarch who might occupy the throne. As a stranger, Ittai was not bound by loyalty to take either side.

23 the brook Kidron. The ravine between Jerusalem and Olivet (30), deepening down to the Dead Sea. In winter there is a torrent running through it: see 1 Kings ii. 37; xv. 13; John xviii. 1. It is now called the Valley of Jehoshaphat.

27 Art [not] thou a seer? Should read, "Behold, do thou return," etc.

28 in the plain. The Heb. text has, "at the crossings," *i.e.*, where the Jordan was crossed ("at the fords," R.V.).

30 his head covered. By wrapping it in a cloth or robe, as a sign of intense grief; a custom prevalent among ancient nations.

32 where he worshipped God. "Where God was worshipped" (R.V.); one of the "high places" that remained in the land.

33 unto whom David said, etc. While David humbles himself before God, and seeks His aid by prayer, he at the same time, with great sagacity and self-possession, adopts measures for baffling the designs of his enemies. The stratagem is characteristic of the imperfect morality of the time. For the public as well as the private life of to-day, Macaulay's words hold good: "The entire history of British rule in India is an illustration of great truth that it is not prudent to oppose perfidy to perfidy, and that the most efficient weapon with which men can encounter falsehood is truth" (*Essay on Lord Clive*).

CHAPTER XVI

14 came weary. Perhaps "came to Ayephim" (R.V. marg.).

21 Ahithophel said unto Absalom, etc. The adoption of this wicked advice would tend to decide the waverers, by showing that Absalom was prepared to go all lengths in his unnatural contest. Thus, however, Nathan's prediction (xii. 11) was literally fulfilled.

CHAPTER XVII

3 the man whom thou seekest, etc. "You only need one man's life, in order to have all the troops at peace" (*Moffatt*).

7 The counsel, etc. Rather, "The advice which Ahithophel has given this time is not good" (R.V.).

8 a bear robbed of her whelps. Whose fury is proverbial: see Prov. xvii. 12; Hosea xiii. 8.

14 The counsel of Hushai, etc. Hushai's advice was likely to take with a vain man, just elated with his first success, and, if adopted, would give David time to collect his adherents.

the good counsel of Ahithophel. That is, counsel well adapted to his object.

16 in the plains. Rather, "at the fords" (R.V.): see on xv. 28.

17 En-rogel. Near the junction of the valley of Hinnom with that of the Kidron.

a wench went and told them. Rather, "the handmaid" of one of the high-priests "used to go and tell them" (R.V.), keeping them constantly informed.

20 the brook of water. "Over the water." An intentionally ambiguous phrase, which might mean the water of the well, or of the Jordan. So the followers of the Stuarts in Scotland used to toast "the king over the water."

21 over the water. *i.e.*, the river Jordan.

22 they passed over Jordan. Psalms xlii., xliii. were probably composed on this occasion: see notes on their titles.

23 hanged himself. Ahithophel could not brook the disregard shown to his advice, and he probably foresaw that Absalom's vanity and folly would ruin his cause. This is the first instance recorded in the Bible of suicide committed by any one outside the battle-field.

25 Ithra an Israelite. Ithra or Jether is said, in

1 Chron. ii. 17, to be an "Ishmaelite." But some scholars think the word here is "Jezreelite."

28 brought beds. The bed was a rug, skin, or carpet.—**basins.** Or, "bowls."

29 cheese of kine. The Hebrew phrase, which occurs here only, has been rendered by some translators, "fat calves."

CHAPTER XVIII

1 captains of thousands, etc. David's army seems to have received large accessions (see also ver. 4). Absalom's arts of insinuation had been practised chiefly at Jerusalem, and his influence was less in the distant districts.

3 the city. That is, Mahanaim (xvii. 27).

5 Deal gently, etc. While Absalom would have *only* David smitten (see xvii. 2–4), David would have Absalom spared.

6 against Israel. The mention of Israel here, and in ver. 7, and xix. 41–43; xx. 1, 2, shows that the Ten Tribes were not thoroughly loyal to David, but were ready to take any opportunity of weakening the power of the tribe of Judah.

the wood (R.V., "forest") **of Ephraim.** This forest appears to have been on the east of the Jordan, not in the territory of Ephraim. In *Hastings' Dict. Bible* it is suggested that it may have been a settlement of Ephraimites.

8 devoured more people. That is, in their flight through forests and swamps.

9 And Absalom met. Rather, "chanced to meet," R.V.

a great oak. Heb., "the great oak," or "terebinth"; a tree well known in after times.

14 three darts. Or "spears."

17 a great pit. Rather, "the great pit," R.V.—another well-known place. So in next verse, "the pillar."

18 Absalom's place. Literally, "hand," as in 1 Sam. xv. 12 (see note thereon). Josephus says that the pillar was of marble, and called "Absalom's *hand.*" It must have been erected either before the birth or after the death of Absalom's sons.

22 Cushi. This word has the article, and probably means "the Cushite," or Ethiopian (so R.V.). Joab may have preferred employing him to carry the news of Absalom's death, as being a foreigner, and perhaps a slave to whom the anger of the king would be of less consequence than to Ahimaaz.

23 the way of the plain. The low land along the Jordan. He thus avoided the ascent and descent of numerous ravines on the shorter route taken by the Cushite.

25 If he be alone, etc. His coming *alone* indicated that he was simply a messenger or courier.

29 Ahimaaz answered, etc. Deliberately concealing the bad news.

CHAPTER XIX

8 sat in the gate. That is, he resumed his public duties, and welcomed the returning army.

for. This should be rendered, "And Israel," etc., and should begin a new paragraph: see R.V.

13 of my flesh. David probably wished to win over Amasa, as the leader of a numerous party, and to supersede Joab, whom he disliked for his overbearing manner, and his severe treatment of Absalom.

14 he. That is, Amasa.

20 all the house of Joseph. *i.e.*, the Ten Tribes, of which Ephraim was chief. Shimei himself belonged to Benjamin.

25 when he was come to Jerusalem, etc. There is no preposition in the original: it may be rendered, "to meet the king *at* Jerusalem."

35 between good and evil. "And bad," R.V.; *i.e.*, between what is pleasurable and the reverse.

37 Chimham. The Syriac and Arabic have, "my son Chimham." We find David afterwards specially recommending him and his brothers to Solomon's regard: see 1 Kings ii. 7; and an allusion in Jer. xli. 17 (on which see note) makes it likely that they received an inheritance near Bethlehem.

CHAPTER XX

6 David said to Abishai. David appears to have commissioned Abishai only (in the absence of Amasa: see xix. 13), wishing not to employ Joab again; but Joab went with his brother, and was, in fact, the commander: see vers. 11–22.

8 went before them. Rather, "came to meet them," R.V.

it fell out. Joab probably managed to let his sword fall from its sheath, so as to have to pick it up and hold it in his hand, without exciting suspicion.

14 unto Abel. "Abel of Beth-maachah," or Abel-maim, in Galilee; now 'Abil Kamḥ'. See 1 Kings xv. 20; 2 Kings xv. 29; 2 Chron. xvi. 4.

18 They shall surely ask [counsel] at Abel. It should be rendered, "In old time they clearly spoke [or 'commanded,' see Matt. v. 21, 27], saying, They will surely ask at Abel, and so conclude." It may be taken as claiming, on behalf of the city, an application of the merciful law in Deut. xx. 10, which Joab appears to have disregarded by commencing the siege without first inquiring whether the people of Abel adhered to Sheba or not.

19 I am, etc. The words *peaceable* and *faithful* being here plural in Heb., "We are peaceable and faithful."

a mother. So called as the central city of the district. The word *metropolis* has the same meaning.

23 Joab was over all the host. Now reinstated as commander-in-chief, although evidently disliked by David.

24 the tribute. Usually referring to forced labour.

CHAPTER XXI

1 he slew the Gibeonites. In doing this, Saul had not only shed innocent blood, but had violated a solemn national covenant: see Josh. ix. 15.

4 We will have no silver nor gold. R.V., "It is no matter of silver or gold," *i.e.*, the blood-guiltiness is not to be expiated by money.

any man in Israel. That is, "in the nation at large," as distinct from Saul's house.

6 we will hang them up. According to the principle of blood-avengement, which was universally allowed and acted upon, the Gibeonites had a right to make this demand, and David was not at liberty to refuse it.

8 Michal. This appears to be an error of the transcriber for Merab (see 1 Sam. xviii. 19), unless the word *sister* has been omitted, as our translators conjecture: see marginal reading.

16 Ishbi-benob. From a comparison of these verses with xxiii. 8–22, and 1 Chron. xi. 11, etc., xx. 4–8, it is evident that there are errors in copying some of the names of persons and places which can now hardly be certainly rectified. The names in 1 Chron. seem to be the most correct.

three hundred [shekels]. About nine pounds avoirdupois.

18 Gob. In 1 Chron. xx. 4 it is "Gezer." The same place is mentioned in 2 Sam. v. 25.

CHAPTER XXII

This chapter contains David's song of praise, which re-appears in Psalm xviii., on which see notes.

CHAPTER XXIII

The following Psalm is probably called "the last," as indicating David's last hopes and desires. It contains: 1, An emphatic declaration that what he speaks is inspired by Israel's God; 2, that there shall be a just ruler on his throne, bringing blessedness to his subjects; 3, that all evil, however dangerous and mischievous, shall be utterly destroyed.

1 said. R.V., "saith." The Hebrew word implies an inspired saying (see Numb. xxiv. 3).

3 He that ruleth, etc. This glowing picture displays the aged king's expectations for his royal successors; but it may be applied to the rising of the Sun of Truth, the Light of the World, under whose sunshine the beautiful fruits of truth and goodness are formed and ripened.

It should be compared with Psa. ii., lxxii., cx.

8-39 The names and exploits of David's chief heroes are now recorded (8-23), with a list of the thirty distinguished warriors (24-39). The list differs considerably from that in 1 Chron. xi. Of those here mentioned, Asahel and Uriah were already dead, and their places were doubtless filled up by others. In some cases the same person appears under different names, one probably personal, the other titular.

8 eight hundred. In 1 Chron. xi. 11 the number is *three* hundred.

10 the Lord wrought a great victory that day. This and the next exploit mentioned (11, 12), occurred probably while David was acting as general under Saul against the Philistines. The actions recorded of these men evince not only martial prowess, but also truly generous feeling, elevated sentiment, and nobleness of mind.

15 of the water of the well of Beth-lehem. A soldier's natural exclamation; David either forgetting that the Philistine garrison was there, or not expecting that his followers would attempt to gratify his wish. As Bethlehem was his native town, this water was well known to him.

17 Be it far from me, etc. Thus he would show his concern for the lives of his soldiers, and honour God by pouring out as a drink offering what he regarded, on account of the risk at which it had been procured, as too precious for his own use: see Deut. xii. 16.

[is not this] the blood, etc.? The R.V. supplies the words, "*shall I drink* the blood," as in 1 Chron. xi. 19.

20 two lionlike men of Moab. R.V. translates "the two sons of Ariel of Moab." Moffatt, however, taking a different reading in the Hebrew, has "two lion cubs in their lair."

in time of snow. He may have taken shelter in a cave which was the haunt of a lion, or the lion may have been driven by the snow to an empty cistern. The lion is not now found west of the Euphrates, but was well known in ancient Palestine.

CHAPTER XXIV

1 again. Referring to the previous instance, recorded xxi. 1.

He moved David. In 1 Chron. xxi. 1, we read, "Satan provoked David." God is said to do what He permits to be done.

2 the king said to Joab, etc. Whatever might be the exact point of David's offence it is plain that this census had a military object (see ver. 9), for which reason Joab and "the captains of the host" (4), not the priests, were commissioned to take it. It did not include any under twenty years of age, nor any of the tribes of Levi and Benjamin: see 1 Chron. xxi. 6; xxvii. 23. The numbers in 1 Chron. differ much from those here given.

5 Aroer. A town on the river Arnon, the south frontier town of the tribe of Reuben.

the right side. *i.e.*, the south, the observer facing the east.

the river of Gad. Rather, "the valley of Gad" (R.V.).

10 David's heart smote him. The king's *own conscience* recognised that a sin had been committed. This sin was undoubtedly vain-glory, probably with a view to unauthorised military aggressions on other lands.

14 let me not fall into the hand of man. David preferred any of those evils which, coming directly from the hand of God, would best assure him that the chastisement was gracious in its design, and regulated by mercy in its infliction. The punishment of which he made choice was one to which he and his family would be exposed as well as the poorest of his subjects.

15 to the time appointed. A more correct translation is: "So David chose the pestilence. And at the time of the wheat harvest, the plague began among the people, and there died," etc.

16 the Lord repented Him of the evil. See note on Gen. vi. 6.

17 these sheep, what have they done? David takes all the blame to himself; but the nation also had been guilty of pride.

18 the threshingfloor. A round level plot of ground in the open air, where the corn was trodden by the oxen. This is supposed to have been on Mount Moriah, which was afterwards occupied by the Temple.

23 All these things did Araunah, as a king, etc. Rather, as R.V., "All this, O king, doth Araunah give."

24 that which dost cost me nothing. Had Araunah's offer been accepted, the sacrifice would have been *his*, not David's.

1 KINGS

INTRODUCTION

As in the case of 1 and 2 Samuel, the two Books of Kings were one book in the Hebrew Bible. The Septuagint translators, however, divided them into two, calling them the 3rd and 4th Books of Kings. This arrangement was followed by the Vulgate and various Continental versions.

The most important of the monarchs whose lives are recorded in 1 Kings after the death of David (i., ii.) is Solomon (ii.–xi.), who raised the influence of Israel to its highest point and extended its territory so that it reached from the Mediterranean to the Euphrates and from the Red Sea to the utmost Lebanon (iv. 21), and whose learning and wisdom became proverbial. But with national glory, national decay and downfall are closely connected. After Solomon's death the kingdom became divided into two, under Rehoboam and Jeroboam (xii.). The former was followed by Abijam (xiv. 31–xv. 8), Asa (xv. 9–24), Jehoshaphat (xv. 24–xxii. 41–51), and Jehoram (xxii. 51) in the kingdom of Judah. Jeroboam was followed in the kingdom of Israel by Nadab (xiv. 20; xv. 25–31), Baasha (xv. 27–xvi. 7), Elah (xvi. 8–14), Zimri, Omri (xvi. 10–28), Ahab (xvi. 29–xxii. 40), Ahaziah (xxii. 40, 52–54). Through all the narratives of these reigns there is something more than the story of battles and conquests of which human history is made up. There is the constant reminder of Another King, to whom all earthly sovereigns and nations must give account. Reign after reign is summed up in the concise and potent sentence, "he did that which was right" or "he did evil *in the sight of the Lord.*"

But the hero of the Book is Elijah. His simple faith, the faith which he inspired in others (xvii. 5, 6, 14, 15), and his unflinching courage (xviii. 18, 22; xxi. 18–20) are an example for all time. And God's vindication of His servant is an encouragement to all who put their trust in Him.

CHAPTER I

1 King David was old. As David became king in his thirtieth year, and reigned forty years (2 Sam. v. 4, 5), he must now have been about seventy.

3 and found Abishag. This incident is introductory to the subsequent narrative with reference to Adonijah, who forfeited his life by asking for Abishag to wife.

5 Adonijah the son of Haggith. Adonijah does not appear to have intended to depose his father, but to assert his claim to succeed to the crown after his death, as being the eldest surviving son: see 2 Sam. iii. 2–4. Amnon, Chileab (Daniel, 1 Chron. iii. 1), and Absalom were older; but we know that Amnon and Absalom were dead, and Chileab, of whom nothing is recorded, probably died young. God had promised the kingdom to Solomon, the "man of peace," who was to build the Temple (1 Chron. xxii. 9; xxviii. 5); and Adonijah was aware of this decision: see ii. 15.

6 had not displeased him. Showing the same laxity of parental discipline which had produced such disastrous consequences in the instances of Amnon and Absalom.

his mother bare him after Absalom. This means only that Adonijah was next in age to Absalom; for they were not sons of the same mother (R.V., "he was born after Absalom").

8 Benaiah. Benaiah was the fifth of David's mighty men, the captain of twenty-four thousand men for the third month (1 Chron. xxvii. 5), and commander of David's body-guard; and was consequently a man of great influence. He succeeded Joab as commander-in-chief under the reign of Solomon.

Shimei. Not Shimei of Bahurim; but probably the son of Elah, and the same who was afterwards one of Solomon's officers (iv. 18). Josephus calls him "the friend of David" (*Antiq.* vii. 14).

9 Zoheleth. "The Serpent's Stone." This was on the eastern side of Zion, by the fountain En-rogel and the King's Gardens, at the junction of the King's Dale with the Valley of Hinnom.

10 Solomon his brother he called not. The omission to invite Solomon showed that Adonijah considered him as his rival.

12 that thou mayest save, etc. See note on 1 Sam. xxiv. 21.

13 Didst not thou . . . swear? The oath is nowhere recorded: but no doubt there was a solemn declaration by David to Bath-sheba of the Divine promise.

18 Adonijah reigneth. *i.e.*, claims the direct succession, the chief ecclesiastical and military authorities (19) being on his side.

25 God save king Adonijah, Heb., "Let king Adonijah live."

28 Call me Bath-sheba. She had probably retired during the interview between David and Nathan: cp. ver. 22.

33 the servants of your lord. *i.e.*, the royal body-guard.

Gihon. Gihon was a fountain in the valley on the west of Zion; consequently on the opposite side of the city to En-rogel, where Adonijah and his party were (9); and was probably chosen on that account.

36 the Lord God of my lord, *i.e.*, "the Eternal, the God of my lord the king": see R.V. So ver. 48, "the Eternal, the God of Israel."

38 the Cherethites and the Pelethites. See note on 2 Sam. viii. 18.

39 a horn of oil. R.V., "the horn," reserved for such occasions. The "tabernacle" is in R.V. "the tent": not the great Tabernacle in Gibeon, but the tent erected by David on Mount Zion.

42 a valiant man. Or, "good," "worthy" (R.V.); as in ver. 52, and Prov. xii. 2.

43 Verily. Rather, "Nay, but"; intended at once to check Adonijah's confidence.

51 to-day. Rather, "first of all" (R.V. marg.).

CHAPTER II

2 of all the earth. That is, *all mankind* (Gen. xi. 9; Josh. xxiii. 14). A fuller account of the closing scenes in David's life is given in 1 Chron. xxviii., xxix., a narrative which is probably to be placed between the preceding and the present chapters.

3 statutes. Ceremonial laws; *commandments*, moral laws; *judgements*, civil laws; *testimonies*, laws for special services in memorial of Jehovah's dealings with the people.

4 may continue. Rather, "may establish" (R.V.).

5 shed the blood of war in peace. *i.e.*, he shed in peace blood which should only be shed in war, or "taking vengeance during peace for blood shed during war" (*Moffatt*).

6 let not his hoar head, etc. *i.e.*, although his grey hairs might otherwise entitle him to honour, let him not go unpunished.

7 show kindness, etc. The dying king felt the claims of gratitude to be not less sacred than those of justice.

came. This word is used of showing kindness. See the narrative in 2 Sam. xix. 31–40.

8 Bahurim. Between Jerusalem and the Jordan (2 Sam. iii. 16; xvii. 18).

Shimei. David's injunction evidently amounts to this—that Shimei was so dangerous a person that he must be closely watched, and on the first act of disobedience be put to death. Shimei might have preserved his life on certain conditions, which he acknowledged to be reasonable, and yet violated on a very slight pretext: see vers. 39, 40.

9 but . . . bring thou down. Rather, "and . . . thou shalt bring down" (R.V.).

19 a seat. The same word has just before been rendered "throne": see R.V.

on his right hand. The place of honour among the Israelites (see Psa. xlv. 9; cx. 1), as also among the Greeks and Romans.

20 one small petition. Bath-sheba, no doubt, was interested in the personal aspects of the case, and did not understand the gravity of such a request.

22 ask for him the kingdom also. See note on 2 Sam. iii. 7. Adonijah's former offence had been overlooked; but it seems that, after his first alarm had subsided, his hopes revived; and Solomon saw in this application (see ver. 15) the first development of a further design upon the crown, between his brother and the two great officials mentioned.

24 hath made me a house. "House" here means "family"; the *royal succession.*

26 thou art worthy of death. As an accomplice in Adonijah's treason.

hast been afflicted, etc. In the hardships and dangers which he had shared with David: see 1 Sam. xxii. 20–23; 2 Sam. xv. 24–29.

27 that he might fulfil the word of the Lord. This passage (which is similar to many others) does not mean that Solomon did this *in order* to fulfil the prophecy; but that, being led to do it by Abiathar's rebellion, he thus fulfilled the word of the Lord.

28 Then tidings came, etc. Rather, "And the tidings came" (R.V.).

tabernacle. *i.e.*, tent (R.V.), as in i. 39.

30 Nay; but I will die here. Joab probably supposed that Solomon would be unwilling to shed blood in a holy place. But by the law (Exod. xxi. 14) even the altar could not protect a murderer.

34. the wilderness. *i.e.*, the Wilderness, or great open pasture-lands, of Judah, mentioned in the Gospels. Joab's being buried with his fathers seems out of respect to his past achievements.

37 Kidron. Solomon specifies the brook Kidron by way of example, meaning the *immediate neighbourhood:* see ver. 42. The road to Gath was in the opposite direction; but the spirit of the prohibition was violated.

44 shall return. Heb., "hath returned": the doom being spoken of as already inflicted.

CHAPTER III

1 Solomon made affinity, etc. Solomon had already married, more than a year before his accession to the throne, Naamah an Ammonitess, the mother of Rehoboam: cp. xi. 42 with xiv. 21. Which of the kings of Egypt was Solomon's father-in-law is not known; probably he was one of the latest in the twenty-first (Tanitic) dynasty.

2 the people sacrificed in high places. Mountains and hills were favourite places of idolatrous worship among all the heathen nations of antiquity. The Israelites were expressly commanded to destroy "the high places" (Deut. xii. 2), and to offer sacrifice only in the place which God should appoint for the purpose (Deut. xii. 13, 14). But so long as the sanctuary was only a movable tabernacle, and Jehovah had not yet chosen any fixed place for His worship, this law could not be carried into full effect. And accordingly the offering on "high places" is here excused on the ground that the temple was not yet built. Serious efforts to suppress it, however, were made in the time of Hezekiah and Josiah: see 2 Kings xii. 3; xviii. 4, 22.

4 to sacrifice there. This was a public act (see 2 Chron. i. 2), expressive of gratitude for the establishment of the new government, and supplicating the continuance of the Divine protection and blessing.

that was the great high place. So called in distinction from the other "high places," because here was the "Tent of meeting" which Moses had made in the wilderness (2 Chron. i. 3).

5 Ask what I shall give thee. Large as the offer

was, God daily makes to every one of us offers as large and liberal; see Matt. vii. 7, 8; John xiv. 13.

7 I am but a little child. So Jer. i. 6.

to go out or come in. To conduct affairs.

8 that cannot be numbered. *i.e.*, a great multitude: see Gen. xiii. 16; xv. 5; xxii. 17.

10 the speech pleased the Lord. This prayer of Solomon is remarkable for its unselfishness, relating as it did entirely to his kingly duties in administering the law among the people. For himself personally he asked nothing. His prayer, therefore, "pleased the Lord."

14 I will lengthen thy days. The promise of long life was *conditional;* and it was forfeited by Solomon's unfaithfulness, so that he scarcely reached the age of sixty: see xi. 42.

15 a dream. *i.e.*, a divine vision and communication in a dream. Hence, on his return to Jerusalem, Solomon celebrates the event with grateful offerings and festivities "before the ark of the covenant" on Mount Zion.

28 they feared the king, etc. The expedient to which Solomon resorted shows that, with absolute judicial power, he possessed an insight into character imparted by God Himself ("the wisdom of God"), making him quick to discern and punish transgressors.

CHAPTER IV

1 So king Solomon, etc. This chapter describes the state of the kingdom, not at any particular time, but during the whole period of Solomon's greatest prosperity.

2 the princes. *i.e.*, the most eminent men or highest officers of his court.

Azariah. Azariah, "the priest," the grandson of Zadok, stands first, as having been high priest at the dedication of the Temple, and through much of Solomon's reign. (The father of Azariah was Ahimaaz.)

3 scribes. "Secretaries," who drew up the royal edicts.

the recorder. The annalist or registrar of the proceedings of the government.

4 Zadok and Abiathar were the priests. Omit *the* (R.V.). Abiathar, although deposed, retained his title. Two "chief priests" were required by the two tabernacles, until the building of the Temple.

6 the tribute. That is, the tributary service, for which levies were raised among the people. This became very unpopular in the course of the great works which Solomon executed: see xii. 4, 18.

8 The son of Hur. Many persons are known in the East as much by their fathers' name as by their own. In such cases as this it is perhaps better to adopt the patronymic reading, as in the margin, "Ben-hur," "Ben-dekar," etc. (so R.V.).

10 Sochoh. "Sucoh" in the mountains south of Hebron: see Josh. xv. 35, 48.

11 the daughter of Solomon. See note on ver. 1.

12 Taanach. Now called *Tannuk,* on the north-east declivity of Mount Carmel: see Judges v. 19. This district comprised the rich plain and valley of Jezreel.

Megiddo. Now *El-lejjûn,* a little to the east of the preceding.

20 making merry. Enjoying security, prosperity, abundance. In the Hebrew Bible, ch. iv. ends with this verse; ch. v. beginning with verse 21 and ending where ch. v. ends in the English version.

21 Solomon reigned over all kingdoms. They were his tributaries. Thus was fulfilled the promise made to Abraham (Gen. xv. 18) respecting the extent of territory which his descendants should possess; but the sins of the king and the people soon narrowed its limits.

the river. The Euphrates.

22 provision for one day. This was the supply for the whole court, comprising the numerous attendants, body-guards, etc., and all who, according to Oriental custom, received their maintenance from the royal establishment.

thirty measures (cors), etc. About 330 bushels of fine, and 660 of coarser flour. The "cor" was the same as the homer.

24 from Tiphsah, etc. Tiphsah, or Thapsacus, on the western bank of the Euphrates, and Azzah, or Gaza, were the frontier towns on the north-east and south-west of Solomon's tributary dominions, which thus extended, in their greatest length, about 400 miles. The word "Tiphsah" (more properly Tiphsach) means *passage,* or *crossing.* It was at this place that the Euphrates was crossed by the younger Cyrus and by Alexander the Great in their expeditions.

on this side. That is, west of the Euphrates.

25 under his vine, etc. Expressive of security and peace.

26 forty thousand stalls. Or, more probably *four* thousand (see 2 Chron. ix. 25). The word rendered "stalls" may perhaps rather mean "spans" or *pairs.*

horsemen. Rather, perhaps, "riding horses."

28 Barley. Barley, which grows abundantly in Palestine, is still used as food for cattle in the East, where oats are not cultivated.

dromedaries. Should be "swift horses."

where [the officers] were. Or, as R.V. marg., "where he (the king) was." "Officers" is not in the original.

29 largeness of heart. *i.e., great powers of mind;* the word "heart" being often used by the Hebrews for mental capacities generally. "As the sand on the sea shore" indicates extraordinary abundance.

31 wiser than all men. *i.e.*, than all the men *of his time,* the most distinguished of whom are mentioned by name.

32 three thousand proverbs. In the Book of Proverbs, not more than one-third of these have been preserved.

songs. The 72nd, the 127th and the 132nd Psalms have been attributed to Solomon. These, with the "Song of Songs," or "Canticles," are all of his songs that we possess.

33 the hyssop. Dr. G. E. Post, of Beirut, Syria, thinks this was a species of marjoram, probably *Origanum maru* (see article "Hyssop," *Hastings' Dict. of the Bible*).

34 And there came of all people. See particularly the visit of the Queen of Sheba, related in ch. x.

CHAPTER V

3 Thou knowest. David seems to have communicated with Hiram on this subject: see 1 Chron. xxii. 4.

4 neither adversary nor evil occurrent. Rather, "occurrence," such as rebellion, pestilence, famine, or war.

6 Lebanon. The forests of Lebanon were probably Solomon's; but the Hebrews were inferior, as artisans and sailors, to the Sidonians, whose services were therefore required for felling and working the timber, and conveying it by sea to a seaport accessible to Jerusalem. Numerous testimonies to the mechanical and nautical skill and the artistic eminence of the Phœnicians are found in the Greek poets and historians (see also Ezek. xxvii.).

7 Blessed be the Lord. For Hiram's acknowledgment of the Eternal, see also 2 Chron. ii. 11.

9 food for my household. This was an appropriate exchange between an agricultural and a commercial state, Tyre supplying, for the most part, the workmen's skill and labour, and Israel supplying food for Hiram's household. Food was also provided for the men employed on the works: see 2 Chron. ii. 10: see note on 2 Sam. v. 11.

15 that bare burdens. These were not Israelites, but persons belonging to conquered or tributary nations: see ix. 20–22; 2 Chron. ii. 17, 18.

17 the foundation of the house. The remains of the foundations at this day, as described by modern travellers, bear evidence to the accuracy of this description, in the " great stones, costly stones, and hewn stones," which are still to be seen in the sub-structures, along the ground where the Temple stood. To obtain sufficient space for its numerous courts and apartments (which in later times, according to Josephus, covered a space half a mile in circuit), Solomon enlarged the area of the summit of the mount by raising a lofty terrace of great extent from the valley beneath.

18 the stone-squarers. Or, " Gebalites," R.V.; that is, natives of Gebal, a city on the sea at the foot of Lebanon, now called Jubeil. See Ezek. xxvii. 9.

CHAPTER VI

1 the four hundred and eightieth year. This date has caused some difficulty in the chronology, and appears inconsistent with the date given by the apostle Paul, according to either reading of Acts xiii. 20. The Septuagint has " the four hundred and fortieth year "; and Josephus, " the five hundred and ninety-second."

2 threescore cubits. About 90 feet, the breadth being 30 feet, and the height 45 feet. It was built after the model of the tabernacle, but was just twice as large; and the symbolical meaning of its various parts was the same: see Exod. xxv., xxvii., xxxv.–xxxix.

4 windows of narrow lights. Perhaps, " with lattice closed," *i.e.*, so that they could not be opened (see R.V.). Other explanations are " windows broad within, and narrow without" (marg. A.V. and R.V.), or " windows with gratings" (*Moffatt*).

5 he built chambers, etc. Rather, " and he built upon the wall of the house a storied part round the walls of the house, around the temple and the oracle; and he made side chambers round about" (see R.V.).

the oracle. That is, the most holy place.

6 chamber. Rather, " storey " (R.V.).

7 made ready before it was brought thither. Or, as R.V., " made ready at the quarry."

10 chambers. Rather, " the storied part." In the second clause the plural " they " refers to its division by floors into three tiers of rooms.

12 which I spake. See the promise made to David in 2 Sam. vii. 13–16.

20 twenty cubits in length, etc. An exact cube of about 30 feet.

21 made a partition by the chains of gold. Rather, as R.V., " drew across chains of gold." " Overlaid it," *i.e.*, the oracle.

22 that was by the oracle. Rather, as R.V. " that belonged to the oracle."

23 two cherubim. These cherubim were distinct from those which covered the mercy-seat, and which were inseparable from it, being formed of the same mass of gold; these were colossal figures about 15 feet high, made of olive wood plated with gold, standing on the ground, on each side of the ark, and spreading their wings across the most holy place.

31 a fifth part. Or " pentagon " (see marg.).

33 the door. *i.e.*, " the entering " (R.V.) from the porch into the holy place.

38 seven years. Or exactly *seven years and a half*, the odd months not being reckoned in the text (" Zif " was the second month). The building was very quickly completed. It was not, however, very large; and besides this a vast number of workmen were employed in it, and the materials were prepared in Lebanon before it was begun.

CHAPTER VII

2 the house of the forest of Lebanon. Probably a palace in Jerusalem, to which this name was given on account of the large quantity of cedar-wood employed in its construction. This edifice and the " king's house " (1), and " the house of Pharaoh's daughter " (8), were different parts of one large pile of building, according to the usual style of Oriental palaces; and all are included in the statement in ver. 1.

3 And it was, etc. Rather, " And it was covered with cedar above, upon the side-chambers, which were upon the pillars, forty-five, *being* fifteen in a row."

5 And all the doors, etc. Rather, " And all the doors (between the chambers) and posts were square, with beam " (not arched), etc. The house seems to have had three rows of galleries, formed not by arches, but by beams laid upon pillars, and giving an outlook into the central court.

14 of the tribe of Naphtali. In the parallel passage (2 Chron. ii. 13) Hiram is called " the son of a woman of the daughters of *Dan*." His mother, who had married a Tyrian, was probably descended from the colony of Danites who seized upon Laish, which lay on the border of the tribe of Naphtali (see Judg. xviii 2, 28, 29); and she might therefore be spoken of as belonging to either tribe.

15 eighteen cubits high. 27 feet. Here, and in Jer. lii. 21, the height of the pillars alone is given. In 2 Chron. iii. 15 (thirty-five cubits high) that of the capitals and of the pedestals on which they stood is included.

20 the belly. Probably the swell of the leaf of the lily (cf. " bellying sails ").

24 knops. *i.e.*, " buds " (cp. German *knospe*), perhaps of fruit, or wild cucumber.

26 two thousand baths. About 16,000 gallons. In 2 Chron. iv. 5 the number is *three* thousand, with which Josephus agrees. The *brazen sea*, with the smaller lavers, was for the use of the priests, in washing themselves, in conducting the sacrifices, and in keeping the courts of the Temple clean. The duty of filling it was performed by the Gibeonites, or Nethinim, who drew water for the house of God. Its typical significance was the same as that of the laver of the tabernacle: see Exod. xxx. 17.

29 additions made of thin work. Framework.

30 plates of brass. Read " axles."

40 lavers. Pots.

41 bowls of the chapiters. They are called "pommels" in 2 Chron. iv. 12. "Capitals on the tops of the columns" (*Moffatt*).

46 Zarthan. Mentioned also in Josh. iii. 16. Near Succoth, in the valley of Jordan (west), where the clay was good for moulding.

51 among the treasures. Rather, "in the treasure-rooms" or "store-rooms."

CHAPTER VIII

1 Then Solomon assembled the elders. The services at the dedication of the Temple consisted of three parts—the solemn transference of the ark of the covenant from the city of David to the Temple (1–21), Solomon's dedication prayer (22–61), and the sacrifice of peace offerings (62–66).

2 the feast in the month Ethanim (otherwise Tisri). This was the Feast of Tabernacles. The building had now been finished nearly a year, and its furniture and utensils were probably prepared in the meantime.

4 the tabernacle of the congregation. The Tent of meeting constructed by Moses, was brought from Gibeon and deposited in some part of the Temple. The poles and curtains were perhaps laid up in the treasury.

8 they were not seen without. The ends of the staves were visible within the holy place, but not outside of it.

unto this day. The time when the narrative was originally written, before the destruction of the Temple by the Chaldeans under Nebuchadnezzar.

9 There was nothing in the ark. In Heb. ix. 4 several things are spoken of as being in the ark which are not mentioned here; but that passage seems to refer to the tabernacle as it existed in the time of Moses. Now that the ark had been brought to its permanent resting-place, "the golden pot that had manna, and Aaron's rod that budded," are removed from the interior of the ark, and placed beside it.

10 the cloud. This was the symbol of the presence of the Eternal, testifying that He had accepted the Temple as His own house. The Temple, with which so many hallowed associations were connected in the mind of the Jew, is used in the New Testament as variously representing Christ (John ii. 19–21), the individual believer (1 Cor. iii. 16; vi. 19), and the universal Church (Eph. ii. 19–22).

12 Then spake Solomon. Having taken his place on a raised platform, where he could be seen and heard by the assembly: see 2 Chron. vi. 13.

13 for Thee to abide in for ever. This alludes to the fixed and more permanent structure of the Temple, compared with the materials of the tabernacle, and its frequent change of place: see 2 Sam. vii. 6, "I have not dwelt, but have walked," etc.

22 Solomon stood before the altar. It appears from ver. 54 and 2 Chron. vi. 13 that Solomon kneeled down when he began to offer prayer.

31 the oath come before Thine altar. "And he [*i.e.*, the accused] come (and) swear," etc.

33 When Thy people Israel, etc. The various cases are taken almost verbally from Lev. xxvi. and Deut. xxviii.

38 plague of his own heart. In 2 Chron. vi. 29, the Hebrew word here rendered "plague" is translated "sore"; it is called "his own sore," with the addition, "and his own grief."

41 a stranger. The Temple was to be "a house of prayer for all people," which shows that the old covenant did not confine the privileges of religion to one particular nation, to the exclusion of all others.

47 We have sinned, etc. This form of confession of sin was afterwards adopted by the Jews: see Psa. cvi. 6; Dan. ix. 5.

48 See Dan. vi. 10. The direction of the face in prayer towards the Temple was intended to denote faith in the presence of God there.

51 the furnace of iron. See Deut. iv. 20.

63 offered a sacrifice. Probably not all at one time, but during the festival. The "peace offerings" furnished forth a feast for the immense concourse of people gathered to the dedication.

65 a feast. Rather, "the feast" (R.V.), *i.e.*, the Feast of Tabernacles.

from the entering in of Hamath. That is, from one extremity of the land to the other.

CHAPTER IX

8 shall be astonished, and shall hiss. "Shall whistle in amazement" (*Moffatt*).

13 Cabul. Josephus says (*Ant.*, viii. 5) that these were towns of Galilee, in the neighbourhood of Tyre; and that "Cabul," in the Phœnician language, signifies *unpleasing*. Conder (*Hastings' Dict. Bible*) identifies them with the large village of Kabûl, east of Acco.

14 six score talents of gold (over $3,500,000). This no doubt was in accordance with the bargain by which Hiram supplied labour and money to Solomon, being repaid in produce (v. 11; 2 Chron. ii. 10), and, in part, by these cities. From 2 Chron. viii. 2 it has been concluded that the twenty towns were restored to Solomon.

15 (the) **Millo.** See note on Judges ix. 6

Hazor, and Megiddo, and Gezer. Hazor would command the northern district (see Josh. xi. 1, 10–13), Megiddo would protect the great plain of Jezreel and the centre of the land, and Gezer the line of road from Egypt along the western lowland plain.

17 Beth-horon the nether. The two Beth-horons were about twelve miles north-west of Jerusalem, at the upper and lower ends of the main pass leading from the western plain to the hill country and the metropolis.

18 Baalath. The site is uncertain.

Tadmor. Tadmor, or Tamar (R.V.), which means a palm-tree, was formerly supposed to have been the original site of the celebrated city of Palmyra, nearly midway between Damascus and Thapsacus, on the Euphrates, a place of great commercial importance under the Roman empire. But Sir G. A. Smith (*Hist. Geog. of the Holy Land*) thinks it was a frontier village of Judæa, now known as Hazazon-Tamar. See Ezek. xlvii. 19.

24 Pharaoh's daughter came, etc. For the reason of this, see 2 Chron. viii. 11.

26 Ezion-geber. Ezion-geber was at the head of the north-eastern arm of the Red Sea, now called the Gulf of Akaba. The possession of this harbour, which Solomon obtained by his sovereignty over Edom, gave him the use of the Red Sea, and access to the Indian Ocean.

Eloth. Eloth or Elath (called by the Greeks and Romans Ailah and Elana) is close to the modern Akaba. It was taken by David from the Edomites; but lost again by Joram about one hundred and fifty years later. It was retaken by Azariah; but, in the reign of Ahaz, became again subject to the Edomites.

27 And Hiram sent, etc. As the countries through which the important trade with India and the East was carried on were now under Solomon's dominion, the Tyrians were naturally anxious to cultivate a friendly connexion with him.

28 Ophir. The situation of Ophir can only be conjectured. The opinions fix it either in the south of Arabia, or on the east of Africa, or in some part of India. Dr. Ira M. Price, Professor of Semitic languages in the University of Chicago, after weighing up all the arguments for the various sites, concludes that south-eastern Arabia was the most probable situation (*Hastings' Dict. Bible*).

CHAPTER X

1 the queen of Sheba. "Sheba" was Saba or Sabæa, in South Arabia: a country whose inhabitants were well known to the Hebrews and the Greeks for their extensive traffic in the spices, gold, and precious stones which there abounded. The productions here described (2) are identical with those of the kingdom of Sabæa, as given by Strabo, the elder Pliny, and other authorities. During the last fifty years, much light has been thrown on the ancient civilisation of Saba by the discovery of coins and inscriptions. For a detailed account, see *Hastings' Dict. of the Bible* (article by Professor D. S. Margoliouth).

5 his servants, and . . . ministers. The "servants" seem to be the ministers of state, seated in their places at the king's table; the "ministers," the attendants of the palace, waiting, in the royal liveries, upon him and his guests.

his ascent. The Hebrew word here used is generally translated "burnt offering"; and the Septuagint and some other versions render the clause, "and the burnt offerings which he offered (or caused to ascend) in the house of the Lord."

12 almug trees. Or, algum-tree (2 Chron. ix. 10, 11). Sandalwood.

19 stays. "Arms" of the chair or throne.

22 Tharshish. The situation of Tarshish has been much debated. The prevailing opinion is that it was the celebrated Phœnician colony of Tartessus on the Atlantic coast of Spain, not far from the modern Cadiz. But some recent scholars, including Cheyne, and Professor Max Müller of Philadelphia, favour the view that it was in Italy and that its people were the Tyrrenians or Etruscans.

24 all the earth. That is, the neighbouring nations. Cp. French, *tout le monde.*

28 and linen yarn, etc. The Hebrew word here and in Chronicles translated "linen yarn" does not bear this meaning elsewhere. The R.V. renders the clause, "the king's merchants received them (the horses) in droves, each drove at a price."

29 And a chariot, etc. In "multiplying horses," Solomon violated an express injunction of the law (Deut. xvii. 16). See also Isa. xxxi. 1. It is worthy of notice that horses and chariots, however serviceable in a plain country, were ill suited for warfare in a mountainous region, such as Palestine. Consequently this law, which discouraged the use of horses, in fact compelled the Israelites to employ the kind of force best suited to the defence of their country.

six hundred [shekels] of silver. This, which included the horses and harness, would be equivalent to about £75; and that of a cavalry horse about £20.

CHAPTER XI

5 Solomon went after Ashtoreth, etc. It appears surprising that a man so eminent for wisdom should fall into idolatry. But his too intimate connexion with neighbouring nations, the enervating influence of prosperity and luxury, the debasing power of sensual indulgence—all probably combined to draw away his heart from the Eternal. Such is the folly of the wisest of men, when he forgets God.

11 the Lord said. Perhaps by the prophet Ahijah: see vers. 29, 30.

26 Jeroboam the son of Nebat, etc. Ahijah's prophecy (31) was no excuse for Jeroboam's conduct; for he was told at the same time that the disruption of the kingdom was not to take place till after Solomon's decease (34). But Jeroboam seems to have been too eager to seize the promised prize, and unwilling to wait till the appointed time.

28 made him ruler. Jeroboam was overseer either over the levies of men for the royal works, or over the collection of the tribute (or perhaps both).

29 Shilonite. That is, a native or inhabitant of Shiloh: see xiv. 2; see also 2 Chron. ix. 29.

30 caught the new garment. The Septuagint has, "Ahijah had clad himself." Probably the outer garment.

32 he shall have one tribe. The taking away of ten tribes would leave two: but Simeon was so incorporated with Judah as almost to be regarded as one with it.

39 but not for ever. For in Christ the kingdom of David is established in far greater glory.

40 Shishak. This is the first time that we find the proper (not the titular) name of an Egyptian sovereign in the Scriptures; unless *Rameses,* in Gen. xlvii. 11, be the name, not of a district, but of the king. Shishak or Sheshonk was the first king of the twenty-second Bubastite dynasty. In the temple at Karnak may be seen his sculptures recording the names of the conquered cities in Palestine.

CHAPTER XII

1 Shechem. Shechem, in the tribe of Ephraim, was a meeting-place of the *ten* tribes as distinguished from Judah. It was afterwards fixed upon by Jeroboam as the capital of his kingdom. The people seem to have assembled without any design to revolt, but with a determination to obtain relief from the requirements of Solomon's reign.

2 dwelt in Egypt. The Septuagint has the same reading here as in the parallel passage in 2 Chron. x. 2, namely, "Jeroboam *returned out of Egypt.*"

4 made our yoke grievous. In carrying on his great public works, Solomon had made his own people overseers and rulers, the heavier and servile work being done apparently by the Canaanites: see ix. 22. The reference is, no doubt, partly to the taxation laid upon the people for these public works, and for the maintenance of Solomon's court and retinue.

6 that stood before Solomon. That is, as his chief officers and counsellors.

7 If thou wilt be a servant, etc. That is, "If thou wilt be compliant now for once, thou mayest be their master ever after."

8 the young men, etc. It was the custom in some Eastern countries for the heir-apparent to be brought up with young men of rank, who might, on his accession, fill the chief civil and military offices. These young men were probably about Rehoboam's age.

15 the cause was from the Lord. All the parties to these transactions, whilst following out their own purposes, were unintentionally accomplishing the designs of God: see Acts ii. 23.

17 which dwelt in the cities of Judah. That is, the priests and Levites, and persons belonging to other tribes residing in the cities of Judah, who were soon afterwards joined by many others: see 2 Chron. xi. 13–17.

18 and all Israel stoned him. Adoram, having been superintendent of the levies of money and of men which had been required for Solomon's great works (iv. 6; v. 14), was probably the most unpopular man that the king could have sent.

20 the tribe of Judah only. Including part of the tribes of Benjamin and Simeon, which had been closely connected with Judah, and probably also a few towns in Dan. The close alliance between these tribes had been promoted by their mutual contiguity, and by the proximity of them all to the Temple; whilst Judah and Benjamin had a further bond of sympathy as being the two royal tribes, and sharing the honour and advantage of Jerusalem as the capital.

22 Shemaiah. See also 2 Chron. xii. 5, 7.

25 built Shechem, etc. Doubtless fortifying Shechem and Penuel in order to secure his new kingdom by a stronghold on the east as well as the west of Jordan.

26 Jeroboam said in his heart, etc. Though Jeroboam knew that he owed his elevation to God, and that, if he were faithful and obedient, his new kingdom was secured to him and to his family by the Divine promise, yet he chose to rely rather upon measures of worldly policy than upon the protection of Jehovah, disowning His authority and perverting His worship. But he found, as all will find who follow his example, that the very plans by which he hoped to secure his safety caused his ruin: see xiv. 7–16.

28 the king took counsel, etc. To effect his political object, Jeroboam not only violated the second commandment, but proceeded to set aside the Divine institutions with respect to the *place*, the *ministers*, the *times*, and the *manner* of worship. Although that which he introduced was a pretended worship of Jehovah under these symbols, and not that of heathen gods which was afterwards established by the dynasty of Omri (from which, indeed, it is always distinguished both in the history and in the prophets), yet he is called the man "who made Israel to sin" (2 Kings x. 29, etc.). The ten tribes, from this time to the subversion of the kingdom, were a nation of idolaters, although a few individuals, amidst great discouragement, adhered to the service of Jehovah, and His prophets were feared and respected even by the worst of their kings.

behold thy gods, O Israel, etc. These words are identical with those of the Israelites in the wilderness when Aaron made the golden calf, Exod. xxxii. 4; and, like those words, contain a bold defiance of Him who spoke by Moses. Like the Israelites, Jeroboam doubtless was led to the adoption of this form of worship by his residence in Egypt.

29 Beth-el . . . Dan. Beth-el and Dan were at the southern and northern extremities of the kingdom. Beth-el was, in consequence of this desecration, called by the prophets "Beth-aven," *i.e., house of vanity*, or, *of idols*, instead of "*Beth-el,*" *house of God* (Amos i. 5; Hos. iv. 15; v. 8: x. 5, 8). At Dan, idolatry had been established at a former period (Judges xviii.).

31 of the lowest. *i.e.*, from the people at large (see R.V.), as distinguished from the Levites, to whom alone, by Divine right, the priestly function belonged. This accounts for the statement in 2 Chron. xi. 13, 14.

32 the feast that is in Judah. *i.e.*, probably the Feast of Tabernacles, which was to be observed on the fifteenth of the seventh month, the month being altered by the will of Jeroboam —"of his own heart," v. 33.

33 he offered. Not satisfied with other innovations, Jeroboam acted as high priest, constituting himself the spiritual as well as temporal head of his kingdom.

CHAPTER XIII

2 he cried against the altar, etc. This prediction was delivered three hundred and sixty years before the event (see 2 Kings xxiii. 15).

3 the ashes. The ashes of the sacrifices.

6 Intreat . . . the Lord thy God. Jeroboam looks for help now, not to the objects of his worship, but to Him whose law and services he had set at nought; but, like Pharaoh in a similar case (Exod. x. 17), he cares only for the removal of the judgement.

9 Eat no bread, nor drink water. To do this would have been a symbol of peace and friendship. The command to return by a different route was an additional precaution against forming any acquaintance by the way. The near vicinity and relation of this apostate people exposed the inhabitants of Judah to peculiar danger of infection from their sin.

11 an old prophet. This old prophet at Beth-el, though a worshipper of Jehovah, and endowed with prophetic inspiration, seems, like Balaam, not to have been a faithful and godly man (see ver. 18).

19 did eat bread . . . and drank water. Not duly considering that, while the prohibition which he had received came immediately from God, he had only this man's word in opposition to it. His conduct showed a too easy credulity in compliance with his own inclination.

24 slew him. This judgement on the disobedient prophet vindicated his message, the authority of which had been compromised by his conduct. And the impression of the event upon the people was deepened by the miraculous restraint upon the lion: see ver. 28.

32 Samaria. This word shows that the book was compiled after Omri had built and named Samaria: see xvi. 24.

33 the lowest of the people. See note on xii. 31.

34 this thing became sin. And thus in after times Jeroboam was known as the king "who did sin and made Israel to sin": see xiv. 16; xv. 30, 34; and 2 Kings x. 31; xiii. 6, etc.

CHAPTER XIV

1 At that time. The predicted evils begin at once to fall on Jeroboam's house.

5 feign herself to be another woman. A striking instance of the folly of attempting disguise before God, who could as easily reveal to the prophet the name and rank of the applicant as make known the result of her child's illness.

10 him that is shut up and left. Some translate this "the bond and the free." It means that not one of the family of Jeroboam should escape.

11 shall the dogs eat. To lie unburied was to the Israelites and other ancient nations a horrible fate, and the greatest insult that could be shown to a slaughtered foe.

14 but what? even now. The sense seems to be, " But why do I speak of it as a distant event? Even now the sentence is beginning to take effect."

17 Tirzah. The pleasant situation of Tirzah had early attracted the Israelitish monarchs, so that it shared for some time with Shechem the honours of the capital (xv. 33; xvi. 8). Its site is uncertain.

22 And Judah did evil. The account in vers. 22-24 indicates a rapid and deep degeneracy, such as is described in Rom. i. 23-32. Man can never rise above the objects of his worship.

23 images and groves. On " images" see Gen. xxxi. 19; Exod. xxiii. 24; Lev. xxvi. 1; 2 Kings iii. 2. And on " groves" see Exod. xxxiv. 13; Judges iii. 7; 2 Kings xxiii. 4, 6. How extremely prone the whole nation was to these forms of idolatry appears also from ver. 15.

25 Shishak king of Egypt, etc. See note on xi. 40. A fuller account of this invasion and of its causes and results is given in 2 Chron. xii. 2-12: on which see notes.

CHAPTER XV

2 Three years. A comparison of vers. 1 and 9 shows that Abijam reigned but part of the third year.

Maachah. " Abishalom" is the same name as " Absalom." In 2 Chron. xi. 20, Maachah is called " the daughter of Absalom"; and in 2 Chron. xiii. 2, " Michaiah, the daughter of Uriel of Gibeah." Jewish writers suppose that Absalom the son of David is here intended, that his daughter Tamar was married to Uriel, and that consequently Maachah was his granddaughter. The term " daughter" is used in a wide sense, like " father" in ver. 3, and " mother" in vers. 10 to 13, where it means *grandmother*.

6 Rehoboam. Several manuscripts, with the Targum and the Arabic version, read " Abijam." The Syriac has " Abia the son of Rehoboam."

13 Maachah. As the king's mother, she had been, during Abijah's reign, the chief lady of the land, and would have still retained her rank under her grandson Asa, but for the cause here stated.

an idol in a grove. Literally, " an abominable thing for an Asherah" (R.V.). The use of this word, found only here and in the parallel passage in Chron., seems to intimate something peculiarly hateful.

14 the high places. The high places devoted to *idolatrous* worship were destroyed (see 2 Chron. xiv. 3); but there were others apparently used in the worship of the true God, though sacrifices could legally be offered only in the place which God had appointed for the purpose (Deut. xii. 13, 14). These were not generally suppressed till the time of Hezekiah (see 2 Kings xii. 3; xviii. 4).

Asa's heart was perfect with the Lord. This refers not to his whole conduct, in which there were some serious blemishes, but to his sincere adherence to the appointed worship of God.

15 the things which his father had dedicated. Perhaps booty obtained in the war with Jeroboam.

17 and built Ramah. Ramah was six miles north of Jerusalem, just on the confines of the two kingdoms, in the great Gophna pass, which formed the only highway between Jerusalem and the central portion of Israel. The town existed long before; but Baasha *repaired* and *fortified* it.

18 king Asa sent them to Ben-hadad. We find, from 2 Chron. xvi. 7, that Asa incurred the Divine displeasure by this application to Syria, which showed a want of trust in Jehovah, and a disposition to rely on human aid.

20 Ijon. This was the extreme north of Palestine, afterwards ravaged by Tiglath-pileser (see 2 Kings xv. 29; Isa. viii. 22, and note). *Cinneroth* or *Chinnereth* lay on the west of the Sea of Galilee, and was another name for Gennesaret.

22 Mizpah. On the northern spur of Olivet, near the modern *Shafat*. In the time of Jeremiah (xli. 9), there was still existing near Mizpah a pit, or fosse, " which Asa the king had made across the valley for fear of Baasha king of Israel."

27 Gibbethon. Gibbethon was a Levitical city in the tribe of Dan (see Josh. xix. 44; xxi. 23). The Philistines had probably taken possession of it recently, upon its being abandoned by the Levites, who were supplanted by the priests of the golden calves (see 2 Chron. xi. 14-17). It has been identified with the modern Kibbiah.

CHAPTER XVI

1 Hanani. There was a prophet Hanani about the same time, who was sent to Asa king of Judah (see 2 Chron. xvi. 7). The Jehu mentioned here wrote the history of Jehoshaphat's reign (2 Chron. xx. 34).

7 the work of his hands. This refers not so much to his general conduct as to the setting up of idols.

because he killed him. Exterminating his family. Although the destruction of Jeroboam's family had been threatened, it was not, on Baasha's part, an act of obedience to the will of God, but one of treasonable ambition, for which he was amenable to the Divine justice.

23 twelve years. In these twelve years are included the five in which Omri was at war with Tibni, who reigned as rival king. With the accession of Omri to the throne of Israel, hostilities ceased between the two kingdoms for about a century, till renewed by Amaziah: see 2 Kings xiv. 8.

24 the hill Samaria. The palace at Tirzah having been destroyed (18), Omri founded a new capital. He called it, after his own name, *Shomeron* (Samaria). It was situated on an oblong hill, rising from the midst of a valley enclosed by hills, save where a narrow opening communicates with the western plain. It thus equalled Jerusalem in the natural strength of its position, but far surpassed it in the fertility and beauty of its surrounding country. This city subsequently gave its name to the central part of Palestine, the inhabitants of which were called *Samaritans*. It was given by the Emperor Augustus to Herod, who rebuilt it, and called it Sebaste, now *Sebustiyeh*.

25 Omri wrought evil. The prophet Micah (vi. 16) speaks of " the statutes of Omri," the keeping of which brought Israel to desolation.

34 Abiram . . . Segub. It is generally supposed that Hiel lost all his sons, the eldest when he began the work, and the youngest when he finished. If this were so, his conduct presents a course of foolhardy defiance to the God of Israel. The fulfilment of the prophecy (Josh. vi. 26) was an impressive manifestation of the power of the true God in an idolatrous age.

CHAPTER XVII

1 Elijah the Tishbite. There is something appalling in the sudden appearance of this extraordinary prophet of Divine vengeance, just at the time when the wickedness of Ahab and his people had reached its greatest height. But amidst all the stern severity which the sins of the nation required on the part of a preacher of repentance, a tender regard for the rebellious monarch and people is discernible.

inhabitants. Josephus and the Septuagint take the word translated "inhabitants" as a proper name; and render the clause, "the Tishbite *from Thisbe* of Gilead." Gilead was in eastern Palestine between Moab and Hauran.

before whom I stand. That is, whose servant I am.

there shall not be dew nor rain. This terrible visitation was designed to make the people see the evil of forsaking the Lord God for the idols of Egypt and Tyre. It was needful that a nation so deeply sunk in ungodliness should be aroused, even at the expense of suffering. See Jas. v. 17 and Rev. xi. 6.

3 the brook Cherith. This was probably one of the winter torrents flowing into the Jordan from the eastern highlands; but it has not been identified.

4 I have commanded the ravens, etc. Elijah had honoured God by his faith and obedience: now God is pleased to honour him by His extraordinary aid; using for this purpose creatures the most unlikely, and controlling their natural instinct, so as to make the prophet the more conscious of His care.

9 Zarephath. A place between Sidon and Tyre, named in the New Testament "Sarepta" (Luke iv. 26), where there is still a village called *Sarafend.* The command to go to a place within the territories of Jezebel's father must have required strong faith on the part of Elijah.

I have commanded a widow. Not by a distinct message from heaven, but by disposing her to supply Elijah with food (4), because he was a prophet of Jehovah. This incident, and the cure of Naaman the Syrian (2 Kings v.), are referred to by our Lord (Luke iv. 25–27) to illustrate God's sovereignty in bestowing His favours and His mercy on the Gentile world. Elijah was the first "apostle to the Gentiles."

12 a (the) **barrel.** This word is elsewhere rendered "pitcher"; an earthen jar.

two sticks. That is, a *few* sticks.

13 make me thereof a little cake first. When God puts faith and self-denial to a severe test, He designs to follow it with a proportionate blessing.

18 to call my sin to remembrance. Referring probably to the general sinfulness of her heart and life, rather than to any specific sin. From the teaching of the "man of God" she had learned something of the nature and evil of sin; and now this trial awakened conscience.

19 a loft. Rather, "the upper chamber."

24 I know that thou art a man of God. Her faith in his prophetic authority was now fully assured by this fresh and convincing proof. This is, so far as we know, the first instance of any one being raised from the dead.

CHAPTER XVIII

1 In the third year. This was the third year of Elijah's residence at Zarephath, or the fourth of the famine, which lasted three years and six months: see Luke iv. 25; James v. 17.

2 Elijah went to show himself unto Ahab. As Elijah had said to Ahab that the return of rain was to be according to the prophet's word (xvii. 1), it was necessary that he should announce it to him, that it might not be regarded as a mere natural event, or as being brought about by the priests of Baal.

10 hath not sent to seek thee. Ahab had probably desired to get Elijah into his power, with the view either of inflicting vengeance upon him, or of endeavouring to compel him to procure the rain.

13 the Lord's prophets. See note on 1 Sam. x. 5.

21 if Baal, then follow him. Though the people worshipped Baal, they had never formally renounced Jehovah; nor had they ceased to regard themselves as His people. They therefore "limped on both sides." "The Lord" should here be "The Eternal."

26 they leaped upon the altar. Rather, "they danced about the altar."

27 Elijah mocked them. Ridicule is not a test of truth, but it may sometimes help to expose a mischievous absurdity.

either he is talking, etc. The heathen supposed that such things might happen to prevent the god hearing their prayers. Homer represents Thetis as waiting twelve days to ask a boon from Jupiter, when he should return from a journey (*Iliad,* i. 426).

28 they . . . cut themselves. Similar self-inflictions by heathen priests, on urgent occasions, are mentioned by Herodotus and Plutarch.

30 Come near. That the people might be satisfied that there was no deception, and become witnesses of what would follow, and prompt executors of the prophet's commands.

31 Elijah took twelve stones. To impress upon the assembled multitude the essential unity of their nation, as God's chosen people, and the proper unity of their wor[illegible]

33 he put the wood in order, etc. Elijah was not of the priestly race; but, as a prophet, he was acting under a special and direct commission from heaven: see 1 Sam. vii. 9.

Fill four barrels. By this means all suspicion of fraud was prevented.

36, 37 In this prayer Elijah expresses the great design of all the miracles which he and other prophets had performed.

38 the fire of the Lord. A similar Divine interposition had occurred on the occasion of Aaron's first sacrifice (Lev. ix. 24). As, in that instance, the Eternal solemnly accredited the *institution* of the Mosaic ritual, so here He sanctioned, in a similar manner, the prophet's attempt to restore His worship in opposition to that of Baal. See also Ex. xix. 16; 1 Chron. xxi. 26; 2 Chron. vii. 1.

40 and slew them there. It is unnecessary to suppose that Elijah did this with his own hand; for assistants would be found among the people who had seized them. These idolatrous prophets, who had been clearly convicted of deceiving the nation, were condemned to death by the law (Deut. xiii. 5, 15, 16; xvii. 5).

42 his face between his knees. A posture expressive of the profoundest reverence.

43 look toward the sea. The summit of Mount Carmel commands a very extensive view of the Mediterranean Sea.

44 a little cloud. A small black cloud on the

verge of the horizon is often the precursor of a violent storm.

46 the hand of the Lord. After his great exertions during a whole day, without time for food or rest, it would require that strength should be specially given to the prophet in order to keep pace with the king's chariot.

ran before Ahab. This proof of Elijah's humility and respect as a subject would be calculated to make a favourable impression on the king's heart; and to convince him that the prophet, in his zeal against idolatry, had been actuated by no personal disrespect or ill-will towards himself, but only by a principle of obedience to God, and an anxious concern for his country's good.

CHAPTER XIX

2 Jezebel sent a messenger unto Elijah. Jezebel s object probably was to induce Elijah to flee, not daring at present to carry her threat into execution. It is a striking evidence of the weakness of the strongest hearts that Elijah should now give way to fear.

3 And when he saw that. Some Hebrew manuscripts, with the Septuagint and Vulgate, read, "And he feared and arose," etc.

4 the wilderness. *i.e.*, of Paran; the "desert of wandering."

a juniper tree. The *retem*, a species of broom, which abounds in this district, and grows large enough to afford protection from snow and rain: see note on Gen. xxi. 15.

take away my life. The prophet, whom in the preceding chapter we have beheld on the very summit of Divinely-imparted power, now comes before us in the deepest depression. After eminent success in the service of God, we are in danger of thinking too much of ourselves; and then it is a mercy to be shown our weakness, that so we may be kept humble (see 2 Cor. xii. 8, 9). See F. W. Robertson's fine sermon on this subject, with its closing sentence: "Not in the jubilee of the myriads on Carmel, but in the humble silence of the hearts of the seven thousand, lay the proof that Elijah had not lived in vain."

6 a cake baken on the coals. "On hot stones" (R.V. marg.). This is a common repast of the Bedouin in the present day.

7 the journey is too great. Horeb is nearly two hundred miles from Beersheba; and evidently the prophet wandered in the desert with scanty supplies, if any.

8 Horeb. Horeb, as "the mount of God" (see Exod. iii. 1; xix. 10, 12), had many ancient associations calculated to revive the prophet's faith and courage.

10 Thine altars. These altars had probably been used by pious Israelites of the ten tribes, when unable to go to Jerusalem: see xviii. 30.

12 a still small voice. Elijah perhaps thought that all the work was to be done by him. He now learned that Israel had to be acted upon by other ministry besides his. He is taught also that though force and terror have their place, the still, small voice of God's word and God's Spirit is a more potent influence upon the hearts and consciences of men.

15 Go, return on thy way, etc. The answer to Elijah's complaint is this: Hazael shall be king of Syria, and shall chastise the Israelites for their iodlatry (see 2 Kings viii. 12); Jehu shall be king of Israel, and shall utterly destroy the idolatrous house of Ahab; and Elisha shall help thee whilst thou art on earth, and, when thou art gone to thy rest, shall carry on thy work.

16 Abel-meholah. "Meadow of the dance." In the valley of the Jordan, south of the Sea of Galilee: see Judges vii. 22; 1 Kings iv. 12.

18 I have left Me seven thousand. Rather, as R.V., "I will leave Me": after the fearful visitations described. "Seven thousand" may be an indefinite number. In the darkest times there may exist a hidden remnant of true servants of God.

19 twelve yoke of oxen. It would appear from this statement that Elisha was a wealthy man, who gave up his worldly possessions to consecrate himself to the Lord's service, and thus was eminently fitted for the office to which he was called by a self-denying faith.

cast his mantle upon him. This was an act of investiture with the prophetic office.

CHAPTER XX

9 this thing I may not do. Ben-hadad's first message was understood by the king of Israel merely as a demand of vassalage, and to this he tamely consented. But the second, which required the actual and immediate surrender of whatever Benhadad chose to take, was too much even for the passive Ahab, and, stimulated by his chief men, and by the general voice of the people, he resolved to make a stand.

10 if the dust of Samaria, etc. A figurative description of the numbers of his army, and the utter destruction which he would inflict upon Samaria. Ahab's pithy reply to this proud boast has become a proverb.

14 by the young men. The soldiers.

Who shall order the battle? Rather, "Who shall begin the battle, the Syrians or I?"

18 take them alive. This unusual command would greatly embarrass his troops, and contribute to the success of their assailants.

22 the return of the year. In the early spring, when the winter rains had ceased.

26 Aphek. There were two or more places named "Aphek," and it is not certain which this was; but it was probably the modern *Fik* or *Afik*, east of Jordan, overlooking the sea of Galilee (*Hastings' Dict. of the Bible*).

27 were all present. Rather, as R.V., "were victualled."

30 a wall. Rather, "the wall" (R.V.); *i.e.*, of the city.

31 are merciful kings. This is a noteworthy answer to the accusations of cruelty towards conquered enemies which are sometimes brought against the Hebrew kings.

33 Now the men, etc. Or, "And the men took it as a good omen, and they hastened and caught up what fell from him" (see R.V. marg.).

34 thou shalt make streets for thee in Damascus. *i.e.*, he gave permission to establish an Israelitish quarter in the Syrian capital.

he made a covenant with him. This conduct of Ahab arose not from any real benevolence, but from mere weakness and vanity. To liberate this faithless enemy of Israel was cruelty to his own subjects, and disobedience to the command implied in the curse: see vers. 28, 42. Cp. 1 Sam. xx. 23.

35 sons of the prophets. The phrase "sons of the prophets" occurs here for the first time. But the idea is contained in 1 Sam. x. 11, 12.

neighbour. Or "companion": one of the

sons of the prophets, like himself, who should therefore have understood " the word of the Lord."

38 with ashes. The Septuagint and the Chaldee read, " with *his headband* over his eyes," R.V. This requires a change of only one letter in the Hebrew.

42 appointed to . . . destruction. Heb., " a man of My curse." For the fulfilment of the following sentence, see xxii. 35.

CHAPTER XXI

3 the inheritance of my fathers. Naboth's refusal to part with his vineyard was avowedly grounded on religious principle. He regarded the law as forbidding him to part with his patrimony. But even if that were not so, Ahab had no right to compel the sale or exchange.

4 would eat no bread. Ahab's childish fretfulness was perhaps indulged the more in order to engage the sympathy of his wife, whom he allowed to act for him in the matter ; and she resolutely made her way to her object through the fourfold guilt of deceit, perjury, robbery, and murder.

11 And the men of his city, etc. An instance of the servility produced by high-handed despotism : cp. 2 Kings x. 1–7.

13 blaspheme. Or, " curse," as R.V. : cp. Job i. 5.

stoned him . . . that he died. That there might be no heir or avenger, his sons also were put to death : see 2 Kings ix. 26.

16 to take possession of it. He seems to have gone with some state (2 Kings ix. 25).

18 which is in Samaria. That is, " who lives at Samaria." He was not there then, for it was at Jezreel that Elijah met Ahab.

19 Hast thou killed ? A man is not the less guilty because, through weakness of character, he can act the part only of an accomplice. Ahab, in his eagerness, took possession the very day after Naboth's death.

20 sold thyself to work evil. He had surrendered himself completely to evil as its slave.

27 went softly. The severe threatening denounced against him made so much impression that, for a while at least, he behaved humbly and carefully ; and on account of this, the infliction of the full punishment was delayed till after his own death : see 2 Kings ix. 25.

CHAPTER XXII

3 Ramoth in Gilead is ours. Ramoth-gilead was one of the cities which Ben-hadad had promised to restore (xx. 34), but on regaining his freedom he had not done so.

8 Micaiah. Micaiah's name has not occurred before : but Ahab's language implies that he had previously received from him messages of rebuke and warning.

Let not the king say so. Jehoshaphat's tame rebuke of Ahab's impious speech, his silent connivance at the treatment of Micaiah (24–27), and his continued willingness to go with Ahab, show great feebleness of principle. He encouraged Ahab in his evil course. His conduct and its results present an impressive warning to those who would seek to benefit others by concessions inconsistent with their own principles.

11 horns of iron. Representing Ahab's strength and success.

15 Go, and prosper. This ironical reply, repeating the very words of the false prophets, was as much as to say, " You favour and believe your prophets who bid you go ; then go by all means, for you have their assurance of success." It is plain that Ahab saw Micaiah's real meaning, probably from his tone of voice, countenance, and gesture.

17 sheep that have not a shepherd. A proverbial expression, derived from Numb. xxvii. 17.

19 I saw the Lord, etc. This may have been either the account of an actual vision, or a parable, describing in figurative language the events shortly about to take place, under the permission of God. Compare the narrative in the first and second chapters of Job.

23 the Lord hath put a lying spirit, etc. " Not by any sudden stroke of vengeance," says Dean Stanley, " but by the very network of evil counsel which he has woven for himself, is the King of Israel to be led to his ruin." And Bishop Wordsworth says : " God punishes Ahab by means of his own sin. He ' chooses ' Ahab's ' delusions ' as the means of Ahab's destruction, and makes Ahab's own backslidings to reprove him. Ahab had preferred lies to Him who is the Truth ; and He who is the Truth will make the lies which Ahab prefers to be the instruments of punishing him who loves them, and of avenging the cause of Him who is the Truth."

30 put thou on thy robes. Although Ahab had overcome the scruples of his ally, he was evidently himself alarmed ; and, in the hope of escaping the predicted danger (17), cunningly proposes to resign the post of honour to his too easy friend ; who narrowly escaped paying the penalty of his foolish confidence ; but in the moment of extremity was saved through faith and prayer : see 2 Chron. xviii. 31.

31 Fight . . . only with the king of Israel. Such was Benhadad's return for Ahab's misplaced kindness : see xx. 34.

34 smote the king of Israel. While wicked men are calculating on the success of their devices (see 30–32), the hand of God often reaches them, and inflicts their predetermined doom.

36 every man to his own country. The Israelites appear to have made a successful retreat after their king was slain. Thus Micaiah's prophecy (17) was exactly fulfilled.

38 they washed his armour. Rather, " and the harlots bathed," see R.V. So that even his blood was treated as polluted.

39 the ivory house. That is, coated or inlaid with ivory. See Psa. xlv. 8.

43 the high places were not taken away. See xv. 14 ; 2 Chron. xv. 17.

48 the ships were broken. Probably by a storm.

49 Jehoshaphat would not. On comparing this with 2 Chron. xx. 36, 37, it appears to refer to a *second* proposal on the part of Ahaziah. Jehoshaphat, having been reproved and punished for entering into this league, would not consent to renew the attempt.

51 Ahaziah. There is a remarkable identity of names in the two royal families of Israel and Judah, during several generations, arising, no doubt, from the connexion between them by the marriage of Jehoshaphat's son with Ahab's daughter.

2 KINGS

INTRODUCTION

WHAT has been said in the Introduction to 1 Kings applies largely to this Book also. It records the reigns of fifteen kings of Judah, beginning with Ahaziah and ending with Zedekiah, and of eleven kings of Israel, beginning with Jehoram and ending with Hoshea. Of the former, Hezekiah (xviii. 1–xx. 21) and Josiah (xxii. 1–xxiii. 30) are the most notable. Jehu (ix. 2–x. 36), with his strange mixture of zeal for the Lord and following the bad example of Jeroboam, is the most memorable among the kings of Israel.

But once more it is a prophet who is the real hero of the Book. After Elijah's ascension (ii. 11) he was succeeded by Elisha. The contrast between the two great religious teachers and leaders has been well drawn by Professor Strachan (*Hastings' Dict. of the Bible*, art. "Elisha"): "Elisha is no son of the desert. Brought up at a peaceful farm in the Jordan Valley, amid the sweet charities of home (1 Kings xix. 20), he always prefers human companionship. He is generally found in cities, sojourning at Jericho among the sons of the prophets, or dwelling in his own house at Samaria or at Dothan (2 Kings vi. 13, 32). . . . Elijah's short career was memorable for a few grand and impressive scenes, Elisha's long career is marked by innumerable deeds of mercy. . . . He enters palaces not as an enemy, but as a friend and counsellor. . . . Even more than in palaces is he welcome in the homes of the people. . . . Most of his miracles are deeds of gracious and homely beneficence. . . . Yet he has his master's sternness when it is needed (iii. 13; vi. 32)."

This Book records the first invasion by the Assyrians (xv. 19) and the beginning of Jewish captivities (xvii. 6), the capture of Jerusalem by Nebuchadnezzar, the destruction of the city and temple, and the second captivity in Babylon (xxiv. 18–xxv. 21).

CHAPTER I

1 Moab rebelled against Israel. The Moabites had been subdued by David; but when the Hebrew power was weakened by the division of the kingdom, they had in great measure regained their independence. But they were subdued by Omri and Ahab, and compelled to pay a heavy tribute. Upon Ahab's ill-success and death they revolt again.

2 Baal-zebub. Literally, "Lord of flies"; *i.e.*, the Fly-god; the tutelary god of Ekron; so called because he was worshipped either under the form of a fly (like the beetle-god of the Egyptians), or as the supposed protector against such annoying insects.

3 Is it not, etc. Rather, "Is it because," etc. (R.V.); and so in vers. 6, 16.

6 a man. Though they seem not to have known Elijah, his authoritative message and manner caused them to return without further inquiry.

8 a hairy man. This refers to his dress, a garment of coarse camel's hair, like that worn by John the Baptist: see Matt. iii. 4; Mark i. 6; cp. Zech. xiii. 4.

10 consumed him and his fifty. This was a severe but well-merited rebuke of the king and people for their impious rejection of Jehovah; and a solemn admonition of His absolute control over life. The spirit of the Gospel is different (Luke ix. 55).

17 the second year of Jehoram. The chronology of this period has not at present been arranged satisfactorily.

CHAPTER II

1 Gilgal. Not the Gilgal in the valley of the Jordan (Josh. v. 9), but in the hill country of Gilgal. Here was a college of the prophets (iv. 38), also at Bethel and at Jericho. Elijah makes his final visitation to the three.

3 sons. Disciples.

7 stood to view. More literally, "stood opposite them." So in ver. 15.

8 mantle. The outward badge of the prophetic office and power (see 1 Kings xix. 19) is used here as Moses used his rod in dividing the Red Sea.

9 a double portion of thy spirit. Literally, "a double share *in* thy spirit." Apparently in allusion to the "double portion" which the first-born received in his father's inheritance (see Deut. xxi. 17). Elisha asks for himself, as inheriting Elijah's office and work, the share of a first-born in his spirit: *i.e.*, twice as much as any other "son of the prophets."

10 a hard thing. "Hard," not because of any limitation of the power and grace of God, but because of the spiritual attainments it required in the recipient: see Matt. xvii. 21.

if thou see me. This would keep Elisha's attention awake to every word and action of his departing master.

11 And it came to pass, etc. This triumphant departure (so different from what the prophet had once passionately desired, 1 Kings xix. 4) testified God's approval of Elijah's singular and devoted piety; and, like the ascension of Enoch, must have greatly helped to revive and confirm a faith in the resurrection and future glory of the saints.

12 the chariot of Israel, etc. The war chariot and its riders, which were deemed the strength of earthly kingdoms, are an emblem of the protection which God had afforded to Israel by Elijah. Elisha rightly regarded the courage, watchfulness, prayers, and Divine gifts of his predecessor as a better defence to Israel than any military force.

13 the mantle of Elijah. The prophet's mantle, transferred to his successor, becomes a pledge to Elisha of the granting of his request (10), and a visible sign to others that he was endued with the spirit, and called to the office of Elijah.

14 Where is the Lord God? etc. Literally, "Where is the Eternal, the God of Elijah?" A confident appeal to God to show His presence with him. By this miracle Elisha's commission as Elijah's successor was made known.

16 seek thy master. See 1 Kings xviii. 12. They had expected Elijah's removal; yet, remembering his sudden appearances and disappearances, they were unwilling to believe that he was really gone until they had done all they could to find him.

21 cast the salt in. In this, as in other cases, the action was only symbolical; the power being wholly in the word of the Eternal.

23 there came forth little children, etc. Rather, as R.V. marg., "young lads." The Hebrew word rendered "children" is used with an extended meaning; being applied to the reapers of Boaz (Ruth ii. 15), and to Absalom (2 Sam. xviii. 5).

CHAPTER III

2 the image. Or obelisk (R.V., "pillar").

4 sheep-master. There is an extensive grazing district in the highlands of Moab. Mesha is mentioned on the "Moabite Stone" (about 850 B.C.) discovered in 1868; where his conflicts with Israel are described from the days of Omri, forty years.

rendered unto the king of Israel, etc. Most likely the tribute consisted of the *wool* of 100,000 lambs (see Isa. xvi. 1) and of 100,000 rams: see R.V. In Eastern countries it is still customary for tribute to be paid in kind: cp. Isa. xvi. 1.

8 through the wilderness of Edom. If they had attacked Moab from the north, they would have been exposed to the Syrians in the rear and the Ammonites on the flank. By advancing from the south, through the desert that lay between Mount Seir and the Dead Sea, they would avoid these dangers, and make a junction with the king of Edom.

11 which poured water, etc. That is, who *waited on* Elijah.

13 Nay. The meaning is, "Speak not so, for the Lord has led not me only, but these other two kings also into this danger, from which He alone can deliver us."

15 bring me a minstrel. The use of music is mentioned on other occasions in connexion with Divine impulse: see 1 Sam. x. 5, 6, 10, 11.

16 Make this valley full of ditches. While the kings could do nothing to procure the supply of water, they were directed to make trenches for its reception. It was a test of faith. And so God still chooses the most unlikely places and the most unlikely persons for the operations of His grace.

19 fell every good tree. According to the law laid down in Deut. xx. 19, fruit-trees were usually spared; but in the present case no exception of this kind was to be made.

20 when the meat offering, etc. R.V., "about the time of offering the oblation"; *i.e.*, at the hour when the morning offering was presented in the Temple.

25 Kir-haraseth. The same as "Kir of Moab" (Isa. xv. 1), "Kir-haresh" (Isa. xvi. 11), and "Kir-heres" (Jer. xlviii. 31); since called *Kerak,* a strong mountain fortress celebrated in the wars of the Crusaders.

26 he took with him, etc. The king of Moab had probably at this time retreated, and shut himself up in his capital, whence he made this unsuccessful sally.

27 indignation against Israel. It is not easy to explain this. The phrase is used elsewhere of *God's* anger against a people. In this place, however, it seems to signify anger on the part of the armies of Judah and Edom that the expedition into which Israel had drawn them had led to so horrible a deed. Josephus says that these allies of Israel, shocked with the spectacle, and moved with pity, raised the siege immediately, and retired from the country (*Antiq.* ix. 3).

CHAPTER IV

1 sons of the prophets. See note on 1 Sam. x. 5. An important difference may be observed in the condition of the prophets in the kingdoms of Judah and Israel. In Judah they are mostly scattered and isolated; but in Israel they have a more compact organisation. This prophetic body in the northern kingdom, like the body of priests in the southern, counteracted, to some extent, the prevalent idolatry.

4 Shut the door. Partly perhaps to guard against intrusion, and partly to avoid display. Cp. ver. 33; Luke viii. 51, 54, etc.

8 a great woman. That is, as in the old translations, "a *rich* woman." Cp. 1 Sam. xxv. 2; 2 Sam. xix. 32.

Shunem. Where the Philistines encamped opposite Mt. Gilboa, and not far from Nain, where Christ raised the widow's son to life.

10 make a little chamber . . . on the wall. Rather, "a little wall-chamber," or "a chamber with walls."

stool. This should be "chair," or "seat," a mark of respect, as the Easterns generally sit on the floor, on a mat or carpet.

candlestick. "Lamp."

13 Wouldest thou be spoken for, etc.? *i.e.*, Hast thou any request that I can present to them for thee? The king and his general were under great obligations to Elisha (see iii. 17–25), so that he might with propriety ask a favour.

I dwell among mine own people. The meaning is, I have nothing to look for from such persons. I only desire to live quietly at home.

16 do not lie, etc. *i.e.*, Raise no hopes that must be disappointed.

23 Wherefore wilt thou go? Clearly thinking that there was not much the matter with the child.

neither new moon, nor sabbath. This indicates that it had become a custom to resort to the prophets on Sabbaths and other particular days for instruction, or to join in religious worship.

It shall be well. The Hebrew is simply " Peace." She wished to stop his inquiries, and obtain her request without giving a definite reply.

24 Slack not thy riding for me. Rather, " Slacken me not *the* riding " (R.V.), *i.e.,* my riding; for the mistress alone rode.

25 to mount Carmel. About 20 miles from Shunem.

27 hath hid it from me. The gift of prophecy did not include the supernatural revelation of every event.

28 Do not deceive me. This was enough to suggest to the prophet that the anguish of the mother arose from the loss of her son.

29 he said to Gehazi, etc. By sending Gehazi with his staff Elisha probably intended to assure the mother that he expected through the prayer of faith to be permitted to restore her son (34).

answer him not. Oriental salutations are tedious, and interfere with prompt attention to business: see Luke x. 4.

31 neither voice, etc. *i.e.,* no sign of life in the body.

35 Then he returned. Note the contrast with our Lord's miracles in the repeated efforts and prayers of the prophet: see 1 Kings xvii. 21.

39 a wild vine. Literally, " vine of the field." It is supposed to have been the colocynth-gourd (*Cucumis colocynthis* or *Cucumis prophetarum*). Its fruit is like a small water-melon.

42 Baal-shalisha. A place only mentioned here. It was to the north of Lydda. From 1 Sam. ix. 4 we gather that the " land of Shalisha " was contiguous to Mount Ephraim.

firstfruits. Carrying out the spirit of the law in Numb. xviii. 13; Deut. xviii. 4, 5; and presenting to the prophets what, if circumstances had allowed, would have been brought to the priests.

44 did eat, and left. This event faintly foreshadows two of our Lord's miracles. Elisha, however, did not perform, but predicted, this miracle, which teaches the lesson of trust in God.

CHAPTER V

2 brought away captive, etc. This is a suggestive illustration of the social miseries which idolatry had brought upon the Israelites. The subsequent narrative shows how God can honour a humble sufferer by making her, through her very calamity, an instrument for displaying His supremacy and goodness. On the leprosy, see Lev. xiii., xiv.

5 ten talents of silver, etc. Conceiving, no doubt, that his royal recommendation and his valuable presents would ensure the prophet's attention. It was therefore necessary that he should be taught that he must receive the boon he desired as God's gift, in God's way.

changes of raiment. *i.e.,* costly clothing for state or festal occasions.

7 he rent his clothes. The letter was not so unreasonable as Jehoram imagined, as the king of Syria seems to have intended only that his brother monarch should employ the power of the prophet, who would naturally be regarded by heathens as subject to his authority. Jehoram, not thinking of Elisha, sees in the letter of the Syrian king only a pretext for hostilities.

10 Go and wash. The simplicity of the means prescribed shows that it was merely a sign of the cure, and a trial of his obedience.

11 I thought, etc. Naaman expected Elisha to come out to one so high in rank and perform the cure, like the heathen conjurors, by solemn invocation and manipulations. He was therefore to be taught the superiority of the prophet of Jahveh, and to learn that he owed his cure, not to a magical touch, but only to the power of Jahveh.

12 Abana and Pharpar. The modern *Barada* and *Awaj,* the waters of which are purer and clearer than those of the Jordan.

13 some great thing. As a long pilgrimage, or the application of a heroic remedy. Naaman is a type of those to whom God's way of salvation is an offence because so simple. So the " greater things " have often been attempted, but in vain.

14 went he down. That is, from Samaria to the Jordan.

15 Behold, now I know, etc. The cure convinced him of the superiority of the Eternal, both in power and in beneficence. God thus uses the discipline of life to lead men's hearts to Himself.

16 he refused. Naaman ought, according to Eastern etiquette, to have offered his presents before he made his request; but the peculiarity of the circumstances had prevented this (see ver. 10): and now Elisha might, without any breach of courtesy, decline receiving them. It was more for the honour of God that he should show that, unlike the false prophets, he was actuated by no mercenary or selfish motives.

17 two mules' burden of earth. It is not easy to say with what particular views Naaman made this request; but in the East, *sacred ground* is most highly appreciated, and as such Naaman doubtless regarded the land of Israel, and thought that the worship of Israel's God would be most acceptable on a portion of its soil.

18 In this thing, etc. Naaman seems to have desired to obtain the prophet's sanction to this act, which he should in future perform only as one of civil service to his king, not of religious worship. There is the suggestion also of an excuse for the bowing down, the outward act being represented as inevitable when the king leaned on his hand. Such plea for outward conformity, without real consent of the heart, has not infrequently been made. The prophet neither approves nor condemns. He leaves it to Naaman's own conscience (" Go in peace " is simply " Good-bye ").

24 the tower. Heb., " the hill " (R.V.); probably a well-known hill near the prophet's house.

26 Went not mine heart [with thee]? *i.e.,* " Was I not there in spirit ? " thus intimating that the whole affair was known to him.

Is it a time to receive, etc.? The time of his country's disgrace and defeat.

oliveyards, etc. Gehazi hoped to purchase land with the property which he fraudulently obtained.

27 The leprosy, etc. This punishment was not too severe for the offence, which besides involving covetousness, fraud, and lying, tended to obscure the glory of God's grace, and to compromise the prophet's character for disinterestedness. It is affecting to see one who had been so intimately associated with such a man as Elisha manifesting a spirit so opposite: but the case of Judas is strikingly similar.

CHAPTER VI

1 the sons of the prophets. No doubt at Jericho, in the college nearest to the Jordan.

6 the iron did swim. Rather, "he made the iron to swim" (R.V.). The "stick" cast in was the sign of the miracle which was wrought by the power of God. God cares for the smaller troubles and apparently trivial details of life. The story also shows the poverty of the "sons of the prophets," and the simplicity of their habits.

13 that I may . . . fetch him. The king of Syria strangely failed to perceive that the God of Israel could disclose *this* plan to His prophet as easily as the others, and could as well protect him against it.

Dothan. See Gen. xxxvii. 17.

17 and he saw. This was, doubtless, a real and supernatural though spiritual manifestation, revealing God's protecting power.

19 This is not the way. Elisha's words must be condemned or approved by the same rule as any other stratagem by which an enemy is deceived.

20 they were in the midst of Samaria. This would show the Syrians that they could effect nothing against a prophet of the Eternal.

22 wouldest thou smite, etc.? The sense is, If you would spare those whom you have taken prisoners in battle, much more ought you to spare those whom you have not so taken. From a political point of view, this treatment of them was eminently wise, as the event showed.

23 came no more. The inroad of marauding bands ceased for some considerable time.

25 an ass's head. The ass was an unclean animal; but necessity acknowledges no law. Plutarch mentions that an extravagant price was paid for this same article by the soldiers of Artaxerxes.

dove's dung. That such revolting food has been eaten in famine may be seen in Josephus's *Wars of the Jews*, v. 13. But the meaning of the words is very doubtful. Bochart says that the Arabs give this name to a kind of pulse or pea, which was very common in Judæa, and which was preserved by being parched and dried. Linnæus supposes that it was a plant called the *Star of Bethlehem*. A "cab," or "kab," R.V., a measure nowhere else mentioned, being the sixth part of a *seah*, or about two quarts of our measure, so that the amount here mentioned was about a pint.

27 If the Lord do not help thee, etc. Or (as R.V. marg.), "Nay, let Jehovah help thee," etc.

29 boiled my son. This and other miseries had been foretold by Moses as the consequences of apostasy (Deut. xxviii. 53–57). Similar things happened during the sieges of Jerusalem by Nebuchadnezzar (see Lam. iv. 10; Ezek. v. 10) and by the Romans (Josephus's *Jewish Wars*, vi. 3, 4).

30 sackcloth. *i.e.*, in token of humiliation and repentance.

31 if the head of Elisha, etc. Because the king thought that Elisha had brought on this calamity, or that he did not exercise his power to remove it. He may, too, have advised the king not to surrender the city, promising deliverance if he would penitently "wait for the Lord" (33).

32 this son of a murderer. Jehoram, both by birth and disposition, was a genuine son of Ahab, the murderer of the prophets and of the innocent Naboth.

hold him fast at the door. R.V., "hold the door fast against him."

the sound of his master's feet behind him. The language of Elisha makes it appear probable that the king followed close upon his messenger, and that the unbelieving inquiry in the next verse was addressed by him to the prophet, to which the words of Elisha in the first verse of vii. are the direct answer: see also vii. 17.

CHAPTER VII

1 a measure of fine flour for a shekel, etc. That is, about a peck of fine flour for half-a-crown, and two pecks of barley for the same.

in the gate. Where the market was held.

2 if the Lord, etc. The language, it is plain, of incredulous scorn, with apparent allusion to the expression in Gen. vii. 11.

3 at the entering in of the gate. Lepers were excluded by law from walled cities and towns, as they had been from the camp during the journeys in the wilderness (Lev. xiii. 46).

6 Hittites. See note on 1 Kings x. 29.

Egyptians. This is now generally understood to be a mistranslation, the original word being *Muzrim* (a tribe in Cappadocia, and therefore neighbours of the Hittites in the North) and not *Mizrim* (Egyptian).

10 porter. Or, "guard," which, as the next clause implies, was composed of more than one sentinel.

13 behold, they are, etc. The meaning is, "If the men sent out to reconnoitre be taken and slain by the Syrians, they meet with no worse fate than those who are still left in the city to encounter death by famine." Some Hebrew manuscripts (and the Septuagint) omit the first clause in the parenthesis, "behold . . . in it."

14 two chariot horses. Or, "two teams of horses" (yoked to two chariots): see R.V. Moffatt has "two men on horseback."

17 charge of the gate. Holding this post, he seemed less likely than others to lose the benefit of the promised plenty.

the people trode upon him. In their eagerness to reach the Syrian camp and share in its spoils.

CHAPTER VIII

1 Then, etc. Rather, "Now Elisha had spoken" (R.V.). It would seem that Elisha said this before the events related in the two preceding chapters, and that it is mentioned here in consequence of what occurred upon the woman's return, after the restoration of plenty. From the mention of Gehazi in ver. 4, it may be inferred that these events occurred before the cure of Naaman, as afterwards Gehazi would have been in no condition to converse with a king.

the Lord hath called, etc. The famine was a Divine punishment for the idolatry of the people.

2 in the land of the Philistines. If the famine was caused by drought, the lowlands near the sea were less likely to suffer from it than the mountainous districts, and they might also obtain supplies by sea. If it was occasioned or aggravated by Syrian invasion, the Philistines in the south might be exempt.

9 forty camels' burden. To display the king's wealth and to honour the prophet.

10 Thou mayest certainly ("shalt surely," R.V.) *recover*. It means that his disease was not mortal, and would not be the cause of his death; but that nevertheless he would die.

11 until he was ashamed. This verse seems to mean that Elisha "set his eyes (*upon him*, R.V.), and kept them fixed, until [Hazael] was ashamed" at finding his purposes detected.

13 is thy servant a dog? This expression has often been interpreted as an outbreak of indignant horror at being thought capable of such atrocities.

But, considering the character and conduct of Hazael, and the spirit of the warfare of that age, it is more natural to understand the exclamation as self-depreciation, and as expressing a doubt whether a person so *inconsiderable* as he was could ever have it in his power to do such a *great* (as he himself calls it, not such an *evil*) thing. The Hebrew text stands thus: " But what! thy servant! the dog! that he should do this great work!" The R.V. translates, " But what is thy servant, which is but a dog, that he should do this great thing?" The prophet's answer is plainly calculated to remove his surprise.

15 a thick cloth. R.V., " the coverlet." " If the king's disease was, *e.g.*, erysipelas of head and face, the act, by inducing metastasis to the brain, might render the disease mortal, which otherwise it might not have been " (*Sir J. Risdon Bennett*).

16–29. Care must be taken to distinguish the Jehoram and Ahaziah of *Israel* from the kings of the same name in *Judah*.

16 Jehoshaphat being then king of Judah. This clause is not found in several ancient manuscripts and versions and appears inconsistent with 2 Chron. xxi. 1, 5. The Hebrew words are the same as the last three in the verse, " Jehoshaphat king of Judah," and were probably a transcriber's repetition.

21 This narrative is brief and obscure. It seems likely that Jehoram, advancing incautiously into the fastnesses of Edom, was surrounded, and only by a vigorous night assault broke through his enemies, so that his people regained their tents. " Zair " is thought by many expositors to be another form for *Seir*.

22 Yet (R.V. " So ") **Edom revolted.** It appears that the dominion of Judah over Edom was never completely restored. Thus was fulfilled the second part of Isaac's prediction respecting Esau in Gen. xxvii. 40. This cut off the Indian trade from Ezion-geber on the Red Sea.

Libnah. Libnah lay in the south-western lowlands. It was one of the priests' cities (see Josh. xxi. 14), and its revolt was probably caused by the introduction of the worship of Baal (see 2 Chron. xxi. 10). It was besieged by the king of Assyria in the time of Hezekiah (2 Kings xix. 8).

24 Jehoram slept with his fathers. See a fuller account of Jehoram's death and burial in 2 Chron. xxi. 18, 19.

CHAPTER IX

1 children. R.V., " sons " (disciples).

2 his brethren. *i.e.*, his comrades, his brothers in arms.

6 went into the house. *i.e.*, out of the courtyard where the council would be seated.

8 shut up and left. Rather, as R.V., " shut up and left at large "; a phrase implying *every one*: see on 1 Kings xiv. 10.

11 Ye know the man, etc. An evasive reply: " You call him a *madman*, and he speaks like one." R.V., " and what his talk was."

13 took every man his garment. It is an ancient custom to honour royal and other illustrious personages by covering the ground over which they have to pass. If there was no time for preparation the robes and mantles of the persons present were used for this purpose: see Matt. xxi. 8.

on the top of the stairs. Rather, " on the bare steps " (R.V. marg.); promptly converting the outside staircase of the house into a temporary throne.

14 had kept Ramoth-gilead. Rather, " was keeping guard at Ramoth-gilead," which the Syrians wanted to recover.

16 So Jehu rode, etc. Neither Ahaziah nor Joram knew anything of what had taken place at Ramoth-gilead, because Jehu and his captains had not allowed any one to leave the city.

18 What hast thou to do with peace? That is, What matters it to thee whether there be peace or war?

21 went out against Jehu. Rather, as in vers. 17, 18, " to meet Jehu " (R.V.).

22 whoredoms . . . witchcrafts. Referring to the licentious and superstitious practices connected with the idolatries which Jezebel had patronised.

23 turned his hands. That is, his reins, so turning his chariot round.

between his arms. Between his shoulders behind.

25 laid this burden. Rather, " pronounced this sentence "; cp. Isa. xiii. 1; xv. 1, etc.; Nahum i. 1.

27 he fled to Megiddo. From the account in 2 Chron. xxii. 9, it appears probable that Ahaziah, when wounded, fled first to Samaria, that being on the way to his own kingdom (the LXX adds, " to be healed "); and that, when discovered there, he was taken, or perhaps fled, to Megiddo, where he was slain.

29 the eleventh year. The difference of a single year between this statement and that in viii. 25 is readily explained by the different modes of computing the respective dates.

30 she painted her face. Literally, " put her eyes in paint." It is a common custom among Eastern women to tinge the edges of the eyelids with powder, prepared from antimony, which makes the eyes appear brighter and larger.

31 [Had] Zimri peace, etc.? R.V., " Is it peace, thou Zimri, thy master's murderer?" The reference is to Elah, slain by Zimri, as Jehoram was slain by Jehu.

33 trode her under foot. That is, by driving over her corpse.

CHAPTER X

1 sons. The term " sons " is often used to include all male descendants.

unto the rulers of Jezreel. The Septuagint has, " to the rulers of Samaria." Other ancient versions have, " the rulers of the city."

3 fight for your master's house. Jehu determined at once to test these officials of the court. If they opposed him, he would trust to the enthusiasm of the troops, and fight them; if they were submissive, he would use them as his tools in completing the destruction of Ahab's family.

7 slew seventy persons. R.V., more exactly, " slew them, even seventy persons."

12 the shearing house. The Septuagint and Eusebius take this to be the name of a town, *Beth-eked*.

13 We are the brethren of Ahaziah. So expeditiously had Jehu executed his measures, that even the relatives of the two kings who had been slain had not heard of their death. All the *sons* of Jehoram, excepting Ahaziah (or Jehoahaz), had been slain by the Arabians (see 2 Chron. xxi. 17; xxii. 1); but these persons were probably *nephews*, who, as belonging to the family of Ahab, fell within Jehu's commission.

14 pit. Or, " tank ": a receptacle for rainwater in which the sheep were washed before shearing. The words have also been translated "at the well of Beth-eked."

15 Rechab. The Rechabites were a branch of the Kenites (see 1 Chron. ii. 55), to whom Jethro the father-in-law of Moses, belonged; see Judges iv. 11; Jer. xxxv. *Jehonadab* is elsewhere called *Jonadab.*

Is thine heart right, etc.? *i.e.,* "Art thou as fully with me, as I am with thee?"

give me thine hand. As a pledge of amity and co-operation. Jehu was evidently glad to have the support of a man of such character and influence; and Jehonadab probably hoped to engage Jehu to restore the pure worship of Jehovah.

16 see my zeal for the Lord. Jehu was one of a large class of men, who are willing to serve God so far as they think to be consistent with their own temporal interests, and shut their eyes to commands which do not agree with their policy or inclination; see vers. 28, 29. God sometimes sees fit to use such persons for His purposes, though they have not His approbation, and obtain from Him only a temporal reward.

19 all his servants. Rather, "all his worshippers," R.V.

23 Search, etc. This order would not excite suspicion, as it seemed to indicate the greatest zeal for the worship of Baal.

25 the city of the house of Baal. Probably, with a slight variation in the Hebrew, "the shrine of the temple."

29 who made, etc. R.V., "wherewith he made."

32 cut Israel short. Literally, "to cut off in Israel," *i.e.,* to rend away parts of the kingdom; as instanced in the next verse. "Coasts," as usual, means "borders": those mentioned being wholly *inland.*

32, 33 Hazael smote them, etc. At this time, probably, Hazael inflicted the cruelties predicted by Elisha in viii. 12, 13. The territory now lost comprised nearly half of the kingdom. It was afterwards recovered by Jehoash and Jeroboam II.

CHAPTER XI

1 destroyed all the seed royal. Athaliah determined to seize the royal power; and her daring measures unwittingly fulfilled a part of the sentence (see ix. 8) against the house of Ahab which Jehu would not execute; for through her the taint of Ahab's blood had been given to the house of David.

2 Jehosheba. The wife of Jehoiada the priest (2 Chron. xxii. 11).

4 And the seventh year, etc. A fuller account is given in 2 Chron. xxiii.

the captains and the guard. R.V., "the Carites and the guard," answering to David's "Cherethites and Pelethites," "executioners and runners."

8 within the ranges. That is, within the ranks of the guards set outside the Temple.

9 every man his men, etc. The priests had been divided by David into courses, which attended at the Temple by turns. Upon this occasion those whose weekly term of service was ended were retained, in addition to those whose week of duty was beginning. So that two courses of priests, singers and porters were in the court of the Temple together: see 2 Chron. xxiii. 8.

12 the testimony. *i.e.,* The Book of the Law. The words "gave him" are not in the Hebrew, which runs "he put the crown upon him and the testimony," *i.e.,* laid it on his head, to show that he was to be "not above but beneath, the law of his country" (Dean Stanley: *Jewish Church,* ii. 397).

God save the king. Literally, "Let the king live."

16 they laid hands on her. Some render, "they made way for her" (R.V.).

the way by the which the horses came, etc. R.V., "by the way of the horses' entry into the king's house," *i.e.,* the gate leading to the stables of the palace: not the Horse gate of the city (Jer. xxxi. 40).

17 Jehoiada made a covenant. As the people had, under the preceding kings, openly forsaken Jehovah and worshipped Baal, it was necessary to renew the covenant, which both king and people had violated. At the same time the king engaged to govern the people according to the law of the Lord; and the people engaged to obey the king whom the Lord placed over them.

CHAPTER XII

4 All the money. Two kinds of dedicated money are here mentioned; namely, 1, the half-shekel paid by every one who "passed over," *i.e.,* was numbered among the people (see ver. 4, R.V. marg.); and 2, the free-will offerings.

5 the breaches of the house. The Temple had suffered, not only from neglect, but still more from injuries maliciously committed by the sons of Athaliah, who had pillaged it to enrich the temple of Baal (see 2 Chron. xxiv. 7). This holy place had been the asylum and nursery of Joash in his childhood; and, in grateful remembrance, he was now zealous for its maintenance and honour.

7 receive no [more] money, etc. The income which had been ordained for repairing the Temple had been retained by the priests and Levites.

9 Jehoiada the priest, etc. According to Chronicles, this change in the plan of collection was "at the king's commandment."

13 there were not made, etc. All the money thus collected was spent in repairs of the edifice; none of it was applied in providing vessels for the Temple service. In 2 Chron. xxiv. 14, it is stated that after the repairs were finished the offerings were again devoted to the latter purpose.

15 they reckoned not, etc. *i.e.,* no account was required of the overseers of the work, as their integrity was undoubted.

16 The trespass money and sin money. R.V., "the money for the guilt offerings and the money for the sin offerings."

17 Hazael set his face to go up to Jerusalem. This was the first appearance of the Syrian power in the southern kingdom. This invasion occurred long after the events related in the preceding part of this chapter; and during the interval, the king, with his people, had revolted from God, and he had even murdered his cousin, the son of Jehoiada, for his faithful reproofs: see 2 Chron. xxiv. 18–24.

20 which goeth down, etc. The R.V. correctly reads, "*on the way* that goeth down." "Silla" has not been identified.

CHAPTER XIII

3 all [their] days. This should be rendered "continually" (R.V.), as in 1 Sam. xviii. 29 and elsewhere; for Ben-hadad was conquered by Joash, the son of Jehoahaz.

5 a saviour. This may refer either to the victories of Joash (25), or to the invasion of Syria by the Assyrians, which caused the invading army to withdraw from Israel.

dwelt in their tents. The fear of hostile inroads had driven the country people to live in the walled towns: they now returned to their rural homes.

6 the grove. R.V., "the Asherah": see note on 1 Kings xiv. 23. This idol had probably remained from the time of Ahab (1 Kings xvi. 33), as its destruction by Jehu is not mentioned.

[Vers. 12, 13 come more naturally at the close of this chapter.]

14 over his face. *i.e.*, "over him" (R.V.). In the prospect of Elisha's departure, the king's conscience was aroused. Hence this visit, and this salutation in the very words which the dying prophet had himself addressed to the ascending Elijah.

16 Put thine hand upon the bow. As a sign that God had appointed Joash to the work of which the shooting was symbolical, and would assist him in it.

17 eastward. Towards Syria, which lay on the north and east of the kingdom of Samaria.

18 and stayed. After Elisha's encouraging assurance (17), Joash could not be ignorant of the meaning of the symbol; and his conduct showed his want of faith and perseverance.

21 cast. Terrified at the approach of the Moabites.

stood up on his feet. As the dead were only wrapt in linen and laid in the tomb, one body might touch another, and, on returning to life, would not be hindered from moving. This miracle showed that the Divine power was still operating among Israel, even after Elisha's death; and it was a pledge of the fulfilment of his dying promise of victory over the Syrians, as recorded in the following verses. It was the last manifestation of the power of God through His prophet, foreshadowing Him by whose death we live.

CHAPTER XIV

6 shall not be put to death. As would have been done according to the general practice of the surrounding nations.

7 the valley of salt. See note on 2 Sam. viii. 13.

Selah. Better known by its Greek name, Petra, which was then the metropolis of Edom or Mount Seir. "Selah," which, like Petra, signifies *a rock*, became afterwards the capital of Arabia Petræa. The houses were mostly excavations in the rock; and hence the name of the city. It is called "the strong city" (Psa. cviii. 10). See also Jer. xlix. 16; Ezek. xxxv. 7; Obad. 3. Its very remarkable ruins are still to be seen in a valley near Mount Hor, called *Wady Mousa*, or the Valley of Moses. See Professor Hull's *Mount Seir, Sinai and Western Palestine* (1889).

Ioktheel. Which means, "subdued by God." This name was retained as long as the place remained under the dominion of the kings of Judah.

8 saying, Come, etc. Amaziah's challenge appears to have been prompted partly by revenge for the outrages committed by the Israelitish soldiers whom he had dismissed (see 2 Chron. xxv. 13), and partly by the elation consequent upon his victory over Edom; and he was given up to his pride and folly as a punishment for his idolatry: see 2 Chron. xxv. 14–20.

14 hostages. Probably as pledges of Amaziah's good conduct, instead of retaining him prisoner. This is the only instance of hostages in Scripture, but the practice was in use among the Persians, Greeks, and Romans.

21 Azariah. Often called Uzziah (xv. 13, etc., and Chron.). The two names, though derived from different words, are nearly synonymous; Uzziah referring to the *strength*, and Azariah to the *help* of Jahveh.

22 built. "Rebuilt." See 1 Kings ix. 26.

23 Jeroboam. The reign of Jeroboam II. was the longest, and outwardly the most prosperous, of any of the kings of Israel, for he regained possession of the land on the north and east (25), and made the Syrians tributary (28). Before its close, the prophets HOSEA and AMOS were sent to the people of Israel (see Hos. i. 1; Amos i. 1; vii. 10), reproving them for their sins, especially their idolatry, warning them against relying upon foreign help, and foretelling captivity under the Assyrians, if they persisted in their wickedness; yet inviting them to repentance by offers of mercy.

24 who made, etc. Rather, as R.V., "wherewith he made." So xv. 9, etc.

25 Hamath. On the Orontes. It had belonged to Israel in the time of David and Solomon.

the Sea of the Plain. "Of the Arabah" (R.V.); the Dead Sea.

the Lord God of Israel. More literally, "the Eternal, the God of Israel," as elsewhere.

Jonah. Evidently that prophet, the account of whose mission to Nineveh has come down to us. His errand to the Assyrians manifests the same Divine forbearance which is here shown towards the Israelites.

Gath-hepher. Near Nazareth, probably at the place now called *El-Meshad.*

CHAPTER XV

5 a several house. It probably means "detached." The Jewish writers conclude that this was outside the city, according to the law. The cause of this infliction is stated in 2 Chron. xxvi. 16–20. Jotham his son seems to have occupied the palace, and to have acted as regent from the commencement of his father's leprosy to his death.

10 before the people. "At Ibleam" (Sept.).

14 Menahem. Josephus says that Menahem was commander-in-chief: *Antiq.* ix. 11, 1. He seems to have been a vigorous general, who, after gaining the throne, made a successful raid upon Syria, as far as Tiphsah, or Thapsacus, on the Euphrates (see 1 Kings iv. 24). But this brought upon him the Assyrians, who had for some time been pushing their conquests westward.

19 Pul. Pul, or Pulu, was a military adventurer of low origin, who seized the throne of Assyria 745 B.C., and assumed the name of Tiglath-pileser III. (see Sayce's *Assyria: its Princes, Priests, and People*, pp. 43, 44). His reign, however, was one of great progress. He inaugurated many reforms in administration and in the army. For his new name see ch. xvi, 10. A corrupt form of the name, "Tilgath-pilneser," appears in 1 Chron. v. 26 and 2 Chron. xxviii. 20.

25 Argob and Arieh. These seem to have been two of the king's officers who were killed with him by the conspirators.

29 carried them captive to Assyria. According to the policy pursued by the Eastern conquerors, the flower of the newly-conquered nation was sent beyond the Euphrates, to people the thinly-inhabited parts of the Assyrian empire; and when this process was completed, new settlers were brought from the East to occupy the land (xvii. 24). The facts mentioned in ver. 29, and in xvii. 6, 24, agree remarkably with the cuneiform inscriptions discovered at Nineveh, which contain accounts of the campaigns of the Assyrian kings; describing them always as first invoking their gods, then defeating the enemy, subjugating the country, carrying off the inhabitants with their most valuable effects to Assyria, replacing them with colonists drawn from their immediate subjects, and appointing their own officers to take charge of the colonists and to govern the country. This was the *first* captivity, or exile of Israel, which included the tribes east of Jordan and the northern part of Canaan; but it was not sufficient to humble the "pride and stoutness" of the inhabitants of Samaria: see Isa. ix. 9. The Assyrian inscriptions fix the date of this captivity at 734 B.C.

32 Jotham. In his reign MICAH and ISAIAH exercised their prophetic ministry, which continued through the reigns of Ahaz and Hezekiah. The first five chapters of Isaiah seem to belong to the reign of Uzziah: see notes, Isa. i. 1; vi. 1.

35 built. He *repaired* it, for it existed long before.

37 Rezin . . . Pekah. Their confederacy against Judah forms the subject of Isa. vii.

CHAPTER XVI

2 Twenty. In the parallel passage, 2 Chron. xxviii. 1, the Vatican manuscript of the Septuagint, with the Syriac and Arabic, read *twenty-five*, which is more probable.

3 to pass through the fire. Some suppose this phrase to indicate not a sacrificial act, but a ceremony of purification; but from xvii. 31; Psa. cvi. 38; Jer. vii. 31; Ezek. xvi. 20; xxiii. 37, it appears that children were actually sacrificed, being sometimes first slain, and then burned: see note on Lev. xx. 2. Ahaz not only followed the worst kings of the house of Omri in worshipping Baal (2 Chron. xxviii. 2), but he practised the cruel rites of Moloch.

4 he sacrificed, etc. The first five chapters of Isaiah throw much light upon the state of the people at this period.

5 Then Rezin, etc. Further particulars of this invasion are given in 2 Chron. xxviii. 6–15.

6 recovered Elath. Elath on the Red Sea.

Jews. This is the first instance in which we find the name Jews; literally *Judæans, i.e.*, men of Judah.

the Syrians. Better read "Edomites." The two words differ in Hebrew only by the similar letters, ד and ר. There is no evidence that the Syrians had ever owned Elath.

7 I am thy servant. That is, "I will be tributary to thee, and place myself under thy protection," preferring to apply to any one rather than to God. But his sin brought its own punishment; for, while he purchased a temporary deliverance from the Syrians, he only changed his oppressor.

9 Kir. See Amos i. 5; ix. 7. "Kir" has not been absolutely identified. There is no mention of it in the cuneiform inscriptions. Professor Max Müller thinks it may have been east of the Lower and Middle Tigris (*Hastings' Dict. of the Bible*).

11 built an altar. It is not said that this new altar was used for idolatrous purposes. It appears at first to have been employed for the offerings prescribed by the law; but it was an unauthorised innovation in the worship of Jehovah. From 2 Chron. xxviii. 23, however, we learn that Ahaz actually "sacrificed unto the gods of Damascus"; proceeding to suspend the Temple worship, and multiplying altars, both in Jerusalem and throughout Judah.

16 Thus did Urijah. Obeying the king rather than God. A contrast with the noble conduct of his predecessor, Azariah, 2 Chron. xxvi. 17, 18.

18 covert. "The covered way for the Sabbath" (R.V.).

from. Rather, "unto" the house of the Lord, as R.V. The approaches to the Temple were "turned," or perhaps "changed," "because of the king of Assyria."

20 in the city of David. According to 2 Chron. xxviii. 27, not in the royal tombs.

CHAPTER XVII

2 not as the kings, etc. Of all the other Israelite kings (Shallum excepted, whose reign was only thirty days), it is expressly stated that they maintained the calf-worship of Jeroboam; but this sin is nowhere attributed to Hoshea, though he was otherwise a bad man.

4 So king of Egypt. It is generally believed that "So" is a form of Sabako or Shabaka, a king of the Ethiopian (25th) dynasty of Egypt. Moffatt substitutes "Seve" for "So." Other scholars think that instead of *Mizraim* (Egypt) the Hebrew should read *Muṣri*, part of North Arabia, and identify "So" with "Sibi," a king of that people.

5 besieged it three years. We have no particulars of this siege; but the character of the invaders, as described by prophets (see Hos. x. 14; Nah. ii. 12, 13; iii. 1) and historians, and the sculptures discovered in the remains of Assyrian cities, combine to show that it must have been a time of extreme suffering; especially when the city was captured, and given up, according to the usual practice, to indiscriminate pillage and slaughter.

6 the king of Assyria. It was by Sargon (Isa. xx. 1) that the city was taken, and he records its capture in the great inscription given by Botta. Sargon was succeeded by his son Sennacherib. See Sayce: *Assyria: its Princes, Priests and People.*

carried Israel away. This was the second captivity of Israel (721 B.C.), which included chiefly the inhabitants of the central part of Canaan: see also xviii. 11. For the former captivity, see xv. 29.

the river of Gozan. The word "by" is not in the Hebrew, which has "on Habor the river of Gozan," Habor or Khabour being a well-known river in Upper Mesopotamia, running into the Euphrates.

7 For so it was, that, etc. Rather, as R.V., "And it was so, because," etc. The inspired writer, in concluding the history of the northern kingdom, carefully traces this awful catastrophe to its cause—the obstinate wickedness of the people. The evil began with Jeroboam's political idolatry, from which the people had gone on to the grosser worship of Baal and Ashtaroth; and had in consequence committed (as the writings of the contemporary prophets show) the most scandalous sins—oppression and robbery, violence and cruelty, gluttony and debauchery. They had continued in this downward course for more than two hundred years; though often checked by startling and even miraculous interpositions of Divine Providence. Famine, war, and pestilence had been repeatedly inflicted upon them; and a long succession of faithful men of God had warned them of the impending danger; but all had been in vain.

And now that the people had utterly failed to accomplish the great object for which Jehovah had separated them for Himself, and instead of being witnesses to the world of the spirituality and perfection of His nature, had dishonoured His holy name, He gave them up into the hand of their enemies, and removed them out of their place. This is a solemn lesson to other nations, to whom God has given a still fuller and clearer revelation of His character and will.

10 images and groves. R.V., "pillars and Asherim:" see notes on Judges ii. 13; iii. 7.

13 and against Judah. A brief intimation that Judah, sharing the sins and rebukes, would have to share the punishment; as the following narrative soon shows.

15 against them. Rather, as R.V., "unto them."

vanity. See Deut. xxxii. 21, and note.

16 a grove. Rather, "an Asherah" (R.V.): see note on 1 Kings xiv. 23.

23 unto this day. They were there also at the time when the Book of Chronicles was written (see 1 Chron. v. 26), which was probably much later than this book. Since that time the people of Israel have never reappeared in a national character as distinct from Judah. Some of their descendants joined the Jewish exiles who returned to Jerusalem after the Babylonish captivity; but the greater portion of them remained (as did also many of the people of Judah) scattered among the nations in the countries to which they had been carried: see Acts ii. 5, 9). Jerome, in the fifth century of the Christian era, who resided for twenty years in Palestine, and was well acquainted with the East, says, "Unto this day the ten tribes are subject to the kings of the Persians; nor has their captivity ever been loosed: they inhabit at this day the cities and mountains of the Medes." Many of them appear to have been brought as settlers to Antioch, and other cities in Asia Minor.

24 Cuthah. "Cuthah" is mentioned as *Kuti*, in the Assyrian inscriptions. It has been identified with the modern Tell-Ibrâhim, near Babylon, and a temple of Nergal (see v. 30) has been found there. An image of Nergal is in the British Museum.

Avah has not been identified.

Hamath, on the Orontes, was called Epiphaneia by the Greeks and Romans. See Numb. xxxiv. 8; 1 Kings viii. 65; 2 Chron. viii. 4; Amos vi. 2.

Sepharvaim. "The two Sippars." Sippar of the Sun-god was discovered in 1881 by Rassam at Abu-Habba on the Euphrates, 16 miles S.E. of Baghdad.

instead of the children of Israel. This does not mean that *all* the Israelites were carried away, but that they were no longer the principal inhabitants of the land. It is evident, from 2 Chron. xxxiv. 6, that many of them were left, as was afterwards the case in the kingdom of Judah: cp. xxiv. 12–16 with xxv. 12, 22. Their descendants became incorporated with those of the heathen colonists; and this mixed population was afterwards known by the name of *Samaritans.* They became bitter enemies of the Jews: see Ezra iv. and Neh. iv.

25 the Lord sent lions among them. The lions, which had always existed in the land (see Judges xiv. 5; 1 Sam. xvii. 34; 1 Kings xiii. 24), became so numerous through its depopulation as to terrify the colonists. The author speaks of this as a Divine judgement (see Lev. xxvi. 22; Deut. xxxii. 24; and cp. Exod. xxiii. 29).

27 one of the priests. This was apparently not a priest of the race of Aaron, but one of those who had ministered at the high places. The result of this proceeding was a mixed worship of false gods and of Jahveh. In later times the Samaritans gave up idolatry, and professed to worship Jahveh, and to regard His law as given by Moses; but they rejected all the later sacred writings. In these respects, and in the annual offering of the paschal lamb on Mount Gerizim. the remnant of the people, who still inhabit *Nablous,* the ancient Shechem, resemble their ancestors.

32 of the lowest of them. Rather, "from among themselves" (R.V.): see note on 1 Kings xii. 31.

33 from thence. Literally, "from whom they were removed": see R.V.

34 they fear not the Lord. The first clause here is explained by the second. These people did not fear and worship the Lord *only,* according to His law: but, joining their own idolatry with His worship, might be truly said not to fear Him.

41 unto this day. This book, therefore, must have been compiled before the inhabitants of Northern Palestine had given up their idolatries, and had fully submitted to the law of Moses. They wished to join in rebuilding the Temple after the return from Babylon (Ezra iv. 2); and they established a rival worship on Mount Gerizim about 409 B.C., when they probably finally gave up idolatry: see note on Neh. xiii. 28.

CHAPTER XVIII

4 brake in pieces the brazen serpent. The destruction of so venerable a memorial of a remarkable fact in the national history shows the wisdom and energy of Hezekiah's piety. "The superstitious veneration paid to sacred relics in the Christian Church, especially the adoration paid to the form of the cross, and even in express words to the wood and the nails of it, with all the impostures which have arisen from that absurd idolatry, have been exactly parallel to the worship of the brazen serpent; and Hezekiah's example fully authorises the total abolition or disuse of everything of that kind in religious worship."—*Scott.*

he called it. Rather, "it was called." *Nehushtan* means "a copper thing."

5 none like him. A usual phrase for remarkable excellence; the same expression being used respecting Josiah (xxiii. 25). David is commonly represented as the model of a Hebrew king.

7 served him not. Entering into the spirit of the theocracy, and depending upon the help of the Eternal (ver. 5), he refused the submission which his father had yielded to the king of Assyria. To do this, when that monarch's power was growing and his attention was directed to Palestine, was an act of unusual faith.

10 they took it. *i.e.,* the Assyrians under Sargon: see note, xvii. 6.

13 the fourteenth year of king Hezekiah. On the chronological difficulty of this statement, see note on Isa. xxxvi. 1. The invasion by Sennacherib was probably in the *twenty-fourth* year of Hezekiah's reign. In the fourteenth, Sargon, father of Sennacherib, appears from the Assyrian inscriptions to have been still upon the throne.

Monumental inscriptions discovered at Kouyunjik (the probable site of Nineveh), and now in the British Museum, record Sennacherib's campaigns against Judah. "Hezekiah, king of Judah," says the Assyrian king, "who had not submitted to my authority, forty-six of his principal cities and fortresses, and villages depending upon them, of which I took no account, I captured, and carried away their spoil. I shut up himself, like a bird in a cage, within Jerusalem, his royal city," etc. He says further, that he added a tribute, and also took from Hezekiah the treasure he had collected in Jerusalem, thirty talents of gold, and eight hundred talents of silver, the treasures of his palace, besides his sons and his daughters, and his male and female servants or slaves, and brought them to Nineveh (2 Kings xviii. 14–16). (See Sayce: *Assyria : its Princes, Priests and People.*) One chamber of the palace contains a sculptured representation of the king, and above his head this inscription: "Sennacherib, the mighty king, king of the country of Assyria, sitting on the throne of judgement, before (or at the entrance of) the city of Lachish; I give permission for its slaughter." And on the bas-reliefs are represented captives, whose physiognomy is apparently Jewish, in an attitude of supplication, bare-footed, and half-clothed.

and took them. In 2 Chron. xxxii. 1, it is said that he "thought" to subdue them unto himself. He certainly did not take *all* the fenced cities; for Jerusalem and Libnah, at least, were not taken.

14 Lachish. Lachish was identified by Flinders Petrie in 1890 as Tel-el-Hesy. It is between Jerusalem and Gaza. Sennacherib was now besieging this place (2 Chron. xxxii. 9); and, while there, he sent part of his forces to Jerusalem, to summon Hezekiah to surrender.

15 Hezekiah gave him, etc. Hezekiah's faith, when put to a severe test, at first failed; and he purchased an expensive and ignominious peace, becoming again a vassal of the Assyrian king; but his faith soon regained its power: see 2 Chron. xxxii. 2–8.

17 And the king of Assyria, etc. This invasion by Sennacherib followed that by Sargon at an interval of some years; and it is supposed that the illness of Hezekiah, related in xx. 1–19, occurred in the interval.

Tartan and Rabsaris and Rab-shakeh. These three names are *official*, not *personal.* "The Tartan," was the general commanding the royal body-guard; "the Rabsaris" the chief eunuch, or chamberlain; and "the Rab-shakeh" the chief cupbearer.

21 this bruised reed. That is, not broken, but cracked; *really* though not *apparently* injured, and thus incapable of yielding the support expected from it. The *reed* was a peculiarly fit symbol of Egypt, as it grew plentifully in that country.

22 hath taken away. This refers to the removal of the "high places," which had been effected by Hezekiah, and which to the heathen must have appeared an act of impiety towards the God of the land.

23 give pledges. Or, "make a bargain: if you can find the horsemen I will find them horses." A taunt aimed at their military feebleness.

25 The Lord said to me, etc. The Rab-shakeh may have heard that the prophets had announced the Assyrian invasions as a judgement on Judah; or he may have made the false boast to terrify the people into submission.

26 the Syrian language. Or, "Aramaic." Through a great part of the Assyrian monarchy, especially on the west of the Euphrates, the Aramaic or Syriac was spoken by the people; and the Assyrians must have been familiar with it.

the Jews' language. That is, the Hebrew.

27 that they may eat, etc. The utmost extremities of famine, to which the people should be reduced in the threatened siege.

30 neither let Hezekiah, etc. The Assyrian had before endeavoured to excite fears of Jehovah's anger; he now insinuates mistrust of Divine protection. The enemies of God's people can only succeed by shaking their confidence in His grace and power.

34 Hamath, and of Arpad. See xvii. 24.

37 their clothes rent. See note on Gen. xxxvii. 34.

CHAPTER XIX

1 went into the house of the Lord. Hezekiah's faith prompted him to refer this cause to the Eternal, whom he had always acknowledged as his Sovereign, and had made it his chief care to serve and honour (see 2 Chron. xxix.–xxxi.), and against whom Rab-shakeh's blasphemies were directed.

2 Isaiah. The first mention in this history of the great prophet's name. But he had evidently before this taken an active part in counselling king and people.

3 rebuke. Rather, "chastisement"; *i.e.,* Divine correction: see 2 Chron. xxxii.

4 the living God. In contrast to the gods of the surrounding nations, with whom the Assyrian had blasphemously confounded Him.

for the remnant. This expression probably refers to Jerusalem, and the few fortresses, with their inhabitants, which had as yet escaped the general desolation: see Isa. i. 8.

7 I will send a blast. The Hebrew word here used is generally rendered "wind" or "spirit." "I will put a spirit in him" (R.V.); *i.e.,* "I will make him alter his feelings and purposes."

a rumour. This is generally supposed to refer to the report of Tirhakah's approach (9). As Sennacherib only took occasion from that to utter fresh blasphemies (10–13), God inflicted upon him, as He had formerly done upon Pharaoh, a most terrible punishment.

8 Libnah. Its site has not yet been identified.

9 Tirhakah. Tirhakah was the last king but one of the Ethiopian or 25th dynasty of Egypt.

10 Thus shall ye speak, etc. Sennacherib wished to induce Hezekiah to capitulate before the Ethiopians arrived, or perhaps before the Jews heard of their approach.

12 my fathers have destroyed. See xvii. 5, 24.

Thelasar. "The Hill of Asshur." The exact site, though probably on the Euphrates, has not been identified.

13 Hamath, etc. See note on xvii. 24.

14 spread it before the Lord. Implying that childlike confidence which impels the believer to lay open all his concerns before the all-seeing God.

15 And Hezekiah prayed. In this prayer Hezekiah, like Solomon (1 Kings viii. 23), recognises at once God's special protection of His people, and His universal presence and sovereignty over all things.

18 cast their gods into the fire. A frequent practice of the Eastern conquerors, unlike the policy of the Romans, who admitted the gods of the nations whom they conquered among their own. See Psa. cxv.; Jer. x. 3, 9, 15.

21 hath shaken her head. In token of scorn and exultation: see Psa. xxii. 7; xliv. 14; Lam. ii. 15; Matt. xxvii. 39.

23 and hast said, etc. A specimen is given, in the prophet's words, of the vaunting language which Sennacherib dared to employ. No obstacle had hitherto impeded him in his progress.

the lodgings, etc. R.V., "his farthest lodging-place, the forest of his fruitful field." *Carmel* means *orchard* or *fruitful field* as in Isa. xxix. 17.

24 all the rivers of besieged places. Better, "all the rivers of Egypt" (R.V.). The proud king boasts that he can easily overcome the obstacles which opposed his expedition against Egypt. In the wilderness he digs, and drinks foreign waters; and the rivers of Egypt are to dry up under the tramp of his feet. The past tense is used only to denote the assumed certainty of the anticipated event.

25 Hast thou not heard, etc. Read, "Hast thou not heard? Long ago I have done it; and from the days of old I have fashioned it." God's answer to the boastful monarch. "Be not proud of thy victories: thou art merely an instrument in My hand by which I have punished wicked cities, as I long ago had determined and have predicted by My prophets": see Isa. x. 5, 6.

27 thy abode, etc. These expressions signify *all the actions of his life*, as in Psa. cxxxix. 2, etc.

28 thy tumult, etc. Rather, "thy arrogance," see R.V.

hook. Or, "ring." It was customary to put a ring in the nose of wild animals, and is still done in our own country with bulls, for the purpose of curbing and governing them: see Job xli. 1, 2; and some Assyrian and Babylonian sculptures represented prisoners as so treated.

29 a sign unto thee. God's message now turns from the invader to Hezekiah and his people, promising them an entire deliverance from the Assyrians, and assuring them, as a sign or pledge of that event, that there should be an abundant supply of provisions for two years, from the spontaneous productions of the land.

30 bear fruit upward. Like an olive, which, when cut down, sends up fresh and fertile shoots.

32 nor shoot, etc. The sculptures at Nineveh contain representations of the Assyrian methods of conducting a siege, which are in exact accordance with these words.

35 the angel of the Lord went out. Some have supposed that this destruction was effected by a pestilence, some by a storm of hail, and others by a destructive wind; see note on ver. 7. But it seems best to understand the term "angel" as meaning a celestial agent, divinely commissioned to accomplish this work of judgement and deliverance, who may, however, have made use of some secondary cause (see 2 Sam. xxiv. 15, 16; Acts xii. 23). The Egyptians (to whom also this supernatural interposition was a timely deliverance) preserved the tradition of it, though in a greatly corrupted form: see Herodotus, b. 2, c. 41. This event appears to be commemorated in Psa. lxxvi.: see note on its title. Where the Assyrian army was, is not ascertained. The inscriptions at Nineveh take no notice of Sennacherib's unsuccessful attempt upon Jerusalem, or of the catastrophe. Naturally, the Assyrians do not record their own defeat.

when they ("men," R.V.) **arose early in the morning.** That is, *at the time of rising* in the morning. See Byron's poem on "The Destruction of Sennacherib's Host."

36 dwelt at Nineveh. According to the Assyrian chronology he reigned eighteen years after this time; and the records show that he made many expeditions, but not into Judæa.

37 Nisroch. This name is believed by Mr. T. G. Pinches, of the British Museum, following Schrader, to be a corruption of Asshur or Asuraku.

Armenia. In the original, "Ararat," so R.V. (see Gen. viii. 4).

CHAPTER XX

1 In those days. As Hezekiah survived this sickness fifteen years, and reigned altogether nearly twenty-nine, this must have been in the fourteenth year of his reign, about the time of the Assyrian invasion under Sargon: see on xviii. 17. The chapter falls naturally at the end of ch. xviii.

thou shalt die. Implying that Hezekiah's disorder was *in itself* incurable, and must have terminated in death, but for the miraculous cure which was granted in answer to his prayer.

3 with a perfect heart. Hezekiah's general conduct was thoroughly consistent with his knowledge and professed piety. He probably refers here especially to his public conduct, and his efforts to establish and maintain the worship of Jehovah.

7 lump of figs. Poultices of figs have long been used, especially in the East, for the cure of inflammatory swellings. Thus God gave an extraordinary effect to the use of ordinary means.

boil. The Hebrew word means, literally, an inflammation (Job ii. 7); in this case, as has been suggested by high medical authority, perhaps an abscess in the throat, or "quinsey," symptoms of which are pain in the bones (Isa. xxxviii. 13) and hoarseness (14): see *Diseases of the Bible*, by Sir J. R. Bennett.

11 dial. The same Hebrew word is translated "degrees" in vers. 9, 10, and in other passages "steps." Hence it is supposed that the "dial" consisted of a kind of *staircase* with a pillar on the top, so constructed that the step on which the shadow fell indicated the hour of the day. Similar step-dials may be seen at Delhi and Benares. The recession of the shadow, in whatever way it was effected, was clearly miraculous. God alone could foretell or effect it. Herodotus states that the Greeks obtained the knowledge of the dial, and the division of the day into twelve parts, from the Babylonians. It is not at all unlikely that Ahaz, who appears to have been fond of foreign objects of art (see xvi. 10), obtained a dial amongst them.

12 Berodach-baladan. He is called, in Isa. xxxix. 1, "Merodach-baladan," deriving his name from a Babylonian deity, Bal or Bel (see Jer. l. 2; Isa. xlvi. 1).

sent letters. We learn from 2 Chron. xxxii. 31 that an account of the miracle just narrated had reached Babylon. Such a wonder was peculiarly fitted to excite the curiosity of a scientific people like the Chaldeans.

13 hearkened unto them. Or, "was glad about them" (see Isa. xxxix. 2). The words in Hebrew differ by only one letter, ע and ח, very similar in sound. This embassage and present from Babylon proved too powerful an assailant for Hezekiah's heart, and put him off his guard: see 2 Chron. xxxii. 31.

the silver and the gold, etc. If the embassy from Babylon preceded Sennacherib's invasion, as seems likely, there is no difficulty in accounting for these treasures. Hezekiah's vanity was particularly culpable, as this embassy afforded a good opportunity of honouring Him who had wrought the miracle and the cure; but this he neglected to do.

17 shall be carried into Babylon. The punishment was to be inflicted through the very people who had occasioned his sin. This is the first explicit prediction of the Babylonian exile, although it had been hinted at before. It was partly fulfilled in the captivity of Manasseh (2 Chron. xxxiii. 11), and in the reign of Zedekiah it was fully accomplished (2 Chron. xxxvi. 18).

19 Good is the word. While the king acquiesces in the judgement as righteous and deserved, he gratefully acknowledges the mercy shown in the postponement of the catastrophe.

CHAPTER XXI

3 Baal. See notes on Judges ii. 11, 13; 1 Kings xv. 13. The worship of stars seems to have been of Chaldean origin. Manasseh not only restored the high places, and imitated Ahab in the worship of Baal, but introduced the star-worship of the Sabæans and the cruel rites of Moloch; and, worst of all, he placed an obscene Asherah image in the Temple of Jehovah.

a grove. "Asherah" (R.V.); see note on 1 Kings xiv. 23.

6 observed times. Or rather, "practised augury" (R.V.): see Lev. xix. 31.

7 a graven image of the grove. Rather, "the image of Asherah, or Astarte": see R.V.

9 Manasseh seduced them. This national relapse into idolatry, so quickly after Hezekiah had laboured earnestly to root it out, indicates that the reformation was in most cases only external, without a real change of heart Every true revival is accompanied by much superficial amendment, followed by collapse.

10 the prophets. Besides Isaiah, some of the "minor prophets" were living in this reign, and perhaps others whose messages have not been preserved.

13 the house of Ahab. As the king and people of Judah had followed Ahab's sins (see ver. 3), so they should share the doom of his family and kingdom.

I will stretch over Jerusalem the line, etc. "I will measure Jerusalem for destruction" (*Moffatt*).

will wipe Jerusalem. This expression denotes its complete desolation and destruction.

14 forsake. Rather, "cast off," as R.V.

the remnant of Mine inheritance. *i.e.,* the kingdom of Judah, as the only remaining portion of God's peculiar people.

16 shed innocent blood. Apostasy is usually accompanied by a fierce and persecuting spirit. The Jews have a tradition that the prophet Isaiah was sawn asunder by the king's command. Josephus says that "Manasseh cruelly slew all the righteous men among the Hebrews; nor would he spare the prophets, but every day slew some of them: so that Jerusalem was overflowed with blood" (*Antiq.* x. 3).

17 the acts of Manasseh. We learn from 2 Chron. xxxiii. 11 that Manasseh was taken prisoner by the Assyrians, and carried to Babylon, and that there he repented and sought God, and was afterwards restored to his kingdom, probably as a tributary to the king of Assyria (see xxiii. 29). Manasseh's name appears on Assyrian inscriptions.

23 slew the king. This private assassination, probably the result of court intrigue, was evidently displeasing to the people at large, who still venerated the royal line of David.

CHAPTER XXII

2 turned not aside. A strong commendation given to none but Josiah: cp. 1 Kings xv. 5.

3 in the eighteenth year. Probably the eighteenth year is here mentioned as the date of the most prominent event in this reformation, which must have occupied a considerable period. It may have been the time when the Book of the Law was brought to the king.

8 the book of the law. This may have been the original copy of the law of Moses (see 2 Chron. xxxiv. 14), or of the covenant which was renewed with the people in the plains of Moab; for they were laid up beside the ark (see Deut. xxxi. 24-26). It is probable that during the reigns of Manasseh and Amon the reading of the Scriptures had been prohibited, and generally given up. "The suggestion that Hilkiah forged the book and pretended to discover it is unworthy of consideration" (Dr. Foakes Jackson in *Peake's Commentary*). The narrative plainly shows that the existence of the book was known, and its character at once recognised.

11 he rent his clothes. The passages read to the king were probably, among others, the threatenings and curses of the law against its transgressors (Lev. xxvi., or Deut. xxviii.). It would seem that Josiah had never before heard them, though many copies of the law had been made under the direction of Hezekiah. To account for this, it is supposed that the people generally at that time were satisfied with abstracts, containing only a sort of ritual directing them in the outward observances of religion.

14 in the college. Literally, "in the second." R.V., "in the second quarter": *i.e.* of the city.

17 they have forsaken Me. From the whole tenor of the history, as well as from the testimony of the prophets JEREMIAH and ZEPHANIAH, who lived at this period, it is evident that the zealous reformation of Josiah had not been heartily complied with by the people, especially by the chief men, and that the nation generally were impenitent, and ripening fast for judgement. The earlier prophecies of Jeremiah, which were probably delivered during the time of Josiah, give us much insight into the moral and religious state of the kingdom of Judah at a time when the worship of God was maintained by the authority of the crown, and idolatry was punishable with death.

20 in peace. That is, before the destruction of Jerusalem and the overthrow of the kingdom. None of Josiah's successors had a royal funeral in Jerusalem. These predictions seem to have further quickened the king's zeal: see xxiii.

CHAPTER XXIII

3 stood to the covenant. *i.e.,* they gave their assent and adhesion to it.

4 This purification appears, from 2 Chron. xxxiv., to have been begun before the finding and public reading of the law; but it was probably not completed till afterwards, and therefore the whole is placed together here.

of the second order. The inferior priests.

the grove. ("Asherah," R.V.): see 1 Kings xiv. 23, and note; and so vers. 6 and 7.

unto Beth-el. Sending the impure to a place which had long ago been polluted by the calf-worship.

5 the idolatrous priests. Heb., *Chemarim:* see Zeph. i. 4.

to the planets. The Hebrew word here used, *Mazzaloth* (also *Mazzaroth,* Job xxxviii. 32), means "the resting-places" of the sun, *i.e.*, the twelve signs of the Zodiac.

7 hangings. Literally, "houses"; probably meaning the tents in which the Asherah were placed.

8 the high places of the gates. Altars with pagan images were probably erected at the city gates, that passers-by might be induced to worship and make offerings there.

10 Hinnom. Sometimes called simply "Gai Hinnom" (the valley of Hinnom), whence the Greek *Gehenna*. The name "Topheth" is understood by the best authorities to mean a place of *burning*. This place having been the scene of the cruel worship of Moloch, Josiah caused it to be polluted by throwing into it the dead bodies of animals and the offal of the city. This practice being continued afterwards, fires were lighted in the valley to consume the carcases, and thus prevent the noxious effects which might otherwise have arisen. Hence the place was called the *Gehenna* of fire; and was regarded by the Jews as representing the place of punishment for the wicked, where it is emphatically said by our Lord (quoting from Isaiah), "their worm dieth not, and the fire is not quenched" (Isa. lxvi. 24; Mark ix. 44).

11 he took away the horses. The ancient Persians, who were sun-worshippers, dedicated to the sun white horses and chariots, which were paraded on solemn occasions. The Jews seem to have adopted this practice, together with the sun-worship, from the Assyrians, in the reigns of Ahaz, Manasseh, and Amon.

12 on the top. That is, on the roof (R.V.). The roofs of the houses were used by the Persians for the worship of the heavenly bodies.

13 the mount of corruption. By this designation is meant the southern end of the Mount of Olives, called the mount of corruption, or "of offence," on account of the idolatrous worship practised thereon.

14 with the bones of men. See 1 Kings xiii. 2.

17 title. Rather "stone" or "pillar," marking the place of a sepulchre. (R.V., "monument.")

22 such a passover. This passover is described more fully in 2 Chron. xxxv. 1–9.

24 familiar spirits. See note on xxi. 6; Deut. xxviii. 10.

images. "Teraphim" (R.V.). See Gen. xxxi. 19.

25 like unto him, etc. See note on xviii. 5.

26 Notwithstanding, etc. The frequent interchange of relapse and reformation, according to the will of the sovereign for the time being, shows that the habits of the people had become thoroughly depraved, and that idolatry, whether with or without royal patronage, was deeply rooted in the public mind. Cp. Jer. iii. 10; viii. 3–7, etc.

29 Pharaoh-nechoh. Herodotus (ii. 159) mentions this expedition of Necos (Pharaoh-nechoh), and says that he defeated the Syrians (Jews) at Magdolus (Megiddo), and took a large city, Kadytis (Chald. *Qaditha*, "the holy," *i.e.*, Jerusalem).

Josiah went against him. Josiah probably was compelled, as a tributary to the king of Assyria, to oppose the progress of the Egyptian army.

30 dead. He was mortally wounded. It appears, from the fuller narrative in 2 Chron. xxxv. 24, that when Josiah had been wounded at Megiddo, he was put into another chariot, and brought either dying or already dead to Jerusalem.

Jehoahaz. Jehoahaz is called "Shallum" by Jeremiah (xxii. 11). He appears to have been more popular than his elder brother Jehoiakim.

32 his fathers. Not his own father Josiah, but his more remote ancestors, referred to so often in this chapter; and so in ver. 37.

33 Riblah. Nechoh seems to have had him brought from Jerusalem (2 Chron. xxxvi. 3) to Riblah. Riblah (now *Ribleh*, a small village) lay on the Orontes, near the northern end of the valley between Lebanon and Hermon.

Hamath. See xvii. 24.

34 Eliakim. Eliakim was Josiah's second son (1 Chron. iii. 15). The eldest, Johanan, was perhaps dead. After defeating Josiah's army, Nechoh took Carchemish, and on his return, treating Judæa as a conquered province, he exercised his supremacy by appointing Eliakim as his deputy, and changed his name, to mark him as his vassal. The same was done by Nebuchadnezzar (xxiv. 17). Jehoiakim's character is portrayed in the darkest colours by Jeremiah (xxii. 13–19).

CHAPTER XXIV

6 slept with his fathers. See Jer. xxii. 18, 19, and note.

8 Jehoiachin. In 1 Chron. iii. 16 he is called "Jeconiah," and in Jer. xxii. 24 "Coniah." As he reigned only three months as a mere vassal of the king of Babylon, his reign is scarcely reckoned, and therefore it was said of Jehoiakim his father (Jer. xxxvi. 30), "he shall have none to sit upon the throne of David."

10 the servants. *i.e.*, his generals. When the city was about to surrender, Nebuchadnezzar came himself (11).

13 the treasures of the house of the Lord. The people were assured by the false prophets that these sacred vessels should be brought back; but God told them by His prophet (Jer. xxvii. 16–22) that, instead of these being restored, the rest should follow, as they did (see xxv. 13–17). Nebuchadnezzar spoiled the Temple three times: 1, when he took Jerusalem in the reign of Jehoiakim (see Dan. i. 2); 2, when he came the second time, in that of Jeconiah; and 3, when he captured it in that of Zedekiah (xxv. 13).

14 all Jerusalem. That is, all those specified afterwards. He stripped the city of all its available defenders.

16 men of might. This enumeration is evidently supplementary to that in ver. 14. Combining the two, the total number of persons now transported may be thus summed up: princes, or chiefs, and warriors, 10,000; persons of property, 7,000; craftsmen and smiths, 1,000; making a total of 18,000.

19 he did that which was evil. He appears to have been a man of weak character, and entirely led by his nobles: see Jer. xxxviii. 5, 24.

20 from His presence. Some divide the sentence here, and read, "For through the anger of the Lord came this" (viz., the succession of the weak and wicked Zedekiah) "in Jerusalem and Judah until He had cast them out from His presence." Then the narrative contained in the next chapter begins thus, "And Zedekiah rebelled," etc. (see R.V.).

rebelled. Relying upon the aid of the king of Egypt: see Jer. xxxvii. 7.

CHAPTER XXV

2 the city was besieged. Jerusalem was strong by nature, and had been so fortified by art that Nebuchadnezzar was only able to reduce it by a blockade which lasted eighteen months, causing

famine in the city. The terrible sufferings of the besieged are described in Lam. iv. 3–10; Ezek. iv. 16; v. 10. See also Jer. xxi.; xxiv.; xxvii.–xxxiv.; xxxvii.–xxxix.; lii.

4 the plain. The Arabah (R.V.): see David's flight in 2 Sam. xv. 28, etc.

6 they gave judgement. This was a just retribution on Zedekiah for the breach of his oath, and his disregard of the merciful counsel of God; see Jer. xxxviii. 17; xxxii. 5; xxxiv. 3; Ezek. xvii. 15.

7 they slew the sons. And, according to Jer. xxxix. 6 and lii. 10, all the "nobles" or "princes" of Judah.

put out the eyes. The loss of sight was intended not only as a punishment, but also to incapacitate him from ever being king again. In the king's blindness, two apparently inconsistent prophecies (Jer. xxxii. 4; Ezek. xii. 13) were both literally fulfilled.

8 the seventh day. In Jer. lii. 12 it is the *tenth* day of the month. Josephus says that it was on the same day of the same month that the second Temple was burned by the Romans. From this period to the completion of the second Temple, under Darius Hystaspis, was seventy years.

9 he burnt the house of the Lord. The ark of the covenant was probably burned with the Temple, for it is never mentioned afterwards; showing how little God cares for the outward ceremonial when the inward spirit of religion is gone: see Jer. vii. 4, 13–15. The prophet Jeremiah was present, and beheld the sad accomplishment of his early predictions, in the horrors of the famine and the carnage, and the plunder and destruction of the city and Temple; and has recorded his feelings in his pathetic elegies: see 2 Chron. xxxvi. 17–19, and Lamentations.

11 did Nebuzar-adan . . . carry away. This formed the *third* stage in the captivity of Judah.

12 left of the poor of the land. Poverty is sometimes a protection. The poor ("the poorest," R.V.), formerly oppressed, have now liberty and peace, while their oppressors are sent into captivity.

19 that were in the king's presence ("that saw the king's face," R.V.). That is, his confidential advisers.

22 These events are more fully related by the prophet Jeremiah, who witnessed them: see Jer. xl.–xlv., and notes.

27 Evil-merodach. Son and successor of Nebuchadnezzar; mentioned in Old Testament only here and in Jer. lii. 31. He reigned two years.

did lift up the head, etc. An act of grace at the beginning of his reign.

28 the kings that were with him. Other captive monarchs.

---

1 CHRONICLES

INTRODUCTION

ALTHOUGH the Books of Chronicles record many of the events which are narrated in Samuel and Kings, there are differences in the standpoint and in the emphasis. After the division of the kingdom into two, Chronicles relates only the history of Judah. Considerable attention is given in Book 1 to genealogies (i.–ix.), a fact which those acquainted with the ideas of the East will readily understand. The arrangements made by David for the tabernacle worship are given in detail (xv., xvi.), as, later, those for the services of the Temple (xxiii.–xxv.). David's farewell instructions to Solomon are recorded in chap. xxviii.; his appeal to the people, with their magnificent response, is given in xxix. 1–9; and his impressive prayer before all the congregation in xxix. 10–19.

In the Hebrew Bible, 1 and 2 Chronicles are one book, and are included in the *Kethubim* ("writings") or *Hagiographa*. Most scholars are now agreed that they were written by the author or final editor of the Book of Ezra. This in itself throws light upon the motive and purpose of Chronicles as distinct from the Books of Samuel and Kings. To a people whose national history had been interrupted by the Captivity, it was of importance to link them up again with their own great past. This is done in the genealogies. It was important also to impress upon them the supreme importance of spiritual worship as the centre and bond of their national unity and well-being. This is done in the account of the bringing up of the ark, the worship of the tabernacle, David's plans for the building of the Temple, and the evil results of departing from God (in Book 1, see especially x. 13, 14; xv.–xvii., xxii., xxiii. 27–32; xxviii., xxix.).

CHAPTER I

1 Adam. It is the peculiar glory of Jewish history, that, whereas the earliest accounts of all other nations are involved in obscurity and fable, this can be clearly traced along an unbroken line to the very commencement of the human race. The genealogies which occupy i.-ix. are mostly repeated from other parts of sacred history, though with considerable additions.

5 sons of Japheth. See Gen. x. and notes. The apparent discrepancies between these genealogies and other parts of Scripture seem to have arisen from the following causes. In some instances, errors or omissions have been made in transcribing; in others, grandsons and remoter descendants are mentioned as sons; in others, again, the successor of a man in his property or titles is called his son; sometimes the same person appears with names varying more or less; and sometimes the same Hebrew word has been, by the English translators of 1611, spelt differently in different places. The R.V. has removed most of these discrepancies. In some instances the Hebrew is different in the two lists, similar letters being occasionally interchanged, as ד *d* and ר *r*. Thus we have in many copies "Diphath" and "Rodanim" for "Riphath" and "Dodanim" (see Gen. x. 3). So in v. 41, "Amram" (or "Hamram," R.V.) corresponds to "Hemdan," Gen. xxvi. 26; and in v. 46 "Hadad" is "Hadar" in Gen. xxxvi. 39.

11-16 And Mizraim, etc. These verses correspond exactly with Gen. x. 13-18.

17 sons of Shem. This genealogy agrees substantially with that in Gen. x.; but the words "the children of Aram," in Gen. x. 23 are left out here, so that Uz, Hul, Gether, and Meshech (Gen., Mash), *grandsons* of Shem, appear as his *sons*.

24-26 Shem, Arphaxad, etc. An abbreviation of the genealogy in Gen. xi. 10, etc.

29 These are their generations. Cp. Gen. xxv. 13-27.

32 sons of Keturah. Cp. Gen. xxv. 1-4.

35-54 sons of Esau, etc. The rest of this chapter should be compared with Gen. xxxvi.

CHAPTER II

2 Dan. Dan, the elder son of Bilhah, is placed here after the sons of Leah, and before those of Rachel, apparently because Rachel had adopted him as her own son (Gen. xxx. 6).

6 Zimri. Probably the same as Zabdi, the father of Carmi: cp. ver. 7 and Josh. vii. 17, 18.

18 Caleb. The "Chelubai" of ver. 9; where the Septuagint has "Caleb." This verse is obscure. It seems that only Caleb's children by Jerioth are here mentioned. But the Vulgate, Syriac, and Arabic versions make Jerioth the daughter of Caleb by Azubah, and the persons subsequently named the sons of Jerioth: see ver. 42. From this 18th verse the genealogy is peculiar to Chronicles.

22 Jair. See Numb. xxxii. 41; Deut. iii. 14, 15; Judges x. 3, 4, and notes.

23 towns of Jair. Rather, "Havoth-jair" (R.V., villages).

25 and Ahijah. The "and" is omitted in R.V. Possibly the word *by* should be understood, Ahijah being the first wife, and Atarah (26) the second.

35 gave his daughter to Jarha. This is the only instance recorded in Scripture of the marriage of a foreign slave to his master's daughter. The object doubtless was to preserve the inheritance in the family. It would appear that, though by the law, in Numb. xxvii. an heiress in her own right could not marry an Israelite of another tribe, she might marry a foreigner, if he were a proselyte, as this caused no confusion of inheritances. One of Sheshan's posterity, Zabad, is mentioned in xi. 41 among David's chief men, and is there styled "the son (*i.e.*, descendant) of Ahlai," the daughter of Sheshan, ver. 31.

42 sons of Caleb. This genealogy of Caleb's family is very obscure. It contains names of several places in the hills and in the western lowlands of Judah: cp. ver. 18. The word "father" before the name of a place may mean "founder." Thus, Mesha established a settlement in Ziph, Maon in Bethzur, etc.

50 the son of Hur. This should begin a new sentence, indicating a new line of the family: "The son (LXX 'sons') of Hur, the firstborn," etc. Hur was the son of Caleb, by Ephrath, or Ephratah: see ver. 19; cp. iv. 4.

54 the house of Joab. Instead of "the house of Joab," it should be "Beth-Joab," as it is the name of a place: see R.V.

55 Kenites. We have no information as to the way in which the Kenites, related to Moses' wife, became intermingled with this branch of the tribe of Judah. See Judges i. 16; Jer. xxxv. 2.

CHAPTER III

1 sons of David. This line is now carried on from ii. 17. The descendants of David are more particularly recorded than any others, as being not only the royal family of Judah, but also the family "of whom as concerning the flesh Christ came" (Rom. i. 3; ix. 5).

Daniel. Called Chileab in 2 Sam. iii. 3.

5 these were born, etc. We have two other lists of David's sons, agreeing in the main with this: see 2 Sam. v. 14, 16; 1 Chron. xiv. 4-7. From comparing these lists, it seems likely that the first Eliphelet and Nogah died in childhood.

Bath-shua. A form of Bath-sheba.

15 sons of Josiah. Of Josiah's sons only the three younger appear in the subsequent history; probably the firstborn, Johanan, died early. Some, indeed, suppose that the son of Josiah mentioned in 2 Kings xxiii. 30 is Johanan; but, from Jer. xxii. 11, we learn that it was Shallum who succeeded Josiah, under the name Jehoahaz. He was *third* in age, although here put *fourth*.

16 Zedekiah his son. Zedekiah was *successor* to his nephew Jehoiachin or Jeconiah. The word "son" may be here used, as elsewhere, meaning successor, to keep up the form of the genealogy begun in ver. 10, and only interrupted in ver. 15 to introduce the four sons of Josiah.

17 Assir. As the word "Assir" means *captive*, the sentence may be read thus: "The sons of Jeconiah the captive (see R.V.) were Salathiel," etc. Respecting this king, Jeremiah prophesied, "Write this man childless" (Jer. xxii. 30); which is supposed to mean that no son of his would succeed him on the throne.

Salathiel. "Shealtiel," R.V. In Luke iii. 27 we learn that Salathiel was the son of Neri, of the family of Nathan. But as the royal branch failed in Jehoiachin, he became heir, and is called *son*. He, too, had no son; and therefore Zerubbabel, the son of his brother Pedaiah (19), became heir, and is called his son: see Ezra v. 2.

CHAPTER IV

1 The sons of Judah. Chapter iv. 1–23 contains genealogical fragments connected with families in the tribe of Judah. Most of the names are otherwise unknown; and in some cases there are errors, which cannot at present be corrected. This is also the case in subsequent chapters.

9 Jabez. This remarkable man, whose parentage is not recorded, probably lived soon after the Israelites took possession of Canaan: and when they were greatly harassed by the remnant of the ancient inhabitants, Jabez showed his piety by desiring the full possession of the promised inheritance, and by seeking it from God through prayer.

10 that it may not grieve me. Or " that I may be *sorrowful* no more"; alluding to the signification of his name.

14 Charashim. (R.V., " Ge-harashim.") Founder of the valley of " craftsmen" or " artificers." See Neh. xi. 35. It has been conjectured that it is now *Hirsha*, a ruined town near Lydda.

18 these are the sons of Bithiah. There is some confusion here, which may be removed by a slight transposition thus: " These are the sons of Bithiah the daughter of Pharaoh, which Mered took; she bare him Miriam, and Shammai, and Ishbah the father of Eshtemoa; whose wife the Jewess bare Jered the father of Gedor," etc.

19 his wife Hodiah. Rather, as R.V., " the wife of Hodiah."

23 those that dwelt among plants and hedges. Rather, as R.V., " the inhabitants of Netaim and Gederah."

38 princes. Or, " chiefs."

41 habitations. "The *Meunim*" (R.V.); cp. Judges x. 12 (Maonites); 2 Chron. xxvi. 7.

43 that were escaped. The descendants of those who had escaped in the wars with Saul and David.

CHAPTER V

2 the chief ruler. The two rights of primogeniture—the *sovereignty* and a *double portion* of the inheritance—were divided between Judah and Joseph: see note on Gen. xlviii. 5; xlix. 8.

10 Hagarites. Or, " Hagarenes," descendants of Hagar; a branch of the Ishmaelites, appropriating the maternal name. A further account of a successful raid is given in vers. 18–22. The enmity between Hebrews and Hagarenes appears in Psa. lxxxiii. 5–8.

17 Jotham . . . and . . . Jeroboam. As these two kings were not contemporaries, there were evidently two registrations.

CHAPTER VI

5 Uzzi. Josephus (*Antiquities*, v. 11, 5) says that after Uzzi the high-priesthood went into the family of Ithamar; and his statement is confirmed by the fact that five generations are given from Uzzi and Eli to Zadok and Abiathar, who were contemporary: see note on 1 Sam. ii. 35. The list of the high-priestly family (4–15) is evidently shortened, and the names of some eminent members are omitted: cp. 2 Chron. xxiii.; xxvi. 17; xxxi. 10.

14 Seraiah. Seraiah was high priest at the capture of Jerusalem, and was put to death by Nebuchadnezzar.

22 The sons of Kohath. It appears from Numb. xxvi. 11 that Korah's sons did not perish with him; and from vers. 27–33 below, that among his descendants were Samuel the prophet and Herman the singer.

28 Vashni. The name of " Joel" appears to have been lost out of the text here (see 1 Sam. viii. 2), and the word " vashni," which signifies *and the second*, and applies to Abiah, is made into a proper name: see R.V.

33 Heman. Heman was grandson to Samuel (here called " Shemuel," which is a literal transcript of the Hebrew), the prophet and judge.

39 Asaph. Asaph and Heman were both Levites; but the one was descended from Gershom, the other from Kohath.

54 dwelling places. The race of Aaron all resided in the district allotted to the two tribes of Judah and Benjamin.

castles. Rather, as R.V., " according to their encampments."

60 thirteen cities. Only eleven are here named; two others, Jutta and Gibeon, are mentioned in Josh. xxi. 16, 17. These had perhaps ceased to exist when this book was written. The list of Levitical cities given in the remainder of this chapter should be compared with Josh. xxi., which appears, from internal and collateral evidence, to be the more accurate text.

77 the rest, etc. Rather, "to the children of Merari, the rest *of the Levites*" (R.V.), the Kohathites and Gershonites being already provided for.

CHAPTER VII

6 The sons of Benjamin. On comparing this with Gen. xlvi. 21 and Numb. xxvi. 38, it is evident that the term *son* is applied both to immediate and to more remote descendants.

7 the sons of Bela. Descendants.

14, 15 whom she (R.V., his wife) **bare.** Moffatt translates: " The children of Manasseh, borne to him by an Aramite concubine, were Machir," etc.

24 built. Probably she enlarged or fortified them.

CHAPTER VIII

1 Benjamin. The term *sons* is here employed with the usual latitude of meaning.

28 dwelt in Jerusalem. Probably after the exile at Babylon. It appears from Neh. xi. 1, 2, that residence at Jerusalem was for some time after the return of the Jews reckoned a proof of patriotism, as, in consequence of the unsettled state of the country, the capital was a post of danger. From a comparison of that account with this, it seems that they both relate to the same period—namely, *after* the exile: see note on ix. 2.

33 Ner begat Kish. Saul's pedigree is carried higher in xi. 35–39 and 1 Sam. ix. 1. There Kish is said to be the " son" of Jehiel or Abiel; but he was his *grandson*, as appears from 1 Sam. xiv. 51.

CHAPTER IX

1 kings of Israel and Judah. The verse may best be divided thus . . . " the kings of Israel: and Judah was carried away," etc.: see R.V. This statement ends the enumeration in ch. viii. With verse 2 a new section begins, relating to the post-exilian times.

2 the first inhabitants. This corresponds in the main with the enumeration in Neh. xi. 3; only in the latter is added, " the children of Solomon's servants"; and some of the names differ, either because they are variously written, or because the two writers, in condensing the registers, select different persons from the list of ancestors: cp. ver. 12 with Neh. xi. 12. By "first inhabitants" are evidently meant those who first returned from Babylon, and took up their abode in the cities of Judæa, especially in Jerusalem.

13 very able men. The same Hebrew words are translated in Neh. xi. 14, "mighty men of valour"; but the rendering here is no doubt the correct one, as the phrase is intended to express their capability for the Temple-service, and not for warlike enterprises.

16 Netophathites. Cp. Neh. xii. 28, 29, where it is said, "the singers had builded them villages round about Jerusalem."

19 keepers of the entry. As their fathers had been in the wilderness, at the tabernacle, under the government of Phinehas.

22 Samuel. It seems that Samuel had made some new regulations respecting the attendance of the Levites, before David established that systematic arrangement which was maintained for many ages.

33 the singers. The singers were free from the laborious work of the sanctuary, having to maintain constantly the service of praise. This verse and the next seem a recapitulation of the preceding account. The persons mentioned (vers. 14–16) were "singers." Ver. 34, according to R.V., reads, "These were heads of fathers'-houses of the Levites," etc.

CHAPTER X

6 all his house died together. All his sons who were in the battle were slain; see 1 Sam. xxxi. 6. Ish-bosheth, and some others who were not there, survived.

9 to carry tidings. Or, as in 1 Sam. xxxi. 9, "to publish." The Hebrew words are the same.

10 in the house of their gods. In the house of Ashtaroth (1 Sam. xxxi. 10). So David had deposited Goliath's sword in the tabernacle as a trophy.

13 against the word of the Lord. Saul had broken God's law by offering sacrifice (1 Sam. xiii. 13); and still more by sparing the king and the spoil of the Amalekites (1 Sam. xv. 11).

for asking counsel, etc. Though Saul did at first inquire of the Lord, yet when he received no answer (1 Sam. xxviii. 6), because God was displeased with him, instead of repenting and confessing his past sins, he went to the woman at Endor.

CHAPTER XI

1 all Israel. The narrative of David's reign omits his rule over Judah (2 Sam. ii.–iv.), and begins with the extension of his power over all Israel. Vers. 1–9 correspond with the narrative in 2 Sam. v. 1–10; and vers. 10–47 with the list of heroes in 2 Sam. xxiii. 8–39.

8 Millo. See Judges ix. 6; 2 Sam. v. 9.

10 These also are the chief. See 2 Sam. xxiii. 8.

strengthened themselves with him. Or, "shewed themselves strong with him," R.V. (*i.e.*, on his side).

11 Hachmonite. In xxvii. 2 he is called "son of Zabdiel," who probably was his immediate father, of the family of Hachmoni. R.V., "son of a Hachmonite."

three hundred. The account in 2 Sam. gives 800: another instance of the variation in numbers, due no doubt to copyists.

12 the three mighties. From 2 Sam. xxiii. 8–12 it appears that these three heroes were Jashobeam ("the Tachmonite"), Eleazar, and *Shammah.* But in this place both Eleazar's achievement and Shammah's name have been omitted (probably through an oversight of a copyist, arising from the repetition of the words "the Philistines were gathered together"); so that the exploit which was really performed by Shammah is ascribed to Eleazar.

22 many acts. Rather, "mighty deeds," R.V.

slew a lion. See notes on the parallel passage, 2 Sam. xxiii. 20.

26 the valiant men of the armies. The variations in the two lists (cp. 2 Sam. xxiii. 24–39) may probably be explained by some difference in the period to which they respectively refer. The present (47 names) is the earlier list, that in 2 Sam. (31 names) the later.

CHAPTER XII

1 these are they that came, etc. This chapter contains four lists, not found in 2 Sam.: 1, of those who came to David in Ziklag (1–7), 1 Sam. xxvii. 6, etc.; 2, of the Gadites and others who had previously come to him in Adullam (8–18), 1 Sam. xxii. 1, 2; 3, of those from Manasseh who adhered to him when with the Philistine king Achish, and accompanied him on his dismissal (19–22), 1 Sam. xxvii., xxix.; 4, of the great gathering that afterwards made him king in Hebron (23–40), 2 Sam. v.

kept himself close. When he was unable to appear in public in Israel, on account of Saul.

2 even of Saul's brethren. This was the more remarkable because as Benjamites they were of the same tribe with Saul: see ver. 29.

Benjamin. The Benjamites were noted for being able to use either hand with equal facility; or for using the left hand (as in the case of Ehud, Judges iii. 15) instead of the right (Judges xx. 16).

3 Antothite. From Anathoth, a priests' city: see Jer. i. 1.

8 into the hold to the wilderness. Rather, as R.V., to the hold in the wilderness, doubtless Adullam: 1 Sam. xxii. 1, 2.

buckler. Rather, "spear" (R.V.), as in ver. 24. These were bold and agile, light armed, fit for guerilla warfare.

16 the hold. *i.e.*, Adullam, as in ver. 8.

17 betray me to mine enemies. David probably at first doubted the intentions of the Benjamites, because Saul was of that tribe: see ver. 2. This accession from the tribe of Benjamin appears to have been the earlier of the two.

18 the spirit came upon. Heb., "clothed." In the two similar passages the full phrase "Spirit of God" is used: see Judges vi. 34; 2 Chron. xxiv. 20. Amasai is moved to take David's part because it is God's cause.

19 upon advisement. Or, "by counsel"; *i.e.*, upon deliberation.

22 like the host of God. Rather, "like a host of God"; a common Hebraism denoting a very large and powerful host.

23 came to David. That is, after the death of Ish-bosheth (2 Sam. iv. 5).

26 the children of Levi. The Levites upon this occasion, as upon some others, came out as warriors.

27 Jehoiada. Abiathar was then high priest, and Jehoiada was captain over the warriors of the house of Aaron. Benaiah, the commander of David's body-guard, and chief general in Solomon's army, was his son.

29 had kept the ward. Rather, "had kept their allegiance," as R.V.

32 had understanding. Equivalent to "understanding the signs of the times." Cp. Matt. xvi. 3. The tribe of Issachar seems to have sent only its chiefs; but they were to express the unanimous assent of the people; who appear to have had entire confidence in the political wisdom of their leaders.

33 could keep rank, etc. R.V., "that could order *the battle array, and were* not of double heart." They were well disciplined and had a single purpose.

38 with a perfect heart. *i.e.,* with sincere loyalty.

39 prepared for them. *i.e.,* brought them provisions.

CHAPTER XIII

2 all the congregation. *i.e.,* the assembly of the "captains and leaders," as representing the nation; in accordance with whose decision David afterwards convened the people (vers. 4, 5).

5 Shihor of Egypt. Called elsewhere the "river of Egypt"; the modern *Wady-el-Arish*; the southern boundary of Palestine (see Josh. xiii. 3).

the entering of Hemath. Or, "the pass of Hamath," the northern frontier of the land (Numb. xxxiv. 8).

6–14 David went up, etc. See 2 Sam. vi. 2–11.

CHAPTER XIV

2 because of His people Israel. That is, *for the sake of* His people Israel.

4 his children. This list should be compared with those in 2 Sam. v. 14–16; 1 Chron. iii. 1–9.

9 the valley of Rephaim. See 2 Sam. v. 18, etc.

CHAPTER XV

1 prepared a place for the ark. See 2 Sam. vi. 12, etc., and notes.

2 ought to carry. The fact that the ark was thus carried is briefly recorded in 2 Sam. vi. 13. Here, and in ver. 13, David confesses that it was wrong to carry it in any other way. And accordingly a full account is given of the priests and Levites who took part in the service (vers. 5–24).

20 Alamoth. "On Alamoth" (virgins), *i.e.,* soprano voices: see Psa. xlvi., title.

21 Sheminith. For bass voices. See Psa. vi., title.

22 song. The Hebrew word is almost always rendered "burden." In the literal sense, this would refer to the carriage or transport of the ark and sacred vessels; and this agrees with the next verse.

28 making a noise. Rather, "with sounding cymbals, with psalteries," etc. R.V., "sounding aloud."

CHAPTER XVI

4 to record. Or, "to mention," as in Isa. lxiii. 7; *i.e.,* "to celebrate."

7 delivered first this psalm. Literally, "gave first to praise the Lord into the hand," etc.; *i.e.,* then for the first time committed this duty to them: see R.V. Portions of this psalm reappear in Psa. cv., xcvi., cvi., on which see notes.

37 he left there. See note on 2 Sam. vi. 17. The ark and the tabernacle had been separated ever since the time of Eli. Asaph and his brethren were attached to the ark as singers; while Heman and Jeduthun acted in the same capacity at the tabernacle (vers. 41, 43), which was now at Gibeon.

42 musical instruments of God. That is, *for the praise* of God.

CHAPTER XVII

For notes on this chapter, see on 2 Sam. vii.

5 from tent to tent. This alludes to the various removals of the ark from place to place.

24 Let it even, etc. "And let Thy name be established, and magnified for ever" (R.V.).

27 let it please Thee. Rather, as R.V., "it hath pleased Thee": referring the passage to the Messiah.

CHAPTER XVIII

1 David smote the Philistines. See notes on 2 Sam. viii.

8 Tibhath and . . . Chun. Called "Betah and Berothai" in 2 Sam. viii. 8.

CHAPTER XIX

See 2 Sam. x., and notes.

6 Mesopotamia. Heb., "Aram-Naharaim" (Gen. xxiv. 10). As compared with the parallel passages, this seems to show a westward movement of the Syrian tribes.

17 came upon them. In 2 Sam. x. 17 it is "came to Helam."

18 seven thousand. In 2 Sam. x. 18 the number is "seven hundred."

CHAPTER XX

This chapter contains a brief summary of the *political* events related in 2 Sam. xi.–xiii.; omitting David's personal and family history.

1 the power of the army. *i.e.,* the whole army, all the men available for warfare.

8 by the hand, etc. Perhaps, "by the hand of David, even by the hand of his servants," whose acts are naturally spoken of as his.

CHAPTER XXI

Chapters xxi.–xxii. 1 resemble 2 Sam. xxiv. The likeness is less close than in other narratives of this book, showing that the accounts are independent.

1 Satan. The word "Satan" signifies simply *an adversary;* but it evidently refers to the evil spirit, who tempts men to sin: see 2 Sam. xxiv. 1.

5 Joab gave the sum, etc. See note on 2 Sam. xxiv. 2.

a thousand thousand, etc. The difference between the numbers here and in 2 Sam. xxiv. 9 is not easily explained; but probably some were included in one account who were omitted in the other.

6 Levi and Benjamin counted he not. It appears from xxvii. 24 that the census was not completed, which accounts for the omission of two tribes. From what is said of the strong repugnance of Joab to the measure, it appears likely that he succeeded at length in dissuading David from proceeding with it.

7 therefore. Rather, "and." Not only Joab but God was displeased, and showed His anger by smiting Israel, as will soon be related: see notes on 2 Sam. xxiv. 14–17.

15 Ornan. Also called (with variations in the Hebrew spelling) "Araunah."

25 six hundred shekels of gold. Rather above £1,000 sterling. This sum, specified as given for "the place," was probably paid for the whole estate, which David purchased as the site for the

Temple. The smaller sum, " fifty shekels of silver " (2 Sam. xxiv. 24), if not a corruption of the text, was the value of " the threshing-floor and the oxen."

29 in the high place at Gibeon. Cp. xvi. 39, 40.

30 he was afraid. David had dreaded to go to sacrifice at Gibeon, but was now encouraged by the Divine mark of acceptance of his sacrifice ; and so proceeded to dedicate this spot as the site of the Temple (xxii. 1), and to prepare for the building (2).

CHAPTER XXII

1 This is the house, etc. Meaning, " This is the site of the house," etc.

2 the strangers. *i.e.*, not Hebrews, but chiefly the descendants of the Canaanites. These were gathered in order to be numbered and registered, that they might be employed in preparing for the Temple : see the next clause, and 2 Chron. ii. 17, 18.

5 young and tender. Probably about eighteen years of age.

10 He shall build a house. The circumstance that a *peaceful* prince was appointed to build the Temple (9) reminds us that it was designed to show God's " thoughts of peace " towards sinful man, and carries forward our thoughts to Him who is styled " the Prince of peace " (Isa. ix. 6), and is emphatically called " our peace."

13 be strong, and of good courage. Compare the words of Moses to the Israelites and to Joshua. An inspiring formula, handed down from age to age !

14 in my trouble. Or, " with great pains " (*Moffatt*).

CHAPTER XXIII

1 So when David, etc. These few words comprise the substance of the narrative contained in 1 Kings i.

3 thirty and eight thousand. The Levites had quadrupled since the census in the time of Moses (see Numb. xxvi.). At that time the males above a month old amounted to 23,000 ; now those above thirty years old amounted to 38,000. This great increase in their number, as well as in the population of Israel, required the new organisation which is described in this and the three succeeding chapters, and which was fully carried into effect after the erection of the Temple. The greater part, to the number of 24,000, were engaged in the sacrificial and other duties of the Temple. These served a thousand in each week, so making twenty-four courses in all. Others, to the number of 6,000, were judges and officers in the country districts ; others were porters to guard the Temple ; and others, singers or musicians.

11 Zizah. The same as " Zina " in the preceding verse : the corresponding Hebrew letters closely resemble each other : ז and נ.

14 concerning Moses, etc. We read very little of the descendants of Moses, although it might be expected that they would be held in great honour ; and one of them was in an office of great trust and responsibility (xxvi. 24). From this verse it appears that, unlike the priestly family of Aaron, they took the position of ordinary Levites.

22 brethren. That is, " kinsmen " : see note on Gen. xxix. 12.

took them. According to the law in Numb. xxvii. 8 ; xxxvi. 5–9.

25 that they may dwell, etc. Rather, " And He dwelleth." R.V.

27 from twenty years old. The Levites, being now released from that which had originally been the most laborious part of their office—the transportation of the tabernacle with its furniture—were employed at the age of twenty (instead of thirty, as before) in the service of the sanctuary. The service of the Temple about to be erected would require a greater number of ministers. Under Hezekiah (2 Chron. xxxi. 17), and after the captivity (Ezra iii. 8), the Levitical service began at the age fixed by David. It may be observed that the minute directions respecting the rearing of the sanctuary, which are given in the Pentateuch, afford one incidental proof of its antiquity, as a later authorship would have been likely to frame the law according to the practice existing at the time.

29 all manner of measure and size. The Levites were to take care that the full amount of offerings of every kind was duly presented.

CHAPTER XXIV

3 David distributed them. To prevent all confusion, now that the priests were so much increased in number, David distributed them, as he had done the Levites, into twenty-four courses—viz., sixteen of the descendants of Eleazar, and eight of those of Ithamar.

5 by lot. Though the lot was resorted to, it did not supersede the exercise of judgement in those cases which admitted of it. The object of the lot seems to have been the determination of the order in which the courses should follow each other, which was in itself a matter of indifference, but might, if not decided in this manner, have given rise to jealousies on the question of precedence.

10 Abijah. As the " course of Abia " is mentioned in Luke i. 5, it is evident that the names and order of these courses of the priests were continued, though with some changes, down to the New Testament era.

19 These were the orderings, etc. Or, " their classes for their service, for coming to the house of Jehovah, according to their arrangement by the hand of Aaron," *i.e.*, as determined by Aaron.

23 the sons of Hebron, etc. The words in italics in this verse are supplied from xxiii. 19.

31 over against. Or, " equally with."

CHAPTER XXV

1 captains. This does not mean military commanders. The Hebrew word is the same as that translated " governors " in xxiv. 5. In Numb. iv. 3 the word " host " is applied to the whole Levitical body, and it is probably so used here.

separated to the service of the sons of Asaph. Rather, as R.V., " separated for the service certain of the sons of Asaph," etc.

prophesy. *i.e.*, *to utter* or *sound forth* the praises of Jehovah.

3 the sons of Jeduthun. Shimei's name, omitted here, is found in ver. 17. Each master-singer had in his chorus twelve in number, who were called his " sons," or " brethren."

5 to lift up the horn. This may signify that Heman was a singer of those psalms which celebrated the greatness of David and his family. Others connect it with the following verse thus : " for, to exalt his horn (*i.e.*, to increase his power and influence), God gave to Heman fourteen sons and three daughters."

CHAPTER XXVI

1 porters. The duties of the porters or gate-keepers were to open and shut the gates, to prevent the entrance of improper persons, to preserve order, and to guard the Temple and its treasury and stores both by day and by night: see xvi. 38–42.

5 for God blessed him. See 2 Sam. vi. 10, 11.

10 though he was not the firstborn, etc. This case shows that the father of a family might transfer to a younger son some of the privileges attached to primogeniture: see v. 1, 2.

15 Asuppim. Heb., "gatherings." R.V., "the storehouse."

16 the gate Shallecheth. Or, "the gate of casting forth"; through which the sweepings and offal of the Temple were thrown. The Hebrew word means "casting forth," from which it has been thought that the gate was that through which the sweepings and offal of the Temple were thrown. Sir Charles Wilson, however (*Hastings' Dict. Bible*), thinks it probable that the refuse was thrown out on the east or west side and burned in the Kidron Valley, whereas the gate Shallecheth was on the west side. He favours the Septuagint rendering which suggests that it was a building with chambers.

18 Parbar. Driver and others think this, derived from the Persian, was an open colonnade or sun-lighted portico (*Hastings' Dict. Bible*).

29 the outward business. As distinguished from the work connected with the service of the sanctuary.

CHAPTER XXVII

4 Dodai. Dodai, or Dodo, was father of Eleazar, one of the mighty men. Some think that the words "Eleazar, the son of" have fallen out here.

17 Aaronites. It appears that, although the tribe of Levi had, like the other tribes, its own patriarchal chief or prince, the race of Aaron, which formed a portion of that tribe, being superior in rank and authority to the Levites generally, were exempted from the general authority of the chief or prince of the tribe, and subjected exclusively to that of the high priest, to whom also the whole tribe of Levi were *ecclesiastically* subject.

22 the tribes of Israel. In this enumeration Asher and Gad are omitted: the former, it has been conjectured, was included in Zebulun and Naphtali, and the latter in Reuben and Manasseh.

23 David took not the number, etc. Evidently David wanted to know only the number of fighting men. He did not reckon any under twenty; desiring to show that he trusted in the fulfilment of God's promise.

24 Joab . . . began to number. Not only was the census not completed, but the particulars of the numbers were not inserted in the royal chronicles; although the totals and some items were evidently otherwise preserved.

28 sycomore. That is, the fig-mulberry (leaves like the latter, fruit like the former), which grows abundantly in Egypt and Syria; mentioned, Luke xix. 4. It is not to be confounded with the "sycamine" (Luke xvii. 6), or mulberry proper, or with an English sycomore.

low plains. That is, the Shephelah, or lowlands west of the Judæan hills.

31 rulers. Or, as in xxviii. 1, "stewards."

CHAPTER XXVIII

2 the footstool of our God. *i.e.*, the ark. See Psa. xcix. 5; cxxxii. 7.

11 houses thereof. The buildings for the grand divisions of the Temple, viz., "the holy place," and the inner sanctuary, "the holy of holies."

parlours. Or, "chambers."

12 by the spirit. *i.e.*, all that was *in his mind.*

18 chariot. Some understand this as referring to the "bases" or supports on which they suppose the cherubim to have stood; others to the cherubim themselves, on which Jehovah is figuratively represented as riding: see Psa. xviii. 10; Ezek. i. 5–28; x.

19 said David. The words "said David" are not in the original, but are supplied by our translators; and some expositors regard this verse as a continuation of the narrative which begins at ver. 11, reading it thus: "From the hand of Jehovah upon *him* [*i.e.*, through the wisdom imparted to him by Jehovah], he explained everything in writing, all the works of the pattern." In ver. 11 we are informed that David gave Solomon a pattern or plan of the Temple: ver. 19 tells us that he added explanations in writing. On the words, "be strong, and of good courage," see note, xxii. 13.

CHAPTER XXIX

7 drams. Heb., "adarkon," denoting the Persian coin called "*daric*," derived from the word "Dara," *i.e.*, king (meaning *royal* coin, like the Spanish 'reals," *i.e.*, *royals*).

8 Jehiel the Gershonite. Who had the oversight of the treasures of the house of the Lord (xxvi. 21, 22).

15 strangers. That is, having no right or property of our own, but being only temporary occupiers at the Divine pleasure.

18 keep this for ever. *i.e.*, keep this disposition for ever in their minds.

20 worshipped the Lord and the king. *i.e.*, paid to both the same *outward* reverence.

22 the second time. If this means that Solomon was *anointed* a second time, this must have been done on account of the first anointing having been in haste, upon the occasion of Adonijah's rebellion (1 Kings i. 39).

27 seven years. The exact time, according to 2 Sam. v. 5, was seven years and six months.

29 Samuel the seer. The title given to Samuel, and used almost exclusively in reference to him (*roeh*), differs in Hebrew from that given to Gad (*chozeh*), which is more commonly employed; as of Heman (xxv. 5), Iddo (2 Chron. ix. 29), Asaph (2 Chron. xxix. 30), Amos (Amos vii. 12), etc.

the book of Nathan, etc. The substance of these books is probably contained in the Books of Samuel and of the Kings: see Prefaces to the First Book of Samuel and the First Book of Kings.

30 the kingdoms of the countries. That is, the surrounding nations, whose affairs were mixed up with those of Israel.

2 CHRONICLES

INTRODUCTION

MUCH that is said in the Introduction to 1 Chronicles applies to this Book also.

Solomon is the principal figure in i.–ix. The narrative in these chapters corresponds with that of 1 Kings iii.–xi. with some interesting additions. The sacrifice at Gibeon, for instance (i. 2, 3), was not merely an act of devotion on the part of Solomon, but a great public ceremony, and it was on the night of that sacrifice that God appeared to him (i. 7). A fuller account is given of the request which Solomon made to the king of Tyre (cp. ii. 7–10 with 1 Kings vii. 13). The brazen altar is merely mentioned in 1 Kings; here its construction and dimensions are given (iv. 1–5). The majestic music of the trumpeters and singers which preceded the manifestation of God's glory is mentioned in 2 Chronicles only (v. 12, 13).

The remaining chapters (x.–xxxvi.) deal with the history of the kingdom of Judah from the time of Rehoboam to the captivity and the proclamation of Cyrus permitting the return of the Jews to Jerusalem. The most important additions to the record of Kings are the account of Jehoshaphat's reforms (xix.), his beautiful intercessory prayer and his appeal to the people, with the defeat of their enemies (xx. 1–30); Amaziah's obedience to God's command at apparent loss to himself (xxv. 1–10); the explanation of Jotham's success (xxvii. 6); and the account of Hezekiah's cleansing of the temple, his sacrifices, his keeping of the Passover and destruction of the idols (xxix.–xxxi.).

CHAPTER I

1 was strengthened. Heb., "strengthened (*i.e.*, established) himself"; perhaps with allusion to the opposition to his accession. Cp. xii. 13; xiii. 21; xxi. 4; xxxii. 5, etc.

3 went to the high place. Cp. 1 Kings iii. 4. A few details are here added.

the tabernacle of the congregation. *i.e.*, "the tent of meeting," as in many other passages (R.V.). The chronicler here lays emphasis on the fact that the Sanctuary and the Ark were for the time in different places.

5 he put. Rather, as R.V., "was there."

7 In that night, etc. The account of this vision in 1 Kings iii. 5–15 substantially accords with this: but with verbal differences that betoken a different narrator.

9 Thy promise. This promise is also referred to in Psa. lxxii.

13 from his journey. The Septuagint gives the correct reading: "And Solomon came from the high place in Gibeon," etc.

16 linen yarn. See notes on 1 Kings x. 28, 29. The whole passage in the two books is nearly identical. "Gold," however (15), is not mentioned in Kings.

CHAPTER II

1 a house for his kingdom. *i.e.*, a royal residence, a palace.

2 three thousand and six hundred. This is the number given by the Sept. in 1 Kings v. 16, where the Hebrew text has 3,300.

3 Huram. The form in Kings, *Hiram*, is probably the more correct.

5 great is our God. Huram acknowledged Jahveh at least as the greatest of gods (cp. ver. 12).

6 only to burn sacrifice. Solomon is careful to set right ideas of Jahveh before the Syrian king. "Let it not be supposed that He, like the gods of the Gentiles, dwells in temples made with hands: this house, however magnificent, cannot be a habitation for Him; and is intended only that His priests and worshippers may have a fit place wherein to conduct His service."

10 twenty thousand baths of oil. See 1 Kings v. 11.

13 Huram my father's. In the Hebrew it is "Huram-Abi"; and at iv. 16, "Huram-Abiv." It probably means "master-workman."

16 Joppa. Now called *Jaffa;* the sea-port of Jerusalem, now first mentioned after the account of the partition of the land, Josh. xix. 46. Cp. Jonah i. 3.

17 all the strangers. The remnant of the Canaanites: see 1 Kings ix. 20, 21; and 1 Chron xxii. 2, and note.

18 to set the people a work. Rather, "to make the people work"; keeping them up to it. This verse repeats ver. 2.

CHAPTER III

1 mount Moriah. It is generally supposed (and Josephus says the same) that this was the spot to which Abraham went to offer up Isaac: see Gen. xxii. 2.

3 these are the things wherein Solomon was instructed. "These are the foundations which

Solomon laid" (R.V.), or "the ground-plan drawn up by Solomon" (*Moffatt*).

the first measure. The "first" means the measure in use in Solomon's time, as distinguished probably from the Babylonian measure used after the Captivity.

4 a hundred and twenty. If this is correct, the "porch" must have formed a lofty tower, four times as high as the rest of the Temple. But some ancient versions omit the "hundred"; and this probably restores the ancient reading. The porch would thus be ten cubits lower than the walls; see 1 Kings vi. 2.

5 the greater house. *i.e.*, the Holy Place, as distinguished from the Most Holy (8).

set. Or, "wrought" (R.V.) *chains*, probably "garlands" or "festoons." See parallel in Kings, "open flowers."

6 for beauty. Or, "for ornament."

Parvaim. A name nowhere else occurring. It is thought by some to be the same as Ophir; others identify it with el-Farvaim, near Dharijja, in north-east Arabia.

10 image work. Rather, "carved work."

13 their faces were inward. Or, "towards the house"; standing as attendant upon Jehovah; looking *eastward*, toward the Holy Place. The cherubim were not set there to be worshipped, but as a mark of honour to the invisible God.

14 he made the vail. An addition to the account in Kings.

15 thirty and five cubits. See note on 1 Kings vii. 15.

CHAPTER IV

1 an altar of brass. This altar was four times as long, four times as broad, and about three times as high as that which had been made by Moses; and it formed a large platform about thirty-five feet square, and seventeen and a half feet high. The account in Kings does not give the dimensions of the altar.

3 oxen. See note on 1 Kings vii. 24.

5 three thousand baths. See note on 1 Kings vii. 26.

7 according to their form. "According to the ordinance concerning them" (R.V.).

16 Huram his father. See note, ii. 13.

22 entry. In 1 Kings vii. 50, instead of "entry," it is "hinges"; which is probably correct, a letter in the Hebrew word being here omitted by a copyist.

CHAPTER V

The section from v. 2 to vii. 22 is substantially the same as in 1 Kings viii. 1–ix. 9: on which see notes.

12 the Levites which were the singers, etc. This reference to the service of song as preceding the display of the Divine glory is not in Kings.

CHAPTER VI

5 to be a ruler. God had, on various occasions, appointed temporary rulers of Israel; but He did not, till the time of David, establish a permanent and hereditary monarchy. This clause, and the reference to Jerusalem (6), are absent from Kings.

13 a brazen scaffold. Additional to the account in Kings.

41 Now therefore arise, etc. Vers. 41, 42 are in substance a quotation from Psa. cxxxii., which was probably composed upon this occasion: see note on its title. The verses are wanting in Kings, where also the reference to the sorrow and repentance of the people after captivity is expanded into an affecting conclusion to the prayer (1 Kings viii. 46–53).

Thy resting place. The ark of the covenant had often removed, even after its arrival in Canaan: see Josh. vi. 4–6; viii. 33; xviii. 1; 1 Sam. iv. 4, 11; vi. 12; vii. 1; 2 Sam. vi. 2–10, 17; xv. 24, 25; 1 Chron. xvii. 5.

42 the mercies of David. Not, as in R.V. marg., "the good deeds of David"; but the faithful promises of God to His servant (Isa. lv. 3).

CHAPTER VII

1 the fire came down from heaven. Omitted in Kings, where also the sacred historian gives the benediction of Solomon after his prayer.

6 waited on their offices. "Stood, according to their stations."

15 attent unto the prayer. Much of the answer, as recorded here, is in the very terms of Solomon's prayer: cp. ver. 15 with vi. 40, and ver. 18 with vi. 16.

CHAPTER VIII

The section from viii. 1 to ix. 28 is for the most part the same as 1 Kings ix. 1–x. 27: on which see notes.

2 cities. These were the cities which Solomon gave to Huram (1 Kings ix. 11), but which Huram returned because "they pleased him not." Solomon then "built" (*i.e.*, enlarged or fortified) them, and placed Israelites in them instead of their former inhabitants.

4 Tadmor. See note on 1 Kings ix. 18.

6 Baalath. See note on 1 Kings ix. 18.

11 the daughter of Pharaoh. See 1 Kings iii. 1; vii. 8. She has not been mentioned before in the Chronicles; and, on the other hand, the account in Kings mentions her removal from the city of David (1 Kings ix. 24) without assigning the reason.

12, 13 Then Solomon offered, etc. The meaning is that from this time forth the sacrificial worship prescribed by Moses was regularly carried on in the new Temple. **After a certain rate every day** (13), is better given in R.V., "as the duty of every day required."

18 Ophir. See note on 1 Kings ix. 28. The "ships" sent by the Tyrian king, if they went to Ezion-geber and to Ophir, must have crossed the isthmus of Suez, or have gone round the Cape of Good Hope; neither of which suppositions is probable. All that is said is that Huram's *servants* accompanied the servants of Solomon: the ships, most likely, remaining in the Mediterranean ports for Solomon's traffic with Tarshish and the West.

CHAPTER IX

1 the queen of Sheba. See note on 1 Kings x. 1.

12 beside that which she had brought. The reading in the parallel passage (1 Kings x. 13), is obviously more correct; viz., "beside that which Solomon gave her of his royal bounty."

14 chapmen. Lit., "travellers." The Hebrew word is used of the men whom Moses sent to "spy out" the land (Numb. xiii. 16, 17).

16 the house of the forest of Lebanon. *i.e.*, a hall of his palace.

21 Tarshish. See note on 1 Kings x. 22.

29 the book ("history," R.V.), **. . . the prophecy . . . the visions.** These works, of which now no trace remains, were but a part of a mass of historical and prophetical literature in the hands of the chronicler: see 1 Chron. xxvii. 24; xxix. 29; 2 Chron. xii. 15; xiii. 22; xx. 34; xxiv. 27; xxvi. 22; xxxii. 32.

CHAPTER X

The section from ch. x. 1 to xi. 4 is the same as 1 Kings xii. 1–24: on which see notes.

CHAPTER XI

5 built. That is, *enlarged* or fortified them. This he did probably from fear not only of the rival kingdom of Israel, but especially of its powerful ally Egypt. Hence most of these fortress towns lay in the south-west.

15 devils. The Hebrew word means "hairy ones"; and is often used for *he-goats.* See R.V., and marg., "satyrs." The reference is probably to the Egyptian goat-god, or similar deities—a form of idolatry which Jeroboam would be likely to introduce in connexion with that of the calves: see note on Lev. xvii. 7.

17 made Rehoboam . . . strong. It appears that most of the pious Israelites joined him, out of every tribe, as well as the whole tribe of Levi, who were deprived of their functions in the kingdom of Israel. Thus Jeroboam's religious apostasy, and his idolatrous practices, greatly weakened his own kingdom, and increased the power and prosperity of his rival.

they walked in the way of David and Solomon. Rehoboam seems to have paid some attention to religion as long as his throne appeared to be in danger; but he cast it off when he thought he had nothing to fear from Jeroboam (xii. 1).

18 Abihail. As Eliab was David's eldest brother, probably Abihail was his *grand*-daughter, if not a degree still further removed.

20 Maachah. See note on 1 Kings xv. 2.

22 the chief. *i.e.,* "to be chief," as R.V.

23 dispersed of all his children. Probably to prevent domestic feuds, which might have arisen had they all remained at Jerusalem; and to extend the influence of the royal family over the whole land. For the same reason, probably, he "desired," or rather demanded, many wives for his sons as well as for himself. R.V. reads, "he sought *for them* many wives."

CHAPTER XII

1 he forsook the law of the Lord. Rehoboam's sins are more fully specified in 1 Kings xiv. 23, 24: on which see notes. But the results are given more in detail here.

2 because they had transgressed. This was God's reason, not Shishak's motive for the invasion.

3 Lubim. These were the Libyans of North-eastern Africa. They probably furnished many of the chariots used on this occasion: Herodotus (iv. 189) states that the Greeks learned from them the method of yoking four horses to a chariot.

Sukkim. The Septuagint renders this "Troglodytes," a name given by the Greeks to dwellers in caves; inhabiting the mountains on the western coast of the Red Sea.

Ethiopians. Heb., "Cushim"; a people coming probably from Nubia, on the south of Egypt. In Nahum iii. 9, the Lubim and Cushim are among the allies of Egypt.

6 princes of Israel. The author continues frequently to use the word *Israel* with reference to the kings and princes of *Judah:* see xv. 17; xx. 34; xxi. 2, 4.

8 that they may know My service, etc. They were thus taught how much better it was to live under the wholesome restraints of Jehovah's laws than under the reckless exaction of an invader.

9 Shishak. One of the large palaces at Karnak, in Egypt, was partly built by Shishak, or Sheshonk; and a sculpture was discovered there representing that monarch dragging the representatives of conquered kingdoms. The inscription contains also the names of some cities mentioned in xi. 6–10, with others in the northern parts of the land.

12 things went well. Rather, as R.V., "there were good things *found*": cp. 1 Kings xiv. 13. The nation was not wholly apostate.

14 he prepared not his heart. *i.e.,* did not resolutely apply himself.

CHAPTER XIII

2 Michaiah. See 1 Kings xv. 2.

5 Ought ye not to know? "Surely ye know?"

for ever. Abijah's address, so far as it regarded his claim to reign over all Israel, had much of false colouring. The promise of perpetual sovereignty of which he speaks was conditional on obedience, which David's successors had not rendered. But his reproof of the apostasy and idolatry of the Israelites is full of truth and power.

a covenant of salt. Numb. xviii. 19.

10 the Levites wait upon their business. Literally, "the Levites in the service"; *i.e.,* they perform the service which can only be duly discharged by members of the tribe of Levi.

12 trumpets. See Numb. x. 9.

17 five hundred thousand. Some copies of the Vulgate, and some old Latin translations of Josephus, state the numbers in verses 3 and 17 as 40,000, 80,000, and 50,000. It is probable that in this verse there is some numerical error in copying. The slaughter may not, however, have been all in one day.

19 Jeshanah . . . Ephrain. Not mentioned elsewhere. R.V. reads for the latter, "Ephron," perhaps Ophrah (Josh. xviii. 23).

20 the Lord struck him. That is, Jeroboam; but, though stricken with disease, he did not die till two years after Abijah: see 1 Kings xiv. 20; xv. 9.

21 waxed mighty. Or, "strengthened himself": see i. 1, and note.

CHAPTER XIV

1 the land was quiet. As the result, partly of Abijah's great victory.

3 high places. See note on 1 Kings xv. 14.

the groves. R.V., "the Asherim." See 1 Kings xiv. 23, and note.

9 Ethiopian. Heb., "the Cushite" (and so in ver. 12); a name applicable to all the descendants of Cush the son of Ham. "Zerah" is supposed by some to be Osorkon II., the successor of Shishak; both of whom are thought to have been Nubians. Several modern authorities, however, think that Zerah and the Cushites came from South Arabia.

a thousand thousand. The majority of this vast multitude were not soldiers in the modern European sense of the term, maintained and disciplined to war as a profession, but simply men armed for the occasion. Larger armies than these are mentioned in history. The army of Tamerlane is said to have amounted to 1,600,000 men, and that of his antagonist Bajazet to 1,400,000.

Mareshah. The modern Merlash, one of the cities which Rehoboam fortified (xi. 8), lay between Hebron and Ashdod. It probably occupied the site of some ruins now found south of *Beit-jibrin.* or Eleutheropolis: see Robinson's *Biblical Researches in Palestine,* ii. 422. Zephathah (10) is not elsewhere mentioned.

11 it is nothing with Thee, etc. Rather, as R.V., " there is none beside Thee to help."

13 could not recover themselves. Literally, " until there was no reviving to them "; *i.e.,* they could not rally.

14 the cities round about Gerar. These cities were probably in the possession of the Philistines, who had joined with the Cushites in attacking Asa.

CHAPTER XV

3 for a long season, etc. A forcible description of the general characteristic results of those periods of apostasy when the mass of the nation turned to idols, and the priests neglected to teach the people to observe the law of Jehovah. Azariah probably had in mind the sins and disasters of the eighteen years of Rehoboam's reign, using them as a lesson.

5 to him that went out, etc. A proverb denoting all the various movements of life: see Judges v. 6.

countries. *i.e.,* all districts of the country.

6 nation was destroyed of nation, etc. Not only in former ages (see Judges xii. 4; xx.; xxi.); but especially in recent times in the wars between the two kingdoms.

7 Be ye strong therefore. Rather, " But you, be firm."

8 Oded the prophet. Some versions read the words, " Azariah the son of Oded." But it is quite as likely that the clause " of Oded the prophet " has been inserted in copying.

11 the spoil. The cattle taken from the Cushite invaders: see xiv. 15.

17 the high places, etc. See 1 Kings xv. 13, 14, and notes. *Perfect* indicates Asa's freedom from *idolatry,* not moral perfection.

CHAPTER XVI

1 built Ramah. As Ramah lay half-way between Jerusalem and Beth-el, it is probable that Baasha had recovered Beth-el, which Abijah had taken from Jeroboam (xiii. 19). The passage to ver. 6 is nearly identical with 1 Kings xv. 17–22.

12 yet in his disease. Rather, " and in his disease too "; trusting in that also to man's help instead of God's.

14 sepulchres. Plural, denoting a series of excavations.

CHAPTER XVII

3 David. " David " is omitted in the Septuagint and a few Hebrew manuscripts; and the internal evidence confirms this reading. Such a phrase as " the first ways of *David* " occurs nowhere else; but, as applied to Asa, there is evident propriety in making a distinction as to his conduct between the earlier and the latter parts of his reign.

6 was lifted up, etc. *i.e.,* was emboldened in the service of Jehovah.

9 had the book of the law of the Lord with them. The scarcity of copies made this needful.

went about . . . and taught the people. Great reformations and revivals of religion have generally been effected by missionary agency of this kind; and this course is sanctioned by the example of Christ and His apostles. Josiah did well by causing the law to be read to such of the people as could be assembled at Jerusalem (see xxxiv. 30); but Jehoshaphat is the only king whom we find sending instruction to their *homes.*

14 three hundred thousand. These numbers are evidently erroneous.

CHAPTER XVIII

1 joined affinity with Ahab. *i.e.,* gave his daughter Athaliah in marriage to Ahab's son Jehoram.

2 after certain years he went down to Ahab. The following narrative is almost identical with 1 Kings xxii. 2–37, where see notes.

14 they shall be delivered, etc. See 1 Kings xxii. 15.

18 I saw the Lord, etc. See 1 Kings xxii. 19.

31 the Lord helped him. Though Jehoshaphat did wrong in forming an alliance with Ahab, and was severely chastised for it (see 1 Kings xxii. 2), he was still a sincerely pious man, and as such under God's protection.

CHAPTER XIX

5 he set judges, etc. The account of Jehoshaphat's internal administration is peculiar to Chronicles.

8 when they returned to Jerusalem. Moffatt reads " among the citizens of Jerusalem."

10 between blood and blood. *i.e.,* murder and accidental death or manslaughter. See Deut. xvii. 8.

between law and commandment, etc. *i.e.,* where there seem to be conflicting obligations. The former were cases explicitly provided for in the law of God as given by Moses, and the latter such as had been left to the judgement of the sovereign.

CHAPTER XX

2 the sea. The Dead Sea.

En-gedi. See Gen. xiv. 7.

6 and said, etc. By employing words derived from Solomon's prayer at the dedication of the Temple (vi. 24–30), the king appeals to God to fulfil the promise implied in His answer by fire (vii. 1–3).

16 the cliff of Ziz. " The ascent of Ziz " or Haziz. This is a steep and difficult zigzag road cut in the face of the rock leading up to Tekoa. It is the only pass from Engedi towards Jerusalem.

22 set ambushments, etc. The text is somewhat obscure; but it seems likely that the men placed in ambush against the army of Judah, either by mistake or designedly, attacked their own allies, and that this led to mutual distrust in the whole army; so that the Ammonites and Moabites united against the Edomites, and nearly destroyed them; and then, quarrelling among themselves, destroyed one another.

25 dead bodies. Some manuscripts and versions have " garments "; the two words being somewhat similar in Hebrew (פגרים and בגדים).

26 Berachah. Answering to the *Wady Bereikut,* north-west of Tekoa.

34 who is mentioned. Rather, " which is inserted " (R.V.). See note on ix. 29.

36 ships to go to Tarshish. In 1 Kings xxii. 48 the reading is, " ships of Tarshish to go to Ophir."

CHAPTER XXI

4 slew all his brethren. The murderous spirit of ambition is amply attested by all history. It is not unusual for despots in the East to put to death all who might be competitors for the throne, or dangerous to their power.

6 as did the house of Ahab. Introducing the Phœnician Baal-worship.

11 to commit fornication. Encouraging the people in idolatry, which is frequently described in Scripture by this figure.

12 a writing . . . from Elijah. It is commonly supposed that Elijah's ascension had taken place several years before. Some conjecture that the name "Elisha" should be read for "Elijah." But a simpler explanation seems to be that the account of Elijah's translation is given out of its chronological order; and that he was still on earth in the days of Jehoram: see 2 Kings ii. 1.

CHAPTER XXII

1 Ahaziah. He is called in the preceding chapter, and in xxv. 23, "Jehoahaz," which in Hebrew is synonymous with Ahaziah.

had slain all the eldest. The Arabs took Jehoram's sons captive, probably with the hope of obtaining a ransom for them: but some band of men in their camp slew them; thus defeating their purpose, whilst accomplishing God's design.

2 Forty and two years. In 2 Kings viii. 26 it is "twenty-two years." But, as his father was only forty at his death (xxi. 20), even this seems too great an age for his *youngest* son. The Septuagint has "twenty."

6 Azariah. This should be "Ahaziah," as appears from the context; and is so in the Septuagint and some Hebrew manuscripts.

9 he sought Ahaziah. See 2 Kings ix. 27. The two accounts of Ahaziah's death supplement each other. He was slain at Megiddo, and buried at Jerusalem.

10 destroyed all the seed royal. See 2 Kings xi. 1.

Jehoiada, as related in 2 Kings xi. 1–16, proclaims the young king Joash, when he is seven years old; upon which Athaliah is slain (xxiii. 1–21). Joash urges the repair of the Temple, and restores the worship of God (xxiv. 1–14). But when Jehoiada dies, he is led by the princes into idolatry; and being reproved by the son of Jehoiada, causes him to be put to death (15–22). For this he is punished, partly by a Syrian invasion, and partly by a conspiracy of his servants, who murder him (23–27).

CHAPTER XXIII

1 Jehoiada strengthened himself. See 2 Kings xi. 4.

8 dismissed not the courses. See 2 Kings xi. 9.

11 gave him the testimony. See 2 Kings xi. 12, 13.

CHAPTER XXIV

3 Jehoiada took . . . two wives. This is particularly mentioned, probably as showing the care which Jehoiada took to preserve the regular succession to the throne, all the rest of the royal line of Solomon having been put to death by Athaliah.

6 the collection. The poll-tax of half a shekel; which, by the law of Moses, was paid by every man of twenty years old and upwards, and was devoted to the maintenance of the services first of the Tabernacle and afterwards of the Temple: see Exod. xxx. 12–16.

7 broken up. Or, simply "broken."

14 whereof were made vessels. It appears, from 2 Kings xii. 13, that only the surplus (which was probably unexpected) was so used.

17 made obeisance to the king. The tenor of the narrative suggests the opinion that in the lifetime of Jehoiada the power of the high priest had overshadowed that of the king and the nobility, and had strengthened the repugnance of those who were not truly religious to the worship of Jehovah, whilst it prepared the king to receive more readily their petition for the toleration of idolatry.

18 groves. "Asherim" (R.V.). See 1 Kings xiv. 23.

20 Zechariah. The same person as is mentioned in the New Testament as the son of Barachiah. see note on Matt. xxiii. 35.

22 slew his son. This was a crime of peculiar enormity; for not only was a priest and prophet of God murdered while fulfilling his Divine commission, but the martyred prophet was a near relative of the king, and the son of the man to whom Joash owed his life, his crown, and all his prosperity.

23 at the end of the year. *i.e.*, the year of Zechariah's death.

the princes of the people. The men who had seduced Joash into idolatry (17, 18), and had conspired with him to murder the prophet.

25 sons. The Septuagint and Vulgate read "son."

the sepulchres of the kings. It appears that a more or less honourable place of burial was assigned to the kings, according to the opinion entertained of their characters and conduct: cp. xxi. 20; xxviii. 27; xxxii. 33.

CHAPTER XXV

2 but not with a perfect heart. He kept the high places (2 Kings xiv. 4), and adopted the idols of Edom (14).

5 made them captains, etc. Rather, "ordered them according to their fathers' houses, under captains of thousands and captains of hundreds" (R.V.).

6 a hundred talents of silver. About 8*s*. 3*d*. for each man.

12 cast them down. This mode of punishment was practised by the Greeks and Romans, as also in the persecution of the Christians in Madagascar. The "rock" was Selah (*Petra*), a great extent of cliffs and precipices.

13 from Samaria even unto Beth-horon. After returning to Joash, they started from Samaria on a marauding expedition into Judah, returning into the Israelite territory at Beth-horon.

16 Art thou made of the king's counsel? Literally, "Have we appointed thee to be counsellor to the king?" To which the prophet replies, "True, I am not thy counsellor, but I know that God hath counselled to destroy thee."

17 Come, let us see one another. See note on 2 Kings xiv. 8.

CHAPTER XXVI

1 Uzziah. The name is generally "Azariah" in Kings; always "Uzziah" in Chronicles (except 1 Chron. iii. 12); and always "Uzziah" in the Prophets.

2 the king. Amaziah. His son took and rebuilt it soon after his accession. See 2 Kings xiv. 22.

5 Zechariah. Of course this is not the Zechariah of xxiv., but a prophet who seems to have been a counsellor of Uzziah. Many ancient authorities read, "who instructed him in the fear of God." The Hebrew words for *visions* and for *fear* are somewhat alike, ראות and מורה.

8 gave gifts. *i.e.,* "paid tribute."

9 the valley gate. On the spot now occupied by the "gate of Jaffa."

10 desert. Or, "wilderness" (of Judah). The mention of *wells* (rather "cisterns," as R.V., or reservoirs, *cattle*, etc., shows that the towers were built to shelter the king's shepherds and their flocks in times of danger, as well as his husbandmen and vine-dressers. Read, "he had much cattle *there* (*i.e.,* in the wilderness), in the (maritime) lowland also, and in the plain (or, 'table land')." The last-mentioned pastoral district was in Gilead, beyond Jordan.

Carmel. Not the mountain of that name, which belonged to Samaria, but "the fruitful fields" of the Judæan hill-country: see Josh. xv. 55; 1 Sam. xxv. 2.

14 slings to cast stones. Literally, as R.V., "stones for slinging."

15 engines. These were probably similar to those used by the Greeks and Romans under the names of *catapultae* and *balistae*. Uzziah's engineers are supposed by many to have been the inventors of these machines, which Pliny distinctly states to have been of Syrian origin. They are represented in Assyrian sculptures.

16 he transgressed against the Lord. He was elated by his prosperity; and instead of giving God the glory, assumed a lordship over things sacred, in imitation perhaps of neighbouring sovereigns; and thus incurred the severe chastisement which confined him for life.

17 valiant men. Bold enough to oppose the king.

21 was a leper. This was a very remarkable punishment. Aspiring to undue honour, he was smitten with a degrading disease. Invading the priests' office, he was subjected to their control, and ejected from his kingly functions. Intruding into the holy place, he was expelled even from the outer court.

22 did . . . Isaiah write. The prophecies in the first six chapters of Isaiah were probably delivered when he was a young man, in the latter part of Uzziah's reign.

CHAPTER XXVII

2 entered not into the temple. The meaning appears to be that he imitated his father in all that was good, but did not, like him, profanely enter the Temple.

3 Ophel. Ophel is the lower ridge south of the Temple, between the valley of the Kedron and the Tyropœon. Jotham's buildings enlarged as well as strengthened the city.

4 mountains. Rather, "the hill-country" (R.V.). Cp. Luke i. 39.

7 the book of the kings. This must refer to a more detailed history than our "Book of the Kings"; for in that there is less concerning Jotham's reign than in the Chronicles.

CHAPTER XXVIII

5 they smote him, etc. The two battles to which this verse refers are not mentioned in Kings.

15 expressed by name. More exactly, "which have been expressed by name" (R.V.), *i.e.,* the persons named, ver. 12.

and brought them to Jericho. This touching incident has no parallel in the histories of the wars of heathen nations, or perhaps even of such as are nominally Christians.

they returned to Samaria. It was probably after this that the kings of Israel and Syria made their joint invasion of Judah, for the purpose of deposing the house of David from the throne; which forms the subject of Isa. vii., viii., ix. 1–7

16 the kings of Assyria. Or, as in 2 Kings xvi. 7, "the king"; who was Tiglath-pileser, called Tilgath-pilneser (20).

19 he made Judah naked. Cp. Exod. xxxii. 25. R.V. reads, "dealt wantonly in Judah."

21 he helped him not. Rather, as R.V., "it helped him not"; *i.e.,* the policy of Ahaz was of no real service to him. As a matter of fact, the Assyrian king did interpose on behalf of Ahaz, 2 Kings xvi. 9. But this was of no real service in the end.

24 shut up the doors. The Temple continued shut up till the beginning of the next reign: see xxix. 3.

CHAPTER XXIX

3 opened the doors, etc. This was an auspicious commencement of Hezekiah's reign, and an encouraging pledge of what his after course was to be. As the Temple at Jerusalem was the religious centre of the nation, to which the affections of every pious Jew were drawn; so the conduct of the kings of Judah with respect to this sacred edifice affords a good criterion of their real character.

4 the east street. Rather, "the broad place on the east," *i.e.,* of the Temple (R.V.); an open area on the Temple hill, before the eastern entrance.

8 the wrath of the Lord. Referring to the calamities which had befallen the people under Ahaz: see xxviii.

17 they made an end. First the priests and Levites together cleansed the courts of the priests and of the people, which occupied eight days: and then the priests cleansed the interior of the Temple (which the Levites were not allowed to enter), and brought all the dirt and rubbish to the porch, whence it was carried away by the Levites to the brook Kidron: this occupied eight days more.

21 for a sin offering. These sacrifices were unusually numerous, because they were offered on account of multiplied sins of a wilful and aggravated kind. The sin offerings were presented first for the *kingdom, i.e.,* for the king and the royal family; secondly, for the *sanctuary,* which had been polluted, and the *priests,* who had been negligent and unholy; and finally for *Judah*—for the whole mass of the people, who, following these examples, had committed every kind of wickedness.

24 an atonement for all Israel. Including the ten tribes, though sunk still deeper than Judah in apostasy and idolatry: thus preparing the way for the large-hearted plan which Hezekiah immediately afterwards carried out: see xxx.

30 sang praises with gladness. The gladness of these services forcibly suggests the importance of a cheerful piety.

34 the Levites did help them. Peace offerings, and some others, the Levites might flay and dress; but the whole burnt offerings (*i.e.,* those which were entirely consumed on the altar) could be offered only by the priests, except in the case of necessity such as that mentioned here.

CHAPTER XXX

1 sent to all Israel. This was apparently the first attempt on the part of any king of Judah to bring back the people of the ten tribes to the true faith. It does not appear that either Hoshea or Hezekiah regarded this act of obedience to Jehovah as inconsistent with the allegiance of the people to their temporal sovereign.

2 in the second month. According to the law, the passover was to be celebrated on the fourteenth day of the first month; but if any man was unclean at that time, he might keep it in the second month (Numb. ix. 2, 3, 11). This was the case now in regard to the whole people: see ver. 3.

3 at that time. Or rather, "at *the* time"; that is, the time fixed by the law; for they did keep it in the second month.

5 of a long time. Rather, "in great numbers" (R.V.).

6 are escaped out of the hand of the kings of Assyria. This was prior to the fall of Samaria; but the kings before Sargon had inflicted much harm on Israel. 1 Chron. v. 26; 2 Kings xv. 19; xvii. 3.

11 came to Jerusalem. Those who came to Jerusalem from the kingdom of Israel appear to have belonged, for the most part, to the tribes which were at a distance from the boundary of the two kingdoms: on which account they had probably less of national jealousy than others who lived nearer the frontier of Judah.

12 by the word of the Lord. Or, as in margin of xxix. 15, "in the business of Jehovah."

15 the Levites were ashamed. Referring, no doubt, more especially to the *priests* mentioned above in ver. 3 and in xxix. 34; who, together probably with some of the Levites, had heretofore been remiss in sanctifying themselves.

19 though he be not cleansed, etc. From this and many similar passages we learn that even under the Mosaic dispensation, when outward rites were made so prominent, God regarded more the state and dispositions of the heart than the external purity of the worshipper: cp. Psa. li. 16, 17.

20 and healed the people. Or, "was propitious to the people"; that is, pardoned or accepted them.

22 that taught the good knowledge of the Lord. Rather, as R.V., "that were well skilled in the service of Jehovah."

23 they kept other seven days. This does not mean that they observed seven other days of unleavened bread; but that they offered sacrifices, with praises and thanksgivings, seven other days.

24 Hezekiah . . . did give. etc. As the people in general, and especially those who came out of the kingdom of Israel, might be unprepared for the expense attending these sacrifices, and especially for their continuance beyond the prescribed time, Hezekiah and his princes supplied them with cattle. This open-handed liberality illustrates the generous influence of true religion.

25 the strangers. Israelites dwelling in the land of Judah (xv. 9). They were in one sense "foreigners," being subjects of a different government.

26 there was not the like in Jerusalem. For the first time since the reign of Solomon, many from among the ten tribes came up to join in celebrating the passover, and the feast was unusual for both numbers and duration.

CHAPTER XXXI

1 all Israel. The whole body of worshippers, both from the northern and the southern kingdom.

images . . . groves. Rather, "pillars. . . . Asherim": see 1 Kings xiv. 23, and note.

destroyed them all. It would appear from this that the numbers and zeal of those who went forth for this purpose were sufficient to overpower all opposition, even in the northern kingdom.

2 the tents (R.V., "camp") **of the Lord.** *i.e.*, the Temple precincts, regarded as the encampment of "Jahveh of hosts."

3 for the burnt offerings. Hezekiah took upon himself the expense of all these sacrifices. Some think that this had been done before by the kings who adhered to the worship of Jahveh.

4 be encouraged in. Rather, "hold fast," or "adhere to"; devoting themselves exclusively to their duties as priests ("give themselves to," R.V.).

5 brought they in abundantly. *i.e.*, in generous profusion, even beyond what the letter of the law required; so making up for past neglect.

10 the Lord hath blessed his people. *i.e.*, with an abundant harvest.

this great store. The liberality of the king and people not only provided well for the priests, but seems to have also inspired the priests with the same disposition.

15 in their set office. Rather, "in trust," as R.V. marg., *i.e.*, to distribute the oblations.

16 beside their genealogy of males. Heb., "apart from their register for males from three years old and upwards; for every one that comes to the house of the Lord," etc.

17 genealogy. Rather, as in vers. 16, 18, 19, "register." The general meaning of these verses is, that according to the registered families of priests and Levites the offerings were distributed among them, whether in their own cities or at the Temple: but special provision was made for those actually engaged in sacred duties.

18 in their set office. Rather, "for in [or, 'according to'] their trust they consecrated themselves to the holy work"; *i.e.*, of distributing the offerings for the priests and Levites.

19 the men that were, etc. Rather, "*there were* men expressed," etc. (R.V.); *i.e.*, the well-known heads were entrusted with the offerings.

CHAPTER XXXII

1 the establishment thereof. Rather, perhaps, "this faithfulness" (R.V.); *i.e.*, in restoring the worship of Jehovah. It was this which averted the impending destruction.

to win them. Rather, "to break them up": see Jer. lii. 7. He seems to have conquered most of them: see 2 Kings xviii. 13, and notes.

2 to fight against Jerusalem. In this account of the Assyrian invasion we have a fuller description than in 2 Kings xviii. of Hezekiah's preparations for defence, by enclosing the water-courses and strengthening the fortifications; with the addition of his pious and encouraging addresses to the people, leading them to trust in God.

4 the brook. The brook Gihon: see ver. 30, and note.

5 up to the towers. That is, either he built the wall up to the height of the towers; or, having built the wall, he raised the towers on it: see Isa. xxii. 10; from which it appears that houses were pulled down for material "to fortify the wall."

6 in the street of the gate. That is, in the "*open place* at the gate of the city": see R.V. The "gate" was probably that on the north, now "the Damascus gate."

comfortably. Or, "encouragingly": cp. 2 Kings vi. 16. These words of trust were, however followed by payment of a large sum to Sennacherib as the price of his withdrawal: see 2 Kings xviii. 14–16.

9 After this. Having withdrawn for a time. The full account of this expedition is in 2 Kings xviii. 17–xix. 36.

he himself laid siege against Lachish. Rather, "he was before Lachish," as R.V.

12 taken away His high places; as if in disrespect to Jahveh.

18 Then. Heb. "And." This preceded the letter.

22 guided. Some render, "protected."

26 Hezekiah humbled himself. See Jer. xxvi. 19.

30 stopped the upper watercourse. It is supposed that Hezekiah covered the fountain of Gihon, on the west of Jerusalem, and conveyed its waters by subterranean channels into the city; so as to cut off the supply from a besieging army, and to preserve it for the inhabitants.

32 goodness. Or, "pious deeds."

in the vision, . . . and in the book. Omit "and" (R.V.). The vision of Isaiah was itself a part of the "book."

CHAPTER XXXIII

3 groves ("Asheroth," R.V.). See 1 Kings xiv. 23; 2 Kings xxi. 3.

6 he observed times. Rather, "he practised augury," as R.V.: see 2 Kings xxi. 6.

10 the Lord spake to Manasseh. The words are recorded in 2 Kings xxi. 11–15.

11 the king of Assyria. This was Esarhaddon, the son and successor of Sennacherib.

among the thorns. The Hebrew word may mean either "among thorns" or "with hooks" or "chains." R.V. has "with chains" (marg., "with hooks").

18 his prayer unto his God. A prayer of ancient date has come down to us, purporting to be this prayer of Manasseh. It abounds in pious sentiments; but, not having been found in Hebrew, nor cited by the more eminent fathers, nor contained in any of the catalogues of Scripture drawn up by ancient councils, it has been properly classed among the apocryphal writings.

22 as did Manasseh his father. Amon, having his father's example before him, with astonishing perverseness copied his vices, but did not imitate his repentance.

CHAPTER XXXIV

2 neither to the right hand, etc. Of no other king of Judah is this said.

3 while he was yet young. *i.e.*, in his sixteenth year.

in the twelfth year. In the following year Jeremiah was called to the prophetic office (Jer. i. 2).

6 And so did he, etc. See 2 Kings xxiii. 15.

with their mattocks. The Hebrew should rather be translated "he searched their (*i.e.*, the idolaters') houses."

8 when he had purged the land. See 2 Kings xxiii. 4.

9 and they returned to Jerusalem. This clause should be read, "and of the inhabitants of Jerusalem," R.V.

13 there were scribes. Now first mentioned as a distinct class.

14 found a book. Rather, "*the* book," as R.V.

17 gathered together. Rather, "emptied out," as R.V.

18 Shaphan read it. Literally, as R.V., "Shaphan read therein," *i.e.*, a part of it. On this important discovery, see note on 2 Kings xxii. 8.

19 he rent his clothes. See 2 Kings xxii. 11.

21 them that are left in Israel and in Judah. Indicating the king's desire to restore the national unity: cp. ver. 6, and xxx. 1, 5, etc.

CHAPTER XXXV

3 ark. It is conjectured that the ark had been removed by Amon to make room for idols; or possibly by Hilkiah, while the Temple was undergoing repairs.

5 And stand in the holy place. Probably the best rendering is, "And stand in the sanctuary, according to the classes of the fathers'-houses of your brethren, the people, even [every] division of a father's-house of the Levites," *i.e.*, in such a manner that for every fathers'-house of the people generally, there should be a corresponding portion of a father's-house of the Levites: see R.V.

6 prepare your brethren. Rather, "prepare [it, viz., the *passover*] for your brethren": see R.V.

18 no passover like to that. See 2 Kings xxiii. 22.

20 After all this. *i.e.*, thirteen years after.

Charchemish. A large city on the western bank of the Euphrates, now a heap of mounds, known as Jerablûs. It was identified by Messrs. Skene and Geo. Smith by means of the Assyrian inscriptions. It was the chief city of the Hittites, and was strongly fortified (see Sayce: *The Hittites: the Story of a Forgotten Empire*). It was the centre of the overland trade in Western Asia.

22 Megiddo. See 2 Kings xxiii. 29.

25 in the lamentations. Not the canonical book of "Lamentations," which relates solely to the destruction of Jerusalem, but some other work not now extant.

CHAPTER XXXVI

7 carried of the vessels. See 2 Kings xxiv. 13.

9 eight years old. This should be *eighteen*, as in 2 Kings xxiv. 8.

10 when the year was expired. The rendering, "at the return of the year" (R.V.), is preferable; for only the three winter months intervened.

his brother. "His father's brother": 2 Kings xxiv. 17.

14 transgressed very much. We gain much insight into the awful corruption of the people at this period from the prophecies of Ezekiel, who had been carried captive to Chaldæa, and who received there, for the special benefit of his fellow-exiles, revelations of the impending doom of the holy city and the reasons of God's displeasure, accompanied with disclosures of His ultimate purposes of mercy towards His people: see Ezekiel viii., x., xi. At the same time, the prophet Jeremiah, living in the midst of his people, warned them against vainly hoping (as the false prophets encouraged them to do) for the preservation of Jerusalem; assured them that the king and his court, the city and its wicked inhabitants, were doomed to total ruin, and that the living germ of Hebrew nationality was with the captives in Babylon; cautioned them against indulging the hope of a speedy restoration, by telling them that the captivity should last for seventy years (Jeremiah xix., xxiv., xxv., xxvii., xxix.); predicted their certain restoration at the appointed time, and the great blessings which God had in reserve for them hereafter (xxx.–xxxiii.); and, further, foretold the utter overthrow of Babylon, which was then in the plenitude of her power (l., li.).

15 rising up betimes. Except in this place the phrase occurs only in the Book of Jeremiah: see vii. 13.

16 misused His prophets. "Scoffed at" (R.V.).

20 them that had escaped from the sword. There is reason to believe that, during these national judgements, the most religious portion of the Hebrews were preserved and carried into exile; while the idolatrous and profane were for the most part destroyed: see Ezekiel ix. 2–6; xiv. 13–21. The numbers of the captives are given in Jer. lii. 28–30.

21 she kept sabbath. The years of exile might be represented as a making up the arrears of rest which had been accumulating by the neglect of the sabbatic year—an institution which served perhaps beyond any other to test the faith and obedience of the people; but which they, in their impiety and covetousness, had neglected. The land of Judah was not colonised by foreigners, as that of Samaria had been; so that there was nothing to prevent its entire re-occupation by the Jews at the appointed time.

22 Now in the first year, etc. The Book of the Chronicles closes with ver. 21. Vers. 22, 23, which record transactions many years afterwards, are identical with Ezra i. 1–3.

THE BOOK OF EZRA

The Exiles' Return

INTRODUCTION

The time covered by this Book extends over a period of about eighty years, from 537 B.C. to 458 B.C. It opens with the proclamation of Cyrus (i. 1–4), which was already mentioned in the last two verses of 2 Chronicles, permitting the return of the Jews to Jerusalem and the rebuilding of the Temple. The first section, which ends with chap. vi., represents a period of about twenty-two years, bringing the history down to 515 B.C. Then there is a gap of fifty-eight years between this and the beginning of chap. vii., the arrival of Ezra in Jerusalem in 458.

The Book is full of spiritual teaching. The Divine mercy and faithfulness are shown in God's restoration of Israel and the fulfilment of His promises (iii. 11; cp. Isa. xliv. 28; xlv. 13; Jer. xxv. 12; xxix. 10, 16). How God helps His faithful servants is repeatedly indicated (vii. 6, 10, 28; viii. 31). And Ezra's exhortation to the people to repent, and his courage in carrying out reforms (ix., x.) are an example to all religious leaders.

CHAPTER I

1 Cyrus. Cyrus had led the united army of Persia and Media against Babylon; and, on the capture of the city, he had added the Babylonian empire to the more eastern one of the Medes and Persians. He appears to have given the administration to Darius the Mede, whose identity has not yet been established. After the short reign of Darius, Cyrus came to Babylon, and in the first year of his reign there he issued this edict.

that the word of the Lord, etc. See Jer. xxv. 12; xxix. 10.

a proclamation, etc. A twofold publication of the decree; by heralds, and by written edicts.

2 The Lord God of heaven. Rather, the Eternal the God of heaven: see R.V.

all the kingdoms of the earth. The empire of Cyrus was of vast extent: reaching on the east to the Indus, on the north to the Euxine Sea, on the west to Egypt and the island of Cyprus, and on the south to the Persian Gulf and to Ethiopia.

charged me. This referred probably to the prophecies in Isaiah (xliv. 26–28; xlv. 1, 12, 13), which expressly mention Cyrus as the deliverer of Israel: see notes on those passages.

3 Who is there among you, etc.? R.V., "Whosoever there is among you of His people, his God be with him."

and build the house. This was to be their chief object in returning to the land of their fathers (see the prophecies of Haggai); and as this work was prosecuted or neglected, their prosperity grew or declined.

4 remaineth. R.V., "is left," *i.e.*, survives (of the Israelites).

5 the chief of the fathers. R.V., "the heads of fathers'-*houses*." Many of the Jews had obtained in Chaldæa comfortable settlements, which led them to prefer remaining there. Josephus says that the proclamation of Cyrus was sent to the descendants of the ten tribes living in Media under his dominion; and as it comprehended the whole nation, it is probable that the first caravan which went to Jerusalem comprised persons from all the tribes (see 1 Chron. ix. 3). Others, also, it is likely, hearing of the prosperity of their brethren in Judæa, followed their example, and took up their abode in other parts of the country.

whose spirit God had raised. The language implies that He who "stirred up the spirit of Cyrus" to give them permission (ver. 3), also "*stirred* up the spirit of the people"; for the Hebrew word is the same in both cases: see R.V.

to go up. The distance from Babylon to Jerusalem was between five and six hundred miles.

6 beside all that was willingly offered. This seems to be explained by the last clause of ver. 4. Liberal contributions were made for the use of the travellers, over and above the freewill offerings for the Temple.

7 brought forth the vessels. Some of the vessels of the Temple had been cut in pieces by the Chaldæans (2 Kings xxiv. 13): but many had been preserved through all the succeeding revolutions, and were now restored. The liberality of Cyrus is more fully shown in the recital of his decree given in the subsequent one of Darius Hystaspis in vi. 3–6.

8 Sheshbazzar. Sheshbazzar was by earlier writers identified with Zerubbabel, but recent scholarship regards him as the predecessor of the latter.

9 chargers. "libation bowls."

knives. For preparing the sacrifices.

11 five thousand and four hundred. There may be here an error in copying. The number above given amounts to 2,499.

with them of the captivity that were brought up. R.V., "when they of the captivity were brought up."

CHAPTER II

1 these are the children. The genealogies, after the Captivity, had both a *civil* and a *religious* importance; as proving the rights of the different families to their respective inheritances, and as furnishing evidence of the descent of the Messiah from David and from Judah. In ch. vii. of the Book of Nehemiah, we have another copy of this register. The sum-total is the same in both; but the particulars of the two differ, and each falls far short of the whole amount.

the province. Judæa (see note, iv. 12) had become one of the provinces of the Persian empire: see v. 8; Neh. i. 3.

2 which came with Zerubbabel. These were the chiefs who were to conduct the people. The leader was Zerubbabel, the son of Pedaiah, and nephew and heir of Shealtiel, and therefore called his son. Upon the extinction of the royal line through Solomon, by the death of Jeconiah without issue, the heirship came into the family of Nathan, another of David's sons, at that time represented by Zerubbabel; who stands, therefore, as descendant of Jeconiah: see 1 Chron. iii. 17–19; Jer. xxii. 30; Matt. i. 12; Luke iii. 27. Joshua, the grandson of Seraiah (or Azariah, Neh. vii. 7), who was slain by Nebuchadnezzar, was the high priest. The "Nehemiah" and "Mordecai" mentioned here are not, of course, the well-known persons bearing those names.

3 children. The word translated "children," throughout this chapter, is usually rendered "sons," and it evidently means here *descendants* when it precedes the name of a person, and *inhabitants* when it is followed by the name of a place. In some cases, however, the same name seems to belong both to a person and to a town.

20 Gibbar. Or, Gibeon: see Neh. vii. 25.

25 Kirjath-arim. Or, Kiriath-jearim: see Neh. vii. 29.

36 The priests. About 4,000 priests now went to Jerusalem: a large number in proportion to the rest of the community. Most of the Levites had remained attached to the Temple, from the disruption of the kingdom, instead of being dispersed through the Ten Tribes. But the priests here mentioned appear to have belonged to four only out of the twenty-four courses into which they had been divided by David; the rest either being extinct or remaining behind. But these four were so subdivided that the twenty-four courses were made up again; retaining their original titles.

43 The Nethinims. The Nethinim are supposed to have been originally of the race of the Gibeonites, who were spared by Joshua: see Josh. ix. 22–27. They performed the meaner services of the Temple: see viii. 20; 1 Chron. ix. 2.

55 The children of Solomon's servants. These were probably the descendants of Gentile artificers who were employed in building the first Temple; and who, becoming proselytes, were, with their posterity, retained for the purpose of keeping it in repair.

59 these were they, etc. The persons here mentioned were probably Israelites—descendants of the ten tribes—who, having been carried into exile long before the captivity of Judah, had lost their genealogies, and so could not claim any certain possession in the land. "Tel-melah," etc., were no doubt towns or districts of Babylonia.

61 the children of Barzillai. These descendants of Barzillai (2 Sam. xvii. 27) seem to have valued their relationship to him more than their connexion with the priesthood; and thus their children were deprived of its privileges, which they now desired.

63 the Tirshatha. This is the title given to Zerubbabel and Nehemiah as the Persian governors of Judæa: see Neh. vii. 65–70; viii. 9; x. 2. By the sentence of the Tirshatha, Barzillai's descendants were not to be restored to the priesthood without a Divine oracle to declare that they were of the race of Aaron.

68 to the house. That is, to the *site* of the former Temple.

69 drams. Or, "darics" (R.V.). Sixty-one thousand were about $200,000.

70 all Israel. Some of the exiles of the ten tribes seem to have returned. So that these tribes re-appeared by their representatives, and "Israel" was in fact re-constituted (*Rawlinson*): see 1 Chron. ix. 3.

CHAPTER III

1 the seventh month. Called "Ethanim" (1 Kings viii. 2), in which fell the feasts of Trumpets and of Tabernacles and the fast of the day of Atonement. It is called by the rabbis Tishri, and answers to parts of September and October.

2 builded the altar. The first care of the Jews on their return was the institution of religious worship.

3 upon his (its) bases. Probably the old foundations.

for fear was upon them, etc. They looked to Jehovah for protection, and *therefore* proceeded immediately to rebuild His altar.

7 to bring cedar trees, etc. As had been done for the former Temple: see 2 Chron. ii. 16.

9 Jeshua. Mentioned as head of a Levitical family in ii. 40, which see. He was a different person from Jeshua the high priest.

10 they set the priests. Another reading found

in several MSS. is "the priests stood" (R.V., marg.).

11 they sang together by course. *i.e.*, antiphonally. Some of the psalms are supposed to have been written about this period, particularly Psa. cvii., cxv., cxvi., cxxvi.

12 the first house. Though the second Temple was as large as the first, if not larger, yet it could not approach the magnificence of that upon which the wealth of David and Solomon had been expended; and—what was much more important—it wanted some of those extraordinary marks of the Divine presence and favour which constituted the chief glory of the former Temple; especially the ark of the covenant, with the mercy-seat upon it, and the holy fire on the altar. But the prophet Haggai was commissioned to comfort the people by the assurance that these deficiencies should be abundantly compensated by the coming Messiah, and His presence in this house (Hag. ii. 2-9).

CHAPTER IV

2 they came to Zerubbabel. These were descendants of the heathen colonists who had been sent into the country by the Assyrian kings, and possibly of the few Israelites who had been left in the land: see 2 Kings xvii. 24-41, and notes.

3 Ye have nothing to do with us. As the Samaritans did not worship Jehovah alone, but joined false gods with Him, they could not be admitted to the pure worship of His people.

5 Darius king of Persia. Darius Hystaspis.

6 Ahasuerus. This is not a proper name, but a royal title, supposed to mean the *lion-king.* Xerxes is the king here styled Ahasuerus.

7 written in the Syrian tongue, etc. *i.e.*, written in Aramaic and translated.

8 in this sort. The letters, decrees, etc., recited in this and the two following chapters, are given not in Hebrew, but in Aramaic. They were probably transcribed by Ezra from public records; and are interesting specimens of the form and style of the official correspondence and state orders of that period.

9 the Dinaites, etc. The different tribes that colonised Palestine: see 2 Kings xvii. 24. Little is known of them distinctively.

10 this side the river. Rather, "beyond"; *i.e.*, on the west side of "the River" Euphrates.

and at such a time. Rather, "and so forth" (R.V.). meaning *et cetera*: and so in ver. 11.

12 the Jews. As the greater part of those who returned from Babylon were of the tribe of Judah, the name "Jews" (or Judahites) was now given to the whole nation, although there were many belonging to the ten tribes among them; and the land was for a time called "Judæa," though this appellation afterwards came to be restricted to the southern part of Palestine.

have set up the walls thereof. This was a misrepresentation: see Neh. ii. 13-17.

13 and so thou shalt, etc. "And in the end thou shalt cause damage to kings."

14 we have maintenance, etc. Or, "we have eaten the salt of the palace"; a phrase still in use, as meaning servants dependent on a master.

18 hath been plainly read. *i.e.*, "translated."

22 that ye fail not. R.V., "that ye be not slack"; losing no time.

24 So it ceased. The enemies of the Jews easily prevailed, their opposition being aided by the indifference and worldly-mindedness of the Jews themselves (see Hag. i. 2-9). The rebuilding of the Temple was suspended; but in the second year of Darius Hystaspis (520 B.C.) it was resumed, and was then finished in four years, nineteen years after its commencement: see Zech. viii. 9; Hag. ii. 18.

CHAPTER V

1 the son of Iddo. That is, *descendant;* for he was the grandson of Iddo: see Zech. i. 1. See also the preface to Haggai, and ch. i., ii. These two prophets were raised up at this critical period to arouse the people to a sense of their duty, and to encourage them by assurances of Divine help and of the future glory of the Temple; and their writings are intimately connected with this portion of history.

unto them. R.V. places a stop at "Jerusalem," and reads, "in the name of the God of Israel *prophesied they* unto them."

3 Tatnai. This was about fifteen years after the first opposition (iv. 5). In the interval there had been a change of governors. Tatnai and his associates seem to have discharged their duty with great fairness and candour; giving an impartial statement of the case, very different from that which had been made by their predecessors in office (iv.).

4 Then said we. The Septuagint, with which the Syriac and Arabic versions agree, uses the third person, "And *they* said unto them," etc.

5 that they could not cause them to cease, etc. R.V., "and they did not make them cease, until the matter should come to Darius, and then answer should be returned by letter concerning it"; see note on ver. 3, as to the conduct of Tatnai.

11 set up. Rather, "finished" (R.V.).

17 the king's treasure-house. The "rolls" or records of the kingdom were carefully preserved in a part of the "treasure-house": see vi. 1.

CHAPTER VI

1 rolls. R.V., "archives."

2 Achmetha. Achmetha was the chief city of Media. It was the summer residence of the Persian monarchs; being selected for that purpose to avoid the heat of the plain of the Tigris, where Susa, the seat of the winter palace, was situated (Neh. i. 1). It was called Ecbatana by the Greeks; and its site is now occupied by the city of *Hamadan.*

3 the height thereof, etc. Double the height of Solomon's Temple, and three times the breadth (1 Kings vi. 2, 3).

9 the God of heaven. This decree of Darius seems to imply his conviction that the God whom the Jews worshipped was the true God: see especially ver. 12. Cp. i. 2. The ancient Persian religion was very far from sanctioning the gross idolatries of other nations.

11 be made a dunghill. As a mark of ignominy. For the same reason the Romans pulled down the houses of criminals.

14 Artaxerxes. See note on ch. vii. 1. His name is introduced here, though the Temple was rebuilt before his reign, probably because he contributed to maintain and beautify it: see vii. 12-19.

15 the month Adar. The twelfth month of the sacred year (part of February and March).

16 kept the dedication . . . with joy. It is highly probable that Psa. cxlvi.-cl. were composed on this occasion, or about this period.

17 twelve he goats, in sign of the re-constitution of Israel; although this was as yet incomplete: see note on ii. 70.

18 in the book of Moses. Moses had given laws respecting the ministry of the priests and Levites, and the celebration of God's worship at the place which He should choose; but the courses of the priests and Levites were appointed by David.

21 and all such, etc. Descendants of the Jews who were left in the land at the time of the captivity.

22 the king of Assyria. That is, the king of Persia, as Assyria now formed part of his dominions: see note on i. 1.

CHAPTER VII

1 Artaxerxes. This was Artaxerxes Longimanus, the son and successor of Xerxes I. The history now passes on to a period about sixty years after the Temple had been finished, as related in ch. vi. During the interval, Zerubbabel, Jeshua, Haggai, and Zechariah, had in all probability died; and although the Temple was built and the worship restored, the civil and ecclesiastical state of the Jews was still very unsettled, until Ezra came with a new body of settlers, and a commission to restore the ancient national institutions. It is probable that the events related in the Book of ESTHER occurred during the interval.

3 the son of Meraioth. In this genealogy, between Azariah and Meraioth, six generations are omitted, which are found in 1 Chron. vi. 7. Enough is given here to prove the descent of Ezra from the line of Eleazar, Aaron's eldest son.

6 a ready scribe. That is, *learned* in the law of Moses, and well qualified to instruct others.

the Lord God of Israel. "The Eternal, the God of Israel," as elsewhere: see R.V.

7 And there went up, etc. This was the second great company that returned from Babylon. They went in circumstances much more encouraging than the former; for now the Temple had been rebuilt, and the worship of God restored.

8 the fifth month. Ab, answering to the latter part of July and the former part of August. The distance between Babylon and Jerusalem is between five and six hundred miles.

12 king of kings. Perhaps this means, "having many tributary kings" under him. But the form of the title preserved by the Greek historians ("the Great King") intimates that it is only superlative, like "the heaven of heavens." Rameses II. applies the title "king of kings" to himself in his hieroglyphics on Cleopatra's Needle.

14 his seven counsellors. So in Esther i. 14, "the seven princes." According to Herodotus (iii. 70, 71, 76, 84) the seven nobles who deposed the false Smerdis, and their successors, had the right of private access to the king at all times as his advisers.

23 diligently. R.V., "exactly." Moffatt translates, "in full."

24 it shall not be lawful, etc. By thus exonerating from taxation all who officiated or assisted in the Temple-worship, the Persian monarch showed the favour with which he regarded the Jews. In their present circumstances, this unusual exemption was a seasonable and important encouragement.

25 set magistrates and judges, etc. The king authorised Ezra, as governor of the Jews who lived west of the Euphrates, to appoint subordinate officers, and to provide for the instruction of the people in the law of God; and he even permitted him to seek the conversion of the other inhabitants of the land to the worship of Jehovah.

27 Blessed be the Lord God ("the Eternal, the God of," etc.). With this sudden outburst of gratitude the Hebrew language is resumed, and is continued through the rest of the book.

CHAPTER VIII

1 them that went up. The number of male adults (for such those here numbered appear to have been) amounts only to 1,754 persons; but the whole body who accompanied Ezra, including women and children, would, according to the usual proportions, consist of nearly seven thousand.

7 the sons of Elam, etc. Many from the families mentioned here had previously gone up with Zerubbabel: see ch. ii.

13 the last sons. These are called "the last," probably because part of the family had returned to Judæa before, and all who remained now followed.

15 Ahava. The place and the river (21, 31) seem to have had the same name. It is supposed that the modern *Hit*, on the Euphrates, occupies the site. The river, however, may have been one of the numerous canals of the Euphrates near Babylon (*Hastings' Dict. Bible*).

none of the sons of Levi. That is, none who were simply Levites; for there were several priests.

17 Casiphia. It is uncertain where Casiphia was situated, or who "Iddo the chief" was.

18 a man of understanding. "Discretion," R.V.

22 the enemy in the way. Roving Arab tribes, who lived by plunder.

24 Sherebiah. Read "to Sherebiah," *i.e.*, priests in addition to these two Levites (see 18, 19; Neh. viii. 7; xi. 15, etc.).

31 on the twelfth day. See vii. 9. The interval had been occupied in reviewing the people (viii. 15) and in gathering the Levites and Nethinim.

35 twelve bullocks for all Israel. Cp. ii. 70; vi. 17, and notes.

36 lieutenants. "Satraps," the chief governors of provinces under Nebuchadnezzar and the Persian kings: see R.V.

CHAPTER IX

1 doing according to their abominations. Rather, "as they should have done with respect to their abominations," etc. The accusation is not that they had actually joined in idol-worship, but that they did not keep themselves separate from idolators, allowing their children to intermarry with them: a practice which had always led to idolatry. This is given as the reason for the prohibition in almost every place where it is repeated: see Deut. vii. 3, 4, etc.

2 the holy seed. So the Israelites were called, because of God's covenant with them, by which they were separated from all other nations, specially set apart to Himself, and entrusted with peculiar religious privileges.

3 plucked off the hair, etc. These were the customary tokens of deep grief and displeasure.

6 and said, etc. Ezra was not personally guilty in this matter; but he spoke and acted as the representative of the whole people: cp. Dan. ix. 3.

8 a remnant. The returned exiles were but a remnant of the whole nation, the bulk of the people still remaining in their dispersions; and those who returned were in an impoverished and abject state, compared with their ancestors.

to give us a nail. This refers to the nails or pins by which the Oriental tents were fastened to the ground, and conveys the idea of habitation.

9 we were bondmen. "Are" should be supplied, as R.V. The people were still under foreign masters.

a wall in Judah. The term here translated "wall" signifies the fence of a sheep-fold; and here represents the Divine protection.

12 Now therefore, etc. The language of the first clause is derived from Deut. vii. 3; that of the second closely follows Deut. xxiii. 6, where it is applied to the Ammonites and Moabites. The inducements recall the promises in Deut. xi. 8; Isa. i. 19; Ezek. xxxvii. 25.

13 such deliverance as this. Rather, "such a remnant" (R.V.): see vers. 8, 14.

14 the people of these abominations. More exactly, as R.V., "the peoples that do these abominations."

CHAPTER X

1 when Ezra, etc. Rather, as R.V., "while Ezra prayed and made confession."

2 Shechaniah. Shechaniah appears not to have been implicated himself; but his father and others of his near relatives were: see ver. 26.

hope in Israel. Rather, "hope for Israel," R.V. However great the sin, it is not hopeless when it is seen and lamented, and decisive steps are taken towards a reformation.

3 make a covenant . . . to put away all the wives, etc. This measure, though it was severe, especially in its bearing on the children, was evidently necessary to prevent the influx of idolatry. These cases differ greatly from those for which a milder rule was laid down by the Apostle Paul (1 Cor. vii. 12, 13); for the Jew who married a heathen wife did so in direct violation of his own law; whereas the parties referred to in the New Testament had married as heathens, but one of them had *subsequently* been converted to Christianity.

9 the ninth month. Kislev, about the beginning of December, which in Palestine is the coldest and most rainy season of the year. Ezra had now been in Jerusalem for four months (vii. 9).

the street. The broad space in front of the gate.

14 Let now our rulers . . . stand. That is, let them act as a court of inquiry; summoning before them the parties concerned, together with the judges and elders of their cities. The investigation seems to have occupied three months: see vers. 16, 17.

15 were employed about. Rather, "stood up against" (R.V.), *i.e.*, opposed. But the rest of the assembly assented (16).

16 the first day of the tenth month. Tebeth (Dec.–Jan.), ten days later than the gathering mentioned in ver. 9.

18 among the sons of the priests. Although the law had particularly provided for the preservation of their honour in their marriages (see Lev. xxi. 7); and they, as teachers of the law, were bound, above all others, to set a good example.

19 they gave their hands. A most expressive mode of solemn agreement.

a ram of the flock for their trespass. A sin offering: see Lev. v. 14–16.

25 of Israel. That is, those who were neither priests nor Levites.

44 All these had taken strange wives. The transgression must have been very widely extended, owing probably in part to the small proportion of women who had returned from Babylon. Although this evil among the Jews seemed now to be thoroughly corrected, we find it noticed again some years afterwards: see Neh. xiii. 23; Mal. ii. 11.

THE BOOK OF NEHEMIAH

The Building of the City

INTRODUCTION

NEHEMIAH is one of the great personalities of the Bible. His faith in God, his high character, his courage, his devotion to his country, his perseverance in face of opposition and ridicule, his belief in prayer, his respect for God's laws and especially for that of the Sabbath, make his life an inspiration for every Christian.

The period covered by the Book is from 445 B.C., thirteen years after Ezra's arrival in Jerusalem, to 433 B.C. Nehemiah, cup-bearer in the palace at Shushan, hears of the sad condition of Judæa, and of its people, and how, though the Temple had been rebuilt, the walls of Jerusalem were still broken down (i. 1–3). In his distress he turns to God with fasting, confession, and prayer, asking God to dispose the king's mind in his favour (i. 4–11). Then he proceeds to action. He asks the king, not only for permission to return to Jerusalem for the purpose of rebuilding the walls, but also for letters to the governors of provinces through which he would have to pass. Artaxerxes not only gives him permission and the desired letters, but also provides him with an escort of cavalry (ii. 5–9). Nehemiah's prayer was more than answered.

But his faith is soon tested more severely. Sanballat the Horonite, with his friends Tobiah and Geshem, oppose Nehemiah's project, ridicule it, and lead an army against the city (ii. 10, 19; iv. 10–12). Nehemiah, however, is not discouraged. His trust is in "the God of heaven" (ii. 20; iv. 4–6, 9, 20). Then he has to deal with complaints from the poor of his own people that the rich are oppressing them with usury and slavery. There is a time to be angry, and Nehemiah expressed his indignation to the nobles and rulers in strong terms. Again his faith and courage won the day (v. 1–13). In this victory his own unselfishness (v. 14–18) had an important part, as making the wealthy men ashamed of their greed and unkindness.

New troubles, however, arise. His enemies, foiled in their first attempts to prevent the building of the wall, try what they can do by treachery. But with prayer and determination he again defeats their designs, and the wall is finished (vi.). The gratitude of Nehemiah and the people to God was expressed in a service of glad thanksgiving and dedication (xii. 27–43).

Nehemiah's faith in God shows itself also in the application of God's law to everyday life. He knew that the highest patriotism should aim at something more than material prosperity and security, that true religion is something more than sacrifices offered upon an altar. Hence the Book of the Law is read by Ezra in the hearing of all the people, Nehemiah impressing upon them that the occasion is one for rejoicing and not for weeping (viii. 12), and reviving the Feast of Tabernacles (viii. 13–18).

Having arranged for the government of Jerusalem (vii. 1–5) and bringing in people from the country to occupy the city (xi. 1, 2), he returns to Babylonia (xiii. 6). His stay there is not long, as he again obtains permission of the king to visit Jerusalem. There, once more, he carries out necessary reforms (xiii. 7, 10, 11, 15–30). His work is done, his death is not recorded, and he disappears from the page of history. But his example remains. And some of his great sayings have been watchwords in the Church of God through the centuries. Among these are: "The God of heaven, He will prosper us; therefore we His servants will arise and build" (ii. 20); "I am doing a great work, so that I cannot come down" (vi. 3); and "Should such a man as I flee?" (vi. 11).

CHAPTER I

1 The words of Nehemiah. Or, "the actions" of Nehemiah; that is, the history of his labours for his country: see 1 Kings xi. 41.

Chisleu. Or Kislev, the third month of the civil year (the ninth of the sacred year), answering to parts of our November and December.

the twentieth year. That is, in the twentieth year of the reign of Artaxerxes Longimanus (see note on Ezra vii. 1), 455–444 B.C., and the ninety-first or ninety-second year after the return from Babylon; the thirteenth year after Ezra's journey to Jerusalem.

Shushan. Or *Susa,* in the sunny plains of the Tigris, the winter residence of the Persian kings. Its ruins are now called *Sus.*

3 the wall . . is broken down. As we have no account in the Book of Ezra of the wall being rebuilt, it is most probable that it was still in the state in which it had been left at the destruction of the city by the Chaldæans: see 2 Kings xxv. 10. The former commissions of Zerubbabel and Ezra (Ezra i.; vii. 11–28) did not extend to the fortification of the city.

4 the God of heaven. This was a Persian method of describing the supreme God. Nehemiah would naturally have fallen into it.

5 and said, etc. We have here (5–11) the substance of Nehemiah's constant supplications. Compare the prayers in Ezra ix. 5–15; Dan. ix. 4–19.

O Lord God of heaven. Literally, "O Eternal, the God of heaven."

7 commandments (moral), **statutes** (ceremonial), **judgements** (civil law).

9 though there were of you cast out, etc. R.V., "though your outcasts were in the uttermost part of the heaven."

11 who desire. R.V., more expressively, "who delight."

the king's cupbearer. Rather, "a cupbearer of the king": one of several. The office of cupbearer was one of great honour and confidence, as well as of considerable profit and influence. A person who held it, being in constant attendance on the king, had opportunities of preferring petitions and obtaining favours. Nehemiah appears to have been enabled from his own resources to sustain his government at Jerusalem with great dignity and hospitality, without laying any burden on the people: see v. 14–18. Others also of the Jews were advanced to places of trust and authority under the Babylonian and Persian monarchs; and so were able to assist and protect their brethren.

CHAPTER II

1 Nisan. The seventh month of the civil, first of the sacred year; answering to our March or April; so that four months had elapsed since Nehemiah had learned the afflicted condition of his countrymen at Jerusalem. This may have been his first attendance since that time on the king in private: see ver. 6, and note.

6 the queen also sitting by him. The presence of the queen intimates the privacy of the occasion. Her name was *Damaspia.*

7 may convey me. Rather, as R.V., "may let me pass through." The "letters" were safe-conducts.

8 forest. The Persian word used here and in Eccles. ii. 5; Sol. Song iv. 13, is probably best translated "park."

palace. R.V., "castle." Probably, the "fort"; afterwards, by a slight modification of the word, called in Greek Baris, and named by Herod Antonia: see Josephus, *Antiquities*, xv. 11, 4.

10 Sanballat, etc. Sanballat was probably an Ephraimite or Samaritan of Beth-horon (Upper or Lower). Tobiah the Ammonite had been a slave. The Moabites and Ammonites had been subdued and carried captive by the kings of Babylon; and it is probable that Sanballat and Tobiah, and Geshem the Arabian (19), held appointments under the king of Persia, as governors over the remnant of these nations and the Samaritans, who were all very hostile to the Jews.

14 the king's pool. Solomon's pool.

15 the brook. The brook Kidron.

CHAPTER III

1 Eliashib. The grandson of the Jeshua who had come from Babylon with Zerubbabel.

the sheep gate. In the E. wall of the city, and on the northern declivity of the Temple-hill: see John v. 2.

sanctified it. By offering prayers, and probably sacrifices.

Meah. Rather, Hammeah (R.V.), or "the hundred."

3 the fish gate. This was north-west of Moriah, and was so called because fish from Joppa and Zidon was brought in by it.

Hassenaah. Perhaps the same as Senaah, Ezra ii. 35.

4 Meremoth. Meremoth also repaired another piece (21). So did the men of Tekoa (5, 27), although their "nobles" refused to work: see also ver. 11.

6 the old gate. Probably this corresponded to the modern *Damascus Gate*, the chief entrance to the city on the N.W. side (*Fergusson*).

7 the throne of the governor. This may mean the official residence of the governor of Syria in Jerusalem.

on this side the River. R.V., "beyond the River," *i.e.*, on the west side of the Euphrates.

8 apothecaries. That is, compounders of and dealers in spices and perfumes.

11 the other. Rather, "another": see note on ver. 4.

the tower of the furnaces. Or, "ovens," perhaps in the wall adjoining "the bakers' street" (Jer. xxxvii. 21). The ovens were of clay from the "valley." "Here, too, in all probability, were the potteries which gave their name to the 'gate of the potteries' (Jer. xix. 2, R.V. marg.)."—*Sayce.*

12 and his daughters. Some of the persons mentioned in this list as having repaired certain portions of the wall, probably did so by paying the expense of the work.

13 The valley gate. That is, the valley of Tyropœon, lying between the main city and the Temple hill.

15 Siloah. Or, "Siloam."

16 the house of the mighty. This was, perhaps, the place formerly occupied by David's body-guard (see 2 Sam. xxiii. 8).

21 after him. The two phrases, "after him" and "next unto him," have the same meaning, and denote that the person next mentioned began at that part of the wall where the other left off.

22 the plain. This is explained by xii. 28, on which see note.

26 Ophel. The southern slope of Moriah.

the water gate. So named from the great water-course leading from the heart of Moriah to "the Virgin's Spring," and thence to the Pool of Siloam, outside the walls of the city.

28 every one over against his house. By assigning to each one the execution of the portion over against his own house, where it adjoined the wall, Nehemiah wisely blended the *personal* with the *patriotic.*

29 the east gate. *i.e.*, of the Temple.

32 unto the sheep gate. Thus completing the circuit of the walls: cp. ver. 1.

CHAPTER IV

1 took great indignation. This displeasure and enmity seem to have been entirely unprovoked, and to have been the result of hatred to the religion, and envy at the prosperity of the Jews.

2 will they fortify themselves? "Will they commit themselves to their God?" (*Ryle*).

6 So built we the wall. *i.e.*, amid the taunts of our enemies, yet with steadfast faith in God and earnest prayer.

unto the half thereof. The circuit of the wall was completed to half its *height* (see R.V.).

7 the walls of Jerusalem were made up. Rather, as R.V., "the repairing of the walls of Jerusalem went forward."

9 We made our prayer . . . and set a watch. Sincere faith and prayer will always be accompanied by watchfulness and activity.

12 they will be upon you. The meaning appears to be, that the Jews who dwelt near the Samaritans and other adversaries were constantly ("ten times") coming to Nehemiah with information of contemplated attacks.

14 I looked, and rose up. *i.e.*, I first inspected the arrangements for defence, and then encouraged the defenders.

16 the rulers were behind. Each chief watching, guiding, and encouraging his men from behind; and at the same time ready to meet any attack.

18 he that sounded the trumpet. To give the alarm.

23 saving that, etc. "None of us took off our clothes; each one kept his weapon in his hand" (*Moffatt*).

CHAPTER V

1 there was a great cry. The poor seem to have had just ground of complaint against their wealthier brethren. Although their exile in Babylon had cured the Jews, as a people, of their tendency to idolatry, they were still, like their ancestors, much given to covetousness and oppression. The transactions in this chapter appear to have occurred during the building of the wall, causing probably an interruption of the work.

2 therefore we take up corn, etc. Rather, as R.V., " let us get corn, that we may eat and live."

3 because of the dearth. The cultivation of the land had probably suffered from the difficulties to which the people had been exposed, as well as from other causes. Hence there was a scarcity of food; and the rich men, taking advantage of their brethren's distress, compelled them to part with all that they possessed, and even to sell their children into bondage, in order to obtain the means of procuring food and of paying the taxes.

7 Ye exact usury. The Mosaic law forbade the Israelites to take usury of their brethren (Exod. xxii. 25; Lev. xxv. 36; Deut. xxiii. 19).

redeemed our brethren. That is, from *slavery*, into which some of the poor Jews had been sold.

10 I likewise, etc. R.V., "I likewise, my brethren, and my servants, do lend them money and corn on usury." Nehemiah's confession would thus appear to include himself. But see vers. 6–10. Probably he lent, but not *on usury*.

11 the hundredth part. That is, a *percentage*, whatever the rate might have been. Nothing can be more forcible, touching, and generous than this address; and it seems to have been met on the whole in a similar spirit. The result must have been greatly to strengthen Nehemiah's hold on popular affection.

12 called the priests. The priests were summoned that the oath might be administered with religious solemnity.

13 I shook my lap. The mantle, or outer garment, was often used to carry goods in: see Exod. xii. 34; Ruth iii. 15. Significant actions of this kind have always been common in the East: see Matt. x. 14; Acts xviii. 6

15 beside forty shekels. Claiming not only the expenses of their households and attendants, but also forty shekels a day in money.

16 I continued. Or, " repaired," as in ch. iii. throughout. Probably this means not by taking any one portion, but by the general supervision of the work.

18 required not I the bread of the governor. In the Persian empire, the dues of the government were paid partly in provisions. Nehemiah, on account of the distressed state of the people, would not take from them the usual allowances to which, as governor, he was entitled.

19 Think upon me, my God. Nehemiah is particularly distinguished by his constant recurrence to God: see vi. 9, 10, etc. This verse is literally rendered in R.V., " Remember unto me, O my God, for good, all that I have done for this people."

CHAPTER VI

1 upon the gates. Heb., " in the gates " (R.V.).

2 the villages. R.V. reads, " in *one of* the villages."

Ono, in the Plain of Sharon, north of Lydda.

5 an open letter. Letters sent by Orientals to superiors, and even to equals, are carefully sealed, and enclosed in silken bags. By sending the letter *open*, contrary to the universal practice, Sanballat doubtless intended both to insult Nehemiah and to excite the fears and discontent of the people by making the accusations generally known.

9 made us afraid. Rather, as R.V., " would have made us afraid."

10 within the Temple. The environs of the Temple were secured by walls and gates, while the gates of the city were not yet set up.

11 Should such a man as I flee? In such circumstances, even the preservation of life formed but a subordinate consideration, compared with the importance of setting an example of courageous confidence in God. It is worthy of notice that Nehemiah, whilst he took every reasonable precaution, never allowed fear to hinder his work.

13 and sin. Not only by culpable timidity and distrust, but by seeking refuge in the Holy Place, which was forbidden to all but priests.

14 the rest of the prophets. These pretended prophets having sold their services to the enemies of religion, Nehemiah prays for their confusion and disappointment.

15 fifty and two days. From the third day of Ab, the fifth month (July, August), to the twenty-fifth of Elul, the sixth (August, September). The solemn assembly of the people was held six days later, on the first of Tishri (viii. 3).

17 the nobles. The part which Nehemiah had taken in the defence of the poor (ch. v.) would arouse the enmity of the rich.

18 because he was the son-in-law of Shechaniah. The serious mischiefs resulting from these connexions with the enemies of their country, show that the strong measures which Ezra adopted to prevent them (Ezra x.) were really necessary.

CHAPTER VII

2 Hanani. The same as mentioned in i. 2.

the ruler of the palace. R.V., " the governor of the castle," the Temple-fortress.

3 while they stand by. Rather, as R.V., " while they stand *on guard*." The porters, singers, and Levites were the watchers at the city gates; while the nightly guardianship of the interior was committed to the inhabitants generally. This was especially necessary from the large unoccupied spaces within the walls (4). The late opening of the gates was an unusual precaution.

5 a register. Rather, as R.V., " the book of the genealogy "—the list of those who had come up from Babylon ninety years before (Ezra ii.).

6 the province. Judæa was now a province of the Persian empire.

8 The children of Parosh, etc. There are variations in this transcript from the original in Ezra, in almost every verse; instructively showing the risks to which written documents are subject in the transmission from hand to hand, especially in numerical statements. The total number, however, is the same in both records: ver. 66, compared with Ezra ii. 64. On details, see notes in Ezra.

CHAPTER VIII

1 Ezra the scribe. Ezra, having taken a journey to Babylon after his first coming to Judæa, had now returned.

2 on the first day of the seventh month. On this day of the ecclesiastical year (Tishri), or the new year's day of the civil year, was the Feast of

Trumpets (Lev. xxiii. 24). In the seventh month, also, the Feast of Tabernacles was held; and it was commanded that at this feast, in every seventh year, the law should be publicly read (Deut. xxxi. 10, 11); which may have suggested the people's request.

3 from the morning until midday. Heb., "from the light"; that is, from about six in the morning till noon.

4 a pulpit of wood. The Hebrew word is often used for a watch-tower: here it signifies a large platform, as it was capable of holding fourteen persons.

7 caused the people to understand. The Hebrew was translated for the benefit of the people who spoke Aramaic, and the meaning was also explained by Ezra and his helpers.

9 the Tirshatha. See note on Ezra ii. 63. Nehemiah never gives himself this name in the portion of the book which is written in the first person.

mourn not, nor weep. The Festivals of Trumpets and Tabernacles were to be observed with joy. One element of this joy, as the next verse shows, was that of doing good to others.

14 should dwell in booths. The Feast of Tabernacles was appointed to be held on the fifteenth day of this month: see Lev. xxiii. 34, 42; Deut. xvi. 13. The people, having heard the directions given respecting it in Lev. xxiii., were eager to commemorate it.

15 the mount. The hill-country.

pine branches. Rather, as R.V., "branches of wild olive."

16 the gate of Ephraim. In the centre of the north wall of the city.

17 had not . . . done so. Although the sacred festivals had been greatly neglected during long portions of the Jewish history, instances are expressly recorded of the Feast of Tabernacles having been kept (2 Chron. viii. 13; Ezra iii. 4). This statement must refer, therefore, to the *mode* rather than the *fact* of celebration.

18 he read in the book. See note on Deut. xxxi. 12. This reading is supposed to have given rise to the regular public reading of the Scriptures every Sabbath day, and to the establishment of synagogues in all the cities of the Jews for that purpose; which was probably one principal means of keeping them from ever again relapsing into idolatry.

CHAPTER IX

1 with fasting, etc. This was not the day of Atonement, which fell on the tenth day of this month; but it was a special national fast, introductory to the solemn covenant which followed (ver. 38; ch. x.). One day only had intervened since the last of the Feast of Tabernacles.

15 promisedst. Rather, as R.V., "commandedst."

17 appointed a captain, etc. "And appointed a captain to lead them back": see Numb. xiv. 4.

21 forty years didst Thou sustain them in the wilderness. See Acts xiii. 21, which seems to be formed by combining the Septuagint rendering of this passage and Deut. i. 31.

22 into corners. Heb., "to the side"; *i.e.*, by definite boundaries.

the land of Sihon, and, etc. Rather, "*even* the land of the king of Heshbon" (R.V.); for Sihon was king of Heshbon.

25 of all goods, wells digged. etc. R.V., "of all good things, cisterns hewn out," etc. To find the means of constant water supply ready prepared for them was a most important advantage.

delighted themselves. Or, "gave themselves to pleasure": see Isa. xlvii. 8. They delighted in the gifts they enjoyed, while they forgot the Giver (26).

27 Therefore Thou deliveredst them, etc. These confessions are affectingly illustrated by the whole history of the Israelites, especially by the Book of Judges—the brief summary of which, in ii. 11–23, greatly resembles this passage.

29 withdrew the shoulder, etc. These metaphors are taken from untrained or refractory oxen, which refuse the yoke: see Zech. vii. 11.

36 servants. That is, slaves (as the original denotes) in their own land to a foreign master. "As our fathers would not serve Thee, we have to serve the Persian king."

37 it yieldeth much increase unto the kings. The tribute paid to the king of Persia was not only a heavy burden upon them in proportion to their means, but it was specially injurious to their interests; inasmuch as it was carried out of their own country, and spent in a foreign land.

38 And because of all this. The R.V. rendering, "And yet for all this," is not an improvement. *Because* of past sins and the punishment they had suffered, they now pledged themselves to be faithful to God.

CHAPTER X

1 those that sealed. The name of the high priest Eliashib is wanting among those that sealed: see xiii. 4. The name of Ezra also is absent: his place as governor had been taken by Nehemiah.

29 clave to their brethren. That is, they publicly and solemnly ratified what their representatives had done.

31 and if the people, etc. The articles of the covenant into which the people entered show what portions of the law they had of late most neglected.

32 the third part of a shekel. About a shilling.

34 for the wood offering. In former times it had been the duty of the Nethinim (who were "hewers of wood and drawers of water to the congregation," or servants of the Temple) to provide the wood necessary for the Temple service. But, after the return from the Captivity, this duty was undertaken by the priests and Levites, and the people at large; and they cast lots to determine the order in which the various classes and families should provide the needful supply. In later times, the Jews had an annual festival called *Xylophoria*, or "wood-carrying"; observed on the fourteenth day of the fifth month, Ab (July, Aug.), when they carried with some solemnity the wood for the use of the Temple.

CHAPTER XI

3 these are the chief (R.V., "chiefs"). This enumeration differs considerably from that in 1 Chron. ix.; and various methods of reconciliation have been proposed. The most probable supposition is. that both lists are extracts from the public register, the names in 1 Chron. ix. being selected for genealogical purposes, whilst those here given were chosen on account of their national and political importance.

9 was second. Joel was the governor of the Benjamites in the city, and Judah his deputy.

10 Jedaiah the son, etc. Probably rather, "Jedaiah, Joiarib, Jachin"; three heads of families.

11 the ruler. The high priest's family supplied "the ruler." Some consider this to be the officer who in the New Testament is called the "captain of the Temple" (Acts v. 24), and who had the superintendence of its secular matters.

14 mighty men of valour. The Hebrew term here used sometimes refers to *wealth,* and in other cases to *moral excellence.*

16 the outward business. It is probable that they had the charge of collecting the revenues, and of providing the sacrifices and other necessaries.

22 were. This should not be inserted, and a comma should follow "Micha" (R.V.). The whole verse is one sentence.

24 at the king's hand. "On the king's part." Pethahiah heard all causes in civil matters between the king and the people, such as about his tribute, or any grievance of which they complained.

31 dwelt at Michmash. Rather, "dwelt from Geba to Michmash."

36 divisions. Or, courses. R.V. reads, "of the Levites certain courses in Judah were joined to Benjamin."

CHAPTER XII

1 the Levites. Not all of them, but only the most distinguished are here named. Cp. vii. 39–45, and Ezra ii. 36, etc.

11 Jaddua. We have here a list of the high priests for several generations after the Jews returned from Babylon. If this Jaddua were, as is said by Josephus, and as the best expositors hold, the high priest who went out to meet Alexander the Great on his approach to Jerusalem (a century after the transaction recorded by Nehemiah), then vers. 10, 11, like some other verses, must have been added after Nehemiah's time.

22 were recorded chief of the fathers. *i.e.,* a registry was kept of the heads of families. R.V. renders, "were recorded heads of fathers' *houses.*" If this list of chief priests reaches down only to Nehemiah's days, then the king here mentioned must be Darius Nothus, the immediate successor of Artaxerxes Longimanus; but if (according to the view stated in the preceding note) "Jaddua" in this verse be the high priest of the time of Alexander, then "Darius" must be Darius Codomannus, whom Alexander conquered, 331 B.C. "He is called *Darius the Persian,* as if the Persian empire had ceased to exist when this passage was written."—*Sayce.*

24 over against them. Antiphonally: see Exod. xv. 20, 21; 1 Sam. xviii. 7; Ezra iii. 11; Psa. xx., cxii., etc.

25 thresholds. Rather, as R.V., "storehouses."

28 the plain country. Rather, "the circuit round about Jerusalem." The word (*kikkar*) usually applied to the land round the lower end of Jordan seems here to be used for the environs of Jerusalem. "Netophathi" should be "the Netophathites," R.V. Netophah was near Bethlehem. "The house of Gilgal," R.V., Beth-Gilgal, was about twenty miles north of Jerusalem. "Geba" (now *Jeha*) was seven miles north of the city. "Azmaveth," now called *Hizmeh,* south-east of Gibeah.

31 I brought up. Neheemiah here resumes the first person from vii. 5.

38 the other company, etc. There appears to have been a double procession of the princes and priests; one company, headed by Ezra, going to the right, and the other, with Nehemiah at their rear, going to the left: thus making a circuit of the wall in different directions, until they met on the opposite side of the city, when they marched in a body to the Temple.

44 of the law. That is, "prescribed by the law."

45 kept the ward, etc. Rather, "They observed what related to their God, and what related to their purification."

CHAPTER XIII

4 was allied unto Tobiah. "Related" or "connected with." The enemies of the Jews, finding their open hostility unavailing, had sought to gain their ends by forming alliances with their leading men. Eliashib's lukewarmness had already been shown by the absence of his name from the covenant (ch. x.). Tobiah's influence was so great that the Jews did not venture to enforce the law of separation in his case.

6 king of Babylon. The kings of Persia reigned over Babylon and all the regions which had before been subject to the kings of Babylon.

after certain days. How long Nehemiah remained in Persia is uncertain; but from the height to which these evils had attained during his absence, it seems probable that it must have been for several years. Nehemiah's second administration lasted probably about ten years, till about 405 B.C.

10 for the Levites, etc. Rather, as R.V., "so that the Levites," etc. They had been obliged to support themselves by working on their allotments of land.

11 Why is the house of God forsaken? The prophet Malachi appears to refer to these abuses: see Mal. i. 9–14; iii. 7–12.

gathered them together. *i.e.,* the Levites.

14 my good deeds. This prayer of Nehemiah should be compared with another, in ver. 22, which shows that his consciousness of the service which by Divine grace he had been enabled to render, was accompanied with a humble sense of his need of sparing mercy.

15 treading wine presses on the sabbath, etc. This particular violation of the law no doubt had become prevalent during the captivity, as the heathen masters of the Jews would prevent them from observing their sacred seasons.

17 I contended with the nobles. It was characteristic of Nehemiah to deal directly with the leaders of the people, as chief in blame.

23 In those days, etc. This reform is supposed to have been from twelve to twenty years after the like reform by Ezra: see Ezra x.

24 according to the language of each people. A mixed dialect, partly Hebrew, partly Philistine (akin to the Egyptian).

28 one of the sons of Joiada. Josephus says that this expelled priest was named Manasseh; that he went to his father-in-law, Sanballat, who built a temple for him upon Mount Gerizim, in opposition to that at Jerusalem; and that this was the origin of the religious rivalry and extreme hatred between the Samaritans and the Jews: see John iv. 20.

THE BOOK OF ESTHER

THE STORY OF A GREAT DELIVERANCE

INTRODUCTION

THOUGH this Book follows "Nehemiah" in our Bible, the events described in it took place at an earlier date. The king here called Ahasuerus is known in history as Xerxes, and "there can be little doubt that the series of festivals described in ch. i. was to inaugurate Xerxes' expedition to Greece, and that the marriage with Esther "in the seventh year of his reign" took place after the great defeat at Salamis, Platæa and Mycalé, 480–479 B.C. (*Bible Handbook*, by Angus and Green, 1904, p. 546). Many scholars think that the story itself was written about fifty years later, say between 430 and 425 B.C. The Feast of Purim (ix. 17–22, 26–32), with its universal observance by the Jews to this day, seems to be one of the strongest evidences that the Book is historical. National festivals do not usually arise out of fiction.

The fact that the name of God is not mentioned in the Book has often been alluded to. But this appears to be rather a mechanical criticism. The teaching of the Book is highly religious. The words of Mordecai (iv. 14) indicate confidence in the promises of God and in the Divine guidance. Esther's appeal to the Jews to fast on her behalf (iv. 16) suggests the necessity for invoking God's help. The story shows the downfall of the proud and the vindication of innocence, and, while the vengeance taken by the Jews is severe (viii. 13; ix. 5, 16), it is to be remembered that it was more in the nature of self-defence, as the king's decree had actually gone out for their annihilation (iii. 13; iv. 3; vii. 4).

CHAPTER I

1 Ahasuerus. In Hebrew his name is "Achashverosh," representing the Persian Khsajârsâ, called Xerxes in Greek.

from India even unto Ethiopia. Herodotus expressly mentions the "Indians and Ethiopians" as being subjects of the Persian empire when Xerxes was preparing to invade Greece.

3 in the third year. Herodotus (vii. 8) tells us that about the third year of his reign (483 B.C.) Xerxes held a great assembly of his princes to determine and arrange his war with the Greeks.

4 a hundred and fourscore days. The deliberations continued for about half a year, at the close of which was a week of universal and unrestrained indulgence. According to Herodotus (vii. 20), four years elapsed between the first conception and the execution of the invasion of Greece.

6 white, green, and blue hangings. Read, as R.V., "*there were hangings of* white cloth, *of* cotton, (as marg.), and *of* blue" (*or*, "purple"). White and purple were the royal colours in Persia.

beds. Rather, "couches"; on which the guests reclined at their meals, as was usual among the ancients. R.V. marg. reads, "of porphyry, and white marble and alabaster, and stone of blue colour."

8 the drinking was according, etc. Or it may be rendered, "the drinking according to custom none did compel"; —the numerous guests might feast as they liked.

9 Vashti the queen. The principal wife of Xerxes, married to him early in his reign, was his cousin Amestris, who survived him. Vashti was therefore a subordinate wife, and at this time the royal favourite.

a feast for the women. While the king's feast was in "the court of the garden," Vashti's was in the "royal house," conducted more privately.

11 to bring Vashti the queen. A command out of keeping with Persian customs, but quite in accord with the character of Xerxes.

12 Vashti refused to come. Such an appearance as the king required at a promiscuous and unbridled carouse would be, according to Oriental notions, a degradation to which a woman of reputation would not be likely to submit.

13 which knew the times. That is, men well versed in public affairs: see 1 Chron. xii. 32.

14 seven princes. See note on Ezra vii. 14.

18 which have heard. etc. This clause should be transposed to follow "ladies" (princesses), R.V.

CHAPTER II

1 After these things. How soon this occurred we know not. The intervening time had been spent in the expedition to Greece. The battle of Platæa, in which Xerxes was finally defeated, took place in the sixth year of his reign (480 B.C.). We learn that after his defeat and return from Greece, Xerxes indulged his licentious passions (Herodotus, ix. 108).

2 Let there be fair young virgins. This narrative shows that the higher men are raised in power and wealth, the lower they often sink in subjection to their own sensual appetites. And it shows how much the Gospel of Christ was needed to give woman her right place in society, and to restore marriage to its original purity.

5 the son of Kish. Some infer from this that Mordecai was of the Benjamite royal family of Saul. But it is not unlikely that the names of Saul's family were favourites in the tribe. The word Mordecai means "belonging to Merodach," a Babylonian deity, and was no doubt a substitute by the heathen for some Jewish name. Cp. Daniel i. 7. Note, it was *Kish*, Mordecai's great-grandfather, who was carried away in captivity, not Mordecai himself. That captivity (598 B.C). took place 120 years before this.

7 Hadassah. "Hadassah" (*myrtle*) was her Hebrew name; "Esther" (*star*) her Persian name. Some, however, identify the latter with the Assyrian *Istar*, the Assyro-Babylonian form of the goddess Ashtoreth, symbolising youth and beauty (*Sayce*). In the Hebrew Prayer Book she is described as "Hadassah, the flower blossoming from the palm."

8 Esther was brought. It was not left to the choice of Esther, or of her guardian, whether she should be brought to the palace (3). A disclosure of her lineage might have kept her from being chosen as queen, but would not have saved her from concubinage. Every one whom the king thus took was considered a secondary wife; and her situation was not, according to the custom of those times and of those countries, deemed unlawful or dishonourable.

11 walked . . . before the court, etc. Mordecai appears to have been a keeper of the gate of the harem, an office held only by the highest of "the chamberlains" or eunuchs.

18 he made a release. This is understood by the Septuagint and the Chaldee to mean a *remission of tribute*. This was the practice of the Persian kings on festal occasions, as weddings. Moffatt renders: "he granted a holiday."

20 did the commandment of Mordecai. As a chief guardian of the harem, Mordecai would still have access to his niece, although, after the manner of the Persians, she was now secluded from the outer world.

CHAPTER III

1 the Agagite. Haman is said by Josephus to have been an Amalekite, descended from the ancient kings of that people, whose royal title was Agag: see Numb. xxiv. 7; 1 Sam. xv. 9.

2 reverenced. "Worshipped" or "prostrated themselves before."

6 sought to destroy all the Jews. If Haman was an Amalekite, his personal pique against Mordecai would be connected with feelings of hatred towards the nation who had been commissioned to exterminate the Amalekites.

7 In the first month, etc. It must not be inferred that Haman had recourse to the lot every day during a whole year: but he determined by lot first which month of the year was most auspicious, and then which day of the month; and the lots fell upon the fourteenth day of the month Adar, which was nearly twelve months after the time at which the decision was given. The overruling providence of God was herein strikingly manifested, for this long interval allowed time to take the necessary measures for defeating the plot.

9 ten thousand talents of silver. Over $20,000,000. Haman probably intended to reimburse himself from the spoil of the Jews.

12 the king's lieutenants. "The king's satraps" (R.V.). The 127 provinces of the Persian empire are stated by Herodotus to have been divided into 20 satrapies. Satraps are also mentioned in viii. 9; ix. 3; and Ezra viii. 36.

the king's ring. A seal-ring bearing the cipher of the sovereign, and thus answering the purpose of both seal and signature.

13 to destroy, etc. It appears surprising that the king should have given his consent to so inhuman a proposal; but history shows that when an arbitrary monarch has become the dupe of a wicked favourite, it frequently becomes the chief object of the king to gratify and aggrandise him, without regard to the lives of his subjects or the interests of his empire.

15 The posts. Xenophon states (*Cyrop.* viii. 6, 17, 18) that Cyrus had established a regular system of posts and couriers throughout the Persian dominions; and Herodotus (viii. 98) minutely describes the system as it was maintained under Xerxes between Susa and the most distant provinces.

was perplexed. No one could be sure of his life, when, to please a favourite, the king would sacrifice a whole nation, and then sit down with him to a drinking bout.

CHAPTER IV

2 clothed with sackcloth. Nothing was allowed to enter the palace which did not bear the aspect of joy and pleasure, or which could remind the king of misery or mortality.

6 street. The open square before the palace gates: see Ezra x. 9, and note.

11 one law of his. Heb., "for him"; *i.e.*, the intruder.

the golden sceptre. The golden sceptre of the Persian kings is referred to by Xenophon (*Cyrop.* viii. 7, 13), and appears from existing sculptures to have been a long staff, probably of wood overlaid and tipped with gold.

14 for such a time as this. Subsequent events showed that Mordecai had correctly interpreted the ways of Providence.

16 neither eat nor drink. That is, abstaining from set meals, and from all "pleasant food" (see Dan. x. 3); taking only what might be absolutely necessary to sustain life. Though *prayer* is not specified here, or in ver. 3, it is evidently implied; prayer being always connected with fasting in Scripture. The efficacy of this humble and earnest appeal to their Divine Protector is seen in the next chapter.

I also and my maidens will fast likewise. Joining privately in the palace, as they were unable to attend the Jewish assemblies in the city.

CHAPTER V

1 the third day. That is, the last day of the fast. Esther, having worn the garb of mourning during the fast, now exchanged it for her royal attire.

2 when the king saw Esther. In the Persian palaces, the principal apartment, called the "inner court" (iv. 11), is open in front; so that the king except when the throne was concealed by a curtain, could see any one entering the hall.

touched the top of the sceptre. In token of he thankful acceptance of the king's favour, and of her reverence and submission.

3 to the half of the kingdom. This form of expression probably arose from the peculiar mode in which the ancient kings of Persia bestowed grants on their favourites; not by direct payments from the royal treasury, but by giving them a charge on the revenues of particular cities or provinces; cp. Mark vi. 23 with Matt. xiv. 7 and Herodotus ix. 109.

4 I have prepared for him. Esther's address and prudence appear in the method she took to ensure success. The court of the palace, where the king was surrounded by his attendants, was not a suitable place for the disclosure of so important and delicate an affair; nor was it likely that the king's sudden feelings would be so lasting as was necessary for her object.

7 Then answered Esther, etc. Esther barely alludes to what the king had said, by repeating his words "petition" and "request"; and then, with feminine adroitness, avoids a direct answer, invites him and Haman to a second banquet, and promises *then* to divulge her wishes; a sure mode of keeping alive the king's curiosity; while at the same time it intimated that her petition was upon a matter of no ordinary importance.

8 to-morrow. This postponement gave room for other important steps towards the final catastrophe. See vers. 12–14, and ch. vi. In the meantime, Esther's conduct still further ingratiated her with the king, and lulled the guilty favourite into fatal security.

9 he stood not up. It might have been imagined that Mordecai, when he saw the danger in which he and his whole nation were involved, would have tried to assuage Haman's resentment. But, having no reason to repent of his conduct, he would not thus displease God and dishonour himself: see iv. 14.

10 refrained himself. Divine Providence restrained him, by means of his own passions, from immediate vengeance; his malice insisting upon a sweeter though tardier revenge.

14 gallows. Or stake, set up on a platform or turret; hence the great height, about 80 feet.

CHAPTER VI

1 On that night could not the king sleep. See note on v. 8. In the wonderful providence of God the sleepless night of a king proves the means of the people's deliverance.

the book of records. The Persians took remarkable pains to preserve the remembrance of their exploits by written documents. Many thousands of clay tablets, with cuneiform inscriptions, were found at Nippur between 1893 and 1896, and many more in 1900 and since. Several of these date from the times of Xerxes and Darius.

7 For the man whom the king delighteth to honour, etc. Haman, thinking that he is devising honours for himself, while he cannot be accused of doing so, does it on a grand scale.

12 Mordecai came again to the king's gate. Returning calmly, after these extraordinary honours, to his former duties.

CHAPTER VII

4 I and my people. The fact that his favourite queen was one of Haman's intended victims would tell more on such a king than the destruction of all the Jewish people; to which, indeed, he had before given his consent.

the king's damage. That is, damage in the loss of subjects and of revenue.

8 fallen upon the bed. Or, "by" or "beside the couch"; in abject supplication and agony of spirit. The construction put upon this act by the king was evidently the effect of highly incensed feelings.

they covered Haman's face. A signal for immediate execution.

CHAPTER VIII

1 the house of Haman. That is, all his property, which, upon the owner's condemnation and death, were confiscated to the king.

2 took off his ring, etc. Investing Mordecai with the office of prime minister (see ix. 4; x. 3).

set Mordecai over the house of Haman. Esther appointed him as her steward.

5 to reverse the letters. Haman's death did not invalidate the murderous edict by which all the Jews in the Persian empire were doomed to the sword; and they had many enemies, who were eagerly looking forward to the day fixed by the decree for slaughter and spoliation: see ix. 1.

8 may no man reverse. The king's answer intimates the impossibility of granting literally Esther's request, to *reverse* or revoke the decree; and points out the expedient to be adopted in order to defeat its operation. As it was a fundamental principle of the Persian government that a royal edict when duly registered was irrevocable (i. 19; Dan. vi. 8), the king was obliged to give a supplementary decree, which would be well known to convey his real wishes, authorising the Jews to defend themselves if attacked.

9 Sivan. May and June.

10 riders on mules, etc. R.V. reads, "riding on swift steeds that were used in the king's service, bred of the stud."

11 to destroy, etc. The Jews did not actually proceed so far (see ix. 10, 15, 16), nor probably was it intended they should; but these powers were necessary, both to indemnify them and to intimidate their enemies.

14 being hastened, etc. Two months had elapsed since the issuing of Haman's letters: and it was essential that the provincial satraps should be fully informed of the new state of affairs as soon as possible. Moreover, the preparations which had been made by the enemies of the Jews would have to be met by counter-preparations on their part. Therefore, though nine months remained for the circulation of the new letters, there was no time to be lost.

17 became Jews. That is, they became proselytes to the religion of the Jews. Some doubtless did this from conviction, because they had seen the hand of God so remarkably displayed on behalf of His people, and were led thereby to become sincere worshippers of Jehovah; others probably from interested motives, observing the favour which the Jews enjoyed at court.

CHAPTER IX

1 had rule over them. It might have been supposed that the declared favour of the king, and the elevated position of Mordecai, would have effectually prevented the contemplated attack; but there was probably a large party in the empire who were hostile to the Jews; whilst others would be tempted by the prospect of a rich booty. Trusting, therefore, in their superior numbers, and in their legal impunity for any excesses they might commit, when the appointed day arrived they attacked the Jews, who stood for the most part on the defensive.

6 in Shushan the palace. Not, probably, within the precincts of the palace, but in the fortified city.

10 the ten sons of Haman. As their names are mentioned, it is likely that they had been advanced to high offices during their father's administration.

laid . . . not their hand. This was probably owing to express instructions from Esther and Mordecai; and it reflects honour on their religion, their wisdom, and their humanity.

16 slew . . . seventy and five thousand. The Septuagint gives the number as 15,000, which is probably correct. It is not improbable that the Jews were remarkably preserved in the midst of imminent danger, for there is no mention that any of them were slain on this occasion. As they simply, with the king's sanction, stood in defence of their lives, slaying only those who attacked them, and universally declined to enrich themselves with the spoil, they must be allowed to have acted in an unexceptionable manner.

19 Therefore the Jews of the villages, etc. The Jews throughout the provinces, having obtained a complete victory over their enemies on the 13th, held festivals on the 14th; but those in the capital, being still engaged in hostilities on that day, did not keep their feast till the 15th. They therefore determined, on Mordecai's recommendation, that the festival should in future continue during both those days (ver. 21).

sending portions one to another. It is customary in the East, when a feast is made, to send portions to those who are unable to attend, especially to relatives and friends in affliction (see Neh. viii. 10, 12).

22 gifts to the poor. The Jews have set a praiseworthy example in relieving their poor on occasions of national rejoicing.

26 Purim. "Purim" is the plural of "Pur," which, in the old Persian, signifies *lot;* as is shown by the explanation twice given: iii. 7; ix. 24. Scholars are still divided as to the exact origin of the word. The name was taken from the circumstance of Haman having cast lots to fix the day of their destruction: see note on iii. 7. This national commemoration has been ever since observed by the Jews, being celebrated on the fourteenth and fifteenth days of the twelfth month, Adar (February—March): see iii. 7. This is exactly one month before the Passover. A fast is held on the thirteenth, called "the Fast of Esther," on the evening of which day the whole Book is read in all the synagogues. It is also read on the forenoon of the fifteenth. Certain prayers are offered, prescribed for the occasion; but the Psalms are not read. "Cursed be Haman" occurs in one of the prayers. The passages, on the other hand, which speak of Mordecai and his final victory, are repeated by the people after the officiating minister in a loud triumphant voice. The feast throughout is celebrated with the greatest hilarity; alms are given to the poor; relatives and friends send presents to each other; and it was long held obligatory to contribute a half-shekel per head to the poor Jews in Jerusalem and throughout the Holy Land. The importance attached to this festival is evinced by a Jewish tradition, that in the days of the Messiah all the feasts of Israel shall cease excepting the Feast of Purim.

29 Esther the queen. Her royal authority carried that of Xerxes, in ordaining the observance of the festival; and when the Persian power had passed away, the feast held its ground through its congeniality with the national feeling; in its commemoration of one great deliverance, which brought to mind all the rest. To the ancient Christian Church the name of Esther became a symbol of the martyr-spirit and the victory of faith and patience over the enemies of God's people.

32 written in the book. Probably "the book of the chronicles of the kings of Media and Persia," referred to, ii. 23; vi. 1; x. 2.

CHAPTER X

1 laid a tribute. We have no account here of the purposes to which this tribute was applied, nor of the wars which Ahasuerus carried on against the Greeks and the Egyptians. Scripture history extends to the affairs of heathen nations only so far as they are connected with those of the people of God.

the isles of the sea. The isles of the Ægean Sea had been conquered by Darius Hystaspis, but had been lost by Xerxes in the war with Greece. Cyprus, however, and some smaller islands, as Tyre and Platæa (off the Libyan coast), remained to him.

3 was next unto king Ahasuerus. Like Joseph in the court of Pharaoh, Obadiah in that of Ahab, Daniel in that of Belshazzar, and Nehemiah in that of Artaxerxes. Good men in such a position may not be able to do all they would in preventing evil; but they may keep themselves from sin, and be the instruments of effecting much good.

peace to all his seed. History tells no more of Esther, Mordecai, or their family annals. But we know, as a matter of fact, that the Jews in the Persian empire enjoyed prosperity and peace down to the time of the successors of Alexander the Great.

THE BOOK OF JOB

Problems in Faith and Suffering

INTRODUCTION

The message of this Book is a twofold one. (1) It shows that true religion is not a matter of self-interest. (2) It shows that suffering is not necessarily a punishment, but may be, and is, a test of faith and a purifier of character.

The Book begins with an account of Job (or, preferably, Hiob) and his great wealth, while he was also a man that feared God (i. 1–3). Then comes the Satanic suggestion, so often repeated since, that religion is a form of self-interest (i. 9–11 ; ii. 4, 5). "Doth Job fear God for nought ?"

God permits calamity after calamity to fall upon His servant. He loses his property (i. 13–17), and then his sons (i. 18, 19), but still stands the test (i. 20–22). Then comes the severest test of all, when he is smitten with a painful and loathsome disease (ii. 7, 8). Still he resists the temptation to blame God (ii. 9, 10). But he is sore perplexed by the mystery of his sufferings (iii.), "Wherefore is light given to him that is in misery, and life unto the bitter in soul ?" (iii. 20). His friends come to comfort him (ii. 11–13) and reason with him (iv., v.). But their comfort is "vacant chaff well meant for grain." Although they utter some fine truths, their arguments do not meet the case (iv. 17 ; v. 7), though Eliphaz comes near it (iv. 17). They think that his sufferings must be a punishment for wrong-doing and that his protests of innocence are hypocrisy (viii. 6, 13 ; xi. 3, 6, 14). Job's answers show impatience with their reasoning (xii. 2–9 ; xiii. 1–14), ending with the noble assertion of his trust in God : "Though He slay me, yet will I trust in Him." (But see note on xiii. 15.) From his friends he turns to God (xiii. 21–xiv. 1, 22 ; xvi. 20, 21) : "make me to know my transgression and my sin" (xiii. 23). Deep is the pathos of the suffering man's cry (xix. 9–20), his piteous appeal to his friends (xix. 21), and yet his renewed assertion of confidence in God : "I know that my Redeemer liveth" (xix. 25) and "He knoweth the way that I take ; when He hath tried me, I shall come forth as gold" (xxiii. 10). One of the finest passages in the Bible is his account of the search for wisdom (xxviii.), the value of it (xxviii. 15–19), and God's answer to man's quest (xxviii. 28), followed by Job's account of his own life (xxix.).

Elihu, the youngest of Job's friends, perhaps comes nearest to the solution of the mystery of suffering (xxxiii. 15–30), though even he seems to think that Job has brought it upon himself (xxxiv. 7–11, 31, 32 ; xxxv. 8).

The words attributed to God (xxxviii.–xl. 2 ; xl. 6–xli.) cannot be said to answer Job's questions. The answer is rather given in the book as a whole and the final issue of it. What these chapters do is to assert the Divine supremacy, in an argument from the world of nature. Job, in true humility, acknowledges this, and confesses himself a sinner (xl. 3–5 ; xlii. 1–6). This is the true answer to the problem of suffering—the lesson learned, of perfect trust, humility, and patience.

And the original question of the cynic and sceptic : "Doth Job fear God for nought ?" is answered also. Even when Job had lost everything and was a forsaken and almost solitary sufferer, he still trusted God. And God did not forsake him, but vindicated him (xlii. 7–10). The end of that man was peace.

CHAPTER I

1 the land of Uz. One of three persons mentioned in the genealogics of Genesis may have given his name to this country : see Gen. x. 23 ; xxii. 21 ; xxxvi. 28. The second is generally thought to be intended—a son of Abraham's brother Nahor. The country has not been identified. It was probably either Edom or Mesopotamia.

Job. Heb., "Eyob."

3 substance. Heb., "cattle" ; in which the wealth of nomadic tribes mainly consists. *Horses* are not mentioned, these being used almost exclusively for war.

she-asses. These are very valuable in the East, on account of their milk.

men of the East. A term denoting the tribes between the Jordan and the Euphrates, and extending over the north of Arabia.

4 every one his day. Periodical family festivals were held in one another's houses ; perhaps on their respective birthdays.

called for their three sisters. The sisters lived, according to the custom of the East, with their mother.

5 Job sent and sanctified them. *i.e.*, prepared them to offer sacrifice. He feared that they might forget God while enjoying His bounties.

burnt offerings. A patriarchal form of sacrifice, denoting absolute self-surrender.

cursed. R.V., "renounced."

6 the sons of God. Sometimes called "saints" (holy ones); more generally "angels" (messengers). The first name refers to their *origin* and *nature*, the second to their *character*, the third to their *office*.

Satan. Heb., "the Satan"; *i.e.*, "the Adversary." The evil spirit who opposes God and goodness; "the accuser of the brethren" (Rev. xii. 10. Cp. Zech. iii. 1). A fine study of the representations of Satan by Dante, Milton, and Goethe is to be found in *The Expositor's Bible*, "Job," by Dr. R. A. Watson.

7 Whence comest thou? For a similar mode of representation, see 1 Kings xxii. 19, and note: and Zech. iii. 1. These passages teach us that even Satan is subject to the control of God.

9 Doth Job fear God for nought? This question introduces the first part of the great controversy—the possibility of *disinterested* goodness.

11 curse Thee to Thy face. Or, "renounce Thee openly": see on ver. 5. The original is very emphatic—"[see] if he will not renounce Thee!"

15 the Sabeans. Heb., "Sheba." These appear to have been a mixed race, partly Cushite (Gen. x. 7) and partly Shemite, of the families of Joktan (Gen. x. 28) and Abraham (Gen. xxv. 3), found in connexion with "the sons of Dedan." They probably made their attack from the south. Dr. D. S. Margoliouth (*Hastings' Dict. Bible*) thinks they came from Central Africa; others trace them to Arabia.

16 The fire of God. *i.e.*, lightning (Exod. ix. 23).

17 The Chaldæans. Predatory inroads of the Chaldæans from the north are mentioned in Gen. xi. 28: see also Hab. i. 6–11.

made out three bands. For the purpose of surrounding the camels: see Gen. xiv. 15; Judg. vii. 16, 21; 1 Sam. xi. 11.

19 from the wilderness. Rather, "from *beyond* the wilderness"; having had all the desert to blow over. Such winds are very violent: see Isa. xxi. 1; Jer. iv. 11; Zech. ix. 14. This, as it "smote the four corners of the house," was of the character of a whirlwind.

young men. Or, "young people"; both sons and daughters.

21 blessed be the name of the Lord. Job looked beyond the immediate instruments or second causes of his afflictions, and found consolation in the belief that an infinitely wise and merciful Sovereign presided over his affairs. What a triumph over Satan's devices!

CHAPTER II

4 Skin for skin. Job may be willing to surrender his property and his children, so long as he is permitted to retain what is equivalent to all—his own life. Satan's inference is, that Job's piety had not yet been subjected to the severest test.

7 boils. Supposed to have been *elephantiasis Græcorum*. See Sir J. R. Bennett's *Diseases of the Bible*, p. 97. The nature and effects of the disease are indicated in other passages of the book: see ii. 6; vii. 4, 5; xiii. 14, 28; xvi. 8, 16; xvii. 1; xix. 20; xxx. 17, 30.

10 one of the foolish women. The epithet often means "wicked" (R.V. marg., "impious"): see Gen. xxxiv. 7.

shall we not receive evil? That is, "Shall we recognise God only with gratitude for the blessings which He gives, and not also with submission to the sorrow which He sends?"

11 Eliphaz the Temanite. These personal and geographical names, as well as those in i. 1, 15, 17, give some clue to the scene of the history: Teman (*south*) was in the land of Edom; the Shuhites were descendants of Shuach, a son of Abraham by Keturah; their home was probably west of Chaldæa, bordering on Arabia; the Naamathites and their locality are nowhere else mentioned in Scripture. There was, however, a Naamah in the Valley (*Shephelah*) of South-west Palestine, Josh. xv. 41. These friends of Job seem to have been not only persons of distinction but also men of wisdom and piety, though they expressed many erroneous views.

12 knew him not. So altered was his appearance by disease and suffering.

13 seven days and seven nights. A usual time of mourning among Orientals: see Gen. l. 10; 1 Sam. xxxi. 13.

none spake a word. They were astonished at Job's sufferings, and unable to offer any consolation in consequence of the views they entertained of their cause.

CHAPTER III

Job's Complaint

The patriarch breaks the long silence by bewailing his very birth and life. Better, he cries, never to have been born (1–10), or to have died at his birth or in infancy (11–19). Then follow general reflections on the profitlessness of life to the miserable (20–26).

1 cursed his day. Overcome by his sufferings, Job uttered expressions which cannot be vindicated: see his own confession, xlii. 3. We must remember that the light he enjoyed, and the sources of comfort open to him, were far inferior to ours.

3 the night in which it was said. Literally, as R.V., "the night which said"; a bold personification.

5 shadow of death. A single word (in Heb.), denoting the deepest darkness. It occurs very frequently in this book.

stain it. Rather, "claim it for their own," as V.R.

7 solitary. Or, "barren," unable to produce a succeeding day or a new life.

8 ready to raise up their mourning. Rather, "skilful in calling up Leviathan"; *i.e.*, by their incantations. Two kinds of magicians are alluded to in this verse: (1) Those who professed to "curse the day," making certain days unlucky; and (2) Those who professed to "rouse Leviathan," the dragon who was popularly supposed to devour the sun or the moon, making eclipses, which were occasions of great terror.

9 the dawning of the day. Heb. (and R.V.), "the eyelids of the morning."

12 prevent me. That is, "anticipate me," or "welcome me."

14 desolate places. Or, "lonely places." Perhaps tombs, in allusion to the vast sepulchral structures built by departed monarchs.

17 There, etc. *i.e.*, in the grave; where the tyrant and his victim, the captive and the taskmaster (18), the small and the great, the slave and his master, rest together. Job lingers mournfully over the thought of the equality of all in death.

23 Why is light given? Words supplied from ver. 20 to complete the sense.

24 my sighing cometh before I eat. Or, "my sighing comes in the place of my daily food"; *i.e.*, is my daily food (Psa. xlii. 4; lxxx. 6).

25 For the thing which I greatly feared. Literally, "For I fear a fear, and it cometh upon me, and what I dread cometh to me. (26) I have no peace, and I have no quiet, and there cometh trembling."

CHAPTERS IV, V

First Speech of Eliphaz

After apologising for speaking, Eliphaz expresses his surprise at hearing complaints from Job, who had so often encouraged others (2–5); asks why he does not confide in his uprightness, since it is not the innocent but the wicked, however powerful they may be, who perish (6–11); refers to a communication made to him in a vision, to show how wrong Job was in arraigning his Maker (12–21); asserts that man has no reason to complain, since the cause of affliction is in himself (v. 1–7); and concludes by exhorting Job to cast himself upon God, whose greatness and goodness are shown both in Nature and in the government of the world (8–16), and by showing the happy consequences of submission to Divine chastisements (17–27).

CHAPTER IV

Is not this thy fear. etc.? Rather, "Is not thy fear (*i.e.*, thy piety) thy confidence? thy hope, is it not also the uprightness of thy ways?" See R.V. "Your blameless life, let that encourage you" (*Moffatt*).

7 who ever perished, being innocent? This sentence contains the essential principle on which the whole argument of Job's friends is based.

8 Even as I have seen. Rather, "So far as I have seen."

10 The roaring of the lion, etc. Unjust, cruel men are often compared in the Scriptures to wild beasts: see Psa. x. 9, etc. In this and the next verse five different names are given to the lion in the Hebrew; showing how common those animals once were in that region.

11 the stout lion's whelps. Rather, as R.V., "the whelps of the lioness."

12 Now a thing, etc. Or, "And to me a word came stealing; my ear caught a whisper of it."

17 Shall mortal man, etc.? Whoever censures the course of Providence by complaining of his own lot (as Job had done) claims to be more just than God, the equity of whose government he thus arraigns. (*Conant.*) All that is spoken in this vision is true in itself; but the use made of it by Eliphaz is wrong.

18 His angels He charged with folly (or, "error"). As even the most exalted spirits are imperfect, compared with the infinite perfection of the Deity, how much more so is man!

19 How much less. Rather, "How much more" (R.V.).

houses of clay. That is, bodies made of dust.

crushed before the moth. This may mean either, "sooner than is the moth", or, "just as the moth is crushed."

21 Doth not their excellency, etc.? Or, "Is not their tent-cord plucked up within them?" (R.V.); referring to life under the figure of a tent (as in Isa. xxxviii. 12).

CHAPTER V

1 Call now. To whom then can you venture to appeal in support of your cause?

saints. Or, "holy ones"; meaning probably the angels.

2 envy. Or, "indignation." Some suppose the meaning to be, that complaints against God are destructive to the complainant. Others apply the words "anger" and "indignation" to God.

3 suddenly I cursed his habitation. That is, "I felt sure that the wicked man, however prosperous he may appear, would be quickly cut down."

4 crushed in the gate. That is, in the *place of judgement,* which was usually held at the gate of the city. They were ruined by litigation, or "oppressed in judgement."

5 the robber, etc. Literally, "the snare gapeth for their substance" (wealth), R.V. *i.e.*, intriguers or robbers seek to rob them (Davies-Gesenius: *Hebrew Dictionary*).

6 Although affliction, etc. Rather, "For" (R.V.); and so in ver. 7, for "yet" read "for."

13 He taketh the wise, etc. St. Paul quotes these words of Eliphaz (1 Cor. iii. 19), not because of the speaker's authority, but of their own truth. Their application by Eliphaz to Job was a mistake.

15 From their mouth. That is, the mouths of their enemies. The figure is taken from rapacious animals, to which unjust and oppressive rulers are frequently likened. R.V. reads, "from the sword of their mouth," following another MS. reading.

19 in seven. That is, in any succession of troubles; a definite number being put for an indefinite.

21 the scourge of the tongue. A *slanderous* tongue, which inflicts a severe wound on the peace and reputation.

23 in league, etc. A poetic expression, meaning that both animate and inanimate creation should be at peace with him.

24 shalt not sin. This probably means "thou shalt miss nothing." Thus the whole line may be read, "Thou shalt visit thy fold" (R.V., or "farm"), "and shalt miss nothing."

26 cometh in. Literally, "cometh up" to the threshing-floor, on some eminence, to catch the breeze.

CHAPTER VI

Job's Reply to Eliphaz

In his reply, the patriarch attempts to justify his complaints on the ground of his severe sufferings (2–7): repeats his desire for death, asserting that his strength was insufficient to bear his trials (8–13); charges his friends with aggravating his afflictions (14–23); and calls upon them to reconsider his case (24–30). Turning from them, he complains of the misery of life (vii. 1–6); entreats God to consider its brevity (7–10); and remonstrates with Him for so deeply afflicting him (11–21).

2 my grief. Eliphaz had used the same word, rendered "wrath" in v. 2. "Vexation," R.V. Moffatt rightly translates Job as repeating the word used by Eliphaz, thus: "'Passion?' Compare my passion of despair with the full weight of my calamity."

laid in the balances together. My complaining would not be found greater than the case warrants.

3 For now it would be heavier, etc. Rather, "For now it (my calamity) is heavier than the sand of the sea; hence my words were vehement," or, "rash" (R.V.).

4 The poison whereof drinketh up my spirit. Here are two images; the shower of poisoned arrows, and the assailing host.

5 Doth the wild ass bray, etc.? This means, Does any one complain in prosperity? Think not that I am impatient without cause.

6 Is there any taste in the white of an egg? The meaning is, Can any one take delight in what is tasteless? Much less can I feel satisfied with misery.

10 I would harden myself in sorrow. Rather, "And it shall still be my consolation; yea, I will exult in unsparing anguish, that I have not denied the words of the Holy One."

11 prolong my life. Or, "be patient" (R.V.); as the Hebrew phrase usually means.

13 Is not my help in me, etc.? This may be better read, "Is not my help in me nothing" (see R.V.), "and soundness (*i.e.*, vigour of constitution) driven from me?"

14 he forsaketh. Or, "lest he forsake," etc.

15 have dealt deceitfully. Or, "disappoint me."

as a brook. Job compares his friends to streams which are abundant in the winter, but are dried up in the heat of summer, and so have least water when it is most needed. The scene so graphically described in the following verses is often witnessed in Arabia.

as the stream, etc. Rather, as R.V., "as the channel of brooks that pass away," referring to the watercourses or *wadys* that intersect the region.

18 The paths of their way, etc. This verse should be translated, "Caravans turn aside in their way (*i.e.*, in search of these streams); they go up into the desert, and perish."

19 Tema . . . Sheba (districts in Arabia). "The troops of Tema and the companies of Sheba" were the merchant-caravans which carried goods from those regions to the western parts of Asia. They knew well all the streams on their route, and directed their journeys by them (ver. 18).

20 were ashamed. That is, at having hoped in vain, like Job himself, in counting upon his friends' sympathy.

21 ye are nothing. In other words, Ye are useless, like them.

22 Did I say, Bring unto me, etc.? These interrogations mean, Did I ask any assistance from you, either a gift or an effort?

25 what doth your arguing reprove? *i.e.*, what force is there in such upbraiding as yours?

26 to reprove words. That is, *mere* words. The second clause should be read, as R.V. marg., "Seeing that the speeches of one that is desperate are for the wind"; *i.e.*, not to be taken into serious account.

27 ye overwhelm . . . ye dig. Rather, as R.V., "ye cast lots for . . . ye make merchandise of," taking advantage of utter helplessness to secure your own gain.

28 be content, etc. Or, "be pleased to look upon me; to your face surely I shall not lie": see R.V.

29 Return, etc. Or, "Return, I pray (*i.e.*, from your unfair judgement); let there be no iniquity (or injustice); yea, return, yet my right is herein"; *i.e.*, my case is good.

CHAPTER VII

1 an appointed time. Or, "a warfare": man's life is a hard service; his days are days of labour.

2 As a servant earnestly desireth the shadow. "As the slave panteth for the shade," *i.e.*, the evening, which will bring refreshment and rest.

5 My skin is broken, etc. Rather, "closeth and melteth," referring to the sores contracting and running alternately.

9 to the grave. Heb., "to Sheol," the world of the departed.

10 He shall return no more. No future life shall be for him *on earth*. The ancient Egyptians taught that this was possible on certain conditions.

12 a whale. Or, "monster." That is, restless and ungovernable; to be restrained by power only.

15 my life. Literally, "my bones"; *i.e.*, my emaciated form.

17 What is man, etc.? Compare the eighth Psalm. The Psalmist contemplates man as honoured by the Divine notice; to the suffering patriarch this notice is for the infliction of deeper suffering.

set Thine heart. Rather, "fix Thine attention upon him."

18 visit him. That is, with sufferings.

19 till I swallow down my spittle. A colloquial expression for a moment of time.

20 I have sinned, etc. Or, "I have sinned, [yet] what [evil] have I done to Thee, O Thou Watcher of men?" meaning that his sins were not so flagrant as to require exemplary punishment.

a mark against Thee. Rather, "a mark to Thee"; *i.e.*, to Thy attacks.

21 Thou shalt seek me in the morning. Rather, "early," or "diligently" (as R.V.). If any favour be shown me, it must be done soon. It is observable that Job here acknowledges himself a *sinner*, while maintaining his general integrity.

CHAPTER VIII

First Speech of Bildad

Bildad infers, from the heavy calamities of Job and of his children, that they had been heinous sinners (2–7); appeals to the testimony of antiquity to prove the close connexion between sin and suffering (8–19); and describes, in contrast, the happiness of the righteous (20–22). There is truth in his affirmation that God always deals justly both with the upright and with the wicked, as well as force in his appeal to the experience of mankind, as in that of Eliphaz to a Divine communication; but his argument also rests upon an unsound foundation, and the implied application to Job and his family was unjust and cruel.

2 a strong wind. Spurning all restraint. Bildad alludes to Job's apology (vi. 26).

3 Doth God pervert judgement? The bold appeals of Job seem to Bildad to arraign the justice of the Almighty. "Judgement" denotes the procedure which springs from "justice" as a principle.

4 If thy children, etc. As Job himself had surmised (i. 5). Bildad now hints that Job may possibly be suffering on account of transgressions that had brought about their doom.

6 If thou wert. Or, perhaps, "If thou *be*"; that is, If thou join reformation with prayer.

8 to the search of their fathers. Rather, "to what their fathers (*i.e.*, a still more remote generation) have searched out." See R.V.

10 Shall not they teach thee? Referring to Job's words (vi. 24). "Words out of their heart" are those which spring from their *deepest* experiences and thoughts. "Heart" in Scripture language expresses intellect as well as emotion.

11 Can the rush, etc.? Vers. 11–19 probably give some well-known adages of the ancients, referred to in vers. 8, 10.

the rush. The papyrus. See notes on Gen. xli. 2; Exod. ii. 3. This proverb probably originated in Egypt; it illustrates the luxuriant prosperity and sudden destruction of the ungodly.

the flag. The Nile-grass; Gen. xli. 2.

13 the hypocrite's hope. Rather, "the hope of the polluted," or "impure." R.V. renders "godless."

16 in his garden. Rather, "over his garden" (R.V.); taking possession of the whole.

17 His roots, etc. The Heb. word *gal*, translated "heap," may also mean "well" or "spring," from the rolling or welling-up of water. It is used in Psa. xlii. 7, in plural meaning "billows." The figure is that of a plant which springs up luxuriantly and overspreads the garden (16), thriving even in stony ground, but, being plucked up, is soon forgotten (18), and others come up in its place (19).

18 If He destroy him. Rather, "it one destroy him";—"if he be destroyed," R.V.—when it is rooted up he will be forgotten, as though the place where he grew were ashamed of him.

19 this is the joy. Evidently sarcastic: Such is his joy in its outcome and result! For "grow," read "spring" (R.V.). The word denotes luxuriant and prosperous growth.

21 Till He fill thy mouth, etc. If therefore you are right, God will not leave you until He has made you rejoice. Read with R.V., "He will yet fill thy mouth," etc.

22 They that hate thee, etc. The parallelism shows that the *wicked* are here intended. Bildad himself and his companions *criticised* Job, but did not *hate* him.

CHAPTERS IX, X

Job's Reply to Bildad

Job, in his answer to Bildad, admits the justice as well as the omnipotence and supremacy of God, and the sinfulness, weakness, and subjection of man (2–20); but maintains that in this life affliction equally befalls the righteous and the wicked; passes to the contemplation of his own trials, desiring, yet fearing to discuss them with God (21–35); expostulates with Him (x. 1–17); and concludes by wishing for death (18–22). The reply of Job displays contending emotions. Fear, hope, confidence, despair, and a sense of the severity of his sufferings, by turns agitate his mind. Thus expressions of acquiescence in the Divine supremacy (ix. 4–15) are succeeded by the language of fretfulness (16–21; also x.).

CHAPTER IX

2 I know it is so. Alluding to the general position which had been maintained, that God would not pervert justice. And yet, he adds, in face of God's omnipotence, how can a man hope successfully to maintain his righteousness before Him?

3 one of a thousand. That is, "for one of his innumerable offences," or "for one of God's thousand questions."

5 and they know not. A poetical form of expression, meaning *suddenly;* as in Psa. xxxv. 8. In the sublime description which follows, the earth (5, 6), the heavenly bodies (7–9), universal nature (10), and lastly man (11–13), are declared to be under God's control.

6 the pillars thereof. A poetical conception; as though the earth were a vast structure supported by columns.

7 it riseth not. *i.e.,* does not appear through the clouds.

sealeth up the stars. *i.e.,* hides their light. Where we use locks, the ancients often employed seals (Dan. vi. 17: Matt. xxvii. 66). So in xxxvii. 7, to "seal up the hand" of men is to hinder them from any development of activity.

9 Arcturus. Heb., *Ash,* or *Ayish* (xxxviii. 32), perhaps "group"; the constellation "Ursa Major"; the four stars of which were regarded by the Arabians as a bier, and the three of the tail as mourners, hence called "sons" (xxxviii. 32).—**Orion.** Heb., *Chesil,* meaning the "rebel" or "fool," supposed to be a giant chained up in the sky. Hence the expression in xxxviii. 31.

Pleiades. Heb., *Kîmah,* "cluster." The reference to these three constellations is now generally conceded, although Jewish authorities and ancient versions greatly differ.

the chambers of the south. The vast spaces, with their constellations, such as the Southern Cross, in the opposite hemisphere.

10 great things past finding out. Job here repeats the language of Eliphaz (v. 9): but lays a deeper emphasis upon the absolute power of God.

13 If God will not withdraw His anger. Rather, affirmatively, "God withdraweth not His anger": see R.V. The "proud helpers" (Heb., "helpers of Rahab") may be men who, relying on their own strength, take part with the enemies of God.

15 to my judge. Or, "adversary," as R.V. Though my cause be just I will entreat Him, as recognising His authority.

16 Yet would I not believe. I could not venture to conclude that it was *I* who induced Him to reply. It would be still of His sovereign will.

17 breaketh. Rather, "crusheth" (the same word as in Gen. iii. 15, rendered "bruise").

21 Though I were perfect. Literally, "I am blameless, [yet] I know not (do not understand) myself! I despise my life": see Gen. xxxix. 6; Psa. i. 6.

22 This is one thing. Probably, "it is all one," whether a man is innocent or guilty; "therefore I said it—for He destroyeth," etc.

23 He will laugh at the trial of the innocent. In this language of Job he seems to have reached the very depth of agonising doubt.

24 Where, and who is he? "He blindeth the eyes of its judges. If it be not He, who, I pray, is it?" Job here asserts that *God* inflicts calamities on the innocent, and exalts the wicked and unjust: see Psa. lxxiii. for a similar state of feeling and its corrective.

25 a post. A runner, or courier. In this and the following verses we have the types of swiftness in *earth, sea,* and *air.*

26 the swift ships. The "boats of reeds," of papyrus (see Isa. xviii. 2), which were used on the Nile, and were celebrated for their swiftness.

hasteth to the prey. Rather, "swoopeth on the prey," as R.V.

27 I will leave off my heaviness. Or, "I will put off my [sad] countenance, and brighten up": see R.V., and marg.

29 If I be wicked, etc. Rather, "I am held guilty; why then labour I [to prove my innocence] in vain?"

30 snow water. Presumed by the Orientals to have specially whitening properties.

32 He is not a man. That is, the contest is unequal.

33 Neither is there any daysman. This word

signifies an arbiter, or umpire, appointed to decide in a disputed cause. The laying his hand upon both refers probably to some ancient ceremony, expressive of his relation to both parties. Job alludes to this to show the inequality of the contest. This cry for a Mediator is at once an expression of the soul's deepest need, and, as it has well been called, " an unconscious prophecy."

35 But it is not so with me. Rather, " For I am not so in myself " (R.V.). *i.e.*, in myself I have no fear, it is only that He overpowers me.

CHAPTER X

2 I will leave my complaint upon myself. Literally, " I will let loose my complaint over myself," *i.e.*, I will freely indulge it : see R.V.

3 Is it good unto Thee. That is, " Is it *pleasing* to Thee to oppress ? " Three causes of complaint are here indicated: oppression of the innocent; disregard by God to His own work; and favour shown to the wicked.

7 Thou knowest, etc. Rather, " Although Thou knowest that I am not wicked (*i.e.*, guilty of great crimes), and none can deliver," etc. This completes the series of questions.

8 fashioned me together round about. Referring to the mode in which the potter forms and finishes an earthen vessel. So, " the clay," in the next verse ; *i.e.*, the potter's clay.

10 poured me out as milk, etc. This is a description of the origin and growth of the human frame : cp. Psa. cxxxix. 14–16.

11 fenced. Or, " interwoven." R.V., has " knit me together."

13 this is with Thee. Rather, " *was* with Thee," *i.e.*, Thou didst purpose to inflict all these things upon me, even when bestowing all these favours.

15 If I be righteous. A contrasted supposition ; but even then I should not be approved. The last part of the verse is rendered in R.V., " being filled with ignominy, and looking upon mine affliction." These words appear to denote Job's own contemplation of his sufferings, described in the next verse by an expressive figure.

16 for it increaseth, etc. Rather, " If it (my head) should lift itself up, Thou wouldest hunt me as a fierce lion " watching the movements of its prey.

17 Thy witnesses. *i.e.*, these inflictions and judgements, called " witnesses " because testifying to Job's guilt : see xvi. 8 ; Mal. iii. 5.

Changes and war. Or, " Changes and a host ! " *i.e.*, host after host.

18 Oh that I had given up the ghost, etc. ! Job here returns to his first wish, uttered then in passion, now in calm despair.

20 cease then. An appeal to be permitted to have a little rest from agonies before death, so speedily approaching.

22 A land of darkness, etc. Literally, " A land of gloom, like dense darkness, of death-shade, and confusion ; and the light is as dense darkness." This is a poetical description of the region of departed spirits, according to the ideas prevailing at the time.

CHAPTER XI

First Speech of Zophar

Zophar, the third of Job's friends, is more vehement than the others. He severely censures Job's self-justification, asserting that his sins deserve severe punishment (2–6); shows the vanity of opposing Him whose knowledge and power are infinite (7–12); and urges Job to repentance (13–20).

3 thy lies. Or, perhaps, " boastings," as R.V.

4 I am clean in Thine eyes. This is exaggerated. Job admitted his imperfection, while he maintained his innocence of the charges laid against him.

6 That they are double, etc. Perhaps the best rendering is, " And that He would show thee secrets of wisdom, for there are intricacies of [His] fixed purpose ; then shouldest Thou know that He hath caused to be forgotten for thee [part] of thine iniquity." (See R.V., marg.) If Job better understood God's doings, he would see that *all* his sins were not remembered against him, great as his punishment had been.

7 Canst thou by searching, etc. ? Rather, " Canst thou reach the depth of God ? canst thou reach unto the perfection of the Almighty ? "

8 It is as high as heaven, etc. The words in the original are an exclamation : " Heights of heaven ! . . . deeper than Sheol ! "

hell. Heb., " Sheol," the invisible world ; which is usually represented as of inconceivable depth and extent : see Isa. xiv. 9.

10 If He cut off, etc. Rather, " If He pass by (ix. 11), and arrest, and call an assembly for judgement, then who can hinder Him ? " (ix. 12).

13 prepare thine heart. Or, " Set thine heart aright " (R.V.).

15 without spot. Or, " without stain or shame." The words are a reply to those of Job (x. 15).

17 And thine age shall be clearer, etc. Rather, " And thy life shall arise [clearer] than noon ; darkness shall be as the morning " : cp. R.V., and see Isa. lviii. 10.

18 thou shalt dig. Rather, as R.V., " search " ; without finding any cause of alarm.

20 their hope shall be, etc. Or, "and their refuge vanisheth from them ; and their hope is a giving up the ghost," *i.e.*, death is the only hope of the wicked, and thine, if thou remainest as thou art.

CHAPTERS XII–XIV

Job's Reply to Zophar

Job, in replying to Zophar, refers also to the arguments of Eliphaz and Bildad. He begins by expressing contempt for his friends, who, though not wiser than himself, had presumed thus to teach him (2–5) ; affirms again that God deals sovereignly with men (6), shows that he can speak of God's might and supremacy in strains as sublime as those of his friends (7–25 ; xiii. 1, 2) : appeals from their charges to the Almighty (3–27) ; and closes with a touching description of the brevity of life (28 ; xiv.).

CHAPTER XII

4 Who calleth upon God, etc. That is, I whom God once heard and answered am treated with scorn.

5 a lamp despised. " An unfortunate man is despised like an extinguished torch." Read, " There is contempt for misfortune, in the thought of the secure, ready for those who waver in their steps " : cp. R.V.

6 Into whose hand God bringeth abundantly. Or, " who have God in their hand " ; *i.e.*, who have no other God than their own will and power : see R.V., marg.

11 Doth not the ear, etc. ? Or, " Doth not the ear try words as the palate tastes food ? " and so I will exercise my own judgement upon the wise sayings you have quoted.

13 With Him. That is, with God. The connexion seems to be, that whereas man acquires knowledge by long experience, the wisdom of God belongs to Him essentially and always.

16 The deceived and the deceiver are His. All are alike under His control.

17 spoiled. Rather, "stripped"; *i.e.*, captives (Isa. xx. 4). And so in ver. 19.

19 princes. Or, "priests"; see Gen. xli. 45. The word in ver. 21 is different.

21 weakeneth the strength of the mighty. Literally, "looseth the girdle of the strong": see ver. 18, and Isa. v. 27. The loosened girdle meant loss of power for action.

22 discovereth. *i.e.*, revealeth.

23 He increaseth . . . He enlargeth. "Increaseth" refers to *power;* "enlargeth" to *extent.*

24 the heart. Or, "understanding"; the heart being spoken of as the seat of intellect.

CHAPTER XIII

8 Will ye accept His person? That is, Will ye be partial? The principles of truth and justice need never be neglected in vindicating God.

9 Is it good, etc.? Or, "Will it be good for you if He shall search you out? or, as men are deceived, can you deceive Him?" *i.e.*, Will your motives in condemning me, under pretence of vindicating Him, bear His scrutiny? Surely He will condemn you (10).

12 Your remembrances, etc. Rather, "Your memorable sayings are like ashes; your bulwarks (*i.e.*, of argument) as bulwarks of clay": cp. R.V.

14 take my flesh in my teeth. That is, "incur every danger." The figure is taken from wild beasts that carry off their prey in their teeth.

put my life in mine hand. Job is willing to risk all consequences to have the cause of his sufferings cleared up.

15 Though He slay me, yet will I trust in Him. The present Heb. text should be rendered, "Lo! let Him slay me; I have no hope ('What else can I expect?' (*Moffatt*)); yet I will defend my ways before Him": *i.e.*, I have no hope of prolonged existence; but I desire to vindicate my character before I die.

16 He also, etc. Some render, "This also will be to me for salvation; for an ungodly man will not come," etc.: cp. R.V.

19 I shall give up the ghost. Job had nothing left to sustain him but the consciousness of his integrity; and if he yield that, he must expire. Some render, "Who is He that can convict me [in judgement?] for then would I be silent, and expire."

26 Thou writest. *i.e.*, judicially. Accusations, or indictments, were produced in writing: see xxxi. 35.

to possess. Or, "inherit." The sorrows of age are a legacy from the sins of youth.

27 Thou puttest my feet in the stocks. Rather, "fastenest logs to my feet," as was done with prisoners to prevent their escape, or as horses are "hobbled."

Thou settest a print, etc. This obscure clause may mean "Thou makest a mark for the roots of my feet," or "watchest my steps."

28 he, as a rotten thing, consumeth. R.V. reads, "Though I am like a rotten thing that consumeth."

CHAPTER XIV

3 dost Thou open Thine eyes. That is, observe or watch closely, so as to bring to account.

4 Who can bring, etc.? As, then, perfection of character is impossible, the source being polluted, why should God be strict in judgement?

9 the scent of water. The plant is represented as inhaling the vital influence from the water.

11 As the waters fail from the sea. The term "sea" is applied, in the Hebrew Scriptures, to the Lake of Tiberias, the Dead Sea, and the flooding rivers Nile and Euphrates. The figure here used is peculiarly applicable to inland waters in the parched countries of the East. For "flood," read "river," as R.V.

12 Till the heavens be no more. Evidently meaning, they shall never appear again *on earth.* The form of words appears to indicate a belief in the general resurrection (see xix. 23–27). For *when* "the heavens are no more," the dead shall live. Cp. note on ver. 14.

13 the grave. Heb., "Sheol." The language is that of earnest longing for a second life, with at least the hope that there may be a happy deliverance from the "under-world."

14 my appointed time. Rather, "my warfare." Job here likens his condition in Sheol to that of a soldier on duty, waiting to be relieved from his post.

will I wait, etc. Rather, "would I wait," if this were so.

15 Thou shalt call, etc. Rather, "Thou shouldest call, and I would answer Thee," etc., as R.V.

16 For now. Or, "But now," as R.V.

17 sealed up in a bag. See note on ix. 7, and 2 Kings xii. 10. The sense is, that Job's sins were accurately estimated, so that none might be omitted in the reckoning.

18 surely the mountain falling, etc. This dissolution of what is firmest and most solid in Nature is illustrative of the transiency of human strength and hope (ver. 19). "*So* Thou destroyest the hope of man."

19 Thou washest away the things that grow out of the dust. Rather, as R.V., "The overflowings thereof wash away the dust."

22 his flesh upon him. etc. This may be translated, "But his flesh suffereth for himself, and his soul mourneth over himself"; *i.e.*, he notices not the grief or sufferings of others. So R.V. marg.

CHAPTER XV

Second Speech of Eliphaz

Another series of the controversy now begins, in which the speakers become more excited and violent, but say little against Job that is new. Eliphaz commences by charging Job's effusions with vanity and impiety (2–13); he opposes Job's affirmation of his innocence and of the too great severity of his punishment (14–16); and describes, in the sayings of wise men of former times, the overwhelming misery of the wicked (17–35).

4 thou castest off fear, etc. Rather, "Yea, thou makest void the fear of God, and restrainest devotion before God": meaning that Job's principles were fatal to holiness and piety; perhaps referring to ix. 22–24; xii. 6.

5 thy mouth uttereth thine iniquity. Rather, "Thine iniquity teacheth thy mouth" (R.V.), *i.e.*, What you say is prompted by your wickedness.

8 the secret of God. *i.e.*, "the secret counsel" (as R.V.). Or, "In the council of God hast thou listened, and hast thou restricted wisdom to thyself?"

11 Is there any secret thing with thee? Rather, "And words gently spoken towards thee": cp. R.V. The meaning of the whole verse is, Do you regard as of small account the Divine consolations and gentle reproofs which I have addressed to you?

12 what do thy eyes wink at? An expression of pride and insolence.

13 That thou turnest thy spirit, etc. Or, "For against God thou turnest thy spirit (*i.e.*, directest thy wrath), and lettest words go forth from thy mouth."

15 His saints. Meaning, probably, *angels*.

19 the earth. Rather, "the *land*": before they had become intermingled with and corrupted by other nations. Now follows a series of "wise sayings," quotations from "the wisdom of the fathers."

20 The wicked man travaileth, etc. Or, "All the days of the wicked man he is in pain, and a number of years is hidden (*i.e.*, secretly destined) for the oppressor." A life of wickedness is *wretched* and *limited*.

22 He believeth not. To "darkness," *i.e.*, calamity, is added despair. He is "waited for," *i.e.*, so it seems to his own apprehension. So "wandereth," in the next verse.

25 For he stretcheth out, etc. Or (as in 27), "Because he hath stretched . . . hath strengthened himself," *i.e.*, "behaved himself proudly" (R.V.).

26 He runneth upon Him, even on His neck, etc. Rather, "with his (*i.e.*, the sinner's) neck, with the thick bosses of his bucklers"; *i.e.*, with his head erect (Psa. lxxv. 5), and confiding in his strength. This is a very significant image of daring impiety.

27 he covereth, etc. Rather, "he hath covered . . . and made" (R.V.); giving himself up to a life of luxury.

28 he dwelleth in desolate cities. Rather, "hath dwelt," etc. His insatiable ambition has caused desolation around him: see Isa. v. 8. He has dispossessed the lawful owners and occupiers, and has brought down a curse upon the very buildings." "Heaps" are *ruins*.

29 Neither shall he prolong the perfection thereof. Probably, "Neither shall their produce bend to the earth" (R.V.), *i.e.*, like heavy crops of corn in harvest or richly-laden trees.

30 the flame. *i.e.*, the scorching sun; or sultry wind.

31 Let not him that is deceived, etc. Rather, "Let him not trust in evil; he is deceived, for evil shall be his recompense."

33 He shall shake off, etc. The grape in its early stages is peculiarly liable to disease, and the olive blossom is so delicate as to be shaken off by the slightest wind.

34 the congregation of hypocrites, etc. "The company of the godless shall be barren" (R.V.), referring to the pictures of blight already given.

CHAPTERS XVI, XVII

Job's Second Reply to Eliphaz

Job finds fault with the friends for distressing rather than comforting him (2–5); renews his complaint and protestations of uprightness, and his request to argue with God (6–22, xvii. 1–10); and closes by saying that his only hope is in the grave (11–16).

CHAPTER XVI

3 emboldeneth. Rather, "provoketh," as R.V.

4 heap up words. Or, as R.V., "join words together" in rhetorical artifice.

7 He hath made . . . Thou hast made. Job turns, in the passion of his speech, from his friends to God in direct appeal.

8 Thou hast filled me with wrinkles, etc Rather, "Thou hast laid hold on me; this testifieth against me; and my falsehood (*i.e.*, the illness, that deceives men) riseth up and testifieth in my face." Thy fearful inflictions are like a false witness testifying against me.

10 They have gaped upon me. Job now turns from God to his earthly persecutors, as the meaner brutes that follow in the lion's track. There were men besides Job's "friends" who derided him (xxx. 1). These especially are "the ungodly," ver. 11.

12 I was at ease, etc. A sudden and unexpected attack.

13 poureth out my gall. Piercing the vitals.

14 giant. Rather, "warrior." The figure is now that of a beleaguered city.

15 I have sewed sackcloth. Not merely "put it on," but enveloped myself closely with the sign of mourning.

my horn. See 1 Sam. ii. 1.

16 foul. Or, "inflamed"; the tears and the inflammation were a symptom of Job's disease.

18 O earth, cover not thou my blood. Job, regarding himself as persecuted to death, claims the supposed right of a murdered person, calls on the earth not to conceal the crime (see Gen. iv. 11), and appeals to God as the vindicator of the victim.

no place. No resting-place; let it always be heard. In Sophocles (*Philoc.*, 1293) the same word as the Septuagint uses here is found in an appeal to the gods.

19 Also now. Rather, "Even now." "Witness" is *personal*.

my record. Or, "eye-witness"; one who knows and sees. R.V., "He that voucheth for me."

20 poureth out tears unto God. When faith is most severely tried by man's unkindness and the darkness of providence, it will still turn, though with tears, to God.

21 O that one might plead! Perhaps, as R.V., "That he (the witness) would maintain the right of a man with God, and of a son of man with his neighbour!"

CHAPTER XVII

1 My breath is corrupt. Rather, "My spirit (or vital power) is spent."

The graves are. Rather, "the grave is."

2 doth not mine eye continue in their provocation? *i.e.*, it is always obtruded on my sight. The connexion is, My friends scorn me (see xvi. 10), and mock and continually provoke me; wherefore I pray God to bring me to trial (3).

3 Lay down now, etc. Rather, "Lay down, I pray, a pledge; be my surety [in the cause pending] with Thee; who [else] is there that will strike hands with me?" viz., as a token of suretyship: see Prov. vi. 1; xvii. 18; xxii. 26. Job here appeals to God to prove his innocence, as his friends could not understand, and do him justice.

4 For, etc. The words imply an answer to the foregoing question. These friends, at least, will not undertake for Job.

6 And aforetime I was as a tabret. Rather, "I am become as one in whose face they spit." *i.e.*, as R.V., "an open abhorring."

8 shall be astonied at this. At this treatment of an upright man by his friends.

shall stir up himself, etc. Or, "shall be roused against the wicked."

9 The righteous also. That is, Yet the righteous shall not be intimidated, but rather strengthened. Job probably includes himself, determining to hold fast his integrity.

10 do ye return. *i.e.*, Return to the charge, repeating your accusations; "and I shall not find," etc.

12 They change the night into day. *i.e.*, by their delusive representations: see xi. 17.

13 If I wait, etc. Rather, "Surely I wait for Sheol [as] my house."

14 to corruption. Or, "the grave."

16 They. That is, *my hopes.* "The bars of the pit" are "the bars of the gates of Sheol," or Hades.

when our rest together, etc. Rather, "Surely together in the dust is rest"; *i.e.*, for me and my hopes.

CHAPTER XVIII

Second Speech of Bildad

Bildad answers Job with great severity (2–4), and describes the fate of the wicked man (5–21).

4 He teareth himself in his anger. Rather, "O thou that tearest thyself in thine anger" (R.V). Bildad charges Job with wishing that the settled principles of the Divine administration should be made to give way to his anger. But, adds Bildad (ver. 5), this shall not be: however the wicked may dislike it, they must suffer.

6 his candle shall be put out with him. Rather, "his lamp [suspended] above him shall be put out."

9 the robber shall prevail against him. Literally, "the snare shall lay fast hold on him." The language of vers. 7–11 is taken from the modes then practised of catching animals; six different words being used to describe various kinds of nets and snares.

13 the strength of his skin. Literally, "the bars of his skin"; *i.e.*, his limbs.

the firstborn of death. That is, the most dreadful disease; as the "first-born of the poor" (Isa. xiv. 30) are the *poorest.* It was doubtless intended that Job should apply all this to himself; the facts in his case being supposed by his friends to be just such as are here described. It is not surprising, therefore, that he was stung to the quick, as his reply shows.

14 His confidence shall be rooted out of his tabernacle. Rather, "He shall be torn from his tent, his security ('wherein he trusted,' R.V.) and it (*i.e.*, his calamity) shall bring him," etc.

15 It shall dwell in his tabernacle, etc. Rather, "There shall dwell in his tent they that are not his"; *i.e.*, strangers shall possess his dwelling (17, 19).

Brimstone, etc. A frequent Scriptural image of desolation, akin to "sowing with salt," to prevent all growth.

19 nephew. Rather, "descendant": see Gen. xxi. 23. "Nephew" in seventeenth-century English meant *grandson.*

20 They that come after. *i.e.*, men of future ages; "they that went before," being his seniors, or contemporaries. Some, however, render (R.V. marg.), *the men of the West*, and *they of the East* According to the former rendering, the astonishment and fear are said to be *perpetual;* according to the latter, *universal.*

CHAPTER XIX

Job's Second Reply to Bildad

Job again complains of his friends, maintaining that the cause of his affliction must be found in God's supremacy (2–6); describes his sufferings, and calls for pity (7–22); and declares his assurance of deliverance, and blessedness with God in a future life (23–29).

3 ten times. Many times.

that ye make yourselves strange to me. Or, "that ye crush me."

4 Mine error remaineth with myself. The meaning is, It is I who suffer by it; and I should therefore have your sympathy.

5 my reproach. That is, my sufferings with which ye reproach me.

10 He hath destroyed me. Literally, "He hath broken me down."

12 His troops. My numerous calamities attack me like an army, prepare their approaches and surround my tent.

15 dwell. Rather, "sojourn," as guests.

16 I called. Rather, "I call . . . and he giveth me no answer, *though* I intreat him with my mouth"; a crowning humiliation.

17 Though I intreated, etc. Literally, "And my intreating." Or, the word rendered "my intreating" may mean "I am loathsome": see R.V. marg.

18 young children despised. Or, "Young lads despise." An extreme indignity in Oriental countries: xxix. 7–10. The latter clause should read (R.V.), "If I arise, they speak against me."

19 my inward friends. Heb., "men of my council"; *i.e.*, intimate friends.

22 satisfied with my flesh. *i.e.*, with having "devoured" me by your calumnies. In Syriac a calumniator is termed "an eater of flesh."

23 printed. Rather, "inscribed," as R.V.

24 an iron pen and lead. The "iron" or stylus carved the letters in the rock; the "lead" was melted and poured into the cavities.

25 For I know. Rather, "But I know" (R.V.).

my Redeemer liveth. Job now turns for comfort under the harsh judgement of men, to his assured belief. He had given up all hope of deliverance in this world, and regarded himself as a man who had been slain: see ch. xvi. 16–19; xvii. 11–16. And this is confirmed by his use of the word "Goel," or *Redeemer*, the designation of the nearest kinsman, who was in Eastern usage "the avenger of blood." It is, therefore, to his hope of vindication in a *future life* that he must here refer, in the conviction that after death he should joyfully behold his ever-living Vindicator, who would publicly appear and decide in his favour. This suggests an analogy between the present passage and some in the Book of Genesis; though the terms employed are so general that their full meaning is recognised chiefly by the help of later indications, such as that in Heb. xi. 13–16: see Gen. iv. 4; xlix. 10, 18, and notes. The references in this book are in harmony with its character and age, and with the distant vision which the early partriarchs had of gospel blessings; for they "saw them *afar off.*"

26 In my flesh. Rather, "without my flesh," probably meaning, "set free from the flesh."

27 not another. "Not a stranger"; "I shall see Him as no stranger to me," *i.e.*, as no more estranged.

my reins. The "reins," or kidneys, were regarded in the East as the seat of deepest longing.

28 But ye should say, etc. In these words, Job seems to declare that the appearance of his Vindicator will bring judgement on his calumniators; see R.V. "If ye say, How we will assail him, seeing that the root of the matter is found in him! be ye afraid," etc. The "root of the matter" is the ground, the real cause for Job's troubles. This, his friends alleged, was found in Job himself.

29 wrath bringeth the punishments of the sword. Literally (as R.V. marg.), "wrath (or wrathful) are the punishments of the sword," the Divine penalty on calumniators.

CHAPTER XX

Second Speech of Zophar

Zophar replies with great heat; taking no notice of Job's professed confidence in God, but describing the accumulated calamities which will certainly overwhelm the wicked (2–29); especially the wealthy and rapacious oppressor. The picture drawn is vivid, in parts coarse; and the speaker leaves its application to be made by Job himself.

2 And for this I make haste. Rather, "Even on account of my hasting within me," *i.e.*, because of my inward emotion.

3 the check of my reproach. Moffatt translates: "to listen to your insults and excuses—an empty answer to my arguments."

6 excellency. Or, "exaltation."

10 His children shall seek to please the poor. R.V. marg., "The poor shall oppress his children."

their goods. Rather, "his goods," or wealth (R.V.) acquired by violence or fraud.

11 His bones are full of the sin of his youth. Rather, "His bones are full of his youth, yet with him it shall lie in the dust"; *i.e.*, he shall be cut off prematurely. The rendering, "*sin of* his youth," seems due to the Vulgate.

13 and forsake it not. Rather, "let it not go"; *i.e.*, swallow it not at once; carrying out the figure of the enjoyment of a sweet morsel.

17 see. Literally, "look upon" (R.V.). That is, possess and enjoy. So in Psa. xxxiv. 12; Lam. iii. 1.

The floods, the brooks. Rather, "the flowing streams," as R.V.

18 According to his substance, etc. Literally, "As the wealth of his restitution [*i.e.*, wealth belonging to others, and soon to be restored] *shall this be*": "and he shall not rejoice."

20 Surely he shall not feel, etc. Literally, may be rendered thus: "Because he knew no rest in his belly (*i.e.*, his greed); in his rapacity nothing escaped."

21 There shall none, etc. Better rendered in R.V., "There was nothing left that he devoured not; therefore his prosperity shall not endure."

23 When he is about, etc. Rather, "It shall come to pass that to fill his belly [God] shall send upon him the fury of His wrath, and shall rain it upon him for his food."

24 steel. Rather, "copper," probably wood strengthened with this metal. The bow was a deadly weapon to the fugitive.

25 It is drawn. Rather, "He draweth it (*i.e.*, the arrow, a natural act on the part of a wounded man), and it cometh out of the body."

the glittering sword. Literally, "the glittering thing," *i.e.*, the *arrow*.

26 All darkness shall be hid in his secret places. R.V., "All darkness is laid up for his treasures." They are destined to be engulfed and lost.

A fire not blown. *i.e.*, *by man.* Some explain this as implying self-ignition, others refer it to lightning. It seems sufficient to understand the phrase as denoting the self-avenging nature of sin.

It shall go ill, etc. Or, "It (the fire) shall devour him that is left in his tent."

28 The increase of his house. *i.e.*, the wealth laid up in his house.

29 This is the portion, etc. These words are repeated, xxvii. 13; where see note.

CHAPTER XXI

Job's Second Reply to Zophar

After a short appeal to the feelings of his friends, Job replies again to their main argument; maintaining that the wicked are often eminently prosperous in this world, and that man is incompetent to judge of the dispensations of God from present appearances (7–34). In closing this second part of the great colloquy, the patriarch has in view not only the insinuations of Zophar, but the reasonings of the other two.

2 let this be your consolations. Comfort me, not by speaking, but by listening.

3 mock on. Literally, "do *thou* mock on," an address to Zophar. "Suffer me," in the former part of the verse, is "Suffer ye me," including all three.

4 should not my spirit be troubled? "My controversy is not so much with you as with God; and having such an antagonist it is not surprising that my spirit is impatient." The added words in italics, *it were so*, are not in the original, and obscure the sense.

5 Mark me. Or, "Look at me"; in silent amazement at the sufferings which have come upon me, the remembrance of which makes me tremble (6).

7 Wherefore do the wicked live, etc.? Job directly controverts the assertions of his friends, adducing facts of human experience, and in affecting contrast with his own lot: see xv. 21–24; xviii. 19; xx. 9, 10, 27, 28.

12 They take the timbrel, etc. Rather, "sing to the (accompaniment of) the timbrel." The word rendered "take" literally means "lift up"; *i.e.*, *the voice.*

organ. Properly, "pipe."

13 wealth. Or, "prosperity."

in a moment go down to the grave (Sheol). Without lingering disease like Job's, or the dread and pains of death.

14 Therefore, etc. All this they enjoy, and *yet they have said unto God*, etc. There is here assigned a twofold ground for irreligion—a perverse will, "we desire not," etc., and a sceptical spirit, as shown in the questions, ver. 15.

16 Lo, their good is not in their hand, etc. Rather (as a reply to his friends), "Lo! is not their good in their hand?" (*i.e.*, have they not here constant prosperity?) but, though this is the case, "far from me be the counsel of the wicked."

17 How oft, etc.? A *question*, not an *exclamation;* implying that this seldom happens. Having described the prosperity of the wicked, Job asks how often the ills which his friends had spoken of, and which he enumerates in vers. 16–21, did in fact befall them. The words "How often" may be supplied before each clause of these verses: cp. R.V.

19 God layeth up his iniquity, etc. "*Do ye say,* 'God is storing up his iniquity for [requital to] his children?' Let Him requite the man himself, that *he* may know it: let *his own* eyes see, and let *him* drink of the Almighty's wrath. For what concern hath he in his house after him?" etc.: cp. R.V.

22 Shall any teach God knowledge? Job implies that his friends had irreverently attributed their opinions to God. He then states his view, that God varies His proceedings in various cases.

those that are high. The *high-minded.* Some commentators less probably understand *the angels.*

23 in his full strength. Literally, "in his perfection," either of strength or of prosperity.

24 His breasts. Delitzsch renders: "His vessels," *e.g.*, pails, pans, are full of milk (from the flocks).

26 They shall lie down, etc. Rather, as R.V., "They lie down alike in the dust, and the worm covereth them." Dissimilar in life, they are alike in death.

28 the prince. Both here and in Isa. xiii. 2, the word rendered "prince," or "noble," is used in a bad sense for *tyrant.*

29 their tokens. Or, "proofs." You may inquire of travellers, who have had many opportunities of observation, for the proofs of what I say.

30 the wicked is reserved, etc. Rather, as R.V., marg., "the wicked is spared in the day of destruction, and led away in the day of wrath"; intimating that the wicked are not punished here, as Zophar and his companions had asserted.

31 Who shall declare his way to his face? *i.e.*, Who dares to accuse and resist him?

32 Yet shall he be brought, etc. Rather, "And he, he is borne to the graves (*i.e.*, the family burial-place), and over the tomb he keepeth watch"; *i.e.*, either his memory shall be preserved by a sepulchral monument, or, "watch shall be kept over his tomb." This is opposed to Bildad's assertion in xviii. 17. The prosperity of the wicked in this world sometimes outlasts his life. He may be brought with funeral honours to the tomb of his fathers, and his monument remain amidst the verdure of the garden (33): cp. 1 Kings xvi. 6, 28; 2 Kings xxi. 18; and note on 1 Sam. xxv. 1.

33 every man shall draw after him, etc. Referring to the long procession of a public funeral.

CHAPTER XXII

Third Speech of Eliphaz

In the third series of the controversy, which commences here, Job's friends seem to have become greatly exasperated. Eliphaz passes from the insinuations of former speeches to the direct charge of specific sins on account of which, he says, these calamities have come upon Job (2–11); then refers him to signal Divine judgements (12–20); and exhorts him to repentance, the advantages of which he states (21–30).

2 As he that is wise may be profitable unto himself. Or, "Nay, for the wise man profiteth *himself,*" not God. Eliphaz *with truth* asserts that as God can be neither profited nor injured by men, it cannot be for any such reason that He favours some and afflicts others; but he thence *erroneously* infers that the cause of the difference in treatment must be found in their difference of character.

4 Will He reprove thee for fear of thee? Or, "punish thee for thy religion." Eliphaz asks sarcastically whether God punishes men for their piety.

5 And thine iniquities infinite. This is the first *direct* accusation of Job by Eliphaz.

6 for nought. Or, "without cause."

8 the mighty man. Heb., "the man of arm"; *i.e.*, might: see ver. 9. Job is here charged with having obtained land unjustly, by force or undue partiality, or with having helped others to do so. The "honourable man" is literally "he whose person is accepted." Such acts are especially condemned in the law of Moses (Exod. xxii. 21; Deut. xxiv. 17, 19; xxvii. 19).

12 Is not God in the height of heaven? Eliphaz now declares what he regards as the source of Job's crimes—the practical atheism of regarding God as a Being too exalted to observe human affairs.

14 He walketh in the circuit (or, *on the vault*) **of heaven.** Not noticing the earth and its affairs (Ezek. viii. 12).

15 Hast thou marked? Or, "Wilt thou keep?" (R.V.).

16 cut down out of time. That is, before the time; prematurely.

Whose foundation was overflown with a flood? Rather, as R.V., "whose foundation was poured out as a stream?" The historic reference to the Deluge is here recognised by the best critics.

17 what can the Almighty do for them? Or, "And what does the Almighty to them?" This seems to be a sarcastic reference to Job's words in xxi. 14–16. Eliphaz adduces the foregoing case to refute Job's assertion that God makes the wicked prosperous in the present life. The R.V., however, makes the clause part of the impious language of the wicked: "What can the Almighty do for us?"

18 yet He filled, etc. These were Job's words (xxi. 16), which Eliphaz repeats, apparently as being in his opinion more agreeable to the doctrines maintained by himself.

20 Whereas, etc. This is given as the language of the "innocent" (as R.V., which prefixes *saying*): and may be better translated, "Truly our enemies are destroyed, and their residue (*i.e.*, goods) the fire devoureth."

21 good shall come unto thee. This exhortation to godliness is based upon an appeal to the sense of the advantages which it will secure. Finely wrought as it is, the argument discloses the essential defect in the character of Eliphaz.

23 thou shalt put away, etc. Rather, "If thou put away iniquity from thy tabernacles, and cast to the dust precious ore, and gold of Ophir to the stones of the brooks, then the Almighty shall be thy precious ore, and treasures of silver to thee." *I.e.*, If thou wilt despise and reject riches as thy portion, then thou shalt have all-sufficiency in the Almighty: cp. R.V.

25 thy defence. Or, "thy treasure," as R.V.

27 thou shalt pay thy vows. Implying that the prayer would be favourably answered. Worshippers were accustomed to vow some sacrifice or gift to God if the prayer should be granted.

28 decree. Or, "determine"; "resolve upon": and the thing will be done.

30 the island of the innocent. For "island" read "coast," *i.e.*, country.

the pureness of thine hands. An expression signifying integrity and uprightn

CHAPTERS XXIII, XXIV

Job's Third Reply to Eliphaz

Job repeats his desire to bring his cause before God; but is in fear and darkness, and knows not where to find Him (2–9); reasserts his innocence (10–12); yet shrinks from appealing to God, because He hides Himself and pursues His unalterable plans (13–17). He then replies to Eliphaz, describing the open oppressions of the wicked, and their secret sins: and asserts that, though destined to future punishment, they are not treated in this life according to their deserts (xxiv.).

CHAPTER XXIII

3 Oh that I knew where I might find Him! This language (3–5) describes the feelings of one who, when his character is attacked, conscious of uprightness, appeals to the Divine tribunal ("His seat"), as Job had already done (xiii. 3; xvi. 21).

6 Will He plead against me, etc.? Or, "Would He confound me by His omnipotence? No, He would give heed unto me" (R.V.): showing clearly that Job still trusted in God.

7 Moffatt translates: "There I might argue with Him as one innocent."

12 more than my necessary food. Some of the best versions render "in my bosom."

14 He performeth the thing that is appointed for me. Or, "He maketh an end of my purpose" (see ver. 12), etc.; *i.e.*, it is useless to oppose my wishes and purposes to His unalterable decree (13).

16 soft. That is, "faint" (R.V.): see Deut. xx. 3; Isa. vii. 4.

17 Because I was not cut off, etc. Or, perhaps, as R.V., marg., "For I am not dismayed because of the darkness, nor because thick darkness covereth my face." The meaning seems to be, I am not so much terrified by my calamities, dreadful as they are, as by my ignorance of the reasons why God afflicts me.

CHAPTER XXIV

1 Why, seeing times, etc.? Or, "Why are not seasons (*i.e.*, of judgement) appointed by the Almighty, and [why] do not those who know Him behold His days?" (*i.e.*, of vengeance). Job rightly regards the delay of the punishment of the wicked as being part of the same mysterious arrangement, which delays his own vindication.

2 remove the landmarks. See Deut xix. 14.

4 hide themselves together. That is, all the poor are compelled to hide from them.

5 go they forth, etc. Rather, "They go forth in their work, seeking eagerly for food (Heb., 'prey'); the wilderness [giveth] to them food for their children." Meaning probably the houseless poor, mentioned in ver. 4, who nave to seek food in the wilderness, from roots and herbs, like wild animals.

6 They reap every one his corn, etc. The description of the destitute poor is continued. Such coarse food as the open field supplies, and the scanty gleanings of the vineyards, are their only sustenance.

7 They cause the naked, etc. Rather, "Naked, they pass the night without clothing, and have no," etc.

9 They pluck. That is, the wicked do so. Not less cruelly are those treated who have not fled to the desert.

take a pledge of the poor. Or, "What is on the poor (*i.e.*, his only garment) they take for a pledge," leaving him naked (10); see Exod. xxii. 26, 27.

10 They cause him to go naked, etc. Rather, "Naked they go without clothing, and hungry they carry the sheaf; within their walls (those of the oppressors) they press out the oil; they tread their winepresses, and suffer thirst." They famish in the midst of the abundance of others: see Luke xv. 16 and Jas. v. 4.

12 God layeth not folly to them. Rather, "God regardeth not the wrong."

13 They are of those that rebel against the light. Job now turns to another class of evil-doers, who need darkness to conceal their purposes.

14 rising with the light. At the very earliest dawn.

15 disguiseth. Or, "putteth a veil over."

16 they dig through houses. Eastern houses are often made of mud or unburned brick; and thieves enter by digging through the walls; see Matt. vi. 19, 20.

Which they had marked for themselves in the day-time. Rather, "In the day-time they shut themselves up," as R.V.

17 if one know them, etc. Or, "For each one knoweth the terrors of death-shade" (thick darkness). They love the darkness which favours their crimes, and fear the light as much as others fear darkness.

18 He is swift as the waters. "Swift is he on the face of the waters (rapidly passing out of sight); cursed is their portion in the land; he shall not return the way of the vineyards" (to look after his estate), *i.e.*, he shall pass away for ever.

20 The womb. *i.e.*, his own mother.

21 He evil entreateth. Referring to the preceding. All this shall befall the man who "devoureth (R.V.) the barren," etc.; cp. Matt. xxiii. 14.

22 He draweth also the mighty. Thus far, Job has reiterated the popular creed. Now he gives by contrast his own views: "Nay, God by His power maketh the mighty to continue; they rise up when they believed not that they should live" (see R.V. marg.). The oppressor thrives and prospers, even unexpectedly to himself.

23 Though it be given him, etc. Rather, "He (God) giveth him (*i.e.*, the wicked) security whereon he relieth; and His eyes are upon their ways": *i.e.*, God guards and defends them.

24 They are exalted for a little while, etc. Or, "They are exalted; a little while, and they are not; they are brought low; like all [others] they are gathered; and as the heads of corn they are cut off." A call to patience, and to consider the end, as in Psa. lxxiii.

25 who will make me a liar? That is, who will convict me of untruth? etc. This is a challenge to any to prove the contrary.

CHAPTER XXV

Third Speech of Bildad

This short closing speech of Bildad gives no answer to Job's arguments; nor does it contain any new charge against him except an implied rebuke for having justified himself before God. But it is gentler in tone than the former, and it expresses sentiments on the power of God and the sinfulness of man which are in the main correct. That it is so brief seems to indicate that the case against Job is exhausted.

5 Behold even to the moon, and it shineth not. More exactly, as R.V., "Behold, even the moon hath no brightness"; *i.e.*, in comparison with His light.

CHAPTER XXVI

Job's Third Reply to Bildad

Job taunts Bildad with the feebleness of his answer (2–4); and then proves himself not behind his opponents in appreciating the power of God, whose operations he magnificently describes in the world of departed spirits, as well as on earth and in the material heavens (5–14).

3 the thing as it is. Rather, "sound knowledge," R.V., as v. 12.

4 To whom. Rather, "With whom"; *i.e.*, by whose assistance.

5 Dead things are formed, etc. Rather, "The Rephaim (*i.e.*, the mighty dead) tremble beneath the waters and their inhabitants." The underworld, Sheol, is regarded as lying deep beneath the ocean and all its teeming life.

6 Hell. Heb., "Sheol," the under-world. The word rendered *destruction* is "Abaddon," which occurs in Rev. ix. 11. It here means the place of destruction.

7 the empty place. Or, "emptiness," the vast space between earth and stars. "The north" appears to mean the northern sky.

9 He holdeth back the face of His throne. A slight difference in the pointing of the Hebrew letters gives the word "moon" instead of "throne." It would then read, "He hideth the face of the moon."

10 Until the day and night come to an end. Rather, "to the confines of light and darkness" (R.V.): referring to the horizon of the earth, supposed to be encircled with water.

11 The pillars of heaven. The loftiest mountains, which seem to sustain the heavens.

12 He divideth the sea with His power, etc. Rather, "By His power He controlleth the sea, and by His wisdom He smiteth its pride (lit., 'Rahab,' ix. 13). By His breath the heavens become bright; His hand pierceth the fleeing serpent."

14 Lo, these, etc. A magnificent close: "Lo! these are but the outskirts of His ways; and what a whisper of a word have we heard of Him! but the thunder of His power who can understand?"

CHAPTERS XXVII, XXVIII

Continued Address of Job

Job apparently pauses for Zophar to reply; but, as the latter is silent, continues his discourse, the scope of which seems to be as follows: Job first denies the two charges which had been brought against him—that he was ungodly and unholy (2–6), and that he maintained the impunity of the wicked (7–23). Then (xxviii.) he describes what man can do in discovering the secrets of the earth, only to show that in Providence there are deeps which no human endeavour can penetrate, leaving practical piety the only possible and certain wisdom for man.

CHAPTER XXVII

1 parable. Poetic discourse.

2 my judgement. Or, "my right" (R.V.).

5 God forbid that I should justify you. That is, I will not on any account acknowledge you to be in the right. I am innocent of these charges.

6 My heart shall not reproach me, etc. Rather, "My heart doth not reproach me as to one of my days": cp. the Apostle Paul's declaration, "I have lived in all good conscience before God unto this day" (Acts xxiii. 1).

7 as the unrighteous. Their wicked calumnies deserve to be punished as they say the wicked are punished.

8 what is the hope, etc.? Or, "what is the hope of the impious, when God cutteth him off, when He taketh," etc.? see R.V., marg.

11 by the hand of God. Or, "concerning" what God has done.

12 Why then are ye thus altogether vain? Or, "Why then do ye thus cherish foolish notions?"

13 This is the portion, etc. Many supply the word *saying*, after the end of ver. 12; and regard vers. 13–23 as Job's account of the opinions of his opponents. The difficulty is that Job appears now to unsay all that he had maintained before respecting the condition of the wicked, and to concede to his friends their whole case. Then this verse is a quotation from Zophar (xx. 29, see note). May not those that follow be a rapid enumeration of what the friends of Job had maintained? It has been suggested that as there is no third speech of Zophar, and this paragraph is so much in his style, it is actually his, so completing the cycle of speeches; the words, *Zophar answered and said*, having dropped out of the text by some accident of transcription.

15 in death. This is probably the generic for the specific term, "pestilence": as Jer. xv. 2; xliii. 11; Rev. vi. 8; xviii. 8.

16 as the clay. That is, in quantity as the clay.

18 his house, etc. Frail and temporary, like the dwelling which the moth makes in a garment, or the watchman in a vineyard (Isa. i. 8).

19 The rich man shall lie down, etc. The Septuagint reads otherwise, and renders, "he lieth down rich, but shall do so no more; he openeth," etc.

He openeth his eyes, and he is not. He is suddenly cut off.

21 And as a storm hurleth him. More exactly, "And it sweepeth him" (as R.V.).

22 shall cast upon him. *i.e.*, His arrows.

CHAPTER XXVIII

1 Surely, etc. Rather, "For there is" (R.V., marg.). The connexion with the preceding chapter is difficult; the general truth, however, inculcated being plain—that man, with all the wonders of his research and skill, cannot comprehend the secrets of the Divine government. Practical, not speculative wisdom is his highest possible attainment.

a vein. Rather, "a mine" (R.V.).

fine. "Refine."

2 brass is molten out of the stone. Rather, "they melt stone into copper"; *i.e.*, from the heated ore melted copper runs forth. In this graphic description of ancient mining, there may have been a reference to the mines in Idumæa, in the Sinaitic peninsula, and in Egypt, which appear from existing monuments to have been worked as early as the time of Joseph. From Gen. iv. 22 we learn that even iron, the most difficult to work of all these metals, had been in use before the Deluge.

3 He setteth an end to darkness. Man penetrates into the darkest mines.

And searcheth out all perfection, etc. Rather, "and searcheth to the farthest limit stones (ores) of darkness and the deathshade"; piercing to the darkest recesses of the earth.

4 The flood breaketh out, etc. "He diggeth a channel [*or,* shaft] away from [the place] where men sojourn: forsaken of the foot (*that passeth by,* R.V.) they are suspended; they are far from men." A forcible description of the perilous and gloomy life of the miner.

5 And under, etc. *i.e.,* not only is the surface tilled, but the earth underneath is upturned and shattered as if by fire.

7 There is a path which no fowl knoweth. Rather, "the way (*i.e.,* to these subterranean regions) no rapacious bird knoweth," etc. To obtain these hidden treasures, men penetrate into places which the acute vision of birds of prey has never seen, and which the feet of wild beasts have never trodden (ver. 8).

9 the rock. Or, "flint"; perhaps quartz, in which gold is commonly found.

10 He cutteth out rivers. Channels to take off the water.

11 He bindeth the floods from overflowing. He keeps the water from oozing into the mine.

12 where shall wisdom be found? The earth's riches, and man's labour and skill, great as they are, cannot produce true wisdom, which must be sought from God's teaching.

15 weighed. *i.e.,* "paid." Before coinage, payments were made by weight: cp. Gen. xxiii. 16.

17 crystal. This probably means glass, of which the ancients had some very costly kinds. Glass-blowing is distinctly represented in the paintings of Beni-Hassan, which are supposed to have been executed about the time of Joseph.

18 pearls. Rather, "crystal," R.V.: a different word from that in ver. 17.

22 Destruction. "Abaddon": see xxvi. 6, note. Earth, air, and the realms of the dead are alike without a knowledge of the great mystery. Only a "rumour" of its meaning has gone forth.

23 God understandeth. Therefore only He can reveal it.

25 He weigheth the waters by measure. He has adjusted even the most unstable things with admirable skill.

27 prepared. Or, "established it and searched it out," so as to make it thoroughly clear to man, who otherwise would never have known it.

28 And unto man He said, etc. This is the great result of the whole.

CHAPTERS XXIX-XXXI

Concluding Speech of Job: His Lament

Job appears to have again looked for a reply to his argument; and, receiving none, he proceeds to utter his feelings in a discourse full of beautiful images: pathetically contrasting his former prosperity (xxix.) with his present state of misery, arising both from the insults and ill-treatment of the most abject of men (xxx. 1-15), and from his bodily sufferings (16-31); and then earnestly protesting his innocence of the sins laid to his charge, particularly licentiousness (xxxi. 1-12), injustice (13-23), avarice, idolatry, etc. (24-40).

CHAPTER XXIX

3 candle. Rather, "lamp"; a beautiful image of the Divine favour.

4 youth. Rather, "ripeness"; *i.e.,* my prime.

When the secret of God, etc. "When I enjoyed God's friendship"; or when God was protecting my home.

6 When I washed my steps with butter, etc. Rather, "When my steps were bathed in milk, and the rock beside me streamed with oil." These are ordinary images of abundance.

7 in the street. The broad place near the city gate, where he sat as an elder or chief. Vers. 7-10 indicate the courtesy of Oriental manners.

14 diadem. "Turban."

16 the cause which I knew not. Ready to attend to an applicant, although a stranger.

22 dropped. Like refreshing rain: cp. Deut. xxxii. 2.

24 If I laughed on them, etc. Or, "I smiled on them [who] had not confidence"; *i.e.,* I cheered the dejected, and was not infected with their despondency.

25 I chose out their way. I led their enterprises.

CHAPTER XXX

2 In whom old age was perished. Rather, "full age"; *i.e.,* who were too feeble to attain matured strength.

3 desolate and waste. Rather, "Emaciated by want and famine; gnawing in the wilderness yesternight, the utterly desolate land"—persons who sought the roots of the desert for food.

4 Who cut up mallows. Or, "pluck up salt-wort" (*salsola*) or "orache." For the juniper or *retem,* see Gen. xxi. 15 and note.

5 They were driven forth. Outcasts on account of their habits and crimes.

6 clifts. Or, clefts. Ordinary editions of the A.V. here read *cliffs,* perhaps an early misprint.

7 under the nettles. Heb., *charul.* There is a plant called by the Arabs *khardul,* a species of wild mustard, like our charlock, which springs up in uncultivated places, and is tall enough to conceal a horse and his rider.

8 They were viler than the earth. Rather, "They were expelled from the land."

12 the youth. Rather, "a brood"; *i.e.,* a worthless rabble.

they raise up, etc. Or, as R.V., "they cast up against me their ways of destruction."

14 They came upon me as a wide breaking in, etc. Rather, "Like a wide breaking-in they come; in the midst of the desolation they roll in." As through a breach in a wall.

15 my soul. Literally, "my honour."

17 my sinews. Rather, "my gnawings" (see ver. 3); *i.e.,* my gnawing pains.

18 By the great force, etc. Literally, "With great force my garment is disguised; as the opening of my tunic it girdeth me." Instead of falling gracefully like the folds of an Oriental dress, it has become misshapen and squalid.

20 Thou regardest me not. Rather, "Thou lookest upon me"; with apparent unconcern.

22 to ride upon it. That is, to be borne upon it, like chaff.

24 Howbeit he will not, etc. Rather, "Doth not he who is in adversity (lit., a heap, *i.e.,* of ruin: not *grave,* as A.V.) stretch out his hand [for aid]? If any one is in desolation, is there not consequently a cry [for help]?" May not I, then, look for help, who have always extended it to others (25), and had good reason to expect prosperity (26)?

27 prevented me. Or, "are come upon me" (R.V.). The tenses here and in the following verses should be *present.*

28 I went mourning without the sun. "I wail, with none to comfort me" (*Moffatt*).

29 dragons. "Jackals," R.V., the animals of the desert; as are the "ostriches" (not *owls*) in the next clause.

30 My skin is black upon me. Literally, "becomes black from upon me," *i.e.*, blackens and falls from me.

31 my organ, etc. Or, "pipe"; my joy is turned into grief.

CHAPTER XXXI

1 I made a covenant with mine eyes. He who knows his own heart will not only watch its feelings, but will also guard every avenue of temptation.

why then should I think? Rather, "how then should I look?"

2 For what portion of God is there from above? Or, "What is [would be] the portion of God from above, and the inheritance," etc.; *i.e.*, if I had indulged wanton thoughts?

3 a strange punishment. Or, "and estrangement," *i.e.*, from God's favour.

5 to deceit. The connexion (see vers. 1, 9) suggests especially the hateful artifices of the seducer.

8 my offspring. Rather, "my productions"; *i.e.*, the produce of my ground.

10 grind unto another. *i.e.*, "become another man's slave."

12 consumeth to destruction. Heb., "to Abaddon." So fearful are the effects of licentiousness.

16 the eyes of the widow to fail. Being disappointed of my help.

18 I have guided her. That is, the widow (16). Some regard 16, 17 as a question, to which 18 is the answer. But it is more natural to suppose that Job's earnestness led him to interpose a parenthetic assertion (18) before he had finished his sentence.

21 when I saw my help in the gate. *i.e.*, when I knew that my intimacy with the judges would secure for me impunity.

22 let mine arm fall, etc. "Let my shoulder fall from its socket."

23 by reason of His highness, etc. Rather, "and on account of His majesty I am powerless."

27 my mouth hath kissed my hand. Wafting kisses was an ancient mode of expressing veneration: cp. 1 Kings xix. 18; Psa. ii. 12; Hos. xiii. 2. The worship of the heavenly bodies was one of the earliest forms of idolatry.

29 If I rejoiced, etc. The sentiment of this verse is in beautiful accordance with the teaching of the New Testament.

31 Oh that we had of his flesh! etc. Rather, "Who can show [a person who] is not satisfied with his food?"

33 as Adam. R.V. marg.: "after the manner of men." Moffatt: "from men."

35 Oh that one would hear me! etc. The terms of this verse are all judicial, and are best rendered thus: "Oh that I had one to hear me! Lo! this is my mark (or signature); let the Almighty reply to me; and let my opponent write an accusation!" or, as R.V., "and that I had the indictment which my adversary hath written!"

37 As a prince. That is, "boldly": "freely." This shows a confidence in God's justice and a consciousness of his own rectitude. It is thought by the best commentators that this solemn avowal of Job's willingness to meet God in judgement is the true conclusion of his speech, the verses that follow having been misplaced in transcription. The latter undoubtedly fall naturally into the long series of challenges by which the patriarch vindicates his conduct, and should perhaps follow ver. 22.

38 If my land cry against me. Having been wrested from its owners (39).

40 thistles. Or, "thorns." "Cockle," *i.e.*, weeds.

CHAPTER XXXII

Speeches of Elihu

2 the Buzite. Buz is mentioned in Jer. xxv. 23, with Tema and Dedan, as a part of Arabia. Some refer the name to a son of Nahor (see Gen. xxii. 21), which would agree with the opinion that Job lived not long after the time of Abraham. Elihu is not mentioned as having been present during the previous discussion; but it is very probable that he, as well as others, had been attracted by the controversy going on between Job and his friends.

4 had waited till Job had spoken. Rather, "had waited (until the three had finished) to speak unto Job." R.V.

First Speech of Elihu

Ver. 6–XXXIII. Elihu was dissatisfied with the state in which the previous debates had left the argument; neither party having set God's providence in the right light. After rendering due respect to the claims of seniority, he gives his reasons for speaking, promising to be impartial (6–22). He then addresses Job; blames him for his strong assertions of his own innocence and his complaints against God; and lays down as his first proposition the important principle, that suffering is disciplinary and corrective (xxxiii.).

9 Great men. Probably, "The aged"; as in Gen. xxv. 23. Wisdom is not necessarily an attribute even of age and experience; it is the gift of God.

12 convinced. *i.e.*, "confuted"; according to the Old English meaning of "convince."

14 he hath not directed his words against me. Elihu was therefore free from any such bias or unfriendly feeling as those might have who had been excited by dispute.

15 They left off speaking. More expressively, as R.V., "They have not a word to say." Heb., "Words are gone from them."

16 When I had waited. Rather, "And shall I wait, because they speak not, because they stand still, and answer no more? I also will answer," etc. R.V.

18 matter. Literally, "words."

19 My belly. "My mind."—**new bottles.** New wine-skins": see Josh. ix. 4, and Matt. ix. 17.

20 may be refreshed. Heb., "get breath," *i.e.* be relieved.

CHAPTER XXXIII

3 clearly. Rather, "purely," "sincerely."

6 I am according to thy wish, etc. Rather, "You and I are equal before God."

10 He findeth occasions against me. Cp. xiii. 24, 27; xix. 11; xxx. 21.

14 God speaketh once, etc. Though God gives no reasons for His conduct (13), yet its practical designs are evident. He communicates with man individually in two ways—by inward suggestions, of which dreams are an example (15–18), and by outward afflictions (19–22).

perceiveth. Rather, "regardeth."

16 sealeth their instruction. He impresses instruction on their hearts. Several examples of Divine truth communicated supernaturally during sleep are recorded in Scripture.

17 from his purpose. *i.e.*, from an evil course of action.

23 If there be a messenger with him. Probably indefinite, applying to any messenger of peculiar faithfulness and skill whom God sends to explain to the afflicted His righteous dealings and merciful designs. When such a message is received with submission and penitence, the chastening has answered its end, and will be withdrawn.

his uprightness. *i.e.*, " what is right for him," R.V.

24 I have found a ransom. It is clear from i. 5, xlii. 8, that Job and his friends well knew that an atonement was necessary if repentance was to be acceptable to God.

26 He will render unto man, etc. Rather, " He restoreth unto man his righteousness" (R.V.). The whole passage is a beautiful foreshadowing of the Gospel.

27 He looketh, etc. Rather, " He (*i.e.*, the restored penitent) will sing before men and say, I sinned, and perverted that which was right, and it was not requited me."

28 He will deliver his soul, etc. Rather, " He hath delivered my soul from the pit; and my life shall see the light."

33 If not. *i.e.*, If thou hast nothing to say in thy defence.

CHAPTER XXXIV

Second Speech of Elihu

Receiving no reply, Elihu commences his second speech by addressing Job's friends (2–4); then states the views of the sufferer (5–9); which he refutes by showing that God cannot govern unjustly, since, being under subjection to no one, He is absolute Sovereign (10–30): and concludes by appealing to Job (31–37). The main object of this speech is to show that God does make a difference between the righteous and the wicked.

4 Let us choose to us judgement. As the result of this trial and testing (3), " Let us choose for ourselves what is right."

5 my judgement. Rather, " my right."

6 My wound is incurable without transgression. R.V., more correctly, " My wound is incurable, *though I am* without transgression."

8 And walketh with wicked men. *i.e.*, He takes their part, by his sentiments, referred to in ver. 9.

9 he hath said. Elihu's interpretation of Job's words.

14 If He set His heart, etc. This may be rendered, " If He set His heart upon Himself (*i.e.*, care only for Himself), and gather to Himself His spirit and His breath (*i.e.*, cease to sustain the life of His creatures), all flesh," etc. God is under no obligation to maintain His creatures; and were He to cease to do so, they would perish.

17 wilt thou condemn Him that is most just? Or, " the Just, the Mighty One." The same argument is continued. It is contrary to our ideas that the Supreme Ruler should be unjust; and contrary to our observation also, for He rebukes unjust rulers: see next verse.

18 Is it fit to say to a king, etc.? Or, better, " He (*i.e.*, God) saith to a king, 'Wicked man!' to princes, 'Ungodly!' (19). Who accepteth not," etc. There is no reason why God, who is infinitely above both, should regard the rich more than the poor.

20 shall they die. That is, ungodly princes and rich men as well as others.

taken away without hand. That is, suddenly, and without any perceptible human agency.

23 He will not lay upon man, etc. " For He appointeth no set time for a man that he should go before God in judgement" (*Duhm*).

24 without number. Or, " without searching out": see note on ver. 23.

29 who then can make trouble? Or, " who then can condemn?" as R.V.: cp. Rom. viii. 33, 34.

against a nation, etc. Or, " both in respect of a nation and a man alike."

30 Lest the people be ensnared. Rather, " nor ensnare the people."

31 Surely, etc. This is the application of the preceding argument. " For hath any said unto God, I have borne *chastisement*, though I offend not?" (R.V., marg.). This supposition expresses Job's own case. So in the appeal, ver. 32.

33 Should it be according to thy mind? etc. Rather, " Shall He recompense according to thy opinion? for thou hast found fault; therefore thou shalt choose, and not I." Some scholars read " thou shalt choose and not God."

34 Let men of understanding tell me, etc. Better, " Men of understanding will say to me,—even a wise man who has heard me; 'Job hath spoken without knowledge,'" etc.

37 clappeth his hands. A mark of triumph and derision (xxvii. 23).

CHAPTER XXXV

Third Speech of Elihu

In this speech Elihu first states Job's supposed opinions (2–4); and then replies to them. He asserts that men, by their sins or by their uprightness, do not injure or profit God, but themselves; and therefore God has no interest in being partial (5–8); and that, though many cry out and are not heard, it is because they find fault with God, instead of seeking His help (9–16).

2 My righteousness is more than God's. Better: " My righteousness is before God"; *i.e.*, I am upright in His sight.

3 For thou saidst, etc. Or, " For thou saidst, What advantage will it (*i.e.*, uprightness) be to thee (*i.e.*, Job); what profit shall I have [by it] more than by my sin?" See R.V.

4 And thy companions with thee. *i.e.*, persons like-minded with Job (not the three friends).

9 they make the oppressed to cry. Rather, " men cry aloud": referring to xxiv. 12; xxx. 20.

10 But none saith, etc. The cry (ver. 9) is the natural utterance of sorrow, not a yearning after God. " Songs in the night": consolation in adversity: see Acts xvi. 25.

12 There they cry. Read, " Then they cry, because of the pride of evil men; but none giveth answer."

14 Although thou sayest, etc. This and the following verses may be rendered thus: " How much less if thou sayest thou dost not regard Him! the cause is before Him, and thou shouldest wait for Him. But now, as there is no infliction of His anger, and he taketh no note of [Job's] great arrogance, therefore Job openeth his mouth rashly; without knowledge he multiplieth words."

CHAPTERS XXXVI, XXXVII

FOURTH SPEECH OF ELIHU

To show how far God is above our comprehension, Elihu proceeds to take an extensive view of God's providential dealings, especially in the protection and deliverance of the poor and afflicted (5–15). After applying this to Job (16–21), he celebrates the power, wisdom, supremacy, justice, and eternity of God (22–26). He then refers to various remarkable displays of Divine power and majesty in the natural world. And he concludes by asserting that God's moral attributes are perfect, though we may be unable to understand His more mysterious dispensations (23, 24).

CHAPTER XXXVI

4 perfect. That is, correct. Elihu means himself. **in knowledge.** Rather, "in strength of heart" or "mind."

7 But with kings are they on the throne, etc. Rather, "And He setteth them (*i.e.*, the righteous) with kings upon the throne for ever," etc.: figuratively expressing the honours and rewards of righteousness.

9 that they have exceeded. "That they have dealt proudly" (R.V.).

12 without knowledge. Or, "by want of knowledge."

13 But the hypocrites in heart. "And the godless in heart" (R.V.).

heap up wrath. Cherishing anger against God.

15 oppression. Rather, "distress."

17 But thou hast fulfilled, etc. The general meaning of this difficult passage (17, 18) probably is, Thou hast taken the part of the wicked, with which God has connected punishment. When His anger comes upon them, take care lest thou be cut off with the same stroke; for then there will be no redemption.

20 Desire not the night, etc. Or, "Long thou not for the night of death (see John ix. 4), when the peoples are cut off in their place" (*i.e.*, suddenly). The thought of death is associated with that of sweeping, overwhelming destruction; and Job is warned not to invoke such calamity upon himself.

22 God exalteth. Rather, "God is exalted," or, "doeth loftily" as R.V.

24 Which men behold. The Heb. means "sing"; *i.e.*, *praise* ("whereof men have sung," R.V.). See note on xxxiii. 27.

27 He maketh small. Rather, "draweth"; by evaporation.

29 the noise of His tabernacle. Literally, "the crash of His tent"; the thunder; the clouds being regarded as God's tent or pavilion: see Psa. xviii. 11.

31 by them judgeth He the people (peoples). That is, by the rain, tempest, etc., He dispenses both punishment and blessing.

32 With clouds He covereth, etc. Rather, "He hideth the light in His hands (*i.e.*, He graspeth the lightning as a concealed weapon), and giveth it charge against the enemy (*or*, as to hitting the mark)." His thunder-clap tells of Him; the cattle also of His approach. This and the following verses suggest a thunderstorm then in progress.

CHAPTER XXXVII

3 He directeth it. Some render, "He letteth it loose."

6 Likewise to the small rain. Heb., "and the shower of rain; yea the shower of the rains in his strength." The rains in hot countries are sometimes excessively heavy—far exceeding anything that is known in our climate.

7 He sealeth up. That is, He restrains. Such storms stop the labours of the field, and keep the beasts in their dens (7, 8).

9 Out of the south. Literally, "From the chamber": see ix. 9.

11 Also by watering, He wearieth, etc. Rather, "Also with moisture He loadeth the cloud; He spreadeth out the thunder-cloud of His light (or lightning). And it (the lightning) turneth itself about by His counsels to do them; *even* all that He commandeth on the face of the whole earth."

16 the balancings of the clouds. How they are suspended in the air.

17 How thy garments are warm, etc. Referring to the sultry stillness of summer heat, and its unpleasant effects upon the body.

18 strong, and as a molten looking-glass. Or, "*Firm* as a molten mirror"; made of polished metal. The sky is often represented in ancient poetry as a vast solid concave mirror.

20 If a man speak, surely, etc. Or, perhaps, "Or shall a man say (*i.e.*, ask) that he may be destroyed?" To contend with the Almighty is to court destruction.

21 And now men see not, etc. Rather, "And now they see not the light that is bright in the skies; and the wind passeth, and cleareth them (the skies). (22) From the north cometh gold (perhaps a golden splendour): upon God (*i.e.*, as His robe) is terrible glory." It is possible that these phenomena were now occurring—a presage of the rising storm.

23 He will not afflict. Or, "oppress"; *i.e.*, He will not deal unjustly.

24 Men do therefore fear Him, etc. "Therefore men should fear Him; for He will not regard any that are wise" [in their own opinion].

CHAPTERS XXXVIII–XL

FIRST ANSWER OF JEHOVAH OUT OF THE STORM

At length, God Himself, to whom Job had repeatedly appealed (see xxxi. 35), interposes to put an end to the protracted controversy; but it is remarkable that, in this sublime discourse, He *gives no explanation* of the difficulties which had so much embarrassed Job and his friends. He does not vindicate His proceedings, or state why the wicked often prosper and the righteous suffer; nor does He refer to the retributions of a future world. The great truth held up to view is, that there ought to be entire confidence in a Being whose works prove Him to be infinitely great and wise. Various Divine operations in nature are introduced, relating to the earth and the ocean (xxxviii. 4–18), the heavens (19–38), and the animal creation (39–41; xxxix. 1–30); and, as man is unable to give an explanation of these, it is declared to be awfully presumptuous to arraign God's moral government, and to complain of His secret counsels and purposes.

CHAPTER XXXVIII

2 Who is this, etc.? Probably referring to Job: see ver. 1.

3 Gird up now thy loins like a man. As one who is preparing for some great effort.

6 fastened. Or, "sunk." The earth is poetically represented, in 5, 6, as a building.

7 the morning stars. This word may be taken

literally, as in Psa. cxlviii. 3; or figuratively, as in Isa. xiv. 12; and may refer to angels, "the sons of God," and to the acclamations with which the foundation or completion of great edifices were celebrated: see Ezra iii. 10; Zech. iv. 7.

10 And brake up for it my decreed place. Rather, "when I apportioned to it my limit."

12 since thy days. This means, "in thy lifetime."

13 might be shaken out of it. That is, out of the earth. The light, spreading to the ends of the earth, disperses the wicked (xxiv. 13–17).

14 It is turned as clay, etc. Rather, "It (the earth) changeth itself as the clay of a seal, and [things] stand out as a garment." The objects upon the earth, before enveloped in darkness, at the return of light are rendered visible and prominent, like the impression formed by a seal, and clothe it in a robe of beauty.

15 their light is withholden. The night being the daytime of the wicked (*i.e.*, their time for action), the light is to them as darkness, and "the uplifted arm is broken," their plans being thwarted: cp. xxiv. 13–17.

16 in the search of the depth. Rather, as R.V., "in the recesses of the deep."

19 Where is the way, etc.? Or, "Where is the way to the abode of light?"

21 Knowest thou it, because thou wast then born? Or, as irony, "Thou [surely] knowest it, for then thou wast born, and the number," etc.

22 treasures. *i.e.*, "treasuries," or storehouses.

25 the overflowing of waters. Or, "torrents of rain."

26 where no man is. Consequently, neither by man's agency, nor immediately for his use.

30 as with a stone, etc. Rather, "as a stone; and the face of the deep is congealed."

31 sweet influences. Or, "bands"; referring to the "cluster" of the Pleiades, consisting of seven stars: see note on ix. 9. For a notable chapter on this passage, see Hugh Macmillan: *Bible Teachings in Nature.*

32 Mazzaroth. See note on 2 Kings xxiii. 5.

Arcturus with his sons. The "sons" of Arcturus or "the Bear" are the "train" (R.V.) of its stars: see note on ix. 9. It is to be remembered that, if modern discoveries seem to explain some of these things, they only advance our knowledge a few steps further, and then we are met by questions as difficult to us as these were to Job.

36 Who hath put wisdom, etc.? Some render this, "Who hath put wisdom in the dark clouds? or who hath given to meteors intelligence?"

37 in wisdom. Or, "with wisdom"; *i.e.*, who, by his wisdom, can determine their proper number?

who can stay, etc. Or, "lay down." *i.e.*, empty. The Arabs still compare heavy clouds to water-skins.

38 groweth into hardness. Rather, "is molten into mire"; the effect of rain.

39 Wilt thou hunt the prey? Or, "Dost thou?" There is here a transition from the inorganic to the organic creation—the region of life, instinct, and appetite, in which creatures are governed by other laws than those of matter. This deepens our impression of the littleness of man, in comparison with Him who made and sustains them all.

CHAPTER XXXIX

1 Knowest thou, etc.? "Knowing" seems to be used here, as elsewhere, in the sense of *watching over* and *providing for* them; and to "number the months" means to *appoint* the number.

3 they cast out their sorrows. Or, "cast away their pains."

4 are in good liking. Rather, "grow fat," or "robust."

7 the multitude. Rather, "the tumult," or "noise."

9 the unicorn. *i.e.*, the wild ox: see note on Numb. xxiii. 22.

13 Gavest thou the goodly wings unto the peacocks, etc.? Rather, "The wing of the ostriches exults! Is it a kindly pinion and plumage?"

14 Which leaveth, etc. Rather, "For she leaveth," etc. The ostrich forms a nest in the sand of the desert, the heat of which supplies the want of continuous incubation.

17 neither hath He imparted to her understanding. The folly of the ostrich is proverbial in the East.

18 She scorneth the horse and his rider. The ostrich is so swift that it is scarcely possible to capture it by direct pursuit.

19 Hast thou clothed his neck with thunder? Rather, "with trembling"—the nervous tremor in every part of the neck when the warhorse is roused for action.

20 Canst thou make him afraid as a grasshopper? Or, "make him leap as a locust?" (R.V.): cp. Joel ii. 4.

The glory of his nostrils. Or, "The majesty of his snorting."

23 the shield. Rather, "javelin."

24 Neither believeth he, etc. Like a person overjoyed.

25 Ha! ha! Or, "At every trumpet-blast he says He-ah!" *i.e.*, he neighs exultingly.

26 stretch her wings towards the south. Referring to the migratory habits of the bird.

CHAPTER XL

2 Shall he that contendeth with the Almighty instruct Him? etc. Rather, "Will he who censured the Almighty contend? Will he who reproved God reply to this?" *i.e.*, to the interrogations of the foregoing chapters.

Answer of Job

Vers. 3–5. Job replies to the demand of God by a penitential confession.

5 Once . . . twice. That is, "repeatedly": cp. xxxiii. 14, 29. This confession of Job shows that a right view of the glorious perfections and wonderful works of God is fitted to produce a deep sense of our own sinfulness: see Isa. vi. 5. To Job personally this quickening of the sense of sin, accompanied as it was by entire submission to God, was the turning-point in his life.

Second Answer of Jehovah out of the Storm

Ver. 7–XLI. God again addresses Job, rebuking him (7, 8); and continuing the argument in proof of His own majesty and power as displayed in executing His judgements (9–14), and in the formation of the behemoth (15–24) and leviathan (xli.). God has wrought in Job's mind conviction of sin, but does not give peace and joy at once. He still "speaks out of the whirlwind," and deepens the sense of unworthiness.

11 Cast abroad the rage of thy wrath. Better, "Pour forth the overflowings of thine anger" (R.V.).

15 behemoth. This is generally thought to be the hippopotamus.

which I made with thee. That is, "equally with thee."

16 the navel. Or, "the muscles" or "sinews."

17 like a cedar. Probably alluding to the elevation and rigidity of the tail when the animal is enraged.

The sinews, etc. Rather, "The sinews of his thighs are firmly twisted."

18 strong pieces of brass. Or, "tubes of copper."

19 the chief of the ways of God. That is, chief in size and strength. So the words are used in Numb. xxiv. 20; Amos vi. 1, 6.

He that made him can make, etc. Rather, "He who made him gave him his sword"; *i.e.,* the means of attack and defence.

21 the shady trees. The wild lotus, or Egyptian water-lily, which grows in marshy places.

23 Behold, he drinketh up a river, etc. Rather, "Lo! a river overflows [but] he is not alarmed: he is unmoved, should the Jordan rush upon his mouth."

24 He taketh it with his eyes, etc. Rather, "Will any one, in his eyes (*i.e.,* when he is on his guard), take him? Can any one pierce his nose with 'snares' or 'hooks'?" *i.e.,* insert a cord or ring to tame or lead him (Isa. xxxvii. 29).

CHAPTER XLI

1 leviathan. Most probably the crocodile.

Or his tongue with a cord which thou lettest down. Rather, "or compress his tongue with a cord."

2 a hook. Rather, "a rush-rope."

a thorn. Or, "a hook" (R.V.).

6 Shall the companions, etc.? This verse may be rendered, "Do the companies [of fishermen] dig [pitfalls] for him," or, "make traffic of him?" (R.V.).

8 do no more. Or, "thou wilt not do it again."

9 the hope of him. That is, of any one who attempts to attack him.

11 prevented me. Or, "anticipated me"; *i.e.,* in good offices, so as to lay me under obligation.

12 his comely proportion. Or, "the beauty of his array."

13 Who can discover, etc.? Or, "Who can slip off the surface of his clothing [of scales]? Within the doubling of his bridle [*i.e.,* his rows of teeth] who can enter?"

18 By his neesings a light doth shine. "His neesings flash forth light" (R.V.). This highly figurative language (18–21) describes the respiration ["sneezings"] of the animal rising out of the water, when the sunlight falls on the spray ejected from his nostrils.

22 In his neck remaineth strength, etc. Rather, "Strength dwelleth in his neck, and terror danceth before him" (R.V.).

24 the nether millstone. The nether or lower millstone was of harder material than the upper.

25 By reason of breakings they purify themselves. Rather, "By terrors they are bewildered."

26 cannot hold. That is, can effect nothing.

29 Darts. Rather, "clubs."

30 Sharp stones are under him, etc. Rather, "Under him are sharp potsherds; he spreadeth his threshing-sledge upon the mire": alluding to the marks made by his scales on the mud.

31 like a pot of ointment. A shining, oily track.

34 He beholdeth all high things. He looks down on every thing as inferior to himself. The "children of pride" are the stronger and fiercer animals.

CHAPTER XLII

Conclusion of the Book

This closing chapter contains Job's confession (2–6); the Divine decision against his friends, and Job's intercession for them (7–9); and his own restored prosperity (10–16).

3 Who is he that hideth counsel without knowledge? This is quoted from the words of Jehovah in xxxviii. 2 (as ver. 4 is from xxxviii. 3; xl. 7); Job thus acknowledging the truth of the charges. The language of contrite confession in reply contrasts beautifully with the authoritative tone of the quotations themselves, and as strikingly with the presumptuous manner in which Job had formerly spoken of God.

6 Wherefore I abhor myself. Or, "Therefore do I retract," viz., my former words. The work of the new birth is now complete. After this, there is "no condemnation." "Out of the trial Job comes, still on God's side, more on God's side than ever, with a nobler faith more strongly founded on the rock of truth."—R. A. Watson in *Expositor's Bible.*

8 My servant Job shall pray for you. This is a beautiful instance of the duty and acceptableness of intercession for others. It also illustrates the nature of patriarchal worship; and shows that in the earliest ages sacrifice was known to be essential to the acceptableness of prayer: see note on xxxiii. 24. After the charges they had brought against Job, it was an appropriate humiliation to them to be indebted to his prayers.

10 turned the captivity of Job. He restored Job to his former prosperity. The phrase is proverbial for renewed freedom and happiness: see Psa. xiv. 7; cxxvi. 1.

11 a piece of money. Or, *hesîtah.* See note on Gen. xxxiii. 19; Josh. xxiv. 32. The mention of this ancient coinage has been taken as an indication that the life of Job belonged to patriarchal times.

12 the latter end of Job. The double compensation was an *outward* and *visible* token of God's remembrance and love, and of the purpose of His discipline—"the end of the Lord," Jas. v. 11. The *truth* would have been the same had Job passed from his dung-hill to the heavenly rest. But it would have been *concealed* from the world. The great lesson of the history applies to cases in which earthly prosperity does not return.

13 seven sons and three daughters. The flocks and herds are *doubled:* the number of children is *the same* as before.

14 Jemima. Meaning, "a dove"; or, according to some, "daylight."

Kezia. That is, "cassia"; an aromatic bark (Psa. xlv. 8) of most agreeable fragrance.

Keren-happuch. Meaning, "horn of antimony," or eye-paint; probably on account of her beautiful eyes.

15 gave them inheritance among their brethren. An evidence of Job's peculiar regard for them, and of his great wealth. Among the Hebrews, the daughter inherited only when there was no son (Numb. xxvii. 8).

16 a hundred and forty years. His age therefore at death must have been nearly 200: further evidence that he belonged to patriarchal times. Terah lived 205 years, Abraham 175, Isaac 180, Jacob 147.

17 So Job died, etc. The Septuagint adds, "It is written that he will rise again with those whom the Lord raiseth."

THE BOOK OF PSALMS

INTRODUCTION

THE Psalms are their own best introduction. Few words are, therefore, necessary here. Believing, as we do, with Dr Alexander Maclaren, that "the deepest and most precious elements in the Psalms are very slightly affected by the answers to questions of date and authorship," we do not here enter upon their discussion. Such answers are occasionally given below, under the head of individual Psalms.

No book in the Bible so completely unites the world's divided Christendom. Roman Catholic and Protestant, Anglican and Non-Anglican, use it in public and private devotion. No book so completely expresses the varied needs of the human heart.

As Archbishop Alexander has so well shown in his Bampton Lectures on *The Witness of the Psalms to Christ and Christianity*, Christ is a frequent subject of their praise, in His sufferings, in His victory, and in His universal reign. We may specially mention here the 2nd, 22nd, 72nd, and 110th ; but those who desire a fuller account of Messianic Psalms will find it wisely treated by Professor W. T. Davison in *Hastings' Bible Dictionary*, article "Psalms." The Psalms were more than once quoted by our Lord Himself (Matt. xxi. 16, 42 ; xxii. 43 ; John ii. 17 ; xiii. 18 ; xv. 25) and are constantly applied to Him by the Apostles in the Acts and in the Epistles.

Many a student of Scripture has had a similar experience to that which Bishop Horne expresses in the Preface to his *Commentary on the Psalms* : "Every Psalm improved infinitely upon his acquaintance with it, and no one gave him uneasiness but the last ; for then he grieved that his work was done. Happier hours than those which have been spent on these meditations on the songs of Sion, he never expects to see in this world."

PSALM I

Psa. i. exhibits the connexion between piety and true happiness ; describing the *characteristics* of the godly man, both what he is not (1), and what he is (2) ; and his *blessedness* (3), which is contrasted with the state of the ungodly (4–6).

1 Blessed. "Happy !" With such a benediction the words of Moses *end* (Deut. xxxiii. 29), and those of Christ, in the Sermon on the Mount, *begin* (Matt. v. 3–11).

that walketh not, etc. The terms here employed seem to denote a *progression* in wickedness ; first, regard for the views and maxims of the ungodly, then the active practice of sin, and, at last, deliberate profanity.

2 the law of the Lord. In Scripture generally, and especially in the Psalms, the "law" frequently means the *whole revealed will of God.* Habitual delight in God's Word is an evidence of real piety, and a source of spiritual vigour.

5 shall not stand in the judgement. *i.e.*, at the bar of God. "Stand" is a forensic term, denoting *to stand acquitted.*

nor sinners in the congregation of the righteous. The time is coming when an entire separation shall be made between the righteous and the wicked.

6 the Lord knoweth. In Scripture to "know" often signifies *to regard with interest, approbation, or affection* : see Matt. vii. 23.

PSALM II

This Psalm is perfectly appropriate to our Lord, the true "Messiah," acknowledged by Peter to be "the Christ, the Son of the living God" : cp. vers. 2, 7 with John vi. 69. And to Him it is expressly referred in Acts iv. 25 ; xiii. 33 ; Heb. 1, 5 ; v. 5 ; Rev. ii. 27.

1 the heathen. Or, "the nations." In the next clause the word is also in the plural : "peoples" meaning large communities, or masses of mankind.

2 the kings of the earth set themselves, etc. In Acts iv. 25–27 this passage is applied to the union of Herod and Pilate—Jew and Gentile—against Jesus Christ ; but the terms are general, and may be applied to every combination against Christ and His religion.

His Anointed. Or, "His Messiah" ; which is a modified form of the Hebrew word here used. "Christ" is its Greek equivalent. *Anointing* was used to inaugurate priests (Exod. xxx. 30), kings (1 Kings i. 39), and in some cases prophets (1 Kings xix. 16).

4 He that sitteth in the heavens shall laugh, etc. This highly figurative language must not be taken to represent the Most High as exulting over the sins or miseries of men. It is a vivid expression of the tranquillity with which Jehovah regards all the opposition of His enemies, however formidable it may appear to us. It suggests, too, the cheerful confidence with which the Christian should view all attacks upon the Gospel and the kingdom of God.

7 I will declare the decree. More precisely, "I will tell of a decree." These are the words of the Anointed King.

This day have I begotten Thee. That is, I have announced Thee as my only begotten Son. Hence the Apostle Paul (Acts xiii. 33; Rom. i. 4) applies these words to the resurrection of Christ; that being the time when His humiliation was terminated, and He was "declared to be the Son of God with power": see also Heb. i. 5; v. 5; and cp. Col. i. 18.

12 Kiss the Son. *i.e.*, "Do Him homage as your Sovereign": a kiss being an ancient mode of expressing veneration: see 1 Sam. x. 1; 1 Kings xix. 18; Hos. xiii. 2.

from the way. Rather, "*in* the way"; the way of error which ye have chosen.

when His wrath, etc. Or, "*For* His wrath will within a little (*i.e.*, in a *little while*, or *easily*) be kindled."

PSALM III

The superscription of this Psalm is confirmed by its contents. Psalms iii. and iv. were probably composed as evening and morning hymns, with reference to the first night of David's flight from Absalom (2 Sam. xvi., xvii.), when his life seemed to hang by a hair: for, had not God heard his prayer and defeated Ahithophel's counsel, he could hardly have escaped.

2 Selah. "Selah" is probably a musical term, meaning *pause*, in which a symphony was probably introduced; and, as the pauses in music generally agreed with the pauses in sense, it often assists in rightly dividing a Psalm.

3 a shield for me. "About me" (R.V.); a protection on every side.

4 I cried . . . He heard. Rather, as R.V., "I cry . . . He answereth": a *constant* experience.

5 sustained. Or, "sustaineth" (R.V.): see on ver. 4.

7 broken the teeth, etc. The Psalmist's enemies are like wild beasts, eager to devour; but God will take away their power to injure him.

PSALM IV

See prefatory note on Psalm iii.

TITLE. **To the chief Musician.** Fifty-five Psalms have this inscription; all but two (lxvi., lxvii.) being ascribed to David, Asaph, or the sons of Korah. The meaning undoubtedly is, "for the use of the Precentor," or leader of the Sanctuary choir.

Neginoth. That is, "stringed instruments": see Habakkuk iii. 19.

1 O God of my righteousness; that is, "Vindicator of my righteous cause."

enlarged. *i.e.*, "set me at large," R.V.

2 my glory. This probably refers to David's royal dignity, which God had given him, and of which his foes were seeking to deprive him.

leasing. An old English word for "falsehood."

3 him that is godly. Rather, "pious"; one who lives under the influence of Divine love. The psalmist describes himself.

4 Stand in awe, and sin not. This clause is rendered in the Septuagint, "Be ye angry, and sin not": and is so used by the Apostle Paul in Eph. iv. 26. Whether this translation or that of the text is adopted, the verse seems to have been addressed to David's comrades, exhorting them to restrain their just indignation.

upon your bed. That is, during the silence of the night.

6 The light of Thy countenance. See Numb. vi. 24–26.

7 their corn and their wine increased. Corn, wine, and oil, being the principal products of Canaan, are often used to represent all earthly good: see Deut. xxxiii. 28; Hos. ii. 8.

8 For Thou, Lord, only, etc. Some render this, "Thou, Lord, makest me to dwell alone in safety"; supposing the words to allude to Numb. xxiii. 9; Deut. xxxiii. 28. "The expression of confidence gains much if 'alone' be taken as referring to the Psalmist" (*Alexander Maclaren*).

PSALM V

TITLE. **Nehiloth.** This word is probably derived from a root signifying to *perforate*, denoting some kind of wind instrument, such as a flute. A Psalm, therefore, for the accompaniment of wind instruments.

3 look up. Rather, "look *out*"; as a watchman expecting deliverance. True faith is not content with the mere act of supplication, but waits with earnest expectation for an answer: see Micah vii. 7; and Hab. ii. 1, where the same word occurs.

5 foolish. Or, "boasters."

8 in Thy righteousness. *i.e.*, in Thy character as a righteous God, be my Guide.

9 their throat is an open sepulchre. *i.e.*, they are waiting to devour me, like a sepulchre opened to receive its victim.

10 Destroy. Rather, "Hold them guilty" (R.V.), *i.e.*, punish them. These maledictions were expressions, not of a malignant spirit, but of a righteous indignation against flagrant sin, and a deep sympathy with the cause of justice.

11 let all those, etc. Or, "So shall all those that put their trust in Thee rejoice; they shall ever shout for joy; and Thou shalt defend them; they also that love Thy name shall be joyful in Thee": see R.V., marg.

13 a shield. The larger shield, covering all the body: see 1 Sam. xvii. 7, 41.

PSALM VI

This Psalm is commonly reckoned as one of the penitential Psalms of David, of which, according to the Jews, there are seven.

TITLE. **Sheminith.** The term "Sheminith" means *eighth*, and may denote an instrument with eight strings; or, which is more likely, music played with the lower notes: see 1 Chron. xv. 20, 21, where "Alamoth" and "Sheminith" clearly signify different parts of music; the former answering probably to our *treble*, and the latter to the *bass*, or, perhaps, an octave below the treble.

1 in Thine anger. I do not plead against correction; only let the correction be *loving*.

2 my bones are vexed. Heb., "affrighted," or "amazed"; and so in vers. 3, 10. The "bones" are mentioned as the strength and framework of the body. The Psalmist's suffering was so intense as to affect his whole frame.

3 how long? That is, "How long wilt Thou delay to help?" This incomplete form of the sentence expresses strong emotion.

5 For in death there is no remembrance of Thee. The Psalmist contemplates death, not as the close of his existence, but as a mark of God's anger, and as putting an end to all opportunity of praising God among his fellow-men: see Isa. xxxviii. 18.

the grave. Heb., "Sheol"; the under-world, or Hades.

6 to swim. That is, "with tears": denoting long and severe distress.

7 consumed. Or, "grown dim," with weeping.

8 the Lord hath heard the voice, etc. This abrupt change from sorrow to joy shows the psalmist's confidence that his prayer had been heard, and would be answered. Many of the plaintive Psalms end thus triumphantly: see Psa. xiii., xxxi.

10 Let all mine enemies, etc. Rather, "All mine enemies shall be ashamed," etc.; "they shall return," etc. (see R.V.).

PSALM VII

TITLE. **Shiggaion.** That this word denotes some particular kind of poem is evident from its use by Habakkuk (iii. 1); but its meaning is doubtful. Some think it is merely "a song"; some, a dithyrambic or irregular ode.

Cush. "Cush" is the Hebrew name for Ethiopia. No person of this name is mentioned in the history of David; but some regard it as applying to Shimei, who was "a Benjamite."

3 if I have done this. That is, the wickedness with which my enemies charge me; referring to the charge made by Shimei of being "a man of blood" (2 Sam. xvi. 7). Spurgeon calls the Psalm "The Song of the Slandered Saint."

4 I have delivered him, etc. "And [if] I have spoiled him that without cause is mine enemy."

7 So shall the congregation, etc. Or, "Let the assembly of the nations [for judgement] surround Thee; and over it (the assembly) return Thou to the lofty [throne]." In the preceding verse God had been invoked *as a judge;* and His delay in interposing is compared to a king's absence, for the purpose of repose (6), from his tribunal, to which He is here entreated to return.

8 according to my righteousness. That is, *in this particular matter*—according to my innocence of the charges brought against me. The confessions of unworthiness made elsewhere plainly show that the Psalmist laid no claim to absolute sinlessness.

11 God judgeth the righteous, etc. The verse may be rendered, "God is a righteous judge (R.V.), and a God who is angry every day." It is obvious that the object of God's anger, though not expressed, is the enemy (5), the wicked (9); of whom it is said, "If he turn not, He (God) will sharpen His sword": cp. Deut. xxxii. 41, 42.

13 He ordaineth His arrows, etc. Or, "His arrows He hath made to be burning"; *i.e.,* inflammable, so as to burn when they wound; "fiery *shafts,*" R.V.

15 He made a pit, etc. Alluding to the method of catching wild beasts by pits covered over slightly with reeds or branches of trees.

17 His righteousness. That is, His *justice.*

PSALM VIII

The allusions in ver. 3 have led many to suppose that David wrote this Psalm in his early life, when his nightly watches as a shepherd gave him frequent opportunities of observing the wonders of the heavens. The subject is the glory of God as manifested in Nature, and especially in the capacities and the dignity which He has bestowed on man; who is here contemplated in his true ideal, apart from his sinfulness, such as he was before he fell, and such as he is to be when restored in Christ. To Him, as the great representative of perfect human nature, the Psalm is emphatically applicable: see Heb. ii. 6–9.

TITLE. **Gittith.** The word "Gittith" is derived from "Gath," a *winepress.* The reference is probably to a tune used at vintage-festivals.

1 O Lord, our Lord. O Eternal, our Lord (Adonai).

2 the avenger. Or, "the vindictive." "Babes and sucklings" may be understood as meaning, the instinctive admiration of Thy works which is shown even by very young children rebukes those who would question Thy being, or obscure Thy glory: see Matt. xxi. 16; 1 Cor. i. 27. "Thou hast *perfected praise*" in the former of these passages is from the LXX translation of the Hebrew.

3 the work of Thy fingers. Expressing the skill and delicacy of the work.

5 a little lower than the angels. Perhaps, "but little lower than God" (R.V.). But the Hebrew word "Elohim," rendered "God," when applied to the Supreme Being, and also "gods," when applied to idols, is supposed by some to be used here, and in a few other places, so as to include any superhuman beings: see 1 Sam. xxviii. 13; Zech. xii. 8.

6 Thou madest him to have dominion, etc. See Gen. i. 26.

7 oxen, etc. "Oxen" is a generic term for *larger cattle.* "Beasts of the field" are always, in Scripture, *wild beasts.*

PSALM IX

In the Russian Psalter ("Orthodox" or "Greek Church"), following the Septuagint, Psa. ix. and x., are united in one. The numbering of the subsequent Psalms is therefore altered, down to the 146th. This ends with ver. 11 of the 147th Psalm in our version, and the Russian 147th begins with ver. 12 of Psa. cxlvii, A.V.

TITLE. **Muth-labben.** Some take "labben" in this title as an anagram of *Nabal,* and render it *on the death of the fool* (see 1 Sam. xxv. 25); others, slightly changing the Hebrew vowels, suppose the ormer part of the compound word to denote *female voices,* or soprano; and the latter to mean, "for *Ben,*" or "[the children of] Ben," a Levitical singer mentioned in 1 Chron. xv. 18.

6 O thou enemy, etc. Or. 'As to the enemy, they are consumed, ruins for ever": cp. R.V. "Thou," in the second clause, probably means Jahveh (as in ver. 5), to whom David always ascribes his victories.

7 shall endure. Rather, "shall sit," *i.e.,* as king (see R.V.): cp. Heb. i. 3.

14 In the gates of the daughter of Zion. The "daughter" is a metaphorical expression for the *inhabitants* of a city viewed collectively ("metropolis," *i.e., mother*-city). The "gates" were the place of public concourse for the inhabitants of Jerusalem.

I will rejoice, etc. Rather, "That I may rejoice," etc.

16 Higgaion. The word "Higgaion" may mean *meditation,* being a direction (stronger than "Selah" alone) to *pause,* reverently and thoughtfully. But the use of the word in Psa. xcii. 3, with reference to the sound of the harp, makes it likely that it was also designed to call for instrumental music whilst the singers paused.

17 The wicked shall be turned into hell. Rather (as R.V.), " The wicked shall return to the underworld " (Sheol). The figure is derived from an army turned back to destruction.

PSALM X

3 And blesseth the covetous, etc. Perhaps, " And the covetous renounceth " (see note on Job i. 5), " [yea] contemneth Jehovah " : see R.V.

4 The wicked, through the pride, etc. Or, " The wicked [saith] in his pride, He (*i.e.,* God) will not make inquisition : 'No God' [are] all his thoughts " : see ver. 13 ; Psa. ix. 12. All sin is practical atheism.

5 grievous. The Hebrew word probably means " enduring," or " firm " (R.V.) ; and describes the sinner's false security.

7 under his tongue, etc. An allusion to the poison of serpents, which is concealed beneath their teeth : see Rom. iii. 13, 14.

9 as a lion, etc. The wicked man is compared first to a lion, and then to a hunter, to show that he employs *craft* as well as *force.*

10 His strong ones. *i.e.,* probably, his strong *claws* or *teeth.*

12 the humble. Or, as in ver. 9, " the poor," *or,* " the afflicted."

17 prepare. Or, " establish."

18 That the man of the earth may no more oppress. The word for " man " used here means " frail man." The phrase indicates the essential weakness of all tyranny : " that man, which is of the earth, may be terrible no more," R.V. : see Psa. ix. 20.

PSALM XI

2 For lo, the wicked bend their bow, etc. These words, and those in ver. 3, are still the words of the Psalmist's friends, warning him of his peril.

3 If the foundations be destroyed, etc. *E.g.,* the foundations of social order ; the principles of justice, and laws based upon them.

4 The Lord is in His holy temple, etc. This is David's animated reply to his desponding friends, and it well suggests the source of consolation amid trials or persecutions in every age. This is specially emphasised by the Hebrew word used, which is *Jahveh,* " The Eternal."

6 snares. Some render this word " burning coals " ; " fire and brimstone " are familiar types of sudden and complete destruction ; and refer doubtless to the great historical example of Sodom and Gomorrah : see Job xviii. 15 ; Ezek. xxxviii. 22. The " horrible tempest," or, rather, " scorching blast," is probably the deadly sandstorm of the desert, the Simoom.

7 His countenance doth behold the upright. Or, more probably, as R.V., " the upright shall behold His face " : see Psa. xvii. 15.

PSALM XII

4 Our lips are our own. The meaning perhaps is, We will utter what we please, flattery or insolence (3) as suits our purpose.

5 I will set him in safety from him that puffeth at him. Or, " I will place in safety him that panteth for it " : see R.V. marg.

PSALM XIII

1 for ever ? Not a second question, but a part of the first : " How long, O Jehovah, wilt Thou continually forget me ? "

3 lighten, *i.e.,* " enlighten." See 1 Sam. xiv. 27, where the same expression is used.

5 But I. The word " I " is emphatic : " And as for me, in Thy mercy I have trusted ; let my heart rejoice in Thy salvation."

PSALM XIV

With some slight variations, Psa. liii. is the same as this.

1 in his heart. To *himself,* if not to others.

corrupt. See Gen. vi. 12.

2 understand. Or, " act wisely." It is the proof of wisdom to seek God : see Psa. cxi. 10 ; Deut. iv. 6 ; Job xxviii. 28 ; Prov. i. 7 ; ix. 10 ; Eccles. xii. 13.

3 There is none that doeth good, no, not one. Here the Septuagint adds four verses, taken from other parts of Scripture (Psa. v. 9 ; x. 7 ; xxxvi. 1 ; cxl. 4 ; Isa. lix. 7, 8). These verses are quoted by the Apostle Paul, Rom. iii. 10–12 ; and appear in the Prayer Book version of the Psalms.

4 who eat up My people. That is, " who oppress and persecute them " : cp. Prov. xxx. 14 ; Micah iii. 3.

5 in the generation. Or " with the generation," as their Helper.

6 Ye have shamed the counsel of the poor. Or, " ye would shame," etc. ; despising the invisible resources on which he relies.

PSALM XV

1 who shall abide. Rather, " sojourn " ; coming as a welcome guest, and there " dwelling," as in the father's home.

4 and changeth not. That is, he keeps all his promises and agreements, whatever they may cost him.

5 usury. The Israelites were forbidden to lend money on usury (or interest) to their brethren, though they might do it to foreigners : see Exod. xxii. 25 ; Deut. xxiii. 20.

reward. Or, " gift " (*i.e.,* bribe), as in Exod. xxiii. 8.

PSALM XVI

TITLE. **Michtam.** This word is derived from a root which means to " hide " or " treasure up," and is applied to gold. Some critics suppose this title to be given to certain Psalms either on account of their *peculiar excellence,* or because they were written in *golden* letters.

2 thou hast said. Probably, " I have said," etc.

my goodness [extendeth] not to Thee. Rather, " my good is not *besides* Thee " ; *i.e.,* There is no good for me without Thee : see R.V.

3 But to the saints, etc. Or (continuing ver. 2), " *I have said* to the saints," etc., " all my delight is in them." My " trust " is in Jehovah alone (1, 2), my " delight " is in His people (3).

4 that hasten [after] another [god]. Literally, " who change for another," *i.e.,* exchange Jehovah for idol-gods.

7 in the night seasons. See note on Psa. iv. 4. The same subject occupied the Psalmist's thoughts by night as by day.

8 He is at my right hand. That is, as my guard or protector.

9 my glory. Rendered in the Septuagint version

(quoted Acts ii. 26), "my tongue." Cp. "honour," Gen. xlix. 6; Psa. vii. 5.

in hope. Or, "in safety," as R.V.

10 Thou wilt not leave my soul in hell (Sheol). Rather, "Thou wilt not leave my soul *to* Sheol" (R.V.), to the power of the unseen world.

Thine Holy One. A reference to the Psalmist's hope of his own resurrection and immortality. But the language connects his own future life, and the hope of God's Israel, with the resurrection of Christ, who, though He died, yet "saw no corruption," because God did "not leave" Him in the state of the dead. Such a prophetic reference is required also by the reasoning of the Apostles Peter and Paul in Acts ii. 25–32; xiii. 35–37. See also Matt. xxviii. 1–10.

corruption. This word, in other passages, is generally translated "the pit" (so R.V. marg.), in which case the meaning of the phrase would be "to abide in the grave."

PSALM XVII

1 Hear the right, O Lord. Or, "Hear righteousness," a righteous *cause*, and a righteous *prayer*.

4 the works of men. Their sinful courses: see Hos. vi. 7.

5 Hold up my goings, etc. Or (continuing ver. 4), "By my steps keeping fast in Thy paths my feet have not swerved": cp. Job xxiii. 11.

8 Keep me as the apple of the eye. Rather, "as the pupil of the eye"; an often-recurring figure, expressing constant and tender care. See Deut. xxxii. 10–12.

10 They are inclosed in their own fat. Literally, "they have closed up their fat"; *i.e.*, "their heart." The image denotes moral and spiritual insensibility: cp. Psa. cxix. 70; Isa. vi. 10.

11 bowing down to the earth. Or, "to cast us down to the earth" (R.V.).

13 which is thy sword. Rather, "*by* Thy sword" (R.V.). So in the next verse, "*by* Thy hand."

They are full of children. More emphatically, as R.V., "They are satisfied with children" (sons). *Treasures* and *children* are the sources of earthly satisfaction.

15 I shall, etc. Or, "Let me," as R.V. marg.

satisfied. The same word as that rendered "full" in ver. 14. David evidently designs to contrast his own choice and his better portion with those of his enemies.

likeness. Rather, "form" or "presence," the word used (Numb. xii. 8) of God's manifestation of Himself to Moses. The phrase is therefore to be interpreted of *beholding* rather than of *bearing* that likeness; although 1 John iii. 2 and 2 Cor. iii. 18 show the connexion of the two. The phrase, "when I awake," is referred by Ewald and others to ver. 3. The solemn heart searchings of the night are succeeded by the morning joy of conscious communion with God. But many understand the language as expressing David's hope of awaking from the sleep of death.

PSALM XVIII

TITLE. **the servant of the Lord.** This is an official title, borne by David (Psa. lxxxix. 3, 20, etc.) in common with others commissioned to do the work of the Eternal.

2 my buckler, and the horn, etc. The "buckler" was the symbol of defence: the "horn" that of attack; the "high tower" of refuge.

4 sorrows. Or, "waves" (*Moffatt*). The images employed are taken partly from a thunderstorm and partly from an earthquake: cp. Psa. civ 6–8.

floods of ungodly men. Heb., "floods of Belial," *i.e.*, of wickedness.

5 The sorrows of hell, etc. Rather, "The cords (see ver. 4) of Sheol surrounded me, the snares of death were beforehand with me," *i.e.*, surprised me, like a net or snare; and so in ver. 18.

11 He made darkness His secret place, etc. Read, as in R.V.,

"He made darkness His hiding-place,
His pavilion round about Him,
Darkness of waters, thick clouds of the skies."

14 He shot out lightnings. Or, "And lightnings in abundance"; "lightnings manifold," R.V.

16 many waters. Those mentioned ver. 4, on which see note.

18 prevented me. Or, "came upon me," R.V.

19 He brought me forth also into a large place. Relief from distress is often represented as a coming forth into an open place: see Psa. xxxi. 8; cxviii. 5.

25 With the merciful, etc. This is an emphatic mode of saying that God's dealings with men correspond to their characters and behaviour; cp. Matt. vii. 2; Gal. vi. 8.

28 candle. Or, "lamp." A lamp lighted in the house is a common Hebrew figure for prosperity, as its extinction is for distress: see Job xviii. 5, 6; xxi. 17; Prov. xxiv. 20.

29 have I leaped over a wall. Or, "do I leap," a general expression, referring to the walls of cities. Both clauses of this verse are descriptive of military triumphs.

30 The word of the Lord is tried. Meaning especially, that the promise of God, when tried, stands the test.

33 like hinds' feet. That is, very swift. See 2 Sam. ii. 18: 1 Chron. xii. 8.

34 So that a bow of steel is broken, etc. Rather, "a bow of brass (or copper) is *bent* by my arms" (see R.V.). This is mentioned as an indication of extraordinary strength. In Homer's *Odyssey* Ulysses is represented as leaving a bow behind him at home which none but himself could bend.

35 Thy gentleness. That is, "condescending kindness"; the kindness of a superior to his inferiors. The Prayer Book has "Thy loving correction."

40 Thou hast also given me the necks, etc. Or, as in Exod. xxiii. 27, "Thou hast made mine enemies turn their backs unto me" (Prayer Book and R.V.).

43 Thou hast delivered me, etc. Part of this description was doubtless intended by the Spirit to refer to the future triumphs of Christ and His Gospel; and it is so used by the Apostle Paul in Rom. xv. 9.

45 shall fade away. Like plants withered before the blast of some destroying wind. Referring to those of "the strangers" who refused submission: see ver. 44.

be afraid, etc. Or, "come trembling out of their hiding-places" (see R.V.).

49 the heathen. Or, "the nations" (R.V.).

PSALM XIX

This Psalm is used by the Jews in Sabbath and festival services.

2 uttereth. Literally, "poureth forth"; marking the fulness of the testimony. The idolatry of the heathen is therefore inexcusable: see Rom. i. 19–21.

3 There is no speech, etc. Or, "No speech, no words; unheard is their voice": *i.e.*, they bear a silent, though most significant, witness. Addison's well-known paraphrase is true to the original, "What though in solemn silence all," etc.

4 Their line. Some, following the ancient versions, regard this word as meaning a musical chord, and render it "sound" or "voice." So the LXX quoted by St. Paul, Rom. x. 18.

7 The law of the Lord. The variety of names given to the Word of God in vers. 7, 8, 9—*law, testimony, statutes, commandment, fear, judgements*—is evidently intended, as in Psa. cxix., to bring out its value as a whole, and in all its parts and bearings; but it is unnecessary to limit too precisely each of the words employed.

converting the soul. Rather, "*restoring* the soul" (R.V.); as the Hebrew word is rendered in Psa. xxiii. 3: see also Ruth iv. 15; Lam. i. 11, 16.

the simple. Literally, "the open-minded."

8 pure. Free from all taint of error or iniquity.

11 in keeping of them. Not merely as the *consequence* of keeping them. Obedience itself is blessedness.

12 errors. The Hebrew word here rendered "errors" denotes sins of inadvertence or infirmity, as distinguished from known and wilful sins, mentioned in the next verse: see Lev. iv. 2, 27; Numb. xv. 27, where a kindred word is used.

from the great transgression. Rather, "from great transgression" (R.V.); referring, not to some offence in particular, but to any wilful sin.

PSALM XX

3 Remember all thy offerings. The Israelites were accustomed, when entering on a campaign or a battle, to offer sacrifices to Jehovah: see 1 Sam. xiii. 8, 9. Both the "burnt sacrifice" and the "meat offering" are here mentioned as being presented on such occasions: see Lev. i., ii.

9 Let the king hear us, etc. The Septuagint and Vulgate render, "O Lord! save the king: may He hear us when we call."

PSALM XXI

3 Thou preventest him, etc. That is, "Thou anticipatest his desires"; see Psa. xviii. 18.

10 Their fruit. That is, their posterity.

PSALM XXII

TITLE. **Aijeleth Shahar.** That is, "the Hind of the Morning" or "Deer of the Dawn" (*Moffatt*). Of the numerous explanations which have been given of this title, the most probable is that which takes it as the designation of a song to the melody of which the Psalm was to be sung. But some critics suppose the words to be a description of the subject of the Psalm; the "hind" being a figure for *persecuted innocence* (1–21), and the "morning" for *deliverance* after long distress (22–31).

1 My God, my God, why hast Thou forsaken me? Our Lord appropriated these words to Himself when on the cross (see Matt. xxvii. 46), substituting for the Hebrew verb the corresponding word in the Aramaic dialect then in use among the Jews.

Why art Thou so far, etc.? *i.e.*, my cry to Thee seems unavailing to save me: see ver. 2.

3 But Thou art holy. "And Thou art holy, sitting [enthroned, Psa. ix. 11; xcix. 1] in the praises of Israel." Although apparently unheard, the psalmist remembers that God's people have ever praised His holiness (His truth and uprightness, Deut. xxxii. 4) as the sure basis of their faith and hope.

6 But I am a worm. A worm in the estimation of those who are worms themselves (see Job xxv. 6; Isa. xli. 14).

8 He trusted on the Lord, etc. Or, "*Saying,* 'Commit thyself unto the Eternal; let Him deliver him; let Him save him, since He delighteth in him'" (see R.V.). These were almost the very words derisively addressed to our Saviour on the cross: see Matt. xxvii. 43.

12 Strong bulls of Bashan. Bashan was celebrated for producing wild cattle and other beasts of extraordinary size. My enemies are fierce and powerful; wild beasts, rather than men.

14 I am poured out like water. Descriptive of extreme debility and exhaustion.

15 my tongue cleaveth to my jaws. From excessive fever and thirst; such as commonly attended the agonies of crucifixion: see John xix. 28.

16 dogs. The word is used to represent the worst of men: see Job xxx. 1.

They pierced my hands and my feet. This is the rendering of many ancient versions, and is, on the whole, the best sense which can be given to the passage.

18 They part my garments, etc. See Matt. xxvii. 35.

20 My darling. Heb., "My only one"; which is perhaps poetically put for "*my life.*"

21 For Thou hast heard me, etc. "Hearing" often includes answering, and therefore *delivering.* The Hebrew word "reëm," here and elsewhere translated "unicorn," probably means the oryx ("the wild oxen," R.V.): see Job xxxix. 9, and notes.

22 I will declare Thy name, etc. The sufferer, now delivered, sees that both his agonies and his release will be productive of perfect satisfaction to himself, of eternal benefit to his brethren of mankind, and of the highest glory to God. This verse is quoted in Heb. ii. 12 to show the intimate relation between the Saviour and His people.

26 Your heart shall live for ever. Rather, as R.V., "Let your heart live for ever"; the welcome and benediction of the giver of the feast: cp. John vi. 51. "A spiritual banquet is prepared in the Church for the meek and lowly of heart; the bread of life and the wine of salvation are set forth in the word and sacraments; and they that 'hunger and thirst after righteousness' shall be 'satisfied' therewith: they 'that seek' the Lord Jesus in His ordinances ever find reason to 'praise Him,' while, nourished by these noble and heavenly viands, they live the life, and work the works, of grace, proceeding still forward to glory; when their 'heart shall live for ever' in heaven."—*Bp. Horne.*

27 All the ends of the world (earth). The inhabitants of the most distant lands shall reap the benefit of the sufferings and the deliverance thus commemorated: see Isa. xxv. 6.

29 All they that be fat. That is, all the rich and noble. The Divine provision is for the rich as well as the poor.

All they that go down to the dust, etc. None, not even the poorest and most abject, shall be excluded from this rich repast.

30 A seed shall serve Him, etc. Rather, "Posterity shall serve Him; [this] shall be told of the Lord to the [next] generation. They (the next generation) shall come, and shall declare," etc. The praises rendered to God for this great work shall be handed down from age to age. The close of this Psalm, after its utterances of deep sorrow, bears a striking resemblance to Isa. lii.

PSALM XXIII

1 my shepherd. This figure is frequently used in the Old and New Testaments with reference both to individual believers and to the people of God collectively: see Psa. lxxx. 1; Gen. xlix. 24; Isa. xl. 11; Jer. xxiii. 3, 4; Ezek. xxxiv. 11, 12, 23; Heb. xiii. 20; 1 Pet. ii. 25; Rev. vii. 17. It is also applied by our Lord to Himself as "the Good Shepherd," who not only knows and feeds and protects, but even "gave His life for the sheep": see John x. 2–18.

3 He restoreth my soul. That is, from *depression* or *wandering*. He reanimates it when exhausted, and recalls it when straying: see note on Psa. xix. 7.

for His name's sake. For an erring man to be kept in the way of righteousness brings honour to God as his protector and guide.

4 the valley of the shadow of death. This phrase refers to any season of extraordinary distress: see Job iii. 5, and note.

Thy rod and Thy staff, etc. The "rod" was probably for defence, the "staff" for the guidance of the flock: see Zech. xi. 7. The two together were badges of the shepherd's office.

5 Thou preparest a table. The Psalmist here changing the figure celebrates God's bounty in supplying his wants and filling him with joy.

in the presence of mine enemies. Notwithstanding their enmity, and even though they may enviously look on.

Thou anointest my head with oil. Oil was used at festive entertainments, and was therefore a common token of joy. Some take the figure here to be that of the shepherd anointing with ointment the bruised head of the sheep.

6 I will dwell in the house of the Lord for ever. That is, as an inmate of His family; constantly enjoying His protection, bounty, and communion: see note on Psa. xv. 1.

PSALM XXIV

There can be little doubt that different parts of this Psalm were sung responsively by different choirs of singers. Vers. 1–6 may have been sung as the procession ascended the hill towards the gates of the city, within which the tabernacle had been erected; and vers. 7–10 when it arrived at them. The application of the Psalm to the ascension of Christ to heaven is very ancient, and may be accepted, although its immediate occasion was obviously connected with the earthly Tabernacle. According to the Talmud, this Psalm was sung in the Temple on the *first day of the week*, as if in "unconscious prophecy" of Christ's resurrection.

1 the fulness thereof. That which fills it; all that it contains. This verse is the motto over the front of the Royal Exchange, London.

4 who hath not lifted up his soul, etc. That is, "who hath not given his heart to anything that is false."

6 that seek thy face, O Jacob. The reading of the old versions and R.V., "O [God of] Jacob," appears better.

7 ye everlasting doors. The word "everlasting" is sometimes used to express very long duration, either past or future: see Gen. xlix. 26; 1 Kings viii. 13; Eccles. i. 4; Isa. xxxii. 14. The ancient gates of Zion are poetically called on to raise their heads, in token of reverence to Him whose entrance is an act of condescension.

10 The Lord of hosts. In Exod. xii. 41, the Israelites are termed the "hosts" of Jahveh: but the word is more frequently applied to the hosts of heaven; by which are sometimes meant the heavenly bodies (see Deut. iv. 19; xvii. 3; 2 Kings xvii. 16), sometimes the angels (see 1 Kings xxii. 19; Psa. ciii. 21; cxlviii. 2). In all these senses the Eternal may be appropriately described as "the LORD OF HOSTS."

PSALM XXV

This Psalm is the second of the acrostic or alphabetical Psalms (Psa. ix. being the first), in which the first words of the several verses begin with the different Hebrew letters in their order. The series of the letters in this and some similar Psalms is imperfect, either through errors of copyists, or more probably because the author made the form subordinate to the full expression of his thought. Psalms of this class generally have a single theme or idea, which is repeated under various forms.

4 Thy ways. That is, the ways of conduct ordained and approved by Thee.

7 the sins of my youth. These (cp. Job xiii. 26) are contrasted with the "transgressions," more deliberate and culpable, of his later life.

11 for it is great. Man would naturally say, "Pardon mine iniquity, for it is *trifling*"; taught by God, he uses the opposite plea—so great that no other can help.

13 at ease. Or, "in good," *i.e.*, prosperity.

the earth. Rather, "the *land*." As peaceful possession of Canaan was one chief promise of the law (see Exod. xx. 12), it came afterwards to include the other blessings of the Jewish covenant; and it is so used by our Lord in Matt. v. 5. The term, "his soul," is commonly used in the Bible for *himself*; hence the verse means, his own life shall be happy, and his posterity shall be blessed after him.

14 The secret of the Lord. That close communion with God which leads to the higher spiritual knowledge of His truth and will ("His covenant").

22 Redeem Israel, etc. This verse is not in the alphabetical order, which closes with ver. 21. It may have been added for liturgical use, in a time of national disaster.

PSALM XXVI

1 I have walked. The pronoun I is emphatic; putting the Psalmist in the strongest contrast with the wicked in character (4, 5) and in destiny (9).

I shall not slide. Some render, "without wavering" (R.V.).

4 I have not sat, etc. The description in this and the next verse of the successive stages of sin may be compared with that in Psa. i. 1.

6 I will wash mine hands, etc. Such ablutions betoken the removal of all that would unfit a man for the service of God.

so will I compass thine altar. "A picturesque way of describing himself as one of the joyous circle of worshippers" (*Alexander Maclaren*).

12 in an even place. On level ground, and, therefore, safe.

PSALM XXVII

3 In this. Or, " even then," R.V.

4 the beauty of the Lord. Or, " graciousness " ; whatever renders Him an object of affection and delight.

8 [When Thou saidst]. These words are not in the original. Literally the verse reads, " To Thee my heart hath said, ' Seek ye My face '—Thy face, Lord," etc. The " heart " quotes the Divine call, and echoes it in its own resolve, meeting the general summons—*ye*, by an individual response—*I*.

10 When my father and my mother forsake me. Or, " leave me."

11 plain. *i.e.*, level, as Psa. xxvi. 12.

12 false witnesses are risen up against me. See 1 Sam. xxii. 9, 10 ; Matt. xxvi. 59, 60.

PSALM XXVIII

Bishop Hannington, the martyr-bishop of Eastern Equatorial Africa, records in his diary that, in the hourly expectation of death, he was much comforted by Psa. xxvii., xxviii., and xxx.

2 toward Thy holy oracle. The Prayer Book version is " towards the mercy-seat of thy holy temple." See 1 Kings vi. 16 ; viii. 27, 30.

4 Give them, etc. See note on Psa. v. 10.

8 their strength. The strength of God's people (9), of whom David was the " anointed " head.

PSALM XXIX

It was used in the synagogue service of the Day of Pentecost, in commemoration of the giving of the Law.

1 ye mighty. Heb., " sons of the mighty," or " sons of gods " ; either " kings " or " angels," as in Psa. lxxxix. 6.

2 the beauty of holiness. " In holy array," R.V. marg. This represents that real " holiness, without which no man shall see the Lord."

6 Sirion. *i.e.*, Hermon.

7 divideth the flames of fire. Describing the peals of thunder coming between the quickly-recurring flashes of lightning.

9 maketh the hinds to calve. The effect of the tempest upon the animate as well as the inanimate creation. Some scholars translate this " maketh the oaks to tremble." Cheyne has, " pierceth the oaks."

And in His Temple, etc. Rather, " And in His Temple everything saith, Glory ! " (R.V.). As if every peal of thunder were a proclamation of God's glory, echoing through His universal Temple of heaven and earth : cp. Isa. vi. 3.

10 flood. The Hebrew word is used elsewhere only with reference to the Deluge (Gen. vi.–xi.). The verse may be rendered, " Jehovah was enthroned on the Deluge, yea, Jehovah is enthroned king for ever " : cp. R.V.

11 peace. In all perils God gives His people strength, and when the storms have passed, a blessed peace. The occasion of this exquisite concluding stanza was no doubt the passing away of the tempest, and the breaking forth again of the sunshine over Temple and city.

PSALM XXX

2 Thou hast healed me. Perhaps intimating that David himself had been among the stricken.

5 but a moment. The Prayer Book rendering is " but the twinkling of an eye."

12 my glory. That is, my soul : see Psa. vii. 5 ; xvi. 9, and notes.

PSALM XXXI

2 my strong rock, etc. For similar variety of words describing a fortress, see Psa. xviii. 1, 2.

5 Into Thine hand. See Luke xxiii. 46 ; Acts vii. 59. This verse was the dying utterance of John Hus amid the flames.

6 lying vanities. This means both *idols* and all other professed sources of help and happiness which draw men away from God, and deceive those who trust in them (Jonah ii. 8).

8 room. That is, " place " ; setting me at liberty.

10 mine iniquity. Rather, " my affliction."

11 a fear, etc. Or, " a terror." My acquaintance are afraid of being known to be connected with me.

13 they took counsel together against me. See 1 Sam. xix. 10–17 ; xxiii. 19, 20 ; Matt. xxvii. 1.

20 from the pride of man. Or, " from the plottings of man " (R.V.) : see ver. 13.

21 in a strong city. Or, " a fortified city " ; representing the perfect security of one who is under Divine protection.

PSALM XXXII

TITLE. **Maschil.** Or, " Didactic " : a Psalm for instruction. This title is borne also by twelve others.

1 whose transgression, etc. In this verse and the next, three words are used for sin ; three also for the Divine redemption. " Transgression," a breach of law, is " forgiven " ; " sin," or antagonism to right, is " covered " or atoned for ; " iniquity " —the corruption of the nature, is " not imputed " —is met by the grace of justification.

3 When I kept silence. That is, So long as I did not acknowledge my sins to God, " my very bones were consumed," etc.

6 For this. " Because of this," *i.e.*, Thy mercy. The Psalmist, like the Apostle Paul, regards his own experience of forgiveness as designed to be an example and encouragement to others : see 1 Tim. i. 16.

shall every one. Or, as R.V., " let every one " : an exhortation.

11 Be glad in the Lord, etc. The key-note, as it were, of the following Psalm.

PSALM XXXIII

2 the psaltery [and] an instrument etc. Rather, as R.V., " the psaltery of ten strings."

3 Sing unto Him a new song. Every fresh contemplation of God supplies new subjects of praise.

4 all His works [are done] in truth. Omit *done*. Truth is the element in which His works exist.

7 a heap. The word here used is elsewhere applied to water only in passages which refer to the dividing of the Red Sea and the Jordan (Exod. xv. 8 ; Josh. iii. 13, 16 ; Psa. lxxviii. 13). The ordinary and the miraculous are alike evidences of the Divine working (*Hengstenberg*).

15 He fashioneth their hearts alike, etc. Rather, " He who fashioneth their heart together (*i.e.*, one as well as another), He who understandeth all their doings " : cp. R.V.

PSALM XXXIV

This Psalm, like Psa. xxv., is alphabetical or acrostic, with precisely the same peculiarities in the omission of one letter and repetition of another as in Psa. xxv., which it resembles in some other respects. It is one of the Psalms still used by the Jews in their morning service for Sabbaths and festivals. Luther calls it, "Thanksgiving for God's kindness."

TITLE. **Abimelech.** The hereditary title of the Philistine kings, as Pharaoh of the Egyptian. The name of this king was Achish, 1 Sam. xxi. 10. The correctness of the title is, however, seriously questioned.

5 They looked unto Him, etc. That is, the "humble" sufferers mentioned in ver. 2. Looking to God in prayer, they were enlightened or gladdened by a gracious answer.

7 The angel of the Lord, etc. For remarkable illustrations of this truth, see Gen. xxxii. 1, 2; Exod. xiv. 19; 2 Kings vi. 17; xix. 35; Dan. vi. 22; Zech. ix. 8. "The Angel" in the singular (not simply "angels") suggests "the Angel of the Covenant."

21 shall be desolate. Rather, "shall be guilty" ("condemned," R.V.), *i.e.*, shall be punished. The evil they commit shall destroy them, while the sufferings of the righteous are but temporary (22), not issuing in condemnation.

PSALM XXXV

6 the angel of the Lord. See note on xxxiv. 7.

7 For without cause, etc. A slight transposition improves the sense and rhythm of this verse; "For without cause they have hidden for me their net, without cause they have dug a pit for my soul," *i.e.*, for me.

12 To the spoiling of my soul. Heb., "bereavement to my soul." This is the "evil" with which he was rewarded.

16 With hypocritical mockers in feasts. Lit., "with profligate cake-jesters," or parasites: time-serving flatterers, who frequented the tables of the great, to gain a living by buffoonery.

17 My darling. See note on Psa. xxii. 20.

19 wink. Secretly rejoicing in the success of their plot.

27 let them say. Let signal mercy cause them so to say.

PSALM XXXVI

1 saith, etc. The best translation appears to be, "The utterance of wickedness (or 'the wicked') saith within my heart," etc. *i.e.*, it produces in me the conviction that he does not fear God.

9 For with Thee is the fountain of life, etc. Thou alone art the inexhaustible source of all blessedness; in Thy favour only shall we realise true happiness. Light is thrown on the darkest subjects and events.

11 remove me. Or, "*expel* me" from my home.

PSALM XXXVII

This Psalm is alphabetical: differing, however, from Psa. xxv., xxxiv., in that the successive letters recur at more distant intervals.

3 So shalt thou dwell in the land, etc. Rather, as imperative, "Dwell in the land, and feed on (or enjoy) truth": R.V., "follow after faithfulness." (Luther: "earn an honest living.")

5 Commit thy way unto the Lord. This was David Livingstone's favourite text. Paul Gerhardt based on it his well-known hymn "Befiehl du deine Wege" ("Commit thou thy ways").

6 thy judgement. The Prayer Book version is "thy just dealing."

7 Rest in the Lord, etc. Lit., "Be silent to Jehovah"; *i.e.*, Await patiently His doings.

9 shall inherit the earth. Rather, "the land." This expression, which is repeated four times in this Psalm, refers to the enjoyment of God's promised favours: see Psa. xxv. 13.

13 his day. His day of exposure and punishment: see Job xviii. 20.

14 conversation. Heb., "way," *i.e.*, mode of life: see R.V. The translators of 1611 use the word "conversation" in this sense, except in Phil. i. 27; iii. 20.

20 the fat of lambs. Or, more probably, "the excellency of the pastures," R.V.; "the beauty of the pastures" (*Alexander Maclaren*). See ver. 2; Psa. xc. 5; Isa. xl. 6–8; "the grass which to-day is, and to-morrow is cast into the oven."

25 Nor his seed begging bread. This is not to be understood absolutely, but generally. See Goldsmith's reference to this verse in *The Vicar of Wakefield*.

30 talketh of judgement. Rather, "uttereth judgement," or rectitude.

PSALM XXXVIII

This Psalm is used by the Jews in the service of the Day of Atonement.

1 O Lord, rebuke me not, etc. This verse is nearly the same as Psa. vi. 1.

4 are gone over mine head. Like a flood of waters.

6 I am troubled. Or, "I have writhed," *i.e.*, with pain.

7 with a loathsome disease. Or, "with burning," or fever (so R.V.).

8 feeble. Rather, "I am chilled and bruised exceedingly"; a description probably of the cold collapse and pains in all the limbs which follow the burning stage of fever (7).

PSALM XXXIX

TITLE. **to Jeduthun.** Jeduthun was one of the leaders of sacred music in the time of David: see 1 Chron. xvi. 41; xxv. 1.

4 mine end. The end of my *sufferings*, and, coincident with these, of my life. Or, perhaps, the *issue* or purpose in view.

6 a vain show. Or, "as a shadow" (R.V. marg.), as an unsubstantial thing.

11 to consume away like a moth. Either (as in Job iv. 19) as a moth *perishes*, or (as in Job xiii. 28) as a moth *consumes* a garment.

13 O spare me, etc. Rather, "O turn from me, that I may be comforted"; *i.e.*, Do not look upon me to chastise me any more.

PSALM XL

Vers. 13–17 of this Psalm are repeated in Psa. lxx., having been detached, perhaps, for separate use in religious worship.

2 Out of a horrible pit. Or, "from a pit of roaring"; *i.e.*, of *roaring waters*: see Psa. lxix. 2. But many render, "a pit of destruction."

5 Many, O Lord my God, etc. Or, "Many things Thou hast done, even Thou, Jehovah my God, Thy wonders and Thy thoughts toward us; nothing can be compared unto Thee: I will declare and speak of them, [but] they are beyond numbering." This verse was quoted by Oliver Cromwell in his address to Parliament, 1654 (see Prothero: *The Psalms in Human Life*).

6 Sacrifice and offering, etc. See notes on Psa. li. 17, 19.

Mine ears hast Thou opened. Lit., "Ears hast

Thou digged for me"; a phrase which may refer either to the removal of deafness, or (as some have thought) to the command in Exod. xxi. 6; in either case implying attention and obedience (Isa. l. 5). It is clear that God has always set a higher value on the submission of the heart than on the numerous sacrifices and offerings of the law, and that His thoughts or purposes (5) contemplate the superseding of these by the voluntary obedience of Him to whom the great work of salvation had been already assigned in God's revealed will (7, 8). And in this sense the passage is quoted and commented on in Heb. x. 5–10: where the Septuagint version, "a body hast Thou prepared me," is used, as its very remarkable variation from the Hebrew does not affect the general sense, or interfere with the object of the quotation.

7 In the volume of the book it is written of me. The "volume," lit., "roll," is the written word of God: the "Law." Probably the latter part of the sentence should be rendered (as R.V. marg.), "it is prescribed to me": *i.e., my duty* is there "written."

8 I delight to do Thy will. Obedience is not only conformity to the written word, but an expression of the heart's desire.

PSALM XLI

1 that considereth the poor. Or, "who regardeth (*i.e.*, with kindly care) the helpless."

2 Thou wilt not deliver. Rather, as R.V., "deliver Thou not"; a prayer.

6 if he come to see me, etc. This seems to point to one who, abusing the Psalmist's confidence, was plotting his ruin, whilst he spoke falsehood. It applies well to Ahithophel (see 2 Sam. xv.).

8 An evil disease. This phrase is elsewhere rendered "a wicked thing" (Deut. xv. 9; Psa. ci. 3), and may refer to some disgraceful report.

9 hath lifted up his heel, etc. Like a horse which kicks at its master. Our Lord applies the latter part of this verse expressly to Judas (see John xiii. 18); omitting the former part, for He had not trusted in the traitor (see John vi. 64).

12 and settest me before Thy face for ever. Thou makest me continually the object of Thy compassionate care.

13 Blessed be the Lord God of Israel. "The Eternal, the God of Israel." This doxology is to be regarded not as a part of the Psalm itself, but as marking the close of the First Book, or division, of the Psalms.

PSALM XLII

Either Psalms xlii. and xliii. were at first one (as they are still in more than forty ancient manuscripts), and were separated perhaps for liturgical use; or the second was a later continuation of the first.

Title. **Maschil.** See note on title to Psa. xxxii.

sons of Korah. The sons of Korah were a Levitical family of singers (see 1 Chron. vi. 31–37), who continued in that employment from the time of David as late as the reign of Jehoshaphat: see 2 Chron. xx. 19.

2 appear before God. In His sanctuary: see Psa. xliii. 3, 4.

5 Why art thou cast down, etc.? In this soliloquy, repeated at intervals as a *refrain*, the Psalmist chides and yet encourages himself in his God.

the help of His countenance. Many of the best critics follow the ancient versions, and some copies of the Hebrew, in joining the next word in the Hebrew to this verse. Thus, without altering a single letter, they read, "*who is* the health (Prayer Book version: 'help') of my countenance and my God:" so making all the three verses (5, 11, xliii. 5) alike.

6 of the Hermonites. Rather, "of the Hermons"; the mountain-range of which Hermon, with its three summits (hence the plural), was the crown. This was on the east of Jordan; and it is put here for the whole of the district on that side of the river. The "hill Mizar," or "the little hill," is probably a spur of these mountains: see Psa. cxxxiii. 3.

7 Deep calleth unto deep, etc. A succession of calamities: one wave summoning another to succeed it.

8 in the day-time, etc. The joy that "cometh in the morning" is anticipated by "songs in the night."

the God of my life. The God to whom my life belongs, and upon whom it depends.

PSALM XLIII

This is the Psalm, part of which was sung at the famous meeting in Tanfield Hall, Edinburgh, 1843, when the "Disruption" took place and the Free Church of Scotland was formed.

1 ungodly. Or, "unmerciful."

3 send out Thy light and Thy truth. There may be an allusion here to the "Urim and Thummim," light and truth (so Bishop J. J. S. Perowne). That is, "Manifest Thy faithfulness" by fulfilling Thy promises.

tabernacles. Plural, intimating the two parts of the sanctuary.

4 my exceeding joy. Lit., "the joy of my exultation."

PSALM XLIV

Title. **Maschil.** See note on title of Psa. xxxii.

2 cast them out. Or, "and didst cause them (viz., our fathers) to *spread abroad*"; answering to the "planting" in the preceding line; whilst "the people" (or rather "peoples") answer to "the heathen."

4 my King. Or, "Thou Thyself (emphatic) art my King"; so that the shame of my defeat and the glory of my deliverance are Thine. The speaker throughout the Psalm being the Jewish nation personified, the singular and plural numbers are used indifferently: cp. vers. 6, 7.

12 for nought. Without advantage to Thyself.

19 dragons. Perhaps "jackals" (R.V., see Job xxx. 29); wild animals of the deserts.

22 for Thy sake. On account of our attachment to Thy service and worship. The Apostle Paul (Rom. viii. 36) applies these words to the sufferings of himself and his fellow-Christians.

PSALM XLV

Title. **Shoshannim.** "Shoshannim" signifies *lilies*, and is probably the name of a tune. Some, however, apply the work to the subject of the Psalm, and remark that lilies are a natural emblem of female beauty.

A Song of loves. "A song concerning lovely and gracious things" (*Delitzsch*).

1 My heart is inditing, etc. Rather, "My heart overfloweth with a good thing. I speak—a work for a king": see R.V. and marg.

4 truth and meekness and righteousness. See Matt. xi. 29; John i. 17; xiv. 6. The threefold power which subdues the world.

6 Thy throne, O God, etc. In their true and complete significance the words are applied to Christ, Heb. i. 8.

above Thy fellows. More than Thy fellow-kings. The perfect fulfilment of these words is again in the Messiah, who, being Divine as well as human, is "higher than the kings of the earth." He is "King of kings": cp. Heb. i. 8, 9; Rev. xix. 11, 16.

8 out of the ivory palaces, etc. Or, "From palaces of ivory stringed instruments have made Thee glad." (The Hebrew word rendered *whereby* is better taken as a noun meaning "stringed instruments." So Gesenius, Delitzsch, Lange.) By "ivory palaces" are meant palaces whose chambers were inlaid or ornamented with ivory.

10 Forget also thine own people. Alluding to the law of marriage in Gen. ii. 24, and perhaps to the calling of Abraham in Gen. xii. 1. So the Church is required to come out from the world, and to be exclusively devoted to her Lord.

12 the daughter of Tyre, etc. According to the Hebrew idiom, the "daughter of Tyre" denotes the *city* or its inhabitants, personified as a virgin. So the "daughter of Zion," Psa. ix. 14. In the times of David and Solomon, and long after, the Tyrians were the most commercial people in the world: and with them the Israelites had most trading intercourse. Hence Tyre—"the rich ones of the people"—was naturally used as a type for the wealth of the world, brought literally as a tribute on this festive occasion to the king and his bride.

13 within. Probably, *within the palace.* The bride is described as awaiting her removal from her father's to her husband's house.

16 Thy children. Lit., "Thy *sons.*" This vision of a long and illustrious posterity shall receive its highest fulfilment in the numerous spiritual progeny of the Messiah, and the perpetuity of His reign over the whole earth: cp. Isa. liii. 10; liv. 1–4; lx. 4–9.

17 the people. Rather, "the peoples," as R.V.; all nations of mankind.

PSALM XLVI

This Psalm has been a frequent source of comfort to God's people in times of trial and persecution. Luther, in dark days, said to Melanchthon, "Come, Philip, let us sing the 46th Psalm." Luther's famous version, "Ein' feste Burg" was translated into English by Thomas Carlyle.

TITLE. **Alamoth.** "Trebles": see note on title to Psa. vi.

2 though the earth be removed. Or, "change" (R.V.). Amidst the greatest convulsions, whether of Nature or of society.

4 There is a river, etc. A peaceful, never-failing, refreshing stream, like that by which Jerusalem was supplied, forms a natural contrast to the turbulent and threatening sea described in ver. 3. It is a frequent Scriptural emblem of the favour of God and the blessings of His gospel: see Psa. xxxvi. 8; Isa. viii. 6; Zech. xiv. 8; Rev. xxii. 1. The water-supply proceeding from the Temple hill was the dependence of the city in times of siege: see 2 Chron. xxxii. 4. The "streams" were its "conduits," supplying the great reservoirs of the city, and communicating with the Pool of Siloam: cp. Isa. viii. 6, 7: see *A Century of Excavation in Palestine,* by Professor R. A. S. Macalister.

5 right early. Or, "when the morning appears."

7 The Lord of hosts. Rather, "Jahveh [God] of hosts," declared in the latter part of the verse to be "the God of Jacob"—the *omnipotent* and the *covenant* God. This verse was among the dying words of John Wesley.

9 maketh wars to cease. In these words, the prophet's inspired thought comprehends the future era of universal peace so often foretold in Scripture: see Isa. ii. 4; Micah iv. 3, 4. The League of Nations in our time is a step towards its fulfilment.

PSALM XLVII

This second "Triumph-song," like the preceding and the following, was probably composed after the destruction of Sennacherib, which must have been a relief to other nations (see ver. 1) besides the Jews.

1 all ye people. Lit., "all ye peoples": an address to the nations of mankind.

2 terrible. Rather, "to be feared" (Prayer Book version); or, "to be venerated."

4 The excellency of Jacob, etc. These words probably mean the sacred territory, called in prophecy "the glory of all lands" (Ezek. xx. 15).

5 God is gone up, etc. A poetical description of God's return to heaven, after having come down to deliver His people.

7 Sing ye praises, etc. Rather, "sing a Maschil," or, "skilful strain": see on Psa. xxxii. title.

9 The princes of the people are gathered together. Rather, "Princes of peoples are gathered [to be] the people of Abraham's God." The designation "God of Abraham" probably refers to the promise made to that patriarch that he should be a blessing *to all the families of the earth.*

the shields of the earth. So the princes or rulers are called, as the protectors of their people.

PSALM XLVIII

1 the mountain of His holiness. That is, "His holy mountain"; so called on account of the Temple, which stood upon it.

2 for situation. Rather, "in elevation" (R.V.).

on the sides of the north, etc. This probably refers to the situation of the Temple as upon the north (strictly N.E.) of the city.

4 the kings were assembled. If the Psalm refers to the invasion of Sennacherib, these would be the satraps or chieftains under him.

5 They saw [it]. The word *it* is not in the Hebrew. "They saw," *i.e.,* the Holy City towering on its height before them.

hasted away. Rather, as R.V. marg., "they were stricken with terror."

7 ships of Tarshish. On "Tarshish," see note on 1 Kings x. 22.

8 As we have heard, etc. That is, What we have heard of as occurring in other times and places we have now experienced ourselves.

14 unto death. The Septuagint and Vulgate rendering, "for ever," does not require the change of a single letter in the Hebrew, and agrees better with the first clause of the verse.

PSALM XLIX

4 a parable. The Psalmist intimates that his poem is to contain a moral lesson on that difficult subject which had exercised the minds of good men, the present prosperity of the wicked. To this lesson, taught by God, he will "incline" or bend his "ear," that he may listen to the oracle which He will then communicate to man.

5 my heels. Or, "my pursuers."

8 precious. That is, " costly."

13 This their way is their folly. Or, " Such is the way (perhaps the destiny) of the foolish, and their posterity," etc.

14 Like sheep, etc. " Like sheep (perhaps meaning without foresight) they gather to Sheol; death tends them; and the upright," whom they now despise, " shall soon rule over them; and their strength is for Sheol to consume out of its dwelling. But God will redeem me from the hand of Sheol, for He will take me." The word "take" is that applied to Enoch in Gen. v. 24, and to Elijah in 2 Kings ii. 3, 5.

18 doest well to thyself. That is, " takest care of thyself."

PSALM L

Title. **Asaph.** Asaph was one of the chief musicians whom David set over the service of song in the house of the Lord; he was also an inspired Psalmist: see 1 Chron. vi. 31, 39; xv. 17, 19; 2 Chron. xxix. 30; Neh. xii. 46. There are twelve Psalms which bear his name: eleven of them being in the Third Book.

1 The mighty God, even the Lord. In Hebrew a threefold title, *El Elohim Jahveh.* This combination of Divine names occurs also in Josh. xxii. 22. "El speaks of God as mighty; Elohim as the object of religious fear; Jehovah [Jahveh] as the self-existent and covenant God" (*A. Maclaren*).

2, 3 Out of Zion, etc. Compare with this the sublime description of God's appearance on Sinai in Exod. xix. and Deut. xxxiii. 2.

5 Gather My saints together. Or, " Gather unto Me My godly ones."

8 or thy burnt offerings, etc. Rather, " and thy burnt offerings are continually before Me," R.V. They are not accused of neglecting these, but of practical ungodliness.

10 the cattle upon a thousand hills. Lit., " the cattle on hills of a thousand"; which most probably means, " hills where the cattle rove by thousands": see R.V. marg.

12 the fulness thereof. All that it contains: see Psa. xxiv. 1.

14 Offer. Rather, " sacrifice"; *i.e.,* Let not the sacrifices which you offer be regarded either as needed by God, or as meritorious actions of yours; but let them be expressions of humble thankfulness: cp. ver. 23. " Then call upon Me," etc. (15).

18 When thou sawest a thief, etc. Refer to the seventh, eighth, and ninth commands of the Decalogue.

21 I kept silence. God is described as " keeping silence" when He does not openly show His displeasure by reproof or punishment.

23 Whoso offereth praise. Lit., " sacrificeth" praise: cp. ver. 14.

conversation. See note on Psa. xxxvii. 14. The offering of praise refers to the *worship* (see 14, 15), the ordering of the conduct to the course of *life* which God approves.

PSALM LI

Called the *Miserere,* from the first word of the Psalm in the Latin version.

3 For I acknowledge, etc. Those to whom God gives grace to confess their sins may expect His mercy in forgiving them. As Alexander Maclaren wells points out, the psalmist realises his personal responsibility: " *My* transgression, *my* iniquity, *my* sin." See also Carlyle: *Heroes and Hero-Worship.*

4 Against Thee, etc. The Psalmist's mind is wholly occupied with his sin as ungrateful, disobedient, and offensive and dishonouring to God. This reflection seems to absorb for the time the thought of the other aspects of his sin, as against Uriah and Bath-sheba herself. That he did not forget these aspects appears from ver. 14.

That Thou mightest be justified, etc. This may mean either, So that Thou art just in passing sentence upon me, and clear in condemning me; or, " I acknowledge my transgressions," etc. (3), in order that it may appear that Thou art just.

6 in the hidden part. In my inmost soul.

7 Purge me, etc. This may be rendered, " Thou wilt purge," etc.; " Thou wilt wash," etc.; " Thou wilt make," etc. (8). So in ver. 15, " Thou wilt open," etc. Here is confidence in God's merciful intentions: cp. 1 Thess. iv. 3; v. 23.

hyssop. See note on 1 Kings iv. 33. Hyssop was much used in sprinkling the blood of purification under the Mosaic law: see Exod. xii. 22; Lev. xiv. 4, 6; Numb. xix. 18; Heb. ix. 19. To " purge with hyssop," therefore, suggests the idea of a purification from guilt; whilst the washing " whiter than snow" (see Isa. i. 18) introduces the idea of sanctification.

10 right. Or, " firm"; *i.e.,* constant, stedfast in Thy service: the result not only of " washing," vers. 2, 7, but of " creation" and " renewal." This passage, and others in the Old Testament, so clearly teach the need of regeneration by Divine power, even though a man might be an Israelite after the flesh, that our Lord expressed surprise at the ignorance shown by " a master in Israel" on this important subject: see John iii. 3–10.

13 Thy ways. This may mean either God's method of dealing with men (see Psa. xviii. 26, and note), or the ways in which He requires us to walk (see Psa. cxix. 37). In both these senses the Psalmist might desire to teach others the Divine ways.

be converted. Rather, " return" (as R.V.). By Thy mercy to me I will encourage those who fall to return: cp. 1 Tim. i. 15, 16.

17 The sacrifices of God, etc. A really contrite spirit is worth all, and more than all, the numerous sacrifices of the ritual: see Psa. xl. 6; 1 Sam. xv. 22. The Psalm thus *begins* and *ends* with the language of deepest penitence. " The joy of forgiveness does not banish sorrow and contrition for sin" (*Perowne*).

19 bullocks. These are mentioned as the finest and choicest victims. He who brings to God a contrite heart (17) will bring with it his most costly offerings.

PSALM LII

1 The goodness of God endureth continually. As if he had said, Mighty and malicious as thou art, the might and mercy of Jehovah are far greater.

4 O thou deceitful tongue. Or, " And the deceitful tongue" (R.V. marg.). " Thy deceitful tongue deals in," etc. (*Luther*).

5 likewise. Bringing upon thee the destruction thou hast brought on others.

6 shall laugh at him. Add " *saying,*" as R.V.

9 good. That is, Thy name is good: see R.V. for altered punctuation. Prayer Book version has, " I will hope in Thy Name, for Thy saints like it well."

PSALM LIII

This Psalm is another edition of Psa. xiv.: on which see notes. The chief variations are in the use of the word "God" instead of "Jahveh," and in ver. 5, which represents those who in Psa. xiv. are said to treat the pious with contumely, as having themselves become objects of contempt.

TITLE. **Mahalath.** This word probably indicates a *tune*, so named from the first word (meaning "sickness") in some popular poem, probably of a mournful character: see lxxxviii., title.

PSALM LIV

TITLE. **when the Ziphims came,** etc. The Ziphites gave this information twice: see 1 Sam. xxiii. 19, and xxvi. 1.

3 oppressors. Or, "terrible ones"; who are also connected with "strangers" in Isa. xxv. 5.

5 reward evil. Or, "cause to return the evil" upon them which they have done to me.

in Thy truth. That is, agreeably to the tenor of Thy promises.

6 it is good. *i.e.,* Thy name is good. "It is so comfortable" (Prayer Book version).

7 mine eye hath seen, etc. Lit., "mine eye hath looked on mine enemies." *His,* as supplied in the text, is for *its*: cp. xcii. 12.

PSALM LV

3 iniquity. "Calumny."

6 "Wings like a dove." See Browning in Pompilia's speech (*The Ring and the Book*: "Pompilia," l. 991 and foll.).

9 divide their tongues. "Confound their counsels."

17 evening and morning, etc. "When our window is opened towards heaven, the window of heaven is open to us" (*C. H. Spurgeon*).

18 there were many with me. More correctly, "in great numbers were they round me."

PSALM LVI

1 would swallow me up. "Pants after me"; like a wild beast longing for my blood.

3 What time I am afraid, I will trust in Thee. "Faith dissolves doubts, as the sun drives away the mists" (*John Bunyan*).

4 His word. The promise which He has made to me.

6 my soul. That is, "my life."

8 my wanderings. In flight from my enemies, who incessantly harass me.

put Thou my tears, etc. That is, "preserve them in Thy memory": see the next clause. "Tears" are here compared to a precious liquor, which is carefully preserved in a skin "bottle."

10 In God. As the element in which I live. The repetition of the phrase is to be noted: see vers. 10, 11.

13 the light of the living. Or, "the light of life" (John viii. 12).

PSALM LVII

TITLE. **Al-taschith.** This phrase means, "Destroy not" (also in the titles to lviii., lix., lxxv.). It has been conjectured that the Psalm with this title forms part of an old vintage-song (see *Hastings' Dict. Bible,* article "Psalms").

the cave. Perhaps the cave at En-gedi, in the limestone ridge west of the Dead Sea; or that of Adullam.

4 them that are set on fire. Rather, "flaming ones"; *i.e.,* persons breathing out flame; cp. Acts ix. 1.

7 My heart is fixed. It is fortified against all fear by reliance on Thee.

8 my glory. This may mean, "my *soul*": see note on Psa. vii. 5.

I . . . will awake early. Lit., "I will awake the dawn"; a bold figure of poetry, as if the writer had said, The morning shall not awake me to praise; but my songs shall anticipate and "awake the dawn."

PSALM LVIII

TITLE. **Al-taschith.** See note on title of preceding Psalm.

1 O congregation. The Hebrew word here used is variously interpreted. Professor Plumptre thinks it an interpolation by a transcriber, as it does not appear in early translations. Some translate it, "O ye gods"; others, "mighty ones" or "rulers."

2 Ye weigh the violence, etc. These wicked rulers, instead of "weighing out" or dispensing justice to the people, dispensed the most violent injustice.

3 are estranged. That is, estranged from God and goodness. For similar expressions, see Eph. v. 18; Col. i. 21.

5 will not hearken to the voice of charmers. In countries where serpents abound there are professed enchanters, who exercise a remarkable influence over them, chiefly by means of musical instruments. Any species which should remain unaffected by such incantations would be regarded as peculiarly malignant.

"So much of adder's wisdom I have learn'd
To fence my ear against thy sorceries."
(Milton: *Samson Agonistes.*)

charming never so wisely. Or, "the skilled weaver of spells" (*A. Maclaren*).

7 let them be as cut in pieces. Or, "as if cut off"; *i.e.,* blunted.

8 melteth. This word seems to refer to the slimy track which the snail leaves behind it.

9 both living, and in His wrath. Rather, "both living and burning": meaning, perhaps, both the fresh thorns just gathered for fuel, and those which have been already set on fire. Or the words may be used with reference to the *contents* of the vessel, rather than the fuel (so Bickell, Cheyne and others); and may be translated, "whether raw (as the word means in 1 Sam. ii. 15) or heated," *i.e.,* cooked. In either case the idea intended is that of a sudden destruction, which frustrates men's plans and often carries themselves away.

10 He shall wash his feet in the blood, etc. As the victorious survivor of a conflict, walking over the battle-field, might be said to do. So Psa. lxviii. 23.

11 that judgeth. It is observable that this is one of the few passages where *Elohim* is joined to a plural; the thought being of *manifold* Divine agencies—Those that judge—in contrast to the "mighty ones" (1): see note.

PSALM LIX

TITLE. **Al-taschith.** See note on title of Psa. lvii.

1 Defend me. Lit., "Set me on high," *i.e.,* out of their reach (*Calvin*).

4 They run. Perhaps used as a military term: see Psa. xviii. 29.

6 They return at evening. The verse seems to describe the disappointment of the enemy, who, after the unsuccessful search of the morning (1 Sam. xix. 12), come back at nightfall and prowl about the place like the gregarious untamed dogs which haunt the streets of Eastern cities: cp. on ver. 14.

7 belch out. "Pour out [words]" or "foam at the mouth."

9 Because of his strength, etc. If this reading be correct, it seems to mean the strength *of the enemy.* But some of the ancient copies and versions read as in ver. 17, "*my* strength": so that the rendering would be, "O my Strength, I will wait upon Thee." The Prayer Book version has, "My strength will I ascribe unto Thee."

10 The God of my mercy shall prevent me. He will give me speedy and timely succour: see note on Psa. xviii. 5.

11 Slay them not, etc. That their humiliation may be a warning to all others: cp. Exod. ix. 16.

14 let them return. Rather, "they return," as ver. 6.

15 grudge. Rather, "tarry all night." As Saul's messengers had done.

16 But I will sing. The words are emphatic, "But I, I will sing," etc.

PSALM LX

Title. **Shushan-eduth.** That is, "Lily of testimony"; probably the name of a tune, or the title of an ode, to the music of which this Psalm was set.

Aram-naharaim. "Aram," or "Syria, of the two rivers"; *i.e.,* Mesopotamia.

Aram-zobah. The Tsubité of the Assyrian texts which place it eastward of Hamath. (*Hastings' Dict. Bible:* article "Aram.")

the Valley of Salt. The sterile region south of the Dead Sea.

2 the earth. Rather, as R.V., "the land"; the national disaster being compared to an earthquake.

4 because of the truth. Either, "in the cause of Thy truth" which we maintain; or, "according to Thy veracity": *i.e.,* "Thou hast given a banner, etc., agreeably to Thy promise." But most of old versions, following a slightly different Hebrew text (קֶשֶׁת for קֹשֶׁט), render, "out of the reach of the bow," *i.e.,* of the enemy's archers.

5 Thy beloved. That is, "Thy beloved people"; as in Deut. xxxiii. 12.

6 God hath spoken, etc. Some attribute to God the words that follow; but it is more probable that they express the joyful expectations which the Psalmist founded upon the Divine promise.

divide. Or, "portion out."

Shechem, etc. Shechem, Ephraim, Judah, Succoth, Gilead, and Manasseh, represent the *whole land,* both west and east of the Jordan.

7 strength. Or, "defence" (R.V.).

8 Moab is my washpot. That is, used for the meanest purposes. The "proud" Moab (Isa. xvi. 6) is to be reduced to the most abject subjection.

over Edom, etc. I will treat it with contempt.

triumph. Rather, "shout aloud"; receive me, thy conqueror, with shouts of applause.

9 Who will bring me, etc.? In reliance on God's promise, the people are ready to go forward into the very heart of their enemies' country. "The strong city" is probably Petra, the famous capital of Idumea, hewn in the rock, and almost impregnable.

PSALM LXI

Title. **Neginah.** The singular of "Neginoth": see note on title of Psa. iv.

2 the rock that is higher than I. That is, Thou wilt set me upon a place of security which I could not reach without Thy assistance; "too high for me" (R.V. marg.).

6 many generations. In a perpetual kingdom. The Targum applies the passage to the King Messiah.

7 He shall abide. Rather, "He shall sit" as king.

PSALM LXII

Title. **Jeduthun.** See note on title of Psa. xxxix.

1 Truly my soul waiteth upon God. Or, "Only for God my soul waiteth silently." The first word may be rendered "only" (as in vers. 2, 4, 5, 6), intimating that the Psalmist's only feeling is that of quiet rest in God. (This word *only* is the keynote of the Psalm.)

3 Ye shall be slain, etc. Rather, "How long will ye assault a man? will ye all [seek to] slay him, [as if he were] like a bowing wall and a tottering fence?"

4 excellency. Rather, "elevation": the figure of the preceding verse being followed out.

5 wait. See ver. 1 and note.

9 Surely. Rather, "only," as ver. 1. They are nothing but vanity!

a lie. Deceiving the expectations of those who trust in them.

To be laid in the balance, etc. Rather, "In the balance they go up," as the lighter scale: see R.V.

PSALM LXIII

1 thirsty. Or, "weary"; as in 2 Sam. xvi. 2; xvii. 2, 29. David's bodily privations are doubtless here alluded to, though the phrase may have a figurative application to his spiritual wants.

2 To see Thy power, etc. Rather, "So in the holy place I have gazed on Thee, to see Thy power and Thy glory": see R.V.

6 in the night watches. The ancient Hebrews divided the night into three watches, which are severally mentioned (Lam. ii. 19; Judges vii. 19; Exod. xiv. 24). The number of divisions was afterwards increased to four (as in the Gospels), and then to six.

7 the shadow of Thy wings. Another reminiscence of the Sanctuary. There, the "wings" of the cherubim shadowing the mercy-seat were an *emblem* of Jehovah's presence; but here, even in the wilderness, the Psalmist has the *reality.*

8 followeth hard after Thee. Rather, "keepeth close after Thee;" or, "hangeth upon Thee" (*Prayer Book version*).

10 foxes. Or, "jackals": see the account of the defeat and destruction of Absalom's army in 2 Sam. xviii. 6–8.

PSALM LXIV

3 And bend their bows to shoot their arrows. More simply, "And bend [*i.e., aim,* or *direct*] their arrows," etc. This figure suggests the poignant pain produced by calumny.

6 They search out, etc. Rather, "They search for iniquities; [they say] we are ready; the search is completed."

7 God shall shoot at them, etc. The arrow of God is here contrasted with the arrow of the wicked (3, 4). He makes the injuries which they intended to inflict on others recoil on themselves.

8 So shall they make their own tongue, etc. Rather, "And they (*i.e.,* men) shall cast them down, their own tongue is against them; they (*i.e.*, men) shall shake the head, every one who looks at them."

9 shall declare, etc. That is, "shall declare it to be His work"; "His doing" (see next clause).

10 shall glory. "Shall be glad."

PSALM LXV

1 waiteth. Or, "is silent": see Psa. lxii. 1, and note. But the calm thankfulness soon becomes exultant (8–13).

2 shall all flesh come. The words pass beyond the restriction of Israelite worship, and represent the whole world at the feet of God.

3 Thou shalt purge them away. Rather, "Thou, even Thou, coverest them"; as in Psa. xxxii. 1. See also Exod. xxix. 37; xxx. 10; Mark ii. 7.

5 By terrible things, etc. By astonishing and awe-inspiring deliverances, as in Deut. x. 21; 2 Sam. vii. 23, where the same word is used.

8 Thy tokens. The signs of Thy presence and power.

the outgoings of the morning and evening. That is, the places from which they appear to come; a poetical representation of the east and the west (Psa. lxxv. 6).

9 the river of God. "A stream" divided for irrigation; here a figure for the rain, the streams which God pours down.

11 Thou crownest the year with Thy goodness. Or, "Thou crownest a year of Thy goodness"; *i.e.*, A year otherwise marked with Thy goodness, Thou crownest with a plentiful harvest.

12 They drop. Rather, "The pastures of the wilderness drop [fatness], and the hills gird themselves with joy."

PSALM LXVI

3 How terrible. See note on Psa. lxv. 5.

submit themselves. Lit., "lie"; *i.e.*, render feigned obedience; as Psa. xviii. 44. "If even His enemies must render a forced and tardy and hypocritical submission, what should they do to whom He has manifested Himself in love!" (*Perowne*).

6 He turneth the sea, etc. A twofold allusion, to the passing of the Red Sea, and of Jordan; the *beginning* and the *end* of the Desert-wandering.

there did we rejoice. Or, "we will rejoice." For His former help we will still and ever praise Him.

11 into the net. The word often means "a stronghold," and may therefore be used here for a prison, *i.e.*, the troubles of life.

12 through fire and through water. Distress and danger.

into a wealthy place. Or, "to abundance." The same Hebrew word is translated "runneth over" in Psa. xxiii. 5.

15 the incense. Or, the "sweet savour"; the ascending smoke and steam of the offering.

PSALM LXVII

This Psalm, like the 65th, appears to have been composed in connexion with one of the great festivals, probably the Feast of Tabernacles (see note on ver. 6, and Lev. xxiii. 34), by one who entered fully into the spiritual designs of those services; looking beyond the temporal privileges and prosperity of the Hebrew nation to the blessings which would be conferred upon the whole world by the Messiah.

1 cause His face to shine upon us. The words are suggested by the priestly blessing (Numb. vi. 24–26); but as the prayer embraces all nations, the word *God* is substituted for the covenant-name, *Jahveh.*

2 Thy saving health. Rather, "Thy salvation."

3 the people. Rather, "peoples: the peoples, all of them." Three words are used in this Psalm for the nations of mankind: giving emphasis to the idea of universality.

6 Then shall the earth yield, etc. Rather, "The earth hath yielded her increase" (R.V.). Probably the Psalmist regarded the natural harvest as a pledge of the ingathering of the nations to the Church of God.

PSALM LXVIII

This Psalm begins with the formula used in the wilderness at the removal of the ark (Numb. x. 35), and contains throughout allusions to that sacred symbol of Jehovah's presence; describing a solemn procession, in which the northern and southern tribes unite, to the sanctuary at Jerusalem. The language in which the Psalmist describes the entrance of the ark into Zion is employed by the Apostle Paul as typical of Christ's Ascension, Eph. iv. 8–11. So also the victories of Israel prefigure the triumphs of the Church.

By the Jews this Psalm was used on the Day of Pentecost, probably because of its references to Sinai; the Giving of the Law being commemorated on that festival. (The harvest thanksgiving was held at the same time: see vers. 9, 10.) The Huguenots under Coligny sang it, in Beza's version, on their battlefields. Its words were on the lips of Cromwell at the battle of Dunbar.

1 Let God arise, etc. "God" is here used for "Jahveh" in the ancient formula.

4 Extol Him that rideth upon the heavens. Rather, as R.V., "Cast up a highway for Him who rideth through the deserts," etc. The word here used is always appropriated to the lower part of the valley of the Jordan and the long desert valley (still called *El-Arabah*) which the Israelites traversed, between the Red Sea and the Dead Sea, on their way to Canaan. The imagery is taken (as in Isa. xl. 3) from the custom of Eastern princes, who sent pioneers before their armies to prepare the roads.

Jah. Rather, "Jah is His name." This name is an abbreviation of *Jahveh;* and it expresses God's faithfulness and unchangeableness: see Exod. iii. 14.

6 He bringeth out those, etc. Rather, "He bringeth out those who are bound into prosperity" (see R.V.).

7 when Thou wentest forth before Thy people, etc. This and the next verse are taken, with little alteration, from the song of Deborah in Judges v. 4, 5. See also Exod. xiii. 21; xix. 10, 18.

9 Thine inheritance. That is, "Thy people": see Deut. xxxii. 9.

10 therein. *in the wilderness* mentioned in ver. 7.

11 Great was the company, etc. Rather, "Great was the company of the *women* announcing the joyful news"; alluding to the ancient custom of females celebrating victories with song and dance: see Exod. xv. 20; 1 Sam. xviii. 6, 7. (R.V., "The women that publish the tidings are a great host.")

13 Though ye have lien, etc. This verse is very obscure, and many widely different renderings have been given of it. Some translate it "When ye shall lie down among the sheep-folds." Or, the suggestion may be, as in R.V., that of abiding in luxurious ease, away from the field of toil and struggle, "Will ye lie among the sheep-folds," etc.? Moffatt has, beginning with ver. 12, "Their spoil is divided by Israel the fair Dove at home, till her wings are covered with silver," etc.

14 white as snow in Salmon. This may mean white with the bones of the slain. Zalmon ("the Dark Mountain") was a hill near Shechem: see Judges ix. 48. The literal rendering is, "When the Almighty scattered kings in it (the land), it snowed in Zalmon."

15 the hill of Bashan. Rather, "A hill of God (*i.e.*, a *great* hill, as a similar phrase is rendered in Psa. xxxvi. 6) is the hill of Bashan; a high hill is the hill of Bashan." The mountain-range of Anti-libanus formed the northern boundary of Bashan. See Shakespeare's reference in *Antony and Cleopatra*, "Oh that I were upon the hill of Basan" (the Prayer Book form of the word).

16 Why leap ye? Rather, "Why look ye askance?" (R.V.), *i.e.*, with envy, at the honour put on Zion.

17 thousands of angels. Rather, "many thousands."

as in Sinai, in the holy place. Rather, "Sinai is in the sanctuary" (R.V. marg.); *i.e.*, the ancient honours of Sinai are transferred to the sanctuary on Zion. The glorious presence of God, once witnessed there, is now vouchsafed here: cp. Heb. xii. 18–24.

18 Thou hast led captivity captive. That is, "Thou hast taken a multitude of captives."

Thou hast received gifts for men. Lit., "Thou hast taken gifts in the man": probably a concise expression for, Thou hast taken spoil which Thou mayest distribute as gifts among men. So that the Apostle's quotation in Eph. iv. 8 agrees exactly with the sense, though not with the words of the Psalm "When a King takes, he takes to give" (*Perowne*).

19 who daily loadeth us with benefits. Or, "day by day He beareth [our burden] for us; [even] the God [who is] our salvation." Luther's version is perhaps the best: "God lays a burden upon us, but He also helps us."

20 the issues. *i.e.*, "the means of escape."

22 [my people]. Rather, "mine *enemies;*" for they are the persons spoken of in vers. 21, 23. God would discover and triumph over them: so that whether they were on the heights of Bashan or in the profoundest depths of the sea, they should not be able to escape: cp. Amos ix. 3.

23 That thy foot may be dipped, etc. See on lviii. 10.

26 from the fountain, etc. That is, "ye who are of the fountain of Israel"; *i.e.*, the offspring of Israel.

27 little Benjamin, etc. Rather, "little Benjamin, their ruler." Benjamin was the youngest son, and the tribe had but a small portion, and had been almost extirpated (Judges xx. 44–47; I Sam. ix. 21), but it gave the first king to Israel. Zebulun and Naphtali are specially praised for their bravery in the Song of Deborah (Judges v.).

30 Rebuke the company of spearman. Rather, as R.V., "Rebuke the wild beast of the reeds"; meaning either the crocodile or the hippopotamus; as a symbol of Egypt, the most powerful heathen kingdom then existing: see next verse. "Bulls" (lit., "strong ones") and "calves" are the *rulers* and the *masses* of the people.

31 stretch out her hands, etc. In token of submission, expressed by the offering of tribute. The princes and people of this mighty and often hostile country shall acknowledge the supremacy of the God of Israel.

33 His voice. The thunder, as xxix. 3–9, etc.

PSALM LXIX

TITLE. **Shoshannim.** See on the title of Psa. xlv.

4 Then I restored, etc. This is an emphatic manner of expressing the causelessness of the enmity complained of. So far from having wronged any of those who thus persecute me, I have gone beyond the demands of justice in endeavouring to satisfy them. "I paid them the things that I never took" (*Prayer Book*).

5 Thou knowest my foolishness, etc. The meaning is, Thou, who knowest all my folly and guilt, knowest that I am guiltless of the crimes imputed to me. The Psalmist maintains that he is suffering rather for his piety than for his sins: see ver. 7.

9 the zeal of Thine house. That is, a jealous regard for the honour of Thy sanctuary. This verse is quoted in John ii. 17; Rom. xv. 3. That which is true of all God's chosen witnesses applies pre-eminently to the Redeemer.

10 fasting. This sign of grief, like "sackcloth" in ver. 11, was probably a token of sorrow for the general neglect of religion.

12 speak against me. Rather, "talk of me." These are probably not *idle loungers* who frequented the gate, but "The [nobles] who sit in the gate," etc. (see Deut. xxv. 7; Job xxix. 7; Jer. xxxix. 3); so that, connecting this with the second clause of the verse, the meaning would be, I am an object of hatred and scorn to the *highest* and the *lowest*.

20 Reproach. Including calumny and insult. To no one has the remainder of this verse ever been more applicable than to the Redeemer; whilst the next verse was circumstantially verified at His crucifixion; see Matt. xxvi. 56; xxvii. 34; John xvi. 32; xix. 28–30. The drink here mentioned being that of the most abject, to offer it to any other was an insult.

22 And [that which should have been], etc. Rather, "And to them when in peace (*i.e.*, when they think themselves safe) let it be a trap": see R.V.

25 This is quoted in Acts i. 20, in reference to Judas, as resembling the enemies of the Psalmist in crime and in punishment. See also Jer. vii. 14, 15; Matt. xxiii. 38.

26 talk to the grief. Rather, as R.V., "tell of the grief."

27 Add iniquity unto their iniquity. Some explain this, Let punishment (the consequence of sin) follow sin; others, Leave them to themselves, so that they may go on to sin more and more.

let them not come into Thy righteousness. *i.e.*, justify them not.

32 your heart shall live that seek God. Rather, "Ye who seek God, let your heart live."

PSALM LXX

This Psalm is the same, with a different use of the Divine names and some other small variations, as the last verses of Psa. xl. It is a prayer to God for speedy deliverance from imminent danger.

PSALM LXXI

3 my strong habitation. Lit., "for a rock of habitation."

6 Thou art He that took me out, etc. Or, "Thou hast been my preserver from," etc.

8 Let my mouth be filled, etc. Rather, "My mouth *shall* be filled," etc. (R.V.). See ver 6

12 O God, be not far from me, etc. This and the next verse contain phrases from Psalms xxii., xxxviii. and xl.

15 I know not the numbers thereof. *i.e.*, the blessings of "Thy righteousness and Thy salvation" are incalculable.

18 old and greyheaded. Lit., "unto old age and grey hairs." The Psalmist anticipates, but has not actually reached, old age.

Thy strength. Rather, "Thine arm," its guidance and protection as well as its strength.

20 me. Rather, "us" (R.V.), in all three clauses. The Psalmist connects his own experience with that of all God's people.

quicken. Or, "revive," give us new life.

21 comfort me on every side. Rather, "turn again and comfort me" (R.V.).

PSALM LXXII

TITLE. **for Solomon.** This should be rendered as in other titles, "of Solomon." One other Psalm is attributed to Solomon (cxxvii.).

1 Give the king Thy judgements. Impart to him right decisions, as the result of the inward principle of "righteousness."

the king's son. Evidently "the king" of the preceding clause; as king's son inheriting the promises made to his father. The best translations continue the form of a *petition* instead of *prediction*, through most of the Psalm; thus, "May he judge," "may the mountains," etc.

3 bring peace. Or, "bear peace" as fruit. The mountains and hills, being the prominent points of the country, are used to represent the whole land, as being in peace.

by righteousness. The connexion of "peace" with "righteousness" is more fully stated in Isa. xxxii. 17; and the union of the two is repeatedly mentioned as the grand characteristic of Messiah's reign: see this enlarged upon in Heb. vii. 2, etc.

4 Judge. Administer justice, maintaining their rights and redressing their wrongs.

5 They shall fear Thee. *i.e.*, Jahveh. The people, governed in "righteousness," will be God-fearing.

6 like rain, etc. With a gentle, refreshing and fertilising influence: see Deut. xxxii. 2; Prov. xix. 12; Hos. vi. 3.—**upon the mown grass.** *i.e.*, upon the cut meadow from which the grass has been taken.

7 so long as the moon endureth. Lit., "till the moon be no more" (R.V.). The "days" of this King thus extend through all time

8 the River. *i.e.*, the Euphrates; which was the eastern boundary of the kingdom of Israel under Solomon: see Exod. xxiii. 31; Deut. xi. 24. The extent of Solomon's kingdom suggests the idea of the universal dominion of the coming King.

10 Tarshish. On Tarshish, see note on 1 Kings x. 22; on "Sheba," see note on 1 Kings x. 1. "Seba" was probably in Nubia. The whole passage means that the wealth of the world shall be made tributary to the Messiah: see note on Psa. xlv. 12.

14 deceit. Or, "extortion."

precious. Their life is protected as a costly treasure: see Psa. xlix. 8.

15 And he, etc. Or, "And he (the redeemed one: v. 14) shall live, and he shall give to Him (*i.e.*, the Redeemer) of the gold of Sheba; and he shall pray for Him continually; daily shall he praise Him."

16 a handful. The Hebrew word here used occurs nowhere else. But it probably means "plenty," or abundance, as R.V.; reaching even to "the top of the mountains," naturally the least fertile part of the land. Every height, with its rustling luxuriance, will seem like the waving cedar-tops of "Lebanon."

they of the city. The town population, completing the picture of prosperity.

grass. Every kind of herbage. The word in ver. 6 is different.

17 men shall be blessed in him. Rather, "shall bless themselves," as the highest good they can desire or enjoy: see Gen. xxii. 18; Acts iii. 26; Gal. iii. 14.

shall call him blessed. Or, "happy," prosperous; a different word from the preceding.

20 The prayers of David, etc. This verse is the *finis* of the First and Second Books, vers. 18, 19 being the doxology of the Second Book. No further compilation had as yet been made.

PSALM LXXIII

TITLE. **Asaph.** See note on title to Psa. l.

1 God is good to Israel. The Prayer Book version has "is loving unto Israel." The French version is very expressive: "Si est-ce que Dieu est très doux," "gentle" or "kind." These were the words that cheered Coligny when he was being borne wounded off the battlefield of Moncontour (see Prothero: *The Psalms in Human Life*).

3 the foolish. Or, "the arrogant," as R.V.

4 For there are no bands in (or, to) **their death.** That is, there is nothing to drag them down to death.

6 a chain. That is, an ornamental chain for the neck (see Prov. i. 9); probably referring to their haughty bearing.

7 They have more than heart could wish. Rather, "The thoughts of their hearts overflow" (R.V. marg.); namely, in the wicked and proud speeches mentioned in the next verse.

8 and speak wickedly, etc. Rather, "They scoff and speak with evil; they speak oppression loftily"; *i.e.*, they speak words tending to the injury of others: cp. Isa. lix. 13.

9 against the heavens. Rather, "in heaven": they give unlimited range to their arrogant language.

10 are wrung out to them. Rather, "are drunk down by them." The "waters" here spoken of are not those of affliction, but of prosperity.

12 Behold, these are the ungodly, who prosper in the world. Rather, "Behold these wicked ones, and [yet] they prosper perpetually, they increase power" (or "wealth").

15 If I say, etc. That is, If I make my misgivings known, I shall suggest injurious doubts to Thy sincere worshippers. The Psalmist could not adopt the sceptical and undevout language of the half-hearted; for in so doing he would "deal treacherously" (R.V.) with God's faithful servants.

16 When I thought to know this, etc. This verse describes the Psalmist's unsuccessful attempt to solve the perplexing problem by meditation and independent reasoning. He gained neither light nor rest until, by communion with God in His house, he was led to look from the present to the future, and from man to God (17–20). See a fine sermon on this passage by Bishop Phillips Brooks (*The Mystery of Iniquity and other Sermons*).

20 As a dream, etc. Of the various meanings given to this verse, the best perhaps is, "As a dream after awaking, so, O Lord, when Thou arousest [them], Thou wilt put to scorn their image"; *i.e.*, the unsubstantial appearance of their prosperity. They awake, to find their happiness gone, as the "baseless fabric of a vision."

21 Thus my heart was grieved. Or, "For my heart became bitter." Connect in thought with ver. 16: I was embittered by my trouble, and therefore did not understand.

22 So foolish was I, etc. Rather, "And I, even I was brutish, and knew not," etc.

25 beside Thee. "In comparison with Thee."

28 But it is good, etc. Rather, "And as for me, nearness to God is my good."

PSALM LXXIV

Title. **Maschil.** See note on titles of Psa. xxxii. 1.

3 Lift up Thy feet. *i.e.*, "hasten Thy steps." Note the frequent use of "Thou," "Thy" throughout this Psalm. God's honour was at stake.

4 their ensigns for signs. "Their signs as signs"; *i.e.*, displacing the symbols of Jehovah's presence as sovereign, they erect their insignia of sovereignty in the sanctuary itself.

5 A man was famous, etc. *i.e.*, the enemy treats the sanctuary as ruthlessly as a woodman the forest-trees.

8 synagogues. The same word in ver. 4 is translated "congregations." The "synagogues" strictly so called, were introduced after the Captivity.

9 our signs. That is, the tokens of Thy presence (see ver. 4).

11 Pluck it out of Thy bosom. "[Draw it] from Thy bosom [and] consume [them]"—the hand being placed sometimes in the bosom when not employed.

13 Thou didst divide, etc. In the Hebrew the pronoun, "Thou," is emphatically repeated through vers. 13–17.

dragons. Or, "sea-monsters." These and "leviathan" are symbols of the Egyptian monarch and his hosts, who were drowned in the Red Sea: see Isa. li. 9; Ezek. xxix. 3; Exod. xiv. 21, 28. By "the people inhabiting the wilderness" (14) some understand wild animals which frequent the shore, and feed on the dead bodies cast up by the sea.

19 Thy turtledove. This beautiful metaphor suggests the idea of innocence, affection, and weakness. The verse may be rendered, "Give not to the beast the soul (or life) of Thy turtledove, the life of Thine afflicted forget not for ever."

20 the covenant. That is, the covenant made with our forefathers: see Gen. xvii. 8.

23 increaseth. Rather, "ascendeth" (R.V.): cp. Exod. ii. 23; Isa. xxxvii. 29.

PSALM LXXV

Title. **Al-taschith.** See note on title of Psa. lvii.

1 For that Thy name is near, etc. Ver. 1 describes the approach of Jehovah, marked by wonders of which men talk; and vers. 2–5 are His proclamation.

8 red. Probably "turbid," foaming as poured out. "The wine foameth" (R.V.). A "cup" often means, in Scripture, the portion allotted to a person. It may be one of prosperity and blessedness (see Psa. xvi. 5; xxiii. 5); or of suffering and wrath, as here and in Jer. xxv. 15; Rev. xiv. 10; xvi. 19.

mixture. Alluding to the spices mingled with wine to increase its stimulating properties.

PSALM LXXVI

This Psalm is entitled in the Septuagint, "A Song for the Assyrian"; and its whole tenor agrees well with the supposition that it refers to the miraculous destruction of Sennacherib's army (2 Kings xix. 35). It should be compared with Psa. xlvi.–xlviii.

Title. **On Neginoth.** *i.e.*, "to the music of stringed instruments": see Psa. vi., *Title*.

1 Israel. The northern kingdom having been destroyed, Hezekiah had endeavoured to unite the remnant of Israel with Judah in the worship of Jehovah (2 Chron. xxx. 1).

2 Salem. "Salem" was probably the ancient name of Jerusalem (see Gen. xiv. 18).

3 battle. Or, "There He shattered the bolts of the bow, shield and sword and battle-gear."

4 Thou art more glorious, etc. This verse may be rendered either, "Thou (Jehovah) art glorious and excellent, from the mountains of prey," a poetic description of the heights where the Assyrians had encamped: see R.V.

5 they have slept their sleep. "They have slumbered [into] their [last] sleep," the sleep of death.

10 restrain. Rather, "gird [about Thee]" as if it were Thy sword. The very passions which excite men to oppose God shall not only be made completely subservient to His purposes, but shall be used as the instrument of punishing His enemies.

PSALM LXXVII

Title. **Jeduthun.** See note on title of Psa. xxxix.

1 I cried unto God. Rather, "My voice is unto God, and I will cry out; my voice is unto God, and may He hearken unto me." The Psalmist carried his sorrows to God's mercy-seat.

2 My sore ran in the night. Rather, "My hand was stretched forth in the night"; *i.e.*, in an attitude of supplication.

3 troubled. Rather, "groaned."

complained. Rather, "mused"; and so in ver. 6 for "commune," and in ver. 12 for "talk."

6 my song. The praises which I once sang, and the Divine benefits which excited me to sing.

10 This is my infirmity, etc. Turning abruptly from his own trouble, the Psalmist, in broken phrase, calls to mind seasons of God's unfailing power and mercy. This explanation is in harmony with ver. 5.

13 in the sanctuary. Rather, "in holiness"; *i.e.*, is most holy. God's "way" here means His mode of dealing with His creatures.

14 the people. Rather, "the peoples" or nations.

19 Thy way is in the sea, etc. Rather, "Thy way *was* in the sea, and Thy path in the great waters, and Thy footsteps *were* not known" (*i.e.*, such as could not be tracked). The words are a poetical description of the passage of the Hebrews through the Red Sea, the fury of the elements being depicted in impressive contrast with the image of a shepherd's guidance and care.

PSALM LXXVIII

2 dark sayings. Or, "riddles": see note on Psa. xlix. 4, where the same words occur.

4 We will not hide them, etc. Religious privileges received by one generation from the preceding are a sacred deposit to be transmitted to the next.

9 The children of Ephraim, etc. During the ascendency of Ephraim, the Israelites had failed, through unbelief and fear, to complete the conquest of Canaan, although fully equipped for the purpose; and to this neglect might be traced the national calamities which followed: see Judg. i., ii.

12 did He. Or, "He had done." This passage recounts the marvellous works which should have awakened gratitude: see Exod. vii.–xii.

Zoan. Or, Tanis, now *Sân;* a very ancient city (Numb. xiii. 22) on the east of the Tanitic branch of the Nile. It was the capital of a district or nome, here called a "field"; and the seat of some of the native dynasties of Egyptian kings. It is mentioned here probably because the Pharaohs who oppressed the Hebrews dwelt there.

13 He divided the sea. See Exod. xiv.

14 In the day time, etc. See Exod. xiii. 21, 22.

15 He clave the rocks, etc. See Exod. xvii. 5–7.

16 the rock. Or, "the cliff"; see Numb. xx. 8–11. The *two* occasions on which the smitten rock yielded water are thus brought to mind.

17 And they sinned yet more, etc. Rather, "Yet they went on to sin yet more against Him, to provoke," etc.: see Deut. ix. 8, 22.

18 they tempted God, etc. See Exod. xvi. 3, 8; Numb. xi. 4–6.

20 Can He give bread also? The supplies which they had already received ought to have precluded all such doubts.

21 a fire was kindled, etc. See Numb. xi. 1–3.

23 Though He had commanded, etc. Rather, "And [yet] He commanded," etc. Though they distrusted Him, He did not withdraw the supply.

24 rained down manna. See Exod. xvi. 4, 14, 15.

25 Man did eat angels' food. Lit., "bread of the mighty ones did each eat"; perhaps meaning the best food, fitted to sustain the powers of the strongest. "Angels" is taken from the old versions.

27 He rained flesh. See Exod. xvi. 8, 12, 13; Numb. xi. 31, 32.

32 believed not for. Rather, "believed not in," R.V. See Numb. xvi., xx., xxi., xxv.

33 trouble. Or, "terror"; as the punishment of their unbelief. See Numb. xiv. 29, 35; xxvi. 64, 65. Their lives were worn out in the wilderness; and their desire to enjoy the promised land was not gratified: see the application of this to the Christian in Heb. iii., iv.

34 they sought Him. See Numb. xxi. 7.

44 their rivers. See Exod. vii. 19–25.

45 divers sorts of flies. See Exod. viii.

46 the locust. See Exod. x.; and cp. Joel i. 4.

48 He gave up their cattle, etc. See Exod. ix. 23–25.

49 By sending evil angels among them. Lit., "a mission of angels of evils."

50 He made a way to His anger. Or, "He levelled a path for His anger": *i.e.*, He gave it free course.

51 And smote all the first-born. See Exod. xii.

55 And divided them an inheritance, etc. See Josh. xiii.–xxi.

57 like a deceitful bow. An untrustworthy bow, whose arrows fall wide or short of the mark.

58 their high places. Referring to the idolatry into which the Israelites fell after the death of Joshua and his contemporaries: see Judges ii. 11, 12, 17.

61 And delivered His strength into captivity. When He permitted the capture of the ark by the Philistines: see 1 Sam. iv. 11, 21; and cp. Psa. cxxxii. 8.

63 And their maidens were not given to marriage. Heb., "and their maidens were not praised"; *i.e.*, in nuptial songs, "their maidens had no marriage song," R.V. This was owing to the slaughter of the young men in war: cp. Isa. iii. 25–iv. 1.

64 Their priests fell, etc. Alluding probably to the death of Hophni and Phinehas. See 1 Sam. iv. 11, etc.

66 smote His enemies in the hinder parts. Rather, "He smote (or drove) back His enemies," cp. R.V.

69 like high palaces. Or, "high places"; like the mountains. See 1 Chron. xxix. 1–19; 1 Kings vi.

70 took him from the sheepfolds. See 1 Sam. xvi. 11, 12; 2 Sam. iii. 17–21.

PSALM LXXIX

1 Thy holy temple have they defiled. To a pious Israelite, the *desecration* of the sanctuary was the worst of evils; even its *destruction* could add little to this. See 2 Kings xxiv. 13.

6 Pour out Thy wrath, etc. This petition, which reappears with a little variation in Jer. x. 25, seems to be designed humbly to represent that those who neither know nor worship Jehovah are fitter subjects of His exemplary vengeance than His own people.

8 former iniquities. Or, "the iniquities of our forefathers," as R.V.

prevent us. Or, "quickly meet (*i.e.*, reach) us."

9 for the glory of Thy name. A frequent ground of appeal: see Numb. xiv. 13–21; Josh. vii. 9.

10 Let [Him] be known, etc. Rather, "Let the avenging of the blood of Thy servants which is shed be made known," etc.: see R.V.

12 Let the sighing of the prisoner come before Thee. The Prayer Book version has "the sorrowful sighing." This verse is the motto on the title-page of John Howard's *Account of Lazarettos.*

PSALM LXXX

TITLE. **upon Shoshannim-Eduth.** *i.e.*, perhaps "to the tune of 'Lilies: a Testimony.'" See notes on titles to Psa. xlv., lx.

1 O Shepherd of Israel. The descendants of Joseph being specified here, his dying father's benediction is appropriately alluded to: see Gen. xlix. 24.

Thou that dwellest between the cherubim. See Exod. xxv. 22; Numb. vii. 89; 2 Sam. vi. 2; 2 Kings xix. 15; Psa. xcix. 1.

3 Turn us again. Rather, "*restore* us."

6 a strife. The object of their hatred and scorn.

11 She sent out her boughs, etc. A beautiful description of the prosperity of the chosen people during the reigns of David and Solomon, when the kingdom extended from the Mediterranean "sea" to the "river" Euphrates.

15 And the vineyard, etc. Some render this, "And protect what Thy right hand," etc.

the branch. Heb., "son."

18 Quicken us. That is, give us new life; see Psa. lxxi. 20.

PSALM LXXXI

This Psalm was apparently intended to be sung at one of the great sacred festivals, or perhaps at all of them.

TITLE. **Gittith.** See note on title of Psa. viii.

2 Take a psalm, etc. "Raise a song, and sound the timbrel."

3 in the new moon. Some render these words, "in the month": *i.e.*, the Passover month, which was constituted the first of the year: see Exod. xii. 2; xiii. 4. But others, following the rendering of the A.V. (and R.V.), suppose the reference to be to the Feast of Trumpets, on the first day of the seventh month, Tisri, the beginning of the civil year, and translate the next clause, "in the full moon," as applying to the Feast of Tabernacles; which followed on the fifteenth day of the same month. See Lev. xxiii. 23–25, 33–43.

5 in Joseph. The nation is so called, as in lxxx. 1, from the most favoured son of Israel.

I heard a language that I understood not. Israel (or, as some think, the Psalmist) speaks, referring to the speech of God, whose words are thus poetically rendered (a full point should be placed at "Egypt," and the italicised *where* should be omitted), "I heard a voice which I knew not, *saying*," etc.

6 the pots. Or, "baskets"; any vessels for holding and carrying materials. This may refer to baskets used by the Hebrews in carrying clay and bricks during their bondage in Egypt. Such baskets are depicted in the sepulchres at Thebes.

7 I answered thee in the secret place of thunder. These words perhaps refer to the cloud in which God interposed, during the passage of the Red Sea, between the Israelites and the Egyptians (see Exod. xiv. 19–24), or to that which overhung Sinai at the giving of the law (see Exod. xx. 18; Heb. xii. 18, 19).

I proved thee at the waters of Meribah. See Exod. xvii. 6, 7; Numb. xx. 13.

12 their own hearts' lust. Or, "to the hardness of their heart."

13 Oh, that My people had hearkened. Or, "would hearken," etc., and "would walk" (R.V.) The words which follow declare the blessings which Jehovah was still prepared to grant.

15 their time. Their national existence and prosperity.

PSALM LXXXII

1 in the congregation of the mighty. Lit., "in the congregation of God" (of "El," the mighty one). God is here represented as the universal Sovereign, who has assembled His vicegerents and inferior governors for the purpose of inquiring into their administration.

5 are out of course. Heb., "are moved," or "totter." Just judges and rulers are the firmest pillars of the social state; but when law and justice are perverted the state itself is shaken; and the only resource of the oppressed is to betake themselves to Him who can and will, in due season, avenge their cause and His own: see Psa. xi. 3, and note.

6 I have said, Ye are gods. Our Saviour refers to this passage as one in which the term "gods" is applied to judges, even though they might be unjust, because they were appointed to act for God on earth: see John x. 34.

7 like one of the princes. Like any heathen prince, who could not claim the same relation to Jehovah, the King of Israel.

PSALM LXXXIII

3 Thy hidden ones. Those whom Thou keepest under Thy merciful protection: see Psa. xxvii. 5; xxxi. 20.

6 the Hagarenes. Respecting the Hagarenes, and the occasions of their enmity, see 1 Chron. v. 10, 19–22.

7 Gebal. South of the Dead Sea, and now called Jebâl.

8 Assur. Assyria.

the children of Lot. Moab or Ammon, who had organised the confederacy: see 2 Chron. xx. 1, 10.

10 En-dor. Endor was not far from the plain of Jezreel (see 1 Sam. xxviii. 4–7), in the neighbourhood of which were fought the two decisive battles in which Barak destroyed the army of Jabin under Sisera, and Gideon that of the Midianites; see Judges iv. 15–24; vii. This plain has always been, even to our own times, the great battle-field of Palestine; and is so referred to in Rev. xvi. 16, under the name of Armageddon (Hill of Megiddo: see Judges v. 19).

12 the houses of God. "The habitations of God."

13 like a wheel. Rather, "like a whirl": *i.e.*, like the whirling chaff which the wind scatters, or "the whirling dust" (R.V.).

15 persecute. Or, "pursue."

18 that Thou, etc. Rather, "That Thou alone, whose name is Jehovah, art Most High," etc.

PSALM LXXXIV

TITLE. **Gittith.** See note on title of Psa. viii.

1 amiable. Rather, "beloved" or "lovely."

5 In whose heart are the ways [of them]. Rather, "In whose heart are (*i.e.*, who love) the highways"; meaning the way to Zion.

6 Who passing through, etc. "Passing through a valley of weeping, they make it a fountain; also the autumn rain covereth it with blessings," or "Who going through the vale of misery use it for a well" (*Prayer Book version*).

9 Behold, O God, our shield, etc. "Shield" is here an epithet of God. "O God our shield, behold! and look upon the face of Thine anointed one." The reference is to the king, or to the high priest, in whose time this Psalm was written, probably to the former.

10 I had rather be a door-keeper, etc. Lit., "be at the threshold." The sons of Korah kept the door of the Temple (1 Chron. xxvi. 1, etc.). The Psalmist prefers the lowest office in God's house to the greatest honour elsewhere.

11 a sun and shield. The source of life and joy, as well as of security.

PSALM LXXXV

1 brought back the captivity of Jacob. See Ezra i., ii.

2 forgiven . . . covered. These two expressions for forgiveness are also combined in Psa. xxxii. 1.

4 Turn us, etc. God is reconciled; and yet the Psalmist mournfully acknowledges how much needs to be wrought before the effects of the Divine displeasure are removed. The people are *restored*, yet need to be *renewed*. Nothing could more exactly describe the condition of the people at the end of their captivity; and the application to the Divine work on the individual soul is not less appropriate.

9 That glory may dwell in our land. That is, the special manifestation of God's presence and favour. This evidently includes the glory of the Messiah as described in Hag. ii. 7–9. It is spoken of in the beautiful allegory of the following verses as the perfected harmony between heaven and earth.

10 truth. Here used in the sense of "faithfulness."

13 And shall set us, etc. Or, "And set His steps for a way"; *i.e.*, teach us to follow Him: "make His footsteps a way to walk in," R.V. "The perfection of man's character and conduct lies in his being an 'imitator of God.' God's Righteousness is revealed from heaven to make men righteous" (*A. Maclaren*).

PSALM LXXXVI

The repeated use of "Lord" (*Adonai*) in this Psalm as a Divine name is noticeable.

2 holy. Rather, "godly" (R.V.).

9 All nations. An inference from the foregoing verse: confessing the nullity of their "gods," they will bow down before Thee. A prediction of the universality of the true religion. Note the optimism of faith.

11 Unite my heart, etc. Let there be no distraction of thought, no division of feeling: cp. ver. 12, and Psa. xii. 2; James i. 8; so Jer. xxxii. 39, "one heart." "Knit my heart unto thee" (*Prayer Book version*).

13 from the lowest hell. Rather, "from Sheol beneath": see note on Deut. xxxii. 22.

15 full of compassion (in *feeling*), **and gracious** (in *act*). The Prayer Book version of this verse is quoted by Tennyson in *Rizpah*:

> "'Full of compassion and mercy, the Lord'
> —let me hear it again."

17 token. That is, a proof of Thy favour. The Psalmist desires this in order that all the world may see that God's servant has not trusted Him in vain.

PSALM LXXXVII

1 His foundation. That is, the city which He [Jehovah] has founded: see Isa. xiv. 32. The abruptness of the commencement adds greatly to the effect and impression of the Psalm.

in the holy mountains. Jerusalem was built on and surrounded by mountains: see Psa. cxxv. 2.

4 I will make mention. The first three verses are the prophet's utterance; now the Eternal speaks.

Rahab. Or, "pride." That is, Egypt.

to them that know me. Rather, "amongst them," etc. These nations shall all be added to the number of Jehovah's people: cp. Isa. xix. 24, 25.

This man was born there. And therefore a citizen. The mystery of the new birth is thus shadowed forth.

5 And of Zion, etc. R.V., "Yea, of Zion," etc.; the prophet's response to the Divine word.

This and that man. More exactly, "This one and that one" (R.V.), *individualising* the great promise of the new birth in Zion.

7 As well the singers, etc. Rather, "And singers as well as players on instruments (or, as some render, dancers), *shall say*: All my springs are in thee [O Zion]," *i.e.*, every conceivable enjoyment.

PSALM LXXXVIII

5 Free among the dead. Like them, "dismissed from the pursuits and enjoyments of life."

9 mourneth. Or, melteth.

11 in the grave. See note on Psa. vi. 5.

13 prevent. Or, "come before Thee"; as in Psa. xcv. 2.

18 mine acquaintance into darkness. Or, "My friends are darkness"; *i.e.*, darkness is now his sole companion.

PSALM LXXXIX

"The majestic Covenant Psalm which, according to the Jewish arrangement, closes the third book of the Psalms" (*C. H. Spurgeon*).

1 I will sing, etc. This outburst of cheerfulness, coming between the complaints in Psa. lxxxviii. and those in ver. 38, etc., shows us that it is the remembrance of God's faithful love which will enable us to "rejoice in tribulation."

3 I have sworn unto David. God's own words are here referred to as the ground of confidence: see 2 Sam. vii.; 1 Chron. xvii.

5 Thy faithfulness, etc. That is, Thy faithfulness is praised or acknowledged.

8 Or to Thy faithfulness round about Thee. Or, "And Thy faithfulness is round about Thee" (R.V.).

10 Rahab is Egypt. See Psa. lxxxvii. 4. This refers to the overthrow of the Egyptian power in the Red Sea: see Isa. li. 9.

12 Tabor and Hermon. Tabor's wooded beauty and Hermon's snowy majesty display the Divine power.

14 the habitation. Either, "the settled place," from which it cannot be moved; or, "the foundation," on which it rests.

15 the joyful sound. Lit., "the trumpet-sound"; the joyous sound by which the people were summoned to the great religious festivals: see Lev. xxiii. 24.

18 For the Lord is our defence, etc. Or, "For *to* the Eternal [belongs] our defence, and *to* the Holy One of Israel, our king." Our protectors are themselves protected by Jehovah: cp. R.V.

19 in vision. So the communication made to David through Nathan is called (1 Chron. xvii. 15).

The holy one. All the versions, and many Hebrew manuscripts, read, "The holy ones"; the prophets.

20 See 1 Sam. xvi. 1, 12, 13.

22 exact. Lit., "harass"; as a creditor his debtor. The words immediately following are taken from the promise recorded in 2 Sam. vii. 10; 1 Chron. xvii. 9.

27 My firstborn. Applicable to the king as representative of the nation, God's "firstborn" (Exod. iv. 22).

35 Once. *i.e.*, "Once *for all*."

37 a faithful witness in heaven. These words perhaps allude to the rainbow (see Gen. ix. 12–17), or to Job xvi. 19.

40 hedges. Or, "fences."

44 glory. Or, "brightness": see Exod. xxiv. 10.

48 Shall he deliver, etc. Rather, "That can deliver," etc., in continuance of the former clause.

from the hand of the grave. Or, "from the power of Sheol," R.V.

52 Blessed, etc. This doxology marks the conclusion of the Third Book of the Psalms.

PSALM XC

This Psalm still forms part of the Jewish morning service. It is part of the Burial Service in most English-speaking Churches. Newman uses it effectively in *The Dream of Gerontius.*

1 our dwelling-place. The Jewish Prayer Book translates "our stronghold of defence"; the English Prayer Book version has "our refuge."

3 Thou turnest man to destruction. Or, "Thou turnest frail man to dust" (that which is crushed); an allusion to Gen. iii. 19: see R.V., and marg. The Jewish Prayer Book has it: "Thou turnest men to contrition."

Return. "Come again" is the beautiful rendering of the Prayer Book version. So also Luther's version.

as a watch in the night. See note on Psa. lxiii. 6. The group of images of the brevity of life in vers. 4–10 is peculiarly impressive.

5 as a sleep. As short as the hours spent in sound slumber appear to be on awaking.

7 troubled. Rather, "affrighted."

9 as a tale. Rather, "as a thought"; as quickly as a thought passes through the mind. Another rendering is, "a sigh": see R.V. marg., and Moffatt.

10 it is soon cut off. Rather, "it passes swiftly by," like birds borne on the wind: see Numb. xi. 31, where the same word is used.

11 Even according, etc. Rather, as R.V., "And Thy wrath according to the fear that is due unto Thee?" Our estimate of God's wrath should be enhanced by a sense of His majesty.

12 that we may apply, etc. Rather, "and [then] we will bring a heart of wisdom"; *i.e.,* as an offering to God: cp. Rom. xii. 1.

13 how long? That is, "How long wilt Thou be wroth with us?"

let it repent Thee. "Have compassion on Thy servants)," or "be gracious unto Thy servants" (*Prayer Book version*).

17 the beauty of the Lord. Or, "graciousness": see note on Psa. xxvii. 4.

the work of our hands. That is, all we undertake or do.

PSALM XCI

3 snare of the fowler. A figure for insidious and complicated dangers. The variety of terms employed suggests dangers of every description, both seen and unseen; perils arising both from human enmity and craft, and from dangerous epidemics.

9 Because, etc. Rather, "For Thou, O Jehovah, art my refuge" (R.V.); a parenthetical soliloquy, like Gen. xlix. 18. Or (as R.V. marg.) the sense may be, "For *thou hast said,* Jehovah is my refuge." C. H. Spurgeon (*Treasury of David*) tells how, during an outbreak of Asiatic cholera in South London in 1854, he was weary in body and sick at heart in his incessant visitation of the suffering. Returning one day from a funeral, he read on a paper in a shoemaker's window the 9th and 10th verses of this Psalm, and they inspired him with fresh courage and calm.

10 thy dwelling. Lit., "thy tent" (R.V.).

11 In all thy ways. That is, the ways along which God's providence leads the believer. To apply such a promise to acts of rashness, vanity, or self-gratification, would be, as our Saviour has taught us in His reply to Satan, to "tempt the Lord our God": see Matt. iv. 6. 7.

13 the lion and adder. *i.e.,* open violence and secret treachery.

14 Because he hath set, etc. The trusting soul has hitherto been addressed by the Psalmist; God Himself now speaks.

PSALM XCII

4 Thy work. Lit., "Thy doing"; *i.e.,* in the government of the world.

7 spring. Or, as in vers. 12, 13, "flourish."

8 But Thou, etc. Or, "And Thou art on high for ever, O Eternal."

10 my horn, etc. See Psa. lxxv. 10; lxxxix. 17.

unicorn. See Job xxxix. 9; Psa. xxii. 21, and notes.

anointed with fresh oil. An emblem of festal gladness.

12 like the palm tree, etc. The palm and cedar are among the noblest specimens of vegetable nature in Palestine. Both trees are long-lived, and flourish during all seasons: the palm being remarkable for its productiveness, the cedar for its size and stateliness. Taken together, they well represent the moral excellency, usefulness, and enduring happiness of the godly in contrast with the short-lived prosperity of the wicked (7).

13 Those that be planted, etc. Rather, "Planted in the house of the Lord, they shall flourish," etc.: *i.e.,* the righteous, under Divine culture in the Church of God, shall grow in grace, like healthy trees planted in a congenial soil: see Psa. i. 3.

PSALM XCIII

3 The floods have lifted up their voice. God's control of the violent forces of Nature is used probably to represent His power over the mightiest enemies of His people (see Isa. viii. 7; xvii. 13; Jer. xlvi. 7, 8); enemies attacking the nation or disturbing its peace.

4 The Lord on high, etc. Render, as R.V.:

"Above the voices of many waters,
The mighty breakers of the sea,
Jehovah on high is mighty."

5 Thy testimonies. The law and the promises of God (Psa. xix. 7).

PSALM XCIV

4 [How long] shall they utter, etc.? Rather, as an assertion, "They utter," etc.

5 They break in pieces. Or, "grind"; "crush."

9 He that planted the ear, etc. Whatever powers any creatures possess are all derived from the Creator, and must therefore belong to Him in perfection. This might in modern phrase be called the argument from causation.

10 the heathen. Or, "nations." The antithesis is not between Israel and the Gentiles, but between *entire nations* and *individual offenders.*

shall not he know? Rather, "[Even] He that teacheth man knowledge" (R.V.).

13 That Thou mayest give, etc. Rather, "To give him rest from," etc. Both protection and the restfulness of a chastened soul.

17 in silence. That is, in the grave: see Psa. cxv. 17.

19 my thoughts. That is, my *distracted, anxious* thoughts.

20 Which frameth mischief by a law. This expression is singularly applicable to the conduct of tyrannical governments in issuing persecuting edicts against the Church of God.

22 defence. Or, "fortress," "high tower" (R.V.).

23 He shall bring upon them. Rather, "shall bring *back*," *i e.*, requite. High-handed tyranny may succeed for a time, but it prepares its own punishment.

PSALM XCV

4 The strength of the hills. Or, "the *heights* of the hills."

7 the sheep of His hand. Whom He leads and provides for.

8 Harden not your heart, etc. This verse is made more emphatic by being spoken in the person of God Himself.

as in the provocation, etc. Rather, "As at Meribah, as in the day of Massah, in the wilderness": see Exod. xvii. 7.

PSALM XCVI

1 a new song. To celebrate new displays of God's perfections, when "He cometh" to reign.

5 idols. Properly, "things of nought"; nothings: see Jer. xiv. 14; 1 Cor. viii. 4.

9 the beauty of holiness. See note on Psa. xxix. 2.

PSALM XCVII

1 the multitude of isles. The regions of the Gentile world.

2 habitation. See note on Psa. lxxxix. 14.

7 all ye gods. The heathen deities are required to bow down before the majesty of the Eternal: cp. Numb. xxxiii. 4; Isa. xlvi. 1.

11 Light is sown, etc. As the seed, though hidden for a time, springs up and brings forth its fruit in its season, so shall real happiness sooner or later be the portion of the pious sufferer. "Righteous" in the Hebrew is *singular, i.e.,* "the righteous man"; "upright" is *plural.*

12 at the remembrance of His holiness. Or, "to His holy memorial," *i.e.*, His name: see Exod. iii. 15; and cp. Psa. xxx. 4. See R.V.

PSALM XCVIII

1 hath gotten Him the victory. Or, "hath wrought salvation for Himself."

3 All the ends of the earth, etc. See Isa. lii. 10, where the same words are used to predict the glorious redemption of mankind by Christ from sin and all its evils.

6 trumpets. Mentioned only here in the Psalms: the long straight trumpets of the priests.

PSALM XCIX

Spurgeon says that this may be called THE SANCTUS or THE HOLY, HOLY, HOLY PSALM, for the word "holy" is the conclusion and the refrain of its three main divisions.

1 let the people, etc. Rather, "The peoples tremble; He sitteth above the cherubim, the earth is moved."

3 For it is holy. Rather, "Holy is He" (R.V.). The final clauses of vers. 3, 5, 9 may have been sung by a separate choir. This threefold ascription of holiness to Jehovah, in the last verse made still more emphatic, is the earthly response to the praises of heaven: see Isa. vi. 3; Rev. iv. 8.

6 Moses and Aaron among His priests. The word "priest" is applied to Moses probably as having ratified the covenant (Exod. xxiv.) and consecrated Aaron (Lev. viii.), but chiefly as being himself a prevailing Mediator between Jehovah and Israel (Exod. xvii., xxxii., etc.).

8 Thou wast a God, etc. Rather, "A forgiving God Thou wast to them, and taking vengeance on their doings."

PSALM C

This Psalm in its metrical form, to the tune "Old Hundred," is familiar wherever the English language is spoken. One metrical version, however, alters the joyousness of the original by rendering part of ver. 2 as "Him serve with fear." Both the A.V. and the Prayer Book version have "Serve the Lord with gladness." This Psalm was sung by the vast assemblage in front of St. Paul's Cathedral when Queen Victoria went to give thanks there at her Diamond Jubilee.

3 and not we ourselves. The marginal reading seems preferable: "and we are His" (R.V.). The two readings in Hebrew are alike in sound, but differ by one letter: see note Isa. ix. 3.

PSALM CI

2 a perfect way. Making his life consistent with his knowledge and professed piety: see Job i. 1; and cp. 1 Kings xi. 4, 6, etc.

O when wilt Thou come unto me? See the promise in Exod. xx. 24. One reason why David desired to have the ark, the symbol of Jehovah's presence, fixed in the capital of the nation, doubtless was, that he might be "blessed" in his efforts to establish a just and holy government.

4 I will not know a wicked person. See note on Psa. 1. 6. The clause may be rendered, "I will know no evil thing" (R.V.).

8 early. Rather, "in the mornings"; probably a reference to the administration of justice every morning at the city gate: see Jer. xxi. 12.

PSALM CII

3 burned as a hearth. Or, "as a firebrand" (R.V.). All my bodily vigour is gone.

4 So that I forget, etc. His grief made him neglect his food.

7 I watch. That is, I am sleepless through anxiety.

8 are sworn against me. Or, "swear by me"; *i.e.*, they refer to me as an example of the evil they imprecate: cp. Jer. xxix. 22.

9 ashes. "Ashes" are put for "grief," of which they were the outward token.

10 Thou hast lifted me up. Or, "Thou hast taken me up" (Prayer Book and R.V.); *i.e.*, as a whirlwind takes anything up, only to dash it to the ground with the greater violence.

11 a shadow that declineth. Or, "a lengthened shadow"; indicating the close of day.

12 But Thou, O Lord, etc. From the thought of his individual sorrow the Psalmist passes to the thought of God's faithfulness to His people. The consolation is two-fold. Whatever becomes of me, the cause of God is safe; and also, as one of God's people, I am a sharer in His promises.

13 the set time. See Jer. xxv. 11; xxix. 10; Dan. ix. 2.

14 favour the dust thereof. That is, the ruins. The Prayer Book version has "it pitieth them to see her in the dust."

16 When the Lord shall build, etc. Rather, "For the Eternal hath built Zion, He hath appeared, etc., He hath turned to the prayer, etc., and not despised," etc.: see R.V.

18 This shall be written, etc. Future generations shall be taught to trust and honour God by the records of His mercy and faithfulness.

22 the people. Rather, "peoples," as R.V.; a forecast of His universal reign.

25 Of old hast Thou laid. etc. Quoted in Heb. i. 10–12, with express application to our Lord Jesus Christ; who is thus identified with the Eternal (cp. Isa. vi. 1–10 with John xii. 41) as possessing eternity and immutability, the attributes of supreme Deity.

PSALM CIII

1 all that is within me. Parallel to "soul," and an amplification of the idea: "every thought, faculty, power: the heart with all its affections, the will, the conscience, the reason; in a word, the whole spiritual being" (*Perowne*).

2 forget not all His benefits. *i.e.*, not *any of* them, according to a well-known Hebrew idiom.

4 destruction. Lit., "the pit," including the grave and Sheol.

5 like the eagle's. Rather, "like the eagle," as R.V. The eagle retains its vigour to a very old age.

6 for all that are oppressed. Gratitude to God for personal mercies passes on to adoration of Him who is the source of all good to all His creatures.

11 as the heaven is high above the earth, etc. God's mercy to them that fear Him is *infinite;* illustrated by the vastest measurements in the material universe; His forgiveness is *complete* (12). The threefold repetition of the words "upon them that fear Him" (11, 13, 17, *Heb.*) reminds us that it is only the penitent believer who really profits by God's fatherly mercy.

12 hath He removed our transgressions. The thought of forgiveness, or rather, of justification, is in the foreground; that of moral and spiritual renovation is also implied in the idea of healing. "He breaks the power of cancelled sin" (*Charles Wesley*).

14 He knoweth our frame. However severe God's chastisements may be, we may be sure that He both knows and remembers our weakness, and will apportion to it His discipline and His grace.

15 his days are as grass. In this beautiful figure, suggested perhaps by Psa. xc. 5, 6, the description of man's frailty is so carried out as to be most forcibly contrasted with God's everlasting mercy (17, 18): cp. Isa. xl. 6–8.

17 unto children's children. Agreeably to the promise made in the second commandment (Exod. xx. 6). But vers. 17, 18 show that these blessings can be enjoyed only in connexion with personal holiness.

PSALM CIV

2 Who stretchest, etc. The Psalmist poetically represents the sky as a canopy, resting on pillars or beams placed around the horizon, in the waters of a great circumambient sea.

4 Who maketh, etc. Rather, "Who maketh winds His messengers, His ministers a flaming fire" (R.V.). The Hebrew words for "angels" and "spirits" have double meanings; the former denoting also *messengers,* the latter *winds.*

5 Who laid the foundations of the earth. Rather, 'He founded the earth on its basis, that it should not be moved for ever and ever."

8 They go up, etc. Rather, "The mountains rose, the valleys sank": see R.V. marg.

12 By them. etc. Rather. "Over them dwell the birds of heaven, from among the leaves they utter their voice."

16 full of sap. Lit., "are satisfied," *i.e.*, fully supplied; *i.e.*, with moisture. The "trees of the Lord—which He hath planted," are indigenous trees, which have not been planted by man or tended by him. So in Psa. lxxx. 10, the Hebrew is "cedars of God."

17 fir trees. Rather, "cypress." The stork builds in high places

18 conies. The "coney" is probably the wabar (*hyrax syriacus*), an animal about the size of a hare, resembling the Alpine marmot: see Lev. xi. 5; Prov. xxx. 26.

26 leviathan. Probably the whale.

28 That Thou givest them they gather. Rather, "Thou givest to them, they gather"; meaning not only that they gather what God gives, but also that God gives all that they gather.

35 Let the sinners, etc. Or, "Sinners shall be consumed from the earth"; perhaps with reference to Numb. xiv. 35.

Praise ye the Lord. "Hallelujah." The first "Hallelujah" in the Psalter.

PSALM CV

1 people. Rather, "peoples" (R.V.); the nations of the world.

5 the judgements of His mouth. His judicial *sentences,* as well as His legislative *enactments.*

6 Ye children of Jacob His chosen. Read, "ye children of Jacob, His chosen ones" (R.V.).

14 He reproved kings for their sakes. As Pharaoh (Gen. xii. 17), and Abimelech (xx. 3). The "anointed ones" and "prophets" (15) are the patriarchs (see Gen. xx. 7), who were admitted to confidential intercourse with God, and received direct revelations from Him.

16 He called for a famine. See Gen. xli. 1–36, 54; xlvii. 13–26.

17 [Even] Joseph, [who] was sold. Rather, omitting the words supplied, "Joseph was sold for a slave": see R.V. This may be adduced as showing by what unlikely means God can fulfil His purposes. On vers. 17–24, see Gen. xxxvii. to l.

18 He was laid in iron. Lit., "his soul entered into the iron." The Prayer Book version following the Vulgate, "the iron entered into his soul," is inadmissible, as the gender of the Hebrew verb shows "his soul" to be the subject. Luther has, "his body had to lie in iron."

19 his word came. That is, "Joseph's word" to his fellow-prisoners, which "came to pass." The next clause probably means that the "word of the Eternal" or Divine prediction (see Gen. xl.) which Joseph spoke, by its fulfilment, vindicated his character, showing that he enjoyed the Divine favour.

25 He turned their heart, etc. See Exod. iv. 21.

27 They. *i.e.*, Moses and Aaron.

28 they rebelled not against His word. Meaning either, as in the preceding verse, *Moses* and *Aaron,* who faithfully executed God's commissions; or *Pharaoh* and *his people,* who, terrified and subdued by repeated judgements, yielded at last to God's command, and let the people go: see the history of these plagues in Exod. vii.–xii. But some ancient versions read, "they rebelled against His words"; referring the passage to the controversy with Pharaoh and his court. The Prayer Book version reads, "and were not obedient," etc. (following the LXX).

darkness. The ninth plague, mentioned first. The fifth and sixth plagues are omitted.

34 caterpillars. Rather, "locusts," hairy (Jer. li. 27), and winged (Nahum iii. 16).

37 not one feeble person. Or, "none that stumbled"; not one who was unequal to the hardships of the journey: cp. Isa. v. 27. This is a remarkable instance of God's providential care.

39 He spread a cloud for a covering. See Exod. xiii. 21, 22.

40 He brought quails. See Exod. xvi. 12, 13.

bread of heaven. See Exod. xvi. 4, 14, 15.

41 He opened the rock, and the waters gushed out. See Exod. xvii. 5, 6; Numb. xx. 7–11; 1 Cor. x. 4.

44 the labour of the people (peoples). That is, the produce of their labour: see Deut. vi. 10, 11.

45 Praise ye the Lord. "Hallelujah": see note civ. 35. The first word of the next Psalm repeats the phrase.

PSALM CVI

1 Praise ye the Lord. "Hallelujah." The first Psalm which begins with this ascription. The other "Hallelujah Psalms" are cxi.-cxiii., cxvii., cxxxv., cxlvi.–cl.

4 with the favour [that Thou bearest], etc. Or, omitting the words supplied: "in the favouring of Thy people," *i.e.*, answer my prayer in showing favour to them.

7 Our fathers understood not Thy wonders in Egypt. Or, "Our fathers in Egypt understood not," etc.

12 Then believed, etc. They believed and praised only when they saw the wonders; but (13) "they made haste, they forgat His works," instead of patiently waiting for Him.

14 lusted. See Numb. xi. 4.

15 leanness. A wasting sickness, which ended in death: see Numb. xi. 33, 34.

16 Aaron the saint of the Lord. "The holy one of Jahveh," so called in reference to his priestly dignity, which was the object of Korah's envy: see Numb. xvi. 10, 11.

18 their company. That is, the company of Levites who offered incense with Korah: see Numb. xvi. 35.

19 They made a calf. See Exod. xxxii. 4–8.

20 their glory. The true and living God, was "their glory."

23 stood before Him in the breach. To defend them from imminent peril of destruction.

24 They despised, etc. See Numb. xiii., xiv.

26 He lifted up His hand. "He sware in His wrath," etc. Psa. xcv. 11. So in Exod. vi. 8; Gen. xiv. 22; Deut. xxxii. 40.

27 to scatter them. Cp. Ezek. xx. 23.

28 They joined themselves unto Baal-peor. See Numb. xxv. 2, 3; and cp. Rev. ii. 14.

the sacrifices of the dead. Some suppose "the dead" here to mean lifeless gods, and refer to Psa. cxv. 4–7; 1 Cor. xii. 2. But the worship of deceased ancestors or heroes has always been one principal form of idolatry.

29 their inventions. Rather, "deeds," *i.e.*, of wickedness. And so in ver. 39.

30 executed judgement. The act of Phinehas was a judicial infliction, was counted as an atonement for the people, and as righteousness to him: cp. ver. 31, and Numb. xxv. 7–13; where the reward promised is a perpetual priesthood.

32 at the waters of strife. "Of Meribah": see Numb. xx. 2–13; Deut. xxxii. 49–52.

33 provoked. Rather, 'rebelled against his spirit": see R.V., and cp. Isa. lxiii. 10.

34 They did not destroy the nations. Or, "peoples," as R.V.: see Josh. xvi. 10; Judges i. 21, 27–36.

37 devils. Rather, "lords," or "destroyers"; probably meaning *idol-gods*. The Septuagint renders "demons" (so R.V.), a word which the heathen applied to *inferior deities*, the Jews to *evil spirits*: see Deut. xxxii. 17; 2 Kings xvi. 3; xvii. 17.

39 went a whoring. *i.e.*, Spiritually, in departing from God.

inventions. Rather, "practices."

41 the heathen. Or, "nations," as R.V.

42 oppressed them. See Judges i. 34; iii. 30; iv. 3; viii. 28.

43 Many times did He deliver them. See Judges ii. 16–19, etc.; 1 Sam. xii. 11, etc. "Yet they rebelled against Him in their counsel."

47 Save us, O Lord our God. This verse fixes the date of the Psalm (and of the preceding) to the period of the Captivity: see prefatory note to Psa. cv.

48 Blessed be the Lord God of Israel, etc. The doxology at the close of the Fourth Book.

PSALM CVII

This regular and beautiful poem was probably composed after the return of the Jews from Babylon, and appears to have been designed to celebrate the Divine mercy in all the circumstances of that auspicious event.

1 O give thanks unto the Lord, etc. The opening words of Psa. cvi. See Ezra iii. 11; Jer. xxxiii. 11.

3 from the south. A correct interpretation of the Heb., "from the sea," *i.e.*, here the Red Sea. Usually the Mediterranean in the west is meant by "the sea," but the west has been mentioned before.

7 the right way. Rather, "a straight path" (see R.V.); a contrast to the "wandering in a desert way," ver. 4.

8 men. Rather, "they," *i.e.*, those whom God has thus heard and saved. And so in vers. 15, 21, 31.

10 Such as sit in darkness. Another scene. The darkness of a dungeon.

11 Because they rebelled. The sufferings of the Captivity are always represented as the result of the people's sin.

17 Fools, etc. This third scene depicts the pangs of sickness brought on by sin, as, *e.g.*, by vicious self-indulgence.

20 their destructions. That is, from death, which threatened them.

23 They that go down, etc. In this fourth picture, that of shipwreck, the Psalmist appears to pass from the remembrances of the Captivity for perils of a more general kind.

27 And are at their wit's end. The Hebrew here is very emphatic, "all their wisdom is swallowed up." Luther has "und wissten keinen Rath mehr" ("and they knew not what to do").

34 into barrenness. Lit., "into *saltness*": see Gen. xiii. 10; xiv. 3; xix. 24–26; Deut. xxix. 23.

35 turneth the wilderness, etc. See Isa. xli. 18.

39 Again, they are. Rather, "And they were"; referring probably once more to the exile in Babylon. Those who are now so prosperous (35–38) are the very persons who before were in abject misery.

40 princes. Persons the most exempt, in ordinary times, from destitution and want. The two parts of this verse are taken from Job xii. 21, 24.

43 Whoso is wise, etc. Or, "Who is wise? Let him observe these things, and let them understand," etc.: cp. the close of Hosea xiv. 9.

PSALM CVIII

See notes on Psa. lvii. and lx., of parts of which this Psalm is composed.

9 Over Philistia will I triumph ("shout," R.V.). Psa. lx. has "Philistia, shout thou because of me."

PSALM CIX

2 are opened. Rather, "they have opened."

4 For my love. That is, "in *return* for my love."

But I [give myself unto] prayer. Lit., "But I pray." This was his *constant*, his *only* resource.

6 Set Thou a wicked man over him. That is, as his judge. He is unjust to others; let him feel what injustice is. In vers. 7, 28, 31, similar judicial metaphors recur: see note on Psa. v. 10.

Satan. Rather, "an adversary," or "accuser," who stood by the accused (Zech. iii. 1). He accuses me, let him have a severe accuser. But Jehovah will defend His servant (31).

7 let his prayer become sin. Let his prayer to his judges for favour, or perhaps to God for help, be construed as an aggravation of his crime.

10 out of their desolate places. That is, creeping forth, in search of food, from amidst the ruins of their habitations.

11 his labour. See note on Psa. cv. 44.

17 let it come. Rather, "and it came," etc., "and it was far," etc.; "it came within him like water" (18), etc.

23 like the shadow, etc. See note on Psa. cii. 11.

tossed up and down. Rather, "shaken out," as from a garment, an allusion to the violence with which a cloud of locusts is scattered by the wind.

28 Let them curse, etc. Rather, "They curse, Thou blessest; they stand up (to accuse me), they are ashamed, Thy servant rejoiceth."

31 To save him, etc. "The contrast between this closing thought and that in ver. 6 is unmistakeable. At the right hand of the tormentor stands Satan as an accuser; at the right hand of the tormented one stands God his vindicator. He who delivered him over to human judges is condemned; and he who was delivered up is 'taken away out of distress and from judgement' (Isa. liii. 8), by the Judge of the judges, in order that as we hear in the next Psalm, he may sit 'at the right hand' of the Heavenly King" (*Delitzsch*).

PSALM CX

This Psalm is distinctly ascribed to David by our Lord; and is no less distinctly claimed by Him and His apostles, without any opposition from the Jews, as referring to the Messiah: see Matt. xxii. 43; Acts ii. 34; 1 Cor. xv. 25, 27: Eph. i. 20, 22; Heb. i. 13. Many of the highest Jewish authorities, as has been proved by numerous Rabbinical citations, interpret the Psalm as a prophecy of the Messiah. It has been called the crown of all the Psalms. Luther says that it is worthy to be overlaid with precious jewels (*Edersheim*).

1 The Lord said, etc. Rather, "An oracle (see Psa. xxxvi. 1, and note) of Jahveh to my Lord (Adonai)."

until I make Thine enemies Thy footstool. An ancient symbol of conquest often found in the paintings on Egyptian tombs: see Josh. x. 24. Ancient thrones were so raised as to need a footstool.

2 the rod of Thy strength. A rod, or staff, in Scripture, is an emblem of power; which may be exercised either to correct or to conquer. Here the reference is Christ's victorious rule.

3 Thy people, etc. Perhaps the best rendering of this verse is as follows: "Thy people [shall be] freewill offerings in the day of Thy might, in ornaments of holiness: from the womb of the dawn to Thee [shall be] the dew of Thy youthful ones." It represents the voluntary and cheerful service, the attractive piety, and the perpetual rise of new generations for the service of the Messiah. Calvin says: "The youth, which like the dew-drops are innumerable, are here designated *the dew of childhood, or of youth.*"

4 After the order of Melchizedek. *i.e.*, King as well as Priest. For an inspired exposition of this verse as applied to our Lord, see Heb. vii.; cp. Gen. xiv. 18; Zech. vi. 13.

6 the heads over many countries. *i.e.*, the *chiefs* of the nations.

7 He shall drink, etc. As a conqueror refreshed by a hasty draught at a brook continues the fight and pursuit till his foes are completely subdued; so the Messiah's strength shall never fail until the last enemy is destroyed.

PSALM CXI

Psalms cxi., cxii. ("Hallelujah Psalms"), are precisely similar in construction. Both are acrostics or alphabetical, having the successive Hebrew letters at the beginning of the successive clauses. There are two such clauses in each of the first eight verses; and three in each of the last two, making 22 clauses in all, for the 22 letters of the Hebrew alphabet.

1 assembly. Or, "company." The word denotes a select society, in distinction from a collection of people. In the general community, the *righteous* formed a smaller company.

5 He hath given meat (food), etc. This and the four following verses doubtless *include* the gift of manna and quails, the deliverance from Egypt, and the conquest of Canaan; but they must not be *restricted* to these things, which are only some of the many proofs that Jehovah is "mindful of His covenant."

7 sure. Or, "faithful." As God's *works* are true and just, so are His *commands.* The words in the next verse, "They stand fast," etc., refer to both the "works" and the "commandments."

10 the beginning. That is, the first principle. This verse is the inference from all that has gone before. As all God's dealings are faithful and gracious, and all His commands good and faithful, it must be true wisdom to worship and obey Him.

PSALM CXII

This Psalm is a companion to the preceding, on which see note. The beginning and the ending of the present Psalm closely resemble those of Psa. i.: "Blessed is the man . . . the desire of the wicked shall perish."

1 Blessed is the man. At the close of the preceding Psalm, the fear of the Lord is declared to be the first principle of all true wisdom; here it is commended as the source of all true happiness.

3 And his righteousness, etc. The same expression which is applied to God in Psa. cxi. 3. Human righteousness has its root in the Divine, and is therefore an everlasting possession. The thought is repeated, ver. 9.

4 light in the darkness. Guidance in seasons of perplexity, and relief in time of trouble. This verse was the text of Dr. Thomas Chalmers' famous sermon at the Disruption in Scotland when 470 ministers resigned their livings in the cause of spiritual independence and formed the Free Church of Scotland.

5 A good man, etc. Rather, "Good (*i.e.*, happy, prosperous) is the man who showeth favour and lendeth; he shall maintain his cause in judgement"; he shall come out unharmed from all conflicts with litigious adversaries: cp. R.V.

7 his heart is fixed. "Lives rooted in God are never uprooted" (*A. Maclaren*).

9 He hath dispersed. He hath distributed munificently: see 2 Cor. ix. 9.

PSALM CXIII

According to a Jewish usage, which is thought to have existed even in the time of Christ, Psalms cxiii.–cxviii. constitute the HALLEL, sung at the annual festivals, especially at the Passover and the Feast of Tabernacles. It is believed that the "hymn" which our Saviour and His disciples sang after the Passover (Matt. xxvi. 30; Mark xiv. 26), was the latter portion of these Psalms (cxv.–cxviii.), which the Jews used before the fourth cup at the Passover meal. Psa. cxiii., cxiv. were sung before the second cup.

5 Who is like unto the Lord our God? A terse and forcible antithesis. God is represented as combining majesty with condescending attention to all.

8 That He may set him with princes. That is, make him to *sit* with them as their equal and associate.

9 He maketh the barren woman, etc. See the history of Hannah (1 Sam. ii. 8), from whose song most of the expressions in vers. 7, 8 are borrowed.

PSALM CXIV

4 The mountains skipped, etc. Referring to the shaking of Sinai: see Exod. xix. 18; Judges v. 4, 5; Psa. xxix. 6; lxviii. 16; Hab. iii. 6.

8 Which turned the rock, etc. This refers to the miraculous supply of water: see Exod. xvii. 6; Numb. xx. 11.

PSALM CXV

This is a responsive or antiphonal Psalm for temple worship, some of the verses being sung by a single voice (*e.g.* vers. 9–11), while others are the response of the congregation.

1 Not unto us, etc. *i.e.*, Glorify not us, but Thyself, in completing our deliverance. The restoration of God's people would remove the shade which their captivity seemed to cast over His mercy and truth as well as power.

3 our God is in the heavens. Not like idols seen and handled, but exalted above all: cp. 1 Tim. vi. 15, 16.

8 are. Rather, "will be." Men become like the objects of their worship.

9 O Israel, etc. Vers. 9–13 were probably sung in responses by Levites and people; vers. 14, 15, by Levites or one of them, and vers. 16–18 by the people.

their help and their shield. That is, of those who trust in Him: see Psa. xxxiii. 20.

16 The heaven [even] the heavens, etc. Or, "The heavens are heavens for the Eternal": cp. R.V.

PSALM CXVI

3 of hell. Heb., "of Sheol": cp. Psa. xviii. 4, 5.

7 unto thy rest. To thy former tranquil confidence in God.

9 I will walk before the Lord, etc. That is, aiming to serve Him and to do His will on earth. Vers. 8, 9 are taken from Psa. lvi. 13; ver. 3 is from Psa. xviii. 4, 5.

10 I believed, therefore, etc. Rather, "I believed, when I spake," *i.e.*, my calling upon God (2, 4) is the result and evidence of my faith.

11 All men are liars (a "lie," R.V.). That is, they disappoint the hopes placed in them. Reliance on human aid is vain.

13 the cup of salvation. Perhaps referring to the cup of *thanksgiving* for salvation; which, as Jewish writers say, commonly accompanied the thank-offerings after deliverance. The Passover cup had a similar meaning. Cp. Matt. xxvi. 27; 1 Cor. x. 16. This and the remaining verses of this Psalm in its metrical form are very generally used in the Communion Service of the Presbyterian Churches.

15 Precious in the sight of the Lord is the death of His saints. "Right dear in the sight of the Lord," etc. (*Prayer Book version*). This is the same as saying, their *life* is precious: see Psa. lxxii. 14. God so highly values the lives of His holy and faithful servants, that He will not lightly permit their death.

16 O Lord, truly I am, etc. Or, "I beseech Thee, O Lord, for I am," etc.

Thou hast loosed my bonds. The assurance of pardon is followed by obedience and faithful service. "Made free from sin—servants of righteousness."

PSALM CXVII

This very short Psalm was perhaps designed to be a chorus or doxology. Many think it was used at the close of the public services of the Temple.

1 praise the Lord, all ye nations. This exhortation to all nations is quoted in Rom. xv. 11 as a prophetic intimation of the future calling of the Gentiles into the Church of Christ.

PSALM CXVIII

This Psalm has been attributed to various authors and occasions, but the best supported opinion seems to be that it was composed for the great celebration of the Feast of Tabernacles in the Second Temple (Neh. viii. 13–18), after the completion of the walls of Jerusalem. The formula of praise with which it opens was that of the Jews after the Captivity (see Jer. xxxiii. 11; etc.). Some allusions in the Psalm harmonise with such a reference—as "the tents of the righteous" (15). The "Hosanna" (25), we know from Jewish writers, was the joyous cry with which the people daily encompassed the altar of burnt offering during the feast; and the Septuagint translators seem to show that such an application of the Psalm was recognised in their time by their translation of ver. 27, "Decorate the festival with leafy boughs." The Psalm is applied in the New Testament to the Messiah (Matt. xii. 10; xxi. 42; Luke xx. 17; 1 Pet. ii. 7; Acts iv. 11): and cp. Matt. xxi. 9. The form of the Psalm is antiphonal; different parts being sung in the names of different persons, and probably by different voices.

Luther, in dedicating his translation of this Psalm to Abbot Frederick of Nürnberg, said: "This is my Psalm, my chosen Psalm." It was the Psalm sung by the troops of William III, Prince of Orange, on their landing at Brixham in 1688.

2 Let Israel now say. Rather, "Oh let Israel say!" "Now" is not an adverb of time. And so in vers. 3, 4.

5 [and set me] in a large place. See note on Psa. xviii. 19.

12 fire of thorns. A fire of thorns is soon kindled, and burns fiercely; but is speedily extinguished.

13 Thou. The "nations" (ver. 10), who had harassed the people of God, are here apostrophised as an individual. So also with Israel, as again in vers. 17–21.

15 the tabernacles of the righteous. See prefatory note to the Psalm.

17 I shall not die, but live. Words quoted by Wycliffe to the friars as he lay dying at Lutterworth.

19 the gates of righteousness. Probably the Temple gate, which only "the righteous" (the worshippers of Jehovah) might enter: ver. 20; Psa. xxiv.; xxvi. 6.

22 The stone which the builders refused, etc. The Jewish people, once outcast and contemned, are now placed in honour and made the cornerstone of God's kingdom upon earth. But the emblem applies with the fullest meaning to our Lord Jesus Christ; who, though rejected by the Jewish authorities, was nevertheless destined to unite both Jews and Gentiles in one vast and glorious spiritual building: see Matt. xxi. 42; Acts iv. 11; Eph. ii. 20; 1 Pet. ii. 4, 7.

24 This is the day which the Lord hath made. The meaning is, It is God who has wrought for us the deliverance which we this day celebrate. This applies well to the feast.

25 Save now, I beseech Thee. Rather, "Save, I pray." These words, contracted into *Hosanna*, are addressed to Jesus as Son of David (Matt. xxvi. 9).

26 He that cometh in the name of the Lord. This was afterwards given as a standing appellation to the Messiah, in allusion either to this passage or to Mal. iii. 1: see Matt. xi. 3; xxi. 9; Heb. x. 37.

27 hath showed us light. That is, Jehovah has granted us a season of extraordinary joy, such as none but God could give.

Bind the sacrifice, etc. *i.e.*, bind it with cords, *and lead it to* the horns of the altar. These words of the "hymn," sung by our Lord and the apostles, immediately preceded the scene in Gethsemane (*Goulburn*).

PSALM CXIX

This Psalm is an alphabetical poem consisting of twenty-two divisions, which are severally headed, in the English Bible, by the successive letters of the Hebrew alphabet. Each part comprises eight verses, all beginning with the Hebrew letter which forms the heading. It is mostly composed of short detached sentences; though occasionally the same thought is pursued through two or more verses. Like other Psalms of this class, it is entirely occupied with one subject. Its one simple theme is *the excellence of the word of God*, which is presented in every variety of form. We find here, as in Psa. xix. 7–9 (on which see note), various terms employed, as almost synonymous, to designate the law, or revealed will of God; and one or more of these occurs in nearly every verse; the only exceptions being vers. 122, 132, and perhaps 84, 90, 91, 120, 121. Of these terms, *Word* denotes generally the expression of God's mind and will; *Law*, this expression as contained in a body of teaching setting forth the code of duty. *Testimonies* are the Divine injunctions regarded as witnessing to God's character and against man's sin. *Statutes* and *ordinances* imply legislative sanction. *Commandments* are more general, being based upon any kind of authority. *Precepts* are a charge entrusted to be kept. *Ways* denote the course of practical conduct; and *judgements* imply account and retribution. All that is here said of the value and use of the ancient Scriptures may be applied, with far greater force, to the complete revelation which we now possess.

Luther's heading of the Psalm is "The Christian's golden ABC of the praise, love, strength and use of God's word."

Ruskin said that it had become "of all the most precious to me, in its overflowing and glorious passion of love for the law of God."

2 His testimonies. God's commandments, as testifying to His holiness and goodness, and against sin.

5 directed. Rather, "fixed," "established."

9 By taking heed [thereto] according to Thy word. Or, "so as to keep it according to Thy word." The whole Psalm is the answer to this question. Prayerful meditation on God's word is the best corrective of youthful passions.

19 I am a stranger in the earth, etc. As a traveller in a strange land needs the guidance of sign-posts or of map, so does a pilgrim on the earth need the guidance of God's truth.

26 I have declared my ways. I have made known to Thee all my affairs and anxieties.

29 the way of lying. This seems to refer particularly to all insincerity and unfaithfulness towards God and His revealed will: see next verse.

grant me thy law graciously. The Prayer Book version has "cause me to make much of Thy law."

32 I will run, etc. My obedience shall be earnest and zealous, "for Thou shalt enlarge (*or*, expand) my heart," freeing it from restraint.

34 Give me understanding. Or, "Make me understand it"; as in ver. 27.

36 covetousness. Or, "gain." That the love of gain is opposed to a faithful observance of the Divine testimonies is taught by our Saviour, in Matt. xiii. 22; Luke xvi. 13; and by the Apostle Paul, in 1 Tim. vi. 10. It is a fact of every-day experience.

38 Stablish Thy word unto Thy servant, etc. Or, "Establish to Thy servant Thy word, which is for (tendeth to) the fear of Thee": see R.V.

45 I will walk at liberty. Or, "at large": see note on ver. 32 and on Psa. xviii. 19.

48 My hands also will I lift up. A symbol of earnest desire, derived from the raising of the hands in prayer.

54 my pilgrimage. Or, "my sojournings." A description of human life derived from the habits of the early patriarchs: see Gen. xlvii. 9.

56 This I had. *i.e.*, this cheering remembrance of Thy name.

60 I made haste, etc. Love of our work is shown by promptitude in setting about it. Cp. v. 32.

61 The bands of the wicked, etc. Or, "The cords (*i.e.*, snares) of the wicked have been cast about me": see R.V.

62 At midnight I will rise, etc. Thus showing the ardour of his love to God. So our Lord spent the night in prayer: see Matt. xiv. 23; Luke vi. 12.

64 The earth, O Lord, is full of Thy mercy. The Divine mercy displayed all around us is a pledge of God's willingness to give the instruction that we need for our souls.

67 Before I was afflicted, etc. This was strikingly exemplified in the religious life of the Jewish people, before and after the Captivity. For a powerful modern study of the discipline of trial, see Dr. A. C. Benson's *Altar Fire.*

70 as fat as grease. See note on Psa. xvii. 10.

74 when they see me. Seeing in me a living proof of the good of trusting in Thy word.

79 Let those that fear Thee turn unto me. Learning with me to trust Thy word.

80 sound. Or, "perfect," entirely devoted to them.

83 like a bottle in the smoke. The skin-bottles of the East (see Josh. ix. 4) are often hung up near the roof, where they become blackened with smoke, and sometimes shrivelled with heat: hence they well represent one whom affliction has made an object of pity rather than of attraction.

84 How many, etc.? This question is equivalent to, "Remember how *few* my days are." The shortness of his life is urged by the Psalmist as a reason for imploring speedy succour.

88 Quicken me after Thy lovingkindness. Or, "According to Thy mercy revive me."

89 For ever, etc. The stability and order of the material universe are a guarantee of the certainty of all God's purposes and promises: cp. vers. 89–91 with Jer. xxxi. 35–37, xxxiii. 19–21.

96 I have seen an end of all perfection, etc. The absolute perfection of the Divine law is here contrasted either with the real incompleteness and frailty of the (apparently) most perfect works of men, or with the deficiency which is found in all human goodness when brought to this standard. Luther's version has: "I have seen an end of all things." The Prayer Book version is similar.

98 Thou through Thy commandments, etc. Or, "Thy commandment (*i.e.,* Thy law, as a whole) hath made me wiser than mine enemies: for it is for ever mine"; *i.e.,* my inalienable possession. God's truth, received with simplicity and cordiality, confers upon its humblest possessors a Divine wisdom which will foil the cunning of their enemies (98), will surpass all merely human endowments and attainments (99), and will be more available than the maxims of long experience, or the greatest knowledge of the world (100). "The ancients" are probably "the aged" (R.V.).

104 I hate every false way. Or, "every path of falsehood."

105 lamp, by night ("lantern," Prayer Book version); **light,** by day.

106 will perform. Rather, as R.V., "have confirmed."

108 the freewill offerings of my mouth. My prayers and praises.

109 My soul. Rather, "My life." The meaning of this expression is, My life is always in peril: see Judges xii. 3; 1 Sam. xix. 5; xxviii. 21; Job xiii. 14.

113 I hate [vain] thoughts. The Hebrew is, "I hate divided *persons* or *things.*" It refers either to persons of unsettled opinions and purposes, or to vacillating, inconsistent conduct, probably to the former. R.V., "I hate them that are of a double mind": cp. 1 Kings xviii. 21: James i. 8.

120 My flesh trembleth. Or becomes rigid with fear. God's penal inflictions are awful, even to those who, being restored to His favour, have no reason to fear for themselves.

122 Be surety. *i.e.,* take up my cause, as Advocate: cp. 1 John ii. 1.

126 It is time, etc. Or, "It is time for Jehovah to act"; in order to vindicate His broken law. Delitzsch renders: "It is time to work for Jehovah."

127 Therefore. That is, because of the *excellence* of God's commandments, as celebrated in many preceding verses.

130 entrance. Rather, "The opening" (R.V.), probably meaning the unfolding. The Spanish version of de Valera has

"El principio de tus palabras alumbra."
("The beginning of thy words gives light.")

"When thy word goeth forth, it giveth light," etc. (*Prayer Book version*).

131 panted. Like an eager runner. Or, "like a wild creature panting open-mouthed for water" (*A. Maclaren*).

133 Order my steps, etc. Or, "Confirm my steps by Thy word."

140 pure. Heb., "fire-proved."

147 prevented. That is, "anticipated"; "was beforehand with." So intent was the Psalmist on devout meditation, that he arose before the dawn for that purpose.

149 Thy lovingkindness . . . Thy judgement. God's mercy and justice both engage Him to hear His people.

151 Thou art near, etc. My enemies are near to injure (150); but Thou art near to save.

152 Concerning Thy testimonies. Rather, as R.V., "From Thy testimonies." They are their own best witness.

156 Great. Rather, "Many"; in opposition to the "many persecutors" in the next verse.

160 Thy word is true from the beginning. Or, "The head (meaning probably 'the sum') of Thy word is truth": see R.V.

164 Seven times. That is, many: a definite for an indefinite number: see Gen. xxxi. 7.

165 And nothing shall offend them. Heb., "and [there is] to them no stumbling-block," or occasion to sin: see Ezek. vii. 19; Matt. v. 29, 30. Love to God's word is one of the best preservatives from stumbling in the path of *faith* or of *duty.*

172 speak. Rather, "sing."

176 I have gone astray, etc. "Is there not something striking and, we had almost said, unexpected in the conclusion of this Psalm? To hear one who has throughout been expressing such holy and joyful aspirations for the salvation of his God, such fervent praises of His love, . . . that we seem to shrink back from the comparison with him, as if considering him almost on the verge of heaven, to hear this man . . . sinking himself to the lowest dust under the sense of the evil of his heart and his perpetual tendency to wander from his God, is indeed a most instructive lesson. It gives an accurate view of the conflict that must be sustained to the end in the believer's heart, and of the opposite graces which meet and flourish there" (*Bridges*).

The Songs of Degrees

This title (lit., "a Song of Goings-up." R.V., "a Song of Ascents"), is prefixed to fifteen Psalms (cxx.–cxxxiv.), which appear to have been composed at various periods by different authors.

Some suppose the term "songs of degrees" to refer to a peculiarity of structure observable in some of them; a phrase of one sentence being repeated in the next with some addition, so as to form a *progression*, or gradation, of thought and language. This is the view taken by Gesenius, Delitzsch and others. But this is found only in one or two of these Psalms.

The Jews say that it means "songs of the steps"; and that these Psalms were sung at the Feast of Tabernacles (at the time when the water was brought up from Siloam to be poured out on the Temple courts) either on the steps of the Temple or during the procession. According to Jewish writers, there were fifteen steps between the Court of the Women and the Court of Israel.

But it is more probable that the title refers to *going up* to Jerusalem, either on the return of the exiles from Babylon, or at the annual festivals. The frequent allusions to the exile (cxx. 5), and to the degradation (cxxii. 3, 4) and almost complete extinction of the nation (cxxiv. 1–5), and to their preservation and restoration (cxxvi., etc.), as well as the mingling of sadness with joy in these Psalms, suggest the supposition that they were first arranged in this manner for the solemn services described in Neh. viii. They may thus be called "Pilgrim Psalms," with a secondary but obvious application to the pilgrimage of life.

PSALM CXX

4 juniper. The "juniper" is the *retem*, a species of broom which grows largely in some districts in Palestine. Its roots are regarded by the Arabs as yielding the best charcoal. The verse may either describe the *enmity* of the slanderers, keen arrows and hot coals representing the cutting and irritating words of a malignant tongue (see Psa. lvii. 4; lxiv. 3; James iii. 6); or the *retribution* coming upon them (in answer to ver. 3), the phrase, like "sword and fire," intimating the punishments by which the guilty are exterminated. Perhaps both ideas are included.

5 Mesech. Mesech and Kedar, in the extreme north (east of Cilicia and later by the Black Sea) and south (in Arabia), are taken as typical of barbarous enemies.

7 I am [for] peace. Lit., "I am peace." This is my very nature.

PSALM CXXI

This was the "travelling Psalm" of Bishop Hannington, which he repeated every morning on his last journey on the way to Uganda.

1 the hills. This means, perhaps, the mountain-land of Judæa generally; and especially the height on which Jerusalem and the Temple stood. To this the Israelites were taught to look as the place where Jehovah displayed His grace to His people: see 1 Kings viii. 47–49; Dan. vi. 10.

From whence cometh my help. Or, "Whence shall my help come?" (R.V.) a question, expressive of the longing in the look; and answered in the next verse.

3 He will not, etc. Or, "May He not," etc. To this, ver. 4 is the affirmative response, "Lo! He shall not slumber," etc.

4 He that keepeth Israel. The frequent mention of *Israel* in these "Songs of Degrees" is characteristic of the restoration, when the people was ideally reconstituted, as in the days of David and Solomon.

5 thy shade. etc. Thy protector. This image would be well understood and felt in the East, where the beams of the sun are often more scorching than among ourselves.

8 thy going out and thy coming in. A common phrase for all the affairs and occupations of life: see Deut. xxviii. 6.

PSALM CXXII

2 shall stand. Rather, "are standing" (R.V.).

3 Jerusalem is builded, etc. Rather, "Jerusalem, thou that art built," etc.: see R.V.

unto the testimony of Israel. Or, "according to the precept for Israel" (that all the males were to go up three times a year): see Exod. xxiii. 17; Psa. lxxxi. 3–5. Luther has "zu predigen dem Volk Israel" ("to preach to the people of Israel"). The Prayer Book version is: "to testify unto Israel."

5 are set. Rather, "were set."

thrones of judgement. Jerusalem was the political as well as the religious metropolis.

9 thy good. That is, "the good of the *city*." The Psalmist would pray for, and strive to promote, its *civil* interests, because of his deep concern for its *religious* interests. A model for the Christian in relation to municipal life. The motto of Glasgow used to be, "Let Glasgow flourish by the preaching of the word."

PSALM CXXIII

2 as the eyes of servants, etc. In the East, orders are rarely given to an attendant in words, but commonly by signs. These are often so slight as to escape notice unless the eyes of the servant are kept fixed on the master or mistress. Just so (says the Psalmist) our expectations are *constantly* fixed upon Jehovah.

3 exceedingly filled with contempt. The scorn and hatred with which our well-to-do luxurious oppressors (4) regard us engross our thoughts and exclude all happiness from our lives.

PSALM CXXIV

This Psalm, in its metrical form,

"Now Israel may say,
And that truly,"

was often sung in times of persecution in Scotland. The most notable occasion was perhaps on the release of John Durie, a faithful minister who had been imprisoned. When he was set free in 1582 and entered Edinburgh, the people came out to meet him, and, to the number of two thousand, sang as they moved up the High Street, the 124th Psalm.

3 quick. That is, "alive": see Numb. xvi. 30, 33.

7 and we are escaped. Lit., "we—we are escaped"; the emphasis of grateful joy.

8 Our help, etc. Corresponding with cxxi. 2. The recurrence marks these Psalms as belonging to a series, probably referring to the same chain of events.

PSALM CXXV

2 As the mountains, etc. Jerusalem, seated on hills, is surrounded by hills still higher, which appear to inclose and shelter it, while "the distant line of Moab would always seem to rise as a wall against invaders from the remote East" (*Stanley*).

3 shall not rest. That is, "shall not always remain." "Shall not lie heavily" (*Perowne*). The God of the righteous will not suffer the power ("rod," or sceptre) of wickedness permanently to oppress them.

But peace, etc. Rather, "Peace be upon Israel": cp. Gal. vi. 16.

PSALM CXXVI

In this Psalm the grateful joy of the restored exiles (1–3) leads to the prayer of assured faith for the complete restoration of Israel (4–6). It was evidently written about the time of Ezra, and perhaps, as was anciently thought, by him.

1 turned again the captivity. Or, "brought back the returned ones," as R.V., marg.

2 The Lord hath done great things for them. The language of ancient prophecy (Joel ii. 21) here twice repeated, to give emphasis to the declaration of its fulfilment.

4 Turn again our captivity. Only a small part of the nation had as yet returned.

as the streams in the South. The word "Negeb," rendered "South," means *dry*, and is applied especially to the southern highlands of Palestine: see Josh. xv. 19. The land, deprived for a time of its inhabitants by the Captivity, and then replenished by the return of the exiles, is compared to the streams in the southern deserts, which dry up in the summer, but are filled again after the rains: see Job vi. 15.

6 He that goeth forth, etc. The word rendered "precious" should rather be "handful"; the verse literally reads, "Going he goeth and weepeth, bearing [his] handful of seed; coming he cometh with singing, bearing his sheaves."

PSALM CXXVII

1 Except the Lord, etc. "On the lintel of the door in many an old English house, we may still read the words *Nisi Dominus frustra*—the Latin version of the opening words of this psalm" (*Samuel Cox*). The same words are the motto of the city of Edinburgh.—**waketh.** Or, "keepeth awake."

2 so He giveth His beloved sleep. The rendering now generally accepted is, "He giveth to His beloved in their sleep." Those who cast their care upon Him repose in peace: while they are slumbering He is giving.

4 children of the youth. That is, sons born while their parents were still young, who, having grown up, will be able to protect their declining years.

5 But they shall speak with the enemies in the gate. Rather, "when they shall speak" they will confidently defend their father's rights against unjust litigation; the city gate being the place where the judges sat.

PSALM CXXVIII

1 Blessed. Or, "Happy"; as in the last verse of the preceding Psalm, which this carries on.

2 the labour. That is, the fruit of thy labour, as in Psa. cv. 44.

3 by the sides of thine house. Some translate, "*in* the inmost parts of thy house," cp. R.V. But "the sides of thy house" seems an appropriate reference to the vine. The Prayer Book version has "upon the walls of thy house."

olive plants. The young olive plants springing up (from the fallen fruit) round the aged tree were a familiar sight in Palestine.

5 thou shalt see the good of Jerusalem. National and family blessings would be closely associated.

6 [And] peace upon Israel. Rather, as a separate sentence, "Peace be upon Israel!" (R.V.) as cxxv. 5.

PSALM CXXIX

1 Many a time. Or, "Much."

from my youth. The Jewish nation is here *personified*, as in Psa. cxviii. 18; Jer. ii. 2; Hos. ii. 15. In its youth—the earliest period of its history—it was oppressed in Egypt.

3 plowed. With the scourge of slavery.

4 the cords. The bonds of slavery.

6 afore it groweth up. Or, "before it shoots forth," *i.e.*, rises to a stalk. On the flat roofs of Oriental houses, covered with a compost of mortar mixed with ashes or sand, grass often springs up in the rainy season; but quickly withers, yielding nothing useful: cp. Isa. xxxviii. 27.

8 say. That is, to the reapers and the gleaners (7): see Ruth ii. 4.

We bless you in the name of the Lord. "We wish you good luck in the name of the Lord" (*Prayer Book version*).

PSALM CXXX

This Psalm, often termed the *De Profundis*, from its opening words in the Vulgate, is one of the "Seven penitential Psalms."

4 But there is forgiveness, etc. Rather, "For there is," etc. It cannot be that Thou shouldest thus mark iniquities, for with Thee is forgiveness, in order that Thou mayest be reverenced.

6 they that watch for the morning. Perhaps referring to the Temple watchmen, who looked out for the dawn. The repetition expresses earnestness.

8 He. Emphatic, implying that none else can: cp. Matt. i. 21.

PSALM CXXXI

2 I have behaved . . . myself, etc. Rather, "I have calmed and hushed my soul, like a weaned child with his mother: like a weaned child with me is my soul"; *i.e.*, I have learned submission to Thy will: the quiet renunciation of what was sweetest in life, in the fond embrace of love.

3 Let Israel hope in the Lord. Repeated from the preceding Psalm, ver. 7.

PSALM CXXXII

1 remember David [and] all his afflictions. Rather, "Remember for David (*i.e.*, so as to fulfil the promise made to him) all his trouble."

6 Ephratah. The ancient name of Bethlehem, Gen. xxxv. 16, 19; xlviii. 7; Ruth iv. 11; Micah v. 2. But the ark never was in Bethlehem. Hence it has been supposed that "Ephratah" is the *district* where the ark was heard of and found. In this district it is further supposed that Kirjath-jearim was situated; the link of connexion being found in the family of Caleb, 1 Chron. ii. 50, 51. Some writers, however, from the resemblance between Ephratah and Ephraim (*Ephrathite* in 1 Sam. i. 1; 1 Kings xi. 26, meaning Ephraimite), less probably regard *Shiloh*, in Mount Ephraim, as the Ephrathite district where the ark was "heard" to be, it being subsequently removed to Kirjath-jearim. Yet another explanation, taking Ephratah as literally Bethlehem, is that the Psalmist in his younger days at home had heard of the ark: "at Ephratah we heard of it: at Kirjath-jearim we found it."

in the fields of the wood. Or, "in the lands of Jaar"; a poetical abbreviation of "Kirjath-jearim," which signifies *Town of the Woods*.

7 We will go into His tabernacles. Or, "Let us go," etc.

8 the ark of Thy strength. This is the only place in which the ark is mentioned in the Psalms.

9 Let Thy priests be clothed with righteousness. "The Psalmist prays that the symbol of the pure vestments may truly represent the inner reality" (*A. Maclaren*).

10 Thine anointed (one). David or his successors.

11 The Lord hath sworn, etc. See 2 Sam. vii. 12; xxiii. 3–5; Isa. lv. 3; Jer. xxxiii. 15, 25, 26.

13 Zion. The name appears to be used, in an extended sense, for the city of Jerusalem. The Temple-mountain was *Moriah.*

14 my rest for ever. My permanent resting-place, after all the changes of its locality (Bethel, Judges xx. 18 n., 26, 27; Mizpeh; Shiloh; Kirjath-jearim; the house of Obed-edom).

17 There will I make the horn, etc. Rather, "There will I make *a* horn to bud *for* David: I have prepared a lamp," etc. The "horn" is an emblem of power and glory (see Ezek. xxix. 21; Luke i. 69); and the "lamp," of joy and prosperity (see Psa. xviii. 28; 1 Kings xi. 36; xv. 4; 2 Chron. xxi. 7; Job xxix. 3).

PSALM CXXXIII

2 the skirts of his garments. Heb., "the mouth," or "the opening," *i.e.*, the edge or border, of the garment, which might be the upper border as well as the lower: the former, *i.e.*, the collar round the neck, is probably intended: see Exod. xxviii. 31, 32. "The Elder Brother is our common anointed High Priest. It is the bond of His priesthood which joins us together as brethren" (*Alfred Edersheim*).

3 As the dew of Hermon, [and as the dew] that descended, etc. Rather, as R.V., "Like the dew of Hermon that cometh down upon the mountains of Zion." The dew of the lofty Hermon is referred to as diffusing fertility through the lands which lay at its feet, even as far as the hills of Zion.

There the Lord commanded the blessing. Calvin points out that the same sentiment is expressed by St. Paul (2 Cor. xiii. 11; Phil. iv. 9), "Live in peace, and the God of peace shall be with you."

PSALM CXXXIV

1 by night. A nightly service in the sanctuary is intimated in 1 Chron. ix. 33.

3 Bless thee. A response that *individualises* each member of the dispersing company as they leave the temple courts.

PSALM CXXXV

6 Whatsoever the Lord pleased. Rather, "All that Jehovah willeth He hath done," etc.

7 vapours, etc. Cloud-masses ascending from the horizon.

lightnings for the rain. *i.e.*, to occasion the rain.

14 the Lord will judge His people. He will *do justice* with respect to them: see Deut. xxxii. 36.

PSALM CXXXVI

This Psalm is a companion to the preceding, and was probably composed at the same time. It differs, however, from Psa. cxxxv., in adding to each sentence or clause a response (borrowed from the ancient psalmody), probably designed to be sung in full chorus by the people. It uses many words and figures derived from the Books of Moses as well as from other Psalms. By some it is called the Great Hallel. Milton's version of it,

> "Let us with a gladsome mind
> Praise the Lord, for He is kind,"

was written when he was a student at Cambridge.

PSALM CXXXVII

1 the rivers of Babylon. Besides the Euphrates, there were in the *land* of Babylon the Tigris, the Chebar (Ezek. i. 1; iii. 15), and the Ulai (Dan. viii. 2), with their branches as well as canals.

2 harps. Instruments generally used on joyful occasions (Job xxx. 31; Psa. lvii. 8; xcii. 3). Hence to hang them up was a sign of grief.

3 they that wasted us. Perhaps, "our tormentors" or "plunderers."

5 Let my right hand forget! Our translators supply the words *her cunning*. The abrupt close of the original is in harmony with the strong excitement of the poet.

7 Remember, O Lord, the children of Edom etc. Rather, as R.V., "Remember, O Lord, against the children of Edom the day of Jerusalem." That is, the day of the great catastrophe of Jerusalem. The Edomites had expressed, in the most indecent and insulting manner, the joy they felt at the downfall of their rival: see Ezek. xxv. 12–14; Obad. 10–14, and the indignation against them is deeper because of their kindredship with Israel.

8 O daughter of Babylon. See note on Psa. xlv. 12.

who art to be destroyed. Or, "who art the destroyed"; for God has pronounced thy doom.

PSALM CXXXVIII

1 Before the gods. Heb., "In the presence of the gods."

2 Thy word. Here meaning particularly "Thy promise."

5 in the ways of the Lord. The words may be better rendered, "sing of the ways (or doings) of the Lord."

PSALM CXXXIX

2 afar off. The Prayer Book version has "long before."

3 Thou compassest, etc. Rather, "Thou winnowest" or "siftest."

5 laid Thine hand upon me, etc. Thou hast me completely in Thy power.

8 in hell. Rather, "in Sheol," the under-world.

9 the wings of the morning. Flying as quickly as the light of dawn shoots from the *east.* "The uttermost parts of the sea": the extreme *west.* "As far as the east is from the west," is the symbol of immeasurable distance.

13 Thou hast possessed my reins. Some render, "Thou hast formed," or "created."

15 My substance. Or, "My strength"; meaning probably the bones and sinews, as the strong framework of the body. The words "curiously wrought" refer to the art of embroidering (Exod. xxviii. 8), and beautifully depict the fine tissues and complicated texture of the human frame. "The lowest parts of the earth" are a figure for what is hidden or mysterious.

16 And in Thy book, etc. Or (as R.V. marg.), "And in Thy book they were all written: [even] the days that were ordained when [there was] not one of them," etc. All these days (their number and changes) were ordered and known by Thee.

17 How precious also are Thy thoughts, etc.! The Psalmist now turns to God's kind and watchful care of him ever since his birth; so that every morning brings fresh occasion to adore Him who knows and supplies all his wants (18).

18 When I awake. "He awakes from sleep, and is conscious of glad wonder to find that, like a tender mother by her slumbering child, God has been watching over him, and that all the blessed communion of past days abides as before" (*A. Maclaren*).

22 I count them mine enemies. Thy enemies must be mine.

24 any wicked way. "A good man desires to know the worst about himself" (*M. Henry*).

PSALM CXL

7 Thou hast covered my head in the day of battle. See 1 Sam. xvii. 45–51; 2 Sam. viii. 6.

9 Let the mischief of their own lips cover them. While my head (see ver. 7) is covered by the Divine protection, let the heads of those who attack me be covered with the consequences of their own calumnies.

PSALM CXLI.

2 set forth. Or, "established"; referring probably to the Divine appointment and the daily offering of this oblation: "So let my constant prayers, in conformity with Thine own appointment, be acceptable."

3 Set a watch, etc. "Nature having made my lips to be a door to my words, let grace keep that door, that no word may be suffered to go out which may any way tend to the dishonour of God or the hurt of others" (*Matthew Henry*).

5 Let the righteous, etc. This and the next two verses are peculiarly obscure.

my prayer also shall be in their calamities. The Prayer Book version has, "I will pray yet against their wickedness." Luther translates "denn ich bete stets, dass sie mir nicht Schaden thun" ("for I pray always that they may not do me harm").

8 leave not my soul destitute. Many render, "pour Thou not out my life"; *i.e.*, let me not die, R.V. marg.

PSALM CXLII

3 Thou knowest my path. Thou (emphatic) who knowest all, knowest all my difficulties, and the way of deliverance.

4 I looked on my right hand, etc. Rather, "Look on the right hand, and see; but none acknowledgeth me; refuge hath failed me," etc.: see R.V.

7 out of prison. A figurative representation of trouble and distress.

The righteous shall compass me about. Sympathising in the joy of my deliverance.

PSALM CXLIII

1 In Thy faithfulness, etc. God's "faithfulness" refers to His covenant engagements; His "righteousness," probably, to His vindication of those who are unjustly oppressed.

3 those that have been long dead. Who are no longer remembered or cared for.

10 the land of uprightness. Rather, "in a land of directness" or "evenness"; along a straight and plain path. So "let Thy Spirit, who is good, lead me," that I may find the path of obedience to "Thy will" plain and clear.

12 I am Thy servant. I hope for aid from Thee, as one who is engaged in Thy service.

PSALM CXLIV

This Psalm is composed chiefly of passages taken from various Psalms of David, especially viii. and xviii.

7 great waters. See note on Psa. xviii. 16.

strange children. Or, "of strangers"; as the same phrase is translated in Psa. xviii. 44, 45.

8 right hand of falsehood. That is, "of *perjury*"; the right hand being lifted up in taking an oath; and so in ver. 11.

9 Upon a psaltery and an instrument of ten strings, etc. Rather, "On a ten-stringed harp will I,'' etc.

12 That our sons, etc. A new theme seems here to be introduced. The R.V. renders, "When our sons," etc., understanding *when* at the beginning of vers. 13, 14, and making ver. 15 the conclusion of the passage.

grown up. Rather, "grown *large*," *i.e.*, *vigorous*. The blessings desired in vers. 12, 13 are those promised in Deut. xxviii. 4.

corner stones. Or, "corner *pillars*"; well suited to express female *beauty*; as the flourishing "plants" represent manly *strength*. "Daughters unite families as corner stones join walls together" (*C. H. Spurgeon*). The pillars also are *within* the house, in sheltered loveliness: the plants *outside* are exposed to the sunshine, the breezes, and the rain.

14 oxen strong to labour. The Hebrew means, rather, "burdened," *i.e.*, "heavy with young."

PSALM CXLV.

This is an alphabetical or acrostic Psalm (see note on title of Psa. xxv.).

1 I will extol. "Magnify" (Prayer Book version) or "exalt." The idea is that of adoration and praise.

5 I will speak. Rather, "I will meditate," or "rehearse [in song],'' a different word from *speak* in ver. 6.

7 abundantly utter. Lit., "pour forth," as from a fountain.

15 in due season. Rather, "in its season."

17 holy. Rather, "merciful" or "kind." Justice and mercy are united in Jehovah's government: cp. Psa. lxxxv. 10; Rom. iii. 26.

19 them that fear Him. Or, "that reverence Him."

PSALM CXLVI

This Psalm, and all that follow it, each beginning with *Hallelujah*, are evidently hymns of public praise, and appear to have been composed for the service of the second Temple. In the Septuagint this Psalm is ascribed to Haggai and Zechariah.

3 put not your trust in princes. The words used by Strafford when Charles I. signed his name to the bill of attainder.

4 his thoughts perish. Even with the best intentions, men are often unable to assist others, or are cut off in the midst of their efforts.

5 Blessed, etc. "The last of the twenty-five 'Blesseds' in the Psalter. Taken together, as any concordance will show, beginning with Psalm i, they present a beautiful and comprehensive ideal of the devout life" (*A. Maclaren*).

8 openeth the eyes of the blind. See Isa. xxxv. 5; Matt. ix. 30; xi. 5; John ix. 7–32.

9 turneth upside down. Rather, "turneth aside," or "thwarts."

PSALM CXLVII

See note at top of Psalm ix. above.

2 The Lord doth build up Jerusalem, etc. Rather, "The Lord is building up Jerusalem: He is gathering together the outcasts of Israel." A grateful acknowledgement of the present fulfilment of the promises in Isa. xi. 12; xliv. 26, 28; lvi. 3. It is possible that this Psalm and the others to the end of the Book were anthems composed for the dedication of the city walls restored under Nehemiah.

4 He telleth the number of the stars. It is a beautiful and precious thought that He who counts and names the stars is He who heals the broken-hearted (ver. 3).

10 the strength of the horse . . . the legs of a man. Describing *cavalry* and *infantry*, as forming the military strength of nations. It is not to those who trust in such resources that Jehovah shows favour, but to those who rely on His protection (11): cp. Isa. xxxi. 1. The care which He takes of those who trust in Him is illustrated in vers. 13, 14.

15 His word runneth very swiftly. The authoritative word of God is here personified as His messenger or agent, whose "swift running" signifies the prompt execution of His will.

17 ice. Probably the *hail.*

PSALM CXLVIII

The *Benedicite*, or apocryphal "Hymn of the Three Children," is based upon this Psalm. Cp. also Milton, *Paradise Lost*, Book V, 153–199, and Newman's hymn in *The Dream of Gerontius*, "Praise to the Holiest in the height."

6 for ever and ever. The immutability ascribed, in passages like this, to the works of Nature is not absolute, but relative to the will—the "decree"—of the Creator. No created powers can revoke the laws which He has imposed on their being.

7 dragons. Rather, "sea-monsters."

9 Fruitful trees. That is, "*fruit* trees"; in distinction from *forest* trees, which are represented by "cedars."

PSALM CXLIX

2 Him that made him. God made the Israelites a nation, formed for His praise; and on their deliverance from Babylon, by a kind of new creation, He restored them to their Temple to worship Him: cp. Isa. xliii. 1–7.

4 will beautify. The Prayer Book version has "and helpeth the meek-hearted."

5 in glory. Meaning either "gloriously," or, "on account of their present glorious state."

6 Let the high praises of God, etc. That is, uniting devotion with watchfulness and courage: see Neh. iv. 17–18.

7 vengeance upon the heathen ("nations," R.V.). Not their own vengeance, but that of God, to whom all "vengeance belongeth." This was partially fulfilled in the successes of the Jews under the Maccabees; and in a far nobler sense may be said to be realised in the spiritual triumphs of the servants of Christ, the weapons of whose warfare are not carnal (2 Cor. x. 4).

PSALM CL

A doxology which marks the end of the Fifth Book of Psalms and of the whole Psalter. It was probably intended to be sung with all the musical instruments used in the Temple worship.

1 His sanctuary. "His sanctuary" is His Temple on earth: "the firmament of His power" is the heavenly Temple. According to a Jewish tradition, this Psalm was sung by persons who came to present the first-fruits as an offering to God, while the Levites met them, singing Psa. xxx.

4 organs. Rather, "the pipe" (R.V.); denoting the whole class of *wind* instruments; the "timbrel," all of the pulsatile kind.

6 everything that hath breath. Lit., "the whole of breath"—all living beings. The Psalmist, in this concluding strain, thus passes beyond the bounds of Israel, and summons the whole animate and intelligent creation to praise Jehovah.

Praise ye the Lord ("Hallelujah"). "The Psalms," says Dr. Chalmers, "have their final and most appropriate outgoing in praise, that highest of all the exercises of godliness." "As the life of the faithful," says Hengstenberg, "and the history of the Church, so also the Psalter, with all its cries from the depths, runs out in a hallelujah." "The first Three Books of the Psalter," remarks Dr. Kay, "ended with *Amen and amen*, the firm expression of faith's reliance on God's truth. The Fourth Book ended, *Amen, hallelujah.* Now faith has been lost in joyful realisation: God's salvation has been completed: henceforth there is only the ever-during anthem, *Hallelujah.*"

THE BOOK OF PROVERBS

Divine Wisdom for Human Life

INTRODUCTION

As the Psalms are the great devotional book of humanity, so the Proverbs may be called its great practical book for daily life. It is a book for youth, with its warnings against youth's special temptations (i. 4, 10; ii. 16–19; iii. 14, 15; vii. 6–27; ix. 13–18; xv. 5, 20), a book for middle life of both men and women, with its exhortations to religion, fidelity, honesty, purity, diligence, temperance, patience, and kindness towards others (i. 19; ii. 9; iii. 5, 6, 9, 27, 28; vi. 6–11, 19, 29; x. 4, 12; xi. 1, 22; xii. 4; xiii. 11; xiv. 31; xvi. 32; xxii. 1, 4, 29;

xxiii. 29–32 ; xxiv. 29 ; xxv. 21, 22 ; xxviii. 27) ; a book for the family and the home, for parents and children (i. 8 ; iv. 1, 31 ; viii. 17 ; x. 5 ; xii. 4 ; xiii. 1 ; xiv. 1 ; xv. 17 ; xvii. 6 ; xix. 13, 14 ; xx. 11 ; xxi. 9, 19 ; xxii. 6 ; xxiii. 22–25 ; xxix. 15 ; xxxi. 10–31).

Its great message for our time, as for the times in which it was written, is that *religion is the highest wisdom.* "The fear of the Lord is the beginning of knowledge" (i. 7), "the beginning of wisdom" (ix. 10).

While it is evident from xxv. 1 that others besides Solomon had a share in the making of the Book as we have it, there is much to show that a great portion of it was his work, and that there are in it selections from the three thousand proverbs with which he is credited in 1 Kings iv. 32.

There are several quotations from Proverbs or allusions to it in the New Testament (cp., for instance, Luke xiv. 10 with Prov. xxv. 7 ; John iii. 13 with Prov. xxx. 4 ; Rom. xii. 20 with Prov. xxv. 21 ; Heb. xii. 5, 6 with Prov. iii. 11, 12 ; Heb. xii. 13 with Prov. iv. 26).

A most interesting connexion of Proverbs with Christian teaching, especially in St. John's Gospel, is noted by Dean Plumptre in his Introduction to Proverbs (*Speaker's Commentary*). He shows how Philo, in his desire to bring the teaching of the Law into harmony with the language of Plato, chose the word *Logos* (the Greek for "word") rather than *Sophia* (the Greek for "wisdom"), as the name of the creative Energy. This prepared the way for the teaching of St. John (cp. John i. 1, etc.), and thus "we may trace, in the highest aspects of Christian theology, the influence of the personified *Sophia* of the Proverbs." He also notices the emphasis which St. Paul lays on the fact that Christ Jesus was made our Wisdom (*Sophia*), and that He is "the Wisdom (*Sophia*) of God (1 Cor. i. 24, 30).

CHAPTER I

2 To know. That we may know, etc.

understanding. More precisely, "discrimination," the power of discerning between truth and falsehood, *intellectually ;* right and wrong, *morally.*

3 To receive the instruction of wisdom. Here the Hebrew word means *prudence* or circumspectness, "wise dealing," R.V.

justice. Rather, "righteousness," as R.V.

4 To give subtilty to the simple. Or, "To give wariness to the inexperienced";—to the young man who is liable to be led astray.

5 A wise man will hear. It is the part of wisdom to be willing to learn. It is the conceited who refuse to profit by the counsels of the more experienced.

wise counsels. From a word signifying to *steer :* maxims of conduct are like the helm of life. The word is used later on in a bad sense (xii. 5).

6 To understand a proverb, etc. Or, "To understand proverb and figure (R.V.), the words of wise men and their riddles" (lit., knotty sayings).

7 The fear of the Lord. This fear is not terror, but that affectionate reverence with which the children of God regard His law : hence the appropriateness of the language in ver. 8. And this spirit of reverence is the primary essential of true wisdom.

9 an ornament. "A chaplet," as R.V., or "garland."

11 Come with us. The picture is that of a robber-band, inviting the young and adventurous.

12 And whole. Lit., "and perfect"; probably meaning, while in full strength.

17 Surely. Rather, "For" (R.V.), as in the preceding verse. Another argument against association with the wicked. You would be more foolish than a bird, who never would fly into a net which he could plainly see !

18 And they lay wait. The "net" (17) ensnares those who lay it. See ver. 11, "Let us lay wait for blood." Yes ; but the blood is *their own !*

19 So are the ways, etc. That which is most strikingly illustrated in the case of violent robbery, is true in reference to all unjust gain. It ruins the life of those who seek it.

20 Wisdom crieth without, etc. This personification of wisdom (feminine) is here in plural form, as if to suggest its all-comprehending character and variety of application. In contrast with the *secret* enticement of the wicked, Wisdom is represented as *publicly* appealing to men. In the lack of books, oral teaching was largely employed in places of popular resort. The deeper application of these words to the Great Teacher has been noted by many expositors. He speaks of Himself as "the Wisdom of God" (Luke xi. 49, cp. with Matt. xxiii. 34).

22 simple ones . . . scorners . . . fools. If by these different terms different classes are intended, the first may denote the thoughtless, the second those who mock at religion, and the third the hardened enemies of truth and goodness : cp. Psa. i. 1.

23 I will pour out my spirit unto you. Or, "I will freely utter my mind to you."

24 stretched out my hand. Or, "beckoned." This is a gesture of entreaty : see Acts xii. 17 ; xxi. 40. The gracious call in vers. 22, 23 being disregarded by many, Wisdom appeals again, but in a sterner tone: cp. Psa. xviii. 25, 26.

26 I also will laugh, etc. Scorn for scorn. It is as if, in the self-inflicted ruin of the "fools," the appeals of Wisdom come back to the memory and conscience in tones of bitter mockery.

27 desolation. Or, "a storm" (R.V.); as in Ezek. xxxviii. 9.

28 They shall seek me early. That is, "earnestly," or "diligently," as R.V. "Early" in this connexion is literally "early *in the morning*": a symbol of activity and industry: cp. Psa. lxiii. 1.

32 the turning away. Or, "backsliding," as R.V.

the prosperity. Or, "careless ease," as R V. marg.; "security."

CHAPTER II

1 And hide. Or, "and lay up," as a valuable possession.

3 if thou criest after knowledge. This and the following metaphors represent an earnest and laborious search: cp. ver. 3 with Matt. vii. 7, and ver. 4 with the description of the miner's hardships and perils in Job xxviii., where also wisdom is defined as "the fear of Jehovah," and declared to be His gift. For the parallel to "hid treasure," see Matt. xiii. 44.

12 from the way of the evil man. Either "perverse," or "false things"; the sophisms of error, and the seductions of vice: and so in ver. 14.

16 the stranger. Though the term here translated "stranger" generally signifies a "foreigner," yet ver. 17 shows that the writer does not refer particularly to such persons, but to any one not a lawful wife.

17 the guide of her youth. Or, "the *companion* of her youth" (see Psa. lv. 13; the husband to whom in youth she had been united, with all the sanctions of religion, according to the ordinance, or "the covenant of her God."

18 inclineth. Or, "sinketh down."

19 Neither take they hold of the paths of life. Unchastity often shortens life. But there is here probably a further reference to its destructive effects upon the moral nature. As the dead return not to life, so the licentious are rarely restored to purity. For this sin, more rapidly and certainly than any other, pollutes the imagination, deadens moral sensibility, paralyses conscience, and destroys all that conviction might effectually fasten upon.

21 the upright shall dwell in the land. A long life in the land of Canaan was one of the chief earthly blessings promised to the faithful Israelite: see Exod. xx. 12. Hence it was used to represent the highest good, as in Matt. v. 5.

22 the earth. Rather, "the land," as in the previous verse.

CHAPTER III

2 long life. See note on ii. 21. The double expression, "length of days," and "long life" (lit., "years of life," as R.V.), may intimate not merely prolonged duration, but *life*, really so named, in its energy and joy; while "peace," the characteristic Bible blessing, crowns the series.

4 good understanding. Some render "good reputation" (see R.V. marg.); others, "good success": see Josh. i. 8; 1 Sam. xviii. 5.

5 unto. Rather, "upon," as one leans upon a staff.

8 It shall be health, etc. "Health for your body and fresh life to your frame" (*Moffatt*).

9 thy substance . . . thine increase. Thy *property* and thine *income*. Obeying the law of tithes and first-fruits: see Exod. xxiii. 19; Mal. iii. 8–10.

10 presses. Rather, "vats" (see R.V.).

11 chastening. The same word as "instruction," i. 2.

13 getteth. Lit., "draweth forth" (as R.V. marg.), *i.e.*, from the Divine store.

14 merchandise. Cp. the imagery in ii. 4—the search as in the mine or the field: here, the quest by means of commerce.

17 ways . . . paths. Alike the broad open roads and the sequestered by-ways.

18 a tree of life. This no doubt alludes to the tree of life in Paradise (Gen. ii. 9; iii. 22), as an emblem of constant and durable happiness, which has been forfeited by sin, but may still be regained by heavenly wisdom.

20 the depths are broken up. Or, "By His knowledge were the abysses cleft"; probably referring to the preparation of the ocean-depths for the reception of the waters: see Gen. i. 9, 10; vii. 11; Job xxxviii. 8–11.

21 Let not them depart from thine eyes. *i.e.*, wisdom and discretion.

25 Be not afraid. Or, "Thou needest not be afraid."

the desolation of the wicked. The sudden and overwhelming judgement in which the wicked shall be taken.

27 them to whom it is due. Lit., "its owners." Kindness is *due* from one man to another, and cannot be withheld without violating the law of God.

29 securely. Or, "trustingly"; not expecting harm from you.

31 Envy thou not, etc. Even when his wrongdoing appears to succeed, for God abhors him (32).

32 His secret. That is, "His confidential friendship."

34 He scorneth the scorners. Or, "Scorners He treats scornfully"; *i.e.*, He will make their punishment correspond with their sin: see i. 24–31. The Greek version of this verse is quoted in James iv. 6; 1 Pet. v. 5.

CHAPTER IV

3 only beloved. That is, beloved *like* an only child.

8 Exalt her, etc. All the love and honour paid to wisdom will be abundantly repaid with honour and dignity.

9 an ornament. Rather, "a chaplet," as i. 9.

12 goest . . . runnest. A climax. Running increases the danger.

17 they eat the bread of wickedness. Their enjoyments are unlawfully procured.

18 the shining light. "The light of dawn" (R.V. marg.). "Como la luz de la aurora" (*Spanish version*).

the perfect day. The noontide.

23 with all diligence. Lit., "more than all keeping"; *i.e.*, keep it with the greatest possible care.

25 Let thine eyes look right on. That is, avoid all crooked and tortuous policy.

CHAPTER V

2 that thy lips may keep knowledge. So as to retain wisdom as well as to impart it to others.

3 drop as a honeycomb. Rather, "drop honey," as R.V.

4 her end. The destruction in which she involves her victims with herself.

5 hell. Heb., "Sheol": see notes on Deut. xxxii. 22; Job xi. 8.

6 Lest thou shouldest ponder, etc. Or, "She is far from treading the way of life; her paths waver."

8 come not nigh the door of her house. Those who would avoid sin must keep as far as possible from the haunts of sinners.

9 thine honour. Either, "thy comeliness," as in Dan. x. 8; or "thy vigour." Some apply the passage to the extortions practised by the confederates of unchaste women. But we may understand the whole as referring to the ruinous effects of vice, entailing disease, poverty, and remorse.

12 How, etc.! Astonishment at his own conduct, but too late!

14 I was almost in all evil. This probably means, I was well nigh brought to the extreme of evil; alluding to the public trial and punishment of his sin; see Lev. xx. 10; Ezek. xvi. 40; John viii. 5.

15 Drink waters out of thine own cistern, etc. The previous warnings against impurity are not to be understood as an injunction to celibacy or asceticism.

16 Let thy fountains, etc. Some render this verse as a remonstrance against conjugal infidelity: "Shall thy fountains be dispersed abroad?" etc. (R.V.).

19 the loving hind and pleasant roe. The figure is now changed for one which the Orientals often use for a gentle and elegant woman. Hence the name *Tabitha* or *Dorcas*, *i.e.*, gazelle.

21 before the eyes of the Lord. A warning specially needed in reference to sins which are from their nature *secret*.

22 he shall be holden with the cords of his sins. Like a wild beast caught in the toils of the hunter. It is true of all sins, but most strikingly so of sensual lusts, that they enslave and punish the man who indulges them.

CHAPTER VI

1 thy friend. Rather, "thy neighbour," as in iii. 28, 29. In very early times suretyship was practised, and was entered into by striking or joining hands. It brought the surety's person and property into all the liabilities of the man for whom he bound himself. Cp. Gen. xliv. 32, 33; Job xvii. 3. Such engagements were, therefore, commonly very imprudent.

2 Thou art snared, etc. Rather, "If thou art snared with the words of thy mouth; if thou art taken," etc.

3 When thou art come, etc. Rather, "Since thou hast come into the power of thy neighbour, go, prostrate thyself, and urge thy neighbour"; *i.e.*, seek to be released from the engagement.

6 Go to the ant, etc. The ants in labouring for a common object exhibit a provident industry which men rarely display except under the guidance and oversight of a ruling mind (ver. 7).

11 as one that travelleth. Probably, "like a highwayman," unexpectedly.

16 These six things, etc. Such enumerations as this are not uncommon in Arabian and Persian writings, and are found in Prov. xxx. and other places in the Bible. They are intended to show some point of resemblance between certain well-known things and the subject in hand, which is commonly mentioned last, as the climax. Here the sin of *sowing discord* by words or signs is said to be as hateful to Jehovah as all the six other sins which He had emphatically denounced.

22 it shall lead thee. That is, "the commandment," "the law" (20), will be to thee a guide, a protector, and a companion.

31 he shall restore sevenfold. That is, he shall make *full* restitution, though he may thereby be deprived of all that he has.

32 But whoso committeth adultery, etc. The argument appears to be this: The thief, driven by hunger to steal, is regarded with pity rather than contempt, and yet for the protection of society is compelled to "restore sevenfold": how much more, then, shall the adulterer be despised, as one who "lacketh understanding," and visited for his crime, which admits no reparation.

35 ransom. That is, compensation. No "gifts" will be accepted as an equivalent for the injury he has suffered.

CHAPTER VII

3 Bind them upon thy fingers. As an amulet, or a precious ring, on which some memento is engraved.

4 Say unto wisdom, etc. Cultivate the most endearing intimacy with her.

6 I looked through my casement. Rather, "lattice": see Judges v. 28. This lifelike narrative or parable, affords to the young and inexperienced an impressive warning against the dangers which beset the loiterer or the pleasure-seeker.

11 stubborn. Moffatt translates "restless and restive."

14 I have peace offerings with me. Or, "upon me"; *i.e.*, peace offerings were due from me, and I have just paid my vows by offering them. I have therefore come out to find some one to partake of them with me. See note on Lev. iii. 1. This description strikingly exhibits the woman's character—her levity and falsehood, with her shameless impiety in making her pretended religious observances a prelude to sin.

16 carved works. Rather, "striped [coverings]."

19 goodman. In Hebrew simply "the man," meaning, of course, "my husband."

20 a bag of money. Provision for a long absence.

at the day appointed. Or, as R.V., "at the full moon."

26 many strong men have been slain by her. Rather, "and mighty [hosts] are all her slain." Her victims are not only many, but mighty; not only wounded, but slain outright. Then, how can the young and inexperienced hope to escape?

CHAPTER VIII

2 in the top of high places, etc. Rather, "At the top of high places by the way; at the meeting of paths, she takes her stand"; like a herald making proclamations; not like the temptress, in secret.

6 excellent. Or, "princely"; upright, straightforward, and open, without duplicity.

8 froward. Lit., "twisted" or "crooked," as R.V.

10 and not silver. That is, rather than silver: see Job xxviii. 15–19.

12 witty inventions. Or, "skilful plans." All that tends to the due ordering of life is, so to speak, the discovery of Wisdom.

17 those that seek me early, etc. Or, "diligently." This promise is the counterpart of the threatening in i. 28, where see note.

20 lead. Rather, "walk."

21 That I may cause, etc. Or, "I have wherewith to enrich those that love me."

22 possessed me. Rather, "got" or "produced me (see Gen. iv. 1), as the beginning of His way."

26 the highest part. Heb., "the head"; meaning probably the "*first clod* of the earth" (the "beginning," R.V.).

27 set a compass. Or, "drew a circle"; alluding to the curved appearance of the boundary of the sea or of the arch of heaven.

28 When He established, etc. Or, "When He fixed the clouds on high": see Gen. i. 6, 7, and note; Job xxvi. 8.

29 When He gave to the sea his decree, etc. Rather, "When He put to the sea its limit, so that the waters should not pass its shore."

30 as one brought up with Him. Some render, "as an architect," or "a master-workman" (R.V.). But perhaps the best meaning is *a foster-child;* cp. Numb. xi. 12; Isa. xlix. 23; lx. 4.

rejoicing always before Him. The personality of the Creator is here strikingly shown. The creation is not soulless development of nature.

36 love death. They court destruction: see i. 29–32.

CHAPTER IX

1 her seven pillars. "Seven" was the number of completeness or perfection: see Rev. i. 4, and cp. James iii. 17. As the beloved daughter of the Universal King, Wisdom builds her royal pavilion (1), provides a magnificent banquet, and publicly invites all who are inclined to partake of it (2–5): cp. Matt. xxii. 2, 3; Luke xiv. 16, 17.

2 she hath mingled her wine. Either flavouring it with spices, or diluting it with water.

3 she crieth. By means of her messengers.

6 Forsake the foolish. Or, "Leave off [your folly], ye simple ones."

shame. Or, "reproach"; *i.e.,* shameful and insulting treatment; so that wisdom is necessary to teach us when and to whom reproof should be given.

10 the knowledge of the holy. Rather, "of the Moss Holy" ("the Holy One," R.V.).

12 thou shalt be wise for thyself. That is, the advantage will be thine own.

thou alone shalt bear it. Neither personal responsibility nor the penalties of transgression can be shifted on others: see Ezek. xviii. 1–22.

13 A foolish woman, etc. Some translators read "Folly," an abstraction personified, in contrast with Wisdom (R.V. marg.).

16 Whoso is simple, etc. Imitating the language of religion (see ver. 4); as the tempter has done in every age.

17 Stolen waters are sweet. This proverb has peculiar force in Eastern countries, where water is often scarce and dear.

18 But he knoweth not that the dead are there. The "Rephaim" (the dead) and "Sheol," are, as it were, in the background of the tempting scene: and the sudden transition from sin's delights to its punishment makes this closing warning most forcible.

CHAPTER X

The Proverbs of Solomon

Here begins the more ancient collection of *Proverbs* or *Maxims,* properly so called, which extends to xxii. 16. For the most part, these proverbs are disconnected; but occasionally there is an evident train of thought uniting two or more in a series. The language of the proverbs is very concise, and marked by certain peculiarities. Every proverb consists of two parts, containing commonly, in the Hebrew, from three to five words each; and it has a meaning complete in itself. The requisite point and vividness are obtained by a parallelism either of *correspondence* or of *antithesis.* All these proverbs have reference to the standard of religious and moral duty, as it existed among the Israelites in their best times; so that their contents fully confirm the title which attributes them to the "wise king."

3 He casteth away the substances of the wicked. Or, "disappointeth the cravings of the wicked."

6 violence covereth the mouth, etc. Moffatt renders: "the bad man's face shall be darkened with disaster."

9 shall be known. *i.e.,* Shall be detected and exposed.

10 He that winketh with the eye. A sign may be an instrument of mischief. See vi. 13.

But a prating fool shall fall. According to some ancient versions, this second clause reads, "But he that rebuketh openly maketh peace," the contrast being between the covert sneer and the faithful reproof.

11 Violence covereth the mouth of the wicked. See note on ver. 6.

12 Love covereth all sins. Love to others, instead of publishing their sins, casts a veil over them: see 1 Pet. iv. 8.

13 But a rod, etc. His mischievous talk can be restrained only by severity.

15 The rich man's wealth is his strong city. Helps to ward off many evils which the poor cannot avert, and therefore suffer doubly. This is one side of the truth; another is given in xviii. 11.

16 The fruit of the wicked. Rather, "revenue," or "gain."

18 He that hideth hatred, etc. Rather, "He that hideth hatred is of lying lips"; *i.e.,* is a liar. Hatred concealed is deceit, hatred outspoken is folly.

19 In the multitude of words, etc. Cp. Eccles. v. 1–7.

24 The fear of the wicked. That is, what he fears.

25 As the whirlwind. Or, "When the whirlwind," etc. (R.V.). He is swept away by the storm: cp. Matt. vii. 24–27.

28 gladness. That is, shall be fulfilled to his joy.

29 The way of the Lord, etc. Rather, "A bulwark to the upright [man is] the way of the Eternal: but [it is] destruction to the workers of iniquity": cp. Hosea xiv. 9.

30 the earth. Or, "the land."

31 bringeth forth, etc. Or (as R.V. marg.), "buddeth with," as a blossoming shrub. The "froward tongue," on the other hand, is compared to one that shall be "cut down."

32 know what is acceptable. *i.e.,* have opportune words always ready.

CHAPTER XI

3 transgressors. The word here and elsewhere so rendered, means more precisely, "the treacherous" (R.V.); so ver. 6, etc.

4 in the day of wrath. That is, in the day of the wrath of God; see Ezek. vii. 19; Rom. ii. 5.

8 cometh in his stead. That is, he falls into the

troubles from which the good man is delivered: see Esther vii. 9, 10; Dan. vi. 23, 24.

12 He that is void of wisdom despiseth his neighbour. Rather, "He that despiseth his neighbour is void of wisdom," R.V. The man who treats others with disrespect disgraces himself. On the contrary, a "man of understanding" keeps his opinion of others to himself, not setting himself up as a censor; Matt. vii. 1.

14 counsel. Or, "wise guidance" (R.V.).

18 The wicked worketh a deceitful work. Or, "The wicked obtaineth a delusive gain; but he that soweth righteousness [obtaineth] a real reward." In the Hebrew there is an emphatic alliteration.

21 [Though] hand [join] in hand. Lit., "Hand to hand." This may be simply a strong assertion, as if to say, "assuredly."

26 blessing. That is, benedictions of the people. In times of scarcity some men hoarded corn, in order to obtain exorbitant profit. This has not been unheard of in modern times.

29 He that troubleth his own house, etc. The first clause probably refers to the niggardly and exacting, the latter to the careless and mismanaging. Both are impoverished.

30 he that winneth souls is wise. Rather, "he that is wise winneth souls" (R.V.).

31 recompensed. Rather, "requited"; *i.e.,* even the righteous, if he sins, shall be chastised; much more shall the wilful and habitual sinner. This sense is supported by the free rendering in the Septuagint version, which is quoted in 1 Pet. iv. 18.

CHAPTER XII

1 instruction. See note on i. 2.

4 a crown. A garland of beauty and gladness.

rottenness in his bones. Destroying all comfort, and wasting health and life.

11 vain [persons]. Or perhaps, "vain *things*," as R.V. marg.

12 The wicked desireth the net of evil men. Or, "vice proves a net for vicious men" (*Moffatt*).

14 the recompense of a man's hands, etc. Every man's words and deeds shall bring back to himself good or evil.

16 a prudent man covereth shame. That is, he suppresses his feelings under shameful treatment. This is put in contrast to the conduct of the indiscreet man in the preceding clause.

17 He that speaketh truth, etc. That is, a true witness aids justice.

23 A prudent man concealeth knowledge. "No cautious man blurts out all he knows" (*Moffatt*). Another of those proverbs which dwell on the advantages of silence.

24 tribute. Or, "taskwork," as R.V. Slothfulness leads to the forfeiting of independence.

26 The righteous is more excellent than his neighbour. Rather, "The righteous showeth the way to his neighbour"; "is a guide to his neighbour," R.V.

27 the substance of a diligent man is precious. Or, "There is valuable wealth for the diligent man" (*Prof. S. H. Hooke*).

CHAPTER XIII

3 he that openeth wide his lips. That is, he that speaks inconsiderately.

5 a wicked man is loathsome, and cometh to shame. Or, "the wicked man acts foully and disgracefully." R.V. marg., "causeth shame and bringeth reproach."

7 maketh himself rich. Or, "pretendeth that he is rich." Outward appearances often deceive, because men try to conceal their real condition.

8 rebuke. "Accusation" or "threat." The rich are more exposed than the poor to such troubles.

9 rejoiceth. That is, "shineth cheerfully."

10 Only by pride cometh contention. Rather, as R.V., "By pride cometh only contention."

11 Wealth gotten by vanity shall be diminished, etc. *i.e.,* wealth won in haste or folly.

12 when the desire cometh. That is, "cometh to pass," is fulfilled.

13 the word. The "word" here is the same as "the law of the wise" in ver. 14.

15 the way of transgressors is hard. Rather, "the way of treacherous men is rough": see R.V. Crafty dealings draw down resentment on a man, and so make his path difficult.

16 dealeth with knowledge. *i.e.,* acts with deliberation.

19 The desire accomplished, etc. The gratification of a man's desire is sweet to him; and [therefore] fools cannot bear to depart from the evil on which their minds are set.

20 shall be destroyed. Or, "shall smart for it," R.V., as xi. 15.

23 for want of judgement. That is, justice. The poor, by honest industry, often attain competence, whilst the unjust come to ruin.

24 He that spareth his rod. That is, refrains from due correction. This is illustrated in God's dealings with His children (Heb. xii. 6–8).

CHAPTER XIV

1 Every wise woman. Rather, "wisdom." "The foolish" is in Heb. literally "folly."

2 He that walketh, etc. True piety produces correct behaviour.

3 a rod of pride. His proud speeches bring their own punishment.

4 Where no oxen are, etc. Useful labour of every sort has its inconvenient and unpleasant side, but to forgo the work for this reason would be folly.

7 Go from the presence, etc. That is, Thou mayest go from the presence of such a person, "and thou hast not perceived lips of knowledge"; *i.e.,* thou hast found that he hath none to give.

8 deceit. Aiming to deceive others, they are deceived themselves.

9 Fools make a mock at sin. Some render this, "Guilt mocketh fools" (R.V. marg.), deceiving and ruining them; but the verse is not very clear.

13 the end of that mirth. Rather, "of mirth itself." Beneath apparent joy, grief may be concealed; and earthly joy surely ends in the grief of disappointment.

14 The backslider in heart. Or, "He whose heart is turned [from God]."

16 the fool rageth, and is confident. Or, "But the fool is haughty and confident."

17 soon angry. The Septuagint reading gives better sense for the second part of the verse: "a prudent man will be patient" (*Moffatt*) or "a man of thought endures" (*Hooke*).

21 happy is he. Or, "Blessed be he"! This verse seems intended as a counterpart to the statement in ver. 20.

22 Do not they err? That is, "Do not they wander"? like drunken men, who miss their way and hurt themselves.

23 In all labour, etc. Working without talking may make men rich; but talking without working will make men poor.

24 The crown of the wise, etc. Better (with the Septuagint), "The crown of the wise is their wisdom; the chaplet of fools is their folly."

25 delivereth souls. That is, persons endangered by false accusation. The second clause of the verse may be read as in R.V., "He that uttereth lies *causeth* deceit."

28 In the multitude of people. This being commonly a mark of good government: see 1 Kings iv. 20.

29 exalteth folly. "The height of folly is to be quick-tempered" (*Moffatt*).

30 A sound heart. Either, "A healthy heart," or, "A quiet heart." Bodily health is greatly promoted by spiritual health—by the self-control, contentment, and peace which religion gives.

31 he that honoureth Him, etc. Rather, as R.V., "He that hath mercy on the needy honoureth Him."

32 in his death. Better "in his integrity" (*Septuagint*).

33 But that which is in the midst of fools, etc. Rather, "But in the midst of fools it is made known." The contrast seems to be between those who have a fund of unspoken wisdom, and those who utter all the little they have.

35 that causeth shame. Or, "that acteth disgracefully."

CHAPTER XV

4 A wholesome tongue. The same word is applied to the heart in xiv. 30, where see note.

a breach in the spirit. Rather, "a wound in the spirit."

7 [doeth] not so. "Does not understand."

8 The sacrifice of the wicked, etc. The costliest offering from one who is leading a wicked life is hateful to God; while the *prayer* of the good man, though he may have no sacrifice to offer, is acceptable to Him.

10 Correction is grievous, etc. Rather, as R.V., "There is grievous correction for him who forsaketh the way."

11 Hell and destruction. Heb., "Sheol and Abaddon"; the under-world and the abyss: see Job xxvi. 6 and note, and Rev. ix. 11.

15 the afflicted. In contrast to him "that is of a merry (cheerful) heart." A gloomy disposition rather than outward affliction, seems therefore meant.

19 is made plain. Rather, "is banked up" as a high-road. The slothful finds hindrances where the honest worker finds helps.

21 walketh uprightly. Or, "goeth straight forward."

24 to the wise, etc. Or, "The path of life [leads] upward for the wise," towards life and happiness: in opposition to the way of sin, which leads downward to destruction (Sheol).

25 will establish the border of the widow. "Establishing the border," means protecting the property or interests.

26 [the words of] the pure are pleasant words. Or, "But pleasant (*i.e.*, kindly) words are pure (in the sight of God)": see R.V.

27 gifts. That is, as bribes.

30 The light of the eyes. "As the light of the eyes (the pleasure derived through the eyes or, perhaps, 'sunshine') rejoiceth the heart; so do good tidings make the bones fat."

31 the reproof of life. "Reproof of [his] life," *i.e.*, of his conduct.

32 instruction. Rather, "discipline," and so in the next verse: see on i. 2.

33 the instruction (discipline) of wisdom. That is, that which leads to wisdom.

before honour is humility. "Humility is the way to honour" (*Moffatt*).

CHAPTER XVI

1 The preparations of the heart in man, etc. Rather (as R.V.), "To man [belong] the preparations of the heart; but from Jehovah [is] the answer of the tongue," or, "A man may think what he will say, but at the moment the word comes to him from the Eternal" (*Moffatt*).

4 The Lord hath made all things for Himself. More literally, "God has made everything for its (or his) correspondency"; *i.e.*, so that one thing answers to, or corresponds with, another. Thus, "even the wicked [corresponds] to the day of evil"; *i.e.*, by Divine arrangement the punishment is not only *connected with*, but is *adapted to*, the sin.

5 Though hand join in hand. See note on xi 21.

6 purged. Or, "expiated"; *i.e.*, forgiven: see Dan. iv. 27; Matt. xxiii. 23. A warning to those who misused Divinely-appointed sacrifices, supposing that these might exonerate the offerer from personal holiness: see Jas. ii. 14–26.

11 All the weights of the bag. Just weights are said to be the work of the Eternal, because He has prescribed them, and has condemned all fraud in respect of them (see Lev. xix. 36), and in respect of all our dealings with others.

12 an abomination. These proverbs (12, 13) suppose the king to be what he should be, but too often is not.

15 as a cloud of the latter rain. That is, producing joy and prosperity: see Deut. xi. 14.

19 to divide the spoil. Implying victory, with the consequent exultation.

20 He that handleth a matter wisely. Or, "He who giveth heed to the word (*i.e.*, the word of God) shall find good," or, success.

21 the sweetness of the lips, etc. He who is wise will gain respect; but if he should also impart his wisdom pleasantly, he will be a more efficient teacher.

22 the instruction of fools, etc. Or, "the correction of fools is *their* folly" (R.V.); *i.e.*, their folly is its own punishment.

26 He that laboureth laboureth for himself. Or, "The soul of a working man worketh for him"; *i.e.*, his own appetite urges him to work to satisfy his hunger: see Eccles. vi. 7.

27 An ungodly man. Heb., "a man of Belial," *i.e.*, a worthless or mischievous man. He digs a pit for others to fall into, and his words are destructive as fire.

31 [If] it be found, etc. Rather, "In the way of righteousness, it is found"; *i.e.* a venerable old age is one of the rewards of righteousness.

32 the mighty. That is, the warrior or hero.

than he that taketh a city. Self-conquest is the greatest of victories. "Self-reverence, self-knowledge, self-control, These three alone lead life to sovereign power" (*Tennyson*).

33 the whole disposing thereof. Rather, "all the decision of it."

CHAPTER XVII

1 a house full of sacrifices. A house full of good provision: see vii. 14; Lev. iii. 1.

2 A wise servant. The "servant" here is the slave: cp. the history of Ziba, 2 Sam. xvi.

5 reproacheth his Maker. Who has placed him in poverty: see xiv. 31.

8 of him that hath it. Of him who has it *to give,* and counts upon its power to secure favour. In the latter part of the verse there is an allusion to the sparkling of a cut jewel whichever way it is turned.

9 he that repeateth a matter. Rather, as R.V., "he that harpeth on a matter alienateth his friend." What is here meant is not breach of confidence, but that insisting upon old offences which will not "let bygones be bygones."

11 An evil man seeketh only rebellion. Or, "A rebel (Heb., 'rebellion') seeketh only evil."

16 Wherefore is there a price, etc.? Rather, "Why is this price in a fool's hand? Is it to get wisdom?" etc. Wisdom cannot be purchased at any price when the capacity for it is wanting.

17 And a brother is born for adversity. Or, "but he is born a brother for adversity"; *i.e.,* a true friend becomes a *brother* (bound in still closer ties) in adversity.

18 in the presence of his friend. Not, *for* his friend; but with his friend (or "neighbour," as R.V.) as a witness. Referring to suretyship.

19 he that exalteth his gate. In the East, the gate being the only external part of a house on which decoration is bestowed, and even this being usually small, a lofty and handsome gate is a mark of pride and ostentation. A figurative expression for pride.

22 doeth good like a medicine. Or, "makes a good cure": see notes on iii. 8; and xiv. 30.

drieth the bosom. "Saps vitality" (*Moffatt*).

23 a gift out of the bosom. That is, a secret gift (see xxi. 14), to bribe the judge or the witnesses. Money and other things of value were often carried in the folded bosom of the robe.

24 Wisdom is before him, etc. Wisdom is close at hand to the intelligent, but the fool seeks it in vain at the greatest distance (see xix. 6).

26 to strike princes for equity. Perhaps "to smite the noble is against justice" (*Hooke*).

27 a man of understanding is of an excellent spirit. Rather (as R.V.), "And he who is of a cool spirit (not easily excited) is a man of understanding."

CHAPTER XVIII

1 Through desire, a man, etc. The verse may better be rendered, "A man separating himself for his desire, seeketh it; with all counsel he quarrelleth"; *i.e.,* the man who selfishly pursues his own desires and interests, acts at variance with the best advice: cp. R.V.

2 But that his heart may discover itself. Or, "But rather [hath delight] in his heart revealing itself." His vanity leads him to self-display.

3 When the wicked cometh, etc. Wickedness is followed by contempt, baseness by shame: see xi. 2.

4 The words of a man's mouth, etc. Men's words are often obscure, but true wisdom is clear and bright.

8 as wounds. This may be rendered either, "like dainty morsels" (R.V.); meaning that slanderous whispers are dangerous, because they are eagerly listened to.

9 a great waster. Or, "squanderer." Laziness and waste are brothers; and both lead to ruin.

10 is safe. Heb., "is set on high," beyond his enemies' reach.

11 his strong city. This verse derives additional force from contrast with the foregoing. The righteous man wisely makes God his refuge and trust: the rich man looks for safety to his wealth.

12 before honour. To be humble is the way to honour. R.V., "before honour *goeth* humility": see xv. 33.

14 will sustain his infirmity. That is, of body. The best comment on this verse is that of Cowper

"No woes like those a wounded spirit feels;
No cure for such till God, who makes them, heals."

15 The heart getteth . . . the ear . . . seeketh. By the inlet of the senses is *perception;* by the reflection of the heart (the mind) this becomes, in the true sense, *knowledge.*

16 A man's gift, etc. See xvii. 8, 23, and notes; and Gen. xxxii. 20.

17 He that is first in his own cause, etc. A warning against *ex parte* decisions. He who states his case first seems right; but the other party will test his assertions and arguments.

19 A brother offended [is harder to be won], etc. Or, simply, "A brother is more obstinate than a strong city." Family quarrels are hard to appease There are, however, other renderings of the text, which is by no means clear.

20 the fruit of his mouth. His words. So in the next clause: "the increase of his lips." These will be food (or poison) to his life; cp. Matt. xv. 11.

21 they that love it. They who indulge and give it license: cp. vers. 20, 21 with Matt. xv. 11.

22 Whoso findeth a wife. There is no reference here (as there is in xix. 14) to a wife's *goodness.* It seems, therefore, that this passage speaks of the marriage relation, in itself considered, as an ordinance and blessing of the Lord: see Gen. ii. 18, etc., and note.

24 A man [that hath] friends, etc. Rather, "A man of [many] associates will ruin himself"; "He that maketh many friends *doeth it* to his own destruction," R.V. But there is a true and valuable friendship; and its bonds are closer than those of the nearest relationship.

CHAPTER XIX

2 that the soul, etc. This may be rendered, "Also in thoughtlessness of soul is no good, and the hasty of feet goeth astray"; condemning rashness of feeling and action.

3 his heart fretteth against the Lord. Men often murmur against God as the author of evils which their own folly has brought upon them.

6 will intreat the favour. Lit., "will stroke the cheeks."

the prince. Or, "the liberal man," as R.V.

7 brethren . . . friends. The contrast is between the relatives and the mere acquaintances of the poor man.

He pursueth them with words, etc. Perhaps, "He follows their promises. They are gone!" But the passage is obscure.

10 Delight. Or, "luxury" (R.V., "delicate living"). It is unseemly for a man to affect a mode of life for which he is naturally unfitted.

11 it is his glory to pass over a transgression. This sentiment is beautifully enforced by our Lord in Matt. v. 38–44.

13 contentious. Nagging.

14 And. Rather, "But." Fathers may bestow material comforts, but a prudent wife must be sought as the gift of God: see xviii. 22.

16 he that despiseth. Or, "is careless of his ways," R.V.; is reckless in his behaviour.

17 will He pay him again. That is, the Eternal will repay him, treating the interests of the poor as if they were His own. So our Lord pledges Himself to reward the smallest service rendered to the humblest of His disciples (Matt. x. 42; xxv. 40).

18 let not thy soul spare for his crying. Rather, "set not thy heart on his destruction" (R.V.); *i.e.*, do not cause his ruin by failing to inflict punishment: see xxiii. 13, 14.

20 in thy latter end. Lit., "in thy after life."

21 Nevertheless. Rather, as R.V., "But." The contrast is between the Divine "counsel," one and unchanging, and the "many" various "devices" or plans of men

22 The desire of a man is his kindness, etc. Or, "The charm of a man is kindness." But perhaps the best rendering of a difficult text is, as R.V., "The desire of a man is *the measure of* his kindness; and a poor man" (who can only give kindness) "is better than a man of deceit" (who fails to do what he professes).

23 And he [that hath it], etc. Lit., "Satisfied, one spendeth the night, not visited by evil." A beautiful picture of rest in the Lord.

24 A slothful man hideth his hand in his bosom. More properly, "The slothful man hideth his hand in the dish": alluding to the Oriental manner of eating: see Matt. xxvi. 23. This is a sarcastic description of lazy habits: cp. R.V.

25 Smite a scorner, etc. Although the hardened sinner may not himself be reclaimed by punishment, others may take warning and amend; but reproof alone is sufficient for those who are well disposed.

26 He that wasteth his father, etc. Rather, "A son who causeth shame and reproach, wasteth his father and chaseth away his mother."

28 An ungodly witness. Heb., "A witness of Belial"; *i.e.*, worthless.

CHAPTER XX

1 whosoever is deceived thereby. Or, "erreth thereby." "Quiconque en fait excès n'est pas sage" ("whoever goes to excess with it is not wise") (*French version*). Wine not only leads to boisterous insolence, but has led even good men (such as Noah and Lot) into folly and sin: see Gen. ix. 21; xix. 33; also Dan. v. 4; Hos. vii. 5; Hab. ii. 5.

2 sinneth against his own soul. Endangers his life.

3 meddling. Rather, "quarrelsome"; the same word as in xvii. 14; xviii. 1.

4 by reason of the cold. Lit., "because of the winter" (November-December); when the weather breaks, and the rains set in.

5 Counsel in the heart of man. Or, "a purpose in a man's heart."

6 goodness. Rather, "kindness." The second part of the verse intimates "that with much promise there may be little performance."

8 Scattereth away. Or, "winnoweth out"; *i.e.*, discovers and removes.

9 Who can say, etc.? This humiliating inquiry has a response in Eccles. vii. 20, and 1 John i. 8–10

10 Divers weights, and divers measures. Heb., "A stone and a stone, an ephah and an ephah." One set to sell with, and another to buy with, for the purpose of fraud.

12 The Lord hath made even both of them. He can therefore hear and see all things, and takes account of our use of the faculties which He has given: see Psa. xciv. 9.

13 Open thine eyes. Be watchful and diligent.

16 for a strange woman. Or, according to the present Hebrew text, "for strangers." The R.V. reads, "hold him in pledge that is surety for strangers."

17 Bread of deceit. Food gained unlawfully.

18 with good advice. Or, "by wise guidance." The injunction corresponds with that in Luke xiv. 31.

19 that flattereth with his lips. Rather, "him that openeth wide his lips" (R.V.); *i.e.*, a gossiping person.

22 shall save. Rather, "shall help": see Rom. xii. 19.

25 who devoureth that which is holy. Rather, "who rashly uttereth holy words": cp. R.V. The proverb refers to solemn promises hastily made.

26 A wise king, etc. Rather, "A wise king winnoweth the wicked, and turneth on them the wheel" (of his threshing-wain). As, in threshing, the wheel separates the grain from the straw, so a wise king will distinguish between the righteous and the wicked.

27 the candle (lamp) of the Lord. As a lamp is intended to light the inmost chambers of a house, so the conscious soul of man is designed by God to enlighten his whole nature.

28 Mercy and truth preserve the king. By securing the respect and love of the people, and bringing down the blessing of God.

30 The blueness of a wound, etc. Or, "Strokes of a wound (stripes that wound, R.V.) are a cleansing evil; and stripes [reach] the inward parts of the body."

CHAPTER XXI

1 as the rivers of water. "Watercourses," R.V. The complete control which God exercises even over men in the highest stations is illustrated from irrigation by means of small canals or watercourses, into or from which the cultivator turns the water at his pleasure: see note on Deut. xi. 10.

2 pondereth. *i.e.*, "weigheth," as R.V.

3 more acceptable to the Lord than sacrifice. This declaration has "a special significance as coming from the king who had been the builder of the Temple, and had offered sacrifices that "could not be told nor numbered for magnitude" (1 Kings viii. 5) (*Plumptre*).

4 the plowing of the wicked. Rather, as in the ancient versions and R.V., "The lamp of the wicked (either their prosperity or their delight) is sin."

5 of every one that is hasty. Eager haste is here opposed to steady industry. Cp. the German *Ohne Hast, ohne Rast*, "Unhasting, unresting," and the similar Latin proverb, *Festina lente*, with the English, "More haste, worse speed." The French version has for "hasty," *étourdi* ("stupid").

6 a vanity tossed to and fro of them that seek death. Or, adopting another reading (R.V.), "They *that seek them* seek death"; *i.e.*, such treasures quickly disappear, and ruin those who acquired them.

7 The robbery of the wicked. Rather, as R.V., "The violence of the wicked."

8 The way of man is froward, etc. Or, "Crooked is the way of a sin-burdened man; but the pure, his work is straight."

9 in a corner of the housetop. See note on Deut. xxii. 8.

a wide house. Rather, "a family-house." The Hebrew is literally "a house in common."

12 The righteous [man], etc. Both clauses refer to the same person, the "righteous one" who is probably "the Righteous God." He "wisely observeth the house of the wicked, [and] overturneth wicked men to ruin."

15 It is joy to the just to do judgement, etc. Rather, "The doing of justice is joy to the righteous; but it is destruction to the workers of iniquity": cp. Luke xxi. 28.

16 the dead. Heb., "the Rephaim": see ii. 18, and note; also ix. 18; Psa. lxxxviii. 10; Isa. xiv. 9.

18 a ransom. Cp. xi. 8. A similar thought is contained in Isa. xliii. 3. Jewish writers illustrate the sentiment by the exchange of places between Haman and Mordecai; Esther vii. 10.

20 There is treasure to be desired, etc. Rather, "There is precious treasure and oil in the dwelling of the wise; but a foolish man squanders it."

24 Proud and haughty scorner, etc. This may be rendered, "As for the proud and haughty man, scoffer is his name; he acteth with excess of presumption."

25 The desire of the slothful, etc. His desire for ease keeps him from working, and so brings him to want.

27 abomination. See note on xv. 8. The former clause is general; the second refers to the special impiety of an attempt to sanctify or to cover some wicked design by ritual observances.

28 speaketh constantly. Or, "shall speak for ever." The French version interprets this of a man who is faithful to his oath: "qui écoute son serment." The Vulgate (Latin version) has: "vir obediens loquetur victoriam."

29 he directeth his way. The wicked man is obstinate, the righteous man is circumspect.

CHAPTER XXII

1 A [good] name. Lit., "a name"; "good" or "honourable" being implied. This verse is inscribed on the cupola which lights the Manchester Exchange.

loving favour. That is, the goodwill of others.

4 By humility, etc. Rather, "The reward of humility and the fear of Jehovah is," etc. (R.V.), as in Psa. xix. 11.

6 Train up a child, etc. Or, "Initiate a child according to his way"; *i.e.*, begin with him according to his capacity and disposition. In other words, train him suitably. "Old" here is not merely *grown-up*, but *aged.*

7 the borrower is servant to the lender. He is obliged to consult his creditor's will and convenience. This is a warning against contracting debts.

8 vanity. Rather, "calamity," as R.V.

10 Cast out the scorner. "If in a company, a circle of friends, a society, a man is found who treats religious questions without respect, moral questions in a frivolous way, serious things jestingly, and in his scornful spirit, his passion for criticism, his love of anecdote, places himself above the duty of showing reverence, veneration and respect, there will arise ceaseless contentions and conflicts. Such a man one ought to chase away" (*Delitzsch*).

11 He that loveth, etc. He who unites integrity with courtesy, will be loved and trusted by his sovereign.

12 preserve knowledge. The meaning is (as R.V.), "preserve *him that hath* knowledge."

of the transgressor. Or, "of the treacherous man" (R.V.).

13 saith, There is a lion without. Imagining difficulties, and inventing ridiculous excuses for his negligence.

14 He that is abhorred of the Lord. Or, "with whom the Eternal is angry": cp. Josh. xi. 20, and 1 Sam. ii. 25. It is a sign of God's righteous anger, when He abandons the sinner to his own lusts.

The Words of the Wise

Ver. 17—XXIV. 34. The verses from 17 to 21 form an introduction to the Third main division of this Book. The "proverbs" in this part are, in general, somewhat longer than in the Second division; some of them extending over several verses. As the word "wise" is in the plural, both here and in xxiv. 23, it appears that the proverbs which followed were collected from different sages.

18 They shall withal be fitted, etc. Or, "[if] they be established together upon thy lips"; *i.e.,* if the convictions of the heart find firm and decided utterance.

20 Have not I written to thee, etc.? The present Heb. text reads, "Have not I written to thee heretofore, concerning counsel and knowledge?"

21 That I might make thee know, etc. Or, "To teach thee truth, even words of faithfulness; that thou mayest carry back faithful words to those who send thee"; *i.e.,* perhaps to those who send thee *to be instructed.*

22 in the gate. That is, by legal process; the law being administered "in the gate": see note on Gen. xxii. 17.

23 And spoil the soul, etc. Or, "and despoil of life" (R.V.) those that spoil them. The poor may appear to be friendless, but they have the Eternal for their protector: cp. xxiii. 10, 11.

25 get a snare to thy soul. That is, lest thou become like him, and so involve thyself in difficulties.

27 Why should he take away thy bed? See notes on vi. 1; xx. 16; and Exod. xxii. 26, 27.

28 Remove not the ancient landmark. See Deut. xix. 14, and note.

29 shall stand before kings. As their servant or minister. Steady and persevering industry is the true pathway to success.

CHAPTER XXIII

1 what is before thee. Some versions render, "*who* is before thee"; *i.e.*, in whose presence thou art. But the A.V. may be quite correct.

4 Cease from thine own wisdom. Do not believe the suggestions of worldly prudence, that wealth is a certain means of attaining happiness.

6 of him that hath an evil eye. Both the French and the German versions, following the Septuagint and the Vulgate, understand "the evil eye" to refer to an envious man. Moffatt has "niggardly."

7 as he thinketh in his heart. The meaning seems to be that as the man is in heart so he will really prove himself to his guest.

11 their redeemer. Or, "their avenging kinsman (*Goel*)": see Numb. xxxv. 12; Job xix. 25, and notes. Cp. also xxii. 22, 23; Psa. lxviii. 5.

13 he shall not die. He shall be saved from those evil courses which lead to premature death: see next verse.

14 hell. Heb., "Sheol," the under-world. Thou shalt save him from dying before his time, and in his sins.

16 my reins. The very depths of my being; see Psa. lxxiii., note.

18 an end. Or, "an hereafter." The expectation of a blessed eternity may well reconcile us to any temporal self-denial for which the service of God may call.

23 Buy the truth, and sell it not. Spare no pains or cost to obtain and to keep it.

28 as [for] a prey. Or, "as a robber," R.V.

transgressors. Heb., "the treacherous": perhaps "the seducers."

29 woe . . . sorrow. Heb., *oh . . . aho.*

babbling. Rather, "anxiety."

redness. Or, "dimness." Bloodshot eyes.

31 his (its) colour, etc. Or, "when it gleams in the cup, [and] goes down rightly," *i.e.,* smoothly and pleasantly: see R.V.

33 behold strange women. Or, "look upon." Drunkenness leads to lust, as well as to filthy and foolish language.

34 that lieth down in the midst of the sea. The drunkard, giddy and reeling like a rolling vessel, and exposed to imminent danger, of which he is unconscious (34), yet reckons himself happy in his insensibility, and determines again to drown all thought and feeling as soon as he awakes from his stupor (35). A striking picture of the physical, mental, and moral evils of drunkenness.

CHAPTER XXIV

5 A wise man is strong, etc. Very similar is our maxim, "Knowledge is power": see Eccles. ix. 14–16.

7 in the gate. The place of deliberation and judgement, where wisdom is most important.

9 The thought of foolishness, etc. Perhaps the meaning is, that the very *purpose* of evil is sinful in the sight of God; but the bold and insolent transgressor is also odious to man.

10 small. Or, "straitened." Alarm and despondency destroy the strength which is needed to bear adversity.

11 If thou forbear to deliver, etc. Rather, "Deliver those who are dragged forth to death; and those who are tottering to the slaughter, oh, keep thou back!" cp. R.V. The reference is to the custom of making proclamations before a prisoner, when he was led forth to execution, that any person able to prove his innocence should come forward and do so.

14 So [shall] the knowledge, etc. Rather, "So learn thou wisdom for thy soul."

16 falleth seven times, and riseth up again. This evidently refers to falling, not into sin (which the Hebrew word never means), but into trouble or suffering.

19 Fret not thyself, etc. This is almost word for word the same as Psa. xxxvii. 1.

20 no reward. In contrast with ver. 14, xxiii. 18.

21 fear thou the Lord and the king. See xvi. 10.

them that are given to change. Heb., "changers"; men who foster irreligion and rebellion.

22 the ruin of them both. Intimating the suddenness and mystery of the destruction of the impious and the disloyal.

23 These things also belong to the wise. Or, "These [words] also [belong] to the wise." A new section in this part of the Book: see note on xxii. 17.

25 to them that rebuke him. That is, that rebuke the wicked (see ver. 24).

26 [Every man] shall kiss his lips, etc. Rather, "He that giveth right words kisseth the lips." Such words are as pleasant as the welcome of a friend: see R.V.

28 without cause. Latin (Vulgate): *frustra.* The case is not precisely that of *false,* but of *unnecessary* adverse testimony, due, not to a regard for truth, but to private malice, and so having the nature of falsehood or deceit.

29 Say not, etc. This verse forbids retaliation, and anticipates the Sermon on the Mount.

30 the field of the slothful. The narrative has an evident spiritual application. "The field and the vineyard are more than the man's earthly possessions. His neglect brings barrenness or desolation to the garden of the soul" (*Plumptre*).

34 So shall thy poverty come, etc. See note on vi. 11.

CHAPTERS XXV–XXIX

Second Book of Solomonic Proverbs

These "Proverbs of Solomon" form the Third Part of the Book. The "men of Hezekiah" were undoubtedly scribes appointed by that monarch, who copied out the proverbs which follow, probably selecting them from others with which they had been connected in oral tradition. Hezekiah, in addition to his other reforms, appears to have aimed to complete and preserve as much of God's Word as had then been written (see 2 Chron. xxxi. 21), probably availing himself of the aid of the prophets of his time.

CHAPTER XXV

2 It is the glory of God, etc. It is the prerogative of Him who is Supreme and Infinite to conceal the reasons of His conduct. An earthly king may have his state secrets (3): but his judicial decisions should be pronounced only after full and public inquiry.

3 unsearchable. That is, they are all alike unsearchable.

4 the finer. Rather, "the founder," as in Judges xvii. 4: or "the silversmith." As silver cannot be made into vessels fit for use or ornament unless the dross be removed; so a king cannot be a blessing to his people unless all bad counsellors are removed from his presence (5).

6 Put not forth thyself, etc. "Put not thyself forward," etc. "Ne fais point le magnifique devant le roi" ("Do not swagger before the king") (*French version*).

8 Lest [thou know not] what to do. Or "what will you do in the end thereof?" Hasty litigation involves men in unexpected difficulties; and in the heat of contention they will sometimes betray confidence (9); which is sure to prejudice their cause with the cool and impartial (10). Compare with ver. 9 our Lord's words in Matt. xviii. 15.

11 pictures of silver. Or, "picture-work of silver"; referring to silver filigree basket.

13 the cold of snow in the time of harvest. Snow from Lebanon was used for cooling drinks in hot weather like iced water.

14 a false gift. That is, one who promises much, and performs nothing.

15 By long forbearing, etc. The power of *patience* and *gentleness.*

16 so much. That is, *only* so much. This teaches moderation in things which are agreeable.

18 a maul. A club, a sledge-hammer.

20 taketh away. Rather, "taketh off," as R.V.

22 thou shalt heap coals of fire, etc. The reference is to the melting of metals by covering them with charcoal, and means that kindness will melt the hard heart in self-accusing penitence: cp. Matt. v. 43, 44; Rom. xii. 20.

23 The north wind driveth away rain, etc. Rather, "The north (*i.e.*, north-west) wind bringeth forth rain"; see R.V. So Plumptre, Moffatt, and others.

26 falling down before the wicked. This perhaps means "cringing" or "vacillating" in his conduct through fear (cp. R.V.). He is as unfit to be useful to others as a fountain, at which the traveller hoped to quench his thirst, when it is trampled upon and polluted.

27 So [for men] to search, etc. The words "is not" are supplied by our translators. Perhaps the best rendering is, "But the pursuit of what is honourable (or, "difficult") to one is an honour."

CHAPTER XXVI

1 rain in harvest. Between the "latter" and the "early rains," *i.e.*, from March to October, rain is an unusual and unseasonable phenomenon: cp. 1 Sam. xii. 17.

a fool. Dr. R. F. Horton (*Expositor's Bible*) points out that there are three Hebrew words, all rendered by the one English expression, fool or folly. One signifies weakness, another depravity, and the third, which is the one uniformly used in this chapter, suggests grossness, a dull and heavy habit. The word "fool" here means, he thinks, "the senseless man."

2 So the curse causeless shall not come. A curse unmerited, like these wandering birds, shall not *settle*—shall not take effect; "lighteth not," R.V.

3 a bridle for the ass. The ass, in the East, is often quite as spirited an animal as the horse.

4 Answer not a fool, etc. Vers. 4, 5 may mean that a smart answer, though generally undesirable, may sometimes be useful. But it is more probable that the phrase "according to" has a different meaning in the two clauses; signifying in the former *similitude*, so as to be like him, and in the latter *fitness*, so as to rebuke him. Proverbs often present two sides of the same truth in apparently contradictory forms.

6 He that sendeth, etc. He fails in his purpose, and suffers injury.

7 are not equal. Rather, "hang loose" (R.V.); *i.e.*, have no force or utility.

8 As he that bindeth a stone in a sling. This is the most ancient rendering of the words; and it means that he makes no better use of it than a slinger would of a stone bound or fastened to his sling.

9 As a thorn goeth up, etc. Or, "As a thorn-stick (*i.e.*, a cudgel) goes up in the hand of a drunken man"; *i.e.*, is lifted up by him. This means that it is used injuriously to himself and others.

10 The great [God] that formed all [things], etc. The word "God" is not in the original. The verse is difficult. Moffatt renders, "An able man does everything himself; a fool hires the first passer-by."

15 The slothful, etc. See note on xix. 24, a similar proverb.

17 He that passeth by, etc. Lit., "He who is excited by a quarrel that is not his, seizeth the ears of a dog passing by (a stray dog)." His hands are full for the time, and when he lets go he will probably be bitten.

19 Am not I in sport? Deceit in sport is always dangerous, often fatal.

21 As coals are to burning coals. Or, "as charcoal [added] to hot embers," etc.

22 wounds. See note on xviii. 8.

23 Burning (or **fervent**) **lips and a wicked heart,** etc. Glowing expressions of love and regard, if joined with a malevolent mind, are like potsherds silvered over with dross: cp. x. 20.

25 seven abominations. That is, a multitude of evil thoughts.

28 A lying tongue, etc. A man hates those whom he has injured.

CHAPTER XXVII

4 envy. Rather, "jealousy": cp. vi. 34, 35.

5 secret love. Which never shows itself in faithful words (even of rebuke) or helpful acts: "love that is hidden," R.V.

6 deceitful. Or, "profuse" (R.V.); *i.e.*, in order to deceive: see 2 Sam. xx. 9, 10; Matt. xxvi. 49. Luther's translation is forcible: "das Küssen des Hassers (the kiss of an enemy) ist ein Gewäsche," *i.e.*, "nonsense" or "humbug."

8 that wandereth from her nest. Unsettled and exposed.

13 And take a pledge of him, etc. Rather, "And hold him in pledge [*i.e.*, as surety]."

14 It shall be counted a curse to him. Loud and eager professions are regarded as insincere, and taken as a curse rather than a blessing. There may be a suggestion of the harm done to the person so praised: "When others speak of us above what is meet, we are apt to think of ourselves above what is meet" (*M. Henry*).

15 A continual dropping. See xix. 13.

16 Whosoever hideth her hideth the wind. Or, "He who restraineth her restraineth the wind, and his right hand cometh upon oil": *i.e.*, she is as subtle as wind, as slippery as oil.

20 Hell and destruction. "Sheol and Abaddon." So R.V.

21 So is a man to his praise. Some render this, "So [let] a man [be] to the mouth that praiseth him"; *i.e.*, let him carefully test all the praise that he receives, that he may not be misled by flattery.

22 Though thou shouldest bray (pound) a fool in a mortar, etc. A reference to the most searching and effective process known for separating the wheat from the chaff, or the fine flour from the husk. No amount of "grinding" will get rid of the ingrained folly.

23 Be thou diligent, etc. Vers. 23–27, which together form one ode of eleven lines, encourage careful attention to daily duties, having reference particularly to agricultural pursuits.

25 The hay appeareth, etc. Rather, "When the

hay passes away (*i.e.*, has been gathered in), and the aftergrowth appears."

26 the price of the field. Perhaps to repay the price of the land already purchased, or to buy more.

27 for thy food, etc. Goat's milk is a chief article of food in the East.

CHAPTER XXVIII

2 The transgression of a land. Better, "rebellion." "A revolt against a ruler leads to rapid changes of dynasty" (*Plumptre*).

the state [thereof] shall be prolonged. More literally, "order" or "stability shall long continue."

4 praise the wicked. A sign of conscience dulled by sin (cp. Rom. i. 32).

5 understand not judgement. Their moral sense is deadened; whilst that of the godly is alive to "all" that is right and good: cp. 1 John ii. 20.

6 perverse in his ways. Rather, "perverse in double dealing."

8 He that by usury, etc. Or, "He that by usury and gain increaseth his wealth, gathereth it for him," etc. In spite of the laws in Lev. xxv. 35, Deut. xxiii., a ruinous rate of interest was often exacted of their brethren by Hebrew money-lenders. This gain would eventually go into the hands of those who would use it better.

10 the upright shall have good things in possession. Rather, "the perfect shall inherit good," R.V.

12 When righteous men do rejoice. Rather, "When the righteous triumph, there is much splendour; but when the wicked rise, men will (must) be searched for"; *i.e.*, hide themselves, or their wealth, for fear of injustice.

13 shall not prosper. No concealment can hide sin from Him who alone gives prosperity: cp. Psa. xxxii. 3–5; 1 John i. 8, 9.

14 Happy is the man that feareth alway. A sensitive, tender conscience is necessary to happiness and to safety. As penitent confession precedes (13), so godly fear always accompanies the enjoyment of pardon.

17 A man that doeth violence, etc. Rather, "A man burdened with the blood," etc. He cannot escape, nor can any avert, his doom.

18 Whoso walketh uprightly, etc. Or, "He that walketh blamelessly shall be delivered; but he that is perverse in double ways shall fall in one (of them)."

20 A faithful man. One who fulfils his obligations; which he who hastens to be rich often disregards, and "shall not be unpunished" (R.V.): cp. 1 Tim. vi. 10.

21 for a piece of bread, etc. A man who takes bribes will come at last to violate his conscience for the most trifling advantage.

22 He that hasteth to be rich hath an evil eye. Rather, as R.V., "He that hath an evil eye hasteth to be rich": cp. Matt. vi. 22, 23. The envious or selfish man is alluded to.

23 He that rebuketh a man afterwards, etc. Rather, as R.V., "He that rebuketh a man shall afterwards find more favour," etc.

24 the companion of a destroyer. That is, of the deliberate villain, who is prepared for any crime: cp. Matt. xv. 4–6.

25 a proud heart. Rather, "a greedy spirit," as R.V. The contrast is between an insatiate ambition for ever leading to collisions and quarrels with others, and peaceful, contented trust in God.

27 he that hideth his eyes. Who turns them away from the wants of others.

CHAPTER XXIX

1 hardeneth his neck. Like a stubborn and refractory animal.

2 When the righteous are in authority. Rather, as R.V., "are increased," in numbers, wealth, or power.

4 he that receiveth gifts. Or, "a man of gifts," *i.e.*, one who exacts bribes. His injustice causes discontent, and his example is pernicious.

7 regardeth not to know [it]. "Does not trouble to know it." Want of sympathy prevents even his understanding it.

8 Scornful men bring a city into a snare. Rather, "Scoffers kindle a city into a flame"; *i.e.*, excite discords: see R.V.

9 Whether he rage or laugh. Or, as R.V. marg., "He (the fool) rageth and laugheth, and there is no rest"; so that he cannot be reasoned with. With such a man argument is useless.

10 the just (upright) seek his soul. "The upright seek to preserve his life."

11 his mind. Heb., "his spirit": probably meaning anger, as R.V. "But a wise man keepeth it back and stilleth it."

12 are wicked. They will seek his favour by flatteries, and will follow his example.

13 the deceitful man. Probably, "the oppressor," as R.V.: cp. xxii. 2. God makes His sun to rise upon both: see Matt. v. 45.

16 shall see. Rather, "shall look upon," as R.V., implying some degree of satisfaction.

17 delight. Very expressive in the Hebrew, where the word is plural, "delights"; joys in great number and rich variety.

18 the people perish. Or, "become disorderly": see note on Exod. xxxii. 25. "Vision" means inspired vision or revelation.

19 A servant will not be corrected by words. That is, by words *only*. "He will not answer," *i.e.*, will not yield responsive obedience.

20 more hope of a fool. Because the hasty word evinces either a self-confidence which will not brook the suggestions of others, or a superficial habit of mind which forms conclusions without weighing the reasons.

21 Shall have him become his son. *i.e.*, he will presume upon his master's kindness, and take undue freedoms. Too great indulgence is sure to be abused.

22 aboundeth in transgression. A passionate man will be led to commit almost any crime.

23 But honour shall uphold the humble in spirit. Rather, "But the humble in spirit shall obtain honour": cp. xv. 33; Matt. xxiii. 12: see R.V.

24 cursing. Or, "the curse"; the adjuration pronounced not only against the thief himself, but against those who do not tell what they know of his crime: see Lev. v. 1, and cp. Judges xvii. 2. The accomplice of the thief "hateth his own soul," *i.e.*, is cruel to *himself*, aggravating his fault and danger by concealment.

26 But [every] man's judgement, etc. More literally, "But a man's judgement," etc. (R.V.). "God, the Supreme Ruler, allots the destinies of men most justly and equitably; with Him one obtains the desired judgement more certainly than with any human ruler whatsoever: cp. xvi. 33" (*Zöckler*).

27 an abomination. There is more than disapproval; there is antipathy.

CHAPTER XXX

THE WORDS OF AGUR AND LEMUEL

This and the next chapter form the Fifth Part of the Book, and contain the teaching of sages otherwise unknown. It is believed by some that Agur was a public teacher, and that Ithiel and Ucal were two of his disciples. Agur means "Collector," and the names of the disciples may be symbolical—Ithiel, "God is with me," and Ucal, "I am able."

Some critics, however, make slight changes in the Hebrew points, and render the verse thus: "The words of Agur, the son of her who was obeyed in Massa. Thus spake the man: I have toiled for God (*i.e.*, to comprehend God), I have toiled for God, and have ceased. For I am" (2), etc.

1 the prophecy. Or, "oracle," R.V. The Hebrew word for the oracle or "burden" of a Divine message is *massa :* see note above.

spake. The word elsewhere applied to Divine communications is here used; see Gen. xxii. 16; Psa. cx. 1.

more brutish. Or, "stupid." Agur speaks thus humbly of his own acquisitions, in contrast with the "word of God" (5).

3 the holy. Either, "the Most Holy"; or, "holy things."

5 pure. Or, "tried" (R.V.); or, Heb., "purified."

6 Add thou not. The "purity" just mentioned cannot be sullied by human admixture.

8 food convenient for me. Lit., "the bread of my portion," as in Gen. xlvii. 22; or, "my due," Lev. x. 13, 14; *i.e.*, what is sufficient for me. "Nourris-moi du pain de mon ordinaire" ("Feed me with bread for my ordinary use") (*French version*).

9 take the name of my God in vain. Heb., "handle the name of my God"; *i.e.*, profane it. Wealth often produces self-sufficiency, and thus leads to forgetfulness of God; while poverty frequently leads to dishonesty and impious murmuring against Him.

11 a generation. Or, "class of men." This and the three following verses point out four hateful vices prevalent in Agur's day: filial ingratitude, hypocrisy, pride, and oppression or extortion.

15 The horseleech. This and the next verse may be an illustration of the insatiableness of the oppressors just mentioned. The word *crying* is not in the Hebrew, and the sense is probably that of R.V. marg., "The horseleech hath two daughters [called] Give, Give." The horseleech haunts the Syrian lakes in countless millions, and was often taken as a personification of rapacious greed.

16 The grave. Heb., "Sheol."

17 The eye that mocketh at his father, etc. By the law of Moses, an obstinately disobedient son was to be punished with death.

that is heir to her mistress. One who supplants her mistress in the affections of her husband.

25 prepare their meat (food). Cp. vi. 7, 8, and note. Ants are called "a people," as if in reference to their organised action. So locusts, Joel ii. 2.

26 conies. Rather, "rock-badgers" (*Hyrax Syriacus*): see note on Lev. xi. 5; cp. Psa. civ. 18.

28 The spider. Or, "the lizard" (R.V.). The Hebrew word is one that is only used here.

29 which go well. Or, "which are stately in their march; yea, four which are stately in going" (R.V.).

31 A greyhound. Lit., "compressed of loins": an epithet which some apply to the war-horse; others (particularly the ancient versions) to the cock; others to the greyhound; and others to a human warrior girt for fight.

a he-goat. The large Oriental he-goats at the head of a flock march along with much stateliness.

a king, against whom, etc. Or, "when his army is with him" (R.V., marg.).

33 Surely the churning, etc. Rather, "For the pressing of milk brings forth cheese, and the pressing of the nose brings forth blood; so the pressing of anger brings forth strife." Therefore (see preceding verse), do not open your mouth when you are angry, for otherwise strife will follow: see xvii. 14.

CHAPTER XXXI

Lemuel. Who Lemuel was is unknown. In the A.V., "prophecy" again stands for "oracle" (*massa*) (R.V.). But some render the passage thus: "Lemuel, king of Massa" (see note on xxx. 1), and suppose him to be the brother of Agur.

1 taught him. Or, "that he learned."

2 What, my son? etc. That is, "What shall I say unto thee?" These are the passionate exclamations of a mother addressed to a beloved son, for whom she had prayed and vowed (see 1 Sam. i. 11), and for whose future welfare she is most anxious. The name Lemuel means "(devoted) to God."

3 to that which destroyeth kings. Some render, "to those (fem.) that destroy kings"; *i.e.*, the numerous women of the royal harem.

6 Give strong drink, etc. Regarding it not as a luxury, but a remedy.

8 In the cause of, etc. Or, "For the cause of the bereaved."

THE PERFECT WIFE

VERS. 10–31. This is a perfect alphabetical poem, probably by a different writer from the foregoing, and an entirely different section; delineating the excellencies of a Hebrew matron. It is interesting also as exhibiting the domestic customs of that age, and the elevated social position of woman among the Hebrews, as compared with that which she held among other ancient nations, or with that which she enjoys among Eastern people to-day.

10 a virtuous woman. Heb., "woman of strength"; *i.e.*, moral power and excellence.

rubies. Rather, "pearls": see Job xxviii. 18.

11 no need of spoil. Rather, "no lack of gain," *or* "treasure": see R.V.

13 And worketh willingly with her hands. Women of rank among the Greeks and Romans, as well as among the Hebrews, were engaged in such industries; by which they not only supplied their own households with clothing, but also obtained other commodities (ver. 14). Professor Plumptre quotes Livy's description of Lucretia (*Livy*, I, 57).

14 the merchants' ships. This comparison, like the reference in ver. 24, shows that the poem belongs to a period of commercial intercourse with other countries, as in the days of Solomon, 1 Kings x. 22.

16 she planteth a vineyard. Her industry and economy not only provide for the household, but even add to her husband's possessions.

18 her merchandise. Or, "her profit"; and

therefore "her lamp goeth not out," etc.; for she works on to increase her gains.

20 She stretcheth out her hand, etc. Her energetic industry is combined with generosity to the poor. In the New Testament, the possession of the means of doing good is adduced as a motive to industry: see Eph. iv. 28.

21 scarlet. A costly dye, which would be used for the richest and most durable clothing. Thus she unites splendour with comfort.

22 silk. Rather, "fine linen," R.V.; the byssus of Egypt: see Gen. xli. 42, and note.

23 known in the gates. Through her thrift he has wealth and leisure to appear, suitably dressed, among the rulers of the land.

24 fine linen. Rather, "garments": see Judges xiv. 12, 13. "Girdles," richly wrought by women, are of high price in the East.

25 Strength and honour are her clothing, etc. Her chief ornaments are her strong mind and good name, which enable her to look forward cheerfully to the future. "She laugheth at the time to come," R.V. "She can afford to laugh, looking ahead" (*Moffatt*).

26 She openeth her mouth with wisdom. Not so absorbed in domestic activities as to neglect higher and more spiritual things.

in her tongue is the law of kindness. Or, "on her tongue," etc. Her activity is not made (as diligence too often is) an excuse for a harsh and bustling manner.

29 Many daughters, etc. The description of the virtuous matron is now changed into a direct address, in which the husband himself "praiseth her." The R.V. shows this by adding the word *saying* to ver. 28.

virtuously. Or, "bravely"; the same word as in ver. 10.

30 Favour. Or, "gracefulness," *i.e.*, of person. This often disappoints expectation.

a woman that feareth the Lord. Godliness is at once the source and the crowning grace of all her excellencies. Thus this beautiful delineation of female virtue is connected with the main subject of the Book; and the fear of the Lord is shown to be, in woman as in man, "the beginning" of all wisdom and goodness.

ECCLESIASTES; OR, THE PREACHER

INTRODUCTION

There is no more striking case of the misuse or careless use of words than the application of the word "pessimist" to the author of this book. Yet this and the word "sceptic" are applied to him by various commentators and other well-known writers.

A pessimist is one who sees no hope in human life. An optimist is not necessarily one who closes his eyes to the dark side, but rather one who, seeing life at its worst, still has hope for the world.

The writer of this book sees the vanity of earthly things (i. 2); of toil (i. 3); of pleasure and indulgence (ii. 1, 2); of riches (ii. 8–11; v. 10–15; vi. 2); of the administration of justice (v. 8); of human friendship (vii. 28). And is it not the experience of many who try to find their happiness apart from God?

But there are other things in life which are satisfying and enduring. Happiness is still to be found (iii. 12, 13; v. 18, 20). Above all human injustices, there is the Divine justice (iii. 16, 17; v. 8). In the midst of human life, yet pointing men above its follies and vanities to the Eternal, stands the house of God, calling them to reverent worship and grateful dedication (v. 1–7). Questions are asked (vi. 11, 12), but they are answered. A good name is an enduring possession (vii. 1). Even sorrow is transmuted and becomes helpful (vii. 3). Wisdom is an abiding inheritance (vii. 11), and is a source of strength (vii. 19). It shall be well with them that fear God (viii. 12). Life is a gift of God to be glad in (viii. 15). There is an end to the activities of this life, but this is a reason for diligence (ix. 10. Cp. the words of Christ, John ix. 4). Even the risks of life are justified (xi. 1, 6). And so this "pessimist" bids his readers to rejoice (xi. 9).

It is said, too, that there is nothing in this book about a future life. But it is hard to see any other meaning in the references to the Judgement (vii. 17; xii. 14) and to the spirit returning to God who gave it (xii. 7). And the practical conclusion of it all is clear. No pessimist could say, with any sense of reality, "Fear God, and keep His commandments" (xii. 13).

CHAPTER I

1 the Preacher. The Hebrew word (*Koheleth*) means "one who collects" or "assembles" people for the purpose of addressing them.

king in Jerusalem. Rather, "*at* Jerusalem." Solomon's name is not mentioned here or elsewhere in this book, as it is in Prov. i. 1; Song of Songs i. 1.

2 Vanity of vanities. A Hebraism for utter vanity. This is the great subject of the discourse: the utter insufficiency of all earthly things to make man happy.

5 where he arose. Rather, "where he ariseth (R.V.); *i.e.*, on the new day. The idea is of a long and hurried journey. "Hasteth" is rendered by Dr. Samuel Cox "panteth."

6 according to his (its) circuits. "Circuits (lit., 'turnings') of the wind." The words rendered "turneth," "whirleth," "returneth," "circuits," are all from the same root.

7 thither they return again. The waters return to their fountains and streams. The suggestion is that of filtration through the earth, rather than of evaporation; the laws of which were then imperfectly known.

8 All things are full of labour, etc. Or, "All [one's] words are wearisome, so that one cannot utter [it; *i.e.*, the wearisomeness]."

9 there is no new thing under the sun. It would be some compensation for this incessant change, if some new sources of human happiness were discovered; but towards this there is no progress. This is still more strikingly illustrated in the present day, in which the wonderful discoveries of science and inventions of art have greatly multiplied human comforts, but still have failed to secure true and lasting happiness.

11 There is no remembrance of former things, etc. Supply *persons*, not *things.*

13 I gave my heart. Or, as R.V., "I applied my heart." "Heart," in Scripture, represents the intellect as well as the affections.

14 vexation of spirit. Or, as R.V., "and a striving after wind," *i.e.*, fruitless effort. Some prefer the rendering, "feeding on wind" (R.V. marg.). Cp. Hos. xii. 1. So in ver. 17; ii. 11, 17, etc.

16 Lo, I am come to great estate, etc. Or, "I have increased and added wisdom above all that were before me over Jerusalem (*i.e.*, as rulers), and my heart has seen very much wisdom and knowledge."

17 to know wisdom, and to know madness and folly. Trying to learn more and more of "wisdom" by contrasting it with "folly."

18 in much wisdom is much grief, etc. The "wisdom" and "knowledge" here spoken of must be understood as sought for the sake of personal gratification and satisfaction. Here they fail, because of their limitation, of the vexations encountered in their search, of their inability to meet the deeper needs of the soul. There is a more excellent wisdom, which is not a source of grief, but the fountain of pure and everlasting joy (John xvii. 3).

CHAPTER II

1 Go to now. Rather, "Come now." This was his next experiment.

2 I said of laughter, etc. The pleasures of sense may intoxicate for a time, but what can they do to satisfy?

3 Yet acquainting mine heart with wisdom. Rather, "And my heart guiding me with wisdom." In the midst of self-indulgence he kept in view his inquiries.

6 pools of water. There still remain near Bethlehem three large pools, supplied with fine fresh water, which are attributed to Solomon. From "the Pools of Solomon" the British troops on the way to Jerusalem and in it were supplied with water during the Great War (1914–1919).

7 I got. That is, "I bought," in addition to those "born in my house."

great and small cattle. Or, as R.V., "herds [of oxen] and flocks" [of sheep].

musical instruments, and that of all sorts. Rather, "a wife, and wives": see 1 Kings xi. 1–3.

9 my wisdom remaineth with me. In the midst of sensual delights he analysed his own pleasure, and calmly judged its value.

10 this was my portion. That is, I certainly did get some pleasure from my labour; but (he adds, ver. 11) that was all, and it was soon over.

12 what [can] the man [do] that cometh after the king? No one can put this great question to the proof with greater advantages than I have had; the utmost he can hope to do is to repeat my experiments; and if he does, it will be with the same sad result.

13 wisdom excelleth folly, etc. Here is *part* of the truth—to be sadly neutralised to the student of life, by the melancholy fact mentioned in the close of the next verse.

14 The wise man's eyes are in his head. That is, where they should be, in order that he may guard against danger, or foresee advantages. And yet, for all this, "one event happeneth to them all."

16 Seeing that which now is, etc. Or, "Inasmuch as in the days to come all (*i.e.*, both wise and fool) will have been long ago forgotten."

how. The word "how" here is an interjection of grief and astonishment, as in Psa. lxxiii. 19. "How doth the wise man die even as the fool!" R.V.: cp. i. 11.

19 over all my labour, etc. That is, all that my toil and wisdom have acquired.

21 whose labour is in wisdom, etc. That is, who has laboured "with sagacity and skill." The word "equity" implies more of the *moral* element than was in the writer's mind.

24 There is nothing better, etc. The meaning is that the unsatisfactoriness attending earthly toil should lead a man cheerfully to accept God's gifts, and enjoy them in a spirit of devout submission to all His unalterable arrangements (24–iii. 15), without the travail and care which cause the sinner vexation (26).

25 who else can hasten [hereunto]? Rather, as R.V., "who can have enjoyment?"

more than I. The Hebrew really means "apart from Him" or "without Him," *i.e.*, apart from God's gift; so introducing the thought in ver. 26.

26 He giveth travail. God in His providence allows the sinner to enrich those for whom he himself never meant to work.

This also is vanity. *i.e.*, this travail of the sinner.

CHAPTER III

1 To every thing there is a season. According to the view given in note on ii. 24, the proverbial sayings in vers. 1–9 refer not to the purposes of man, but to the counsels and designs of God (see 2), who allots to all men a season for all that He has appointed for them.

purpose. Or, "undertaking."

2 A time to be born, etc. "This catalogue appears to be given as an enumeration of the various particulars which make up human life from its commencement to its close, or, so to speak, as a kind of syllabus of human life" (*Tyler*).

3 A time to kill. In ver. 2, natural death was spoken of; here, that which comes by violence or accident.

5 A time to cast away stones. Or, "to cast stones abroad." Stones are thus thrown when land is to be made unfit for cultivation (see 2 Kings iii. 19, 25), as they are "gathered," or collected, when the land is to be restored to use.

7 A time to rend. A time of "rending clothes" would be equivalent, in Oriental phraseology to a time of *affliction*.

9 What profit hath he that worketh, etc.? Since things are thus ordered unalterably by God, of what use is this labour? The writer, in his disappointment, seems to have carried this sentiment to the verge of fatalism; but he corrects this in the 11th verse.

11 beautiful in his (its) time (or, season). "Beautiful" here seems to mean "appropriate" or "harmonious." Whatever takes place by Divine appointment is in beautiful accord with the universal system, however unable man may be to discern that it is so.

He hath set the world in their heart. A preferable rendering seems to be (as R.V. marg.), "He hath put eternity in their heart, only that man doth not find out," or "comprehend," etc., referring to man's consciousness of eternity joined to his inability to discern the whole scheme of things. "Eternity is like a sea without a shore, so that man's vision cannot stretch to its horizon and scan God's works from the beginning to the end" (*Wordsworth*).

12 I know that there is no good, etc. Rather, as R.V., "I know that there is nothing better for them than to rejoice, and to do good as long as they live," *i.e.*, to do good makes "life worth living."

14 God doeth it, that men should fear before Him. The perpetual recurrence of similar events (see also v. 15) proves the permanence and consistency of the Divine purpose.

16 wickedness was there. As the impartial administration of justice is one of the highest blessings that a country can enjoy, so its opposite is one of the heaviest curses; a source of numerous, extensive, and aggravated miseries.

17 for every purpose and for every work. And therefore for retribution, which must be an essential part of God's arrangements: see note on ver. 1. It would seem, from what follows, that the writer expected some retribution in the present world.

18 I said in mine heart, etc. Disappointed of any adequate present retribution, he is tempted to think that God designs to prove man to be altogether like the brutes (18–20), even questioning whether there is any difference in their ultimate destiny (21); and thus he nearly sinks into Epicurean self-indulgence (22).

That God might manifest them. Rather, that this state of prevailing injustice was permitted, "for God to prove them, that they might see for themselves that they are beasts": see the preceding note.

19 one breath. Or, "one spirit" (Heb. *ruch*).

no pre-eminence. That is, in respect of death, which befalls them both.

21 Who knoweth the spirit of man, etc.? Or, "Who knoweth whether the spirit of man goeth upward?" etc. (R.V.). This question implies that he had held the belief that there is a difference after death; and that, whilst a beast has no other than a lower earthly life, man has a life which, at death, "goeth upward." But this belief of his is now sorely shaken.

CHAPTER IV

1 I returned, and considered. "I turned to consider once more." A state of doubt (iii. 21) cannot give satisfaction to a mind earnestly seeking after truth; and the inquirer will therefore review again and again the appearances which led to it.

on the side of their oppressors, etc. Or, "and from the hand of their oppressors was power." used to oppress.

2 I praised the dead. *i.e.*, I called them happier who died long ago.

4 every right work. "Every skilful work." Whilst the poor are oppressed (ver. 1), the successful are envied; so that both have their "vexation."

5 eateth his own flesh. Rather, "eateth his meat (or, food)." So that contentment with moderate means is best (6), if it can be attained.

6 Better is a handful with quietness. Or, "Better is a handful of quiet, than both fists full of," etc.

7 Then I returned, and I saw, etc. Rather, "And again I observed," etc.

8 [there is] not a second. Toiling to acquire wealth, although there is no one connected either by blood or by particular friendship to inherit it.

9 they have a good reward. Men may effect unitedly what singly they could not accomplish, whilst they enjoy their earnings better together than they could alone.

10 For he hath not, etc. Rather, "and hath not," etc.

12 And if one prevail against him, etc. Rather, "And if any overpower one [alone], two will stand against him," *i.e.*, the assailant.

13 Better is a poor and a wise child, etc. The Preacher now turns to political changes, as illustrating his position.

child. Rather, "youth," as R.V. The same word is used for Joseph at the age of 17 (Gen. xxxvii. 30; xlii. 20), and of Rehoboam's companions (1 Kings xii. 8, 10).

14 becometh poor. *i.e.*, the old and foolish hereditary king "becometh poor" by his impolitic measures; whilst a captive or slave from his prison, like Joseph (Gen. xli. 40–45), rises to power.

15 I considered all the living, etc. Vers. 15, 16 should be rendered, "I saw all the living who walk under the sun with (*i.e.*, on the side of) the young man, the second (*i.e.*, successor) who stood up in his stead: there was no end of all the people, even of all before whom he was (*i.e.*, as their leader); yet they that come after shall not rejoice in him," etc. Though he has been borne into power by the favour of the multitude, he shall soon find his popularity decline, and perhaps be thrust out by some new idol. The history of modern nations, Western as well as Eastern, supplies many illustrations of this.

CHAPTER V

1 be more ready to hear, etc. Or, "draw nigh to hear": *i.e.*, to attend and obey. See 1 Sam. xv. 22, where to "hearken" is forcibly contrasted with formal sacrifices offered without true devotion, such as are here said to be a "doing evil."

2 to utter any thing. Rather, "a word." Let the recollection of God's majesty deter you from multiplying words in your addresses to Him.

3 For a dream, etc. Rather, "For a dream cometh with a multitude of business." "Wo viel Sorge ist, da kommen Träume" ("Where there is much care, there come dreams") (*Luther's version*).

4 He hath no pleasure in fools. Those who make thoughtless, rash vows, which they are unwilling to perform. The Hebrew, however, is capable of another interpretation: "there is no steadfast purpose in fools," *i.e.*, it is fools who have not steadfast purpose, who make promises and do not keep them.

6 thy flesh. *i.e., thyself,* considered as frail, in refusing the self-denial which the vow uttered by thy mouth required.

an error. "A mistake"; I made the vow inconsiderately, and therefore have not kept it.

destroy the work of thine hands. *i.e.*, frustrate the undertakings for the success of which thy vows were made.

8 For He that is higher, etc. Lit., "for the high is watching over the high, and high ones over them." This probably refers to the various grades of earthly rulers.

9 The king himself is served by the field. Or, "the king is subject to (*i.e.*, is dependent on) the field." It is a consolation to think that oppression must have its limits, since without the cultivation of the ground the king could not get his revenue; so that in one view the king is more dependent on the ploughman than the ploughman on the king.

14 by evil travail. Or perhaps, "in some untoward affair": either by improvidence and vice, or by ill-judged undertakings, or by the fraud and treachery of others, or by misfortune.

17 All his days also, etc. Rather, "All his days he ate in darkness, and increased [his] anxiety, and his sorrow and vexation."

20 For he shall not much remember the days of his life. Or, "He remembers not much the days of his life"; *i.e.*, he does not look at the past with regret, nor at the future with uneasiness (cp. 16, 17); but gratefully enjoys the blessings which God bestows in answer to his desires.

CHAPTER VI

1 And it is common among men. Rather, "And it is great (*or*, heavy) upon man."

2 an evil disease. Or, "a sore evil."

3 good. Lit., "the good": meaning not enjoying the good in his possessions.

that he have no burial. Or, "even though the grave did not wait for him" (*Dr. Samuel Cox*).

4 he cometh in. *i.e.*, the untimely-born, that has neither name nor remembrance.

5 This hath more rest than the other. The untimely-born sees less, indeed nothing, of the troubles of life.

6 Yet hath he seen no good. Rather, "And yet enjoy no good" (R.V.). If it be objected that a life greatly prolonged is better than untimely birth, because life itself is a blessing, the Preacher replies that such a life, without enjoyment, is protracted misery, and, after all, ends in death.

7 All the labour, etc. Perhaps the meaning of these difficult verses (7–11) may be as follows: All man's toil is to supply his wants, yet his desire is not satisfied. For in this respect what advantage over the fool has the wise man, or the humble man who knows how to conduct himself among his fellow men? It is true that what the eye sees (as a present possession) is better than what the desire goes out for (9); yet even this is vanity and windy effort. "Whatever is, long ago its name has been called (*i.e.*, its nature and condition settled); and it is known (*i.e.*, determined) what man himself is, and he cannot contend with Him that is mightier than he. Since there are many things which [promise satisfaction but] increase vanity, what is profitable to man?"

CHAPTER VII

1 A [good] name, etc. Heb., "A name." The words "name" and "ointment" are alliterative in Hebrew (*shem* and *shemen*): cp. Song of Songs i. 3.

2 the living will lay it to his heart. Since affliction is the common lot of all men, it is better to frequent the place where we may learn how to endure and to improve it, than to associate continually with the gay and luxurious. None ever go to the house of mourning in a right state of mind without feeling the truth of these words.

6 as the crackling of thorns, etc. Making noise and smoke; but useless, because they give little heat, and soon go out.

7 oppression maketh a wise man mad ("foolish," R.V.). This probably means that the practice of oppression maddens, or demoralises the *oppressor*. Even wise men have been intoxicated by the possession of power; so that they have become tyrannical as rulers or corrupt as judges. But even this must be endured patiently, and the "end" must be awaited (ver 8).

9 anger resteth in the bosom of fools. Irritability, soon roused and long indulged, is a characteristic of a fool.

10 Say not thou, etc. Patience is here recommended, in opposition to that querulous spirit which contrasts its present lot with the supposed advantages of former times.

11 Wisdom is good with an inheritance. Rather, "as good as an inheritance," R.V.; yea, it is a gain (*i.e.*, better than an inheritance) to them that see the sun.

to them that see the sun. *i.e.*, "those who lead an active life" (*Dr. Samuel Cox*).

13 the work of God. *i.e.*, what God does in the circumstances of man's life. This is a reason for patience, derived from the thoughts in iii. 1–11.

14 God also hath set the one, etc. God has so arranged the alternations of good and evil, and kept them so entirely under His control, that we can never predict the future with certainty.

15 in the days of my vanity. *i.e.*, "in this my unsatisfying life."

16 Be not righteous over much. The writer here seems to derive his maxims from his observation of life. Whether in irony, as some think, or for the moment in sad earnest, he counsels abstinence from extremes—from over-enthusiasm on the one side, or from rash wickedness on the other. The law of calculating prudence may be violated in different ways by both saint and sinner. To the maxim of worldly common sense which asks, "Why shouldest thou destroy thyself?" the Great Teacher replies, "He that shall lose his life for My sake and the gospel's, shall find it."

17 Be not over much wicked. Still the prudential maxim: a wise and important warning: yet very different from the protest against sin as sin.

18 It is good that thou shouldest take hold of this. Rather, "Take hold of *this;* yea, from *that* withhold not thy hand"; *i.e.*, the two maxims in vers. 16, 17. "He that feareth God" will, according to the Preacher, be guarded against both extremes, and their bad results.

19 Wisdom strengtheneth, etc. This is the wisdom of him that is patient, and fears God. It fortifies the soul, and elevates it above every other fear.

more than ten mighty men, etc. Rather, as R.V., "more than ten rulers which are in a city." "Ten" denotes *completeness*—"a fully-organised government."

21 Also take no heed, etc. Another maxim of common sense; not to care what people say. The words rendered "curse thee" may be taken to mean "speak evil of thee."

22 thine own heart knoweth, etc. The consciousness of our own sins against others should keep us from being angry with their faults against us.

24 That which is far off, etc. Or, "Far off is that which is, and deep; deep, who shall find it out?" cp. R.V.

15 to know and to search, and to seek out. These various terms "to *know*, to *search*, and to *seek out*," express intense application to discover wisdom and its result.

26 the sinner shall be taken by her. See note on Prov. xxii. 14.

27 the account. Or, "result."

have I not found. The example and teaching of the Lord Jesus Christ have altered this Eastern view of woman.

CHAPTER VIII

1 the boldness of his face shall be changed. Or, "and the harshness (or 'hardness,' as R.V.) of his face is changed"; *i.e.*, if his aspect was gloomy wisdom makes it serene and bright.

2 in regard of the oath of God. Referring to the oath of allegiance, in which the name of God was invoked: see 2 Kings xi. 17; 1 Chron. xi. 3; xxix. 24; and cp. Ezek. xvii. 13–16, where Zedekiah is denounced for breaking his oath to the king of Babylon.

3 to go out of his sight. Or, to depart from him; *i.e.*, by rebellion.

4 Where the word of a king is, etc. Rather, "Inasmuch as the word of a king is powerful," etc.

5 a wise man's heart discerneth, etc. The meaning may be, that he keeps in view the season of judgement and retribution.

6 Because to every purpose, etc. Rather, "For to every undertaking there is a season and judgement, for the evil ('misery,' R.V.) of man is great upon him."

8 There is no man that hath power over the spirit, etc. "[As] there is no man who has power over the wind to restrain the wind, and there is [to man] no control over the day of death, and there is no exemption in war, so wickedness will not deliver its possessor." Wickedness, however high-handed, will have its punishment.

9 to his own hurt. Rather, "to his hurt"; *i.e.*, the hurt of the person ruled.

10 And so I saw, etc. Referring to these hurtful tyrants who went on till they died. "And so I saw [these] bad men buried, and they came [to the grave]; and they that had done right departed from the holy place, and were forgotten in the city": cp. R.V. and marg.

11 Because sentence, etc. This apparent failure of justice emboldens transgressors to continue in their course.

14 There is a vanity, etc. In this and the next verse there is a recurrence to the topic on which so much has been said already—the inexplicable inequalities in human life, and the wisdom of temperate enjoyment rather than of unavailing speculation.

15 of his labour. Rather, "in his labour," as R.V.

17 I beheld all the work of God. *i.e.*, His administration of the affairs of the world.

CHAPTER IX

1 by all that is before them. Rather, "all [is] before them" (R.V.); *i.e.*, signs of God's love and displeasure [seem to] await them indiscriminately. It is impossible, from the events which befall a man in this life, to determine his real character in the sight of God. Such statements must be understood only as criticisms of life from a human point of view: the Preacher is contemplating life and death apart from the future judgement of which he afterwards emphatically speaks (xi. 9).

2 he that sweareth. *i.e.*, who swears lightly and falsely; while "he that feareth an oath" is one who takes it seriously and keeps it faithfully.

4 For to him that is joined, etc. Rather, "For who is there that is chosen out (*i.e.*, excepted)? To all the living there is hope: a living dog is better than a dead lion."

5 the living know that they shall die. If they know nothing else, they know this; whereas the dead "know not anything."

any more a reward. Any further advantage.

6 now. Or, "long ago."

7 For God now accepteth, etc. Or, with R.V., "For God hath already accepted," etc. The hearty but moderate enjoyment of the good things of life is again recommended, as a wise alternative to restless speculation: cp. ii. 24; iii. 12, 22; v. 18.

8 Let thy garments be always white, etc. White garments and perfumed oil were signs of festivity amongst the Hebrews.

10 Whatsoever thy hand findeth to do, etc. Whatever appears to thee desirable or important to be done, do it promptly and earnestly, remembering that the period for doing it will soon have passed for ever: cp. John ix. 4. "The grave" in the Hebrew is Sheol, "the under-world."

11 the race is not to the swift. Wisdom and energy often fail of present success.

nor yet favour to men of skill. The esteem and respect of mankind are not always gained by such men; sometimes neglect, envy, and contempt are their portion.

chance. What to men appears accidental. The absolute control of Divine Providence over all events has been repeatedly asserted: see iii. 1–11.

12 man also knoweth not his time. Or, "time of calamity." Calamity and death come upon him as if by chance (11); as unexpectedly as "net" or "snare" upon fishes and birds.

13 This wisdom have I seen, etc. Or. "This also have I seen, [as] wisdom under the sun, and it seemed great unto me." The "wisdom" is that of the poor man in ver. 15; and the whole narrative (which may be that of an actual occurrence) illustrates (16) both the value of wisdom, and the maxim of ver. 11, that "favour" is not "to men of skill."

17 The words of wise men are heard in quiet, etc. Rather, "The words of wise men heard in quiet [are better] than the outcry of a ruler among fools," *i.e.*, a foolish ruler. The "poor wise man" (15) seems to be still thought of.

CHAPTER X

1 the ointment of the apothecary. Rather, "the fragrant oil of the perfumer." A slight indiscretion which would pass without observation in other men, would be marked in a wise man. This maxim applies very forcibly to the Christian, whose profession should be without a blemish.

2 at his right hand. The right hand, being more used, is more quick and apt than the left. So a wise man can use his thoughts promptly and aptly; whilst a fool is confused and unable to act.

3 when he that is a fool, etc. He exhibits his folly to every one, and in all his conduct. According to some interpreters, the meaning of the second clause is that he stigmatises those whom he meets as fools, showing thus his vain self-sufficiency.

4 leave not thy place. *i.e.*, "Do not rebel": see viii. 3, and note.

7 servants upon horses. Horses are often mentioned as appendages of rank: see Esther vi. 8, 9; Jer. xvii. 25; Ezek. xxiii. 12.

8 whoso breaketh a hedge. Rather, "breaketh down a wall." Serpents hide in the crevices of walls. Vers. 8, 9 refer to various modes of injuring others (see Gen. xlix. 6; 2 Kings iii. 19, 25; Prov. xxvi. 27), which are here represented as recoiling upon the perpetrators. Wisdom teaches a man that what does harm to another will in the end be mischievous to himself.

10 to direct. Rather, "to give success." Science and skill often save hard labour, as well as much time and money.

11 Surely the serpent will bite without enchantment, etc. Rather, "If the serpent bite because he is not charmed, then there is no advantage to the master of the tongue" (*i.e.*, the charmer): cp. R.V. An enchanter must be quick in his art, or the serpent will bite before his song has lulled it. So a wise man will be prompt.

12 are gracious. *i.e.*, they are conciliatory; whereas the fool's words are provoking, and begin with folly, to end in rage (13), which will destroy himself and others too.

14 after him. Perhaps this should be, "after *that*."

15 he knoweth not how to go to the city. *i.e.*, he cannot find out the broad and frequented highway, and therefore goes a long way round to get to his object. Cp. Isaiah xxxv. 8.

16 a child. Rather, "a youth," and therefore too often deficient in wisdom, experience, and skill.

thy princes eat in the morning. The morning repast of the East, like that of the French, is very light, the principal meal being late in the afternoon. Therefore, to eat, *i.e.*, *to feast*, in the morning was regarded as luxurious and intemperate, and as wasting time which ought to be devoted to business.

17 the son of nobles. And therefore educated in the knowledge of the duties of his high station.

18 the house droppeth through. Or, "falleth in."

19 But (R.V., "And") **money answereth all things.** This appears to refer to the rich and luxurious, by whom the feast is made for merriment, and wine gladdens the living, and money supplies the whole.

20 a bird of the air shall carry the voice. A proverbial expression, indicating the unexpected way in which secrets often come out. Detraction even of those who seem most removed from us may reach their ears.

CHAPTER XI

1 Cast thy bread upon the waters. Vers. 1-3 appear to be intended to show that it is often wise to deal generously, inasmuch as liberality to those who cannot repay, though it appears like casting bread upon the waters, is never lost. Some suppose that there is an allusion to the practice in Egypt of sowing corn before the Nile, after overflowing the land, has entirely receded to its channel. Bullock (*Speaker's Commentary*) points out that in Isa. xviii. 2, the phrase "upon the waters" refers to ships. Moffatt renders, "Trust your goods far and wide at sea till you get good returns after a while."

2 Give a portion to seven. "Seven" is a number of completeness; and therefore this is a command to be most extensively liberal. The expression, "Give a portion," is perhaps borrowed from the practice of distributing food to the needy on festive occasions (Neh. viii. 10; Esther ix. 22).

thou knowest not what evil, etc. Thou knowest not but that thou mayest become needy. The same sentiment, but with its application extended to eternal things, is illustrated by our Lord in the parable of the unjust steward (Luke xvi. 1–12).

3 they empty themselves upon the earth. As the clouds arise from the sea, and empty themselves upon the earth, whence the water returns again to the sea (see i. 7), they form an apt illustration of the sentiment of these verses, that good returns to him who does it.

4 He that observeth the wind shall not sow, etc. As the farmer who refuses to sow or to reap unless the weather be favourable, will not prosper, so the man who waits for opportunities such as he would desire, will be likely to live in vain. So in all the work of life: Be guided not by transient phenomena, but by eternal principles and laws.

5 As thou knowest not, etc. The Preacher is still enforcing the same exhortation. Because we know so little of the purposes of God respecting both ourselves and others, every present opportunity of doing good should be diligently used.

the spirit. Many (as R.V.) prefer the rendering "wind" to "spirit," and refer to ver. 4. But the next clause and the use of a similar expression in John iii. 8, seem to show that here, as elsewhere, there is an intended transition from one meaning of the word to the other.

6 In the morning sow thy seed, etc. Go on constantly in the way of duty, and be assured your wise activity shall not fail of a blessing. This sentiment is applicable to all our labours, and especially to efforts for the spiritual good of others; to which, in addition to the general encouragement here given, special promises are annexed; cp. Isa. lv. 11–13; Gal. vi. 7–10.

8 But if a man live many years, etc. Rather, "For if a man live many years, he shall rejoice in them all, and shall remember," etc. He should connect present pleasure with thoughts of the coming "darkness." For the man who never anticipates the future will be ill-prepared to meet it when it comes.

9 But know, etc. Rather, "And know." This is not intended as a bar to the enjoyment already mentioned. "It is certainly used here as an incentive to cheerfulness. We are to be happy *because* we are to stand at the bar of God, because in the Judgement He will adjust and compensate all the wrongs and afflictions of time" (*Dr. Samuel Cox*). It also becomes a safeguard and a defence.

10 remove sorrow, etc. Sorrow here (as R.V., marg.) is more literally "vexation," or colloquially "worry." Do not look at the dark side of things, nor practise unnecessary mortification ("evil" to "the flesh").

childhood and youth are vanity. They will soon be gone for ever: wisely therefore make the best of them.

CHAPTER XII

1 Remember now. Rather, "And remember." Religion is the most effectual preservative of youth, and the best preparative for infirmity and age. This life, so full of vanity and vexation, will be best understood and used if it is regarded as God's gift and trust, to be spent in doing His will (13).

thy Creator. A plural form in Hebrew, like *Elohim*, expressive of majesty. Father, Son, and Spirit, are all concerned in the creation of man.

2 While the sun, etc. All this (2–5) is a highly figurative and very beautiful description of the approach of death. Dr. Samuel Cox (*Expositor's Bible*) takes a view of the passage which seems less far-fetched than the explanations of many commentators. According to him, the description is that of a tempest breaking upon an Eastern city. "Such and so terrible is death to the godless and sensual."

the mourners go about the streets. Mourners were hired to bewail the deceased.

6 Or ever the silver cord be loosed, etc. The Preacher proceeds by another set of images to represent the process of death. Some suppose the metaphors to be taken from various parts of the human body—the "cord of silver" breaks, and the "golden bowl," or lamp suspended by a "silver chain," is broken, and "the lamp of life" is extinguished. And then death is represented by the images of the "broken wheel" and the "broken pitcher" of a well.

7 Then shall the dust return, etc. Rather, "And the dust returneth," etc.

the spirit shall return, etc. The inspired Preacher regarded the body as the organ of the indwelling spirit, which, though acting by means of the body while connected with it, is yet capable of separate existence and activity.

10 The Preacher sought to find out, etc. Rather, "The Preacher sought to find out words of pleasantness, and writing of uprightness, words of truth"; aiming to join what is agreeable and interesting with what is true and useful.

11 and as nails fastened, etc. "As nails driven in," or "spikes driven home by the Shepherds as they pitch their tents" (*Dr. Samuel Cox*). All these words of the wise, he says, have been suggested and inspired by one Teacher, *i.e.*, by God Himself.

12 Of making many books there is no end, etc. This is not an attack on books and reading but a plea for concentration. The Preacher urges his readers to be satisfied with a few good writings which shall act as goads and nails, rather than to perplex themselves either with reading many books or with making new ones.

for this is the whole [duty] of man. Or, "for this is [the duty of] every man." Without true practical religion no man can be happy, whatever be his rank or advantages; with it, he who has little earthly good may possess a pure and real blessedness. The same truth is, in every variety of form, taught by Him who is "greater than Solomon"; and who not only illustrated and enforced all His precepts by His own perfect example, but Himself opened for us the closed gates of paradise.

THE SONG OF SONGS

INTRODUCTION

THE interpretations of this book are many and varied. The simplest and most natural appears to be that which regards it as a poem or drama of pure wedded love. As such it was enshrined in the Jewish Scriptures, and is still part of the service of the Passover, as one of the five *Megilloth* or rolls which are read at different festivals. That it is capable of a typical application can hardly be denied.

We content ourselves with giving a summary of the drama, taken from *The Bible Handbook*, by Angus and Green.

Scene I. *In Solomon's Gardens.*—The damsels of Jerusalem, as chorus, celebrate the praise of the royal bridegroom (i. 2–4). The Shulamite excuses her rusticity, and asks where she may find the bridegroom: the damsels reply (i. 5–8). Solomon enters, and an affectionate dialogue ensues (i. 9; ii. 7).

Scene II. *The Shulamite, alone.*—She describes first a happy visit from her beloved; and then a dream, in which he appears as lost and found (ii. 8; iii. 5).

Scene III. *The Royal Espousals.*—Inhabitants of Jerusalem describe the approach of the King and Bride (iii. 6–11). A scene of mutual endearment follows (iv. 1; v. 1).

Scene IV. *The Palace.*—The Shulamite narrates a dream to the damsel chorus (v. 2–8). They reply (v. 9). She responds, extolling her beloved (v. 10–16). The chorus responds (vi. 1). The Bride replies (vi. 2, 3). Solomon enters and descants upon her charms (vi. 4–9).

Scene V. *The Palace* (continued).—Dialogue between the damsel chorus and the Bride (vi. 10–13). Damsels continue (vii. 1–5). Solomon enters and again expresses his delight (vii. 6–9). The Bride invites her beloved to visit her childhood's rural home (vii. 9 ; viii. 4).

Scene VI. *The Shulamite's Home.*—Inhabitants of the country (viii. 5); Solomon (viii. 5) ; the Bride (viii. 6, 7) ; her Brothers (viii. 8, 9) ; the Bride (viii. 10–12) ; Solomon (viii. 13) ; the Bride (viii. 14).

CHAPTER I

1 Let him, etc. This opening chorus, to ver. 4, is probably throughout the language of the virgin-choir, who alternate from the singular to the plural, speaking now in the character of the bride, now in their own. Some, however, prefer to regard it as a dialogue between the virgins and the bride.

4 We will remember, etc. Rather, " We will praise thy love above wine ; rightly do they love thee." The latter clause is a refrain corresponding to the end of ver 3.

5 the tents of Kedar. See Gen. xxv. 13 ; Psa. cxx. 5. The Arabs still use dark-coloured tents, covered with a coarse canvas, made from the hair of their black goats. The points of comparison are : " Black as the tents of Kedar . . . comely as the curtains of Solomon."

6 Look not, etc. Or, " Look not upon me [*i.e.*, in disdain], because I am swarthy, because the sun has glared upon me." She had been subjected by her brothers to coarse and rustic toil, accounting for her dark complexion.

mine own vineyard. *i.e.*, my personal beauty : see viii. 12. The words are often used in a spiritual sense as a warning against neglect of one's own inner life, or one's own family, while being engrossed in social or public duties.

7 Where thou feedest, etc. *i.e.*, " Where thou feedest [thy flock], where thou makest it to rest at noon [when shepherds usually take their flocks to the shade], lest I should be as one straying among," etc. ; or, " as one veiled " ; *i.e*, treated as a harlot (Gen. xxxviii. 14).

9 I have compared thee. Solomon now enters upon the scene, and accosts the bride with this simile. The " company of horses," etc., should rather be " my mare in [one of] Pharaoh's chariots " ; *i.e.*, in a chariot sent by Pharaoh : see 1 Kings x. 29.

10 rows . . . chains. The words " jewels " and " gold " have been supplied by our translators. The " rows " (" plaits," R.V.) were probably of hair, braided over the cheeks ; the " chains," a necklace such as country maidens wear. Solomon promises to replace these simple ornaments by more costly ones. See next verse.

11 borders. The word rendered " rows," in ver. 10, " plaits." " Studs," or beads, " of silver," would be interspersed with wreathed gold.

spikenard. Or, " nard." A costly perfume (see John xii. 3, 4), produced from an Indian plant. It is impossible not to think of the spikenard which filled the room with odour while the King reclined at His table.

13 He shall lie all night, etc. The Hebrew conveys no reference to night. The words should read, " It (the bag of myrrh) abideth between my breasts " ; an allusion to the custom of wearing some precious perfume suspended from the neck. On " myrrh " see Exod. xxx. 23. Pleasant is my Beloved to me as a bag of myrrh worn in my bosom.

14 camphire. Heb., " copher " ; the henna shrub, the flowers of which are both beautiful and fragrant. Its leaves also yield a deep orange dye, with which Eastern women tinge their nails and part of their hands and feet.

En-gedi. See note on 1 Sam. xxiii. 29. En-gedi, from its tropical climate, was, and still is, a very fertile spot.

15 Thou hast doves' eyes. Rather, as R.V., " thine eyes are [as] doves " ; *i.e.*, loving, gentle.

16 our bed is green. Rather, " our couch is verdant ; the beams of our house are cedars, our fretted ceilings cypresses " : referring to the trees overhanging the grass. Cp. *Paradise Lost*, iv. 692, etc.

CHAPTER II

1 the rose. Rather, " a rose." The bride in her humility compares herself to the wild flowers among the grass. This " rose " is a bulbous plant —probably the white narcissus or the autumn crocus (R.V. marg.).

Sharon. The low-lying wooded and pasture land north of Joppa, well described by Thomson, *The Land and the Book* (xxxiii., xxxiv.).

the lily. Rather, " a lily." Our " lily of the valley " does not grow in Palestine. The lily here mentioned is probably the iris. To this wild flower our Lord refers (Matt. vi. 28).

2 As the lily among thorns. Rather, " As a lily," etc. The bridegroom turns the bride's modest self-depreciation into a beautiful compliment, which the bride reciprocates in the next verse.

3 the apple tree. A tree uniting delicious fruit with refreshing shade.

5 flagons. Rather, " raisin-cakes " : see 2 Sam. vi. 19.

7 roes. Or, " gazelles." These elegant creatures are mentioned here as emblems of female beauty, as well as of shyness and timidity.

That ye stir not up, nor awake my love. The sense is, " nor awaken love," *i.e.*, the passion of love, which she begs her attendants not to say or do anything to excite.

until it please. Love awakens spontaneously. This verse is repeated at the end of the bride's soliloquy (iii. 5), and again at the close of the Fifth part of the Song (viii. 4).

9 He looketh forth at the windows, etc. Rather, " He looketh through the windows, glanceth through the lattices."

13 The fig tree putteth forth, etc. Or, " The fig tree is sweetening her green figs, *i.e.*, the late figs, which continue to grow through the winter, and ripen in the spring ; the vines in blossom send forth their fragrance."

14 the secret places of the stairs. Rather, " the hiding-places of the cliff." He complains that, like a dove on a high cliff, she is inaccessible, behind the lattice, in her chamber on the wall.

15 Take us the foxes, the little foxes. The bride is detained by her duties in the vineyard. She quotes the charge addressed to her as the reason why she cannot yet have the companionship of her beloved. Foxes abound in Judæa, and do much injury to vineyards and gardens. Another interpretation of the verse is that the bride, whom the bridegroom had begged to let him hear her voice, sings to him this couplet of a vineyard song.

16 He feedeth. This means, "He feedeth his flock": see i. 7.

17 Until the day break, etc. Rather, "Until the day becomes cool, and the shadows flee away" (*i.e.*, stretch away, or lengthen); meaning the evening. And so in iv. 6.

the mountains of Bether. Or, "of division"; meaning either "mountains which separate us," or perhaps, as Conder thinks, a range of that name, where the village of Bittir stands, south-west of Jerusalem.

CHAPTER III

2 I will rise now. That is, "*I said,* Come, let me rise"; speaking to herself.

4 my mother's house. The fitting residence for the daughter.

5 nor awake my love. See note on ii. 7.

6 Who is this, etc.? The Hebrew words rendered "this," and "perfumed," are in the feminine gender, referring to the bride.

the wilderness. From the country, in contrast with the city.

pillars of smoke. From the incense which was burnt before the marriage procession.

powders. That is, costly aromatic powders.

7 bed. Or, "couch"; a litter or palanquin. It was Solomon's, *i.e.*, provided by the king himself for his bride's comfort and dignity. So by the guard of warriors, "all of them armed with a sword," he secured her safely against night attacks on the journey.

9 a chariot. Palanquin (R.V.).

10 covering, etc. Rather, seat (R.V.), of purple cushions.

The midst thereof being paved with love, etc. Perhaps, "its interior decorated, [a work of] love from daughters of Jerusalem." Moffatt and others render "inlaid with ebony."

11 With the crown. Or, "garland."

CHAPTER IV

1 Thou hast doves' eyes. "Thine eyes are doves (see i. 15) behind thy veil"; and so in ver. 3.

Thy hair is as a flock of goats. The figures of Eastern poetry are peculiarly bold and luxuriant. Here the dark hair of the bride, hanging down in tresses over her shoulders, is compared to a flock of goats (which in Palestine are commonly black) "lying outspread from Mount Gilead" down the mountain side.

2 Thy teeth are like a flock. The teeth are white, even and complete.

3 thy speech. Rather, "thy place of speech"; thy mouth.

. . . within thy locks. Rather, ". . . behind the veil."

4 the tower of David. It was customary on the outside of towers to hang shields (Ezek. xxvii. 10, 11). This allusion is suggested by the bride's necklace of jewels.

5 two young roes. Rather, "two fawns, twins of a gazelle."

6 Until the day break, etc. The bride modestly interrupts the glowing description of her charms, and longs for solitude till the evening (ii. 17, and note); which makes the king admire still more her perfect loveliness.

8 Come with me from Lebanon. The home of the bride was in Northern Palestine, of which the chief mountain-peaks are mentioned. The appeal is in the spirit of Psa. xlv. 10, 11: "Forget thine own people and thy father's house, so shall the king greatly desire thy beauty."

spouse. Or, "bride." The word used here and in vers. 9, 10, 11, 12, and v. 1, is always applied elsewhere to a married woman.

Look (or, "go," R.V. marg.) **from the top of Amana,** etc. "Amana," or "Abana," was probably the name of a part of Shenir or Hermon, from which the river of the same name flowed to Damascus: see Deut. iii. 9; 2 Kings v. 12. On these hills lions were formerly found, and the Syrian panther (or "leopard") is still sometimes seen.

9 one of thine eyes. Rather, "one of thy glances."

12 A garden inclosed etc. Better, "shut up," as in the next clause (R.V.). A garden with its choicest productions, and a spring with its refreshing streams, are described as being "shut up" and "sealed": with reference perhaps to the bride's modesty and chastity.

13 Thy plants, etc. The image of a garden is here followed into detail. For "pleasant," the R.V. has more accurately, "precious," as in Deut. xxxiii. 14.

Camphire. Rather, "henna": see on i. 14. The plants here mentioned were mostly exotics. "Calamus" is the sweet or aromatic cane (see Groser's *Trees and Plants mentioned in the Bible*, p. 206).

15 A fountain of gardens. That is, as R.V., "*Thou art* a fountain of gardens."

streams (R.V., "flowing streams") **from Lebanon.** Like one of those mountain streams fed by perennial snows, which diffuse life, fertility, and beauty where they flow.

16 Awake, O north wind. The bride replies to her husband's praises, desiring that "the garden" which he so much admires may yield for him its richest delights. The "north wind" clears the air; the "south" warms and ripens. In Palestine the east and west winds are stormy.

that the spices thereof may flow out. The breezes diffuse the fragrance of the plants.

CHAPTER V

2 my undefiled. Heb., "my perfect one."

3 coat. The inner garment. She will not arouse herself or take trouble for his sake.

4 by the hole. Through which a person might thrust his arm to open the door. He naturally expected to be able to unfasten the door; but it appears to have been purposely secured by an additional fastening.

5 sweet-smelling myrrh. Rather, "flowing myrrh," which is the best. Perhaps "he had come prepared as if for a festival, and the costly ointment which he had brought with him had dropped on the handles of the bolts" (*Delitzsch*).

7 They smote me, they wounded me. They treated me as a tramp. The same thing is intimated by the taking away of the veil, which is one of the greatest indignities that can be inflicted on a woman in Eastern countries.

8 I charge you. The recital of the dream is

over, and the bride's passionate appeal to her companions shows the impression it had left.

9 What is thy beloved, etc. ? This inquiry of the daughters of Jerusalem, suggested by the bride's passionate adjuration to them, is skilfully introduced by the poet, to lead to the description which immediately follows.

12 His eyes are as the eyes of doves, etc. Rather, "His eyes are doves by streams of water, bathing in milk, dwelling in fulness." This latter clause applies to the doves. The whole is meant to depict the soft, loving expression of the full, dark eyes.

13 sweet flowers. Rather, as in marg., "towers of perfumes." The "towers" may stand for elevated banks (R.V.) covered with fragrant bloom.

14 His belly, etc. Rather, as R.V., "His body is [as] ivory-work overlaid with sapphires"; referring to the white robe of royalty, and the bright-coloured girdle.

15 sockets. Denoting the richly ornamented sandals.

His countenance, etc. Rather, "His aspect"; the manly dignity of his appearance.

16 His mouth. His words: "that which he speaks, and the manner in which he speaks it" (*Delitzsch*). "Most sweet," and "altogether lovely," are, in the original, "sweetnesses" and "preciousnesses": the plural denoting abundance.

CHAPTER VI

1 Whither is thy beloved gone ? This inquiry by the bride's companions leads towards the scene of re-union.

4 beautiful . . . as Tirzah. Solomon now sees the bride approaching, and repeats his words of admiration and love, heightening the picture by new details. Tirzah (see note 1 Kings xiv. 17) and Jerusalem are mentioned as the fairest cities in the land.

Terrible as an army with banners. This figure, which is carried out in the next verse, represents the bride as irresistible in captivating those who behold her. The praises which follow are the same as in iv. 1–3, where see notes.

8 There are threescore queens. Not one of them can compare with the bride: even they unite in extolling her as unique (10).

9 the only one of her mother. Not her only child, but her "choice one" or "darling."

11 To see the fruits of the valley. Rather, "To look at the verdure of the valley, to see the vine sprout, and the pomegranates blossom."

12 the chariots of Ammi-nadib. "The war-chariots of my noble people." The spiritual interpretation is that of "the soul carried away directly, irresistibly, rapidly toward her bridegroom and her king" (*Moody Stuart*).

13 Return, return. She is on the point of retiring, when her attendants entreat her to come back.

O Shulamite. Or, "Shulamith." The Septuagint reads *Shunamite*, or "native of Shunem."

we. That is, the daughters of Jerusalem, desirous still to contemplate and praise her beauty.

What will ye see in the Shulamite ? etc. "See" is the same word as "look" in the appeal of the maidens. "Why will ye look upon the Shulamite, as upon the dance of Mahanaim ?" R.V. "Company" in A.V., should be rendered "dance"; and "Mahanaim" (two armies) seems to be a proper name, designating the place where the angel-host met Jacob on his return to Canaan (Gen. xxxii. 1–3).

CHAPTER VII

1 How beautiful, etc. ! The bride, in her rich attire, is here described, from her richly embroidered sandals to her luxuriant tresses. It must be remembered that the speakers are of the bride's own sex. Solomon has not yet appeared.

3 young roes. See note on iv. 5.

4 as a (the) tower of ivory. That is, white, straight, and slender.

fishpools. Rather, "pools." The eyes were moist, dark, and sparkling. Mr. A. T. Chapman (art. "Heshbon" in *Hastings' Dict. of Bible*) says that the site is now covered with extensive ruins, chiefly Roman, and that a stream issues from a cave near by. There appears to be now no reservoir such as former travellers mentioned.

Bath-rabbim. "Daughter of multitudes," probably a poetical designation of Heshbon.

the tower of Lebanon. Straight and symmetrical.

5 Carmel. An emblem of stateliness and beauty.

held in the galleries. Rather (as R.V.), "held captive in the tresses *thereof*."

6 O love. This probably refers not to the bride, but to the passion of love which she has awakened in the king.

7 like a palm tree. Upright, graceful, and stately.

8 smell. Or, "breath."

9 And the roof of thy mouth. Or, "And thy palate (*i.e.*, thy speech, as in v. 16) is like," etc.

For my beloved, etc. The true order is, "that goeth down sweetly ('smoothly,' R.V.) for my beloved," etc., an interruption by the bride. If her words *were* like wine, they were all for him. Let them linger with him even in his slumbers, while he murmured their meaning

12 if the vine flourish, etc. Rather, "Whether the vine hath budded, whether the vine-blossom hath opened": see R.V.

13 mandrakes. See Gen. xxx. 14, etc.

CHAPTER VIII

1 as my brother. *i.e.*, one whom she might caress in public as well as in private, without impropriety.

2 Who would instruct me. Perhaps, "thou shouldest teach me": see R.V. marg.

the juice of my pomegranate. The sherbet made with pomegranate juice is particularly esteemed for its agreeable and cooling acidity.

5 Who is this that cometh up, etc. ? See note on iii. 6.

I raised thee up. Rather, as R.V., "I awakened thee." The words of the bridegroom recall the first hours of their love, under this tree, and by her own early home.

6 Set me as a seal. Denoting intimate and inviolable union.

jealousy. It is evident, from the connexion, that the word "jealousy" is only used here to express strong and intense love. Love is strong as death, inasmuch as it conquers all; and it is tenacious (Heb., "hard," not precisely "cruel," as A.V. and R.V.), like the grave, which never relaxes its hold.

7 it would utterly be contemned. Or, "with scorn should he (the man who would propose such an exchange) be scorned."

8 sister. The brothers of the bride (i. 6), to whom the disposal of their sister belonged (see

Gen. xxiv. 50), are now introduced as having objected to her marriage (8, 9); to which she replies that she has arrived at maturity, and has pledged herself to Solomon (10–12). All this is related by the bride, to show the determination and constancy of her affection from the beginning.

when she shall be spoken for. *i.e.*, when she shall be asked in marriage.

9 if she be a wall. *i.e.*, if she be inaccessible—unwilling to receive suitors—we will ornament her in reward for her modesty.

if she be a door. *i.e.*, If she be disposed to give a ready reception to suitors, we will keep her in strict seclusion.

10 I am (or " was," R.V. marg.) **a wall.** She replies to the brothers in their own style; and asserts that the modesty and reserve which rendered her inaccessible to the addresses of others had the more surely won the favour of her accepted suitor.

as one that found favour. The bride here uses the word from which the names Solomon and Shulamith (or rather Shelomith) are derived—" peace."

12 My vineyard, which is mine. See i. 6, and note. The bride employs the Baal-hamon vineyard as a parable of her own case, " My vineyard is before me," *i.e.*, is in my charge. But Solomon, she declares, is welcome to the profits of his vineyard. She yields to him her affection disinterestedly and in return for his love.

two hundred. This is probably a plea that her brothers may have some reward for their former care of her.

13 hearken to thy voice. Rather, " are listening for thy voice."

14 Make haste, my beloved. At the bridegroom's desire, the bride sings a verse which shows that she cannot forget the incidents of their earlier love (see ii. 15, and note). The song repeats that in ii. 17: only the hills of separation exist no more.

THE BOOK OF ISAIAH

INTRODUCTION

UPON this book, more than any other in the Old Testament except perhaps Deuteronomy, the searchlight of criticism, or critical scholarship, has been directed. The result has been to make clearer than ever two main facts about it: (1) Its prophetic, or Divinely inspired character, and (2) The Messianic nature of many of its predictions. Even accepting the view that there was a second writer, who composed the later chapters of the book—a view now taken by the great majority of Christian scholars—the latest date at which any of the book was written is not less than 530 years before Christ. Isaiah himself prophesied from 740 to 701 B.C., more than 120 years before the Babylonian captivity which he foretold (xxxix. 5, 7). Such a prediction and its fulfilment can only be explained by a supernatural vision revealed to him. And the predictions of Emmanuel (vii. 14), of the Prince of Peace and His unending dominion (ix. 6, 7), of the Servant of the Lord (xlii. 1–7), of His sufferings and final victory (liii.), and of His message of salvation (lxi. 1–3), however much they may have had partial fulfilment in persons or in the nation, have found their complete fulfilment only in the Lord Jesus Christ. This complete picture of the Saviour, be it remembered, was drawn, even accepting the latest date above indicated, more than 500 years before Jesus lived on earth.

It was the 61st chapter that our Lord applied to Himself in the synagogue at Nazareth (Luke iv. 17–19), and it was from the 53rd chapter that Philip, conversing with the Ethiopian treasurer, " preached unto him Jesus " (Acts viii. 32–35).

The contents of the book may briefly be summarised under three heads:

1. *Practical exhortations.*—Isaiah takes no narrow view of the preacher's office. He is a true preacher of righteousness. He denounces wickedness, individual and national (i. 4, 21, 23). Even the vanities of feminine attire do not escape his notice (iii. 16–24). The covetousness of the rich and their oppression of the poor he exposes unsparingly (v. 7, 8). Religion, with him, is something more than ritual observances and temple worship; it is above all, as God instructed him, a matter of conduct and right dealing between man and man (i. 13–17). But amid all rebuke of sin, he speaks of mercy for the sinner (i. 18;

iv. 4–6; xii. 1, 2; xxix. 24; lv. 7), and of hope and comfort for all faithful servants of God (xxv. 4, 8; xxvi. 3, 4; xxxii. 17, 18; xxxv. 1, 2, 10; xl. 29–31; xlii. 16; xliii. 2; li. 11).

2. *Predictions about the nations.*—These are principally given in the chapters or passages entitled "Burdens"; Babylon (xiii.–xiv. 23); Philistia (xiv. 28–32); Moab (xv., xvi.); Damascus, for Syria (xvii.); Ethiopia and Egypt (xviii.–xx.); Babylon, "the Wilderness of the Sea" (xxi. 1–10); Edom or "Dumah" (xxi. 11, 12); Arabia (xxi. 13–17); Jerusalem, or Judah, "the Valley of Vision" (xxii.); and Tyre (xxiii.). Further predictions are given in chapters xxxiii. and xxxiv. against Assyria and Edom.

3. *Prophecies of the Messiah and His Kingdom.*—In addition to those already indicated above, the character of His reign and its results are predicted in ii. 4; ix. 2; xl. 11; lii. 13–15.

[Apart from the exposition given below, the reader who desires to study questions of authorship, date, and fuller summaries of the contents of the book may be referred to *The Bible Handbook*, by Angus and Green, or to *The Progress of Prophecy*, by Prof. W. J. Farley, chaps. vii. and viii. (1925).]

CHAPTER I

1 The vision, etc. Ewald terms this chapter appropriately, "The Great Arraignment." From ver. 7 it has been argued that the chapter cannot be earlier than the time of Ahaz, when foreign invasions began. See 2 Kings xvi. 5, 6; 2 Chron. xxviii. 5–8. Or the picture may be that of the desolation caused by the Assyrians.

2 Hear, O heavens, etc. See Psa. l. 4. The appeal is repeated from Deut. xxxii. 1, being as applicable in Isaiah's day as it had been centuries before.

they have rebelled. The word "they" is emphatic in Hebrew: even my *children*, whom I have *reared*, have rebelled.

3 his owner. If the fatherly relation was too high to grasp, Israel might at least have risen to the level of the irrational animals, and recognised its Master.

4 A seed of evildoers. *i.e.*, "a race *who are* evildoers," not *descended from* evildoers. The Spanish version is "gente pecadora" (sinful race).

the Holy One of Israel This appellation is found almost exclusively in Isaiah. It suggests God's inherent holiness along with His covenant relation to His people.

5 Ye will revolt more and more. R.V., "Why will ye be still stricken, that ye revolt more and more?" Cp. Ezek. xviii. 31: "Why will ye die?"

6 From the sole of the foot, etc. Comp. Deut. xxviii. 35; Job ii. 7.

7 desolate. Lit., "a desolation." There were at least three invasions of Judah by "strangers" during Isaiah's ministry: one by the combined forces of Syria and Israel (vii.), and two by the Assyrians (xxii., xxxvi.).

8 the daughter of Zion. A personification of the city and inhabitants of Jerusalem: see 2 Kings xix. 21 and Psa. xlv. 12. "Sometimes, however, it seems to mean the city without the inhabitants (Lam. ii. 8); sometimes the inhabitants without the city (Mic. iv. 10)."—*Cheyne.*

a cottage in a vineyard. A temporary hut erected for the fruit-watcher of the vineyard or cucumber ground: see note on Job xxvii. 18. A picture of loneliness.

9 We should have been as Sodom, etc. *i.e.*, We should have been totally and justly destroyed.

12 to tread. Rather, "to trample," *i.e.*, insultingly; your attendance upon these outward rites, whilst your hearts and lives are ungodly and impure, is an insult to Me.

13 vain oblations. Lit., "the *minchah* (meal-offering) of vanity."

Incense is an abomination, etc. Rather, "Incense is abomination to Me; [and so are] new moon, sabbath, calling of assembly: I cannot endure iniquity, and the solemn meeting"; *i.e.* I cannot bear these services when coupled with iniquity: see R.V.

14 appointed feasts. The Hebrew term here used is appropriated in Scripture to the Sabbath, the Passover, the Pentecost, the Day of Atonement, the Feast of Tabernacles, and the Feast of Trumpets. Though these were appointed by God, yet when so kept they became hateful to Him.

15 blood. Heb., "bloods" (bloodstains).

16 Wash you, etc. This refers to *personal reformation*, which, although not the ground of forgiveness, is repeatedly commanded, as being indispensable to it; see lv. 7; Ezek. xviii. 30–32.

18 let us reason together. Listen to reason: hear what I am ready to do for you. "Isaiah lays more stress on this intellectual side of the moral sense than on the other, and the frequency with which in this chapter he employs the expressions *know* and *consider* and *reason*, is characteristic of all his prophesying."—*G. A. Smith.*

23 Thy princes. The corruption of the ruling class is always a main feature of Oriental misrule.

24 ease Me. Or, "rid Myself," as a man would do, of those who thus annoy Me.

25 purely purge. *i.e.*, thoroughly. Lit., "as with alkali," or lye. Metaphor from smelting. The "tin" (rather, lead) was used in alloying silver.

26 as at the first. As in the earlier and better times of the nation.

27 her converts. *i.e.*, those who return to God by true repentance.

29 the oaks. Or, "terebinth-trees"; meaning groves of such trees. These were favourite places of idolatrous worship.

31 the maker of it. Rather, "and his work" (R.V., so also Luther's version).

CHAPTER II

2 the mountain of the Lord's house. Mount Moriah, on which the Temple was built. It is here predicted that the true and spiritual worship of the Eternal God shall prevail over all systems of false religion, and that all nations shall be gathered under the righteous government of Zion's Divine King, that they shall renounce the arts of war, and shall learn and practise only those of peace. Christianity has already done much to mitigate the horrors of war, and to ameliorate, in various ways, the political and social state of mankind. (See Gladstone's *Letters on Church and Religion*: Letter to Sir A. Panizzi.) And we who live in the twentieth century have seen "what prophets and kings desired to see" and did not see—the gathering together of many nations in the League of Nations.

3 people. Rather, "peoples"; or, nations (R.V.).

He will teach us of His ways. The language of the "peoples" who go up to seek Jehovah, expecting to learn *part of* "His ways"—enough for practical duty: "we will walk," etc.

Zion. It was at Jerusalem that the doctrines and precepts of the Gospel were first preached, and thence they were diffused through the world: see John iv. 22; Luke xxiv. 47, 49.

4 among the nations. Rather, "between the nations." The peoples will appeal to Him as umpire on international questions. Disputes will be settled no longer by the senseless arbitrament of war, but by the Word of God.

6 Therefore. Rather, "For" (R.V.). In this declaration of God's displeasure the reason is given why the people must return to God (5), if they would have the foregoing prophecy fulfilled to them. Then follow the causes of this displeasure—their connexion with foreigners, and imitation of them in their superstitious practices (6), their reliance on pecuniary and martial resources (7), and their worship of idols (8).

replenished from the East. Rather, "filled *with customs* (or *superstitions*) from the East" (see R.V.).

please themselves in. Rather, as R.V., "strike hands with"; *i.e.*, make a compact with "the children of strangers," *i.e.*, the heathen.

8 idols. Lit., "nothings"; "gods which are yet no gods" (Jer. ii. 11).

9 boweth down . . . humbleth himself. In voluntary degradation before their idols.

Therefore forgive them not. Or, "And Thou dost not forgive them": a return to the statement in ver. 6.

10 Enter into the rock. *i.e.*, into the caves of the rock. The Jews had been accustomed to do this in times of hostile invasion: see Judg. vi. 2; 1 Sam. xiii. 6.

for fear, etc. Rather (as R.V.), "from before the terror of the Lord, and from the glory of His majesty." The phrase is quoted, 2 Thess. i. 9.

13 cedars. Lowth remarks that in Hebrew poetry certain images are regularly appropriated to particular subjects: *e.g.*, "cedars" and "oaks" to kings and princes: "mountains" to kingdoms; "towers" to protectors.

15 every high tower, etc. Referring possibly to the great works of Uzziah: 2 Chron. xxvi. 9–15.

16 ships of Tarshish. See note on 1 Kings x. 22.

all pleasant pictures. Upon all visible objects of desire; *i.e.*, upon all that is beautiful to the sight.

18 the idols He shall utterly abolish. Rather, "The idols shall utterly pass away" (R.V.), a vivid prophetic outburst.

20 To the moles and to the bats. The idolaters, finding their idols unable to deliver them, would fling them, in the terror of their flight, to these pests of the field and of the house.

21 into the tops of the ragged rocks. Rather, "into the fissures of the cliffs." The next words, "for fear," or "from before the terror," etc., are repeated from ver. 19. Such refrains are common in Isaiah.

22 Cease ye from man. *i.e.*, cease to trust in him.

CHAPTER III

1 from Judah. Not only from the capital, but from the whole kingdom.

the stay and the staff. Two genders of the same noun are used here, as in Eccles. ii. 8; Nahum ii. 13, according to a Hebrew idiom to represent *all*, *i.e.*, every *kind* of support: first, support of food (1); then, of order and government (2, etc.).

2 the ancient. Rather, "the elder."

3 the eloquent orator. Heb., "the skilful of whispering"; *i.e.*, "the expert enchanter": comp. viii. 19; and see Eccles. x. 11; Jer. viii. 17, where the same word is used.

4 babes. Lit., "childishnesses" or puerilities. Appropriate to the days of Ahaz.

6 clothing. This may be a strong representation of universal poverty in the land—a man who could still dress himself decently being distinguished above his fellows—a picture of misery heightened by the reply (7).

8 their tongue and their doings. That is, "their words and deeds"—their whole conduct.

10 to the righteous. Or, "of the righteous" (R.V.).

12 they which lead thee. That is, the prophets, who should be the people's teachers.

destroy. *i.e.*, they efface the traces of the way in which thou shouldest walk.

13 to plead. That is, "to accuse." He who accuses will also "judge," or condemn. For "people," read "peoples."

14 ye have eaten up, etc. Emphatic: "ye—ye have eaten." The words of God Himself. The "ancients," or elders, and "princes," have abused their trust to purposes of selfish indulgence.

15 grind the faces. "Crush" or "pound." A figure for cruel oppression.

16 the daughters of Zion are haughty, etc. A striking exposure and reproof of female luxury. The mention in vers. 18–23 of the things to be taken away shows the length to which extravagance was carried. Having depicted with dramatic vividness the scene of judgement, the prophet breaks off abruptly to announce a Divine threatening against the women of Jerusalem, whose influence had become so great (12), and who were now given to reckless luxury and extravagance: see on 23.

tinkling. That is, with their ankle-rings.

17 smite with a scab. And so make bald.

18 In that day, etc. With the increased knowledge now possessed of Eastern customs and dress, the following translation seems preferable: "In that day the Lord will remove the ornaments of the anklets, the tasselled tresses, and the crescents; the ear-pendants, and the bracelets, and the small veils; the turbans, and the ankle chains, and the girdles, and the perfume boxes and the amulets; the finger-rings and the nose-jewels, the festival robes and the mantles, the cloaks and the satchels; the mirrors and the fine linen vests, the headdresses (or turbans: the Hebrew word is only used here), and the large veils." Comp. R.V. A description of Egyptian ladies' dress and ornaments, illustrating this passage, may be found in Lane's *Modern Egyptians,* vol. i. ch. i., and App. A.; and one fulfilment of the prophecy is shown in Layard's *Discoveries in Nineveh and Babylon,* pp. 152, 153, where the sculptures commemorating Sennacherib's invasion are depicted.

24 a rent. Rather, "a rope" (R.V.). The rope thrown over them as prisoners.

stomacher. Or, "flowing robe."

burning. Perhaps a "brand" inflicted by the conquerors.

26 her gates shall lament and mourn. Bereaved as it were of the crowds who once met there for counsel or pleasant fellowship.

sit upon the ground. Sitting on the ground was a posture which denoted deep mourning and distress. Thus, in a medal of Vespasian, a woman is represented in a sitting posture, under a palm-tree, with the inscription, "Judæa Capta."

CHAPTER IV

1 seven. That is, *several*; the number "seven" being used indefinitely. Such would be the carnage of the war, that there would be few men left. In unnatural self-humiliation, the daughters of Jerusalem would not only seek for husbands, but would renounce their ordinary legal claim as wives, for food and clothing.

2 the Branch of the Lord, or "sprout of the Eternal." This prophecy is clearly referred to by the later prophets Jeremiah (xxiii. 5; xxxiii. 15) and Zechariah (iii. 8; vi. 12), in a manner which shows that the word "Branch" must be applied to a person who is a righteous judge, a king of the family of David, a servant of God. And this can be no other than the Messiah, who is justly called "beautiful, glorious, excellent, comely." So through belief in God and in His inexhaustible mercy "from the blackest pessimism shall arise new hope and faith, as from beneath Isaiah's darkest verses that glorious passage suddenly bursts like uncontrollable spring from the very feet of winter."—*G. A. Smith.*

3 Shall be called. The kingdom of the Messiah shall realise what the former theocracy symbolised —the moral purity of those whom God acknowledges as His people.

written among the living. Lit., "written down for life."

4 the filth. That is, their moral defilement.

the spirit of judgement, etc. The reformation and holiness of Zion is distinctly attributed to a Divine influence, convincing, correcting, and purifying like fire: comp. i. 25. That this is the work of the Holy Spirit we learn from John xvi. 8–15.

5 upon all the glory [shall be] a defence. Or, "over all the glory [shall be spread] a canopy" (R.V.), like the pillar of cloud and of fire over Israel in the wilderness.

CHAPTER V

1 my well-beloved. Or, "my Friend," meaning God. This introduction is adapted to secure a ready hearing for the prophet's communication.

In a very fruitful hill. Lit., "Upon a horn, a son of oil (or fatness)," *i.e.,* a fertile peak. The sunny sides of rocky precipitous hills have always been selected for the cultivation of the vine.

2 fenced it. Rather, "digged it thoroughly."

a tower. Serving to protect the vineyard, to accommodate the owner and his labourers, and to contain the implements of cultivation and wine-making.

4 wild grapes. "Uvas silvestres" (*Spanish version*).

5 it shall be eaten up. Lit., "it shall be for consuming," *i.e.* for a grazing-ground. Instead of being inclosed, it shall be thrown open for the pasturing and trampling of cattle.

6 no rain. This startling threat, which man could not enforce, prepares the way for the application of the parable in vers. 7–10. There can be no longer any doubt who the Lord of the Vineyard is. He is the Lord of the whole earth.

7 for judgement, but behold oppression. In this and the following verses the wild grapes are specified. Here and throughout the writings of the prophets we see how the sins of the past are repeated in our own time.

8 in the midst of the earth. Rather, "within the land."

10 ten acres of vineyard, etc. The tenth part of a "homer" was called a "bath" in liquid and an "ephah" in dry measure, and contained about seven and a half gallons. It is therefore threatened that an acre of vineyard should yield less than a gallon, and that the produce of arable land should be only a tenth of the seed. The acre (as much as a man with a yoke of oxen could plough in a day) was about two-thirds of an English acre.

12 But they regard not, etc. Cp. Psa. xxviii. 5.

13 because [they have] no knowledge. R.V., "for lack of knowledge."

14 hell. Heb. "Sheol," or Gr. "Hades": the grave (see Job xi. 8).

17 after their manner. Rather, "as in their pasture" (R.V.); *i.e.,* the whole land, even the domains of the rich (see 8, 9), shall become a mere pasture-ground for wandering shepherds. For "strangers" the R.V. has, more correctly, "wanderers."

18 a cart rope. That is, a strong rope. These men are represented not as being led away insensibly by sin, but as earnestly and perseveringly working at it with much labour: harnessed to it.

22 mighty to drink wine, etc. That was their only heroism, the heroism of the sot. In defence of right they were very cowards; unable to stand against the temptation of a bribe, *ib.:* see 23, and comp. i. 23.

24 the fire. Lit., "the tongue of fire" (R.V.).

the flame consumeth the chaff. Rather, "and as the burning grass falleth."

25 the hills did tremble. The natural and immediate reference is to coming invasions of the Assyrian forces, whose fierceness and violence, as illustrated by the monuments, are vividly described (vers. 27–29). Their onset, however, was eventually to be succeeded by the yet more terrible and fatal attack by the king of Babylon.

their carcases were torn. Rather, as R.V., "their carcases were as refuse"—unburied, like common street sweepings.

26 will hiss unto them. Or "whistles unto them," *i.e.,* summoning the invading nations.

28 are sharp. Rather, "are sharpened," on purpose to destroy.

30 against them. *i.e.,* against the nation of Judah. The imagery is now changed for that of an advancing angry sea, over which there settles impenetrable gloom.

CHAPTER VI

1 I saw also the Lord (Adonai). The Divine essence is declared to be invisible (John i. 18; Exod. xxxiii. 20), yet the phrase to *see God* is sometimes employed in Scripture to denote either an extraordinary display of His glory, or His appearance in a human form: see Exod. xxiv. 10. It is here evidently used in the latter sense: comp. Ezek. i. 26. The vision was that of the Son of God, John xii. 41.

His train. That is, the train of His royal robe.

2 the seraphim. "Seraphim" signifies, according to some scholars, burning ones, but others translate it "exalted" or "noble ones." The "cherubim" seen by Ezekiel, and the "four living creatures" of the Apocalypse, correspond with the delineation. Comp. ver. 11, and Heb. xii. 29. They *stood* "above Him" (R.V.), poised on their wings.

3 one cried unto another. They sang responsively; "the one (rank) called to the other."

Holy, holy, holy. A repetition of this kind elsewhere indicates emphasis: see Jer. vii. 4; xxii. 29; Ezek. xxi. 27.—"The intensity of recoil from the confused religious views and low moral temper of the prophet's generation. . . . The Trisagion rings, and has need to ring, for ever down the Church. . . . The vision of God—this is the one thing needful for worship and for conduct."—*G. A. Smith.*

The whole earth is full of His glory. Lit., "The fulness of the whole earth is His glory."

4 the posts of the door. Rather, "the foundations of the thresholds." (R.V.)

5 a man of unclean lips. See Job xl. 5, and note. The *lips* are mentioned probably because Isaiah felt his unworthiness in prospect of the call to declare God's judgements.

7 purged. Or, "atoned for." Fire here represents purifying influence (Mal. iii. 2, 3), which is shown to be connected with pardon, by the fire being taken from the altar.

9 Hear ye, etc. An idiom which probably means here, "Go on hearing," "Go on seeing."

11 Lord, how long? That is, "How long shall this blindness continue?" To which the answer in effect is, "Until it ruins them, and causes them to be removed from the country."

12 And [there be] great forsaking. Or, "And great is the desolation in the midst," etc. R.V., "the forsaken places be many."

13 yet in it [shall be] a tenth. Rather, "Yet in it (the land) [shall be] a tenth (a remnant), and it (the tenth) shall again be consumed; but as a terebinth and an oak, in which, when felled, there is a stock (to send forth new shoots), so a holy seed is the stock of it (the land)." This is a declaration that even the remnant of the nation should be persecuted, yet should be indestructible. A "holy seed" should be the germ of God's true Israel. See Rom. ix. 27; xi. 5.

CHAPTER VII

1 Rezin . . . and Pekah. See 2 Kings xvi. 5, 6; 2 Chron. xxviii. 5–8, and notes. The prophet's message seems to have been delivered at some time between the first successes of the allied enemies and their final retreat.

2 Syria is confederate with Ephraim. Lit., "Syria resteth on Ephraim." The name of the leading tribe of Israel signifies the whole kingdom. Syria had made it the "base of operations" against Judah.

3 Shear-jashub. This name means "A remnant shall return"; and is afterwards used (x. 21), not as a name, but as a promise which the child's presence was designed to convey.

the upper pool. This pool is a large tank or reservoir at the lower end of the Tyropœon valley. It is full in the rainy season; and its waters are then conducted by a "conduit," or aqueduct, to the pool of Hezekiah, within the walls. See *A Century of Excavation in Palestine*, by Professor R. A. S. Macalister (R.T.S., 1925), p. 184. The "highway," or rather "causeway," probably ran along the stone wall which formed the lower end of the pool, and beside it the fullers—cleaners of woollen cloth—plied their trade: see xxxvi. 2, 11, 12.

4 the two tails of these smoking firebrands. More exactly, "these two tails (or stumps) of smoking firebrands." Once mischievous, but now powerless.

6 the son of Tabeal. Nothing more is known of this person, who was probably a Syrian, as the name is Aramaic. Comp. Ezra iv. 7.

8 within three score and five years. The period thus defined includes the three successive strokes by which the power of the kingdom of Israel was annihilated; namely, the two invasions of Tiglath-pileser and Shalmaneser (2 Kings xv. 29; xvii. 6), and the introduction of foreign colonists by Esarhaddon (2 Kings xvii. 24). See, on these kings, Budge: *Babylonian Life and History* (R.T.S., 1925).

9 If ye will not believe. That is, Ahaz and his attendants, who probably showed signs of distrust, which led to this additional message, offering and giving a sign.

11 a sign. A "sign" is a sensible pledge, not necessarily miraculous, of the truth of something else. Here it is a token of the truth of what the prophet had promised in God's name.

12 neither will I tempt the Lord. When Ahaz was expressly commanded to ask for a sign, this was mere hypocrisy.

13 O house of David. Other princes of the royal family may have been in attendance upon the king.

will ye weary my God also? Will ye try His patience?

14 a (the) **virgin shall conceive, and bear a son.** Like so many prophecies of the O.T., this has clearly a double reference. The language of vers. 15, 16 points to an early deliverance, within the lifetime of the child. The second and complete fulfilment was in the birth of the Messiah (see Matt. i. 22, 23). As to the kingdom referred to (chap. vii. 18; viii. 8, etc.), Delitzsch has well said: "If Isaiah here, in chaps. vii.–xii., looks upon Assyria absolutely as the universal empire, this is so far true, seeing that the four empires from the Babylonian to the Roman are really only the unfolding of the beginning which had its place in Assyria. And if, here in chap. vii., he thinks of the son of the virgin as growing up under the Assyrian oppressions, this is also so far true, since Jesus was actually born in a time in which the Holy Land . . . found itself under the supremacy of the universal empire, and in a condition which went back to the unbelief of Ahaz as its ultimate cause."

15 butter and honey. (The word translated "butter" means thickened milk, curds or cheese.) These products are those of the desert, or of a country which has been depopulated and turned into pasture. Comp. ver. 21.

16 The land that thou abhorrest, etc. Or, "The

land whose two kings thou fearest shall be forsaken," *i.e.*, by its inhabitants; given up to desolation.

17 Days that have not come. Ever since the days of Ahaz, with the exception of very brief periods, the Jews have been subject to foreign domination.

18 shall hiss. See note on chap. v. 26.

the fly . . the bee. These figures well represent the numbers and destructiveness of their enemies. The *fly* is peculiarly appropriate to Egypt, where the moist heat produces it in abundance.

20 a razor that is hired. Ahaz had hired the help of the king of Assyria with the treasures of God's house: and God would hire or allure him by the plunder and conquest of the land. The head and feet, as the two extremities, represent the whole body, and the beard what was most valued and honoured.

21 a man shall nourish, etc. The people being too few and poor to till the land, should resume pastoral life, and that upon the scantiest scale, the finest and strongest cattle having passed into the enemy's hands. But with the reduced population, even this would supply milk enough and to spare.

22 Abundance, etc. The pasture being rich because of the few beasts to eat it down.

23 silverlings. Lit., "pieces (probably shekels) of silver." A shekel per vine was the rent of a valuable vineyard.

24 With arrows and with bows. Both for their own protection and for the chase, wild animals having now made their homes in the district.

25 There shall not come thither, etc. Rather, "*Thou* shalt not come thither for fear," etc. This verse completes the description of the general desolation; thorns and briers being represented as growing on the terraced hills; and districts once carefully tilled being converted into pastures.

CHAPTER VIII

1 with a man's pen. That is, using common letters, instead of characters which were known only to a few. For the same purpose of legibility the tablet or board (not "roll" as in A.V.) was to be large; and the letters, being few, would be large also. The name inscribed signifies, "Haste, spoil! quick, prey!"

2 Uriah the priest. Uriah (or Urijah) was probably the high priest mentioned in 2 Kings xvi. 10-16, who joined with the king in profaning the temple. Zechariah might be the father-in-law of Ahaz. see 2 Kings xviii. 2.

3 Call his name, etc. The child thus became the symbol of the impending chastisement of Syria and the Ten Tribes.

6 this people refuseth, etc. This probably means the people of both kingdoms (see 14). They compared the trickling "waters of Shiloah" with the mighty Euphrates, in other words their little kingdom with the greatness of Assyria.

7 the River. That is, the Euphrates, which aptly symbolised the Assyrian monarchy, because it overspreads its banks and inundates the surrounding country.

8 And he shall pass through, etc. More vividly as well as accurately rendered in R.V., "And he shall sweep onward into Judah; he shall overflow and pass through," etc.

thy land, O Immanuel. That is, "the land belonging to thee." This brief apostrophe to Immanuel, the Messiah, suggests a future deliverance, and leads on to an ironical invitation to all the enemies of Israel to do their worst, of the failure of which the name Immanuel—"God with us"—was a standing pledge (10). "*God with us,*" says G. A. Smith, "is the one great fact of life."

11 with a strong hand. That is, by a strong prophetic impulse: see Ezek. iii. 14.

12 Say ye not, A confederacy. R.V., "A conspiracy." This may refer to the alliance between Syria and Israel, which was causing so much alarm to Judah, or to the alliance which Ahaz was making with Assyria for his protection. In other words, put your trust in God, honour and reverence Him (ver. 13), and He will be to you "a sanctuary," an asylum from danger, such as the Assyrian monarch cannot afford you; whilst He will be a destroyer, worse than Rezin or Pekah, to those who distrust and disobey Him (14, 15). This involves a general principle, and is therefore applied to Christ and the Gospel: cp. 2 Cor. ii. 16.

16 Bind up the testimony. This was spoken to encourage the faithful Israelites to hold fast (binding and sealing in their hearts) to God's "testimony" (His promise), and keeping God's "law": thus being witnesses to the people of His truth, in opposition to those who vainly sought light by forbidden arts.

I will look for him. In God and in His word is the prophet's unquenchable hope.

18 and the children whom the Lord hath given, etc. Shear-jashub and the infant Maher-shalal-hash-baz. A remnant of God's people shall return: the despoilers shall themselves be spoiled! The "signs" had a universal meaning, and the language is therefore applied to the Messiah. Heb. ii. 13.

19 peep. That is "chirp" like small fowl. So also in x. 14. This feeble sound was supposed to be made by the spirits with whom the wizards professed to deal.

For the living to the dead? That is, Should they resort, in behalf of the living, to the dead? Luther's version has "Soll man die Todten für die Lebendigen fragen?" ("Are we to ask the dead for the living?") This is surely a message for those who are influenced by the spiritism of to-day. No real light has ever come on any subject from that source.

20 [It is] because [there is] no light in them. Rather, as R.V., "Surely there is no morning for them," *i.e.*, they shall have no relief, no prosperity: comp. lviii. 8; Job xi. 17.

21 through it. That is, through the land.

bestead. That is, distressed.

And curse their king and their God. Rather, "curse [their wretched fate] by their king and their God," uttering imprecations against their lot, instead of humbling themselves under God's mighty hand; looking "upward" in despair, and "to the earth" in sullen misery: beholding nothing but "darkness."

CHAPTER IX

3 And not increased the joy. Rather (as R.V.), "Thou hast increased their joy" (two different readings in the Heb., though alike in sound): comp. Psa. c. 3.

4 the staff of his shoulder. The staff with which the shoulder or neck is smitten.

the day of Midian. See x. 26; the point of comparison being the sudden destruction by special Divine interposition of a threatening host: Judg. vii. 2-13; viii. 1-23.

5 For every battle, etc. Rather, "For all the

armour of the armed man in the tumult, and the garments rolled in blood, shall even be for burning, for fuel of fire" (R.V.), *i.e.*, all warlike equipments shall be utterly destroyed, and war itself shall cease.

6 For unto us, etc. This magnificent prophecy, which forms one of the great choruses in Handel's *Messiah*, cannot, without extravagance, be applied to any other sovereign than Immanuel already predicted. The ancient Jews were unanimous in referring it to the Messiah; and, although these exact words are not quoted in the New Testament, the passage is evidently referred to in the annunciation of the birth of our Lord (Luke i. 28–33).

Wonderful. Lit., "Wonder." He is so in all respects, in His person, sufferings, and works.

everlasting Father. Lit., "Father of Eternity": eternal in His own existence, and the Giver of eternal life to others. This prophecy could not be applied in its fulness to any ordinary human being. The combination of this with His birth as a child is a very clear foreshadowing of the union of God and man in the person of Christ (see note on chap. vii. 14).

9 Ephraim and the inhabitant of Samaria. A counterpart to "inhabitants of Jerusalem and men of Judah," in ch. v. 3. The two prophecies are of a similar strain.

10 sycomores. Light and common timber, much used, like sun-dried "bricks" in cheap building.

11 Rezin. The Assyrians, by whom, under Tiglath-pileser, Rezin was slain, would invade Israel also; and the Syrians and Philistines would join the conqueror, and rush into and pillage the country: see 2 Kings xvii. 6.

join. Or, "instigate," "excite"; "stir up" (R.V.).

14 branch. Properly "palm-branch"; which grows at the summit of the tree, and is therefore very appropriately contrasted with the "rush."

15 The ancient. Rather, "the elder"; that is, ruler. The false prophets are called "the tail," because of their base servility to these wicked rulers.

17 shall have no joy in their young men. Shall signify His displeasure by suffering them to be smitten in battle.

19 darkened. Or, "burnt"; or, "consumed."

20 And he shall snatch, etc. That is, the people. These fearful horrors of civil war were doubtless realised in the unsettled period described in 2 Kings xv.

21 Manasseh, Ephraim, etc. There should be intestine strife in the northern kingdom, whilst the rival parties should combine "against Judah."

CHAPTER X

1 that write grievousness which they have prescribed. Rather, "and to writers [professional interpreters of the law] who prescribe oppression."

3 where will ye leave your glory? That is, "Where will ye deposit your honour?" as in a place of security.

4 Without me, etc. Rather as R.V., "They shall only bow down under the prisoners," etc.

VERS. 5–34. The following prophecy refers to an Assyrian invasion of Judah, which has generally been supposed to be that by Sennacherib. Some later expositors, however, have held that the passage applies to an earlier inroad, by Sargon, in connexion with his expedition against Philistia and Egypt (xx.). It would seem from the monuments that at that time Sargon overran the territory of Judah, and at least threatened Jerusalem (see further on xxii. 1–4).

5 the staff in their hand. That is, in the hand of the Assyrians. They who smote the Israelites with their rod were themselves only a rod in God's hand.

6 hypocritical. Rather, "profane," as R.V.

7 Howbeit he meaneth not so. Whilst wicked men form and pursue their plans, God is making them subservient to His purposes: comp. ver. 12, and note on 1 Kings xii. 15.

8 Are not my princes altogether ("all of them," R.V.) **kings?** The Assyrian monarch here asserts his officers to be equal to the kings of other countries. The satraps who led their several contingents were equal to kings in the extent of their government; some of them were really conquered kings: see the title "king of kings," Ezra vii. 12.

9 Is not Calno as Carchemish? That is, "Have they not been equally subdued by me?" All these towns were on the line of march from Nineveh to Jerusalem. Calno (modern *Zerghul*) had fallen under Tiglath-pileser; Carchemish under Sargon himself. Carchemish was the capital of the Hittites, now called *Jerablûs*. For its detailed history see Sayce: *The Hittites* (4th edition, 1925). Hamath is now called *el-Asi*, on the river Orontes. Arpad is now a heap of ruins called *Tel Erfâd*.

10 found. As a man finds and easily takes a nest: comp. ver. 14.

them of Jerusalem and of Samaria. As though Jehovah were a mere tutelary deity of a particular land: comp. 2 Kings xviii., xix.

11 Samaria. Taken by Sargon, 721 B.C.

12 the fruit of the stout heart, etc. That is, the wicked actions resulting from the Assyrian's arrogance.

13 the bounds of the people (peoples). That is, the boundaries of nations, by extending my own empire.

I have put down the inhabitants. Rather, as R.V., "I have brought down them that sit [on thrones]."

14 peeped. Or, "chirped." This comparison of the Assyrian conquest to a mighty "birds-nesting" is the very height of arrogance—sharply and suddenly rebuked in the next verse.

15 As if the rod should shake itself, etc. Rather, "As if a staff should brandish those who wield it! As if a rod should lift up that which is no wood!" This boast of the Assyrian is as absurd as for the staff to talk of using its owner.

16 his fat ones. The "stout-hearted" Assyrian warriors.

17 And the Light of Israel shall be for a fire. Comp. Heb. xii. 29 (where "*our* God" is emphatic).

18 And shall consume. Compare with this the vaunt of the Assyrian messengers in xxxvii. 24. The "thorns" and "briers" (17), the "forest" and the "fruitful field," together represent the battalions of Assyria.

And they shall be as when a standardbearer fainteth. Rather, "And it shall be like the wasting away of a sick man."

20 the remnant of Israel. See Hezekiah's invitation, 2 Chron. xxx. 6.

him that smote them. That is, the Assyrian, whose aid was sought by Ahaz.

21 The remnant shall return. Alluding to the name of the prophet's son: see viii. 3. The reference is still to the people of both kingdoms. "Mighty God," as in ix. 6. The return predicted evidently includes a return to God by true repentance.

22 Yet a remnant. Rather, as R.V., "*only* a remnant."

23 in the midst of all the land. Or, "In the midst of all the earth" (R.V.). The judgements of God are a spectacle and a warning to mankind.

26 And [as] His rod [was] upon the sea. Rather, "And His (Jehovah's) rod [shall be as it was] over the sea, and He shall lift it up after the manner of Egypt" (*i.e.*, the manner in which He punished Egypt): comp. ver. 24, where "the manner of Egypt" means the way in which Egypt *oppressed* Israel.

27 because of the anointing. The best translation appears to be: "The yoke (of Israel) is broken by reason of fatness": (see R.V. marg.), the figure being taken from a fat ox, which bursts and casts off the yoke: comp. Deut. xxxii. 15; Hos. iv. 16.

28 He is come to Aiath. Or, Ai. The prophet here describes, in vivid language, the march of the Assyrian king towards Jerusalem, from the north. (Sennacherib, twenty years later, approached from the south-west.)

he hath laid up his carriages. Rather, "he leaveth his baggage." Michmash was a strong post commanding a "passage," or defile (ver. 29; 1 Sam. xiii. 23), well fitted for a military depôt.

30 Lift up thy voice. Or, perhaps, "Shriek, daughter of Gallim! listen, Laishah! answer her, Anathoth!" representing the terror and sufferings of the captured towns. "Madmenah" (*dunghill*) and "Gebim" (*cisterns*) cannot be identified. They were no doubt suburban villages north of Jerusalem. "Nob" is at the northern extremity of the Olivet range.

32 that day. Or, "This very day" (R.V.), resting there one day, within sight of the city which he threatens with assault on the morrow. But there he shall suddenly fall, like a haughty (or lofty) tree felled by the axe (vers. 33, 34; comp. Ezek. xxxi.).

CHAPTER XI

1 the stem of Jesse. Rather, as R.V., "a shoot out of the stock of Jesse."

a branch. Heb., *netser;* the root of the name *Nazareth:* see on Matt. ii. 23.

shall grow. Lit., "shall bear fruit."

3 and shall make Him of quick understanding, etc. Rather, as R.V., "and His delight shall be in the fear of Jehovah." Delitzsch renders, "And fear of Jehovah shall be fragrance unto Him!" But G. A. Smith gives us a fresh thought here. He says: "The phrase may as well mean *He shall draw His breath in the fear of the Lord. . . .* Christ drew His breath in the fear of the Lord. . . . We too may, by Christ's grace, *draw breath,* like Him, *in the fear of the Lord.*"

the sight of His eyes . . . the hearing of His ears. "His favour or displeasure does not depend upon external qualities: He judges according to the relation of the heart to God."—*Delitzsch.*

4 reprove with equity for. Or, "shall do justice to"; "shall decide with equity for," etc. These just decisions, rigorously enforced, are designated "the rod (*or* sceptre) of His mouth.

5 righteousness . . faithfulness. Nearly synonymous, "justice . . . trustworthiness."

6 The wolf also shall dwell with the lamb. The cause of this reign of universal peace is to be found in the 9th verse. As the knowledge of the Eternal fills the hearts of men, so they shall be kind to one another; and the wild beasts, no longer hunted, but tamed by kindness, shall share the benefit of the Messiah's reign.

9 As the waters cover the sea. That is, *completely filling* its bed.

10 And in that day there shall be a root of Jesse. Rather, "And in that day the root (or sprout) of Jesse which is standing shall be for a banner of the peoples; to Him the nations shall seek, and His dwelling-place shall be glorious."

11 shall set His hand again the second time. This restoration is called the "second," the first being probably the deliverance of God's ancient people from Egypt. The countries specified after Assyria, the enemy then threatening Judah, are named in geographical order as surrounding Palestine, and are therefore to be taken for the *whole earth* (12): see Gen. x.; Numb. xii. 1. The complete fulfilment of the prophecy will be when "all Israel shall be saved": see Rom. xi.

the islands of the sea. Or, the coast-land of the sea"; *i.e.* the Mediterranean Sea: meaning such parts of Europe as were then known.

12 an ensign for the nations. An intimation of the ingathering of the heathen in fellowship with Israel into His Church: cp. lv. 4, 5.

the outcasts of Israel . . . the dispersed of Judah. The word "outcasts" is masculine; the word "dispersed," feminine: thus including all.

13 The envy also of Ephraim. See notes on Judg. viii. 1; 1 Kings xi. 28; and on title of Psa. lxxviii. The "adversaries of Judah" are here the Ephraimites.

14 they shall fly upon the shoulders, etc. That is, "They shall pounce upon" them like birds of prey. The tribes, instead of attacking one another, shall unite, as in David's days, against their common enemies. "The children of the East" are Edom, Moab, and Ammon, the exciters of the great confederacies against Israel mentioned in 2 Sam. viii., x.

15 the tongue of the Egyptian sea. The narrow gulf of Suez, through which a dry passage was made for the Israelites (Exod. xiv.).

in the seven streams. Rather, "*into* seven streams" (R.V.). The "River" is the Euphrates, which shall not be a greater obstacle to the return than the Jordan had been to the entrance into their land (Josh. iii.).

CHAPTER XII

This psalm of the Church of united Jews and Gentiles is a counterpart to Miriam's song in Exod. xv. Only one passage, however, is borrowed from it: comp. ver. 2 and Exod. xv. 2.

3 the wells of salvation. There may be an allusion here to the miraculous supply of water to the Israelites in the wilderness; which was afterwards celebrated with great pomp on the last day of the Feast of Tabernacles: see note on Lev. xxiii. 34; John vii. 37. The blessings of salvation are often compared to water: see lv. 1; John iv. 10; Rev. xxii. 1, 17; Joel iii. 18, "A fountain shall come forth of the house of the Lord." As Israel was miraculously supplied with water in the desert, so will God open manifold sources of salvation, from which ye may draw to your hearts' delight.

4 the people. That is, the peoples. God redeems His people with a view to the salvation of mankind.

Concerning Babylon (Chaps. XIII–XIV 23)

CHAPTER XIII

1 burden. Or, "oracle." This word is most commonly applied to threatenings: but not always: see Zech. ix. 1; xii. 1. It is the word (*massa*) used in Prov. xxx. 1; xxxi. 1. For the latest account of Babylon and its history, see Budge: *Babylonian Life and History* (1925). "Babylon represents civilisation: she is the brow of the world's pride and enmity to God" (*G. A. Smith*).

2 high. Rather, "bare," so that the signal may be clearly seen. "The banner-staff on the mountain, the voice uplifted, and the waving of the hand denoting a violent beckoning, are all favourite ideas with Isaiah."—*Delitzsch.*

the gates of the nobles. That is, of Babylon: see note on Job xxi. 28.

3 My sanctified ones. That is, "*consecrated* ones" (R.V.); My chosen and appointed instruments. The leaders and armies are spoken of as mustering under the command of the Lord.

them that rejoice in My highness. Or, "My proudly exulting ones"

8 Their faces [shall be as] flames. That is, flushed by intense inward agitation.

9 Cruel. That is, in which no mercy can be shown: comp. Jer. vi. 23; l. 42.

10 the constellations thereof. Heb., "its Chesilim" (Orions) (see note on Job ix. 9); *i.e.*, its most brilliant constellations. The extinction of the very sources of light represents complete and irreparable destruction.

12 the golden wedge of Ophir. Rather, "pure gold of Ophir" (R.V.). The terrible slaughter should make men rarer than gold: comp. iv. 1.

14 it shall be as the chased roe. Or, "gazelle which is scared." The flight of the foreign residents from Babylon is here vividly delineated. Babylon, in the days of its pride, was the mart and meeting-place of nations.

17 the Medes. The Medes are mentioned, according to frequent usage, as being at first more numerous and powerful than their allies, the Persians. In Isaiah's day, they were already harassing the Assyrians. Their disregard of wealth, which usually attracts invaders, their skilful archery, and their savage cruelty, are particularly noticed by the historians Herodotus, Xenophon, Diodorus Siculus, and Ammianus Marcellinus. At the time when this prophecy was delivered, the Medes, like the Babylonians, were subject to the Assyrians; but they threw off the yoke soon after Sennacherib's disaster, about 700 years before Christ: see Herod. i. 95, *et seq.*

20 Neither shall the shepherds make their fold there. In 1853 Layard described the site of Babylon as "a naked and hideous waste" (*Nineveh and Babylon*, p. 484). In the time of Strabo (born 60 B.C.) Babylon was a complete desert.

22 And the wild beasts of the islands. Rather, "And their houses shall be full of doleful creatures, and ostriches shall dwell there, and shaggy [goats] shall gambol there, and wolves shall cry in their palaces, and jackals in [their] halls of pleasure," etc.: comp. R.V. For the exact fulfilment of the prophecy, see Newton on the Prophecies, Diss. 15; and Keith's *Evidence of Prophecy.*

CHAPTER XIV

1 For the Lord will have mercy, etc. The R.V. for "mercy" reads "compassion." The reason of the judgement upon Babylon is here given. "Babylon falls that Israel may rise."

4 this proverb. Or, "parable" (R.V.) *mashal.* This triumphal song celebrates the overthrow of the Babylonian tyranny (4–6), which causes the whole earth to rejoice (7, 8), and arouses even the regions of the dead, where the departed kings receive the fallen monarch with astonishment and exultation (9–11). It forcibly contrasts his former pride of power with his terrible fall, and describes his want even of burial, the destruction of his race, and the desolation of his land (12–23).

6 and none hindereth. Rather, "with a tyranny without restraint." Luther's version has "ohne Barmherzigkeit" ("without mercy").

8 the cedars of Lebanon. For similar personifications of inanimate Nature, comp. chap. lv. 12; Zech. xi. 2.

9 Hell from beneath, etc. Lit., "Sheol (the under-world) shuddereth before thee at thine approach, it stirreth up the shades for thee, even the he-goats (the mighty ones) of the earth, it lifteth from their thrones all kings of peoples."

11 the noise of thy viols. Here put for music in general (see v. 12), *i.e., mirth* and *revelry.*

12 Lucifer. The morning-star. A *star* is a symbol of royalty (Numb. xxiv. 17); and the brilliant morning-star is an emblem of peculiar glory (Rev. ii. 28; xxii. 16). It, therefore, well represents the imperial grandeur of the king of Babylon; while it was especially appropriate on account of the pursuit of astronomical studies in Babylon.

Which didst weaken the nations. Rather, "Who didst lay low the nations" (R.V.).

13 in the sides of the north. Rather, as R.V., "in the uttermost parts of the north."

16 They that see thee. The scene has been gradually transferred from Sheol to the earth: this is the language of human onlookers.

19 thou art cast out of thy grave. On the importance attached to burial in the royal sepulchres, see 2 Chron. xxi. 20; xxiv. 16; Jer. xxii. 19.

as the raiment of those that are slain. Rather, "clothed," or "covered with the slain, that have been thrust through," etc.

That go down to the stones of the pit. The picture is that of a pit hastily dug on the field of battle to receive the slain, filled up with stones and trodden down.

21 Prepare slaughter for his children. Let the whole race be destroyed: comp. 2 Kings x. 11, 14, 17. None of the ancient royal family of Babylon ever regained the throne; and the Babylonian empire never rose again.

22 nephew. *i.e.*, grandson, "scion and seed" (*G. A. Smith*).

Saith the Lord of hosts. The manner in which the preceding prophecy received its accomplishment will be seen from the following summary of the more remarkable vicissitudes which Babylon underwent. In the days of Sargon and Sennacherib it was repeatedly humbled by the armies of Assyria 721–681 B.C.), and the strife continued until the reign of Nabopolassar, the Babylonian king, by whom Assyria was eventually crushed (about 609). Babylon attained its highest splendour under Nebuchadnezzar, son of Nebopolassar (died 562 B.C.). About 538 B.C. the city was taken by the Medo-Persian army under Cyrus. In consequence of a rebellion of the inhabitants about the year 517 B.C., Darius Hystaspis ordered its gates to be taken away, and its walls to be lowered. In the year 477 B.C., Xerxes plundered and destroyed the temple of Belus. After its conquest by Seleucus Nicator, 312 B.C., it fell still further into decay, especially in consequence of the erection of Seleucia on the Tigris, which that king made his residence; it was then made a royal park for wild beasts, and was gradually reduced to its present desolate state.

CONCERNING ASSYRIA

VERS. 24–27. These verses contain a solemn reiteration of Jehovah's purpose concerning Assyria. The language is akin to that in x. 24–27.

25 in My land, and upon My mountains. The fatal blow against Assyria was struck in the mountain-land of Judah.

26 This is the purpose, etc. The overthrow of Assyria, like that of the other world-powers, was a part of the righteous judgement of Jehovah upon all idolatries. Hence "the whole earth" and "the nations" are associated here with Assyria. "The words point, as it were, to the idea of a universal history,"—to "a scheme embracing all nations and all ages."—*Plumptre.*

CONCERNING PHILISTIA

VERS. 28–32. The new title and specification of time here given show that the following is a distinct prophecy.

29 whole Palestina. Rather, "Philistia, all of thee" (R.V.). The Philistines are spoken of above (ix. 11; xi. 14), and throughout the historical books of the Old Testament, as the hereditary enemies of Israel. They were subdued by David (2 Sam. v. 17–25; xxi. 15), and paid tribute to Jehoshaphat (2 Chron. xvii. 11); but rebelled against Jehoram (2 Chron. xxi. 16, 17), were chastised and subdued by Uzziah (2 Chron. xxvi. 6), and again revolted from Ahaz (2 Chron. xxviii. 18), and plundered the country of Judah. They are now threatened with severer inflictions by a host from the north (Assyria), which should crush them; whilst Zion, trusting in Jehovah, should be delivered (31, 32; 2 Kings xviii. 13, etc.). See, for much valuable light on the Philistines, *A Century of Excavation in Palestine,* by Professor R. A. S. Macalister (1925).

the rod of him that smote thee. Some interpret this of the sceptre of the royal house of Judah, now for a time "broken in pieces." Others regard it as referring to Assyria. One ruler (Tiglath-pileser) was dead, but a worse should arise—a "cockatrice," or "basilisk," R.V. (great viper), followed by "a winged dragon." Sargon and Sennacherib brought Philistia to ruin.

30 the firstborn of the poor. That is, the very poorest.

31 a smoke. Either the clouds of dust raised by an army, or the smoke of approaching fire—perhaps both—advancing from the north, *i.e.*, from Assyria.

none shall be alone in his appointed times. Rather, "There is no straggler in his hosts"; the picture of a disciplined army.

32 the messengers of the nation. Of any nation which should send ambassadors to Judæa. Whatever revolutions may occur, God is the protector of His people, and His enemies have no cause to rejoice.

the poor of His people shall trust in it. Rather, as R.V., "in her (*i.e.*, in Zion) shall the afflicted of His people take refuge."

CONCERNING MOAB (CHAPS. XV., XVI)

These chapters contain one connected prophecy against the Moabites, who, after the death of Solomon, had transferred their allegiance from the crown of Judah to that of Israel. Soon after the death of Ahab, they refused their annual tribute (see 2 Kings iii. 5); and they appear not only to have maintained their independence, but also to have gained possession of some of the towns of Israel (comp. Josh. xiii. 24–27), until the time of the Chaldæan invasion, when, probably, this prophecy was fulfilled. The sudden capture of Ar, their capital, and Kir, their chief fortress (see note on 2 Kings iii. 25), spreads terror through the other cities, and causes the people to flee to the mountains and the deserts (xv. 1–9). The Moabites are therefore exhorted to renew their submission to the king of Judah, entreating his protection (xvi. 1–5); but this they are too proud to do (6), and must undergo sufferings so dreadful, that the very thought of them makes the prophet weep (7–12). An appendix, afterwards added, announces the near approach of the catastrophe (13, 14).

CHAPTER XV

1 in the night. Rather, "in a night," as R.V.

2 He. That is, the people.

Bajith. "The house," *i.e.*, the temple of Chemosh, their god (comp. xvi. 12; Numb. xxii. 41).

4 His life shall be grievous unto him. Or, "His soul trembleth within him" (R.V.).

7 shall they carry away. That is, the Moabites. The "brook" is one of those flowing into the Dead Sea, probably *Wady-el-Achsa,* the boundary between Moab and Idumæa, "the brook Zered" of Deut. ii. 13. The Moabites, as their last resource, carry their possessions across the Willow-brook to the land of Idumæa.

8 Beer-elim. Perhaps, "the well of the mighty ones" (Numb. xxi. 18). Eglaim and Beer-elim were at opposite extremities of Moab. The cry of wailing passes through the whole land.

9 more. *i.e.* more calamities.

Dimon. Probably the same as Dibon, ver. 2. Here the "Moabite Stone" was found in 1868.

lions. Heb., "a lion"; a symbol of a mighty and cruel foe.

CHAPTER XVI

1 the lamb ("lambs," R.V.). That is, the tribute-lambs: see 2 Kings iii. 4, 5. By acknowledging the suzerainty of the House of David, the Moabites might put themselves under the protection of the Divine King of Israel.

Sela. "Rock" or "cliff." "Sela, *which is* toward the wilderness" (R.V.), is probably put for the Moabite frontier farthest from Palestine.

2 as a wandering bird. Terrified, and fluttering as it were with indecision.

3 Take ("Give," R.V.) **counsel.** This and the next verse (perhaps also the 5th) are best understood as an impassioned entreaty of the fugitive Moabites at the frontier, on the river Arnon, that the Hebrews would give them counsel and protection. The "shadow" is the protecting shade of Zion.

4 Let Mine outcasts dwell with thee, Moab. Rather, "Let My outcasts dwell with thee! Moab—be thou a shelter to it from the face of the destroyer": see the preceding note. The following words, to the end of ver. 5, are most naturally understood as a continuance of the Moabites' appeal. Judah is now in such a state that they have hope of a favourable reception.

5 he shall sit. Or, "One shall sit."

6 his lies [shall] not be [so]. Rather, "False are his pretensions." This verse is the reply of Judah to the Moabites, and gives a reason for rejecting their petition.

7 Every one shall howl. Rather, "All of it" (*i.e.*, of Moab) "shall howl."

the foundations. Or, "the cakes of pressed grapes" ("raisin-cakes," R.V.).

8 They are come even unto Jazer, etc. Rather, "They (the vines) reached to Jazer, they strayed to the desert; its branches were stretched out, they passed over to the sea." "The vine," one of the chief products of the land, is here used to represent its wealth and glory: comp. Psa. lxxx. 8–11.

9 I will bewail. The prophet mourns as a man the prospect of Moab's fate; responding to "the weeping of Jazer" with tears of his own. Jazer was at the northern limit of the territory as Kir-hareseth (Kir-heres, Kir of Moab) at the southern. Heshbon was the capital, Elealeh and Sibmah were close by.

the shouting for thy summer fruits. Or, "alarm (lit., 'battle-shout') is fallen upon thy summer fruits," etc.

10 I have made . . . to cease. These "are God's words. Amidst all his true and deep human sympathy, the prophet is still delivering a message from God."—*Kay.*

12 when it is seen that Moab, etc. Rather, "When Moab hath appeared (*i.e.*, before his gods), when he hath wearied himself on the high-place, and hath gone to his sanctuary to pray, yet he shall not prevail": comp. xv. 2.

13 since that time. Or, "of old." This and the next verse are manifestly an addition at a later time, when God had revealed the speedy fulfilment of the foregoing predictions.

14 the years of a hireling. That is, years exactly computed.

CONCERNING DAMASCUS (CHAP. XVII. 1–11)

Although this prophecy is nominally against Damascus only, it includes the allied kingdom of Samaria. It is evident that the date of this prophecy was early in Isaiah's career. Probably it belongs to the first year of Ahaz, about 735 B.C. It was fulfilled by the invasions of Tiglath-pileser (2 Kings xv. 29; xvi. 9) and Shalmaneser (2 Kings xvii.).

CHAPTER XVII

2 Aroer. There was one Aroer on the river Arnon (Josh. xiii. 16), and another "before Rabbah" (Josh. xiii. 25), not far from Ramoth-gilead. The "cities of Aroer" may be these two, with their dependent towns.

3 They shall be as the glory. See ver. 4. The allied nations shall fare alike.

5 the valley of Rephaim. See note on Josh. xv. 8.

6 gleaning grapes shall be left in it, etc. Rather, "gleanings shall be left in it, as the beating of an olive tree." Olives being gathered (as walnuts are with us) by beating the tree with a stick, a few at the top would frequently remain unobserved: see Deut. xxiv. 20.

8 the groves ("Asherim," R.V.) **or the images.** See notes on Judg. ii. 13; iii. 7. The "images" are "pillars of the sun" connected with the worship of Baal: see 2 Chron. xiv. 5; xxxiv. 4.

10 pleasant plants . . . strange slips. Or, "pleasant plantations and strange vines"—probably associated with heathen rites. For "pleasant plants" some read "plantings of Adonis" (*Cheyne*, R.V. marg.).

CONCERNING ASSYRIA

VER. 12–XVIII. The prophet now suddenly turns to the Assyrians, the instruments of God's judgement, and describes the onset of their hosts, and their instantaneous destruction, which is depicted in language of wonderful force and vividness (12–14). Information of all this is to be given to the messengers of Egypt and Cush, that they may acknowledge God's power (xviii.).

12 Woe to the multitude, etc. Rather, as R.V., "Ah! the uproar of many peoples, which roar like the roaring of the seas; and the rushing of nations, that rush like the rushing of mighty waters!" "So did the rage of the world sound to Isaiah, as it crashed into pieces upon the steadfast providence of God" (*G. A. Smith*).

13 the chaff of the mountains. Threshing-floors were commonly on hills: see 2 Sam. xxiv. 18, and note.

a rolling thing. R.V., "the whirling dust."

14 at eveningtide, etc. A foreshadowing of the destruction of Sennacherib's army. See xxxvii. 36.

CHAPTER XVIII

This short and difficult chapter is a call to Ethiopia and to Egypt to observe the Divine dealings with Assyria. Egypt was at the time under the dominion of Tirhakah, a powerful Cushite or Ethiopian king.

1 the land shadowing with wings. Rather, "the land of the rustling (or whirring) of wings"; Nubia and Ethiopia. The buzzing of innumerable flies is the great feature of this whole region, and may be employed as an emblem of the motley and swarming population.

2 bulrushes. Rather, "of papyrus" (R.V.); of which the Egyptians appear to have made light boats (as the modern Abyssinians still do), resembling the coracles of the ancient Britons.

scattered and peeled. Rather, as R.V., "tall and smooth"; a characteristic description of the Ethiopians. So ver. 7.

A nation, etc. R.V., "A nation that meteth out and treadeth down." Delitzsch renders, "the nation of command on command and treading down."

4 I will take my rest. Jehovah will not at first interfere with the Assyrians, but will even favour their success to a certain point, as dew and sunshine promote the growth of plants; but before their plans are executed He will interpose and destroy them: cp. Psa. l. 21.

5 when the bud is perfect, etc. God will suddenly frustrate the invader's plan when ripening for execution.

6 the fowls shall summer, etc. Indicating the whole year.

7 the present. This may refer to offerings sent from Ethiopia and Egypt to Jehovah: see 2 Chron. xxxii. 23.

CONCERNING EGYPT

CHAPTER XIX

"The first fifteen verses describe judgement as ready to fall upon the land of the Pharaohs. The last ten speak of the religious results to Egypt of that prophecy, and they form the most universal and 'missionary' of all Isaiah's prophecies" (*G. A. Smith*).

2 I will set, etc. Or, "stir up." History tells us that on the death of the king now on the throne of Egypt (Tirhakah) there ensued a time of anarchy, followed by the breaking up of Egypt into twelve petty kingdoms, subject to Assyria, after which Psammetichus re-established for a time the independence of the country, 664 B.C.

3 to the charmers, etc. The Egyptians have been, in all ages, much addicted to the arts of divination.

5 from the sea. That is, from the Nile; which, during its annual inundation, has all the appearance of a sea, and is still called by the people of Egypt by that name.

6 And they shall turn the rivers, etc. Rather, "And the streams shall become putrid, the canals of Egypt shall be emptied and dried up,": alluding to the offensive miasma exhaled by the half-dried canals: comp. R.V

7 The paper reeds, etc. Rather, as R.V., "The meadows by the Nile, by the brink of the Nile, and all that is sown by the Nile, shall become dry," etc. These places would naturally be the last to suffer from a drought.

8 The fishers also shall mourn. The Nile has always been celebrated for the quantity, variety, and excellence of its fish.

9 they that work in fine flax. Both flax and cotton ("networks") abounded and still abound in Egypt, and their cultivation and manufacture afforded support to many of its inhabitants.

10 And they shall be broken, etc. Rather, "And her pillars shall be broken in pieces, all they that work for hire shall be grieved," R.V. The distress affects all classes, both the nobles (or "pillars") and the poor.

11 the princes of Zoan. See note on Psa. lxxviii. 12.

12 Where are the ? This form of challenge characterises the later chapters of Isaiah (xli. 22, 26; xliii. 9; xlv. 21; xlviii. 14).

13 Noph. In Egyptian *Men-nophri,* and in modern Coptic *Men-nouf.* Hence it was called by the Hebrews *Noph* or *Moph* (Hos. ix. 6), and by the Greeks *Memphis.* It was the capital first of Lower Egypt, and then of the whole country, until superseded by Alexandria. Little now remains but vast ruins; much of the materials having been used to build other cities. But the famous recumbent Colossi of Rameses, mentioned by Herodotus, are to be seen there. It is reached from Bedrashên, which is about an hour by train from Cairo. Not far from it is the Serapeum, or burial-place of the sacred bulls.

seduced. Or, "caused to go astray" (R.V.); as in the next verse.

14 hath mingled. The land is compared to a vessel in which an intoxicating draught is mingled.

15 branch. "Palm-branch," as R.V. The labours of the higher and the lower alike shall fail.

18 the language of Canaan. The reception of a language implies the adoption of the customs of a people; and to speak the language of Canaan, *i.e.*, the sacred language used in the worship of Jehovah, denotes conversion to Him. Some interpret the numbers in this verse definitely, but apply them to different cities; others regard "five" as put for an indefinite number.

The city of destruction. Most commentators, following some ancient MSS., which have one Hebrew letter slightly changed (ח for ה) read "the city of the Sun," *i.e.*, Heliopolis (the *On* of Gen. xli. 45), where a temple was erected, 149 B.C., after the model of that at Jerusalem. It was here that "Cleopatra's Needle" once stood, and that its twin obelisk still stands.

19 an altar to the Lord. The honours which they once paid to their idols shall now be paid to the Eternal.

23 a highway. Free communication and intimate union. The way between Egypt and Assyria lay through the land of Israel, which often suffered disastrously in the conflict between the two empires. Now it should be a bond of reconciliation between them.

shall serve. That is, shall serve God.

24 shall Israel be the third. That is, the three nations shall be united as one people. The prophecy must be considered as referring rather to the spread of the true religion and the worship of the true God, than to a political or civil alliance.

25 My people . . . the works of My hands . . . Mine inheritance. Egypt and Assyria having been chief among the enemies of God's people, represent the world-powers in conflict with His true Israel; and the prophecy seems to intimate, not the destruction, but the conversion of those who have opposed God's kingdom, and their admission to the full enjoyment of Gospel blessings.

CHAPTER XX

1 Ashdod. Ashdod, now *Esdud,* one of the five cities of the Philistines (see Josh. xv. 46, 47; 1 Sam. v. 1, the Azotus of Acts viii. 40), was the key to Egypt on the side of Palestine; it was therefore strongly fortified, and was frequently attacked in the wars between Egypt and Assyria. Herodotus says that it sustained a siege of twenty-nine years by Psammetichus, king of Egypt.

Sargon. This king (*Sar-ukin,* "He established the king"), whose name occurs only here in the Bible, is frequently mentioned in the Assyrian inscriptions; which for the first time enable us to understand many historical facts and allusions of Scripture. To several of these the notes on following chapters will call attention (see especially xxi., xxii., xxxvii.). Sargon usurped the Assyrian throne on the death of Shalmaneser IV. At the time of his accession (722 B.C.) the siege of Samaria, begun by Shalmaneser, was in progress; and it was Sargon by whom the city was overthrown and its inhabitants deported (2 Kings xvii. 6). His reign, which was marked by much military prowess, continued for seventeen years, and he was succeeded by his son Sennacherib, 705 B.C. The "year in which the Tartan (title of the Assyrian commander-in-chief) came to Ashdod" seems to have been 711 B.C., when Sargon sent an expedition to the city to subdue a rebellion against the suzerainty of Assyria: see Sayce's *Fresh Light from the Ancient Monuments,* pp. 111, 112; and Budge: *Babylonian Life and History* (1925), pp. 37, 104.

2 naked. That is, without the mantle of "sackcloth" which prophets usually wore: see 1 Sam. xix. 23, 24.

3 three years. That is, either *at intervals* during that time; or (connecting the words, as in the Hebrew text, with what follows rather than with what precedes), *for a three years' sign and wonder* (see R.V. and marg.).

5 they shall be afraid. Those Jews who expected help from Egypt and Ethiopia.

6 this isle. Rather, "coast-land" (R.V.); referring to Palestine, which lay along the coast, here called "*this* coast," to distinguish it from Egypt, mentioned just before.

Concerning Babylon

CHAPTER XXI

1–10. That this prophecy relates to Babylon is evident from ver. 9. The prediction refers to the overthrow of Babylon by Sargon (about 710 B.C.), as shown by the monuments (Sayce's *Assyria: its Princes, Priests, and People,* 1926, p. 52).

1 the desert of the sea. "The continent on which Babylon stood was a *midbar*, a great plain running to the south by Arabia Deserta, and so intersected by the Euphrates, as well as by marshes and lakes, that it floated, as it were, in the sea."—*Delitzsch :* comp. Jer. li. 13.

from a terrible land. *i.e.*, from Assyria: see Introduction to the chapter.

2 Go up, O Elam. The province of *Susis*, or Susiana, south of Assyria and north-west of Persia. It was now tributary to Sargon.

5 Prepare the table, Watch in the watch-tower. Rather, as R.V., "They prepare the table, they set the watch." A picture from the interior of the city: feasting within the palace, sentinels without.

Arise, ye princes, [and] anoint the shield. A sudden cry breaking in upon the festival: *To arms!* The shields were anointed or oiled before going into action, that the weapon of the enemy might have less effect on the slippery surface.

6 Go, set a watchman. The point of view is now changed; the prophet, at a distance from the city, being directed to send a messenger to watch what befalls.

8 he cried, A lion. Rather, "He cried as a lion" (R.V.), as if impatient and angry with long waiting: see Rev. x. 3.

9 here cometh a chariot of men, etc. Rather, as R.V., "here cometh a troop of men, horsemen in pairs."

he answered and said. They answered and said; that is, the troop of men who brought the news of the fall of Babylon.

10 O my threshing, etc. That is, "O my oppressed and afflicted people"; language of tenderness addressed to the Jews. It would have been better news for them that *Assyria*, their great enemy, would be defeated; but the prophet can only declare what had been revealed to him: comp. vers. 3, 4.

CONCERNING EDOM

VERS. 11, 12. **Dumah.** "Dumah" was an Arabian town and district lying south of Edom; but the name is perhaps here used for Edom or Idumæa, as the prophet is represented as interrogated "out of Seir." This prophecy is obscure from its brevity; but its position here, following that respecting Babylon, seems to intimate a connexion with the devastating inroads of Sargon. Would they extend to the desolation of Edom? The word *Dumah* is literally "silence," and the name of the town may be used symbolically.

11 He calleth. Rather, as R.V., "One calleth"—a mysterious voice, from the mountains of Seir, reaching the prophet's watch-tower in Jerusalem.

12 The morning cometh. The only answer that the prophet can give is that intervals of brightness will be followed again by gloom. Luther translates: "If the morning is already coming, yet it will be night."

return, come. R.V. marg., "Come ye again," *i.e.*, to inquire afresh, when some further revelation may be given.

CONCERNING ARABIA

VERS. 13–17. **Dedanim.** The Dedanites (see Gen. x. 7), on the east of Arabia, were a mercantile people, trading with Tyre in ivory, ebony, etc. (see Ezek. xxvii. 15, 20; xxxviii. 13). The interruption of their caravans, and the necessity of lodging in the thickets (out of the beaten track), is a proof of the disturbed state of the country.

14 Tema. A tribe of Ishmaelites (see Gen. xxv. 15) who dwelt in the neighbourhood of Edom, near the present caravan route from Damascus to Mecca.

16 the years of a hireling. See note on xvi. 14.

17 Kedar. "Kedar" (see Gen. xxv. 13) is here put for *Arabia* in general.

CONCERNING JERUSALEM

CHAPTER XXII

1 the valley of vision. That is, Jerusalem; called a "valley" because, though seated on hills, it was surrounded by hills still higher, with valleys between them; and "of vision," as the place where God's presence was manifested. The prophecy relates to some period when the city was besieged, most likely by Sennacherib. The picture of a besieged city, famished and imperilled, yet trusting in its defences, while the inhabitants sought to drown their fears in revelry, is depicted with indignant force.

that thou art wholly gone up, etc. Crowding to every place from which a view of the invading force could be obtained: in eager curiosity, mingled with vain confidence.

2 a joyous city. Full of reckless self-indulgence: see ver. 13.

not slain with the sword. The mortality was most probably from famine and plague, the consequences of the siege: comp. Lam. iv. 9.

3 They are bound by the archers. Or, as R.V. marg., "they are made prisoners without the bow." They make no resistance. Their self-confidence has led to humiliation.

5 crying to mountains. Their cry reaches the surrounding hills, which re-echo it.

6 Elam . . . Kir. Two of the tribes composing the Assyrian force,—Elam (see on xxi. 2) on the east, greatly famed for bowmen (Jer. xlix. 35; Ezek. xxxii. 24), and Kir (Armenia) on the west. These represent the two extremes of Assyria's dominions.

8 he discovered the covering. Rather, "he took away the covering" (R.V.)—"the curtain or covering which made Judah blind to the threatened danger" (*Delitzsch*).

the house of the forest. See note on 1 Kings vii. 2. This palace was intended for, or converted into, an arsenal.

9 the waters of the lower pool. Comp. 2 Chron. xxxii. 3, 4.

10 ye have numbered the houses of Jerusalem. Probably to ascertain how many of them could be spared for the repair of the wall.

11 a ditch. Rather, "a reservoir": (see 2 Kings xx. 20). See on this whole passage, Macalister: *A Century of Excavation in Palestine*, chapter ii., "Topography."

CONCERNING SHEBNA AND ELIAKIM

VERS. 15–25. This section illustrates the character and action of those who at this crisis brought about the national disasters. Shebna, an official in the court of Hezekiah, opposed the calls of the prophets, and encouraged the people in rebellion against Jehovah. He is to be degraded from his office, and sent into captivity (15–19), while his place is to be filled by a faithful counsellor (20–25). To a certain extent, he seems to have regained his position, as he re-appears in the same reign, although in a lower office (xxxvi. 3).

16 What hast thou here? The prophet may be

supposed to have addressed Shebna while superintending the excavation of his superb tomb; and then to have pointed to it, saying, "He is hewing out," etc. "Here" is thrice repeated, as emphatic.

17 will carry thee away with a mighty captivity. Rather, "will hurl thee forth far away with a man's throw."

will surely cover thee. Or, "will lay fast hold on thee" (R.V. marg.)

18 violently turn thee, etc. Lit., "rolling will roll thee [as] a roll, [and toss thee] like a ball": comp. R.V. and marg.

And there the chariots of thy glory, etc. Rather, as R.V., "And there shall be the chariots of thy glory, thou shame of thy lord's house."

20 my servant Eliakim. Nothing more is known of Eliakim than that he afterwards appears in Shebna's post (xxxvi. 3; 2 Kings xviii. 18).

21 a father. The prime minister was so called: see Gen. xlv. 8.

22 the key of the house of David, etc. That is, he shall enjoy high political authority. Our Lord appropriates these words to Himself (Rev. iii. 7), to intimate His power in the Church.

23 a nail in a sure place. A large nail or peg was usually inserted into the walls of Oriental houses to hang things upon. Here it denotes figuratively the security of Eliakim's position, and his ability to confer wealth and honour on his family: see Zech. x. 4.

a glorious throne. Or, "a seat of glory." His father's house, and all of his own family, shall be supported by him.

24 From the vessels of cups, etc. All who belonged to Eliakim, whatever might be their stations or employments, would be benefited by his elevation.

25 the nail that is fastened. These words refer to Eliakim: so making the lesson to the great ones of the land the more impressive and complete.

Concerning Tyre

CHAPTER XXIII

The subject of this chapter is the overthrow of Tyre (1–14); its depression for a period of seventy years, and its subsequent restoration to its former prosperity and wealth, which should be consecrated to God's service (15–18). As Assyria represented military power, so Tyre represented commerce. This ancient city of the Phœnicians (7), a colony of Zidon, was situated on the north coast of Palestine, and was built partly on the mainland and partly on an island near the shore. It was for ages the great centre of the world's commerce; and planted its colonies (among which was the powerful city of Carthage) along the coasts of Asia Minor, Greece, Cyprus, Africa, and Spain.

1 ships of Tarshish. See note on 1 Kings x. 22. The mariners of Phœnicia, putting in at Cyprus on their homeward voyage, hear with consternation the tidings of the fate that has befallen Tyre: the harbour which they joyfully hoped to re-enter has been swept away.

the land of Chittim. See note on Numb. xxiv. 24.

2 the isle. *i.e.*, the coast-land of Phœnicia.

3 the seed of Sihor. "Sihor" (the *black*, or muddy) is a name of the Nile, here also called "the River." Egypt, fertilised by the mud of the overflowing Nile, produced a great abundance of grain, which was exported by the Tyrian merchants "by" (or "on") great waters, *i.e.*, the Mediterranean.

4 the strength of the sea. Or, "the stronghold of the sea"; *i.e.*, Tyre: see Ezek. xxvi. 17. Tyre complains of being left desolate and solitary, like a widow who has never had children.

5 As at the report concerning Egypt. Rather, "When the tidings come to Egypt": see R.V. The Egyptians would be troubled, not only by the loss of trade with Tyre, but by the downfall of a powerful stronghold against invasion from the east: see ver. 14.

7 Her own feet, etc. "Whose feet carried her afar off," etc. (R.V.), alluding to the commercial travels of the Tyrians.

8 the crowning [city]. That is, the dispenser of crowns; many of her colonies being governed by kings under the mother state.

10 Pass through thy land as a river, etc. Rather, "Overflow thy land as the river" (*i.e.*, the Nile).

11 against the merchant [city]. Lit., "against Canaan"; the Phœnicians being Canaanites, dwellers on "the lowland," as the name imports.

12 thou oppressed virgin, daughter of Zidon. The "daughter of Zidon" (or the Zidonians) here means the Phœnicians generally.

Chittim. Cyprus. Here too they would seek refuge, but in vain. Luli, king of Zidon, fled to Cyprus on the approach of Sennacherib (*Records of the Past*, vii. 61).

13 Behold the land of the Chaldeans, etc. The R.V. reads, "Behold the land of the Chaldeans: this people is no more; the Assyrian hath appointed it for the beasts of the wilderness; they set up their towers, they overthrew the palaces thereof; they made it a ruin." The Assyrians had overrun and wasted Babylonia; and the same fate would befall Phœnicia.

15 the days of one king. That is, probably one kingdom or dynasty. Tyre would regain her commercial importance, though not her independence.

shall Tyre sing as a harlot. Or, "it shall be unto Tyre as [in] the song of the harlot." A song of which "the harlot" is the subject rather than the singer. Tyre shall make use of every means to bring herself into notice. The next verse quotes the refrain of the song.

17 shall commit fornication. This term, suggested by the word "harlot" in vers. 15, 16, is used metaphorically, and denotes the commercial intercourse of Tyre with foreign nations, the gains of her commerce being similarly expressed by the word "hire."

18 her merchandise, etc. The wealth of Tyre shall be made to benefit the servants of Jehovah.

that dwell before the Lord. Not only for the priests, who "stand before Jehovah," but for the people of the Holy Land. The renewed commerce of Tyre with the Jews after the captivity is intimated (Ezra iii. 7; Neh. xiii. 16); comp. Psa. xlv. 12.

Isaiah's Apocalypse (Chaps. XXIV–XXVII)

These chapters form one prophecy, consisting of a description of calamities (xxiv.); a song of praise for deliverance from them, and for the spread of the true religion which would ensue (xxv.); another song of praise celebrating the triumphs of this religion (xxvi.); and a prediction of the happy effects of these events on the character of the people of God (xxvii.). The language is so general as to suggest that it does not refer exclusively to any one period or event, but is rather intended to show the extreme measures to which God would resort in order to purify His people and to convert the world, as well as the beneficial results of His judgements. It would thus, in all the calamities which befell the Hebrew nation, point to their Author and design, and supply to the sufferers consolation and hope.

CHAPTER XXIV

1 the earth. Or, "land"; denoting the land of Israel, and so much of the surrounding countries as had their political interests implicated with it. The term "world" (4) is synonymous with "earth," and is applied in xiii. 11 to the Babylonian empire.

turneth it upside down, etc. The image here used is that of a vessel, completely drained by being turned upside down.

6 are desolate. Or, "are found guilty" (R.V.), or "punished" (R.V. marg.).

11 a crying for wine. Rather, as R.V., "a crying because of the wine"; *i.e.* because of the failure of the vine-crop. Comp. Joel i. 5; the likeness between the two prophecies has often been noted.

12 the gate is smitten with destruction. So that the city is left defenceless.

13 When thus it shall be, etc. Rather, "For so it shall be in the midst of the earth among the nations, like the beating of an olive tree," etc.: comp. xvii. 5, 6.

15 glorify ye the Lord in the fires. Some translate the latter phrase "in the [land of] light," *i.e.*, in the *East* (R.V.), as contrasted with "the coasts of the sea," *i.e.*, the West; comp. xlv. 6; lix. 19.

16 glory to the righteous. "Glory (*i.e.*, honour, splendour, as iv. 2; xxiii. 9) to the righteous [man *or* people]."

My leanness, my leanness! "Ruin to me! ruin to me!" etc. (R.V., "I pine away! I pine away!") This mention, from distant lands, of honour and renown as rightfully belonging to the righteous, only forces more painfully upon the prophet's mind the actual state of the land of Israel; which he describes in powerful language, ver. 17, etc.

18 the windows from on high are open. As they were at the Deluge: see Gen. vii. 11. Both heaven and earth are moved, and become the ministers of ruin.

20 shall be removed like a cottage. Rather, "shall be shaken like a lodging-place"; referring to a frail hut of branches.

22 visited. Or, "furnished," as R.V. marg.

23 the moon shall be confounded. Rather, "The silvery moon shall blush"; a bold and beautiful figure, perhaps suggested by the red appearance of the moon when eclipsed.

When the Lord of hosts shall reign. Rather, "For"; marking the cause as well as the time.

ancients. "Elders"; rulers of the tribes. Deut. xxxi. 28.

CHAPTER XXV

Of the chapters xxv.–xxvii., Sir G. A. Smith says that they "stand in the front rank of evangelical prophecy. . . . Perhaps their most signal feature is their designation of the people of God. . . . God's people are described by adjectives signifying their spiritual qualities." He points out that the three Hebrew words translated by two in English "poor" and "needy" (xxv. 4 and xxvi. 6) in their root ideas of *infirmity*, *need* and positive *affliction*, cover among them every aspect of physical poverty and distress, and came to be the expression of the highest moral and evangelical virtues.

2 a city. Perhaps the original allusion was to Babylon. But the reference goes far beyond any single event of the kind, and contrasts the ideal world-city with the ideal Zion, the city of God.

4 against the wall. Raging ineffectually.

5 branch. Rather, "song" (R.V.); *i.e.*, their song of triumph.

6 in this mountain. That is, in Mount Zion: see xxiv. 23. Jerusalem under Jehovah's glorious reign shall be the centre of attraction, and the source of light, life, and joy to the whole world ("unto all peoples"). This beautifully predicts the blessings and glories of the kingdom of Christ.

wines on the lees. Wines which have been left "on the lees," and are then filtered off, are said to possess a superior colour and flavour; "strong clear wines" (Delitzsch).

7 He will destroy, etc. God, by His Gospel, will remove that ignorance of and insensibility to Divine truth, which "covers" the intellects and hearts of men. (See remark at head of notes on this chapter.)

8 in victory. The R.V. reads "for ever," which is the true sense of the Hebrew word here employed.

the rebuke of His people. That is, the reproach cast upon them. The predictions of this verse are applied in the New Testament to the glories of the redeemed in heaven: see 1 Cor. xv. 54; Rev. vii. 17; xxi. 4.

9 Lo, this is our God, etc. "A brief strain from the hymn of the redeemed."—*Cheyne.*

10 under him. Rather, "in his place" (R.V.); *i.e.*, in his own land. There may have been some immediate reference in this prediction to events unrecorded. Moab, often actively mischievous against Judah, may be regarded as symbolising the enemies of God's people in general.

for the dunghill. Lit., "water of the dunghill"; straw trodden down, and left to rot in the pool.

11 in the midst of them. Rather, "in the midst of *it*"; *i.e.*, the pool, ver. 10. Moab may strive to extricate himself; but all the devices (not "spoils") of his hands will be useless.

CHAPTER XXVI

2 Open ye the gates. A call from heaven.

the righteous nation which keepeth the truth. Characteristic of the ideal Israel: "righteous" in allegiance to God; "keeping truth," lit., "faithfulness," sincerity in every form.

3 Thou wilt keep [him] in perfect peace, etc. Lit., "A [man of] fixed purpose Thou wilt guard in peace." Decision for God and confidence in Him ensure true peace.

4 everlasting strength. Lit., "a Rock of ages," *i.e.*, "an everlasting Rock," or Protector.

7 The way of the just, etc. Rather, "The way for the just is right ('smoothness'—*Delitzsch*); Thou, Most Upright, dost make level the course of the just"; *i.e.*, God makes a straightforward and prosperous course for the righteous.

9 in the night . . . early. Emblems taken from the darkness and the dawn. "In the night of affliction, and when the day begins to break."

12 in us. Rather, "for us," as R.V. The great works which Thou *hast* wrought for us assure us that Thou *wilt* give us peace.

14 Therefore. Rather, "For that purpose."

15 Thou hadst removed, etc. Rather, "Thou hast extended for all the borders of the land": a poetical description of the future increase and prosperity of the nation.

16 a prayer. Or, "whisper"; see 1 Sam. i. 13, 14.

18 We have as it were brought forth wind. This is a common metaphor for disappointment. When, instead of casting ourselves submissively upon Thy mercy, we struggled to deliver ourselves, we only aggravated our sufferings.

Neither have the inhabitants of the world fallen. Rather, as R.V. marg., "Neither have inhabitants of the world been born."

19 Thy dead [men] shall live, etc. Rather, "Thy dead shall live; my corpse (*i.e.*, the body of my people) shall arise."

the dew of herbs. Some render, "a dew of lights," light being a symbol of vitalising force. There may be an allusion to the reflection of the sun in the dews of morning.

cast out. Rather, "cast forth," as R.V.: produce men to life.

21 her blood. That is, bloodshed; as in i. 15. See note on Psa. ix. 12; and comp. Gen. iv. 10; also Job xvi. 18. The many unjust deaths which had been occasioned by wars or oppression should now be reckoned for and avenged.

CHAPTER XXVII

1 leviathan. These threatenings against Babylon, and Israel's other foes, are expressed in vivid figures. For "piercing serpent" the R.V. reads, "swift serpent." The best expositors take the emblems as applying respectively to Assyria (the *swift* Tigris), Babylonia (the *winding* Euphrates), and Egypt (Rahab, the dragon): see Psa. lxxiv. 13, 14, and note: Ezek. xxix. 3; xxxii. 2.

2 of [red] wine. Heb. simply, "of wine." In vers. 2–5, Israel is compared (as in ch. v.) to a vineyard, which God protects and rids of all that is noxious: comp. John xv. 1–8.

4 Fury is not in me, etc. Or, "There is no fury in me; yet would that I had the briers and thorns in battle! I would advance against them," etc. I will no more be angry with my vineyard, my people; but I will destroy the briers which have molested them, unless they make peace with Me (5).

5 take hold of my strength. Or, "take hold of My protection."

6 He shall cause them that come, etc. Rather, "In coming days Jacob shall take root."

7 them that are slain by him. Rather, "his slain"; *i.e.*, probably those slain on his account. "Hath God smitten Israel as severely as He hath punished their oppressors? **8** [No, for] in *moderation*, by driving her away, Thou dost contend with her. He sifteth her by His violent blast in the time of the east wind." (The Hebrew word translated "removeth" in A.V. expresses the separating of wheat from chaff or gold from dross.)

9 By this therefore, etc. That is, "By this [chastisement] therefore shall the iniquity of Jacob be expiated; and this is all the fruit (*i.e.*, effect) of taking away his sin: [this will appear] when he makes all the stones of the altar (*i.e.*, of his idols) like broken chalk-stones; [so that] the Asherahs and the sun-pillars shall stand no more": comp. R.V. On "the groves," or Asherahs, see note on Judg. iii. 7.

10 Yet the defenced city, etc. Some regard this as a further description of God's chastisements in the desolation of Jerusalem. Others think that it refers to a city or cities of the Gentiles.

the branches thereof. The branches of the trees growing among its ruins.

11 set them on fire. That is, make fires with them.

12 shall beat off. That is, "shall beat off *the fruit*," as R.V.; shall gather it in; see xvii. 6. The "River" is the Euphrates. As a husbandman gathers in his olives from his trees, so God shall gather in His people from Babylon (on "the river" Euphrates) and from Egypt by "the brook," the boundary between Egypt and Palestine, the *Wady-el-Arish.*

one by one. Carefully and completely.

CHAPTER XXVIII

1 the crown of pride. Or, "the proud crown of the drunkards," etc.; *i.e.*, the haughty capital of the sensualised people of the Ten Tribes. This refers to Samaria, which crowns the summit of a fine round swelling hill encircled by "fat (or rich) valleys": see note on 1 Kings xvi. 24.

2 a mighty and strong one. Probably the king of Assyria: comp. vii. 17–20; viii. 7.

4 the hasty fruit. The early (not "hasty"; the "first ripe," R.V.) fig is eagerly plucked and eaten as a rarity: so the Assyrians would eagerly seize and completely destroy Samaria.

7 they also have erred through wine, etc. The sins which had caused the ruin of Ephraim had deeply infected Judah also.

9 Whom shall he teach knowledge? That is, "Whom [say they] shall he teach?" etc. These are the questions of the demoralised priests and judges (7), who repel with scorn the idea that they should require the plain and repeated teachings of the prophet, which they regard as fit only for children.

10 For precept [must be] upon precept, etc. More exactly, as R.V., "For [it is] precept upon precept," etc. The very sound of the words in Hebrew is expressive of scornfulness: *tsav latsav, tsav latsav; kav lakav, kav lakav; tseyr sham, tseyr sham.*

11 For with stammering lips. etc. This is a response to the preceding taunting language. Since the people refused to hearken to God's messages, which they regarded as adapted only to children, He would teach them by the stammering (*i.e.*, unintelligible) speech of foreigners.

12 This is the rest. In the plain instructions which God gave them, He pointed out the only way to real peace and safety. But "they would not hear"; therefore (13) these instructions have become to them a curse, and not a blessing: comp. 2 Cor. ii. 15, 16.

15 Because ye have said, etc. In thought, if not in word. This was the natural interpretation of their impious disregard of God's threatenings and judgements. The language undoubtedly refers to the various attempts of the politicians of the time to gain the support of heathen powers: see 2 Kings xvi. 7, 9; and comp. Jer. ii. 17, 19.

with hell (Sheol). As though by a private understanding, to escape.

16 A stone. Before announcing the destruction of these sinners and their "refuge of lies," the prophet points to Zion, and reminds God's people of that ancient promise to the family of David, on which, amidst all God's judgements, they were to build their peace and security. This passage, therefore, like many others, directed them to look forward for comfort to our Lord's coming. The prophecy is more than once quoted in the New Testament; see Rom. ix. 33; x. 11; 1 Pet. ii. 6 (where it is specifically referred to Christ).

shall not make haste. "Shall not flee away." "Wer glaubet, der fliehet nicht" (*Luther's version*).

17 Judgement also will I lay to the line, etc. God would make strict justice the rule of His proceedings, as the builder regulates his work by the line and plummet.

19 From the time that it goeth forth. Rather, as R.V., "As often as it passeth through."

it shall be a vexation only to understand the report, or "message." The "doctrine" (9), which they had derided as only fit for babes, shall become "a terror" to them when they once learn its meaning.

21 as in Mount Perazim, etc. God will treat His rebellious people as He formerly treated their heathen enemies: see Josh. x. 10, 11; 2 Sam. v. 17–25; 1 Chron. xiv. 8–17.

22 bands. "Bands" often represent penal suffering.

23 hear my speech. The following parable is a vindication of God's severe and "strange" chastisements. As the farmer varies his operations according to the soil, the season, and the nature of the crop, so does God change His treatment of men according to their spiritual condition.

24 Doth he open? That is (as R.V.), "Doth he *continually open?*" He is not content to be always ploughing.

25 When he hath made plain, etc. Rather, "When he has levelled its surface, does he not cast abroad the fitches (or fennel), and sow cummin broad-cast, and plant wheat in rows, and barley marked out (perhaps drilled), and spelt in its border?" The two modes of sowing are clearly distinguished.

27 the fitches are beaten out, etc. Four modes or threshing are here described. Fitches and cummin are threshed with a *flail*, bread-corn with a *sledge* armed with sharp stones or iron teeth, other corn with the *wheels of the wagon*, and the *trampling of horses*. So God, from whom the farmer's knowledge comes (v. 29), adapts His treatment to the needs of men.

CHAPTER XXIX

1 Ariel. This name, as applied to Zion or Jerusalem, may denote either *lion of God, i.e.*, a city of heroes; or, preferably, *fire-place* (*i.e.*, altar) of God, as in Ezek. xliii. 15, 16; where "Ariel" is twice rendered "altar" ("altar hearth," R.V.).

where David dwelt. Lit., as R.V., "where David encamped."

Let them kill sacrifices. Rather, "Let the festivals go round," *i.e.*, year by year. Though they have done so through a long period, yet the city shall not escape God's chastisements (2).

2 it shall be unto me as Ariel. That is, it shall correspond to its name; it shall be a place of sacrifice an altar-hearth.

4 thy speech shall be low, etc.: see note on viii. 19. Jerusalem would be greatly weakened and humbled, and would speak as one in fear.

5 Moreover the multitude, etc. Or, "But the multitude of thy strangers, or foes" (R.V.). Though much distressed, the city should not now be taken.

9 Stay yourselves, and wonder. Rather, "Stupefy yourselves, and be stupid: blind yourselves, and be blind"; addressed to Jerusalem, whose spiritual sottishness and blindness are depicted, 10, 12: comp. vi. 10.

11 the vision of all. Rather, as R.V., "all vision."

12 I am not learned. Rather, "I know not writing"; *i.e.*, I cannot read. Every one, learned or ignorant, has his own excuse for not attending to God's word, though all profess to honour Him (13).

13 taught by the precept of men. That is, their very religion is a matter of human authority, and merely learned by rote: see R.V. marg. The description is applied by our Lord to the traditionalists of His time: Matt. xv. 8, 9.

15 that seek deep, etc. Or, "seek to hide their plans deep." The politicians of Jerusalem endeavoured to act independently of God.

16 Surely your turning of things, etc. Rather (as R.V. and marg.), "Oh, your perversity! Shall the potter be counted as clay?" Is he not superior to it? Does he not know all about it? Surely, then, God sees through the hearts of His creatures.

17 Lebanon shall be turned, etc. A proverbial phrase, meaning that the wild and the cultivated shall change places (comp. xxxii. 15, and note). It points, probably, to the future casting off of the Jews, and the admission of the Gentiles to the privileges of God's people: comp. Matt. xxi. 43; Rom. xi. 7–24.

18 shall the deaf hear the words of the book. An allusion, probably, to the figure in vers. 11, 12. The Gentiles, who had been in real, not pretended, darkness, shall hear and see the words of life.

20 the terrible one . . . the scorner . . . all that watch, etc. The proud, scornful, and ungodly. To "watch" or to keep awake for a thing is to pursue it eagerly.

22 Jacob shall not now be ashamed. Jacob is poetically supposed to be looking on his children. Instead of observing with shame and sorrow, as in times past, their sins and sufferings, he rejoices, both in the accession of a new spiritual progeny, the special workmanship of God (ver. 23; Eph. ii. 10), and in the restoration to saving wisdom of his own natural descendants (ver. 24; Rom. xi. 11–15, 31, 32).

CHAPTER XXX

1 that cover with a covering. "Weave a web," referring to the proposed treaty.

not of My spirit. Contrary to the warnings of My prophets.

4 his princes. The princes, or nobles, of Judah. They wait on the frontier while their envoys go forward to the interior: see note on "Zoan," Psa. lxxviii. 12. "Hanes" is probably "Hnés," or "Ehnés," in Middle Egypt, on the west side of the Nile; called by the Greeks Heracleopolis.

6 The burden (oracle) **of the beasts of the south.** The title of the brief prediction that follows. The prophet sees the Jewish messengers going down to Egypt with their gifts, to secure a favourable reception, and exclaims, "Through the land of trouble and anguish," etc. The asses and camels carry the presents through the desert, and to no good purpose at the end.

7 Therefore have I cried concerning this, etc.

The best expositors render this, "Therefore I have named her Rahab that sitteth still." The name "Rahab," meaning "pride" or "arrogancy" (Job ix. 13; xxvi. 12), is used poetically for Egypt (see Psa. lxxxvii. 4; lxxxix. 10; Isa. li. 9). "*Blustering and inactivity, blustering and sitting still*, that is her character" (*G. A. Smith*).

9 That this is a rebellious people. Rather (as R.V.), "For this is a rebellious people. The reason why the oracle (6, 7) was to be written down, to witness against their perversity.

12 this word. That is, the messages of the prophets (9, 10), in particular the warning against invoking Egyptian aid: a policy stigmatised as "iniquity" (13).

13 Swelling out. Or, bulging like an Eastern wall of unburnt bricks: comp. "a bowing wall" (Psa. lxii. 3).

14 And He shall break it. Rather, "and its breaking shall be as the breaking of a potter's vessel, a shattering unsparingly," etc. The punishment will be sudden (13) and complete (14).

a sherd. A fragment of pottery: see Job ii. 8.

15 In returning and rest. That is, in returning obediently to the precepts, and quietly confiding in the covenant of the Holy One of Israel: see ver. 11. "Isaiah preached no submission to fate, but reverence for an all-wise Ruler, whose method was plain to every clear-sighted observer of the fortunes of the nations of the world, and whose purpose could only be love and peace to His own people" (*G. A. Smith*).

16 we will flee upon horses. For which Egypt was famous (xxxi. 1): see note on 1 Kings x. 29.

17 One thousand [shall flee], etc. The opposite of the promise in Lev. xxvi. 8, etc.

as a beacon. Heb., "a pine tree"; hence "a beacon," "a signal-post," or "a mast": solitary, a mere remnant and memorial.

18 therefore will the Lord wait. That is, Since God has determined to chastise you for good, He will "wait" (as one who expects a beneficial result) "that He may be gracious to you." Thus He will display His "mercy" as well as His "judgement," or justice.

20 Yet shall not thy teachers be removed. Though God might still afflict them outwardly, He would not deprive them of their religious privileges; but whenever they attempted to go astray, He would follow them with admonitions to return (21).

22 Ye shall defile. That is, You shall regard them as polluted and unclean. The images of idols were usually made of wood or clay "covered" or plated with gold or silver. So for "ornament" the R.V. has "plating."

24 ear. Or, "plough": see note on Gen. xlv. 6.

clean. Or, "savoury," R.V. Heb., "salted." The word rendered "provender," means literally *mixed* food: various kinds of grain, duly seasoned, and "winnowed" from all useless or injurious elements.

25 Rivers [and] streams of waters. Plentiful irrigation, one of the blessings of peace in a country at rest.

28 To sift the nations with the sieve of vanity. That is, so as to sift them to nothing. The three metaphors of a flood (see viii. 8), a sieve, and a bridle to restrain, describe God's dealings with the nations.

29 the night when a holy solemnity is kept. The Passover, which was celebrated at night (see Exod. xii. 42; Deut. xvi. 1–6), and at which hymns were sung: see Matt. xxvi. 30, and note on Psa. cxiii. 1.

when one goeth with a pipe. Like the companies who came up with music of flutes to the annual festivals at Jerusalem.

the mighty One of Israel. Lit., as R.V., "the Rock of Israel."

31 For through the voice of the Lord, etc. Or, "He (the Eternal) shall smite [him] with a rod. And every stroke of the ordained rod, which Jehovah will lay upon him, shall be with tabrets and harps"; *i.e.*, with rejoicings on the part of those whom Assyria had oppressed (32).

33 Tophet. Rather, as R.V., "a Topheth": see note on 2 Kings xxiii. 10.

"for the king." Rather, "for Moloch," as for a sacrifice to him. The force and pride of Assyria shall be utterly consumed.

CHAPTER XXXI

1 horses . . . chariots . . . horsemen. See notes on Deut. xvii. 16; 1 Kings x. 29.

2 Yet He also is wise. A stroke of refined irony.

evil. That is, "calamity"; the punishment, which "His words" had threatened against "the house of evil-doers," the race of wicked, unbelieving Jews; and against Egypt, whom they regarded as their "help."

6 Turn ye unto Him. The promises of Divine interposition are here used to enforce repentance.

8 not of a mighty man . . . not of a mean man. The Assyrian army shall be destroyed by God's direct interposition.

shall be discomfited. Rather, "Shall become enslaved," "shall become tributary," R.V.

9 And he shall pass over, etc. Or, "And his rock (*i.e.*, strength—his host) through fear shall pass away, and his princes shall flee from the standard"; representing the remnant of his army, even his generals, as fleeing panic-stricken from their ensigns: see R.V.

whose fire (light) **is in Zion.** See note on "Ariel," xxix. 1.

CHAPTER XXXII

2 a man. That is, the King spoken of in ver. 1. To a traveller in the East, shelter from the winds of the desert, with their suffocating clouds of dust, water to quench thirst, and shade from the scorching sun, would be inestimable blessings. "Temptations keep far away from the heart that keeps near to Christ" (*G. A. Smith*).

4 the rash. Or, precipitate. **Stammerers,** hesitating. Two extremes.

5 The vile person, etc. *i.e.*, there will be a due discrimination of character; and persons and things will be called by their right names.

7 The instruments. The *means* which he uses to increase his wealth.

8 by liberal things shall he stand. Or, "and to liberal things he will stand"; *i.e.*, he will persevere in them.

12 They shall lament for the teats. "They (masc.) shall smite upon their breasts" (R.V.), in token of grief.

13 houses of joy. "Happy homes."

14 The forts and towers. Rather, "Ophel and the watch-tower": see note on 2 Chron. xxvii. 3.

15 the fruitful field be counted for a forest. See note on xxix. 17. Here the thought is that "the whole would be so glorious that what was now valued as a fruit-garden would be thrown into the shade by something far more glorious still, in comparison with which it would have the appearance of a wild domain" (*Delitzsch*). The "breath" which makes the wilderness fruitful is an emblem of the power by which moral and spiritual renovation is produced.

17 quietness and assurance. As the effusion of the Spirit produces righteousness, so the prevalence of righteousness causes universal peace amongst men: see note on Psa. lxxii. 3. For "assurance" the R.V. has "confidence."

19 When it shall hail. Rather, as R.V., "But it shall hail, at the downfall of the forest." The "forest" denotes Sennacherib's army; and the "city" is either Nineveh, the metropolis of Assyria, or the ideal fortress of the world-power: comp. xxv. 2; xxvi. 5, 6.

20 Blessed are ye that sow beside all waters. Those who expect the fulfilment of these glorious promises are thus encouraged to patient obedience in the dark and difficult times that must intervene.

CHAPTER XXXIII

1 that spoilest, etc. Sennacherib.

2 Be Thou their arm. That is, Thy people's, who "have waited for Thee."

3 the people. Rather, "the peoples" (R.V.), different tribes represented in Sennacherib's army.

4 And your spoil. Addressing the Assyrians, whose collected spoils the Jews would clear off as locusts strip the fields.

6 And wisdom and knowledge. Or, as R.V., "There shall be stability in thy times"—an address to Zion—"abundance of salvation, wisdom, and knowledge: the fear of Jehovah is his (Israel's) treasure." Luther's version gives a slightly different connexion and meaning to the Hebrew: "There shall be faith in thy time; and power, salvation, wisdom, knowledge (or skill), and the fear of God shall be thy treasure."

8 The highways lie waste. The presence of Sennacherib's army had stopped all peaceful intercourse through the country.

9 Lebanon . . . Sharon. The richest districts are now desolate. For "hewn down" read "withereth away" (R.V.). The plain of Sharon lay along the sea-coast between Carmel and Joppa, and was proverbial for fertility and beauty. For "*their fruits*," read "*their leaves*," the wooded heights of Carmel and the oaks of Bashan being alike stripped of their beauty.

11 Your breath, [as] fire, shall devour you. That is, your proud and angry spirit shall cause your destruction, O Assyrians.

12 the people (peoples) **shall be,** etc. The destruction shall be *complete* (lime-burnings) as well as *sudden* (brushwood).

14 the hypocrites. Rather, "the godless."

15 He that walketh righteously. The judgements which terrify sinners shall not harm the upright (15, 16), but shall restore to them the glory of better days (17).

blood. *i.e.*, plotting of bloodshed.

17 They shall behold the land that is very far off. Rather, perhaps, "They (thine eyes) shall behold a far-stretching land" (R.V.). The Hebrew means "a land of distances," and suggests a fair expanse of open country, unencumbered by its foes.

18 Thine heart shall meditate terror. That is, Thou shalt thankfully look back upon thy recent terror from the Assyrian officers, who are now gone. The three mentioned are probably an accountant, a tax-collector (he that weighed *the tribute*, R.V.), and a military surveyor.

19 that thou canst not understand. See note on xxviii. 11.

21 A place of broad rivers and streams. A source of fertility and wealth, with security from all danger from enemies. The "galley with oars," and the "gallant ship," signify ships of war.

24 the inhabitant shall not say, I am sick. Suffering shall cease when sin, which is its cause, ceases: see Psa. ciii. 3. The words are only applicable in their fullest sense to a state of things still future, either in heaven or on earth.

CHAPTER XXXIV

2 He hath utterly destroyed them. Or, "He has devoted them to destruction."

4 as a scroll. Like an ancient volume or book-roll, which used to be rolled round a stick, as maps often are now.

5 bathed in heaven. That is, saturated, soaked with the wrath of heaven, which it is to execute upon Edom. Compare this prophecy with lxiii. 1–6; Jer. xlix. 7–22; and Obad. 1–21.

6 the Lord hath a sacrifice. Sacrifice being connected with slaughter as an expression of God's anger against sin, it furnished a significant representation of deserved punishment. comp. Ezek. xxxix. 17–20.

Bozrah. Not the Moabite city in the Haurân, now called *Buzra*; but another town south-east of the Dead Sea, represented by the modern village *El-busaireh.*

7 shall come down. That is, shall come down to the slaughter. On "the unicorns" ("wild oxen," R.V.) see note on Numb xxiii. 22. These large, strong animals represent the nobles or princes of Edom.

9 the streams thereof. That is, the streams of Edom. The figure is derived from the volcanic nature of the district, as well as from the destruction of the neighbouring cities Sodom and Gomorrah: see Gen. xix. 24–28; and comp. Jer. xlix. 18.

11 the cormorant and the bittern. Rather, as R.V., "the pelican and the porcupine" (or hedgehog). The "owl" is probably the eagle-owl, a large species inhabiting the ruins and caves of the district. These wild animals shall be the sole occupants of the land: see note on xiii. 21.

the stones of emptiness. That is, the *plummet-stones* of desolation: comp. 2 Kings xxi. 13. The words for "confusion" and "desolation" (*tohu* and *bohu*) are the words used to describe chaos, Gen. i. 2.

12 They shall call the nobles, etc. Edom was an elective monarchy. But there shall be no eligible candidates left.

13 dragons . . . owls. Rather, as R.V., "jackals . . . ostriches."

14 The wild beasts of the island. Heb., "howling creatures," wolves (R.V.), or hyænas (*Cheyne*). For "the satyr" see on xiii. 21. The "screech owl," Heb., the *lilith*, "night monster," R.V.

15 the great owl. Probably "the arrow-snake"; so called from the suddenness with which it springs on its prey. It abounds in Arabia, and its wound is deadly.

16 Seek ye out of the book of the Lord, etc. The prophet calls upon all who should live after the devastation of Idumæa to compare these predictions in "the scroll of Jehovah" with the event.

it hath gathered them. That is, the wild animals previously spoken of.

17 hath divided it unto them by line. By measuring-line and lot. As Canaan was allotted to the Israelites, so is Edom allotted to these creatures, for a perpetual inheritance. "It has never since regained its former state of cultivation, and swarms with serpents; only wild crows and eagles and great crowds of flying-cats give life to the desolate heights and barren plains" (*Delitzsch*).

CHAPTER XXXV

1 shall be glad for them. Or, simply "shall be glad" (R.V.).

the rose. The narcissus.

2 They shall see, etc. Lit., "The wilderness and the solitary place shall see."

3 Strengthen ye, etc. An address to the people of Israel generally.

5 Then the eyes of the blind, etc. Not only shall external Nature be renewed, but man shall share the blessing. By His miraculous cures our Lord not only in part fulfilled this prophecy, but also showed Himself to be the great Deliverer by whom it was to be accomplished in all its fullness.

7 the parched ground. Or, "mirage." The glowing sands of the desert appear at a little distance like a sheet of water, and thus deceive the thirsty traveller. It is here beautifully contrasted with the reality, which vivifies and refreshes: see the contrast to these verses in xxxiv. 9, 10, 13.

the habitation of dragons (jackals). The driest places.

8 it shall be for those. That is, for "the redeemed" afterwards mentioned. The main idea here is, that the way of access to these blessings shall be free and plain to all.

9 Nor any ravenous beast shall go up thereon. The people of God shall enjoy their blessedness, secure from every enemy and danger. The image is that of a raised causeway, too high for wild beasts to climb.

10 shall return, and come to Zion, etc. The connexion of the sentence is made clearer by R.V. arrangement, "The ransomed of Jehovah shall return, and come with singing unto Zion; and everlasting joy shall be upon their heads."

CHAPTER XXXVI

On this and the three next chapters, see the notes on the parallel passage in 2 Kings xviii.–xx., to which those which here follow are merely supplementary.

1 in the fourteenth year of king Hezekiah. This chronological note as it stands is difficult, as it appears from the Assyrian monuments that Sennacherib succeeded to Sargon on the throne of Assyria, 705 B.C., *i.e.*, in the twentieth year of Hezekiah, and that the expedition against Judah took place 701 B.C., or Hezekiah's twenty-sixth year. Various explanations have been suggested by scholars, but none of them seems quite to meet the case. But, as Professor Sayce points out, the events of Hezekiah's reign are not arranged in chronological order. His sickness and the embassy from Merodach-baladan which followed it, instead of taking place after the campaign of Sennacherib, occurred more than ten years before. The king of Assyria from whom Hezekiah and Jerusalem were to be delivered (2 Kings xx. 6) was not Sennacherib but Sargon (*The Higher Criticism and the Monuments*, 1894, p. 446).

2 the highway of the fuller's field. See note on vii. 3.

3 Shebna the scribe. A lower office than he had previously held; one step probably in his degradation and ruin: see on xxii. 15–19.

6 Egypt. There was some ground for the charge that the ruling party in Jerusalem was seeking an Egyptian alliance; a policy against which Isaiah had uttered his indignant protest: see xxx. 1–7; xxxi. 1–3.

19 Hamath, etc. The Assyrian inscriptions show that Hamath (see x. 9), the key to Northern Palestine, was destroyed by Sargon soon after the fall of Samaria. "Sepharvaim" (*Abu Habba*) is a short distance south-west of Bagdad. Sennacherib vaunts his father Sargon's conquests as his own.

CHAPTER XXXVII

12 Telassar. "Hill of Asshur"—"the Til-Assuri of the inscriptions, on the eastern side of the Tigris" (*Schrader*).

32 a remnant. The characteristic doctrine of Isaiah: see iv. 3, etc., and the name of his son Shear-jashub. Those who by their abode at Jerusalem had escaped the invader shall "go forth" to occupy and cultivate the ravaged land.

36 the angel of the Lord went forth. See on 2 Kings xix. 35. The account in 2 Chron. xxxii. 20 is simply that "all the mighty men of valour, and the leaders, and the captains" were cut off. Herodotus relates that the disaster to the Assyrian army happened at Pelusium (*Sin*, Ezek. xxx. 15, 16), on the east frontier of Egypt, and was caused by an immense number of *mice* that gnawed the *bowstrings* of the army in the night, and so rendered them ineffective. This was no doubt the too literal reading of a hieroglyphic record, the mouse being an Egyptian emblem of *death*, and the bow of *war*. The Egyptian priests attribute the interposition to their own gods, and place the judgement in their own territory.

CHAPTER XXXVIII

1–8. The dangerous illness and wonderful recovery of Hezekiah is related more fully in 2 Kings xx. 1–11; where see notes.

9 The writing of Hezekiah. This beautiful plaintive psalm records the king's feelings in the prospect of death. His depression may be in part accounted for by the unsettled and dangerous state of the nation (see note on 2 Kings xx. 1), and perhaps by the circumstance that he had not yet an heir to the throne: comp. 2 Kings xx. 6, with xxi. 1.

10 in the cutting off of my days. Or, "in the quiet of my days"; "when life seemed to be going on undisturbed" (*Delitzsch*).

my years. That is, those which are usually allotted to man.

11 I shall not see the Lord ("Jah"), etc. For the sentiment, comp. Psa. xxvii. 13. To "see Jah" is to have fellowship with Him.

12 As a shepherd's tent. That is, quickly, as a shepherd's tent is removed.

with pining sickness. Rather, "from the thrum"; *i.e.*, the ends of the threads by which the web is fastened to the loom (see R.V. marg.).

From day even to night. Or, "within the space of a day."

13 I reckoned till morning, etc. Or, "I composed [myself] until morning; [and] like a lion did He crush all my bones."

14 chatter. Or, "twitter"; uttering the feeble broken sounds of one in pain.

mine eyes fail [with looking] upward. Or, "Mine eyes look languishingly towards the height," or "longed heavenwards." "A half-despairing look is for some time all he is equal to" (*Cheyne*).

undertake for me. "Be Thou my surety," R.V.

15 What shall I say? Sudden grateful surprise.

I shall go softly. That is, solemnly and humbly, as one who remembers his own dependence and God's great mercy towards him: see next verse.

17 Behold, for peace I had great bitterness, etc. Rather, "Behold! my great bitterness [is turned] into peace, and Thou," etc. These words describe Hezekiah's restoration to health, not his affliction.

Thou hast cast all my sins behind Thy back. To cast a person or thing "behind the back" is an Oriental phrase expressing entire *oblivion.* In reference to offences, it means *to forgive.*

18 They that go down into the pit, etc. See note on Psa. vi. 5.

20 we will sing my songs. That is, "my *family* and *nation* will sing them." This song of Hezekiah, like other psalms, was designed not merely as a personal record, but to be used in celebrating the praises of God, and probably in the public service of the Temple.

21 boil. This word means an inflamed ulcer; perhaps the eruption produced by the plague, which threatened death.

CHAPTER XXXIX

On the embassy here described, see notes on 2 Kings xx. 12–17. Merodach-baladan probably made this visit of congratulation a cover for his design of forming a league against the power of Assyria: see note on chap. xxxvi. 1, and Sayce's *Fresh Light from the Ancient Monuments*, p. 110.

8 For there shall be peace and truth in my days. Or, "peace and stability." This is not to be understood as the language of selfish satisfaction that *he* at least was to be spared the suffering that his descendants would endure. Hezekiah felt the coming distress as *his own;* and yet is thankful for the respite.

The Restoration of Judah

CHAPTER XL

The fortieth chapter is the Introduction to the Second portion of the Book, which is by many eminent scholars regarded as the work of a "second Isaiah." (For the arguments for and against, see Angus and Green's *Bible Handbook*, 1904, pp. 499–503.) The prophet is directed to comfort God's captive people by the assurance that the Lord will soon appear to end their humiliation (1, 2). The New Testament authorises the application of the prophecy to the advent of the Divine Redeemer (see Matt. iii. 1–3, etc.), and this alone fully meets the requirements of the language; but other great interpositions of God on behalf of His Church may be included.

1 Comfort ye. An address to God's messengers and ministers everywhere. All are to combine in the high mission of comfort to His people.

2 Speak ye comfortably to Jerusalem. Lit., "Speak ye to the heart of Jerusalem." Jerusalem is here put for the chosen people, whose metropolis it was.

warfare. Or, "hardship," suffering: see note on Job vii. 1 (R.V. marg.).

double for all her sins. "Double" probably means *ample* or *abundant:* see note on Job xi. 6.

3 of him that crieth. Rather, as R.V., "of one that crieth."

Prepare ye the way of the Lord. This refers to the Eastern custom of sending pioneers to prepare the way for the march of the monarch through a wild and uncultivated region. Such was the character of the ministry of John the Baptist, who came to "make ready a people prepared for the Lord" (Luke i. 16, 17).

6 The voice said, Cry, etc. Or, as R.V., "The voice of one saying, Cry. And one said." Two voices, one responding to the other: both different from the "voice" in ver. 3.

goodliness. All that is human is perishing; and that which is most attractive, "the flower thereof," is the most frail. But God's word, especially His "exceeding great and precious promises," are everlasting and sure: comp. 1 Pet. i. 24, 25. *Verbum Dei manet in Æternum* was the motto of John the Steadfast, Elector of Saxony and friend of Luther. Carlyle says: "The letters V. D. M. I. Æ. were engraved on all the furniture of his existence, standards, pictures, plate, on the very sleeves of his lackeys, and I can perceive on his own deep heart first of all."

7 the spirit. This should be rendered "breath" (R.V.), or "wind."

10 will come with strong [hand]. Rather, "will come as a mighty one" (R.V.).

His work. *i.e.,* the *result* of "His work" of deliverance; "His reward" (R.V.).

11 He shall feed His flock like a shepherd. These exquisitely beautiful figures, borrowed from pastoral life, and now enshrined in the sweet music of Handel's *Messiah,* express the benignant and tender care of the "Good Shepherd"; who provides for all His sheep, but shows peculiar compassion to the weak: comp. John x. The word translated "*gently* lead" is the same that is rendered "leadeth" in Psa. xxiii. "Those that are with young," should read, as in R.V., "those that give suck."

13 Who hath directed the Spirit of the Lord? The appeal in ver. 12 is to the omnipotence of God, in this verse to His omniscience; in ver. 14 to His infinite wisdom. The questions apply to all His arrangements; but especially to the Gospel and its application to men, to which it is referred in Rom. xi. 34.

15 Behold, the nations, etc. From what God is in Himself, the prophet passes to what He is in His government of the world, which is infinitely easy to Him. The symbols (a drop hanging to a bucket, a grain of sand adhering to a balance) represent the extreme of lightness.

16 Lebanon is not sufficient, etc. The utmost conceivable sacrifice is immeasurably short of what we owe to God.

18 To whom then will ye liken God? If God is thus infinitely great, how foolish must it be to regard a piece of metal, or a block of wood, fashioned "by art and man's device," as being in any way a representation of Him!

20 He that is so impoverished, etc. The sense is better given by the R.V., "He that is too impoverished for [such] an oblation"; *i.e.*, as that of verse 19.

21 from the foundations of the earth. Delitzsch interprets, "Have ye not gained insight into the foundations of the earth?"—"has no understanding (such is the sense of the four questions) dawned upon you, namely, how they originated?"

24 they shall not be planted. Rather, as R.V. marg., "Scarcely are they planted, scarcely are they sown, scarcely hath their stock taken root in the ground, when He bloweth upon them, and they wither," etc.

27 Why sayest thou, O Jacob, etc.? God's people ought cheerfully to trust in Him, though the fulfilment of His promise appears to be delayed.

My way. *i.e.*, My troublous, thorny way. Does not He see it?

my judgement. *i.e.*, My right, disregarded by my oppressors. Is He indifferent to it?

28 There is no searching of His understanding. Therefore He knows all your wants, though you cannot understand all His doings.

31 They shall mount up with wings as eagles. "Put forth pinions like eagles" (*G. A. Smith*); "lift up their wings like eagles" (*Delitzsch*).

They shall walk and not faint. Courage, steadfastness, perseverance in the routine tasks or drudgery of everyday life.

CHAPTER XLI

1 let the people (peoples) **renew their strength.** This verse is God's challenge to the world.

2 Who raised up the righteous [man] from the east, etc.? Rather, as R.V., "Who hath raised up one from the east, whom He calleth in righteousness (or, 'whom righteousness calleth') to His foot?" Cyrus is thus described as God's agent for punishing idolaters and for delivering Israel: see xliv. 27, 28; xlv. 1–7. Persia lay to "the east" of Babylon.

Called him to His foot. That is, to march after Him: see Judg. iv. 10.

4 Calling the generations from the beginning. That is, calling them into existence. Part of the language here applied to the only true God is used of our Lord, in Rev. i. 17; ii. 8; xxii. 13.

5 The isles saw [it], and feared, etc. A graphic description of the terror caused by the victorious march of Cyrus.

7 saying, It is ready for the sodering. Rather, as R.V., "Saying of the soldering, It is good." The different craftsmen are sarcastically represented as encouraging themselves, on the approach of the foe, to trust in the idols which their own hands had made. They are furbishing up the old images, and preparing new ones for the emergency! "The irony is severe, but true to the facts as Herodotus relates them, . . . and then hark how the voice of Jehovah crashes across it all!" (*G. A. Smith*).

8 But thou, Israel, [art] my Servant. Rather, "But thou, Israel, my Servant," etc.

9 from the chief men thereof. Rather, as R.V., "from the corners thereof." Abraham had been called from what, in a Palestinian point of view, was the extremity of the world.

10 Fear thou not; for I am with thee. This was quoted by Lord Roberts in a message he sent through the Religious Tract Society to the cadets of New Zealand in 1910 for inscription in New Testaments presented to them by the Auckland Scripture Gift Association.

14 thy Redeemer. See note on Job xix. 25; and Lev. xxv. 24, 25.

15 I will make thee. That is, "I will make thee to be," etc.: see note on xxviii. 27. Weak as thou art, by My power thou shalt destroy thy mightiest enemies.

19 the shittah (acacia) **tree.** See note on Exod. xxv. 5. The word rendered "box" probably means the cypress. The whole series of figures expressively represents the refreshing consolation and help which were to burst all at once on those who were apparently forsaken of God.

21 Produce your cause, etc. "In the first stage of the argument, Jehovah appealed in support of His Deity to the fact that it was He who had called the oppressor of the nations upon the arena of history (2, 3); in this second step He appeals to the fact that He only knows or can predict the future."—*Delitzsch.*

22 the latter end of them. Or, "their issue"; *i.e.*, their fulfilment. The idols are challenged to adduce in support of their claims, predictions already verified by the event, or prophecies yet to be accomplished.

23 do good, or do evil. "Do *something*, either good or evil." Show some sign of life and activity, whatever it may be!

25 I have raised up one from the north. This prophecy refers to the Medo-Persian empire. Media lay to the north of Babylonia; Persia to the east, "the rising of the sun." The father of Cyrus was a Persian, his mother a Mede.

shall he call upon My name. Or, as R.V., "one that calleth upon My name. This may mean either "calleth upon" (Zeph. iii. 9; Jer. x. 25), or "calleth out" (comp. Exod. xxxiii. 19, xxxiv. 5, with xxxv. 30); "invokes." Thus Cyrus does make use of it in the edict setting the exiles free (Ezra i. 2).

there is none that heareth your words. The address is to the imaginary idol deities: comp. v. 23.

27 The first [shall say] to Zion, etc. Rather, "I am the first [to say] to Zion," etc.: comp. R.V.

29 vanity. The pretensions of their oracles are false, and the whole system of idolatry mere imposture.

CHAPTER XLII

1 Behold My Servant, etc. The "Servant of Jehovah" is a phrase denoting Israel in its ideal character, as chosen by Himself, to execute His commission, and to show forth His praise. This character, in its perfection, belongs to the Son of God alone. Hence the present passage is quoted in Matt. xii. 18–21, with direct application to our Lord.

3 the smoking flax. Or, "dimly burning wick" (R.V. marg.).

He shall bring forth judgement unto truth ("in truth," R.V.). That is, He shall fully vindicate His righteous cause: comp. Matt. xii. 20.

4 He shall not fail. The words just applied to the wick and the reed are here emphatically repeated: "He shall not be dimmed nor be bruised." Gentle as he is, he is not feeble.

6 have called thee in righteousness. Addressed to the "Servant of Jehovah," called to accomplish God's righteous purposes.

8 I am the Lord. "I am the Eternal": see note on Exod. iii. 14.

10 a new song. See note on Psa. xcvi. 1. The "new things" (v. 9) furnish material for a "new song."

11 The villages that Kedar doth inhabit. See note on xxi. 17.

the inhabitants of the rock. Or, perhaps, "of Sela," the stronghold of Edom: see note on 2 Kings xiv. 7.

13 He shall stir up, etc. Rather, "like a warrior He will rouse His zeal."

14 I will destroy and devour. Or, "I will gasp and pant at once": see R.V. Expressing solitary yearning and effort (*G. A. Smith*).

18 A new aspect of the subject is here presented. Israel's blindness and sin (18–20) are adduced, to show that God's great work of salvation is altogether undeserved, and intended to display His righteousness and to honour His word (21).

19 as he that is perfect. R.V., "at peace *with Me*"; *i.e.*, My covenanted friend.

21 The Lord is well pleased for His righteousness' sake, etc. Rather, as R.V., "It pleased the Lord, for His righteousness' sake, to magnify the law and make it honourable" (or, to make the teaching great and glorious). "But," etc. That is, their present condition is in melancholy contrast with their high privilege, as the possessors of such a revelation.

CHAPTER XLIII

2 When thou passest through the waters, etc. "Water" and "fire" are emblems of troubles and dangers, amidst which Israel shall enjoy perfect security; whether in Babylon, or in the journey home, or after re-settlement in their own land.

3 I gave Egypt for thy ransom, etc. Or, as R.V., "I have given Egypt," etc. The declaration probably refers to the coming subjugation of Egypt and the neighbouring kingdoms by the rising imperial power of Persia, the empire through which the people of God were to regain their liberty.

4 honourable. Rather, "honoured," *i.e.*, by My love to thee. The preferable arrangement of the sentence is as in R.V.: "Since thou hast been precious in My sight, and honourable, *and* I have loved thee; therefore will I give men for thee, and peoples for thy life."

6 I will say to the north, etc. That is, I will gather My scattered people from all parts of the world.

7 For I have created him for My glory, etc. Rather, "Whom I have created for My glory, whom I have formed and made": see R.V.

10 And My Servant whom I have chosen. That is, "And [ye are also] My Servant," etc.

12 I have declared, and have saved. Announced salvation and brought it.

14 For your sake I have sent to Babylon. Babylon, like Egypt (3, 16, 17), is to be devoted to destruction for Israel's deliverance.

have brought down all their nobles. Rather, as R.V. (by a slightly altered reading), "will bring down all of them as fugitives."

whose cry [is] in the ships. Or, "whose shout," etc.; *i.e.*, of exultation or pride. (R.V., "in the ships of their rejoicing.")

16 Which maketh a way in the sea, etc. The method of Israel's deliverance from Egypt was a type and pledge of God's future help.

22 But thou hast not called upon Me, etc. The humbler creation renders praise to God (v. 21), but Israel has failed to honour its Creator and Redeemer.

24 sweet cane. Sweet cane was an ingredient in the holy oil (Exod. xxx. 23), and was an article of commerce often brought from a distance (Jer. vi. 20).

26 Put Me in remembrance. Remind Me of My promises, that thou mayest gain thy cause.

27 Thy first father. Probably referring to Jacob, as distinguished from Adam, the father of the human race as a whole. For "teachers," read "mediators" or, as R.V., "interpreters"; the term denoting all, as prophets and priests, who were the channels of communication between Jehovah and His people. The "princes of the Sanctuary" (28), or "holy princes" (R.V. marg.), are the spiritual heads of the people as distinguished from the temporal.

CHAPTER XLIV

2 Jesurun. This term is also applied to Israel in Deut. xxxii. 15; xxxiii. 5, 26; and probably means "the upright one," referring to the object for which Israel was "created" a nation.

3 I will pour water. The "water" and "floods" here, as elsewhere, denote the influences of the Holy "Spirit."

7 shall declare it. That is, the future.

Since I appointed the ancient people. The earliest inhabitants of the world.

8 there is no God. Lit., as R.V., "there is no Rock." The gods of the nations will be unable to protect them; but the Eternal is a sure defence, His people being witnesses.

11 all his fellows. The makers and worshippers of the idol, as being equally senseless ("all that join themselves thereto," R.V. marg.).

12 The smith with the tongs, etc. Rather, as R.V., "The smith [maketh] *or* [sharpeneth] an axe, and worketh in the coals," etc.

he is hungry. Suggesting the thought, How can that which is made by one who suffers from hunger and thirst be compared with the self-sufficient God?

13 He marketh it out with a line. "Draws lines on a block, marking them out with a pencil" (*Moffatt*).

15 Then shall it be for a man to burn. Vers. 15–19 show the absurdity of worshipping an idol made from the very material which is applied to the lowest domestic uses.

19 an abomination. See Exod. viii. 26.

20 He feedeth on ashes. That is, he looks for life and support to that which is worthless and disappointing.

Is there not a lie in my right hand? "Is not this, about which I am busied, and upon which I am spending my strength and resting my hope, a deception?"

25 the liars. That is, impostors, or false prophets. Their "tokens" are their pretended proofs of Divine influence.

And maketh their knowledge foolish. He shows them to be fools.

27 That saith to the deep, Be dry. This is generally supposed to refer to the stratagem by which Cyrus took Babylon, diverting the Euphrates from its course through the city, and effecting an entrance for his soldiers along the empty channel.

28 [He is] My shepherd. Kings are often called "shepherds"; but the name may be specially given to Cyrus as the gatherer and restorer of

Israel, "the sheep of God's pasture." The future deliverer of the Jews from Babylon, who had been already referred to (xli. 25), is here first mentioned by name. Josephus (*Ant.* xi. 1, § 2) says that Cyrus had this prophecy shown him on his conquest of Babylon, and thereupon resolved to fulfil it: see Ezra i. 2–4.

CHAPTER XLV

1 His anointed. Cyrus is called the *anointed of Jehovah*, because God had solemnly set him apart to perform an important public service in His cause.

To subdue nations. See Ezra i. 2.

I will loose the loins of kings. As the girding of the loins was necessary to active exercise, so the "loosening" or ungirding them represents lassitude or weakness. God says that He will weaken the enemies of Cyrus.

3 the treasures of darkness. Hidden in vaults and "secret places." The countries which Cyrus conquered were among the richest in the world. The wealth of Crœsus, king of Lydia, was proverbial, and that of Babylon was probably greater (see Xenophon, *Cyrop.* vii. 2, 11).

5 I girded thee. See note on "loose," ver. 1.

7 I form the light, and create darkness. According to the Persians there were two coeternal beings, who divided the government of the world between them. One of these, called Ormuzd, was regarded as the principle of *light*, the source of all good; while the other, Ahriman, was thought to be the principle of *darkness*, and the fountain of all evil. Jehovah is the only God independent and sovereign. The "evil" and the "darkness" here are shown by the context to mean penal judgements.

8 let righteousness, etc. "Let her (the earth) cause," etc., R.V.

9 Woe unto him, etc. The R.V. renders, more literally and expressly, "Woe unto him that striveth with his Maker! a potsherd among the potsherds of the earth."

11 command ye Me. Or, "ask of Me"; that is, instead of arrogantly doubting My proceedings, inquire humbly respecting My designs, and leave the care of them to Me.

13 I have raised him up. That is, Cyrus; who will be led to these generous acts not by any prospect of remuneration, but by a regard to the command of God: see Ezra i. 2.

14 the Sabeans. See note on xliii. 3. The extraordinary stature of the Sabeans is mentioned by Herodotus, b. 3, c. 20. It seems to be introduced here to enhance the glory of Israel's superiority, and the submission of the Gentile nations.

15 Verily Thou art a God that hidest Thyself. The prophet utters his feelings of admiring awe at the view granted to him of God's great plan of purifying, delivering, and honouring Israel, by their exile in Babylon and restoration by Cyrus. God's work of redemption and restoration of His people calls forth from the apostle Paul a similar exclamation (Rom. xi. 33–36).

17 in the Lord. "By the Eternal."

19 I have not spoken in secret. Not like the dark and doubtful responses of heathen oracles, to which men resorted in vain; but in plain, exact, circumstantial language, which should always be verified by the event.

20 ye that are escaped of the nations. Surviving the desolating judgements upon the idolaters. These are invited to come and observe the uselessness of trusting in idol gods.

that set up. Rather, "that carry" (R.V.); a sarcastic reference to the fugitives carrying their helpless gods.

22 All the ends of the earth. "The ends of the earth" includes all nations: see Psa. lxxii. 8; xcviii. 3. In this verse "the first imperative exhorts, the second promises" (*Delitzsch*).

23 I have sworn by Myself. Vers. 23, 24 contain a fuller statement of the truth intimated in ver. 22, that the benefits of salvation shall be extended to the whole world. That there is here a primary and direct reference to the Messiah is evident from Rom. xiv. 11; Phil. ii. 10, 11.

24 Surely. Or, "Only," as R.V.

25 all the seed of Israel. That is, all the true children of God; His Israel gathered out of the whole human race.

CHAPTER XLVI

1 Bel boweth down, etc. Thrown down ignominiously by the conqueror. "Bel" (another form of Baal) was the principal god of the Babylonians (see Budge, *Babylonian Life and History*, 1925, p. 102). There was in Babylon a splendid temple erected to him, the ruins of which are still visible. His name appears in the compound proper names of the country; such as *Bel*shazzar, *Bel*teshazzar. "Nebo," the other idol specified, is supposed to have been the symbol of the planet Mercury; corresponding to Hermes among the Greeks, and Anubis among the Egyptians. This name is likewise found in many of the compound names of the Chaldæans; *e.g.*, *Nebo*nassar, *Nebu*chadnezzar (Budge, as quoted, p. 105).

Your carriages were (are) **heavy loaden.** The word "carriages" is always used, in the Bible, in the old English sense of *things carried*, or burdens. "Your burdens are packed, a load to the weary [beast]": see R.V.

3 which are carried from the womb. The argument is, Babylon carries its gods; but your God carries you! The expressions used point back to the infancy of the nation, when Jehovah had manifested a more than maternal care and tenderness, which He would continue to exercise until the latest period of their history.

6 They lavish gold. This expression is appropriately applied to the idols of Babylon, many of which appear to have been very costly: see Dan. iii. 1.

7 They bear him upon the shoulder. From the workshop to the shrine.

8 show yourselves men. That is, "act rationally; stand fast" (see R.V. marg.). The address is to waverers between the worship of Jehovah and heathenism.

11 a ravenous bird. This ravenous bird represents Cyrus; and the image denotes rapidity, strength, and destructive power. It is worthy of notice that Cyrus had an eagle as his standard (Xenophon, *Cyrop.* vii. 1, 4).

12 ye stouthearted. Addressed to those who have gone yet further in the direction of idolatry than the "transgressors" (8).

CHAPTER XLVII

1 Come down, and sit in the dust. Babylon is represented here as a queen, reduced from the luxury and elegance of a palace to servitude and shame.

Sit on the ground : [there is] no throne. More literally, as R.V., " Sit on the ground without a throne."

2 Take the millstones. See note on Exod. xi. 5.

Uncover thy locks, etc. Rather, " Raise thy veil ; lift up the skirt." The exposure endured by the lowest class of slaves in doing their work.

3 I will not meet [thee as] a man. " I will make peace with no man " (" will accept no man," R.V.). Luther's version, similarly Cheyne, has " no one can resist Me." Delitzsch translates : " I will take vengeance and not spare men."

4 [As for] our Redeemer, etc. A joyful exclamation of the Church, recognising in the Lord of hosts all-conquering might, and a will to carry on the work of redemption.

6 I was wroth with My people. Although employed to chastise Israel's sins, Babylon is to be dealt with according to her own purposes of cruel ambition : see notes on x. 7, and 1 Kings xii. 15.

8 that dwellest carelessly. The Babylonians trusted in their defences and provisions, and mocked Cyrus when he besieged their city.

I shall not sit as a widow. " A widow " in the loss of all alliances, " childless " in the loss of population.

9 In a moment in one day. Literally fulfilled ; on the third of Marchesvan (Nov.), 539 B.C. The fall was sudden and complete.

thy sorceries . . . thine enchantments. The value which the Chaldeans set upon soothsaying appears from Dan. i. 20 ; ii. 2, 10 ; iv. 7 ; v. 11, etc.

10 Thy wisdom and thy knowledge. The Chaldeans were celebrated for their astronomical science and philosophy.

11 Thou shalt not know from whence it riseth. Lit., " Thou shalt not know the dawning thereof." Moffatt translates, " You know not how to evade."

13 Let now the astrologers. The astrologers professed to make their calculations of the future by " dividing the heavens " into houses, watching the stars in their conjunctions and oppositions, and " studying the new moons " as to their times, etc.

14 There shall not be a coal to warm at. This may mean, " It shall not be a coal to warm one's self at," etc., but a fire intolerably hot and destructive : see Heb. xii. 29.

15 Thus shall they be unto thee, etc. Rather, " Thus shall the things be unto thee wherein thou hast laboured ; they that have trafficked with thee from thy youth shall wander," etc., R.V. All who have carried on commercial intercourse with the great trading city are scattered, regardless of its humiliation.

CHAPTER XLVIII

1 are come forth out of the waters of Judah. Out of a stream branching into many channels : see Psa. lxviii. 26. Judah is mentioned probably because, as the royal tribe of the Messiah, it was to give its name to the whole nation.

4 an iron sinew. Intractable and insensible.

6 Thou hast heard, see all this, etc. *i.e.*, " Thou hast heard [the prediction] ; behold it all [fulfilled]. And will ye not confess it ? "

8 from that time [that] thine ear was not opened. Or, " From of old thine ear was not opened " (R.V.), *i.e.*, thou wouldest not attend to My communications.

10 I have refined thee, but not with (or as, R.V.) silver. I have long tried thee (R.V. marg.) with afflictions—a melting of a higher sort than that of silver—but have not found thee pure ; so that thy deliverance is for My glory, not for thy merit (v. 11).

13 When I call unto them. See xl. 26.

14 The Lord hath loved him. Referring to Cyrus.

16 And now the Lord God, and His Spirit, hath sent me. Or, " And now the Lord God hath sent me, and His Spirit " ; comp. R.V., which leaves the construction ambiguous. Calvin and others regard the whole clause as a parenthesis, in which the prophet emphatically asserts that he was commissioned by God, and inspired by the Holy Spirit, to make this communication.

21 And they thirsted not, etc. God repeats in the experiences and redemption of His people still the refreshing and renewal which He bestowed in the desert-march of Israel.

22 There is no peace. Lest any should forget the connexion between peace and righteousness (18), it is emphatically added that none of the promised blessings would be enjoyed by the wicked.

CHAPTER XLIX

1 Listen, O isles, unto Me. The message of God's Israel (3) to the world ; and in its highest sense the language of the Messiah as the spiritual Deliverer both of Jews and Gentiles.

My name. Israel : a prince with God, prophetic of the nation's calling and destiny. There may also be an allusion to the names of the Messiah ;—Immanuel, " God with us," Jesus, " He shall save " ; see Matt. i. 21 and Heb. v. 5.

2 My mouth. *i.e.*, " my speech," or teaching.

4 Then I said, etc. The accomplishment of the Divine design begins in apparent failure. " Israel " seems far from accomplishing its destiny. Even Christ in His ministry would be despised and rejected (comp. ver. 7 with liii. 3). But notwithstanding this, His rightful claim (" judgement ") would be maintained by the Eternal, with whom also " His work " (*i.e.*, " recompence," as R.V.) would be secure.

5 Though Israel be not gathered. The true reading of the passage is probably that of R.V., " And that Israel be gathered unto Him," continuing the description of the Messiah's mission. The following clause is a parenthesis (" for I am honourable in the eyes of Jehovah, and my God is become my strength ").

6 It is a light thing, etc. " Not only is the restoration of the remnant of Israel the work of the Servant of Jehovah, but God has appointed Him for something higher than this, a mission extending to all mankind."—*Delitzsch.*

7 the nation abhorreth, etc. The object of contempt and abhorrence to the Jewish people.

to a servant of rulers. He who once subjected himself to the power of unjust rulers shall receive the homage of kings.

8 In an acceptable time. Or, " a time of favour." This passage is applied by the apostle Paul to the times of the Messiah ; whom it represents as pleading successfully for the extension of Gospel blessings to all who seek to be " reconciled to God " through Him : see 2 Cor. v. 18–vi. 2.

to establish the earth. Or, as R.V., " to raise up the land." The restoration of the cities and inhabitants of Palestine ; " the prisoners " " in darkness " being the exiles, to whom the mighty word of the Eternal brings the light of liberty; but the prophecy in its highest meaning refers to the restoration of man by the Gospel: see xlii. 7.

9 They shall feed in the ways, etc. The allusions to the return from captivity are here continued. The people returning home are represented as a flock, able to obtain sufficient pasture (even upon bare sandy hills) without being obliged to go a long way round. The mirage ("the heat,"ver. 10) shall not hurt them, by leading them astray, nor the sun by its oppressive heat; for He who has compassion on them in their misery shall lead them by springs of refreshing water (see xxxv. 7), and open for them a way through the most pathless regions (ver. 11, comp. xl. 4). The description is applied in Rev. vii. 16, to the blessedness of the redeemed.

12 these from the land of Sinim. Converts shall flock into the Church from the more distant quarters. "Sinim" has been variously interpreted; but the prevailing opinion is that it denotes *China,* which was known to the ancients under the name of "Sina" or "Sinim."

14 But Zion said, etc. The language of dejection at the delay of God's deliverance.

16 I have graven thee upon the palms of My hands. As men make marks upon some part of the flesh, as a memorial of some absent object of regard. A mark of this kind on the hands is constantly in sight. So the *picture* of Zion (not merely the *name,* as the next clause shows) is represented as drawn in the inside of Jehovah's hand. Zion and her walls are thus continually before Him: and even if for a time broken down, their eternal *idea* remains with Him, to be realised again and again in an increasingly glorious form.

20 The children which thou shalt have, after thou hast lost the other. Lit., "The children of thy bereavement," as R.V.; born to thee in thy state of bereavement.

21 seeing I have lost my children, etc. Or, "Seeing I was bereaved and barren, an exile and an outcast."

23 lick up the dust of thy feet. A figurative expression, meaning, "they shall be completely subject to thee": see Psa. lxxii. 9.

24 Shall the prey be taken from the mighty? A question of momentary scepticism, implying that such deliverance appears impossible. But God will effect it, driving the oppressor to desperate rage.

CHAPTER L

The appeal is that of the Servant of Jehovah, in the person of the Messiah.

1 Where is the bill, etc.? It is not God who has broken up the relationship, but Israel itself.

4 The Lord God hath given me. The Servant of Jehovah is qualified to instruct and comfort His people (4); is obedient and meek (5), yet confiding in God (6), and therefore fearless and successful (7-9). All this is strikingly applicable to Christ.

the learned. Lit., in both parts of the verse, "learners," or "the taught": see R.V. I hear and speak in the spirit of discipleship: comp. John viii. 26.

6 to them that plucked off the hair. Plucking the beard and spitting in the face are, in the East, regarded as the greatest insults. The fulfilment of these words in our Lord's sufferings will appear from Matt. xxvi. 67; xxvii. 26, 30; John xviii. 22.

7 Therefore have I set my face like a flint. I can go unflinchingly through all my sufferings; for God will vindicate me (8) by delivering me from them: see Luke ix. 51; John xvii. 1-5; Rom. i. 4. Ver. 8 seems to be referred to in Rom. viii. 33, 34, and to be applied to the believer, who is justified through Christ.

9 they all shall wax old. *i.e.,* my enemies.

11 that compass [yourselves] about with sparks. R.V., "That gird yourselves about with firebrands."

CHAPTER LI

1 the pit whence ye are digged. The quarry from which were brought the stones composing your national edifice; *i.e.,* your progenitors Abraham and Sarah.

2 I called him alone. As a single individual.

4 I will make My judgement to rest. *i.e.,* I will establish it.

9 Rahab. See notes on xxx. 7, and on Psa. lxxiv. 13.

11 Therefore the redeemed of the Lord, etc. Comp. xxxv. 10 in its connexion.

12 I, even I. This emphatic reduplication implies that Jehovah alone is all-sufficient to deliver from the mightiest oppressor (13). The address (fem.) is to Zion.

14 The captive exile hasteneth, etc. Rather, "The bent-down [prisoner] hasteneth to be loosed, and he shall not die [and go down] into the pit; his bread shall not fail. For I am," etc. God's salvation shall reach even him who, bent under heavy chains in the dungeon, is perishing with hunger. It shall therefore relieve the most extreme and hopeless suffering.

17 Which hast drunk at the hand of the Lord. This figure forcibly represents a state of helpless misery under Jehovah's anger: see Ps. lxxv. 8.

19 These two things. Desolation by famine, and destruction by sword.

20 As a wild bull. Rather, "as an antelope" (R.V.).

23 Bow down. See Josh. x. 24, and note.

CHAPTER LII

1 there shall no more come into thee, etc. A promise and a reminder of the purity which should characterise the Church: comp. Rev. xxi. 26, 27.

2 sit down. *i.e.,* arise and take possession of thy throne.

3 Ye have sold yourselves, etc. Rather, "Ye were sold for nought" (R.V.). As Israel's oppressors gave nothing for him, so they can claim nothing when he is "redeemed," or delivered from them.

4 My people went down aforetime into Egypt. Pharaoh and Sennacherib were mighty, yet the Eternal freed Israel from their tyranny; and surely He can save him from other enemies: see next verse.

5 what have I here? Or, "what do I here?" (R.V.); *i.e.,* in Babylon. What is to be My course of action? God is represented as deliberating with Himself; enumerating the reasons for His interposition in the wanton tyranny and blasphemy of their oppressors.

for nought. *i.e.,* "gratuitously," as in ver. 3; without any compensating result.

make them to howl. Omit "make them to." It is the oppressors who "howl" or shriek in triumph.

every day. "All the day" (R.V.).

6 Therefore, etc. The answer to the question of ver. 5. Because My people are oppressed and

My name is blasphemed, I will assert Myself, and appear for their deliverance.

7 How beautiful, etc.! The expected herald now appears "upon the mountains" of Judah; the watchmen on the walls of Zion announce His rapid approach. The representation is ideal. The literal Zion was in ruins. The Church in captivity was the true Zion, and to her "watchmen" the herald came.

8 Thy watchmen, etc. Rather, as R.V., "The voice of thy watchmen! They lift up the voice. Together do they sing."

8 they shall see eye to eye, etc. More exactly, "They shall see, eye to eye, how Jehovah returneth to Zion" (R.V., and marg.). They see Jehovah bringing back Zion as clearly and distinctly as when one man looks into the eye of another. "They see the Eternal face to face as He returns to Zion" (*Moffatt*).

10 hath made bare His holy arm. The image is that of a warrior throwing back the loose sleeve of his robe, to have his arm free.

11 Depart ye, depart ye. Comp. Exod. xiii. 21, 22; xiv. 19, 20; Ezra viii. 22, 23, 28, 31. All are to march now the Divine Leader is at hand; their exodus, however, is not to be a flight (Exod. xii. 11), but a march of triumph.

Touch no unclean [thing]. Take with you no idolatrous symbols or Babylonian spoils.

13 This verse, as Calvin pointed out, is really the beginning of a new section, which includes chap. liii. The whole section is the description of the Suffering Servant of God. It is a unique portrait. Whether the earlier or later date of the prophecy be accepted, it is a portrait drawn centuries before Christ appeared in human form. And, however particular features of it may be found in other personalities, it is only in Christ that they are all combined.

14 As many were astonied. At the mean and suffering appearance of the expected deliverer.

15 So. Corresponding to *As* in the previous verse. In proportion to the astonishment caused by His humiliation shall be the effect of His work.

shall He sprinkle many nations. But, for "sprinkle," many expositors read "startle"; literally, "make to spring," an interpretation which seems to agree better with the context.

The kings shall shut their mouths. In amazement and awe.

CHAPTER LIII

1 Who hath believed our report? The prophet, in the name of the people, confesses their unbelief. "Report" signifies, not the *message* delivered *by* us, but "that which we have heard" (R.V. marg.), *i.e.*, the message delivered *to* us. The *our* in this verse, and the *we* in ver. 2, alike denote the people of Israel.

2 as a tender plant. A weakly shoot from a decayed trunk, giving no promise of beauty or value: see note on xi. 1.

a root out of a dry ground. There was nothing in the time or surroundings of the Saviour's birth to account for Him.

4 Surely He hath borne our griefs. The quotation of these words in Matt. viii. 17, with reference to some of the effects of sin, seems to point to Christ's work in the removal of all. The words "borne" and "carried" imply taking *upon Himself* and taking *away*: comp. John i. 29; 1 Pet. ii. 24.

we did esteem Him stricken. That is, by Divine judgement. The word is applied especially to the infliction of such diseases as the plague or the leprosy: see note on Lev. xiii. 2; Luke xiii. 2; John ix. 2.

5 He was wounded for our transgressions. "It was not His own sins and iniquities, but ours which He had taken upon Himself, that He might make atonement for them in our stead, that were the cause of His having to suffer so cruel and painful a death."—*Delitzsch.* The "chastisement of our peace" means the chastisement by which our peace (with God) was effected.

healed. Cured of the malady of sin, not merely delivered from its consequences.

6 have gone astray. That is, astray from God.

the Lord hath laid on Him the iniquity of us all. "Nothing could be plainer than these words. The speakers confess that they know that the Servant's suffering was both vicarious and redemptive" (*G. A. Smith*).

8 And who shall declare His generation, etc.? Of the different renderings given to this clause, the best seems to be that of the R.V.: "And as for His generation, who *among them* considered that He was cut off out of the land of the living?"

9 He made His grave with the wicked. Rather, "And His grave was *appointed* with the wicked; *but* He was with," etc. The Jewish rulers intended our Saviour to have the disgraceful burial of a criminal; but Divine Providence wonderfully ordered it otherwise: see Matt. xxvii. 57–61. Some interpreters, however, for *Because* read *Although* (R.V.), and regard both the preceding lines as referring to our Lord's humiliation.

10 it pleased the Lord to bruise Him. The use of the word "pleased" here conveys to English readers a meaning which is not in the Hebrew, the idea of the original being "it was God's purpose."

He shall see [His] seed. As a consequence of His being put to death ("*when* Thou shalt make," etc.), He lives again. His "seed," or posterity, is the Church of the redeemed.

He shall prolong His days. See Rev. i. 18, "alive for evermore."

the pleasure of the Lord. The work of salvation.

11 He shall see of the travail of His soul. That is, "He shall see the fruit of His sufferings, and shall be satisfied." The good resulting from His great sorrows shall abundantly compensate Him for all that He endured.

By His knowledge. That is, "by the knowledge of Him"; such a knowledge as leads to faith in Him, and thus saves the soul. Many, however, take the phrase as referring to Christ's own knowledge, "His insight into the dealings and purposes of the Eternal," an essential element in His qualification as Saviour.

justify many. Or, "make the many righteous": comp. Rom. v. 19.

12 made intercession. Rather, "maketh intercession" continuously; applying to them all the blessings which flow from His atoning death.

Of the whole of this wonderful chapter Delitzsch says: "The banner of the cross is here set up."

CHAPTER LIV

2 lengthen thy cords, and strengthen thy stakes. This beautiful metaphor is taken from the pastoral life of the East. As more room is needed by a growing family, the whole tent must be enlarged, the cords extended, and the pegs strengthened.

4 the shame of thy youth. *i.e.*, of the Egyptian bondage: "the reproach of thy widowhood," *i.e.*, of the Babylonian captivity in which Israel was left like a widow.

6 a wife of youth. One of whom there was early and constant love, which had not been destroyed even by her sins.

when thou wast refused. R.V., "when she is cast off": a continuance of the description, a wife, for a time separated and unhappy, but now recalled.

8 In a little wrath. Rather, as R.V., "In overflowing wrath"; or, better still, with *Cheyne*, "in a gush of wrath."

9 the waters of Noah. Whatever may be the troubles of the Church, it shall never be swept away and perish. The promise recorded (Gen. viii. 21; ix. 11), here appears as an oath.

11 with fair colours. Rather, "in stibium"; a paint formed from antimony, with which the Hebrew women tinged their eye-lashes. This seems designed to suggest the costliness and beauty of the building. The black stibium would richly set off the splendour of the sapphires, the agates (or "rubies," R.V.), and the carbuncles (or diamonds): comp. the description of the New Jerusalem, Rev. xxi. 19, 20.

13 all thy children shall be taught of the Lord. Our Lord quotes this prediction in proof of the necessity of that Divine teaching by which the Holy Spirit both enlightens the mind and influences the heart (John vi. 45).

15 shall fall for thy sake. Or, "shall fall (*i.e.*, come over) to thee" comp. R.V. marg.

CHAPTER LV

1 Ho, every one that thirsteth. The adaptation, richness, and freeness of Gospel blessings are contrasted with the costly and unsatisfying attempts of men to obtain happiness from other sources.

2 Hearken diligently. Lit., "Hearken, O hearken!"

3 the sure mercies of David. The blessings surely promised to David: see note on 2 Sam. vii. 10; and compare 2 Chron. vi. 42; Psa. lxxxix. 1, 3, 28. It is evident that the main and ultimate subject of the promise is the Messiah and His saving work; and to Him the Apostle Paul applies these words in Acts xiii. 34.

4 a witness to the people. This refers to the Messiah, who is to "the peoples" a "witness" bearing testimony to God's truth, both condemnatory and saving (John xviii. 37; Mal. iii. 5; Rev. i. 5); and a "leader and commander" (Dan. ix. 25; Heb. ii. 10), ruling His followers and leading them on to victory.

9 So are My ways higher than your ways. Man's forgiveness is arbitrary, partial, imperfect, and often reluctant; but God "delighteth in mercy," and is ever ready to forgive all sin.

12 ye shall go out with joy. The joyful salvation of those who trust God's "word" of grace, to whose happiness everything ministers. And this joy is accompanied with a moral change, which converts the wilderness into "the garden of the Lord": comp. Psa. xcvi. 11; xxxv. 1, 2.

13 Instead of the thorn shall come up the fir tree, etc. "The change is compared to the transition from the wilderness (*i.e.*, the misery of the exile), with its monotonous dwarf shrubs, to a park of beautiful trees (comp. xli. 18, 19), in the midst of which Israel is to walk "in solemn troops and sweet societies" (as in xxxv. 9)."—*Cheyne.*

CHAPTER LVI

2 that keepeth the Sabbath. The observance of the Sabbath appears to be particularly mentioned, partly because it could be maintained, at least in spirit, by the Jews even during their exile, and partly because of its great and permanent importance to the maintenance of religion among men (see also lviii. 13, 14).

3 the son of the stranger . . . the eunuch. These two classes had been expressly excluded by the law from the congregation of the Hebrews: see Deut. xxiii. 1–8. No doubt many among the Jews, taken to be eunuchs in the court of Babylon (xxxix. 7; comp. Dan. i. 3, etc.), would be despised by their brethren on their return to Palestine, and this word was needed to reassure them. But it contains the deeper lesson that the Gospel has removed all external barriers to religious privileges.

5 an everlasting name. A remarkable illustration of this promise is found in the case of the Ethiopian eunuch (Acts viii. 26–39), who had obtained in the Church of Christ "a place and a name" of honour far higher than he could have attained as the progenitor of an illustrious race.

8 Beside those that are gathered unto Him. Rather, "Besides His own gathered ones" (Psa. xlvii. 9; John x. 16).

9 All ye beasts of the field. God's people being regarded as His flock, their leaders and teachers are called "watchmen" and "watchdogs": whilst the agents of Divine correction and punishment are appropriately spoken of as "wild beasts."

10 watchmen. There were prophets during the Babylonian exile (Jer. xxix. 15, etc.).

Sleeping. More literally, as R.V., "Dreaming."

11 from his quarter. Rather, "from every quarter," R.V.

12 Come ye, etc. One of the unfaithful "shepherds" thus invites to a two days' banquet.

CHAPTER LVII

1 The righteous perisheth. While the unfaithful "watchmen" are thus rioting in self-indulgence, the good and true pass away unnoticed.

merciful. Rather, "godly," as R.V. marg.

the evil [to come]. The removal of the righteous from impending calamities is at once a mercy to themselves and a warning to the ungodly.

2 Each one walking. That is, each one "who walks." This peaceful rest is the end of all who live uprightly. "Their beds" are their graves.

5 with idols. Rather, "among the terebinths" (*or*, "oaks," as R.V.).

slaying the children. See notes on Lev. xx. 2; 2 Kings xvi. 3.

6 Among the smooth [stones]. The reference is probably to anointed stones, such as were set up by the patriarchs for memorials (see Gen. xxviii. 18; xxxv. 14), and by the heathen as objects of worship. Such idols were the chosen "portion" and "lot" of the idolatrous Jews.

Should I receive comfort in these? Or, "Shall I be appeased for these things?" See i. 24.

7 Upon a lofty and high mountain. Vers. 7, 8 show the extent, publicity, and grossness of Jewish idolatry. They had crowned their hills and filled their houses with memorials of it; and felt no shame on account of their sins.

9 thou wentest to the king. "The king" probably denotes the foreign monarchs with whom the Israelites were seeking forbidden alliances (see xxx. 2; Hos. v. 13; xii. 1).

even unto hell (Sheol). That is, the lowest degree of debasement.

10 the greatness of thy way. "The length of thy journey." It cost her great sacrifices to purchase the favour of her heathen rulers. Yet she persisted.

Thou hast found the life of thine hand. That is, "thou hast found a quickening of thy strength" (R.V.).

11 of whom hast thou been afraid? Why have you reverenced other gods whilst you falsely professed to be My people, encouraging yourselves in your hypocrisy by My forbearance? I will show what your professed righteousness is by your works, and they shall not avail you (ver. 12).

13 thy companies. The hosts either of idols or of allies, or of both, on which the Israelites relied.

14 And shall say. Or, "And one shall say," etc. "Another of those mysterious voices which fill the air round about the prophet" (*Cheyne*). Every obstacle shall be removed from the path of those who put their trust in God: see note on xl. 3.

16 For the spirit should fail before me. The frailty of man is adduced as a reason for the exercise of Divine mercy: comp. Psa. ciii. 14.

17 covetousness. "Eagerness after worldly possessions, selfishness, worldly-mindedness in general" (*Delitzsch*). This was one of the prevailing sins of the Jewish people, which drew down upon them Divine vengeance.

19 I create the fruit of the lips. "The fruit of the lips" is used in Heb. xiii. 15, in the sense of thanksgiving. God is the author of praise by bestowing as the theme of it "peace on him that is far off, and to him that is near," *i.e.*, on Gentile and on Jew.

20 when it cannot rest. Or, "for it cannot rest" (R.V.). Their own passions, the accusations of conscience, and the anger of God, make it impossible for the wicked to enjoy "rest"—real, satisfying peace: see note on xlviii. 22.

CHAPTER LVIII

2 Yet they seek Me daily, etc. They showed much zeal for the ceremonies of religion, and even took a certain pleasure in the punctual observance of them; while they had no delight in spiritual religion, or even practical morality. Their worship is but self-seeking.

3 [Wherefore] have we afflicted our soul? That is, by fasting. Where professed austerities are a cloak for selfishness, they are most displeasing to God: see 1 Kings xxi. 9–13.

ye find pleasure, etc. You carry on business, and make your servants perform their full tale of work. A double mark of hypocrisy.

4 To make your voice to be heard on high. Even during a fast, men's passions may remain unsubdued and display themselves in violent language and conduct.

6 Is not this the fast that I have chosen? The fast which God accepts includes the self-denial shown in the exercise of justice, kindness, and charity: comp. 1 Cor. xiii. 3.

the heavy burdens. Lit., "the bands of the yoke" (R.V.).

7 from thine own flesh. That is, "from thine own kindred." Thou shouldest not be ashamed of them because they are poor, nor withhold from them needful help.

8 The glory of the Lord shall be thy rereward. Alluding to the manner in which the Israelites came up out of Egypt: see Exod. xiii. 21; xiv. 19; and note on lii. 11. By obeying the Divine laws they would now be as effectually secured and protected as they then were by the pillar of cloud and fire.

9 the putting forth of the finger. Pointing with the finger: the sign of contempt.

vanity. Or, "wickedness."

11 and make fat thy bones. See Prov. xv. 30, and note.

12 shall build the old waste places. The children of the exiles will begin, as soon as they return home, to build up again the ruins of olden times; receiving in consequence these honourable titles.

13 If thou turn away thy foot. "If thou dost not tread its holy ground with the foot of week-day work."—"The Sabbath, above all other institutions appointed by the law, was the true means of uniting and sustaining Israel as a religious community, more especially in exile, where a great part of the worship necessarily fell into abeyance on account of its intimate connexion with Jerusalem and the Holy Land."—*Delitzsch.* "Six days of the week I am *your* man: on the seventh I am *God's* man only," was the answer of Cairns, afterwards Lord Chancellor of England, to a friend who offered him, when a young and struggling barrister, a brief which would have required the giving up of the day of rest to master it.

14 to ride upon the high places of the earth. See Deut. xxxii. 13.

CHAPTER LIX

2 your sins have hid His face. Heb., "the Face."

4 None calleth for justice, etc. Rather, as R.V., "None sueth in righteousness, and none pleadeth in truth." All transactions between man and man are tainted by insincerity and hypocrisy.

5 They hatch cockatrice' (or adders') **eggs** Their purposes are mischievous; they hurt others, and they do no good to themselves (6).

9 Therefore is judgement far from us. Being opposed to all peace and justice (8), they lose the benefits of God's salvation (11).

10 in desolate places. Or, "in dark places": comp. Lam. iii. 6.

11 like bears . . . like doves. The more violent and the more gentle expressions of grief.

12 our transgressions, etc. The language of the people now takes the tone of penitence.

14 truth is fallen in the street. For a similar impressive personification, see Psa. lv. 9–11. So entirely were truth and honesty banished from all public and private transactions, that every one who would not conform to the wicked practices of the multitude exposed himself to ruin (15).

16 no intercessor. Rather, "none interposing." Just when the wickedness and the misery of the people have reached a most alarming height, and evidently cannot be arrested by any human power, God interposes.

brought salvation unto Him. He *for* Himself (or *by* Himself—*all alone*) wrought salvation.

17 He put on righteousness, etc. The figure of a warrior arming himself for battle, here carried out into striking detail. But there are no offensive weapons: He wars and conquers by His Spirit alone.

19 When the enemy shall come in like a flood. Or, "For He shall come as a rushing stream, which the breath of the Lord driveth" (R.V.).

20 the Redeemer. "A redeemer," R.V.; *i.e.*, He shall come to Zion as a redeemer (Goel).

that turn from transgression in Jacob. The promise is not for the literal, but the spiritual Israel: see Rom. xi. 26.

21 upon thee. Words addressed to the true Israel, the witness and messenger of Divine truth to all generations.

CHAPTER LX

1 Arise, shine. The Septuagint adds, "O Jerusalem."

the glory of the Lord, etc. Zion has lain prostrate in the darkness of night. But the sun arises, she springs upwards as with new life, and reflects the light which she receives. The verse is not only an encouragement, but a call to activity: comp. Rom. xiii. 11, 12.

4 shall be nursed at [thy] side. Rather, "shall be carried at the side": see R.V. The Eastern mode of carrying children on the hip.

5 Then shalt thou see, etc. This verse describes the joyful excitement with which Zion would witness the vast accession made to her numbers. It may be rendered thus: "Then shalt thou see, and become radiant (with joy), and thy heart shall throb and swell; because the abundance of the sea shall be turned unto thee, the strength of nations shall come to thee"; referring to the multitudes and the wealth of distant lands, which should be poured in like a flood upon her.

6 Midian . . . Ephah . . . Sheba. On these tribes, see Gen. xxv. 2, 4, 13, 14; and note on Psa. lxxii. 10.

8 as the doves to their windows. This image (probably referring to the ships crowding the Mediterranean to bring the exiles home) conveys the idea of vast numbers as well as of eagerness in flight. The swiftness and the cloud-like appearance of a distant flock of pigeons in full flight has been often observed.

11 thy gates shall be open continually. Implying a state of security, which encourages the influx of strangers. Suggesting also a readiness to welcome them.

brought. *i.e.*, led in triumph, as willing captives.

12 For the nation, etc. "The state of every nation is henceforth to be determined by its subjection or otherwise to the Church of God."

13 The glory of Lebanon, etc. As the cedar and other forest-trees were employed in the erection of the Temple, so all that is best and richest in the world shall be brought to the service of the Sanctuary. "But when God became man, and did indeed tread with human feet this world of ours, what then were the *places of His feet?* Sometimes, it is true, the Temple, but . . . far more often where the sick lay and the bereaved were weeping . . . the city gateways where the beggars stood, the lanes where the village folk had gathered their deaf and dumb, their palsied and their lunatic" (*G. A. Smith*).

14 The sons, etc. As though the oppressors themselves had perished.

16 suck the milk. etc. States and rulers imparting their vitality to the Church.

17 I will also make, etc. Like "Salvation" and "Praise" in the next verse, "Peace" and "Righteousness" seem here to be personified. I will make Peace thy magistracy, and Righteousness thy police. Here is the security for national rights and freedom.

22 in his time. Or, "in *its* time." When God sees that the proper time is come, there shall be no delay: see Heb. x. 37.

CHAPTER LXI

1 The Spirit of the Lord God (Adonai Jahveh) **is upon me.** The speaker is the Servant of the Eternal, who announces His own saving work (3).

the Lord hath anointed me. See note on Exod. xxx. 25, and refs.

2 the acceptable year of the Lord. "A year of the Lord's good pleasure."

the day of vengeance of our God. God's work of deliverance illustrates His justice as well as His mercy, and therefore involves "vengeance" upon the oppressors of His people, as well as salvation for those who humble themselves before Him.

3 beauty. Or, "a garland" (R.V.) *or* "turban." Mourners laid aside their head-dress and other ornaments, abstained from using the "oil of joy," and put dust and ashes on their heads: see Josh. vii. 6, and refs.; and 2 Sam. xii. 20. "For (instead of) ashes." For a modern and practical application of this, see the *Life of George Cadbury*, by A. G. Gardiner, where he quotes it in reference to his founding of the garden city.

4 they shall build the old wastes. See notes on xlix. 8; lviii. 12.

5 strangers shall stand and feed your flocks. The Church, imparting spiritual blessings to the world (6), shall receive its services and wealth.

6 the Priests of the Lord. The ancient ideal (Exod. xix. 6) fulfilled in the universal priesthood of believers (1 Pet. ii. 5, 9).

7 For your shame, etc. See note on xl. 2.

8 I hate robbery for burnt offering. R.V. renders, "I hate robbery *with* iniquity; and I will give them their recompense in truth"; *i.e.*, I hate rapine, accompanied, as it always is, with iniquity; and I will give My people an ample recompense for all they have suffered: see note on xl. 10.

11 as the earth bringeth forth her bud. Messiah's coming shall be to the world like rain to the earth, making it bring forth the fruits of righteousness and praise: comp. Psa. lxxii. 6, 7.

CHAPTER LXII

2 a new name. Significant of God's favour and of Israel's advancement to higher dignity: see Gen. xvii. 5, 15; xxxii. 28.

4 Forsaken . . . Desolate . . . Hephzi-bah . . . Beulah. See liv. 4, 5. The four names here used, "Azubah" (*forsaken*), "Shemamah" (*desolate*), "Hephzibah" (*my delight is in her*), and "Beulah" (*married*), were all probably not unfamiliar female names: for the first and third occur in 1 Kings xxii. 42; 2 Kings xxi. 1; and men's names corresponding to the second are found in 1 Chron. ii. 28, 44; iv. 17; vii. 37.

5 thy sons. That the sons are also spoken of as husbands is simply a combination of the literal and figurative.

6 watchmen. Those whom God had appointed to be the instructors of His people; to whom in the Old Testament the name of "watchmen" is often applied: see lvi. 10; also Ezek. iii. 17; xxxiii. 7.

7 Ye that make mention of the Lord. Rather, as in xliii. 26, "ye that put in remembrance," or *remind* Jehovah: comp. Luke xviii. 1–7. "Ye that are the Lord's remembrancers" (R.V.).

10 Prepare ye the way of the people. See note on xl. 3.

11 His work before Him. See note on xl. 10.

CHAPTER LXIII

1 dyed. Rather, "crimsoned" (R.V. marg.).

2 wine-fat. Or, "wine-vat," into which the grapes were put to be trodden with the feet, whilst the juice flowed off into a reservoir. A person so employed would naturally be splashed with the red juice, and thus resemble one who was covered with blood.

3 alone. As the Messiah is here taking "vengeance" on His foes, and "their blood," not His own, is "sprinkled on His garments," this passage cannot refer, as sometimes understood, to His bearing alone the guilt of man, in which He could not have expected any human help.

6 and make them drunk, etc. *i.e.*, made them drink to the full the cup of wrath.

7 This verse begins a new section, in which the prophet breaks out into thanksgiving and prayer. In Luther's version it begins the sixty-fourth chapter.

8 Children [that] will not lie. Rather, "Children that will not be false to Me."

9 the angel of His presence. See note on Gen. xvi. 7; and comp. Exod. iii. 21 with xiv. 19.

He bare them. See note on xl. 11.

10 vexed His holy Spirit. See Exod. xxiii. 20, 21; Psa. lxxviii. 17, 40; cvi. 43; 1 Cor. x. 9.

11 Then he remembered the days of old. The word "he" refers to Israel, who remembers the past, and uses it as a plea for renewed mercy: see li. 9, 10.

12 That led [them] by the right hand of Moses, etc. Rather, as R.V., "That caused His glorious arm to go at the right hand of Moses," ready to uphold him.

14 a beast. Rather, "cattle." This comparison appears to be drawn from the custom of cattle descending from their summer pastures in the mountain to their permanent home in the valley. The passage refers to the end rather than the course of God's leadings. He brought them into valleys with green pastures and still waters; *i.e.*, into the "rest" of Canaan.

15 The sounding ("yearning," R.V.) **of Thy bowels.** That is, "Where is Thy former pity for Thy people in their distress?" In Hebrew phraseology the "bowels" are spoken of as the seat of the tender emotions. We should say, "the longing of Thy heart."

16 Doubtless. Or, "For" (R.V.). The plea is, the Fatherhood of God.

17 Why hast Thou made us to err from Thy ways? See note on Exod. iv. 21. It cannot be supposed that God exerts any positive influence to harden the hearts of men; but He may, because of their wickedness, withhold from them His grace, and leave them to pursue their own ways. Israel pleads that it has been put into such a position.

CHAPTER LXIV

1 that Thou wouldest come down. See note on Judg. v. 5.

2 As when the melting fire burneth. Or, "as the fire kindleth the brushwood" (R.V.).

3 When Thou didst terrible things, etc. The wonders of Sinai authorise such a prayer as that just offered.

4 Neither hath the eye seen. Or, "Neither hath the eye seen a God beside Thee [who] will act for one who trusteth in Him": comp. R.V. See 1 Cor. ii. 9.

5 in those is continuance. One rendering refers the "continuance" to the people's sins, and ends the verse with a question: "In them have we been for a long time, and shall we be saved?" See R.V. and marg. Luther's version has much in its favour: "Thou wast angry because we sinned and continued long therein; and yet we are saved."

8 we all are the work of Thy hand. Another appeal to the Divine Fatherhood, as in lxiii. 16. Thou wilt not, therefore, reject those who are so entirely dependent upon Thee: comp. Psa. cxxxviii. 8.

10 Thy holy cities. Read, "Thy holy cities are become a wilderness, Zion is become," etc. (R.V.).

11 all our pleasant things. All the objects of our desire; see 2 Chron. xxxvi. 19, where the same word is used.

12 for these things. *i.e.*, in such a state of things." Will not these things lead Thee to interpose?

CHAPTER LXV

1 I am sought. Rather, "I am inquired of," *i.e.*, successfully: see R.V. "Sought," in the second part of the verse, is a different word. That the "nation" here means the Gentile world, in opposition to the Hebrews, who were called by God's name, appears from Rom. x. 20.

2 a rebellious people. To the people of Israel: see Rom. x. 21.

3 that sacrificeth in gardens. Or, "groves": see i. 29. Not in places set apart for worship, but in scenes of sensuous gratification.

4 which remain ("sit," R.V.) **among the graves.** Probably for the purposes of necromancy; seeking to obtain a knowledge of future events from the spirits of the dead, which they imagined to hover about their tombs. The "monuments" are the "secret places" (R.V.), vaults, or crypts in which they hoped that supernatural visions would come to them.

which eat swine's flesh. The eating of swine's flesh was expressly prohibited by the law.

5 Stand by thyself. In our Lord's time, the Pharisees and their disciples, who formed a large part of the nation, displayed much of this self-righteous pride.

These are a smoke in My nose. As offensive as smoke is to the nostrils. Or perhaps the meaning is, "They are fuel for the wrath of God, which manifests itself, as it were, in smoking breath": comp. Deut. xxxii. 22.

8 As the new wine is found in the cluster. While the corrupt mass is destroyed, whatever is good shall be carefully preserved as the seed (9) of a future nation.

Destroy it not. Perhaps a quotation from a vintage-song, "*Al-taschith*" (Psa. lvii., lviii., lix., *titles*).

10 the valley of Achor. This was a valley near Jericho, where Achan was put to death: see Josh. vii. 24. Sharon lying on the west, and Achor on the east of the kingdom of Judah, the blessing shall cover the whole land. Respecting "Sharon," see note on xxxiii. 9.

11 But ye [are] they that, etc. Rather, "And as for you who forsake the Eternal, who forget My holy mountain, who prepare for Gad a table.

and who fill for Meni a mixed draught." Gad and Meni represented Fortune and Destiny, for whom the idolatrous Jews held sacrificial feasts: see R.V., and comp. Jer. vii. 18; xliv. 17. The rebuke is one for the gambler of to-day, who "prepares a table for Fortune."

12 will I number you. There is here an allusion to the name of the idol "Meni," just mentioned; as if God said, "You worship *Destiny*, and I have *destined* you to the sword."

14 But ye shall cry for sorrow of heart. These verses forcibly display the difference which God will make "between the righteous and the wicked": comp. Mal. iii. 17–iv. 3.

15 ye shall leave your name for a curse. That is, their punishment would be so awful and irremediable, that it would become a formula of curse for those who wished to utter the most terrible imprecations.

16 in the God of truth. That is, the God of faithfulness; so called here because He had fulfilled His threatenings and promises. The very Hebrew word here used (*Amen*) is applied to Christ, with this explanation of it, in Rev. iii. 14.

17 I create new heavens and a new earth. This new creation signifies a great moral and spiritual revolution, which shall bring to an end the former confusions, iniquities, and miseries of the human race, and shall fill the Church with perpetual joy; comp. vers. 17–19 with Rev. xxi. 1–5.

22 as the days of a tree. This refers to the great age which certain trees attain. The olive, the oak, the cedar, and the terebinth, among the trees of Palestine, are said to live for centuries.

23 for trouble. Heb., "for the terror"; perhaps meaning, "for sudden death": see Lev. xxvi. 16.

24 before they call, I will answer. With these encouraging assurances of God's readiness to hear and answer His people's prayers, comp. Dan. ix. 20, 21; Matt. vi. 8; Acts ii. 1, 2, etc.

25 The wolf and the lamb shall feed together. We have here an almost verbal repetition of the beautiful picture of universal harmony in xi. 6–9. Under the reign of the Messiah, the evil passions and propensities of men, and all other hurtful influences, will be subdued, and peace and concord shall universally prevail.

And dust shall be the serpent's meat (food). (Gen. iii. 14; Rom. xvi. 20.) "The serpent will then no longer lie in wait for man's life. It will still creep in the dust, but without injuring man" (*Delitzsch*).

CHAPTER LXVI

1 Where is the house that ye build unto Me? These words plainly declare that the Mosaic ritual shall no longer be acceptable to God. Some, who regard this as written during the Captivity, suppose the reference to be to the Temple which the returning exiles were purposing to build in Jerusalem. The passage rebukes self-righteous and hypocritical formalists, as those of our Lord's days, who gloried in the rebuilding of the Temple at the very time when God was superseding it: see John ii. 20.

2 For all those things hath Mine hand made. That is, heaven and earth (1). I need no temples made with hands; all creation is My dwelling. But My temple, the "place of My rest," is the humble and obedient heart: comp. lvii. 15.

3 He that killeth an ox, etc. The various offerings of the Mosaic law are here classed with the sacrifices of heathenism. The most regular outward service, if the heart and life be not right, is as offensive to God as flagrant idolatry.

4 their delusions. Or, "calamities."

5 said, Let the Lord be glorified. The words of the persecutors should probably be rendered as ironical, "Let Jehovah be glorified, that we may see your joy" (R.V.). Upon which the prophet adds, "But they shall be ashamed."

6 from the city. That is, from Jerusalem. The prophet hears the roar of war in the city, even in the Temple itself. Jehovah, like a warrior (see xlii. 13), is taking vengeance on His enemies, who have cast out their brethren (5). This powerfully depicts the confusion and horrors which prevailed in Jerusalem (and even in the Temple) during its siege and capture by the Romans.

7 Before she travailed, she brought forth. *i.e.*, the true Jerusalem, the Church of the Messiah, by which, even before the convulsions of the great crisis, a new spiritual Israel shall spring suddenly to life. At the first preaching of the apostles three thousand were converted in one day; and the Gospel was speedily propagated over almost the whole of the known world. And this was only a partial fulfilment of the prophecy.

11 That ye may suck, and be satisfied. Those who have sympathised with Zion in her sorrows shall partake of her abundance and her glory; nourished by the same truth, and comforted from the same sources of consolation.

12 be borne upon [her] sides. That is, as a child is by its mother: see xlix. 22; lx. 4.

17 purify themselves in the gardens. *i.e.*, by idolatrous rites: see lxv. 3, 5. In the following clause, instead of the word "tree," we should read, "the one in the midst"; the allusion being to an idolatrous procession, with the priest as the leader, through the midst of the garden or grove where the rites were celebrated.

the abomination. This term comprehends whatever was held as abominable in the law of God, such as creeping things and reptiles: see Lev. xi. 10.

18 I [know] their works and their thoughts. More probably, "And I [will punish] their deeds and their thoughts." The verb is omitted, probably to give terseness and force to the sentence.

19 those that escape. *i.e.*, those who shall have survived the judgements predicted; and who, by what they shall have witnessed, shall have been brought to acknowledge and receive the Messiah. These are to become missionaries to the world—"to far Spain, and the distances of Africa, towards the Black Sea and to Greece, a full round of the compass" (*G. A. Smith*).

20 upon horses, and in chariots. The description represents the ingathering of the Jews to the Church through the agency of the Gentiles.

23 from one new moon to another. Indicating the regularity and constancy with which the whole human family shall worship the true God.

24 And they shall go forth. The spiritual Israelites, offering perpetually their pure worship in the New Jerusalem, shall look down from its height upon Tophet, and see with abhorrence the death-fires and corruption of the apostate Israel of former days. Such is the solemn contrast with which the prophecy closes: selected by the Great Teacher Himself as His warning to the impenitent (Mark ix. 44).

THE BOOK OF JEREMIAH

INTRODUCTION

It was about seventy years after the death of Isaiah that the call of God came to the young Jeremiah (i. 4–6). Josiah, King of Judah, was then in the thirteenth year of his reign, 628 B.C. He had already begun, when he was sixteen years old, to "seek after the God of David his father," and in the twentieth year of his age to cleanse the land of idols (2 Chron. xxxiv. 3, 4). It was an encouraging time for those who had at heart the highest interests of the people, and the work of reformation was strengthened by the finding of the Book of the Law in the Temple in the eighteenth year of Josiah's reign (2 Kings xxii. 1–xxiii. 30; 2 Chron. xxxiv. 8–xxxv. 27).

At first Jeremiah shrinks from the great task of being God's messenger to the people, but God encourages him by His promises of help and support (i. 7–12). It is evident that there were many of the people who had not accepted Josiah's reformation, or only sullenly acquiesced in it, for the first message given to Jeremiah is one of judgement for their sins (i. 14–16). The earlier chapters contain the stern words, spoken partly at Anathoth, his native place, and partly at Jerusalem, in which he denounced the wickedness of his time. The finding of the law is referred to in chap. xi. 2–8.

The death of Josiah in battle against Pharaoh-Necho, at Megiddo, made Jeremiah's task still more difficult. Josiah's son and successor, Shallum or Jehoahaz, only reigned three months, and is only once mentioned in this book (xxii. 10, 11; cp. 2 Kings xxiii. 31–33). He was succeeded by Jehoiakim, to whom many of Jeremiah's rebukes are addressed (xix. 3–5; xxii. 1–19; xxxvi. 30, 31). Jeremiah suffered the penalty of his courage and faithfulness. He was more than once arrested and imprisoned under Jehoiakim and Zedekiah (xx. 2; xxxvii. 15, 16; xxxviii. 6–28).

When Jerusalem was taken by the Assyrians, Nebuchadrezzar gave special instructions that he was to be well treated (xxxix. 12), and Nebuzar-adan the captain of the guard gave him the option of coming with him to Babylon or remaining in his own country (xl. 4). Jeremiah chose the latter, but when the remnant decided to take refuge in Egypt, contrary to his remonstrance (xlii. 7–22), they compelled him to go with them (xliii. 5–7). There he still spoke to the people, and foretold the Divine judgements upon other nations (xliii. 10–13; xliv.; xlvi.; li.). And there, according to the tradition, he died.

"But for Jeremiah," says Dr. W. H. Bennett (*Expositor's Bible*), "the religion of Jehovah might have perished with His Chosen People. It was his mission to save Revelation from the wreck of Israel. Humanly speaking, the religious future of the world depended upon this stern, solitary prophet." Even Renan says that, before John the Baptist, Jeremiah was the man who contributed most to the foundation of Christianity. "The sufferings of the Prophet," says Elvet Lewis, "have become one of the noble heritages of the human race" (*Devotional Commentary:* Jeremiah).

CHAPTER I

1 Anathoth. Anathoth was a city of the priests (Josh. xxi. 18), in the tribe of Benjamin, less than three miles north-east of Jerusalem; now called *Anata*.

3 unto the end of the eleventh year of Zedekiah. In this enumeration of kings, Jehoahaz (Jehoiakim's predecessor) and Jehoiachin (his son and successor) are omitted. Each of them lasted only three months; and none of the prophecies contained in the Book appear to belong to either of these reigns.

The ministry of Jeremiah, also, continued some years after "the carrying away of Jerusalem captive" (see xl.–xlv., etc.), but this latter period is not here mentioned.

5 knew thee. *i.e.*, favourably; implying choice.

unto the nations. Not merely to the Jews: see xlvi.–li. To this office Jeremiah was "sanctified" or set apart in God's purposes before his birth: cp. Gal. i. 15.

6 I am a child. The Hebrew word here used may denote any period of youthful life: cp. Gen. xxxiv. 19; xli 12. Jeremiah may have been about twenty years old.

8 of their faces. *i.e.*, as R.V., "because of them."

10 to root out, and to pull down, etc. That is, to *announce* these things: see Ezek. xliii. 3.

11 a rod (shoot) of an almond tree. The almond tree, which flowers very early in the year, derives its Hebrew name ("wake-tree") from its *watching*, as it were, for the first dawn of spring. Hence this shoot of an almond tree represented the speedy fulfilment of these predictions, of which God says, "I am watching over My word to perform it."

13 toward the north. Rather, "from the north" (R.V.).

15 they shall come. Cp. xxxix. 3. In ver. 16, God speaks of the heathen conquerors as uttering His sentence.

they shall set every one his throne, etc. Shall sit in judgement upon the people's crimes.

17 gird up thy loins. Prepare thyself resolutely for thy work. The phrase is derived from the Eastern custom of tucking up the skirt in the girdle, before undertaking any laborious employment, as a journey (Exod. xii. 11), a race (1 Kings xviii. 46), a conflict (Job xxxviii. 3).

18 I have made thee this day a defenced city. Thou shalt be as strong as a fortified city. The emblem is in strong contrast with Jeremiah's natural disposition.

CHAPTER II

2 The kindness of thy youth. This probably means "thy piety and love towards Me"; and may refer to that faithful generation who, after being led through the wilderness, took possession of Canaan: see Joshua, especially Josh. xxii. 1.

3 Israel [was] holiness unto the Lord. Rather, "Israel was holy to Jehovah, [being] the first-fruit of His (*i.e.*, God's) produce: all who eat him will [therefore] be held guilty," etc. God regarded Israel as consecrated, like the first-fruits, to Himself (see Exod. xxiii. 19). No stranger was allowed to partake of the first-fruits (Lev. xxii. 10, 16). So God would severely punish all who attempted to injure Israel, as in the cases of the Amalekites and the Amorites: see Exod. xvii. 14–16; Deut. ii. 30, etc.

5 and have walked after vanity, etc. Or, "after emptiness and become empty themselves." These words are quoted from 2 Kings xvii. 15. Men assimilate themselves to the object of their worship.

6 a land of deserts. See Numb. xi. 1; xxi. 4, and notes.

8 The pastors. Or, "shepherds." This may mean kings or rulers (so R.V.), as distinguished from priests and prophets; see 1 Kings xxii. 17.

9 will I plead. "The Hebrew word is that of the plaintiff setting forth his accusation in a law-court" (*Dean Payne-Smith*).

10 over. Or, "over to" (R.V.). "Chittim" (Cyprus) and "Kedar" (Arabia Deserta) are put for *west* and *east*.

11 Hath a nation changed [their] gods? While the heathen cling to their idols, though they obtain from them no good, Israel has exchanged truth for error—the ever fresh, full, accessible fountain of life for the "cistern," laboriously excavated, which would become stagnant, if it were not "broken," and therefore dry (13). So to the *one* evil which the heathen commit—that of idolatry, the Jews have added a *second*—that of apostasy.

16 Noph and Tahapanes. See note on Isa. xix. 13. Noph is *Memphis*. Tahapanes was called by the Greeks *Daphne*, near Pelusium; see xliii. The prophetic vision was fulfilled when Josiah was defeated and slain by the Egyptians at Megiddo (2 Kings xxiii. 29).

have broken the crown of thy head. Or, "have stripped thee."

17 Hast thou not procured this, etc.? More exactly, "Is not this (thy present calamitous state) what thy forsaking Jehovah, even while He guided thee in the way, has brought about?"

18 to drink the waters of Sihor. The same figure as in ver. 13. Instead of seeking supply from Me, you have gone to the Nile or the Euphrates—to Egypt or Assyria. "Sihor" is the Nile: see Isa. xxiii. 3.

19 Thine own wickedness shall correct thee. The alliances with foreign powers, into which the Jews had been led by their mistrust of God and disobedience to Him, were both the cause and the means of their punishment: see ver. 36.

20 I have broken. The ancient versions, followed by Luther, read, "Thou hast broken thy yoke, and hast burst thy bonds; and hast said, I will not serve (or obey); for upon every high hill," etc. This agrees better with the latter clause.

22 nitre. R.V., "lye," in which "natron" or carbonate of soda was used.

soap. Or, "potash"; an alkali obtained from the ashes of plants.

marked. With a stain.

23 See thy way in the valley. "Way," for "conduct." Alluding to the worship of Moloch in the valley of Hinnom; see note on 2 Kings xxiii. 10.

dromedary. Or, young she-camel.

traversing her ways. That is, running hither and thither.

24 at her pleasure. Or, as R.V., "in her desire."

in her occasion . . . in her month. At the pairing season.

25 Withhold thy foot from being unshod, etc. "Do not so recklessly follow thy wicked ways; do not so thirst after idols."

There is no hope, etc. That is, It is useless to oppose me: I say "No" to all thine entreaties, for I have loved strange gods, etc.

26 So is the house of Israel ashamed. The suggestion is, that where there is shame there may yet (notwithstanding ver. 25) be repentance.

29 Wherefore will ye plead with Me? *i.e.*, Why do you complain of Me as if I had wronged you?

33 Therefore hast thou also taught the wicked ones (fem.) **thy ways.** Or, "Thou hast taught thy ways wickednesses;" *i.e.*, Thou hast made sin a study and an art, in which thou hast attained such proficiency that thou canst openly practise the most atrocious cruelties (34), and yet call them innocent or venial (35).

34 I have not found it, etc. "I have not found it by digging through, *i.e.*, by laborious search, but everywhere." The sin is open, flagrant. Some ancient versions read, "but upon every oak" or "terebinth," an allusion to idolatrous practices.

36 to change thy way. The description of a vacillating policy in seeking alliances.

37 thine hands upon thine head. As one in the deepest shame and grief: see 2 Sam. xiii. 19.

thy confidences. Thy supports, those in whom you trust: formerly Assyria, and now Egypt.

CHAPTER III

1 They say, etc. This verse may be connected with the preceding, thus: "Jehovah hath rejected thy supports," etc., "saying, Lo (or suppose), a man shall put away his wife, . . . And hast thou played the harlot with many lovers, and [yet thinkest] to return unto Me! saith Jehovah." The passage so read is an exposure of the fallacy of the people's hopes. On the laws of divorce here alluded to, see Deut. xxiv. 1-4.

2 In the ways hast thou sat. See Gen. xxxviii. 14, 21.

the ("an," R.V.) **Arabian.** The Arabs of the deserts around Palestine are notorious for lying in wait for travellers.

4 Wilt thou not from this time cry unto Me? Some render vers. 4, 5 as follows: "Dost thou not already cry unto Me, 'Thou art my Father, the husband of my youth: will He keep [His anger] for ever, will He retain it perpetually?' Behold thou sayest this, and yet thou doest evil." Jehovah thus accuses the people of claiming the privileges of their covenant with Him whilst continuing to speak and do evil: see ii. 27.

5 as thou couldest. "Persistently" (*Payne-Smith*).

9 lightness. Rather, "infamy." This of course refers to *Israel* and her idolatries.

11 The backsliding Israel hath justified herself. "Hath shown herself more righteous" (R.V.). Great as were the sins of Israel, she might be almost called "righteous" when compared with Judah; because Judah had possessed the Temple of God, with His Divinely-appointed worship and priests (see 2 Chron. xi. 13–17, and note), with many zealous prophets, and had been solemnly warned by the defection and the punishment of Israel. If, in spite of all these advantages, she persisted in her idolatry, she was even more culpable than Israel, and deserved to be treated more severely.

12 toward the north. Towards the countries in which the exiles of the Ten Tribes were dispersed—Mesopotamia, Assyria, and Media (2 Kings xvii. 6).

I will not cause Mine anger (countenance) to fall upon you. "I will not look in anger upon you" (R.V.).

13 hast scattered thy ways. Hast gone in all directions.

14 a family. Or, "a tribe." Though in a whole city or nation there should be only one or two of My people, I will not forget even these, but will bring them back with the rest: see Deut. xxx. 1–5.

I will bring you to Zion. This prophecy was fulfilled, in part, when many from the Ten Tribes joined themselves to the people of Judah on their return from Babylon, and at many subsequent periods. But it cannot be regarded as completely fulfilled till "all Israel shall be saved": cp. Acts xxvi. 7; Rom. xi. 26.

15 pastors. "Shepherds," as R.V. See note on ii. 8.

16 The ark of the covenant of the Lord. The ark was the most sacred of all the religious symbols, and the second Temple was regarded as having far less glory than the first, because it had not this. But the prophet declares that the ark shall not be needed or even desired; for Jerusalem—the Church—into which all nations shall be gathered shall be Jehovah's throne: cp. Rev. xxi. 22.

17 imagination. Or, "stubbornness," as R.V.

18 the land of the north. A general expression for the great Mesopotamian region—the land of the captivities.

19 How shall I, etc.? Rather, "And I shall."

21 upon the high places. As the customary places of lament (cp. Isa. xv. 2). Upon those high places also idolatry had been practised: where the sin had been committed there the cry of penitence is heard.

23 the multitude. Or, "the tumult," as R.V. Read "[In vain is] the tumult on the mountains." Moffatt translates, "orgies on the mountains."

24 shame. Heb., "the shame": probably meaning the shameful idols. *Bosheth*, the Heb. word, is often used, as in Ishbosheth, as an equivalent for *Baal*.

25 We lie down. Rather, as R.V., "Let us lie down," in the attitude of contrition. So in the following clause: "let our confusion cover us."

CHAPTER IV

1 If thou wilt return. Or, "If thou wouldest return, O Israel, saith Jehovah, to Me thou must return" (in repentance). A sincere return in righteousness to God's service is the condition of His blessing.

2 And thou shalt swear, etc. That is, thou shalt publicly profess and adhere to His service, the token of this being the form of oath, "As the Eternal liveth": see R.V. See Deut. vi. 13; Isa. xix. 18.

3 Break up your fallow ground. The two metaphors in vers. 3, 4 show that there must be a thorough putting away of all sin from the heart and life; otherwise reformation will be as fruitless as a sowing among thorns.

5 Declare ye in Judah, etc. The prophet now sees the threatened punishment as if it were actually present (see Isa. x. 28, etc.); he beholds the northern invader entering and ravaging the land. This may refer to the Scythians, who overran great part of Western Asia about this time: see Herodotus, i. 103. It may allude also to the Babylonians, who shortly afterwards destroyed Jerusalem, and carried away the princes and many of the people.

the trumpet. That is, the trumpet of alarm.

6 Set up the (a) standard. A signal or flag, pointing out the place of refuge.

Retire. Or, "flee for safety" (as R.V.), *i.e.*, to Zion.

the north. See note on iii. 18.

7 The lion, etc. Rather, "A lion . . . and a destroyer of nations." So R.V.

without an inhabitant. See xliii. 5–7.

9 shall perish. Or, "shall fail"; *i.e.*, with fear.

10 Surely Thou hast greatly deceived this people. The best rendering of this passage appears to be that which prefaces this sentence by the words, "They will say," instead of, "Then said I."

11 A dry wind of the high places. Rather, "a hot wind of the barren heights in the wilderness," etc. God says that He will sweep the land, not with the cool breeze which winnows the grain, but with the deadly Samûm and its clouds of scorching sand—a reminiscence of an Eastern wind at Anathoth. This represents the terrible invaders who shall sweep over the country: see Hab. i. 9.

12 a full wind from those [places]. Rather, "a wind fuller (*i.e.*, stronger) than these shall come for Me"; *i.e.*, to do My bidding.

13 Woe unto us! The people's cry, as the terrible invader draws near.

14 O Jerusalem. The response of God through the prophet.

15 a voice declareth from Dan, etc. This may mean, There is no time to be lost; for the invader has passed the northern frontier, and is already at Mount Ephraim (not more than ten miles from Jerusalem).

16 Make ye mention to the nations. That is, "Report it to the nations." God's chastisement of His people is to be public and exemplary.

watchers. That is, "besiegers"; so called to agree with the figure in ver. 17.

17 As keepers of a field. The tented plain is like a great pasture land covered with shepherds' and herdsmen's booths.

19 My bowels! my bowels! Or, "My heart! my heart!"

21 the standard, etc. The standard of Zion, as in ver. 6. The "trumpet" is typical, generally, of war.

22 For My people, etc. God's answer to the people's cry.

23 I beheld, etc. The prophet now speaks.

27 Yet will I not make a full end. When all seems to be destroyed, God has yet a reserve in mercy: cp. Rom. xi. 5.

29 The whole city. Rather, "The whole land."

30 Though thou rentest thy face. Rather, "distendest thine eyes" (*i.e.*, with antimony). See note on 2 Kings ix. 30. The figure of ch. ii. is resumed, to show how useless shall be all the efforts of the people to obtain help in their distress.

31 is wearied. "Fainteth," R.V., *i.e.*, with exhaustion.

CHAPTER V

1 I will pardon it. "I will pardon her," R.V. The representation is not to be taken literally, for there were good men in Jerusalem, such as Baruch, etc. (cp. xxiv. 4, 5); but it is designed to show that Jerusalem, like Sodom, was guilty as a whole; and yet that God was willing to carry His long-suffering and clemency farther, if possible, than in that case: see Gen. xviii. 23–31.

2 The Lord liveth. *i.e.*, "As the Eternal liveth"; the most solemn form of oath being used as the sanction of falsehood.

6 of the evenings. Probably "of the deserts," as R.V. marg. The two words are very similar in Hebrew.

A leopard shall watch. That is, shall watch for prey.

7 adultery. Evidently *idolatry*, not without a reference to its licentious accompaniments.

10 battlements. Or, "branches" (R.V.), *i.e.*, leave only the root or stem. The metaphor is that of a vineyard (ii. 21): cp. Isa. vi. 13.

13 And the prophets shall become wind. This is the language of the scoffing Jews. They said, The gloomy predictions of the prophets shall turn out to be wind, and shall return on their own heads.

16 Their quiver is as an open sepulchre. See note on Psa. v. 9. The "open sepulchre" is here equivalent to a storehouse of death, *i.e.*, death-dealing arrows. The words are, however, omitted in the Septuagint version.

17 shall impoverish. Rather, "shall beat down," as R.V.

19 So shall ye serve strangers. The punishment like the offence. As they had served strange gods, so they should serve a strange people.

22 Fear ye not Me? Man's reverence is due to God, as the Creator, Controller, and beneficent Sustainer (24) of all things. The power of so slight a thing as sand to resist the might of the ocean is a striking illustration of creative might and wisdom. But the Jews had utterly disregarded even these natural claims.

23 a revolting and a rebellious heart. Not only departing from God but actively opposing His will.

24 That giveth rain. As the preceding appeal had been to God's creative power, so this is to His providential goodness. The "former rain" marked the autumn, the "latter" the spring. The "appointed weeks of harvest" were the interval between the Passover and the Pentecost, which latter was called the "Feast of Weeks."

28 Yet they prosper. Rather, as R.V., "that they (*i.e.*, the fatherless) may prosper."

31 by their means. Lit., "on their hand," *i.e.*, under their guidance: see 1 Chron. xxv. 2, 3.

CHAPTER VI

1 O ye children of Benjamin. The Benjamites are addressed, most probably because, when assailed from the north, they would naturally seek shelter in Jerusalem; which they are here instructed to leave, and to flee southwards to the mountain fastnesses. Tekoa, on a hill about twelve miles from Jerusalem, still retains its name. Beth-haccerem, "the house of the vineyard," is thought by Condor to be *Ain Karim*, west of Jerusalem.

3 The shepherds with their flocks. The Babylonian and other generals (see xxv. 34) and their armies, who will cover the land like sheep and cattle, and devour everything.

4 Prepare. Lit., "Sanctify"; *i.e.*, by the sacrifices usually offered before a battle, to propitiate the Deity: see Ezek. xxi. 21–23. This is the language of the enemy generals.

at noon. The two impatient exclamations of the soldiers in this verse were made at different times of the day.

Woe unto us! Or, "Alas for us!" The soldiers, eager for plunder, regret the close of day; but resolve to renew the attack at night (5).

8 depart. Rather, as R.V., "be alienated."

9 Turn back thine hand. *i.e.*, Put it again and again into them; do the work thoroughly. The phrase refers, probably, to the successive removals of the people. See 2 Kings xxiv. 14; xxv. 11. An address to the invaders.

10 uncircumcised. Unprepared to listen to God's word.

14 slightly. They treat it as a light matter.

15 they were not at all ashamed. Rather, "They have been put to shame because they have committed abomination; yet surely they are not at all ashamed, nor do they know how to blush": see R.V. marg. They are so hardened as to be utterly insensible to the disgrace which they have brought upon themselves.

16 ask for the old paths. Act as travellers would when they find themselves going wrong: ask for the "old paths," which God marked out in His law, and in which your ancestors found peace and happiness.

17 watchmen. The prophets: see Ezek. iii. 17–21.

18 what is among them. *i.e.*, "what is going

on among them"; their evil doings and My punishments (19).

21 stumblingblocks. *i.e.*, causes of overthrow or ruin.

22 sides. Or, "extremities"; *i.e.*, from a distant land.

23 They shall lay hold on bow and spear. This description of the Babylonian cavalry is illustrated by sculptures still remaining.

24 We have heard the fame thereof. The prophet speaks in the name of the people on hearing the tidings.

27 I have set thee [for] a tower. Rather, "I have appointed thee a trier among My people, an assayer (or separator), that thou," etc.: see 28–30. The Vulgate, followed by Luther, has "Probatorem dedi te in populo meo."

28 Walking with slanders. *i.e.*, "going about as slanderers."

brass and iron. "Copper and iron," the baser metals; no silver or gold in them.

29 The bellows are burned. Or, as R.V., "The bellows blow fiercely." Yet the dross could not be separated. The severest measures of correction have been used in vain.

CHAPTER VII

4 these. *i.e.*, these buildings of the Temple, to which Jeremiah would point as he spoke. The "lying words" or "deceptive phrases" ("paroles trompeuses," *French version*), are not so much the statement here made, as the inference drawn from it, that God would always favour and protect the Temple and city which were called His own. A warning against relying on the mere externals of religion.

10 We are delivered. This probably means, "We are set free by this punctilious discharge of religious duties to go on sinning."

11 a den of robbers. On the application of these words by our Lord, see Matt. xxi. 13.

12 which was in Shiloh. See note on Josh. xviii. 1; also 1 Sam. iv. 12, 22; Psa. lxxviii. 60. The fate of Shiloh is referred to in order to destroy the people's false confidence in the possession of the Temple, and other national privileges.

13 rising up early. *i.e.*, speaking with prompt and earnest solicitude.

16 I will not hear thee. Jeremiah is forbidden to pray, not for the reformation of the people, but for the removal of the impending chastisement; the absolute necessity for which is shown in the following description of their public and shameless idolatry.

18 the queen of heaven. Probably the goddess Ishtar or Astarte. For this goddess, see Sayce, *Primer of Assyriology* (1925), and Budge, *Babylonian Life and History* (1925).

19 [Do they] not [provoke] themselves? The sinner's rebellion hurts not God, but it ruins himself, for he cannot live without God's favour.

21 Put your burnt offerings, etc. Or, "Add your burnt offerings," etc. (R.V.). The meaning is, "Multiply your sacrifices as you may, so long as you do not bring an obedient heart, they have no value in God's sight, and therefore you may as well eat them as offer them." By the law in Lev. i. no part of a burnt offering could be eaten.

22 I spake not unto your fathers. Jeremiah elsewhere expressly recognises sacrifice as an ordinance of God (xxxiii. 18). The phrase here rendered *concerning* strictly means *on account of* or *for the sake of*. The law was not given for the sake of the ritual, which indeed was enjoined after the Ten Commandments, and had no place, like them, in the Ark of the Covenant. From the outset, therefore, the legislation of Sinai made the ceremonial distinctly subordinate to the moral. Orelli's is one of the best explanations of this verse: "We should say, 'I have not so much given you commands in respect of sacrifice as rather enjoined you this.'"

23 Obey My voice. The fundamental principle of the whole law was *obedience* to all that God enjoined: see 1 Sam. xv. 22.

24 imagination. Rather, "stubbornness," as R.V.

28 Truth is perished. Fidelity to God is extinct.

29 Cut off thine hair. Prepare thyself for mourning: see Isa. xv. 2. The "high places" here should rather be rendered "bare heights."

31 Tophet. It is doubtful whether this is a proper name, and it may mean generally a place of uncleanness.

to burn their sons and their daughters. In honour of Moloch, the fire or sun-god. The victims were first slain (Ezek. xvi. 21), then consumed.

32 till there be no place. No place *to bury any more*: see R.V. But some interpreters read, "for want of room *elsewhere*": see R.V. marg.

33 fray. *i.e.*, "frighten": cp. *affray, afraid.*

34 desolate. A waste (R.V.). The word is used only of places once inhabited now laid waste.

CHAPTER VIII

1 They shall bring out the bones, etc. This might be done partly to obtain the jewels and treasures buried with the dead, but chiefly to insult the conquered people, by dishonouring the remains of their rulers and priests.

3 this evil family. The whole "house of Israel."

4 Shall they fall, etc. Will not those who fall try to rise? Will not one who has taken a wrong road turn back? How irrational, then, is this persistence in sin, and refusal to repent!

7 her appointed times. For her migrations in spring and autumn. See Tristram: *Natural History of the Bible.*

the crane and the swallow. Rather, "the swift and the crane." With these contrasts cp. Isa. i. 3.

the judgement. Rather, as R.V., "the ordinance"; given to the birds as an instinct, to men as a command; obeyed in the former case, disregarded in the latter.

8 How do ye say, etc.? An appeal to the recognised expounders of the law.

Lo, certainly in vain made He [it], etc. Rather, "But, behold, the false pen of the scribes hath turned it into falsehood": cp. R.V.

the pen of the scribes. The first mention of scribes as a literary class dates from Hezekiah's day: they are called "men of Hezekiah" (Prov xxv. 1). For the word see 2 Chron. xxxiv. 13, 15 (in Josiah's time). The claim made by the scribes, "The law of the Eternal is with us," shows that the Pentateuch or Torah existed in Jeremiah's day as a recognised standard of religion. Hence its antiquity may be fairly presumed. As Dr. Payne-Smith, Dean of Canterbury, has well said: "The Torah must have existed in writing before there could have been an order of men whose special business it was to study it."

10 Therefore will I give, etc. This and the following verses contain a solemn repetition of the charge and threatening in vi. 12–15.

that shall inherit. Or, as R.V., "that shall

possess." The idea is that of a forcible possession, as by invaders.

13 And [the things that] I have given them shall pass away. Rather, as R.V. marg., "And I have appointed them those that shall pass over them"; their enemies, like a devastating flood.

14 let us be silent there. *i.e.*, let us cease from all resistance, as God has made it useless. The language is that of the people, one to another.

17 Which will not be charmed. Implacable enemies: see Psa. lviii. 5.

18 When I would comfort myself. "My sorrow is past healing" (*Moffatt*).

19 of the daughter of My people because of them that dwell, etc. Rather, as R.V., "of the daughter of my people from a land that is very far off." This is the cry of the future exiles, which is answered immediately by God's complaint of their sins: "Why have they provoked Me?" etc.

20 The harvest is past. The reply of the exiles, meaning that all seasons of hope and opportunities of deliverance have passed away. "Summer" is literally "the fruit-gathering," after the corn-harvest.

21 For the hurt, etc. The prophet himself now takes up the strain.

I am black. In the garb of mourning.

22 Gilead. Over which the sun rose at Anathoth. East of the Jordan, where the balsam-tree (*opobalsamum*) abounded. Some writers say that the balm was *mastic*, but Dr. G. E. Post, a recognised Oriental scholar and traveller, says the tree which produces it has not been found east of Jordan (*Hastings' Dict. of Bible*: article "Balm").

CHAPTER IX

2 Oh that I had in the wilderness, etc.! So detestable are their lives, that the most desolate lodging-place would be preferable to their company.

3 they are not valiant for the truth upon the earth. Rather, "and they are grown strong in the land, but not for truth" (R.V.).

7 How shall I do for the daughter of My people? How otherwise can I reclaim them?

8 an arrow shot out. Rather, as R.V., "a deadly arrow."

And for the habitations of the wilderness. Rather, "And for the pastures of the wilderness a lamentation, because they are desolate," etc.

11 dragons. Rather, "jackals" (R.V.); and so in x. 22.

12 for what the land perisheth, etc. Better as another question, "Wherefore is the land perished and burned up?" (R.V.)

14 imagination. Rather, "stubbornness," as R.V.

17 cunning women. *i.e.*, skilful in mourning; persons who had been taught to utter laments at funerals: see Eccles. xii. 5.

19 our dwellings have cast [us] out. Rather, "They (*i.e.*, our enemies) have cast down our habitations": cp. R.V.

21 death is come up into our windows. Death is personified as entering the house or raging in the streets to kill the people.

23 Let not the wise man glory, etc. By such awful judgements God teaches that nothing human or earthly can give security; and that true safety and honour can be gained only by knowing, obeying, and trusting Him. That the lessons here taught by God's judgements may also be learned from His mercies is shown by the use of this passage in 1 Cor. i. 17–31.

25 I will punish, etc. Lit., "I will punish all them which are uncircumcised in [their] uncircumcision" (R.V.). They have the outward sign of the covenant, but are "uncircumcised in heart" (Rom. ii. 29).

26 all that are in the utmost corners. Rather, "all that are cut as to the corner [of the beard]": cp. R.V. As this practice was forbidden to the Jews (see Lev. xix. 27; xxi. 5), this description would designate Gentiles. The Jew who forsakes God's covenant shall be treated like the heathen, for he is like them "in heart."

CHAPTER X

2 the signs of heaven. Uncommon phenomena, such as eclipses, or comets, which men have usually regarded with alarm: cp. Shakespeare, *Julius Cæsar*, Act I, Scene 3; Act II, Scene 2.

3 of the people. Rather, "of the peoples"—the heathen nations.

5 They are upright as the palm tree. Rather, "like a palm tree of turnery work" (see R.V.); a mere carved pillar, stiff and lifeless. Luther translates, "Säulen" (pillars).

6 [Forasmuch as]. These words are not in the Hebrew. The verse begins with the emphatic exclamation, "There is none at all like unto Thee, O Jehovah."

7 O King of nations. R.V., "O King of the nations": not the tutelary God of Israel only.

8 The stock is a doctrine of vanities. Or, "The wood itself is a teacher of vanities": and therefore its votaries can only be foolish: cp. R.V.

9 Tarshish. See note on 1 Kings x. 22.

Uphaz. Uphaz is supposed by some to be the same as Ophir: see 1 Kings ix. 28. But others regard it as a different name, signifying "gold coast": cp. Dan. x. 5. There is no certainty on the subject.

11 Thus shall ye say unto them, etc. This verse is in Chaldee or Aramaic, a dialect which Jeremiah uses nowhere else. It is found, however, in the oldest versions; and it is supposed to be intended for the Jewish exiles as a reply to the Chaldean idolaters by whom they were to be surrounded.

14 Every man is brutish in [his] knowledge. This may mean, "Every one is too brutish to know" (R.V. marg.); *i.e.*, to know the true God.

Every founder is confounded by the graven image. Rather, as R.V., "Every goldsmith is put to shame by [his] graven image"—"put to shame," because after all his skill and labour, it is nothing more!

15 errors. Mockeries; delusions (see R.V., and marg.).

their visitation. *i.e.*, for testing and judgement.

16 the rod. Probably, "the tribe," as R.V.

17 wares. "Packages," or "bundles"; the few things which captives might be permitted to carry with them. "Gather" [and take them] "out of the land."

the fortress. That is, the *besieged* fortress, or city.

18 at this once. "At this time" (R.V.).

that they may find it so. "That they may feel it" (R.V.), *i.e.*, distress; or, "that they may find out by experience."

19 Woe is me, etc.! The cry of Zion in her desolation.

21 they shall not prosper, etc. Rather, as R.V., "they have not prospered, and all their flocks are scattered."

22 the noise of the bruit. That is, "the voice of a rumour," *i.e.*, of the approaching enemy: see R.V. For "a den of dragons," read "a dwelling place of jackals."

23 It is not in man that walketh to direct his steps. Therefore Zion is encouraged to pray that her correction may be "in measure" ("in judgement," ver. 24).

CHAPTER XI

3 this covenant. The covenant made with your ancestors (4), and recently renewed by Josiah (2 Kings xxii. 8–xxiii. 25). Much of the language of these verses is derived from the Book of Deuteronomy, which had just been publicly read in the hearing of the people: see Deut. iv. 20, 23, 24; v. 2; xi. 26–28; xxvii. 26; xxviii. 1; xxix. 13, etc.

4 From the iron furnace. Or, "Out of the iron furnace," *i.e.*, Egypt.

5 So be it. "Amen." This appears to be the prophet's response to the covenant just repeated, as prescribed in Deut. xxvii. 15, 26.

6 Proclaim. A command to the prophet, showing that he took an active part in the proceedings of Josiah (2 Kings xxiii. 2, etc.).

8 I will bring upon them, etc. Rather, "I brought upon them," etc. (R.V.).

9 A conspiracy. This was no secret confederacy (see ver. 13), but an almost universal return, as if by agreement, to the sins which Josiah's reformation had checked for a time.

13 according to the number of thy cities, etc. Among the heathen, every city, street, and house had its tutelary deity.

15 she hath wrought lewdness [with] many. This verse is difficult, and the ancient versions appear to have had different readings. Driver translates, "What hath my beloved to do in mine house, seeing she bringeth evil devices to pass? Will vows and holy flesh remove thine evil from off thee? then mightest thou rejoice."

16 a great tumult. The tumult of on-rushing foes.

18 knowledge of it. Rather, "knowledge of them," *i.e.*, of "their doings."

19 a lamb [or] an ox. Rather, "a pet" or "house lamb," see 2 Sam. xii. 3. "A gentle lamb," R.V.: cp. Isa. liii. 7.

with the fruit thereof. Rather, "in its food," or "fruit"; *i.e.*, when fruit-bearing: meaning Jeremiah whilst prophesying.

23 no remnant. None should be left in Anathoth. We find from Ezra ii. 23 that 128 returned from exile.

CHAPTER XII

1 Righteous art Thou. Whatever difficulty we may find in understanding parts of God's ways, we should always hold fast the conviction that He is righteous. On the subject of the prosperity of the wicked, cp. Psa. xxxvii.

4 The beasts are consumed, etc. The animate and inanimate creation suffer through the prevalence of wickedness.

He shall not see our last end. That is, the prophet's threats will not be fulfilled.

5 the swelling of Jordan. Rather, "the pride of Jordan"; or "the jungle of Jordan" (*Moffatt*), as in Zech. xi. 3; a poetic expression for the dense and luxuriant thickets on its banks, affording shelter to lions and other wild beasts; see xlix. 19; l. 44. The meaning is, "If thou art afraid of ordinary dangers or perplexed by a difficulty like that (v. 1), how wilt thou endure greater?" It refers to the severer sufferings which Jeremiah would have to bear.

10 pastors. "Shepherds": see note on **ii. 8.** Nomad shepherds are meant.

12 high places. Rather, as R.V., "bare heights."

14 mine evil neighbours. The Ammonites, Moabites, etc., "the birds and beasts of prey" (9), which had joined in spoiling God's heritage: see 2 Kings xxiv. 1–4; Psa. cxxxvii. 7.

16 they. That is, the neighbouring nations, who had so often enticed Israel to idolatry. There is a future even for these heathen people, if they will acknowledge the true God. The fulfilment of this is in the Church of Christ; cp. Ezek. xvi. 53–63.

CHAPTER XIII

1 a linen girdle. The girdles now most common in the East consist of long pieces of linen, cotton, or silk, wound in numerous folds round the waist.

6 after many days. During which the girdle is represented as rotting.

10 good for nothing. The girdle was thus an emblem, first, of the close relation between God and the Jewish people, and then of their utter depravation and consequent degradation and ruin. "Surrendered to the Babylonish captivity because of their impurity" (*Orelli*).

12 Every bottle. In this case the words mean "every jar." The jars knocked against each other, so as to be burst and shattered, and therefore destroyed. As the Jews mocked at the symbolic instruction ("Do we not certainly know," etc.?), the prophet explains it in a fearful threatening.

13 with drunkenness. That is, with God's wrath (see Psa. lxxv. 8).

16 before your feet stumble upon the dark mountains. That is, "before you are involved in ruin."

18 your principalities. This should read, "your head-dresses." "The queen" is probably the queen-mother (so R.V.), whose influence is always powerful in Oriental courts: see 1 Kings xv. 13, and note. The king at this time was probably Jehoiachin, who was still very young: see 2 Kings xxiv. 8; 2 Chron. xxxvi. 5.

19 The cities of the south, etc. "An army entering from the north would march along the Shefêlah, or fertile plain near the sea-coast, and would capture the outlying cities, before it attacked Jerusalem . . . Cp. the actual march of Sennacherib, 2 Kings xviii. 13" (*Payne-Smith*).

20 given thee. The address is to Zion, under a feminine personation. The "flock" denotes the towns, among which there was the metropolis, or "mother-city."

21 when He shall punish thee? For thou hast taught them, etc. Rather, "when He shall set thy friends over thee as head, seeing thou thyself hast instructed them against thee"? (R.V.). These "friends" are the heathen allies of Judah, now become her masters.

22 made bare. Or, "violently stripped," as those of a captive.

23 Can the Ethiopian, etc.? It is interesting to note that both the French and the German versions translate the Hebrew word as "the Moor." This means, that the depravity of the people was so inveterate that there was no hope of reformation, and therefore there must be punishment.

25 the portion of thy measures. That is, "the portion to be measured out to thee." Thy punishment shall be proportioned to thy sin.

26 Therefore will I, etc. Lit., "And I also will,"

etc. As thou hast dishonoured Me, so will I dishonour thee.

27 Wilt thou not be made clean? etc. Lit., "Thou wilt not be made clean—after yet how long!" Cp. R.V.

CHAPTER XIV

1 the dearth. Or, "the drought," as R.V.

2 the gates thereof. That is, the gates of its cities: meaning those who assemble there: see Job xxix. 7.

They are black unto the ground. *i.e.*, "They sit in black (the garb of mourning) upon the ground," as R.V.

3 their little ones. Rather, "their servants."

covered their heads. Like mourners: see Esther vi. 12.

4 the ground is chapt. Rather, "the husbandmen are dismayed."

plowmen. They could not till the hard earth, nor hope for a harvest if they did so.

6 no grass. No herbage (R.V.) generally: a different word from "grass," in ver. 5.

7 Do Thou [it]. Rather, and more expressively, "Act Thou."

8 as a stranger in the land. Who feels no particular interest in it.

10 Therefore the Lord doth not accept them. Words of an earlier prophet (Hos. viii. 13).

12 oblation. Meal offering: *minchah*, as in the Levitical ordinances.

16 their wickedness. That is, the *consequences* of their wickedness.

18 go about into a land that they know not. This may be rendered, "go trafficking into the land, and regard not," *i.e.*, they carry on their deception regardless of God's judgements: cp. R.V., and marg.

22 that can cause rain. A question suggested by the drought.

CHAPTER XV

1 Moses and Samuel. Whose intercessions formerly prevailed (Exod. xxxii. 11, 12; 1 Sam. vii. 9).

3 four kinds. That is, four kinds of destroyers.

4 I will cause them to be removed, etc. Rather, "I will cause them to be a terror among all the kingdoms of the earth."

7 I will fan them with a fan, etc. That is, scatter them like chaff as they are driven out. The R.V. more correctly reads the words in the past, "I have fanned . . . I have bereaved . . . I have destroyed."

8 I have brought upon them, etc. Of the various meanings given to this verse, perhaps the best is this: "I have brought upon them, even upon the mother of the choice youth, destruction at noon (*i.e.*, unexpectedly); I have caused anguish and terror to fall upon her suddenly. She that hath borne seven droopeth with grief; her sun is gone down," etc.

10 every one of them doth curse me. The unwelcome truths which the prophet delivered, caused his countrymen to dislike him as much as they would hate the hard-hearted usurer, or the importunate borrower.

12 Shall iron break the northern iron and the steel? Rather, "Can one break iron, even iron from the north, and brass"? (bronze) (R.V.). "Northern iron" was probably a sort of steel, prepared by the Chalybes, who lived near the Euxine Sea. This probably means the Chaldean power, which was to bring "evil" and "affliction" (11).

15 Thou knowest, etc. Again the prophet's words.

Take me not away in Thy long-suffering. That is, in Thy long-suffering towards my persecutors, do not leave my life in jeopardy.

16 I did eat them. The Hebrew idiom implies that, *as soon as* the words of God came to the prophet, he eagerly received them.

17 of the mockers. Rather, "of the mirthful": cp. R.V. He denied himself even innocent enjoyment.

because of Thy hand. See note on Isa. viii. 11.

18 as a liar. Lit., "a lie." The sense is as in R.V., "a deceitful [brook]" (Job vi. 15), a dried-up watercourse, bitterly disappointing the thirsty and expectant traveller. So the prophet keenly laments the apparent failure of his mission.

19 If thou return. *i.e.*, to the fearless discharge of duty. God replies to the prophet, that if he will return to his work, he shall again be entrusted with a message; and if he will boldly defend the right and condemn the wrong, his words shall be found to be of Divine authority.

Let them return unto thee. Rather, as R.V., "They shall return unto thee"; *i.e.*, as suppliants, to seek thy favour and good offices. Those who in standing up for the truth will not give way to the world, will often have the world come round to them.

20 a fenced brasen wall. See note on i. 18. The promise repeats the very words in which Jeremiah was first summoned to his work.

CHAPTER XVI

6 nor cut themselves. This was one of the heathen customs adopted by the Jews, in opposition to the law in Lev. xix. 28.

7 Neither shall men tear, etc. Rather, Neither shall men "*break* [*bread*] for them" (R.V., so also the Septuagint, the Vulgate, and the French and German versions), alluding to the funeral feast which was usually provided for mourners cp. Deut. xxvi. 14; Ezek. xxiv. 16, 17; Hos ix. 4. So "the cup of consolation."

9 In (before) your eyes, and in your days. As if to correct the feeling, "These judgements will not come at any rate in *our* time."

13 there shall ye serve other gods day and night. The meaning appears to be ironical, "Ye shall have your fill of your idol-worship."

14 the days come, etc. A promise of signal deliverance inserted in the midst of threatenings.

15 that brought up the children of Israel from the land of the north. The restoration of the Jews from Babylon, though not accompanied by miracles, as the deliverance from Egypt had been, was likely to make a greater impression upon the world; partly as being a manifest fulfilment of prophecy, and partly because of the extensive dispersion of the people.

16 I will send for many fishers, etc. There shall be no hiding-place by sea or land for these sinners, where God will not find them.

18 first. Before the deliverance promised in ver. 14.

because they have defiled My land, etc. Or, "For they have polluted My land with the carcases of their abominations (*i.e.*, their lifeless idols), and they have filled My inheritance with their detestable things": cp. R.V.

CHAPTER XVII

1 a pen of iron. A small chisel, used for engraving inscriptions upon rocks (Job xix. 24).

graven upon the table of their heart. Deep in their moral nature, and showing itself in their multiplied idolatries.

your altars. The remaining altars of the Baalim.

2 their children remember. *i.e.*, the children *retain* and *practise* the sins which they have learned from their fathers.

their groves. See note on Judg. iii. 7.

3 O My mountain in the field. Or, "O My mountain, with the *open country*"; meaning Jerusalem, with the whole land of Judah. "For sin" means because of sin.

6 the heath in the desert. Meaning, probably, "a bare (or dry) tree"; as the Hebrew word signifies "naked," or "destitute."

8 shall not see. Rather, according to another reading, "shall not fear."

11 As the partridge, etc. Perhaps, as R.V., "As the partridge that gathereth [young] which she hath not brought forth." It was anciently supposed that the partridge took the eggs of other birds, and hatched them, but was afterwards abandoned by the young birds; and thus had nothing to compensate her for her trouble. So he that procures riches by unfair means shall find that he has laboured in vain.

12 A glorious high throne, etc. The throne of Jehovah "[set] on high from the beginning," R.V.; called "the place of our sanctuary," to show that He is always at hand to help those who seek His protection.

13 written in the earth. "Written in the dust"; *i.e.*, consigned to oblivion. Contrast Job xix. 23, 24.

16 to follow Thee. Rather, "after Thee" (R.V.). I have not shrunk from obeying Thy call to be a teacher of this people; nor, on the other hand, have I desired the calamities which I predicted. I have spoken under Thy influence, and as in Thy presence.

VERS. 19–27. This prophetic message consists of a command to observe the Sabbath, having reference to profanations of it which were probably particularly prevalent at the time (19–23). Great national blessings are promised in case of obedience (24–26); and the destruction of Jerusalem is threatened if the desecration is continued (27).

19 the gate of the children of the people. It is not known what gate is here intended. Orelli translates "gate of the (thy) countrymen," and explains that Jeremiah's countrymen are the Benjamites.

26 the plain. "The lowland" (R.V.), called the *Shephelah*. This was west of Jerusalem. "The Mountains" were the hill country of Judah; the South, or *Negeb*, the arid region south of Hebron.

CHAPTER XVIII

3 on the wheels. Lit., "on the two stones." Some suppose moulds to be meant; but the reference is probably to the turning instrument, which consisted of two wheels, like those of a hand-mill, on the upper and smaller of which the vessel to be formed was placed Similar wheels were used in Egypt · see Wilkinson's *Ancient Egypt*, iii. 165.

8 I will repent. See notes on Gen. vi. 6; 2 Sam. xxiv. 16. Moffatt has, "I will change My mind."

11 I frame evil. "I am shaping." The word for *frame* is the same as that used for the potter's art; so keeping up the figure. The Septuagint has ἐγω πλάσσω ἐφ' ὑμᾶς κακά ("I am moulding evils against you").

12 And they said. Rather, as R.V., "But they say."

There is no hope. See ii. 25. "We have gone too far to mend."

13 The virgin of Israel. An appellation of the people collectively: see xiv. 17.

14 Will [a man] leave the snow of Lebanon, etc. ? The word for "a man" is not in the Hebrew, and R.V. renders the verse, "Shall the snow of Lebanon fail from the rock of the field ? [or] shall the cold waters that flow down from afar be dried up ?" The emblem is that of *perennial* flow, the "rock of the field" describing the lower cliffs facing the open country, down which fall the cascades fed by the melting snows. The Jews had forsaken the cool and "living waters" for channels of their own digging: cp. ii. 13.

15 a way not cast up. A road not properly constructed.

16 desolate. Rather, as R.V., "an astonishment."

18 nor the word from the prophet. *i.e.*, Jeremiah is not the only true priest or prophet, nor are all the others ignorant or deceitful, as he declares them to be.

let us smite him with the tongue. Let us accuse him to the rulers.

CHAPTER XIX

1 the ancients. *i.e.*, "the elders" (R.V.).

2 the east gate. More probably, "the pottery-gate": "the gate Harsith," R.V., not mentioned by that name elsewhere. Nehemiah (iii. 14, 15) mentions two gates leading from the city to the Valley of Hinnom. This may have been one of them, or a postern used for casting out refuse.

4 have estranged this place. *i.e.*, have alienated it to the worship of idols.

7 I will make void. Emphatic in Heb., "I will empty out."

8 desolate. Rather, "an astonishment," as xviii. 16.

9 to eat the flesh. A repetition of the threatening in Deut. xxviii. 53, which was fulfilled speedily (see Lam. iv. 10), and repeatedly, as appears from Josephus's account of the siege of Jerusalem by Titus. See *Wars*, vi. 3, § 8.

13 upon whose roofs, etc. See 2 Kings xxiii. 12.

CHAPTER XX

1 Pashur. Another person of the same name is mentioned, xxi. 1. "Chief governor," should rather be "chief officer," as R.V.

2 smote. Inflicted stripes.

and put him in the stocks. The strokes and the torture which Pashur inflicted show his extreme malignity against Jeremiah. The "stocks" were an instrument of torture, in which the neck, hands and feet of the prisoner were so fastened as to hold the body in a painfully distorted position. Cp. Acts xvi. 24.

the high gate of Benjamin. The gate of the Temple corresponding to the Gate of Benjamin in the north wall of the city.

3 Pashur. "Pashur" is supposed to mean *prosperity* (or safety) *around*. "Magor-missabib" means *terror on every side*. The latter word occurs ver. 10, and vi. 25; xlvi. 5; xlix. 29 (Psa. xxxi. 13).

5 the labours thereof. That is, all the possessions gained by labour.

6 thou, Pashur, etc. Another priest appears in Pashur's place (xxix. 25). It appears that in the days of the Captivity the descendants of Pashur became numerous (Ezra ii. 38).

7 deceived. Rather, "allured," as in Hos. ii. 14: or, "persuaded," as in Prov. xxv. 15: see R.V. marg. The following words should also be in the past tense: "Thou *wast* stronger than I, and *didst* prevail." Thy representations and urgent commands overcame my reluctance to undertake this office: see i. 4–10.

8 daily. Rather, "all the day," as R.V.

9 [His word] was in mine heart, etc. Rather, There was in mine heart as it were a burning fire, etc. (see R.V.).

I could not [stay]. I was tempted to renounce an office so unthankful and perilous; but then an inward impulse would not let me rest, and I was constrained to persevere.

10 Report [say they], and we will report it. Or, "Denounce, and we will denounce him." Only you begin, and we will support the charge. This was the language of the prophet's "familiar friends" to one another (see R.V.).

11 for they shall not prosper, etc. Rather, as R.V., "because they have not dealt wisely."

14 Cursed be the day, etc. Vers. 14–18 have been thought to be out of place immediately after an ascription of praise to God, and to come in better after ver. 7. But in violent emotion the transitions of feeling are often great and sudden, particularly when personal interest appears to be in conflict with the urgent claims of duty. It should be remembered that the feelings here expressed are not justified (cp. Job iii., and note on ver. 1): but this record of them shows the prophet's lively sensibility, whilst denouncing the most awful punishments.

CHAPTER XXI

2 Nebuchadrezzar. This is frequently written "Nebuchadnezzar." In some words the Hebrew dialect prefers *n*, and the Aramaic *r*. The latter is in this case the nearer to the original form of the name, which has been found on some Babylonian cylinders. It is the spelling adopted by Sayce (*Primer of Assyriology*, 1925).

5 I myself will fight against you. *i.e.*, with pestilence.

9 his life shall be unto him for a prey. This expression means, to escape with life, as a person does with plunder or spoil which he carries off with great risk and difficulty.

13 the valley [and] rock of the plain. A description of Jerusalem, which was situated partly in a valley and partly on rocky hills; so that the people thought it almost impregnable.

CHAPTER XXII

6 Thou art Gilead. This may mean, Though for beauty thou (O royal palace) art like Gilead, and for majestic height like Lebanon, yet I will have thee desolated by invaders; as Gilead and Lebanon have been: see 2 Kings x. 32, etc.

10 Weep ye not for the dead. Referring to Josiah, the good and patriotic king of Judah, who died deeply lamented (see 2 Chron. xxxv. 24, 25), being spared the pain of seeing and sharing the disgrace and suffering of his country: see 2 Kings xxii. 20.

him that goeth away. Shallum (see ver. 11); who, though a younger son of Josiah, was raised by the people to the throne under the name of Jehoahaz, but was soon carried captive into Egypt, never to return: see 2 Kings xxiii. 31–35.

11 king of Judah. Referring to Shallum.

13 Woe unto him. That is, Jehoiakim, the reigning prince; who is first described (13, 14), then addressed (15–17), and finally named (18).

14 vermilion. The ancient vermilion was a bisulphuret of mercury.

15 Did not thy father eat and drink? Your father Josiah enjoyed what he needed, without all this pomp; and distinguished himself, not by his splendour, but by the justice of his government.

18 They shall not lament for him. You shall not be lamented like your father; your corpse shall not be cared for more than that of an ass who dies on the road: cp. xxxvi. 30. Of the circumstances of Jehoiakim's death we have no record. Nebuchadrezzar appears to have designed to carry him to Babylon, but he probably died on the way: see 2 Chron. xxxvi. 6. "The prophet quotes the *verba ipsissima* of the usual wail for the dead. Hence the apparently unsuitable *Alas! sister!*" (*Lange*).

20 Go up to Lebanon. This is addressed to Jerusalem, bidding her to watch from mountain heights, and to bewail the progress of the conquering Babylonians.

from the passages. Rather, "from Abarim" (R.V.): see note on Numb. xxvii. 12.

22 shall eat up. Or, "consume," as a parching wind withers the grass. There is here a play upon words, "shall make pasture of thy pastors."

23 O inhabitant of Lebanon. Referring to ver. 14. Thou tenant of the cedar palace!

How gracious, etc.! Rather, "How wilt thou groan!"

28 a despised broken idol. Rather, "a despised broken vessel." This is the inquiry of those who witness his degradation.

29 O earth, earth, earth! Or, "O land!" The repetition is emphatic, as in vii. 4; Ezek. xxi. 27.

30 Write ye this man childless. Not as a man, for he had children (see 1 Chron. iii. 17); but as a king, for none of his children became king, "sitting upon the throne of David." Jehoiakim and his brother Zedekiah were the latest of David's descendants who reigned in Judah. The promise of the temporal kingdom is here abrogated. Thus the royal line (Matt. i.) was not a line of actual kings from Salathiel onwards.

a man that shall not prosper. He spent thirty-seven years in imprisonment; and though he was then liberated and treated kindly by Evil-Merodach, he was retained to attend the court of his superior monarch (2 Kings xxv. 27–30).

CHAPTER XXIII

1 the pastors. "The shepherds," R.V. The kings just mentioned, and their subordinate officers. With these are contrasted more righteous rulers (4), and especially the King Messiah (5), the "Good Shepherd" (John x. 11, 14).

3 I have driven. Cp. ver. 2, "ye have driven." The same calamity may be regarded as due to human unfaithfulness or to Divine displeasure.

4 Neither shall they be lacking. "Neither shall any be lacking," R.V.

5 a righteous Branch. This name of the Messiah is evidently derived from Isa. iv. 2, on which see note. To comfort God's people under the tyranny of their kings, the debasement of their country, their sufferings from the Babylonians, and the division and dispersion of their tribes, the prophet dwells upon the justice, prosperity, unity, which shall be enjoyed under Messiah's reign.

and a King shall reign and prosper. "And He shall reign as king, and deal wisely," R.V.

6 The Lord our Righteousness. Or, "The Eternal [is] our Righteousness": see R.V. The same title is applied to Jerusalem (xxxiii. 16), and is used here (as in Isa. lxii. 1, etc.) as one leading characteristic of the Divine salvation.

8 the north country. See note on xvi. 15.

9 because of the prophets. Rather, according to the Hebrew, "Concerning the Prophets" (a title to the section: see R.V.). "My heart within me is broken—all my bones shake," etc. Jeremiah is deeply grieved at the profanity and deceit of the false prophets in Judah, who rival those of Samaria in their sins, and shall share their punishment (9–40).

like a drunken man. That is, overpowered by my emotions.

10 because of swearing. Or, "because of the curse."

13 And I have seen folly, etc. Rather, "As I saw folly in the prophets of Samaria, etc.; so I have seen a horrible thing in the prophets of Jerusalem."

in Baal. Better, as R.V., "by Baal."

18 For who hath stood, etc.? That is, Who among these false prophets has been admitted to His confidence, and heard Him declare His purposes? They are mere impostors.

Who hath marked His word? Moffatt has "or grasped a word of his?" The French version is: "qui a aperçu ou entendu sa parole?" ("Who has noticed or understood his word?").

20 In the latter days. The time "of your visitation" (12). Experience will convince you of the truth of my predictions, and the falsehood of your own.

27 have forgotten. Better, "forgot."

28 The prophet that hath a dream, etc. This seems to mean, Let the false prophet tell his mere dreams, and let the true prophet faithfully declare God's word; and it will soon be seen which is straw and which is wheat; for God's word has a mighty power (29).

the chaff. Rather, "the straw," as R.V.

30 I am against the prophets, etc. Three species of deception practised by false prophets are here specified: 1. They sometimes borrowed Divine oracles from the true prophets (30); 2. They delivered mere human utterances to the people as of Divine authority (31); 3. They invented dreams, to give currency to their delusions (32).

33 What is the burden of the Lord? This appears to be a scoffing play upon the Hebrew word (which means both "a burden" and "a prophecy"), taunting Jeremiah with announcing only grievous calamities. God will put an end to this profanity, making every such scoffing "word" a "burden" of woe to him who utters it (36). The chief ancient versions, instead of "What burden?" read, "Ye are the burden."

39 I will utterly forget you, etc. This should read, "I will take you up like a burden and I will cast you off, and the city that I gave unto you and to your fathers, away from My presence."

CHAPTER XXIV

Two baskets of figs of opposite qualities are employed to represent the different fates of those who have submitted to Nebuchadrezzar, and have been taken by him to Babylon, where they shall be blessed (1–7), and of those who, remaining in their own land or going to Egypt, meditate resistance to him (8–10). Cp. xxxvii.; 2 Kings xxiv. 12, 20.

1 before the temple of the Lord. Probably as first-fruits for offerings: see Exod. xxiii. 19; Deut. xxvi. 2.

carpenters ("craftsmen," R.V.) **and smiths.** The artisans were taken away partly for the service of the Chaldean monarch, and partly to deprive the Jews of the means of rebellion: see 1 Sam. xiii. 19, and note.

2 first ripe. The early figs were considered the best. There are three sorts of figs; the first, which is the fig here mentioned, comes to maturity about the middle or latter end of June: this is deemed a great delicacy (see Isa. xxviii. 4). The summer or dry fig is ripe about August; and the winter fig not till November.

naughty. *i.e.*, "bad."

8 them that dwell in the land of Egypt. Either taken captive by Necho, or fugitives from the Chaldeans.

CHAPTER XXV

The captivity awaiting the Jewish nation in Babylon is explicitly foretold, and its duration assigned (1–11). This chastisement of the Jews shall be followed by severer punishments of the Chaldeans (Babylonians), and other heathen nations (12–14). As a symbol of this, the prophet speaks of the cup of wrath (15–29), and the ravening lion (38).

1 in the fourth year of Jehoiakim. This was the year in which Nebuchadrezzar, having defeated the Egyptians at Carchemish, came to Jerusalem, and imposed a tribute on king Jehoiakim. These events occurred about the end of the third and beginning of the fourth year of that king, 605–4 B.C. On Carchemish, see Sayce: *The Hittites* (1925).

3 the three and twentieth year. *i.e.*, of Jeremiah's ministry.

4 rising early. See note on vii. 13.

9 My servant. See note on Isa. xlv. 1. The construction is: and [I will send unto] Nebuchadrezzar, etc.: see R.V.

10 the sound of the millstones, etc. As the corn for the family was ground every day, and every house had its night-lamp, the absence of this sound and of this light betokened utter desolation: see Deut. xxiv. 6; Job xviii. 6.

11 seventy years. Considerable diversity of opinion exists as to the right manner of reckoning these seventy years: but it is most probable that they began when Nebuchadrezzar defeated the Egyptians at Carchemish and made Jehoiakim tributary, 606–5 B.C., and ended in the first year of Cyrus, 536 B.C., when Babylon ceased to be the capital of a kingdom: see notes on 2 Kings xxiv. 1; xxv. 11. But it is not wise to press figures too literally. "Seventy" is a round number.

14 shall serve themselves of them. *i.e.*, "shall exact service of them." The "nations" and "kings" are those which were confederate with Cyrus.

15 the wine cup. See Psa. lxxv. 8; Isa. li. 17–23. The taking of the cup is evidently a metaphor representing the utterance of a threat of punishment.

19 Pharaoh king of Egypt, etc. The various nations here mentioned (18–26) are grouped around the Holy Land, which is the starting-point, according to the closeness of their connexion with the Jews. The "Pharaoh" of the time was Necho, defeated at Carchemish: see on ver. 11.

20 the mingled people. Foreigners resident in Egypt, chiefly Ionians, Carians and Phœnicians, mercenaries in the Egyptian armies (*Lange*).

Azzah. The same as Gaza (see R.V.).

the remnant of Ashdod. Ashdod had been much reduced during the twenty-nine years' siege by Psammetichus. "This is one of the pregnant sentences which none but a contemporary writer could have used" (*Dean Payne-Smith*).

22 the isles. "The isle" or "coastland"; referring to the Mediterranean coasts and islands.

23 [that are] in the utmost corners. "That have the corners [of their hair] shorn." See note on ix. 26.

24 the mingled people. Various tribes of different races inhabiting the Arabian deserts: see note on Gen. xxxvii. 25.

25 Zimri. Nowhere else mentioned; probably an Arabian tribe.

26 Sheshach. "Sheshach" means Babylon, as appears from li. 41; and it has been found on Assyrian sculptures as the name of a Babylonian idol. The word is made by a system of secret writing, which substitutes the last letter of the Hebrew alphabet for the first, the last but one for the second, and so on (as if in English, Z answered to A, Y to B, X to C, etc.). According to this, the three letters for Babylon, B. B. L., correspond to Sh. Sh. Ch.: see note on li. 41.

34 like a pleasant vessel. Like a beautiful vase (*French version*: "comme un vase de prix," "as a costly vase") irreparably shattered by a fall.

37 peaceable habitations. "Peaceable folds," R.V., or "peaceful meadows" (*Moffatt*).

cut down. Or, "brought to silence," R.V.

38 the fierceness of the oppressor. Or, "the fierceness of the destroying [sword]": see R.V.

CHAPTER XXVI

2 all the cities of Judah. By their representatives, probably on some feast-day.

6 like Shiloh. See note on vii. 12. It is a probable supposition that the present narrative is to be connected with that chapter; these six verses being a summary of what is there given in greater detail, repeated as introductory to the narrative that follows.

10 came up. The princes, hearing of the tumult, came to the Temple, to bring the matter to a regular trial.

the new gate. Perhaps the gate built (or repaired) by Jotham: see 2 Kings xv. 35.

16 not worthy to die. There is a striking resemblance between this trial and that of our Lord before Pilate, as to the nature of the charge, the malignity of the priests, and the declaration of His innocence by the civil magistrate.

17 the elders of the land. Sustaining by argument the decision of the "princes and all the people." The princes (or rulers) were the heads of the chief families, the elders were the representatives of the people at large.

18 the Morasthite. See Micah iii. 12, and notes.

20 there was also a man that prophesied, etc. This appears to be mentioned by Jeremiah himself to show that he was in imminent danger of falling a victim to the anger of his enemies. From this, however, he was saved by the kindness of an influential man (24) whose father had probably been the royal secretary (2 Kings xxii. 12–14), and who was himself the father of the noble and faithful Gedaliah (xl. 7).

Urijah. Nothing more is known of this prophet. The incident suggests the many unrecorded servants of Jehovah, who witnessed and suffered for Him.

CHAPTERS XXVII, XXVIII

These chapters refer to the fourth year of Zedekiah, when the Jews and the neighbouring nations appear to have conspired to throw off the Babylonian yoke. Jeremiah is therefore commanded to make yokes and bonds, the symbols of vassalage, and send them to these nations, with a command to submit to Nebuchadnezzar (1–11). He also addresses Zedekiah and the Jewish people to the same purport (12–15); and bids those who oppose his predictions to pray for the preservation of the sacred vessels remaining in the Temple, and to see whether they will prevail (16–22). One of these false prophets contradicts his message (xxviii. 1–4); upon which Jeremiah refers him to ancient prophecies of calamity already in part fulfilled (5–9); but as Hananiah persists in his falsehood, and breaks the yoke which the prophet wears, Jeremiah repeats the prediction, and adds a personal threatening against Hananiah, which is speedily fulfilled (10–17).

CHAPTER XXVII

1 Jehoiakim. This reading, though very ancient, is clearly an error in copying, and the name should be "Zedekiah," as in the Syriac version, and vers. 3, 12; xxviii. 1. (The Septuagint omits the verse.) See R.V., marg.

6 the beasts of the field, etc. See note on xxviii. 14.

7 his son, and his son's son. Evil-Merodach and Nabonidus (with whom Belshazzar was associated).

many nations and great kings. See note on xxv. 14.

9 diviners. Some of the various kinds of divination are noticed in Isa. xliv. 25; xlvii. 13; Ezek. xxi. 21; Hos. iv. 12.

16 the vessels of the Lord's house shall now shortly be brought again from Babylon. Whither they had been carried in the two preceding reigns: see 2 Chron. xxxvi. 7, 10. Jeremiah, in opposition to the statement of the false prophets says that not only should they remain there for a while, but the rest would follow (21, 22).

20 which Nebuchadrezzar king of Babylon took not. See note on 2 Kings xxiv. 13.

CHAPTER XXVIII

1 in the beginning. That is, in the early part of Zedekiah's reign; for it was the fourth year.

of Gibeon. A priestly city (Josh. xxi. 17). Hananiah was therefore probably a brother-priest to Jeremiah, as well as a rival prophet.

4 I will bring again to this place Jeconiah. The plot was evidently to depose Zedekiah and to restore the banished king, probably by the aid of Egypt.

10 the yoke. Which Jeremiah was wearing by Divine command: see xxvii. 2. The action of Hananiah was intended to impress the people.

11 And the prophet Jeremiah went his way. Further argument would be useless. The prophet calmly awaits the issue of events.

13 for them. That is, instead of them.

14 I have given him the beasts of the field. "The words simply emphasise the absolute sovereignty of the Babylonian king" (Professor H. Wheeler Robinson in *Peake's Commentary*).

17 in the seventh month. In the second month after his doom had been denounced: cp. ver. 1.

CHAPTER XXIX

I the residue. etc. Some had probably succumbed to the hardships of the journey; others may have died in Babylon.

2 the queen. The queen-mother (2 Kings xxiv. 15): cp. chap. xxiii. 18.

3 by the hand of Elasah, etc. These were ambassadors, sent by the king of Judah to do homage to Nebuchadrezzar. That they also carried Jeremiah's letter seems to show that this letter had official sanction. Elasah, son of Shaphan, was brother to one of the prophet's most influential friends (xxvi. 24), and Gemariah was probably the son of Hilkiah the high priest of Josiah's day.

5 Build ye houses, etc. Expecting soon to return to their own country, the captives seem to have neglected their personal and social duties and interests in Babylonia.

7 seek the peace of the city. Though you are unwilling exiles in a foreign land, discharge the duties of good subjects and citizens. "The city"; not necessarily Babylon, but any city where their lot might be cast. Every Christian ought to be a good citizen.

8 neither hearken to your dreams. Namely, by making inquiries of these prophets as to the meaning of your dreams. The people might be said to "cause" their own dreams, by the excited and restless state of mind from which they sprang, and giving credit to their responses.

10 after seventy years. Not from the date of the letter, but from the time previously assigned (xxv. 11).

11 an expected end. Lit., "a hereafter and an expectation." The Vulgate has "ut dem vobis finem et patientiam" ("that I may give you an object and patience" to reach it). R.V., "hope in your latter end." These promises extend far beyond the return of the Jews from Babylon.

18 to be removed to all the kingdoms, etc. Rather, as R.V., "to be tossed to and fro among all the kingdoms," etc. The French version has "et je les abandonnerai pour être errants par tous les royaumes de la terre" ("and I shall abandon them to be wanderers among all the kingdoms of the earth").

21 Ahab . . . Zedekiah. Nothing more is known of the false prophets here named.

22 roasted in the fire. That the Babylonians were accustomed to inflict this cruel punishment is evident from Dan. iii. 6, 20.

24 to Shemaiah the Nehelamite. Rather, as R.V., "Concerning Shemaiah," etc.

25 in thy name. "In thine own name," R.V.

26 in the stead of Jehoiada. This Jehoiada was probably one who had held office between Pashur (see xx. 6) and Zephaniah.

for every man that is mad, etc. That is, such persons as madly take on themselves to be prophets.

in prison, and in the stocks. Rather, as R.V., "in the stocks and in shackles," or, "the collar."

31 he caused you to trust in a lie. Shemaiah had evidently succeeded in persuading many of the exiles to anticipate a speedy deliverance, against Jeremiah's distinct assurances.

CHAPTER XXX

5 a voice of trembling, etc. This seems to refer to the Medo-Persian invasion of Babylon; which, though necessary to the restoration of the Jews, threatened them, as well as other subjects of the king of Babylon, with severe sufferings.

8 I will break his yoke. The yoke of the king of Babylon.

9 David their king. As the Jews have never since their return from Babylon had a king named David, nor indeed any king, this must refer to the Messiah. The Targum has "the son of David their king."

13 That thou mayest be bound up. Moffatt translates: "there is none to bandage you, no salve for your bruise."

14 thy lovers. The allies whom Israel had made.

16 Therefore, etc. This is really the continuation of vers. 10 and 11, where the restoration of Israel is promised. The parenthesis vers. 12–15 indicates what their sufferings have been. Now their punishment is complete, and "they that devour thee shall be devoured."

18 and the city shall be builded, etc. "Towns shall be built on their own sites, and buildings stand where once they stood" (*Moffatt*).

20 as aforetime. As they were in the prosperous days of David: see note on ver. 9.

21 And their nobles, etc. Rather. "And their Prince shall be from themselves, and their Ruler shall come forth from the midst of them" (R.V.). This also evidently must refer to the Messiah, as the restored Jews were no more governed by a ruler of their own nation in Palestine than in Babylon, where they appear to have had a "Prince of the captivity."

23 Behold, the whirlwind, etc. See xxiii. 19. The judgement there denounced against sinners in Israel is here threatened to Israel's enemy.

a continuing whirlwind. R.V., "a sweeping tempest."

24 ye shall consider. Or, "ye shall understand," R.V.

CHAPTER XXXI

2 the wilderness. The "wilderness" may perhaps mean the land of exile; for this would be as a wilderness to those who pined for their own land, which they are here assured they shall revisit.

3 The Lord hath appeared, etc. Israel's response to Jehovah's words.

of old. Or, "from afar" (R.V., marg.), as in xxx. 10.

5 shall eat [them] as common things. Or, "shall enjoy the fruit." This implies *abiding* security, as four years had to elapse between the planting and the eating (Lev. xix. 23–25).

6 the watchmen. Men stationed upon the mountains to proclaim the festival: see Isa. lii. 7, 8. The proclamation of the feasts in Zion by watchmen on Mount Ephraim indicates the re-union of the nation: cp. Isa. xi. 13.

O Lord, save, etc. "Hosannah" (Psa. cxviii. 25; Matt. xxi. 9). The next verse contains Jehovah's answer to this invocation.

8 the blind and the lame, etc. None shall be left behind, not even those who appear to be most unfit to undertake the journey. For "the north country," see on iii. 12. "The coasts" mean "the ends of the earth."

9 Ephraim is My firstborn. Not by birth, but by choice: see Gen. xlviii. 14–20. So complete should be the re-union that the birthright should be recognised.

14 I will satiate the soul of the priests. This refers to the priests' share in the abundance of offerings.

15 A voice was heard in Ramah, etc. By a beautiful figure, Rachel (Rahel) is introduced as mourning in her grave near Ramah (Gen. xxxv. 16; 1 Sam. ix. 6; x. 2) over the destruction of her descendants, the people of Ephraim and Benjamin; but she is comforted by the promise of their return (16, 17): cp. Isa. xlix. 20, 21. The language, being figurative, is susceptible of other applications, and is used in Matt. ii. 18 as a type of the grief caused by Herod's cruelty.

16 thy work shall be rewarded. The meaning is, Thou shalt not have brought forth and brought up children in vain.

17 in thine end. *i.e.*, in the future.

18 Turn Thou me, and I shall be turned. Real conversion requires Divine aid.

19 I smote upon my thigh. Among the Hebrews, Persians, Greeks, and other nations, smiting on the thigh was a common mode of expressing indignation and grief: see Ezek. xxi. 12.

the reproach of my youth. The reproach brought upon me by the sins of my youth.

21 high heaps. Or, "sign-posts"; *i.e.*, to mark the way for the exiles to return through the deserts.

22 A woman shall compass a man. Commentators are greatly divided as to the meaning of these words. Calvin's explanation, however, seems the best: "the feeblest of them shall be more than a match for the strongest of their foes."

24 And there shall dwell in Judah itself, etc. Rather, as R.V., "And Judah and all the cities thereof shall dwell therein together."

26 Upon this I awaked. This is probably inserted to keep the reader in mind that all these bright prospects were presented in a dream to the prophet, and would certainly be fulfilled.

29 The fathers have eaten a sour grape (R.V., "sour grapes"), etc. A proverbial expression (see Ezek. xviii. 2), the meaning of which appears from Lam. v. 7. The thought ("they shall say no more," etc.) is that in the new order of things there would be a quickened sense of personal responsibility. Consciousness of personal guilt is the first step toward recovery.

31 a new covenant. Vers. 31–34 are a clear announcement that the old Jewish economy would be superseded by one of a personal and spiritual character; and they are accordingly quoted for this purpose in Heb. viii. 8–12. In the connexion in which they stand here, they predict not only the Gospel covenant, but also the enjoyment of its blessings by the Hebrew race: cp. Rom. xi. 25–32.

32 although I was a husband unto them. Many follow the Septuagint in rendering these words, "for I *rejected* them": a translation adopted in Heb. viii. 9. The Vulgate, followed by Luther, has "I ruled over (or subdued) them" ("dominatus sum eorum").

33 and write it in their hearts. There will not be a mere slavish observance of ceremonies; but the knowledge, love, and zealous fulfilment of God's commands: cp. Ezek. xi. 19, etc.; John iv. 23.

35 the ordinances of the moon, etc. The laws which regulate these bodies.

36 a nation. God here promises not merely that the Hebrew people shall never be extinct, but also that they shall share the blessings of the Gospel: see note on ver. 31.

38 the tower of Hananeel. At the north-east angle of the city walls; as "the gate of the corner" was at the north-west. See Neh. iii. 1; Zech. xiv. 10.

39 Gareb . . . Goath. These places are not now known; but the general meaning of the passage is, that the new city shall be larger than the former, including places now waste or unclean. An expressive type of the spiritual Jerusalem: see Ezek. xl. 2; xlv. 6. This "valley of the dead bodies" is the valley of Hinnom; that "of the ashes," the place where the ashes from the altar were cast; "the fields" were the cultivated land between the city walls and the brook Kidron.

CHAPTER XXXII

2 was shut up. See the more extended detail in ch. xxxvii.

5 until I visit him. This phrase is used sometimes in a favourable sense (see xxvii. 22), sometimes the contrary (see v. 9).

7 my field. Though the Levites (including the priests) could not hold other land, they possessed the suburbs of their cities (see Numb. xxxv. 4); which, however, could not be alienated, as other town property might (Lev. xxv. 32–34). The nearest of kin had the right of purchase (Lev. xxv. 25). But this transaction was merely a transfer from one member of a family to another, as in Ruth iv.

8 Then I knew, etc. By the coincidence with the prediction, 6, 7.

9 and weighed him the money. The Jews do not appear to have had a national coinage before the exile; but they made use of pieces of silver of a certain weight (220 grs.), called shekels. The purchase-money of this property was equal to only $11.50. The field itself may have been small; and its value was diminished by its being then in the possession of the Chaldeans.

11 the evidence ("deed," R.V.) **of the purchase.** This is the first record of the use of written documents in the purchase of land; and it shows a near approach to the caution and completeness of similar modern transactions. The deed, being duly signed by the contracting parties and by witnesses, was sealed up, that it might be carefully preserved; while an "open" copy was made for occasional reference.

[according to] the law and custom. Or, as R.V. marg., "[containing] the terms and conditions."

12 Baruch. Baruch was the friend and helper of Jeremiah on various occasions in his public ministry (see xxxvi., xliii.), and honoured by a special promise of Divine protection (see xlv.).

14 these evidences. "These deeds," R.V., as before.

in an earthen vessel. A frequent mode of securing valuable things in the East. This sealed duplicate was made for reference, in case the open copy were lost or tampered with.

15 shall be possessed again. Rather, as R.V., "shall yet again be bought."

24 the mounts. These were works raised by the besiegers, partly to cover their engines, and partly to elevate the soldiers to a level with the battlements of the city.

31 from the day that they built it. Solomon, who completed the city of Jerusalem, introduced into it that idolatry which afterwards caused its ruin: see 1 Kings xi. 4.

35 Molech. See notes on 2 Kings xvi. 3; xxiii. 10.

40 that I will not turn away from them, to do them good. The words mean, "that I will not cease from showing them favour."

CHAPTER XXXIII

2 the Maker thereof. "Who made the earth" (*Moffatt*). The Eternal here pledges that unchanging faithfulness which His name implies (see note on Exod. vi. 3) for the fulfilment of His promises.

3 mighty. Rather, "inaccessible"; "des choses grandes et cachées" ("great and hidden things") (*French version*).

4 which are thrown down by the mounts, etc. Rather, as R.V., "which are broken down [to make a defence] against the mounts and against the sword."

5 They come to fight with the Chaldeans, etc. "The Chaldeans are come to fight and to fill them (*i.e.*, the houses) with the corpses of the men, whom I have slain," etc.

9 And it shall be to Me, etc. *i.e.*, the city, Jerusalem, shall be, etc.: see R.V.

11 Praise the Lord of hosts, etc. A formula of praise: see Psa. cxxxvi.

13 telleth. "Counteth." Cp. Milton, *L'Allegro*, "Every shepherd tells this tale."

16 The Lord our Righteousness. *i.e.*, descriptively, and supplying the substantive verb, "Jehovah [is] our Righteousness." The city is thus honoured with a title derived from her Divine King: see xxiii. 6.

24 this people. The people of Jerusalem in their despondency.

The two families, etc. Meaning, perhaps, the two kingdoms of Israel and Judah.

25 If My covenant [be] not with day and night. Rather, as R.V., "If My covenant with day and night [stand] not." The invariableness of natural phenomena should sustain our faith in the promises of God.

CHAPTER XXXIV

2 Behold, I will give this city, etc. See notes on 2 Kings xxv. 6, 7.

5 thou shalt die in peace. *i.e.*, by a natural death. Josephus says that Nebuchadrezzar honoured his remains with a magnificent funeral (*Antiq.* x. 8, § 7).

8 to proclaim liberty unto them. By the law (Exod. xxi. 2; Deut. xv. 12), the Israelites were required to let their Hebrew bondsmen go free after having served six years; but this law had fallen into disuse. To revive it now was a measure of policy, as the emancipated people would have the greater interest in defending their country.

9 should serve himself of them. Should employ them for forced labour.

11 turned, and caused to return. *i.e.*, into slavery.

17 a liberty for you, etc. By these words the people were taught to connect the subsequent horrors of the siege and sacking of Jerusalem with their disobedience to God's law regarding the poor.

18 when they cut the calf, etc. A mode of confirming a covenant (see Gen. xv. 10). The ceremony implied the consent of the parties covenanting, if they broke their engagement, to be themselves thus cut asunder, and made a sacrifice to Divine justice.

21 which are gone up from you. The Chaldean army had raised the siege of Jerusalem for a time, owing to the appearance of a force from Egypt.

CHAPTER XXXV

The Rechabites were a family of the Kenites (see 1 Chron. ii. 55), probably descended from the father-in-law of Moses (Judges i. 16). Jonadab (see ver. 6) chief of the tribe in the days of Jehu, was held in high esteem for wisdom and piety (2 Kings x. 15). The self-denying observance of his commands by his people, during a period of nearly 300 years, is used as a rebuke to the Israelites, who had repeatedly broken Jehovah's laws; and a curse is pronounced upon the Israelites, and a blessing on the Rechabites.

7 neither shall ye build house, etc. The character of Jonadab renders it probable that this was intended to preserve them from the luxury which was enervating and debasing the Hebrews.

the Syrians. These continued to harass the country of Judah, after Damascus had fallen before the power of Assyria: see 2 Kings xxiv. 2.

19 shall not want a man to stand before Me for ever. The perpetuity of the race, not distinct nationality, is here promised. The approbation which God here expresses shows with what favour He regards obedience to parental and other rightful authority, and how He rewards it in this world: see Exod. xx. 12, and note.

CHAPTER XXXVI

The fourth year of Jehoiakim, the date of the occurrences recorded in this chapter was also the first year of Nebuchadrezzar.

2 a roll of a book. Or, "a scroll"; such as books were made of. At one end of the parchment roll, or, if it were long, at each end, a stick was attached, around which it was rolled and unrolled in order to read the contents: see Luke iv. 17. The text was not written in lines across from one end to the other, but in compartments or columns (improperly translated "leaves" in ver. 23); so that only a portion need be unrolled at a time.

4 Baruch. See xxxii. 12, and note.

5 shut up. "Hindered." French version: "je suis retenu," "I am detained."

6 the fasting day. Rather, "on *a* fast day" (as R.V. marg.; see 9); a day which had been appointed for the purpose by the people, who were alarmed at the conquests of Nebuchadrezzar and the prospects of the country.

10 the new gate of the Lord's house. Where he was most likely to attract their attention.

16 We will surely tell the king. They seem to have done this with a good intent (see ver. 25); hoping that the impious king and his favourites might be alarmed, as they had been.

22 the winterhouse. Or, "the winter apartment"; see Amos iii. 15. The "hearth" was probably a sort of movable brazier (see R.V.). At the time of this fast, which was in December, the weather is often very cold for a few days at Jerusalem, and in the hilly districts of Palestine.

23 leaves. "Columns," as R.V. marg.: see note, ver. 2.

29 to Jehoiakim. "Concerning Jehoiakim," R.V. Jeremiah was not now admitted to the royal presence.

30 He shall have none to sit upon the throne of David. See note on 2 Kings xxiv. 8.

CHAPTER XXXVII

1 whom. *i.e.*, Zedekiah: see 2 Kings xxiv. 17. "Coniah" is Jehoiachin (xxii. 24).

5 Pharaoh's army, etc. This king was Hophra (Apries in Herodotus).

10 and there remained but wounded men among them, etc. A forcible expression of the important truth that God can never be at a loss for means to accomplish His purposes: cp. Matt. iii. 9.

12 to separate himself thence. Or, perhaps, "to obtain from thence his portion," *i.e.*, his inheritance (see R.V.).

13 Thou fallest away. *i.e.*, Thou art a deserter: see xxi. 9. In predicting the Chaldeans' success the prophet may have seemed to be taking their side.

15 in the house of Jonathan. In Eastern countries, a part of the house of a public functionary is often employed as a prison.

16 cabins. Or, "vaults" (R.V., "cells"). The "dungeon" was probably a deep pit (see xxxviii. 6) in the midst of the inner court of the house, having vaulted recesses round it near the bottom, in which the prisoners were lodged.

21 out of the bakers' street. *i.e.*, from the bakers' shops. It is much more customary in the East than in Europe for persons of the same trade to carry on their business in the same street. The prophet was thus supplied with food at the king's expense; and the whole passage affords an illustration of the truth contained in Prov. xxviii. 23.

CHAPTER XXXVIII

2 he that goeth forth to the Chaldeans. Jeremiah was no deserter (xxxvii. 13), but he did counsel a policy of surrender to the Chaldeans (see 17, 18).

5 the king is not he, etc. Zedekiah was evidently a weak prince (see 24). His history shows how moral imbecility may involve a man in crime and ruin: see notes on 1 Kings xxi. 19; xxii. 2.

6 Malchiah the son of Hammelech. As the word "hammelech" in Hebrew means "the king," some (as R.V.) translate "Malchiah the king's son."

no water. These "dungeons" or "pits" were probably used as cisterns during part of the year. Jerusalem was supplied with water by large cisterns hewn in the rock under the houses.

7 Ebed-melech. *i.e.*, "the servant (slave) of a king." It has long been the practice in Eastern courts to entrust the guardianship of the royal harem to foreign slaves, the chief of whom derives great power from his opportunity of gaining access to the king at all times. In the present case, this influence was possessed by a kind negro (9, 12), who was afterwards rewarded by Divine protection when others were punished (xxxix. 18).

11 old cast clouts, etc. "Old torn and worn-out garments."

15 wilt thou not hearken? Rather, "thou wilt not hearken," as R.V.

16 that made us this soul. *i.e.*, "who gave us this life."

17 the king of Babylon's princes. Because Nebuchadrezzar himself was absent, at Riblah: see xxxix. 5.

19 that are fallen to the Chaldeans. Those who had already surrendered themselves would only taunt the king for at last following their example.

22 the king of Judah's house. *i.e.*, in *thy* house. Instead of escaping the mockery which he dreads, he shall be reproached by the women of his own palace.

26 I presented my supplication. This we find he had done (see xxxvii. 20). It was a part of the truth; the whole they had no right to know.

27 for the matter was not perceived. The French version has "car on n'avait rien su de cet affaire" ("for nothing was known of this affair"). Moffatt translates: "For the interview had been quite private."

28 and he was [there] when Jerusalem was taken. Rather, as the commencement of a new paragraph, continued in the next chapter: "And it came to pass when Jerusalem was taken." Then follows a parenthesis to the end of ver. 2; see R.V.

CHAPTER XXXIX

3 in the middle gate. Probably a gate which led from the lower city to the fortress on Zion. Zedekiah fled by an opposite gate on the south, leading to the king's garden, near the junction of the valleys of Kidron and Hinnom.

Rab-saris . . . Rab-mag. "Rab-saris" means *chief of the eunuchs;* and "Rab-mag" *chief of the Magi.* These were the *titles* of the officers whose *names* precede them: see ver. 13 and 2 Kings xviii. 17.

14 Gedaliah. The son of the nobleman who had before befriended Jeremiah (see xxvi. 24).

15 Now the word of the Lord came, etc. These verses, to the end of the chapter, are an appendix to the history, describing what had taken place before the capture of the city: see xxxviii. 13.

CHAPTER XL

1 from Ramah. By comparing this account with that in xxxix. 11–14, it appears that Jeremiah, contrary to the king's command, was carried as a prisoner as far as Ramah (only six miles from Jerusalem); the prophet being then set at liberty, and, on his choosing to remain in his own country, being placed under the protection of Gedaliah.

6 Mizpah. This was the Mizpah in Benjamin, about four miles north-west of Jerusalem, now called Nebi Samiil.

10 to serve the Chaldeans. Lit., as R.V., "to stand before the Chaldeans," *i.e.*, to serve in an official capacity, a different phrase from that in ver. 9.

gather ye wine, etc. Betokening a state of security. Corn is not mentioned, as the harvest season was past; Jerusalem having been taken in the fourth month (June-July).

CHAPTER XLI

1 of the seed royal, and the princes of the king, etc. Rather, as R.V., "of the seed royal, and [one of] the chief officers of the king, and ten men with him."

5 from Samaria. In the reign of Josiah many persons from the Ten Tribes, who were left in the land, had attended the worship at Jerusalem; and some of these probably brought gifts for the service re-established among the ruins of the Temple.

having cut themselves. These signs of mourning were most likely adopted on account of the destruction of the city and Temple. Cutting the flesh was forbidden to the Hebrews (see Lev. xix. 28), but seems to have been practised by them.

6 weeping all along. In pretended sympathy.

8 treasures in the field. Rather, as R.V., "stores hidden in the field." Such methods of storing grain (practicable in a dry country) in places undiscoverable save by the owners, are not uncommon in the East.

9 because of Gedaliah. R.V. has "by the side of Gedaliah." But there are various readings.

which Asa the king had made. See note on 1 Kings xv. 22. The "pit," although not mentioned in the history, was no doubt a part of the works, perhaps a cistern.

14 cast about. *i.e.,* "turned about."

17 the habitation of Chimham. Or, "the lodging-place of Chimham" ("Geruth Chimham," R.V.), probably a khan or caravanserai: cp. Gen. xlii. 26, and note. Chimham was son of Barzillai (2 Sam. xix. 37, 38).

CHAPTER XLII

1 Jezaniah. Called Azariah, xliii. 2. There was another Jezaniah, xl. 8.

6 Whether it be good, or whether it be evil. Whether it be pleasing to us or not.

12 I will show mercies unto you. Or, as R.V., "I will grant you mercy." Nebuchadrezzar's mercy—a gift from God.

cause you to return to your own land. Rather, "to dwell, or remain in." They were already in the land.

16 the sword which ye feared. . . Egypt, etc. These denunciations were fulfilled when Egypt was invaded by the Chaldeans.

19 The Lord hath said, etc. Hitherto God had spoken (ver. 15), now the prophet himself speaks.

that I have admonished you. More precisely, as R.V., "that I have testified unto you."

20 ye dissembled in your hearts. Or, "ye have done evil against your own souls"; *i.e.,* to your ruin.

CHAPTER XLIII

3 Baruch the son of Neriah, etc. Jeremiah is charged with mistaking the counsel of a designing friend for a Divine oracle.

9 in the clay. Rather, "in mortar."

in the brickkiln. Or, "in brickwork," as R.V. The stones to be hidden, or laid, in mortar, signified the foundation of Nebuchadrezzar's throne.

12 he shall burn them. He shall burn the temples, and carry off the idols.

as a shepherd putteth on his garment. He shall get possession of it as easily "as a shepherd throws his cloak around him when going forth to watch his flock by night" (*Dean Payne-Smith*).

13 the images. Perhaps *obelisks,* with which the approaches to the temples were adorned: cp. 2 Chron. xxxiv. 4. There is one now remaining at Matariyeh, near the site of the ancient Heliopolis, which is formed of a block of red granite from sixty to seventy feet high, covered with hieroglyphics. Its twin obelisk, "Cleopatra's Needle," is on the Thames Embankment. They both stood in front of the Temple of the Sun.

CHAPTER XLIV

1 Migdol . . . Tahpanhes . . . Noph . . . Pathros. These four places are mentioned in geographical order. "Migdol" is probably Magdolum, at the north-east of Egypt, towards the Red Sea. On "Tahpanhes," see note on ii. 16. On "Noph," see note on Isa. xix. 13. "Pathros" is the Thebaid in Upper Egypt, often distinguished from "Egypt" (see Isa. xi. 11).

8 might cut yourselves off. Rather, "may be cut off," R.V.

15 their wives had burned. Rather, as R.V., "their wives burned."

17 our own mouth. Or, as R.V., "our mouth"; meaning their vow to serve the queen of heaven.

the queen of heaven. See note on vii. 18.

19 cakes to worship her. R.V. marg., "cakes to portray her"; "cakes in the shape of her" (*Moffatt*). They were, perhaps, star-shaped (*Prof. Wheeler Robinson*).

without our men. *i.e.,* "without our husbands" (R.V.). Our husbands did not hinder, but joined us. On the introduction of idolatry by female influence, see 1 Kings xi. 1-8; xv. 13; 2 Kings xi. 3, 18.

25 ye will surely accomplish, etc The Hebrew here is feminine; showing that this clause is addressed to the women. The R.V. reads the words as an ironical address: "Establish then your vows, and perform your vows."

26 My name shall no more be named, etc. *i.e.,* the Jews would become practically extinct.

30 Pharaoh-hophra. The Apries of the Greek historians, the grandson of Necho. He was defeated and dethroned by Amasis, who headed a revolt of the troops (see Herodotus, ii. 161, 169). Amasis after some years handed him over to his enemies, by whom he was put to death.

CHAPTER XLV

3 I fainted in my sighing. "I am weary with my groaning," R.V., as Psa. vi. 6.

5 seekest thou great things, etc. In the midst of such terrible calamities, do not seek for any special prominence, as a deliverer or a prophet. Be content that your life is secured to you. Baruch, who was of distinguished family, his grandfather Maaseiah having been governor of Jerusalem in the time of Josiah (2 Chron. xxxiv. 8), might have expected to play some important part in the present crisis: his ambition, however, is repressed, and he is bidden patiently to endure. It is a counsel of general and modern application.

CHAPTER XLVI

The rest of the prophecies in this book are concerned with foreign nations; beginning with Egypt and ending with Babylon. They should be compared with the corresponding predictions of Amos and Isaiah, many of which they repeat; as well as with those of the contemporary prophets, Ezekiel and Obadiah.

1 against the Gentiles. Rather, as R.V., "concerning the nations." So in the next verse, "Of Egypt; concerning the army," etc.

2 Pharaoh-necho. The son and successor of Psammetichus, one of the most powerful kings of Egypt. His expedition to the Euphrates, when king Josiah was slain, is mentioned in 2 Kings xxiii. 29-35. The rout of the Egyptian king at Carchemish changed the whole course of Oriental history.

4 the brigandines. The "coats of mail," as R.V.

5 Wherefore have I seen them dismayed, etc.? More vividly and literally, "Wherefore have I seen it? They are dismayed and are turned backward."

7 Who is this that cometh up as a flood? The R.V. translates, "Who is this that riseth up like the Nile, whose waters toss themselves like the rivers?" It is a metaphor for the advance of the Egyptian army.

8 the city. Put collectively for "the cities."

9 Come up. Or, as R.V., "Go up." The prophet's words.

rage. Rather, "rush wildly."

the Lydians. Rather, "the Ludim"; one of the Egyptian tribes (Gen. x. 13).

12 the land. Rather, "the earth": see R.V.

13 The word, etc. With this second prophecy concerning Egypt, cp. xliii. 10–13.

15 Why are thy valiant [men], etc.? Another reading gives the singular: see R.V. marg., "Why is thy mighty one swept away? he stood not," etc. The Septuagint understands this of Apis, the god of Egypt.

16 and they said, Arise. etc. This refers to the mercenaries (21). Payne-Smith points out that there is here one of those minute touches which so often occur in Scripture as evidences of its truth. Herodotus tells us that the strength of Apries (Hophra) consisted in mercenaries, and that his favouritism towards them was finally the cause of his ruin.

17 They did cry there, etc. Or, according to the ancient versions, "They cried, The name of Pharaoh king of Egypt [is] a noise"—an empty sound. The Hebrew words for *name* (*shem*) and *there* (*sham*) are identical in consonants.

19 daughter. The usual collective term for *inhabitants;* so ver. 11.

20 destruction. Or, "the gadfly" (R.V. marg.), stinging and maddening the "heifer."

21 fatted bullocks. Rather, "calves of the stall," R.V. When the warlike mercenaries of Egypt, Ethiopians, Libyans, and Ludim (9), were destroyed or scattered, their place was taken by the more effeminate inhabitants of Asia Minor, who settled in the fertile land of Lower Egypt, and became too pampered to fight (Herodotus, ii. 163).

22 as hewers of wood. The Chaldean hosts, devastating the numerous and populous cities of Egypt, are compared to woodmen felling the forests and thickets, and thus disturbing the serpents, who show their anger by a furious hiss, while they flee away.

23 though it cannot be searched. Rather, "impenetrable though it be."

25 the multitude of No. Rather, "Amon of No" (R.V.). Amon was the principal Egyptian deity, here called Amon of No, or Thebes, because that city was the chief seat of his worship. Hence it was called, in Greek, Diospolis—the city of Zeus Ammon.

26 afterward it shall be inhabited. See note on Ezek. xxix. 13.

27, 28. Fear thou not, etc. A repetition of xxx. 10, 11.

CHAPTER XLVII

1 Pharaoh. This was probably Pharaoh-necho, after his victory at Megiddo; and if so, the prophecy would be the more remarkable, as there was no likelihood of a Chaldean invasion at that time.

3 shall not look back to [their] children for feebleness of hands. So unstrung shall they be that not even fathers will stay to rally their children.

4 every helper. The Philistines, allies with Phœnicia.

the country ("coastland," or "isle") **of Caphtor.** That the Philistines came from Caphtor is clear from Deut. ii. 23; Amos ix. 7. Ebers and other scholars place it in the Egyptian Delta, but more recent authorities (*e.g.* Sayce) consider that it was Crete or some part of that island (see *Hastings' Dict. of Bible*).

5 Baldness. "Baldness" may mean intense sorrow; or utter loss of all that was valuable.

valley. Or, "lowland": the Philistines inhabited the plain country along the shore, the "Shephelah." The word *with* should be omitted; "the remnant of their valley" being a description of Ashkelon.

CHAPTER XLVIII

1 Against Moab. Rather, "Concerning Moab," as R.V.

Nebo . . . Kiriathaim. . . . Misgab (or, "the high fort"), etc. Many of these cities belonged at first to the Emim (Gen. xiv. 5), then to the Moabites, and afterwards to the Amorites (Numb. xxi. 24–30), who were speedily dispossessed by the Hebrews (Numb. xxxii. 37). After the Assyrians subdued Israel, they fell again into the hands of the Moabites.

3 Horonaim. "The two caverns": see Isa. xv. 5.

6 be like the heath, etc. See note on xvii. 6. Choose poverty and desolateness to save your life.

7 thy works. Or, the product of work; thy *resources.*

Chemosh. See Numb. xxi. 29, and note.

8 the plain. The table-land: see Josh. xiii. 9, 17, 21.

10 that doeth the work of the Lord. The work of punishment to be inflicted on the Moabites. "Deceitfully" should rather be "negligently" (R.V.).

11 he hath settled on his lees. A figure denoting that Moab had enjoyed great prosperity, as well as tranquillity, in consequence of her freedom from foreign wars: see note on Isa. xxv. 6. Here "taste" is an emblem of national character.

12 wanderers that shall cause him to wander. Lit., "tilters that shall tilt him up." Moab, which has just been represented as a jar of old wine, is here described as being tilted, or raised at one end, in order to be completely "emptied," *i.e.,* to be devastated and depopulated, every smaller vessel that held the wine being at the same time exhausted of its contents.

13 ashamed of Chemosh. Chemosh shall defend the Moabites no better than the golden calf at Bethel had protected the Israelites.

15 and gone up [out of] her cities. Rather, "and her cities are gone up [in smoke]," as R.V. marg.

17 rod. Or, "sceptre"; the ensign of dominion.

18 in thirst. That is, in a parched place or in the dust. This expression is emphatic, as Dibon was remarkable for its well-watered situation: see note on Isa. xv. 9.

19 Aroer. Vers. 19–25 represent strongly the consternation of the Moabites and the desolation of the whole country; judgement falling on every place. Some of the places cannot now be identified.

20 for it is broken down. *i.e.,* Dibon, her strong fortress.

24 Bozrah. To be distinguished from the Edomite Bozrah (Isa. lxiii. 1).

26 Make ye him drunken. That is, with the cup of fury and trembling; see xxv. 15; Isa. li. 17, 22.

27 since thou spakest of him, etc. Rather, as R.V., "as often as thou speakest of him, thou waggest the head"; a mark of contempt.

29 We have heard the pride of Moab, etc. The passage to ver. 36 seems an expansion of Isa. xvi. 6–12.

30 but it shall not be so. It will be powerless.

31 will I howl. The prophet here speaks in his own person. In Isaiah it is Moab who laments (xvi. 7); Isaiah himself afterwards (9, 11).

32 Sibmah. Two miles from Heshbon. The

same as Sebam (see also Numb. xxxii. 38). The whole region was famed for its vineyards.

the sea. No doubt an upland lake, now dried up.

33 from the plentiful field. Heb., "from Carmel"; a general term applied to fruitful fields: cp. Isa. xvi. 10.

[Their] shouting shall be no shouting. These joyous shoutings shall give place to the war-cry, or the death-wail.

34 [As] a heifer of three years old. See Isa. xv. 5.

39 They shall howl [saying]. Rather, as R.V., "How is it broken down! [how] do they howl!"

40 he shall fly ("swoop"). *i.e.*, the enemy, Nebuchadrezzar.

45 because of the force. Or, "without force"; in vain.

a fire shall come forth out of Heshbon, etc. See note on Numb. xxi. 28; xxiv. 17; from which these words are taken.

47 bring again the captivity. *i.e.*, restore the prosperity, as in other passages.

CHAPTER XLIX

1 their king. For "their king," read "Milcom" (R.V., "Malcam"), or Molech, the chief deity of the Ammonites: see 1 Kings xi. 7, 33.

2 Rabbah. "Rabbah" (which means *the great*) was the capital of the Ammonites: see 2 Sam. xii. 26.

3 Ai. An Ammonite town not mentioned elsewhere. The Ai in Canaan (Josh. vii. 2) was a different place.

by the hedges. *i.e.*, the fences of the vineyards: see R.V. The remainder of the verse is nearly identical with Amos i. 15.

VERS. 7–22. The Edomites, notwithstanding their acuteness, and the strength of their position, shall be utterly destroyed, and made a byword among the nations. The phraseology of certain parts of this prophecy so closely resembles that of Obadiah, as to make it evident that one of these prophets had read the work of the other (cp. 9, 10, 14–16 with Obad. 2–6). The more probable opinion is, that Obadiah was the earlier of the two, and that Jeremiah borrowed from him, as he has done from the books of Numbers and Isaiah.

7 Teman. A city and district in the east of Edom; so called from Teman, a grandson of Esau: see Gen. xxxvi. 11. Its inhabitants were celebrated for wisdom: see Job ii. 11; Obad. 8, 9.

8 Dwell deep. Hide yourselves from the enemy, either by retiring into caverns, or by fleeing into the depths of the desert.

Dedan. The Dedanites were probably descendants of Abraham, dwelling among the Edomites: cp. xxv. 23, and see Gen. xxv. 2.

9 Would they not leave, etc.? Rather, as R.V. marg., "they will leave no gleaning grapes; if thieves by night, they will destroy till they have enough" ("their fill").

11 Leave thy fatherless children, etc. If these words are to be taken as they stand, they appear like mingled threatening and promise; implying that there shall be no one left to protect the widows and orphans; for the land shall be stripped of men, as it had been before (1 Kings xi. 16). Only God, therefore, can protect them.

13 Bozrah. See note on Isa. xxxiv. 6.

14 I have heard a rumour ("tidings," R.V.) **from the Lord.** The words correspond with the beginning of Obadiah.

unto the heathen. Better, "among the nations," as R.V. So next verse.

16 thou that dwellest in the clefts of the rock. Or, "in the fastnesses of Sela" (Petra), the rock-city. See note on "Sela," 2 Kings xiv. 7. The position of the city in an almost inaccessible chasm shows how appropriately it is compared to an eagle's nest; and its complete desolation, after it had been rebuilt, is a clear fulfilment of this and other predictions: see Mal. i. 4.

19 Behold, he shall come up like a lion, etc. Or, "Behold, one (*i.e.*, the invader) cometh up as a lion from the pride of Jordan (see note on xii. 5) to the sheepfold of the strong; for I will suddenly make him (*i.e.*, the strong) run away from it. And who is the chosen one? I will appoint [him] against it; for who is like me? and who will meet me? and who is the shepherd that will stand before me?" God compares the rock-hewn city to a sheepfold (see 1 Sam. xxiv. 3, and note), and sends an enemy against it, like a lion, whom the strongest shepherd cannot resist; for he is chosen and appointed by God.

20 Surely the least of the flock, etc. Or, "Surely they shall drag them away, like the little ones of the flock; surely one shall make their sheepfold desolate (*or*, dismayed) over them": a continuation of the figure of the preceding verse.

21 at the cry, etc. Rather, as R.V., "There is a cry, the noise whereof is heard," etc.

23 Hamath. See note on 2 Sam. viii. 9. "Arpad," now called Tell Arfad, an uninhabited ruin, north of Aleppo.

23 sorrow on the sea. The best commentators regard "the sea" here as figurative, either meaning "like the unrest of the waves," or "in the sea of human hearts."

25 How is the city of praise not left, etc.! Or, "How is it that the city of praise is not forsaken, the city of my joy?" An exclamation of surprise that the population had not saved themselves by flight. They remain only to be massacred.

VERS. 28–33. The Chaldeans, in their conquering progress, will also harass the Arabian tribes, and chase them from their haunts. On "Kedar," see note on Isa. xxi. 17. Of "Hazor" we know nothing. Kedar denotes the nomad tribes, and Hazor those who had fixed abodes (from Heb., *hazer*, a village).

31 Arise. *i.e.*, "Arise, O ye Chaldeans": see 28.

the wealthy nation. Lit., as R.V., "a nation that is at ease."

which dwell alone. Separate from others, and therefore fancying themselves secure from attack: see Numb. xxiii. 9.

32 [that are] in the utmost corners. See note on ix. 26.

VERS. 34–39. This prophecy "concerning Elam" appears from the date assigned to have been given some years later than the preceding. No particular historical fulfilment of the predictions can be assigned. Elam was once subject to Assyria (Ezra iv. 9). It was now doubtless to be engulfed in the destruction which the victorious progress of Nebuchadrezzar brought upon the peoples of the East.

34 Elam. See notes on "Elam," in Gen. xiv. 1, and Isa. xxii. 6.

36 the four winds. *i.e.*, enemies from every quarter.

38 set My throne. A throne of judgement.

CHAPTER L

2 confounded . . . broken. Or, as R.V., "put to shame . . . dismayed." On "Bel": see note on Isa. xlvi. 1. "Merodach" is frequently mentioned in the Assyrian cuneiform inscriptions as *Mar-u-duk*, and is described sometimes as the supreme god. The name is contained in those of two Babylonian kings, "Evil-merodach" (lii. 31) and Merodach-baladan (Isa. xxxix. 1).

3 out of the north. The Medes.

They shall remove, they shall depart. More literally and vividly as in R.V., "They are fled, they are gone!"

5 They shall ask their way to Zion. Or, as R.V., "They shall inquire concerning Zion."

6 from mountain to hill. From one idolatrous haunt to another.

their resting-place. Their proper fold.

7 the habitation of justice. Or, "the fold of righteousness," *i.e.*, the true source of good and safety. The argument of Israel's enemies was, It cannot be counted impiety towards Jahveh to oppress those who have rebelled against Him.

8 be as the he goats. "Lead on." March with boldness and energy.

9 raise. Or, "stir up," as R.V.

An assembly of great nations. The Medo-Persians with their allies; see li. 27, 28.

None shall return in vain. Perhaps meaning, None shall miss their mark.

11 the heifer at grass. The R.V. reads, "the heifer that treadeth out [the corn]."

12 Your mother. Your mother *country*.

the hindermost of the nations [shall be], etc. Rather, as R.V., "She [shall be] the hindermost of the nations, a wilderness," etc.

15 She hath given her hand. That is, she has surrendered. Ancient Oriental sculptures frequently indicate the submission of the conquered by the stretching out of the hand. Cp. Virgil, *Æn.* xii. 936.

foundations. Rather "battlements" or "bulwarks" (R.V.).

16 Cut off the sower from Babylon. In ancient times the plain of Babylon was so fertile that, according to Herodotus (i. 193), the seed yielded from two to three hundredfold. It is now an utter waste, with here and there a patch of cultivation.

every one to his people. Cp. Isa. xiii. 14. The reference is to immigrants settled in Babylonia, who will now hastily return to their own countries.

19 his habitation. Rather, "his pasture," as R.V.

20 whom I reserve. Or, "whom I leave as a remnant," as R.V.

21 Merathaim . . . Pekod. Symbolic names for Babylon; vengeance or visitation (Pekod), the doubly rebellious (Merathaim).

Waste. Or, "Slay," as in ver. 27.

23 hammer. The term has often been applied to redoubtable conquerors, as Charles *Martel* of France, and Edward I. of England, *Malleus Scotorum*.

24 I have laid a snare for thee. Predicting the stratagem of Cyrus, who took the city by surprise: see note on Isa. xlv. 1. Cp. Herodotus, i. 191.

25 this is the work of the Lord God of hosts. Or, "For the Lord God of hosts hath a work to do."

26 from the utmost border. "From every quarter." R.V. marg.

27 her bullocks. Her strong men.

28 of them that flee. Of the Jews set free from bondage.

31 O thou most proud. Heb., "O Pride!" Moffatt translates, "Queen Insolence." So in next verse, "the proud one shall stumble."

33 [were] oppressed. Better, "*are* oppressed," as R.V., and so in the following clauses.

34 to the land. "To the earth," as R.V.: cp. Isa. xiv. 7.

A sword is, etc. There is no "is" in the Hebrew, and the force of the passage is strikingly and correctly brought out by Moffatt, who begins each of the vers. 35–38, "Sword, strike," etc.

36 liars. The soothsayers.

they shall dote. Shall appear fools (*Orelli*).

37 mingled people. Auxiliaries: see note on xxv. 24.

39 wild beasts . . . owls. Rather, wild cats . . . wolves . . . ostriches.

41 a people shall come from the north. See note on ver. 3. The whole picture is a companion to that in vi. 22–24; where the attack upon Jerusalem is described. Now the same ruin befalls her great enemy.

44 Behold, he shall come up, etc. This and the two following verses predict the same calamities for Babylon as were threatened to Edom in xlix. 19–21.

CHAPTER LI

1 in the midst of them that rise up against Me. Perhaps, as R.V., "in Leb-kamai." After the method of the cryptogram in xxv. 26, this Hebrew word represents *Casdim*, or "Chaldeans."

2 fanners. Who would fan or winnow her.

7 Babylon hath been a golden cup, etc. Cp. xxv. 15, 16. The epithet "golden" indicates the wealth and splendour of Babylon: see the spiritual application of the words, Rev. xvii. 4, 5.

9 We would have healed Babylon. The appeal to her allies (or, perhaps, to the Jewish exiles in Babylon) in the preceding verse, and this their reply, forcibly show the hopelessness of her restoration.

10 our righteousness. The justice of our cause.

11 Make bright the arrows. "Make sharp the arrows."

gather the shields. The Hebrew word translated "gather" really means "fill." The idea is to put on the shields.

12 upon the walls. Rather, "against the walls" (R.V.). The address is to the besiegers.

the ambushes. See note on l. 24.

13 many waters. The Euphrates and its numerous canals, which passed through and near the city.

20 battle axe. As the verbs are in the past tense in Hebrew, they should be rendered, "I have broken in pieces," "I have destroyed," etc.; and thus they apply to Babylon: cp. Isa. x. 5, 15. Some, however, regard them as the prophetic past, and refer them to the future and to Cyrus.

25 O destroying mountain. Lit., "mountain of destruction." The Mount of Olives, when defiled by idolatry, is called by the same name (2 Kings xxiii. 13). A similar phrase occurs in Prov. xxviii. 24, "man of destruction," *i.e., destroyer*. Lange (*Commentary*) thinks that the reference is to the destroying influence of Babylon in spiritual relations.

27 Ararat, Minni, and Ashchenaz. The mountainous countries towards the Caucasus and the Black Sea.

the rough caterpillars (locusts). Representing the bristling spears of the riders.

30 have forborne. Have *ceased ;* giving up their cause as lost.

her bars. Her " bars of iron " : see Isa. xlv. 2.

31 at [one] end. Or, " on every quarter " (R.V.). Herodotus (i. 191) states that, owing to the great extent of Babylon, those who dwelt in the outskirts were taken prisoners by the Persians before the people in the centre of the city knew of the attack.

32 are stopped. Rather, " are taken." The " passages " are probably the ferries across the river, which would naturally be guarded. But the channel of the river being dried, and the reeds or palisades burnt, to clear the way, the city was captured.

33 The daughter of Babylon, etc. Rather, " The daughter of Babylon is like a threshing-floor at the time when it is trodden " (R.V.). See notes on Isa. xxi. 10 ; xli. 15.

34 hath devoured me, etc. The speaker is " the inhabitant of Zion " : see next verse.

36 her sea. " Probably the great lake dug by Nitocris to receive the waters of the Euphrates " (*Payne-Smith*) ; see Herodotus, i. 185.

37 dragons. " Jackals," as R.V.

39 In their heat. *i.e.,* while they are heated with wine, I will prepare for them another sort of wine—the wine of my indignation : see note on Isa. xxi. 4.

41 Sheshach. " Babel " : see xxv. 26, and note.

42 The sea is come up, etc. The country is inundated with invaders.

44 that which he hath swallowed up. *i.e.,* the riches of his temple, consisting of the spoils of conquered countries ; especially the sacred vessels from Jerusalem, which had been placed there.

46 And lest your heart faint, etc. Rather, " *And let not* your heart faint, nor fear ye," etc. : see R.V. The prophet gives to the Jews the signs of Babylon's approaching end, as our Lord gave His disciples signs of the end of the Jewish state : see Matt. xxiv. 6–22. The chief sign is that of internal commotions and revolts in the different parts of the empire.

48 shall sing for Babylon. Shall rejoice over her ruin : " shall sing for joy over Babylon," R.V.

49 As Babylon [hath caused] the slain, etc. Or, " Both Babylon is to fall, O ye slain of Israel ; and with Babylon shall fall the slain of all the country " : see R.V., marg.

50 afar off. " From afar " (R.V.), *i.e.,* while still in Babylon. Set free, bethink yourselves of your proper home, and set out on your return.

51 We are confounded (ashamed), etc. The reply of the exiles.

55 hath spoiled . . . and destroyed. Rather, as R.V., " spoileth . . . destroyeth."

when her waves do roar, etc. " The noise of their voice is uttered " : refers to that of the invaders, silencing " the great voice " of the city ; *i.e.,* the hum of city life in days of peace.

58 The broad walls of Babylon. There were two walls. According to Herodotus, there was space enough for a four-horsed chariot to drive along between them. See *Babylonian Life and History* by Sir E. Wallis Budge (1925, pp. 67, 68).

VERS. 59–64. These verses form an appendix to the prophecy concerning Babylon, and describe the method of its communication to the exiled Jews. The oracle was not to be communicated at once to all the people, but to one individual (cp. xxx.).

59 when he went with Zedekiah. Nothing more is known of this journey, which may have been to render homage.

a quiet prince. Lit., " prince of the resting-place." Probably marshal of the caravan, who arranged the halting-places (" quartermaster," R.V. marg.). The French version has " principal chambellan," " principal chamberlain ").

61 and shalt see, and shalt read, etc. Rather, " then see that thou read all these words, and say," etc.

64 Thus far are the words of Jeremiah. This note is appended, probably to show that the next chapter is by a different hand.

CHAPTER LII

This chapter is almost verbally identical with 2 Kings xxiv. 18–20 ; xxv. 1–21 ; 27–30 (on which see the notes) ; but it gives some particulars of the history rather more fully.

10 he slew also all the princes of Judah in Riblah. This is additional to the account in 2 Kings.

11 and put him in prison till the day of his death. Not in 2 Kings.

28 This is the people whom Nebuchadrezzar, etc. These three verses are not given in the Septuagint. Niebuhr, followed by Lange, thinks they are a gloss. " Seventh year " (v. 28) should be " seventeenth year."

31 Evil-merodach. Son and successor of Nebuchadrezzar.

THE BOOK OF LAMENTATIONS

INTRODUCTION

THE Hebrew title of this Book, in its earlier form, is *Hichah,* " How ! " from the first word of the first chapter. As the same word begins chaps. ii. and iv., it was a characteristic expression of the writer's grief, an exclamation of surprise and sorrow. But the later Hebrew edition and commentators called the Book *Kinoth,* dirges, elegies (cp. the Irish *keen* or *caoin,* the weeping for the dead). This title was followed by the Septuagint and the Vulgate, using respectively the Greek and Latin equivalents, " Lamentations." It is one of the " Kethubim " or hagiographa, and is one of the *megilloth* (" rolls ") which is still read in the Synagogues on the anniversary of the destruction of the Temple. The Roman Catholic Church uses lessons from it in the services for Maundy Thursday, Good

Friday, and the Saturday of Holy Week. In the Book of Common Prayer, "Lessons proper for Holy Days" are taken from it for the Monday, Tuesday, and Wednesday before Easter (chaps. i., 1-15 ; ii. 13 ; iii. and iv. 1-21).

The author's name is not mentioned in the Book. It has, however, been generally ascribed to Jeremiah, though this authorship is questioned by some eminent authorities. The references to invasion, captivity, desecration of the Temple, and desolation of the city (i. 1, 2-4, 10 ; ii. 6, 7, 9, 15, 19, 20 ; iv. 4, 15) seem to point to the siege and capture of Jerusalem by Nebuchadrezzar, 599-588 B.C. And it is in keeping with the tenderness of Jeremiah, as revealed in the Book that bears his name, that he should pour out his patriotism and his sorrow as is done in Lamentations. (Note especially Jer. viii. 18, 21 ; ix. 1 : "Oh that my head were waters," etc., and cp. Lam. iii. 48, 49.)

Yet the Book is not one of lamentation merely. There are messages of encouragement, exhortations to repentance, and promises of the Divine mercy (iii. 22-26, 31-33, 40, 41, 57, 58 ; iv. 22 ; v. 19, 21).

CHAPTER I

The first part of the chapter (1-11) contains, for the most part, the words of the prophet ; in the second part (12-22) Jerusalem herself is the speaker.

1 How doth the city sit solitary ! See Isa. iii. 26.

2 her lovers . . . her friends. The allies in whom she trusted.

3 because of great servitude. This probably refers to the long-continued Chaldean oppressions, which had driven many of the people from the country into exile (rather than "into *captivity*" : see R.V. marg.), before the fall of Jerusalem (see Jer. xl. 11).

the straits. The figure is that of hunted animals driven into a contracted space. The French version has, "l'ont saisi dans son angoisse."

4 The ways of Zion. That is, the ways *to* Zion.

her virgins. The female choirs, accustomed to take part in the services and festivals : see Psa. lxviii. 25.

5 the chief. *i.e.*, they have acquired the ascendancy : see Deut. xxviii. 13, 44.

6 beauty. Or, "glory."

7 remembered. Rather, as R.V., "remembereth."

8 removed. That is, is treated as unclean.

9 behold my affliction. Here, as in vers. 12-22, Jerusalem is introduced as the speaker.

11 to relieve the soul. "To make the soul to come again" ; to restore or sustain life. The French version has, "afin de reprendre du cœur" ("in order to renew the heart").

14 wreathed. That is, "twisted" ("knit together," R.V.).

15 an assembly. More emphatically in R.V., "a solemn assembly" ; as though the Chaldeans made a festival of their destroying work. "A triumphant host" (*Moffatt*).

as in a winepress. See Isa. lxiii. 1-6, and notes. The destruction there foretold of Israel's enemies is now suffered by Israel himself.

17 Jerusalem, etc. R.V., "Jerusalem is among them as an unclean thing."

18 The Lord is righteous, etc. Righteous in His judgements, for they have been merited by my sins.

20 is turned. That is, "sorely agitated."

at home there is as death. That is, death by pestilence or famine.

21 called. That is, "announced" (or "proclaimed," R.V.).

CHAPTER II

1 His footstool. The ark of the covenant ; see 1 Chron. xxviii. 2.

2 the habitations . . . the strong holds. The rural homes and city fortresses.

3 all the horn of Israel. All her power and glory : see note on 1 Sam. ii. 1.

6 His tabernacle, as if it were of a garden. Rather, "His booth, as of a garden" ; the allusion being to the lodge in a garden where the vine-dresser or watchman lodged ; hence, "the tabernacle."

11 My liver is poured, etc. See note on i. 20. The liver was regarded as the seat of emotion. "My soul is wretched" (*Moffatt*).

13 What thing shall I take to witness for thee ? Rather, as R.V., "What shall I testify unto thee ?" to relieve thy sorrow.

thy breach is great like the sea. Thy destruction is as vast as the sea.

14 have seen. Foreseen ; foretold.

false burdens. "Burden" is used, as so often in Isaiah, for the vision or message of a prophet.

15 The perfection of beauty, etc. For these epithets, see Psa. l. 2 ; xlviii. 2.

18 Their heart. The heart of the Jews.

O wall of the daughter of Zion. The wall of Jerusalem, like the city itself, is personified : cp. ver. 8.

19 in the beginning of the watches. *i.e.*, all the night through.

20 Shall the women eat their fruit ? See note on 2 Kings vi. 29.

[and] children of a span long. Rather, as R.V., "the children that are dandled in the hands."

22 my terrors round about. Thou hast collected all kinds of fear and suffering in great numbers around me. The Heb. here recalls Jeremiah's frequent phrase, "magor-missabib" : see Jer. vi. 25.

CHAPTER III

3 Surely against me is He turned, etc. The arrangement of the sentence should be, "Surely against me He turneth His hand (*i.e.*, turneth it again and again)" : see R.V.

all the day. The French version has, "chaque jour de nouveau" ("each day afresh").

5 He hath builded against me. As a besieger builds mounds to attack a city.

6 He hath set me, etc. A repetition of Psa. cxliii. 3. "He hath made me to dwell in dark places, as those that have been long dead," R.V.

14 I was a derision. Rather, as R.V., "I am become a derision."

16 He hath also broken my teeth, etc. *i.e.*, with gritty bread.

19 Remembering mine affliction. Or, "Remember my affliction," etc.

27 the yoke. That is, of chastisement.

28 He sitteth alone, etc. Rather, "Let him sit alone. . . . Let him put his mouth. . . . Let him give his cheek. . . . Let him be filled."

He hath borne it upon him. Rather, "because He (God) hath laid it upon him."

29 He putteth ("Let him put") **his mouth in the dust.** The same spirit of humility is indicated in the following verse. Indignities from our fellow-men are patiently submitted to when we regard them as deserved Divine chastisements: see 2 Sam. xvi. 11.

40 Let us search and try our ways. Acceptable confession requires not only sincerity, but knowledge of our own hearts, as tested by God's Word.

43 Thou hast covered. Probably, "Thou hast covered Thyself" (R.V. marg.): see next verse.

49 trickleth. Better, "poureth," as R.V.

53 and cast a stone upon me. Closing my dungeon with a stone (see Dan. vi. 17).

54 Waters flowed over mine head. Figurative, for the extreme of misery.

63 I am their music. "I am their song," R.V.: cp. Job xxx. 9. "I am the burden of their satire" (*Moffatt*).

64 Render unto them. The words in this and the two following verses should be rendered as future: "Thou wilt render . . . Thou wilt give . . . Thou wilt pursue": see R.V.

CHAPTER IV

1 How is the gold become dim! The Israelites, now sadly tarnished in character and reputation.

3 the sea monsters. Rather, "the monsters," or "jackals" (R.V.): see note on Job xxx. 29.

ostriches. See note on Job xxxix. 14.

7 Nazarites. Correctly, "Nazirites": see note on Numb. vi. 2.

polishing. Heb., "division"; meaning either the shape or the veining of the body.

8 blacker than a coal. Or, "blacker than blackness."

10 pitiful. Or, "tender-hearted": showing how extreme must have been their destitution.

12 into the gates of Jerusalem. See note on 2 Kings xxv. 2. Two reasons might be assigned for this incredulity—the strength of the fortress, as renewed by Uzziah and his son (2 Chron. xxvi. 9; xxvii. 3); and the protection of Jehovah, as shown in the destruction of Sennacherib and his army (2 Kings xix. 34, 35).

13 For the sins, etc. "[It is] because of the sins," etc.

14 wandered. Or, "staggered."

15 [it is] unclean. Rather, "Unclean!" the leper's cry.

They said among the heathen. Rather, as R V., "men said among the nations"; so in ver. 16, "men respected not."

16 hath divided. That is, "hath scattered or dispersed them."

17 our eyes as yet failed for our vain help. Or, as R.V., "Our eyes do yet fail [in looking] for our vain help."

a nation that could not save [us]. Probably referring to Egypt.

CHAPTER V

4 for money . . . sold. Our wells and forests are no longer ours.

5 Our necks [are] under persecution. Rather, as R.V., "Our pursuers are upon our necks"; closely pressing on us.

6 We have given the hand, etc. See note on Jer. l. 15: see also Ezek. xvii. 18.

8 Servants. "Slaves," referring to the ignoble origin of many of the Chaldeans.

9 We gat. "We get," R.V. "The perils of the wilderness" refer to the hordes of wild Arabs that made the pastures insecure.

10 Our skin was (is) **black.** Rather, "is fiery red with" the "burning heat of famine."

13 They took the young men to grind. Or, as R.V., "The young men bare the mill": meaning the hand-mill. See notes on Exod. xi. 5; Judges xvi. 21.

the children fell ("stumbled," R.V.) **under the wood.** The carrying of wood was as menial as grinding at the mill, and for children it was oppressively laborious.

14 The elders have ceased from the gate. See Job xxix. 7, and note.

17 our eyes are dim. See note on 1 Sam. xiv. 27.

19 Thou, O Lord, remainest for ever. "Thou, O Eternal, sittest [as King] for ever." The unchangeableness and supremacy of God encourage the sufferers in asking that they may not be cast off for ever.

21 Renew our days as of old. That is, Restore to us what we enjoyed in former days—our religious ordinances, Temple, etc.

22 But Thou hast utterly rejected us, etc. Rather, "Unless Thou hast utterly rejected us, [*and*] art very wroth against us": thus suggesting that there is room for hope.

EZEKIEL

INTRODUCTION

EZEKIEL was one of the prophets of the Captivity, and his prophecies covered a period of twenty-two years. (For particulars as to place and date, see notes on i. 1, below.) It is interesting to compare his visions with those of the Apocalypse of St. John, whose writings have traces of the language and ideas of the Old Testament prophet. Both were exiles. Both lived in times when the pagan powers seemed triumphant. Both found it necessary to rebuke the unbelief and deadness of the professed people of God. And both spoke of the final victory of righteousness.

At the beginning of his prophetic work Ezekiel is encouraged, as Isaiah and Jeremiah were, by the vision of God's glory and the promise of His help (i. 1, 28). Like them, he needed encouragement. He shrank from the task (iii. 14). His earliest messages were those of rebuke and warning to Israel (ii. 3–7; iii. 7–9; iv. 17–21; v. 7–17; vi. 3–10; vii. 3, 4, 20). He gives graphic pictures of the idolatry and licentious rites into which the people had fallen (viii. 6, 9, 10), and proclaims the judgements of heaven against them (ix. 4–10; xii. 15, 16). He vindicates, against objectors, the justice and fairness of the Divine judgements, and emphasises individual responsibility (xviii. esp. 2, 3, 9, 20, 23, 25, 29). His warnings to Israel at this stage reach a climax in his prophecy of the doom of Zedekiah and the downfall of his throne (xxi. 25–27), and, spoken at the commencement of the siege of Jerusalem, his prediction of its fall (xxiv. 2, 6, 13, 14).

Then follow his prophecies against Ammon (xxv. 1–7), Moab (xxv. 8–11), Edom (xxv. 12–14), Philistia (xxv. 15–17), Tyre (xxvi.–xxviii. 19), Sidon (xxviii. 20–24), and Egypt (xxix.–xxxii.). These may be compared with Jeremiah's predictions (Jer. xlvi.–lii.).

The news of the fall of Jerusalem eighteen months after Ezekiel had foretold it, is brought to the prophet in Babylonia by a fugitive who had escaped from the doomed city (xxxiii. 21). Contrary to the false prophets (xxxiii. 24), Ezekiel tells Israel that they must still suffer for their sins (xxxiii. 27–29), but goes on to hold out hope of restoration (xxxiv. 11–16, 29–31). This hope is vividly illustrated by the vision of the dry bones (xxxvii.), a vision which, with its testimony to the power of the Spirit of God, has often been an inspiration and encouragement to God's true servants in times of spiritual deadness.

The closing chapters of the Book (esp. xliii.–xlviii.) are aglow with the light of a new day and with the vision of the city whose name shall be, "The Lord is there" (xlviii. 35).

"There are many things in Ezekiel," says Dr. Skinner, "which give him a high place amongst the heralds of Christ in the Old Testament. His clear assertion of the value of the individual soul and of the efficacy of repentance, his profound sense of sin as ingratitude, and of the need of a new heart in order to fulfil the law of God, his impassioned vindication of the character of God as merciful and eager to forgive, are among the brightest gems of spiritual truth to be found in the pages of prophecy" (*Hastings' Dict. Bible*, art. "Ezekiel").

CHAPTER I

1 the thirtieth year. Perhaps the 30th year of the prophet's life. He commenced prophesying in the fifth year after the captivity of Jehoiachin (ver. 2), that is, in the reign of Zedekiah. This was 592 B.C.

the fourth [month]. Nearly corresponding with our July.

Chebar. This was formerly supposed to be the "Chaboras" of the Greeks: now the *Khabour;* a river which joins the Euphrates about two hundred miles north of Babylon. But the best opinion now is that the Chebar must have been nearer Babylon and was probably one of the canals in the neighbourhood of that city.

4 out of the north. The quarter from which Divine judgements had fallen upon Zion: see Jer. i. 14.

infolding itself. Or, "flashing"; perhaps meaning unintermitted. The Hebrew expression occurs only in one other passage, Exod. ix. 24. The appearance seems to have been that of a dark storm-cloud, in which was an incessant blaze like lightning, the centre being a clear, intense light. This august vision was designed to prepare Ezekiel for his prophetic office. As many of its duties would expose him to the hostility of his fellow-men, it was most important that his mind should be deeply impressed with the reality, majesty, and power of the living God.

and out of the midst thereof, etc. Rather, "and it (*masc.*, the cloud) had a brightness around, and from the midst of it (*fem.*, the fire) like an eye of gold alloy (*i.e.*, a clear centre of golden light), from the midst of the fire."

5 four living creatures. On the cherubim see notes on Gen. iii. 24; Exod. xxv. 18; also Rev. iv. 6, 7. The four faces and four wings, and other variations, were probably intended to suggest intelligence and energy, corresponding with the rest of the vision.

6 every one had four faces. The "living ones" in the Apocalypse had each its own special form; here all the "faces" are combined in each. These varying details do not affect the general correspondence of the symbols.

9 they turned not when they went. Having a face in every direction, they had no need to turn.

10 the face of a man, etc. *i.e.*, the face of a man [in front], that of a lion to the right, of an ox to the left, and of an eagle [at the back]. The punctuation here adopted slightly differs from that in the ordinary English Bible.

11 Thus [were] their faces, etc. Rather, as R.V., "And their faces and their wings were separate above."

two covered their bodies. In token of humility.

2 whither the spirit was to go, they went. They were moved by an immediate Divine impulse.

13 lamps. Or, "torches."

15 one wheel. *i.e.*, one by each of the living creatures. Each wheel being composed of two rims intersecting each other, four semicircular parts or "faces" were thus formed, and the wheels seemed to move in any direction without turning. Their astonishing height, numerous eyes, power of rapid motion, and sympathy with the living creatures, greatly heighten the impression of Divine intelligence and omnipotence which the whole vision conveys.

16 beryl. Heb., "tarshish"; probably topaz.

18 their rings. The circumference of the wheels.

they were so high that they were dreadful. Rather, as R.V., "they were high and dreadful."

22 the likeness of the firmament. Rather, as R.V., "the likeness of a firmament."

as the colour of the terrible crystal. Rather, "as a glance of the terrible (dazzling) crystal"; cp. Rev. iv. 6.

24 the voice of speech. Or, "a noise of tumult" (R.V.).

25 from the firmament. Rather, "above the firmament."

26 as the appearance of a man. God was pleased to appear in human form also to Daniel (Dan. vii. 9). These manifestations of Jehovah might serve to prepare the minds of His people for the incarnation of our Lord.

28 the bow that is in the cloud. The memorial of God's promise and the emblem of mercy. Cp. Rev. iv. 3, 4.

CHAPTER II

1 Son of man. This phrase is applied only to Ezekiel and Daniel (viii. 17), both of whom prophesied in Chaldea, where it was a common mode of address, equivalent to "O man!"

5 yet shall know. If the warning did not profit them, it would yet vindicate the justice and mercy of God.

6 thou dost dwell among scorpions. Though thou shouldest be exposed to malice and injury: cp. Matt. x. 16.

8 eat that I give thee. Receive its whole contents, so as to make them thine own: see iii. 10.

9 sent unto me. Rather, "stretched out to me."

a roll of a book. See note on Jer. xxxvi. 2.

10 written within and without. Ancient rolls were usually written on the inside only; but this is represented as full to overflowing of its dreadful contents: see Rev. v. 1.

CHAPTER III

2 to eat that roll. See note on ii. 8.

3 as honey for sweetness. Denoting, probably, the inward satisfaction flowing from simple obedience to God's commands. The nature of the work, however, soon made him feel its bitterness (14): cp. Rev. x. 9, 10.

6 many people. Or, "many peoples," as R.V.—speaking various languages.

12 from his (its) place. The sound of praise came from the place where the chariot of the Almighty was.

13 that touched one another. Or, "as they touched," etc., see R.V. *i.e.*, when expanded for flight; otherwise they were separate (i. 11).

14 the hand of the Lord was strong upon me. I was under a powerful Divine impulse.

15 Tel-abib. Probably the chief colony of the Jews on the Chebar. *Tel* signifies "hill"; *abib*, "ears of corn."

and I sat where they sat. This was the common attitude of grief; and seven days was the usual period of deep mourning (Job ii. 13). This proof of the prophet's sympathy with his exiled brethren ought to have gained their confidence and their attention to his message.

astonished. Or, "in deep silence."

19 hast delivered thy soul. Art clear from the guilt of his sin.

20 When a righteous man. The best of men is safe only as he keeps constantly in mind his liability to fall; watching over himself, and praying and striving against all evil.

I lay a stumbling-block, etc. Allowing him to be placed where his principles are put to a severe test.

his righteousness. Lit., "his righteousnesses"; *i.e.*, his good deeds.

23 into the plain. Again into solitude; that, after having received his commission, he might be again fortified by the heavenly vision.

24 and spake with me, etc. The same Spirit which at one time prompts to speak, at another commands silence.

25 and shall bind thee with them. It is probable that the reading should be, "I will put bands upon thee and bind thee," a figurative expression for God's restraint, of which the following verse is a continuation.

26 And I will make thy tongue, etc. In retribution for their treatment of the prophet.

27 But when I speak with thee, etc. There would be times when the prophet's enforced silence would be broken by Divine impulses so strong that he could not but speak.

CHAPTER IV

1 a tile. Rather, "a brick." Such bricks, on which inscriptions and designs were portrayed by stamping or engraving when moist, were much used in Nineveh and Babylon; and are found in great numbers in their ruins. Many inscriptions on bricks are to be found in the illustrations to *Babylonian Life and History,* by Sir E. Wallis Budge (1925). There can be little doubt that the successive actions here described took place only in vision, like the eating of the prophetic roll mentioned in ch. iii. 1–3.

2 lay siege against it. Pictorially.

the camp. Rather, "encampments," denoting different points of attack.

3 pan. Or, "plate," on which bread was baked.

4 upon thy left side. In one unmoving position, symbol of a fettered or disabled condition. Similarly ver. 6.

thou shalt bear their iniquity. This phrase always means to bear the *punishment* due to sin (see Numb. xiv. 33; Lev. xix. 8; Isa. liii. 11; Ezek. xviii. 19, 20; xxiii. 35). But it is difficult to determine what are these periods of 390 and 40 years. The Septuagint has 190 years for 390. The 190 is made up of two periods of 150 and 40. "This 150 years is apparently intended to represent the period between the fall of Samaria and the destruction of Jerusalem (722–588 B.C.), while the 40 years are, in round numbers, the years from the fall of Jersualem to the Decree of Cyrus, though the Captivity was generally reckoned to have lasted 70 years which was reckoned from Jehoiakim's reign, 606–536 B.C." (Dr. H. A. Redpath in *Westminster Commentaries*). Dr. Currey, Master of the Charterhouse, says (*Speaker's Commentary*) that "it seems more in accordance with the other *signs*, to suppose that the years represent not that which has been, but that which shall be."

7 set thy face. That is, "turn thine attention."

thine arm shall be uncovered. So as to be unencumbered for action—for the action of the siege.

8 I will lay bands upon thee. A Divine constraint.

10 thy meat (food) **. . . shall be,** etc. The mixture of all sorts of meal in one cake, the small quantity prescribed (giving less than a pound of food a day), the revolting cookery at first ordered, and the stinted allowance of about a pint and a half of water daily, were evidently combined to show the extreme destitution to which God would reduce the luxurious Jews.

15 cow's dung. In many parts of Asia, at the present day, dried animal dung is used as fuel.

CHAPTER V

I take thee a sharp knife, take thee a barber's razor. Rather, as R.V., "Take thee a sharp sword; [as] a barber's razor shalt thou take it."

upon thine head and upon thy beard. A symbol of calamity and mourning.

5 in the midst of the nations. Palestine, at the centre of the ancient world, with Assyria and Chaldea to the east, Syria and Phœnicia to the north, Egypt and Ethiopia to the south, Arabia to the south-east, and the coastlands of "the Gentiles" to the west, occupied a position fitted for the diffusion of holy influences, had Israel been faithful to its calling; and at the same time especially liable to attack when they were weakened by sin.

6 she hath changed My judgements into wickedness. Or. "She hath wickedly rebelled against My judgements." She had sinned against God's commandments.

7 ye multiplied. Rather, as R.V., "ye are turbulent." The same word is used, Psa. ii. 1, "rage."

neither have done according to the judgements of the nations. Who had held to *their* gods, while you have been unfaithful to Jehovah: see Jer. ii. 10, 11.

12 A third part of thee. For this threefold woe, see Jer. xv. 2.

I will draw out a sword after them. The exiles shall continue to feel the severity of the Divine judgements.

13 I will be comforted. That is, I will be *appeased.* The French version has: "je me satisferai" ("I shall be satisfied").

CHAPTER VI

3 Ye mountains of Israel. The mountains and hills are first addressed, probably as being the scenes of idolatry: cp. vers. 3, 4, with 1 Kings xii. 31, etc. So with the "rivers"; rather ravines or wadys, also often polluted by idolatry: see Isa. lvii. 5, 6.

4 I will cast down your slain men before your idols. That all might see what was the sin which had caused the ruin of the people, and how helpless were the gods in whom they had trusted. The "images" are *sun-images* (R.V.).

9 Because I am broken, etc. Rather, "Because I have broken their wanton heart that departeth from Me, and their eyes," etc.: see R.V. marg.

11 Smite with thine hand. Expressing grief and indignation.

14 Diblath. Read "Riblah," on the right bank of the Orontes and north of Damascus.

CHAPTER VII

4 thine abominations shall be in the midst of thee. That is, thy sin shall be brought home to thee.

5 an only evil. "Evil on evil!" (*Moffatt*).

6 watcheth. Or, "awaketh" (R.V.). In the original there is a play upon two very similar Hebrew words signifying "end" and "watch"; and the second introduces the impressive figure of the dawning of a day of trouble.

7 The morning. Rather, "The circle"; *i.e.*, cycle (see Eccles. i. 6); meaning, "Thy turn has come."

the sounding again of the mountains. The joyful shouts with which the hills resounded on festive occasions.

10 The morning. See note on ver. 7.

The rod hath blossomed, etc. The rod *of Judah* has blossomed into proud luxuriance. Judah has become proud and self-willed in her iniquities, and (11) the violence of her enemies has risen into "a [chastising] rod of, or for, [her] wickedness": see Isa. x. 5.

12 Let not the buyer rejoice, nor the seller mourn. He who buys an estate will not enjoy it: he who sells it would soon have lost it otherwise; nor will there be a jubilee of restitution; for the Chaldeans are at hand.

13 Neither shall any strengthen himself in the iniquity of his life. Or, "And none that liveth in iniquity shall prosper."

16 But they that escape of them shall escape. Rather, "And their fugitives have fled, but they are on the mountains," etc. Having spoken of the uselessness of defence, the prophet now depicts the miseries of flight.

19 They shall cast their silver, etc. In the hurry of flight.

because it is the stumblingblock. Their gold and silver had been used to procure their luxuries and their idols.

20 the beauty of his (the people's) **ornament.** The "ornament" was the *gold and silver* just mentioned, which they "used in pride, and made the images and their abominations and detestable things thereof."

22 My secret [place]. The sanctuary, which was not to be entered by any one but the priests, shall be spoiled by invaders.

23 Make a (the) **chain.** An emblem of the approaching captivity.

24 the worst of the heathen. A description of the ruthless Chaldeans.

CHAPTER VIII

1 the elders of Judah sat before me. The posture of reverent attention. Their hostility to the prophet (see ii. 5–8) had now evidently ceased.

3 He put forth, etc. A vision, or figurative language.

the image of jealousy. An idol: see Exod. xx. 5. Skinner (*Ezekiel* in *Expositor's Bible*) thinks it was the *asherah* set up by Manasseh in the Temple (cp. 2 Chron. xxxiii. 7 and 2 Kings xxi. 7).

6 that I should go far off from My sanctuary. Where idols are admitted Jehovah cannot dwell: cp. 2 Cor. xiv. 14–18.

10 behold every form of creeping things, etc. This description applied exactly to the Babylonian and Egyptian temples, the walls of which were covered with representations of gods in the forms of animals and men, and monstrous combinations of both.

11 seventy men of the ancients (elders). Seventy had on more than one occasion been the number chosen to represent the whole people: see Exod. xxiv. 1; Numb. xi. 16.

12 in the chambers of his imagery. That is, in his image-painted chambers: see ver. 10.

14 women weeping for Tammuz. The Babylonian legend and festival of Tammuz resembled those of the Grecian Adonis; whose death was first lamented, and his restoration to life afterwards celebrated with licentious rejoicings. See Milton, *Paradise Lost,* i. 446–457; Budge, *Babylonian Life and History* (1925), pp. 106, 138. These fables represented the diminution and increase of the sun's vital heat in winter and spring.

16 between the porch and the altar. The place where the Jewish priests on special occasions invoked the mercy of Jehovah for the people: see Joel ii. 17.

five and twenty men. The chiefs of the twenty-four classes of priests (1 Chron. xxiv. 4–18), with the high priest at their head.

they worshipped the sun. This sun-worship is expressly mentioned, 2 Kings xxiii. 5, 11.

17 they put the branch to their nose. Referring to the practice of holding before the face a branch of myrtle or some other tree. See J. G. Frazer's *Adonis,* etc., and Moulton's *Early Zoroastrianism,* both quoted by Peake (*Commentary*).

CHAPTER IX

2 by his side. That is, suspended from his girdle, as is still the custom in the East.

3 was gone up. Arising from "between the cherubim"; *i.e.,* from the mercy-seat, to scatter His enemies (Numb. x. 35).

clothed with linen. As a priest. The presence and commission of this messenger of protection shows the care which God takes of His people amidst apparently indiscriminate sufferings.

6 the ancient men. The five and twenty men mentioned, ch. viii. 16.

7 Defile the house. These men had polluted it with their sins; and God had withdrawn from it (3), and left it to be openly defiled with their blood.

CHAPTER X

2 He spake. That is, He that sat on the throne.

the man clothed with linen. The same messenger who lately acted as the minister of God's mercy to His servants being now employed to execute His vengeance upon His enemies.

scatter them over the city. The inhabitants being slain, the city is to be burned.

5 was heard. As they began to move.

13 O wheel. Rather, "A whirling": probably a command to move rapidly, which is obeyed in ver. 19.

19 and [every one] stood. Rather, as R.V., "and they stood": the cherubim halting, as if in suspense, whether God would leave the city: see xi. 22.

20 I knew that they were the cherubim. "In this departure the seer recognises for the first time the full meaning of the vision which he had seen on the banks of the Chebar" (Dr. G. Currey in *Speaker's Commentary*).

CHAPTER XI

1 five and twenty men. Different from the persons mentioned in viii. 16; those being *priests,* these *princes.*

3 [It is] not near; let us build houses. This may be rendered as the saying of the exiles, "The time is not near for us to build houses" in Chaldea, as the prophet directs: see R.V., and Jer. xxix. 5–28. Moffatt, on the other hand, translates it, "Houses have been recently rebuilding; all is well!" Similarly Skinner, following the Septuagint.

this [city] is the caldron, and we be the flesh. "We are safe inside the cauldron." There is perhaps a derisive allusion to the image of Jeremiah (i. 13).

10 in the border of Israel. Literally fulfilled at the frontier-town of Riblah in Hamath (Jer. li. 9, 10). See chap. vi. 14.

11 neither shall ye be the flesh in the midst thereof. Your purpose of remaining in this city shall not be realised.

16 a little sanctuary. Perhaps, "a sanctuary for a little while," as R.V. The Temple might be destroyed, and its worship interrupted; but to His sincere and humble worshippers, even in a heathen land, God would be as a temple: cp. Isa. lxvi. 1, 2.

23 from the midst of the city. Deserting it in displeasure. This withdrawment of the Divine presence was gradual, as if it were reluctant. First, the Divine glory comes forth from the interior of the holy place to its external threshold (x. 4); then it removes to "the door of the east gate" (x. 19); and now it leaves the city altogether.

CHAPTER XII

3 stuff for removing. That is, whatever is necessary for a long journey.

4 thou shalt go forth at even. By secret flight: see 2 Kings xxv. 4. The flight of Zedekiah was thus graphically foretold among the exiles by the Chebar.

6 in the twilight. Rather, "in the dark," as R.V.

13 yet shall he not see it. Zedekiah being blinded by order of Nebuchadrezzar: see 2 Kings xxv. 7, and note.

16 that they may declare all their abominations. *i.e.,* that they may confess what their sins have been.

18 eat thy bread, etc. Another sign; the prophet thus dramatically picturing the fear of the approaching siege.

19 the people of the land. The Jewish exiles in Chaldea.

22 The days are prolonged, and every vision faileth. Time passes on, and these prophecies of evil are not fulfilled.

23 the effect of every vision. That is, the *fulfilment* of every vision.

27 he prophesieth of the times that are far off. The same spirit of unbelief still produces the same false security; and is declared in the New Testament to be one characteristic of "the last times" (Matt. xxiv. 38, 39; 2 Pet. iii. 3–10).

CHAPTER XIII

3 that follow their own spirit, and have seen nothing. The false prophets are described as those who, having received no Divine message, follow their own guesses or inclinations, and utter that which has no reality. The true prophets spake "as they were moved by the Holy Ghost." These false prophets were numerous at this time both in Judæa and in Babylon, and greatly misled the people: see Jer. xxiii.

4 like the foxes in the deserts. These men were only mischievous and destructive.

5 Ye have not gone up, etc. An indignant address to the prophets, who, caring only for themselves, were of no value for the defence of the people. The imagery is that of a besieged city.

6 They have made [others] to hope that they would confirm the word. Or, "they have hoped for the fulfilling of the word." Beginning with deluding others, they have even deceived themselves.

9 neither shall they be written, etc. That is, They shall be cut off from all the privileges of My people. The words are a climax. Not in the congregation, not in the register of genealogies, not even in the land!

10 with untempered [mortar]. Rather, "with whitewash" or stucco. One of these false prophets would rear some unsubstantial fabric of hope; and others would strive to give this fabric an attractive appearance, and to disguise its defects.

17 the daughters of thy people, etc. This is the only Old Testament passage that speaks of false prophetesses.

18 pillows to all armholes. "Amulets on everybody's wrist" (*Moffatt*).

and make kerchiefs upon the head of every stature ("[persons of] every stature," R.V.). Or, "head-veils for every size," *i.e.*, to suit every one's size. These were the superstitious charms, the "mascots" of that time.

Will ye hunt the souls, etc.? Rather, "Shall ye hunt the souls (persons) of My people, and keep your own souls alive?" (see R.V., marg.), *i.e.*, make a living for yourselves by deluding others.

19 to slay the souls that should not die, etc. That is, to corrupt and ruin people who deserve a better fate, and to sustain your own worthless lives. So the Eternal was "polluted," or dishonoured among His people, for these false prophets' paltry fees.

22 ye have made the heart of the righteous sad. Their lies perplexed the good and emboldened the wicked. The R.V. translates the latter part of the verse, "that he shall not return from his wicked way, and be saved alive."

CHAPTER XIV

1 sat before me. See viii. 1, and note.

4 I the Lord will answer him that cometh, etc. Rather, "I Jehovah will answer him according to it, according to the multitude," etc. The emphasis of repetition.

7 and cometh to a prophet to inquire of him, etc. Rather, "and cometh to a prophet to inquire for himself concerning Me, I the Lord will answer him concerning Myself": cp. R.V. The answer follows in ver. 8.

9 I the Lord have deceived that prophet. See note on 1 Kings xxii. 23.

13 the land. Rather, "a land," as R.V.

14 Daniel. At this time Daniel had been at least fourteen years in Babylon, and had held for nearly ten years the high posts to which his gifts had caused him to be elevated: see Dan. i., ii. There was, therefore, ample time for his extraordinary worth to be generally recognised. Noah had been permitted to save his family, Daniel his associates, and Job his friends; but not all of them together could save idolatrous Israel: cp. Jer. vii. 16; xv. 1. It has been well suggested that the mention of a contemporary, together with the saints of older days, would show that neither *past* nor *present* worthies could avail in such a case. (So Calvin.)

22 ye shall be comforted. When you see the wickedness of the remnant whom I will bring into exile, you will be fully satisfied that the punishment which I have inflicted was not too severe.

CHAPTER XV

2 [or than] a branch. Rather, "[even] the vine branch."

4 burned. Rather, "scorched." Is it (the scorched part that remains) fit for any work? The allusion is to the impoverished and reduced state of the covenant-people.

7 they shall go out from [one] fire, and [another] fire shall devour them. Rather, as R.V., "they shall go forth from the fire, but the fire shall devour them." The brand plucked from the burning shall itself be consumed!

CHAPTER XVI

3 an Amorite . . . a Hittite. The Hittites and Amorites were two of the chief Canaanite tribes; and Israel is here connected with them to show how she had manifested the very propensities to evil which had caused their extermination. For the same reason Sodom is called her "sister" (46, 49).

4 supple. Rather, "cleanse," as R.V.

thou wast not salted. Salt was anciently applied to new-born infants; partly, perhaps, to harden the skin.

5 to the loathing of thy person. Rather, "with contempt of thy life."

6 polluted. Better, as R.V., "weltering."

7 whereas thou wast naked and bare. Rather, "and thou (still) wast naked and bare." This part of the description refers to the sojourn of the Israelites in Egypt, when they were greatly increased in numbers, but were much distressed.

8 I spread My skirt over thee. A phrase expressive of entering into the marriage relation (Ruth iii. 9). The reference is to Sinai and to the covenant into which Jehovah then entered with the people.

12 a jewel upon thy forehead. R.V., "a ring upon thy nose": a prized ornament in the East.

15 because of thy renown. Instead of regarding all their privileges as God's unmerited gifts, and using them for His glory, they looked upon them as their own, prided themselves in them, and perverted them into occasions of sin.

24 an eminent place. Or, "a vaulted chamber," as R.V., marg.

26 fornication with the Egyptians. This refers probably as much to political alliances with Egypt as to the adoption of its idolatry; both of which involved the guilt of unfaithfulness to God (Isa. xxxi.).

27 the daughters of the Philistines. Here put for the Philistines. Wicked as they are, they have not apostatised like you: see Jer. ii. 10, 11.

31 thou scornest hire. You persist in your wicked courses, not because there is anything to be gained by them, but from love to the sins themselves.

33 thou givest thy gifts, etc. The conduct of king Ahaz in purchasing aid from Assyria by the gold and silver of the Temple has been cited as an apt illustration of this passage.

37 I will even gather them round about against thee. Your associates in sin shall be the instruments of your punishment.

38 I will give thee blood in fury and jealousy. Or, as R.V., "I will bring upon thee the blood of fury and jealousy."

42 make . . . to rest. *i.e.*, "satisfy." So R.V.

46 thy left hand . . . thy right hand. *i.e.*, looking eastward from the Temple hill.

47 thou wast corrupted more than they. Having sinned against fuller knowledge and greater privileges (see ver. 27).

51 hast justified thy sisters. See Jer. iii. 11, and note.

53 When I shall bring again their captivity. See note on Job xlii. 10. The fulfilment of such predictions is not in the literal restoration of Sodom and Samaria, but in the ingathering of the heathen into the Church. "A divine mercy which embraces in its sweep those communities which had reached the lowest depths of moral corruption" (*Skinner*).

56 was not mentioned by thy mouth. It was not mentioned, as being unworthy of thy notice.

57 of [thy] reproach. Rather, "of *the* reproach" (R.V.); *i.e.*, the disgrace which they inflicted on thee by invading the land.

59 the oath. The oath of fidelity to Me: see Exod. xxiv. 3, 8; Josh. xxiv. 22.

61 thine elder and thy younger. That is, thy elder *ones* and thy younger *ones.* Both the words are plural; referring not to Samaria and Sodom merely, but to the nations in general which shall be admitted into the Church: see Isa. ii. 2–4; liv. 1–3.

not by thy covenant. Not by such alliances as thou hast wickedly formed of old; but according to Jehovah's covenant.

CHAPTER XVII

2 a riddle. See note on Prov. i. 6.

3 a great eagle. Assyria.

Lebanon. An emblem of Jerusalem, as the crowning city of the land.

4 a city of merchants. Babylon; so called on account of its extensive commerce: see Isa. xliii. 14; xlvii. 15.

6 under him. *i.e.*, the king of Babylon; who gave the kingdom of Judah to Zedekiah as his vassal.

7 another great eagle. Egypt.

by the furrows of her plantation. Or, "from the beds where it was planted": cp. R.V.

8 It was planted. *i.e.*, "*And yet* it was planted." The rule of the king of Babylon during the reign of Zedekiah appears not to have been oppressive, but rather mild and liberal; notwithstanding which, Zedekiah was continually intriguing with Egypt.

9 all the leaves of her spring. Rather, as R.V., "all its fresh springing leaves."

17 by casting up mounts. Rather, "When they (*i.e.*, the enemy, the Assyrians) shall cast up mounts," etc.

19 Mine oath that he hath despised. Zedekiah had sworn allegiance to Nebuchadrezzar in the name of the Lord: see 2 Chron. xxxvi. 13.

22 I will also take, etc. The Eternal Himself interposes. Earthly powers had hitherto carried out His purposes regarding Israel. Now He appears to plant the Tree which shall cover the earth with its shade.

CHAPTER XVIII

3 ye shall not have [occasion] any more, etc. This does not indicate any change in God's government, but only that He will make it clear that every individual is held responsible for his own conduct.

4 the soul of the son is Mine. Although children are often implicated in the temporal consequences of the sins of their parents, no one will be condemned hereafter for any but his own sins. Skinner rightly calls attention to the distinction between national and individual retribution.

6 hath not eaten, etc. At idol feasts.

8 usury. Interest of money. "Increase," payment for the loan of goods. The Israelites, as brethren, were to help one another without expectation of gain; but they might take usury of foreigners: see Lev. xxv. 36; Deut. xxiii. 19, 20. "The placing out of capital at interest for commercial purposes is not taken into consideration at all. The case is that of money lent to a brother in distress, in which no advantage is to be taken, nor profit required" (*Currey* in *Speaker's Commentary*).

16 hath not withholden the pledge. Rather, as R.V., "hath not taken aught to pledge."

19 Why? doth not the son, etc. Punctuate, "Why doth not the son bear the iniquity of the father?" see R.V.

24 All his righteousness that he hath done shall not be mentioned. Rather, as R.V., "None of his righteous deeds (righteousnesses) that he hath done shall be remembered." It is wrong, therefore, to found any judgement as to our character before God on our past experiences, when these are not in harmony with our present conduct.

31 make you a new heart and a new spirit. Although it is God who works in us to will and to do what is good, and is the first mover in our regeneration; we must yet work together with Him, not resisting the influences of His Spirit, nor receiving His grace in vain.

CHAPTER XIX

1 Israel. The whole nation.

2 A lioness. The lion was the ensign of Judah: see Gen. xlix. 9.

3 one of her whelps. Jehoahaz; see 2 Kings xxiii. 33. His tyranny is described in the words, "it devoured men."

4 he was taken in their pit. An image taken from lion-hunting. "Chains": lit., *nose-rings*, keeps up the figure.

5 another of her whelps. *i.e.*, Jehoiachin: see 2 Kings xxiv. 6. He succeeded regularly to the throne, Jehoiakim, his predecessor, having been appointed by the king of Babylon, and being counted therefore as a usurper, during whose reign the people "waited."

6 he went up and down among the lions. Acting like the kings of heathen nations.

9 they brought him into holds. At the date of this prophecy, Jehoiachin was still a prisoner in Babylon.

10 Thy mother. *i.e.*, Jerusalem. The words are addressed to Jehoiachin. "In thy blood," *i.e.*, in this family, the city was fruitful, like a far-spreading vine.

11 among the thick branches. Rather, as R.V. marg., "among the clouds."

CHAPTER XX

1 the seventh year. *i.e.*, in the seventh year of Jehoiachin's captivity.

the elders of Israel. See note, xiv. 1.

4 Wilt thou judge them? This is a command rather than a question. Or it may be read, with the Septuagint and Vulgate, "If thou wilt judge them, then cause them to know," etc.

5 lifted up Mine hand. An act accompanying an oath or solemn pledge.

8 neither did they forsake the idols of Egypt. This passage is important, as showing that the Israelites in Egypt fell in some measure under the temptations of the country's idolatry. It may also be inferred from such incidents as the worship of the golden calf.

9 I wrought. *i.e.*, I interposed on their behalf.

for My name's sake. To vindicate My character and power, as the One God: cp. Exod. xxxii. 12.

12 a sign. The Sabbath, and the other appointed rests (see Lev. xxv. 1–16), were both a sign of their special relation to God, and an important means of preserving it.

13 My Sabbaths they greatly polluted ("profaned," R.V.). Indicating a disregard of the Sabbath, greater than shown in the incidents of Exod. xvi. 27; Numb. xv. 32.

25 statutes that were good. As the people rebelled against these "life-giving" statutes (13), God gave them up in punishment to the death-dealing observances of idolatry: cp. Psa. lxxxi. 12; Rom. i. 24.

28 when I had brought them into the land. The sins of a *third* generation are now brought to mind.

29 Bamah. Lit., "What go they to?" *i.e.*, high place. The meaning is, Notwithstanding my remonstrance, the place is notorious for idolatrous practices unto this day. The original suggests a contemptuous play upon words.

30 Are ye polluted, etc.? The prophet now passes from "the fathers" to his own contemporaries, whose representatives are now seated before him.

32 that which cometh into your mind. Viz., amalgamation with the Babylonian people. This was an impossible fancy. Never could they escape from their responsibility as a nation.

35 the wilderness of the people (peoples). Into some dreary and distressful place of the Gentile world, which should be to the Jews of that time what the wilderness had been to their fathers on their departure from Egypt: see Hos. ii. 14, and note. Their wish to be incorporated with the heathen (see 32) should not be gratified; but God, in His providence, would rather insulate them, and discipline them for their good.

37 to pass under the rod. The shepherd's staff (see Lev. xxvii. 32, and cp. Jer. xxxiii. 13; Micah vii. 14); *i.e.*, I will treat you as My flock.

39 serve ye every one his idols. *i.e.*, "Renounce me or renounce your idols." God abhors half-heartedness and indecision in religion: cp. Josh. xxiv. 20; 1 Kings xviii. 21; Rev. iii. 16.

VER. 45–XXI. 27. The twentieth chapter ends in the Hebrew Bible with ver. 44; a better arrangement than that of the English versions, as the remaining verses of the chapter belong to what follows.

46 set thy face toward the south. Ezekiel was in the northern part of Chaldea, and therefore Judæa lay to the south.

the forest. The land is so described as to prepare the way for the emblem of the devouring fire.

47 every green tree in thee, and every dry tree. This fearful visitation will involve the better part of the people as well as the worst.

from the south to the north. From one end of the land to the other.

49 Doth he not speak parables? *i.e.*, "Doth he not speak unintelligibly?" Therefore, the same message is delivered plainly in the words which follow (xxi. 1–5).

CHAPTER XXI

3 My sword. Nebuchadrezzar and his army, the instrument of God's judgement.

6 with the breaking of thy loins. The loins were regarded as the seat of strength (Job xl. 16), and the expression indicates the prostration due to intense grief.

10 It contemneth the rod of My son. According to the rendering in the text, the clause means that the sword shall not spare even royalty ("the sceptre") more than others. Cp. ver. 13.

13 Because [it is] a trial, etc. "For it is a trial, and what if the contemning sceptre shall be no more?" The sword did, in fact, humble the royalty of Judah.

14 smite thine hands together. A sign of indignation.

let the sword be doubled the third time. Let the stroke be repeated twice and thrice; *i.e.*, often (see Job xxxiii. 29).

It is the sword of the great [men], etc. "It is the sword of the great one pierced through, the sword of the great one pierced through; it encompasseth them": see R.V. marg. The "great one" is probably the royal house, now to be smitten; hence the plural in the second clause.

16 Go thee one way or other. Rather, "Unite thyself (*i.e.*, concentrate thy powers) on the right hand, turn to the left, whithersoever thine edge is appointed." The words are addressed to the sword.

17 I will cause My fury to rest. *i.e.*, by satisfying it, by inflicting severe punishment.

19 both twain shall come, etc. *i.e.*, both ways or roads shall proceed from the same point. This the prophet exhibits in some graphic portrayal, as he had depicted the siege of Jerusalem on a tile, or brick, iv. 1.

choose thou a place. Rather, "make a hand," *i.e.*, a finger-post, pointing to Rabbath and Jerusalem.

20 Jerusalem the defenced. Jerusalem is so called because the people of Judah confided in its natural strength and its fortifications.

21 the king of Babylon stood at the parting of the way. The prophet was to represent in his sketch the position of Nebuchadrezzar looking down the two roads from the point where they met. Shall he march upon Jerusalem to the right, or upon Rabbath to the left? He resorts to auguries to decide his course.

he made [his] arrows bright. Rather, "He shook the arrows to and fro" (R.V.). Jerome tells us that the Chaldeans, before a warlike expedition, marked several arrows with the names of the cities which they intended to assault, put them together in a quiver, shook them and drew them out, as lots are drawn. They then marched against the city whose arrow was first drawn, believing that their gods had directed them to destroy it.

images. Lit., "the teraphim," R.V.

he looked in the liver. A mode of divination familiar to the Greeks and Romans, as well as to the Orientals. The liver of the animal sacrificed was the first part inspected; and if this presented very unfavourable signs, no further observations were made.

22 to open the mouth in the slaughter. *i.e.*, to raise the war-cry of death.

battering rams. These instruments of war are represented in many of the sculptures discovered at Nineveh. They are often placed on inclined planes of stone.

23 unto them. *i.e.*, to the Jews. They shall despise as vain the auguries of the Assyrians.

to them that have sworn oaths. *i.e.*, who have sworn oaths of submission to the Assyrians (see xvii. 13 and 2 Chron. xxxvi. 13). These oaths are referred to in the next clause: "But he (Nebuchadrezzar) will call to mind the iniquity (*i.e.*, treachery which the Jews have practised), that they may be taken."

24 ye shall be taken with the hand. *i.e.*, with the well-known hand or power of Nebuchadrezzar.

25 And thou, profane wicked prince of Israel. Or, "And thou, O pierced, wicked prince of Israel." See R.V. Moffatt translates, "O prince of Israel to be slain."

when iniquity [shall have] an end. *i.e.*, "when [thine] iniquity shall have its appropriate *issue*"; its appropriate recompense or retribution: see xxxv. 5.

26 the diadem. Rather, "turban"; or, "mitre" (R.V.); the head-dress of the high priest: see Exod. xxviii. 36–38.

this [shall] not [be] the same. Lit., "This shall not be thus"; *i.e.*, the glory of priest and king shall cease.

him that is low, etc. Or, as R.V., "that which is low," etc. Cp. the words of the *Magnificat*, Luke i. 52.

27 whose right it is. The nation shall be unsettled, until the appearing of Him to whom the dominion ("the crown," ver. 26) belongs. Thus the prophecy against Jerusalem and its wicked king Zedekiah ends with a declaration of the Messianic hope.

28 the Ammonites. Although the divining lot had determined Nebuchadrezzar to proceed first against Jerusalem (see 22), the turn of the Ammonites would also come.

their reproach. *i.e.*, the reproach which the Ammonites cast upon the Jews in their distress: see xxv. 3, 6; Zeph. ii. 8.

to consume because of the glittering. Rather, "to consume, to flash" (as lightning); see 10.

29 Whiles they divine a lie unto thee. *i.e.*, "while they utter false prophecies *for* thee," *i.e.*, to buoy up thy hopes.

To bring thee upon the necks. *i.e.*, "To add thee to the number of those who are already slain in Judæa (see 14), and to make thy condition like theirs."

30 Shall I cause it to return into his [its] sheath. Or, as some render, "Return it (*i.e.*, the sword) into its sheath"; *i.e.*, make no resistance, for it will be of no avail: cp. R.V.

CHAPTER XXII

2 wilt thou judge. See note on xx. 4.

4 and art come even unto thy years. *i.e.*, to the years appointed for thy punishment.

5 [which art] infamous [and] much vexed. Or, "as infamous and full of confusion." Even the heathen round about the Jews would insult them under their troubles.

6 to their power. *i.e.*, every one employed his power in violence and bloodshed.

7 In thee. These charges refer to the various specific precepts which the people had violated; and they are made the more emphatic by the fact that the sins were committed *in Jerusalem*, the city which God had chosen for His residence, and had favoured with His ordinances and oracles.

9 they eat upon the mountains. They hold idolatrous feasts: see xviii. 6.

12 usury and increase. See note, xviii. 13.

13 I have smitten My hand. *i.e.*, with grief and indignation: cp. xxi. 17.

16 thou shalt take thine inheritance, etc. Rather, as R.V., "Thou shalt be profaned in thyself, in the sight of the nations."

18 they are [even] the dross of silver. They are not only alloyed with baser metals, but their very silver is turned to dross: see Isa. i. 22.

19 I will gather you. As into a furnace, to consume you: see ver. 20. Jerusalem was the centre of the great trying process.

28 daubed them with. Rather, as R.V., "daubed for them."

untempered [mortar]. See note on xiii. 10.

30 and stand in the gap. Like Moses, Psa. cvi. 23.

CHAPTER XXIII

3 in Egypt. The Israelites had been greatly contaminated with idolatry in Egypt: see note, xx. 8.

4 Aholah . . . . . Aholibah. "Oholah," "Oholibah" (R.V.). *Oholah* means, "her own tent," or "tabernacle"; *Oholibah*, "my tabernacle [is] in her." Recent scholarship, however, regards the words as practically identical (*Oxford Hebrew Lexicon*; Gray's *Hebrew Proper Names*; J. A. Selbie in *Hastings' Dict. of Bible*, and Skinner, *Expositor's Bible*). Samaria (or the kingdom of the Ten Tribes) openly deserted the sanctuary of Jehovah, which was in Jerusalem, and set up "her own tabernacle" for the worship of the golden calf. "The key to all the realistic language of the chapter is to be found in the last words of ver. 7, 'with all their idols she defiled herself,'" (Dr. H. A. Redpath in *Westminster Commentaries*).

5 on the Assyrians [her] neighbours. Or, "on the Assyrians drawing near to her." This alliance was first the disgrace and then the ruin of the Ten Tribes.

6 riding upon horses. The employment of cavalry was a main distinction between the Assyrian and the Israelite armies.

10 famous. Rather, "notorious"; *i.e.*, infamous. "She became a byword among women," R.V.

11 she was more corrupt. *i.e.,* in the days of Manasseh (2 Kings xxi. 1–16).

12 She doted upon the Assyrians [her] neighbours. As in the friendly intercourse between Ahaz and Tiglath-pileser (2 Kings xvi.).

14 men pourtrayed upon the wall. Either *deified men,* such as most of the gods of the nations were—in other words, Babylonian gods painted in human form; or *Babylonian princes,* with whom the Jews were led to form alliances, and by whom they were allured to idolatry: see viii. 10.

pourtrayed with vermilion. At Khorsabad, among other sculptures, there are figures in a sacerdotal dress, supposed to be diviners or magicians, which have more of the vermilion and of the black pigment in their hair than any others on the walls (15). See Bonomi's *Nineveh and its Palaces,* p. 206.

15 girded with girdles. The Assyrians generally wore flowing robes, mantles of various shapes, long fringed scarfs, and embroidered girdles.

16 sent messengers unto them. There was alliance and friendly intercourse between Chaldea and the kings of Judah (2 Kings xx. 12; xxiv. 1).

17 alienated. *i.e.,* through satiety, and the wish to have other lovers in their room.

23 Pekod, and Shoa, and Koa. Most translators regard these words as proper names, of Babylon itself or of some of its provinces. But others, with the Vulgate, render them, "powerful, and rich, and noble." (For *Pekod,* see Jer. l. 21.)

24 with chariots, wagons, and wheels. Perhaps, "with weapons, chariots, and wagons," as R.V.

25 thy nose and thine ears. In Egypt the noses of adulterers were cut off; and in Babylonia both their ears and noses.

34 break. Rather, "gnaw" (R.V.), or "scrape"; *i.e.,* thou shalt completely exhaust the "cup."

pluck off. Or, "tear," R.V.

35 thy lewdness and thy whoredoms. *i.e.,* the consequences of these sins.

36 wilt thou judge Aholah, etc.? See note on xx. 4.

39 the same day into My sanctuary. The treating of the Eternal as one of the deities of polytheism was in the worst spirit of idolatry.

40 that ye have sent for men, etc. They not merely yielded to temptation, but courted it. The imagery here is that of a stately and voluptuous feast. The "bed" is the divan or couch on which the feasters reclined.

42 Sabeans. Mentioned in Isa. xlv. 14 in connexion with Ethiopia. The rendering of R.V. and Moffatt, though supported by the Septuagint, "drunkards," is not generally accepted.

45 the righteous men. The nations whom God would employ as the instruments of His righteous purposes.

46 to be removed. Rather, as R.V., "to be tossed to and fro."

CHAPTER XXIV

This chapter is dated on the very day on which Nebuchad**rezzar** began his last siege of Jerusalem (cp. ver. 1 with 2 Kings xxv. 1; Jer. xxxix. 1; lii. 4), and announces that important event (2).

1 the tenth month, etc. This day was afterwards annually observed as a solemn fast (Zech. viii. 19).

3 a pot. "The caldron" (R.V.), a reference to xi. 3.

5 burn also the bones under it. All classes of the people must be involved in the calamity.

6 scum. Or, "rust" (R.V.); or "verdigris"; *i.e.,* wickedness. Verdigris is *poison.* The complaint is, that former judgements have not in any degree purified the city.

let no lot fall upon it. *i.e.,* Let all the inhabitants, without distinction of age or station, be the prey of the enemy. The lot was frequently used on the capture of a city, to determine which of the inhabitants should be slain, and which should be spared: see 2 Sam. viii. 2.

7 she set it upon the top of a rock. Instead of attempting to conceal her iniquities, she had sinned without shame, pouring the blood upon a "bare rock" (R.V.), where it could not be absorbed or hidden; therefore her punishment shall be public (8).

10 spice it well. "Pour out the broth" (*Moffatt*).

12 She hath wearied [herself] with lies. Rather, "It (*i.e.,* the caldron) hath wearied [me] with labours"; *i.e.,* with endeavours to cleanse it. The poisonous rust can be removed only by the destruction of the caldron (the city) itself.

16 I take away from thee the desire of thine eyes. The servant of God is called upon, in the very day of the preceding message, to suffer a sorrowful bereavement without showing any outward token of grief. This was to be a sign to the people of the calamities which were coming upon them, so great that they would have no time or desire to lament for the dead. See on ver. 17.

17 the tire of thine head. *i.e.,* the turban, or head-dress. The usual tokens of grief were loud outcries, the removal of the usual head-dress and sandals, whilst the mouth and beard, and sometimes the head, were wrapped in the mantle. To these, on occasion of death, was added the funeral feast: see Jer. xvi. 7; Hos. ix. 4.

27 and be no more dumb. During the siege of Jerusalem the prophet was to await in silence the fulfilment of his last terrible predictions. When they were fulfilled, he would have new messages to deliver to the smitten and humbled remnant. The next prophecy of Ezekial to the Jews was three years later (xxxiii. 21).

CHAPTER XXV

Whilst Ezekiel awaits the fulfilment of his last threatenings against the Jews, he is directed to predict the punishment of their heathen neighbours, who had been the instigators and accomplices of their sins. Four of these, the Ammonites, Moabites, Edomites and Philistines, are marked out in this chapter as the objects of Divine vengeance, on account of their inhuman triumph over the fall of Israel: cp. Amos i.

2 the Ammonites. From 2 Kings xxiv. 2 it appears that the Ammonites and Moabites had joined with Nebuchadrezzar in his attack upon Judah.

4 the men of the east. The Arab tribes of the desert lying between Palestine and the Persian Gulf: see Judges vi. 3; Jer. xlix. 28.

their places. Rather, as R.V., "their encampments."

7 from the people. "From the peoples"; the "heathen" should rather be "nations," R.V.

8 like unto all the heathen. *i.e.,* We see no difference between Israel and other nations; their God has no more power to preserve them than the gods of their neighbours have.

9 I will open the side of Moab. *i.e.,* I will cause his borders to be invaded.

10 that the Ammonites may not be remembered. The Ammonites and Moabites have long lost their national existence, and would hardly have been known but for the Scripture record of their crimes and doom.

13 I will also stretch out Mine hand upon Edom. The sin charged against Edom is that of long-cherished, implacable hatred against Israel. How this was shown may be gathered from Psa. cxxxvii. 7. The subject is resumed in xxxv.; see also Isa. xxxiv., Obadiah, and notes.

and they of Dedan, etc. "From Teman even unto Dedan shall they fall by the sword." *i.e.*, from one extremity of Edom to another.

15 for the old hatred. This hatred dated back from the time when the Philistines began to oppress the Israelites in the days of the Judges: see Judges x. 7; xiii. 1.

16 the Philistines. As Philistia lay on the direct route from Egypt to Chaldea, it suffered exceedingly in the wars between the two rival powers; and before the Christian era it had ceased to be the residence of an independent people. Gaza alone has retained any importance.

the Cherethim. A name or a tribe of the Philistines: see 1 Sam. xxx. 14; 2 Sam. viii. 18. The Septuagint calls them Cretans. Their Hebrew name is from the verb "to slay," so that the words here mean: "I will slay the slayers."

CHAPTER XXVI

Chapters xxvi.–xxviii. form a connected series of prophecies against Tyre and Zidon, divided into five parts.

1 the eleventh year. It is remarkable that this was the year in which Jerusalem was taken. The month is not mentioned; but it was probably the fifth—the month immediately following that of the fall of Jerusalem (Jer. lii. 6–12). Tyre has scarcely uttered its proud taunts against Zion, when Jehovah, by the mouth of His prophet, announced its own doom.

2 [that was] the gates of the people. Rather, as R.V., "the gate of the peoples." Referring to the great confluence of people from all parts to Jerusalem, not only for worship, but for trade.

she is turned unto Me. Her commerce and wealth will now be transferred to Me.

3 many nations. The Babylonians under Nebuchadrezzar, the Macedonians under Alexander, the Crusaders, and the Saracens.

4 and make her [like] the top of a rock. "And make her a bare rock," R.V. Her destruction shall be complete.

5 a spoil to the nations. See note on Isa. xxiii. 1. When Ezekiel uttered these predictions, Tyre had attained the highest prosperity, as head of the Phœnician cities and colonies. Skinner (*Ezekiel*) has a fine passage on the greatness and the extensive commerce of Tyre, and quotes in illustration Matthew Arnold's *The Scholar Gipsy*. The island-town had successfully resisted a siege of five years by Shalmaneser, king of Assyria; and it is doubtful whether Nebuchadrezzar succeeded in taking that part of the city after besieging it for thirteen years. He, however, destroyed the other part, and reduced the whole to dependence; and thus gave the first blow to its power. Alexander captured it, 332 B.C., by constructing a mole from the mainland. This has, during a long series of ages, aided the accumulation of sand; so that the port is now almost useless; whilst the rocky island is literally (as Dr. Robinson found) a "place for the spreading of nets"; and a little town of miserable hovels marks the site of ancient Tyre.

These prophecies and the subsequent story of Tyre are a perpetual warning to the individual and the nation against a success that is purely material. "The commercial spirit is indeed but one of the forms in which men devote themselves to the service of this present world; but in any community where it reigns supreme we may confidently look for the same signs of religious decay which Ezekiel detected in Tyre in his day" (*Skinner*).

6 her daughters which are in the field. That is, the dependent towns on the mainland.

9 engines of war. R.V., "his battering engines."

11 thy strong garrisons. Or, "pillars of thy strength" (R.V.). The Hebrew word is commonly used for consecrated pillars. Herodotus (ii. 24) mentions two pillars, one of emerald, the other of gold, in the temple of Hercules at Tyre.

12 and they shall lay thy stones, etc. This was done when Alexander used the materials of the town on the mainland to make a mole for approaching the island.

20 I shall set thy glory in the land of the living. The Septuagint, whose reading Moffatt here follows, has, "thou shalt exist no more in the land of the living." This seems the more intelligible rendering.

CHAPTER XXVII

The second part of this prophecy is a lamentation over Tyre; describing her beauty and resources. The full and lively picture here drawn of Tyre's wealth and glory in the prophet's time illustrates the Divine foreknowledge, as well as the Divine power, in making her what she has become. This chapter is deeply interesting also, as being the most extended account which we possess of the commerce of the world at that early date. Skinner says that from a literary point of view this and the 28th are amongst the most beautiful chapters in the whole book.

3 the entry of the sea. Heb., "the entrances of the sea," probably referring to the two ports of the island.

5 Senir. Or, "Shenir"; a name of Hermon: see note on Deut. iii. 8, 9.

6 The company of the Ashurites have made thy benches of ivory. Rather, "They have made thy planking of ivory, inlaid in box from the isles of Chittim" (Cyprus): cp. R.V., and marg.: see note on Numb. xxiv. 24.

Elishah. "Elishah" probably means the coastlands and islands of Greece (Hellas). In these was found the shell-fish murex, from which purple dye is obtained.

that which covered thee. *i.e.*, "thine awnings."

8 Arvad. An island on the northern part of the Phœnician coast, now *Ruad*: see Gen. x. 18.

9 Gebal. Called by the Greeks, Byblos, and now *Jebeil*: see note on 1 Kings v. 18.

to occupy. Rather, "to deal in."

10 They of Persia, etc. An enumeration of the mercenary troops engaged by Tyre. "Lud," a tribe of Egypt: see Isa. lxvi. 19, note. "Phut," the Libyans: see Jer. xlvi. 9, note.

they set forth thy comeliness. That is, "they contributed to thy glory." After the destruction of Tyre as an independent power by Nebuchadrezzar, she contributed her quota of ships and men to the service of Persia (Herod. vii. 89; Arrian, ii. 15).

13 Javan, Tubal, and Meshech. "Javan" signifies probably the Ionian Greeks of the western coasts of Asia Minor; "Tubal," the Tibareni, on the north coast of Pontus; "Meshech," the Moschi in the Caucasus and the shores of the Black Sea. The two latter names seem to survive in *Tobolsk* and *Muscovy*.

14 Togarmah. Armenia: cp. Gen. x. 2, note.

15 Dedan. See note on Isa. xxi. 13.

for a present. Rather, "for a price"; *i.e.*, in exchange (R.V.).

horns of ivory. Elephants' tusks.

16 Syria. Some manuscripts and versions read "Edom," which suits the arrangement better. The difference in the Hebrew letters is that between ר and ד.

emeralds. Probably "carbuncles" (R.V. marg.). "Agate," rather, rubies (R.V.).

17 Minnith. A place belonging to the Ammonites: see Judges xi. 33.

pannag. Perhaps, "cake" (see R.V.). Fürst, however, in his *Heb. Lexikon* thinks Pannag is the name of a place.

18 Helbon. Probably Chalybon, north-west of Damascus, now Helbûn, which produced the favourite wine of the Persian kings.

19 Dan also. Heb., "Vedan," probably the name of a tribe. "Javan" usually denotes the Greeks; and the word rendered "going to and fro," rather means "from Uzal." Read, "Vedan and Javan," Arab and Greek merchants, "traded from Uzal in thy markets," or, "for thy wares." Uzal is the modern *Senea*, capital of Yemen in Arabia.

21 the princes of Kedar. See note on Isa. xxi. 17.

22 Sheba and Raamah. Cushite nations mentioned in Gen. x. 7.

23 Canneh. Probably the same as Calneh or Calno, since *Ctesiphon*, on the Tigris. These three places were in Mesopotamia: see Isa. x. 9; xxxvii. 12. "Sheba" in this verse is probably the Shemite Sheba of Gen. x. 28. "Chilmad" is unknown.

25 The ships of Tarshish did sing of thee. Rather, as R.V., "The ships of Tarshish were thy caravans for thy merchandise." The Vulgate has, "naves maris, principes tui in negotiatione tua," "the ships of the sea, your leaders in your business." A different reading of the Hebrew gives "ministered unto thee" (*Redpath*).

26 the east wind hath broken thee. Cp. Psa. xlviii. 7; Jer. xviii. 17.

27 occupiers. Or, "exchangers," or "traders." Cp. "Occupy till I come" (Luke xix. 13).

28 The suburbs. The surrounding seas and coasts.

34 In the time [when] thou shalt be broken. Or, "now that thou art broken."

CHAPTER XXVIII

2 the prince of Tyrus. This king was Ithobal (or Ethbaal) II. The first king of that name was the father of Jezebel (1 Kings xvi. 31).

in the seat of God. In a place divinely beautiful: cp. ver. 13.

3 wiser than Daniel. See xiv. 14, and note.

9 thou [shalt be] a man. Better, "thou art man," as R.V.

10 Thou shalt die the deaths of the uncircumcised. In the lips of a Jew this was a term of contempt (see Exod. vi. 12, and note; 1 Sam. xvii. 36).

12 Thou sealest up the sum. That is, Thou exhibitest human nature in its complete perfection: and, like a perfect and unfallen man, thou dwellest in Eden (13). The proud monarch of Tyre is ironically represented as a kind of model man—his own idea of himself.

13 Every precious stone was thy covering. Oriental monarchs were accustomed to adorn themselves heavily with jewellery.

14 the anointed cherub that covereth. The king of Tyre is compared to the cherubim which covered the ark, being set there by God's command (Exod. xxv. 20); "anointed" as kings were, as if he were exalted by God Himself to the highest dignity.

thou wast upon the holy mountain of God. Like the cherubim in the holy place upon the Temple hill.

in the midst of the stones of fire. Perhaps the fire of God's justice (cp. ver. 16 and Exod. xix. 18).

16 I will cast thee as profane. The king is here identified with the city, in which wealth had led to oppression and cruelty.

17 Thou hast corrupted thy wisdom by reason of thy brightness. Thy prosperity made thee proud and infatuated.

VERS. 20–26. The prophet denounces punishment upon Zidon, the mother-city of Tyre; reverting again to the injuries she had inflicted on Israel, to whom deliverance, restoration, and peace are promised.

22 I will be glorified. By revealing My power and justice.

24 there shall be no more a pricking brier. Alluding to the language of Moses in Numb. xxxiii. 55.

CHAPTER XXIX

The series of prophecies against Egypt comprises six several predictions delivered at different times, extending over a period of seventeen years. In ch. xxix., God threatens Pharaoh for his self-sufficient pride, with destruction to himself, and all the horrors of a desolating war through his country (2–12); yet a promise is given of some relief after forty years, though the kingdom shall then be enfeebled and debased (13–16). The prophecy was in part fulfilled by the revolt against Hophra, who was dethroned and put to death (see Jer. xliv. 30), and by the subsequent civil war, which led to the invasion of Nebuchadrezzar, who overran the country.

3 The great dragon. See note on Psa. lxxiv. 13.

in the midst of his rivers. The Nile, with its numerous channels.

7 and madest all their loins to be at a stand. Or, "and madest all their loins to shake."

10 From the tower of Syene, etc. Or, "from Migdol even to Syene, even to the border of Ethiopia"; the former being at the northern, the latter at the southern boundary of Egypt: see R.V. marg.

11 forty years. Some regard "forty years" as a symbolic number for a period of chastisement and affliction.

12 I will scatter the Egyptians. According to Josephus (*Ant.* x. 9, § 7; *Cont. Apion.* i. 19), Nebuchadrezzar slew the king of Egypt (Pharaoh-Hophra), and carried many of his subjects to Babylon. Others would find refuge in Lybia, Ethiopia, and other regions.

14 Pathros. Upper Egypt.

habitation. Rather "birth," as R.V.

a base kingdom. Reduced to vassalage.

16 And it shall be no more the confidence. Or, "And they shall no more be to the house of Israel for a confidence, bringing to mind [their] iniquity in their turning after them (the Egyptians)," etc. Egypt, once so powerful, shall be so weak that the Israelites shall no more look to it for assistance.

VER. 17–XXX. 19. This prophecy, although standing second in order, is the latest in date of the series, being more than sixteen years after the preceding section. It announces Nebuchadrezzar's renewed invasion of Egypt (see Sayce: *Primer of Assyriology*, 1925, p. 72); and it adds a promise of Israel's restoration (17–21). It then more fully describes the fear and desolation caused by the Chaldean invasion through all the cities of Egypt, and even in Ethiopia (xxx. 1–19).

18 every head was made bald. This description shows the severity as well as the length of the service. The "bald" heads and the "peeled" shoulders describe the result of much carrying of burdens (*Oxford Heb. Lex.*). It is believed that Nebuchadrezzar began the mole which Alexander afterwards completed (see note on xxvi. 12). The siege of Tyre lasted for thirteen years: see xxvi. 5.

yet had he no wages, nor his army. Or, "There were not wages to him and his army from Tyre," etc. The words do not imply complete failure, but only that the booty was not proportioned to the time and labour expended. Jerome says that Nebuchadrezzar took Tyre, but found that the inhabitants had fled with all their wealth.

21 I will give thee the opening of the mouth. See note on xxiv. 27.

CHAPTER XXX

2 Woe worth the day! "Woe be to the day!" ("worth"=German *werden*). Cp. Scott, *Lady of the Lake*, i. 9.

3 the time of the heathen. The time of God's judgements against idolatrous nations.

5 Ethiopia, and Libya, and Lydia. Heb., "Cush, and Put, and Lud."

Chub. Recent scholars, following the Septuagint, read "Lub" or Libya.

6 from the tower of Syene. Rather, "from Migdol to Syene": see on xxix. 10.

9 the careless Ethiopians. The Ethiopians on the Upper Nile thought themselves secure from danger.

12 the rivers. *i.e.*, the canals, on which Egypt depended for its irrigation.

of the wicked. That is, "of cruel," or destructive men," as in v. 16, 17: see Isa. xix. 4. This epithet has been justly applicable to the successive conquerors and oppressors of Egypt through all subsequent ages, Chaldeans, Medo-Persians, Greeks, Romans, Mamelukes.

13 Noph. Memphis. See note on Isa. xix. 13.

no more a prince, etc. That is, no *native* ruler.

14 No. Thebes. See notes on Psa. lxxviii. 12 and Jer. xlvi. 25.

15 Sin, the strength of Egypt. Sin, or Pelusium, is called the "strength," or in other writers the "key" of Egypt, because of its position and fortification as a frontier-town.

17 Pi-beseth. Aven or On (now Heliopolis; see note on Gen. xli. 45), Pi-beseth or Bubastis, and Tehaphnelles or Tahpanhes (see note on Jer. ii. 16), all lay in Lower Egypt between Pelusium and Memphis.

18 the yokes of Egypt. The yokes imposed by her.

VERS. 20–26. This short prophecy declares that the reverses which the Egyptians have suffered (perhaps in their unsuccessful attempt to relieve Jerusalem, 2 Kings xxiv. 7; Jer. xxxvii. 7, 8) are only the beginning of the destruction of their power by the Chaldeans. The prophecy was uttered between three and four months before the fall of Jerusalem.

21 I have broken the arm, etc. One "arm" had been "broken" at Carchemish. The other was now to be shattered.

roller. Or, "bandage."

23 I will scatter the Egyptians, etc. (also in ver. 26). See xxix. 12, note.

CHAPTER XXXI

In this chapter a threatening is addressed to Pharaoh. The reference to Assyria is a doubtful reading, and all the subsequent references appear to apply to Egypt.

3 with a shadowing shroud. Or, "and an overshadowing thicket."

among the thick boughs. Or, "among the clouds" (R.V., marg.): see on xix. 11.

4 The waters made him great, etc. Read, as in R.V., "The waters nourished him, the deep made him to grow; her rivers ran round about her plantation; and she sent out her channels unto all the trees of the field."

8 the garden of God. See xxviii. 13.

chestnut. Rather, "plane-trees," R.V.

11 the mighty one of the heathen. Or, "a mighty one of the nations" (*i.e.*, the king of Babylon, now rising into power).

15 I covered the deep for him. As a mourner wears a covering of sackcloth.

16 shall be comforted. Rather, "*are* comforted." The conquered nations are consoled by finding that a kingdom once so mighty has become like themselves: cp. Isa. xiv. 10.

CHAPTER XXXII

This chapter contains two prophetic songs of lamentation over the king and people of Egypt; uttered probably at an interval of a fortnight from each other, and more than a year after the fall of Jerusalem.

2 a whale. A "dragon," R.V., or "crocodile."

5 with thy height. Or, "with thy hugeness."

7 I will cover the heaven. That is, as with funereal garments: see note on xxxi. 15.

14 Then will I make their waters deep. Rather, "make their waters *to subside*"; *i.e.*, to become clear and calm. Egypt shall no more be able to disturb the tranquillity of neighbouring states.

VERS. 17–32. In this second prophetic lamentation, the Egyptian monarch is represented as being taken to the mouth of a vast pit opened for the carcases of the slain; is told to contemplate the dishonoured burial of other mighty princes and people conquered by Nebuchadrezzar; and is assured that his doom will be the same as theirs. "One of the most weird passages in literature" (*A. B. Davidson*).

17 the twelfth year. Also in the twelfth month, as ver. 1.

21 hell. Heb., "Sheol"; the place of the departed. The figure employed in Isa. xiv. 9–14, etc., is here greatly amplified, according to the peculiar style of Ezekiel.

23 In the sides. Rather, "in the inmost parts (see Psa. cxxviii. 3, and note) of the pit."

24 Elam. "Elam," the name of a country south of Assyria.

26 Meshech, Tubal. See note on xxvii. 13.

27 they shall not lie. Or, "Shall they not lie," etc. (R.V. marg.).

upon their bones. As we say "upon their heads." But some read "their shields" instead of "their iniquities."

28 thou shalt be broken. That is, "Thou, O Egypt."

29 with their might. *i.e.*, "for all their might," as R.V. marg.

31 shall be comforted. See note on xxxi. 16. Pharaoh may comfort himself, if he can, by knowing that he is not without companions in destruction.

32 My terror. A better reading is, "*his* terror." I have allowed him to cause terror; but now I will lay him in the pit.

CHAPTER XXXIII

2 their watchman. Cp. vers. 6, 7. "There is nothing in Ezekiel's ministry that appeals more directly to the Christian conscience than the serious and profound sense of pastoral responsibility to which this passage bears witness" (*Skinner*).

10 If our transgressions and our sins, etc. This is the language of those who murmur under Divine punishment, instead of humbly confessing guilt and entreating God's mercy.

11 I have no pleasure, etc. See xviii. 28–32.

VERS. 21–33. Ezekiel now recommences his ministry to his own people, by warning them against the delusive hopes still prevailing among the remnant in Judea (21–29), and by exposing the folly of his fellow-captives in neglecting the warnings of him who was now proved to be a true prophet (30–33).

21 one that had escaped out of Jerusalem came unto me. As had been foretold in xxiv. 26. The date here given allows a year and five months to have elapsed since the fall of Jerusalem. But the Syriac Version and some MSS. read "the eleventh year of our captivity," which is much more probable. The Septuagint has "the tenth year."

22 was upon me. Rather, "had been upon me" (R.V.): in the solemn charge preceding this renewal of the prophet's testimony to the people (1–9). For three years Ezekiel had delivered no direct messages from God to his own countrymen: cp. xxiv. 1.

24 Abraham was one. That is, one only; a single individual: see Isa. li. 2. "If Abraham," they argued, "when thus alone, was so greatly multiplied, much more shall we, who are many."

26 Ye stand upon your sword. *i.e.*, "Ye trust to your swords"; to might rather than right.

27 they that are in the wastes, etc. No place shall be a security—the solitary wastes, the open country, the natural fastnesses among the hills.

30 Also, thou son of man, etc. Rather, "And thou, son of man—the children of thy people, who talk about thee," etc. This is the beginning of a long and rather unconnected sentence, which ends in ver. 33 with the words, "And when this comes—lo! it is come—then they know that a prophet hath been among them."

CHAPTER XXXIV

2 prophesy against the shepherds of Israel. The rulers and kings are meant. See note on Jer. ii. 8. (Cp. Jer. xxiii. 1–8.)

6 My sheep. The emphasis is to be noted. Jehovah expressly claims the flock as His own: see 11, 12.

16 the fat and the strong. The rich and powerful, who, under the misgovernment of the rulers, had greatly oppressed the poor.

17 as for you, O My flock. The "judgement" is not only for the "shepherds," but for different portions of the flock.

18 ye must foul the residue with your feet. A reproach most applicable to those who oppress the poor in civil matters; or who, in religious, would debar them from pure instruction in Divine truth, and set before them mere human traditions.

24 My servant David. "A Messianic prediction in the fullest sense of the word" (*Skinner*). For the employment of David's name to designate the royal line in its spiritual aspect, and so pointing to the Messiah, cp. xxxvii. 24; Jer. xxx. 9; Hos. iii. 5.

29 a plant of renown. Some refer this to the Messiah, comparing xvii. 22 and Isa. xi. 1, on which see note. The word, however, more properly means a *plantation* (so R.V.), *i.e.*, a place richly planted; "a right fertile soil" (*Moffatt*), so that "they shall be no more consumed with hunger."

31 ye My flock, the flock of My pasture. The contrast is between the flock and the Shepherd: "men" and God.

CHAPTER XXXV

In this section (to xxxvi. 15) the opposite destinies of Israel and of her enemies are forcibly depicted. Her restoration involves their destruction: cp. Isa. xlvi. 1; lxiii. 1, and notes.

2 mount Seir. That is, the mountainous country of the Edomites, extending from the Dead Sea to the Elanitic Gulf: see Gen. xxxvi. 9; Deut. ii. 8.

5 thou hast had a perpetual hatred, etc. See notes on xxv. 13, and xxi. 25.

6 sith. An old English word for "since."

10 These two nations and these two countries. Israel and Judah.

15 Idumea. Heb., "Edom." So R.V.

CHAPTER XXXVI

2 the ancient high places. Or, "everlasting heights": cp. Gen. xlix. 26; Deut. xxxiii. 15.

3 an infamy. "An evil report," R.V. "La moquerie du peuple" (*French version*).

8 shall shoot forth your branches, etc. As though inanimate Nature held out a hand of greeting to welcome the Return. "Israel," as in other passages of the prophecy, includes the whole covenant people.

13 Thou [land] devourest up men. The position of the land of Canaan between the great continents and monarchies of Asia and Africa, was highly advantageous to a nation which enjoyed Jehovah's favour and protection, but peculiarly dangerous if these were withdrawn.

VERS. 16–38. In this section Ezekiel is instructed to remind the people of their continued sins, which show that the restoration promised is entirely undeserved (17–21); and to tell them that, as they have profaned God's name by their sins, He will glorify it by connecting their return to holiness with renewed prosperity (22, 23). He will therefore give them His Spirit to soften and purify their hearts.

20 they profaned My holy name. That is, they caused it to be profaned; even to be blasphemed, through the wickedness of those who bore it: see Rom. ii. 24. "These," said the heathen, "are the people of Jahveh," regarding Him as a national god, and attributing to Him a character like that of "His people."

25 Then will I sprinkle clean water upon you. An allusion to the methods of purification under the law: see Numb. xix.

37 I will yet for this be inquired of. Cp. xiv. 3. There was a moral state of the people in which

God would *not* be "inquired of" by them. Now He welcomes their approach, as one result of the "new heart" and "new spirit"; teaching them the further lesson that the people must seek by earnest prayer for the fulfilment of the promise, if they would enjoy it. This suggests a reason why the Jews were not more prosperous after their return from Babylon, and why the Church of Christ is still so depressed.

38 the holy flock (Heb., "flock of holy things"). The animals designed for sacrifice.

CHAPTER XXXVII

Chapters xxxvii.-xxxix. contain three expressive symbolical descriptions of the restoration, union, and triumph of the chosen people.

1 full of bones. The bones of slain men (9); as on some battlefield of past days.

4 Prophesy. "Speak in the name of God."

5 breath. The repeated words in this section, "breath," "wind," and "spirit," are in Hebrew the same (see R.V. marg.), and must be rendered according to the context

7 a shaking. Or, "a rattling."

9 Prophesy unto the wind. The emblem of the Spirit of God (see John iii. 8), the Author and Giver of life (Gen. ii. 7).

11 we are cut off for our parts. Rather, as R.V., "we are clean cut off."

13 when I have opened your graves. Although the blessing here promised is plainly a national and moral resurrection, yet the imagery employed assumes that the people were familiar with the doctrine of a personal resurrection (cp. Isa. xxvi. 19, and note).

VERS. 15-28. The first blessing which flows from the Divine communication of spiritual life is the union of Israel, hitherto divided, under the rule of the true David. This is symbolised by two rods, the emblems of authority, becoming one; so that the two kingdoms of Judah and Ephraim shall be no more divided (15-22); but shall be obedient, safe, and prosperous, as in David's days, with God's sanctuary in the midst of them, and His glory resting upon them (23-28): cp. Isa. xi. 13.

16 one stick. Cp. Numb. xvii. 1, etc. The name of "Ephraim" was given to the kingdom of the Ten Tribes: see Hosea.

for the children of Israel his companions. That is, such portions of the other tribes as remained with or passed over to the kingdom of Judah: see 2 Chron. xi. 13-17; xv. 9.

17 they shall be one in thine hand. "Where God is least, is least union; where He is most, is perfect oneness" (Elvet Lewis: *By the River Chebar*).

25 My servant David shall be their prince for ever. "As the 'David' of this promise is Christ, so the covenant-people are no longer the Jews distinctively, but the faithful in Christ; and the territory of blessing is no longer Canaan, but the whole earth; and only when it becomes His actual possession can the prophecies concerning Him, as the New Testament David, reach their destined accomplishment" (*Dr. P. Fairbairn*).

CHAPTER XXXVIII

Expositors have differed much in opinion as to the interpretation of this section of prophecy. Some understand it as referring to a literal prodigious armament of many nations for the purpose of attacking the Jews after their restoration to their own land, which will be defeated by the immediate judgements of God. But it appears more consistent with the whole scope of scriptural prophecy, and especially with the visions which immediately follow in chs. xl.-xlviii., to give it a more enlarged meaning, understanding it as describing the consummation of the great conflict which has always been going on between the kingdoms of God and of Satan in the world, and which will end in the universal establishment of the Saviour's spiritual reign: see note on ver. 17. "It is the same struggle which is depicted in the Book of Revelation (xx.7-10), where St. John adopts words and phrases of Ezekiel, indicating thereby that he is predicting the same event which Ezekiel had foretold" (Currey in *Speaker's Commentary*).

2 Gog, the land of Magog, etc. Rather, "Gog of the land of Magog, the prince of Rosh, Meshech, and Tubal" (R.V.). Magog was a son of Japhet. On "Meshech and Tubal," see note on xxvii. 13. "Rosh" is not mentioned elsewhere, and may possibly have the same origin as the word "Russians." All these are the northern nations of the Caucasus, and of the Black and Caspian Seas, who were known to the Greeks as Scythians.

5 Persia, Ethiopia, and Libya. The *extremities* of the great confederacy are here enumerated: "Magog," N.; "Persia," E.; "Ethiopia" (Cush), S.; and "Libya" (Phut), W A symbol of universal heathendom.

6 Gomer. Probably the Cimmerians, or people of the Crimea and the adjacent regions, though some scholars identify Gomer with Cappadocia.

Togarmah. The people of Armenia.

7 a guard. More properly, "commander," as R.V. marg.

8 thou shalt be visited. Rather, "thou shalt be appointed," *i.e.*, to lead them.

brought back from the sword. Rather, "restored"; *i.e.*, from the ravages of invasion.

12 in the midst of the land. Or, "in the centre of the earth." Expressively describing the position of Palestine among the nations.

13 the merchants of Tarshish. Hoping to profit by the sale of the booty which these marauders had taken.

17 of whom I have spoken in old time. It is evident, then, that these are the enemies and this is the war which had been predicted, with other names and circumstances, both by Balaam (Numb. xxiv. 17) and by the earlier prophets of Israel: see Psa. ii., cx.; Joel iii.; Isa. xxv., xxvi., xxxiv., etc. The one struggle between good and evil, embodied in various forms, is the great theme of prophecy.

20 the steep places. Walls or towers.

22 I will plead against him. Rather, "I will have a controversy with him"; *i.e.*, will bring him to justice for his sins.

CHAPTER XXXIX

2 and leave but the sixth part of thee. Rather, "and I will lead thee on" (R.V.).

6 that dwell carelessly in the isles. Rather, "that dwell securely in the coastlands."

9 they shall burn them with fire seven years. "They shall make fires of them seven years" (R.V.). "Seven," the number of completeness.

11 the valley of them that pass through. Rather, "the valley of Abarim," east of the Dead Sea.

12 seven months. See ver. 9, note.

14 And they shall sever out men of continual employment. Or, "And they shall set apart regular men, passing through the land, burying the stragglers that are left over the face of the land, to purify it. After the end of seven months they shall search, and the passers through shall pass through the land; and when one seeth a man's bone, then he setteth up a signal by it," etc. Thus every remnant of the dead bodies would be swept away from the face of the land.

16 And also the name of the city shall be Hamonah. Or, "And also the name of a neighbouring city shall be Hamonah" ("multitude").

17 Speak unto every feathered fowl, etc. Cp. Rev. xix. 17, 18.

20 chariots. Rather, "horsemen," as in Isa. xxi. 7.

26 they have borne their shame. Rather, "they shall forget their shame." Their restoration shall be complete.

CHAPTER XL

Ezekiel's predictions had begun with a vision of the Eternal on His chariot-throne, soon withdrawing from the Temple (x., xi.), which is shortly afterwards utterly destroyed; whilst Jerusalem is laid in ruins, the land desolated, the prince dethroned, and the people exiled. They now close with another vision, in which he beholds the restoration of the Temple, the renewal of worship, the re-establishment of royalty, a new partition of the land, and settlement of the people. Commentators differ greatly in the interpretation of this vision. The most prevalent view in the Christian Church has been that this vision is an elaborate symbol of the blessings which God designs to bestow upon His Church under the Gospel dispensation. The prophecy begins with a description of an ideal temple drawn from that of Solomon, but on a far larger scale. The prophet was writing for Jews, familiar with the details of temple buildings and sacrifices. But if we bear in mind its symbolical character and its spiritual meaning, as summed up in the closing words of the book, "The Lord is there," much of the detail which seems uninteresting to the modern mind will be lit up with a new light or inspired with a new message.

2 by which. Rather, as R.V., "whereon." The "very high mountain" represents the ideal exaltation of the mountain of the "Lord's house" "above the hills": cp. Isa. ii. 2; Micah iv. 1.

on the south. *i.e.*, of the prophet's position, entering the land from Chaldea.

3 like the appearance of brass. That is, bright and sparkling: see i. 7; cp. Rev. i. 15. The "man," evidently, was an angel.

5 by the cubit and a hand-breadth. This cubit, the same as the cubit of Solomon's Temple, was about twenty inches long. Hence the reed, or rod, would be about ten feet long.

7 little chamber. Or, "lodge"; or "guard chamber" (R.V. and marg.). There were three on each side, bordering the avenue that led up to the porch and east gate.

16 narrow windows. Or, "closed" (R.V.); *i.e.*, with bars or lattices, which, being let into the walls or beams, could not be opened and shut at pleasure.

palm trees. Probably pilasters resembling palm-trees; the trunks forming the shafts, and the branches the capitals.

31 utter. That is, "outer"; and so in ver. 37, and xlii. 1, 14.

43 hooks. Rather, "edging boards"; *i.e.*, borders to the tables.

46 the sons of Zadok. That is, of the family of the high priest: see note on xliv. 15.

48 And he, etc. From the court to the house, *i.e.*, the Temple.

CHAPTER XLI

1 the temple. The body or nave of the Temple.

4 before the temple. Not admitting the prophet into the most holy place.

6 three. Rather, "in three stories," as R.V.

that they might have hold, etc. R.V., "that they might have hold [therein], and not have hold in the wall of the house"; cp. 1 Kings vi. 6, and note.

8 six great cubits. Or, "six cubits to the joining," or corner (R.V. marg.). Currey (*Speaker's Commentary*) translates: "The floor of the side-chambers to the ceiling six cubits."

12 the separate place, etc. An annexe; a place for storage or for ashes, etc.

CHAPTER XLII

1 the chamber. "The chambers."

5 the galleries were higher than these. The upper storeys had corridors, the breadth of which was taken out of the rooms themselves, making them so much the narrower: see next verse.

6 therefore [the building] was straitened, etc. "The top storey was contracted" (*Moffatt*).

10 in the thickness of the wall. In the *breadth* of the wall; *i.e.*, the breadth of the ground which that wall enclosed. The Septuagint reads "south" for "east."

11 according to their fashions. Like the chambers already described.

14 those things which are for the people. *i.e.*, to the outer court.

16 five hundred reeds. A "reed" being about 10 feet (xl. 5), 500 of these would make a length of 5,000 feet, or nearly a mile: and give a circumference of more than four miles.

CHAPTER XLIII

3 to destroy the city. That is, to predict its destruction.

6 I heard [Him] speaking. Rather, "I heard *one* speaking, etc.

the man. Rather, "a man" (R.V.). Probably another messenger from God.

7 nor by the carcases of their kings. This perhaps alludes to the burial of some of the kings, close to or perhaps even within the Temple area, which was regarded as a profanation.

8 and the wall between me and them. R.V., "and there was [but] the wall between me and them." The palace of the kings, where idolatry was practised, was separated by only this slight partition from the Temple of the true God.

13 the bottom. Either the hollowed base of the altar, or the cavity for the fire.

14 the lower settle. Or, "ledge"; perhaps for standing upon.

15 the altar. "Ariel," translated "altar," in the next clause and the next verse: cp. Isa. xxix. 1.

18 These are the ordinances of the altar, etc. The rites to be observed, not statedly, but on the day of the altar's dedication.

CHAPTER XLIV

3 [It is] for the prince. This is most naturally understood of the "David" foretold, xxxiv. 24, *i.e.*, the Messiah. An additional proof that all these details are symbolical. The Rabbis interpret the passage of the Messiah.

VERS. 4–31. In this section the officers of God's house are appointed, and are enjoined to sanctify themselves for His service; and not only to put away from among them all foreigners and strangers, but to degrade those of their own body who had profaned themselves. The ceremonies which are here prescribed are for the most part found in the Levitical institutions; only they are much more strict; the things formerly required of the high priest being here extended to all the priests. These minute specifications, like those of the Mosaic laws, show the standard of character and conduct which God expects on the part of all His people, since He has granted to them the privilege to approach Him as a "holy priesthood, to offer up spiritual sacrifices, acceptable to God by Jesus Christ" (1 Pet. ii. 5).

4 the north gate. This part of the Temple had been desecrated by the "image of jealousy," viii. 3.

6 let it suffice you. That is, Let these things cease. Cp. 1 Pet. iv. 3.

11 ministering to the house. They shall be employed in the menial offices of the sanctuary.

15 the sons of Zadok. Zadok had succeeded to the high priesthood when the line of Ithamar forfeited that honour, see 1 Sam. ii. 35; 1 Kings i. 7; ii. 26, 27, and notes.

16 My table. See chap. xli. 22, 23.

CHAPTER XLV

6 the city. *i.e.*, the city with its suburbs, and with the space reserved for supplying the necessary means of sustenance: see xlviii. 15–20.

7 for the prince. See note on xlviii. 21.

10 Just balances. Just weights and measures (for the need of which see Amos viii. 5)—this is the essential point in vers. 10–12. The dry homer was about 11 bushels; the liquid homer about 90 gallons. The shekel would probably be equal now to about £1 5*s*. But the shekel varied very much.

18 thou shalt take, etc. Vers. 18–25 are directed to the prince. He is commanded to provide the sacrifices, and the priest is to offer them.

29 for him that is simple. *i.e.*, for sins of ignorance. See Lev. iv. 2, 13, 27.

23 seven bullocks and seven rams. The Mosaic ordinance was for "two young bullocks and one ram and seven lambs": Numb. xxviii. 19, 24.

25 In the seventh month, etc. The service for the Feast of Tabernacles is the same as that for the Passover. The Pentecost is not mentioned.

CHAPTER XLVI

17 the year of liberty. *i.e.*, the year of jubilee; when slaves were set at liberty, and land returned to its original owner (Lev. xxv.).

18 by oppression. As Ahab did to Naboth: see 1 Kings xxi. 3–16.

CHAPTER XLVII

1 eastward. *i.e.*, into and along the valley of the Kidron.

7 at the bank of the river. Cp. with this, and vers. 9 and 12; Rev. xxii. 2.

8 the desert. Heb., "Arabah"; the name of the depressed "plain" (Gen. xiii. 10, 12) or valley in which the Jordan and the Dead Sea lie.

the sea. The Dead Sea.

9 a very great multitude of fish. No fish can exist in the Dead Sea. Hence the blessings which the Gospel brings are most appropriately represented in the healing of this sea of death by the waters of life which flow from under the mercy-seat of God.

10 from En-gedi even unto En-eglaim. *i.e.*, from one side of the lake to the other. For "En-gedi," see note on 1 Sam. xxiv. 1. "En-eglaim" (or, *calves' fountain*) was probably on the other side of the sea, in the land of Moab.

the great sea. The Mediterranean.

11 they shall be given to salt. *i.e.*, for reservoirs of salt, as before. The Dead Sea and its cliffs and salt marshes furnish salt for commerce. This is not therefore a curse, but the contrary. Sterility and death shall be removed; but so much salt shall be left as may serve all useful purposes.

15 Hethlon. Its site, like those of other places mentioned here, is unknown.

16 Hauran. "Hauran" is a district east of the Sea of Galilee, south of Damascus, and north-east of Bashan. It still bears the same name, probably derived from the numerous caves, which the inhabitants use as dwellings: see Gen. xiv. 6, and note.

19 strife [in] Kadesh. Rather, "Meribah-Kadesh" (Deut. xxxii. 51).

the river to the great sea. Or, "to the brook [of Egypt], to the great sea," R.V. Currey (*Speaker's Commentary*) translates: "riverward to the great sea." The French version gives a different suggestion: "le long du torrent, jusqu' à la grande mer" ("along the torrent, as far as the great sea").

CHAPTER XLVIII

8 oblation. Sanctified portion or reservation.

11 [It shall be] for the priests that are sanctified. Or, "The sanctified [portion shall be] for the priests," as R.V., marg.

15 profane. *i.e.*, common; not sacred. The city is holy, as compared with other cities; but, in comparison with the sanctuary, it is common.

18 they that serve the city. *i.e.*, those who perform the various labours which a great city needs.

21 on the one side and on the other. *i.e.*, on the west side and on the east, of the square of 25,000 reeds, which is to be set apart for sacred purposes.

over against the portions for the princes, etc. Rather, as R.V., "answerable unto the portions, it shall be for the prince: and the holy oblation and the sanctuary of the house shall be in the midst thereof."

28 to the river, etc. See note on xlvii. 19.

30 four thousand and five hundred measures ("[reeds] by measure," R.V.); *i.e.*, about 8½ miles. Cp. the 12,000 furlongs in the measurement of the New Jerusalem, Rev. xxi. 16.

35 from that day. That on which the glory returned, xliii. 4.

The Lord is there. Namely, by His powerful and gracious presence, which would be to the inhabitants the source of all peace, security, felicity, and holiness. There is probably an allusion to the Shekinah, the symbol of Jehovah's presence, which was the glory of the former Temple. In the Church of the future the reality would fill not the Temple only but the whole City of God (see Rev. xxi. 2, 3).

Such visions as those of Ezekiel and of John of Patmos have inspired many thinkers and philanthropists since. May they bring us not only bright hopes for the hereafter but a new inspiration for our civic life to-day.

"I will not cease from mental strife,
Nor shall my sword sleep in my hand,
Till we have built Jerusalem
In England's green and pleasant land."

"'The Lord there.' Neither city nor soul can ever gain a better name" (Elvet Lewis: *By the River Chebar*).

THE BOOK OF DANIEL

INTRODUCTION

THE story of Daniel presents many analogies with that of Joseph. Both belonged to a captive race. Both were young men in the court of a heathen king. Both were exposed to strong temptation. Both found help in prayer. Both suffered for their faithfulness to God and conscience. And both won the respect of the monarch and reached the highest place under him in the government of the State.

The Book opens with the siege and capture of Jerusalem by Nebuchadrezzar in the time of King Jehoiakim, 605 B.C. Amongst the captives taken to Babylon was Daniel, who was at once selected as one of the youths of royal blood and of the princes, good-looking and well-educated, to be trained in the language and literature of the Chaldeans (i. 1–7). Very soon Daniel is confronted with the temptation to compromise with his religious convictions, in partaking of food which had been offered to idols. This temptation he successfully overcomes (i. 8–16), and rises to a foremost place among the learned men at the court (i. 17–20).

Nebuchadrezzar's dream gives Daniel his first great opportunity (ii. 1–16), and in his need he betakes himself to God in prayer (ii. 17, 18). The meaning of the dream is revealed to him (ii. 19), and he does not forget to return thanks to God (ii. 20–23). Then he gives to the king the memorable interpretation of the four great kingdoms, and the kingdom which shall never be destroyed (ii. 31–45). Of this vision and its teaching, Melanchthon says that "this short narrative embraces the whole sum of the Gospel."

Daniel's friends are again tested, this time by a question of worship. As they refuse to worship the golden image which Nebuchadrezzar has set up, they are cast into the fiery furnace, from which they are delivered unharmed, the result being that their religion is protected by a royal decree (iii.).

Another dream of Nebuchadrezzar—the destruction of the great tree—is interpreted by Daniel as a prediction of the king's madness (iv.).

One of the most impressive passages in the Book is the account of Belshazzar's feast and Daniel's interpretation of the mysterious writing on the wall (v.), an interpretation which results in his promotion to the third highest place in the kingdom.

Once more Daniel's faith and conscience are tested, as the result of a conspiracy among the other high officers of government (vi. 3, 4). A royal decree is issued that none shall ask, for thirty days, a petition of any one but the king. Daniel, continuing to pray to God and making no concealment of it (vi. 10), is cast into the den of lions. Again God's care protects and rescues His servant, and wins from the king, as it did previously from Nebuchadrezzar, a recognition of the living God.

For the interpretation of the apocalyptic visions contained in chapters vii.–xii., the reader is referred to the detailed exposition below. Daniel's beautiful prayer of confession (ix. 3–19) is one of the finest things in the Book.

CHAPTER I

I the third year of the reign of Jehoiakim. Many suggestions have been made to remove the apparent discrepancy between this date and that given in Jer. xxv. 1: "the fourth year of Jehoiakim"; the simplest of which seems to be the following. After the conquest of Nineveh, Nabopolassar, the king of Babylon, wishing to recover Syria and Palestine from Pharaoh-Necho, but feeling himself too old for fresh expeditions, gave a share in the kingdom to his son Nebuchadrezzar. The young king speedily set out, a little before the end of the third year of Jehoiakim; and early in the fourth year of that prince, and before the first year of his own reign had expired, he defeated the Egyptians at Carchemish (Jer. xlvi. 2), and laid siege to Jerusalem.

2 into his hand. *i.e.,* into his power. Jehoiakim occupied the throne some years after this, but as Nebuchadrezzar's vassal.

Shinar. The ancient name of Babylonia, Gen. x. 10; retained in poetry, Isa. xi. 11; Zech. v. 11.

the house of his god. Probably the temple of Belus, described by Herodotus (i. 181). The "treasure-house" was the depository of consecrated vessels and votive offerings.

3 the master of his eunuchs. Eunuchs were anciently, as they are now, much employed and trusted in Eastern courts; and some of them rise to high political and military offices. Both Sennacherib and Nebuchadrezzar were accompanied in their invasions by a "Rab-saris," or chief eunuch: see 2 Kings xviii. 17; Jer. xxxix. 3, 13.

of the king's seed. According to Josephus (*Ant.* x. 10, 1), Daniel and his three companions were related to the new king Zedekiah. They were certainly of high rank.

4 children. Rather, "youths," as R.V.; for the word includes persons of different ages: see Gen. xxi. 15; 1 Kings xii. 8, 10, 14. They were probably about fifteen to seventeen years old.

well favoured. Good looking.

cunning. *i.e.,* "skilled": see Exod. xxxviii. 23.

the learning and the tongue, etc. Or, "the literature and the language." The language of the country at this time was Eastern Aramaic, which we find in ii. 4, etc.: see 2 Kings xviii. 26, and note.

5 the king's meat. "Delicate" or "lordly" food.

6 Daniel, Hananiah, Mishael, and Azariah. All these four Hebrew names contained the name of God ("God my Judge"; "Jah (or Jahveh) is gracious"; "Who is like God?" "Jah (or Jahveh) is Helper"), and were calculated to remind those who bore them of Him. The new names given to them had reference to some Babylonian deities; in "Abednego"—"nego" is a copyist's error for "Nebo." For Nebo see Budge: *Babylonian Life and History* (1925), p. 105.

8 he would not defile himself. The food was probably such as the Mosaic law forbade (Lev. iii. 17; xi. 4); and which had been, according to heathen custom, offered to idols (1 Cor. viii. 10).

9 God had brought Daniel into favour. All that is here told us of Daniel shows that he was at once amiable, modest, and conscientious; and these virtues, no doubt, had conciliated the affection of his governor. For "tender love," R.V. has "compassion": Moffatt has "pity."

11 (the) **Melzar.** "Melzar" is probably a Persian word, meaning "the steward," as R.V.

12 pulse. Rather, "vegetables" generally.

19 the king communed with them. *i.e.,* he examined them. The four Hebrews were so far superior to the rest, that they were immediately appointed to be personal attendants on the king.

20 astrologers. Rather, "enchanters" (R.V.).

21 Daniel continued, etc. "Simple words, but what a volume of tried faithfulness is unrolled by them! Amid all the intrigues indigenous at all times in dynasties of Oriental despotism, amid all the envy towards a foreign captive in high office . . . the insanity of the king and the murder of two of his successors, in that whole critical period for his people, Daniel *continued*" (Pusey: *Daniel*).

CHAPTER II

1 In the second year of the reign of Nebuchadnezzar. Three years at least must have elapsed (see i. 5, 18) since the date of the occurrences recorded in i. 1, 2, where Nebuchadrezzar is called "king." The date in this verse is probably reckoned from the commencement of his sole reign, at his father's death, about two years after he had undertaken the expedition against Palestine. This would allow an interval of nearly four years.

2 the Chaldeans. "The diviners" (*Moffatt*) or dream-interpreters.

4 in Syriac. Aramaic. See note on i. 4.

[*Here the Aramaic portion of the book commences, and it is continued to the end of vii.*]

5 The thing is gone from me. Meaning either, "The dream has escaped my memory"; or, "The decree has gone from me," and is irrevocable.

cut in pieces. Lit., "made pieces"; a severe but not uncommon punishment: see 1 Sam. xv. 33. Assyrian sculptures represent the infliction of it, by the cutting off the various limbs of the criminal.

8 gain the time. *i.e.,* you desire to gain advantage by delay.

9 there is but one decree for you. Or, "one fate awaits you."

till the time be changed. Until you can secure a favourable day for your purposes.

14 the captain of the king's guard. See note on Gen. xxxvii. 36.

16 that he would give him time. The narrative implies that his request was successful. The king's passion may have cooled, or Daniel's demeanour may have pleased him; but we must not fail to observe in it God's all-controlling hand; see i. 9.

18 that they would desire mercies, etc. It was evident that none could help them but God, and that this could only be expected in answer to prayer.

the God of heaven. God—not one of many deities, but supreme. The title is found in Gen. xxiv. 7; but was more usual after the Captivity.

20 Blessed be the name of God. Every answer to prayer should call forth praise: cp. Phil. iv. 6.

wisdom and might are His. Daniel's mind was evidently occupied not only with the mercy shown to himself and his friends, by the dream being made known to him, but also with the great subjects of the dream itself, as illustrating God's power and wisdom in the change of empires from age to age.

23 O Thou God of my fathers. The order of words in the original is emphatic: "To Thee, O God of my fathers, I give thanks and praise."

25 I have found a man of the captives of Judah, etc. Haughtily ignoring the fact that Daniel was already known to the king.

27 Daniel answered, etc. Cp. Joseph's language on a similar occasion, Gen. xl. 8; xli. 16.

30 for [their] sakes that shall make known, etc. Rather, as R.V., "but to the intent that the interpretation may be made known unto the king."

31 a great image. This dream accords perfectly with its great object. A colossal image in which heterogeneous materials were combined to make one human form, aptly symbolises the great empires of the world, which, with all their differences, are in nature alike, and all earthly and human. That they appear combined in one form, while in reality successive, suggests the identity which subsisted through all changing eras—the one idea of *world-empire.* And a mountain rock, detached, moved, expanding by a mysterious, inward, unseen power, beautifully represents the origin, progress, and final universality of that kingdom which is not of this world.

the form thereof was terrible. Rather, "its aspect (R.V.) was terrible." Among the monuments of Egypt and Assyria, colossal statues of monarchs are found.

35 that no place was found for them. *i.e.*, they utterly disappeared: cp. Psa. xxxvii. 10; ciii. 16; Rev. xx. 11.

36 we will tell, etc. Daniel modestly includes his companions.

38 ruler over them all. The word "all," like other absolute terms, is frequently used in Scripture with a limited sense: see Deut. ii. 25; Matt. iii. 5. But Nebuchadrezzar, or the Babylonian empire, as supreme over the whole realm of Asiatic civilisation, was the first fitting representative of the world-power, "the head of gold."

39 another kingdom inferior to thee. The Median kingdom. There has been, and is, considerable diversity of opinion as to the identity of all the four kingdoms. But, in the words of the late Dean Farrar (*Expositor's Bible*: Daniel), written thirty years ago and confirmed by recent scholars, "it may be regarded as a certain result of exegesis that the four empires are: (1) the Babylonian; (2) the Median; (3) the Persian; (4) the Greco-Macedonian."

another third kingdom of brass. The Persian.

40 the fourth kingdom shall be strong as iron. The Greco-Macedonian kingdom.

41 the feet and toes. The feet probably represent the kingdoms of the Selucidæ in Syria and of the Ptolemies in Egypt, the two most important of the kingdoms into which the Greco-Macedonian empire was broken up. The toes represent the minor kingdoms.

miry clay. Rather, "earthenware clay." The clay and iron were evidently intermingled (see ver. 43), though they were "divided," so that they would not coalesce; and thus the strength of the iron was useless through the brittleness of the clay.

43 they shall mingle themselves, etc. Rather, "They shall be mixing themselves among the race of man, but they shall not be cleaving one to another"; *i.e.*, there shall be mixture, but not union.

44 shall not be left to other people. That is, it shall not be transferred to another people, as the previous kingdoms had been.

46 and worshipped Daniel. That Nebuchadrezzar did not treat Daniel as a god is clear from the next verse; for he attributes the revealing of the secret to Daniel's God. "To worship" is used in the sense of bow down to; to honour. The French version has "se prosterna devant Daniel" ("prostrated himself before Daniel").

47 your God is a God of gods. Nebuchadrezzar was evidently convinced of the wisdom and supremacy of Jehovah; yet he remained an idolater, as the sequel shows.

48 the whole province of Babylon. The district around the capital.

all the wise men of Babylon. The "wise men" appear to have been arranged in certain orders or classes, each having its head. Daniel was placed over the whole as the president.

49 over the affairs of the province. Governors of the province under Daniel. Daniel did not forget, in his prosperity, the companions of his captivity.

Daniel [sat] in the gate of the king. Nebuchadrezzar retained him at court, as one of his confidential advisers.

CHAPTER III

1 an image of gold. From the descriptions which are given of the fabrication of idols in Isa. xl. 18–20; xli. 6, 7; xliv. 10–13; xlvi. 6, 7, it appears that golden idols were made of plates of gold covering a mass of wood or stone; and many ancient monuments are found which have evidently been thus plated with metal.

whose height was threescore cubits, etc. About 90 feet high and 9 feet broad. It was an image dedicated to Bel, the chief deity of Babylon. The whole narrative has received confirmation from the excavations carried on by Mr. C. L. Woolley at Ur in 1922–1924. "Nebuchadnezzar," says Mr. Woolley, "introduced a new plan of building to accommodate a new form of worship." "There can be no doubt," says Sir E. Wallis Budge, "that Nebuchadrezzar provided a statue of Bêl-Marduk, and had it set up in the open court of the temple where all worshippers could see it" (*Babylonian Life and History*, 1925, pp. 230, 231).

2 the princes, etc. Some of these titles are of Persian, and some of Aramaic origin; but the exact meaning of each cannot now be ascertained. They are thus translated in the R.V.: "satraps," or viceroys of subject-kingdoms; "deputies," the lieutenants of the satraps; "governors" of provinces; "judges" (or "chief soothsayers"); "treasurers"; "counsellors," or judges; "sheriffs," or "lawyers"; "and all the rulers of the provinces."

4 O people (peoples), **nations, and languages.** The Babylonian empire was now at the height of its greatness. It contained "within its vast area representatives from the east and west, north and south; the Greek and the Mede, the Phœnician and the Assyrian, the 'captive of Judah,' and the Arab of the South."

5 the cornet, flute, etc The "cornet" was a straight horn; the "sackbut" a kind of small harp; the "psaltery" a lyre; the "dulcimer," perhaps, bagpipes.

6 the same hour. Lit., "in the glance of an eye"; *i.e.*, immediately.

12 Shadrach, Meshach, and Abed-nego. Why these three were selected by the accusers we are not told, and it is useless to inquire. Daniel's character assures us that he would not comply with the king's command; but he may have been absent, or the accusers may have feared to lay a charge against him.

16 we are not careful. Rather, "we do not need." It is needless to enter into the matter: we are determined at all risks to worship none but God, who is able to deliver us.

19 the form of his visage was changed. Showing the most violent anger.

one seven times more. The word "seven" is often employed to denote completeness. The furnace was to be heated to the greatest intensity.

20 the most mighty men. That is, in bodily strength.

21 in their coats, etc. Moffatt translates: "in their mantles, their trousers, their turbans and their other clothes." This is substantially the Assyrian and Babylonian dress shown on the monuments (see also Herodotus, i. 190).

C

22 the flame of the fire slew those men, etc. Hurried by the king's peremptory command, the men could not consult their own safety; and therefore, when they "carried up" the three Hebrews to the opening at the top of the furnace, they were burnt. The apocryphal "Song of the Three Children" is inserted here in some editions of the Bible.

25 like the Son of God. Lit., "like to a son of the gods": see R.V. Nebuchadrezzar calls this personage "an angel" (28): and Luther, Calvin, and Coverdale, in common with the majority of commentators, take this to be the meaning: cp. Job i. 6; Psa. lxxxix. 6, and notes. The heathen monarch probably thought only of a majestic superhuman being.

26 the mouth. Rather, "the door"; for the use of those who attended to the furnace.

28 changed. "Frustrated."

CHAPTER IV

8 But at the last, etc. Daniel seems to have kept himself aloof from the soothsayers, whose pretensions and artifices he could not countenance.

the spirit of the holy gods. Nebuchadrezzar here speaks like a polytheist, but in vers. 3, 34, 35, he shows belief in the One God.

12 meat. Rather, "food"; as it should be rendered in almost every instance in which the word "meat" occurs in the English Bible.

13 a watcher and a holy one. That is, "a watcher [who was] also a holy one." A phrase for an angel, taken from the Babylonian mythology, and occurring frequently in the Apocrypha, especially the Book of Enoch.

15 even with a band of iron and brass. As a fence around it, that it should be carefully guarded and preserved.

let his portion be with the beasts. Here is a change from the *tree* to a *person* represented by it.

16 let his heart be changed. The desires and sympathies of a man shall be exchanged for the propensities of a beast.

seven times. The term is quite indefinite.

17 This matter. Or, "sentence." "Demand" means "requirement."

to the intent, etc. To show the supreme power of the Most High God over the mightiest potentates.

the basest of men. A person of humble condition.

19 Astonied. Terrified at the import of the dream.

for one hour. Rather, "for an instant": see iii. 6.

the dream be to them that hate thee, etc. A loyal utterance. I could have wished that these calamities had befallen thy foes rather than thyself.

25 They shall drive thee, etc. Rather, "thou shalt be driven," etc.; "thou shalt be made to eat," etc.; "thou shalt be wetted," etc. The threatening seems to be that, by a Divine visitation for his pride, he should become a maniac (see vers. 34, 36), affected by what is generally called *lycanthropy,* imagining himself a beast, and constantly endeavouring to act accordingly, by ranging among the animals in the parks connected with the royal residence.

27 break off thy sins by righteousness. Cp. Jer. xviii. 7, 8; Jonah iii. 10. Daniel spoke with faithfulness, courtesy, and generous feeling.

29 he walked in the palace. "He was walking upon the royal palace": (see R.V. and marg.), *i.e.,* on the flat roof.

30 great Babylon that I have built. Parallel cases in history of great monarchs whose pride preceded their swift downfall are those of Alexander the Great, Philip II of Spain, and Napoleon.

33 like eagles' [feathers], etc. These words are, of course, like those in vers. 11, 12, 22, tinged with Eastern hyperbole. Farrar translates: "rough like eagles' feathers." But it seems not unlikely that the king's fancies were gratified as far as was safe; whilst his kingdom was preserved for him when his reason should return.

CHAPTER V

1 Belshazzar the king. From the Scriptures (2 Kings xxv. 27; Jer. lii. 31) we learn that the son and successor of Nebuchadrezzar was Evil-Merodach (561 B.C.). Belshazzar was the son of Nabonidus, and so far no satisfactory explanation has been given of his appearance here as king. "But the cuneiform inscriptions have proved that he is no figment of the imagination. He was at one time heir to the throne and the commander of the Babylonian army." (See Sayce: *The Higher Criticism and the Monuments,* Fourth Ed., 1894, p. 527).

2 his wives and his concubines. The Babylonians differed from the Persians and other Oriental nations (see Esther i. 10, 11) in admitting females to their banquets.

5 over against the candlestick. The writing being over against the chandelier would be very conspicuous.

6 the king's countenance, etc. Lit., "the king's brightnesses; *i.e.,* his bright looks grew pale. The pallor, faintness, trembling, and loud outcry, showed the extreme terror of the conscience-stricken king.

7 the third ruler. See note, ver. 1.

8 they could not read the writing. It is likely that the meaning rather than the actual words was what they could not understand, as the language, Aramaic, was well known to them.

10 the queen. The queen mother. Some suppose "the queen" to be Nitocris, a woman of great energy and wisdom, mentioned by Herodotus, i. 185-188. She was probably either daughter to Nebuchadrezzar, or, as some think, widow of Neriglissar.

11 there is a man in thy kingdom. Daniel appears always to have avoided connecting himself very closely with the *magi;* and he probably lost his office as their chief at the death of Nebuchadrezzar; and thus ceased to be connected with the king's court, though employed in some department of the government (viii. 27). It might therefore easily happen that Belshazzar had little or no personal knowledge of him.

[I say] thy father. The repetition is emphatic, reminding Belshazzar that his royal ancestor Nebuchadrezzar, who was eminently wise and successful, had honoured and trusted Daniel above all his other advisers.

13 Jewry. Or, "Judea."

25 Mene, Mene, Tekel, Upharsin. "Mene, Mene"; *numbered, numbered*: "Tekel"; *weighed*: "Upharsin"; U *and:* Pharsin (meaning the same as "Peres") *divided,* but perhaps thus modified, to suggest the name of the "Persians," whose empire was to supersede that of Babylon: see ii. 39. The words are Aramaic.

26 hath numbered thy kingdom. That is, the years of its duration.

27 weighed in the balances. This is a frequent metaphor, representing judicial decision: cp. 1 Sam. ii. 3; Job xxxi. 6.

28 divided. That is, *torn away* from thee, and given to others.

31 Darius the Median. Authorities differ greatly as to the identity of this Darius.

CHAPTER VI

2 was first. Or, "was *one*" (R.V.).

3 was preferred, etc. This awakened the jealousy of his colleagues.

6 assembled together. This word, which recurs in vers. 11, 15, implies eager and even tumultuous haste. Luther has *häufig*, "often."

7 to establish. That is, to advise the king to establish. The ostensible object of the decree was "probably to obtain from the Babylonians and other provinces a recognition of the king as the representative of the Supreme God, invested with his delegated power. The decree was for thirty days; for those who, for such a space, had so recognised that divinity of the king would have admitted the principle of submission to him as a Divine authority" (*Pusey*).

8 which altereth not. See Esther viii. 8, and note.

10 his chamber. Rather, "upper chamber"; an apartment used for retirement (2 Sam. xviii. 33), and therefore for prayer: see Acts i. 13; x. 9.

toward Jerusalem. It was customary with the Jews, in prayer, to turn the face toward Jerusalem, where were the symbols of God's presence and favour toward His people: see 1 Kings viii. 30–48; Psa. v. 7; xxviii. 2; Jonah ii. 4.

three times a day. Cp. Psa. lv. 17.

as he did aforetime. He made no change in his religious habits on account of the king's decree, though he knew that he exposed himself to the loss of office and dignity, and even to a dreadful death. He presents an instructive example not only of constancy in God's service at all risks, but also of firm avowal of religious principle, as opposed to all subterfuge and concealment.

11 these men assembled. They evidently expected to find Daniel praying. "He was probably out of ordinary sight in his retirement; so that, while not even in appearance denying his faith for the sake of the king's command, his devotion was unostentatious" (*Pusey*).

12 Hast thou not signed a decree, etc.? Daniel's enemies follow up their plot with skill and determination. They obtain an acknowledgment of the edict from the king; they represent the disregard of it as a personal insult, aggravated by Daniel's being a foreign captive; and, when the king hesitates, they vehemently urge the execution of the sentence.

14 he laboured till the going down of the sun. He tried earnestly to find some expedient, until the evening, beyond which the execution of the penalty could not be delayed.

16 He will deliver thee. The heathen believed in the interposition of the gods on behalf of their worshippers; and Darius had probably heard of the events recorded in ch. iii.

17 a stone was brought. Such stones were generally used for closing caves and sepulchres (Josh. x. 18; John xi. 38, 39), and when fastened, were sometimes sealed (Matt. xxvii. 66). The king's seal kept Daniel's enemies, and the lords' signet his friends, from interfering.

18 instruments of music. The word here translated "instruments of music" is by some rendered "dancing girls." Luther, following the older versions and the Septuagint, translates it "food."

22 innocency was found in me. Daniel was conscious of uprightness before God and man. His disobedience to an impious law he declares to be "no hurt" or wrong.

24 their children and their wives. This extension of punishment to the children and other relatives of criminals was a widely-spread ancient custom. In the Mosaic law there is a merciful provision against it (Deut. xxiv. 16).

28 Cyrus the Persian. Cyrus conquered Babylon in 538 B.C.

CHAPTER VII

1 In the first year of Belshazzar. See note, v. 1.

2 strove upon. Chaldee, "rushed to," or towards. R.V., "brake forth upon." The French version has "se levèrent avec impetuosité" ("rose up impetuously").

the Great Sea. The Mediterranean. All the empires here symbolised ruled over the countries near the eastern part of this sea.

3 four great beasts. As the prophet observed one of these beasts after another, they were probably successive in their origin. It has always been customary to symbolise kings and kingdoms by different animals. This is very observable in the sculptures at Nineveh, and in the coins of many nations, both ancient and modern. The four kingdoms of Daniel's vision correspond with the four parts of the image in that of Nebuchadrezzar, ch. ii.

4 eagle's wings. The addition of the eagle's wings to the lion represents ferocious strength widely and rapidly pursuing its victims. The removal of the wings refers, probably, to Nebuchadrezzar and the temporary loss of his greatness (v. 33), and in some degree to the kingdom of Babylon itself.

5 like to a bear. The bear is remarkable for greediness and cunning; and appears here, whilst devouring its prey, to be maintaining an attitude of cautious watchfulness for a fresh victim. It symbolises the Median Empire kingdom, which, at the time of the vision, was watching its opportunity to seize on Babylon, and was soon to be commanded to "arise and devour," for the fulfilment of God's purposes against that empire.

6 like a leopard. The leopard, or panther, with four wings, probably represents the Persian kingdom. On this interpretation the four heads are Cyrus, Darius, Astyages or Artaxerxes, and the four wings the rapidity and extent of its conquests.

7 a fourth beast, etc. What empire is here meant is much disputed: see on ii. 40. The earlier commentators mostly hold the fourth beast to be the Roman empire. The generally accepted view of scholars now is that it is the Greco-Macedonian kingdom. The small horn represents Antiochus, whose assumption of the title "Epiphanes" (the illustrious) was in harmony with the expression here used, "a mouth speaking great things." He took Jerusalem 170 B.C., and three years later set up the statue of Zeus in the Temple there.

8 eyes like the eyes of man. Intelligence and sagacity (Ezek. i. 18).

9 till the thrones were cast down. Rather, as R.V., "till thrones were placed." This judicial proceeding goes on in heaven, whilst the beasts appear on earth; and when the last has been punished, the Son of Man receives the kingdom, which, whatever be its vicissitudes, is never to pass away.

the Ancient of days. An expression equivalent to *the Eternal.* The Judge of these transitory monarchies is He whose dominion is "from everlasting to everlasting."

whose garment was white as snow. The royal robe of the Hebrew sovereign was white; indicating purity and honour.

His throne was [like] the fiery flame. Cp. Ezek. i. 4–26, and notes.

13 one like the Son of Man. Lit., as R.V., "one like unto a son of man": throwing emphasis upon the Incarnation.

15 in the midst of my body. Lit., "in the midst of my sheath"; the image being that of a sword wearing out its scabbard: a symbol of restless anxiety.

18 the saints of the Most High shall take the kingdom. The spiritual influence of the Gospel being spoken of as the kingdom of the Messiah, or the kingdom of heaven, which is to be extended over the whole earth, the "saints," or people of God, are represented as possessing the world, and reigning with Christ over it: cp. Isa. lx.

24 another. Namely, the little horn, vers. 8, 11, 20.

25 and think to change times and laws. This was attempted by Antiochus Epiphanes, who tried to abolish the Jewish feasts and worship (see note on ver. 7).

they. That is, the saints of the Most High.

a time and times and the dividing of time. The plural, "times," means *two* times; thus the whole will be three times and a half, which mean three years and a half. Antiochus Epiphanes interrupted the worship of the Temple for three years and a half. This interpretation does not, however, exclude a further fulfilment, as in the case of so many of the prophecies.

[*Here ends the Aramaic portion of the Book, the remainder being written in Hebrew.*]

CHAPTER VIII

2 Shushan. See note on Neh. i. 1.

the palace. Of the Persian kings.

Elam. "Elam" is often put for Persia. When this book was completed (i. 21), Elam, with its capital Susa, was a "province" of the vast empire of Cyrus.

Ulai. The Eulæus, on the banks of which Susa stood. It is now called *Karûn.*

3 the higher came up last. The Median kingdom was the older, but the Persian became the more mighty, and swallowed up the other.

4 westward, and northward, and southward. The Persians pushed their conquests chiefly in these directions, comprehending, in the west, Babylonia, Mesopotamia, Syria, Asia Minor; in the north, Colchis, Armenia, Iberia, and the regions round the Caspian Sea; and in the south, Palestine, Egypt, Ethiopia, and Libya: cp. vii. 5, and note.

5 a he-goat. The goat is said to have been the national emblem of Macedonia. His "notable (or conspicuous) horn" is Alexander (21).

from the west. That is, from Europe.

and touched not the ground. Alexander's conquests were both extensive and extraordinarily rapid, being completed within twelve years.

7 he was moved with choler against him. The Greeks were eager to revenge themselves upon the Persians as their ancient foes.

8 when he was strong, the great horn was broken. Alexander died, 323 B.C., at the very summit of his power, at the age of 32.

four notable ones toward the four winds of heaven. After some years of contest among Alexander's successors, Cassander obtained the western or European provinces; Lysimachus the northern, on the shores of the Euxine; Seleucus the eastern, including Persia, Babylon, Syria, etc.; and Ptolemy, Egypt, and the rest of Africa, with Palestine, which, however, was the subject of frequent warfare between the two kingdoms of Egypt and Syria.

9 a little horn. This "little horn" is thought by the best interpreters to be Antiochus Epiphanes, who sprang from one of the four kingdoms into which Alexander's empire was divided, being a successor of Seleucus.

toward the south. Antiochus conquered Egypt 170 B.C. (1 Macc. i. 17–20).

toward the east. Persia, whither he went (1 Macc. iii. 29–37) to replenish his treasury.

the pleasant [land]. Rather, "the glorious land," *i.e.*, Palestine: see xi. 16, 41; Ezek. xx. 6, 15: cp. 1 Macc. i. 21, 24.

10 to the host of heaven. The "host of heaven" and "the stars" probably represent the leaders of the Jews, especially the priests. Antiochus, having gained possession of Jerusalem, committed the most cruel and wanton excesses: see 1 Macc. i. 21–64; 2 Macc. ix. 4.

11 by him. Rather, "from him," *i.e.*, from the Prince of the host, God Himself.

12 And a host was given, etc. Rather, as R.V., "And the host was given over [to it] together with the continual [burnt offering] through transgression; and it cast down truth to the ground, and it did [its pleasure] and prospered."

13 one saint. "A holy one," *i.e.*, angel: see Job v. 1.

the transgression of desolation. This may mean either, "the desolating wickedness"; or, as both Luther and the French version have it, "the sin which causes the desolation."

14 days. Heb., "evening morning": cp. Gen. i. 5.

then shall the sanctuary be cleansed. The sanctuary was cleansed (or vindicated) by Judas Maccabeus, December 25th, 165 B.C. (see 1 Macc. iv. 41–56; 2 Macc. x. 1–5).

15 the appearance of a man. Evidently an angel in human form: see Gen. xviii. 2; and cp. ix. 21; Luke i. 19, where, as in ver. 16, he is named Gabriel, which means "hero of God."

17 I was afraid. See note on Gen. xv. 12, and cp. v. 18.

at the time of the end [shall be] the vision. Rather, "to the time of the end the vision" reaches or refers. By "the time of the end" may be meant the time of the coming of the Messiah, which was to finish the Jewish dispensation, and to introduce "the last times." But the words may have had a temporary fulfilment in the cleansing of the sanctuary.

19 at the time appointed the end [shall be]. Or, "for the appointed time there is an end"; these sufferings shall not be perpetual.

21 Grecia. Heb., "Javan"; *i.e.*, the Ionians, by which name the Greeks were mostly known in the East. "King" is put for *kingdom:* see vii. 17, compared with vii. 23

the first king. Alexander was the founder of the Grecian dominion over the Jewish people.

22 not in his power. None of Alexander's successors equalled him in power.

23 dark sentences. Rather, "dissimulation" or "stratagems." The whole reign of Antiochus was marked by a combination of cruelty and fraud.

24 and practise. *i.e.*, "and do his pleasure," as in ver. 12.

the mighty and the holy people. Rather, "the mighty ones and the people of the saints"; *i.e.*, the princes and the pious among the Jews.

25 by peace. Rather, "in peace"; *i.e.*, when none suspect him.

against the Prince of princes. Against God; see note on v. 11.

without hand. That is, not by human power, but by God's stroke. Two different accounts are given of the death of Antiochus (1 Macc. vi. 1–16: 2 Macc. ix. 4–28). It is certain that he died in the East of a mysterious and incurable disease.

26 the evening and the morning. See v. 14, and note.

shut thou up the vision. Having written it, seal it up, that it may be preserved (cp. Jer. xxxii. 14); for the events are yet distant. The R.V. renders the latter part of the verse, "for it belongeth to many days [to come]."

The preceding notes have proceeded upon the supposition that vers. 9–12, 23–25, refer to Antiochus, which is the usual, and appears the most natural interpretation of them: though doubtless he is to be regarded (like Edom in Isa. xxxiv., lxiii.) as a representative of the enemies of the people of God. Jerome, and others of the fathers, considered him to be a type of Antichrist. But some apply this portion of the prophecy to the Roman dominion. Others understand it as referring to Mohammed and his followers, who have triumphed and reigned in the regions which formed the scene of the empire, first of Persia, and then of Alexander and his successors; and they consider this little horn to represent the great *Eastern* apostasy and spiritual tyranny, as distinguished from the *Western*, which they suppose to be represented by the little horn of the fourth beast in vii. 8.

CHAPTER IX

1 Darius the son of Ahasuerus.

2 I Daniel understood by (the) **books.** That is, by the sacred books. Jeremiah had sent a letter to Babylon, in which he had been commanded expressly to foretell seventy years from the deportation of Jeconiah as the duration of the captivity of Judah (Jer. xxix. 10).

3 I set my face, etc. Daniel well knew that the mercy which God promised to His people must be sought by humiliation and prayer (Ezek. xxxvi. 37).

4 I prayed unto the Lord my God. In this "effectual fervent prayer," the prophet thoroughly identifies himself with his people; humbling himself most deeply for their sins, whilst he pleads earnestly for national mercies. The short ejaculations so often repeated show the strength of his feelings. The whole prayer is a model for private as well as public confession and supplication.

9 though. Lit., "for" (R.V.).

20 whiles I was speaking. This is an encouraging instance of God's readiness to answer prayer: cp. Psa. xxxiv. 4; lxv. 2.

21 the man Gabriel. See note on viii. 16.

about the time of the evening oblation. About three o'clock in the afternoon.

24 Seventy weeks. Or, "seventy sevens." Daniel's prayer was founded on the promise respecting the "seventy years" (Jer. xxix. 10); the answer makes known a period of "seven times seventy," or 490 years.

are determined upon thy people, etc. "Are decreed respecting thy people," etc.; *i.e.*, as the period in which these predictions regarding thy people shall be fulfilled.

to finish the transgression, etc. Some commentators apply this verse to the restoration of the people, and the rebuilding of the city, after the exile in Babylon; but others regard it as referring to the coming and work of Messiah. It is not, however, easy to give with certainty the meaning of each clause. Perhaps the best translation is, "to shut up the transgression, and to seal up the sins; and to expiate iniquity, and to bring in everlasting righteousness; and to seal up vision and prophet, and to anoint the holy of holies."

25 to restore and to build Jerusalem. Though Cyrus had been foretold as the rebuilder of Jerusalem (Isa. xliv. 28), yet the period here spoken of cannot be reckoned either from his decree, or from its subsequent confirmation by Darius Hystaspis. The whole question of dates must be left undecided.

the Messiah the Prince. Rather, "an Anointed One, a Prince." (See R.V. marg.) "There can be no reasonable doubt," says Farrar (*Daniel*, p. 280), "that this is a reference to the deposition of the high priest Onias III, and his murder by Andronicus (171 B.C.)."

26 but not for Himself. Lit., "and nothing for Him": see R.V. and marg. Here both the old versions and more modern translations vary greatly. Moffatt renders: "leaving no successor."

the end thereof. Heb., "his end"; perhaps the end which the prince will bring on the city and sanctuary.

and unto the end of the war desolations are determined. Rather, "and unto the end [will be] war, a determined measure of desolations" ("Statuta desolatio," *Vulgate*): see Matt. xxiv. 21, 22; Luke xxi. 22–24.

27 He shall confirm the covenant. Rather, as R.V., "He shall make a firm covenant." This verse refers to the history of the one "seven" of years which completes the "seventy sevens." But commentators differ greatly in their interpretations. If it refers to the tyranny and overthrow of Antiochus, the half of the week ("week" being seven years) would be the three and a half years during which Antiochus suppressed the Jewish worship.

and for the overspreading of abominations He shall make [it] desolate. Rather, "and over the wing of abominations [shall be] a desolation," or "[shall come] one that maketh desolate." The "wing" is supposed by some to be a pinnacle of the Temple; by others it is regarded as referring to the image, probably winged like so many Babylonian figures, which Antiochus set up there.

that determined shall be poured upon the desolate. If the last word be translated "desolator" (see R.V.), then it intimates that this future enemy of Israel, after being used by God as the instrument of His justice, shall himself be punished: cp. Isa. x. 7, and note.

CHAPTER X

1 In the third year of Cyrus. See note on i. 21. This vision followed a fast of three weeks (see 2, 3), with which the prophet had begun the year, probably on account of the condition of his people, whose efforts to rebuild the Temple were for a time successfully opposed by their enemies: see Ezra iv. 5.

but the time appointed was long. Rather, as R.V., "even a great warfare": see note on Job vii. 1. This perhaps means that the vision related to a severe conflict.

4 Hiddekel. The Tigris. Daniel had probably now ceased to reside at court, and taken up his abode among some of his people, near this river.

5 a certain man clothed in linen. See note on viii. 15. White linen was an emblem of *purity* (Rev. vii. 14; xix. 8), and was therefore appointed to be worn by the priests (Lev. vi. 10; Ezek. xliv. 17, 18). Hence the seven ministers of God's punitive justice appear clothed in it (Rev. xv. 6).

fine gold of Uphaz. See note on Jer. x. 9; and compare with the whole description Rev. i. 13–16.

6 like the beryl. See note on Ezek. i. 16.

8 my comeliness was turned in me into corruption. The bright looks of health were changed for the paleness of death.

10 which set me upon my knees, etc. Rather, "which placed me tottering upon my knees and the palms of my hands."

13 the prince of the kingdom of Persia. The interference of Michael, here called "one of the chief princes" and prince of Israel (21), and elsewhere "the archangel" (Jude 9), appears to lead to the conclusion that "the prince of Persia" and "the prince of Grecia" represent superhuman beings acting as patrons of those nations, and devoted to their particular interests.

one of the chief princes. That is, of the archangels. "Michael" (meaning, *Who like God?*) always appears as the leader and patron either of ancient Israel (as here and in ver. 21; xii. 1; Jude 9); or of the true Israel (as in Rev. xii. 7).

I remained there with the kings of Persia. Charles translates: "I left him alone there with the prince of the kings of Persia."

14 in the latter days. This may mean, in future times.

touched my lips. See Isa. vi. 6, 7.

16 one like the similitude of the sons of men. An angel; as ver. 5, and again, ver. 18. There is thus in this vision a threefold angelic ministration. The angel appears now as a man, without majesty and that splendour which had appalled the prophet.

17 the servant of this my lord. That is, "I"; an expression of humility.

20 and now. As soon as he had made the promised discoveries, which occupy xi., xii.

the prince of Grecia shall come. The patron of "Javan," or Greece (see viii. 21), will need the same vigilance, as he is not friendly to the interests of Israel (21).

21 and there is none that holdeth with me in these things. Rather, "and there is not one strengthening himself with me against these," etc. This clearly teaches the prophet not to trust in the apparently favourable dispositions of princes or dynasties, but to look to God alone for the protection of His people.

CHAPTER XI

1 in the first year of Darius the Mede. (See note on Ezra i. 1.) This verse really belongs to chap. x.

2 three kings in Persia, and the fourth. The three being Cyrus, Cambyses, and Darius Hystaspis; and the fourth Xerxes, who invaded Greece with a vast army (Herodotus, vii., viii., ix.), and thus led to the overthrow of the Persian empire by the "mighty king," Alexander (3).

4 his kingdom shall be broken. See viii. 8, and note.

nor according to his dominion. None of Alexander's successors obtained an empire so extensive as his.

his kingdom shall be plucked up. By his death, which brought to an end the kingdom which he founded and sustained.

even for others beside those. *i.e.,* given to others than his posterity.

5 the king of the south. The kingdom of Egypt under Ptolemy Soter, which was one of the most powerful of the monarchies arising out of the division of Alexander's empire. The Jewish people, lying between this kingdom and that of the Seleucidæ in Syria on the north, were subject for a long period to one or the other, and suffered alternately from each.

[one] of his princes. Seleucus Nicator, who founded the mighty kingdom of Syria, had been a governor under Ptolemy.

6 in the end of years. That is, after some time. The prophecy passes on to the time of Ptolemy Philadelphus and Antiochus Theos. In order to end the wars between these kingdoms, Ptolemy gave his daughter Berenice in marriage to Antiochus; who for this purpose divorced his wife Laodice, and excluded her children from the succession. But Antiochus soon afterwards restored Laodice; who then poisoned him, that her son Seleucus Callinicus might reign. By the order of Seleucus, Berenice was put to death.

the power of the arm. That is, her *strength,* or influence.

neither shall he stand. That is, the king of the south and his power.

he that begat her. Some, by a slight change, render it, "her son," who in fact was put to death with her. (So Luther, followed by Charles and Moffatt.)

7 out of a branch of her roots. One who sprang from the same root as Berenice. Her brother Ptolemy Euergetes avenged her death, by slaying Laodice, and overrunning Syria and Cilicia with an army, taking the "fortresses," and carrying off an enormous booty: see Polybius, l. 5.

10 his sons. The sons of the king of Syria were Seleucus Ceraunus (who soon died), and Antiochus the Great, who then carried on the war alone.

his fortress. Perhaps Gaza.

12 And when he hath taken away the multitude. Or, "And the multitude (*i.e.,* of the Egyptian army) shall be elated": see R.V.

14 the robbers of thy people. Or, "the violent among thy people."

16 which by his hand shall be consumed. Rather, "and in his hand shall be destruction" (R.V.).

17 and upright ones with him. A better rendering is, "and he shall make treaties with him."

the daughter of women, corrupting her. This perhaps means Cleopatra, daughter of Antiochus, whom her father instructed to betray the interests of her husband, Ptolemy Epiphanes.

18 without his own reproach he shall cause [it] to turn upon him. Rather, "and a general shall cause his reproach against him to cease, beside that he shall turn his reproach upon himself." Antiochus dishonoured the Roman arms by invading their allies; Scipio not only wiped off that disgrace, but inflicted upon Antiochus one more severe.

19 fort. Rather, "fortresses."

20 in his estate, etc. *i.e.*, as his successor. A brief reference is made to Seleucus Philopator, who was poisoned after a short reign, chiefly distinguished by the taxes which he imposed for the purposes of paying tribute to the Romans (20); and then the prophecy appears to describe at length the reign of Antiochus Epiphanes. Some expositors, however, do not agree in applying vers. 31–45 to Antiochus; but consider that there is here a transition to other subjects: see note on ver. 31.

22 with the arms of a flood. "The overflowing wings of Egypt were swept away before him" (*Farrar*).

the prince of the covenant. *i.e.*, bound to him by treaty.

27 they shall speak lies at one table. Each party aiming to deceive the other by an appearance of friendship.

but it shall not prosper. This perhaps refers to the scheme of Antiochus to obtain possession of the whole of Egypt; in which Ptolemy concurred. But this was not accomplished. Antiochus left Egypt, and attacked Jerusalem.

the end shall be at the time appointed. All these intrigues shall not accomplish the objects of the kings, but in God's time they shall subserve His purposes.

28 he shall do [exploits]. Rather, "he shall accomplish his purpose." Antiochus took Jerusalem, and ravaged it, and entered and polluted the Temple (2 Macc. v. 15–21; 1 Macc. i. 21–28).

29 but it shall not be as the former, etc. The latter invasion shall not be successful like the former.

30 the ships of Chittim. See note on Numb. xxiv. 24. Ptolemy obtained the aid of the Romans, who imperiously required Antiochus to retire from Egypt.

31 And arms shall stand on his part. "And arms (*i.e.*, forces, 6, 11) from him shall stand up, and shall profane the sanctuary, the fortress," etc. The Temple itself was fortified, as well as the city.

they shall place the abomination that maketh desolate. Cp. 1 Macc. i. 57.

32 the people that do know their God. etc. This probably refers to Mattathias and his sons and followers, the history of whose labours and sufferings is found in 1 Maccabees: see also sketch of the history of the Jews between the Old and New Testaments, at the end of the Old Testament.

35 to try them, and to purge, and to make them white. "To make trial among them, and to purify and to make white" (or clean). Suffering tends both to test and to purify.

36 And the king shall do according to his will. The Romans checked the ambitious projects of Antiochus, but not his arbitrary despotism; so that he interfered with the religion as well as the civil rights of his subjects.

37 Neither shall he regard the god (gods) **of his fathers.** Antiochus was under none of the restraints by which men are usually influenced: see note on ver. 36; Jer. ii. 10, 11; Mic. iv. 5.

nor the desire of women. That is, the object of their desire. Probably referring to Tammuz-Adonis, to whose worship the Syrian women were devoted. (See Milton, *Paradise Lost*, i. 446–452.) The Græco-Syrian monarchs had adopted the Eastern deities, Baal and Ashtoreth; but Antiochus regarded not "the gods of his fathers," nor "any god," even "the God of gods"; but aimed to establish the worship of the Roman Jupiter. It was after a baffled attempt by Antiochus to plunder the temple of Astarte (under the name of Anaitis) at Elymais, that he was attacked by his fatal illness.

38 in his estate. Or, "in his stead"; *i.e.*, instead of another god.

the god of forces. Or, "the god of fortresses." *i.e.*, Jupiter Capitolinus, whose worship Antiochus introduced from Rome and enforced in Syria, and even in Judæa, where he placed his statute and altar in the Temple: see Livy, lxii. 6; xli. 20; 1 Macc. i. 39, 62.

39 Thus shall he do in the most strong holds, etc. Or, "And he does [his will] to fenced fortresses with a strange god; whoever acknowledges him he will greatly honour, and cause them to rule over many, and will divide the land for a reward."

40 at the time of the end. This is apparently the end either of this tyrant's reign, or of these appointed trials; and these nearly coincide. In the imperfect histories that we have of Antiochus there is no account of another war with Egypt; but Porphyry asserts the circumstantial agreement of all this description with the facts of the history, and Jerome quotes his assertion without questioning it. Some regard vers. 40–45 as a summary of the events of his reign, viewed in relation to its close.

43 the Libyans. The Libyans were almost always connected with Egypt by subjection or alliance: see 2 Chron. xii. 3.

shall be at his steps. That is, they shall follow him as his subjects.

44 tidings out of the east and out of the north. The Parthians on the east (Tacit. *Hist.* v. 8) and the Armenians on the north (Appian, 45) assailed the dominions of Antiochus, and compelled him to return (1 Macc. iii. 27–37).

45 the tabernacles of his palace. The royal tents.

between the seas. The clause may be better rendered, "between the seas and the beautiful holy mountain" (*i.e.*, between the Mediterranean and Jerusalem). Antiochus Epiphanes died in 164 or 163 B.C. (see 1 Macc. vi. 1–16).

CHAPTER XII

1 And at that time. When God's people are oppressed, their guardian shall interpose; but in the efforts for their freedom there shall be a struggle and suffering of unexampled severity. Yet there shall be a glorious deliverance and resurrection, in which those who were their faithful leaders and teachers in their time of depression shall have the highest honours (1–3). For use in that time this vision is to be preserved (4).

Michael. See notes on x. 13.

written in the book. Cp. Exod. xxxii. 33; Rev. xx. 12–15.

2 many of them that sleep in the dust of the earth shall awake. These words, like so many prophetic utterances, have both an immediate and a further, complete fulfilment, referring in the first instance to the national revival and in the second place to the final resurrection of the just and the unjust.

4 seal the book. See note on viii. 26.

many shall run to and fro. If this translation

be accepted, it perhaps refers primarily to the extensive diffusion of religious truth by the Jewish people before the coming of Christ. But the form of the Hebrew verb is used of scrutiny or inspection, as of God's all-seeing eyes (2 Chron. xvi. 9) and has therefore been translated by some scholars "many shall peruse the book." Charles and Moffatt give a different reading, suggesting that "many shall apostatise."

5 other two. That is, two angels.

7 and sware by Him that liveth for ever and ever. Thus indicating the importance and the certainty of the announcement.

a time, times, and a half. See notes on vii. 24, 25.

all these things shall be finished. When for "a time, times, and half a time" the power of God's people has been broken, then this vision shall be completed. Such was the case under the persecutions of Antiochus. But it may also refer to a future period.

8 I heard, but I understood not. As these prophecies have been so variously interpreted, notwithstanding all the light of subsequent events and revelations, it is not surprising that they were mysterious to Daniel.

9 Go thy way, etc. Make no further inquiry; the prophetic communication is now completed. Look rather to the practical end of all, the purifying and instructing of those who are willing to learn.

10 the wise shall understand. Or, "the teachers shall understand" (see R.V. marg.).

11 from the time that the daily [sacrifice] shall be taken away, etc. It is clear from these words that some forcible interruption of the Temple-service is the date from which the 1290 days begin. This period is supposed by some to be the space of time between the issuing of the command of Antiochus to rifle and pollute the Temple, and the restoration of its sacred rites by Judas Maccabeus. Others think that these "days" signify *years*, and apply the predictions to the papacy, or to Mohammedanism.

12 Blessed is he that waiteth, etc. A further addition is here made of 45 days; closing with a happy consummation, in which he who shall reach it will be blessed, for the long struggle shall have passed completely away.

13 thou shalt rest, etc. With this cheering assurance of his personal acceptance and everlasting safety and happiness, the prophet's message is concluded.

HOSEA

INTRODUCTION

HOSEA, himself a native of the kingdom of Israel — the Ten Tribes, as distinguished from Judah—exercised his prophetic ministry among his own people. His work began in the time of Jeroboam II, and lasted at least about forty years, from about 780 to 740 B.C. He prophesied at the same time as Isaiah, Joel, Micah, and Amos.

The Book begins with the story of his unhappy marriage, which became a parable of the faithlessness of Israel in departing from God and going after strange gods, as the prophet's forgiveness was a type of the Divine mercy (i. 2; ii. 12, 13; iii.). The moral and spiritual condition of Israel at that time is then described (iv.), and the prophet urges the people to repentance (vi. 1–3), with promises of God's forgiveness. But his remonstrances and exhortations seem to meet with no response, and he again proclaims the Divine judgements upon their sins (viii., ix.), repeating his appeal for repentance and amendment (x. 12; xii. 6). He depicts God as yearning, with tender pity, over Israel (xi. 8). He closes with another earnest invitation to return to God, and God's gracious promise to "heal their backsliding and love them freely," restoring them to joyous and fruitful life (xiv. 5–7).

"In Hosea," says W. J. Farley (*The Progress of Prophecy*, p. 63), "we stand beside the fountain-head of that gracious doctrine—God is Love. . . Very specially he anticipates the New Testament in emphasising three things—*The necessity of knowledge of God* (iv. 1, 6); *the necessity for repentance* (vi. 1; xiv. 1, 2); and *the love of God* (iii. 1; xi. 1–4)."

CHAPTER I

2 children of whoredoms. The intention clearly is to exhibit in the strongest light the unfaithfulness of the people of Israel to the covenant of Jehovah. It has been much questioned whether all this is a parable, or a description of a vision, or a narrative of actual occurrences. If the more literal interpretation is taken, it should be borne in mind that the unchastity of the wife was openly shown *after marriage.* Hosea was not, in any case, commanded to espouse a woman notoriously profligate, but one who afterwards became unfaithful and deserted him. It is in her subsequent repentance and her forgiveness by the man she had wronged that the great message of the book consists. Cp. the story of Lancelot and Guinevere in the *Idylls of the King.*

3 Gomer the daughter of Diblaim. The names "Gomer," signifying *consummation,* and "Diblaim," meaning *cakes of preserved figs* (which were deemed a luxury in the East), are probably chosen to intimate the consummate wickedness of the people, and their devotedness to the sensual gratifications which accompanied the practice of idolatry.

4 Call his name Jezreel. The name "Jezreêl" appears to be selected partly on account of the historical associations connected with the city (see next note); and partly because of its etymological meaning, "God will sow." It may thus be both symbolical (4, 5) and prophetical (ii. 23).

I will avenge the blood of Jezreel, etc. Jezreêl was a royal residence in the great plain of Jezreêl at the head of the valley which bears the same name: see ver. 5, and note on 1 Sam. xxviii. 4. The city was implicated in the murder of Naboth and his sons (1 Kings xxi), and the punishment of Ahab in his posterity (2 Kings ix. 21–37; x. 11) by Jehu.

5 I will break the bow of Israel, etc "The bow" is the emblem of military power.

6 Lo-ruhamah. "Not having obtained mercy," or, "the Unpitied." Moffatt gives the name as "Nomercy."

but I will utterly take them away. Rather, as R.V., "that I should in any wise pardon them."

7 and will save them, etc. Fulfilled in the destruction of Sennacherib's army (2 Kings xix.).

9 Lo-ammi. "Not My people."

10 Yet the number of the children of Israel, etc. An allusion to the promises in Gen. xxii. 17; xxxii. 12.

in the place where it was said unto them. That is, *wherever* these words of judgement had been spoken, in Palestine, or in the lands of captivity.

[Ye are] the sons of the living God. The Apostle Paul (Rom. ix. 25, 26) applies this passage to the whole body of the faithful, both Jews and Gentiles. Thus, though the Israelite has lost his national pre-eminence, all the blessings of the Gospel are still within his reach, and he shall share them with the Gentiles: see Isa. xlii. 6.

11 and appoint themselves one head. In their reunited state thankfully choosing as their King the Messiah whom God has appointed for them; cp. iii. 5.

they shall come up out of the land. This may allude to the coming up of the Israelites from Babylon, regarded as representative of higher blessings.

great shall be the day of Jezreel. That is, memorable shall be the season of God's sowing to produce a harvest, "which cannot be measured nor numbered," of those who, "having obtained mercy," are "the sons of the living God." In ch. ii. 1, the symbolic names of the prophet's three children are employed to express the restored privilege. "Jezreel," unchanged in form, appears with new meaning; "Lo-ammi" and "Lo-ruhamah," by losing the negative ("Lo"), have their significance reversed.

CHAPTER II

2 Plead with your mother. "Mother" here, and in iv. 5, signifies the Israelitish community, the individual members of which might be regarded as her children. Those who are alive to the sin and danger of the nation are called upon to join the prophet in his efforts to arouse and reform it.

she is not my wife. By her base conduct she has forfeited her right to the name and advantages of a wife.

out of her sight. Rather, "from her face."

3 Lest I strip her naked, etc. Lest I reduce her to a state of utter destitution and misery.

5 my lovers. The idols which I have worshipped. So infatuated had the Israelites become, as to ascribe their prosperity or adversity to these divinities: cp. Jer. xliv. 17–19.

6 I will hedge up thy way with thorns, etc. The "thorns" and the "wall" represent the restraints and sufferings by which God mercifully checks the fatal pursuit of sin.

7 follow after. The Heb. word denotes hot, eager pursuit.

8 Corn . . . wine . . . oil . . . silver and gold. The products of the soil and the fruits of commerce.

they prepared for Baal. Or, "used for Baal," as R.V.: cp. Isa. xliv. 17. The very gifts which Jehovah bestowed upon His people they devoted to their idols.

9 in the time thereof . . . in the season thereof. Just when she is most confidently counting upon these things as her own (see ver. 5), I will make her feel that they are Mine, by taking them away.

10 In the sight of her lovers. The heathen gods are represented as witnessing the disgrace of their worshippers, without being able to relieve them.

11 her feast days, her new moons, and her sabbaths. The yearly, monthly, and weekly festivals (still observed, as this passage shows, in the northern nation), were designed to be seasons of holy joy; but the people had deprived them of their sacredness, and had turned them into occasions of sinful pleasure; and now God will deprive them of their joyfulness.

13 the days of (the) **Baalim, wherein she burned incense to them.** Or, as R.V., "unto which she burned incense." That is, the days of the *worship* of Baalim, as opposed to the festivals of Divine appointment (11).

14 Therefore. This word seems to refer to vers. 6, 9. As My people have sinned against Me, *therefore* I will first check them, then correct them, and lastly will draw them by My long-suffering mercy back to Myself.

15 her vineyards. Her own forfeited heritage: "from thence"; *i.e.,* from the wilderness.

the valley of Achor for a door of hope. As the wanderings of Israel in the wilderness, and the occurrences at Ai and Achor, however painful, had been in reality a most merciful preparation for the conquest and possession of Canaan, so shall the chastenings just mentioned be a preparation for the enjoyment of spiritual blessings: cp. Deut. viii. 2–6; Josh. vii.; viii. 1, 2. So in every human life where there is repentance and trust in God, the valley of trouble becomes the door of hope.

shall sing. Lit., "shall make answer" (R.V.); gratefully responding to God's kindness. Many regard this as alluding to the song of the Hebrews at the Red Sea: see Exod. xv. 21.

16 Baali. The term *Baal,* in its common use, signified "lord," and was usually applied to the husband by the wife: see 1 Pet. iii. 6. But this name had been so connected with idolatrous worship, that God refuses any more to be called by the title. *Ish* means "husband"; and the termination *i* stands for "my."

20 thou shalt know the Lord. The meaning probably is, Thou shalt learn by thine own experience that I am, as My name Jahveh implies, unchanging and faithful: see notes on Exod. iii. 14; vi. 3.

21 I will hear (answer) **the heavens,** etc. "All creation" has groaned under the curse caused by Israel's sin (ver. 9: cp. Rom. viii. 22); but now, by a beautiful figure, each link in the chain of natural agencies is personified, as calling for vivifying power to that which is above it, and the highest, "the heavens," as invoking the Eternal. And they no longer ask in vain for the blessing needful to fertility; for He who alone possesses the power will now bless His repentant people. The highest natural causes are but instruments by which the supreme First Cause works out His designs; and all are subordinated by Him to the purposes of His moral government.

22 Jezreel. The name of the restored Israel, "whom God soweth": see next verse.

23 I will have mercy, etc., "I will have mercy on Nomercy" (*Moffatt*).

CHAPTER III

1 beloved of [her] friend. The word "friend" is probably here used for *husband;* who loved her even in her unfaithfulness. Gomer (i. 3) is the woman indicated.

flagons of wine. Rather, "raisin-cakes" ("love-cakes of raisins," R.V.): see notes on i. 3, and on Isa. xvi. 7.

2 fifteen pieces of silver. The price appears to have been paid half in money and half in corn; and thus the whole amount is equal to the value of a slave: see Exod. xxi. 32; Zech. xi. 12, 13. This suggests the degraded condition of Israel at the time when God interposes for his restoration.

3 Thou shalt abide. Lit., "Thou shalt sit," *i.e.,* "sit *still*": lead a secluded life, not yet restored to full conjugal intercourse. So the clause, "Thou shalt not be for [another] man," should be rendered, as R.V., "Thou shalt not be any man's wife." The words, "So will I also be for thee," represent the husband also as waiting for the time of renewed conjugal and perfect union.

4 the children of Israel. Primarily, the Ten Tribes, although the prophet has in view the destiny of the whole united nation: see i. 11.

without an image. Or, as R.V., "without pillar," the mark of a consecrated place.

without an ephod. See Exod. xxviii. 6, and note.

[without] teraphim. See note on Gen. xxxi. 19. The whole verse describes a period during which the Israelites would have no political independence, no legitimate sacrifices or priest, and no idolatrous statue or deity. Such was their state during some of their earlier captivities, and such it has been during the long period which has elapsed since the last destruction of the Temple. For more than eighteen centuries they have kept from idolatry.

5 David their king. A forecast of the Messiah and the acceptance of Him by Israel.

CHAPTER IV

1 ye children of Israel. The northern kingdom: cp. ver. 15.

2 By swearing, etc. Or, as R.V., "There is nought but swearing," etc.

blood toucheth blood. "Bloodshed follows bloodshed."

3 Therefore shall the land mourn. See note on ii. 21.

4 let no man strive, etc. This is rather a statement of fact, "No man strives or rebukes another."

5 the prophet also shall fall (stumble) **with thee in the night.** By day and by night the common people, the prophets, yea, the whole nation (see ii. 4), shall feel My anger.

thy mother. The nation or the tribe.

6 thou hast rejected knowledge. This is addressed to the priests of Israel. They have rejected the knowledge of God and He refuses to acknowledge them as His priests.

8 They eat up the sin of My people. Probably, "the sin-offering." These false priests earnestly upheld the wicked image-worship of the people for the sake of their own profit.

9 like people, like priest. The one shall share the fate of the other: see Isa. xxiv. 2.

11 Whoredom and wine and new wine. The prophet now turns from the priests to the people: cp. Prov. ii. 19; xxiii. 29–35, and notes. Licentiousness and drunkenness are the causes of that stupidity which leads Israel to take a stock for his god, and a stick for his prophet (12).

12 their staff declareth unto them. Some have understood this to refer to rod-divination, but it seems better to regard "staff" as meaning "twig," referring to the tree-cultus (see *Peake's Commentary*).

13 elms. Rather, "terebinths."

your spouses (*or,* daughters-in-law) **shall commit adultery.** Omit "shall" (R.V.). The idolatrous worship to which the Israelites were prone was connected with gross licentiousness: cp. Judges ii. 13.

14 I will not punish, etc. I will not single them out for punishment, as though they were the chief offenders: the whole people are implicated, and shall "fall," or "be overthrown" (R.V.).

15 let not Judah offend. To make his appeals more impressive, the prophet enjoins Judah to have nothing to do with the debased sister-kingdom.

Gilgal . . . Beth-aven. The sacred associations connected with Gilgal and Bethel in the history of the Israelites (Gen. xxviii. 10–22; xxxv. 1–7; 1 Sam. x. 3, 8; xi. 14, 15; xv. 21, 33) seem to have led to the establishment of false worship there. Hence the prophets denounce these places (see ix. 15; xii. 11; Amos iv. 4, 5); and, instead of calling the latter "Bethel," *the house of God,* they transfer to it the name of a neighbouring village, "Beth-aven," *the house of vanity,* referring to the unprofitableness of sin.

16 Israel slideth back as a backsliding heifer. Rather, "Israel is stubborn, as a stubborn heifer"; as in Deut. xxi. 18.

as a lamb in a large place. They wish to range at large; they shall do so, unprotected.

17 Ephraim is joined to idols. Ephraim, as the leading tribe, gives its name to the kingdom of Israel.

18 Their drink is sour, etc. Rather, "Their carousal is over, they commit whoredom (*i.e.,* they turn from wine to lewdness); her shields (or rulers) desperately love shame. [Therefore] the wind binds her (the nation) in its wings (*i.e.,* to carry it away), and they shall be ashamed," etc.

CHAPTER V

1 Mizpah . . . Tabor. Mizpah of Gilead, and Tabor, well-wooded hills which afforded covert to game. The "snares" and "nets" represent the seductions to idolatry of the kings and priests of Israel: see 1 Kings xii. 26–33.

2 And the revolters are profound. Or, "And the apostates have deepened (*i.e.*, increased) slaughter, and I [will increase] punishment to them all."

4 They will not frame their doings, etc. Rather, as R.V., "Their doings will not suffer them to turn unto their God."

6 with their flocks and with their herds. *i.e.*, with the costliest sacrifices.

to seek the Lord. To entreat His help in their trouble.

7 strange children. *Spurious* children: see i. 2; ii. 4.

now shall a month devour them. Perhaps put for "new moon" (see R.V.); the meaning of the clause being that their hypocritical feasts shall be their ruin.

8 Blow ye the cornet. That is, "Sound *an alarm.*"

After thee, O Benjamin. Or, "[the enemy] is behind thee, O Benjamin": having conquered the North, he now threatens the Southern capital.

10 like them that remove the bound (landmark). That is, they are grasping and fraudulent: see Deut. xix. 14.

11 walked after the commandment. "The commandment" is, perhaps, the institution of image-worship by Jeroboam, which the people readily adopted (see 1 Kings xii. 28–32).

13 Then went Ephraim to the Assyrian. This refers to the vassalage to the Assyrian king, which both Israel and Judah promised, in the hope of gaining his protection: see 2 Kings xv. 19 (the embassy of Menahem); xvi. 7 (the embassy of Ahaz).

Jareb. Lit., the adversary; it is evidently a symbolical name for Assyria, like "Rahab" for Egypt.

15 I will go and return to My place. God's withdrawal involves the deprivation of that all-sufficient protection and aid which His presence implies.

early. That is, "earnestly" (R.V.). The verse should be connected with the next, "will seek Me earnestly, [saying] Come," etc. (R.V., marg.).

CHAPTER VI

2 After two days. That is, after a very brief period, as we say, "in a couple of days." For this indefinite use of "two," see 1 Kings xvii. 12; Isa. vii. 21.

3 Then shall we know, etc. Or, "And let us know, let us follow on (*i.e.*, eagerly strive to know Jehovah); [for] His coming forth is sure as the morning" (R.V.), etc.; *i.e.*, it is as certain as the cheering dawn and the fertilising rain (see Gen. viii. 22), and therefore we cannot be disappointed.

4 your goodness. Lit., "your mercy"; or, "your love": a phrase designating religion: see Isa. lvii. 1. The French version has "votre piété."

5 have I hewed them. I have threatened them severely: cp. Isa. xi. 4; Heb. iv. 12.

thy judgements. Most ancient versions read, "my judgement goeth forth as the light (lightning)."

6 I desired (desire) **mercy and not sacrifice.** See the quotation of this passage by our Lord in Matt. ix. 13; xii. 7.

7 like men. Better, "like Adam" (R.V.): cp. Rom. v. 14. The word *there* presents difficulties. Several leading commentators regard it as referring to Palestine, which was to Israel as Paradise to Adam.

8 polluted with blood. Rather, "tracked with blood." This was probably Ramoth-Gilead, the chief city of the district; which, though a priests' city, and one of the cities of refuge, had become notorious for idolatry and bloodshed: see 2 Kings xv. 25.

9 in the way by consent. Rather, "in the way *towards Shechem*" (R.V.); another city of refuge. It is probable that the privilege of sanctuary had been abused, so that these cities on the two sides of Jordan had become nests of banditti.

11 He hath set a harvest for thee. A harvest of punishment. Render, with R.V., "there is a harvest appointed for thee."

when I returned the captivity of My people. Or, "When I would bring back the captivity of My people, when I would heal Israel, then the iniquity," etc.

CHAPTER VII

2 their own doings have beset them about. Their evil doings and their consequences compass them about.

4 until it be leavened. That is, *only* for a little while, until the dough is leavened. The Israelites would not brook more than the very slightest interruption to their licentiousness: see 2 Pet. ii. 14.

5 In the day of our king. A birthday or coronation-day, celebrated with riotous excess.

with bottles of wine, etc. Or, "the heat (or fever) of wine; [so that] he held out his hand with mockers." The reference is to those who drink together, holding out their cups to each other.

6 like an oven. As no signs of the heat of an oven appear when the door is closed, so do the princes (see ver. 5) hide their machinations till they are ready to destroy their king.

7 all their kings are fallen. Zechariah was slain by Shallum, Shallum by Menahem, Pekahiah by Pekah, and Pekah by Hoshea; and of all of them it is recorded that they "did that which was evil in the sight of the Lord."

8 the people. Rather, "the peoples," R.V., by alliances with the heathen.

Ephraim is a cake not turned. As a cake not turned in baking would be half bread and half dough, so their religion was a mixture and their character weak.

9 he knoweth it not. The sadness of moral declension is here indicated.

11 without heart. That is, without understanding: see note on iv. 11. As the dove in its alarm often rushes into the danger which it fears, so the Israelites foolishly court those foreign alliances which will ruin them.

12 as their congregation hath heard. By the public warnings of the prophets.

14 when they howled upon their beds. Or, as R.V., "But they howl," etc. Their cry of fear and anguish, not that of penitence.

they assemble themselves. That is, to pray to their *idols.*

15 have bound. Or, "admonished them."

16 rage. Or, "insolence."

CHAPTER VIII

1 [Set] the trumpet to thy mouth, etc. The brevity of the language expresses the nearness of the danger: "To thy mouth the trumpet! Like an eagle to the house of Jehovah!" "The house of Jehovah" probably means His land and people.

4 but not by Me. That is, without consulting Me.

I knew it not. *i.e.*, it was without my approval.

5 Thy calf, O Samaria, hath cast [**thee**] **off.** Rather, as R.V., "He hath cast off thy calf, O Samaria."

6 For from Israel [**was**] **it also.** Perhaps referring to ver. 4. Israel, who has set up kings and princes of his own, has *also* made this calf, which is no God.

7 It hath no stalk. Perhaps, as R.V., "He hath no standing corn." There is no produce of his sowing; or if there is, it yields no meal; or if it does, he has no benefit from it.

9 a wild ass alone by himself. Like the "wild ass" in its untractableness and waywardness.

hath hired lovers. Sending presents to foreign nations to obtain their alliance.

they shall sorrow a little, etc. Rather, "they shall soon cease to elect kings and princes." Luther has "they shall soon be weary of the burden of," etc.

11 hath made many altars. This sin was expressly prohibited in Deut. xii. 13, 14, with the threat that those who committed it should be left to serve idols in a foreign land: see Deut. iv. 28.

CHAPTER IX

1 thou hast loved a reward (hire) **upon every cornfloor.** The meaning may be, "Thou hast loved to see thy floor full, and hast attributed thy plenty to thy idols, rejoicing before them at the ingathering of thy corn": cp. ii. 12; Jer. xliv. 17.

2 shall fail in her. *i.e.*, shall disappoint their expectations.

3 they shall eat unclean things in Assyria. As they have preferred unclean things in their own holy land, they shall soon be forced to eat their food in a foreign country, where all is defiled. Cp. Dan. i. 8.

4 as the bread of mourners. See note on Ezek. xxiv. 17.

for their bread for their soul, etc. Rather, "Their bread shall be for their soul (*i.e.*, for themselves only); it shall not come into the house of Jehovah." It shall be only for the satisfaction of their appetite: lacking the consecration imparted by offering to God.

6 they are gone because of destruction. Rather, as R.V., "they are gone away from destruction."

Egypt shall gather them up. For burial.

the pleasant [**places**] **for their silver.** Or, "their pleasant things of silver," R.V., *i.e.*, decorations, utensils, perhaps idols. These shall be buried in the earth, and nettles shall grow over them.

7 the prophet is a fool. This and the following clause are Hosea's quotation of what the people say, and then he goes on "for the multitude of thine iniquity," etc.

10 like grapes in the wilderness. Israel was at first as acceptable to Me as grapes are to a traveller in the desert, or as the earliest figs are to the eater: see note on Jer. xxiv. 2. But the people soon gave themselves up to idolatry and licentiousness: see Numb. xxv. 1–5.

separated themselves unto [**that**] **shame.** "Consecrated themselves unto the shameful thing" (R.V.).

And [**their**] **abominations,** etc. *i.e.*, they became as abominable as the impure gods which they loved.

11 their glory shall fly away. Their "glory," or prosperity, shall be destroyed by the failure of population; for they shall have few children, and those few shall be slain (12, 13). "From the birth," etc., should be rendered, "There shall be no birth," etc.

13 Ephraim, as I saw Tyrus.

14 Give them a miscarrying womb. Some suppose this to be the prophet's intercession. Rather, inflict upon them barrenness than let them bring forth children "for the murderer": cp. Luke xxiii. 29.

15 All their wickedness is in Gilgal. See iv. 15.

Mine house. Meaning probably the land of Israel: cp. viii. 1.

CHAPTER X

1 Israel is an empty vine. Or, "Israel is a luxuriant vine; he maketh his fruit equal to himself"; *i.e.*, putteth forth fruit according to his luxuriance: cp. R.V. The "luxuriance" is outward prosperity; the "fruit" is the sin (in this case, idolatry) to which men are so prone to pervert the gifts of Providence.

2 Now shall they be found faulty. Rather, "now shall they be punished."

3 to us. Rather, "for us" (R.V.). They shall be made to acknowledge that their king cannot save them without Jehovah's help: cp. 1 Sam. viii., and notes.

4 Thus judgement springeth up as hemlock. See note on Deut. xxix. 18. Punishment shall spring up as quickly and luxuriantly as weeds do in the field.

5 the priests thereof [**that**] **rejoiced.** This should be, "And the priests shall grieve because of its departed glory." Respecting the word here rendered "priests," see note on 2 Kings xxiii. 5.

6 king Jareb. The king of Assyria: see on ch. v. 13.

7 as the foam. Perhaps "as a chip"; *i.e.*, on the water.

8 Aven. Probably used for Beth-aven: cp. iv. 15.

they shall say to the mountains, Cover us. Cp. Isa. ii. 19; Rev. vi.

9 there they stood. Or, "there they have stood," or remained.

10 when they shall bind themselves in their two furrows. Or, "When I shall bind them for their two transgressions"; probably the two calves.

11 I will make Ephraim to ride. That is, I will take her away (see Job xxx. 22) from the easy work of treading corn; and, having put a yoke upon her neck, I will set her to plough and harrow. The comfort and liberty which Israel has abused shall be exchanged for servitude and suffering.

14 Shalman spoiled Beth-arbel. "Shalman" seems to be an abbreviated form of *Shalmaneser*. "Beth-arbel" was probably a fortress which he took in his first campaign. It is identified by many with Arbela in Galilee (now *Irbid*) and by others with Irbid, in the north of Gilead.

15 So shall Beth-el do unto you. Your idolatrous worship at Bethel is the first cause of your sufferings.

In a morning. That is, "suddenly." R.V. has, "at daybreak."

CHAPTER XI

1 And called My son out of Egypt. These words are quoted in Matt. ii. 15, and are applied to the childhood of the Son of God, which was partly spent in Egypt. The fatherly love and purposes of mercy, which led God to deliver Israel from Egypt, led Him also to protect our Lord in His infancy by sending Him thither.

2 As they called them. That is, "the prophets," my messengers, called the people; but the more they called, the more did Israel turn away.

4 with cords of a man, etc. Not by violence, but by gentleness; like one who, instead of urging his cattle to the utmost, lifts the yoke from their necks, lest it should heat and gall them, whilst he feeds them. Expressive of God's tender regard to the circumstances and wants of His people.

5 refused to return. *i.e.*, to God.

6 his branches. Or, "his bars" (R.V.); *i.e.*, fortresses.

7 though they called them. See on ver. 2.

would exalt [Him]. Rather, as R.V. marg., "will lift [Himself] up." In cold apathy the call to arise is disregarded.

8 Admah . . . Zeboim. Admah and Zeboim were allies of Sodom, and involved in its destruction (Deut. xxix. 23). These questions show the tenderness of the Divine compassion, even towards the impenitent and the backslider: cp. Ezek. xxxiii. 11; Luke xix. 41.

9 I will not enter into the city. The meaning may be either, "I will not come against the city (*i.e.*, the city of Samaria), as I did against Admah and Zeboim": or, "I will not come with wrath," or "terror," as in Jer. xv. 8.

10 They shall walk after the Lord, etc. The "roar" is a potent summons, like the "great trumpet," Isa. xxvii. 13.

10 shall tremble. Rather, "shall flutter"; *i.e.*, fly hastily. Israel shall follow the Lord obediently, and shall hasten from all quarters to enjoy their long-lost privileges; and then will God show His anger against their oppressors; see Isa. lx. 8.

12 Judah yet ruleth with God. The rendering in the text is hardly consistent with ch. xii. 2. The clause is more correctly translated thus: "And Judah still wandereth (see Jer. ii. 31, last part) with respect to God, and to the Most Holy, the Faithful One": see R.V. marg. The faithlessness of Israel stands in marked contrast to the faithfulness of God. In the Hebrew text this verse is the first of ch. xii.

CHAPTER XII

1 feedeth on wind, etc. An unprofitable task. He will obtain no real help from Egypt or Assyria.

desolation. Rather, "violence."

oil is carried into Egypt. As a present, to obtain the aid of the Egyptians. Oil was one of the most valuable products of Canaan.

3 He took his brother by the heel. This incident seems to be alluded to as showing, before the birth of their ancestor, God's purpose to give the nation superior power: cp. Rom. ix. 11-13. God's special love to His chosen people, and His readiness to hear and answer their humble and penitent prayers, are here connected with the sacred associations of the four names, "Jacob," "Israel," "Bethel," and "Jahveh."

4 he had power over the angel. See note, Gen. xxxii. 24. The "weeping and supplication" no doubt refer to Jacob's prayers in Gen. xxxii. 9-11, 24-30.

He found him in Beth-el. This refers to the promises both in Gen. xxviii. 10-22, and in Gen. xxxv. 9, 14; which were given, says the prophet, not only to Jacob, but to "us."

5 the Lord. Rather, "Jahveh": see Exod. vi. 3, and note.

7 [He is] a merchant. He is not *Israel*, a successful wrestler with God; but *Canaan*, a deceitful trafficker, like those whom he was commissioned to expel from the land.

to oppress. *i.e.*, by extortion.

8 none iniquity in me that were sin. That is, "none that involves me in guilt": see Zech. xi. 5. Men are prone to harden themselves in impenitence by the false notion that God regards them with favour because they are successful in their sinful courses: cp. Deut. xxix. 19.

9 And I [that] am the Lord, etc. This is better translated, "And yet," etc. The meaning is: Sinful as thou hast been, yet, if thou wilt repent and listen to the teachings and warnings of My prophets, I will repeat the deliverance which thy festival commemorates.

11 [Is there] iniquity [in] Gilead? "Gilead" and "Gilgal" probably represent all the tribes on the two sides of the Jordan, and are particularly specified with reference to iv. 15; vi. 8.

12 And Jacob fled. Vers. 12, 13 show how God had raised the Hebrew nation from a low condition to great prosperity, and had faithfully kept His promises to them; thus making their ingratitude the more sinful.

14 his blood. That is, the guilt of bloodshed.

CHAPTER XIII

1 When Ephraim spake trembling, etc. This clause is very obscure. R.V. renders it, "When Ephraim spake there was trembling; he exalted himself in Israel"; and they apply it to the predominance of that tribe.

when he offended in Baal. By introducing the worship of Baal. Then "he died," *i.e.*, lost the principle of national life. That great act of apostasy sealed the downfall of the kingdom.

2 Let the men that sacrifice kiss the calves. See note on Job xxxi. 27. This verse appears to refer to the establishment of the calf-worship by Jeroboam. Having made their images, they say, "Let those who wish to perform religious service worship the calf, instead of going to Jerusalem": see 1 Kings xii. 28.

3 the chimney. Or, "the opening" in the wall; the lattice.

5 I did know thee. I regarded thee with favour.

6 According to their pasture. The meaning is, "According as they were fed, they were also satiated": cp. Deut. xxxii. 13-15.

8 the caul of their heart. The pericardium, or membrane which contains the heart; put for the heart itself.

9 O Israel, thou hast destroyed thyself, etc. Rather, as R.V., "It is thy destruction, O Israel, that [thou art] against Me, against thy help." Canon Box (*Peake's Commentary*) translates the last three words as "who can help thee?"

10 I will be thy king, etc. Rather, "Where now is thy king, that he may save thee in all thy cities?" (R.V.).

11 I gave thee a king in mine anger. Referring to their kingly government in general.

12 The iniquity of Ephraim is bound up. See Job xiv. 17, and note.

hid. Rather, "laid up in store," as R.V.

13 The sorrows of a travailing woman. This metaphor represents the extreme folly of the impenitent Israelites, who endangered their existence by delaying to comply with God's design in laying upon them their sufferings. The "unwise son" is the child who cannot emerge into birth.

O death, I will be thy plagues, etc. Many slightly alter the pointing, and render (as in ver. 10), "Where is thy plague, O death? Where is thy destruction, O grave (Sheol)?" See R.V., and cp. 1 Cor. xv. 55. The words intimate Jehovah's power and readiness to restore the nation to life if they repent: cp. Isa. xxvi. 19; Ezek. xxxvii. 13, and notes.

Repentance shall be hid from Mine eyes. Meaning, perhaps, "My purposes are unchangeable."

15 Though he be fruitful. Alluding to the name "Ephraim": see Gen. xli. 52.

He shall spoil. That is, the Assyrian enemy, symbolised by the east wind.

(This 15th verse is in the Hebrew followed by the Septuagint and the Vulgate, the 1st verse of ch. xiv.)

CHAPTER XIV

2 receive [us] graciously. Lit., as R.V., "accept that which is good."

the calves of our lips. That is, the sacrifices of thanksgiving with our lips; cp. Heb. xiii. 15.

3 Asshur shall not save us, etc. In these words they renounce their three chief sins: dependence upon *Assyria*, recourse to *Egypt* (riding upon horses), and *idolatry*.

5 grow. Or, "blossom," as R.V. So in ver. 7.

Lebanon. The trees of Lebanon.

7 the wine of Lebanon. Lebanon has long been celebrated for the excellence of its wines. These varied images, depicting beauty, strength, fragrance, and usefulness, show the blessed results of God's restoring grace.

8 a green fir tree. "The *berosh*, one of the large genus of the pine or fir, or (as others translate) the cypress, was a tall stately tree (Isa. lv. 13), in whose branches the stork could make its nest (Psa. civ. 17); its wood precious enough to be employed in the Temple (1 Kings v. 8, 10; vi. 15, 34); fine enough to be used in all sorts of musical instruments (2 Sam. vi. 5): strong and pliant enough to be used for spears (Nah. ii. 3). It was part of the glory of Lebanon (Isa. xxxvii. 24; lx. 13)" (*Pusey*).

9 who is wise, etc. A postscript to the whole series of Hosea's prophecies.

the just shall walk in them. The plainest Divine instructions, and the most urgent Divine appeals, will profit those only who prayerfully study God's Word, and obediently follow His will.

JOEL

INTRODUCTION

THE central message of this Book is the promise of the Spirit. This, too, is its great link with the New Testament and with the Christian Church of to-day.

It was a promise made in an unpromising time. The exact date of the Book is not known. Some authorities put it as early as the time of Joash, of the Kingdom of Judah, about 830 B.C. (cp. 2 Kings xi. 4–21; 2 Chr. xxiv. esp. v. 19). In favour of this date is the fact that, while the prophet mentions the Phœnicians, Philistines, Egyptians and Edomites (iii. 4, 19), he makes no reference to the Assyrians or Babylonians, and there is no mention of kings or princes, but rather of elders and priests (i. 14; ii. 16, 17). Others consider that the Book was written after the exile, as late as 444 B.C. But whatever the time was, it was a time of famine and drought. Wave after wave of desolation and destruction had swept over the land (i. 4). The harvest had perished; the fruit-trees were withered; the very seeds rotted in their clods, and the cattle were perplexed because there was no pasture (i. 10–12, 17–20). In that dark hour the promises of God flashed out: "I will restore to you the years that the locust hath eaten"; "I will pour out My Spirit upon all flesh" (ii. 25, 28). There is no hour in life so dark, for the individual, the nation, or the Church, that the promises of God cannot brighten it.

It was a promise repeated and fulfilled upon the day of Pentecost (Acts ii. 16–21). To the very men whom St. Peter accused of crucifying the Saviour he also says, "The promise is unto you and to your children" (cp. Acts ii. 36 with Acts ii. 39). No one is so far from God that the Spirit of God cannot reach him.

The Book is also a call to repentance, both personal and national (i. 14; ii. 13, 15. Cp. Acts ii. 38). It is a message for our own time as well as for the days of Joel.

The closing chapter deals with the future of the nations. Some of it has already been fulfilled (*e.g.* iii. 4, 19). Much of it awaits fulfilment (iii. 12–14). But the final issue is clear. "Judah shall dwell for ever," and "the Lord dwelleth in Zion" (iii. 20, 21).

CHAPTER I

2 the land. Of Judah.

4 palmerworm . . . locust . . . cankerworm . . . caterpillar. These four words are all different names for the locust, expressing respectively the *gnawing*, the *swarming*, the *licking*, and the *consuming* insect; all expressive of its destructiveness.

5 Awake, ye drunkards. The destruction of the vines will particularly affect those who are given to excess in drinking.

6 a great lion. Rather, "a lioness." The invasion of a country by a swarm of locusts is a fearful calamity. They sometimes cover the earth for several miles; and wherever they spread the verdure of the country entirely disappears, the corn is consumed, the trees and plants are stripped of their leaves, and the rind is peeled from the young shoots.

7 My vine . . . my fig tree! This is the exclamation of the people.

8 Lament. The land (mentioned in ver. 6) is here addressed. The figure employed, that of a betrothed maiden, expresses the bitterest lamentation.

9 The meat (meal) **offering.** So complete was the devastation that there could not be found sufficient fine flour, oil, and frankincense for the *minchah*, or gift accompanying the daily burnt offering. So with the wine for the drink offering. This interruption in the course of worship was regarded as a serious calamity—ominous of Jehovah's withdrawal from His people.

13 Gird yourselves. *i.e.*, with sackcloth.

15 the day of the Lord is at hand. Cp. Isa. xiii. 6, and note.

18 the cattle are perplexed. This is perhaps the most pathetic touch in the whole picture of desolation.

19 the fire hath devoured, etc. This may be a figure for scorching drought, or it may refer to the actual kindling of the herbage either through extreme heat, or else by design, that the flame and smoke might hinder the advancing locust-pest.

20 cry. Rather, "pant" (R.V.), as in Psa. xlii. 1.

CHAPTER II

1 the trumpet. Or, "the cornet"; employed to summon the people to a solemn fast.

2 darkness . . . gloominess . . . clouds . . . thick darkness. Here, as in i. 4, four nearly synonymous words are used to depict this terrible visitation, the darkness of which shall spread as irresistibly and widely as the morning light does over all the land.

4 as the appearance of horses. Locusts have heads much resembling those of horses, so that they are called by the Italians *cavalette*, or *little horses*. So in German, *Heupferde*.

5 Like the noise of chariots, etc. The loud noise made by locusts, both in flying and in feeding, has been noticed by many travellers.

6 shall gather blackness. Rather, as R.V., "are waxed pale."

7 they shall not break their ranks. They shall advance in a dense and unbroken phalanx: see Prov. xxx. 27.

8 when they fall upon the sword, they shall not be wounded. Rather, as R.V., "And they burst through the weapons, and break not off [their course]." Weapons or missiles are useless to stay their progress.

11 the Lord shall utter His voice, etc. The rolling thunder heightens the terror of the scene: and the mind is led onward to a more fearful day of the Eternal, in prospect of which the exhortation to repent acquires new force. Cp. Mal. iii. 2.

13 rend your heart, and not your garments. Not the outward expression only, but the inward repentance is required.

14 a meat (meal) **offering,** etc. Removing the visitation which had caused these offerings to cease: see i. 9.

16 elders. The old men.

gather the children, etc. Those who would commonly be excused from appearing in public congregations should now come forth: see Deut. xxiv. 5. Even the infants are to be carried in their parents' arms.

17 between the porch and the altar. *i.e.*, in the priests' court, between the altar of burnt offering and the holy place.

18 Then will the Lord, etc. Rather to be read as historical, introducing what follows: "Then the Eternal was jealous for His land, and had compassion upon His people (19). And the Eternal answered and said."

20 the northern [**army**]. Coming into Palestine (as locusts sometimes do) from Syria.

the east sea. *i.e.*, the Dead Sea.

the utmost sea. Rather, "the hinder (*i.e.*, the western) sea"; the Mediterranean.

his stink. Referring to the putrid heaps of dead locusts.

he hath done great things. He hath dealt proudly. But God will be exalted over him (21).

21 Fear not, O land. The prophet, in a striking and beautiful climax, calls first on the land, then (22) on the animal creation, and lastly (23) upon men, to welcome the return of blessing.

23 For He hath given you the former rain moderately. Rather, "For He giveth you the former rain in due measure": see R.V.

in the first [**month**]. Better "as of old" (so Luther, the French version, and Moffatt, following Septuagint and Vulgate). The "early rain" in the autumn, causing the seed to germinate, and the "latter rain" in the spring, ripening the crop.

25 the years. Generally speaking, an invasion of locusts is for one year only; but the effect of it continues unto the next, the seed having been destroyed with the crops. Cp. ch. i. 4.

28 I will pour out My Spirit. God's Spirit had been with His Church from the beginning; but His influences were to be extended in the Church itself and beyond it, to Gentiles as well as Jews, to "all flesh." On this whole passage, see Acts ii. 16–21.

29 upon the servants and upon the handmaids. Male and female slaves. The most despised classes in society shall participate in these Divine influences.

31 The sun shall be turned into darkness, etc. Imagery taken from eclipses. Cp. Matt. xxiv. 29 and Rev. vi. 12.

32 shall be deliverance. Rather, "shall be the escaped"; referring to those who "call upon the name of Jehovah," and are "saved"; see R.V.

CHAPTER III

2 the valley of Jehoshaphat. This name has been affixed by Jewish tradition to the valley of the Kidron, between Jerusalem and the Mount of Olives. But some suppose it to be the valley in which Jehovah destroyed the combined hosts of the Ammonites, Moabites, etc., when arrayed against Jehoshaphat, and which, in 2 Chron. xx.

26, is called "the valley of Berachah." It is probable that this place and event are alluded to here, but only as representing the final destruction of all the worldly powers which oppose God's kingdom. Hence the king's name, "Jehoshaphat" (signifying *Jehovah judges*) is substituted for "Berachah" (*blessing*).

3 a boy for a harlot, etc. Making a boy the price of a harlot's company, and a girl the price of a draught of wine. No language could more forcibly express the reckless and contemptuous way in which their oppressors had treated them.

4 what have ye to do with Me? Or, "What are ye [doing] to Me?" What injury have I done to you, that you treat My people as if you had something to retaliate? If you do so, I will avenge them upon you.

the coasts of Palestine. Rather, as R.V., "the regions of Philistia."

5 My goodly pleasant things. These, as well as the "silver" and the "gold," may be part of the spoils of the Temple.

6 unto the Grecians. Heb., "unto Javan." The Greek colonies in Asia Minor are probably meant.

8 the Sabeans. See Job i. 15, and note on Isa. xlv. 14.

9 Proclaim ye this among the Gentiles (the nations), etc. A summons to the enemies of the chosen people to come in all the pride of warlike array to receive their overthrow.

10 Beat your plowshares into swords. The result of the establishment of Messiah's kingdom is just the reverse of this; see Isa. ii. 1–4, and notes. But the introduction of it into a sinful world excites the most deadly hostility of man.

13 Put ye in the sickle. The prophet now turns his address to God's people.

the harvest. See note on Hosea vi. 11.

fats. "vats" of the winepresses.

14 the valley of decision. The valley where the great conflict is decided. See note on ver. 2.

18 the valley of Shittim. "The Valley of Acacias." The Moabite plains near the mouth of the Jordan: see Numb. xxv. 1. Perhaps "Shittim" is mentioned because it was the scene of Moab's temptation and of Israel's sin and punishment (cp. Micah vi. 5). The grace of God shall extend to the most unlikely places and persons.

19 Egypt . . . And Edom. The Egyptians, as the earliest oppressors of Israel; and the Edomites, who cherished their hostility to the last, and showed it especially at the fall of Jerusalem (see Psa. cxxxvii. 7), are repeatedly brought forward by the prophets as representatives of the most inveterate enemies of the Church: see Isa. lxiii. 1. The world-kingdoms shall perish, while the Church rejoices in the eternal presence of her God.

21 will cleanse their blood. Will wipe out their blood-guiltiness.

AMOS

INTRODUCTION

AMOS, like Hosea, prophesied to the Ten Tribes, although he was a native of the kingdom of Judah, having been born in the wilderness (or "bush") of Tekoa, south of Bethlehem. There he was a shepherd (i. 1) and a dresser of sycomore, or wild fig trees (vii. 14, 15), and country life has left its impress on his imagery (i. 13; ii. 4, 5, 12; v. 19; vi. 12; viii. 1; ix. 13). His time was about 760 B.C. "Rome was not yet founded, and the principal Greek states, Athens and Sparta, were only gradually forming their laws, and preparing for the great part they were to play during the next few centuries" (*The Work of the Prophets*, by R. E. Selfe, 1904).

But though he lived in the country, he was acquainted with the life of the city, and had a message, which he fearlessly delivered, for the nation as a whole. He notices how the rich dwell in their palaces of ivory (iii. 15) and oppress the poor (ii. 6, 7; iv. 1); the dishonesty of the merchants and their disregard, in their covetousness, of God's day (viii. 4–6); the general idolatry (viii. 14); and the corruption and bribery that prevailed even in the administration of justice (v. 12). Like Isaiah (Isa. i. 11–17), Amos, in view of all this, shows the hollowness and unreality of their observances (iv. 4, 5; v. 21, 22).

In five visions God proclaims through him His judgements upon Israel—the grasshoppers or locusts (vii. 1); the fire (vii. 4); the plumbline (vii. 7–9); the basket of summer fruit (viii. 1, 2); and the terrible and searching doom announced by the Lord standing at the altar (ix. 1–4).

But mercy, as ever, shines through the clouds of judgement. The Book closes with promises of Divine pardon and restoration (ix. 14, 15).

CHAPTER I

1 herdmen. More properly, *shepherds* or *sheep-breeders.*

Tekoa. Now *Tekua,* situated on an elevated hill five miles south of Bethlehem. "The slopes on which Amos herded his cattle show the mass of desert hills with their tops *below* the spectator, and therefore displaying every meteoric effect in a way they would not have done had he been obliged to look *up* to them. . . . No one can read his book without feeling that he haunted heights, and lived in the face of very wide horizons." (G. A. Smith, *Historical Geog. of the Holy Land,* 1894, p. 315.)

the earthquake. As Jeroboam II died in the fifteenth year of Uzziah's reign, this earthquake could not have happened later than the seventeenth year of Uzziah. Palestine is subject to such convulsions; but this was peculiarly awful, so that it was known as "*the* earthquake," and is alluded to again in Zech. xiv. 5.

2 will roar, etc. The words are taken from Joel (iii. 16). The metaphor probably refers to the roar of the lion: cp. iii. 8.

Carmel. "Carmel by the sea" (see Isa. xxxv. 2; Jer. xlvi. 18), the promontory at the mouth of the Kishon, which has always been celebrated for the luxuriance of its woods and herbage (ix. 3, and note). There was another Carmel, Josh. xv. 55.

3 For three transgressions . . . and ("yea," R.V.) **for four.** Because of its *multiplied* or *repeated* transgressions. This expression is repeated at the commencement of each of the following denunciations; and then one offence on the part of each of the guilty nations is specified as being peculiarly aggravated.

I will not turn away, etc. Or, "I will not reverse it"; *i.e.* the decree of punishment.

Gilead. "Gilead" here signifies the tribes east of the Jordan: see 2 Kings x. 32; xiii. 3, 7, where both Hazael and his son Ben-hadad are mentioned, and their cruel oppression is described as "threshing."

5 the bar. That is, the fortifications.

the plain of Aven. "Aven," or "On," is the Egyptian name for the city of the sun, Heliopolis (see Gen. xli. 45; Ezek. xxx. 17), and the name is here used for the Syrian Heliopolis, the celebrated city of Baalbek, which lay in the Bukáa or valley (Cœle-Syria) between Lebanon and Hermon.

the house of Eden. "Beth-eden," *the house of pleasure,* is probably the name of a royal residence in the mountains of Lebanon, called by Ptolemy (v. 15) "Paradise."

Kir. See note on 2 Kings xvi. 9.

6 Gaza. Gaza was the most important city of the Philistines. The old site has long been forsaken, but the modern town is still large and populous. It was taken from the Turks by the British forces during the Great War of 1914–1919. The other ancient Philistine cities are now small villages; and the exact site of Gath is not known: see note on Isa. xiv. 29.

the whole captivity. They swept off all that were within their reach. This is probably the invasion which is recorded in 2 Chron. xxi. 16, 17.

9 the brotherly covenant. The covenant which had subsisted between David and Solomon and the king of Tyre: see 2 Sam. v. 11; 1 Kings v. 12; ix. 11.

11 transgressions of Edom. See notes on 2 Sam. viii. 13; Isa. xxxiv.: Obadiah 10.

12 palaces of Bozrah. See notes on Jer. xlix. 7; Isa. xxxiv. 6.

13 That they might enlarge their border. The Ammonites aimed utterly to exterminate the Israelites, that they might extend their own territory.

14 I will kindle a fire, etc. See note on Jer. xlix. 2.

CHAPTER II

1 he burned the bones of the king of Edom. According to an uncertain tradition preserved by Jerome, these were the bones of that king of Edom who was allied with Jehoshaphat and Jehoram (2 Kings iii. 9). This disinterment was an act of cold-blooded revenge.

2 I will send a fire. The instrument of his revenge shall be the means of his punishment.

4 their lies. Probably "their idols"; see note on Psa. xxxi. 6.

6 a pair of shoes. Rather, "a pair of sandals"; mere soles fastened by thongs; things of the smallest value: cp. Ezek. xiii. 19. The word "sold" is to be understood here in the sense of selling *into slavery,* which was frequently done: see Lev. xxv. 39; 2 Kings iv. 1.

7 That pant after the dust, etc. Rather, "that trample the head of the poor in the dust." (So Septuagint, Vulgate, Luther, and recent translations.)

To profane My holy name. It is not unlikely that, as the Israelites professed to honour Jehovah in their image-worship, they even pretended to do so in the licentious practices associated with pagan worship.

8 they lay themselves down, etc. They not only appropriated to their own use the garments which had been pledged (see Exod. xxii. 26), and the fines which had been levied; but to this injustice they added the impiety of using these things at their idol-feasts.

9 the Amorite. See note on Gen. xv. 16. The reference is to the destruction of the Canaanite nations, of whom the Amorite was the most powerful. The form of expression here and in ver. 10 is emphatic: "It was I who destroyed—I who brought you up."

11 Nazarites ("Nazirites," R.V.). See note on Numb. vi. 2.

13 Behold, I am pressed under you. Rather, "Behold, I will press [you] down," etc. (*i.e.,* I will over-power you with punishment), "and flight shall fail," etc.

14 Therefore. The Heb. is simply, "And."

16 Shall flee away naked. That is, the bravest shall throw off his armour and flee.

saith the Lord. Professor Gandell (*Speaker's Commentary*) points out that the Hebrew word used here has more significance than the English word "saith" suggests. It means the *utterance,* perhaps the *oracle,* of God to His prophet, and by Him delivered to others.

CHAPTER III

2 therefore I will punish (visit) **you.** Because they had enjoyed remarkable Divine favours and sinned against special obligations.

3 Can (shall) **two walk together, etc.?** The point of the question is that Judah, having ceased to "agree" with God, can no longer expect His favour and help. "Think not to have God with thee unless thou art with God" (*Pusey*).

4 Will a lion roar, etc.? The lion roars, when eager for his prey, or when exulting over it. He does not roar in the forest, or cry (growl) in his den without cause; so God does not threaten and punish where there is no sin.

5 Shall [one] take up a snare from the earth, etc.? Rather, as R.V., "Shall a snare spring up from the ground, and have taken nothing at all?" The emblems, taken from rural life, convey the same general meaning: no effect without a cause.

6 and the people not be afraid. It was no vain alarm which the prophets were sounding in the ears of their countrymen; and, whoever might be the instruments, God was the author of the chastisement.

Shall there be evil, etc.? The word "evil" here means *calamity*, as in Gen. xix. 19. "Evil which is sin, the Lord hath not done; evil which is punishment for sin, the Lord bringeth" (*Augustine*, quoted by Pusey).

7 but He revealeth, etc. Before God inflicts His strokes, He mercifully warns men by His prophets.

9 in the palaces at Ashdod, etc. Or, "upon the palaces," etc., making proclamation from the flat roofs, and summoning the heathen nations (Philistines and Egyptians) to note the humiliation of Israel: cp. 2 Sam. i. 20. For "Ashdod" the Septuagint has "of the Assyrians."

12 Two legs, or a piece of an ear. No more than the mere fragments of God's flock shall be left, to show how they have been devoured.

That dwell in Samaria in the corner of a bed, and in Damascus [in] a couch. This should be translated, "That sit in Samaria in the corner (*i.e.*, the place of honour) of a sofa, and in the damask of a couch"; referring to the luxurious habits of the people: cp. R.V.

13 in the house of Jacob. Rather, "against the house of Jacob."

15 the winter with the summer house, etc. Descriptive of extreme domestic luxury. "So wealthy were they," writes *Jerome*, "as to possess two sorts of houses, the "winter house" being turned to the south, the "summer house" to the north, so that, according to the variety of the seasons, they might temper to them the heat and cold." The "houses of ivory" were houses *decorated* or *panelled* with ivory.

CHAPTER IV

1 ye kine of Bashan. See note on Psa. xxii. 12. In this passage, masculine and feminine forms are intermingled, as some think, to designate the effeminacy of the courtiers and companions of the king of Israel (cp. Hosea vii. 5), who is called "their master" (masters). Others, however, think that women only are meant, and by other commentators both women and men are supposed to be indicated.

2 hath sworn by His holiness. It was His holiness which their sin had outraged.

with hooks, etc. An expressive image of sudden disaster and helplessness, as that of a fish lifted out of the water.

3 And ye shall go out at the breaches, etc. Perhaps the best rendering of this verse is, "And at the breaches (of your walls) ye shall go forth, each straight before her; and ye shall throw yourselves [down from] the citadel, saith Jehovah." The figure is derived from the headlong rush of frightened cattle: cp. R.V., where the word for "palace" or "citadel" is given, according to the Heb. form, as a proper name "[into] Harmon." "Harmon" is supposed by some to be "Hermon"; by others "Armenia."

4 your tithes after three years. The Heb. literally reads, "every three days" (so R.V.), indicating extreme punctiliousness of religious observance. The whole language is that of irony: You may maintain your worship carefully, but you only provoke Me; for I have forbidden your calf-worship, and have chosen Jerusalem, not Beth-el, for My sanctuary.

5 a sacrifice of thanksgiving with leaven. See Lev. vii. 13, and note.

this liketh you. It is your own way of approaching God, not His way. *Keil* remarks on the whole description, that it shows the worship in the kingdom of the Ten Tribes to have been conducted *generally* according to the precepts of the Mosaic law; but with exaggerated formality and zeal.

6 cleanness of teeth. This is the same as "want of bread."

7 When there were yet three months to the harvest. The "latter rain," which falls in Palestine about February, is necessary for the growth of the corn: see note on Deut. xi. 14. This was not yet absolutely withheld, but was very partial.

10 after the manner of Egypt. That is, as I formerly did to the Egyptians.

11 I have overthrown [some] of you, etc. This refers to some awful catastrophe, not noticed elsewhere, by which some of the cities of Israel were burnt, whilst others narrowly escaped, like a brand plucked from the fire: cp. Zech. iii. 2; 1 Cor. iii. 15.

12 Prepare to meet thy God, O Israel. Famine, pestilence, earthquake, were Jehovah's *messengers.* These having failed of their effect, Israel is summoned to meet God HIMSELF, in some yet more dread revelation of His power and justice, and also of His love. The words point to the "day of the Lord," for which repentance and submission are the only "preparation."

13 He that formeth the mountains, etc. This sublime description gives emphasis to the preceding words, "thy God." The Eternal, the Searcher of hearts, is the Covenant God of Israel.

CHAPTER V

1 against you. Or, "over you," as a funeral lamentation: see R.V.

2 The virgin. A mode of personifying a people, like "daughter." Cp. Isa. xlvii. 1–5.

forsaken. Or, "cast down."

3 that went out [by] a thousand. To war.

shall leave an hundred. "Shall have an hundred left."

5 Beer-sheba. A city of Judah (1 Kings xix. 3), on its southern frontier. Like Bethel and Gilgal, it appears to have been at this time a place of idolatrous resort, ch. viii. 14.

6 the house of Joseph. The kingdom of Ephraim, or the Ten Tribes.

7 and leave off righteousness in the earth. Rather, "And who cast righteousness down to the ground": see R.V.

8 the seven stars. The Pleiades: see notes on Job ix. 9; xxxviii. 31.

9 That strengtheneth the spoiled, etc. Rather, as R.V., "That bringeth sudden destruction upon the strong; so that destruction cometh upon the fortress."

10 him that rebuketh in the gate. This may mean the prophets who uttered their rebukes "in the gate," the most frequented part of the city.

11 burdens. Or, "presents"; or "forced tributes."

13 the prudent shall keep silence. In such a time, the wise and pious can only wait in silence for God's interposition to check the overwhelming power of public and private wickedness.

16 skilful of lamentation. See Eccles. xii. 5; Jer. ix. 17, and notes.

18 the day of the Lord. "The day of the Eternal" may be either *the day of His anger*, which these men boldly despise, as if they said, "Let Him do His worst"; or, more probably, *the day of His interposition;* which they thought must be to them, as Israelites, a time of blessing; but which, because they were faithless to His covenant, would bring to them only darkness and misery.

21 I despise your feast days, etc. See Isa. i. 10–15, and notes.

23 viols. "Harps."

25 Have ye offered unto Me, etc.? Rather, "Did ye offer unto Me, etc.? and (yet, *i.e.*, at the same time) ye bore," etc. Taken with the next verse the meaning is: "Were ye really offering sacrifices unto Me in the wilderness?" The Israelites are accused of having, from the earliest periods of their history, mixed idolatrous observances with a professed attention to the ritual observances of the Mosaic law.

26 ye have borne the tabernacle of your Moloch, etc. This is rendered by some, "Ye carried the tabernacle of your king (or, of Moloch), and the shrine of your images, the star of your gods": see R.V. marg. But the word "Sakkut," which is translated "tabernacle," and occurs nowhere else, is thought by some to be, like "Chiun" or "Kairvan," the name of an Assyrian god. Those who adopt the rendering of the text suppose "Chiun" to be the planet Saturn, of which they think Remphan to be the Egyptian name. The text is quoted in Acts vii. 43 nearly according to the Septuagint, which has "Raiphan."

27 beyond Damascus. Even to Babylon: see Acts vii. 43.

CHAPTER VI

1 [Which are] named chief of the nations. Rather, "The notable men of the chief of the nations" (R.V.); *i.e.*, the princes of the two kingdoms of Israel and Judah, who, trusting in the strength of their capitals, set the people, who "came," or looked up to them, an example of confident ease and recklessness of Divine warnings. The same epithets are applied by Isaiah (Isa. xxxii. 9, 11) to the luxurious women of Israel.

2 Calneh. Or, *Calno* (Isa. x. 9), probably Ctesiphon; situated opposite Seleucia, and for a time the capital of the Parthians (R.V.).

Hamath. See notes on Numb. xiii. 21; 2 Sam. viii. 9.

Gath of the Philistines. Gath was one of the principal cities of the Philistines, the residence of Goliath. Uzziah, in whose reign Amos prophesied, took it and destroyed its wall (2 Chron. xxvi. 6).

[Be they] better than these kingdoms? Of the various explanations given to this question the most probable is, See how these mighty cities are humbled and reduced, and learn to fear My judgements.

3 Ye that put far away the evil day. Banishing all fear of the threatened punishment, men hold fast to their iniquities.

the seat of violence. The judgement-seat, where injustice was practised.

5 That chant. Rather, as R.V., "That sing idle songs."

[and] invent to themselves, etc Cultivating merely for their own diversion an art which David consecrated to the service of God.

7 And the banquet of them that stretched themselves, etc. Rather, "And the revelry of those that recline (on couches) shall pass away": see R.V. Having been chief in sin, they shall be chief in punishment.

8 the excellency (*or*, pride) **of Jacob.** See note on Psa. xlvii. 4; and Ezek. xxiv. 21.

10 a man's uncle shall take him up, etc. Or, "A man's uncle, even he who burneth him, shall take him up," etc. This probably means that the mortality (of pestilence following famine) will be so great as to throw the care of the dead upon their more distant relatives; who, to prevent infection, will burn the bodies instead of burying them.

Hold thy tongue, etc. Or, "Hush! for [it is not a time] to mention the name of Jehovah." The meaning is not very obvious, but perhaps it is this: that one of the household, confined to the chamber (the "sides" or "innermost parts" of the house) by the disease, says that he is the sole survivor; and he is told that it is of no use now to call upon God, for his case is hopeless.

12 Shall horses run upon the rock? *i.e.*, "Is your conduct more reasonable who have violated the eternal laws of God?" (*Gandell*).

13 horns. That is, *power.* Some scholars, however, regard the Hebrew words *Lo-debar* ("a thing of nought") and *Karmaim* ("horns") as the names of two towns, Lo-debar being mentioned in 2 Sam. ix. 4, and Karnaim in Gen. xiv. 5.

14 the river of the wilderness. Rather, "the brook of the Arabah" (R.V.); *i.e.*, of the Jordan valley.

CHAPTER VII

1 grasshoppers. Rather, "locusts."

the king's mowings. "The king's mowings," or *croppings*, may refer to the exaction by the monarch of the first growth of the grass for his own cattle (see 1 Sam. viii. 14). If locusts destroyed the aftercrop, there was no hope of any grass till the summer was passed.

4 a part. Rather, "*the* part"; *i.e.*, the other part; the dry land as well as the deep. The "fire" denotes a heavier judgement than the "locusts."

8 I will set a plumbline, etc. The application of the line and plummet to a completed building implies that its correctness and stability are being tested, and that, if found faulty or dangerous, it will be taken down. This symbol therefore represents God's trial of a people, which often results in their condemnation: cp. Isa. xxviii. 17; 2 Kings xxi. 13.

10 Amaziah. Probably the high priest of the idolatrous sanctuary. The charge of treason was connected with the fact that Amos belonged to the southern kingdom. In the northern, therefore, he was regarded as an interloper and a spy; perhaps as an emissary from the rival monarch.

12 there eat bread, and prophesy there. Gain thy living by prophesying there. The idolatrous priest apparently regards Amos as merely a hireling, like himself, doing his work for the maintenance which the king of Judah gave him.

13 the king's chapel. Rather, "the king's sanctuary" (R.V.).

14 neither was I a prophet's son. *i.e.*, I was not a disciple of the prophets. See note on 1 Sam. x. 12.

a gatherer. Perhaps, "scraper": alluding to the practice of scraping or making incisions in the sycomore fruit, to promote its maturity.

sycomore fruit. Luther translates, "mulberries." The French version has "wild figs." Professor Canney (*Peake's Com.*) translates, "fig-mulberries."

17 divided by line. Divided among the victorious enemies.

a polluted (unclean) **land.** A foreign heathen land, polluted by idol worship. We have no historical record of the fulfilment of these predictions regarding Amaziah.

CHAPTER VIII

1 summer fruit. *i.e.*, fruit fully ripe, which soon rots; representing Israel as ripe for judgement: cp. Rev. xiv. 15, 18.

2 the end. This word in the original nearly resembles that for *summer fruit* (*qayitz, qetz*). Such play upon words is not uncommon in the prophets.

pass by them. *i.e.*, "pardon them."

3 the temple. Rather, "palace" (R.V. marg.).

with silence. Without the usual wailings, either for fear of the enemy, or because none were left to mourn.

5 making the ephah small, and the shekel great. By diminishing the measure they gave, and at the same time increasing the weight by which the money was reckoned, they were guilty of a double fraud. The spirit of covetousness leads men to rob both God and man. Like other Old Testament rebukes, this language might be used as a description of many in the twentieth century.

6 That we may buy the poor. *i.e.*, reduce them to bondage. See note on ii. 6.

7 the excellency of Jacob. God Himself.

8 it shall be cast out and drowned, etc. Or, "and shall subside, as the river of Egypt does," when its flood is exhausted.

9 I will cause the sun to go down at noon. Your prosperity shall be suddenly eclipsed by the deepest and darkest sorrow (10): cp. Jer. xv. 9.

11 a famine . . . of hearing the words of the Lord. Those who despise God's faithful messengers shall have none to guide and comfort them in perplexity and distress.

12 from sea to sea. The Dead Sea lay south, and the Great Sea west, of the kingdom of Israel; and the north and east are added in the next line. In no quarter shall they find Divine help and guidance.

14 the sin of Samaria. This peculiar designation of the golden calf, founded on the words of Deut. ix. 21, shows the aggravation of their crime, as being a repetition of that which had brought upon their ancestors severe punishment.

Thy god, O Dan, liveth. *i.e.*, "*As* thy god, O Dan, liveth" (R.V.); a formula of swearing (see 1 Sam. xx. 3). "The manner (way) of Beer-sheba" is an elliptical phrase for the idol whose worship was practised there: see v. 5.

CHAPTER IX

1 the altar. Probably the altar in "the king's sanctuary" at Beth-el (vii. 13). Already had Jehovah smitten Jeroboam's altar there (1 Kings xiii. 5); and He now appears, to demolish utterly the idol-temple and destroy its worshippers.

Smite the lintel of the door, etc. Rather, "Smite the capitals ("chapiters," R.V.), and the thresholds shall shake, and smite them upon the head of all of them," etc. Bring down the temple upon the heads of those who worship in it; cp. Judges xvi. 22–30.

2 hell. Heb., "Sheol"; the state or place of the dead. See note on Job xi. 8.

3 in the top of Carmel. Carmel was well adapted for concealment, not only on account of its woods and copses, but because of its numerous caves, of which there are four hundred in one part of the mountain. See note on i. 2.

5 He that toucheth the land, and it shall melt. The least token of God's displeasure is sufficient to put the whole frame of Nature out of order.

the flood (river) **of Egypt.** The Nile: see note on viii. 8.

6 He that buildeth His stories, etc. Or, "He who buildeth in the heavens His upper-chambers, and His vault on the earth, He hath founded it."

7 as children of the Ethiopians. By your sins you have forfeited your privileges as "sons of Israel," and are become "sons of Cushites," a race known of old for enmity to God: see Gen. x. 8, 9. Israel's deliverance was nothing more than a migration like that of the Philistine or Syrians. Respecting "Caphtor" and "Kir," see notes on Jer. xlvii. 4 and 2 Kings xvi. 9.

9 yet shall not the least grain fall upon the earth. Not one sinner shall escape, nor one faithful Israelite perish. This shall be fully evident at the last judgement.

11 the tabernacle of David that is fallen. "The fallen hut of David"; indicating the ruined state of David's house, impoverished and decayed.

12 the remnant of Edom. The Edomites had been subjects, but were now, as ever, the bitterest enemies of Israel. Yet these, with other "heathen," are to be blessed through Him who fills the throne of David. The Apostle James partially quotes this prophecy from the Septuagint (Acts xv. 15–17), expressly to show that the blessings of the covenant of mercy were to be extended to the Gentile world; and that thus the "kingdom of David" would be re-established in brighter, because spiritual glory.

13 the plowman shall overtake the reaper, etc. In consequence of the swiftly-ripening and abundant harvest: see Lev. xxvi. 5.

the mountains shall drop sweet wine. Vineyards were generally planted on terraces constructed upon the hillsides.

shall melt. Dissolving, as it were, into streams of milk and honey. Cp. with the whole verse Joel iii. 18.

14 I will bring again the captivity, etc. "The raising up of the fallen hut of David commenced with the coming of Christ and the founding of the Christian Church by the apostles; and the possession of Edom and all the other nations upon whom Jehovah reveals His name, took its rise in the reception of the Gentiles into the Kingdom of Heaven set up by Christ. The founding and building of this Kingdom continue through all the ages of the Christian Church, and will be completed when the fulness of the Gentiles shall one day enter into the Kingdom of God, and the still unbelieving Israel shall have been converted to Christ. The land which will flow with streams of Divine blessing is the domain of the Christian Church, or the earth so far as it has received the blessings of Christianity. The people which cultivates this land is the Christian Church, so far as it stands in living faith, and produces fruits of the Holy Spirit" (*Keil*).

OBADIAH

INTRODUCTION

NOTHING is known of the author of this Book. He is not to be confounded with the Obadiah mentioned in 1 Kings xviii. 3–16, who hid a hundred prophets in a cave and fed them. Another of the same name is mentioned in 2 Chron. xvii. 7, but there is no evidence to connect him with the prophecy.

The message of the Book is almost entirely one of judgement. And it is interesting to compare the judgements here announced upon Edom with those proclaimed by Isaiah (Isa. xxi. 11, 12), Ezekiel (Ezek. xxv. 12–14; xxxv.), Jeremiah (Jer. xlix. 7; Lam. iv. 21, 22). These judgements were inflicted because of the action of the Edomites in assisting the Babylonians against Jerusalem (verses 10–13). Their doom is an illustration of the eternal principle enunciated by our Lord Himself, "With what measure ye mete it shall be measured to you again" (cp. verse 15 with Luke vi. 38).

But for Zion the prophet's vision is one of hope. "Upon mount Zion shall be deliverance" (17). And in his words "the kingdom shall be the Lord's" (22), we hear the far-off prelude of the triumph-song of heaven: "He shall reign for ever and ever"; "Hallelujah! for the Lord God omnipotent reigneth" (Rev. xi. 15; xix. 6).

1 concerning Edom. Edom, or Idumea, was the territory of the descendants of Esau (see Gen. xxv. 30; xxxvi. 8), who drove out the Horites and took possession of Mount Seir, the mountainous tract south of the Dead Sea, between the valley of the Arabah (now *El Ghor*) and the eastern desert (see Deut. ii. 12). On its capital Sela (*Petra*), see 2 Kings xiv. 7; Jer. xlix. 16, and notes.

We have heard a rumour. The prophet speaks in the name of his countrymen.

an ambassador. Or, "messenger." For "heathen," read "nations."

Arise ye. The address of the messenger to the peoples. "Let us rise up"; their response, addressed one to another.

5 cut off. *i.e.*, utterly stripped; nothing is left. Robbers leave something behind; grapegatherers leave "gleanings"; but *these* destroyers leave nothing!

6 [the things of] Esau. The most carefully concealed treasures of the Edomites.

7 Have brought thee even to the border. Or, "Have sent thee to the frontier": refusing to receive the messengers whom thou hast sent to ask for help.

and prevailed against thee. Taking the conqueror's side; a retribution for Edom's conduct towards Israel (11).

have laid a wound under thee. *i.e.*, "have given thee a secret blow." But many substitute "snare" for "wound": see R.V.

7 There is none understanding in him. *i.e.*, Edom had allowed himself to be befooled by the promises of his pretended friends.

10 thy brother Jacob. The word "brother" is inserted to aggravate the sin of the Edomites, to whom the Hebrews had been instructed to show peculiar kindness (Deut. xxiii. 7).

12 spoken proudly. *i.e.*, in mockery.

14 the crossway. "The ravine," or narrow pass.

15 the heathen. "The nations."

16 as ye have drunk, etc. The heathen invaders had desecrated Mount Zion by impious revelry; and in retribution shall drink the cup of God's wrath.

17 deliverance. Cp. Joel ii. 32.

18 the house of Jacob. . . . And the house of Joseph. Probably the two kingdoms of Judah and Israel (cp. Isa. xlvi. 3). Fulfilled in the days of John Hyrcanus (130 B.C.), by whom the Edomites were utterly subdued, being henceforth absorbed into the Jewish community.

19 they of the South. *i.e.*, of the southern part of Palestine.

they of the plain. Or, of the "Shephelah"; "the lowland" (R.V.).

20 the captivity of this host, etc. Read, with R.V., "the captivity of this host of the children of Israel which are [among] the Canaanites [shall possess] even unto Zarephath." The exiles of the Ten Tribes were very numerous; their deportation from their own land having been more complete than that of Judah. They are to spread northwards. On Zarephath, see note on 1 Kings xvii. 9.

Sepharad. Probably a district in the north of Asia Minor (*Sayce*).

21 saviours. Or, "deliverers." All who deliver God's people are "judges" of His enemies. But Isaiah points more distinctly to the Messiah in this twofold character: see Isa. lxiii. 1–5, and notes. The whole prediction figuratively represents the extension and triumph of the Church.

JONAH

INTRODUCTION

THE only other reference we have to Jonah in the Old Testament is in 2 Kings xiv. 25, where it is said that he foretold the restoration of Israel by Jeroboam II, and that he was the son of a prophet, Amittai of Gath-hepher (see i. 1). The date of it has been variously fixed as in the ninth or as late as the third century B.C. Apart from linguistic considerations, the principal argument for the later date is the statement that "Nineveh *was* an exceeding great city" (iii. 3).

Whether the Book is entirely historical or in part at least an allegory, is a point on which good men have differed. But whether it be history or allegory, there is general agreement as to the lessons it is meant to convey—the lesson of the Divine mercy, and a rebuke to Jewish exclusiveness and all human efforts to limit the Divine forgiveness and favour. Our Saviour used the story as a symbol of His own death and resurrection (Matt. xii. 39, 40), and in holding up the heathen of Nineveh as an example of repentance confirmed its rebuke of Jewish narrowness (Matt. xii. 41 ; Luke xi. 32). The Book is, indeed, a great plea for "foreign missions."

Jonah is not willing to obey the call of God that he should go and preach to the people of Nineveh, and takes a ship going from Joppa (now Jaffa) to Tarshish or Tartessus, in Spain or Italy (i. 1–3). But he cannot thus escape from God's presence (cp. Psa. cxxxix. 7–10). A storm comes on, and the sailors in their terror, after casting lots, throw Jonah into the sea (i. 4–15). There he is swallowed by a "great fish" (i. 17), and it may here be pointed out that neither in the Hebrew nor in the Greek of our Lord's reference does the word necessarily mean "whale." His prayer for deliverance was heard, and he was cast out upon the dry land (ii.).

God does not cast off His disobedient servant, but gives him another chance (iii. 2) and sends him again to Nineveh. This time the prophet obeys, and proclaims that the city shall be overthrown within forty days (iii. 3, 4). The result was the repentance of the king and the whole people (iii. 5–9). The anger of God was averted and He spared the city (iii. 10).

But Jonah is still a reluctant messenger. Formerly he had refused to convey the message of doom ; now he is displeased at the Divine mercy (iv. 1–3). God reasons with him and teaches him, by the symbol of the gourd, that the Divine mercy is greater than all human pity (iv. 4–11). So once more, the lesson comes through Jonah to us all that God's ways are not as our ways nor His thoughts as our thoughts.

CHAPTER I

1 the son of Amittai. This note of parentage identifies Jonah with the prophet mentioned 2 Kings xiv. 25 : see Introduction.

2 Nineveh. Nineveh, the ancient capital of the Assyrian empire, lay on the eastern bank of the Tigris, opposite to the site of the modern town of *Mosul.* As the capital of a large empire, and a great *entrepôt* of commerce between the East and the West, it became extremely wealthy and luxurious. It was besieged and taken by Cyaxares and Nabopolassar about 606 B.C. ; after which it never regained its imperial power.

3 But Jonah rose up to flee. There is nothing strange in Jonah's reluctance to undertake a mission to a distant heathen city, which appeared likely to expose him to great peril both from the king and from the people. Moses (Exod. iv.), and even the bold Elijah (1 Kings xix.), had shrunk from similar dangers ; and there are few of God's servants who have not quailed before smaller difficulties. He alleges, however, an additional reason in iv. 2, on which see note.

Tarshish. In the far west : see note on 1 Kings x. 22. The word of God commissioned the prophet to the east : he would flee to the far west.

from the presence of the Lord. *i.e.*, from his place as a prophet of God ; one who stood near Him as a king's servant does.

Joppa. Joppa (now *Jaffa*) lies on the east coast of the Mediterranean, about 30 miles distant from Jerusalem, of which, though an insecure harbour, it was for a long time the only seaport: see 2 Chron. ii. 16; Ezra iii. 7. The railway now runs from Jaffa to Jerusalem.

4 a great wind. This sea is subject to sudden and violent storms: cp. the "Euraquilo" of St. Paul's voyage, Acts xxvii. 14 (R.V.).

5 every man unto his god. This was probably a Phœnician vessel, manned by sailors of various nations, who worshipped different idols.

the wares. "The tackle," but may include the cargo.

5 into the sides. Rather, "into the innermost parts" (R.V.).

7 the lot fell upon Jonah. See notes on Josh. vii. 14, and Prov. xvi. 33.

8 Tell us, we pray thee, etc. The sailors were unwilling to condemn Jonah without a personal confession.

10 exceedingly afraid. They were alarmed by this proof of the omniscience of God, and of the ease with which He could discover and reach any who were seeking to shun Him.

Why hast thou done this? More precisely, "What is this that thou hast done?"

11 wrought, and was tempestuous. Or, "grew more and more tempestuous" (R.V.): so ver. 13.

13 rowed hard. The Heb. here is very expressive: they "dug" the sea.

14 they cried unto the Lord. Worshipping Jahveh, Jonah's God, and not their own.

lay not upon us innocent blood,etc. That is, Do not punish us as murderers of an innocent man; for we are only following the indications of Thy will.

16 Then the men feared the Lord exceedingly. Under the overpowering conviction of Jehovah's justice and power, which were shown both in raising and in so suddenly quelling the storm. These foreign sailors appear in favourable contrast to the erring prophet, in respect to both humanity and reverence. This is in itself an indication of the purpose of the book—to show, as St. Peter afterwards had to learn, that "in every nation he that feareth God and worketh righteousness is accepted of Him."

a sacrifice. Of some animal on board.

This 16th verse is the last of the 1st chapter in the Hebrew, the 17th verse being the 1st of chap. ii.

17 the Lord had prepared a great fish. That there are fishes in the Mediterranean capable of swallowing a man whole has been fully proved by credible testimony. But the event is clearly related as a miraculous Divine interposition: and though God is not said to have "created," but to have "appointed" a fish, it is not necessary to inquire further of what kind it was. It was doubtless fit for the purpose. It may, however, be remarked that there is nothing, either in the Hebrew of this passage, or in the Greek of St. Matthew (xii. 40), to show that it was "a whale," as some have supposed.

CHAPTER II

2 hell. Heb., "Sheol"; the place of the dead; here used metaphorically, to denote the prophet's desperate condition.

3 In the midst [heart] **of the seas.** Cp. "*heart* of the earth," Matt. xii. 40.

4 out of Thy sight. That is, from Thy *notice* and *care.* He who had attempted to flee from God's presence now feels how necessary to his life and happiness is the compassionate regard of that Divine Providence which watches over all.

5 to the soul. The seat of physical life.

The weeds were wrapped about my head. In his struggles before he was swallowed by the fish.

6 the bottoms of the mountains. Lit., "cuttings off of the mountains," where the mountains ended, or were cut off, in the depths of the sea.

corruption. Heb., "the pit."

8 lying vanities. Idol gods. See note on Psa. xxxi. 6.

their own mercy. God, the source of mercy. In Psa. cxliv. 2, "my goodness" is expressed in Heb. by the same word.

9 Salvation. This deliverance, type of a greater.

10 upon the dry land. Probably in the neighbourhood of Joppa.

CHAPTER III

3 exceeding great. Lit., "great to God": see note on Gen. x. 9.

three days' journey. *i.e.*, in circumference; sixty miles. A quadrangle 150 stadia (furlongs) by 90.—(*Diodorus Siculus.*) The walls enclosed large open spaces: parks, farms, and pastures.

4 a day's journey. As far as he could go in a day whilst proclaiming his message: see note on i. 2. Up and down in the city; not in a direct line across.

Yet forty days, etc. An unconditional announcement in *form;* yet, as the sequel shows, conditioned by the people's conduct.

5 the people of Nineveh believed God. They believed in the supremacy of the God of Israel, in the certainty of His judgements, and in His willingness to pardon the repentant. Our Lord (Matt. xii. 41) reproaches the Jews of His own day with being less open to impression than the Ninevites.

6 the king of Nineveh. It is not as yet ascertained who this king was. Possibly Shalmaneser II: see Chronological Table in Sayce's *Assyria.*

7 let them not feed, nor drink water. The Easterns, when fasting, abstain from all food until the evening: see 2 Sam. i. 12.

8 let them turn every one from his evil way. If outward acts of humiliation are to be acceptable to God, they must be accompanied with the putting away of cherished sin.

9 Who can tell if God will turn and repent? Rather, as R.V., "Who knoweth whether God will not turn and repent?" Cp. Joel ii. 14.

10 God repented, etc. See note on Gen. vi. 6.

CHAPTER IV

2 Therefore I fled before unto Tarshish, etc. Or, as R.V., "Therefore I hasted to flee," etc. Jonah's want of sympathy with God's sparing mercy was due partly to a selfish regard to his own safety and reputation, and partly to national exclusiveness which made him unwilling that the doom of a heathen city should be averted.

3 take, I beseech Thee, my life from me. The language has been compared with that of Moses (Numb. xi. 15) and Elijah (1 Kings xix. 9–18; where see note), who both had been weary of their lives, but in how different a spirit! They mourned over the people's hardness of heart: Jonah resents the sparing mercy of God.

5 Jonah went out of the city. Apparently before the forty days had expired. Had he remained in the city, and fulfilled his ministry of repentance, the reformation of the Ninevites might have been more thorough and lasting.

6 a gourd. This plant, in Hebrew "kikayon," is probably the *ricinus communis*, or *palma christi*; a broad-leaved plant, rapid both in its growth and in its decay, but now made to grow with extraordinary quickness, for Jonah's shelter.

8 vehement. Rather, "sultry," as R.V.

9 I do well to be angry, even unto death. Rather, "I am exceedingly vexed, even to death." The excessive grief, like the excessive joy (ver. 6), was the sign of a morbid disposition.

11 that cannot discern, etc. That is, children of a tender age, incapable of personal transgression. Reckoning these, according to the usual calculation, as a fifth part of the population, the city would contain 600,000 inhabitants.

These two closing verses (10 and 11) are an excellent summing up of the meaning and message of the book—fitting it "to be through all ages a standing reproof of every form of bigotry" (Prebendary Huxtable in *Speaker's Commentary*).

MICAH

INTRODUCTION

MICAH is one of the best instances of the twofold office of the prophet. He was the messenger on behalf of God, speaking God's message to his own time. He was the messenger of the future, foretelling the doom of nations and the final victory of righteousness and peace.

With no uncertain sound he attacks the vices prevalent around him, the covetousness of the rich (ii. 2) and the evictions of the poor from their homes and their lands (ii. 4, 9); the corrupt government (iii. 1–3; vii. 3); the dishonest trading (vi. 10, 11; cp. Amos viii. 5); the unworthy prophets and priests (iii. 5, 11); the universal ungodliness (vii. 2).

With equal courage he depicts the coming judgements upon his people (i. 3, 6, 16; iii. 6, 12). Jeremiah's narrative shows us how courageous such faithful preaching was, as, referring to Micah's prophecy (iii. 12), that Zion should be "plowed as a field," certain of the elders reminded the people that Micah had been in danger of his life (Jer. xxv. 18, 19). Thus Micah's courage and Hezekiah's defence of him had their influence in saving the life of the later fearless prophet.

So also he predicts the judgements that were to fall upon their oppressors, Assyria and others (v. 5, 6, 9, 15).

But Micah was more than a prophet of doom. He was also a preacher of righteousness. No finer definition of religion has ever been given than his words, "He hath showed thee, O man, what is good; and what doth the Lord require of thee but to do justly, and love mercy, and walk humbly with thy God?" (vi. 5).

He was also a forerunner of Christ and His kingdom. He who, under the Divine inspiration, foresaw the wars and desolation that human wickedness was to bring upon the nations, foresaw also the coming of a better day, when war shall be no more, and the world's Ruler shall arise in Bethlehem (iv. 3; v. 2–5). Mercy shall once more prevail (vii. 18–20).

CHAPTER I

1 the Morasthite. Micah is called a "Morasthite," as being a native of Moresheth-Gath, a village in the west of Judah, in the maritime plain, near Eleutheropolis.

which he saw. In a vision.

2 Hear, all ye people (peoples). The Judge of the whole earth summons all nations to hear His testimony and sentence against Israel, whom He immediately addresses. This description of the Divine judgements resembles Nah. i. 2–6.

His holy temple. *i.e.*, heaven (cp. Isa. lxiii. 15).

4 the valleys shall be cleft. The remembrance of the great earthquake in the days of Uzziah (Amos i. 1) must still have been vivid; and the event serves as an emblem of God's further judgements.

5 Samaria . . . Jerusalem. The national sins of the two kingdoms are traced to their respective capitals; which, instead of being centres of holy influence, were only sources of corruption.

what are the high places of Judah? The Septuagint reads, "what is the *sin* of Judah?"

6 as plantings of a vineyard. By the stones of its buildings being used to form terraces for the growth of the vine on its hillsides: see notes on 1 Kings xvi. 24; Isa. xxviii. 1.

discover. "Lay bare."

7 the hire of a harlot. The Israelites had regarded their possessions as the gifts of their false gods (cp. Hos. ii. 5; Jer. xliv. 17). "Once the prize of faithless living, now the prey of faithless foes" (*Moffatt*).

8 Therefore I will wail and howl. The prophet, while denouncing judgement as a messenger of God, intensely feels the coming sorrow, as a man and a patriot.

naked. Without the outer garment: see Isa. xx. 2, and note.

dragons . . . owls. Rather, "jackals . . . ostriches" (R.V.).

9 He is come. *i.e.*, "the enemy." The R.V., however, reads, "it is come . . . it reacheth," *i.e.*, the wound. The prophet sees the invader entering Judah (9), attacking its northern towns and villages, destroying Jerusalem (10–12), and passing on to places in the south of Judah (13–15): cp. Isa. x. 28–32.

10 Weep ye not at all. Or, as many render, "In Accho, weep ye not." There is evidently an allusion here to David's lament over Saul and Jonathan (2 Sam. i. 20). This indicates a triumph of Israel's enemies over the kingdom and family of David similar to that of the Philistines over the kingdom of Saul. Throughout this passage the verbs are adapted to the meanings and sounds of the proper names; giving by this play upon names, which cannot be fully represented in English, a peculiar emphasis to the denunciation. A good paraphrase, showing this play on words, is given in the *Speaker's Commentary*, and a similar one is given in Moffatt's translation. These are to be preferred to either the A.V. or the R.V., as bringing out the meaning. Thus "the house of Aphrah," or Beth-le-Aphrah (R.V.), signifies *house of dust.* Other instances are given in the notes to the following verses.

11 inhabitant. The word in this and the following verses is feminine: "inhabitress," R.V., and stands collectively for the population.

Saphir. Fair-town.

Zaanan. Outlet. There shall be no freedom of egress.

[In] the mourning of Beth-ezel (neighbour-town), etc. Rather, "The mourning of Beth-ezel takes from you his standing" (*Pusey*); *i.e.*, keeps him from standing beside you to help you; for "Ezel" means "by the side of." In both places the people are themselves in such distress that they can give no help.

12 Maroth. Bitter-town.

waited carefully for good. "Have writhed with pain, waiting for something good" (*Speaker's Commentary*).

13 Lachish. Perhaps, Horse-town.

She is (was) **the beginning of the sin,** etc. Of this fact we have no other record nor any further explanation. The city Lachish, which was strongly fortified, suffered from both the Assyrians and the Chaldeans: see Isa. xxxvi. 1; Jer. xxxiv. 7.

14 shalt thou give presents. Rather, "Thou shalt give a parting-gift," R.V.; *i.e.*, thou shalt give her up, as unable to protect her any longer.

Achzib. False-town.

shall be a lie. (Heb., *achzab*). All hope of aid from them shall prove vain.

15 an heir. A "master"; or, "possessor." The enemy (Sennacherib) shall possess Mareshah (heir-town).

He shall come unto Adullam the glory of Israel. Or, "The glory of Israel shall come even unto Adullam," R.V.; perhaps meaning, The princes shall be reduced to the same straits into which David was formerly brought: see 1 Sam. xxii. 1, 2.

16 as the eagle. Rather, "as the vulture," which has a bald head. The address is to Judah personified as a mother bereaved of "her delicate children," or "the children of her delight" (*Fr. vsrsion:* "tes fils qui faisaient tes délices," "thy children who caused you delights").

CHAPTER II

1 devise . . . work evil . . . practise. Sin is here traced through three stages—the purpose, the elaboration of a plan, and the execution.

3 For this time [is] evil. Or, "for it is an evil time," R.V.

4 Turning away He hath divided our fields. Or, "to a rebel (*i.e.*, an enemy) He hath divided our fields": see R.V.

5 thou shalt have none, etc The land which was once apportioned among you (see Josh. xiv. 1, 5; Judges i. 3) shall now be possessed by strangers.

6 Prophesy ye not, etc. Perhaps the best rendering of this verse is, "Prophesy not, [they say]. They shall prophesy. If they prophesy not thus, shame will not depart."

7 Is the spirit of the Lord straitened? etc. Can the spirit of prophecy speak only of evil? Are these punishments things in which God delights? Are they not rather the necessary consequences of your sins? Are not my words benignant to the upright? But my people have long resisted me (8).

8 Even of late. Heb., "yesterday."

Ye pull off the robe with the garment. The "garment" is the cloak mentioned in Exod. xxii. 26, 27 (see note); the "robe" is probably an ornamental addition; cp. Josh. vii. 21.

9 my glory. *i.e.*, the inheritance, God's glorious gift to Israel (cp. ver. 2). Hence, by a righteous retribution, the oppressors are driven into exile; for the land which their crimes have "polluted" cannot be their "rest" (10).

11 a man walking in the spirit and falsehood. *i.e.*, a false prophet; R.V., "walking in wind and falsehood."

He shall even be the prophet of this people. So corrupt had the people become, that no prophet was acceptable to them who did not sanction their voluptuous habits.

12 I will surely gather the remnant of Israel. A reference to the restoration from Babylon, and of the greater salvation to be wrought by Christ.

Bozrah. There were two Bozrahs, one in Edom and the other in Moab, both celebrated for their large flocks. It is probably Bozrah in Edom that is here meant.

13 The breaker is come up (gone up) **before them.** This "breaker" is a *deliverer.* "They were confined before, as in a prison, and the gate of the prison was burst open to set them free" (*Pusey*): cp. Isa. xliii. 6; lxii. 10.

CHAPTER III

1 judgement. "Justice."

3 Who also eat the flesh of My people, etc. A figurative expression for oppression.

5 that bite with their teeth, etc. These men predicted "peace" to those who pampered them, but became enemies of those who refused to do so.

7 cover their lips. A sign of mourning.

10 They build up Zion with blood, etc. See Jer. xxii. 13: vi. 13: viii. 10, where the same charges are brought against the leaders of a later period.

11 yet will they lean upon the Lord, etc. They were so insensible of their sinfulness that they still expected His protection.

12 plowed as a field, etc. From Jer. xxvi. 17–19 we learn that this prophecy was delivered in the days of Hezekiah, that the king and people, so far from resenting the prophet's indignant words, received them in the spirit of penitence and prayer, and that "the Lord repented Him of the evil which He had pronounced upon them."

CHAPTER IV

1 But in the last (latter) **days,** etc. See notes on Isa. ii. 1–4. These lines were perhaps derived both by Isaiah and Micah from a prophecy of an earlier date, which Micah quotes the more largely (see 4). Otherwise, Micah's is most probably the original.

the law shall go forth, etc. The light of truth from Christ's teaching diffused from this centre through the whole world.

4 under his vine and under his fig tree. See 1 Kings iv. 25.

5 we will walk in the name of the Lord. To "walk in His name," means to act as one who reverences and trusts Him because of His character and word. The honour and confidence which "all the peoples" give to their idols we (says the prophet) will yield to the Eternal alone, in whom we shall never be disappointed.

6 In that day. *i.e.* (ver. 1), in the "latter day," the day of the Messiah.

7 I will make her that halted, etc. I will not destroy her that was feeble, but will save a "remnant," and make it the germ of "a strong nation."

8 O tower of the flock. This appears to be the fortress of Zion; from which the kings of Judah, as "shepherds" of the people, watched and succoured their flock. Such was to be the work of the Good Shepherd (St. John x. 11).

the first dominion. Rather, as R.V., "the former dominion," of the glorious days of David and Solomon; whose prosperous reigns represent that of Messiah: see note on Isa. lx. 1. Read, "The former dominion shall come, the kingdom of the daughter of Jerusalem."

9 as a woman in travail. This figure, with a similar application, occurs in John xvi. 20, 21.

10 to Babylon. The prophet seems here suddenly to overleap more than a hundred years to that which would be the end and climax of all present disasters. But it is evident that the verse has also a wider and more distant application in the sufferings and final deliverance of the Church of God.

11 defiled. Or, "profaned."

look. Or, "see its desire."

13 Arise, and thresh. See Isa. xxviii. 28; xli. 15.

I will make thine horn iron, etc. The figure of an ox threshing corn is followed by a further description of the power which God will give to His people, in order that all which they thus acquire may be consecrated to Him.

I will consecrate. etc. Rather, according to the most approved reading, "Thou shalt consecrate," etc.

CHAPTER V

1 Now gather thyself. Rather, as R.V., "Now shalt thou gather thyself."

daughter of troops. An appellation of Zion, perhaps derived from the military spirit and skill shown by the people in the obstinate defence of their city.

he hath laid siege. That is, the enemy.

the judge of Israel. Probably meaning "king."

2 Beth-lehem Ephratah. See Psa. cxxxii. 6.

[Though] thou be little (which art little). The littleness of Bethlehem is referred to probably as forming a link of connexion between the past and the future deliverance of Israel, through the fact that the "Ruler" in each case would spring from an origin so despised. The Sanhedrin (Matt. ii. 6) quote the words, "art *not* the least," etc., keeping to the general sense of the passage:—little, indeed, in size and estimation, yet in spiritual importance and greatness not least.

thousands. Districts.

Whose goings forth [have been] from of old, etc. The word rendered "goings forth," is the noun derived from the verb meaning to "come forth," used in the former clause; and it indicates that the Ruler, who hereafter shall "come forth" from Bethlehem, had already repeatedly gone forth in ancient times, "from everlasting," in the exercise of the same beneficent authority. And this clearly proves the personal pre-existence of the Messiah as the Lord of all: cp. John i. 1–3; Col. i. 16, 17; Heb. i. 2, 3.

3 Therefore will He give them up. In the accomplishment of His great purpose, Jehovah will for a time suffer His people to fall under the power of their enemies.

she which travaileth. Some commentators, including Hengstenberg, suppose this to be the mother of our Lord, and connect the passage with the prediction in Isa. vii. 14, on which see note. Others, among whom are Theodoret and Calvin, think that the allusion is to *the Church*, which has shortly before been represented (iv. 9, 10) as being in the pangs of suffering, but which shall be delivered and blessed by the coming of the Messiah.

4 and feed. *i.e.*, "and feed [his flock]."

5 [the] (our) **peace.** That is, "the author of peace": cp. Isa. ix. 6; Eph. ii. 14.

seven shepherds. "Seven" and "eight" are used, as in Eccles. xi. 2, to signify *an abundance*—enough and more than enough. As the degradation of Israel is represented by a lack of governors (see Isa. iii. 1–12), its strength and safety are shown by the large number of rulers and defenders.

6 waste. Rather, "rule." Lit., "feed," *i.e.*, "be shepherds over," as ver. 4.

the land of Assyria. The enemies who threatened Israel in the prophet's time (cp. Isa. x.) represent all future foes of the people of the Messiah.

the land of Nimrod. So called because Nimrod had taken possession of it: see marginal reading of Gen. x. 11.

13 standing images. Or, "pillars" (R.V.).

14 thy groves. R.V., "Asherim": see note on Judges iii. 7.

CHAPTER VI

1 contend thou before the mountains. Call them to listen to this controversy between Jehovah and Israel: cp. Deut. xxxii. 1; Isa. i. 2.

2 ye strong foundations. Better, as R.V., "ye enduring foundations."

3 what have I done unto thee? For similar expostulations, showing the reasonableness of God's commands, see Isa. xliii. 23; Jer. ii. 5, 31.

4 Moses, Aaron, and Miriam. Miriam was a prophetess: see Exod. xv. 20, and note.

5 what Balaam the son of Beor answered him. Being compelled to bless instead of cursing Israel.

from Shittim unto Gilgal. The meaning appears to be, And remember what happened to Israel from Shittim (where you might all justly have perished for your sin) to Gilgal (the headquarters of your nation upon your first entrance into Canaan).

6 Wherewith shall I come before the Lord, etc. ? The language of the people personified, addressing the prophet.

7 the fruit of my body, etc. See Lev. xx. 2; 2 Kings xvi. 3.

8 to do justly, etc. These things had always been insisted upon as the weightier matters of the law (see Deut. x. 12, from which these words are partly derived; 1 Sam. xv. 22 and Isa. i. 11–15).

9 shall see Thy name. Or, " and wisdom is theirs who regard (or fear) Thy name " ; *i.e.*, it is the part of wisdom to attend. Attend, then, to the rod (*i.e.*, the threatened chastisement), and to Him who has appointed it.

10 the scant measure (ephah). See Amos viii. 5.

11 Shall I count [them] pure, etc. ? Lit., as R.V., "Shall I be pure," etc.? An ellipsis must be supplied: " Shall I [sayest thou]," etc. ? The French version has "Est il innocent, celui qui a de fausses balances?" (" Is he innocent, who has false balances ? ").

14 and thy casting down, etc. Or, " and emptiness shall be within thee " ; *i.e.*, thy food shall not nourish thee.

and thou shalt take hold. Rather, " And thou shalt put away but shalt not save."

15 And sweet wine, etc. Rather, " And [thou shalt tread out] the grape-juice (' the vintage,' R.V.) ; but shalt not drink wine " : cp. Amos v. 11.

16 the statutes of Omri. See 1 Kings xvi. 25.

CHAPTER VII

1 Woe is me ! The prophet here speaks as the representative of the remnant of the faithful.

as when they have gathered the summer fruits. I look in vain for a godly man, as one looks in vain for fine grapes or early figs when the fruit has been gathered.

my soul desired the first-ripe fruit. Rather, "no early fig which my soul desireth " (see R.V. marg.).

3 That they may do evil with both hands earnestly. Or, " They prepare their hands for evil."

they wrap it up. Or, " they weave it together " ; *i.e.*, elaborate their scheme.

4 the day of Thy watchmen. That is, the day of calamity predicted by Thy watchmen, the prophets : see Hos. ix. 7.

5 Trust ye not in a friend, etc. This warning shows the faithlessness of the people in all the relations of life. For " guide," R.V. marg. rightly has " familiar friend."

7 Therefore (But as for me), **I will look unto the Lord.** So desperate is the depravity, that God's people can find solace only in Him and His purposes of saving mercy.

9 until He plead my cause. See Psa. lxxii. 3.

10 [she that is] mine enemy. A hostile *people* : hence the feminine.

11 shall the decree be far removed. This may be rendered, " the line shall be extended " ; *i.e.*, the city shall be enlarged to admit those who come from Assyria, etc. (12). The Church shall be greatly increased : cp. Isa. liv. 2.

12 In that day [also] he shall come, etc. Rather, " In that day shall they come unto thee from Assyria and the cities of Egypt, and from Egypt even to the River," *i.e.*, the Euphrates (R.V.) : cp. Isa. xix. 18–23, and notes.

and from sea to sea, etc. The seas may be the Mediterranean and the Persian Gulf ; the mountains, Lebanon and Sinai. Or the sense may be more general, indicating all parts of the world.

13 Notwithstanding the land shall be desolate, etc. For " land " read " earth," *i.e.*, the world that is condemned for its sons.

14 thy rod. The shepherd's crook.

which dwell solitarily. The solitariness of Israel among the heathen was one mark of their being Jehovah's people : cp. Numb. xxiii. 9 ; Deut. xxxiii. 28.

Carmel . . . Bashan . . . Gilead. Every fertile district of the land, from west to east, and on both sides of the Jordan.

15 According to the days, etc. This is God's answer to ver. 14.

16 at all their might. Because reduced to impotence.

17 They shall move out of their holes. Rather, as R.V., " They shall come trembling out of their close places," *i.e.*, their fastnesses.

18 Who is a God like unto Thee ? There may here be a reference by the prophet to his own name. The whole passage is a lyric " outburst of emotion," in the review of God's faithfulness and mercy.

20 Thou wilt perform the truth (or, wilt show Thy faithfulness) **to Jacob,** etc. This verse is applied with slight variation, in the inspired song of Zacharias, on the birth of his child, to Him whose herald and forerunner that child was to be (Luke i. 72, 73).

NAHUM

INTRODUCTION

THE men of Nineveh repented at the preaching of Jonah. But Nahum's prophecy shows that their repentance had not lasted, and it is with Nineveh that his Book is almost entirely concerned. The date of it is partly fixed by the reference to the fall of Thebes (No or No-Amon), which took place in 663 B.C. and is mentioned by Nahum as a past event (see note on iii. 8) ; and partly by the date of the fall of Nineveh, which took place about 606 B.C., after Nahum's prophecy (see for fuller details the account of Scheil's discoveries in 1895 in *Hastings' Dict. Bible* : article " Nahum "). He prophesied, therefore, at a time when Israel was subject to the Assyrian yoke, and his message is appropriate to his name, Nahum or "Comforter."

To the oppressed and afflicted people his first words are those of comfort and hope. God will not allow iniquity to go unpunished (i. 2, 3, 6). He is a stronghold in the day of trouble (i. 7). He will therefore break the yoke of Assyria (i. 11–13). The feet of the messengers of deliverance and peace may already be seen upon the distant mountains (i. 15 ; cp. Isa. lii. 7, and Rom. x. 15).

For Nineveh, the prophet's message is one of judgement. Its wickedness is described. It is a bloody city, full of lies and robbery, of vice and supersitition (iii. 1, 4). Its fall shall be complete (ii. 6, 9, 13 ; iii. 7, 18). And the nations which the mighty power of Assyria had oppressed shall rejoice in their deliverance from its despotism (iii. 19).

CHAPTER I

1 burden. "Oracle" : see Isa. xiii. 1. "Vision," the future revealed to his "inner eye."

the Elkoshite. This Elkosh was most probably near Eleutheropolis, in the same region from which Micah came.

2 jealous. Jealous for His own honour, which means jealous for holiness, justice, truth ; and jealous for His people, whose cause He will defend and vindicate.

3 slow to anger. His judgements are not hasty or capricious.

4 Bashan . . . Carmel . . . Lebanon. Imagery from the prophet's own country.

5 is burned. Or, "is upheaved," as R.V.

8 of the place thereof. That is, of Nineveh.

9 What do ye imagine against the Lord ? If this be addressed to the Assyrians, the meaning is, that all their plots shall be vain, and that God will cut them off by a stroke which shall not need to be repeated.

10 as thorns. This probably alludes to the impenetrability of a closely-planted thorn hedge, as the next represents the careless security of the drunkard. Unassailable and secure as the Assyrians may appear, they "shall be consumed, like dry stubble, utterly."

11 There is one come out of thee, etc. Addressed to Nineveh, from which the Assyrian king went forth upon his expedition against Jerusalem.

12 quiet. Rather, "perfect" ; *i.e.*, "in full strength" : so R.V. Whatever be their power and their numbers, they shall be cut down ; and he (*i.e.*, their mighty monarch) shall pass away (not "pass through").

Though I have afflicted thee. That is, Jerusalem, or Judah.

14 concerning thee. The Assyrian monarch. His race shall become extinct.

15 the feet of him that bringeth good tidings. See notes on Isa. xl. 9 and lii. 7.

keep thy solemn feasts. The destruction of the Assyrian invaders allowed the Israelites to resume their national festivals, to which the people could not come up on account of the enemy occupation.

the wicked. Heb. "Belial," *i.e.*, "the wicked one," the Assyrian.

CHAPTER II

1 He that dasheth in pieces, etc. This appears to be addressed to Nineveh, against which the invader is coming. Fulfilled in the campaign of the Median Cyaxares against Nineveh about 606 B.C.

2 For the Lord hath turned away, etc. Rather, "For Jehovah restoreth (*i.e.*, will restore) the excellency of Jacob as the excellency of Israel" : see R.V. "Jacob" is used as the original name of God's people, and "Israel" as their covenant name. He will give to the race of Jacob all the blessings conveyed in the promises to Israel.

their vine branches. Cp. Psa. lxxx. 8–16 ; Isa. v. 1–7. The Assyrian spoilers had laid waste the vineyards.

3 of his mighty men. Of the Median army which should come against Nineveh.

is made red. The shields as the monuments show, were painted red.

The chariots [shall be] with flaming torches, etc. "Gleam like fire" (*Luther*). Chariots were commonly strengthened and decorated with polished steel or brass, which flashed in the sunlight.

4 shall rage. Rather, "rage." The whole description is best rendered in the present tense, a vivid picture of the siege.

5 He shall recount. Heb., "He remembereth" ; *i.e.*, he calls up. But in vain ; for, through fear or weakness, "they stumble in the ways" ; "in their march," R.V.

the defence. Rather, "the covert" ("mantelet," R.V.) ; meaning perhaps the engine called by the Romans *testudo ;* a shed to protect the besiegers and their battering-ram, in attacking the wall ; or in the case of the besieged, a kind of breast-work to shield them from the missiles of the enemy.

6 The gates of the rivers, etc. Some take this to be a figurative description of the invasion, and the consequent dissolution of the Assyrian empire ; but it may perhaps refer to the entrance of the invaders through the river-gates, or to an actual inundation of the Tigris.

7 And Huzzab shall be led away captive, etc. The best commentators regard Huzzab as the name of the queen of Nineveh, though the name has not been identified. "Led away captive," is literally "uncovered."

tabering. "Beating." The Heb. word is used Psa. lxviii. 25, "playing with timbrels."

8 like a pool of water. Water, especially in large quantities, is a frequent emblem of abundant population and prosperity, such as Nineveh had long enjoyed. But this is now rapidly flowing away, and cannot be stopped : cp. Hos. xiii. 15 ; Rev. xvii. 1, 15.

10 She is empty, and void, and waste. Or, more emphatically, "emptiness, and a void, and

a waste !" The Hebrew has a striking alliteration, of which Moffatt gives the effect in his translation : "desolate, dreary, drained."

13 thy messengers. Such as the Rabshakeh, 2 Kings xviii. 17.

CHAPTER III

2 of a whip. Rather, "of the whip" (R.V.), a signal of the on-coming host.

8 populous No. No-Amon : cp. Isa. xx. 3 ; Jer. xlvi. 25, and notes. This city (called by the Egyptians, Tapé, *i.e.*, the *head ;* and by the Greeks, Thebæ) was one of the mightiest of the ancient world. It was celebrated even in the Homeric age for its warriors and its magnificence (*Il.* ix. 381–384), and still retains in the grandeur of its ruins, Karnak and Luxor, proofs of its former splendour. The argument of Nahum plainly shows that No had already been overthrown. This event is recorded in the Assyrian inscriptions : Assur-bani-pal, son and successor of Esarhaddon, invaded Egypt, then under king Urdamani, son of Tirhakah the Ethiopian, capturing, pillaging, and destroying No, 663 B.C.

the rivers . . . the sea. The artificial channels of streams for irrigating the country ; and the Nile, denominated a sea from its vast expanse of waters : see note, Isa. xix. 5.

her wall was from the sea. *i.e.*, the Nile was as a wall to the city.

9 Put. The name of an African people, sometimes rendered "Libyans" : see Gen. x. 6, 13, and note on Ezek. xxvii. 10.

Lubim. The Nubian tribes.

11 Thou also shalt be drunken. See Psa. lxxv. 8 ; Isa. li. 17–23, and notes.

Thou shalt be hid. That is, "Thou shalt disappear."

strength because of the enemy. Rather, "a defence against the enemy" (R.V. marg.).

14 Draw thee waters, etc. An ironical summons to make all preparations against a siege. The clay or mortar for building was kneaded by treading with bare feet. Let the Assyrians do what they would, it would now be vain (15).

15 the fire . . . the sword. Whilst the people shall fall by the sword, the buildings will be destroyed by fire ; as the ruins of Nineveh show was the fact.

the cankerworm. Or, "locust." From these animals three illustrations are here derived : their devastations represent the utter destruction of Nineveh, their vast swarms its numerous merchants and princes, and their sudden flight its strange depopulation : cp. Joel i., and notes.

16 Thou hast multiplied thy merchants. On the commerce of the Assyrians with Tyre, see Ezek. xxvii. 23, 24.

17 Thy crowned. Nobles, who wore a kind of diadem ; or perhaps priests.

18 Thy shepherds slumber, etc. Thy shepherds, or chieftains, slumber in death ; thy worthies are at rest : cp. 1 Kings xxii. 17.

19 the bruit. That is, "report." The surrounding states will express their joy at the ruin of an empire whose rule has been so oppressive.

thy wickedness. The "wickedness" for which Nineveh was to be punished is attested by her own sculptures, which have been brought to light after being buried nearly 2,500 years. In these are portrayed the burning of cities, and the impalement, decapitation, and flaying alive of prisoners, besides other cruel modes of torture : see Layard's *Nineveh and Babylon.* One more denunciation was uttered against this wicked city some years later by Zephaniah (ii. 13–15) ; and shortly afterwards the whole was fulfilled, 606 B.C.

HABAKKUK

INTRODUCTION

THE Book gives us no particulars as to the personality of Habakkuk, except that he is called a prophet (i. 1), and it would appear from iii. 1, 19 (see notes in exposition), that he had some part in the Temple service. The date of his prophecy is variously fixed by different writers as between 625 and 600 B.C., perhaps during the reigns of Jehoahaz and Jehoiakim, and at the same time as Jeremiah.

Like the other prophets, he laments the wickedness of his time, the prevalence of violence (i. 3), and the corruption of justice (i. 4). He proclaims God's judgements upon his nation for their sins, and particularly announces the invasions by the Chaldeans (i. 6), whose character he describes (i. 6–11) in words the truth of which is confirmed by history and the monuments. Against the Chaldeans also he pronounces the judgements of God, for their pride, idolatry, covetousness, drunkenness, and cruelty (ii. 5, 8, 12, 15, 18, 19).

Filled with awe at the Divine judgements, which it was his office to proclaim (iii. 2–16), he appeals for the Divine mercy (iii. 2) and expresses his trust in God and the joy which comes of faith (iii. 17–20).

As to the final issue he has no doubt. "The earth shall be filled with the knowledge of the glory of the Lord, as the waters cover the sea" (ii. 14). He, too, is linked up with the New Testament and with the Reformation by his great message of justification by faith (cp. ii. 4 with Rom. i. 17 ; Gal. iii. 11 ; Heb. x. 38).

CHAPTER I

1 burden. "Oracle." See Isa. xiii. 1; Nahum i. 1.

2 cry out unto Thee of violence. Some regard this as an anticipation of the dreadful oppressions of the Chaldeans: but it probably represents the tyranny and disorders prevailing in the kingdom of Judah, which were recompensed by a punishment resembling the crime: see vers. 6–11.

3 grievance. Or, "trouble." Sept. has πόνος: Vulgate, "laborem."

4 the law is slacked. "Benumbed" or paralysed.

5 Behold ye, etc. The prophet addresses the Jews, announcing a wonderful and fearful work of Jehovah which shall be accomplished in their own days—namely, the elevation of the Chaldean power, and its rapid and extensive conquests (6–10). The words are quoted by the Apostle Paul, Acts xiii. 40, 41, of the perverseness of the Jews in his day.

6 I raise up the Chaldeans. See note on Isa. xxiii. 13.

7 Their judgement and their dignity, etc. A slight variation in the reading gives, "Out of them goeth destruction."

8 swifter than the leopards. See note on Dan. vii. 6.

shall spread themselves. *i.e.*, they spread themselves over the country for plunder. The description throughout should be rendered in the present tense, a vivid description of Chaldean warfare.

9 Their faces shall sup up [as] the east wind. Rather, "The eagerness of their faces is [as] an east wind," cp. R.V. G. A. Smith has "the set of their faces is forward." Similarly *The Speaker's Commentary*.

they shall gather the captivity. Rather, "they gather captives" (R.V.).

10 dust. Rather, "earth"; *i.e.*, mounds: see Jer. xxxii. 24.

11 Then shall [his] mind change, etc. Rather, as R.V., "Then shall he sweep by [as] a wind, and shall pass over, and be guilty, [even] he whose might is his god."

12 for judgement. *i.e.*, as the *instruments* of Thy judgements for our "correction."

O mighty God. Heb., "O Rock": cp. Deut. xxxii. 4.

13 more righteous. Though the Jews were wicked, the Chaldeans were much more deeply sunk in guilt.

14 no ruler. No chief to guard or defend them.

16 they sacrifice unto their net, etc. The victims of the Chaldeans being called "fishes," the "hook" and "net" are the policy and power by which their conquests were effected; and to which alone, instead of to God's permission, they ascribed their success: see 11, and note.

17 empty their net. As fishermen do, in order to cast it again for a fresh draught.

CHAPTER II

1 and set me upon the tower. As a watchman looking for help.

when I am reproved. Rather, "in regard to my remonstrance," namely, that in i. 12–17.

2 Write the vision, etc. Not, "that he who runs may read," but "that he who reads may run"; *i.e.*, "that one may read it at a glance" (*Moffatt*).

tables. "Tablets."

3 at the end it shall speak. Rather, as R.V., "it hasteth (Heb., 'panteth') toward the end." The purposes of God, though apparently delayed in their accomplishment, are sure to be fulfilled.

4 Behold, his soul [which] is lifted up, etc. Rather, "Behold [the man of] presumption, his soul is not right in him; but the just by his faith shall live." The latter clause is taken by the Apostle Paul as the very motto of the Gospel: Rom. i. 17; Gal. iii. 11. It was the text that made clear to Luther the great doctrine of justification by faith.

5 Yea also, because he transgresseth, etc. Or, "And moreover wine is treacherous; the mighty man is proud, and cannot rest" (keep at home). The arrogance was evidently inflamed by strong drink.

6 with thick clay. Rather, "with a mass of pledges or debts": see R.V. The Chaldean, like a rapacious usurer, gathers what is "not his." But "how long" shall he be suffered to do this? Shall he not "suddenly" be punished? (ver. 7).

7 Shall they not rise up, etc.? Rather, "Shall not thy creditors arise suddenly?" The suddenness appears to point to the unexpected rise of the Medo-Persian power.

8 the violence of the land. *i.e.*, the violence which thou hast done in it.

9 from the power (hand) **of evil.** From all chances of calamity.

11 the stone shall cry out of the wall, etc. By this bold personification, the very materials used in the sumptuous buildings of Babylon are described as accusing the king of the rapine by which they have been procured, and the crimes which they have witnessed.

13 shall labour in the very fire. R.V., "labour for the fire." See Jer. li. 58.

14 the earth shall be filled, etc. The punishment of the Chaldean oppressors shall not only display the glory of a righteous and holy God, but shall prepare the way for the new manifestation of His glory in the Gospel: see Isa. xi. 9.

15 That puttest thy bottle to [him]. Rather, "Who pourest out thy heat (*i.e.*, thy wrath), and makest him drunken." The allusion is taken from the well-known drunken habits of the Chaldeans; but it refers figuratively to the ignominy to which they reduced the conquered nations (see Isa. li. 17, 21, 22).

17 the violence of Lebanon. *i.e.*, the violence *done to* Lebanon. See Isa. xxxvii. 24.

18 a teacher of lies. All idols give false notions of the Deity.

19 to the dumb stone, etc. Rather, "to the dumb stone, 'Arise!' Shall this teach? Behold, it is overlaid with gold and silver." Who can imagine that such a thing can teach?

20 But the Lord is in His holy temple. Idols have no "breath," and their pretended oracles are "lies"; but the Eternal is present "in His Temple," and speaks there with truth and authority.

CHAPTER III

1 upon Shigionoth. After the manner of the "Shiggaion," or dithyrambic ode, "a lyrical poem composed under strong mental excitement." (See note on title of Psa. vii.) Ewald thinks that this poem was composed for public use in the Temple, vers. 2 and 16–19 being sung by the prophet, and the second or principal part by the choir of Levites.

2 Thy speech. The revelation contained in the preceding chapters.

revive Thy work, etc. *i.e.,* during the time of the threatened chastening, do Thou repeat and "make known" "Thy work" of "mercy" by delivering Thy people.

3 God came from Teman, etc. Rather, "God will come from Teman," etc.; *i.e.,* He will renew His "work," interposing for Israel as He did in those ancient manifestations celebrated in Deut. xxxiii. 2; Judges v. 4, 5; Psa. lxviii. 7, 8. "Teman" and "Paran" (see Gen. xxi. 21; Jer. xlix. 7) are together put for the desert through which the Israelites pass on their journey from Egypt to Canaan.

4 [His] brightness was as the light, etc. The coming of God is compared to the sun rising over the hills of Edom and Sinai, His rays ("horns") streaming forth, as it were, "from His hand," and lighting up the heavens and the earth. Yet this glorious appearance is not God Himself; it is but the veil in which He wraps His omnipotence: cp. Psa. civ. 2.

5 burning coals. Rather, "burning fever"; as in Deut. xxxii. 24.

6 He stood, and measured the earth, etc. Rather, "He standeth, and shaketh the earth; He looketh, and agitateth the nations."

His ways are everlasting. "His goings are [as] of old," R.V.: cp. Micah v. 2.

7 the tents of Cushan, etc. Referring to the deliverances of the Hebrews from their oppressors in ancient times (see Judges iii. 8–10; vi., vii.), which are introduced here as pledges of future salvation.

9 made quite naked. Drawn out from its case, for use.

[according] to the oaths of the tribes, [even Thy] word. Various renderings have been given of this clause, of which the best appears to be, "The tribes were sworn [to Thy] command. But some scholars favour the translation, "Thy quiver is filled with shafts."

10 lifted up his (its) hands on high. See Psa. lxxvii. 16–19.

13 for salvation with Thine anointed. Rather, "for the salvation *of* Thine anointed" (R.V.). The reference is not to the unworthy Jehoiakim, but to the anointed *people.*

the foundation unto the neck. Not only the "head" of the building, but all the rest, from "the foundation up to the neck," is destroyed.

discovering. Laying bare.

14 Thou didst strike through with his staves, etc. Or, "Thou hast pierced with his own spears (*i.e.,* of his own followers) the head of his scattered tribes."

to scatter me. The prophet speaks in the name of the people.

15 the heap. Or, "the boiling up"; "surge," R.V. marg.

16 my belly trembled. Calvin thinks that the prophet here returns again to the fear which he had entertained (see ver. 2) on account of God's threatenings; and that what he now represents himself as hearing are the actual judgements which God had announced.

that I might rest, etc. Or, "Because I must wait for the day of calamity, for the invader to come up against my people."

17 Although the fig tree shall not blossom, etc. An emphatic or detailed description of the ruin brought upon an agricultural community by invasion.

18 I will rejoice in the Lord. This triumphant close to the prophet's song illustrates the power of true religion to sustain the soul in the absence or loss of every earthly good.

19 The Lord God. "The Eternal, the Lord."

to walk upon mine high places. See 2 Sam. i. 19.

To the chief singer (musician). The inscription at the beginning of many of the Psalms, here placed at the close.

ZEPHANIAH

INTRODUCTION

Apart from the personal references in the Book itself, we have no record of the life of Zephaniah. But these references are of great interest. That he was of royal blood is generally recognised as clear from his mention of Hezekiah ("Hizkiah") as one of his ancestors (i. 1). As Dr. Selbie has pointed out (*Hastings' Dict. Bible*, art. "Zephaniah"), this gives an additional point to his strictures upon the princes and the king's sons (i. 8, 9). Zephaniah also gives us the time at which he prophesied, which was during the reign of king Josiah (i. 1), and as he speaks of the worship of Baal (i. 4) this supplies a still more definite indication, as the altars of Baal were destroyed in the eighteenth year of that king (2 Kings xxii. 3; xxiii. 4), the Chemarim or idolatrous priests (i. 4) being also mentioned in 2 Kings xxiii. 4. Zephaniah's date, then, was from about 625 to 620 B.C.

All this has its bearing on his message. The work of the earlier prophets had been largely undone during the reign of Manasseh, and idolatry, with its accompanying evils, had again become rampant. As the former judgements had not proved effective, God announces, through His servant, more drastic methods. This time He will search Jerusalem with lanterns (i. 12). It shall be "a day of wrath, a day of trouble and distress" (i. 15).

Then follow predictions of doom upon other nations, such as the Philistines (ii. 4–6), predictions which, as Dr. Keith has shown in his *Evidences of Prophecy*, have been fulfilled in remarkable detail. The same is true of the judgements on Nineveh (ii. 13–15).

But Zephaniah, like the other prophets, closes with a message of exultant hope. Israel shall be restored (iii. 20). " Sing, O daughter of Zion . . . be glad and rejoice with all the heart, O daughter of Jerusalem " (iii. 14).

CHAPTER I

1 Hizkiah. That is, Hezekiah.

3 the stumblingblocks with the wicked. That is, the idols with their worshippers: cp. Ezek. xiv. 3.

4 the Chemarim with the priests. See notes on 2 Kings xxiii. 5 and Hosea x. 5. The " priests " were probably corrupt members of the house of Aaron.

5 upon the housetops. From the housetops the objects of their worship were clearly seen. The worship of the heavenly bodies had become very prevalent among the Jews, imitating the Assyrians: see 2 Kings xxiii. 5; Jer. vii. 17, 18; xliv. 17–19, 25.

Malcham. *i.e.*, " their king," or " Molech ": see Amos v. 26. These persons seek to combine the worship of Jehovah with idolatry.

7 the day of the Lord. See on Joel i. 15.

He hath bid His guests. Rather, " He hath consecrated His called ones "; *i.e.*, the Chaldean invaders: cp. Isa. xiii. 3; xxxiv. 6, or " prepared those whom He has invited."

8 the king's children. The various members of the royal family, who indulged in foreign fashions and luxuries.

9 those that leap on (over) **the threshold.** This may refer to the violence and fraud of the retainers of the nobles, who invaded other men's houses to seize their property. But some think that a superstitious practice is indicated.

10 from the second (quarter). See note on 2 Kings xxii. 14.

11 Maktesh. " Maktesh " signifies a hollow place (Judges xv. 19), a mortar (Prov. xxvii. 22); and here it probably means the Tyropœon valley: cp. Jer. xxi. 13.

the merchant people. Heb. (and R.V.), " the people of Canaan " (see Hos. xii. 7); the Jews being so called, because they were like the heathen in their eagerness for wealth and luxury.

12 candles. Or, " lamps." With the closest scrutiny.

The Lord will not do good, etc. He will take no notice of men's conduct.

15 That day. The famous Latin hymn of the 13th century, *Dies iræ, dies illa*, which is entitled *De novissimo judicio*, took its first words from the Vulgate version of this verse.

16 A day of the trumpet. To the gloom and distress portrayed in ver. 15 the terrors of war are superadded.

CHAPTER II

1 Gather yourselves together, etc. Or, " Bend yourselves, yea, bend, O unfeeling nation." Addressed to the Philistines.

4–15. The prophet enforces his call to repentance by predicting the fate of the Philistines (4–7), the Moabites and Ammonites (8–11), the Cushites (12), and the Assyrians (13–15).

4 at the noon day. At an unexpected time: see 2 Sam. iv. 5; Jer. xv. 8.

Ekron. It has been identified with *Akir*, now a station on the railway from Jaffa to Jerusalem (*Hastings' Dict. of Bible*).

5 the Cherethites. See 1 Sam. xxx. 14.

8 Moab . . . Ammon. See notes on Isa. xv. 1; Jer. xlix. 1; Amos i. 13.

11 He will famish all the gods. By depriving them of their sacrifices.

13 will make Nineveh a desolation. See notes on the Book of Nahum.

14 the cormorant and the bittern. " The pelican and the porcupine " (R.V.): cp. Isa. xiii. 21; xiv. 22; xxxiv. 11–15.

CHAPTER III

1 filthy. Rather, " rebellious," as R.V.

2 the voice. The voice of God's messengers, the prophets.

3 till the morrow. Rather, " for the morning "; *i.e.*, They leave nothing for the morrow, but greedily devour all immediately.

5 He faileth not. A motto of encouragement for to-day and every day. A good morning text.

6 I have cut off the nations. Rather, as R.V., " I have cut off nations." By their punishment the Jews should have taken warning: see ii. 4.

their towers. " their battlements," R.V.

7 So their dwelling should not be cut off, etc. The better reading appears to be that of the Septuagint and Syriac, which give " from her eyes " (an almost identical word in the Hebrew letter) instead of " their dwelling." Moffatt translates, " she will never lose sight of My orders."

9 For then will I turn to the people (the peoples), etc. The rest of this chapter is very similar to Isa. xi., xxxv., lx.; Ezek. xxxvi., xxxvii.; and the same general principles are applicable to its interpretation: see the notes on those chapters.

10 the daughter of My dispersed. *i.e.*, " My scattered people."

11 shalt thou not be ashamed. Thy punishment and disgrace shall have ceased.

12 afflicted. Or, " humble "; " poor in spirit " (Matt. v. 3).

17 He will rest in His love. Rather, " He will be *silent* in His love "; *i.e.*, in His mercy He will mention thine iniquities no more: see Jer. xxxi. 34; Micah vii. 19. G. A. Smith reads: " He will renew His love." This is a various reading of the Hebrew.

18 them that are sorrowful for the solemn assembly. That is, those who mourned the loss of public worship.

19 I will get them praise and fame, etc More exactly, as R.V., " I will make them a praise and a name, whose shame hath been in all the earth."

HAGGAI

INTRODUCTION

THE date of this Book is definitely fixed by its opening words. The actual year was the second year of Darius I, *i.e.*, 520 B.C., and it was on the first day of the sixth month that Haggai began to deliver his message to Zerubbabel the governor of Jerusalem and to Joshua the high priest (i. 1).

Like Joel, he spoke in an unpromising time. Lethargy had fallen upon the people. Fifteen years before, the foundation of the Temple had been laid, under the leadership of the two men above mentioned, amid great rejoicing, after the return from the Captivity (Ezra iii. 6, 8–13). But there it stopped. The Samaritans, to whom Zerubbabel had refused permission to help in the building, set themselves to frustrate his purpose (Ezra iv. 4, 5). They invoked the help of king Artaxerxes, and the work was stopped (Ezra iv. 7–24).

But the opposition of the enemy was not the only cause. The early enthusiasm of the people had faded, and in its place were apathy and selfishness. It was against these forces that Haggai spoke. "The time is not come," they said (i. 2). How often this has been a hindrance to progress, a barrier to religious and social reform! They could not build the house of God, but they dwelt in their own cieled houses (i. 4).

And their selfishness had not profited them (i. 6–11). They had much labour with little result (cp. Prov. xi. 24).

Haggai's message was effective. The leaders and the people "obeyed the voice of the Lord their God," and the building of the Temple was resumed (i. 12–15 ; cp. Ezra v. 1, 2). It was completed in about four years, and dedicated in the sixth year of Darius, 516 B.C. (Ezra vi. 14, 15). The faithfulness and fearlessness of the prophet had their reward.

Haggai not merely rebuked them for their selfishness and apathy, but continued to encourage the leaders and people to persevere. "Be strong and work, for I am with you, saith the Lord of hosts" (ii. 4). He puts before them the great privilege of building this new Temple, the glory of which was to be greater than that of the old one (ii. 9). Here is a prediction of the presence in it of the Messiah (cp. Luke ii. 22, 46).

And beyond the fulfilment in the earthly temple, there lies the fulfilment in the spiritual and enduring city of God, when the kings of the earth shall bring their honour and glory into it (cp. ii. 7, and note on this verse, with Rev. xxi. 22–24). So shall the shaking of the nations and the overthrow of despotisms (ii. 7, 22) lead to the world's peace and the final establishment of the kingdom which cannot be shaken (cp. ii. 6, 21, with Heb. xii. 26–28).

CHAPTER I

1 Darius the king. That is, the king of Persia, of whose empire Judea was a province. This Darius was the son of Hystaspis, and reigned 521–486 B.C. The events here referred to are related in Ezra v., vi.

in the sixth month. Of the Hebrew year, the month of Elul (Septuagint).

Josedech (Jehozadak). Josedech was son of Seraiah, the high priest who was slain when Jerusalem was taken: see 2 Kings xxv. 18–21.

4 for you, O ye. As a contrast to the spirit here condemned: see 1 Chron. xvii. 1 ; Psa. cxxxii. 1–5.

cieled houses. Panelled ; lined with timber.

5 Consider your ways. Consider your past conduct and to what it has led you.

8 the mountain. To the hill country generally, whence timber could be obtained. It needed only that *wood* should be collected : the *stones* of the ruined Temple were still there lying "in every street" (Lam. iv. 1).

9 I did blow upon it. R.V. marg., "I did blow it *away*."

ye run every man unto his own house. You hasten forward your own buildings.

12 all the remnant of the people. The few who had returned to Judæa.

13 I am with you. To protect you from your enemies, and give you favour with the king, and success in your work: cp. Ezra v., vi.

15 in the four and twentieth day, etc. In less than a month after Haggai's first message.

CHAPTER II

I the seventh month. Ethanim or Tisri, answering to Sept.–Oct.

3 Who is left among you? "There might be some aged men still living, who had seen Solomon's temple. Eighteen years before, there had been many such" (Ezra iii. 12: Canon Drake, in *Speaker's Commentary*). The 70 years of exile were now completed.

as nothing. "The Holy of Holies was empty. The Ark, the Cherubim, the Tables of stone, the vase of Manna, the Rod of Aaron, were gone. The golden shields had vanished. Even the High Priest, though he had recovered his official dress, had not been able to resume the Breastplate with the oracular stones" (*Stanley*).

6 I will shake the heavens, etc. This figure is often used to signify great commotions and changes, political, social, or religious. Cp. Heb. xii. 26.

7 the desire. Heb., "the desire" (a feminine noun denoting *collectiveness,* "that which is most desired," or, "the treasure") "of all nations—they shall come." Some regard this as applying to the Messiah *personally;* but the plural form of the verb in the Hebrew, as well as the feminine noun, forbids such an explanation of the passage. The obvious meaning is that the wealth (8) which they delight in "shall come" as an offering to Jehovah (cp. Isa. lx. 5; lxi. 6). The R.V. translates, "the desirable things of all nations shall come." The French version has "les délices des toutes les nations." In its largest application, the prediction is that all the richest of the world's store, material, intellectual, and spiritual, shall be made tributary to the kingdom of God.

9 The glory of this latter house, etc. Rather, "The latter glory of this house shall be greater than the former" (R.V.), pointing to the spiritual glory which would arise from the presence of the Christ.

And in this place will I give peace. The worship now being re-established shall prepare the way for the Gospel of peace.

10 the ninth [month]. Chisleu, Nov.–Dec. Two months after the preceding message.

13 It shall be unclean. The holy offering does not sanctify whatever touches it; but the unclean pollutes anything that comes in contact with it: so your good works do not compensate for your neglect of My Temple; but this neglect makes everything else that you do unacceptable. Hence comes your want of that success which would be a mark of Divine favour towards you: cp. Jas. ii. 10.

15 upward. Rather, "forward," or "onward." So in ver. 18. The future has better things in store.

16 to draw out fifty [vessels]. Or, "to draw out fifty vats," or, "barrels"; a measure doubtless large, but probably indefinite.

19 Is the seed yet in the barn? If this is to be read as a question the meaning is probably that which is suggested in Moffatt's translation: "Will your seed be lying idle in the barns?" But some think that the original should read as a statement of fact, "Lo, the seed is still in the barn." (So Luther.) But the harvest is sure.

21 I will shake, etc. See ver. 6.

22 of his brother. "Of his fellow."

23 and will make thee as a signet. The seal, on which the owner's name was engraved, was of the highest value to him, and kept with jealous care. Cp. Jer. xxii. 24. So, amidst all the convulsions of the nations, God will preserve His faithful servant Zerubbabel. This promise, like that in Matt. xxviii. 20; Mark xvi. 16, 17, may be regarded as having a further application to all God's servants who are called to posts of difficulty or danger.

ZECHARIAH

INTRODUCTION

ZECHARIAH was the contemporary and fellow-worker of Haggai and prophesied for two years, 520 to 518 B.C. (For the conditions of the time and place, see Introduction to the Book of Haggai, above.) But his Book is more full of picturesque imagery, of inspiring visions, and especially of passages that had their fulfilment in the human life of the Lord Jesus Christ.

He begins with a call to repentance (i. 2–6). Then follows a series of seven visions. The vision of the horsemen among the myrtle-trees (i. 8–17), with its "comfortable words," is to reassure the people generally in regard to God's mercy and the fulfilment of His promises. The vision of the four horns and the four carpenters or smiths (i. 18–21) is a specific assurance of the overthrow of their oppressors. The vision of the man with the measuring line (ii. 1–8) foreshadows the growth of Jerusalem, the presence of God as her real defence, and her preciousness in His sight. In the fourth vision, which represents Joshua the high priest as being accused by the Adversary, God gives to His servant and to the people the assurance of His pardon and cleansing (iii.). The fifth vision, of the golden candlestick with the olive-trees supplying the oil through the golden pipes (iv.) has its lesson of encouragement for the Church of God, in all its history, that no difficulties can hinder it (iv. 7), that its strength is not in material resources or human power but in God's Spirit (iv. 6) ; and that small beginnings may have great endings (iv. 10). In the sixth vision, that of the flying roll, the woman and the ephah (v.), is shown the necessity for national righteousness and the punishment and removal of dishonesty and perjury. The last vision, that of the four chariots and the horses of different colours (vi. 1–8), is one of a more general and universal character and indicates the world dominion of " the Lord of all the earth " (v. 5).

Then comes the first of Zechariah's great prophecies of the Messiah, who is here described as the Branch, and who shall be crowned as priest and king (vi. 12, 13).

In words that recall those of Isaiah (Isa. i. 12–17), and of Micah (Micah vi. 6–8), Zechariah answers a question about fasting. He does not tell the people not to fast, but shows its futility and hypocrisy unless there be right dealing with their neighbours, especially the widow, the fatherless, the stranger and the poor (vii. esp. 5, 6, 9, 10), with truthfulness and justice (viii. 16, 17). Then shall there be joy and gladness, children playing in safety in the streets, and men and women living to old age because Jerusalem shall be a city of truth, a holy mountain, attracting the homage of all nations (viii. 3–5, 19–23).

The remaining chapters (ix.–xiv.) differ so much in style and substance from the earlier ones, that some commentators regard them as being by a different hand from Zechariah's. They contain prophecies about Hadrach, Damascus, Hamath, Assyria, Egypt and Greece as well as some about Tyre and Sidon and the cities of Philistia (ix. 1, 2, 3, 5, 13 ; x. 10). But in them as in the earlier chapters, there are predictions of the coming of the Messiah (cp. ix. 9, with John xii. 14, 15). A fountain shall be opened for sin and for uncleanness (xiii. 1 ; cp. Heb. ix. 14) ; the whole life of city and home shall be consecrated to God (xiv. 20, 21) ; and " the Lord shall be king over all the earth " (xiv. 9).

CHAPTER I

1 In the eighth month, etc. Marchesvan (Oct.–Nov.). Just two months after Haggai began to prophesy, and about one month after the Temple was recommenced.

in the second year of Darius. See note on Hag. i. 1.

the son of Berechiah. Ezra (v. 1) and Nehemiah (xii. 16) call him the son of Iddo, " son " there meaning descendant. He was the grandson of Iddo.

5 Your fathers, where are they? The generation to whom God's word was revealed has passed away ; but that word has still its bearing upon you : cp. Isa. xl. 6–8.

6 statutes. Rather, " decrees." The things which I had decreed, " took hold of " (*i.e.*, overtook) your fathers.

they returned and said. That is, to God.

7 the four and twentieth day of the eleventh month. About three months after the former message. " Shebat " was the Babylonian name of the eleventh month (Jan.–Feb.).

8 a man riding upon a red horse. Or, " chestnut horse." Similar representations of God's controlling and protecting providence are given in Gen. xxxii. 1 ; Josh. v. 13 ; 2 Kings vi. 17.

in the bottom. Or, " in the deep valley," where the myrtle is chiefly found.

12 these threescore and ten years. See note on 2 Kings xxv. 8.

15 they helped forward the affliction. Luther's version best brings out the meaning : " I was a little angry with Israel, but they help to destroy it."

16 a line shall be stretched forth, etc. The measuring line for rebuilding it.

17 My cities through prosperity, etc. Rather, " My cities shall yet overflow with prosperity " (R.V. marg.).

18 four horns. Indicating that the hostile nations were on all sides.

20 carpenters. Rather, " blacksmiths " : *i.e.*, to shatter their enemies (ver. 21).

CHAPTER II

4 this young man. The measurer.

towns without walls. " Unwalled villages," as Ezek. xxxviii. 11, not needing outward defences.

5 a wall of fire. Within which she shall be perfectly secure : cp. Psa. lxxxiv. 11.

7 O Zion. That is, O ye that belong to Zion.

8 After the glory. Probably meaning, after (*i.e.*, in addition to) the glory promised (see ver. 5).

toucheth the apple of His eye. Cp. Deut. xxxii. 10.

12 shall inherit. Shall take as His own possession.

13 Be silent, etc. Cp. Hab. ii. 20.

CHAPTER III

1 Joshua the high priest. See Hag. i. 1; Ezra ii. 1.

Satan. The Adversary or "the accuser"; who, in ancient courts of justice, stood at the right hand of the accused: see Psa. cix. 6. The Evil One is not necessarily meant here.

2 a brand plucked out of the fire. That is, a remnant rescued from destruction: see Amos iv. 11.

3 Joshua was clothed with filthy garments. Denoting the sins and pollutions of the people, and especially of the priesthood.

5 And I said. If this reading is correct, the prophet seems to interpose a request. But the Chaldee, Syriac, and Vulgate read "he said," which agrees better with the context.

mitre. "turban."

7 I will give thee places to walk, etc. I will give thee a place among those who are My helpers ("who stand by").

8 men wondered at. Rather, "men of wonder," or of sign; *i.e.*, men intended for signs and tokens: see R.V., and cp. Isa. xx. 3; Ezek. xii. 11; xxiv. 24. You and your brethren, now restored to your country and to your priestly functions, are a sign and pledge of the fulfilment of My great promise of the Messiah. Hence He is here spoken of as "the Branch," or, "Scion," a title intimating the revival in Him of Israel's glory: see Isa. iv. 2; xi. 1, and notes.

9 seven eyes. Perhaps seven facets.

10 call. "Invite": the communion of saints.

CHAPTER IV

1 waked me. Or, "aroused me," from the meditations suggested by the preceding vision.

2 candlestick. "lampstand."

seven pipes to the seven lamps. The Hebrew idiom is different from ours, and the meaning is "seven pipes to the lamps," or one pipe to each lamp. The seven lamps indicate perfect light.

3 two olive trees. Not as a reservoir of oil, which might be emptied, but a living and inexhaustible supply. Cp. Rev. xi. 4.

6 Not by might, nor by power. Let not your weakness and poverty dishearten you in rebuilding the Temple. His providence and grace will furnish unlooked-for supplies; just as the unseen oil in the trees and in the bowl feeds the lamps. Your difficulties shall vanish, and your work shall be completed with grateful joy (7).

This promise of Divine power to overcome difficulties has often been fulfilled in the lives of individual Christians and in the history of the Church, especially in modern missions. In India, China, Japan, Uganda, Fiji, Madagascar, and many other countries, the mountain has become a plain.

7 headstone. "Top-stone."

10 [with] those seven, etc. Rather, "And those seven eyes of Jehovah, those that run to and fro in all the earth, rejoice and see the plummet in the hand of Zerubbabel": cp. R.V. God's all-watchful providence (iii. 9; Prov. xv. 3) beholds with joy and favour the work of Zerubbabel; and however some may "despise" the small beginning, He will take care that the work shall be gloriously completed.

14 the two anointed ones (Heb., "two sons of oil"). Some suppose these "two who supplied oil" to be Zerubbabel and Joshua—symbolising the civil government and the priesthood. Calvin thinks that they denote, in general, the abundance and constancy with which God supplies grace to His people.

CHAPTER V

2 twenty cubits . . . ten cubits. Making the length more than ten yards, and the breadth more than five. A figurative expression of great size.

3 of the whole earth. Rather, "of the whole *land*" (R.V.); *i.e.*, of Judea.

on this side . . . on that side. The roll was written on both sides (cp. Ezek. ii. 10); containing on one side the crimes against the *second* table of the Law, represented by "theft"; and on the other those against the *first* table, represented by "swearing."

4 with the timber thereof and the stones thereof. Utterly detroying all that he has.

6 an ephah. Or, "barrel." The ephah was one of the largest measures used by the Hebrews, containing about seven gallons. Indicating the full measure which the sins of the Jews had attained before their captivity.

resemblance. Some ancient authorities read *iniquity*, the two words in Heb. being very similar.

8 This is wickedness. That is, This woman represents wickedness.

cast it. Rather, "cast her," the woman. He hides and effectually imprisons her, by the lead cast on the cover.

9 like the wings of a stork. That is, very strong. Some suppose that these two women denote the Assyrians and Babylonians. But they are probably symbols of wickedness generally. All this foreshadows the purification of the Church: see on ver. 11.

11 the land of Shinar. "Shinar" is the country around Babylon: where, as in its appropriate home, the Jews left their propensity to idolatry. In its widest sense Shinar may symbolise the whole sphere of ungodliness, "the world," into which all evil is banished from the Church (*Keil*).

CHAPTER VI

1 mountains of brass. Or, "bronze." This represents solidity. What these "two mountains" mean is doubtful. The Heb. reads, "*the* two mountains," which would seem to suggest Mount Zion and the Mount of Olives.

5 the four spirits of the heavens. Rather, "winds"; indicating the four quarters of the earth. Cp. Rev. vii. 1.

6 go forth into the north country, etc. That the "north" (probably Assyria and Babylonia) is destined to suffer desolation, and then to enjoy peace.

toward the south country. That is, towards Egypt.

8 have quieted My spirit, etc. The future, not the past, is used here. The meaning is that the judgements to be inflicted on Babylon will satisfy God's justice.

10 Take of them of the captivity. Rather, "Take from them of the captivity," etc.; "yea, take silver and gold," etc. (11).

of Heldai, of Tobijah, and of Jedaiah. These were probably a deputation from the Jews still remaining in Babylon, who had sent them with contributions of gold and silver to help forward the rebuilding of the Temple at Jerusalem.

11 crowns. As these were symbols of the priestly and royal dignities, they were probably the kingly crown, and the golden plate, or ornament on the tiara (Exod. xxviii. 36), of the high priest. Whether they were separate or combined into one head-dress is not said.

12 he shall grow up. Lit., "shall *branch* up"; *i.e.*, out of the stem of Jesse, or David; his relation to whom is signified by this title: see iii. 8; Isa. iv. 2; xi. 1.

13 between them both. The meaning probably is, between the two offices just mentioned. The Messiah unites all the functions and honours of the priestly and kingly offices. All this is clearly applied to our Lord in Heb. vii.: cp. also Gen. xiv. 18; Psa. cx.

14 Helem. The same person as Heldai (10). "Hen" may be the same as Josiah (10).

CHAPTER VII

1 Chisleu. Or, "Kisleu." The Babylonian or Chaldee word, used after the Captivity.

2 when they had sent into the house of God, etc. Rather, "when Bethel sent Sherezer, "etc. "They of Bethel," R.V.

3 to speak unto the priests. It was the priest's duty (see Mal. ii. 7) to direct the people in the worship of God, and the observances of His law; see note on ver. 5.

5 in the fifth and seventh month. These two fasts were of merely human appointment; that of the fifth month commemorating the destruction of the Temple by the Babylonians; that of the seventh the murder of Gedaliah: see 2 Kings xxv. 8–10, 25; Jer. xli. 1–3; lii. 12–14. The question was whether, when the seventy years of captivity were expired and the Temple was rebuilt, these fasts should be continued. The Jews still retain them in their calendar.

did ye at all fast unto Me? Have your fasts and your feasts been seasons of true humiliation before God, or of real thankfulness to Him? The answer is indicated in ver. 10; cp. Isa. i. 11–20; lviii. 3–6.

7 the plain. This "plain" is the low country along the coast of the Western Sea, the "Shephelah." These parts were probably at this time almost depopulated, the "lowland" being the track of the great armies passing between Egypt and Asia.

9 Thus speaketh. Rather, "Thus spoke"; *i.e.*, to your ancestors: see Isa. i. 23; lviii. 6, 7; Micah vi. 6–8.

11 and pulled away the shoulder. See Neh. ix. 29.

12 hath sent. Rather, "sent." So ver. 13, "it *came* to pass": see note on ver. 9.

CHAPTER VIII

2 I was jealous. Rather, "I have been jealous"; *i.e.*, against the foes of Zion.

3 I am returned. See Ezek. ix. 3; x. 4, 18, 19; xi. 22, 23; xliii. 1–7.

4 dwell. Rather, "sit"; the aged sitting in the open air, the children playing there: a lovely picture of peace restored. Such scenes are not possible amid the horrors of war.

7 from the east country, etc. From all places, wherever they are dispersed. Lit., "from the sun-rising and from the sun-setting."

10 no hire for man, etc. That is, no reward of labour.

because of the affliction. Rather, "Because of the adversary" (R.V.).

15 fear ye not. My threatenings have been accomplished; fear not, then, that I shall fail to fulfil My promises.

19 The fast of the fourth [month]. The fast of the tenth month commemorated the beginning of the siege of Jerusalem, and that of the fourth month its capture: see Jer. lii. 4, 6, 7. Respecting the other fasts, see note on vii. 5.

23 ten men. That is, many men.

shall take hold of the skirt. In the manner of one who desires to go with another, and will not take a refusal: see Isa. iii. 6.

CHAPTER IX

1 The burden. Or, "oracle": see Isa. xiii. 1.

the land of Hadrach. The name "Hadrach" does not occur elsewhere in Scripture; but it is probably to be identified with *Ha-ta-rak-ka*, near Damascus and Hamath, mentioned in Assyrian inscriptions (*Schrader*).

the rest (resting-place) **thereof.** That is, of the burden; the place on which the impending judgement shall settle. "The goal" (*Moffatt*).

When the eyes of man, etc. Rather, "For the eyes of men and of all the tribes of Israel," etc.; cp. R.V.

2 And Hamath also shall border thereby. Rather, "And Hamath also, [which] bordereth thereby"; *i.e.*, Hamath shall share in the same judgement.

though (*or*, because) **it be very wise.** That is, Tyre: see Isa. xxiii.; Ezek. xxvi.–xxviii., and notes, particularly Ezek. xxviii. 3, 4, 17.

6 a bastard. Meaning, perhaps, a mongrel, degraded race.

7 And I will take away, etc. The remnant of the people shall forsake their idolatrous and abominable practices for the worship of "our God"; and thus be incorporated (like the ancient Jebusites in Jerusalem) with God's people. See Psa. lxxxvii.

8 for now have I seen with Mine eyes. Or, "now I will see." God will guard His own people against the armies that march to and fro, and not suffer any enemy to injure them; for which purpose His eyes will be constantly on the watch.

9 having salvation. Heb., "saved." As to His subjects He is "just"; as to His enemies He is "saved" from all their designs, and therefore He becomes "the Author of salvation" to His people. Yet He does not ride in the chariot or on the horse of the warrior (10); but, as one who is both peaceful and lowly, upon "the foal of an ass": cp. Matt. xxi. 4, etc.

10 And I will cut off the chariot, etc. Warlike equipages and equipments will no more be needed in the Messiah's peaceful reign. Cp. Hosea ii. 18; Micah v. 9–11.

from sea [even] to sea, etc. See Psa. lxxii. 8. From the Dead Sea to the Mediterranean, and from the Euphrates to the South.

11 As for thee also. This is addressed still to Zion.

by the blood of thy covenant. That is, on account of the blood of the covenant which I have made with thee: see Exod. xxiv. 8.

out of the pit, etc. That is, "out of their *prison*"; empty cisterns being often used as dungeons (see Jer. xxxviii. 6).

12 Turn you. Rather, "Return." The "stronghold" is Zion. The people are "prisoners of hope"; prisoners who have hope. Though distressed, they have the prospect of deliverance.

double. That is, abundantly: see note on Isa. xl. 2.

13 When I have bent Judah, etc. Rather, "For I will use Judah as My bow, and Ephraim as My arrow, and raise up," etc.; making My people, now saved and led by the Messiah (14), the conquerors of the world for Him.

14 whirlwinds of the south. See Isa. xxi. 1.

15 subdue with sling stones. Rather, as R.V., "and shall tread down the sling-stones,"crushing these threatening missiles under foot. Cp. Job xli. 28.

they shall drink. That is, the blood of the slain, like a lion: see Numb. xxiii. 24.

like bowls. Rather, "like the bowl," filled with sacrificial blood, which was sprinkled on "the corners of the altar."

16 His land. The earth now subject to Messiah: see Isa. lxii. 3.

CHAPTER X

1 the latter rain. See Deut. xi. 14; Joel ii. 23.

2 the idols. Heb., "the *teraphim*" (so R.V.): see note on Gen. xxxi. 19.

went their way. Rather, "went astray."

3 the goats. The leaders or "chief ones," as in Isa. xiv. 9.

as His goodly horse. That is, bold and powerful.

4 Out of him. That is, out of Judah: cp. Jer. xxx. 21.

the corner. *i.e.,* "the corner *stone,*" R.V.; the chief support.

every oppressor. Rather, "every *ruler*" (Isa. lx. 17).

5 on horses. In which their foes trusted (Psa. xx. 7).

8 I will hiss for them. See note on Isa. v. 26.

as they have increased. As in their most prosperous days (1 Kings iv. 20).

9 I will sow them, etc. "Though I scatter them among the peoples, yet they shall remember Me," etc. If I have to chastise, I will yet cause them to repent.

11 He shall pass through the sea with affliction. Or, "He shall pass through the sea of affliction" (R.V.).

the River. That is, the Nile.

CHAPTER XI

1 Lebanon. Lebanon and Bashan, with their forests, are often put for the princes and nobles (see Isa. ii. 12, 13, and note; x. 34; Ezek. xvii. 3), here called "shepherds" and "lions."

2 the forest of the vintage. Rather, "the 'strong' or 'defenced' forest" (R.V.); *i.e.,* that which seemed least liable to injury.

3 [There is] a voice of the howling, etc. Literally, and more emphatically, as R.V., "A voice of the howling of the shepherds!"

the pride of Jordan. See note on Jer. xii. 5. The "young lions," dislodged by the fire from the brakes and thickets, fill the land with their cry.

4 Feed. An address to Zechariah, who in his relation to the people typifies the Good Shepherd.

the flock of the slaughter (of slaughter). That is, the flock devoted to slaughter, and valued only for that purpose.

6 I will deliver the men, etc. This points to the subjection of the Jews to their oppressors through many ages.

7 And I will feed the flock. Rather, as R.V., "So I fed the flock," carrying out the injunction of ver. 4.

O poor of the flock! Or, "verily a most miserable flock!" See R.V., and marg.

two staves. Shepherds carried "a rod and a staff"—a cudgel for defence against attack, and a crook to tend and guide the flock. Psa. xxiii. 4.

Beauty . . . Bands. Favour and Union. Favour or Goodwill on the part of God and Unity amongst men. The former staff was for defence against the nations, a sign of protection from their attacks, see ver. 10; the latter, an emblem of the unity of the flock.

8 Three shepherds. Rather, "The three shepherds." This probably means "all"; possibly with reference to the three classes of rulers among the Jews—the priests, magistrates, and prophets. All these were unfaithful.

in one month. That is, within a short space of time.

My soul loathed them, etc. "My soul was weary of them (*i.e.,* of the flock, the people), and their soul also loathed Me," R.V.

9 eat every one the flesh of another. That is, Let them suffer the worst consequences of war and famine: see 2 Kings vi. 26–29. During the siege of Jerusalem by the Romans, this was actually done: see Jos. *Wars,* v. 10, § 3; vi. 3, §§ 3, 4.

10 my covenant which I had made with all the people (peoples). Restraining them from dispersing Israel.

11 and so the poor of the flock, etc. The Septuagint has "the Canaanites" (cp. Zech. xiv. 21). Moffatt translates "hucksters." For "waited upon me," read, with R.V., "gave heed unto me."

12 give ye my price. I asked the rulers for my wages. The contemptible sum they offered (less than £4) showed how little value they set both upon the shepherd and upon his work.

13 a goodly price. Ironical, "a goodly price indeed!" The value set on a slave's life (Exod. xxi. 32)! "Cast it" publicly, in the Temple itself, "to the potter," the despised and polluted workman of Tophet (Jer. xviii., xix.). This passage quoted in Matt. xxvii. 9, 10.

14 Then I cut asunder mine other staff. "Favour" with the nations having already been destroyed, "unity" among the people now also perishes.

15 foolish. That is, "wicked." The prophet now personates another kind of shepherd. The "instrument," or equipment, would be the rod and staff, with a knife, flute and scrip, or wallet for provisions.

16 which shall not visit those that be cut off, etc. Rather, "He will not attend to those that are perishing, the strayed he will not seek," etc.; "that which standeth (is healthy) he will not feed," etc. The Good Shepherd being rejected, the people would be given over to selfish deceivers.

nor feed that that standeth still. The sound portion of the flock.

and tear their claws. Rather, "And break their hoofs." *i.e.,* by merciless driving over rough roads (*Speaker's Commentary*).

17 the idol shepherd. Rather, "the worthless shepherd," R.V.

His arm shall be clean dried up, etc. God will justly deprive him of the power and understanding which he has abused.

CHAPTER XII

1 for Israel. "Concerning Israel," R.V.

2 a cup of trembling. Rather, "a cup of reeling" (R.V.), or, "of staggering." The nations eagerly gather around Jerusalem as around a bowl which they hope to drain, but the draught fills them with bewilderment and confusion (Isa. li. 17, 22).

When they shall be in the siege, etc. Lit., "And also in respect of Judah shall it be (a cup of trembling to the nations round about) in the siege against Jerusalem." Luther's version suggests what appears to be the true meaning, that the cause and the triumph of Judah shall be one with those of Jerusalem. Cp. v. 7.

3 a burdensome stone. A stone so heavy, that any who attempt to carry it shall be lacerated or bruised ("sore wounded," R.V.): cp. Matt. xxi. 44.

4 I will open Mine eyes, etc. Rather, "I will open its eyes," in contrast with "the horses of the peoples," which shall be blinded.

6 like a hearth of fire among the wood. Rather, "Like a firepan among logs of wood."

7 the tents of Judah. That is, the rural population. The more obscure and feeble shall be first delivered, that the princes and the citizens may not despise them.

8 as David. The hero of Israel (2 Sam. xvii. 8; xviii. 3).

10 they shall look upon Me whom they have pierced. A better reading is "upon Him." For the further application of the words, see John xix. 37; Rev. i. 7.

11 the mourning of Hadadrimmon. On account of the death of Josiah: see 2 Kings xxiii. 30; 2 Chron. xxxv. 25, and notes. "Hadadrimmon" (an Assyrian word) was the name of a place near Megiddo.

12, 13 David . . . Nathan . . . Levi . . . Shimei. Nathan and Shimei were the son and grandson of David and Levi (see 2 Sam. v. 14; Numb. iii. 18), and are mentioned as representing the subordinate branches of the kingly and the priestly line.

CHAPTER XIII

1 there shall be a fountain opened, etc. This promise includes both the remission of sin, and moral and spiritual healing.

"Cleanse me from its guilt and power."

2 the idols. Though idolatry was not so much a prevailing sin after the Captivity, the lingering spirit of it remained.

3 shall thrust him through. Fulfilling the law in Deut. xiii.

4 a rough garment to deceive. The garb of a prophet, after the pattern of Elijah (1 Kings xix. 13, 19); cp. Matt. iii. 4.

5 man taught me to keep cattle. Rather, "one purchased me," *i.e.*, as his servant. A man will rather be thought a slave than a false prophet.

6 in thine hands. Rather, as R.V., "between thine arms' (hands); scars upon his breast; either superstitious marks or wounds incurred in a private brawl.

7 the man that is My fellow. See note on Psa. xlv. 7. The Messiah is here represented as a Ruler. If He, the Shepherd, is cut off, the sheep and lambs ("the little ones") must expect to suffer. Cp. Matt. xxvi. 31.

CHAPTER XIV

1 the day. Rather, "a day," as R.V.

thy spoil. *i.e.*, the spoil of Jerusalem, portioned out by the enemy in the very midst of the city; so complete was its subjugation.

3 as when He fought in the day of battle. As He formerly fought against the enemies of Israel—the Egyptians, Canaanites, and others. Cp. Exod. xiv. 14.

4 half the mountain shall remove, etc. The marvellous salvation of God's true people from the punishment of the nation appears to be here figuratively represented by the opening of a way through the mountain, as God anciently opened one through the sea.

5 ye shall flee to the valley of the mountains. Or, "Ye shall flee by the valley of *My* mountains" (R.V.); *i.e.*, those which I make by cleaving the Mount of Olives.

Azal. Probably the name of a place close to Jerusalem.

the earthquake. See Amos i. 1. An event so terrible that it abode in memory even after the Captivity.

the saints. Or, "holy ones," as R.V.; perhaps angels, as in Deut. xxxiii. 2.

with thee. Rather, "with him."

6 it shall come to pass in that day, etc. A slightly different reading is rendered in R.V.: "the light shall not be with brightness and with gloom." *i.e.*, there shall be no variation.

7 one day. Unlike any other.

not day, nor night. "And there shall be one day—it is known to Jehovah—not day and night (*i.e.*, day succeeded by night), but at evening there shall be light": referring to an eternal "day" of glory, which shall arrive at a time known only to Jehovah: see Matt. xxiv. 36.

8 Half of them toward the former (eastern) **sea,** etc. Half toward the Dead Sea, and half toward the Mediterranean. No permanent stream flows by Jerusalem; but it is to be the source of living waters flowing in all directions: cp. Ezek. xlvii. 1.

9 one Lord, and His name one. The Eternal alone shall be everywhere acknowledged and worshipped.

10 turned as a plain. "Turned into a plain" (like the Arabah).

From Geba to Rimmon. *i.e.*, from the northern frontier of the land (2 Kings xxiii. 8) to the southern (Josh. xv. 32). The whole territory is to be depressed that Jerusalem may appear exalted: cp. Isa. ii. 2; Micah iv. 1.

10 And it shall be lifted up. Jerusalem, thus exalted, and conspicuous from afar, shall "abide" in her place, "compact together" (Psa. cxxii. 3, from east to west and from north to south. For "the tower of Hananeel" see note on Jer. xxxi. 38. "The king's winepresses" were in the royal gardens on the south of the city (Neh. iii. 15).

11 there shall be no more utter destruction. Or, "there shall be no more curse"; see Rev. xxii. 3.

shall be safely inhabited. Rather, "shall abide in safety."

14 Judah also. The country districts rallying to the defence of the metropolis. Cp. xii. 2.

at Jerusalem. Or, "*in* Jerusalem," against those who in ver. 12 are said to fight "*against* Jerusalem."

16 to keep the feast of tabernacles. They shall join as God's people in His worship. Cp. Isa. lxvi. 23; Micah iv. 1, 2.

17 shall be no rain. One of the heaviest national calamities, entailing famine and lingering death: see 1 Kings xvii.

that [have] no [rain]. Rather, as R.V., "neither [shall it be] upon them." That is, a like deprivation shall be theirs. As it is, Egypt has no rain; and the judgement would be in the withholding of the annual inundation.

20 Holiness ("Holy," R.V.) **unto the Lord.** This was formerly inscribed only on the tiara of the high priest. What has hitherto been common shall now be sacred, and what has been sacred shall be more holy still. And this shall extend to all, even the meanest things in the City of God.

21 and take of them. *i.e.*, of the common vessels in Jerusalem. This intimates (1) that the distinction between sacred and secular is now superseded by the common sanctity of all, and (2) that the number of worshippers is so vast as to press everything into service.

no more the Canaanite. Whom the Israelites were commanded to exterminate. But some render "trafficker" (R.V. marg.). See note on xi. 11.

The imagery and the expressions used in the latter part of this chapter are derived from the Jewish ritual and polity; the rewards and punishments of the New Dispensation being described, as they often are in the prophetic writings, under figures borrowed from the Old.

MALACHI

INTRODUCTION

THE Bible begins with the account of how light dawned upon the natural world (Gen. i. 1–3). The Old Testament closes with the announcement of the coming of the spiritual light, "the Sun of Righteousness" (Mal. iv. 2). It is interesting to note that the New Testament, whose Gospel narratives begin with the star in the East (Matt. ii. 2, 10, 11), the Dayspring from on high (Luke i. 18), and the coming of "the Light of men" (John i. 4–9), ends with the prediction of the time when neither lamp nor sun shall be needed any more, for "the Lord God giveth them light" and "the bright and morning Star" shall for ever shine upon His people (Rev. xxii. 5, 16). So from Genesis to Revelation, the Bible is the messenger of light, scattering the darkness of sorrow and of sin, and bringing to the hearts of men peace, hope, and joy.

Malachi's prophecy was written in a time when the clouds had again gathered over the life of Israel. It was after the Exile, somewhere between 460 and 432 B.C. and was either contemporaneous with the earlier work of Ezra and Nehemiah in Jerusalem or with Nehemiah's second visit. The internal evidence, especially his reference to the Temple as already built (i. 10; iii. 1, 10), seems to indicate the later date. That Malachi's name is not mentioned by any other writer of the period has suggested to some commentators that it was a title expressive of his mission, Malachi meaning "My messenger," or, if it is an abbreviation for "Malachiyah," "the messenger of the Lord." In any case it was a time of many abuses and corruptions.

Against these the earlier chapters of the Book are directed. The prophet denounces the carelessness of priests and people in offering unworthy sacrifices, contrasting their ingratitude with the favour which they had received from God in comparison with Edom (i. 6–10; cp. verses 2 and 3). But even then he sees the vision of a coming day when God's name shall be universally honoured—another Old Testament forecast of foreign missions (i. 11).

He attaches special blame to the priests, who should have been teachers and examples to the people (ii. 1–9). He speaks strongly against intermarriage with the heathen, and particularly where it has led to divorcing of Jewish wives (ii. 11–16). And then come his great predictions of the coming of the Messiah, preluded by the messenger who should "prepare the way before Him" (iii. 1), a prediction applied to John the Baptist in Matt. xi. 10, 14; Mark i. 2; ix. 11, 12; Luke i. 17, 76; vii. 27; John i. 23.

The coming of the Messiah will first of all be for testing and judgement (iii. 2–9; iv. 1), then for restoration and blessing to all who honour Him (iii. 10–16). Under His glorious reign God shall be honoured (iii. 16), distinction shall be made between the good and the evil (iii. 18), generous offerings shall be brought into God's house (iii. 10), God's commandments shall be observed (iv. 4), family life and affection shall be restored (iv. 6), and peace and prosperity shall smile upon the nation (iii. 11, 12).

CHAPTER I

1 the burden. "The oracle": see on Isa. xiii. 1.

3 I hated Esau. From the context it is clear that the posterity rather than the persons of the brothers are here intended. See Rom. ix. 13.

and laid his mountains, etc. Rather, as R.V., "And I made his mountains a desolation, and [gave] his heritage to the jackals of the wilderness": cp. Isa. xiii. 21, 22; xxxiv. 13. According to either rendering, utter desolation (4) is meant. Respecting the agreement of historical facts with this prediction, see notes on Isa. xxxiv.; Jer. xlix. 17–22; and on Obadiah.

4 impoverished. Or, "beaten down," R.V.

will return and build. Or, "will rebuild"; according to the common Heb. idiom. Edom does not seem to have been carried into captivity.

5 from the border of Israel. Or, "beyond the border of Israel"; *i.e.*, in alien territory (R.V.).

6 O priests, that despise My name. The glory of which they were set apart to maintain.

7 polluted bread. One kind of offering is specified as including all. Instead of presenting the best, they give the worst, such as they would not have dared to offer to their earthly ruler (8).

8 if. Rather, "when" (R.V.).

[is it] not evil? Lit., as R.V., "it is no evil?" ironically. Or before this exclamation "ye say" may be supplied.

9 Will He regard your persons? Try now whether such offerings will appease Jehovah's anger, which you have brought upon us. Nay, He will not regard you.

10 Who [is there] even among you, etc.? Or, "Oh that there were one among you that would shut the doors, that ye might not kindle [fire on] Mine altar in vain!" R.V.; *i.e.*, let My worship be discontinued altogether, rather than be conducted in a manner which gives Me no pleasure.

11 incense [shall be] offered unto My name. The spiritual services of the new dispensation are described in figures borrowed from the institutions and worship of the old, which the priests had so grievously perverted. Incense is the symbol of prayer. Cp. John iv. 23, 24.

12 contemptible. Complaining of the inadequacy of the portion assigned for their own maintenance.

13 ye have snuffed at it. You have despised it.

torn. Rather, "taken by violence," R.V.

Thus ye brought an offering. Rather, "Thus ye bring the offering."

14 a corrupt thing. Lit., "a blemished *female*."

CHAPTER II

2 Your blessings. *i.e.*, everything that should have been a blessing to you.

3 I will corrupt your seed. Rather, as R.V., "I will rebuke the seed," *i.e.*, prevent the ground from yielding a crop.

the dung of your solemn feasts. That is, the offal of your polluted sacrifices, which shall be flung back, as it were, into your faces, bringing you only disgrace instead of benefit.

[one] shall take you away. Rather, as R.V., "Ye shall be taken away."

4 And ye shall know, etc. That all these rebukes and chastenings were sent that I might not cast off the house of Levi, but might fulfil the covenant of "life and peace" which I made with the faithful priests of his house: cp. Numb. iii. 5; xxv. 12, 13.

6 iniquity. "Unrighteousness" (R.V.).

7 the priest's lips should keep knowledge, etc. The spiritual duties of the priests (cp. Deut. xxxiii. 10) are here exclusively dwelt upon, as being the most important, and the most opposed to the formalism of the age.

8 to stumble at the law (*or*, "in the law," R.V.). That is, to violate it: cp. Jer. xviii. 15.

9 partial in the law. "Have had respect of persons in the law," *i.e.*, when acting as judges (Deut. xvii. 8–13).

10 the covenant of our fathers. The covenant which God made with our fathers: cp. Ezra ix. 11, 12.

11 the holiness of the Lord which He loved. That is, that which was holy to the Eternal, which He loved: cp. Jer. ii. 3; Ezra ix. 2. They profaned their sacred character by marrying the daughters (*i.e.*, the votaries) of idols.

12 the master and the scholar. Rather (as R.V.), "him that waketh and him that answereth"; a proverbial expression, derived from the calls and replies of watchmen, and signifying *every one*: see Psa. cxxxiv.; Isa. lxii. 6.

13 And this have ye done again. This probably means, "And this *second* thing have ye done"; *i.e.*, beside taking idolatrous wives, ye have divorced your Hebrew wives, whose tears cover My altar, and make your offerings distasteful to Me.

15 And did not He make one? etc.

16 covereth violence with his garment. Rather, "covereth his garment with violence"; *i.e.*, is cruel to his wife by divorcing her. The word "garment" seems to have acquired the meaning of conjugal protection (see Ruth iii. 9; Ezek. xvi. 8), and even to be used for "a wife," as it is among the Orientals now.

CHAPTER III

1 My messenger. The Elijah of the gospel (iv. 5; Matt. xi. 14), John the Baptist, the forerunner of Christ, who came "in the spirit and power of Elijah." On his ministry see Matt. iii.; xi. 7–19; Luke i. 13–17.

the messenger of the covenant. Or, "the Angel of the covenant." On the application of the name "angel" to the Messiah, see Gen. xvi. 7; Judges ii. 1; Isa. lxiii. 9.

whom ye delight in. For whom you eagerly look, expecting Him to give you the full enjoyment of all the blessings of God's covenant with Israel; little imagining that when He comes He will abrogate the national and ceremonial, which alone you value (Jer. xxxi. 31–34; Heb. viii. 6–13); and will establish the moral and spiritual (Matt. v. 17–48), which you despise and hate.

2 like a refiner's fire, etc. Testing all, and separating the precious from the vile, especially among the ministers of the sanctuary (3): see Matt. iii. 7–12.

3 He shall sit. Giving the idea of watchful, sedulous attention.

4 as in the days of old. See ii. 4.

5 sorcerers, etc. The sins here mentioned were very prevalent among the Jews at this time: see Zech. v. 4; x. 2; Neh. v. 3–13; vi. 12–14.

6 Therefore. Lit., " And." The unchangeableness of the Eternal is a ground of hope.

7 ye are gone away. It is you that have changed, not I. For " gone away " R.V. reads " turned aside."

10 That there may be meat (food) **in Mine house.** For My sacrifices and My ministers.

11 the devourer. Locusts and other destructive animals. Cp. Joel i. 4; ii. 25.

16 a book of remembrance was written before Him. As a king records the services of his faithful subjects: cp. Esth. vi. 1; Psa. lxix. 28.

17 in that day, etc. Rather, as R.V. marg., " They shall be Mine . . . in the day that I do this, even a peculiar treasure."

CHAPTER IV

2 shall the Sun of Righteousness arise. The glorious Source of righteousness, whose beams convey spiritual health, showing itself in buoyant and joyful vigour: cp. 2 Sam. xxiii. 4; John i. 9.
grow up. Or, " gambol " (R.V.).

4 Remember ye the law of Moses. The fact that God Himself by His prophet declares " the law " to have been " commanded " to Moses " in Horeb," has an important affirmative bearing on the authenticity of the writings referred to.

5 I will send you Elijah the prophet. See note on iii. 1.

6 he shall turn the heart of the fathers. Family discord was the natural result of these divorces and foreign marriages which the prophet had denounced. Hence its removal is indicated as a preparation for the Messiah's coming and reign. See Luke i. 17.

One of the best sermons of Charles Kingsley is that which forms tne first in his volume of *Sermons for the Times.* It is on these last words of the Old Testament. He points out that the Old Testament ends by saying that God would send to the Jews Elijah the prophet; and the New Testament begins by telling us of John the Baptist's coming in the spirit and power of Elijah. And then he presses home the importance of family life and the duties of fathers to children and children to fathers. The message was needed in the 19th century. It is still more needed in the 20th.

His closing words are worth pondering. " Wheresoever the hearts of the fathers are not turned to the children, and the hearts of the children to the fathers, there will a great and terrible day of the Lord come; and that nation, like Judæa of old, like many a fair country in Europe at this moment, will be smitten with a curse."

THE NON-CANONICAL BOOKS

SOMETIMES CALLED THE APOCRYPHA

INTRODUCTION

A SUMMARY of the contents of these books, covering the period between the Book of Malachi and the New Testament, is given below, the quotations being taken from the Revised Version.

The Christian Church has been divided as to the use of the non-canonical books. There are various reasons for this. The books are not found in the Hebrew Canon, and have never been accepted as authoritative by the Jews. They are never directly mentioned by our Lord and His apostles. Some of them, too, contain elements of obvious legend and superstition.

But they cannot be ignored by any one who wants to know the political and religious history of the Jews for the four hundred years between the close of the Old Testament and the birth of Christ, and the condition of the world into which the Saviour came. They show, amongst other things, the increase of the belief in a future life and in the coming of the Messiah (see, on this, Dr. Salmon's work on "Apocrypha" in the *Speaker's Commentary*).

Though the Apocrypha books are not found in the Hebrew Canon, they are included in the Greek (Septuagint) version of the Old Testament, and were used by the Eastern Church, being quoted as Scripture by the early Christian Fathers such as Irenæus, Clement of Alexandria, Tertullian and Cyprian. The Roman Catholic Church, using as it does the Vulgate, the Latin translation of the Septuagint, has accepted the Apocrypha ever since the Council of Trent (1546) decreed that all the books found in the Vulgate are canonical.

In the Reformed Churches there has been considerable variety of opinion on the subject. Luther included the Apocrypha in his Bible (1534) as "books which are not equal to the Sacred Scriptures but nevertheless are good and useful to read." Calvin included them in his *French Commentary* (1535).

So far as British Protestantism is concerned, it, too, is divided about the non-canonical books. The official statement of the Church of England (*Article VI*) is, after reciting the names of the Canonical Books, that "the other books (as *Jerome* saith) the Church doth read for example of life and instruction of manners; but yet it doth not apply them to establish any doctrine." The Westminster *Confession of Faith* says that "the books commonly called Apocrypha, not being of divine inspiration, are no part of the Canon of the Scripture; and therefore are of no authority in the Church of God, nor to be in any otherwise approved, or made use of, than other human writings."

[For those who want to study the subject more fully, the following books may be mentioned: *Hastings' Dictionary of the Bible*, art. "Apocrypha"; Salmon, as quoted above; Streane, *The Age of the Maccabees;* de Saulcy, *Histoire des Maccabées;* Schürer, *The Jewish People in the Time of Christ.*]

I ESDRAS

Esdras is the Greek form of Ezra, and this book is in the Sixth Article of the Church of England called the Third Book of Esdras. The reason is that in the Vulgate Ezra is called 1 Esdras and Nehemiah 2 Esdras.

1 Es. has many links with the Old Testament, as well as with the history of the pagan nations. Not only are Josiah, Zedekiah, and Jeremiah mentioned in it, but also the Persians, Cyrus, Artaxerxes and Darius, and the Hittite city, Carchemish.

Chapter i. gives an account of the great passover of king Josiah and of his death very similar to that contained in 2 Chron. xxxv.; and of the reigns of Jehoahaz, Joakim (Jehoiachim) and Zedekiah recorded in 2 Chron. xxxvi., with the destruction of Jerusalem by Nebuchadnezzar and the beginning of the Captivity in Babylon. The proclamation of Cyrus in favour of the rebuilding of Jerusalem is recorded in chap. ii. as in Ezra i., and the same chapter relates, as in Ezra iv., the opposition of the enemies of the Jews, a story continued in the closing verses of chap. v.

Chapters iii. and iv. are notable for the discussion as to the strongest force in human life and the conclusion that " great is truth and stronger than all things . . . truth abideth and is strong for ever; she liveth and conquereth for evermore."

In the story of the return from the Captivity and the list of the men who came back to Jerusalem, as given in Ezra ii., chap. v. of 1 Es. adds the interesting detail that " Darius sent with them a thousand horsemen, till they had brought them back to Jerusalem safely, and with musical instruments, tabrets and flutes " (v. 2).

The story of Ezra himself as given in Ezra vii. and Neh. viii. is narrated in chaps. viii. and ix. A variation occurs in the joyous and kindly exhortation of Nehemiah viii. 10. " Go your way, eat the fat and drink the sweet and send portions to them for whom nothing is prepared." In Neh. the verse ends " for the joy of the Lord is your strength "; in 1 Es. ix. 52, it is " the Lord will bring you to honour."

The weight of the evidence points to the date of the book as being in the second century B.C., though some authorities place it somewhat later.

2 ESDRAS

The most notable feature of this book is its reference to the Messiah. In ii. 34 we read, " look for your shepherd, he shall give you everlasting rest; for he is right at hand, that shall come in the end of the world." And in vii. 28, 29, occur the memorable words: " For my son Jesus shall be revealed with those that be with him, and shall rejoice with them that remain four hundred years. After these shall my son Christ die, and all that have the breath of life."

There are other interesting links with the New Testament. Compare " I gathered you together, as a hen gathereth her chickens under her wings " (i. 30) with Matt. xxiii. 37; " I Esdras saw upon the Mount Zion a great multitude whom I could not number, and they all praised the Lord with songs. . . . These be they that have put off the mortal clothing, and put on the immortal, and have confessed the name of God: now are they crowned and receive palms " (ii. 42–45) with Rev. vii. 9–14; and " when there shall be seen in the world earthquakes, devices of nations, wavering of leaders, disquietude of peoples," etc. (chap. ix.) with Matt. xxiv. 7, and Luke xxi. 10, 11.

These identities of language lead scholars to suppose that while the book is mainly the work of a Jewish writer, there were additions by a Christian. The date is further indicated by the Eagle Vision (chap. xii.) and is now generally placed in the reign of Domitian, between A.D. 81 and 96.

The contents of the book are chiefly a picture of Israel's sad condition both in the Babylonian Captivity and in the subsequent persecutions in the Roman period, while the book closes on a note of final victory.

It contains many fine practical exhortations, such as " Do right to the widow, judge the fatherless, give to the poor, defend the orphan, clothe the naked, heal the broken and the weak, laugh not a lame man to scorn, defend the maimed, and let the blind man come unto the sight of My glory. Keep the old and young within thy walls " (chap. ii.); and " therefore be thou no longer curious how the ungodly shall be punished; but inquire how the righteous shall be saved, they whose the world is, and for whom the world was created " (chap. ix.).

TOBIT

The high ideals of the Jewish people at its best are enshrined in this book. Such are the honouring of God and abhorrence of idolatry (chaps. i., iii., iv., xiii.); the purity of domestic life (iv., x.); and the duty of kindness to the poor (i., ii., iv., xii.). Some of the exhortations on the last-named subject are repeated in the Offertory Sentences in the Book of Common Prayer: " Give alms of thy goods " (Tobit iv.).

The language, too, is of exceptional beauty. As an instance of this, the prayer in chap. xiii. may be specially noted, with its glorious concluding words: " For Jerusalem shall be builded with sapphires and emeralds and precious stones; thy walls and towers and battlements with pure gold. And the streets of Jerusalem shall be paved with beryl and carbuncle and stones of Ophir. And all her streets shall say, Hallelujah, and give praise, saying, Blessed is God, which hath exalted thee for ever."

But along with these high and inspiring thoughts there are some crude superstitions as in vi. 4, viii. 2, 3, referring to the exorcism of evil spirits.

As a picture of the life and ideas of the time it portrays, the book is full of interest. It purports to be an account of the condition of Israel in its first captivity at Nineveh in the time of Enemessar (cp. i. 2 with 2 Kings xvii. 3, 23), though it was most likely written at a later date. It may be said with certainty that it was written at least 100 years B.C., while some scholars date it between 200 and 300 B.C.

JUDITH

Piety and patriotism are the two principal features of this book. The reality of God's rule and the power of prayer are clearly taught (iv. 9, 12–15; vi. 18–21; vii. 28–30; ix. 11–14; xvi. 2, 3, 13), and the book hardly merits the statement of some writers that it is conspicuously Pharisaic and ceremonial.

The patriotism of Judith has made her, whether she be a historical character or not, one of the world's heroines, and there is hardly a picture-gallery in Europe where there is not a picture of " Judith and Holofernes."

The graphic picture of the sufferings endured by the besieged Israelites in " Bethulia " (vii. 19–22) has its parallel in the stories of Leyden and Londonderry. All the more brightly shines out the faith and courage of Ozias in standing firm against the multitude who called for surrender (vii. 23–27), and his words are still an inspiration, " Brethren, be of good courage, let us endure five days, in the which space the Lord our God shall turn His mercy toward us; for He will not forsake us utterly. But if these days do pass, and there come no help unto us, I will do according to your words " (vii. 30, 31). And there are no finer words in the Psalms than those of Judith's prayer before she went forth to her great and grim adventure: " For Thy power standeth not in multitude, nor Thy might in strong men; but Thou art a God of the afflicted, Thou art a helper of the oppressed, an upholder of the weak, a protector of the forlorn, a saviour of them that are without hope" (ix. 11).

The book is generally believed to have been written in the time of the Maccabees, somewhat over 100 years B.C.

THE REST OF ESTHER

This book should be read in connexion with the Book of Esther in the Old Testament. It supplements the narrative therein contained. One of the most important additions is the reason given by Mordecai (Mardocheus) for not bowing down to Haman. "Thou knowest, Lord, that it was neither in contempt nor pride, nor for any desire of glory, that I did not bow down to proud Aman. For I could have been content with goodwill for the salvation of Israel to kiss the soles of his feet. But I did this, that I might not prefer the glory of man above the glory of God; neither will I bow down to any but to Thee, which art my Lord" (xiii. 12–14). Esther's statement is also interesting: "Thine handmaid hath not eaten at Aman's table, neither have I honoured the king's feast, nor drunk the wine of the drink offerings" (xiv. 17).

The note at the beginning of chap. ii., which is attributed to St. Jerome, seems to fix the date of this "epistle of Phrurai" (Purim) as about 177 B.C.

THE WISDOM OF SOLOMON

This book, although it bears the name of Solomon, was not written by him, nor even in the Hebrew language. It is as if a painter should describe his work as "after Raphael." It was written in the spirit and after the manner of the Book of Proverbs, and its author was most probably a Jew of Alexandria. The date, however, is quite uncertain, some scholars placing it early in the Christian era and others assigning it to the second century B.C.

Some of its most noteworthy passages are:

"The souls of the righteous are in the hand of God, and no torment shall touch them" (iii. 1);

"And what good have riches and vaunting brought us? Those things all passed away as a shadow, and as a message that runneth by; as a ship passing through the billowy water, whereof, when it is gone by, there is no trace to be found, neither pathway of its keel in the billows" (v. 10);

and the powerful argument against idolatry (xiii.–xv.). The writer speaks of the folly of a man supplicating "for a good journey that which cannot so much as move a step," while "one preparing to sail and about to journey over raging waves, calleth upon a piece of wood more rotten than the vessel that carrieth him" (xiv. 1).

ECCLESIASTICUS

This is a Greek translation, or paraphrase, of a Hebrew manuscript, the original being the work of Jesus the Son of Sirach, about 190 B.C., the translator being his grandson who came to Egypt in the 38th year of Euergetes, *i.e.*, 132 B.C., and made the translation there (Ecclus. Prologue).

The discovery of the Hebrew original, or large portions of it, is due to modern scholarship and enterprise. A fragment was first found in Palestine by Mrs. Agnes Smith Lewis, of Cambridge, and published in 1897, with a continuation which was discovered by Professor Sayce. Most of the remainder of the Hebrew was subsequently secured from Cairo by Dr. Shechter, of Cambridge.

Large sections of this book are prescribed in the Table of Lessons in the Book of Common Prayer for the morning and evening Lessons from November 4 to 16. Chap. xliv., beginning, "Let us now praise famous men" has become a classic form of commemoration.

Some notable sayings of the Son of Sirach may be given here:

Temptation. "My son, if thou comest to serve the Lord, prepare thy soul for temptation" (ii. 1; words quoted by Thomas à Kempis, *Imitation of Christ*).

Father and Son. "My son, help thy father in his old age; and grieve him not as long as he liveth. And if he fail in understanding, have patience with him" (iii. 12, 13).

Kindness. "Incline thine ear to a poor man and answer him with peaceable words in meekness. Deliver him that is wronged from the hand of him that wrongeth him. . . . Be as a father unto the fatherless and instead of a husband unto their mother; so shalt thou be as a son of the Most High, and he shall love thee more than thy mother doth" (iv. 8–10). "Be not wanting to them that weep; and mourn with them that mourn" (vii. 34).

Speech. "Blame not before thou hast examined: understand first, and then rebuke" (xi. 7).

Forgiveness. "Forgive thy neighbour the hurt that he hath done thee; and then thy sins shall be pardoned when thou prayest. . . . Remember thy last end and cease from enmity" (xxviii. 2, 6).

Counsel. "Take not counsel with a woman about her rival; neither with a coward about war; nor with a merchant about exchange; nor with a buyer about selling; nor with an envious man about thankfulness; nor with an unmerciful man about kindliness; nor with a sluggard about any kind of work; nor with a hireling in thy house about finishing his work; nor with an idle servant about much business; give not heed to these in any matter of counsel. But rather be continually with a godly man, whom thou shalt have known to be a keeper of the commandments, who in his soul is as thine own soul, and who will grieve with thee, if thou shalt miscarry" (xxxvii. 11, 12).

BARUCH

Portions of this book (iv. 1–21, iv. 36, and v.) are contained in the Lectionary of the Book of Common Prayer for November 17 and 18.

It may be regarded as a supplement to the book of Jeremiah, much as *The Wisdom of Solomon* is a supplement to *Proverbs*, and if not actually written by Baruch the scribe, Jeremiah's friend (i. 1), is an attempt to reproduce his teaching, as an antidote to idolatry (i. 22; vi. 12) and a preparation for the coming of the Messiah (iv. 22). It was probably written thirty or forty years before Christ.

"It has at least the distinction of being the only book in the Apocrypha which is modelled upon the *prophetic* utterances of the Old Testament, and both in the faithful setting forth of the nation's sin and punishment, and in the cheering hope of deliverance with which the writer concludes, we see at any rate a reflection of the days when the voice of the true prophet had not yet ceased to be heard in the land" (Streane: *The Age of the Maccabees*, p. 169).

THE SONG OF THE THREE HOLY CHILDREN

This short book consists of a Greek addition to the Book of Daniel, given in the Septuagint after

Daniel iii. 23. The "three holy children" are Shadrach, Meshach and Abednego, and their song, the *Benedicite*, has been used in the Christian Church since the fourth century.

THE HISTORY OF SUSANNA

Briefly stated, the story of Susanna and the elders may be said to be a vindication of female purity and a condemnation of false witness. It is also an illustration of the wisdom of Daniel in examining the witnesses, and by taking them apart, getting them to contradict one another. Hence the exclamation of Shylock in *The Merchant of Venice*, "A Daniel come to judgement!"

BEL AND THE DRAGON

Like the two preceding stories, this is associated with Daniel. It enlarges on the narrative of Daniel in the den of lions and says that he was in the den six days, "and in the den were seven lions, and they had given them every day two carcases, and two sheep; which then were not given to them, to the intent they might devour Daniel." Chiefly, however, the story is a condemnation of idolatry. Bel was delivered into Daniel's power, "who overthrew him and his temple," and the brazen dragon, which was also worshipped in Babylon, was burst asunder by Daniel, and it was for this that he was cast into the lions' den.

THE PRAYER OF MANASSES

In 2 Chron xxxiii. 10–13 we read that Manasseh, king of Judah, was taken in chains to Babylon by the king of Assyria's army, and in v. 18 of the same chapter it is stated that "the rest of the acts of Manasseh and his prayer unto his God . . . are written among the acts of the Kings of Israel." This is the prayer which is recorded in the Apocrypha under that name. It is in Greek, and no Hebrew MS. of it has yet been found. But it may well be that the original is in existence and that, as in the case of Ecclesiasticus, it may come to light some day. The prayer is a beautiful example of penitential trust in God's mercy.

THE FIRST BOOK OF THE MACCABEES

While other books of the Apocrypha deal with the history of the Jewish people under the Assyrians and Persians, the Books of the Maccabees bring us into contact with Greece and Rome. They are both of great historical value for the second century B.C.

The First Book gives us the history from 175 to 135 B.C. It begins with the accession of Antiochus Epiphanes, king of Syria, recording his defeat of Ptolemy in Egypt and his conquest of Jerusalem and the cities of Judah (i.). It then records the revolt of Mattathias, son of a priest at Jerusalem, how he and his friends pulled down the pagan altars (ii. 25, 45) and how, before his death, he charged the people to obey the law of God, saying, "None that put their trust in Him shall want for strength" (ii. 61), and telling them that Judas Maccabeus shall be their captain.

Chapters iii. to ix. relate the heroic deeds of Judas Maccabeus, whose story has been wedded to music by Handel in his great oratorio of that name. It is interesting to recall that the air, "Wise men, flattering, may deceive you" in Part II. of *Judas Maccabeus* was the last air that Handel wrote, as "Sion now her head shall raise," with the chorus "Tune your harps," was his last chorus (see Historical Notes on *Judas Maccabeus* by the late Dr. F. G. Edwards). The same oratorio contains the stirring strains of "Arm, arm, ye brave," and "See the conquering hero comes," as well as the duet which celebrates the end of War," O lovely peace."

Chapters ix. to xii. narrate the deeds of Jonathan Maccabeus the brother and successor of Judas, and how he won the respect of Alexander Epiphanes and Demetrius, the successors of Antiochus Epiphanes and obtained from the latter the immunity of Israel from tribute. He, as well as Judas, made friendship with Rome and sent an embassy to the Roman senate.

Under Simon Maccabeus, who succeeded to the leadership on the death of Jonathan, the assertion of Jewish liberty was complete. "In the hundred and seventieth year [about 143 B.C.] was the yoke of the heathen taken away from Israel" (xiii. 41). "And the land had rest all the days of Simon; and he sought the good of his nation. . . . And they tilled their land in peace, and the land gave her increase. . . . The ancient men sat in the streets" (xiv. 4–9). "The law he searched out, and every lawless and wicked person he took away" (xiv. 14). He also confirmed the confederacy with Rome (xiv. 24).

The book ends with the murder of Simon by one of the Ptolemies and the succession, as high priest and ruler, of his son John Hyrcanus (xvi. 24). It was he who first expressly assumed the title of "King of the Jews."

The subsequent history of Israel from Hyrcanus until the birth of Christ (135 B.C.–A.D. 4) is to be found in the pages of Josephus. An excellent summary of it is contained in Angus and Green's *Bible Handbook*, chap. xvii. Between Judas Aristobulus, the successor of John Hyrcanus (106 B.C.) and Herod the Great (37 B.C.) there were seven kings. The glories of the Maccabean period were followed by constant dissensions, sometimes between members of the royal family and sometimes between the Pharisees and the Sadducees. Gradually Palestine became more and more a province of the Roman Empire. And so the way was prepared for the coming of Israel's true Messiah, the foundation of His spiritual kingdom, and the spread of His Gospel throughout the known world. The boast of His great Apostle was that he was a Roman citizen.

THE SECOND BOOK OF THE MACCABEES

This book covers much of the period 175–160 B.C., part of the history narrated in Book I. But it is an independent story, written by Jason of Cyrene, and contains some special features of its own. We may note its preface (i., ii.) going back to the earlier history from the time of Jeremiah; the story of how the attempt of Heliodonus to seize the treasury at Jerusalem was frustrated by a vision (iii.); the influence of the Greeks upon religion and social life (iv. 9–16; vi. 1–9); the Jewish regard for the Sabbath (v. 25); the heroic sufferings and death of Eleazar the scribe (vi. 18–31) and of other persecutions endured for conscience' sake (vii.).

THE NEW TESTAMENT

THE GOSPEL ACCORDING TO ST. MATTHEW

INTRODUCTION

A WORD may be said about the Four Gospels as a whole. The Greek word of which our "Gospel" is a translation means "good news" or "glad tidings." The "good news" is the message of salvation through our Lord Jesus Christ. And what we call "the Gospels" tell us how that salvation came to men through the birth or Incarnation, the life and teaching, the cross and suffering, the death, resurrection and ascension of the Saviour.

Of the four Gospels, there is a marked unity between the first three, which are a record of the Saviour's life and activities, and a marked difference between them and the fourth, which is much more a record of His teaching. Hence the first three are generally called the Synoptic Gospels, because they give the same general view or synopsis, and their writers are known as the Synoptists.

Although St. Matthew's Gospel comes first in our New Testament, it was not the first in order of time—a place assigned to St. Mark. The actual date is not stated in the book itself, but the internal evidence shows that this Gospel as we have it was written some time before the destruction of Jerusalem by Vespasian in A.D. 70, though some put it a little later. It is generally held by Biblical scholars that it was based upon an earlier work of St. Matthew, written in Hebrew.

And then there is the evidence of the early Christian writers in the second century, such as Justin Martyr (A.D. 114–160), Irenæus (born A.D. 140), and Clement of Alexandria, whose Epistle from Rome to the Church at Corinth was written between A.D. 90 and 100.

From their writings, "we have these four Gospels proved to have been circulating in the Church within seventy years of the crucifixion and received as Scripture" (Oliver: *In Defence of the Faith.* Cp. Row: *Manual of Christian Evidences*, and A. B. Bruce: *Apologetics*, Book III, Chap. VIII). Not a few of those who had witnessed our Lord's ministry must have been living in A.D. 70 (Row's *Manual*, 1887, p. 139; cp. *The Jesus of History*, by T. R. Glover, Chap. I).

When we come to St. Matthew's Gospel itself, we are at once struck by some distinctive characteristics. The first is the genealogy with which it commences, tracing our Lord's descent as "the son of David, the son of Abraham." It was clearly written for Jewish readers. The thought of Jesus as the Messiah is prominent in the words of the wise men (ii. 2), and of His kingdom in the words of the Baptist (iii. 2), and in the Saviour's own preaching (iv. 23). Then the Saviour appears as the great Lawgiver, fulfilling and enlarging the old Mosaic Law (v. 17, 27, 28, 33, 43, 44). The miracles (see esp. viii. 1–7, 16) "enforce and explain the position and authority of the Lawgiver" (Westcott, *Introduction to the Study of the Gospels*, Chap. VII). The parables peculiar to St. Matthew, while of world-wide significance, have in many cases their bearing upon Jewish exclusiveness, and are "suited to awaken his own nation to a sense of their sins, to correct their hopes of an earthly kingdom, and to prepare them for the admission of the Gentiles to the Church" (*Bible Handbook*, by Angus and Green, § 449).

The story of the events which led up to the crucifixion again makes prominent the Kingship of Christ (xxvii. 11). He was kingly as He stood before Pilate (xxvii. 14); as King He suffered on the Cross (xxvii. 37); and as King He gave to His disciples the great declaration of His kingly authority and their great commission for the spiritual conquest of the world (xxviii. 18–20).

CHAPTER I

1 The book of the generation. That is, "the genealogy" (see Gen. ii. 4, and note). 1 Chron. i.–ix. shows the care with which family registers were kept (see note on 1 Chron. i. 1). On the difference between the two genealogies in Matthew and in Luke, see note on Luke iii. 24.

St. Matthew, writing for Jews, is at pains to show that Jesus of Nazareth is King of Israel, the long-expected Messiah. Hence the importance of the genealogy. It links together the Old Testament and the New. But while it emphasises the human side of our Lord's nature, this chapter reaches its climax and full meaning in "Emmanuel: God with us" (ver. 23).

Jesus Christ. "JESUS" is the Greek form of "Joshua"; the meaning of which is "he saves." CHRIST or Messiah ("Anointed"), is our Lord's official name (see note on Psa. ii. 2; and cp. John i. 20, 41; iv. 29). The combination of the words "Jesus Christ" (so frequent in the Epistles) is confined in the Gospels, with one exception, to their introductory parts.

2 Judas. The Greek form of the Hebrew name "Judah."

5 Rachab (Rahab). See note on Josh. ii. 1. The fact that the four women included in this genealogy were all either Gentiles by birth or frail in character, may serve to illustrate our Lord's humiliation in taking our nature, as well as the extension of the benefits of His work to all nations, and even to persons whom the world treats as outcasts.

8 Ozias (Uzziah). Three kings of Judah (Ahaziah, Joash, Amaziah) are omitted between Joram and Uzziah: and Jehoiakim (11) between Josiah and Jeconiah (see 2 Kings viii. 25; xii. 1; xiv. 1; xxiv. 6). There seem also to be similar omissions in the other two divisions of the genealogy. The three divisions were reduced to the same numbers, probably in order to aid the memory. In doing this, the compiler omitted the three generations immediately descended from Ahab; and Jehoiakim also, the son of Josiah, who appears, from Jer. xxii. 13–19; xxxvi. 23–31, to have been atrociously wicked.

12 Zorobabel (Zerubbabel), said in 1 Chron. iii. 19 to have been son to Pedaiah and nephew of Salathiel (Shealtiel). He was probably Salathiel's heir.

13 Abiud. Among the sons of Zerubbabel (1 Chron. iii. 19) Abiud is not mentioned. He is supposed to have been the son there named *Hananiah.*

17 fourteen generations. The threefold division corresponds to the periods *before, during,* and *after* the occupation of the throne by David's family.

18 espoused. More correctly, "betrothed," as R.V.

19 her husband. The Jews regarded betrothed persons as man and wife, though the marriage had not been celebrated; and they treated unfaithfulness as adultery.

a just man. Joseph's sense of right led him to decide upon a divorce (Deut. xxiv. 1), though he was unwilling to inflict the further punishment which the law allowed (Deut. xxii. 23, 24), and which a public divorce would have entailed. "Not willing" expresses the *wish;* "minded" the *purpose.*

21 He shall save His people from their sins. The original is emphatic, "It is He" (and none other) "who shall save," etc. He saves them from the power of sin as well as from its guilt and punishment. See Jer. xxxi. 33, 34, as quoted in Heb. viii. 10–12.

22 that it might be fulfilled. With respect to the prophecy, see note on Isa. vii. 14. "Behold, *the* virgin," etc. It is in this higher fulfilment of the prediction that the appropriateness of the term "virgin," and the full meaning of the name "Immanuel" (see Luke i. 35; John i. 14), become apparent.

of the Lord by the prophet. More precisely, "by the Lord (Jehovah) through the prophet" (R.V.).

25 firstborn. See var. read. The word is probably, as in R.V., to be omitted here (though not in Luke ii. 7), but if retained it would indicate that there was nothing repugnant to the views of the inspired writer in the idea that our Lord's mother might have other children; and, indeed, it would afford a *presumption,* though not proof, that she had. The question is, however, to be settled on other grounds: see xiii. 55, and note.

CHAPTER II

1 Bethlehem. A small town about six miles south of Jerusalem, well known as the original seat of the family of David: see Ruth i. 1; iv. 11; 1 Sam. xvi.; Psa. cxxxii. 6; Micah v. 2.

Herod the king. Herod, the son of Antipater, who was an Idumæan, had obtained the kingdom of Judæa from the Romans, to whom Palestine, with all the neighbouring territory, was now subject. He is called Herod the Great, being the most distinguished of his family. But neither his kingly qualities, nor the splendid style in which he rebuilt the Temple, could obtain for him the affection of his subjects. They were prejudiced against him as a foreigner, and hated him for his treatment of the Hasmonean family (the Maccabees' family name); his compliance with heathen customs, and his numerous cruelties.

wise men. Rather, "*Magi.*" This name, originally designating the sacerdotal caste among the Medes, was applied also generally to other Eastern philosophers who followed them in cultivating the sciences. Astronomy, which was always connected with astrology, was one of their chief studies. The chief home of the Magi was in Persia and Babylon. "Heathen wisdom led by God to the cradle of Christ" (*A. Maclaren*).

2 His star. (Not "His star in the East"; but "We have seen in the East." To them the star would be in the *west.*) The East was at this time pervaded by an expectation of a new and universal empire to arise in Judæa (Sueton. *Vesp.* c. 4; Tacit. *Ann.* v. 13); and there were remarkable conjunctions of the planets Jupiter and Saturn the year 6 B.C. (747 A.U.C.), which might awaken the attention of the Magi. But Wieseler states that the astronomical tables of the Chinese actually record the appearance of a new star in 750 A.U.C.

to worship. The Greek word here used is applied to the reverence paid to teachers, and the homage rendered to kings.

3 he was troubled. Herod, as a foreigner and usurper, feared one who was born King of the Jews. The people dreaded fresh tumults and wars, which would be sure to lead to further cruelties on the part of Herod.

4 the chief priests and scribes of the people. The "scribes" were mostly men of the priestly or Levitical families, whose office it was to preserve, copy, and explain the Scriptures and the traditions.

Christ. Rather, "*the* Christ": see note on the name at i. 1.

6 And thou Bethlehem, etc. The passage (Micah v. 2) is quoted rather according to the sense than the exact words. The negative ("*not* the least") is an addition of the scribes, but well suits the prophet's sense. He says, "the least" *materially;* they, "not the least," *morally.*

shall rule. Lit., "shall be shepherd of" (R.V.).

7 inquired of them diligently. Rather, "ascertained from them exactly."

8 search diligently for the young child. The R.V. better represents the force of the original, "Search out carefully concerning the young child."

11 gold, and frankincense, and myrrh. "Frankincense" is a fragrant resin, probably obtained from the *Boswellia serrata,* which grows in the mountains of India. "Myrrh" was a favourite perfume; cp. Gen. xxxvii. 25; Ps. xlv. 8. These valuable offerings, such as would be made to a king, probably afforded to Joseph and Mary the means of support on their journey to Egypt. Herod, the chief priests, and the Magi, afford an instructive representation of the different ways in which men treat the Saviour and the gospel. Some regard Him with malignant hostility; others, and often those who have the greatest religious advantages, with unbelieving indifference; whilst a third class, perhaps having fewer privileges, thankfully look to Him as their Lord, and consecrate what they have to His service: cp. viii. 11, 12.

12 another way. So as to avoid Jerusalem.

13 the angel. Rather, "an angel," as R.V., and ver. 19.

flee into Egypt. Egypt being near, and a Roman province, and much inhabited by Jews, was an easy and convenient refuge.

15 until the death of Herod. Herod died in April of the year 750 A.U.C. or 4 B.C., according to the usual computation. But some careful writers think that he lived until 753.

that it might be fulfilled, etc. See Hos. xi. 1. Egypt, under the Old Covenant and the New, became "the cradle of the Church."

16 that he was mocked (trifled with). That is, as he himself supposed.

all the children. Greek, "all the *boys.*" Bethlehem being a very small town, the number of victims probably was not large. So many and atrocious were Herod's cruelties, that this probably would never have been recorded except for its connexion with the life of our Lord.

the coasts. Or, "borders"; *i.e.,* the immediate neighbourhood; see note on Exod. x. 4.

diligently inquired. Rather, as R.V., "exactly learned." The limit of age (two years old and under) seems to define the time within which the star had appeared.

17 Then was fulfilled, etc. See note on Jer. xxxi. 15.

20 they are dead, etc. There is here a verbal reference to Exod. iv. 19: probably designed to remind Joseph that He who had protected Moses was now watching over "the young child" Jesus.

22 Archelaus. By Herod's last will, which Augustus confirmed, his dominions were divided; and Archelaus somewhat unexpectedly obtained the government of Judæa, Idumæa, and part of Samaria, with the title of "ethnarch"; though he was sometimes popularly called "king." After a reign of about nine years his oppression and cruelty caused the emperor to depose and banish him.

23 Nazareth. A small village in Southern Galilee, about six miles north-west of Mount Tabor. It is first noticed as the residence of our Lord's mother (Luke i. 26). It is now a larger place, containing about 7,000 people. A fine description of Nazareth and its surrounding scenery is given by Geikie: *Life of Christ,* ch. xii.

He shall be called a Nazarene. A prophecy nowhere found literally in the O.T. But in several prophecies it had been foretold that the Messiah should be reproached and despised (see refs. and Psa. lxix. 7, 12; Isa. xlix. 7, etc.). In our Lord's days the people of Nazareth were held in contempt, not only by the inhabitants of Jerusalem, but even by those of the small towns in their own neighbourhood: as appears from the question of Nathanael of Cana (John i. 46). Hence it may be inferred that the evangelist has here condensed the substance of ancient prophecies in a phrase of his own time. This seems intimated in the general phrase, "by (*or,* through) the prophets." The Saviour, brought up in Nazareth, was "a root out of a dry ground" (Isa. liii. 2).

CHAPTER III

1 In those days. This refers to ii. 23, and it means whilst Jesus was still at Nazareth. The expression is otherwise indefinite: cp. Exod. ii. 11. The interval between our Lord's return to Nazareth and John's public appearance was not quite thirty years.

John the Baptist. This appellation of John the son of Zechariah was evidently familiar to the Jews (see Joseph. *Antiq.* xviii. 5, † 2); and it shows that the baptism he administered was distinguished from ordinary proselyte baptism, as Christian baptism was distinguished from his (Acts xix. 3).

the wilderness of Judæa. This "wilderness" was the thinly-peopled district lying between Jerusalem and the Jordan and Dead Sea. Much of it was pasture-land; cp. Josh. xv. 61, 62. It may here be noted that the word "wilderness," which is of frequent occurrence in the Scriptures, does not necessarily mean barren or waste land, but is used as the Australians speak of "the bush" or the South Africans of "the veld," meaning "the country" as distinguished from the town.

2 Repent. The Greek word means change of heart and life.

the kingdom of heaven. The "kingdom of heaven" is a Jewish phrase, used in the New Testament only by Matthew; equivalent to the "kingdom of God." It appears to have been derived from the prophecies which represented

Messiah as a Divine King (see Dan. ii. 44; vii. 13, 14). It embraces the government of Christ on earth and in heaven, in all its aspects.

3 the prophet Esaias. See Isa. xl. 3. The prophet's language is, "In the wilderness prepare ye," etc.

4 of camel's hair. That is, woven from camel's hair. This seems to have been a prophetic garb: see 2 Kings i. 8; Zech. xiii. 4. These peculiarities of John's clothing and food pointed him out as the successor of Elijah.

meat. Rather, "food," as the Old English word *meat* means: see Lev. ii. 1.

locusts. Tristram (*Natural History of the Bible*) says he found them very good, when eaten after the Arab fashion, stewed with butter. Doughty (*Arabia Deserta*) says that the fat spring locust is reckoned a sweetmeat in town and in desert, but later broods are dry and unwholesome.

7 Pharisees and Sadducees. These were the two principal sects of the Jews at that time: see Joseph. *Antiq.* xiii. 5, 9. The Pharisees were distinguished by their punctilious regard to the letter of the law, and the traditional instructions of their teachers. As the result of this, most of them were formal and ostentatious in worship, self-righteous, and bigoted. The Sadducees rejected many important truths of Scripture (see xxii. 23; Acts xxiii. 8); reducing their religious belief almost to a bare Deism, destitute of any sufficient motive to holiness. They were chiefly men of rank and education, who had mixed much with foreigners. But the Pharisees were more numerous and influential with the people.

O generation of vipers. How is it that you, who think yourselves "children of Abraham" (though you are rather "broods of vipers," cunning and malignant), are afraid of the wrath which the prophets always connected with the coming of Messiah? see Isa. lx. 12; lxiii. 1, and note. If you are sincere, alter your conduct, and put away all confidence in hereditary privileges (9); for now every one is to be dealt with according to his individual character (10). This faithfulness repulsed most of them: see Luke vii. 30.

8 meet for repentance. "Worthy of repentance," R.V.

9 of these stones. That is, materials the most unlikely; John perhaps pointed to the shingle of the river.

10 the axe is laid unto the root. Rather, as R.V., "the axe is lying at the root"—not yet upraised to smite, but ready should your unfruitfulness continue.

11 whose shoes I am not worthy to bear. By performing such menial services, a newly-acquired slave was expected to show submission to his master. Hence the loosing, tying, or carrying the shoe or sandal became proverbial to express the humblest service.

He shall baptise you. My office is to call men to repent: it is His to exercise a Divine power upon men's hearts.

with fire. This most probably refers here to that refining process which was the predicted characteristic of gospel times. For the true Israel were to be separated, even by severe measures, both from the ungodly and from their own remaining sins: see Isa. i. 25; iv. 3, 4; Ezek. xx. 38; Mal. iii. 2, 17, 18.

12 fan. Or, "winnowing shovel": see notes on Ruth iii. 2; 2 Sam. xxiv. 18.

13 Then cometh Jesus. Whilst the forerunner is preaching and baptising, Jesus Himself comes to begin His public work. In doing this, He places Himself on a level with man, by submitting first to John's baptism (13–15), by which He obtains a special testimony of His Father's approval (16, 17); and then to the varied assaults of Satan, until the tempter is completely repulsed, and angels come to wait upon Him (iv. 1–11).

14 John forbad Him. Or, "was hindering Him (R.V., 'would have hindered Him'), saying, I have need," etc.

15 to fulfil all righteousness. "To fulfil every ordinance" (*David Smith*); "to fulfil every religious duty" (*Weymouth*). Baptism, in our Lord's case, says Monro Gibson (*Expos. Bible*), was "the symbol of separation from private life and consecration to God in the office of Messiah." He also received an inward anointing for His work: see Acts x. 38.

16 He saw. That is, *Jesus* saw. The appearance was also beheld by John himself (John i. 32).

like a dove. A fit emblem of the gentle and peaceful character of Jesus and His mission: see xi. 29; Isa. lxi. 1, 2. Luke expressly says that the Holy Spirit assumed a "bodily form."

17 my beloved Son. "The Son of God" was one of the titles of the Messiah (Psa. ii. 12), indicating the dignity both of His nature and of His office: cp. Isa. xlii. 1. This testimony to our Lord's sonship and acceptance was repeated at His transfiguration (xvii. 5); and the voice from heaven spoke again in answer to His prayer (John xii. 28).

CHAPTER IV

1 led up. Urged by a powerful Divine impulse.

the wilderness. See note Matt. iii. 1 and Mark i. 12.

to be tempted. This was the express purpose of the Holy Spirit in leading our Lord to retire to the wilderness.

the devil. The temptation is clearly ascribed to the personal agency of Satan. Our Lord's human soul was free from all tendency to evil; but it was accessible to temptation from without. Thus He "was in all points tempted like as we are, yet without sin" (Heb. iv. 15). And He meets every temptation exactly as any one else might meet it, by the simple and appropriate use of God's revealed word.

2 fasted. Abstaining from all food (Luke iv. 2). Moses (Exod. xxxiv. 28) and Elijah (1 Kings xix. 8) had been similarly sustained by Divine power through a fast of equal duration.

forty days. On the length of the temptation, see Mark i. 13.

The three temptations were directly aimed against the mission of the Son of God: first against its chief requirement, self-renunciation and trust in God (see xx. 28; xxvi. 53); then against its principal evidence, the unostentatious usefulness and beneficence which characterise all His miracles (see xi. 4–6; Luke ix. 55, 56); and lastly against its ultimate object, the restoration of God's rightful rule and acknowledged supremacy over the whole world. Had the temptation succeeded, Jesus would have become only the Messiah expected by the worldly-minded Jews. For us, allowing for the difference due to Christ's Messiahship, the similar temptations are those of appetite, of avarice, and of ambition.

4 every word. That is, by whatever God shall appoint: see Deut. viii. 3.

5 Then. This word seems to fix the order of the temptations: see notes on ver. 6, and on Luke iv. 2.

a (the) **pinnacle** (lit., *wing*) **of the Temple.** This was probably the pointed roof of the southern portico, which overhung the valley of the Kedron at a height of more than 250 feet.

6 cast Thyself down. An attempt to pervert the implicit trust in God just avowed by our Lord into presumption. Satan tempts by endeavours to *exaggerate* what is right. He would turn piety into fanaticism.

7 It is written again. Satan's artful misuse of Scripture is met and repelled by Scripture rightly applied: see Psa. xci. 11.

8 the kingdoms of the world. See Milton, *Paradise Regained*, iii. 251, and foll.

9 will I give Thee. Falsely asserting (see Luke iv. 6) that God has given to him the entire disposal of them.

worship me. Rendering me homage as Thy superior, of whom Thy kingdom is held. Satan here (a liar from the beginning) claims that the great objects of human desire are to be gained by worshipping him. Upon this bold disclosure of the tempter's object, our Lord rebukes and repels him.

11 the devil leaveth Him. See note on Luke iv. 13.

12 John was cast into prison. See xiv. 3–5.

He departed into Galilee. See John iv. 1–3.

13 Capernaum. Capernaum was the name of a fountain (Joseph. *Wars*, iii. 10, 8), and of a town, situated on the western shore of the Lake of Tiberias, probably at or near *Khan Minyeh*. It was a meeting-place of many great roads. Its present complete desolation forcibly illustrates our Lord's denunciation in xi. 23.

15, 16. See Isa. viii. 22.

17 From that time. That is, from the time when He heard of John's imprisonment (12). Jesus had preached before; but, now that the ministry of His forerunner had ceased, He took up and carried forward the teachings of John.

18 Sea of Galilee. Called also the Sea of Tiberias (John vi. 1; xxi. 1); the Lake of Gennesareth (Luke v. 1); and, in the Old Testament, the Sea of Chinnereth (Numb. xxxiv. 11). This lake, or inland sea, is about thirteen miles long and less than seven broad.

20 left [their] nets, and followed Him. They had, previously to this, recognised Jesus as the Messiah (see John i. 40, 41), but had continued to follow their occupation as fishermen. They now appear to have left their business, and become constant attendants on Jesus; although, when they were near their homes, they sometimes went out to fish.

22 the ship. Rather, as R.V., "the boat." So in many other passages.

23 synagogues. The synagogues were places in which the Jews, from the time of the Captivity, were accustomed to meet, chiefly on the Sabbaths and new moons, to hear the Law and the Prophets read and explained. They existed in our Lord's time in almost every town both in Palestine and wherever Jews were settled. Each synagogue had a community, with its president and elders (Mark v. 22), who might chastise (x. 17; Acts xxii. 19; xxvi. 11) or expel (John ix. 34) an offender.

24 Syria. In the New Testament, "Syria" is the Roman province, of which Palestine was the south-western part.

torments. Painful maladies.

possessed with devils. In the New Testament, various bodily and mental disorders, often of the most severe and painful kind, are attributed to the agency of the devil (Acts x. 38) or of demons. Some suppose that in thus speaking of them our Lord and the sacred writers used the current language of the Jews, without intending to give any sanction to the opinion on which it was founded. But this hardly accounts for all the references. The subject is too large and mysterious to be dealt with in a single note.

lunatic. "Epileptic" (R.V.).

25 Decapolis. This name, which means *ten cities*, included several towns, lying (with one exception) on the east of the Jordan, and distinguished from the neighbouring districts by a large admixture of Gentile inhabitants.

CHAPTER V

3 Blessed. With these beatitudes compare the blessings promised through Moses to ancient Israel (Deut. xxviii.). As the Jews had come to regard these as their hereditary right, our Lord marks out the *character* of those who are to enjoy the blessings of His kingdom. The full meaning of the beatitudes would be more clearly seen if the word translated "blessed" were rendered "happy." Happiness is here shown by our Lord to consist not in what we have, but in what we are.

theirs is the kingdom of heaven. They enjoy the blessings of the Divine kingdom of Messiah, predicted and partially described in Psa. lxxii.; Isa. lx.; Jer. xxx., xxxi.; Ezek. xxxiv. 22–31; Dan. ii. 34, 44.

5 the meek. In contrast with the spirit in which earthly power and supremacy are generally sought, and especially with the hopes and ambitions of the Jews at this epoch. The conquests of Christ's kingdom are those of gentleness: see Psa. xlv. 4.

the earth. Or, "the land"; meaning the blessings suggested by Canaan: see Psa. xxv. 13; xxxvii. 9, 11, and notes. But the promise is true in its largest sense. The whole world will yet be won by the forces of love.

6 righteousness. "Righteousness" here means the removal of all sin, and the fulfilment of God's will in heart and conduct. "Hunger" and "thirst" symbolise not merely the dictates of the judgement, but the *appetites* of the new life.

filled. The word here used denotes the amplest satisfaction: see Psa. xvii. 15. Weymouth translates, "they shall be completely satisfied."

8 the pure in heart. There is here an evident reference to Psa. xxiv., where purity of heart is declared to be a condition of communion with God in His sanctuary. Our Lord extends the privilege to all places and times. God is seen by the pure now and hereafter (1 John iii. 2, 3).

9 shall be called. That is, "they shall be recognised" as such by God, in being partakers of His moral likeness.

10 which are persecuted. Rather, as R.V., "that have been persecuted." The reference of this verse is to confessors and martyrs of the past; that in vers. 11, 12 to Christ's own disciples.

13 Ye are the salt. There was a remarkable proverb current in our Lord's days, "Nothing is more useful than sun and salt" (Plin. *Hist. Nat.* xxxi. 9). What salt and sunlight are to the material world, preventing corruption and dispelling darkness, Christ's disciples, divinely imbued with the living, saving power of gospel truth, are to be to the spiritual world. But, if there be any in whom the gospel loses its sanctifying and diffusive influence, their lives become useless.

14 Ye are the light of the world. The very title appropriated in John i. 9; viii. 12, to Christ is here given by Him to His disciples, as those to whom He has given His grace and truth, that they may shine forth for the salvation of the world.

15 a candle, etc. Render, as R.V., " a lamp": " the lampstand."

a (the) **bushel.** Rather, "measure," the *modius*, found in every house: containing about two gallons.

16 so shine. Rather, "shine thus"; *i.e.*, like a lamp on its stand.

17 to fulfil. Our Lord, by His life, sufferings, and death, "fulfilled" the types of the ceremonial law, and the predictions of the prophets. But the scope of the whole discourse, and especially the following precepts, make it evident that He here refers to the *completeness* which He gave, both by His teaching and by His example, to the moral and spiritual commands both of the law and of the prophets.

18 jot. Or, "iota" (Heb. *yod*, י); the smallest letter in the alphabet. A "tittle" is a small point or stroke, by which some letters are distinguished from others (as Heb. ד from ר: cp. English E from F).

20 scribes and Pharisees. The scribes were students, public readers, and expounders of the law. The majority of them were Pharisees, though some belonged to other sects.

21-48. The superiority of our Lord's teaching is now shown in regard to several enactments of the ancient law: 1. The law against *murder*, which is now shown to include hatred, and to require a conciliatory spirit (21-26). 2. The law against *adultery*, which applies in principle to lust and to divorce (27-32). 3. The law of *oaths*, intended to lead to simple affirmation (33-37). 4. The law of *retaliation*, which must not be held to permit private revenge, or to exclude a hearty readiness to forgive and to benefit those who have wronged us (38-42). 5. The law of *exclusiveness*. The law to love one's neighbour had been so misinterpreted as to imply hatred to one's enemies. Our Lord shows that the law, rightly understood, leads to a comprehensive and godlike charity (43-48).

21 by them of old time. Rather, "*to* them of old" (R.V.); "to the ancients." For those who lived under a preparatory dispensation, the general precept was sufficient.

22 But I say unto you. A formula not of disapproval, but of exposition: a phrase used by Hebrew teachers to introduce their explanations of the law.

angry with his brother. The words, "without a cause," seem to have been added by some early transcriber "to soften the apparent rigour of the precept" (*Bengel, Alford*). Most modern critics omit the phrase (R.V.). The expressions used (*Raca!* "empty" and *Thou fool!* a term attributing utter mental and moral worthlessness) illustrate the several degrees of anger, incurring corresponding penalties. The "judgement" was a local court of judges or magistrates. The "council" was the supreme central court, or Sanhedrin, who inflicted capital punishment with the disgrace of stoning. "Hell fire" is rather "the Gehenna of fire" (see 2 Kings xxiii. 10, and note), and refers to the burning of the body—the greatest ignominy, which was inflicted only occasionally upon the worst of criminals. By this climax, our Lord shows the guilt and danger of indulging hatred in the heart, even though its expressions may be only those of contempt or petulance.

23 if thou bring. More precisely, as R.V., "If thou art offering"—the remembrance occurring in the very act of presenting the sacrifice.

to the altar. "Gifts," or offerings to God, were commonly presented at the Temple: and in part or wholly consumed upon "the altar." But he who retains enmity to his fellow-man cannot be an acceptable worshipper.

aught against thee. Not only, If thou hast any ground of complaint against him; but if he have any against thee.

25 whiles thou art in the way. Here follows a new illustration, derived from the legal practice of the time, which allowed the settlement of a dispute after a summons had been served, and before the cause had come on for trial. The indulgence of an unkindly spirit places a man in the condition of one who is already summoned; and who, if he do not speedily seek reconciliation, will be irrevocably condemned: see note on Luke xii. 58.

28 looketh, etc. The sense is, "gazeth with impure desire."

29 offend thee. Rather, "causeth thee to stumble"; *i.e.*, to sin (R.V.). "Is a snare to thee" (*Weymouth*).

pluck it out. The "right eye" and "right hand," the most valuable of our members, represent sometimes our strongest propensities and habits, sometimes our most precious earthly possessions. Whenever these become inlets to temptation or the instruments of sin, they must be surrendered, or we perish.

31 It hath been said. See note on Deut. xxiv. 1; also on xix. 3-9, where our Lord further explains this subject.

33 Thou shalt not forswear thyself. A literal rendering of the Third Commandment, which in Hebrew reads, "Thou shalt not lift up the name of Jehovah thy God to vanity" (*or*, "falsehood"). To "lift up the name" is a phrase signifying to swear by it.

34 Swear not at all. An oath is an appeal to God to witness and to judge the truth of a man's words; and therefore brings him under solemn obligation "unto the Lord." But the Jews denied that an oath was binding, unless the name of God, or the gold or the sacrifices of the Temple, were invoked. Our Lord shows the futility of these distinctions; which were originally the resource of fraud, and had the effect of filling common discourse with profane expletives. The spirit of this precept is violated by using the name of God to give emphasis to our language. Some persons in all subsequent ages have regarded this prohibition as extending even to solemn judicial oaths.

37 Yea, yea. A Christian's word should be enough.

cometh of evil (*or*, "of the evil one," R.V.: see note on vi. 13). The need of oaths indicates either want of truthfulness or want of confidence, or both, and therefore is the result of evil. And the frequent use of them increases the evil.

38 An eye for an eye, etc. Exod. xxi. 24.

39 resist not evil ("him that is evil," R.V.). This

by no means warrants (as the Jews held that it did) the practice of private retaliation. On the contrary, the Christian is required to cherish a spirit of forgiveness and generosity; rather foregoing his rights and submitting to injury, than doing anything which might produce a revengeful or unkindly spirit.

A blow on the cheek was a contumelious action.

40 coat . . . cloak. The "coat," or "tunic," is the inner and smaller; the "cloak," the outer and more valuable of the two garments ordinarily worn. The force of this command to yield even the *cloak* will appear from Exod. xxii. 27. In Luke vi. 29 the order is reversed, the outer garment being there regarded as that *first seized*.

41 compel thee to go. The Greek word means "impress you into his service." Impressment by the imperial couriers (a practice which the Romans borrowed from the Persians) was an act of public oppression. Weymouth translates "compel you to convey his goods."

twain. "Two."

42 Give to him that asketh thee. Our Lord emphatically repeats the law of Deut. xv. 1–11 (on which see notes). The people had been often reminded of this law (see Psa. xxxvii. 26; cxii. 5, 9); but they repeatedly violated it (see Neh. v.; Ezek. xxii. 7), and did so in the time of Christ (Matt. xxiii. 14).

43 love thy neighbour, and hate thine enemy. This was a perversion of the law of love in Lev. xix. 18: restricting the meaning of the term "neighbour," and adding the hatred here denounced.

45 He maketh His sun, etc. Even the rays of the sun and the drops of rain read a lesson to the vindictive.

46 the publicans. "Tax-gatherers." The "publicans," or collectors of the revenue under the Roman government, comprised two classes of persons. The higher grade were usually Romans of rank, who levied the revenues of a large district. Under them, the taxes were farmed by numerous local collectors, who are the "publicans" of the New Testament. As they collected the tribute for a foreign heathen power, and often practised extortion, they were extremely unpopular among their countrymen. The children of the benevolent Father in heaven ought to cultivate higher virtues than even such men may practise.

48 perfect. "Complete in goodness" (*Weymouth*).

CHAPTER VI

1 alms. The best Greek manuscripts read "righteousness"; according to which this verse is a general introduction to what follows: almsgiving (2–4), devotion (5–15), and fasting (16–18); in all of which ostentation is condemned.

to be seen of them. Rather, "in order to be observed by them." Our Lord forbids, not publicity, but ostentation: cp. v. 16.

2 do not sound a trumpet. "Do not court attention."

They have their reward. That is, as the original denotes, they have it *in full*. The Greek also emphasises *their*.

5 they love to pray standing. "Standing" was a frequent posture in prayer among the Jews of our Lord's days (Luke xviii. 11, 13) and the early Christians. The same is customary with the modern Jews and in the Reformed Churches of the Continent. It is not the *position* which is condemned, but the spirit of ostentation ("at the corner of the streets").

6 shall reward thee openly. Both here and in vers. 4, 18 the word "openly" is probably an interpolation by some early transcriber. It is not the publicity, but the fact of the reward to which our Lord draws attention. His promise must not be taken as supplying the motive, but as affording encouragement in self-denying virtue.

7 use not vain repetitions. The frequent repetition of ill-understood forms indicates unworthy notions of Him who knows all our wants (8), and is ever ready to relieve them; and it shows a reliance upon the service itself, as giving a claim to His favours.

8 your Father knoweth. "Therefore we do not pray to God to inform Him, but to worship Him" (*Bengel*).

9 After this manner. Let this be the substance, whatever be the form. In Luke xi. 2, the command is more definite, "When ye pray, say": see note on that passage.

Our Father. This relationship is occasionally referred to in the Old Testament (Exod. iv. 22; Isa. lxiii. 16; lxiv. 8; Jer. xxxi. 9); but in its fullest sense it is a truth revealed by Christ. It is the basic thought of the Prayer.

Hallowed be Thy name. A prayer for reverence.

10 Thy kingdom come. See note on iii. 2. And if we pray for it, we must also work for it.

Thy will be done. It is significant that in the Lord's Prayer, spiritual things are put first. Thus we learn to trust our heavenly Father for the temporal things of life.

11 daily bread. Meaning probably, food necessary for our subsistence: cp. Prov. xxx. 8.

12 debts. That is, "faults"; "trespasses." See ver. 14; Luke xi. 4; and xviii. 4, on which see note. The word "trespasses" in the Lord's Prayer as generally used, is from Tyndale's version.

as we forgive. Or (see var. read), "as we have forgiven" (R.V.). This does not intimate that our forgiveness of others is either the ground or the measure of God's forgiveness of us, but the condition of it.

13 lead us not into temptation. In Psa. cxli. 4 there is a similar petition; and both are explained by the promise in 1 Cor. x. 13. He who sincerely and earnestly offers this petition will not wilfully or carelessly go into temptation.

deliver us from evil. Here is trust in our Father's prevailing power. This petition looks forward to a complete deliverance from all sin and all its consequences. The R.V. reads, "from the evil one," from whom "temptation" specially proceeds. The original will bear either sense. But the rendering "evil" seems preferable, as referring not only to promptings from without, but to the sin that arises from within.

14 For if ye forgive. Our Lord here reverts to His words in ver. 12. The forgiveness of injuries is not only a part of His new law of love, but it is essential to the acceptance of our prayers.

17 anoint thine head. That is, dress and appear as usual. Every kind of self-denial in the service of God should be as much as possible concealed from all but God.

19 where moth and rust doth corrupt. In Palestine and other Eastern countries, where fashions rarely change, clothes were laid up in large quantities as treasures by wealthy men. Hence their treasures were in danger from moths.

22 The light. Rather, "the lamp," as R.V.; a different word from that in v. 14.

single. "Sound" (*i.e.*, "clear"); as opposed to "evil," or "diseased." "If your eyesight is good" (*Weymouth*). See note on Luke xi. 34.

24 serve. Or, "be a slave to." The word refers, not to occasional services, but to continued and complete subjection.

mammon. Mammon is an Aramaic word meaning *riches*, which our Lord here personifies. There cannot in any case be single-hearted service of two lords, when they are so opposed as God and the world.

25–34. In these verses we have Christ's cure for care. 1. God has given you life; will He not also give you the means to support it? (25). 2. God feeds the birds, and clothes the flowers. Are not ye much better than they? (26, 28–30). 3. Anxiety does not help you (27). 4. God knows your need (31–32). 5. Put first things first (33).

25 Therefore. The most common and deceptive excuse for laying up treasures is solicitude for the future. Therefore indulge not such anxieties.

Take no thought. That is, "be not *anxious*" (R.V.): see Phil. iv. 6. The word "thought" in Old English often meant anxious care. So Shakespeare: "sicklied o'er with the pale cast of thought."

more than meat (food). That is, of *higher value*. He who has given the greater will not be unmindful of the less.

27 stature. Probably, "age" (R.V. marg.); as in John ix. 21, 23; Heb. xi. 11; for the subject of anxiety is the lengthening of life, and "one cubit," or twenty-one inches (here evidently put as the "least" measure of space: see Luke xii. 26), would be too great an addition to a man's stature to become a common object of desire.

28 the lilies of the field. This term probably includes the many beautiful anemones, cyclamens, etc., which abound in Palestine, and which would now be in their summer beauty.

30 the grass. Or, *herbage* generally, which in the East was used for fuel, being placed below and around the earthen "oven," or portable vessel used for baking bread.

32 the Gentiles. Heathen who know not God.

seek. The word here used means "seek with eagerness." Let it not be so with you.

33 seek ye first. As the one great object of pursuit. The Lord's Prayer teaches the same lesson; see note on ver. 10.

these things shall be added. Lit., given over and above; as an illustration of this, see 1 Kings iii. 11–13.

34 no thought for the morrow. Rather, "Be not anxious about the morrow, for the morrow will have its own anxieties." Luther translates: "Es ist genug dass ein jeglicher Tag seine eigne Plage habe" ("It is enough that each day have its own anxiety").

CHAPTER VII

1 Judge not. Opinions must necessarily be formed, on conduct and character, but must not be formed *censoriously*.

mete. "Measure."

3 mote. The "mote" is a "splinter" or "chip"; *i.e.*, a very *small* thing; the "beam" is a very *large* thing.

5 Thou hypocrite. He blinds himself to the true character of his own sins, and disguises his want of charity for his brother under the garb of sympathy.

6 that which is holy. "This verse inculcates prudence, tact and discernment of character" (*A. Maclaren*).

7 Ask . . . seek . . . knock. The following commands and promises are repeated with more general application in Luke xi. 9–13, on which see notes. Weymouth paraphrases: "Keep asking . . . seeking . . . knocking."

9 what man. "Man" here is emphatic. and strongly marks the contrast between the human and the divine.

11 good things. The variation in Luke xi. 13 shows that the "good things" are the blessings involved in the gift of "the Holy Spirit"; here particularly charity and wisdom.

12 Therefore. Because you hope for the Divine favour in answer to your prayer.

whatsoever ye would. The *negative* part of this command has been taught by others. Our Lord here puts it in a *positive* form. Not only avoid doing to others what you in their position would dislike, but do to them whatever you would reasonably wish them to do to you. For this we need heavenly grace; and nothing short of it is the "fulfilling of the law."

13 at (by) **the strait** (narrow) **gate.** Both to begin and to persevere in such a course of self-denying, spiritual obedience as the foregoing precepts enjoin will be arduous and difficult; and many will choose an easier path; but this alone leads to life.

14 few. But this will not always be the case: see Rev. vii. 9.

15 in sheep's clothing. An allusion, it may be, to the fleecy garb, the "rough garment," of the professed prophet: see Zech. xiii. 4.

ravening. Rapacious, devouring.

16 Ye shall know them. That is, the teachers. Men are too apt to judge the doctrine itself by its unworthy advocates and professors. The "fruits" are those of spirit and conduct: see Gal. v. 22, 23.

21 "Lord, Lord." Professing that Christ is their Master, but not doing His will.

22 in that day. "That day" is a frequent prophetic phrase (see Isa. ii. 11; Mal. iii. 17), referring to a period of Divine manifestation; sometimes the introduction of Messiah's kingdom, sometimes its consummation. Here it is evidently the latter, when the great and final difference shall be made between the righteous and the wicked: 2 Thess. i. 7–10; Heb. x. 25.

prophesied. Or, "preached." Not merely "foretelling," but any "forth-telling" in Christ's name, is included.

23 I never knew you. Or, "acknowledged": see Psa. i. 6, and note, and cp. 1 Cor. viii. 3; Gal. iv. 9; and especially 2 Tim. ii. 19, which seems like an echo of our Lord's words.

24 I will liken him. The germ of these similitudes may be found in Prov. xii. 7; Isa. xxviii. 16, 17; but they are here wrought out with the greatest beauty in a most impressive contrast.

a rock. Rather, "the rock," as R.V.

doctrine. Rather, "teaching," as R.V. His manner of teaching was that of one possessing original "authority." On the scribes, see ii. 4. They were mainly expounders of the law, telling what this or that Rabbi thought about it.

CHAPTER VIII

2 there came a leper. This miracle is more fully related in Mark i. 40–45, on which see notes.

4 for a testimony unto them. As a proof to the priests that he was healed.

5 there came unto Him a centurion. From the fuller account in Luke vii. 1–10 (on which see notes), it appears that the centurion sent the elders of the Jews and afterwards his "friends" to Jesus. The narratives are not inconsistent. It is possible that the centurion's earnestness overcame his modesty, and that he followed his friends.

11 from the east and west. From the most remote heathen lands.

shall sit down. Lit., "recline." A "feast" represents, in prophecy, the blessings of Messiah's reign (Isa. xxv. 6), which were to be extended "to the Gentiles" and "the end of the earth" (Isa. xlix. 6): cp. xxii. 1–14; Luke xiv. 15–24.

12 the children of the kingdom. Those who, trusting in their outward advantages and religious privileges, think themselves the natural heirs of these blessings, shall, for their unbelief, be disinherited: cp. Rom. xi. 7–24. And their disappointment, rage, and misery will be like those of a person unexpectedly thrust out from a brilliant and cheerful banquet hall "into the outside darkness" of the night.

14, 15. See Mark i. 29–31, and note on ver. 31.

17 spoken by Esaias. This quotation from Isa. liii. 4 (on which see note) differs from the Septuagint and from that in 1 Pet. ii. 24; but it is fully accordant with the sense of the prophet.

18 the other side. The eastern side of the Sea of Galilee.

19–22. Cp. Luke ix. 57–62.

20 the Son of man. This title was probably well known among the Jews as an appellation of the Messiah, being derived from Dan. vii. 13, where it is a Chaldee phrase, signifying "a man." The form of expression in that passage, "one like a son of man," was well adapted to suggest the peculiar constitution of our Lord's nature, and may therefore have led Him to the frequent use of this designation.

hath not where to lay His head. If you would be my disciple, you must be prepared to sacrifice even the ordinary comforts of life.

21, 22. See notes on Luke ix. 59, 60.

23 a ship. Rather, *the* ship ("boat," R.V.); *i.e.*, the vessel which the disciples had prepared (18); see Mark iii. 9.

24 was covered. Or, "was becoming covered." The Lake of Tiberias, lying deep among precipitous mountains, is exposed, like all mountain lakes, to sudden gusts from all sides, which sweep down the valleys, and violently agitate the waters. That this was a severe tempest is shown by the fact that four experienced fishermen on board the little barque were greatly alarmed.

He was asleep. This is the only passage where the sleep of Jesus is mentioned.

26 ye of little faith. Although they were of "little faith" (confidence), in so far as they feared to perish with the slumbering Redeemer; yet they were "believing" (trustful), inasmuch as they looked to Him for deliverance.

28 Gergesenes. Rather "Gadarenes" (so R.V.); as in Mark v. 1, and Luke viii. 26. Origen says that Gergesa (now *Kersa*) was a city on the eastern shore of the lake. It was probably included in the district of the more important city, Gadara, on the river Hieromax (*Yarmuk*), one of the cities of the Decapolis, and the capital of Peræa, inhabited chiefly by Gentiles: see map, and *Land and the Book*, p. 375. On this miracle, see notes on Mark v. 1–21; where, as in Luke, only one demoniac is mentioned, his companion being probably less remarkable.

32 and perished in the waters. This case, and that of the barren fig tree (see xxi. 19), are the only instances in which our Saviour's miracles did not promote directly the temporal welfare and happiness of men. There are great moral lessons in both. The affinity of sin with the bestial and impure is here especially and impressively taught.

34 besought (Him) that He would depart. A sad illustration, often still repeated, of the blindness of men to their own best interests.

CHAPTER IX

1 His own city. Capernaum, which He had selected as the place of His residence: see iv. 13.

2 they brought to Him, etc. On this miracle, see notes, Luke v. 17–26.

9 at the receipt of custom. Or, "at the place of toll" (R.V.), or "the custom-house."

he arose, and followed Him. Luke (v. 28) adds, "he left all." This Matthew modestly omits.

10 Jesus sat at meat. Rather, "as he (Matthew) sat (reclined) at meat, many publicans and sinners came and sat down (reclined) with Jesus," etc. (R.V.). Luke records (v. 29) what Matthew omits, with the modesty indicated above, that this feast was provided by Matthew himself; probably in order to bring his former associates into closer intercourse with Jesus; as well as to show honour to the Saviour.

publicans and sinners. Tax-gatherers were regarded as among the worst of sinners: see note on ch. v. 46.

11 when the Pharisees saw it. Perhaps standing outside and watching the guests arriving or departing.

13 go ye. That is, to the synagogue, where will be found a copy of Hosea (*Bengel*).

mercy, and not sacrifce. That is, "mercy *rather than* sacrifice," which is the reading of the LXX: see Hos. vi. 6, and note. Our Lord vindicates Himself, both by proverb and by Scripture, as a public religious teacher, in showing "mercy" to those who were diseased with sin; and He then announces the salvation of sinners as the great purpose for which He came into the world: cp. xviii. 11; Luke xv.

I am not come to call the righteous. If any are truly righteous, they will not need my salvation. If they think themselves so, they will not care to seek it.

14 the disciples of John. See Acts xix. 4, 5. They still clung, like their Master, to the old, while his message was a preparation for the new.

fast. This no doubt refers to voluntary fasting, over and above what the law required: see Luke xviii. 12.

15 children of the bridechamber. See Judges xiv. 11, and note.

as long as the bridegroom is with them. Our Lord thus confirms the intimation of His forerunner (John iii. 29); announcing Himself as the Messiah, who had long ago been represented as the "bridegroom," and His coming as the marriage of Israel: see Psa. xlv.; Isa. lxii. 5. And this figure He employs further to illustrate the difference between the ascetic severity of John as a preacher of repentance only, and Himself as the gracious Author of a joyful salvation. Gladness, not mourning, should distinguish His followers, at least whilst He is with them on earth.

then shall they fast. In token of mourning. Not an injunction of ascetic practices.

17 bottles. Rather, "wine-skins" (R.V.): see Josh. ix. 4. These skin-bottles, when they are old, become dry, and unsuitable for new wine, as they cannot swell when it ferments. They therefore burst. So the forms of the old dispensation were unsuitable to the free and expansive spirit of the new. It is not fasting in itself which is prohibited (see vi. 16, 17; Acts xiv. 23), but the imposition of the burdensome restrictions and observances of the old dispensation upon the Christian.

18 a certain ruler. That is, a ruler or president of the synagogue of Capernaum. His name was Jairus. The events of this section are more fully recorded in Mark v. 22–43, on which see notes.

is even now dead. Matthew, giving only a short account, passes over the fact mentioned by Mark, that the death of the child was reported to the father after his application to Jesus.

27–31. The record of this miracle and the next is peculiar to Matthew.

27 Son of David. By this appellation the blind men acknowledged Jesus to be the Messiah, for it appears to have been the general popular designation of the expected King of Israel (see xxii. 42). But, as this seemed to favour the idea of an earthly reign over the Jewish nation, and so was liable to grievous abuse (as when the people desired to make Jesus a king, John vi. 15), our Lord did not Himself employ it, but preferred to call Himself "the Son of man"—a title of deeper significance, and less liable to perversion.

30 See that no man know it. The charge was strict, even impassioned, as the word employed signifies. The reason was perhaps the desire of Christ to avoid mere notoriety. That the command was disobeyed shows that zeal prevailed over the spirit of obedience.

34 through the prince of the devils (demons). See xii. 23–30 (where the charge is repeated), and notes.

36 fainted. Rather "were harassed" or "distressed" (R.V.): like sheep, each one wearied out, and the flock scattered by the negligence and rapacity of their keepers: cp. Zech. xi. 16, 17. The Jewish teachers, by their burdensome traditions and grievous exactions, had robbed religion of all that could sanctify and comfort; so that the people, wearied with the double oppression of the Romans and of their own leaders, were ready to wander after any one who promised them relief: cp. xxiv. 24.

38 pray. Recognising His power to qualify labourers and His authority to call them forth, and appealing to the interest which He takes in "His harvest." Those who pray earnestly for this blessing will be ready for the call to labour, whenever (as in ch. x.) it is addressed to themselves.

CHAPTER X

1 His twelve disciples. They had been selected before this time (see Luke vi. 13, and note on v. 1); now they are solemnly commissioned *as apostles.* "Disciple" means "learner"; "Apostle," one who is sent, a missionary. Their number corresponded to that of the twelve tribes of Israel, to whom in the first instance their commission was limited (ver. 6): cp. xix. 28; Rev. xxi. 12, 14.

2 The first. Matthew has placed the first four in the order in which they were called to be constant attendants on our Lord, Peter being "first": see iv. 18–21. Two groups follow, each containing four disciples. The arrangement of names differs in each group, as given in the various lists (see Mark iii. 16–19; Luke vi. 14–16; Acts i. 13), with the exception that the name at the head of the group is in all cases the same: Peter, Philip, James.

3 Bartholomew. Bartholomew, or Bar-Talmai (son of Talmai), the patronymic (the father's name carried on by the son, as in Russian, Petrovitch, "son of Peter") of Nathanael, who was brought to Jesus by Philip, with whom he is always associated: see John i. 46; xxi. 2.

Thomas. The Hebrew name "Thomas" (in Greek Didymus) means "the twin": see John xi. 16.

Matthew. Note that the evangelist describes himself as "the tax-gatherer"—the name of reproach.

James. Called also (Mark xv. 40) *the Less;* probably either in age or stature (Greek, *little*). "Alphæus" is probably another form of Cleophas: see John xix. 25. The mother of this James was called Mary.

Lebbæus. Called also "Thaddæus" (Mark iii. 18); probably another form of "Judas" (Jude, the brother of James), Luke vi. 16; John xiv. 22.

4 Canaanite. This surname has no reference to Canaan, and should be "Kananæan," a Hebrew appellation (of which the Greek is *Zelotes*, "the Zealot": Luke vi. 15) given to a sect to which Simon had belonged

Iscariot. "Iscariot" is probably a Greek compound of two Hebrew words, meaning *Man of Kerioth* (Josh. xv. 25). Kerioth was a village in Southern Judæa. Judas appears to have been the only disciple not a Galilæan.

who also betrayed Him. One of the strongest evidences of our Lord's perfect innocence is found in the exposure of His most confidential communications to such a man. How gladly would His enemies have used Judas as a witness against Him, could they have done so! (see xxvi. 59, 60). How gladly would Judas have appeased his own conscience, if he could, by persuading himself that he had not betrayed the innocent!

5 Samaritans. The Samaritans were a mixed race, descended partly from the Ten Tribes, partly from heathen immigrants. They inhabited the central part of Palestine, lying between Judæa and Galilee. There had long been a bitter enmity between them and the Jews. See John iv. 9; and notes on 2 Kings xvii. 24, 27; Ezra iv. 2, 3; Neh. xiii. 28. For the present the gospel was to be preached only to the Jews, "the lost sheep (see ix. 36) of Israel." Our Lord, before His ascension, extended the commission, expressly including Samaria (Acts i. 8) as well as the Gentiles (xxviii. 19): see Col. i. 26–28.

8 freely. That is, you have received your gifts of knowledge and miraculous power gratuitously. Therefore you must not use them for your private advantage.

9–15. The instructions in these verses were repeated by our Lord when He sent forth the Seventy. They are more fully recorded in Luke x. 4–16, on which see notes.

10 scrip. A wallet. Deissmann (*Light from the Ancient East*, 1910, p. 108) shows that the word πήρα here translated "scrip" was that used for a beggar's collecting-bag. The word appears on a Syrian monument of the Roman Empire period.

shoes (sandals). That is, a *change* of shoes.

staves. That is, no other than that which you have actually in use: cp. Mark vi. 8. If you happen to have a staff, you may use it; but do not stay to procure one. Do not make the slightest provision, as for a journey.

worthy of his meat (food). That is, worthy of his sustenance.

11 worthy. That is, deserving of your confidence; devout and well-disposed.

16 I send you forth, etc. Our Lord now passes beyond the immediate commission of the Twelve, and anticipates their whole career as His apostles.

wise as serpents, and harmless as doves. *i.e.*, "Have the good qualities of each." The serpent was believed to be "prudent," but malignant (Gen. xlix. 17): the dove is "guileless," but silly (Hos. vii. 11). Be prudent, but be guileless. "Wisdom without innocency is knavery; innocency without wisdom is foolery" (*Quarles*).

17 councils. The local "tribunals" attached to the synagogues. Their judges could punish by scourging: see Acts xxii. 19.

18 and. Rather, "yea, moreover"; implying severer trial.

governors and kings. Roman "governors" of provinces (Matt. xxvii.; Acts xxiii., xxiv.), and dependent "kings," as Herod, or perhaps the emperors of Rome (Acts xii. 1; xxv. 23; xxv. 11, 12).

a testimony against them. Rather, "to them" (R.V.). The servants of Christ are to bear this "testimony" to the truth of their doctrines, by their calm heroism and forgiving meekness in danger and suffering.

19 take no thought. Rather, "be not anxious" (cp. vi. 25 and note), as they might naturally be, from a remembrance of the interests involved in their "testimony." Look for aid in the emergency to the Holy Spirit, who will so help you that when you speak it shall rather be He who speaks than you, with a wisdom which none can gainsay: cp. Luke xxi. 15. "The disciples of Christ," remarks *Matthew Henry*, "must be more thoughtful how to do well than to speak well; how to keep their integrity, than how to vindicate it."

22 hated by all men. In nothing perhaps has the hardening nature of man's ungodliness been so strikingly displayed as in the bitter hatred which Christians have had to endure, frequently even from their dearest relatives. Those who are tolerant of everything else are intolerant of a vital and active piety.

23 till the Son of man be come. You will have barely time to preach to all Israel before I come to judge and punish your persecutors in the approaching destruction of the Jewish state. Therefore do not linger where you are ill-received.

25 Beelzebub. Rather, "Beelzebul." Baal-zebub, the "lord of the fly," was the god of Ekron (2 Kings i. 2), whose name the Jews had contemptuously altered from *zebub* to *zebul*, from Heb. *zebel*, "dung"; and applied to the chief of the demons (see 1 Cor. x. 20).

26 for there is nothing covered, etc. I charge you to announce publicly all that I have taught you; and I promise you that I will publicly vindicate you from all their aspersions.

27 What I tell you in darkness, etc. Our Lord delivered to His disciples many private instructions in parabolic form; but only that their meaning might be publicly unfolded as their hearers might be able to understand and receive it.

upon the housetops. Where people were accustomed to sit. So that anything thus proclaimed would be widely known.

28 which is able to destroy. Some expositors understand Satan to be meant.

29 a farthing. The *assarion*, the sixteenth part of the denarius, which was worth about 9½*d*. God only is the arbiter of life and death. Fear Him rather than man; trust Him, and fear not man. See Luke xii. 6, where the illustration is strengthened: not the odd sparrow, thrown into the bargain as almost valueless, is forgotten before God. The humblest of God's creatures have their value in His sight: how much more men! especially Christians; but above all, the witnesses of Jesus!

30 the very hairs of your head, etc. Showing God's watchful care over His creatures, even in regard to what is smallest and most trivial in their lives. Cp. Ps. lvi. 8; cxvi. 15.

34 I came not to send peace. His ultimate purpose is not to introduce discord, but peace. Yet, in a world like ours, true peace can be attained only as the result of a severe conflict between the opposing powers of good and evil.

35 to set a man . . . against his father, etc. A free quotation from Micah vii. 6. Cp. ver. 22, and note.

38 he that taketh not his cross. The victim of this Roman punishment, which was most painful and ignominious, was often compelled to carry the cross on which he was to suffer to the place of execution. "Bearing the cross" is a phrase often used by our Lord. His hearers must well have understood Him to refer to the deepest suffering and disgrace. He probably designed to prepare their minds for His own death, and especially to associate it with the great principles of Christian self-sacrifice. This is one of those sayings of which John xii. 16 was eminently true.

39 He that findeth his life. The word rendered "life" and "soul," both here and at xvi. 25, 26, is put, according to a Hebrew idiom transferred to the Greek, for "self," which is substituted for it in Luke ix. 25. It evidently includes all a man's most cherished interests. He who makes his own interests paramount shall lose what he seeks: he whose chief aim is to serve me shall obtain the highest good for himself.

41 a prophet, etc. Three degrees of Christian attainment are here set forth (cp. "fathers, young men, little children," 1 John ii. 12–14), from the highest inspiration to the lowliest discipleship. Each of these is regarded and honoured by the Master.

42 these little ones. Perhaps some children were present. The smallest services rendered to the humblest of Christ's followers shall be recompensed: cp. xviii. 10; xxv. 40.

CHAPTER XI

1 their cities. The cities of the Galilæans.

2 in the prison. Herod had imprisoned John in the fortress of Machærus, on the east of the Dead Sea: see xiv. 3, and Josephus, *Ant.* xviii. 5, § 2.

the works of Christ. Rather, "the works of *the Christ*" (R.V.); for Matthew never uses the word as a proper name. This probably means works characteristic of the Messiah; particularly the recent restoration to life of the widow's son at Nain: see Luke vii.; and cp. ver. 5 with Isa. xxxv. 5; lxi. 1–3 (on which see notes).

3 He that should come. Lit., "He that cometh" (R.V.): a designation of the Messiah, which John the Baptist had adopted (see iii. 11), derived probably from Psa. cxviii. 26, on which see note. It is hardly to be wondered at that John, in his prison, had misgivings whether Jesus, whom he had baptised, was indeed the Messiah. There were no signs of a kingdom being established, such as he no doubt had hoped for. And even though his ideal of a kingdom and of the Messiah was a higher one than that of others of his time (Matt. iii. 11, 12; John i. 29) he saw no evidence of his ideal being fulfilled. "Jesus was neither a Reformer nor a Victim: could he be the Messiah?" (David Smith: *In the Days of His Flesh*, p. 225).

4 those things which ye do hear and see. See Luke vii. 21; where the miracles performed in the presence of John's disciples are recorded. The preaching of the gospel to the poor is, equally with miracle, a sign of the Christ. It is the spiritual manifestation of the Divine power which miracles reveal in the physical realm. This was the answer of our Lord.

6 blessed is he. That is, Happy is he to whom I shall not prove a stumbling-block; whom my condition and my deeds do not lead to reject me. There seems a gentle reference here to the faltering faith of the Baptist. Yet the tribute to this Baptist which follows shows in what high place the Saviour held him.

7 as they departed. "The world praises a man in his presence, blames him in his absence. Divine truth does the contrary" (*Bengel*).

A reed shaken with the wind? This illustration is derived from the reeds which fringed the banks of the Jordan, where John baptised. Did you go to see a feeble, inconstant man? or an effeminate courtier and flatterer (ver. 8)? Nay, you know you went to see a stern and inflexible prophet, one who is in truth superior to all the prophets: for he is the "Messenger" of the Messiah, the predicted Elijah (ver. 14; cp. Mal. iii. 1; iv. 5). In speaking thus highly of John, to whom He had sent a gentle reproof, our Lord shows how He can at once rebuke the failings of His people, and yet approve their works of faith and love.

11 a greater than John the Baptist. John, indeed, as living nearest to the reign of Messiah, was superior to all his predecessors; but the actual subjects of this reign possess still higher privileges: cp. Zech. xii. 8. For "least," read, as in the Greek, "of lower rank" (*Weymouth*).

12 the kingdom of heaven suffereth violence. "It is not your thoughtless, fickle, reed-hunting, sight-seeing people, that get the kingdom, but eager, earnest, 'violent' men" (Monro Gibson in *Expositor's Bible*).

13 all the prophets and the law prophesied. That is, The whole of the Old Testament dispensation was prophetic. John came to introduce the kingdom to which every inspired utterance and ordinance had pointed.

14 if ye will receive [it]. Rather, as R.V., "if ye are willing to receive *it*" or "*him.*"

15 He that hath ears to hear. A call to candid and thoughtful attention. Listen and think; be willing to receive (ver. 14) what I say. John is Elijah: and if so, am not I, to whom both he and these miracles bear witness, the Lord? (Mal. iii. 1; iv. 5).

16 like unto children. The men of this time are like capricious children. John, the preacher of repentance, lived as an ascetic, and called you to mourn for your sins. I, the messenger of salvation, join you in your social enjoyments (John ii. 1–10), and invite you to cheerfulness: but you reject us both. Those, however, who are taught by Divine wisdom recognise and honour its varied exhibition in John and in myself, and receive us both.

markets. The places of public resort.

18 He hath a devil (demon). Referring to the solitary and melancholy habits of demoniacs: see Mark v. 5.

19 a friend of publicans and sinners. Making His condescension and kindness an occasion of reproach. He was a friend, not to their vices, but to their souls: cp. Luke xv. 1, 2.

justified of her children. Heavenly wisdom is recognised and vindicated by all the truly wise. The reading, "by her works," is preferred by R.V. In Luke vii. 35, the word "children" is unquestionably used.

21 Chorazin. Chorazin is placed by Jerome on the Lake of Tiberias, about two miles from Capernaum; and Bethsaida (the birthplace of Peter, Andrew, and Philip) was probably near it. Both seem to have been small towns, and their sites have not yet been identified.

Tyre and Sidon. Respecting Tyre and Sidon, see notes on 2 Sam. v. 11; Isa. xxiii.; Ezek. xxvi.–xxviii.

they would have repented. That some nations and individuals enjoy greater advantages for their well-being than others is an obvious fact in the history of mankind. not a difficulty peculiar to Christianity. The Bible does not profess to explain it, leaving it among "the secret things" which "belong to the Lord." The essential thing is that men will be judged according to their opportunities.

23 brought down to hell. "Heaven" and "hell" (Hades) here stand in contrast with each other: the former denoting a high state of privilege, the latter an extreme of woe and desolation: cp. Isa. xiv. 15. Capernaum had been especially favoured as the chosen residence of Jesus, and the scene of many of His miracles and discourses. The interrogative reading adopted in R.V. is sustained by the best authorities, and gives a vivid sense to the passage.

25 Jesus answered. The word "answered" in the Gospels often means to speak in consequence of what has preceded. Our Lord, meditating on the truths which He had just uttered, breaks forth into an acknowledgment of His Father's sovereign wisdom and goodness in adapting and applying the gospel not to those who rely upon their own wisdom, but to those who, with child-like simplicity, receive His instructions.

because Thou hast hid. The subject of our Lord's praise and thanksgiving is not the failure of the wise of this world to obtain the blessings of His kingdom, but the bestowment of those blessings upon the gentle and humble.

26 it seemed good. More emphatic in the original: "It was Thy good pleasure": cp. 1 Cor. i. 21; 2 Thess. i. 11.

27 no man knoweth the Son. The whole course of thought is analogous to that in John i. 18. "The Son" reveals the unseen Father, and the revelation is one of "grace and truth" (17). So He says, "Come unto me, and I will give you rest."

will reveal [Him]. Rather, as R.V., "willeth to reveal Him."

28 Come unto me. No merely human teacher could utter such a claim as this, and be thought sane.

that labour and are heavy laden. "You toiling and burdened ones" (*Weymouth*).

I will give. Emphatic in original. "And *I* will give."

29 I am meek, etc. "Gentle," not austere, so as to repel; and "lowly," coming down to every sufferer's need. The two form a complete expression of *sympathy*.

CHAPTER XII

1 At that time. On the exact time of this occurrence, see Luke vi. 1.

began to pluck the ears of corn. The law allowed this on other days (see Deut. xxiii. 25); but it was supposed to be forbidden on the sabbath. The act was regarded as a kind of reaping; and the rubbing in the hands (Luke) as threshing.

4 the house of God. The tabernacle at Nob. Before the erection of the Temple this appellation was given to the place of the Ark: see Psa. xxiii. 6.

did eat the shewbread. See Exod. xxv. 30; 1 Sam. xxi. 5, 6, and notes. Our Lord urges first the plea of necessity. His disciples, like David and his followers, were in want of food. David's visit to Nob was on the sabbath: see Lev. xxiv. 5–9.

5 are blameless. The priests were more busily engaged on the sabbath than on other days (see Numb. xxviii. 9, 10). But they were blameless, because they laboured in the service of the Temple. Much more the disciples of Jesus, who were engaged in a "greater" service (see ver. 6). The word rendered "profane," means simply to put to common or secular use.

6 greater than the Temple. The Temple service was greater than the obligation to sabbath-rest: here is One greater than the Temple, much more then supreme over the sabbath (8).

7 what this meaneth. See Hos. vi. 6, and note. In ix. 13, the same words are quoted in reproof of another phase of punctilious ritualism; here we find a second form, in which it shows its hostility to true charity, which is the essence of all acceptable worship. But if, for "sacrifices," the sabbath-rest might be violated, how much more in "mercy" to men's necessities and sufferings! Matthew alone reports this argument founded upon the Temple service. In John v. 17, Jesus takes even higher ground.

8 Lord even of the sabbath day. Mark (ii. 27) records the statement on which this remark is immediately founded. The sabbath and other observances are not an *end*, but means appointed to promote man's good. The Son of man, to whom all things connected with this great end have been entrusted (xi. 27), can therefore dispense with them if He pleases.

9 when He was departed. "On another sabbath" (Luke vi. 6). The two narratives are joined by both evangelists, because of their bearing on the sabbath question.

11 that shall have one sheep. "A single sheep." This simple act of humanity was not then forbidden by the Jewish teachers, though it was afterwards prohibited in the Talmud, as if to confute our Lord's argument. Matthew alone narrates the appeal here made to the Jews respecting their own customs.

12 to do well. "Not to do good when you can is to do evil; and this is the worst violation of the sabbath" (*Bengel*). See Mark iii. 4; Luke vi. 9, where doing evil is expressly stated as the alternative.

13 And he stretched it forth. Believing that He who gave the command would give the power to obey it, the sufferer made the attempt, and in this act of faith the strength was given. By healing the man without any outward action, our Lord made the miraculous power unquestionable, and deprived the Pharisees of all legal ground of objection.

14 held a council. Rather, "took counsel," as R.V.

how they might destroy Him. "They were filled with madness" (Luke vi. 11). From this time they began to plot His destruction: see Mark iii. 6, and note.

15 He healed them all. That is, all the sick whom they brought to Him.

17 spoken by Esaias. See notes on Isa. xli. 8; xlii. 1–7. The quotation is a free rendering of the Hebrew. How forcible the contrast between the gentle and benign "Servant of God" and His cruel and bigoted enemies (14)!

24 by Beelzebub (Beelzebul). See note on ch. x. 25. The argument of the Pharisees was that He who could control the demons must have an understanding with the demons' master. This argument was whispered among the people, the Pharisees themselves not having the audacity to state it openly. But Jesus "knew their thoughts," and effectually replied.

27 your children. Your "disciples," or adherents (see note on 1 Sam. x. 12). Whether they really could do this, or only pretended to do it, the argument is equally valid. Your own pupils profess to cast out devils. Why ascribe my power to Beelzebul more than theirs? Nay, my power is more clearly Divine: for my success is obtained, not in some doubtful instances, and by the use of exorcisms: it is simple, instantaneous, and complete in the most desperate cases. It is the "Spirit" of God; such a display of His power as shows that "the reign of God is already upon you" (28), taking you by surprise.

29 Or else. It follows, then, that I come to bind the strong, and to take his possession from him; a contest so urgent (ver. 30) as to allow no neutrality. This conflict, in which all must take one side or the other, is still going on in the world; and all those who do not take part with Christ are really taking part with Satan.

31 blasphemy against the [Holy] Ghost. To gain a clear idea of our Lord's meaning, observe, 1. That among the spectators on this occasion there might be many who denied the Divine mission of "the Son of man," but who yet might yield to further evidence; while there were others, acute and well-informed, who were determined not to believe, and malignantly ascribed to Satanic power works which showed the presence of "the Spirit of God" (28). To these latter our Lord evidently refers; though He may, perhaps, be understood rather as warning them against a sin to which they were very closely approaching, than as declaring that they had already committed it. 2. That the sin which shall not be forgiven is not so much the particular act which gave occasion to the remark, as a state of heart, the result of a long course of wilful and malignant opposition to known truth. 3. That unpardonable sin is not confined to the attributing Christ's miracles to Satanic agency (cp. Heb. vi. 4–6); nor is it the only sin which ensures final destruction. 4. At the same time, it is certain that every sin of which men truly repent will be pardoned. No *forgiveness*, therefore, means no *repentance*.

32 the [world] to come. "The world to come" was a Jewish phrase for the expected reign of the Messiah. If this be the sense in which it is here used by our Lord, the meaning is, That blessed period which brings pardon and deliverance to others brings none to him; he is irremediably lost.

33 make. In your thoughts: "represent." "Grant the tree to be good" (*Weymouth*).

the tree is known by his fruit. If the fruit is good, the tree must be good. My good works must, then, have a good origin, as your evil works must have a bad one: see ver. 34.

34 O generation (brood) **of vipers.** See iii. 7, and note. The merciful Saviour does not shrink from using the same strong expressions which had been used by the appointed preacher of repentance. The phrase, "brood of vipers," is peculiarly appropriate to the Pharisees; for "the poison of asps was under their lips"; and their "reckless words" of malignant slander hindered the people from believing in the Saviour (xxiii. 13).

36 every idle word. "Idle" means literally "without deed"—doing nothing. Not only premeditated speeches, but careless, unconsidered words will be judged: for they are spoken "out of the abundance of the heart," and are therefore a true index of its real state; and, as such, must be of great account in the judgement: cp. Jas. iii. 2–12.

38 we would see a sign from Thee. The Jews held that only a "sign from heaven" could distinguish a messenger of Jehovah from those who wrought miracles by Satanic agency: alleging that such signs were given by their ancient prophets (Exod. xvi. 4; 1 Sam. xii 16–18; Isa. xxxviii. 8; see also Dan. vii. 13). Hence their repeated demands from our Lord (see xvi. 1). His life was, indeed, remarkable for such signs (see ii. 2; iii. 16, 17; John xii. 28); but He would not sanction superstitious notions, or gratify a cavilling temper; and He therefore refused the demand.

39 adulterous. According to Old Testament usage, this word signifies *faithless to God*, whose people the Jews professed to be: see Exod. xxxiv. 15.

the sign of the prophet Jonas. You, who attribute my miracles to Satan, ask a sign. I will give *you* none. If you want one, look to Jonah in your own Scriptures. His entombment in the fish and his resurrection (40) were "a sign" to the Ninevites (Luke xi. 30): so my entombment and resurrection will be a sign, more wonderful and conclusive, to this generation; who, however, will disbelieve it, and incur a heavier condemnation (41).

40 whale's belly. The word is generic, meaning any large sea-monster. See Jonah i. 17, note.

three days and three nights. The Jews spoke of "a day and a night" as a unit, which, in calculating days, they did not divide into parts. Hence three times "a day and a night" might only be one whole day with parts of two others: cp. Matt. xvi. 21, with Mark viii. 31; 2 Chron. x. 5, with x. 12; Esther iv. 16, with v. 1.

the heart of the earth. The language of Jonah (ii. 3) is. "Thou hadst cast me . . . in the midst (lit., *heart*) of the seas." Our Lord is speaking of His entombment.

41 shall rise in judgement. Rather, as R.V., "shall stand up in the judgement."

42 queen of the south. "Of Sheba": see note on 1 Kings x. 1.

43 he walketh through dry places. The melancholy disposition of the demoniacs, leading them to wander restlessly through desert (lit., "waterless") places, might have suggested the popular notion that the demons themselves had a preference for the wilderness, and were connected with the wild howling creatures which dwelt there. The special point is, the danger of resting in a partial reformation such as had been the conversion of the Jews from their old idolatrous habits to the strict outward worship of the only true God. Where vital godliness does not take the place of confuted error or forsaken sin, the heart is liable to become the prey of errors and sins even worse than the former.

46 His brethren stood without. They "could not come at Him for the press" (Luke viii. 19); which was so great, "that He and His disciples could not so much as eat bread" (Mark iii. 20). They came "to lay hold on Him" (Mark iii. 21); for some of them did not "believe on Him" (John vii. 5), but thought He was "beside Himself."

49 my brethren. We never find any of our Lord's disciples addressing Him as "brother," either before or after His resurrection.

50 the same is my brother, and sister, and mother. Those who most resemble Christ in His love and devotedness to His Father, are truly the most nearly related to Him, and are the objects of His dearest affection.

CHAPTER XIII

1 by the sea. The Lake of Tiberias.

3 parables. "In figurative language" (*Weymouth*). A parable is an illustration of a religious truth by a narrative taken from ordinary life. These narratives are generally fictitious; but in a few instances they relate to real events, which, when so used, are said to be "allegorised": see Gal. iv. 24. In some of our Lord's parables there is a transition made at the close from the image to the thing represented: see xxiv. 51; John x., xv.; and cp. Isa. v. 7. Rightly to understand them, we must look for the central point of the comparison; taking care not to give too much importance to minute particulars, which serve only to complete the story. The seven parables in this chapter illustrate the nature of "the kingdom of God" in its inward principles and its external manifestations.

3–9. THE SOWER. This parable illustrates the different reception which men give to the word of God; as seen in the case of: 1. Those upon whom, through the hardening power of carelessness or aversion, the truth made no impression; 2. The fickle multitude of hearers; 3. Those whose assent to the truth was made inoperative through worldly interests; and 4. The disciples who heartily welcome and faithfully use it. Of the influences which have prepared the "good ground," our Lord here says nothing, His object being to awaken a sense of responsibility as to "how we hear"; for which reason He adds the admonitions preserved in Mark iv. 21–25; Luke viii. 16–18. The main lesson of the story is, however, the encouragement to the Christian worker (vers. 8, 23).

3 a sower. "The sower" (R.V.).

4 by the way side. Lying exposed on the beaten path.

5 stony places. Rocky places; where, the soil being shallow, the plant soon vegetates, but quickly withers.

7 among thorns. Among the seeds and roots of thorny plants, unsuspected beneath the soil.

These are most various and luxuriant in Palestine: see Prov. xxiv. 30, 31 (Stanley, *Sinai and Palestine*, p. 426).

8 a hundredfold. Tennyson (*In Memoriam*) speaks of Nature:

"And finding that of fifty seeds
She often brings but one to bear."

But if that one produces one hundred, sixty, or even thirty fold, the loss is abundantly compensated.

11 mysteries. Or, "secrets." This word in the New Testament means truths which have heretofore been hidden, but are now being revealed. Thus the calling of the Gentiles was "a mystery" (Eph. iii. 3, 4, 9); so the conversion of the Jews (Rom. xi. 25), and the doctrine of the resurrection (1 Cor. xv. 51): see note, 1 Tim. iii. 16.

12 to him shall be given. He who rightly uses the gifts which God has committed to him will be counted worthy of a higher trust; but he who neglects his advantages will be deprived of them; and will be condemned as an unprofitable servant: cp. xxv. 29.

14 is fulfilled the prophecy of Esaias. Lit., "is being completely fulfilled," a partial fulfilment having taken place among contemporaries of the prophet. The passage is quoted from the Septuagint version of Isa. vi. 9, 10; on which see note. The words find a fulfilment wherever men persist in rejecting Divine truth, and are left by God to the spiritual dulness and insensibility which result from such a course. This is the fundamental idea in all the passages in the New Testament in which this prophecy is alluded to (see John xii. 40; Acts xxviii. 26).

19 [then] cometh the wicked [one]. Indifference and neglect deaden the perception of truth; and Satan is ever ready to "take away" from the memory, sometimes by the most trivial suggestions, that which has been so ill-appreciated.

20 anon (immediately) **with joy receiveth it.** A man may be easily excited by the novelty of the gospel, or by its wonderful and attractive disclosures; but he may be destitute of any deep conviction or earnest purpose.

21 he is offended. See note on xi. 6. "By and by," like "anon," means in Old English, "immediately" (R.V., "straightway he stumbleth"). The same Greek word (*euthus*) is used in both vers. 20 and 21.

22 among the thorns. A peculiarly sad case. The soil is good and the growth is genuine: the hindrance is not from within, but from without.

the deceitfulness of riches. The mind may be diverted from religion by anxious cares about earthly things, as well as by the possession of wealth; but the latter is peculiarly "deceitful." Men still are under the deception that wealth in itself brings happiness.

23 good ground. Neither hard (19), nor shallow (20, 21), nor weedy (22): prepared, therefore, by previous culture. Such is "an honest and good heart" (Luke), which is ready to "understand" "and receive" (Mark) the word, to "keep it, and to bring forth fruit with patience" (Luke), in a measure proportioned to the faithfulness with which it is used.

24–30. THE TARES. Whilst, through the gospel, God is multiplying His servants in the world, Satan is increasing the number of false professors (24, 25). Human reason suggests the immediate extirpation of these (26–28); but God has determined, for the sake of His own people, that this mixed state shall continue till the final judgement (29, 30); when the wicked shall be completely separated and punished, and the righteous shall enjoy unalloyed happiness and glory: cp. 36–43.

25 while men slept. That is, in the night (see Job xxxiii. 15).

tares. Probably our darnel, *lolium temulentum;* a noxious weed, which grows also in Palestine, and which on first sprouting from the ground resembles wheat.

30 grow together. "Very commonly the roots of the two are so intertwined that it is impossible to separate them without plucking up both. Both therefore must be left to grow together until the time of harvest."—*The Land and the Book*, p. 420.

30–33. THE MUSTARD SEED; and THE LEAVEN. The parable of the mustard seed probably refers to the diffusive power which God has given to the truth; that of the leaven to its assimilating influence upon the world in which He has placed it. Both may also be applied to individual piety in its gradual development and its all-pervading influence upon the whole man.

31 mustard seed. Some plants producing mustard attain a large size in hot climates; particularly the *khardal*, or *salvadora persica*, which is found in Syria, Arabia, and India, and which, springing from a very small seed, becomes a large and spreading tree.

32 is the least of all seeds. The simple teaching of the despised Man of Nazareth, preached by a few obscure persons, has extended its influence through the world.

33 leaven. Here again is the encouragement of those who believe and spread the gospel. "Jesus knew that the living force of truth in each single heart must diffuse itself, and that, as soul after soul was won, it would silently revolutionise the world, and leaven all humanity" (*Geikie*).

three measures (seahs). Equal to one ephah, the quantity commonly used for one baking ($4\frac{1}{2}$ gallons, English measure): see Gen. xviii. 6; Judges vi. 19.

35 that it might be fulfilled. See note on Psa. lxxviii. 2, ascribed to Asaph. The quotation is made, not from the LXX, but directly from the Hebrew.

38 the field is the world. Now about to have the "children of the kingdom" sown in it, as "good seed."

40 the end of this world. Lit., "the consummation of the age" (R.V. marg.). This may refer to the close of the Jewish dispensation in A.D. 70, or to the end of the Christian era; or to both. In ver. 38 the word for "world" is different.

41 all things that offend ("all stumbling-blocks"). All persons and things whose influence is sinful and injurious.

44–46. THE HIDDEN TREASURE; and THE PEARL OF GREAT PRICE (only in Matthew). The central thought of these two parables is the preciousness of the Gospel. "The pearl of great price" is generally understood to be the kingdom of God, and the "merchant" the sinner seeking it. But it may be interpreted differently, understanding it to teach the preciousness of the human soul, God seeking the goodly pearls, and for man's salvation giving His only begotten Son.

44 treasure hid in a field. In the despotic and frequently disturbed countries of the East, treasure was often buried, and so lost, through the absence or death of the owner, until accidentally found by the husbandman.

he hideth. Lest any one should deprive him of

it. The only point of this man's conduct proposed for imitation is his anxious solicitude to secure, by any trouble and at any cost, the treasure he has found.

buyeth that field. So as to make the treasure legally his own. The purchase of the field is mentioned only as a necessary incident in the parable.

47–50. THE DRAG-NET (only in Matthew). The function of the net is to "gather" (ver. 47). Here, again, is the redemptive work of the Gospel.

47 net. The word in the original (*sagēnē* from which *seine* is derived) means a large drag-net, the ends of which are carried out far apart, then drawn together. It occurs only here in the New Testament.

52 every scribe. As a scribe "well instructed" in the law is qualified to teach it; so you, "if you understand these things," will be prepared, like a competent master of a house, to give to all who look to you for supplies "things new and old" (Song of Songs vii. 13)—truths of every kind, adapted to the need of each.

54 into His own country. On this visit to Nazareth see note on Luke iv. 16.

55 His brethren. It is an ancient and prevalent opinion (derived probably from the dogma of the perpetual virginity of Mary) that these persons were either cousins of our Lord, or children of Joseph by a former wife. But the evidence of Scripture seems to favour the belief that they were Mary's younger children. In every place, except one, where they are mentioned in the Gospels (see Mark iii. 31; Luke viii. 19; John ii. 12, etc.), they are found associated with her; so that it is most natural to conclude that she was their mother. It appears that they did not believe in Jesus (John vii. 5) for some time after the appointment of the apostles; and therefore they could not be of the number of the Twelve; from whom indeed they are particularly distinguished when, at a later period, they are found in company with them (Acts i. 14). They must therefore not be confounded with the sons of Alphæus, although bearing the same names. It is also worthy of notice, that the force of our Lord's declaration in xii. 50 depends greatly upon the fact of those who are there called His "brethren" standing in the nearest possible relation to Him. That the sons of Alphæus, like our Lord's brethren, were named James, Joses, and Judas, proves nothing, these names being among the most common in Jewish families. It is sometimes argued, very plausibly, that Christ would not have committed His mother to John if she had children of her own. But these children did not believe on Him at the time, and were therefore passed by.

58 because of their unbelief. See Mark vi. 5.

CHAPTER XIV

1–12. See notes on Mark vi. 14–29.

1 At that time. That is, while the Twelve were on their journey "two and two" (Mark vi. 7).

the fame of Jesus. "The report concerning Jesus" (R.V.).

2 mighty works do show forth themselves in Him. Lit., as R.V., "These ('the') powers work in Him."

8 charger. Dish, trencher.

15 when it was evening. This was the first evening; extending from three o'clock, "when the day began to wear away" (Luke), till sunset, when the second evening (23) commenced, continuing till it was "dark" (John). On this miracle see John vi., and notes. It is the only miracle narrated by all four evangelists.

17 they say. Andrew, Peter's brother, was spokesman for the rest; John vi. 8.

19 He blessed. Or, "gave thanks" (see John vi. 11), according to Jewish custom, for the provision. A truly thankful heart seeks and gains a blessing with the gift.

21 beside women and children. All the four evangelists say that the five thousand were *men;* and Matthew particularly mentions that women and children were there too.

22 constrained His disciples. The disciples may have been inclined to join the multitude in their wish to "make Him king" (John vi. 15). He therefore "immediately" dismissed the people, and "constrained" the disciples also to leave the place.

a ship. Rather, "the boat" (which belonged to the disciples). So ver. 24 (and xv. 39) "the mountain" (which overhung the lake).

23 when the evening was come. See note on ver. 15. "Tossed," more accurately "distressed," as R.V.

25 the fourth watch. On the Jewish watches, see note on Psa. lxiii. 6. The Romans had introduced into Palestine their division of the night into four parts, which are all mentioned in Mark xiii. 35. The fourth watch lasted, at this time of the year, from about 3 to 6 a.m.

26 a spirit. Rather, "an apparition" (R.V.); or "phantom."

29 He said, Come. Our Lord encourages Peter to make this trial of his confidence; and by the result teaches him that the higher enterprises of faith can be successful only when the mind is simply fixed on the power and will of Christ, disregarding all appearances of difficulty and danger. This incident of Peter's walking on the water is narrated only by Matthew.

31 wherefore didst thou doubt? Our Lord did not reprove Peter's bold proposal, nor his prompt compliance with the permission to "come," but the weakness of his sincere though imperfect faith.

32 ceased. Lit., "grew weary": sank to rest, as though exhausted.

34 the land of Gennesaret. "Gennesaret" is probably a corruption of Cinnereth; a district on the west of the lake.

36 hem. "Fringe," "border," (R.V.), or "tassel," the distinguishing mark of the Israelite (Numb. xv. 38, 39).

CHAPTER XV

1–20. See Mark vii., and notes.

5 But ye say, etc. Rather, "Whoever shall say to his father or mother, That by which thou mightest have derived benefit from me is a gift" [consecrated to God]: cp. Mark vii. 11, 12. This law was bad in principle; for it allowed religious gifts to interfere with the discharge of other obligations; but in practice it became still worse; because it was held that anything so consecrated might still be used for the man's own advantage, though it was sacrilege to apply it to the good of others.

11 Not that which goeth into the mouth, etc. See notes on Mark vii. 14–19.

12 offended. "Shocked" (*Weymouth*).

15 this parable. The figurative expression in ver. 11. That, after all their previous lessons, the disciples did not even "yet understand" this, might result from their strong Jewish views respecting the distinction between clean and unclean meats: see Acts x. 14.

21 coasts. That is, "parts"; so xvi. 13; in ver. 22 "borders" (R.V.).

22 a woman of Canaan. The Phœnicians, a branch of the Canaanites (see Gen. x. 15, 19), had received among them a large admixture of Greeks as conquerors and settlers; and they now belonged to the Roman province of Syria. Hence this woman is called a Canaanite, a Greek, and a Syrophœnician: see Mark vii. 26.

24 of the house of Israel. See x. 5, 6 (Ezek. xxxiv. 6). Such was the purpose of our Lord's personal ministry; yet even this was occasionally broken by such incidents as this. The fountain sealed sometimes broke its banks, in token of the rich flood of grace which should follow (*Alford*).

26 dogs ("the little dogs").

27 Truth, Lord; yet the dogs, etc. Rather, as R.V., "Yea, Lord, for even the dogs eat," etc. Saidst Thou "dogs"? I accept the name, for the dogs, too, have their portion of the meat, "the crumbs which fall" from the table. It is enough for me if I have but their portion.

29 nigh unto the sea of Galilee. Into the district of Decapolis, on the eastern side of the lake, where He cured a deaf man (Mark vii. 31–37).

a mountain. Rather, as R.V., "the mountain"; the highland district.

32 I will not. R.V. more exactly, "I would not," *i.e.*, "I am unwilling to do so."

33 Whence . . . so much bread. The disciples may have forgotten the former miracle (xiv. 15–21; cp. xvi. 9, 10), or perhaps they wondered whether it would be repeated.

37 broken meat. Rather, "broken pieces" (R.V.); *i.e.*, not the crumbs, but the portions prepared for eating.

seven baskets. The Greek word for "basket," used by both evangelists who record this miracle, differs from that used by all four in narrating the former feeding of a multitude. The word used here means a pannier or hamper, sometimes large enough to hold a man; as in Acts ix. 25; the only other place in the N.T. where the same Greek word is used.

38 four thousand men. The people were fewer, and the loaves were more upon this occasion, than upon the former.

39 the coasts of Magdala. Magdala (or Magadan: see var. read.) and Dalmanutha (Mark viii. 10) were probably neighbouring villages on the south-east of the Lake.

CHAPTER XVI

1 The Pharisees also with the Sadducees. These sects were in general strongly opposed to each other: their separate attacks upon our Lord are often noticed, but now they make common cause against Him.

a sign from heaven. See xii. 38, and notes.

3 lowring. Lit., "appearing gloomy." The word is elsewhere used (only), Mark x. 22, "sad." From "glooming" comes the word *gloaming* (*Dr. Morrison*).

the signs of the times? The indications that these are the times of the Messiah.

6 leaven of the Pharisees and of the Sadducees. See note on iii. 7. Mark, instead of the Sadducees, mentions "the leaven of Herod"; probably because most of the political party of Herod ("the Herodians") were Sadducees in religious opinions. Whatever differences there were between these parties, they were all tainted with hypocrisy and worldliness. Formalism and scepticism flourish side by side.

7 because we have taken no bread. They had with them but one loaf (see Mark viii. 14). They seem to have doubted whether our Lord could be referring to this circumstance; but they were at a loss to find any other meaning.

13 Cæsarea Philippi. This place was near, if not on the same spot, as the ancient city Dan (Judges xviii. 27–29) It was formerly called Paneas; but was enlarged and embellished by Philip the tetrach, who named it "Cæsarea"; to which "Philippi" was added to distinguish it from other places of the same name, especially from the Cæsarea on the west coast. It lay in the extreme north of Palestine, near one of the sources of the Jordan. It is now a miserable village called *Banias.*

17 Simon Bar-jona. "Bar-jona," *i.e.*, "Son of John."

18 Peter. "Petros," in Aramaic *Kepha,* signifying "a rock": see next note. This designation had been prophetically given by our Lord to Simon, when he first became a disciple: see John i. 42.

upon this rock. Much controversy has arisen over the meaning of this passage. But the natural and simple interpretation appears to be that, while Christ Himself is the chief corner-stone, Peter, like other apostles, became a foundation-stone of the Church (Eph. ii. 20; 1 Pet. ii. 4). Another possible interpretation is that "this rock" was Peter's confession (ver. 16).

church. The only mention of the Church in the Gospels (except xviii. 17; where see note). The word, *ecclesia,* stands here for the whole body of believers throughout the world.

hell. Lit., "Hades," corresponding with Heb. "Sheol"; "the world of the dead," which insatiably swallows up all the might and glory of the earth (see Isa. xiv. 3–20). The "gates" were the place of council, and the most strongly fortified parts of ancient cities. Hence the emblem is that of governmental or military power (compare the phrase, the Sublime *Porte,* as used formerly of the Ottoman court). The sense is, Even that power which is able to destroy all other things, shall not prevail against my Church.

19 the keys. A key is a badge of power and authority: see Isa. xxii. 22, and note; Rev. i. 18; iii. 7. And the terms "bind" and "loose" were frequently used by the Jews in the sense of "permit" and "forbid," as applied to the authoritative teaching of their Rabbis. Peter, on account of his earnest and prompt avowal, is the first to receive that authority, which was afterwards (xviii. 18; John xx. 23) given also to his colleagues; and for the exercise of which they were endued with power from on high. Of him, too, God made choice that he "should open the door of faith to the Gentiles" as well as to the Jews (Acts ii.; x.).

20 tell no man. Though the apostles were destined to be authoritative teachers of this great truth, the time for its public promulgation was not yet come; nor were they as yet fully prepared for the work.

21 the elders and chief priests and scribes. See note on ii. 4.

22 to rebuke Him. Opposing what He had said; as if it were not true. The phrase, "Be it far from Thee," is in the original, "[God be] merciful to

Thee!" a Jewish form of deprecation: followed by the strongest negative, "This shall never be unto Thee," R.V.

23 Get thee behind me. This is the very rebuke which our Lord had addressed to the tempter (iv. 10). Simon is "a rock" while he sustains the truth: a "stumbling-block" when he endeavours to impede the Saviour's purpose.

thou savourest ("mindest," R.V.). Thy views and feelings do not accord with God's, but with men's.

24 will come. "Wishes to come," etc. (R.V., "would come"); so in the first, but not in the second clause of ver. 25. On vers. 24, 25, see notes on x. 38, 39.

28 coming into His kingdom. In the display of His royal power. Some apply this to the outpouring of the Holy Spirit, and the rapid triumphs of the gospel, recorded in the Acts of the Apostles; others, to the approaching overthrow of the Jewish state. The connexion of our Lord's promise with the Transfiguration, was that the latter was an earnest of the glory to be fully revealed in the "kingdom."

CHAPTER XVII

1 after six days. Probably six *whole* days, with parts of two others; making, according to Luke, "about eight days." The emphasis is in the close connexion of the Transfiguration with the preceding sayings. On the Transfiguration, see notes, Luke ix. 28–36.

a high mountain apart. The word "apart" does not describe the *mountain* as isolated, but intimates the withdrawal of Christ with His three disciples from the rest (Mark ix. 2). The mountain was probably Hermon.

11 Elias truly shall first come. The shortness and secrecy of Elijah's visit on this occasion surprised the disciples, who expected him to "restore all things"; and they were further astonished by the mention of "the rising from the dead" (Mark ix. 10). Our Lord corrects their error as to the person of the forerunner, and derives from John's death a fresh intimation of His own.

restore all things. John the Baptist, like Elijah, was only a *reformer*, having no new revelation to communicate.

14–21. See Mark ix. 14–29, and notes.

20 nothing shall be impossible. See Mark xi. 24, and note.

22, 23. See Mark ix. 30–32, and notes.

24 tribute. Rather, "the didrachma"; the offering of a half-shekel each, which the Jews paid for the support of the Temple (Exod. xxx. 12–16).

25 prevented him. "Anticipated him," by speaking first on the subject ("spake first to him," R.V.). Cp. the use of "prevent" in the Prayer-book: "Prevent us, O Lord."

custom ("toll," R.V.) **or tribute.** The former word denotes a tax on goods, the latter on persons.

26 Then are the children free. Upon this reasoning, our Lord, as Son of God, was under no obligation to contribute to the Temple, because it was His Father's house, and therefore His own. But He waives His right, lest those who do not recognise this truth should think that He disregards the worship of God. How gladly His enemies would have used such a pretext against Him is seen in xxvi. 59–63.

27 a piece of money. Lit., "a stater"; a Roman coin worth a shekel (R.V.), and therefore enough for two persons.

CHAPTER XVIII

1–9. See notes on Mark ix. 33–50.

3 converted. "Except ye turn," *i.e.*, change your attitude and conduct.

7 offences. "Causes of stumbling"; hindrances.

9 hell fire. "Gehenna of fire," see v. 22, note.

10 their angels. Guardian angels.

12–14. This parable occurs, with a different application, in Luke xv. 4–6; see notes thereon. Here it is designed to show the solicitude with which God watches over His children, so that none of them may perish (14).

15 thou hast gained thy brother. This kind, manly, and wise manner of treating injuries, so different from any that is generally adopted, would prevent the growth of many misunderstandings and quarrels.

17 the church. Our Lord shows, in ver. 19, that by "the church" He means those who are "gathered together in His name"; the "congregation" of believers. The words do not prescribe any particular method of organisation or of action.

18 Whatsoever ye shall bind. See note on xvi. 19.

20 in my name. By my authority, and for my service and honour. The subsequent promise shows that He possesses Divine attributes, and bestows Divine influence. The Rabbis had a similar saying, "that where two or three of their doctors were sitting in judgement, the Shekinah was in the midst of them" (*Lightfoot*).

21 till seven times? The Rabbis inferred from Amos i. 3 that forgiveness was to be granted three times. "Seven" seems to be here used by Peter for a large but yet limited number. Our Lord's reply is evidently designed to take away all limits: cp. Gen. iv. 24; Prov. xxiv. 16. The following parable shows that the sins which God forgives us are incalculably more and greater than we are ever called to forgive others.

24 one was brought unto him. One of his chief ministers. Ten thousand talents evidently stands for an immense amount (more than $20,000,000), representing the exceeding greatness of our debt to God.

25 commanded him to be sold. This was a practice of many ancient nations: see Lev. xxv. 39–41; 2 Kings iv. 1; Amos ii. 6.

28 a hundred pence. The Roman "penny," or denarius, being worth about 9½*d.*, a "hundred pence" would be less than £4, a very insignificant sum compared with the other. So trifling are the offences which any one can commit against us, compared with our sins against God!

34 the tormentors. Probably, "the gaolers" (*Liddell and Scott*).

35 So likewise. "An unforgiving man is no son of God" (*David Smith*). Cp. Eph. iv. 32; v. 1, 2; Jas. ii. 13.

CHAPTER XIX

1 beyond Jordan. The evangelist here mentions only the two extremities of a period which He passes over. Our Lord appears to have "departed from Galilee," through Samaria, to Jerusalem; where He attended the Feasts of Tabernacles and of the Dedication; and then to have gone "beyond Jordan," where we now find Him.

3 tempting Him. Whatever answer our Lord might give to this question would displease some: for the Jewish teachers were divided in opinion;

one party (the school of Hillel) holding that anything which displeased a husband gave him a right to divorce his wife; and the other (the school of Shammai) limiting the right to the case of adultery. Both appealed to Deut. xxiv. 1; which, however, was not a "command" to divorce, but rather a restriction upon a practice then prevailing: see notes on Exod. xx. 23; Deut. xxiv. 1. Our Lord, after pointing out the purpose of this national and temporary regulation, refers to the original law (see Gen. ii. 24, and notes); which He traces to the primary creation of the race (see Gen. i. 27), when "He who made them at the beginning made them a male and a female, and said, On this account (*i.e.*, because they were so made) a man shall leave his father and mother, and cleave to his wife, and the two shall become one flesh." Nothing, therefore, but the sin which does in itself vitiate the bond can justify their separation.

11 this saying. That is, "this saying of *yours*," that "it is not good to marry." Our Lord's remarks in vers. 11, 12 plainly show that celibacy is so far from being superior to the married state, that it is rather an exceptional condition, commendable only when maintained from a desire to devote all the energies of life uninterruptedly to God's active service; cp. 1 Cor. vii. 25–28; ix. 5.

13–15. See Mark x. 13–16, and notes.

16 Good Master. This young ruler appears to have regarded Jesus as being merely a man of most eminent virtue; and he asks how he, too, may attain that unusual goodness which shall ensure to him eternal life. Hence our Lord first teaches him that absolute goodness belongs not to man, but to God; and then shows him that, moral (20) and amiable (Mark x. 21) as he was, there was a fatal flaw in his righteousness.

17 Why callest thou me good? The R.V. and Weymouth, following some MSS., read, "Why askest thou me concerning that which is good?" But this is extremely doubtful. It does not harmonise with the next sentence, 'One there is who is good." And both Mark x. 18 and Luke xviii. 19, unquestionably read, "Why callest thou me good?" as though Christ would say, Your ideas of human goodness are wrong. If I am not much more than a "Teacher" according to the sense in which you use that title, I am not entitled to be called "good."

20 The young man. Peculiar to Matthew. It is from Luke that it appears he was a "ruler," *i.e.*, of the synagogue; an ecclesiastical office.

21 Jesus said. Mark has, "Jesus beholding him loved him, and said."

go [and] sell that thou hast. This test was not intended as a universal rule, but was perfectly adapted to the young ruler's case.

22 he went away sorrowful. Feeling that the demand was right, yet wanting courage to comply with it, he had all the unhappiness of one who does not act up to his convictions, added to the bitter disappointment of finding the virtues in which he trusted fatally deficient.

23 shall hardly (with difficulty) **enter the kingdom of heaven.** Wealth, as usually procuring comfort and respect, frequently produces self-sufficiency and self-indulgence; which are inconsistent with the self-denial needed in order to follow Christ.

24 the eye of a needle. The words are to be taken in their simple and obvious meaning, and form a strong hyperbole, similar to some still in use, and signifying the greatest human impossibility (see vers. 25, 26). Some have supposed our Lord to refer to a narrow gate called "a needle's eye"; but this is unnecessary.

25 exceedingly amazed. They took the ordinary worldly view that riches give a man a moral and spiritual advantage.

26 with God all things are possible. God alone can make a man truly humble, heavenly-minded, and self-denying; and He can make any man such, whether he be rich or poor.

27 we have forsaken all. Although the apostles were not rich men, they all had much to give up, in leaving their homes and friends, and the occupations from which they derived their subsistence, to follow their Lord. The sons of Zebedee had hired servants; and Matthew appears to have been a man of some property (see Luke v. 29). Peter's question, "What shall we have therefore?" still shows a failure to apprehend Christ's requirement of self-renunciation.

28 in the regeneration. "Ye, who have followed me in this life, shall, at the completion of the new creation," etc. The reference is to the kingdom of God which Christ was about to establish (cp. Isa. lxv. 17; lxvi. 22; Matt. iii. 2; Rev. xxi. 1, and notes), and in which His apostles should be His chief ministers; whilst every one who should forsake all for Him should share its glory and blessedness, both "in this present time" and "in the world to come" (Luke xviii. 30).

CHAPTER XX

2 a penny. "A denarius," the chief silver coin of the Romans at that period, worth 20 cents of our money; the full daily pay of a labourer.

3 the third hour. About nine o'clock in the morning. Among the Jews, as among the Greeks and Romans, the working day was divided into twelve hours (see John xi. 9): beginning about sunrise, and ending about sunset.

8 when even was come. According to the law in Lev. xix. 13; Deut. xxiv. 15.

11 goodman. "Goodman" is an old English appellation of the master of a house, or householder, as in ver. 1.

12 the burden and heat of the day. R.V., "The burden of the day and the scorching heat."

15 Is thine eye evil? Art thou envious because I act kindly?

19 crucify. In Matthew alone is the mode of death specified. The Sanhedrin would condemn Christ to death, but the Gentiles would crucify Him.

20 the mother of Zebedee's children. Her name was Salome: cp. xxvii. 56 with Mark xv. 40; xvi. 1. It appears from Mark x. 35, that the two sons joined their mother in making this request, which may have arisen, on their part, from our Lord's promise in xix. 28. It shows the truth of the remark in Luke xviii. 34, that the disciples did not understand our Lord's previous announcement, perhaps regarding it as a figurative expression for great obstacles and conflicts, from which He would come off victorious to establish a temporal kingdom.

22 Ye know not what ye ask. This reproof intimates that they were ignorant of the true nature of Christ's kingdom, in which the highest eminence would be the result of the severest labours and sufferings for the good of others (26–28).

to drink of the cup, etc. To share my portion of sufferings: see Psa. lxxv. 8, and note.

We are able. This self-confidence was soon shown to result from a want of self-knowledge (see xxvi. 56): yet, as the profession sprang from love, Jesus graciously accepted it.

23 is not mine to give, etc. The R.V. gives a slightly different turn to the sentence: "is not mine to give, but [it is for them] for whom it hath been prepared," etc. Our Lord does not disclaim the power to dispose of the honours of His kingdom (see Rev. iii. 21); but He says that they can be granted only according to the rule laid down by His Father. What this is appears from vers. 26–28.

24 moved with indignation. An indignation proceeding from the same source as the request of the two, and therefore equally needing to be corrected.

26 it shall not be so among you. All authority in the Church of Christ is to result from the moral influence of eminent service and self-denial.

will be great. "Wants to be great"; or, as R.V., "would be great." "Minister" is servant (Gr. *diakonos,* whence the word "deacon"); "servant" (Gr. *doulos*) is bond-servant.

28 to give His life. Of all the actions by which the Son of man "ministered" to others, this was the chief. He whose life was in the highest sense His own, and was never forfeited by sin, *gave* it (John x. 18) a ransom (the price of life, Exod. xxi. 30; Prov. xiii. 8) for (in the stead of, ii. 22) many (Rev. vii. 4, 9). Here, in words simple and precise, our Lord distinctly speaks of His death as a substitution.

29 Jericho. Jericho (see Josh. ii. 1; 1 Kings xvi. 23) had been captured and rebuilt by Herod, who had there a palace and a fortress. It was placed at a little distance from the ancient site: about seven miles west of the Jordan, and nineteen miles east of Jerusalem. As the Passover was at hand, Jericho was probably filled with people going up to Jerusalem, including many Galilæans, who commonly avoided passing through Samaria, by taking the route through Peræa, on the east of the Jordan, and then recrossing the river near Jericho. Our Lord and His disciples probably fell in with the multitudes here, and proceeded with them towards Jerusalem.

30 two blind men. Here, as in viii. 28 (on which see note), Matthew mentions *two,* whilst Mark and Luke mention only *one.* The two may have been healed at once, or perhaps at different times; but the son of Timæus being the more remarkable, his cure was particularly recorded: see Mark x. 46–52, and notes.

31 rebuked them, because, etc. Rather, "charged them that they should be silent."

CHAPTER XXI

2 an ass tied, and a colt. The colt only was needed; but the ass followed by natural instinct. This circumstance is mentioned only by Matthew, who is about to quote the Scripture which it fulfils: see ver. 5.

4 that it might be fulfilled. This was our Lord's purpose; but the disciples did not at the time think of it (John xii. 16).

spoken by the prophet. See note on Zech. ix. 9. The evangelist quotes just that portion of the prophecy which is seen to be fulfilled by the incidents narrated.

5 the foal of an ass. The Greek is the "foal of a beast of burden."

7 a very great multitude. Rather, as R.V., "the most part of the multitude." The disciples placed their garments on the colt, the people strewed theirs upon the ground.

8 spread their garments. Spreading of garments and branches on the way was a custom observed in token of honour and welcome for a king: cp. 2 Kings ix. 13. Palm branches or leaves (which were used on this occasion: see John xii. 13) were a symbol of joy (Lev. xxiii. 40) and victory (Rev. vii. 9). On the word "strawed," see xxv. 24.

9 Hosanna. This is a direct reference to Psa. cxviii. 25, 26, which the Jews had been accustomed to apply to the King-Messiah; see notes on Psa. cxviii. The word "Hosanna," which was at first a prayer, meaning, "Save, I pray," had come to be addressed in acclamation to the king. "Hosanna to the Son of David," means "God grant salvation to," etc., like "God save the King."

10 moved. The original conveys the idea of being shaken as by an earthquake.

Who is this? The multitude who accompanied Jesus, and for the most part those also who came out of the city to join the procession (John xii. 12, 13), were from Galilee or Peræa. This question of the inhabitants of the city probably expressed scorn as well as surprise.

12 Jesus went into the Temple. Matthew brings together, in 12–16, our Lord's principal *actions* in the Temple; and begins at ver. 23 to detail His *teachings* there. The traders were cast out on the second day (Mark xi. 11–15).

cast out. Our Lord probably designed this action to be an indication that He was the Messiah: see Mal. iii. 1, of which this is one fulfilment. On both the resemblance and the difference between this act and one performed three years before, see John ii. 14, and notes.

all them that sold. At the great festivals there was a large demand for sacrificial victims, which were sold in the court of the Gentiles, after being examined and approved by the priests. The business of the money-changers was to exchange the coins in common use for the Jewish half-shekel, in which the Temple tribute was to be paid; and they received a commission of about four per cent.

13 It is written. See note on Mark xi. 17.

16 Out of the mouths of babes, etc. This follows the Septuagint version of Psa. viii. 2; on which see note. If, as your Scriptures show, God is praised by infantile admiration of His works, surely children's hosannas to the Son of David are not to be rebuked.

17 Bethany. See note on Mark xi. 19. Bethany was a village nearly two miles south-east of Jerusalem, frequently resorted to by our Lord: see John xi. 1, 5, 18.

lodged. Or, "He passed the night."

19 when He saw a (one) **fig tree,** etc. A fuller account of this is given in Mark xi. 12–14; on which see notes.

in the way. R.V., "by the wayside."

23 the chief priests and the elders. Mark and Luke add, "and the scribes." This was probably an official inquiry by members of the Sanhedrin into our Lord's authority for acting as the Messiah by making a public entry into Jerusalem, for casting out the traders from their accustomed place of traffic, and for teaching in the Temple. The question was evidently the result of a plot to destroy Him (Luke xix. 47).

24 I also will ask you, etc. Jesus might have answered by referring to His recent miracles, both the cures in the Temple (14) and the raising of Lazarus (John xi.); but His enemies would probably have evaded the force of such evidence, as they had previously done (xii. 24). He prefers a reply which not only defeats their plot, but compels them to confess their incompetence to judge (27).

25 The baptism of John. "Of men." Rather, "from men" (R.V.) parallel to "from heaven."

27 We cannot tell. Lit., "We know not" (R.V.).

Neither tell I you. If you are unable or unwilling to decide whether John was a true prophet or not, you are clearly unfit to judge me.

28–32. THE TWO SONS. In this parable Jesus divides the Jews, the supposed family of God, into two classes: one, "the publicans and the harlots" (32), who, though once openly irreligious, "believed" the preacher of repentance; the other, ostentatious in their religious professions, but insincere, "believed him not." The latter, by their own confession, are convicted of disobedience; whilst the former "take the lead of" them, for they "did the will of the Father." The parable is applicable to many professed Christians.

32 the way of righteousness. The very way which you profess to follow.

when ye had seen [it]. When ye had seen the beneficial effects which followed John's ministry.

repented not afterwards. "Did not even repent afterward" (R.V.).

33–40. THE LABOURERS IN THE VINEYARD. This parable should be compared with Isa. v. 1–7, where, however, a different illustration is used; the vineyard itself, not the labourers, being there rebuked and threatened.

33 a winepress. Mark has "a winefat," or vat, under the winepress to receive the juice.

a tower. A watch tower for protection.

went into a far country. Lit., "left the country." Luke adds, "for a long time."

34 the fruits. The rental was paid in a certain definite proportion of the produce.

37 he sent unto them his son. See note on Mark xii. 6. This verse contains the real and direct answer to the question of the Pharisees in ver. 23; for it affirms that, "the authority by which Jesus did these things" is that of "the Son."

41 They say. Thus passing upon themselves the sentence that they should be rejected and deprived of their privileges, and that the Gentiles should be called in their place (43). There is in the original a play upon the words: "He will miserably destroy those miserable men," R.V. Luke adds the answer of the people, "God forbid," when they perceived the application of the parable.

42 The stone which the builders rejected, etc. See note on Psa. cxviii. 22. The quotation was specially appropriate, as so soon following the hosannas of the multitude, from this very Psalm. Your rejection of "the Son" cannot injure Him, for God has made Him the head-stone of the spiritual Temple; but it will ruin yourselves (44).

43 Therefore. That is, because you builders reject the corner-stone chosen by God.

The kingdom of God shall be taken from you. Meaning that the Jewish nation should cease to be the visible embodiment of the Divine rule (the "theocracy").

the fruits thereof. The characteristics of God's kingdom: so keeping up the figure of a vineyard.

44 grind him to powder. The former part of the figure ("shall be broken to pieces," R.V.) resembles Isa. viii. 14, 15, the latter ("will scatter him as dust," R.V.) Dan. ii. 44; both of which passages refer to the Messiah. He who takes offence at Christ must suffer for it; but he who persists in his enmity till Christ appears in judgement must be utterly ruined.

46 they feared the multitude. A large part of the multitude who were now assembling from all parts, to celebrate the Passover at Jerusalem, regarded Jesus as a prophet (see John xii. 19). Therefore the rulers resorted to the measure described in Luke xx. 20.

CHAPTER XXII

2 a marriage. Rather, "marriage festivities"; or, more generally, "a festival." The parable greatly resembles that in Luke xiv. 16–24, which was delivered on a different occasion.

3 sent forth his servants. Guests who had been previously invited were summoned by the servants when the feast was ready, and were expected then to be prepared to go. So God had sent His invitations to the Jews by the prophets, who predicted the Messiah's coming; and they ought therefore to have been prepared, when John the Baptist, the Twelve, and the Seventy announced that "the kingdom of heaven is at hand."

4 sent forth other servants. The urgent repetition of the invitation represents God's repeated messages of mercy to the Jews, though they had refused His call. The apostles are no doubt here referred to.

6 the remnant. The greater part were indifferent (3–5); "the remainder," the open enemies of Christ, persecuted His messengers.

9 the highways. The great thoroughfares of the city, the crossroads; "the partings of the highways" (R.V.), the places of chief resort.

12 not having a wedding garment. To appear at a festival without an appropriate dress was a mark of disrespect to the host; particularly when, as was the case in royal feasts, he had provided one for every comer. But the point of the illustration probably lies, not so much in the source whence fitness for the blessings of the gospel is derived, as in the meetness itself, the "putting on the Lord Jesus Christ," as at once the justification and sanctification of the believer: cp. Rom. xiii. 14; Gal. iii. 27; Eph. iv. 24.

13 outer darkness. Or. "the darkness without." See note on viii. 12. As the wedding feast took place at night, the comparison is between the brilliantly lighted banquet hall and the darkness without.

14 many are called, but few are chosen. This moral refers to both parts of the parable. Many hear the call of the gospel, but heed it not; and even of those who feel disposed to welcome its gifts but few are prepared to comply with its requirements. This verse shows that the man without the wedding garment (12) is a type of a numerous class.

15 entangle. Or, "ensnare" (R.V.). The Jewish rulers, greatly enraged by our Lord's rebukes and threatenings, had determined upon His death, but were afraid of the people. They therefore endeavoured to extract from Him something which might afford a plausible accusation against Him, or at least might alienate men from Him. In this plot the different parties united. But His prudence and wisdom baffle and astonish, first, the Pharisees and Herodians, who try to involve Him in a *political* difficulty (15–22); then the Sadducees, who hope to entangle Him in a *theological* one

(23–33); and again the Pharisees, who watch His reply to an inquiring lawyer (34–40). At last He confounds and silences them all by a question respecting the parentage of the Messiah, which they are quite unable to answer (41–46).

16 the Herodians. The Herodians were political partisans of the Herodian family, and consequently of the Roman supremacy. They were, therefore, usually opposed to the Pharisees, who espoused the popular Jewish sentiment, which regarded the payment of tribute to a foreign power as a badge of servitude, and even as a breach of the law of Moses. The question which these two parties now proposed was one that might naturally have arisen between them, and might well appear to result from the conscientious scruples of "just men" (Luke xx. 20). They hoped that they should place Jesus in a dilemma from which He could not escape. An affirmative answer would have destroyed His credit with the common people; and then the Pharisees could have apprehended Him without fear. A negative reply would have enabled the Herodians to denounce Him to the Roman governor as a preacher of sedition.

17 Cæsar. "Cæsar" was the common appellation of the Roman emperors. The emperor at this time was Tiberius.

19 tribute money. The "census money." A poll-tax of a denarius, levied by the Romans in the provinces, was extended to Judæa by Pompey (Joseph. *Antiq.* xiv. 4, § 4). A similar tax had been previously levied by the kings of Syria (Joseph. *Antiq.* xiii. 2, § 3).

21 Render therefore unto Cæsar, etc. Our Lord's reply manifests consummate prudence. So far as it is an answer to the question, it accords with a correct maxim of the Jewish teachers, that "where a king's coin is current, his sovereignty is acknowledged." But His words contain further lessons of deeper wisdom, teaching us that the benefits derived from an orderly government render the payment of its dues imperative; and that, so long as its requirements do not interfere with the paramount claims of God, they are sanctioned by His authority. On the other hand, He excepts from human control the higher things that belong to God, whose "image" man bears, and to whom he owes himself and all that he has.

23 which say (saying) **that there is no resurrection.** The Sadducees denied the whole doctrine of a future life, as well as that of spiritual existences: see Acts xxiii. 8: xxvi. 8.

24 his brother shall marry his wife. This case refers to an ancient Eastern custom, which was followed by the Hebrews, and was regulated by the Mosaic law (see Gen. xxxviii. 8, 26; Deut. xxv. 5; Ruth i. 11; iii. 1–13, and notes). It is probable that this objection was a favourite and successful weapon of the Sadducees in their contests with the Pharisees, who appear to have supposed that the relationships of the present life would continue in the future state. The case that the Sadducees put was impossible.

29 the power of God. "The resurrection of the dead rests upon the power of God; the belief of the resurrection rests upon the Scriptures" (*Bengel*). God's power can make men become "as angels" (30): His word, even the portion given by Moses (which alone the Sadducees received as of Divine authority), says that God is still the God of Abraham, Isaac, and Jacob (Exod. iii. 6).

32 I am the God of Abraham, etc. This phrase and others like it are often used as a brief abstract, including all or any of the blessings of that covenant-relation to God which they imply: cp. Deut. xxvi. 16–19; Isa. xli. 10; Zech. xiii. 9; Heb. xi. 16. "I am their God" implies that Abraham, Isaac, and Jacob are living, as God declares to Moses that, long after their death, He is still their God. They must, therefore, still be capable of enjoying the benefits arising from their relation to Him, and, though dead to this world, they must still "live to Him" (Luke xx. 38); for the fulfilment of His promises can be enjoyed only by the living, not by the dead.

33 doctrine. Rather, "teaching" (R.V.), as in vii. 28.

34 when the Pharisees had heard, etc. Many of the Pharisees would gladly have seen Jesus defeated or entrapped by the Sadducees; but some could not but admire His wisdom; and one of them wished to try it further. His motive might not be bad; but, in asking the question in the presence of vigilant enemies, the inquirer was, in effect, "tempting Him." or testing Him (35): see notes on Mark xii. 28–34. The similar question and reply recorded (Luke x. 25–28) were on a different occasion. The problem was a very common one in the Jewish schools.

42 of Christ. Rather, "of the Christ" (R.V.), or "the Messiah"; particularly as to His parentage.

43 in spirit. "In the Spirit" (R.V.), that is, speaking by the Holy Spirit: see Psa. cx., and preliminary note. Our Lord not only recognises the current belief as to the authorship of this Psalm, but endorses this belief by His own authority, the whole point of His argument resting on the fact that the language is David's own.

45 how is He his son? This difficulty can be satisfactorily solved only by acknowledging that the Messiah is both God and man. But the worldly views of the Jewish teachers respecting His person and kingdom had blinded them to the higher revelations of their own Scriptures.

CHAPTER XXIII

Portions of Luke xi., xiii. (on which see notes) resemble some parts of this chapter; which, however, evidently contains one regular discourse in its right connexion.

2 sit in Moses' seat. Their office is to expound and apply judicially the law of Moses; therefore "all things" which they enjoin out of that law you are to observe. But you are neither to imitate their example, nor to receive their unscriptural traditions.

5 phylacteries. Phylacteries took their name from a Greek word signifying to *keep safely*. They were strips of parchment containing sentences extracted from the law, particularly Exod. xiii. 9, 16; Deut. vi. 4–9; xi. 13–21, on which see notes. The Jews bound these, in leather cases, on the forehead, or on the left wrist; and it seems that the Pharisees made them larger and more conspicuous than others. They did the same with the "borders," "tassels," or "fringes" of their garments; on which see Numb. xv. 37–41, and note.

6 uppermost rooms. Rather, "the highest places." The place of honour at the table was the middle place in the couch at the top; and in the synagogue, it was the seat nearest the "ark" or depository of the law.

7 greetings ("the salutations," R.V.) **in the markets** (places of public concourse). The Jewish teachers liked to be publicly and loudly hailed by their followers with cries of "Rabbi! Rabbi!" meaning, "My master." Our Lord here condemns not only vanity, but also all that assumption of superior authority in religious matters which the terms "Teacher," "Father," "Master" were held to imply; as being derogatory to the claims of their heavenly Father and of their Lord and Saviour, and inconsistent with the fraternal relations of Christians as brethren (10).

8 Master. Or, "Leader." The words, "even (the) Christ," seem to have been added to this verse from ver. 10 by some transcriber.

11 he that is greatest. See xx. 26, 27, and note.

13 neither suffer ye them that are entering. Not only had they by their traditions obscured and perverted their own Scriptures, and so deluded the people; but, when the ministry of John the Baptist and of our Lord had so powerfully affected many of the people that they seemed to be ready to enter "the kingdom of heaven," these false teachers did their utmost to excite their prejudices (see xii. 23, 24; John ix. 24); and with too much success.

15 ye compass sea and land, etc. You make the most strenuous efforts to gain a proselyte. The word "proselyte," as it is used in Scripture, refers to Gentiles who had submitted to the whole Mosaic law.

16 he is a debtor. The same word is rendered in ver. 18, "he is guilty"; but in both cases it means "he is bound" by his oath.

17 sanctifieth. That is, gives it all its sacredness.

23 hypocrites. "Actors."

anise and cummin. "Mint, anise" (rather, "dill"), and "cummin" (which, like dill, somewhat resembles fennel), are small herbs; to which, with extreme scrupulousness, the Pharisees extended the law of tithes (Lev. xxvii. 30), neglecting the "weightier," or more important, requirements: see Micah vi. 8, and note.

24 strain at. Rather, "strain *out*," as the word is printed in some early editions of the English Bible. The gnat and the camel are put for the smallest and the largest animals, both alike unclean (Lev. xi. 4, 20–23, 41, 42). The Jews strained their wine carefully, lest they should be polluted by swallowing an insect; and they whitewashed their graves annually (on the 15th of Adar), lest they should become unclean by treading on them unawares. Our Lord's meaning seems to be, In vain do you cleanse your cup and strain your wine; you leave in it worse impurities, and the liquor itself is bad: your lives are full of extortion and excess. In vain do you whitewash your graves; they are still abodes of pestilent corruption: your hearts "are full of hypocrisy and iniquity." You carefully shun ceremonial uncleanness, and yet disobey the weightiest of God's commandments.

31 ye be (are) **witnesses,** etc. In what you *say* you admit that you are their descendants; in what you *do* you resemble them. Doing this, while you acknowledge their crime in persecuting God's faithful messengers, you must be finally abandoned to fill to the brim their cup of sin and punishment (32), and you must take it and drain it all (35, 36).

33 generation ("offspring," R.V.) **of vipers.** See note on iii. 7. In pronouncing their character and doom, the Judge reminds them of the very words by which the preacher of repentance had sought to convince them of sin.

34 Wherefore. Since you imitate your fathers: see note on Exod. iv. 21.

35 righteous Abel. Abel is the first righteous man whose murder is recorded in the Bible (Gen. iv. 8), and Zechariah the son of Jehoiada is the last (2 Chron. xxiv. 20–22), according to the *Jewish arrangement* of the Old Testament. As all the circumstances of the death of the latter agree with the particulars here mentioned, it is likely that he is the person intended.

36 upon this generation. Within about forty years from this time Jerusalem was destroyed and the nation dispersed, with dreadful sufferings and slaughter.

37 how often, etc.! The words seem most naturally to refer to previous visits of our Lord to the capital. But such visits, prior to this last, are unrecorded in the first three Gospels. St. John, however, relates them (ii. 13; v. 1; vii. 14, etc.); thus supplying the explanation of our Lord's appeal.

38 your house. Your dwelling-place: see Psa. lxix. 25. But some think that the Temple is meant.

39 Blessed [is] He that cometh in the name of the Lord. Acknowledging me to be the Messiah, as my disciples and the children of Jerusalem have already done (see xxi. 9). This, then, is Israel's "song of conversion. With these words the public discourses of Christ to the Jews concludes: with these words their repentance will begin" (*Bengel*).

CHAPTER XXIV

2 that shall not be thrown down. Josephus relates that, when the Romans had taken Jerusalem, they demolished the entire city and Temple, except three towers and part of the western wall; doing this so effectually, that it was hardly credible that such a city had ever stood there. See Macalister: *A Century of Excavation in Palestine*, pp. 94, 202.

3 the sign of Thy coming. "Of thy Parousia" or presence. A comparison of ver. 3 with Mark xiii. 4 and Luke xxi. 7, shows that the disciples regarded the destruction of Jerusalem and of the Temple as a coming of Christ, and as "the end of the world" (lit., "the age," or existing constitution of things); and in this they were partly right. But they probably expected that this would be the beginning of an earthly kingdom, in which their Lord would restore pre-eminence and glory to the remnant of the nation, and reign in peace over the whole world (see Luke xxiv. 21; Acts i. 6).

4 In this discourse our Lord first gives to His disciples four signs of His coming as the Judge of ancient Israel: 1. The appearance of many false Messiahs (5); 2. Civil commotions, wars, and other great sufferings (6–8); 3. Persecutions of His followers by both Jews and Gentiles, notwithstanding which the gospel shall spread (9–14); and, 4. The last sign (on seeing which all His disciples should hasten away), the investing of Jerusalem by the Roman armies (15–18).

5 many shall come in my name, saying, I am (the) **Christ.** ("assuming my name": *Weymouth*). The fulfilment of these predictions (particularly 5–8, 15–22) is found in the *Jewish Wars* of Josephus; who, as a Jew not converted to Christianity, a priest, and not only an eye witness, but to a great extent an actor in these great events, is, notwithstanding some few inaccuracies, an unexceptionable witness to the accomplishment of our Lord's words. He mentions impostors, who "deceived many"; and "wars, and rumours of wars" in Palestine (*Ant.* xx. 8, §§ 6, 7, 10; *Wars*, ii. 12, §§ 1, 2, 3; 13, § 4, etc.); "famine," which is usually the precursor of "pestilence" (*Ant.* iii. 15, § 3; cp. also Acts xi. 28); and "earthquake" (*Wars*, iv. 4, § 5).

7 kingdom against kingdom. Cp. 2 Chron. xv. 2–7; Jer. li. 46, and note.

8 sorrows. "Travail" (R.V.). The death-pangs of Judaism and the birth-throes of the new dispensation: cp. Isa. lxvi. 6–8, and notes.

9 hated of all (the) **nations.** Cp. 1 Cor. i. 23.

10 shall many be offended (stumble), etc. Times of persecution usually produce many apostates, who are often the first to betray those whom they have forsaken.

11 false prophets. False teachers among Christians. In consequence of these apostasies and heresies, "lawlessness" (or licentiousness) abounds, and spreads its blighting influence over "the many," a very large portion of professors of Christianity: see 2 Pet. ii.; 1 John ii. 18–23; iv. 1–3; Jude; Rev. ii. 4, 14, 20.

12 the love of many. Rather, "the love of the many," R.V., a general defection.

14 in all the world. Before the destruction of Jerusalem, the gospel had been preached through "the whole world" then known to or visited by the subjects of Rome. (The word for "world," lit., "the inhabited earth," is the same as in Luke ii. 1.) See Rom. xv. 19, 23; Col. i. 6, 23; 2 Tim. iv. 17. In like manner, before "the end" of the present dispensation, it may be expected that the truth shall be made known "to all nations," as "a witness" to them of the justice and mercy of God.

15 the abomination of desolation. That is, "the abominable thing (or *idol*) that destroys" (Dan. ix. 27). This is clearly connected in time, if not in some other way, with the siege of Jerusalem by the Roman army (see Luke xxi. 20). Hence many suppose it to refer to the eagles, which the Roman legions carried as standards, and worshipped as idols. When these should appear on "the holy ground" near the city, then would be the time for the disciples to flee. One circumstance which is strongly in favour of this opinion is, that the first approach of the Romans to Jerusalem, after this time, with the intention of "desolating" it, was in A.D. 66 under Cestius Gallus; who then withdrew his forces (Jos. *Wars*, ii. 19, § 7), so that the Christians had time to escape before the city was closely invested by Vespasian, A.D. 68. Eusebius (*Ecc. Hist.* iii. 5) says that they availed themselves of this opportunity and fled to Pella and other places beyond Jordan. [For "the holy place," R.V. marg. reads more accurately, "a holy place."]

17 the housetop. The flat roof, on which the Orientals spend much of their time, is reached by a staircase from the court near the gateway; so that a person escaping in great haste need not go through any of the chambers of "the house." When you see this sign (15), do not stay to save any of your possessions, but flee for your lives.

20 not in the winter, neither on the sabbath day. Pray that there be neither natural nor legal impediments to your flight. The Jewish restrictions on sabbath travelling would make many Jewish Christians hesitate to go beyond the prescribed distance, and, apart from any scruples which they might themselves entertain, would render journeying on that day very difficult.

22 there should no flesh be saved. So terrible was the slaughter of the Jewish people in the times of Titus and Hadrian, that, had it been much prolonged, the whole nation must have been exterminated. But for the sake of the "remnant according to the election of grace" (Rom. xi. 5), God "shortened the days."

26 believe [it] not. Some Jewish Christians would be likely to cling to the expectation that their Lord would appear to save the favoured city and nation from utter destruction.

27 shineth. Lit., as R.V., "is seen."

so shall also the coming (lit., "presence") **of the Son of man be.** Sudden and unexpected.

28 there will the eagles be gathered together. Cp. Job xxxix. 30; Hab. i. 8. As quickly and surely as the vulture scents out the carcase, so quickly and surely will the ministers of vengeance find out a people ripe for destruction.

29 Immediately, etc. Some think that our Lord here makes a transition to His final coming to judgement. Others suppose, as this event is to follow "immediately" after the preceding woes, that He refers to the second capture of Jerusalem by Hadrian, about A.D. 135; in consequence of the insurrection of the Jews under Bar-cochba, which brought upon them sufferings even more terrible than any they had endured before. But the prediction may have both a nearer and a more remote fulfilment.

shall fall from heaven. Our Lord here adopts the figurative language in which the ancient prophets predicted the convulsions and overthrow of nations: see Isa. xiii. 10; xxxiv. 4; Ezek. xxxii. 7; Joel iii. 15, and notes.

30 the sign of the Son of man. Some expositors have supposed this "sign" to be an unusual appearance of the heavenly bodies (Luke xxi. 25), or a peculiar star (as in ii. 2), or a cross (the Fathers) or other luminous phenomenon. But the clause more probably refers to the demand in xvi. 1; and means, Then shall this unbelieving generation have "a sign from heaven," even the Son of man Himself coming as Judge (see Dan. vii. 9–14, and notes), to overturn their national system; and, by the proclamation of His chosen messengers, to gather His true Israel from all nations (31).

32 a parable. Or, "its parable" (see R.V.); *i.e.*, the illustration which it affords.

33 it is near. Better, as R.V., "He (the Son of man) is nigh."

36 my Father only. See note on Mark xiii. 32.

41 at the mill. The hand-mills used for grinding corn (see Exod. xi. 5, and note) often required the strength of two women. Vers. 37–41 illustrate the unexpectedness of the visitation; which will overtake men in the midst of their ordinary occupations, and allow but few to escape.

51 cut him asunder. A terrible punishment inflicted on the greatest criminals: see 1 Sam. xv. 33; 2 Sam. xii. 31; Dan. ii. 5, and notes.

CHAPTER XXV

1 Then shall the kingdom of heaven be likened, etc. This parable is founded upon the marriage ceremonies among the Jews and other Eastern nations. The festivities on such occasions sometimes occupied a week. In the evening, the bridegroom, attended by a company of young men (see note on Judges xiv. 11), brought home his bride from her father's house. The young female friends of both parties, who had waited near the house till his return, lighting their lamps, joined the train. With joyful acclamations, they all proceeded to the nuptial entertainment at the bridegroom's house; and, when they had entered, the doors were closed. The great lesson of the parable is the necessity not only of making due provision, but especially of maintaining a constant readiness for the coming of Christ.

lamps. Rather, "torches": wooden stems hollowed at the top, and bearing a piece of cloth steeped in oil.

5 they all slumbered and slept. Our Lord by this incident warns even His most watchful disciples against the least forgetfulness or neglect.

8 are gone out. Rather, "are *going* out" (R.V.). The conduct of many, at the approach of death, resembles that of "the foolish virgins." Having disregarded their duty towards God in the time of health, they now become alarmed, trembling, and solicitous for the aid of others; often when it is too late.

9 [Not so] lest, etc. The original does not express the negative. "Perhaps there will not be enough," etc.

12 I know you not. That is, "I acknowledge you not": see note on Psa. i. 6.

14 For [the kingdom of heaven is], etc. Or, "For [the Son of man, at His coming, will deal with you] as a man who, when going abroad, called his own servants," etc. This parable greatly resembles that in Luke xix. 12–27, on which see notes. Both are founded upon a custom which still prevails in some countries, of entrusting money, or other property, to servants, that they may trade with it on their master's behalf. This parable appropriately follows the preceding. While the former inculcates habitual regard to Christ's expected coming, and constant readiness for it; this enforces habitual diligence (such as love to Him, rather than fear, will prompt) in the discharge of our present duties on earth during His absence.

a far country. Rather, as R.V., "another country" (see xxi. 33).

18 hid his lord's money. His indolence led him to be careless of his lord's wishes and interests, and to think him "harsh" and unjust in his requirements (24); so that he would only do what he thought necessary to escape punishment. But he was "foolish" (2) as well as "wicked," as his lord shows (26, 27).

23 Well done. The same commendation is bestowed on both of the faithful servants. Christ estimates His people's services not by their results, but by their fidelity. Phillips Brooks (*Twenty Sermons*) takes the man with the two talents as "a type of common mediocrity, the average man." But he had high views of duty and responsibility.

24 reaping where thou hast not sown, etc. That is, Thou exactest from thy servants more than they are able, or ought to be required, to perform. Such is the estimate which too many form of Christ's service; magnifying its difficulties and losing sight of His promised help; and forgetting that He condemns as "wicked" not only the positively profane, but the "slothful" too.

hast not strawed. R.V., "didst not scatter." To *straw* is an old form of to *strew* (xxi. 8).

25 thou hast [that is] thine. This was false; for his skill, labour, and time were his lord's, as well as the money. It is robbery of God to neglect His gifts, as well as to abuse them.

26 thou knewest. A question: "Did you know?"

27 usury. Or, "interest," which the "exchangers" or "bankers" (as R.V.) allowed upon money deposited with them. As this might have been done with perfect ease, the idle servant was utterly without excuse. The lesson here may be that those who are conscious of but small ability may seek out helpers able to direct and employ their service.

29 he shall have abundance. See note on xiii. 12. The parable as a whole is a lesson on high and low views of life; and on personal responsibility. God's gifts are fairly distributed; God's reckoning is also fair (cp. Luke xii. 47, 48).

31 When the Son of man, etc. This representation of judgement carries the view beyond the circle of Christ's professed disciples, entrusted with "talents" for His service, and embraces "all the nations." There seems a special reference to forms of *unconscious* service. Those accepted and welcomed did not know that they were ministering to Christ, but "the law written on their hearts" by God's Holy Spirit prompted them to acts of beneficence and charity: see Rom. ii. 7–10.

32 divideth [his] sheep from the goats. An image derived from Ezek. xxxiv. 17. This description suggests that the present mixture of the good and the evil will continue in the world until the final, judicial separation.

34 the King. Our Lord, by here calling Himself "the King," showed His disciples the nature of His kingdom, as opposed to the carnal and earthly views of the Jews. He is indeed a King: but the rewards which He distributes are heavenly rather than earthly; and the punishments which He inflicts are eternal rather than temporal.

37 when saw we Thee an hungred, etc.? Those good deeds which are genuine fruits of Christian faith and love always have the grace of modest self-forgetfulness.

40 ye have done it unto me. Nothing could more strikingly exhibit the Saviour's condescension; nor could stronger motives be presented to active and self-denying benevolence. It is clear that conduct, and especially kindness or the neglect of it, are in the sight of Christ deciding factors in the last Judgement.

46 everlasting . . . eternal. The same word in both cases. So R.V., "these shall go away into eternal punishment: but the righteous into eternal life." That which is predicated of the blessedness also describes the penalty. Such is the solemn declaration by the Divine and compassionate Redeemer: cp. Luke xvi. 23–26.

CHAPTER XXVI

2 after two days. These words appear to have been spoken by Jesus on the fourth day of the week, that is, on the Wednesday. On the day of the Passover, see note, John xiii. 1.

3 the chief priests . . . and the elders. See note on ii. 4.

the palace. Or, "court" (R.V.); the open area in the centre of the mansion: see 58, 69.

Caiaphas. Joseph Caiaphas, a Sadducee, was the high priest during the whole of Pilate's government. He was son-in-law of Annas; who had been deposed from the high priesthood by the Roman procurator Valerius (Jos. *Antiq.* xviii. 2, § 2), but still retained the title and considerable authority, perhaps as *Sagan* or deputy (Luke iii. 2; John xviii. 13; Acts iv. 6).

5 Not on the feast [day]. Rather, "not during the feast" (R.V.): which lasted a whole week. The approaching Passover had drawn to Jerusalem a great multitude of people from Galilee and Peræa, who were favourably disposed towards Jesus; so that the Sanhedrin feared a commotion if He were apprehended now. The offer of Judas (14) changed their plans, and brought about the crucifixion of our Lord at the very time of the Passover, in fulfilment of the Divine purpose.

6 when Jesus was in Bethany. This incident is not to be confused with that recorded in Luke vii. 37.

7–16. See notes on Mark xiv. 3–11.

15 they covenanted with him, etc. Rather, as R.V., "they weighed unto him thirty pieces of silver." Equal to £4 16*s*.

17 [feast of] unleavened bread. The obligation to abstain from leavened bread did not properly commence till the paschal supper, on the 15th of Nisan; but, for fear of transgressing the law, the Jews used to put away all leaven from their houses on the day before, the 14th of the month. Thus the feast might be said to last eight days (see Josephus, *Ant.* ii. 15, § 1). On 17–20, see notes on Luke xxii. 7–30. Whether this was the customary Passover evening, see note on John xiii. 1.

21–25. See notes on John xiii. 21–30.

22 exceeding sorrowful. Sorrowful that He should be betrayed; more so, that the traitor should be one of themselves. Each, save Judas, appears to have been thrown back upon himself, searching himself whether he could be capable of so great wickedness; and "every one of them," Judas not excepted, but he hypocritically "began to say, Lord, is it I?" Meantime, Peter had beckoned to John to ask quietly who it was.

23 He that dippeth his hand. Mark (xiv. 20), says, "He who is dipping [his hand] with me in the dish," *i.e.*, one who is reclining at my side, eating with me. The language seems to allude to Psa. xli. 9, which is noted in John xiii. 18. The fingers of the right hand were used to take the food out of the dish in which it was served; the hands being washed both before and after the meal.

24 goeth. That is, "passeth away"; "dieth"; see Gen. xv. 2; Job x. 21. But God's expressed purpose that Jesus should die could not excuse the malignity of His murderers: see Acts ii. 23.

25 Thou hast said. A Jewish form of assent, equivalent to, "It is as thou hast said." As this answer was unknown to the other disciples (see John xiii. 28, 29), it has been supposed that our Lord did not speak, but gave Judas a sign to this effect; and that Matthew gives the substantial meaning, rather than the precise form of the reply. But some think that He spoke in so low a tone as not to be heard by the rest.

26 as they were eating. John (xiii. 30) seems to intimate that the Lord's Supper was not instituted until Judas had withdrawn. If so, the other evangelists have not regarded the order of time.

blessed [it]. See xiv. 19, and 1 Cor. xi. 24.

this is my body. The verb would not be inserted in such a sentence in Aramaic, the language which our Lord probably spoke: but in the Greek of the New Testament, as well as in other writers and languages, it often signifies *to represent*: see xiii. 37–39; Gal. iv. 24, 25; Rev. i. 20.

27 Drink ye all of it. "As to the bread, we read that He simply said, 'Take, eat.' Why does He expressly bid them *all* drink? And why does Mark explicitly say that *they all drank of it?*" (*Calvin*). Does not this suggest that, if communion in "one kind alone were sufficient, it is the cup which should be used?" (*Bengel*).

28 the new testament. Rather, "the new covenant"; or, omitting "new" (with most authorities), "the covenant," referring evidently to Exod. xxiv. 7, 8, and Jer. xxxi. 31: on which see notes. This covenant, procured and ratified by the blood of Christ, stands firm to all who believe in Him; and of this great truth the Lord's Supper is the appointed sign. As the bread was an emblem of the body of Christ, given to death for us; so the wine was an emblem of His blood shed for us: and so further, the taking and eating and drinking the bread and wine are symbolical of the personal appropriation by faith of the benefits of His sacrifice, especially "the remission of sins."

which is shed ("being shed") **for many.** See xx. 28; Rom. v. 15, 19; 1 Tim. ii. 6, and notes.

29 I will not drink henceforth, etc. Probably a figurative expression (cp. Rev. xix. 9) representing the association of His disciples with Himself in the spiritual worship of heaven at "the marriage supper of the Lamb." Weymouth renders, "When I shall drink the new wine with you," etc. Thus this ordinance becomes anticipative, as well as commemorative.

30 when they had sung a hymn. Psalms cxiii.–cxviii. were usually sung at the Passover: Psalms cxiii., cxiv. after the first cup of wine; Psalms cxv.–cxviii. after the third cup—the "cup of blessing"—which our Lord seems to have used in instituting the Supper; see note on Psa. cxiii., title. Here intervene the deeply interesting discourses and prayer in John xiv.–xvii.

31 for it is written, etc. See Zech. xiii. 7, and notes. Our Lord's frequent quotations of the prophetic Scriptures during His last sufferings show how all that occurred was in full accordance with the purposes of God.

33 [yet] will I never be offended (caused to stumble). Peter had just been forewarned (Luke xxii. 31); but instead of learning his weakness, he was led on by over-confident zeal to more earnest protestations.

34 before the cock crow. See note on the parallel passage in Mark (xiv. 30), who is the most full and precise of the evangelists respecting the warning and the fall of Peter.

36 Gethsemane. Gethsemane signifies *oil-press.* It was an olive-yard lying at the western foot of Olivet, on the way to Bethany.

and pray yonder. Into a more retired part of the garden. "In great trials, solitude is desired; yet so that friends be within reach" (*Bengel*). They might also become witnesses of part, at least, of our Lord's agony.

37 Peter and the two sons of Zebedee. See note on Mark v. 37. It is worthy of remark, that during our Lord's agony, as well as at His transfiguration, His three favoured companions were oppressed with sleep (40, 43), and witnessed only part of the wonderful scene. Of this only the prominent passages are briefly recorded; and that not by John, who was present, but most fully, in both cases, by Luke.

38 sorrowful, even unto death. The three evangelists seem to labour by variety of language to express the *intensity* of our Lord's sufferings. But they go no further. It is easy to see that the outward circumstances and bodily tortures of our Lord's approaching death, full as they were of suffering, from human and Satanic malignity and treachery, from weariness, scourging, and crucifixion, were not the cause of His oppressive anguish; for many of His followers who have not looked forward to martyrdom as calmly as He did, have met it with perfect cheerfulness. The silence of the inspired writers on this subject seems to show that the sufferings of the Redeemer were altogether beyond our comprehension, arising from His peculiar position as the sinless Sufferer of sinful man.

39 fell on His face. The humblest posture of supplication.

if it be possible. This is equivalent to, "If Thou be willing" (Luke), for "all things" that God sees it right to do "are possible unto" Him (Mark). A comparison of ver. 42 with Luke xxii. 43 leads to the inference that our Lord took the coming of an angel to strengthen Him as an intimation that the cup of suffering could not be taken away.

this cup. See note on xx. 22. The "cup" of suffering, called by Mark "the hour," is probably the present almost insupportable conflict of feeling.

41 the flesh is weak. Possibly our Lord mentioned this as an excuse for the past drowsiness; He evidently adduced it as a reason for combined watchfulness and prayer. By some the words are taken to be a statement about Himself and His need for their sympathy and help.

43 again. The word in the best texts follows, *He came;* as R.V.

45 Sleep on now. "Sad irony" (*David Smith*). The Lord instantly adds, "Rise up," etc. The time for action has suddenly come.

47 a great multitude. Some of the chief priests and elders themselves, with their servants, and the captain and officers of the Temple guard, were among the multitude (51; Luke xxii. 52; John xviii. 3). They may perhaps have feared a commotion; they evidently desired to make it appear that Jesus was a dangerous ringleader of sedition. Hence the point of His rebuke (55).

49 hail. The usual salutation. "Our modern Western equivalent would be simply, 'Good evening'" (*Weymouth*).

kissed Him. A strong expression, "Kissed Him eagerly." The traitor overdid his part. Jesus had probably already declared Himself (John xviii. 5, 8), yet the preconcerted signal was necessary, to authorise the officers in taking Him.

50 Friend. The word here used is merely a term of civility (see xx. 13; xxii. 12); not implying friendship, like that employed in John xv. 15.

wherefore art thou come? Rather, as R.V., "[do] that for which thou art come." Our Lord calmly repels the hypocritical embrace. Fawn not upon me, but do your work: cp. John xiii. 27.

51 one of them. Peter (see John xviii. 10).

52 they that take the sword, etc. "If you use the sword, you expose all your lives to danger" (*Geikie*).

53 twelve legions. Instead of the twelve disciples. The Romans commonly kept in Palestine at least one legion, consisting of about 6,000 infantry and 600 cavalry; of which about 1,000, under a tribune or chiliarch, were usually quartered in Jerusalem at the great festivals: see Acts xxi. 31, 32; xxiii. 23. "Twelve legions of angels," therefore, means an overpowering force.

56 all this was done. Either our Lord's words or the comment of the Evangelist.

57 to Caiaphas. He was led first to Annas (see John xviii. 13), shortly after midnight.

the scribes and the elders. This was probably an unofficial, hastily-summoned meeting of some members of the Sanhedrin. A full and formal meeting was held early the next morning (59; Luke xxii. 66). Jewish usage forbade the trial of capital offences by night.

58 palace. Rather, "court": see note on ver. 3.

with the servants (officers). Who had made a fire in the middle of the court: see Mark xiv. 54; Luke xxii. 55.

59 sought (were seeking) **false witness.** Of course they would have preferred *true;* but, having determined to secure His condemnation, they were utterly unscrupulous about the means.

60 two false witnesses. The evidence of two witnesses agreeing in their testimony was requisite in order to convict of a capital crime (Deut. xix. 15). Many were brought to prove the case against Jesus, but utterly failed. These two appear to have been wrong only in their interpretation of our Lord's words (see John ii. 19, and note).

61 I am able to destroy, etc. Words spoken at the *beginning* of Christ's ministry; recorded only by John (ii. 19): cp. Mark xiv. 58.

63 Jesus held His peace. Here, as afterwards before Pilate (xxvii. 12), Jesus made no reply to the false accusations of determined malice. This induced the high priest, who wished to condemn Him by His own words, to adopt another method of inquiry, by solemn adjuration as to His Messiahship. This our Lord at once avows; and, on this ground, He is condemned by the council.

64 Thou hast said. That is, "It is as thou hast said" (see 25). "But (Jesus adds), as I am, so ye shall henceforth (R.V.) see me, who now stand apparently defenceless at your tribunal, seated on the throne of heaven as your Ruler and Judge": cp. Dan. vii. 13, 14.

65 rent his clothes. His ordinary dress. This he did in horror at the "blasphemy," which by the law of Moses (Lev. xxiv. 16) made the offender (as all the rest exclaim) "worthy of death." They totally disregarded the abundant proof which Jesus had given of His Messiahship.

66 guilty. Or, "worthy," as R.V. "He deserves to die."

67 buffeted Him. They smote Him with clenched fists. This was done by the officers, who also blindfolded Him as a condemned criminal (Luke xxii. 63, 64: cp. Esth. vii. 8).

69–75. See 3, 58. Peter's threefold denial is reported by all the evangelists with characteristic variations, which will present no difficulties to those who remember that all writers often give a speaker's meaning rather than his words, and that each denial might include several replies. The first occasion was when Peter, joining the group around the fire in the outer hall, was accosted by the portress. He then went into the porch, and the cock crew. The second was "after a little while"; when he was returning from the porch, and was again assailed by the same maid (Mark xiv. 69), by another (Matt. xxvi. 71), by a man (Luke xxii. 58), and by the company at large, to whom he replied several times. The third denial was about "an hour after"; when "they that stood by" more urgently asserted that he must be a follower of Jesus, for his provincial dialect proved him to be a Galilæan: and a kinsman of Malchus recognised him as having been in the garden. Then the crowing of the cock, and especially his Master's look, brought him to himself, and he hastened away and "wept bitterly." After this Peter has no place in any of the narratives until the morning of the resurrection, when he appears with John (John xx. 3, and note).

CHAPTER XXVII

1 took counsel. The Sanhedrin could condemn a criminal to die, but they could not carry the sentence into execution without the sanction of the Roman governor (John xviii. 31). The right of inflicting capital punishment had been taken away from the Jews at the deposition of Archelaus. The Jewish authorities therefore consulted together to find a political charge which they might put forward against Jesus. Pilate's inquiry and remark (John xviii. 29, 30) brought out this accusation of treason (Luke xxiii. 2), to which they afterwards added (John xix. 7) that of blasphemy. But it was on the political charge that Pilate sentenced Him (John xix. 12–15); and accordingly this was specified in the title on the cross: see John xix. 19, and note.

2 the governor. The Roman governor's residence was at Cæsarea; but he usually came to Jerusalem at the Passover, with a large body of soldiers, to check any popular risings, which were not infrequent at that season.

3–10. These verses are peculiar to Matthew.

3 repented. That this was only an intolerable remorse, not a change of heart, or "repentance unto salvation" (2 Cor. vii. 10), appears from the result (5, compared with John xvii. 12: Acts i. 18). Judas may perhaps not have anticipated the consequences of his treachery. But the consequences of sin are always beyond the transgressor's calculation. The protest and remorse of Judas were a solemn warning to the Jewish rulers against their unjust and cruel action.

5 the Temple. More precisely, "the Sanctuary," as R.V. He flung the money into the Holy Place.

hanged himself. It may seem surprising that such a man should have connected himself with Jesus, so as to be chosen an apostle. He may have been led to it by a strong impression of our Lord's superhuman power, and by a hope of advancement in His new kingdom. But, as this delusive hope was gradually dispelled by his Master's life and teachings, his real character became apparent. "This is the tragedy of his career, that he yielded to the baser impulses of his nature, and suffered them to usurp dominion over him" (*David Smith*).

6 the price of blood. Their objection may have been founded on the principle involved in Deut. xxiii. 18. Their cold and cutting reply to Judas (4), and all their conduct show, how dead may be the moral feelings of those who are most scrupulous about the forms of religion.

7 the potter's field. "In Acts i. 18, it is said that Judas bought the field; in Matthew, that the priests bought it. The apparent difficulty is simply a mistranslation of the word ἐκτήσατο in Acts. Schleusner and Rosenmüller rightly explain it as meaning, 'Judas, by his unholy reward, afforded the means of buying the spot.' Schleusner quotes an apt illustration from *Josephus*" (*Geikie*).

8 unto this day. It long remained a public testimony to the innocence of our Lord and the injustice of His judges.

9 Then was fulfilled, etc. Through the whole of 8–10, the evangelist appears to have had several prophetic passages in view. The name of the ground, the use to which it was applied, and the circumstances attending the purchase, seem to have suggested Jeremiah's appellation of this very valley—"the valley of slaughter"—a name of sin and punishment, connected with "the blood of the innocent" victims immolated by the "elders of the people" and "the priests" (Jer. xix. 2, 4, 6), and with the burying "in Tophet till there be no place" (Jer. vii. 31, 32, and note). And all this is further associated with Zechariah's prophecy (see Zech. xi. 12, 13), of which the sense is given rather than the words. This last prophecy is attributed to Jeremiah. Origen (quoted by David Smith: *In the Days of His Flesh*, p. 487, n.) thought it was either a scribe's error, or a quotation from some secret scripture of Jeremiah. Calvin thought it was an error for "Zechariah," but added "it does not greatly trouble me." David Smith says that the latter part of Zechariah (ix.–xv.) is a collection of prophecies belonging to different periods, and asks, "What if xi. 12, 13 were a prophecy of Jeremiah after all?"

14 He answered him to never a word. R.V., "He gave him no answer, not even to one word." Jesus had answered Pilate's judicial question, but He made no reply to the false and clamorous accusations of the chief priests. His calm silence, whilst His accusers became "more fierce" (Luke xxiii. 5), evidently impressed Pilate "greatly," and confirmed his belief in our Lord's innocence (Luke xxiii. 14, 15; cp. 1 Pet. ii. 23).

15 at [that] feast. Rather, as R.V., "at the feast": a general expression: "at feast-time."

17 Whom will ye that I release? Pilate now weakly tries to save Jesus without offending the Jews, or laying himself open to the charge of acquitting a rebel. Knowing that one great cause of the enmity of the priests was "envy" of our Lord's popularity with the multitude, he turns to the people and proposes to release Jesus. They were allowed at the festivals to demand the freedom of one prisoner: and Pilate offers them the choice of Barabbas, a criminal then in custody, or Jesus (Mark xv. 7), and three times earnestly beseeches them to choose the latter (Luke xxiii. 16–22). But the violence of His accusers prevails. "They persuade the multitude," consisting probably of their own adherents among the lower classes of Jerusalem; they raise an outcry against Jesus, and will not desist until the governor has "delivered Him to their will."

19 his wife. This incident, recorded only by Matthew, illustrates the accuracy of the Gospel records; for the provincial governors had but recently been allowed by the Roman senate to be accompanied by their wives (Tacitus, *Ann.* iii. 33, 34). Pilate's wife is said to have been named Claudia Procula. Both in her dream, and in the effect it produced upon her, leading her to send a message to her husband even on the judgement-seat, the hand of God is to be seen.

22 Let Him be crucified. Crucifixion was the Roman punishment awarded to the crime of which our Lord was accused. The cross consisted of a strong upright post, having a short bar or stake projecting from the middle, and a larger transverse beam at right angles, or a little below the top. It was just high enough to raise the feet a little above the ground. The criminal, stripped of his clothes, was fixed to the cross by nails or spikes driven through the hands, and sometimes through the feet, either separated or united. The weight of the body rested not so much upon the nails as upon a wooden pin or peg attached to the upright beam, and serving for a partial seat; but this, if it diminished the sufferings at first, made them much more lingering: see Mark xv. 44; John xix. 32, 33.

24 this just person. See ver. 19. The emblematical action (which Pilate probably knew to be practised among the Jews, as it was by other nations: see Deut. xxi. 6, 9) made his declaration of our Lord's innocence the more impressive; but it could not cleanse his own conscience from guilt. Pilate wanted to be just, but he allowed himself to be overborne by expediency and fear. Bacon has done him an injustice in calling him "jesting Pilate." Edwin Arnold is nearer the truth in his estimate in *The Light of the World*. See also note on ver. 31.

25 His blood [be] on us, etc. That is, If there be guilt, on us and our children let it rest. See xxiii. 35; Deut. xix. 10. The verse is peculiar to Matthew. This awful imprecation has for eighteen centuries seemed to rest on the Jewish nation. In their subsequent wars with Rome, "wrath came upon them to the uttermost"; and the retribution was the more remarkable, by the crucifixion of such multitudes of them, that room failed for the crosses, and crosses for the bodies. (Joseph. *Wars*, v. 11, § 1.)

26 when he had scourged Jesus. As He had predicted (xx. 19). It was a Roman custom to scourge a criminal before execution; and the infliction was cruelly severe.

27 the common hall. The court of the "prætorium," or governor's residence: see John xviii. 28, and note.

the whole band. Perhaps, "a cohort" or "battalion," about 600 men. The same Greek word is used in Acts x. 1.

28 scarlet. Rather, "crimson"; the red military cloak of a Roman officer. The robe, the bramble crown, and the reed, were mock emblems of the royalty which Jesus was accused of claiming. All these indignities He bore in meek and submissive silence: see Isa. liii. 7.

31 after that they had mocked Him. Before He was actually led away, Pilate brought Him out to the people, and made some final efforts to release Him (John xix. 4–16).

32 as they came out. Rather, "as they were going out"; *i.e.*, out of the city. All executions took place outside the city, as anciently "without the camp": see Numb. xv. 35; 1 Kings xxi. 13; and cp. Heb. xiii. 11–13.

a man of Cyrene. Cyrene (now *Grennah*, part of Tunis) was a city of Libya, on the north coast of Africa. It was an important Greek colony, and contained a large number of Jews; see Acts ii. 10; vi. 9. Perhaps this man was singled out because he showed some sympathy with Jesus; but if it were not so, it is probable that he became interested in the meek and uncomplaining sufferer; for his sons, and probably their mother, were well known among the disciples; see Mark xv. 21; Rom. xvi. 13.

him they compelled (Gr., "impressed," cp. the word "pressgang") **to bear His cross.** At first Jesus bore His own cross, as was usual (see John xix. 17); but His sufferings through the preceding night had probably so exhausted His frame that He could not carry it alone: see Luke xxiii. 26. This kind of "impressment" is referred to, ch. v. 41.

33 a place of a skull. So called, either because it was a rounded knoll, or because the skulls of criminals who had been executed and buried there were frequently found in it. Tradition places it on the west of the Temple, where the "Church of the Holy Sepulchre" is at present situated. Professor Macalister (*A Century of Excavation in Palestine*, 1926, pp. 85–94) does not think that there is sufficient evidence to warrant us in rejecting this site.

34 vinegar. This was a weak acid wine (Mark xv. 23), the common drink of the soldiers; and was mixed with frankincense, myrrh, and other drugs (called "myrrh" in Mark xv. 23), to stupefy criminals before their execution. The words suggest Psa. lxix. 21. Our Lord refused the draught, choosing to retain His powers of consciousness and will unimpaired through all His sufferings.

35 they crucified Him. With a prayer for the soldiers on His lips: see Luke xxiii. 34. "Redemisti crucem passus" ("Thou hast redeemed us by thy suffering on the cross"), *Old Latin Hymn.*

casting lots. See note on John xix. 23.

36 they watched Him. It was usual for the soldiers to remain watching the cross, lest the friends of the crucified should take the body before death.

37 His accusation written. On this inscription see John xix. 19, and notes.

38 thieves. Rather, "robbers," R.V.; who belonged to one of the bands with which the country was infested, and had been reserved, as usual, to one of the great feasts for execution. It was probably to mark our Lord with peculiar infamy that He was crucified between these two men: but it fulfilled (Mark xv. 28) the remarkable prophecy in Isa. liii. 12, which our Lord had applied to Himself (Luke xxii. 37).

40 Thou that destroyest the Temple, etc. Referring to words which our Lord had spoken at the commencement of His ministry (John ii. 19). These words, referred to by the "false witnesses" in ch. xxvi. 61, had evidently impressed themselves strongly on the popular mind.

43 if He will have Him. Derisively quoting the very words of a prophecy which they were unconsciously fulfilling: see Psa. xxii. 7, 8, and note.

44 cast the same in His teeth. Rather, "cast upon Him the same reproach," R.V. For some interesting incidents not related here, see Luke xxiii. 39–43; John xix. 25–27.

45 unto the ninth hour. That is, from noon till three o'clock p.m. "It frequently happens thus in Syria, when the sirocco comes up from the desert; and though the phenomenon generally passes quietly, it is frequently the harbinger of an earthquake" (cp. Thomson: *The Land and the Book*, ch. xix.). "A natural phenomenon, yet the hand of God was in it" (*David Smith*). It has been often noted that during the three hours of darkness our Lord was silent. The following words were uttered as the darkness cleared away.

46 My God! my God! why hast Thou forsaken me? These are the opening words of Psa. xxii., in an Aramaic form. They show how fully our Lord took our place. He was "made a curse for us," and "bore our sins": see note on xxvi. 38. That He knew Himself to be bearing not His own sins, but those of others, is manifest from the filial confidence expressed in His appeal, "*My* God!" as well as in the words afterwards uttered with His expiring breath: see Luke xxiii. 46.

48 vinegar. "Sour wine," but without the drugs mentioned in ver. 34. Our Lord had exclaimed, "I thirst" (John xix. 28). Thirst arising from fever was one of the greatest sufferings attending crucifixion. Our Lord drank of this sour wine, though He refused the narcotic draught (John xix. 30).

50 cried again with a loud voice. The words which Jesus uttered "with a loud voice" are found in Luke xxiii. 46; John xix. 30.

yielded up the ghost. The overwhelming

violence of our Lord's sufferings caused Him to die before the malefactors, and thus accomplished the Divine purpose: see John xix. 32–36.

51 the veil of the Temple. This was the large and thick curtain which separated the holy place from the most holy. As our Lord expired at the ninth hour (three in the afternoon), when the evening sacrifice was offered in the Temple, the priest would be, at the very time, burning incense in the holy place, and the people praying without. The rending of the veil, which laid open the way into the most holy place, indicated the removal of previous restrictions, and the opening of a new and better way of access to God through Christ the great High Priest: see Heb. ix. 7–12, 24–26; x. 12–14, 19–22.

from top to bottom. "A proof that it was not done by human instrumentality" (*Weymouth*).

53 came out of the graves. (Only in Matthew.) The power of death and the grave was vanquished by the death of Christ, a victory completed in His Resurrection.

54 the centurion, etc. The Roman officer who superintended the crucifixion. He had just before heard the taunt, "If Thou be the Son of God"; and his words imply his conviction that the meek but dignified Sufferer is all that He claimed to be. The words as given by Luke (xxiii. 47), "Certainly this was a righteous man," are to the same effect.

55 many women were there. The mother of Jesus had probably retired before the darkness came on, accompanied by the beloved disciple (John xix. 25–27), overpowered by the sufferings of her Son. The others lingered to the end; and two (61) of them watched His burial, intending to embalm the body of Him to whose wants they had largely "ministered" during the last year or two of His life.

56 Mary Magdalene. That is, "Mary of the town of Magdala": see xv. 39; and Luke viii. 2, and notes. On "Mary the mother of James and Joses," see x. 3; xiii. 55, and notes; and John xix. 25. The "mother of Zebedee's children" was named Salome (Mark xv. 40).

57 When the even was come. Just before sunset, when the sabbath would begin. Some intervening events are related in John xix. 31–37.

a rich man. Matthew alone mentions that he was "rich"; indicating a fulfilment of Isa. liii. 9. Mark (xv. 43) calls him "an honourable counsellor," referring to his rank as a member of the Sanhedrin, to whose "counsel and deed" he "had not consented," being "a good man and a just" (Luke xxiii. 50, 51). John mentions that Joseph's discipleship was secret, "for fear of the Jews" (xix. 38).

Arimathæa. Formerly Ramathaim Zophim, the city of Samuel (1 Sam. i. 1), not far from Jerusalem.

58 begged the body of Jesus. The Romans generally left the bodies of crucified criminals upon the cross till they wasted away, or were devoured by birds. But they made an exception in favour of the Jews, on account of the law in Deut. xxi. 22, 23; and usually dispatched those who remained alive towards the close of the day, burying them at the place of execution. Our Lord, having in His death completed His sacrifice, was not to be subjected to this further indignity: see note on Isa. liii. 9.

60 he rolled a great stone. The rock-hewn tombs of the wealthy in Palestine had a carefully-finished portal, closed by a massive stone door, running in a groove. This required great strength to open it (Mark xvi. 3), and it admitted of being fastened and "sealed" (66). The tomb of Joseph was in his garden (cp. 2 Kings xxi. 18), near the place of crucifixion (John xix. 41). It was "a new tomb"; no other burial had taken place in it; proving the identity of Him who rose.

62–66. This paragraph is peculiar to Matthew.

62 the next day, that followed [the day] of the preparation. The R.V. reads more exactly, "On the morrow, which is [the day] after the Preparation." The day before the sabbath (Friday) was called "the preparation," because everything requisite for the sabbath was then made ready: this "next day," therefore, was the sabbath itself, and, as shown in the notes on St. John's narrative, probably the day of the regular Paschal feast.

63 I will rise again. Our Lord's sayings (xii. 40, etc.), imperfectly apprehended and believed by His attached disciples, were eagerly laid hold of by His enemies, whose perceptions were quickened by malice and fear.

64 until the third day. The same as "after three days" (63): see note on xii. 40.

the last error shall be worse. We shall have worse imposture than before.

65 Ye have a watch. Or, "take a guard" (R.V. marg.). The presence of the Roman soldiers at the sepulchre, as well as the other precautionary measures of the Jewish rulers, only served to strengthen the evidence of the resurrection.

66 setting a watch. Or (R.V.), "the guard being with them." This guard was designed to prevent violence, the "seal" upon the fastening to prevent fraud: cp. Dan. vi. 17, and note. The sealing was effected by stretching a cord across the stone, securing the two ends to the rock out of which the sepulchre was hewn. The Jewish priests and rulers have now accomplished their design against the Lord's Anointed; and one thing only is wanting to complete their triumph—to throw open the sepulchre upon the third day, and to find there the lifeless body.

CHAPTER XXVIII

The brief accounts which the four evangelists give of His resurrection and ascension, with the intervening events, contain some apparent discrepancies: arising partly from the different order and aspect in which the same circumstances are presented by the different writers; partly from the selection by each of those occurrences which best suited his plan; and chiefly from the omission of many incidents which were unknown to some or all (John xx. 30; xxi. 25). They all, however, agree in relating the three successive steps by which the doubting disciples were at length convinced that the Lord had risen: first, the empty tomb; secondly, the testimony of the angels; and thirdly, the appearances of the Lord Himself.

Perhaps the different narratives may be blended together as follows. "Last at the cross and first at the tomb," the faithful women from Galilee come very early on the first day of the week to embalm the sacred body, Mary Magdalene taking the lead, and arriving first at the sepulchre. To her astonishment she finds the great stone rolled away from the entrance and the tomb emptied; and she runs back to announce the fact to the apostles. Meanwhile the other women, having reached the sepulchre, see the angel who had removed the stone, and who bids them to go and announce the resurrection to the disciples (Matt. xxviii. 1–8; Mark xvi. 1–8; Luke xxiv. 1–9; John xx. 1, 2).

On the information of Mary Magdalene, Peter and John run to the sepulchre, which they also find empty, but they depart without seeing the angels or the Lord (Luke xxiv. 12; John xx. 3–10). Mary, who has followed them to the tomb, lingers weeping alone; looks within, where she sees the angels; and, turning back, obtains the first view of her risen Lord (John xx. 11–18; Mark xvi. 9); who also appears to the other women, as they were going to carry the tidings to the disciples (Matt. xxviii. 9, 10), and then shows Himself to Peter (Luke xxiv. 34; 1 Cor. xv. 5). In the evening He converses with two disciples walking to Emmaus (Mark xvi. 12; Luke xxiv. 13–31); and then suddenly appears in the midst of the assembled disciples, Thomas alone being absent (Mark xvi. 14; Luke xxiv. 26–49; John xx. 19–23). Eight days afterwards, He again visits their assembly, and reproves the incredulity of Thomas (John xx. 26–29). The disciples now go into Galilee, where Jesus appears to some of them near the Lake of Tiberias (John xxi.), and to a large assembly, comprising "above five hundred brethren" (Matt. xxviii. 16–20; 1 Cor. xv. 6). He then is seen by James, "the Lord's brother," alone (1 Cor. xv. 7); and, lastly, by the apostles on the Mount of Olives, near Bethany, just before His ascension (Luke xxiv. 50, 51; Acts i. 4–9).

2 rolled back the stone. (See note on xxvii. 60.) These things occurred probably just before the women arrived.

3 His countenance. Rather, "appearance" (R.V.): see Dan. x. 6.

5 Fear not ye. The word "ye" is emphatic. "Let His foes and His keepers shake; but fear not *ye*, His faithful followers."

7 He goeth before you (leadeth you as a shepherd) **into Galilee.** Where His disciples were most numerous. He did not, however, go thither for more than a week (John xx. 26), when the Feast of Unleavened Bread would be ended, and those who had come up to Jerusalem might have returned.

8 the sepulchre. The Greek word here is changed from "sepulchre" (the erection over the grave) to "tomb" (the grave itself), as if to intimate that the tomb was empty.

with fear and great joy. Awe, on account of the wonders they had seen; joy, at the tidings they had heard.

9 All hail. The usual formula of greeting. "Peace be to you": "good morning." This appearance of our Lord to the women is recorded only in Matthew.

held Him by (took hold of) **the feet.** By touching our Lord's feet they expressed the deepest reverence, mingled with the most ardent affection; while they obtained a fresh evidence that it was not a phantom which they saw, but the living body of the real Jesus.

10 my brethren. Our Lord may have chosen this appellation to show that neither His disciples' unfaithfulness, nor His own new state of existence, had altered His relation or feelings to them: cp. John xx. 17.

12 when they were assembled. This plan was probably determined upon at a meeting of those who were most hostile to Christ, not a formal sitting of the whole council.

13 while we slept. This pretence was altogether absurd. It was unlikely that the disciples should make the attempt; incredible that men accustomed to martial discipline should one and all sleep at their post, knowing that the penalty was death; and impossible that if they were asleep they should know what others were doing at the time. But those who reject well-accredited truth will often welcome a convenient lie; so "that saying (*i.e.*, that account of the matter) was commonly repeated among the Jews."

14 and secure you. Lit., "rid you of care" (R.V.); "screen you from punishment" (*Weymouth*).

16 into a (the) **mountain.** An appointed place for the great gathering. The last words of Jesus which Matthew records, were delivered, like His first discourses, on a mountain in Galilee.

17 some doubted. Probably not some of the apostles; but some of the large body of disciples ("five hundred brethren at once") to whom He appeared in Galilee, who at first doubted whether it was really He. The frankness with which Matthew mentions this fact indicates conscious truthfulness.

18 All power is (hath been) **given unto me.** For the "power" here intended (strictly "authority," R.V.), see Acts ii. 33–36; v. 31; Rom. xiv. 9; Eph. i. 20–23; Phil. ii. 9–11; Heb. i. 3, 4; ii. 9; Rev. v. 5–14, etc.

19 Go ye. This command, being given to the assembled multitude of disciples, shows that it is the duty and the privilege of every true disciple to endeavour to "make disciples of" others: see Acts viii. 4.

teach. Or, "make disciples of" (R.V.); teach them the doctrine concerning me, and endeavour to lead them to receive it. We have here the threefold object of the preachers of the Gospel—to make men disciples of Christ, by converting them to the faith; to bring them to a public profession of the faith, by baptism; and to train them up in the practice of universal holiness.

all (the) **nations.** Not confining your labours to your own countrymen. Yet it required another express revelation (Acts x.) to teach the disciples that the gospel tidings were not to be confined to the Jews, or to the proselytes, in "all the nations," but to be preached to *all men*.

baptising them. All who are made disciples are to be baptised. Baptism is the solemn rite of admission into the visible Church, and is designed as a profession of faith in the character and the word of God, as revealed in Holy Scriptures.

in the name. Rather, "*into* the name," etc. (R.V.); a formula implying *union with and dedication to*. And it should be observed that it is not into the *names*, but into the *name;* showing that, with a distinct recognition of the different parts which the Father, the Son, and the Holy Spirit take in the great work of salvation, there is joined an equally distinct apprehension of the unity of the Godhead, as the fountain of authority and the source of blessing: cp. 2 Cor. xiii. 14. In the Acts, the recorded instances of baptism are in the name of Jesus only, but the gift of the Holy Spirit is associated with the ordinance: in *promise* (ii. 38) *preceding* the rite (x. 44, 47) or *following* it (viii. 17, xix. 6).

20 I am with you alway ("all the days"). The presence and power of Christ are necessary to success in His service. And they are promised, as an all-sufficient strength and comfort, to His faithful servants, in all their Christian labours, "unto the end of the world," or, as R.V. marg., "the consummation of the age," the accomplishment of all the great purposes which mark and crown the era of redemption.

THE GOSPEL ACCORDING TO ST. MARK

INTRODUCTION

THAT this was the first of the Four Gospels in point of time is generally agreed. The date is not later than A.D. 70, or earlier than A.D. 63, and is most probably 65 or 66. A very early Christian tradition traces it to Mark's connexion with Peter.

The author's full name was John Mark, and it was to his mother's house that Peter went on his deliverance from prison (Acts xii. 12). He accompanied Barnabas and Paul on their first missionary journey (Acts xiii. 5), having been taken with them from Jerusalem to Antioch (Acts xii. 25). His action in leaving them at Perga (Acts xiii. 13), due either to fear of the dangers of the mountainous interior of Asia Minor or to domestic claims, was the cause of sharp division between Barnabas and Paul (Acts xv. 36–40). But the breach was afterwards healed, and Paul speaks in affectionate terms of Mark (Col. iv. 10, 11 ; Philem. 24 ; 2 Tim. iv. 11).

In contrast with St. Matthew, it is evident that St. Mark wrote primarily for Gentiles. Thus he gives explanations of words like "Boanerges," "Talitha cumi," "Bartimæus"; of Jewish customs (vii. 3 ; xiv. 12 ; xv. 42) and of localities (xiii. 6, etc.) which would not be familiar to Gentile readers. He makes no reference to the Jewish Law.

Perhaps the most notable feature of this Gospel is the vividness with which incidents are described. Graphic details are given, such as must have been observed by an eyewitness. Such are the look and gesture and the actual Aramaic words of our Lord (*e.g.*, iii. 5, 17, 34 ; v. 32 ; vii. 34 ; ix. 35 ; x. 23) ; xiv. 36). "Straightway" ("immediately" or "at once") is a favourite word of St. Mark's, occurring about twenty-seven times in the Gospel. More than in any other Gospel, we find descriptions of the impression produced upon the disciples and the people by the words and actions of our Lord (*e.g.*, i. 22, 27 ; ii. 12 ; iv. 41 ; vi. 2, 51 ; x. 24, 26, 32). All these, and many other details, combine to produce a conviction of reality and truthfulness.

CHAPTER I

1 Jesus Christ. An expression not elsewhere found in the Gospels, except in the introductory words of St. Matthew. "Jesus in His humanity, Christ in His office, Son of God in His eternal nature" (*Speaker's Comm.*).

2 in the prophets. Some of the best manuscripts and versions read, "Esaias the prophet" (so R.V.) ; the name of the principal prophet quoted being mentioned alone, although there is also a quotation from Malachi.

4 John did baptise, etc. More literally, "John arose, baptising," or "who baptised" : see R.V.

for (unto) **the remission of sins.** "He enforced *repentance*, and *baptism* as the sign and proof of it : and both had respect *to the forgiveness of sins* ; for which, however, his dispensation made no new provision, gave in fact no new promise ; but the penitent were referred to Him who was to come after John."

7 one mightier than I. Here is the encouragement of every preacher.

latchet (dimin. of *latch*="fastener"). The strap which passed over the instep, and fastened the shoe or sandal : see Matt. iii. 11.

10 He saw. *Jesus* saw : see Luke iii. 21.

opened. R.V., "rent asunder."

12 the wilderness. The scene of our Lord's fasting and temptation is not known. Some think it was the wilderness of Sinai, where Moses and Elijah fasted. Tradition has fixed on a mountain above Jericho, and given it the name of Quarantania ("the hill of the forty days").

13 forty days. It seems that our Lord was tempted during the whole of the forty days (see Luke iv 2), but that the most urgent assaults of the tempter were made at the end of that time.

15 The time (period *or* era) **is fulfilled.** These words, recorded by Mark alone, bring before the mind the long bygone ages of preparation for the coming of "the kingdom of God" : during which full proof had been afforded of the greatness of man's wants, and of his own inability to supply them. This preparation had now been completed by the short ministry and the speedy withdrawal of John, who had pointed to Jesus as the expected Saviour.

and believe (in) **the gospel.** John had preached "repentance." To this our Lord adds faith in "the good tidings": comp. Acts xx. 21.

19 James. Evidently the elder brother.

20 with the hired servants. A point noted by Mark only. They were not called to leave their father without help.

22 astonished at His doctrine (teaching). See Matt. vii. 28, 29. Our Lord began to teach "immediately," and continued teaching frequently (Luke iv. 31) in the synagogue at Capernaum.

not as the scribes. They simply taught the traditions they had received.

24 Let [us] alone. The word is rather an exclamation, *Ah!* the cry of the evil spirit. But the best editors omit it here. It occurs Luke iv. 34.

I know Thee who Thou art, etc. This testimony was not that of believing confidence, which Jesus delights to receive. The demons knew Him to be "the Son of God" (Luke iv. 41). But our Lord, by His command, "Hold thy peace," shows that He would reserve in His own hands the publication of this fact: revealing it to His immediate disciples first.

26 had torn him. Or, "had convulsed him"; though without being allowed permanently to injure him (Luke iv. 35).

31 she ministered. Having none of that protracted weakness which attends a natural recovery from severe fever. The preceding descriptive details, "He came and took . . . and lifted her up," are all peculiar to Mark.

32 when the sun did set. They waited till sunset, when the sabbath ended (21), before they brought their sick. All the three evangelists who relate this mention the great numbers that came and were healed at the close of this first sabbath spent in Capernaum Only Mark records, in his graphic way, that "all the city was gathered together at the door" (33). He also alone notices the presence of those "possessed."

35 He went out. That is, out of Peter's house (29). For His return, see ii. 1. There were many "solitary" (R.V., "desert") places on the bare hills, or in the ravines bordering the lake.

and there prayed. It appears to have been our Lord's habit to prepare for the activities of the day by giving part of the night to prayer: thus in His life showing "that union of energy and rest, of active labour and deep devotion," which He would like to characterise His followers (*Stanley*).

30 followed after Him. Emphatic in original; "pursued Him eagerly"; "hunted him out and discovered him" (*Moffatt*).

37 All men seek for Thee. Many of the people came also, and entreated Him to remain with them (Luke iv. 42). All this portion of the narrative shows His great popularity at the beginning of His work in Galilee (see ver. 45).

38 towns. A word used only here, meaning literally, "village-towns," with which parts of the Gennesaret district were thickly studded: Joseph. *Wars*, iii. 3, § 2.

therefore came I forth. Some take the Saviour to mean "into this world": as in Luke iv. 43; John xvi. 28. But others think that He referred to His coming forth from Capernaum.

40 a leper. Respecting the leprosy, see notes on Lev. xiii., xiv. For the incident, comp. Matt. viii. 1-13.

beseeching Him, and kneeling down to Him. Peculiar to Mark.

43 straitly charged him. The word employed denotes a strong, peremptory command. R.V. marg. has "sternly."

44 say nothing to any man. Our Lord appears to have frequently given such prohibitions as this; for which He might have various reasons. In this instance He probably desired that the cure should be acknowledged by the priest, the appointed judge in such matters, before anything could occur to create a prejudice.

for a testimony unto them. That this cure would be to the priests who saw and acknowledged it a testimony of the Messiahship of Jesus, which would condemn their unbelief.

45 the (a) **city.** That is, any city. The result of the man's publication of the cure showed the wisdom of our Lord's prohibition.

CHAPTER II

See Luke v. 17-26.

3 borne of four. A graphic touch, peculiar to Mark.

4 the bed. Pallet or thin mattress.

press: the crowd.

5 Son (lit., "Child"), **thy sins be forgiven thee.** As the word *be* is ambiguous (apparently expressing a *wish*), the translation *are* is preferable: so R.V.

14 [son] of Alphæus. This Alphæus (mentioned only by Mark) is a different person from the father of James (Matt. x. 3).

21 else the new piece, etc. Or, "That which filleth (*or* should fill) it up taketh away from it, the new from the old." See Matt. ix. 14-17.

26 Abiathar. Abiathar is named (only by Mark) as the high priest; but in 1 Sam. xxi. 1-6, we find that his father Ahimelech was then in the office. Some suggest that Ahimelech may have had also the name of "Abiathar"; others that the words mean, "in the days of Abiathar, *who was afterwards* the high priest."

27 The sabbath was made for man, etc. Only in Mark: comp. note on Matt. xii. 8. This saying of our Lord rebukes equally all superstitious regard to the sabbath, and all neglect of the opportunity which it was designed to give for spiritual culture.

CHAPTER III

See notes on Matt. xii. 10-14.

4 to save life, or to kill? He who neglects to save life when he can do so must be held accountable for the loss of it (see Prov. xxiv. 11, 12). The descriptive touches, "They held their peace," and, in ver. 5, "He looked round about on them with anger," are peculiar to Mark.

5 being grieved. A word used only here, implying pity as well as indignation. Holy "anger" against sin is perfectly compatible with holy compassion and "grief" for the sinner.

6 Pharisees . . . took counsel with the Herodians. This was a very remarkable combination; for these two parties were strongly opposed to one another. On the Herodians, see Matt. xxii. 16, note.

7 from Galilee, etc. The enumeration in this and the next verse shows that the fame of our Lord's teaching and miracles had spread through the whole land, and had attracted to Him all classes of the inhabitants.

8 Idumæa. Edom, which reached from the Dead Sea to the Red Sea.

10 plagues. Or, "scourges"; *i.e.* sicknesses; so called because they were regarded as Divine chastisements for sin.

11 when they saw Him. Lit., "whensoever they beheld Him" (R.V.). The word indicates the close connexion between the demons and the human beings whom they "possessed." The demons recognise "the Son of God" in Him whom the demoniacs see, and urge their victims to "fall down before Him," etc.

12 that they should not make Him known. See notes on i. 24, and on Matt. xvi. 20.

13 into a (the) **mountain.** See note on Matt. v. 1.

14–19. See notes on Matt. x. 1–4.

14 ordained. That is, "appointed" (R.V.). Whilst Matthew records at length the commission subsequently given to the apostles, from which we may gather the nature and objects of their office, Mark states the immediate purpose of their designation. They were to be with Jesus; to witness His life, death, and resurrection; to learn by His example, as well as by His public discourses (Matt. v.–vii.) and His private teachings (John xiv.–xvi.). Thus instructed, they were to begin, under His superintendence, that work of preaching and healing which they were further to carry out after His departure.

17 sons of thunder. Some take this name to be an allusion to the vehement and zealous disposition of the two brothers: see ix. 38; x. 37.

19 they went into a house. Wycliffe's rendering, as given in the margin of the A.V., "they came home," is probably the best. But the Septuagint has the verb in the singular, "he cometh" (as R.V.).

21 His friends. That is, His family. They intended to persuade, or even to compel Him to desist from His labours; regarding Him as "beside Himself": see note on Matt. xii. 46. For their arrival, see ver. 31. Their conduct in influencing the mother of Jesus to impede Him in His work accounts for His tone towards her.

22 the scribes . . . from Jerusalem. These, like most of the Scribes, were Pharisees (Matt. xii. 24); and they had come down from Jerusalem probably to oppose the progress of the new teaching. On vers. 22–35, see notes on Matt. xii. 24–50.

He hath Beelzebub (Beelzebul). See note on Matt. x. 25. If Jesus were possessed by Beelzebul, "the prince of the demons," He would have power over inferior demons. Hence the form of His reply.

29 in danger of eternal damnation. The best authorities read, "is guilty of an eternal sin" (R.V.). The phrase is peculiar to Mark: see on Matt. xii. 32.

CHAPTER IV

1–20 (Parable of THE SOWER). See notes on Matt. xiii. 3–23.

11 them that are without. In later phraseology, all non-Christians (1 Cor. v. 12). Here it means all who were outside the circle of the disciples. "It is doubtless a hint of the germ of the opposition between the old and the new communities" (*Lange*).

13 And He said unto them, etc. This question of our Lord is peculiar to Mark. Its ground is, that the parable of the Sower is the simple type of all the rest. Read "all the parables," with R.V.

15 immediately. Peculiar to Mark.

21 a candle. Rather, "the lamp," and "to be set on the lampstand" (R.V.). This simile of the lamp, which is used in Matt. v. 15, Luke xi. 33, in other connexions, teaches the disciples that our Lord's object in now giving to them the explanation of this parable was, that He might qualify them for being the public instructors of the world; for, what He was now teaching them in secret, was in proper time and manner to go widely abroad (21, 22). Therefore they are to attend earnestly to His teaching (23); for, according to the measure of attention that they pay, and the obedience which they render, will be their spiritual growth (24, 25).

24 with what measure ye mete, etc. What is elsewhere applied to persons (Matt. vii. 2; Luke vi. 38) is here applied to "the word." As you treat it, so will it operate towards you. If you believe it, it brings you salvation; if you reject it, it condemns you: see 2 Cor. ii. 15, 16.

25 For he that hath, etc. See note on Matt. xiii. 12.

26–29. THE SEED SPRINGING SECRETLY. Our Lord adds this parable (peculiar to Mark) to fortify His disciples against impatience. As the husbandman labours, in certain assurance that, by the hidden processes of life, God will in due time cause the seed to germinate and ripen, "he knoweth not how"; so do you industriously preach the word of God, calmly expecting that in due time He will give an abundant harvest.

30–32. THE MUSTARD SEED. See notes on Matt. xiii. 31, 32.

33 as they were able to hear it. Gradually enlarging His communications, as they were prepared to understand more; comp. John xvi. 12. The apostles afterwards acted on the same principles as their Lord; adapting their instructions to the ignorant, so as to lead them onwards: see 1 Cor. iii. 1, etc.; Heb. v. 11–14. The reference (peculiar to Mark) to the *private* exposition to the disciples is no doubt one of Peter's reminiscences.

35–41. See notes on Matt. viii. 24–27.

37 was now full. Rather, "was now filling" (R.V.).

38 a pillow. Rather, "the cushion" (R.V.). The bold question, "Carest Thou not that we perish?" is peculiar to this Gospel. Such an appeal was characteristic of Peter.

40 And He said unto them. In Matthew, the reproof is placed *before* the stilling of the storm; but Mark, with whom Luke agrees, is evidently exact.

CHAPTER V

2 a man with an unclean spirit. Matthew (viii. 28) speaks of *two* demoniacs. Perhaps there was something peculiar in the appearance or the character of one of the men, which rendered him more prominent. Luke (viii. 27) mentions only one.

3 dwelling among the tombs. The mountains of Palestine abound with large caverns, often improved by human labour, and adapted for use as sheepfolds, dwellings (Judg. vi. 2), or tombs. Such caves afforded refuge for outlaws and maniacs.

4 he had been often bound, etc. The vivid details in this and the next verse are peculiar to Mark.

7 What have I to do with Thee? Why do you interfere with us? See 2 Sam. xvi. 10; Ezra iv. 3. These demons "believe and tremble" (Jas. ii. 19).

9 Legion. The Roman word "Legion" (see Matt. xxvi. 53, and note) had come to signify a large number; and here it represents the overwhelming power of this demoniacal influence, pervading the man's whole nature. But this narrative shows that the powers of evil are all under the control of Him who "was manifested to destroy the works of the devil," and who now mercifully restrains that power which He will hereafter utterly overthrow: comp. Rom. xvi. 20.

10 out of the country. That is, according to Luke, "into the abyss." See note, Luke viii. 31.

12 Send us into the swine. Why the demons made this request, and why our Lord granted it, we are not informed. The incident may teach us, as Dr. A. Maclaren puts it, "that a spirit in rebellion against God gravitates downwards, and becomes more or less bestialised."

15 clothed. He had "worn no clothes" (Luke viii. 27) while under the power of the evil spirits.

17 to depart out of their coasts (borders). Looking at their own loss rather than at the exhibition of Divine power that they had witnessed. "Their prayer was heard; He did depart; He took them at their word, and let them alone" (*Trench*).

18 when He was come into the ship. Rather, as R.V., "as He was entering into the boat"; in the act of stepping on board.

prayed Him that he might be with Him. The man perhaps feared the return of the ejected demons; but his subsequent conduct shows that he also felt grateful to his Deliverer. Our Lord, however, desired that he should become to his Gentile kindred and neighbours a witness of the Messiah's grace and power.

22 one of the rulers. The ruler or president of the synagogue was a person who presided over the assembly; not only convening it and preserving order in it, but inviting readers and speakers to officiate: see Acts xiii. 15. Only Mark gives his name.

26 and had spent all she had, etc. These vivid descriptions of a hopeless case are peculiar to Mark. Luke, the physician, says, she "could not be healed of any."

27 His garment. The "garment" was the mantle (see note on Matt. v. 40); on the border of which was a fringe (see Numb. xv. 38) or "hem."

28 she said. That is, to herself: she thought.

29 of that (the) **plague.** Of her illness.

30 And Jesus, immediately knowing, etc. Better, as R.V., "And straightway, Jesus knowing," etc.

virtue. Rather, "power" (R.V.). He knew that He had exercised His divine power in rewarding the woman's faith.

34 Daughter. A term of kindness, like the word "son" in ii. 5.

go in (lit., "into") **peace.** This woman's faith was not unmixed with some mistake and infirmity; but it was genuine, and therefore obtained the blessing which she sought.

36 As soon as Jesus heard. R.V. marg., "Jesus overhearing."

37 save Peter, and James, and John. "And the father and mother of the maiden" (Luke). The three disciples here chosen to witness our Lord's power over death were afterwards selected to be present at His transfiguration (ix. 2), and His agony in the garden (xiv. 33). They were also (xvi. 7; John xx. 2; 1 Cor. xv. 7) among the earliest witnesses of His resurrection. It can hardly be doubted that they were thus distinguished in order to complete their fitness to stand foremost in labours and sufferings for their Lord (Acts ii. 14; iii. 4; iv. 3, 13; viii. 14; xii. 2).

38 wept and wailed. It is still customary in the East not only to give vent to grief in loud outcries, but, on occasion of death, to hire professional mourners and minstrels to bewail the deceased in most doleful music and lamentations: see Eccles. xii. 5; Jer. ix. 17; xvi. 6, 7; Ezek. xxiv. 17; Amos v. 16.

39 is not dead. "This is rather a sleep than death" (comp. John xi. 11). The fact that "they laughed at Him" is mentioned to show that she was really dead.

41 Talitha cumi. The exact words are given (as in vii. 34) in the Aramaic, the common speech of the people.

43 that no man should know it. The meaning seems to be, that they should not publish it *immediately*, in order that He might retire before the excitement that it would cause had spread among the people.

[something] should be given her to eat. This detail completes the picture in all its vividness, and indicates our Lord's attention to the smallest as well as the greatest wants of those whom He benefits.

CHAPTER VI

1 He went out from thence, etc. From the neighbourhood of the Lake of Gennesaret our Lord went to Nazareth, the surrounding district being called "His own country (fatherland)."

3 the carpenter. This word implies that Jesus Himself actually worked at the trade of His reputed father. As the people of Nazareth mentioned Him only as "the son of *Mary*," it appears probable that Joseph had died before this time; and that Jesus was therefore known as having helped to support by His labour His widowed mother, with whom He dwelt.

5 He could there do no mighty work. He "could not" do this, without violating His rules of requiring faith as a condition of His help. "The door was, so to speak, shut upon the Saviour by the people's impiety" (*Calvin*).

7 by two and two. Thus regarding their weakness and the social necessities of their nature, and guarding them against the dangers of isolation and of personal ambition. It is observable that, whilst Matthew places their names in pairs in his list, it is Mark who tells us that they were sent out by "two and two."

8 a staff only. In Matt. x. 10 the command is not to take a staff (R.V.), *i.e.*, an *extra* staff. So "no shoes," *i.e.*, no *change of* shoes.

no scrip. Referring probably to the wallet carried by a beggar, like that of the wandering heathen priest (*Deissmann*).

13 anointed. The anointing was not the means of cure; but (like touching with the hand) was a visible symbol of the invisible healing power thus imparted. See James v. 14: see also vii. 33; 2 Kings v. 14; John ix. 6.

14 Herod. This was Herod Antipas, son of

Herod the Great, and brother to Archelaus: see note on Matt. ii. 1, 22. At his father's death, he obtained the government of Galilee and Peræa, with the title of "tetrarch" (Luke iii. 1, 19), which originally meant *a ruler of a fourth part* (of the kingdom), but was afterwards applied more generally, like the name "king." At the time of these events he was probably residing at Machærus, a fortress in the south of Peræa, east of the Dead Sea, where John was imprisoned. He was a very different man from his father—weak, crafty, and temporising, rather than violent and cruel; with some good dispositions, but too much the slave of passion to allow them to have much practical influence.

His name was spread abroad. By the preaching of the apostles as well as His own. The various reports "perplexed" Herod; and his own guilty conscience led him to adopt the supposition which he most dreaded—"It is John." Comp. the scene in Shakespeare's Richard III. (Act v. Sc. 3): "Let me sit heavy on thy soul to-morrow."

therefore mighty works do show forth themselves. Or, as R.V., "therefore do these (the) powers work in him."

17 Philip's wife. Not Philip the tetrarch of Ituræa (Luke iii. 1), but another brother who had no tetrarchy. Herodias was a granddaughter of Herod the Great, and was married to her uncle Philip, whom she abandoned for Herod. To make way for her, Herod had divorced his former wife, the daughter of Aretas, king of Arabia; which involved him afterwards in war.

19 had a quarrel against him. Rather, as R.V., "set herself against him," having "an inward grudge" (A.V. marg.).

20 observed him. This means rather, "preserved him" from the attempts of Herodias against his life ("kept him safe," R.V.). Therefore she resolved to gain her end by stratagem.

did many things. The Greek verb of what was probably the original reading, "was much perplexed" (*ēporei*), is very similar in form to that word translated "did" (*epoiei*). His "hearing gladly" was doubtless due to the fact that John explained some of the points about which Herod was perplexed. He could at least appreciate the preacher's message.

21 a convenient day. For the execution of the queen's designs.

chief [estates] of Galilee. The most distinguished men in that province.

22 the daughter, etc. Salome, the daughter of Philip and Herodias. She afterwards married her uncle Philip, the tetrarch of Ituræa, and then her cousin Aristobulus.

and danced. This was usually done by paid performers. For a princess to assume the part of a professional dancing-girl was the greatest indecorum.

23 unto the half of my kingdom. See note on Esther v. 3. A vain promise, as Herod the tetrarch would have no power to give away any part of his sovereignty! He speaks of his kingdom like Ahasuerus!—*Stier*.

25 by and by in a charger. Or, "at once on a platter." She asks to have it done "at once," lest Herod should change his mind when cool.

26 for his oath's sake. He forgot that to keep an unlawful vow was only adding to the guilt of a hasty word the heavier guilt of a deliberate crime. He was also afraid of being ridiculed as mean or spiritless, which led him, as it has led many others, into wrong-doing.

reject. "Disappoint" or "break faith with."

27 an executioner. A soldier of the guard in attendance. Mark here uses a Latin term.

29 when his disciples heard [of it]. John's death seems to have occurred about three years after he began his public work, and when he had lain in prison nearly a year and a half: for the Passover was now at hand (John vi. 4); and this was the third during our Lord's ministry.

33 afoot. Or, "by land." Seeing the direction which the vessel was taking, the people "ran together" by land round the northern end of the lake, to meet our Lord on His disembarking.

37 two hundred pennyworth. Worth about $40, though some place the value at even a higher sum. See note on Matt. xx. 2. This was Philip's reply (John vi. 7). He probably mentions the amount actually in "the bag," or common purse.

40 in ranks. The word here used properly means "garden-beds"; the orderly grouping of the companies (39), each consisting of fifty or a hundred. By this arrangement the vast multitude could be conveniently served, and accurately counted. The "green grass" is the touch of an eyewitness. During several months of the year the herbage on these slopes is parched and brown. But John (vi. 4) informs us that the Passover was nigh. The whole scene would therefore be verdant in the freshness of spring. See one of the finest passages of Ruskin (*Modern Painters*, Part iv. chap. xiv. § 51).

45 unto Bethsaida. "Towards Bethsaida." They land on the plain of Gennesareth (53); and the next day the multitude follow in boats to Capernaum, seeking for Jesus, and find Him there (John vi. 24, 25, 59).

46 when He had sent them away. R.V., "after He had taken leave of them."

48 toiling. The original word is very expressive: "distressed" (R.V.).

the fourth watch. From "cock-crowing" till sunrise (about 3–6 a.m.). *Three* watches are elsewhere reckoned: the latter being the Jewish method, the former the Roman.

would have passed by them. A touch peculiar to Mark. As though He disregarded their distress. Thus He acted towards the sisters at Bethany (John xi. 6). He often sees fit to try faith, and to elicit prayer, even while He designs to bestow His gracious help: see also Luke xxiv. 28. Mark omits the incident of Peter's walking upon the waves.

52 their heart was hardened. Peculiar to Mark and showing the truthfulness of his narrative.

53 drew. Rather, "moored," as R.V.

56 And whithersoever He entered, etc. Only in Mark.

CHAPTER VII

2 defiled. Or, "common." As the law enjoined washing (Lev. xv. 11) after a person had touched anything ceremonially unclean, the excessive formalism of the Jewish teachers had imposed this ablution whenever there was the least possibility of defilement. It was for reasons not of cleanliness, but ceremonial observance, that they were so strict. In proportion as the spirit of true religion is departing, men usually make its external requirements more numerous and burdensome.

3 For the Pharisees, etc. This explanation is peculiar to Mark, and is no doubt given for the sake of his Gentile readers.

oft. Or, "diligently," R.V. But the literal translation is "with the fist"; which means the whole hand, and not merely the fingers. Ancient writers translate this, "up to the elbow."

tradition of the elders. The interpretation of the Mosaic law by eminent teachers of former times. It was often puerile, and even mischievous; inducing men not only to neglect (8), but also to oppose (9), and virtually to annul (12), the spirit of the law: yet it was enjoined as sacred and authoritative. In our Lord's time it was only an oral tradition, but it has subsequently been collected in the Talmud.

4 wash. The crowded state of an Eastern "market-place," or bazaar, would necessarily cause defilement to the clothes or persons of the Pharisees.

tables. Rather, "couches." But the word is absent from the most ancient MSS., and is omitted in R.V.

6 Esaias prophesied. Isa. xxix. 13, 15. The prophet's descriptions apply not to his own age only, but to "hypocrites" and formalists of all times.

their heart is far from me. No worship in which the "heart" is not engaged can be acceptable: comp. John iv. 24.

9 Full well. Ironical. Luther renders *finely.*

10 curseth. Rather, "speaketh evil of," R.V.

11 It is Corban. Moffatt well translates: "This money might have been at your service but it is Korban." The word "Corban" means an offering, "a consecrated thing" (*Weymouth,* n.).

17 His disciples. Peter was their spokesman, Matt. xv. 15.

19 purging all meats. The word "purging," in accordance with the Greek, is best taken as applying to our Lord Himself. So R.V., "*This He said,* making all meats clean." He purged or purified all food by this deep saying of His: comp. Acts x. 15.

21 evil thoughts. The catalogue of sins proceeding from the depraved heart is given by Matthew according to the order of the commands in the Decalogue (comp. Exod. xx. with Matt. xv. 19). Here the list is longer and the number greater. "Wickedness" means *malice;* "lasciviousness" may include *unrestrained indulgence* of every kind; "an evil eye" is *envy;* "blasphemy" may include *calumny;* and the last sin, "foolishness," seems, as in the Old Testament (see Psa. xiv. 1), to mean *senseless and reckless impiety.* Such are the defiling streams, some of which flow forth from the heart, until it is renewed by Divine grace.

24. See Matt. xv. 21–28. Mark again adds some details not in the parallel account, as that Christ "could not be hid."

26 a Greek. A Gentile.

a Syrophœnician. The *Syrian* Phœnicians were distinguished from the *Libyan* Phœnicians, of North Africa.

27 Let the children first be filled. These words (which Mark alone mentions) show that her application was not refused absolutely. Her faith laid hold of the apparently slight hope.

30 laid upon the bed. These graphic words suggest the contrast between the present quiet repose of the child and her previous rage and restlessness.

32. The miraculous healing of the deaf and dumb man, which follows, is related by Mark only. But, in Matthew's account of the same journey (Matt. xv. 31), "the dumb speaking" is mentioned as one of the miracles which excited the admiration of the multitude.

33 touched his tongue. This and two other passages (viii. 23–26; John ix. 1–7) contain the only recorded instances in which our Lord used other means than speech in performing His miracles.

34 He sighed. The sight of suffering in any form evidently touched the Saviour deeply: comp. John xi. 35, 38.

Ephphatha. An Aramaic word, applicable to the organs of speech as well as of hearing.

36 tell no man. It was in this very region that our Lord had commissioned the restored demoniac to report his deliverance to his family and friends (v. 20). He now enjoins secrecy; as He usually did when He was about to remain some time in a neighbourhood.

CHAPTER VIII

1–9. On these verses, see Matt. xv. 32–39.

3 divers. Several.

10–12. See notes on Matt. xvi. 1–4.

10 Dalmanutha. On the western side of the lake, now *Ain-el-Bareideh;* not far from Magdala or Magadan: see Matt. xv. 39.

12 He sighed deeply. Deeply grieved with the perverseness of these men.

There shall no sign be given. The wording of this refusal is most emphatic.

14–21. See notes on Matt. xvi. 5–12.

14 neither . . . more than one loaf. A point of detail peculiar to Mark.

15 and [of] the leaven of Herod. Only in Mark. The "leaven" or corrupt doctrine of Herod was itself a form of Sadduceeism: worldliness arising from scepticism as to spiritual truths, and leading to alliance with the political power: see on Matt. xxii. 16.

17 have ye your heart yet hardened? Comp. Isa. vi. 9.

22 Bethsaida. On Bethsaida, see note on vi. 45. This miracle is related by Mark alone; and it is remarkable not only for the use of an external application (see note on vii. 34), but also for the gradual process of the cure: illustrating the variety of the Divine methods.

24 I see men as trees, walking. I can distinguish men from trees only by their movements.

Chapters viii. 27–38, ix., closely resemble Matt. xvi. 13–28, xvii., xviii.

31 after three days. On "three days," see note on Matt. xii. 40.

33 looked on His disciples. All of whom probably felt what Peter had expressed. It is observable that, though Mark (with Luke) omits the praise given to Peter, he records (with Matthew) the reproof addressed to the apostle.

34 deny himself. "renounce" or "give up" himself.

and take up his cross. Jesus here puts the hard and yet the heroic aspect of His service in the forefront. To follow Him means the daily sacrifice of self.

38 adulterous. See note on Matt. xii. 39.

CHAPTER IX

2–13. See notes on Luke ix. 28–36, and on Matt. xvii. 1–13.

3 shining . . . [as snow] . . . so as no fuller on earth can white them. Phrases of vivid description, peculiar to this evangelist, and no doubt containing Peter's own reminiscence of the scene. So ver. 6, "he wist not what to answer," and 8, "suddenly when they had looked round about."

10 questioning one with another. The disciples, like other pious Jews, doubtless believed in the soul's immortality and the future general resurrection (see Acts xxiii. 6–8, also John xi. 24); but they found it hard to believe our Lord's declarations concerning His own death and resurrection, as they expected that the Messiah would live for ever (John xii. 34).

14 the scribes questioning with them. The scribes (particularised only by Mark) were probably triumphing over the disciples, and from their failure deducing their Master's inability. How great the change from the Mount of Transfiguration, with the open heaven and the homage of the glorified, to this scene of misery and unbelief!

15 were greatly amazed, etc. Only in Mark. Our Lord's countenance perhaps retained something of the brightness of His recent transfiguration. But the people might well be awe-struck by the suddenness of His appearance, and His calmness and heavenly serenity, as contrasted with the excited faces of the applicant, the sufferer, and the eager disputants.

18 he teareth him. Throwing him into convulsions or violent epileptic fits.

20 he fell on the ground, etc. This description, and the following dialogue with the father, is peculiar to Mark.

23 If thou canst [believe], etc. Rather (see var. read.), "If thou canst!—All things are possible," etc. The full force of the language may be best brought out by a paraphrase: The difficulty is, not whether I can heal, but whether thou canst believe; for all things are possible to him that believeth. Faith in the Saviour is the channel through which all His blessings flow to men.

25 I charge thee. The word "I" is here emphatic: Not my disciples, but I, command you.

29 by prayer and fasting. The higher achievements of Christian holiness and benevolence demand the strongest faith; which must therefore be made and kept vigorous by earnest devotion and self-renunciation. The words "and fasting" are omitted in R.V., but the MSS. authority for them is sufficiently strong.

30 would not that any man should know it. Wishing to continue His instructions respecting His approaching death without interruption from the multitude: see next verse.

32 understood not that saying. Although familiar with the doctrine of atonement, they could not receive the idea that the Messiah was to be Himself the atoning victim.

34 who [should be] the greatest. The honour recently given to Peter (Matt. xvi. 17–19), and the privilege granted to three of the disciples (Matt. xvii. 1), may have given fresh impulse to that earthly ambition which our Lord always aimed to repress.

36 set him in the midst. To impress the lesson more powerfully upon them all.

taken him in His arms. A graphic touch, peculiar to Mark.

38 John answered Him, etc. Note his words "followeth not *us*." This spirit is not yet extinct in the Christian Church. John probably felt himself condemned by our Lord's words; and he interrupts the discourse to ascertain whether what he had done in this instance was wrong. Jesus shows that it was; for the man who had been rebuked was evidently acting in His service, and in reliance upon His power.

39 he that is not against us, etc. This saying is a counterpart to that in Matt. xii. 30; and, like it, shows that there can be no neutrality in the contest between God and sin. The form in which the truth is here put teaches us that differences in views and methods are to be charitably borne with, where there is fundamental agreement of faith. "All those who, notwithstanding outward differences of communion and government, believe in and preach Jesus Christ, without bitterly and uncharitably opposing each other, are hereby declared to be helpers forward of each other's work. Oh that all Christians would remember this!"—*Alford.*

42 shall offend. Rather, "cause to fall." (R.V., "Whosoever shall cause one of these little ones that believe on me to stumble.")

a millstone. The word signifies a stone of a mill worked by an ass, and larger than the common hand-mill; "a great millstone" (R.V.).

43 if thy hand offend thee (cause thee to stumble). See note on Matt. v. 29, 30.

fire that never shall be quenched. See notes on Isa. lxvi. 24 (from which these expressions are taken); and on Matt. v. 22, 29.

44 [where their worm dieth not, etc.] This verse and ver. 46 seem to have been added by some early transcriber, as if to give emphasis to ver. 48, where alone the sentence is found in the earliest copies.

49 salted with fire. There is some difficulty in this passage, arising from a mixture of two closely connected metaphors. The meaning appears to be, Just as every burnt sacrifice offered to God must be seasoned with salt—the emblem of purity (Lev. ii. 13); so every person consecrated to Him must be purified, though it be by a process as painful as fire (*i.e.*, the cutting off the hand, or foot, or eye). [The words "and every sacrifice shall be salted with salt," omitted by most editors, and in R.V., were probably the explanation of a transcriber.]

50 have (be at) **peace one with another.** Referring to the ambitious contention out of which this discourse arose (33).

CHAPTER X

1–12. See notes on Matt. xix. 1–12.

12 put away her husband. The law of Moses did not permit a woman to divorce her husband. But the Jews seem to have adopted the custom from the Romans.

13 And they brought, etc. At some place, unspecified, in our Lord's journey through Peræa.

young children. Properly, "little children" (R.V.), as in 14.

14 much displeased. "Moved with indignation" (R.V.). Peculiar to Mark. That the *disciples* should interpose a hindrance showed how little they yet understood their Master.

for of such. Rather, "to such belongs the kingdom of God."

15 as a little child. These words evidently refer to that humility which is one essential characteristic of Christ's true followers: see 14, and also ix. 33–37, and notes.

16 He took them up in His arms. This action mentioned by Mark only, strikingly displays the condescending affection of our Lord.

17–34. See notes on Matt. xix. 16–30.

17 running, and kneeled. Graphic touches, as of an eyewitness.

19 Defraud not. Only in Mark. The other commands are all from the Decalogue. This is probably "St. Mark's rendering of the Tenth Commandment" (*Hammond*). See also Lev. xix. 13.

21 Jesus beholding him loved him. Only in Mark. There was about this young ruler an engaging openness and sincerity which contrasted very favourably with the hypocrisy and dishonesty of the Pharisees and scribes.

24 for them that trust in riches. These words explain the meaning of ver. 23. Those who *possess* riches are apt to *trust* in them—to regard them as a source of security and happiness. This whole verse is peculiar to Mark: see note on Matt. xix. 23.

30 with persecutions. The addition of these words (only in Mark) shows that the blessings of which our Lord is speaking are chiefly spiritual. Yet, even in this life, those who have willingly lost for Christ's sake have often found unexpected advantages—"houses," where they have been welcomed; "brothers, sisters, mothers," who have made common interest with them (see Rom. xvi. 13) and "children" in the faith (see 2 Cor. vi. 13; Gal. iv. 19).

32 amazed . . . afraid. A vivid description of the disciples' feelings, after the manner of this evangelist. There was a majesty and mystery in His bearing which filled them with awe.

35–45. See Matt. xx. 20–28.

35 James and John. According to Matthew, it was the mother who made this request on her sons' behalf. Both statements are no doubt true.

37 in Thy glory. They evidently referred to a state of earthly glory, which they expected Jesus soon to assume.

38 baptised. "The being immersed and overwhelmed with waters is a frequent metaphor, in all languages, to express the rush of successive troubles" (*Watson*).

42 which are accounted. "They who are acknowledged as rulers," etc.

43 minister. Or, "servant," the word in ver. 44 meaning "bond servant"; a climax.

46–52. See notes on Matt. xx. 29–34.

46 Bartimæus. "*Bar*" is the Aramaic word for *son*. Mark alone gives the name. The case of Bartimæus affords a striking illustration of persevering faith and its reward.

49 And they call the blind man, etc. This part of the narrative, to the end of 50, is peculiar to Mark.

CHAPTER XI

1–11. See notes on Matt. xxi. 1–11.

4 tied by the door, etc. This minute description is peculiar to Mark; "tied at the door without in the open street," R.V.

10 The kingdom of our father David. That is, the promised restoration of David's kingdom by the Messiah: see 2 Sam. vii.; Isa. xi. The multitude had, however, no conception of the spiritual nature of Christ's kingdom; and, before a week had elapsed, a similar multitude in Jerusalem were clamorous for His death.

11 when He had looked round about. Only in Mark. "A look serious, sorrowful, judicial."—*Meyer.*

12–19. See notes on Matt. xxi. 18–22.

13 the time of figs was not [yet]. An explanation peculiar to Mark. The fig tree yielded two and sometimes three crops of fruit in the year. Some of the latest crop remained in sheltered spots till the spring; when the summer figs began to form, and the leaves were put forth. If a tree were early in leafing, it might be expected to have upon it some young fruit forming, and perhaps some old fruit remaining. "The expectation was not founded on the time of year, for as St. Mark observes, it was not yet the season even for young figs . . . but on the fact that the leaves were out" (*Speaker's Commentary*).

14 No man eat fruit of thee. It can scarcely be doubted that our Lord designed the withering of the fig tree to convey other lessons besides that which is enforced in 23, 24. It certainly may be used as an apt emblem of the Jewish people, "wholly a right seed," planted "in a very fruitful hill"; but now "turned into a degenerate plant," bringing no "fruits of righteousness," and therefore soon to be "withered" and "burned": see Isa. v. 1–7; Jer. ii. 21; John xv. 6. It is worthy of notice, that while our Lord symbolised His abundant mercies by many miracles for the good of men, He expressed the severity of His judgements by *one* sign, inflicted on a senseless tree.

16 the Temple. The Temple enclosure (*hieron*), not the Sanctuary (*naos*). Even the Court of the Gentiles was to be held sacred.

17 ye have made it a den of thieves (robbers). See Jer. vii. 11. Formerly our Lord had reproved the unseemly introduction of secular business, with its cares and bustle, into the Temple (John ii. 16); now He rebukes the fraud and extortion which are the natural fruit of the former. Perhaps part of the quotation from Isaiah was designed to reprove the contempt poured upon Gentile proselytes, by the use of their part of the Temple for worldly business.

18 chief priests. See note, Matt. ii. 4.

doctrine. "Teaching," R.V.

19 He went out of the city. Jesus went out of the city every evening, crossing the Mount of Olives to Bethany; probably in part to obtain rest and quiet, Jerusalem being filled at this time with an immense concourse of persons.

23 this mountain. Figurative expression for any great difficulty or obstacle: comp. Zech. iv. 7.

24 believe that ye receive them. This evidently to be understood as meaning, Whatsoever is asked in reliance upon God's promises, and according to His will: see 1 John v. 14. To the prayer of one who thinks and lives in harmony with the will of God, nothing is impossible.

25 when ye stand praying, forgive. This command may have been added, lest, from the withering curse which had been pronounced upon the fig tree, any of the disciples should imagine that they might imprecate curses upon those who opposed them (see Luke ix. 54). Forgiveness of others is a condition of effectual prayer Comp. Matt. vi. 14, 15.

27–32. On these verses, see Matt. xxi. 23–27, and notes.

CHAPTER XII

1 parables. Mark relates only one parable; but Matthew adds several others.

1-12. See notes on Matt. xxi. 33-46.

6 his well-beloved. The language here used defines most clearly the difference in rank and authority between the servants and the son, who is "the heir" of the vineyard (comp. Heb. iii. 5, 6). It also expresses the greatness of that Divine love which, when all other means of recovering men from rebellion were exhausted, did not shrink from this, the greatest possible gift. And, further, it displays the tragic obstinacy of those who reject "the Son."

13-27. See notes on Matt. xxii. 15-33.

26 in the bush. Probably meaning "in the passage relating to the bush": see R.V.

28 one of the scribes. A "lawyer" of the sect of "the Pharisees": see Matt. xxii. 34, 35, and note.

Which is the first commandment? This was one of the "strivings about the law" (Titus iii. 9) warmly contested among the Jews; some giving the preference to the sabbath law, others to sacrifices, others to various ceremonial laws. Our Lord gives the pre-eminence to "the law of love."

30 with all thy heart, etc. Supreme and undivided affection. The terms used express man's moral, emotional, and intellectual nature, with his active powers.

31 the second [is] like. For both are parts of the one great law of love. The R.V. has, "the second is this."

Thou shalt love thy neighbour. The parable of the Good Samaritan (Luke x. 29-35) was spoken to show who is our neighbour.

as thyself. Herbert Spencer caricatures this teaching, though he admires "the religion of amity." His suggestion (*Principles of Sociology*) that Christ's teaching would lead to neglect of one's own affairs, has no foundation.

32, 33 the scribe said, etc. This reply of the scribe ("Of a truth, Master, Thou hast well said," R.V.), which is related by Mark only, shows that he had entered into the true spirit of our Lord's answer: comp. Psa. xl. 6; l. 8-14.

34 discreetly. Lit., "as one having understanding." He saw through the externals of the law to those fundamental principles which are essential to "the kingdom of God." But, unless such perception lead to practical faith, it does not save. "If thou art not far off, enter; better otherwise to have been far off" (*Bengel*).

35-37. See notes on Matt. xxii. 41-46; where it appears that the view of the scribes had been elicited by a question from our Lord.

37 the common people. Rather, "the mass of the people" (see R.V. marg.): no reference being intended to social distinction. *Vulgate:* "multa turba"; *Fr. version:* "une grande foule" (a great crowd).

38 His doctrine. His teaching. Vers. 38, 39 sum up what is given at length in Matt. xxiii.

love. Rather, "desire," as R.V.

40 which devour widows' houses. By pretending to special piety, they insinuated themselves into the confidence of unprotected persons, for their own covetous objects.

damnation. "Condemnation."

41 the treasury. The "treasury" is said to have been a part of the second court of the Temple (the Court of the Women), where thirteen chests with "trumpet-shaped" openings were placed to receive (see 2 Kings xii. 9) the voluntary offerings of the people for the Temple service: see Edersheim, *The Temple and its Services*, p. 27.

42 two mites. "Two mites" (in Old English *minutes*, from their smallness) was the smallest offering that was allowed to be made. The mite (*lepton*) was worth about $\frac{1}{16}$th of our penny.

44 all her living. Her gift was not only far greater than those of others in proportion to her means; but it was also the sacrifice, by one who had very little to live upon, of all that she had to support her, at least for that day. Such self-denial shows not only gratitude, but also genuine faith in God's providence.

CHAPTER XIII

For the whole chapter see notes on Matt. xxiv.

1 And as He went out of the Temple. The interview with "the Greeks who came up to worship at the feast," and our Lord's solemn words that followed it, occurred after the incident of the widow's mite (xii. 41-43; John xii. 20-36).

see what manner of stones. Many of the stones used in the Temple were, according to Josephus (*Wars*, v. 5, § 6), 40 cubits, or, according to the Talmud, 45 cubits long, and of white marble. There are stones still remaining in the wall which measure 24 and 30 feet (Robinson's *Bib. Res.* i. 423). See Macalister, *A Century of Excavation in Palestine*, p. 107.

3 Peter and James and John and Andrew. Mark alone gives the names of the disciples who asked this question.

against them. Rather, "unto them," as R.V.

11 but the Holy Ghost. Comp. Matt. x. 18-20, and note.

14 abomination of desolation. A heathen idol and altar in the Temple (cf. 1 Macc. i. 54).

standing where it ought not. See Dan. ix. 27; xi. 31.

32 neither the Son. In our Lord's person the Divine and human natures were both complete. His human soul was capable of growth in wisdom (Luke ii. 52), susceptible of human emotions (John xi. 35), and dependent upon Divine influence (John iii. 34; Heb. ix. 14), and therefore upon the exercise of prayer (i. 35). His manhood was necessarily finite and progressive in knowledge; and, as "Son" (Heb. v. 5, 8) He had put Himself in subjection, or, in the language of the apostle Paul, had "emptied Himself" (Phil. ii. 7), and therefore might not have had this fact communicated to Him.

34-37. These concluding verses differ from the close of the discourse as given by Matthew and Luke; being a summary of the parables which Matthew relates, with one or two particulars added.

35 at even, etc. See note on Matt. xiv. 25.

CHAPTER XIV

1, 2. See notes on Matt. xxvi. 1-5.

3 Simon the leper. Simon had been a leper, but had probably been healed by our Lord. He was a friend, and perhaps a relative, of the family of Lazarus; who was himself a guest at this supper, whilst his sister "Martha served," and his other sister Mary performed the action here narrated (see John xii. 2, 3). This narrative must not be confounded with that in Luke vii. 36-50, which has many very different circumstances.

spikenard. The meaning of the Greek word here used (lit., *pistic*) is not certain. It is probably "*genuine* nard."

box. Or, "flask"; of which she probably "brake" either the seal or the neck.

on His head. She applied some also to His feet, which she wiped with her hair (John xii. 3).

4 Why was this waste? The peculiar odour of the perfume, which instantly pervaded the whole room, disclosed at once its quality and costliness. It appears, from John xii. 4, that the dissatisfaction was expressed by Judas, but as he made the pretence of charity, others of the disciples may have acquiesced in it.

5 three hundred pence. About $60; which was little less than a labourer's wages for a whole year (Matt. xx. 2). Lightfoot (*Hor. Heb.* ii. 448) puts it as high as $300 in modern value. He who said this soon after sold his Master's life for a paltry thirty shekels, the price of a slave (Exod. xxi. 32), less than a third of this amount.

6 a good work. "A beautiful work."

8 She hath done what she could. This interesting form of eulogium is found only in Mark.

aforehand. The anointing of His body was to take place while He was yet alive, as there would be no time afforded for it after His death. Probably Mary had no more than a general presentiment of His approaching departure. This significant act afforded our Lord another opportunity of announcing His speedy decease.

9 throughout the whole world. This promise clearly indicates our Lord's intention that all the most important facts concerning Himself should be preserved in an enduring form, and circulated throughout "the whole world."

11 they were glad. It was the opportunity of seizing Jesus "in the absence of the multitude" (Luke xxii. 6), that made this proposal so acceptable to the rulers.

money. Matthew alone mentions the sum—"thirty pieces of silver" (shekels); between $15 and $20: see note on ver. 5.

12–16. See notes on Luke xxii. 7–30.

17–21. See notes on Matt. xxvi. 21–25; John xiii. 21–30.

22–25. See notes on Matt. xxvi. 26–29.

30 before the cock crow twice. In relating both our Lord's words and Peter's denial, Mark alone mentions a second cock-crowing. The cock often crows irregularly about midnight, or not long after: and again always, and regularly, about the third hour, or daybreak. When, therefore, "the cock-crowing" is spoken of indefinitely, this last is always meant. Hence the name "cock-crowing" was used for the third watch of the night, which ended at the third hour after midnight (xiii. 35). Mark, therefore, here relates more definitely; the others more generally.

32–42. See notes on Matt. xxvi. 36–46.

33 to be sore amazed. A touch peculiar to Mark.

36 Abba. Mark here, as elsewhere, preserves the Aramaic form: see v. 41; vii. 34.

37 Simon, sleepest thou? Only in Mark. The very words must have lingered in the remembrance of the apostle addressed (see Introduction).

40 neither wist they what to answer Him. Comp. ix. 6.

43–52. See notes, Matt. xxvi. 47–56.

51 a certain young man. It cannot be ascertained who this young man was. Dean Plumptre ingeniously conjectures that he was Lazarus. But others think that he was Mark himself, who thus modestly claims to have been an eyewitness of part of what he relates.

52 naked. This may simply mean, without his outer robe (see Isa. xx. 2, 3; John xxi. 7). The young man, aroused by the tumult, did not wait to dress himself in the ordinary manner, but merely threw on this linen robe. The material of the dress—"linen"—shows that he did not belong to the poorest class.

53–72. See notes on Matt. xxvi. 57–75.

54 at the fire. Lit., "in the light": showing he was recognised by the firelight falling on his face.

56 their witness agreed not together. Or, "their evidence did not agree" (*Moffatt*).

66 in the palace. That is, in the court: see Matt. xxvi. 3. The trial was going on in a room above, which seems to have looked into the court.

69 a maid. "The maid" (R.V.), the same person as before.

72 when he thought thereon. This apostle's fall is a solemn warning to every Christian to "watch and pray."

CHAPTER XV

On this chapter, see notes on Matt. xxvii., Luke xxiii., and John xviii.

16 Prætorium. This was formerly Herod's palace; it was now the residence of the Roman governor, and the court of justice.

21 the father of Alexander and Rufus. Peculiar to Mark: a characteristic note of accuracy. A Rufus is mentioned by St. Paul (Rom. xvi. 13).

25 the third hour. The time here mentioned agrees well with that specified in ver. 33, and in Matt. xxvii. 45 and Luke xxiii. 44; but it appears to be at variance with John xix. 14. John may have adopted a different mode of calculation: see note on the last-mentioned passage.

26 superscription. See on John xix. 19.

39 the Son of God. See on Matt. xxvii. 54.

40 James the less (little). See note on Matt. x. 3.

Salome. See note on Matt. xx. 20.

42 the day before the sabbath. See note on John xix. 31.

43 an honourable counsellor. "A councillor of honourable position."

went in boldly ("boldly went in," R.V.). His "fear of the Jews" (John xix. 38) being overcome by the power of love.

44 Pilate marvelled. The wonder of Pilate that Christ had died so quickly is mentioned only by Mark. The tortures of crucifixion did not cause a speedy death; and the fact that our Lord's death was thus speedy was part of the great mystery of His sacrifice: see notes on Luke xxiii. 46; John x. 18; xix. 30, 34.

CHAPTER XVI

1 anoint Him. See John xix. 40. It is possible that they bought the spices on Friday just before the sabbath began (Luke xxiii. 56), and prepared them after its close on Saturday evening.

4 for it was very great. Its size not only caused their anxiety, but enabled them, "when they looked" from a distance, to see that it was moved.

5 a young man. That is, an angel in human form (see Gen. xix. 15, 16; Acts i. 10).

6 Ye seek Jesus of Nazareth. The Greek is very emphatic: " Ye seek Jesus, the Nazarene, the crucified."

7 and Peter. This particular mention of Peter, found in this Gospel only, would assure the penitent disciple of his Lord's forgiveness: comp. 1 Cor. xv. 5. The reference to Peter seems also to show that the vision of the angel occurred after Peter and John had left the sepulchre: see John xx. 10.

8 they trembled and were amazed. The R.V. more vividly represents the original: " trembling and astonishment had come upon them."

Vers. 9–20. This section is absent from the two oldest MSS., one of which leaves a blank space after ver. 8, as if for the addition of some further matter. Eusebius and other early writers say (probably from Origen) that the " accurate copies " of Mark omit vers. 9–20: and in some later MSS. another and a shorter conclusion is added.* On the other hand, the verses are found in the great majority of existing MSS. as well as in most of the ancient versions, and are supported by Irenæus, as well as by Latin writers from Ambrose and Augustine onwards. It seems certain that vers. 8, 9 are not continuous: in any case there is a break in the narrative, the rest of the chapter being a rapid epitome in great contrast with Mark's usual style of graphic narration. On the other hand, it is impossible to suppose that the Gospel ended abruptly with the words " for they were afraid "; and the omission of a concluding paragraph is well explained by supposing that the transcriber was interrupted in his work. The weight of modern critical opinion on the whole seems to be in favour of retaining the passage as authentic and canonical, but later than the rest of the Gospel. See Westcott, *Introduction to the Study of the Gospels*, p. 338; Westcott and Hort, *Greek Testament*, vol. ii. pp. 29–51; Scrivener, *Introduction to the Criticism of the New Testament*, pp. 583–590; Dean Burgon, *The last Twelve verses of the Gospel according to St. Mark vindicated against recent objectors and established* (1871); Dr. Salmon, *Introduction to the New Testament*, 4th edition, pp. 158–164, and the Commentaries on this Gospel; Dr. James Moffatt's *Translation of the New Testament*, note on St. Mark xvi. 8.

* "And all that had been enjoined on them they reported briefly to the companions of Peter. And after these things Jesus Himself from the East even to the West sent forth by them the holy and incorruptible preaching of eternal salvation."—*First found in MS.* L, *belonging to the eighth or the ninth century.*

9 He appeared first to Mary Magdalene. See John xx. 11–17, and notes.

11 they . . . believed not. Certainly Thomas did not believe (John xx. 24, 25), and possibly some others of the disciples. But all doubt was soon dispelled: see Luke xxiv. 34–47. Most of these narratives end with the words " they believed not." So far were the apostles from being credulous, that we are astonished at their slowness to believe.

12 in another form. He was only recognised upon His breaking and blessing the bread (Luke xxiv. 31–35). Lange explains by saying that He was wearing different clothes (comp. John xx. 15), that He bore traces of His sufferings during the crucifixion; and that, on the other hand, He was more sublime in His appearance.

13 neither believed they them. The two returning from Emmaus were met by the apostles with the tidings, " The Lord is risen indeed," Luke xxiv. 33, 34. " The rest," therefore, who did not believe the two disciples, must have been others of the professed followers of Jesus.

These verses contain an epitome of what our Lord said on various occasions; see Matt. xxviii. 18–20; Luke xxiv. 49; Acts i. 4–8.

15 Go ye into all the world, etc. See note on Matt. xxviii. 19.

to every creature. " By these words the missionary work is bound upon the Church through all ages, till every part of the earth shall have been evangelised."—*Alford.*

16 he that believeth not, etc. Unbelief, *i.e.*, the rejection of the gospel in heart and life, shall condemn a man, whether baptised or unbaptised.—*Alford.*

17 these signs, etc. During the first age of the Church, these extraordinary gifts were not only exercised by the apostles themselves, but were also conveyed by them to others. (See Acts ii. 4; xvi. 18; xxviii. 8.) They were credentials for the authority of the apostles.

18 if they drink any deadly thing. Poisoning was extensively practised at this period. No instance of this Divine interposition is recorded in Scripture; but it is not more wonderful than others which are related.

19 sat on the right hand of God. Peculiar to Mark.

20 the Lord working with them. Thereby fulfilling His promise (Matt. xxviii. 20). This was the secret of their unparalleled success; the Lord wrought with them by His Spirit; fitting them to deliver, and preparing their hearers to receive, the saving truth of His gospel.

THE GOSPEL ACCORDING TO ST. LUKE

INTRODUCTION

RENAN has described this Gospel as " the most beautiful book ever written, the hosanna of the little ones and the humble," and there is a beauty in its language which is all its own. It is evident that its author was a man of education and culture. He is described by St. Paul as " the beloved physician " (Col. iv. 14). He was the companion of Paul in his missionary journeys (Acts xvi. 10–18; xx. 5, 6; xxi. 17, 18, and in his voyage to Rome (Acts xxvii.–

xxviii. 16), and was with him as, in his prison there, he looked forward to his approaching death (2 Tim. iv. 11). The date of the Gospel is uncertain, but it is later than St. Matthew and St. Mark, and may have been written after A.D. 70, perhaps as late as A.D. 80.

The book is full of priceless gems. It is to St. Luke that we owe the *Magnificat* (i. 46–55), the *Benedictus* (i. 68–79), the *Gloria in Excelsis* (ii. 14), the *Nunc Dimittis* (ii. 29–32); the story of the Prodigal Son (xv. 11–32), and the humanitarian story of the Good Samaritan (x. 30–37). Ruskin says of Fra Angelico, "Under every cypress the angels walked; he had seen their white robes, whiter than the dawn, at his bedside, as he awoke in early summer. They had sung with him, one on each side, when his voice failed for joy at sweet vesper and matin time; his eyes were blinded by their wings in the sunset, when it sank behind the hills of Luni" (*Modern Painters*, V., Pt. IX., Chap. VIII., §§ 12, 13, 15). To St. Luke also the heavenly messengers were a reality. An angel appears to Zacharias in his temple ministry, to Mary in her home at Nazareth, and to the shepherds keeping watch over their flocks by night. Thus to the minister of the Gospel, to the wife and mother in the home, to the man attending to his daily toil, angel messengers may still draw nigh. And when the shadows gather round the Saviour, angels come to strengthen Him in Gethesemane, and after the cross and the grave announce to His troubled followers the glad news of His victory over death.

St. Luke's is the Gospel of humanity. Like St. Matthew, he gives us a genealogy of the Saviour, but he traces the descent not from Abraham but from "Adam, the son of God" (iii. 13–38). And his picture of our Lord emphasises His humanity (ii. 12), His home life (ii. 40, 51, 52), His sympathy with the poor and the suffering (*e.g.* iv. 18; v. 12–15), and His compassion on the sinful (v. 31, 32; vii. 36–50; xv. 2). In this connexion it is significant to note that St. Luke is the only evangelist who records the Saviour's prayer for His murderers (xxiii. 34).

CHAPTER I

1 to set forth in order a declaration. Rather, as R.V. "to draw up a narrative"; referring probably to current statements of the leading facts of our Lord's history, taken from the testimony of eye-witnesses for the use of the first Christians. These have not come down to us, being superseded by the inspired records of the four evangelists. The so-called "Apocryphal Gospels" belong to a later age.

which are most surely believed. Rather, as R.V., "which have been fulfilled," or "accomplished."

2 as they delivered, etc. Referring to the apostles, from whose oral testimony these narratives were drawn up.

tho word. That is, "the word of the gospel"; a phrase used by Luke elsewhere: see Acts xiii. 26; xv. 7; xvii. 11; xx. 32.

3 having had perfect understanding. Rather, as R.V., "having traced the course of all things." The word employed suggests "the following the course of a stream from the fountain-head" (*Wordsworth*). The expression "from the very first," makes it not improbable that Luke derived the early part of his Gospel from our Lord's mother or near relatives.

in order. Mainly, but not entirely, chronological.

most excellent. A title of honour, used in addressing persons of rank or authority: see Acts xxiv. 3; xxvi. 25. Nothing more is known of Theophilus. "The point of real importance is that a man of high official authority was a convert at this early period, going through a course of oral instruction and continuing earnest research into the facts" (*Speaker's Commentary*).

4 instructed. That is, "taught by word of mouth"; Greek, *catechised.*

5–ii. 52. The style of the portion which follows, to the end of ch. ii., is in the original so peculiar as to make it probable that Luke is here following very closely some oral or written narratives, one of which supplied ch. i., and another ch. ii.

5 Zacharias. Zechariah, "remembered by Jehovah."

the course of Abia (Abijah). This was the eighth of the twenty-four classes of priests, appointed by David to perform the service in weekly rotation, so that each of the courses attended at the Temple twice in the year (see 1 Chron. xxiv. 1–19; 2 Chron. viii. 14, and notes). On the division made after the Captivity, see Ezra ii. 36, and note.

of the daughters of Aaron. So that John was of the sacerdotal family by both parents. "Elisabeth" is the same as "Elisheba" the name of Aaron's wife (Exod. vi. 23). The Hebrew word literally means "God her oath," and the best rendering is that of Fürst: "the covenant God."

8 in the order of his course. That is, during the attendance of his course (5) at the Temple.

9 to burn incense, etc. Rather, " to enter the sanctuary of the Lord, and offer incense."

10 the whole multitude of the people were praying. See Exod. xxx. 1–10. The pious were accustomed to unite in silent supplication during the offering of the incense, which was the symbol of acceptable prayer (Psa. cxli. 2; Rev. v. 8; viii. 3, 4).

13 thy prayer is heard. Referring to his prayer for a son.

John. Heb., " Jochanan "; meaning, " Jehovah is gracious." The name appears several times in the Old Testament and the Apocrypha.

15 in the sight of the Lord. Though without earthly dignity, he shall be one of the chief of God's servants (Matt. xi. 11); he shall be a true priest (Lev. x. 9) and Nazirite (Numb. vi. 1–21), extraordinarily endowed with the Holy Spirit.

17 the spirit and power of Elias (Elijah). With the zeal and energy which Elijah had shown (see 1 Kings xvii., xviii., xxi.): see Mal. iv. 6. The words of the last of the prophets are thus confirmed by the angel.

18 Whereby shall I know this? There was so much unbelief in this request, that God saw correction to be needed (22). See, for a contrast in a similar case, Rom. iv. 19–21.

19 that stand in the presence of God. As one of His chief attendants. The eminent rank of the messenger shows the importance of his communication: and his name (see note on Dan. viii. 16) might remind Zacharias of Gabriel's former errand to Daniel, when sent to announce the coming of Messiah: see Dan. ix. 21, 25.

21 the people waited (" were waiting," R.V.). The people would not leave the Temple till the priest came out of the holy place, and the benediction was pronounced.

22 he beckoned. Better, as R.V., " he continued making signs."

24 hid herself. That is, she kept herself in retirement; perhaps to devote herself without hindrance to prayer and thanksgiving (25).

26 in the sixth month. Since the announcement to Elisabeth: see ver. 36.

Nazareth. See notes on Matt. ii. 23.

27 espoused. Rather, " betrothed," R.V.

of the house of David. Here, and in Matt. i. 20, this is said of Joseph. That Mary also was a descendant of David is nowhere expressly affirmed in the Gospels; but it is implied in 32–35, where she is informed that she shall be the only human parent of Jesus, while yet David is called " His father": see also Rom. i. 3; Heb. vii. 14; Acts ii. 30; Psa. cxxxii. 11.

28 Blessed [art] thou among women. The words were probably added here by some transcriber from ver. 42.

29 she was troubled. She wondered what message was to follow such a salutation.

33 over the house of Jacob. The announcement of His reign over the whole world might have been incomprehensible to Mary: it lies hidden, however, in the words, " of His kingdom there shall be no end." Cp. Isa. ix. 7; Dan. vii. 14.

35 The Holy Ghost. These words apparently refer to the phrase used in Gen. i. 2 (on which see note): where, as here, the creative energy is attributed to the Holy Spirit.

that holy thing. It was necessary that the Redeemer should be " born of a woman " (Gal. iv. 4), that He might be of the same nature with those whom He came to redeem. It was equally necessary that He should be perfectly holy, as no sinful being could make atonement for others.

36 thy cousin. Or, " kinswoman."

45 blessed. " Happy "; perhaps with an allusion to the affliction resulting from Zacharias' want of faith.

46–55. (The *Magnificat:* Latin for " doth magnify.") This hymn of praise has many expressions borrowed from the song of Hannah (1 Sam. ii. 1–10).

" We can scarcely regard it as accidental that St. Luke, who was certainly a man of culture, alone of the sacred historians preserves the three Evangelical hymns, which the Church has wrought into her services, the *Magnificat*, the *Benedictus*, the *Nunc Dimittis*, and the angelic hymn which has since been developed into the *Gloria in Excelsis* " (*Speaker's Commentary*).

47 my spirit. " Soul " (46) and " spirit " form a climax.

48 blessed. Rather (as the word is rendered in Jas. v. 11), " shall count me happy."

50, 51. On this connexion of judgement with mercy, see Isa. lxiii. 1.

52 the mighty from [their] seats. Lit., as R.V., " princes from their thrones." " Mary," says *Lange*, " would have been no true daughter of David if she could have spoken these words without primary reference to Herod; but no believing Israelite, if she had thought of Herod alone. The overthrow of all anti-Messianic powers seems in her imagination to begin with the fall of the Idumæan usurper."

56 returned to her own house. The events related in Matt. i. 18–24 probably occurred soon after Mary's return.

58 had showed great mercy upon her. Lit., " had magnified His mercy towards her," R.V.; in verbal accord with the *Magnificat.*

59 they called. Rather, " they were naming "; *i.e.*, were about to name him: see R.V.

62 made signs. See note on ver. 22.

63 a writing table (tablet). A tablet whitened or covered with wax, and written upon with a stylus or iron pencil.

66 What manner of child shall this be? Rather, as R.V., " What then shall this child be? " The question relates not to the character of his childhood, but to what he would turn out to be in the future. *Luther* has: " Was, meinest du, wird aus dem Kindlein werden? " (" What do you think will become of this little child? ").

67 prophesied. Thinking of the expected Child, as well as of his own son, Zacharias praises God for fulfilling His promise. Then, addressing his infant son, he declares his mission as the prophet and herald of the Divine Redeemer. From the first word in the Latin version of this song, it is known as the *Benedictus.*

68 redeemed. Lit., " wrought redemption for," R.V.

69 a horn of salvation. See 1 Sam. ii. 1; and Psa. cxxxii. 17.

71 That we should be saved. Rather, in continuance of ver. 69, " [He hath raised up] salvation from our enemies," etc.: see R.V.

72 To perform the mercy [promised] to our fathers. There is no word in the original answering to *promised.* The R.V. is accurate: " to show mercy towards our fathers."

74 being delivered. It has been the policy of

the enemies of God's people, in all ages, to restrict and even put down their public worship. Zacharias may allude to Antiochus Epiphanes and the Romans, both of whom had interfered with the temple services.

without fear. That is, without the dread of enemies.

75 In holiness and righteousness. "Holiness," or piety, the inward spirit, the Godward side of our nature. "Righteousness" or justice, the manward or practical side. The French version has "la sainteté et la justice" ("holiness and justice").

77 To give knowledge of salvation. Teaching them that the "salvation" they needed was not a political, but a spiritual emancipation; beginning with the "remission of their sins," which Messiah was coming to bestow, as the gift of God's "tender mercy."

78 dayspring. See Isa. viii. 22; ix. 2; Mal. iv. 2.

80 deserts. Thinly-peopled districts; as in Matt. iii. 1.

the day of his showing. His entrance on his public ministry.

CHAPTER II

1 the world. Lit., "the inhabited [earth]," *i.e.*, the whole Roman empire. So the French say *tout le monde*, "all the world," without meaning literally the whole world.

taxed. Rather, "enrolled," or "registered," for the purpose of a census: and so in ver. 5.

2 Cyrenius. Dr. A. W. Zumpt (1870), supported by Mommsen, showed it to be probable that Publius Sulpitius Quirinus, the Cyrenius mentioned here, was *twice* governor of Syria, first, at the time of our Lord's birth, and again ten years later; and that the Jews were registered by him on both occasions: so that this was the "first enrolment" of the two which he made. This has now been proved to be historical fact by Sir William Ramsay, the great scholar and archæologist (*Was Christ born at Bethlehem?* and *The Bearing of Recent Discovery on the Trustworthiness of the New Testament*).

4 lineage ("family," R.V.). It was a *Roman* custom to number women and children as well as men (5); and it was a *Jewish* practice to enrol every one at his ancestral home.

6 while they were there. By this apparently accidental circumstance was fulfilled the prophecy in Micah v. 2.

7 her firstborn. See notes on Matt. i. 25; xiii. 55.

a manger. Perhaps a cave or grotto used as a stable or shelter for cattle.

8 in the same country. That is, *in that district;* the district of Bethlehem; whose inhabitants would regard it, rather than Jerusalem, as "the city of David" (11, 15).

shepherds. The heavenly message is sent to men who, like the fishermen of Galilee afterwards summoned to our Lord's service, were diligently fulfilling the duties of their calling.

keeping watch . . . by night. As the flocks were not kept out at night in the open fields between the autumnal rains and the Passover, and as, on the other hand, the pasture is burned up in the summer, it is inferred that our Lord's birth must have occurred in the spring; but the exact time is uncertain. The traditional date of "Christmas" does not appear until the fourth century.

9 the glory of the Lord. A glory such as betokened the Divine presence, "the Shekinah."

10 to all people. Rather, "to the whole people"; namely, of Israel, to whom the gospel was first to be proclaimed.

11 a Saviour, which is Christ the Lord. These three names point to His saving work, His Divine appointment, and His supreme dignity.

12 this [shall be] a sign. Rather, "This shall be the sign to you; ye shall find a babe wrapped," etc. You will recognise the infant by the unusual place in which you will find Him.

swaddling clothes. Linen clothes in which the new-born infant was tightly bound up.

14 peace, good will toward (among) **men.** The translation of the R.V., "peace among men in whom He is well pleased," is a paraphrase of a reading which, literally rendered, is "peace among men of good will." The difference between this and the ordinary text consists in the addition of one letter (*s*) to the word for "good will." The four chief Greek MSS., but no others, have this addition, followed by the Vulgate and the Latin Fathers generally. According to this reading, there are only two clauses in the angels' song:

"Glory to God in the highest,
And on earth peace among men of good will."

The great mass of Greek MSS., however, have the reading of the received text and the ordinary English version, which reading is confirmed by the quotations of the Greek fathers generally. The arrangement in two clauses, apart from the difficulty in translation, destroys the symmetry and spoils the sense of the passage. The angels' song celebrates the incarnation of Messiah, as causing the inhabitants of "the highest" heavens to glorify God; as bringing to the earth "peace"—the reconciliation of man and God; and as thus opening the way for all the blessings which Divine "good will," or benevolence, can bestow.

19 Mary kept. Mary "kept" in memory and carefully "compared together all these sayings" (R.V.) and events regarding her infant.

22 her purification. Some MSS. have "*their* purification"; *i.e.*, of Mary (see Lev. xii.) and the babe.

23 shall be called holy. That is, shall be esteemed specially devoted to the Divine service: see Exod. xiii. 13–15; Numb. iii. 11, 12; viii. 16–18; xviii. 15, 16.

24 to offer a sacrifice. See note on Lev. xii. 8. All this was before the visit of the Magi: see note on ver. 39. The offering shows the poverty of Mary and Joseph.

25 the consolation of Israel. The "consolation of Israel" was a well-known phrase among the Jews; derived from Isa. xl. 1; xlix. 13, and referring to the Messiah.

26 the Lord's Christ. See Psa. ii. 2.

29 Lord. Lit., "Master."

"As the *Magnificat* is charged with personal feeling, and the *Benedictus* with national aspiration, so the *Nunc Dimittis* is the expression of hope for the world" (Principal Grieve in *Peake's Commentary*.

30 Thy salvation. Impersonated in the Messiah. Vers. 30–32 are formed from the very words of ancient prophecy: see Isa. xlii. 6; xlix. 6; lii. 10; lx. 1–3; lxi. 11.

31 all people. "All the peoples," including Israel and the Gentiles, as shown in verse 32.

34 for the fall and rising [again]. There is

perhaps here a reference to Isa. viii. 14, 15; xxviii. 16. If so, the metaphor is that of a stone, by which some may fall, whilst it enables others to rise. So Jesus will prove a cause of blessing to some and of woe to others, according as they receive or reject Him: cp. Isa. xxviii. 16; Matt. xxi. 44; Jas. iv. 6.

35 a sword shall pierce. Mary's faith as well as her maternal feelings, would be most severely tested by the trials, the sufferings, and the death of her Divine Son: see iv. 29; Matt. xii. 46; and especially John xix. 25.

that the thoughts (reasonings) **of** (out of) **many hearts,** etc. Nothing shows more clearly the state of a man's heart than the way in which he regards and treats the Saviour and His work. This is the touchstone of character: see John xv. 23; 1 Cor. i. 23, 24; xvi. 22; 1 John iv. 2, 3.

36 Aser. Asher. Some of the exiles belonging to the ten tribes returned to Palestine with their brethren of Judah and Benjamin, and preserved their genealogies: see note on Ezra i. 5: cp. Acts xxvi. 7; Jas. i. 1.

37 fourscore and four years. Probably the length of her whole life.

prayers. Rather, "supplications," as R.V., a more emphatic word.

39 when they had performed all things, etc. The visit of the Magi (Matt. ii.), the flight into Egypt, and the massacre of the babes at Bethlehem, were probably subsequent to the presentation of Jesus in the Temple. After these events, He would hardly have been taken to Jerusalem. Some, however, think that this journey to Nazareth was taken immediately after the presentation in the Temple; and that after that, Joseph and Mary returned to Bethlehem. They would, therefore, place Matt. ii. *after* ver. 39. But it appears better to regard it as immediately following ver. 38; and to understand the evangelist as saying that after (whether immediately or not he does not say) all these things were done, they went to live at Nazareth. Some months, or even years, may have intervened between this visit to Jerusalem and the residence in Nazareth.

40 the child grew. In His human nature Jesus experienced the development of all His powers, in the degrees proper to every age; "becoming full of wisdom": see note on Mark xiii. 32.

the grace. Rather, the *favour* of God.

41–52. These verses are all the record given in any of the Gospels of the first thirty years in the life of Jesus. "The solitary floweret," says *Stier*, "out of the wonderful 'garden enclosed' of those years, plucked in the very crisis of its blossoming."

41 His parents went to Jerusalem. See note on 1 Sam. i. 4.

42 when He was twelve years old. Among the Jews, when a boy entered his thirteenth year, he was called "a son of the law," and was initiated into its observances. It was therefore a solemn occasion in the life of "the boy Jesus."

43 the child Jesus. Better, "the boy Jesus."

the days. Including, probably, at least, the preparation, the Passover, and the seven days of unleavened bread.

44 in the company. The number of persons quitting Jerusalem for Galilee after the Passover would generally be very large; and they would travel in company, as Eastern pilgrims in the present day usually do, for the sake of security and society. Joseph and Mary, accustomed to the thoughtful obedience of Jesus, would not be likely to seek Him till they missed Him when the caravan halted, and the several families gathered round their evening meal.

46 after three days. This most probably means three days after they had left Jerusalem; a day for their departure; a day for their return; and a day for their search (*Lange*).

in the Temple. In one of its chambers or halls, where "doctors," or teachers of the law, instructed their disciples; to whom they allowed great liberty of question and reply. The attendance of a youth of this age was not in itself strange: but the "understanding and answers" of Jesus surprised the teachers.

49 my Father's business. "In my Father's house" (R.V.). The Greek may be translated by either. The boy's meaning is: To *seek* me was unnecessary; I was sure to be *here*. "A child is to be found at his father's." In the appellation, "my Father," there is, as *Godet* observes, "a delicate but decisive reply to Mary's words, *Thy father and I*. Jesus shows in this, His first recorded utterance, that His consciousness of a Divine nature and mission is beginning to be developed.

50 they understood not. It seems necessary that Mary should not fully understand these things, in order that the maternal instincts on the one hand, and the filial submission on the other, might remain natural.

51 was subject unto them. The high consciousness which had manifested itself (49) did not interfere with His self-humiliation, nor render Him independent of His parents. This voluntary subjection showed itself in working at His reputed father's trade (see Mark vi. 3). From this time we hear no more of Joseph. We next hear only of "His mother and brethren" (John ii. 12), whence it is inferred that, between this time and the commencement of our Lord's public life, Joseph died (*Alford*).

52 stature. Or, "age" (R.V. marg.); the gradual development of his manhood from twelve to thirty. How suggestive is this simple statement! A child in whose heart was bound up no "folly" (Prov. xxii. 15); a young man pure in soul from all "youthful lusts" (2 Tim. ii. 22); a son whose consciousness of His Divine origin abated not His obedience to earthly parents; a man so unpretending and genial that He won the favour of others; a servant of God, ever mindful of His high destiny, yet submissively working at His trade in the obscurity of a secluded village; such we must suppose our Lord to have been during the eighteen years of retirement which His Father saw to be the best preparation for His brief public life. And in all how perfect an example to all His followers!

CHAPTER III

1 the fifteenth year, etc. "The fifteenth year" from the time when Tiberius was associated with Augustus in the empire; A.U.C. 765. The date, therefore, is A.U.C. 780 (A.D. 27).

governor of Judæa. Upon the deposition of Archelaus (see note on Matt. ii. 22), Judæa had been put under the government of a Roman procurator; an officer subordinate to the governor of a province, but in this case possessing the power of life and death. Pontius Pilate had been appointed to the office about two years before the date given in the text; and he held it for ten years. He was then summoned to Rome to answer the complaints of the Jews; and soon afterwards put an end to his life.

Herod (Herod Antipas). See note on Mark vi. 14.

Philip. This Philip (see note on Mark vi. 17) was half-brother of Herod Antipas; and was better than most of the Herodian family; Jos. *Ant.* xviii. 4, § 6. His tetrarchy, comprising Ituræa and Trachonitis, lay south of Damascus, and between the Haûran and the upper waters of the Jordan. Cæsarea *Philippi* was named from him.

Abilene. Abilene was the district round Abila, a town eighteen miles north-west of Damascus.

Annas and Caiaphas. See note on Matt. xxvi. 3.

2–17. See notes on Matt. iii. 1–12.

2 the word of God came. This denotes prophetic inspiration: cp. Jer. i. 2; Ezek. vi. 1.

6 all flesh shall see the salvation of God. This last sentence, quoted by Luke alone, agrees with the universal character of his Gospel.

7 to the multitude (multitudes). These crowds consisted largely of Pharisees and Sadducees, and of persons under their influence, to whom the following words were specifically addressed. This explains the severity of John's language, dealing as he was with formalism on the one hand and unbelief on the other.

8 we have Abraham to our father. "We are Abraham's children."

14 [the] soldiers. Literally, soldiers on service.

15–18. A summary of the events narrated in John i. 19–28; on which see notes.

20 shut up John in prison. John's imprisonment occurred some time later (see on Mark vi. 17–20), but it is mentioned here by anticipation, to show how his public ministry was brought to an end.

21 Jesus also being baptised, etc. Jesus came unostentatiously, like one of John's converts. Luke's aim seems to be to show how our Lord placed Himself on a level with us; and for this reason, probably, he mentions here, as in his narrative of the transfiguration, that Jesus was "praying." On the baptism of Jesus see notes on Matt. iii. 13–17.

23 began to be about thirty years of age. Rather, "Jesus was about thirty years of age when He began" [His ministry]: see Acts i. 22: cp. R.V. This was the age at which the priests and Levites entered fully on their public service, and at which the scribes were permitted to teach (Numb. iv. 3, 43, 47).

(as was supposed). This was the general belief; the fact of the miraculous conception not having been made public.

24–38. This genealogy differs from that in Matt. i., by taking the line of David's descendants through his son Nathan, whereas Matthew gives the line of the kings of Judah and their descendants. Both, however, terminate in Joseph, the reputed father of Jesus, who is called in the one "the son of Jacob," and in the other the "son of Heli." This apparent discrepancy has given rise to much controversy, and many explanations have been proposed. Matthew's purpose, in accordance with the design of his Gospel, is to show that Jesus, being adopted before His birth by Joseph, is the promised heir to "the throne of His father David," and is "born King of the Jews" (ii. 2). He therefore gives the *regal pedigree;* omitting insignificant or obnoxious names, so as to bring it into three fourteens, corresponding to the periods *before, during,* and *after* the possession of the kingdom by the house of David; and suggesting that the old polity ends, and a new era begins, at the birth of Jesus. Luke, on the other hand, traces the line *of natural descent* up to David, and then through Abraham to Adam; showing that Jesus was the promised "seed of the woman," and thus "the Saviour of the world." It is therefore most probable that Joseph was the *son* of Heli, and the *son-in-law* of Jacob by marriage with his daughter Mary: Jacob and Heli being both sons of Matthan or Matthat, and Jacob having adopted Joseph as his heir (Matt. i. 16) in default of sons of his own. Mary as the daughter of Jacob would also be of the house of David (i. 27 (note); 32: see also Acts ii. 30; xiii. 23; Rom. i. 3).

The differences between the two evangelists are not real discrepancies, but are rather indications of the naturalness and truth of their narratives. Had there been any contradiction between the two accounts, it must have been pointed out in the early ages; the Jews especially would have been anxious, if possible, to disprove the descent of Jesus from David; which on the contrary they implicitly recognised.

36 the son of Cainan. The compiler of this genealogy followed the Septuagint version of Gen. xi. 12, 13.

CHAPTER IV

THE TEMPTATION. See notes on Matt. iv. 1–11.

1 full of the Holy Ghost. The Spirit supplied Him with the strength which He needed for it: cp. 1 Cor. x. 13.

2 tempted. Luke has not arranged the temptations in the same way as Matthew, who evidently follows the order of *time:* see Matt. iv. 5, 9, and notes. This is one of many instances of unimportant diversity, united with substantial agreement, between the evangelists, which show the value of their several narratives as independent testimonies to the truth.

4 It is written. It is remarkable that our Lord found within the compass of a few verses Divine truth sufficient to repel all the assaults of Satan.

13 had ended all the temptation. "Satan had assailed the Saviour on every point of His human nature" (*Speaker's Commentary*). Cp. Heb. iv. 15.

for a season. Rather, "until a season," or "opportunity": probably the time mentioned in xxii. 53, if not before.

14, 15 are a summary introducing a new portion of our Lord's life. Between vers. 13 and 16 intervene the narratives in John i. 19–51, ii., iii., iv. 1–42.

16 He came to Nazareth. Many suppose this to be the visit to Nazareth recorded in Matt. xiii. 53–58; Mark vi. 1–6, which is here more fully related, though out of the order of time. They infer this from the similarity of many of the circumstances in the two narratives; particularly the expressions used by the cavilling people, and by our Lord in His reply. They allege also that Nazareth is mentioned, as though Jesus had for some time ceased to reside there (16), and that Capernaum is spoken of (23) as a place where He had for some time dwelt and had wrought many miracles; the fame of which had spread throughout Galilee. On the other hand, it is said that vers. 16, 23 contain nothing to show that Nazareth was not the home to which Jesus "came" from His journeys in Peræa, various parts of Galilee, *including Capernaum,* Judæa, and Samaria (John i. 43; ii. 1, 12, 13; iii.; v.; Mark i. 14).

went into the synagogue. See note on Matt. iv. 23. Our Lord's "custom" of going to the synagogue service for reading and expounding the Scriptures and for prayer is a noteworthy example for His followers.

stood up for to read. Signifying His desire to read. Opportunity was sometimes given in synagogues for strangers to speak a word of exhortation or consolation to the people (Acts xiii. 15).

17 there was delivered unto Him. Lit., "there was further delivered unto Him"; *i.e.*, for the second lesson (*haphtarah*); the first (*parashah*) being always from the Pentateuch. The ordinary *haphtarah* for the day was probably in the prophecies of Isaiah; hence the "roll" containing them was handed to Him.

found the place where it was written. The quotation is chiefly from the Septuagint version of Isa. lxi. 1, 2; on which see notes. Perhaps in the whole of the prophetical writings no passage could be found so suitable as this for the opening of our Lord's commission in the little despised (John i. 46) village of Nazareth. Had the hearts of the people corresponded in any degree with their actual condition, they would have welcomed Him who was anointed with the Spirit of Jehovah, not only to reign as King in Zion, but also to raise the debased, and to comfort the poor and suffering.

18 the poor. See vi. 20, and note.

them that are bruised. This clause is inserted here from the Septuagint of Isa. lviii. 6.

19 the acceptable year of the Lord. From this expression some of the Fathers inferred that our Lord's ministry lasted only a year; a view which has been adopted by some moderns. The Gospel of John, however, proves it to be untenable. The phrase stands for the year of Jubilee (Lev. xxv.), which is regarded as symbolising the privileges of Christ's kingdom.

20 the minister. Better, "the attendant," as R.V., the officer who had charge of the sacred books.

sat down. A Jewish teacher *stood* when reading the Scriptures, but *sat* while expounding them.

the eyes of all. The people would know that this passage in Isaiah was usually applied to the Messiah, and would naturally be eager to see whether Jesus would appropriate it to Himself. And when, delicately referring to their privileges, rather than to His own claims, their fellow-townsman announces its present fulfilment, they are pleased with so "gracious" or attractive a declaration. But, as soon as He suggests the possibility that, through selfishness, familiarity, and pride, they may lose their privileges and see them transferred to others, even to Gentiles, they are filled with wrath, and even attempt to kill Him.

23 Physician, heal thyself. This proverb, with a different application, was addressed to our Lord at the cross. "Here the expression 'physician' is not to be pressed; it is a merely proverbial expression like our 'charity begins at home'" (*Speaker's Commentary*).

Capernaum. Here first mentioned by St. Luke; an instance of the way in which the historian shows his knowledge of facts which he has not explicitly recorded.

24 in his own country. In Matthew it is added, "and in his own house." Not only Christ's fellow-villagers, but even some of His nearest relatives disbelieved in Him (John vii. 5).

25 three years and six months. The history in Kings mentions only three years. In the Epistle of James (v. 17) the time is given as here.

26 save. Rather, "but only"; *i.e.*, not to any Israelitish widow, *but only* to a Gentile. See note on 1 Kings xvii. 9. These two miracles of mercy to Gentile sufferers were most appropriate symbols of the universal beneficence of the true Messiah, as opposed to the narrow feelings and expectations of the Jews.

28 filled with wrath. For a similar instance of murderous rage, see Acts xxii. 22; and cp. Deut. xxxii. 21; Rom. x. 19.

29 the brow of the hill. Nazareth lies on the side of a range of hills forming a basin: the "brow" is *above*, not *below* the city. The cliff from which they intended to precipitate Jesus is probably one which overhangs the present Maronite convent at the south-west corner of the town, and is an abrupt wall of limestone rock about forty feet high.

30 passing through the midst of them. The most natural interpretation of this is, that our Lord so awed them by His majesty and dignity that they made way for Him to pass: cp. John viii. 59; xviii. 6. His hour was not yet come. He departs, not to escape suffering, but to await, in the diligent exercise of His ministry, the sufferings which it was ordained He should afterwards undergo.

went His way. Leaving Nazareth, as it would appear, no more to return: see John i. 11.

31 came down to Capernaum. On our Lord's arrival from Nazareth at Capernaum, occurred the call of Peter and Andrew, James and John. The explanation, "a city of Galilee," is added for St. Luke's Gentile readers.

32 power. Rather, "authority"; as the word is rendered in ver. 36: see notes on Mark i. 22.

33–37. See notes on Mark i. 23–28.

33 an unclean devil (demon). The word "unclean" is peculiar to Luke. To the Gentiles, demons might be good or bad.

36 with authority and power. Our Lord's peculiar *manner* of performing His miracles showed His supreme "authority." He spoke to the demons as one who had "power" Himself to compel their obedience. "Authority" suffers no contradiction; "power," no opposition.—*Lange.*

37 the fame. Rather, as R.V., "a rumour."

38–44. See notes on Mark i. 29–39.

38 a great fever. A phrase peculiar to Luke who being a physician, uses the technical term.

CHAPTER V

2 standing. That is, "lying at anchor."

were washing. Their fishing for the time was over, so that their trouble in obeying the command (4) would be the greater.

3 out of the ship (boat). Our Lord was thus secured from the pressure of the crowd, and was sufficiently raised for them to see and hear Him well.

5 all the night. As night is the usual time for fishing, it was not likely that, having failed in the night, they should succeed by day. But he would obey the Master's word, although with little hope.

6 their net (nets) **brake.** Rather, as R.V., "were breaking"; *i.e.*, beginning to break.

8 for I am a sinful man. All were "astonished" at our Lord's control over creation; but Peter's susceptible mind was deeply affected with that sense of personal sinfulness which other pious men have felt and expressed under a vivid perception of the presence and power of the Most Holy: see Job xl. 4, 5. The signal miracle was, moreover, a rebuke to the hesitancy shown in Peter's words (5).

10 shalt catch men. The Greek means "shall be catching," suggesting continuous labour. The promise had its special fulfilment at Pentecost and shortly after; see Acts ii. 41, etc.

11 forsook all. See note on Matt. xix. 27.

12–16. See notes on Mark i. 40–45.

16 He withdrew . . . and prayed. Lit., "was withdrawing . . . and praying": cp. Mark i. 45, which gives the immediate reason for this retirement. Luke is the most particular of all the evangelists in referring to our Lord's constant habits of devotion.

17 the power of the Lord. *i.e.*, of God.

to heal them. The original seems rather to mean "for Him to heal," or "for His work of healing." "Them" appears to be an incorrect reading.

19 let him down. They would reach the top of the house by the outside staircase (see note, Matt. xxiv. 17). The "tiling" through which they let the man down was probably a covering which projected beyond the parapet over part of the central court, where our Lord was. This would be light and thin, commonly of rafters covered with mud tiles and straw; and in many cases so made as to be readily taken away.

20 thy sins are forgiven. It is probable that the paralytic's suffering was the result of his own sin. But it does not follow that suffering is always the punishment of wrong-doing. Many of the most saintly people have been great sufferers. Anyhow, the Saviour dealt first with the man's greatest need—the healing of the soul.

21 speaketh blasphemies. They justly held that it belonged to God alone to forgive sins; but they did not see that the Saviour was Himself Divine.

24 take up thy couch. The thin light mattresses which were commonly used as beds could easily be carried away.

27, 28. See notes on Matt. ix. 9.

29–39. See notes on Matt. ix. 10–17.

30 their scribes and Pharisees. The scribes and Pharisees of the town.

33 fast often. and make prayers. The claim of some in Christian Churches that the ascetic life is the "religious" life is refuted by the example of our Lord and His disciples.

36 if otherwise, etc. "Otherwise he both rends the new, and the patch of the new does not agree with the old." Each part is spoilt, and the whole is incongruous.

37 bottles. "wine-skins," as R.V.

39 The old is better This verse (which is peculiar to Luke) contains our Lord's final answer to the question in ver. 33. Had John dissuaded his disciples from strict fasting and frequent prayers, he would have been prematurely offering new wine to those who had been accustomed to the old. "It is not easy to pass from a system with which one has been identified from childhood, to an entirely different principle of life. Such men must be allowed time to be familiarised with the new principle that is presented to them" (*Godet*).

CHAPTER VI

See notes on Matt. xii. 1–13, and on Mark ii. 23–28; iii. 1–6.

1 on the second sabbath after the first. Lit., "on the second-first sabbath." The best authorities are so divided as to whether the adjective δευτεροπρώτῳ (*deuteroproto*) forms part of the text, and if it does, what it means, that it seems profitless to discuss it here. It is enough for us that it was a sabbath, as in Matt. and Mark.

11 madness. A senseless rage, which rejects all evidence.

12–49. These verses relate the call of the Twelve and the Sermon on the Mount. On the question whether the substance of this sermon was twice given on different occasions ("The Sermon on the Mount" and "The Sermon on the Plain"), see notes on Matt. v. 1, 2.

12–19. See notes on Matt. x. 1–4, and on Mark iii. 13–19.

12 continued all night in prayer. See notes on ch. v. 16; Matt. v. 1.

17 in the plain. Rather, "on a level place."

19 virtue. power.

20–49. See notes on Matt. v.–vii. The discourse is here given in abridged form; excepting that four "woes" are added to the beatitudes.

21 ye shall laugh. That is, "ye shall rejoice": see Psa. cxxvi. 2.

22 shall separate you. That is, "*excommunicate* you."

24 woe unto you. Our Lord now turns to the classes of men that had shown themselves foremost in opposing and maligning Him, the Pharisees ond Sadducees of the period. They consisted in great measure of the prosperous members of the community.

that are rich. That is, who trust in your wealth: cp. xviii. 24, 25 with Mark x. 24, and see note on Matt. xix. 23.

ye have received your consolation. "You get aii the comforts you ever get" (*Moffatt*).

26 shall speak well of you. Our Lord here points out the danger of seeking popularity at the expense of conscience.

29 thy cloke . . . [thy] coat. The order in which the two garments are mentioned in Matthew is here inverted, the suggestion being of that which would be seized first.

35 hoping for nothing again. Or, as R.V., "never despairing."

36 Be ye therefore merciful. See note on Matt. v. 48.

38 shall [men] give. Luke here preserves a portion of our Lord's discourse not found in Matthew; exhibiting the benefits which a man derives from his charitable treatment of others (38); and then illustrating the incapacity of the censorious man for guiding others aright; because he is "blind" himself (39), and his disciples cannot, at their best, become better than he (40): see note on Matt. vii. 1. Some writers see no connexion between vers. 38 and 39. But surely the exhortation to generosity in 38 is appropriately followed by the warning against the censorious spirit mentioned in 39 and 41.

40 The disciple, etc. A saying used, Matt. x. 24, with a different application.

43–49. The following verses are connected not so much with those immediately preceding, as with the whole foregoing discourse: see Matt. vii. 18.

45 A good man, etc. See Matt. xii. 34, 35, and notes.

48 for it was founded upon a rock. The R.V. prefers the reading, "because it was well built." But a good deal is still to be said for the A.V. text, on the weight of the MSS.

CHAPTER VII

2 centurion. Centurions were Roman officers commanding 100 men. One of them was usually quartered in every important provincial town, to preserve order. This man appears to have become strongly attached to the Jewish worship and people; and to have inferred, from the miracles of which he had heard, that Jesus must be the Messiah, whose authority he humbly acknowledges (7, 8).

3 the elders. Omit "the."

4 instantly. *i.e.,* "urgently."

5 and he hath built us a synagogue. Rather, "and himself built us a synagogue" (R.V.). A striking instance of honour paid by a Gentile to the religion of Israel.

6 the centurion sent friends. See note on Matt. viii. 5.

8 Do this, and he doeth [it]. My authority is but limited; for my power is but human, and my rank subordinate: yet even my word is certainly and promptly obeyed. Who or what can resist Thine?

11 Nain. A village of Galilee (still called *Nein*), lying on the northern declivity of Little Hermon, about eight miles S.W. of Nazareth. This narrative is peculiar to Luke.

many of his disciples. Not only of the apostles, who had been set apart on the preceding day; but of those, generally, who believed in Him.

12 carried out. Among the Jews, all burials were outside the city walls, except those of kings and distinguished persons: see 1 Sam. xxviii. 3; 2 Kings xxi. 18.

13 He had compassion. Our Lord's compassion appears to have been awakened, without any solicitation on the part of the mourners, by the affecting combination;—an only son, a widowed mother, a sympathising crowd.

14 the bier. The corpse was wrapped in folds of linen (John xi. 44), and carried on an open bier.

Arise. The calm dignity apparent in every case in which our Lord raised the dead (viii. 54; John xi. 43) is particularly impressive when contrasted with the manner in which the prophets Elijah and Elisha, and in which also His own apostles Peter and Paul, obtained the restoration of life in the only other instances in which it was granted (1 Kings xvii. 17–24; 2 Kings iv. 31–37; Acts ix. 39–43; xx. 9–12).

15 delivered him to his mother. By this tender and gracious act, Jesus honours maternal love.

16 God hath visited His people. Cp. Luke i. 68.

17 throughout all Judæa. Beyond the limits of Galilee, in which Nain was situated.

18–35. See notes on Matt. xi. 2–19.

21 plagues, and of evil spirits. "Observe that Luke, himself a physician, distinguishes between the *diseased* and the *possessed*" (*Alford*).

29–35. These verses are most probably a parenthetical statement of the evangelist, designed to show that the success of John's ministry, though great, was almost entirely confined to the more despised classes of people, who "justified God" by their faith in His Divine commission and their obedience to His injunctions; whilst the religious teachers rejected Him. The statement serves to introduce the remarks of our Lord which follow in vers. 31–35. The words, "And the Lord said" (31), which seem to indicate the resumption of the discourse after an interruption, are not found in the best manuscripts.

36–50. Peculiar to Luke.

37 a woman. There is no ground for supposing, as some have done, and as is stated in the title often prefixed to the chapter, that this woman was *Mary Magdalene* (mentioned in viii. 2); or Mary *the sister of Lazarus*, who also anointed our Lord's feet shortly before His last sufferings: see note on Mark xiv. 3. Neither of them, so far as we know, had been a person of immoral character. Of this woman we hear nothing more.

brought an alabaster box, etc. It is still customary, in some parts of the East, to allow strangers to enter the house, or the open court in which the meal is often taken. This was probably the best opportunity which this penitent woman could find of expressing personally her gratitude to her Deliverer.

38 stood at His feet behind [Him], etc. The Jews were accustomed to recline at table, with the feet unshod on the couch; so that one who stood weeping behind a guest might easily let her tears fall upon his feet.

39 would have known. The inspiration of a prophet (thought he) would reveal to him this sinner's character; and his sanctity would shrink from her touch. Jesus therefore (he concluded) cannot be a prophet. Our Lord's reply proves the contrary: for He shows His knowledge not only of the woman's life and conduct, but even of the Pharisee's thoughts: and His accurate appreciation of the penitence of the one, and the uncharitable self-righteousness of the other.

41 five hundred pence (denarii) **. . . fifty.** Equal to about £20 and £2 respectively.

44 gavest me no water. Simon probably thought it a sufficient condescension to invite the Nazarene prophet to his table, without adding these customary tokens of hospitality. And the incivility might have passed unnoticed by Him who "came not to be ministered unto, but to minister," had it not afforded an opportunity for a rebuke of the Pharisee for his remark in ver. 39.

47 for she loved much. The word "for" often adduces not a *cause* but a *proof*. Our Lord is speaking not of the *ground* of forgiveness, but of its *evidence;* which evidence is grateful love. Not, "she *is forgiven* because she loved," but "*we know* by her love that she is forgiven." On the contrary, as in the Pharisee's case, little love shows little sense of pardon.

CHAPTER VIII

1–3. Peculiar to Luke.

2 Mary called Magdalene. See note on Matt. xxvii. 56.

seven devils (demons). "Seven" is the number of completeness, and it probably implies here, and in Matt. xii. 45, the thorough subjugation of the whole nature to demoniacal power.

3 Herod's steward. An office of responsibility, and therefore of honour, in the court of Herod Antipas. It is probable that Joanna was now a widow, and thus able to devote her time and property to the service of her Benefactor (xxiv. 10).

4–15. See notes on Matt. xiii. 1–23.

16–18. See notes on Mark iv. 21–25.

19 Then. This word (in ver. 22 rendered "now") is a particle of connexion, not a note of time. See notes on Matt. xii. 46–50.

22–25—ix. 57–62. Cp. Matt. viii. 23–27; Mark iv. 36–41, and notes.

26–40. See notes on Matt. viii. 28–34; Mark v. 1–21.

31 the deep. Lit., "the *abyss*," or "bottomless *place*"; used in Rev. ix. 1, 2, etc., for the abode of malignant spirits, whence, with God's permission, they can come forth on the earth.

39 how great things God hath done unto thee.

Jesus refers the work to God: the man himself to Jesus: a beautiful combination of truths.

46 virtue. power.

41–5 See notes on Matt. ix. 18–26; Mark v. 22–43.

CHAPTER IX

1–6. See notes on Matt. x. 1–15; Mark vi. 7–13.

7–9. See notes on Mark vi. 14–31.

10–17. See notes on Matt. xiv. 13–21; Mark vi. 31–44; John vi. 1–13.

18–27. See notes on Matt. xvi. 13–28; Mark viii. 27–38.

18 alone praying. "While he was praying by himself his disciples were beside him" (*Moffatt*).

23 daily. The self-renunciation signified by "taking up the cross" is to be the constant habit of the soul.

24 will save, etc. "Willeth," or, "wants to" save—expressing deliberate purpose.

26 in His own glory, etc. The threefold glory of the Son of man, arising from personal dignity, official authority, and the attendance of angels.

28–36. See notes on Matt. xvii. 1–9; Mark ix. 2–10.

28 Peter and John and James. See note on Mark v. 37. Peter refers distinctly to this wondrous scene (2 Pet. i. 16–18).

to pray. Mentioned only by Luke.

29 His countenance was altered. Of this change or transfiguration, only the brightness which radiated from His person and garments (cp. Exod. xxxiv. 29–35) is described: the rest was doubtless indescribable.

31 decease. Or, "departure": cp. 2 Pet. i. 15.

32 were heavy. Rather, "Now Peter and his companions had been heavy with sleep; but, having kept awake, they saw," etc. The transfiguration seems to have occurred at night; and they were at first extremely wearied with the toils of the day and the fatigue of the ascent, until the light and glory thoroughly awoke them. The circumstance of their remaining awake is carefully noted, to show that the transfiguration was not a mere vision.

33 tabernacles. "Tents" or "booths." Peter was so confused that he probably had nothing more than the general feeling, "It is good to be here"; and therefore wished to provide for the stay of the heavenly visitants.

34 the cloud. A bright cloud, like the Shekinah, a symbol of the Divine presence, enveloped Jesus and the heavenly visitants, and struck the disciples with awe.

35 This is my beloved Son. Three times during the ministry of Jesus the Father audibly expressed His satisfaction in His Son's work; in every case as a response to prayer, and at a signal crisis in His life and work: see vers. 28, 29; iii. 21, 22; and John xii. 27, 28. The transfiguration, which occurred just before the last journey of our Lord from Galilee to Jerusalem, was a most fitting preparation for the great events which were drawing nigh. It gave the disciples a momentary glimpse of the glory which awaited Him when His work on earth was finished. It was a formal recognition of His supremacy by the Law-giver and the Reformer of ancient Israel. And, when the representatives of the former economy depart, the heavenly voice proclaiming, "Hear Him!" intimates that that dispensation is passing away, and is giving place to another, of which Jesus, by virtue of His work and death, is constituted the Lord and Head.

36 told no man. In obedience to our Lord's commands (Matt. xvii. 9).

37–45. See notes on Mark ix. 14–32.

44 Let these sayings sink down. The great importance as well as the unexpected strangeness of this truth required that they should fix their thoughts upon it: see note on Mark ix. 32.

45 that they perceived it not. More precisely, as R.V., "that they should not perceive it." "It was the *divine purpose* that they should not at present be aware of the full significancy of these words" (*Alford*).

46–50. See notes on Matt. xviii. 1–6; Mark ix. 33–50.

51 when the time was come. Lit., "when the days were being fulfilled"; "when the days were well-nigh come" (R.V.).

received up. This "being received up" points to the glory to which our Lord's work on earth would quickly bring Him. His "setting His face stedfastly," etc., indicates His fixed and determinate resolve.

52 a village of the Samaritans. See notes on John iv. 6, 9.

53 did not receive Him. See note on Matt. x. 5.

to Jerusalem. He was evidently going up to one of the great Jewish festivals. The Samaritans expected that the Messiah when He came would confirm their Gerizim ritual.

54 John. This same John afterwards came down with Peter to Samaria (Acts viii. 14–17) to confer the gifts of the Holy Spirit on the Samaritan believers.

as Elias did. See 2 Kings i. 10.

57–62. See notes on Matt. viii. 18–22.

59 and bury my father. This appears from Matt. (viii. 21, 22) to have been one of the "disciples," who had probably just heard of his father's death. The reply of our Lord, without intending any disparagement of relative claims and duties, was clearly designed to set forth the paramount nature of spiritual obligations. Let those who are (spiritually) dead confine themselves wholly to such works as these; but let nothing be allowed for a moment to direct from their high calling those who are alive to the claims of my kingdom.

62 No man, having put his hand to the plough, etc. The ploughman cannot make a good furrow unless he keeps his attention fixed without distraction upon his work: neither can a Christian, and least of all one who is to "preach the kingdom of God," perform his important work with a divided heart. These three cases show how the Lord adapted His requirements to the characters of His hearers. He bids the rash or precipitate enthusiast to "count the cost" of discipleship: He prompts the time-serving and compromising to decisive action; and He urges the inconstant to unreserved consecration to one high purpose.

CHAPTER X

1 other seventy. Our Lord had Himself preached, and had sent the Twelve, through Galilee. The mission of the Seventy, related only by Luke, was more extensive, although temporary and preparatory.

4 purse. The ends of the "girdle" (Matt. x. 9) were commonly used for purses. "For all things—money, food, and clothing, as well as protection—rely on me, whilst you are doing my work." In its spirit this command is universal; its literal form was but of temporary application (see Luke xxii. 35, 36). Ver. 7 shows that the necessary provision was to be supplied by their Lord through the gifts of their hearers and converts.

scrip. Rather, "wallet" for provisions.

salute no man by the way. See 2 Kings iv. 29, and note. "Everything shows that the Master's business required haste" (*Lange*).

5 Peace [be] to this house. That is, Courteously address to its inmates the customary salutation. The prayer which it implies shall be answered for them, if they are willing to receive the gospel of "peace": but whether they do or not, in any case it shall be answered to you.

6 the son of peace. According to the preferable reading, "*a* son of peace" (R.V.), one susceptible to the blessing. "If there is a soul there breathing peace" (*Moffatt*).

7 in the same house. Or, as R.V., "in that same house," the house of "the son of peace," however poor it might be.

13–15. See Matt. xi. 20–24.

16 He that heareth you, etc. See Matt. x. 40.

17 are subject unto us. They are glad to find themselves able to do what had lately baffled even some of the Twelve (ix. 40).

18 I beheld Satan as lightning fall (fallen) **from heaven.** He saw in their mission and its results a beginning of the final overthrow of the Prince of all evil.

19 serpents and scorpions. See note on xi. 12. This is a well-known figure for malignant powers of evil (Psa. xci. 13; Ezek. ii. 6), which the disciples, under their Lord's safeguard, in prosecuting His work, are to overcome.

20 rejoice not. That is, *comparatively.*

because your names are written in heaven. Cp. Isa. iv. 3, and note. To be enrolled "in the Lamb's book of life" (Rev. xxi. 27) as a faithful subject of the kingdom of heaven is a far more valuable distinction than the possession of supernatural gifts: see Numb. xxii. 8; Matt. vii. 22, 23, and notes.

21 In that hour, etc. See Matt. xi. 25–27, and notes. The passage is evidently in its right place here. Our Lord may have uttered His joyful feelings in these words more than once.

Jesus rejoiced. By the "wise and prudent" (or "understanding," R.V.) must be understood those whom the world regards as such: the "babes" are not necessarily the ignorant, but those who are of simple, child-like spirit. Our Lord rejoices not that the truth was hidden from *any*, but that it was not hidden from all.

25 lawyer. That is, a teacher or expounder of the Mosaic law. For a similar narrative compare that in xviii. 18–30, and Matt. xix. 16–30.

tempted Him. That is, "proved Him": see note on Matt. xxii. 34.

27 he answering said. The correctness of this man's views is proved by our Lord's mention of the same two commands: see Mark xii. 29–31. But with theoretical correctness he appears to have been uniting practical disobedience; and this our Lord brings home to him by His explanation of the word "neighbour."

29 willing. Or, "desiring," as R.V. The lawyer probably felt uneasy in the conviction that our Lord's words in ver. 28 were designed to suggest that he had come short of what he knew to be necessary. The Saviour's answer in the parable suggests that our question should rather be, "To whom can I be neighbour?"

30–37. Parable of the GOOD SAMARITAN. Peculiar to Luke.

30 went down. See note on Matt. xx. 29. The road from Jerusalem to Jericho is a long descent of twenty-one miles. "Sharp turns of the road, and projecting spurs of rocks, everywhere facilitated the attack or escape" of robbers, and made this route, even till recent times, one of the most dangerous in Palestine (Stanley, *Sinai and Palestine*, p. 416).

33 a certain Samaritan. The Samaritans appear to have reciprocated the national hostility of the Jews (see ix. 52, 53); and we may suppose that our Lord selected a *Samaritan* as an example of the loving neighbour who succoured the half-dead Jew, in order to give, in one of the hated and despised race, an illustration of that Divine love which forgets all antipathies in another's distress.

34 oil and wine. "Oil and wine," which were frequently carried by travellers (see Gen. xxviii. 18; Josh. ix. 13), were applied to wounds in the East: see Isa. i. 6.

an inn. The words here rendered "inn" and "host" occur nowhere else in Scripture, and suggest rather a Roman inn than an Eastern khan or caravanserai.

35 two pence. On "pence" see note, Matt. xx. 2.

38 a certain village. The village was Bethany, near Jerusalem (see John xi. 1). This visit probably occurred when Jesus had gone up, in the course of His last journey, for a brief visit to Jerusalem at the Feast of Dedication (John x. 22, 23). The two sisters were both attached disciples of our Lord. The busy, energetic Martha, who seems to have been the elder sister and manager of the household, was not only assiduous in providing for His entertainment, but was so "anxious and harassed" about it as to neglect His spiritual teaching, and to find fault with Mary, whose whole soul was engaged in earnest attention to His "gracious words." The Saviour's gentle rebuke of Martha was called forth by her own complaint. That Martha had a genuine faith is shown by John xi. 20–24.

CHAPTER XI

1 teach us to pray. Our Lord's answer to their request first suggests subjects for prayer (2–4), and then encourages persistency in prayer (5–13).

as John also taught his disciples. The Jewish teachers gave their disciples short forms of prayer. The prayer which follows is substantially the same as that which had already been given in the Sermon on the Mount, Matt. vi. 9–13, where see notes. The form of the prayer as it appears in the R.V. follows the best authorities (see the words enclosed in brackets).

2 When ye pray. Lit., "Whensoever ye pray," etc

5 at midnight. During the hot season, travellers in the East often prefer the cool evening and night for a journey.

7 shut. Rather "locked"; and my family (servants and children), as well as myself, are in bed.

8 importunity. The force of the parable lies partly in the resemblances, partly in the contrasts. God is our Friend, our Father; but in Him there is nothing "evil." If, then, importunity can overcome selfishness (5–8), and if natural affection leads a father to grant his child's requests (11, 12), how surely may we reckon on the grace and wisdom of our Heavenly Friend and Father! Cp. also xviii. 1–8.

9 Ask . . . seek . . . knock. Prayer is to be marked by thoughtful and persevering earnestness; and the corresponding threefold promise gives us the fullest certainty that all such prayer is heard and will be answered. The matter of prayer had been given in vers. 2–4; here the manner of it is enjoined. With verses 9–13 cp. Matt. vii. 7–11.

11 a serpent. To a hungry child a stone would be useless; a serpent, not only useless, but injurious.

12 scorpion. A venomous reptile found in hot countries among the stones of old buildings.

13 the Holy Spirit. See note on Matt. vii. 11.

14, 15, 17–25. On this section and the next, see notes, Matt. xii. 22–45; Mark iii. 22.

18 If Satan also, etc. Our Lord here places Himself upon the standing ground of His opponents. If He really did cast out demons through the power of the devil, it would follow that Satan was at present employed in destroying his own work.

20 the finger of God. Matt. has "the Spirit of God."

21 When a strong man armed, etc. Had I been in league with Satan, I should have left him to keep his power over men "in peace." But what I am doing shows both my superiority and my enmity to him; so that there can be no neutrality (23).

27 Blessed, etc. An Oriental expression of the highest admiration. Contrast 1 Sam. xx. 30. Our Lord, not denying that it was a great happiness to have been His mother, nor reproving the maternal instinct which had prompted the exclamation, points out the far greater blessedness resulting from spiritual relationship to Himself; a principle which seems directly opposed to the religious veneration which has been claimed for our Lord's mother: cp. Matt. xii. 46–50, and notes.

33–35. These verses are found also in the Sermon on the Mount (see Matt. v. 15; vi. 22, 23, and notes); and cp. viii. 16. They are here repeated, with a special application to the preceding discourse. As God made Solomon and Jonah to be a "light" to the queen of Sheba and to the men of Nineveh, so He is making "the Son of man" a "light" "to this generation" (John iii. 19; viii. 12).

33 a candle . . . a secret place . . . a bushel . . . a candlestick. Rather, "a lamp" . . . "a cellar" . . . "the bushel" . . . "the lampstand," R.V.

34 The light of the body. Rather, "The lamp of thy body," R.V. If the eye which admits the light be not healthy (*i.e.,* if the soul be in a wrong state towards God and His truth), you will still be in darkness. "The Jews did not see the significance of our Lord's teaching and miracles, because they shut the eyes of their understanding, which should be the light of their soul" (*Alford*). "Body" here metaphorically expresses man's *spiritual being.*

36 as when the bright shining, etc. Rather, "as when a lamp lights you with its rays" (*Moffatt*).

37 to dine. To take the early or mid-day meal. It is the same Greek verb which is used in John xxi. 12, 15. It really means "to break one's fast"; cp. Fr. *déjeuner.*

38 washed. This was a thorough washing of the hands: see note on Mark vii. 3. "We have no ground for supposing that the Saviour did not commonly wash Himself before a meal. Now perhaps He omitted it because He had just accepted the invitation, or because He was wearied by the day's work which He had hitherto accomplished" (*Speaker's Commentary*).

39 Now do ye, etc. This is one instance in which, etc. On the whole discourse, see Matt. xxiii., and notes. This summary specifies four chief sins: hypocrisy, covetousness, formal legalism, pride.

40 Ye fools. It is *folly* to attend only to the external observances of religion; for God made man with a soul as well as a body.

41 such things as ye have. This may be rendered, "Give as alms the contents" [*i.e.,* of the vessel—yourselves]; meaning, instead of your ostentatious charities, give your hearts to the service of God and man. Or it may mean, "Give as alms the food which the vessels hold."

42 Woe unto you, Pharisees, etc. The performance of one class of duties must not be made an excuse for the neglect of another.

44 graves which appear not. The same figure is found in Matt. xxiii. 27; but with a different application. There, the outward ostentation of the Pharisees is reproved; here, their inward secret wickedness.

49 said the wisdom of God. There is perhaps here a general allusion to 2 Chron. xxiv. 18–22. Cp. Matt. xxiii. 34.

51 It shall be required of this generation. See note on Matt. xxiii. 31.

52 have taken away the key of knowledge. See Matt. xxiii. 13, and note.

CHAPTER XII

1 the leaven of the Pharisees. Their corrupt doctrine. For they say, and do not (Matt. xxiii. 3).

2–9. See notes on Matt. x. 26–33.

8 confess me before men. A firm and consistent avowal before the world of Jesus as the object of worship, love, and trust.

10 blasphemeth against the Holy Ghost. See notes on Matt. xii. 31, 32.

11 when they bring you unto the synagogues. See note on Matt. x. 19.

14 Who made me a judge or a divider over you? It was no part of our Lord's office to administer the laws, or to arbitrate in civil matters. He came to teach men the higher law of love; and to correct the desire of worldly gain, and reliance upon earthly possessions as a source of happiness.

15 a man's life, etc. The meaning is, However large a man's possessions may be, his "life," even his natural life, does not depend upon them; and the higher life, the spiritual and immortal life, may be lost through them.

16 a parable. Only in Luke.

brought forth plentifully. The case is not that of a dishonest man or an extortioner. His riches were fairly acquired; the gift of Providence.

17 no room (place). *Ambrose* well observes, "Thou hast storehouses, the bosoms of the needy, the homes of widows, the mouths of infants."

20 shall be required. R.V., "is required"; literally, "This night they require thy soul of thee": the man awakes to the consciousness that he must surrender this pampered life *at once.*

21 layeth up treasure for himself. As one whose trust and aims terminate in himself. This is the impoverishment, and at length the loss of soul.

22–31. A repetition with variations of what had already been uttered in the Sermon on the Mount: see notes on Matt. vi. 25–33.

24 Consider the ravens. Cp. Job xxxviii. 41; Psa. cxlvii. 9. In the Sermon on the Mount the reference is more general: "the fowls of the air."

26 If ye then, etc. This application of the foregoing lesson is peculiar to Luke, though it is suggested in Matt. vi. 27.

29 neither be ye of doubtful mind. A word peculiar to this passage. Be not agitated, worried.

31 the kingdom. "That state, first internal, then social, in which the human will is nothing but the free agent of the Divine will" (*Godet*).

33 Sell that ye have, etc. Our Lord now passes from precepts respecting the acquisition of riches to counsels as to their worthy use. He speaks to all those who would follow Him. They must give up *all* to do so. Compare the command to the young ruler: Matt. xix. 21, and note.

where no thief approacheth, etc. They are not liable either to violence or to decay.

35 Let your loins be girded. See note on Jer. i. 17; and Matt. xxv. 1. Be ever ready and watchful. The gathering up of the loose Eastern robes was the sign of readiness for immediate active service.

your lights burning. This symbol is similar to that used in the parable of the Wise and Foolish Virgins, Matt. xxv.

37 and serve them. Treating them not as servants (xvii. 7, 8), but as most honoured and distinguished guests: see John xiii. 1–16; Rev. iii. 20, 21.

38 second watch, etc. See note on Matt. xiv. 25. The second and third watches, extending from 9 p.m. to 3 a.m., are selected probably to illustrate unsleeping vigilance, as that is the part of the night in which men would be most drowsy.

39–46. See notes on Matt. xxiv. 42–51.

39 the goodman of the house. The phrase is the same as that elsewhere rendered "master of the house" or "householder."

41 Then Peter said, etc. This question of Peter is peculiar to Luke.

48 he that knew not. All men have some knowledge of God's will; but those who have the light of revelation, and neglect it, are specially guilty: see Rom. ii. 12–16.

49 and what will I if, etc.? Rather, "and what will I? Oh that it were already kindled!" Some regard this "fire" as referring to the power of the Holy Spirit: see Matt. iii. 11; Acts ii. 3, 4. Others think that it refers to the persecutions and dissensions which the spread of the gospel has occasioned (51, 52). But see note on Matt. iii. 11, in accordance with which passage it is best to interpret this. Cp. the traditional saying of our Lord, "He who is near me is near the fire."

50 straitened. Restrained; held back; distressed. The word is used by the apostle Paul, 2 Cor. v. 14; Phil. i. 23.

52 but rather division. See Matt. x. 34, and note.

54–56. See note on Matt. xvi. 3.

55 the south wind. The simoom, from the sultry desert on the south of Judæa. "Heat," *i.e.*, "scorching heat," R.V., or drought.

57 even of yourselves. You ought not to need these signs to awaken you to repentance.

58, 59. Another simile employed in the Sermon on the Mount; see Matt. v. 25, 26, and notes. Here the point of the exhortation is that the Jews should not lose the short season of grace and salvation.

CHAPTER XIII

1 whose blood Pilate had mingled with their sacrifices. Nothing further is known either of this event or of that referred to in ver. 4. The slaughter evidently occurred at one of the great festivals. Fanatical insurrections, repressed by military severities, were too frequent at such times to be always recorded by historians.

2 Suppose ye, etc.? The truth that all suffering is the consequence of our sinful state, and the fact that much suffering is the direct result of particular sins, had been distorted into the common error that every great calamity was a punishment for some flagrant sin: see John ix. 2, and Introduction to the Book of Job. This notion led, on the one hand, to uncharitable judgements; and on the other, to self-complacency on the part of the prosperous; whom our Lord therefore warns, lest they also perish; and He adds a parable (6–9) to teach them to regard the lengthening of their lives as space given them to repent: see Rom. ii. 4, 5.

3 likewise. Rather, "in like manner"; *i.e.*, as certainly and terribly. In fact, some thousands of the Jews did afterwards perish by the Roman sword. But the words bear also a more general application.

4 the tower in Siloam. A tower adjacent to the pool of that name in Jerusalem: see Neh. iii. 15; John ix. 7; and Joseph. *Wars*, v. 4, § 2. Instances from *Galilee* and *Jerusalem*, from the cruelty of man and from so-called accident.

6–9. Parable of THE BARREN FIG TREE. Peculiar to Luke.

7 three years. Sufficient time being given to show that its barrenness is not accidental. There is no need to press this reference as applying to the actual period of our Lord's ministry.

why cumbereth ("why doth it also encumber," R.V.). The Greek verb means "to leave unemployed"; hence "to make barren"; "to render useless" (see *Liddell and Scott*).

11 a woman. Incident peculiar to Luke.

a spirit of infirmity. That is, infirmity inflicted by an evil spirit.

13 He laid His hands on her. A sign of the power that "restored the bodily organism to the control of the emancipated will" (*Godet*).

14 the ruler of the synagogue. See note on Mark v. 22.

15 Thou hypocrite. The best MSS. have "You hypocrites," suggesting that the ruler was representative of his class. He did not speak frankly and honestly: but addressed to the multitude the reproof which he meant for Jesus, and perverted Scripture for his own purpose.

18–21. Parables of the MUSTARD SEED and of the LEAVEN. See Matt. xiii. 31; Mark iv. 30, and notes.

23 Lord, are there few that be (are being) **saved?** The question was one of speculative curiosity. A man truly in earnest would have asked, "What shall I do to be saved?" In reply, therefore, Jesus directs the questioner to practical matters, exhorting him to consider his own personal relation to God's kingdom.

24 Strive. Rather, "struggle"; for the Greek word suggests a combat. The exhortation in ver. 24 is somewhat like that previously given in the Sermon on the Mount, Matt. vii. 13, 14; but the emphasis is here laid, not on the difference between the broad and the narrow way, but on the absolute necessity of *unflinching earnestness* in religion: cp. Matt. xi. 12.

31 Herod will kill thee. "Wants to kill thee." The Greek is not the future of kill, but the verb meaning "wishes." Our Lord's reply, addressed to Herod, makes it likely that this warning was instigated by Herod, who was alarmed at His popularity, and desired to get Him out of his territory, without displeasing the multitude. He replies that He shall not hasten His work or His journey, and that He has nothing to fear from Herod: for it is not in Galilee or Peræa that His labours and sufferings are to be consummated in His death, but in Jerusalem (31–35): cp. ix. 11.

33 to-day and to-morrow. See Hosea vi. 2, and note.

34 O Jerusalem, Jerusalem! See notes on Matt. xxiii. 37–39, where these words, now spoken in Peræa, are repeated in the city itself, with variations to suit the connexion.

CHAPTER XIV

1 on the sabbath day. A usual day for entertainments. For the incident, cp. Mark iii. 1–6.

4 held their peace. They would not acknowledge that it was lawful to heal on the sabbath, and they could not show it to be unlawful.

5 an ass or an ox. Cp. note on the similar question, Matt. xii. 11. Pharisaic casuistry or quibbling decided that an animal might not be lifted from the pit on the sabbath, but that food might be let down to it.

7 chief rooms. Rather, "the chief of *seats*" or "*places*"; and so in vers. 8–10: see note on Matt. xxiii. 6, where the same point is raised on a subsequent occasion.

10 Friend. Two words are so translated: one, a mere title of courtesy (Matt. xxii. 12, where see note), the other a word of confidence and affection (John xv. 14). The *latter* is here employed.

worship. Rather, "honour." The consequence rather than the motive of this conduct.

12 a dinner or a supper. The morning or the evening meal: at noontide or sunset respectively.

call not thy friends. Our Lord condemns, not social hospitalities (Matt. xi. 18, 19), but the selfish spirit which leads men to extend these only to those who can make an adequate return. The Christian spirit prompts us to give, looking for nothing again; although the promise of God assures us of a future reward.

15 shall eat bread in the kingdom of God. Shall be admitted to the resurrection festival: see ver. 14.

16–24. Parable of THE GREAT SUPPER. Peculiar to Luke. A similar parable was afterwards spoken in Jerusalem (Matt. xxii. 1–14).

17 sent his servant, etc. See note on Matt. xxii. 3.

18 began to make excuse. The responsibilities of property, the claims of business, the pressure of domestic cares, are so many inadequate pleas for rejecting the great invitation. Excuses are not reasons.

23 compel [them]. Or, "constrain them." These outcasts would hardly believe that the invitation was for them. The compulsion to be used is only that of earnest persuasion. "Saul, mad for Judaism, *compelled* in one way; Paul, the servant of Jesus, in another" (*Bengel*). Does not the Christian Church too often fail in "going out" (vers. 21 and 23) in order to reach the indifferent and careless?

26 If any man come to me, etc. See notes on Matt. x. 37, 38, where similar words, spoken before, are recorded.

hate. Love and hatred are used to designate strong decided preference: cp. Matt. x. 37. Love to parents is one of the first requirements of ethics; love of life, one of the strongest laws of nature: but even these must not come into competition with the claims of Jesus. *Life* (the same word often rendered *soul*) may include natural affection and desire.

28–33. The two parables which follow (which are given by Luke only) show that the entire self-renunciation which is required of Christ's true disciples should lead every one solemnly to reflect and count the cost of committing himself to a Christian life; especially as the profession of religion without its reality is worthless and offensive.

31 what king, etc.? It is noted by many expositors that Herod Antipas was at this time engaged in a war with Aretas of Damascus, father of the tetrarch's divorced wife, a war which led to Herod's humiliation and crushing defeat.

33 forsaketh. "Renounceth," R.V.; "who will not part with all his goods" (*Moffatt*).

34 Salt is good, etc. Another saying from the Sermon on the Mount: see Matt. v. 13; Mark ix. 50, and notes.

CHAPTER XV

This and the next chapter contain a series of parables peculiar to Luke, directed particularly against the Pharisees; first (in ch. xv.) in reply to their accusation, then (in ch. xvi.) in reproof of their covetous worldliness. In ch. xv., their murmurings at our Lord's reception of publicans (1, 2) are silenced by three beautiful parables, displaying God's love to the greatest sinners. The silly wanderer (see Prov. i. 4, and note) is sought out, brought tenderly back, and rejoiced over (3–7). The smallest coin which has borne God's likeness (Gen. i. 26) is thought to be worth patient search and public joy (8–10). Even the thankless, wayward, wasteful, debased prodigal is still regarded as a son, and is watched for, embraced, restored, and honoured, filling the Father's house with joy; though self-righteous men may refuse to receive him (11–32).

1 drew near. Lit., "were drawing near" (R.V.). It was so *habitually*.

3–7. Parable of THE LOST SHEEP. Here the point seems to be that of foolish, helpless wandering.

4 the wilderness. The open pasture-land: see note on Matt. iii. 1.

5 layeth [it] on his shoulders. Not driving it back. The circumstance is finely expressive of the tenderness shown by the Good Shepherd.

8–10. Parable of THE LOST PIECE OF SILVER. Here the special thought seems to be that of *the Divine ownership*. The strayed sheep excites pity, and is sought for its own sake; the silver coin is lost to its possessor, and for that reason is searched for. There may be the further thought of the "image and superscription" which gives its value to a coin.

8 a candle. Rather, "a lamp"; to enable her to search the darkest corners of the ill-lighted house.

11–32. Parable of THE PRODIGAL SON. This parable has been well called the crown and gem of our Lord's parables. One writer calls it "The Pearl of Parables." In distinction from the other two, it sets forth sin as wilful, purposed wandering. To both the younger and elder sons the father shows the same condescending grace; and the warm welcome and full forgiveness which he gives to the returning outcast are scarcely more touching than the gentle forbearance and tender reproof with which he meets the haughty and self-righteous Pharisee.

12 the portion of goods that falleth to me. By law an inheritance was divided equally among the sons, except the eldest, who took a double share. But this son claims his share before it is due.

14 began to be in want. "He had spent all"; there is left no resource in himself; "there arose a mighty famine"; there is nothing external to satisfy the cravings of the soul.

15 to feed swine. Nothing could more forcibly depict to a Jew the extreme of degradation than the occupation of a swineherd as the servant of a foreigner, which would bear, in his view, the closest resemblance to the condition of the tax-gatherers who collected the taxes for foreign rulers.

16 the husks. Rather, "pods," with the fruit in them, of the carob-tree (*ceratonia siliquosa*): which are used in the East for feeding swine, and are sometimes eaten by the very poor.

17 when he came to himself. He was not his true self while he lived in sin; he becomes conscious that he was made for other things.

How many hired servants, etc.? The lowest place in the father's house is luxury compared with this.

21 I have sinned, etc. The purposed conclusion, "Make me as one of thy hired servants," is *omitted;* the father's love is already so manifested that the son is conscious of the higher privilege.

22 the best robe, etc. The "chief robe," the "ring," and the "shoes," implying freedom and dignity in the person who wore them, were never allowed to servants. Slaves went barefoot.

23 the fatted calf. Already in the stall, as if in readiness for a feast; not unusual in a rich man's house.

24 dead. Alienation from God and from goodness is moral death.

28 and entreated him. God is long-suffering even to the self-righteous. "The parable itself, spoken to the Pharisees, was an entreaty to the elder brother" (*Schaff*).

29 do I serve thee. The unfilial slavish spirit here shows itself; strict obedience, but servile motive. The words that follow are more emphatically rendered in R.V., "and I never transgressed a commandment of thine."

a kid. Even a kid: the smallest of festal gifts.

30 thy son. Not *my brother*. Contrast the answer of the father (32).

31 Son. Lit., child, an appeal of loving, patient earnestness.

32 It was meet. Lit., "There was need." It could not be otherwise.

CHAPTER XVI

1-8. Parable of THE UNJUST STEWARD. This parable has been variously explained and applied. But the key to it is in vers. 8, 9, on which see notes. In a sentence it may be said that the parable teaches that we should exercise prudence and foresight in regard to eternal things, even as men do in regard to their temporal affairs.

8 the lord. "His lord." That is, the steward's lord, who admired the man's shrewdness, though he suffered by it. "The master praised the dishonest factor for looking ahead" (*Moffatt*).

children of light. The "sons of the light" are they who are illuminated by heavenly wisdom: see John xii. 36; Eph. v. 8; 1 Thess. v. 7, 8. They, however, use this wisdom to far less purpose in the pursuit of heavenly things, than the men of the world use their natural shrewdness in earthly pursuits.

9 friends of (by means of) **the mammon,** etc. As the unjust steward, by the use of his lord's money, provided for himself "friends" and "habitations" against his time of need, so do you employ whatever your Lord entrusts to you in such a way that you may have friends and a home hereafter. This includes not only almsgiving, but all use of property in God's service: cp. xii. 33; Matt. xxv. 34-40; Mark ix. 41; Heb. vi. 10.

mammon of unrighteousness. "The mammon which the unrighteous worship." Make money, not your god, but your friend. Our Lord cautions us against two opposite mistakes: (1) idolising money, as if it were a good in itself; (2) supposing it to be so profane and unclean that it cannot be employed in the service of God.

when ye fail. Another reading has "when it fails." When earthly wealth is gone, the eternal home remains. For "everlasting mansions," R.V. translates, "the eternal tabernacles."

they may receive you. The "friends" whom you have thus made will welcome you. It is not the *title* to heaven of which our Lord is speaking, but the *welcome.*

10 in that which is least. Or, as R.V., "in a very little"; in earthly riches. He who faithfully employs these will also make a right use of spiritual gifts.

12 that which is your own. Substantial, enduring, and inalienable possessions. These questions intimate that faithfulness to God is the highest prudence; to which the next verse, reproduced from the Sermon on the Mount, adds that this faithfulness cannot exist with the love of money (Matt. vi. 24).

14 covetous. Better, "lovers of money," as R.V.

15 highly esteemed. The Greek means "lofty."

is abomination. Or, "loathsome." See Exod. viii. 26, and note.

16 until John. This had been already said to the disciples of the Baptist: see note on Matt. xi. 12.

17 it is easier, etc. Reproduced from the Sermon on the Mount: see note on Matt. v. 18.

18 Whosoever putteth away his wife, etc. Another illustration of our Lord's immediate subject—the false principles and teachings of the Pharisees: see notes on Matt. v. 31; xix. 3-9. This verse "combines the first case of Mark x. 11, with the second case of Matt. v. 32, and may be the original form" (*Grieve*).

19-31. Parable of THE RICH MAN AND LAZARUS. The parable is an answer to the sneers of the Pharisees (14). Its main points are: 1. The uncertainty and transitoriness of earthly blessings; 2. The responsibility of rich men, not only for what they do, but for what they do not do, with their wealth; and 3. The supremacy of the Law of God as a guide to eternal life (*Speaker's Commentary*).

19 fared sumptuously. Not to be understood merely of *food;* see R.V. marg., "living in mirth and splendour." There is no intimation that his luxuries were unjustly acquired or squandered profligately. The sin was in the neglect of duty.

20 Lazarus. The name Lazarus (or Eleazar, signifying *one whose help is God*) is probably meant to mark the poor man's character, which is not otherwise designated. Not because he was poor, but because, in his poverty, he made God his trust, he is taken to "Abraham's bosom."

21 the dogs came. Treated by men contemptuously, as little better than a dog; and by dogs compassionately, as like one of themselves.

22 Abraham's bosom. An expression derived from the position of the favoured guest at a feast (see John xiii. 23, 25), implying honour, joy, and intimate association (John i. 18).

and was buried. The rich man's body has a gorgeous funeral on earth, the soul of Lazarus an angelic convoy to heaven.

23 hell. "Hades" (R.V.); the name given to the abode of the departed, both the righteous and the wicked: see Acts ii. 31; Rev. i. 18. It is by the "torments" that the state of the ungodly man after death is characterised.

24 tormented in this flame. The sufferings of disembodied spirits are here and elsewhere metaphorically represented by bodily pain.

25 Son, remember. There is every reason to suppose that, in the future state, the events of the past life will be vividly recalled by the memory, which will thus become a source either of grateful joy or of poignant anguish. The "rich man," as a Jew, was a "son of Abraham." The word employed is one of affection: "Child."

thy good things. What most seemed "good" to thee: thy choice; "receivedst," *i.e.*, to the full: cp. Matt. vi. 2.

26 a great gulf. The image is that of a deep ravine, across which this conversation is held, as from opposite mountain sides. The details of the parable must not be literally pressed. They form its accessories, by which its spiritual lessons are conveyed.

29 Moses and the prophets. That is, their inspired writings, in which sufficient condemnation would be found of self-indulgent luxurious lives.

30 Nay. "Not so"; that is, I know they will not hear them.

31 though one rose from the dead. Lazarus was recalled from the grave, and One greater than Lazarus soon afterwards rose from the dead: but the Pharisees, instead of believing, were only the more exasperated against the truth. The claims of modern spiritism may well be subjected to the light of this parable.

CHAPTER XVII

1 Then said He. Rather, "And He said"; for the connexion with the preceding chapter is not that of *time*, but of *subject*. These verses are similar with a few additions, to several remarks which Matthew has preserved in their connexion: see Matt. xvii. 20; xviii. 6, 7, 15, 21, 22.

offences. That is, "occasions of sin"; "hindrances" (*Moffatt*); see notes on Matt. v. 29; Mark ix. 42.

3 Take heed. Be careful not to cause any one to fall into sin, especially by manifesting an unforgiving spirit (4).

5 Increase our faith. The disciples felt that unusual faith on their part was needed for the fulfilment of the foregoing command.

6 sycamine tree. The "sycamine" is the black mulberry tree, which is found in Palestine: distinct from the "sycomore."

7 will say unto him, etc. Rather, "will say unto him as he cometh in from the field, Go at once," etc.: cp. R.V. The connexion seems to be that "the increase of faith for which the apostles prayed was to come through obedience, outward and inward obedience to their Master's will" (*Plumptre*).

8 afterward thou shalt eat and drink. Do not regard these requirements as a hardship, or think to found on them a claim for God's favour. When a servant comes in from his work, however laborious, the master still requires his attendance, and does not feel that the servant has thereby earned special thanks.

10 unprofitable. Having no claim or merit.

11–19. Peculiar to Luke.

11 through the midst of. That is, "between." This seems to be the journey mentioned in Matt. xix. 1. This incident is perhaps out of the exact order of time, being introduced here as illustrating the anti-Pharisaic spirit of our Lord's actions and teachings, which appears so prominent throughout this section. After healing ten lepers, He particularly commends and blesses the Samaritan, who alone showed any gratitude to his benefactor (11–19).

12 stood afar off. In obedience to the law (Lev. xiii. 45, 46).

14 show yourselves unto the priests. See note on Mark i. 44. This command implied that they would be healed on the way; and their obedience to it showed so much faith in our Lord's power as obtained the cure.

17 Were there not, etc.? Rather, "Were not the ten cleansed?" R.V.

18 this stranger. "This foreigner": see note on John iv. 9.

19 hath made thee whole. Or, "hath saved thee."

20 cometh not with observation. It will be gradual and unobserved.

21 within you. "In your midst," or, "*among* you," as a people (see R.V. marg.). But others think that the preposition means within, as contrasted with what is without (cp. Matt. xxiii. 26).

22 The days will come. "Days" of severe trial "will come, when ye shall desire to see one" such day as these in which ye now enjoy my personal presence among you (21).

23–37. See Matt. xxiv. 23–41, and notes.

25 suffer . . . and be rejected. The coming of the kingdom of God (20) is very different from that which you expect. As to myself, my sufferings must precede my glory; and so it must be as to my disciples (Matt. x. 24, 25; Rom. viii. 17; 1 Pet. iv. 13). As to these unbelievers, it is the coming of a day of vengeance.

31 upon the housetop. See note on Matt. xxiv. 17.

32 Remember Lot's wife. Peculiar to Luke. See Gen. xix. 17, 26. Lot's wife is to all ages a solemn example of the danger of godless company and worldliness.

37 Where, Lord? This question gives our Lord occasion to declare that such punishments may be expected, not in Jerusalem only, but "whereso-ever" sin similarly prevails.

CHAPTER XVIII

1–14. Parable of THE UNJUST JUDGE. Peculiar to Luke. The parable incidentally illustrates the disregard of equity that characterised the courts at this period.

3 Avenge me of mine adversary. Rather, "Exact justice for me from my opponent," in my cause before thee. On the oppression of widows generally, see Exod. xxii. 22; Mal. iii. 5; and by the Pharisees especially, see Mark xii. 40.

5 weary me. Gr. "to give a black eye"; hence "to mortify," "to annoy."

6 Hear what the unjust judge saith. If one who thought only of his own ease and comfort would be induced to do justice to one whom he only knew as a suitor in his court, how much more will He who is infinitely just and loving hear the cry of His own chosen ones!

7 though He bear long with them. Rather (as in James v. 7), "though He hath long patience in regard to them"; delaying in mercy the vengeance which He will inflict for them upon their persecutors.

8 speedily. There is no real delay, though man, in his impatience, may think there is: see 2 Pet. iii. 8–10.

when the Son of man cometh, etc. When this day of vengeance and deliverance comes, how few will be found still confident, and persisting like the widow! The danger is, not that God will be unfaithful, but that His elect, through mistrust, will relax their importunity.

9–14. Parable of THE PHARISEE and PUBLICAN. Peculiar to Luke. This parable, like the former, is introduced by a statement of its purpose.

9 trusted in themselves . . . and despised others. These two traits of character are always connected. Men's estimation of others and feelings towards them are determined by their feelings towards God.

11 other men. "The rest of men," as R.V.

12 twice in the week. The Law required fasting *once a year,* on the great day of Atonement (Lev. xxiii. 27); the Rabbis enjoined a fast on the second and fifth days of every week.

of all that I possess. Rather, "of all that I *gain* or acquire." Not capital, but income: see Matt. xxiii. 23, and note.

13 standing afar off. In the Temple court, most worshippers pressed as near as possible to the entrance of the Holy Place. The publican felt, like the Pharisee, but in the opposite sense, that he was "not as other men." To the Pharisee others were sinners, and he was righteous; to the publican others were righteous, and he "the sinner."

14 justified. These two men represent in their simplest form two opposite principles, of trust in personal merit on the one hand, and humble appeal to God's free mercy on the other. But in actual life the publican's words are often found on a Pharisee's lips; and the conflict goes on even in the true believer's heart.

every one that exalteth himself, etc. A repetition, in a new connexion of xiv. 11: see also Matt. xxiii. 12.

15–17. See Mark x. 13–16, and note.

15 infants. Lit., "the (their) babes."

18–30. See notes on Matt. xix. 16–29, and Mark x. 17–32.

18 a certain ruler. This description of him is peculiar to Luke.

31–34. See notes on Matt. xx. 17–19.

34 they understood none of these things. See Mark ix. 32, and note.

35—xix. 1. See notes on Matt. xx. 29–34; Mark x. 46–52.

35 as He was come nigh unto Jericho. According to Matthew and Mark this was when Jesus and His disciples were *leaving* Jericho. There were two Jerichos, an old and a new town.

43 glorifying God. Luke here, as in some other places (v. 26; ix. 43; xiii. 17), notices particularly the effect of the miracle upon men's minds, leading them to "glorify God."

CHAPTER XIX

1 passed. "Was passing."

2 chief among the publicans. This narrative is peculiar to Luke. On the office of Zacchæus, see note on Matt. v. 46. He either farmed the taxes of a large district, which he sub-let again to the ordinary collectors; or was receiver-general of the taxes of the district from the inferior collectors.

4 a sycomore tree. The Egyptian fig; a tree which resembles the mulberry in appearance and foliage, and grows to a great size and height.

5 at thy house. Jericho was a city of the priests. To select the house of a tax-gatherer for His lodging was in such a place especially significant.

7 they all murmured (were all murmuring). Not only a complaint from the Pharisees, but a *general* dissatisfaction.

8 stood. Indicating resolution and decision. The French version renders: "se présentant devant le Seigneur" (presenting himself before the Lord).

I give to the poor, etc. Not, as some understand the passage, I am in the habit of giving, as a self-vindication: but rather, a vow: I will do so henceforth.

if I have taken any thing, etc. Rather, "Whatever I have exacted from any one by unfair charges." True penitence shows itself in the confession of the particular sin, combined with an effort, as far as possible, to undo its evil consequences.

fourfold. This was much beyond the demands of the law, which in general only required double (Exod. xxii. 4, 9), or sometimes only the addition of a fifth part (Numb. v. 6, 7), upon proof and conviction of the offence.

9 he also is a son of Abraham. Your bigotry denies him the privileges of your nation; my grace confers upon him those of the kingdom of heaven. Abraham was the father of all them that believe.

10 the Son of man. Cp. Matt. xviii. 11. There, love for childhood speaks; here, compassion for the transgressor.

11 because He was nigh to Jerusalem, etc. As our Lord was now within fifteen miles of Jerusalem, and had recently wrought many wonderful miracles, His numerous followers imagined that, on reaching the royal city, He would "immediately" establish His kingdom as Messiah (see 37). He therefore delivers a parable to correct their views, to repress their impatience, and to teach the duty of patiently waiting and actively working for Him.

12–27. Parable of THE POUNDS. This parable, though very similar in some points to that of the Talents, in Matt. xxv. 14–30 (on which see notes), was evidently delivered upon an earlier occasion, and differs from it in some important particulars. In Matthew, the sums of money first mentioned vary according to the ability of the servants. In Luke, a prince commits to each of ten servants the same small sum; he obtains from those who are faithful very different returns, and confers rewards bearing in each case the same proportion to the servants' diligence and success. This parable also, besides the servants, refers to rebellious citizens, evidently representing those who, like the greater part of the Jews, rejected altogether the Saviour's authority.

12 to receive for himself a kingdom. This illustration would be understood by hearers who would remember the journey of Archelaus to Rome.

to obtain from the emperor confirmation in the throne of Judæa.

13 his ten servants. Or, "ten of his servants."

ten pounds. The "pound" (or mina), equalling 100 denarii (a little more than £3 of our money), was therefore but a fraction of the "talent" in Matt. xxv.

Occupy. "Trade with it." Vulgate: "negotiamini"; Luther: "handelt" (both words indicating to trade with). See note on Matt. xxv. 14.

15 how much every man had gained. Or, "what business each had done."

17 authority over ten cities. This alludes to the ancient Oriental custom of assigning the government and revenues of a certain number of cities to a meritorious public officer, as the reward of his services.

25 they said unto him. That is, the servants said to the king.

26 even that he hath, etc. See note on Matt. xiii. 12.

28 He went before, ascending. Advancing determinately to meet His sufferings and accomplish His work. The road from Jericho to Jerusalem is an ascent all the way.

29–46. These verses are parallel with Matt. xxi. 1–22: see note on Matt. xxi. 1. On vers. 29–38, see notes on Matt. xxi. 1–9; Mark xi. 1–10. Luke, as a foreigner, speaks of "the mount *called* the Mount of Olives," or "Olivet,"

33 the owners. A detail peculiar to Luke. Mark has, "certain of them that stood there."

36 clothes. Better, "garments," as R.V., the word being the same as in ver. 35.

37 began to rejoice and praise God, etc. A graphic detail peculiar to Luke. In ver. 38 the "peace in heaven" may be compared with the angels' "peace on earth" (ii. 14, where see note).

39–44. Peculiar to Luke. Some of the Pharisees were offended that such lofty epithets and such great prophecies should be applied to one whom they regarded only as a "teacher."

41 wept over it. As at the grave of Lazarus His friend (John xi. 35).

42 in this thy day. "The time of thy visitation" (ver. 44), when I am come, willing to save thee.

43 a trench. Rather, "a bank" with palisades. In besieging Jerusalem, Titus first surrounded it with a wooden fence (Joseph. *Wars*, v. 6, § 2); and, when the Jews destroyed this, he blockaded the city with a fortified wall. Cp. Isa. xxix. 2–4.

44 the time of thy visitation. That is, of my presence to bring salvation: see i. 68, 78; vii. 16.

45, 46. See notes on Matt. xxi. 12, 13, and Mark xi. 17.

47, 48. These verses, like xxi. 37, 38, contain a general description of the manner in which our Lord spent the last few days before He suffered. Some of the particulars are found in chs. ix.–xxii.

47 the chief of the people. "The principal men of the people," R.V.: cp. Mark xi. 18.

48 were very attentive. Or, "hung upon Him" (R.V.); implying deep interest and admiration.

CHAPTER XX

The events recorded in this chapter are found also in Matt. xxi. 23–46; xxii., xxiii.: see notes on Matt. xxi. 23; xxii. 15; xxiii. 1.

1 preached the gospel. "Proclaiming the good news." A phrase characteristic of Luke, used only by one other evangelist, Matt. xi. 5.

6 will stone us. The rulers had been accustomed to encourage such acts of violence on the part of the people, for their own purposes: and now they fear the weapon they have used.

9–19. Parable of The Labourers in the Vineyard. See notes on Matt. xxi. 23, 33–46; Mark xii. 1–12.

20–26. See notes on Matt. xxii. 15–22; Mark xii. 13–17.

20 they watched him. Rather, "and having watched their opportunity."

27–38. See notes on Matt. xxii. 23–33: Mark xii. 18–27.

36 equal unto the angels. Like them in the enjoyment of immortality; and therefore not needing marriage, which is the means of replacing those whom death destroys.

children of the resurrection. Having obtained the full benefit of their adoption, in the deliverance of *body* as well as soul from the effects of sin: see Rom. viii. 23; Eph. i. 14.

38 for all live unto Him. Peculiar to Luke. The meaning is that in relation to Him those who are dead *to us* are still alive.

39, 40. A summary of the beginning and end of Mark xii. 28–34.

40 durst not ask Him any [question at all]. The question as to the great commandment of the Law (Matt. xxii. 36; Mark xii. 28) was asked at this time, but Luke, who had given its substance on a former occasion (x. 25–28), does not here repeat it.

41–47. See notes on Matt. xxii. 41–46; Mark xii. 35–40.

CHAPTER XXI

1–4. See notes on Mark xii. 41–44.

5–36. This section closely resembles Mark's account of our Lord's prophetic discourse on the Mount of Olives: see notes on Matt. xxiv. 1; Mark xiii. 1.

5 gifts. The "gifts," or votive offerings in the Temple, were very numerous and valuable: see Joseph. *Wars*, v. 5, § 4; *Ant.* xv. 11, § 3.

7 And they asked Him, etc. This was after leaving the Temple: see Matt. xxiv. 3.

8 The time draweth near (is at hand). These are the words of the impostors, who imitate our Lord's own preaching (Mark i. 15).

9 is not by and by. "Is not immediately."

12–19. See notes on Matt. x. 17–22.

13 for a testimony. This public persecution "will turn out an opportunity for you to bear witness" (*Moffatt*). See note on Matt. x. 18, and cp. Phil. i. 19.

18 not a hair of your head. If you patiently trust and obey me, you shall obtain both present deliverance and eternal salvation (ver. 19).

19 possess ye your souls. Though the reading "ye shall win your lives" is accepted by R.V., there is a good deal to be said for the reading of the A.V. The MSS. are not decisive.

21 in the midst of it. That is, of Jerusalem. The "countries" are rather "country places."

22 the days of vengeance. Cp. Isa. xxxiv. 1–8; lxiii. 1, 4, and notes.

24 into all nations. Formerly the Jews had been led captive into Chaldæa; now they were to be dispersed through the whole world. For many ages the Holy City, with apostate Israel, has been trodden down by Romans, Persians, Saracens, superstitious Christian nations, and Turks.

the times of the Gentiles. Ancient Israel has had its time (xix. 42) of merciful probation; the

Gentiles are to have theirs. As the former ends in a day of combined vengeance and redemption, so with the latter.

26 for looking after those things. Better, as R.V., "for expectation of the things," etc.

28 your redemption. This verse is peculiar to Luke. The reference seems primarily to be to the deliverance of the Christians from persecution and peril, by the punishment of their unbelieving countrymen.

The outstanding lessons of this passage (7–28) are well summed up by J. M. E. Ross, whose three volumes on St. Luke in the *Devotional Commentary* are full of devout teaching and practical help. 1. *Our Lord is sure that whatever opposes His kingdom is doomed* (verse 6). 2. *Our Lord is sure that, whatever comes, the patient, trustful soul can afford to be an optimist* (esp. verse 18). 3. *Our Lord is sure that, whatever happens in the welter of circumstances, personality is the thing that matters* (verse 19).

29 and all the trees. A graphic touch, peculiar to Luke, and appropriate to the spring-time in which the trees were in their early foliage.

34–36. This practical exhortation is peculiar to Luke.

35 as a snare. Unexpected.

36 always. Lit., "at every season": so R.V.

worthy . . . to stand. To stand in judgement, uncondemned.

37 abode in the mount. According to Mark xi. 11, He spent these nights at Bethany, which was on the western slope of the Mount of Olives.

CHAPTER XXII

This chapter is for the most part parallel to Matt. xxvi.

3–6. See notes on Mark xiv. 10, 11. Luke omits the supper at Bethany.

3 surnamed. Rather, "called" (R.V.). Iscariot was not a surname, but a local name.

4 captains. That is, "Jewish captains of the Temple"; the officers of the Levitical guard in the building: see Acts ix. 1.

6 promised. Or, "consented." The promise was theirs.

in the absence of the multitude. Or, "without tumult," as marg. A.V. and R.V.

7–14. See notes on Matt. xxvi. 17–19.

7 the day of unleavened bread. That is, the first day of the feast so called. "When the passover must be killed," an addition for the information of Gentile readers.

8 Peter and John. Only Luke gives the names of the two disciples.

12 furnished. Lit., "furnished with couches"; *i.e.*, for reclining at table.

make ready. By sacrificing and preparing the lamb, and providing the bread, wine, and other things necessary for the paschal supper: see Exod. xii.

14–38. The order of the transactions during the paschal supper appears to have been the following: the taking of the places at table (14); the contention for pre-eminence (24–30); our Lord's expression of desire, and the first cup of wine (15–18); the washing of the disciples' feet, and reproof to them (John xiii. 1–20); the pointing out of the traitor (21–23); the foretelling of Peter's denial (31–38); and the institution of the Lord's Supper (19, 20). Luke introduces the institution of the Supper out of its regular order, and connects it with the first cup; apparently that he may exhibit in close connexion the passing of the old economy (18), and the introduction of the new (19, 20).

15 With desire. That is, "I have earnestly desired." Our Lord longed to begin the last conflict which was to terminate His humiliation and to complete His work of mercy; and in this feast He desired both to give to His disciples a fresh proof, and to institute a permanent memorial, of His love to them. On the question whether this was the customary time of the Passover, see note on John xiii. 1.

17 the cup (Greek, "a cup"). This was probably the first cup in the Passover-meal, which was now about to be "fulfilled" (16), and so abrogated, by His death. The cup of the Lord's Supper is not mentioned till ver. 20.

19, 20. See notes on Matt. xxvi. 26–28.

21 with me on the table. Partaking of the same dish. From the account of John (xiii. 30) it would appear that Judas had left the room before the institution of the Lord's Supper, so confirming the order as given above (14–38, note).

24 there was. Or, "there had been." The washing of the disciples' feet (John xiii. 1–17), which, though not related here, is evidently alluded to in ver. 27, was probably designed to correct that self-seeking which caused the dispute (see Matt. xx. 25–28).

25 benefactors. The title "Euergetes" (or benefactor) had been given to and assumed by one of the Ptolemies of Egypt, and some other Eastern princes. Our Lord urges His disciples to become in reality what others are only in name —the *benefactors* of mankind: see notes on Matt. xx. 26, 28.

28 in my temptations. "In my trials."

30 in my kingdom. See note on Matt. viii. 11.

and sit on thrones. A repetition of a promise formerly given (Matt. xix. 28). The words are evidently symbolic of spiritual power.

31 hath desired [to have] you. Rather, "urgently demanded you." Our Lord, though addressing Peter chiefly, includes all his brethren (observe "you" and "thee," vers. 31, 32), as their conduct (ver. 24) showed that Satan, who was permitted to tempt, had already gained some advantage over them. And his "sifting" of them, by putting the genuineness of their faith and love to the severest test, would bring to light the treachery of Judas, the instability of Peter, and the weakness of all. But their Lord, knowing that all but Judas were true-hearted, although cowardly, would pray for them; and especially for that one of them who fell farthest, that when he had "turned again" (R.V.), he might "strengthen" or "stablish" others (1 Pet. v. 10; 2 Pet. i. 12; iii. 17). Luke alone has preserved these touching words of our Lord.

33 I am ready to go with Thee. The order in the original is very emphatic. "With Thee I am ready to go," etc. So R.V.

35–37. The language is figurative, derived from the previous mission of the apostles; but they took it as literal (see vers. 38, 49); and our Lord regarded it as sufficient ("It is enough") to have given them a warning which events would soon teach them to understand: cp. Eph. vi. 13–20.

37 an end. That is, "fulfilment," as R.V.

39–46. See notes on Matt. xxvi. 36–46. Luke's account of our Lord's agony in the garden, while it omits some particulars which the other two Gospels contain, adds the important details in vers. 43, 44, which verses, although omitted by some ancient authorities, and doubted by some modern editors, have preponderating evidence in their support.

41 about a stone's cast. A graphic detail peculiar to Luke.

44 His sweat was as it were great drops of blood. This probably means that the sweat was *like* drops of blood, *i.e.*, highly coloured with blood. Van Oosterzee says of this description that it is "characteristic of the physician." The word "Agony," used by Luke alone, and only here, has become the ordinary designation of the Saviour's conflict.

46 pray, lest ye enter, etc. More precisely, as R.V., "pray that ye enter not," etc.

47–53. See notes on Matt. xxvi. 47–56; Mark xiv. 43–52; John xviii. 2–11. Luke introduces here several minute and striking details which are not found elsewhere.

48 betrayest thou, etc.? The question is only in Luke. The order is emphatic: "Is it with a kiss that thou betrayest?" thus turning a sign of love into an instrument of treachery.

50 one of them. This was Peter, whom John alone names. The act was very characteristic.

51 Suffer ye thus far. This short sentence (peculiar to Luke) is obscure. If addressed to the captors, it may mean, "Excuse what has been done," or, "Allow me so much liberty as to touch the wounded man." "Permit me thus far" (*Weymouth*; similarly, *David Smith*). If spoken to the disciples, it may mean, "Let them do as they please." In the former view, it is a plea for *forbearance;* in the latter, for *patience.*

53 this is your hour, etc. What you have not done before you do now, because God permits and Satan prompts you.

54–62. See note on Matt. xxvi. 69: see also notes on Mark xiv. 66–72; and John xviii. 17, 18.

63–71. See notes on Matt. xxvi. 59–68.

67 If I tell you, etc. I know that neither any reply I may make, nor any questions I may ask, will avail to shake your determination to condemn me. But I avow myself (69) the Messiah—your Judge: see note on Matt. xxvi. 64.

CHAPTER XXIII

On the chapter, see notes on Matt. xxvii.; Mark xv.; John xviii., xix.

1 the whole multitude, etc. See note on Matt. xxvii. 1.

3 Thou sayest [it]. That is, "It is as thou sayest"; see ver. 70. Our Lord's reply, which is given more fully in John xviii. 36, 37, thoroughly convinced Pilate of His innocence (4).

4–16. This account of Pilate's proceedings, and of the trial before Herod, is peculiar to Luke.

5 Jewry. The old English equivalent for "Judæa"; and so in John vii. 1. The "synoptic" evangelists relate very little of Christ's ministry in Judæa, but this and other passages clearly imply it.

6 When Pilate heard of Galilee. Pilate was eager to embrace the opportunity to shift the responsibility of an act which he dared not refuse, yet could not approve. From ver. 12 it would also seem that the Roman governor wished to show courtesy to the Tetrarch.

7 who himself also was at Jerusalem. Herod Antipas, professing conformity to Judaism, would naturally be in the city for the Passover. Usually, Pilate lived at Cæsarea, Herod at Tiberias.

9 answered him nothing. He knew that Herod was not wishing to learn and obey the truth.

11 a gorgeous robe. The Greek word suggests that the robe was *white* (Vulgate, *veste alba;* Luther, *ein weisses Kleid*), which was the royal colour among the Hebrews: cp. Matt. vi. 28, 29. But the imperial colour among the Romans was *purple;* and hence that was the colour of the robe in which Pilate's soldiers arrayed Jesus in their mockery of Him: see John xix. 2.

15 is done unto him. Rather, "hath been done *by* him" (R.V.); *i.e.*, by Jesus.

16 I will therefore chastise him. Pilate wished to treat the affair as a misdemeanour; and to inflict a slight but degrading punishment, which would throw contempt upon the alleged pretensions of Jesus. But the Jews persisted in urging its importance, and prevailed.

26–43. See notes on Matt. xxvii. 31–44; Mark xv. 20–32.

28 Daughters of Jerusalem. These were therefore not the women who had followed Him from Galilee; but inhabitants of Jerusalem, who were attracted by the spectacle, and moved with sympathy for the sufferer.

if they do these things, etc. "If while there is still life in the nation such deeds are possible, what will happen when that life is withered and the hour of doom arrives?" (*Peake's Commentary*).

33 Calvary. In the Greek, as R.V., "the skull." "Calvary" is a Latin word, corresponding with the Hebrew *Golgotha* (see Matt. xxvii. 33, and note).

34 Father, forgive them; for they know not what they do. To Luke we owe this precious portion of the intercession of Jesus, which, although omitted by some ancient authorities (R.V. marg.), has the weight of evidence in its favour. Conscious, whilst He is bearing human guilt, of His Father's unabated love, He pleads already for the pardon of those who were nailing Him to the cross (Isa. liii. 12), turning their very ignorance into a plea for mercy. The plea was in the first instance for the Roman executioners; but no doubt embraced His enemies, who had delivered Him into their hands, and whom excess of bigotry had also blinded to the true nature of the act: cp. Matt. v. 44; Acts vii. 60; 1 Pet. ii. 21–23; also Acts iii. 17; 1 Cor. ii. 8.

39 one of the malefactors. The incident that follows is peculiar to Luke. Matthew and Mark speak of *both* the robbers as reviling Jesus.

If thou be the Christ. The best MSS. have, "Art not thou the Christ?" A bitterly ironical question.

42 into Thy kingdom. Or, "*in* Thy kingdom" (R.V.); when Thou shalt come again in regal power and glory. How this man had obtained his knowledge of Jesus we are not told; but the proofs of his penitence and faith are clear. He acknowledges his own guilt and the justice of his condemnation; he reproves the ungodliness of his companion, attests the innocence of the crucified Jesus, and makes personal application to Him as the Royal and Divine Messiah.

43 To-day. "To-day"; for I am a King already, and my death will but establish my kingdom.

paradise. The word "paradise," from the Persian, originally signifying a *garden,* came to be applied to the garden of Eden (Gen. ii. 8, *Septuagint*), and was subsequently used to designate the abode of the souls of the righteous after death (2 Cor. xii. 4; Rev. ii. 7).

44–49. See notes, Matt. xxvii. 45–54; Mark xv. 33–39.

44 the sixth hour. The hour of noon. So in

Matthew and Mark. According to John (xix. 14) it was "the sixth hour" when Jesus stood before Pilate: see note on that passage.

the earth. Or, as translated in Matthew and Mark, "the land." The word is the same in all three Gospels (and in R.V.). It was now that (Matthew, Mark) Jesus uttered the cry, "My God, my God, why hast Thou forsaken me?"

46 into Thy hands, etc. Only in Luke. The words of Psa. xxxi. 5, with the emphatic word "Father" prefixed. Just before this utterance our Lord had said, "It is finished": see note, John xix. 30.

47 Certainly this was a righteous man. "This man was really innocent" (*Moffatt*).

48 smote their breasts. In remorse for what had been done. In many, doubtless, this prepared the way for the conviction which followed Peter's preaching (Acts ii. 37).

50–56. See notes on Matt. xxvii. 57–66; Mark xv. 42–47; John xix. 38–42.

50 the same had not consented, etc. An addition peculiar to Luke, indicating at once Joseph's position and conduct as a member of the Sanhedrin.

56 rested on the sabbath day. Only Luke mentions this detail, suggesting the quiet sadness of that most memorable day.

CHAPTER XXIV

This chapter is partly parallel to Matt. xxviii.; Mark xvi.; John xx., xxi. See, particularly, note on Matt. xxviii. 1. But Luke alone relates our Lord's conversations with the two disciples whom He joined on their way to Emmaus (13–35), and with the apostles on His first reappearance among them (37–48); and he alone (50–53) gives a detailed account of our Lord's ascension, which Mark simply records (xvi. 19).

4 two men. Matthew and Mark mention only one angel. Different witnesses would report each her own impressions.

5 Why seek ye the living (one) **among the dead?** The form of question is peculiar to Luke.

7 The Son of man, etc. This reference to our Lord's prediction of His sufferings is peculiar to Luke. The angel appeals to the memory of the women, as though they too, with the rest of the disciples, had heard Christ's words.

12 linen clothes. Rather, "cloths," or bandages, in which the body of our Lord was wrapped with the spices.

departed, wondering in himself. Rather, "He went away to his own home (cp. John xx. 10), wondering." John was the companion of Peter in this visit to the tomb (John xx. 3).

13 two of them. Not two of the apostles, but of the "rest" mentioned in ver. 9: see ver. 18, and note, and ver. 33.

Emmaus. Emmaus (which signifies "the hot-baths") lay about seven miles from Jerusalem (Joseph. *Wars*, vii. 6, § 6). Its site is not determined.

16 their eyes were holden. See vers. 31, 37; Mark xvi. 12; Matt. xxviii. 17.

17 as ye walk, and are sad? "They stood still, looking sad" (R.V.). This vivid account of the disciples' demeanour following our Lord's question, is accepted by most modern scholars.

18 Cleopas. Many writers think that Cleopas (contracted from Cleopatros) is a different word from Clopas or Alphæus, the name of the husband of Mary, mother of James the Less, ver. 10 (mentioning John xix. 25, where see note). Lightfoot, however (*Galatians*), thinks that Cleopas is the same as Clopas.

Art thou only a stranger, etc.? The meaning is, surely thou art the only person in Jerusalem (even among the strangers here) who dost not know, etc.: cp. R.V.

21 the third day. See note on Matt. xii. 40. The very mention of "the *third* day" in connexion with what follows ought to have rekindled hope.

25 O fools. Rather, "without understanding."

26 Christ. Rather, "the Christ."

27 Moses and all the prophets. Cp. vers. 44, 45; Acts vii. 21–24; 1 Cor. xv. 3, 4.

30 He took (the) **bread.** He acted as the master of the house; and by this action, as well as by His mode of doing it (cp. ch. ix. 16) revealed Himself to the disciples.

33 the eleven. A phrase for the "apostles"; one of whom, however, was absent: see John xx. 19, 24.

34 appeared to Simon. Cp. 1 Cor. xv. 5, and see note, Mark xvi. 7.

36–49. Cp. Mark xvi. 14–18; John xx. 19–23, and notes.

36 Jesus Himself stood in the midst. "The doors being shut" (John xx. 19). The manner and suddenness of His appearance, after His recent death, excited their alarm (37).

39 Behold my hands and my feet. This would at once convince them of His possession of a material body, and of His identity: see John xx. 20.

43 did eat before them. In condescension to their "slowness of heart" to believe, He multiplies the proofs of His resurrection.

44–49. These verses appear to contain a summary of our Lord's instructions to His disciples, during the forty days that intervened between His resurrection and His ascension.

44 These are the words which I spake. Some of these words are recorded: see xviii. 31; xxii. 37; Matt. xxvi. 56; but doubtless there were very many others, of which we have no account.

in the Law, etc. This was the threefold division of the Old Testament Scriptures among the Jews. "The Psalms" is a general description of the "Hagiographa" an expression meaning "sacred writings" as distinct from the Law and the Prophets.

46 it behoved Christ to suffer. Rather, as R.V., "that the Christ should suffer."

47 beginning at Jerusalem. The apostles obeyed this command literally (Acts ii.–viii.); and they afterwards still further carried out the spirit of it by announcing the gospel first to the Jews in every Gentile city to which they went: see Acts xi. 19; xiii. 5, 46; xvii. 1, 2; xviii. 5, 6, etc.

49 the promise of my Father. "The baptism with the Holy Ghost," which they were to receive "not many days hence" (Acts i. 5).

50 to Bethany. "Until [they were] over against Bethany," R.V. A further account of our Lord's ascension is given by Luke in Acts i. 9–12.

52 with great joy. The account in Acts gives the reason of the joy, in the promise uttered by the angels (i. 11).

53 were continually in the Temple. That is, at all the appointed seasons of prayer: see Acts iii. 1. At other times they appear to have met for converse and prayer in the "upper room" (Acts i. 13). Their daily presence in the Temple would show that the crucified Jesus still had devoted followers, and would enable them to satisfy any inquirers who wished for information respecting the extraordinary occurrences which they had witnessed.

THE GOSPEL ACCORDING TO ST. JOHN

INTRODUCTION

In a letter written to his son at Oxford (1899), Archbishop Temple refers to Coleridge's speculations on the Holy Trinity. He says: "I am obliged to confess that from seventeen to five-and-twenty I indulged largely in such speculations. But I felt all along like a swimmer who sees no shore before him after long swimming, and at last allows himself to be picked up by a ship that seems to be going his way. . . . My passing ship was St. John" (*Life*, vol. ii., p. 690).

There are many who have similarly found this Gospel lay hold of them as no other portion of the New Testament has done. From the words in the first chapter, "we beheld His glory," on through the great conversations with Nicodemus and the woman of Samaria (iii., iv.), the Saviour's profound statement of His relations to the Father (v. 19–36), His words to His disciples about His relation to men as their spiritual Bread of Life (vi. 32–58, 63), His claim to be the Light of the World (viii. 12), His tender picture of Himself as the Good Shepherd (x. 8–18), His tears at the grave of Lazarus (xi. 36), His rapture when they told Him of the Greeks who said, "We want to see Jesus" (xii. 20–24), and His confidence as to the redemptive power of His own death (xii. 31–33; xvi. 33), His practical message of the Vine and its branches (xv. 1–10), His words that point the mourner upwards to the Father's house (xiv. 1–3), the intercessory prayer that reveals the very depths of His heart (xvii.), on to the Prætorium, the scourging and the Cross (xviii. 28–xix. 30), the conviction grows upon us that "never man spake like this Man." "Thou art the King of Glory, O Christ."

Before such a conviction questions of date and authorship are of very secondary importance. Those who desire to study the subject in detail may be referred to Angus and Green's *Bible Handbook*, Buckland's *Universal Bible Dictionary*, the books on St. John's Gospel by Sanday, Luthardt, and Westcott, and a booklet by Dean Armitage Robinson on *The Historical Character of St. John's Gospel.* It is enough to say here that the evidence seems overwhelming that the book was written by John "the beloved disciple," and that its date was probably the last decade of the first century.

"The Synoptic Gospels contain the Gospel of the infant Church; that of St. John the Gospel of its maturity. . . . It is possible, in a more limited sense, to describe the first as historical, and the last as ideal. . . . It is an Epic, because it is the divine reflection of the Life of the Son of God, not taken in a special aspect, but as the Word manifested to men" (Westcott: *Introduction to the Study of the Gospels*, Chap. V.).

CHAPTER I

1 In the beginning. A manifest reference to Gen. i. 1; meaning that before anything was made, the Word already "was." The reference to the creation seems to be kept up in vers. 4, 5.

the Word. John alone employs this term to designate the Son of God; but he employs it without explanation, as one which had already come into use in such a sense as to make it the most suitable word which he could adopt. The term (Greek, *Logos*) is found in the writings of Philo of Alexandria, a Jewish Platonist (about 20 B.C.–A.D. 40), whose writings were exercising a powerful influence in Egypt and throughout the East. Its equivalent in the Aramaic language (*Memra*) was familiar to the Jewish theologians, being constantly employed in the Targums, or paraphrases of the Old Testament, as equivalent to God Himself. Thus the covenant of Jacob at Bethel, according to the Jewish paraphrast, is that "the Word of Jehovah should be his God" (Gen. xxviii. 21). A "word" is the expression, the revelation of thought. So Christ reveals the Father. The *Logos* of Philo was *impersonal;* the *Memra* of the Jewish divines was a *personification* only; the WORD of the evangelist is essentially *personal*.

with God. "The Word" is closely united with the Divine nature, and is partaker of the Godhead absolutely, without restriction or qualification. Yet in this union there is a distinction (2), not in offices and actions only, but subsisting "in the beginning," before any external Divine act—an eternal intercommunion. The words here used are opposed at once to the denial of our Lord's proper Deity (Socinianism), and to the confusion of "Persons" in the Godhead (Sabellianism).

3 by Him. Rather, "through Him"; *i.e.*, by His agency; and so in ver. 17.

4 In Him was life. Life was in Him as in its source, whence all life is derived; and especially man's life. And this life is also light; for without knowledge, purity, and joy (of which light is the symbol) man does not really *live*.

5 the darkness comprehended it not. Another rendering of the passage substitutes the word "overcame" for "apprehended": in which case it would refer to the impotence of darkness to quench the light (*Westcott*).

6 There was. R.V., "There came"; or "there arose, became"; contrasted with *was* in ver. 1. The "man" sent, is further contrasted with "the Word" who was in the world.

John. Never called "the Baptist" in this Gospel. On the other hand, the evangelist never speaks of himself by name.

7 for a witness. "For witness" R.V.; "for the purpose of witnessing" (*Moffatt*).

through him. That is, through *John*.

9 [That] was the true Light, etc. The phrase, "that cometh (coming) into the world" may grammatically refer either to "light," or to "every man." R.V. marg. renders, "The true light, which lighteth every man, was coming into the world." "True," here and elsewhere in John's Gospel, means *original, real,* and therefore also *permanent* and *universal*. John "was the burning and shining lamp" (v. 35); but neither his origin nor his powers fitted him to be "the true Light" of "every man."

10 He was in the world. Contrasted with "He came," in the next verse. In "the world," He was from the beginning, yet unrecognised. Luther translates: "Es war" ("it was") connecting "it" with "light" (v. 9), which is a neuter noun in the Greek.

11 He came unto His own (house or inheritance), **and His own** (people), etc. Referring to His incarnation. His own chosen people of Israel failed to acknowledge Him. Some, however, in all ages and in different nations, not by virtue of human will or human parentage, but under a Divine power, were led to receive Him, and thus obtained the privilege of being "sons of God" (12, 13).

12 power. Or, "the right" (R.V.).

the sons. Rather, "children." The Incarnate Word was the "firstborn among many brethren."

His name. His nature as *revealed;* the expression of which is in the name, "the Christ."

13 born. Lit. "begotten," R.V. marg.

14 was made flesh. Or, "became flesh" (R.V.). Flesh here stands for the human nature generally, including soul as well as body. The words, "dwelt (lit., 'tabernacled') among us," seem to refer to the dwelling of God among men, symbolised by the Shekinah, or visible "glory," in the holy of holies. The glory beheld in Christ Jesus (1 John i. 2) was spiritual, "full of grace and truth."

His glory. For particular instances see ii. 11; xi. 4, 40; and cp. Luke ix. 28–36, but His whole life was a revelation of His glory. This is one of the evangelist's constant references to what he and his colleagues had "seen and heard," as affording indisputable evidence of the truth of his testimony.

as of the only begotten, etc. Lit. (see R.V. marg.), "as of an only begotten from a Father."

grace and truth. Cp. ver. 17, where "grace and truth" are opposed to the Mosaic Law.

15 is preferred before me. Or, "hath come to be before me." Though He was after me in His ministry on earth, He was before me in dignity and pre-existence; and therefore now takes precedence of me.

16 And of His fulness, etc. This and the next two verses are the words, not of the Baptist, but of the evangelist.

grace for grace. "Grace in the place of grace"; one grace after another. This expression beautifully represents the inexhaustible "fulness" of Christ.

17 grace and truth. Truth: "the reality and substance of salvation, in contrast with the shadow" (*Lange*).

18 the only begotten Son. Although there is a variation in the reading here ("one who is God only begotten" or "the only begotten Son"), the sense, as Westcott (*Speaker's Commentary*) sanely points out. is really not affected.

which is in the bosom. Indicating the eternal union between the Son and the Father: see note on Luke xvi. 22; also xiii. 23

19 the Jews. The term, "the Jews," is often used by John for the stricter portion of the Jewish people, as distinguished from "the multitude," the mass of the community. The "Jews" were accordingly in general Pharisees, and opponents of Christ.

21 I am not. In the sense in which the Jews used the word, he was not Elijah, whom they expected to return in person (see Matt. xvii. 10). John came, indeed, in the spirit and power of Elijah (Luke i. 17, and note); cp. Matt. xi. 14; xvii. 11; Malachi iv. 5.

that prophet ("the prophet"). See Deut. xviii. 15–18; from which some of the Jews inferred that one of their prophets would return, either as the Messiah or as His attendant: see Matt. xvi. 14, and note.

27 whose shoe's latchet, etc. See note on Matt. iii. 11.

28 Bethabara. All the best manuscripts have "Bethany," instead of Bethabara. The words, "beyond Jordan," distinguish it from the Bethany near Jerusalem.

29 the Lamb. Isaiah (liii. 7) had likened the Messiah in His death to a lamb, with which the people were already familiar as a Divinely appointed sacrificial victim, both in the daily offering (Exod. xxix. 38, 39), and also in the Passover (Exod. xii.), which the evangelist distinctly connects with our Lord's death (xix. 36). John points out Jesus as the antitype of these types, the fulfilment of this prophecy.

taketh away. Or, "beareth"; probably including both ideas: "taketh away, by Himself bearing": see Isa. liii. 5.

the sin of the world. "Sin" collectively "regarded in its unity, as the common corruption of humanity" (*Westcott*).

31 I knew him not. *I* is emphatic. Even I, although His forerunner, did not know Him. Whether John, living in the hill-country of Judæa, was personally acquainted with Jesus in Nazareth previously to His baptism, is quite uncertain; in any case, it was not until he saw the appointed sign that he was assured that Jesus was the Messiah.

manifest. Partly by the descent of the Spirit upon Him in baptism, partly by John's consequent testimony.

32 it abode upon Him. Implying permanence.

34 the Son of God. Referring to the voice which accompanied the descent of the Holy Spirit (Matt. iii. 17).

35 two of his disciples. One was Andrew (40), the other undoubtedly John himself, who avoids the mention of his own name throughout his Gospel. The whole narrative bears the marks of an eye-witness.

37 followed Jesus. Apparently walking after Him (38), as if they wished to overtake and converse with Him.

38 Master. "Master" is the old English for *Teacher*. Jesus had asked, *What* seek ye? The answer of the disciples makes the object of the quest to be *personal*: 'We are seeking Thee!'"

39 Come and see. A better reading has, "Come, and ye shall see."

the tenth hour. An apparent discrepancy between Mark xv. 25 and John xix. 14 suggests that John reckons the hours from midnight and noon, according to one of the Roman methods, so as to make this ten o'clock a.m.: see notes on iv. 6, 52, and xix. 14. The two disciples seem to have remained with Jesus the greater part of the day. What they then saw and heard confirmed their belief that He was the Messiah (41). Before the day was over, Andrew had found Simon and brought him to Christ.

41 He first findeth. Or, "He is the first to find"; *i.e.*, probably, before John found his own brother James. It is an emphatic statement, that Simon was brought to Jesus originally through his brother's efforts. Andrew is thrice mentioned as bringing others to Christ (see vi. 8; xii. 22); and hardly in any other connexion.

42 when Jesus beheld him. The Greek verb is the same as that which is used in ver. 36, and suggests an intense or penetrating look.

Cephas. The Aramaic name "Cephas," like the Greek name "Peter," means a *rock*. This new name indicated our Lord's Divine knowledge of Simon's character and future service: see note on Matt. xvi. 18.

43 Follow me. That is, Become my disciple. This did not yet involve constant attendance upon Jesus, to which the disciples were afterwards called. The whole foregoing section relates to an earlier call than Matt. iv. 18–22 and parallel passages.

44 Bethsaida. See note on Matt. xi. 21. Peter was shortly afterwards living in Capernaum (Matt. viii. 5, 14).

45 Nathanael. Nathanael is described in xxi. 2 as "of Cana in Galilee"; where Jesus was two days afterwards (ii. 1), and perhaps at this time. Nathanael is generally supposed to have been the same as Bartholomew: see note on Matt. x. 3.

46 Nazareth. See notes on Matt. ii. 23. From the speaker's point of view, the question was not unreasonable.

47 an Israelite indeed. One of the true Israel—a real, faithful, prayerful servant of God.

48 under the fig tree. The suggestion is that of quiet meditation. Cp. 1 Kings iv. 25, and similar passages.

49 Rabbi, Thou art the Son of God, etc. Nathanael's admiring confession shows his certain conviction that no human eye could have witnessed his retirement (50).

51 Verily, verily. The phrase, "Verily, verily" or "truly, truly" (Gr. "Amen, amen") is peculiar to John. "The 'Verily, verily, I say unto you' of the Lord, answers to the 'Thus saith the LORD' of the prophets" (*Stier*).

I say unto you. "You" is plural, meaning all the disciples.

Hereafter. The best authorities omit this word.

heaven open (the heaven opened), etc. These words manifestly allude to Jacob's vision (see Gen. xxviii. 12). You shall behold such a communication opened between heaven and me, the representative of man, the true Israel, as may be illustrated by that supernatural vision; angels "ascending" as though charged with the prayers of the faithful, and "descending" with the answers. On the title, "Son of man," as applied by our Lord to Himself, see note on Matt. viii. 20.

CHAPTER II

1 the third day. That is, the third day after the transactions related in i. 43–51.

Cana. Cana (now *Kena-el-Jelil*), Nathanael's city (xxi. 2), was about eight miles nearly due north of Nazareth. There was another Cana in the tribe of Asher (Josh. xix. 28).

the mother of Jesus was there. Mary seems to have been connected in some way with this family, who were evidently not poor people (5). The disciples, having been gathered during the past few days, would be just at last included in the invitation. Perhaps it was this addition to the guests which caused "wine to be wanting" (or to fail).

2 Jesus (also) **was called,** etc. (bidden, *i.e.*, *invited*). Our Lord's presence at this festival shows that He does not expect His followers to shrink from social intercourse. They should rather improve it by the influence of Christian example.

3 the mother of Jesus saith, etc. (The name of Mary is never mentioned by John.) Appealing to her Son to help out of the difficulty. There is no evidence that she asked for, or expected, a miracle. Only, trusting in Him fully, and recognising His wisdom and greatness, she naturally turns to Him.

4 Woman. "The address is that of courteous respect, even of tenderness" (*Westcott* in *Speaker's Commentary*). Our Lord used the same word to His mother in His tender parting on the cross (xix. 26).

what have I to do with thee? etc. Lit., "what is there to me and thee?"

mine hour. The time for showing my power.

5 His mother saith, etc. Mary still feels assured that Jesus will interpose.

6 six waterpots of stone. The detail is that of an eye-witness.

purifying. See Mark vii. 2, 3, and notes.

firkins. The "firkin" probably contained nearly nine gallons; so that each vessel held at least twenty gallons, and their total contents would not be less than 120 gallons. Some have supposed that the "drawing out," *i.e.*, from the well, as the word used appears to signify, was subsequent to the vessels being filled.

8 governor of the feast. Manager or steward. ("Governor" and "ruler" are the same word in the original; so R.V.)

10 have well drunk. Or, as R.V., "have drunk freely": not implying that it was so in this case; the remark is general.

11 of miracles ("of His signs," R.V.). John almost invariably uses a word which means "signs" rather than "miracles" or wonders; keeping before his readers' minds the significance of our Lord's works. The best wine kept until the last is typical of Messiah's kingdom. It is noteworthy that both at the beginning and at the end of His ministry our Lord used wine at a feast to symbolise the value of His redemptive work—"His glory."

believed on Him. That is, their faith in Him was strengthened and confirmed: see xi. 15.

12 went down to Capernaum. A visit of which no particulars are given. Cp. Matt. iv. 13; John vi. 24.

13 the Passover ("the Jews'" added for the sake of Gentile readers). This, our Lord's first Passover during His public ministry, is mentioned by John alone, though the language of the other evangelists implies that He had gone to Judæa soon after the beginning of His ministry (Matt. iv. 12; Mark i. 14). John connects with this first Passover the cleansing of the Temple and the casting out of the traders; while the other evangelists describe a like transaction at His last Passover (Matt. xxi. 12, 13; Mark xi. 15-17; Luke xix. 45, 46). The two transactions resemble each other so much, that some (*e.g.*, R. H. Hutton, *Theological Essays*) have thought them to be the same. But our Lord's *actions*, as well as His *words* (see note on Matt. v. 1), might well be repeated if occasion arose. And, besides the difference in the language employed on the two occasions, and in other particulars recorded, there is every probability that the act would need to be repeated, for a single reproof would hardly altogether put a stop to a custom which some found so profitable, and many so convenient. See notes on Matt. xxi. 12, 13; Mark xi. 15-17.

14 the Temple. The Temple enclosure (*hieron*), not the Sanctuary, which is expressed by another word (*naos*), ver. 19.

15 small cords. Made, as the Greek word suggests, of the rushes strewn for the cattle to lie on, and used for driving them out. The R.V. reads, "cast all out of the Temple, both the sheep and the oxen." The traffickers, conscious of the unlawfulness of their proceedings, and awed by the authority of our Lord, had fled at once.

16 my Father's house. A phrase similar to that used by Him eighteen years before, Luke ii. 49, and involving a claim to Messiahship.

17 the zeal of Thine house, etc. That is, "zeal for Thy house—for its purity and honour." "The disciples remembered": a personal reminiscence by the evangelist.

18 What sign showest thou, etc.? It was rather for the authoritative mode in which our Lord did this, than for the act itself, that "the Jews" (see on i. 19) required a warrant.

19 Destroy this temple, etc. Neither our Lord's disciples nor the Jews appear to have understood this saying, which was purposely enigmatical, as He had not yet begun to speak openly of His death. It was afterwards employed in a perverted form against Him (see Matt. xxvi. 61, and note). That one evangelist alone records the saying, and two others (see also Mark xiv. 58) relate the malicious use made of it, is a striking case of "undesigned coincidence."

20 Forty and six years, etc. The Temple had already been so long in building; for it was then just forty-six years from the commencement of the work by Herod, in the fifteenth year of his reign: Joseph. *Wars*, i. 21, § 1. It was not completed till about A.D. 63, seven years before its destruction by the Romans, A.D. 70.

22 the Scripture. That is, the Old Testament, which in several passages foretells the resurrection of Christ: see Psa. xvi. 9, 10, and note; cp. also xx. 9; and Luke xxiv. 26, 27.

23 in the feast [**day**]. Rather, "at" or "during the festival": see note on Matt. xxvi. 5.

miracles (signs). These miracles are not recorded, but they were evidently remarkable: see iii. 2.

24 But Jesus did not commit (entrust) **Himself,** etc. He did not entrust Himself and the full meaning of His Messiahship to them, for He knew how imperfect their ideas about Him were.

CHAPTER III

1 a man. Compare the verse preceding. The interview with Nicodemus illustrates, among other things, our Lord's knowledge of human nature.

a ruler of the Jews. A member of the Sanhedrin. It is only from St. John that we know anything of Nicodemus.

2 by night. That Nicodemus "came to Jesus *by night*" through fear is evident from the manner in which his coming is afterwards referred to in contrast with his subsequent open confession: see xix. 39, and cp. vii. 50.

we know. It is not Messiahship, but merely a Divine commission as a *teacher*, which he here acknowledges: "that thou art come from God as Teacher."

3 born again. Lit., "born from above," though the Greek word is sometimes translated "anew." In essence the meaning is the same—the necessity for regeneration or the new, spiritual birth (as in ver. 5).

5 of water and [**of the**] **Spirit.** Baptism and the Spirit. "The words, taken in their immediate meaning as intelligible to Nicodemus, set forth, as required before entrance into the kingdom of God, the acceptance of the preliminary rite divinely sanctioned, which was the seal of repentance and so of forgiveness, and following on this the communication of a new life, resulting from the direct action of the Holy Spirit through Christ" (*Westcott*).

6 That which is born of the flesh is flesh, etc. All that is holy, and fitted for the kingdom of heaven, is in its origin and nature not fleshly, but spiritual; and no agency but that of the Spirit of God can impart it. Hence the terms "flesh" and "spirit" are often used in Scripture to denote respectively the unrenewed and renewed state of man's heart: see especially Rom. vii. 18; viii. 5-9; Gal. v. 16-19.

7 Marvel not, etc. Do not think the change of

which I speak incredible because you cannot understand the way in which it is brought to pass. Powerful effects, which all can see, are produced by unseen causes beyond human control in the natural world: well, therefore, may the like be expected in the spiritual world (8). The beauty and aptitude of this illustration are still more apparent in Hebrew and Greek, in both of which "wind" and "spirit" are expressed by the same word. The Vulgate (Latin) has: "Spiritus ubi vult spirat . . . sic est omnis qui natus est ex Spiritu."

unto thee, Ye must, etc. Our Lord, in changing his address from the singular to the plural, suggests that the error of Nicodemus was that of his class.

10 Art thou a master ("teacher"), etc.? Nicodemus ought to have learned this doctrine from the Old Testament Scriptures (Psa. li. 10; Isa. xi.; lxi.; Ezek. xi. 19, 20; xxxvi. 26, etc.). He would then have been prepared to believe our Lord's words.

12 earthly things. Truths and facts already having place on earth.—**heavenly things;** new heavenly revelations and things (*Lange*).

14 as Moses, etc. Our Lord illustrates his work by referring this "teacher of Israel" to a Divinely commanded act of the great lawgiver whom he venerated (Numb. xxi. 9). The simplicity of the way of salvation through the Cross is here shown.

16 only begotten Son. A phrase used elsewhere by John of our Lord, not by Jesus of Himself: see note on i. 14, and cp. i. 18; 1 John iv. 9. Some commentators regard this and the following verses (to ver. 21) as the evangelist's comments; others consider that they are the Saviour's own words.

18 is condemned already. Better, as R.V., "hath been judged already." Sentence is already passed.

19 this is the condemnation, etc. Read, with R.V., "this is the judgement, that the light is come into the world, and men loved the darkness rather than the light; for their works were evil."

20 reproved. Old English for *convicted:* cp. xvi. 8.

22-36. These verses contain the Baptist's further testimony to our Lord. Jesus begins to baptise before John's ministry had terminated (22-24); and this involves John's disciples in a controversy, which they refer to their Master (25, 26).

22 the land of Judæa. That is, the rural districts of Judæa.

baptised. "Was baptising," through His disciples (iv. 2).

23 Ænon . . . Salim. Conder identifies Ænon with "'Ainûn, Salim being east of Nablûs.

much water. Greek, "many waters." The remark incidentally shows that the locality was not on the Jordan itself.

24 prison. John merely *alludes* to the Baptist's imprisonment; the account of which is to be sought in the other Gospels. From these words, compared with Matt. iv. 12, it appears that the events related in i. 15–iv. 54 occurred between vers. 11, 12 of Matt. iv.

25 the Jews. The best MSS. read, "questioning with a Jew." This conversation is vividly detailed as by a personal witness.

29 friend of the bridegroom. The "friend of the bridegroom" or "groomsman" negotiated the preliminaries of marriage, and arranged the marriage-feast. John represses the jealous zeal of his disciples, by reminding them that he cannot go beyond the bounds of his mission as appointed by God (27), and that he has always declared that he is not the Messiah, but the Messiah's forerunner (28); holding to Him a relation similar to that which the bridegroom's friend holds to the bridegroom (29). See note on Matt. ix. 15.

30 I must decrease. As the morning star at the sun's approach.

31-35. This paragraph is probably by the evangelist: see note on vers. 16-21.

31 is earthly. Lit., an emphatic repetition of the preceding phrase, "is of the earth." So R.V.

32 what He hath seen and heard. One who has merely an earthly human nature cannot speak of heavenly things as He can who has dwelt among them, superior to them all, and intimately conversant with them: see note on ver. 11.

no man receiveth His testimony. That is, almost none: the exaggeration of deep feeling.

33 set to his seal. That is, has set his seal to it, as one who attests a document.

34 God (or, "He": see var. read.) **giveth not the Spirit by measure** [**unto Him**]. The words, "unto Him," are not in the original.

36 hath everlasting (eternal) **life.** As his present and enduring possession.

believeth not. Rather, as R.V., "obeyeth not"; a different word from that in the former part of the verse.

abideth on him. He was under this wrath before; refusing the appointed Deliverer, he remains subject to it.

CHAPTER IV

1 Jesus made and baptised, etc. A continuation of the narrative from iii. 22, 23. "Than John" must mean, than John *had done*, before being cast into prison.

2 Jesus Himself baptised not. Perhaps lest any should pride themselves upon having been baptised by Him; as well as to show that the preaching of the word was of higher importance than any outward rite: cp. 1 Cor. i. 17.

4 through Samaria. A traveller from this part of Judæa to Galilee must pass through Samaria, unless he crossed the Jordan, and went round by Peræa, as Jewish travellers often did: see Luke ix. 52, 53. But the sequel shows that the shortness of the route was not the only reason why our Lord chose it.

5 Sychar. It is now generally held that Sychar was a village near Shechem (*Askar*, two miles E. of Nablous), though it was formerly supposed to be Shechem. G. A. Smith (*Historical Geography of the Holy Land*) devotes a whole chapter to the question of its site, confuting some modern writers who said that there was no such place as Sychar.

that Jacob gave, etc. See Gen. xxxiii. 19; xlviii. 22, and note; Josh. xxiv. 32.

6 Jacob's well. A spring (*'Ain*), called a "cistern" in vers. 11, 12. Called "Jacob's" from the tradition mentioned in ver. 12. G. A. Smith (*op. cit.*) has no hesitation in identifying.

thus. Simply sat. See the line of the old Latin hymn: "Quærens me sedisti lassus."

the sixth hour. Noon, according to the Jewish time. But some think that it was six in the evening.

7 woman of Samaria. Not of the city of Samaria, which was several miles distant, but of the nation. She lived at Sychar.

8 meat. That is, "food" (of any kind). The Greek word here means simply *nourishment.*

9 How is it, etc.? Perhaps the words imply not

only surprise, but also something of triumph, that even a Jew could humble himself in his necessity to ask drink of a Samaritan woman.

For the Jews, etc. The evangelist's remark, not the woman's. But some high authorities omit the clause.

Samaritans. On the origin of the Samaritans, and the bitter enmity between them and the Jews, see note on Matt. x. 5, and other passages referred to there.

10 the gift of God. The blessings which God is now giving to the world. Our Lord's reference is plainly to salvation, and to Himself as the Author of it.

living water. That is, springing water, like that of a fountain; as opposed to the stagnant water of a cistern. The phrase, long ago used to describe the pure, life-giving, healthful blessings of Divine grace (Psa. xxxvi. 8; Isa. xli. 17, 18; Jer. ii. 13), is here figuratively employed, with reference to the special character of this well, fed by living springs. You come hither to get living water, but the true living water, that which fully answers to its name, is what only I can give.

12 Art thou greater, etc.? The Samaritans, although a mixed race, claimed to be descended from Ephraim and Manasseh. Hence the woman's emphasis on "our father."

14 shall never thirst, etc. Shall never be unsatisfied.

in him. His well, therefore, is always at hand.

a well of water springing up, etc. Very vivid in the original: "a spring of water leaping up."

16 Go, call thy husband, etc. Our Lord turns to the facts of her life, so as at once to arouse her conscience and to convince her of His Divine authority.

20 Our fathers, etc. There is no reason to suppose that this was a frivolous remark on the woman's part, to divert attention from more serious things. It is much more likely that her awakened conscience led her to ask in earnest sincerity where she may seek God's mercy with the assurance of obtaining it. By "our fathers," she probably means her Samaritan ancestors, who built a temple on Mount Gerizim (see note on Neh. xiii. 28). This was destroyed about 129 B.C. by John Hyrcanus: but the Samaritans continued to worship on the mountain; and to this day the remnant of the people resort to it.

and ye say, etc. God had chosen Jerusalem as the site of the Temple, and the place for offering sacrifices: see 1 Kings viii. 48; ix. 3; xi. 13; Psa. lxxvi. 2. But the Samaritans contended that Gerizim had been indicated by Moses as the place of Divine worship: maintaining that, in Deut. xxvii. 4, *Gerizim* should be read, as in the Samaritan text, instead of "Ebal." (Cp. Deut. xi. 29; xxvii. 11, 12.)

21 when ye shall, etc. That is, when ye shall worship the Father, but not only in this mountain, or in Jerusalem. It will no longer be a question whether Zion or Gerizim is the right place of worship; for the worship of the comomn Father of all nations will be restricted to no place.

22 Ye worship ye know not what. Rather, as R.V., "Ye worship that which ye know not; we worship that which we know." Though you worship Jehovah, your ideas of Him are incorrect.

salvation is of the Jews. Lit., "the (expected and promised) salvation is from the Jews."

24 God is a Spirit. Or, "God is Spirit," essentially and absolutely; and therefore He "seeks" or desires that that part of man's nature which most nearly corresponds with His own should be especially devoted to His worship. This alone will give the value of "truth" to any outward form of service; and it is quite independent of forms and places (21, 23): cp. Acts vii. 48; xvii. 24, 25. "Dost thou wish to pray in a temple? Pray in thyself; but first become a temple of God" (*Augustine*).

25 I know that Messias cometh. The Samaritans, as well as the Jews, expected the Messiah; resting their expectation on such passages in the books of Moses as Deut. xviii. 15–20 (see Westcott: *Introduction to the Study of the Gospels*, ch. ii., note ii.). The woman's feeling seems to have been, I cannot understand these things; but they will all be made clear when the Christ shall come. And she perhaps already had some suspicion that He who had "told her all things" (see ver. 29) might be the Christ (see ver. 29). It is at any rate a wonderful confession of faith.

26 I that speak unto thee am [He]. This appears to have been the first, and it is one of the clearest, of our Lord's declarations that He was the Messiah. Perhaps He made this disclosure on this occasion partly to show that He was to be the "Saviour of all men." One reason for not declaring His Messiahship openly to the Jews is given in vi. 15. In Samaria there was no such danger. Besides which, He discerned in this woman the moral preparation for such an announcement.

27 with the woman. Or, "with a woman," contrary to the precepts and habits of the Rabbis.

28 the men. Rather, "the people."

29 Is not this the Christ? Rather, as R.V., "Can this be the Christ?"

30 came. Rather, "were coming." They had not yet arrived.

32 I have meat, etc. In fulfilling my Father's will I find refreshment and strength, and I have done so now by teaching this ignorant sinner. Food "that ye know not," R.V. A source of strength to which as yet you are but strangers.

35 Say not ye. "Ye" is emphatic. Such is *human* computation.

There are yet four months, etc. Some think that our Lord here refers to the actual period of the year, as being four months before harvest-time, or about the beginning of January. But it is much more likely that He uses a proverbial saying, derived from the period which usually elapsed between seed-time and harvest, and designed to inculcate patience in waiting for the results of labour. In this case, says our Lord, the spiritual harvest immediately follows the sowing. "Already he that reapeth receiveth wages": R.V. marg.

37 And herein is that saying true. Rather, "For in this case the true saying [is applicable]."

38 other men. The prophets, my forerunner, and myself.

42 not because of thy saying. Rather, "no longer because of thy speaking." The woman's report led many at once to believe, who afterwards found a still surer ground of faith, when they heard Him themselves. It is remarkable that, though the Jews, who saw many miracles, were constantly demanding a sign, and even the disciples were sometimes in doubt, these Samaritans, who witnessed no miracle, readily received our Lord's words as convincingly true.

43 after two days. Rather, "after the two days": see ver. 40.

44 For. Bethlehem of Judæa was His birthplace. And as Judæa contained the religious centre of the people to whom our Lord "came" (i. 11), it is the region most probably meant by "His own country." The Gospel of John deals especially with our Lord's Judæan ministry. As in His human nature Christ was an Israelite, Jerusalem was "His own" metropolis.

46 a certain nobleman ("king's officer"). Probably an officer of the court of Herod the tetrarch (Antipas).

48 ye will not believe. This general charge, which was most just (in great contrast with the ready faith of the Samaritans), was apparently designed to test the courtier's sincerity. The reply shows that he made the request, not because he wanted to see a sign, but because he believed that Jesus could grant his earnest desire and heal his son.

52 at the seventh hour. On the Jewish reckoning, 1 p.m.; on the Roman, 7 p.m. See on i. 39; iv. 6.

53 and his whole house. "The first converted family."

54 second. That is, the second miracle which our Lord wrought *in Galilee*: see ii. 11.

CHAPTER V

1 After this. Rather, "After *these things.*" John appears to use the singular—*after this*—only when he wishes to mark the sequence as immediate (cp. iii. 22; v. 14; vi. 1, etc., with ii. 12; xi. 7, 11, etc.). There was a considerable interval between iv. 54 and v. 1.

a feast. It is quite uncertain what festival it was. Almost every feast has been proposed by various expositors; but the weight of opinion is for Purim, the "Feast of Lots" (Esther ix.).

2 the sheep [market]. Rather, the "sheep-*gate,*" as R.V.: see Neh. iii. 1, 32; xii. 39. No doubt near the Temple, and so called from the sheep for sacrifice; but the precise situation, both of the gate and of the pool, is uncertain. Dr. Robinson identifies the latter with the Pool of the Virgin, the upper fountain of Siloam, intermittent to this day (*Biblical Researches*, i. 433, 508). This view is also taken by Macalister (*Century of Excavation in Palestine*, 1925, pp. 137–142).

Bethesda. Signifying in Aramaic, *House* (or place) *of mercy.* Westcott and others, however, think that the true reading is *Bethzatha,* "house of the olive."

3 impotent folk. Infirm, diseased people.

waiting, etc. From the word "withered" to the end of ver. 4 is wanting in some ancient manuscripts (so R.V.). The passage is probably a very ancient interpolation. Ver. 7 implies that the spring was intermittent; and the intervening words express the early belief as to the cause.

6 Wilt thou be, etc.? "Do you want to be?"

7 while I am coming. This implies that he could move, though very slowly.

8 take up thy bed. See note on Luke v. 24.

10 The Jews. See note on i. 19.

it is not lawful, etc. See Matt. xii. 1–7, and notes.

11 the same, etc. He who can control the laws of Nature may suspend an outward religious ordinance.

12 What man is that, etc.? The form of the question (not, Who healed thee? but, Who told thee to carry thy bed?) shows how the bigoted can shut their eyes even to a Divine work, looking only at some supposed irregularity attending it.

13 had conveyed Himself away. Had retired or got out of the way. Lit., "to bend the head aside, to avoid a blow" (*Westcott*).

14 Jesus findeth him. "Though Jesus had withdrawn from the multitude, He sought the object of His mercy" (*Westcott*).

sin no more. These words seem to imply that the malady was either the effect or the punishment of sin (a different case from that in ix. 3). They are a solemn warning that sin repeated after Divine chastisement and deliverance, will incur "a worse thing"—some more signal and terrible punishment.

15 told the Jews. Partly, perhaps, to justify himself, partly to make known his benefactor.

17 My Father worketh, etc. My Father, who instituted the sabbath, is always ("even until now," R.V.) putting forth His power, on the sabbath as well as on other days; I, His Son, do the same. In accusing me, therefore, you accuse the Father, the Lawgiver Himself, as though He transgressed His own law. The ground which our Lord here takes is peculiar to Himself, and therefore different from that on which He vindicates His disciples in Matt. xii. 3–8.

18 had broken. Literally, "was loosing," or "relaxing."

His Father. Rather, "*His own* Father," in a peculiar sense: cp. Rom. viii. 32. So in ver. 19.

20 that ye may marvel: That *ye* (emphatic) who reject me may yet wonder (see Acts iv. 13), and so, in some instances at least, be led to faith.

22 For the Father, etc. Rather, "For not even doth the Father judge any man"; *i.e., directly.*

but hath committed ("given"), etc. Our Lord is showing His *equality* with the Father. And He is to be honoured, even as the Father; who, indeed, is not truly honoured, unless the Son is honoured too (23).

24 Him that sent me. That is, "who believeth Him as having sent me"; cp. xii. 44; xvii. 3; 1 John v. 9–12.

hath everlasting life. This life eternal is a *present* possession.

shall not come into condemnation. Rather, as R.V., "cometh not into judgement." Already he has "passed over" out of the sphere of "death" into that of "life." The life and death are spiritual.

25 and now is. Referring still to the spiritual resurrection, more fully to be accomplished by the gifts of Pentecost, for which "the hour cometh"; but also, in a measure, a present reality (Eph. v. 14).

26 in Himself. In Himself as its fountain.

27 and hath given Him authority, etc. "The Judge, even as the Advocate (Heb. ii. 18) must share the nature of those who are brought before Him" (*Westcott*). The rendering in R.V. marg. is literally correct: "because He is a son of man."

30 as I hear. My decisions are in perfect accord with what I know the Father's to be: see ver. 19. "These decisions are His acts of absolution or of condemnation, saying to one, 'Thy sins are forgiven thee,' and to another, 'Thy deeds are evil'" (*Godet*).

31 if I bear witness of myself, etc. That is, If my testimony were unsupported, you might reject it as untrue: cp. viii. 14, and see note there.

32 There is another, etc. Or, "It is another that beareth witness," so that my statements are confirmed.

33 Ye sent unto John. Our Lord's hearers might think, when He spoke of testimony, that He meant that of the Baptist; this He corrects; although He might indeed have referred to the forerunner.

34 I receive not testimony from man. Rather, as R.V., "The testimony which I receive is not from man."

that ye might be saved. Yet I appeal even to this imperfect witness, in order that you, who professed to rejoice in his light, may attain salvation by believing in me through his testimony.

35 a burning and a shining light. Rather, "The lamp that is kindled and shineth": French version: "allumée et vivante," "lighted and burning": R.V., "the burning and shining lamp": the great religious luminary of his day, in whom you took a kind of pleasure (Mark vi. 20); yet, after all, he was not "the Light"; see i. 9, and note. He shines only because "kindled"; *i.e.*, his light is *derived*. The word *was* shows that the day of his shining was past.

36 I have greater witness. Better, "The witness which I have is greater" (R.V.).

the same works that I do. The very miracles which I am now doing, and one of which occasioned this discourse. To His miracles our Lord often appealed (x. 25, 37; xiv. 10, 11; xv. 24).

37 the Father. In the law and the prophets, and at the baptism of Christ. But this was only a part of the testimony. He who cannot be discerned by human sense, reveals His truth to prepared souls. This inward revelation is the "abiding word."

39 Search the Scriptures. Or, as R.V., "Ye search the Scriptures." The whole argument of our Lord is to show that while they have the witness, they reject it. So their scrupulous examination of Scripture itself comes to nothing, for they reject Him whom it reveals. "No doubt you search the Scriptures with care, supposing that eternal life is to be found in this kind of study, and yet (40) you will not come unto me that you may have this life." So *Godet.*

44 from God only. Rather, as R.V., "from *the only* God"; the only source of true honour.

45 Do not think, etc. It is no part of my work to accuse you (iii. 17). Nor is this necessary; your own Moses is your accuser. Disbelieving me, you do in fact disbelieve him who "wrote of me."

in whom ye trust. Lit., as R.V., "on whom ye have set your hope." Vulgate: "in quo vos speratis" ("in whom ye hope").

46 for he wrote of me. This is an important testimony to the author of the Pentateuch, and to the correctness of that interpretation of its promises, types, and prophecies which applies them to Christ.

CHAPTER VI

1 went over. To the neighbourhood of Bethsaida (Julias): see Luke ix. 10, and note.

which is the [Sea] of Tiberias. An explanation for John's Gentile readers. The name does not occur in the first three Gospels. On Tiberias see note, ver. 23.

3 a mountain. Rather, "*the* mountain"; probably the tablelands on the east of the lake.

4 a feast. Rather, as R.V., "the feast," preeminently. The words, "of the Jews" are added again for the Gentiles.

5 He saith unto Philip. From the other Gospel narratives it appears that some of the disciples had suggested the necessity of dismissing the people, and had named the sum which it would cost to buy food for them. Philip says, This would not be sufficient (7). The question was addressed to him as knowing the neighbourhood (i. 44).

6 to prove him. To test his faith in the power of Jesus.

7 Two hundred pennyworth. Almost $40 worth: see note on Matt. xx. 2, Mark vi. 37.

9–21. See notes on Matt. xiv. 13–33. The minute references, to Andrew, to the "lad," to the loaves being of "barley," are peculiar to John, and betoken an eye-witness.

10 much grass. The time being spring (4): cp. Mark vi. 39; the grass was freshly green.

12 that nothing be lost. Only St. John mentions our Lord's command. This union of frugality and care with creative power is something so peculiar, that it impresses, beyond all mistake, a heavenly character upon the narrative. Never would such a thing have been invented. Nature, that mirror of Divine perfections, places before our eyes the same combination of boundless munificence and of truest frugality in imparting her benefits (*Olshausen*).

13 baskets. It is likely that each of the disciples took a basket. Thus all would have a lesson against wasting the gifts of Divine bounty, and an evidence how abundant was the miraculous provision.

14 miracle. Rather, "sign": see note on ii. 11.

that prophet. See note on i. 21.

15 When Jesus therefore perceived, etc. This public miracle, of which thousands had shared the benefit, raised the enthusiasm of the people to the highest pitch; and they were already planning to take Him up to the Passover at Jerusalem, and there make Him King. The other evangelists mention His *immediate* dispersion of the people and dismissal of His disciples; John supplies the reason for it. "There is no stronger proof," remarks *Dr. Sanday,* "both of the genuineness and of the authenticity of the Fourth Gospel than the way in which it reflects the current Messianic idea."

16 went down. At Christ's own bidding: Matt. xiv. 22.

17 toward Capernaum. "Unto Bethsaida": Mark vi. 45; in the same direction.

it was now dark, etc. They had probably waited for some time off the shore, expecting that Jesus would soon join them.

18 a great wind. See note on Matt. viii. 24.

19 five and twenty or thirty furlongs. Three or four miles.

21 Then they willingly received, etc. "Then they were willing to receive Him into the boat"; their fears (19) being removed.

22 when the people, etc. Rather, "the multitude, etc., *having seen*"; *i.e.,* on the preceding evening. After the miracle, many of the people on the eastern side of the lake, intent upon their design (15), seem to have watched the departure of the disciples (16); which they did not oppose, as they saw that Jesus remained behind, and that there was no other boat. Missing Him in the morning, they supposed that He had gone round the head of the lake; and therefore put off in some boats which had arrived in the meantime (23), expecting to reach Capernaum first. Hence their question of surprise when they found Him there before them.

23 Tiberias. Tiberias (now *Tabariyeh*) is a town on the south-west coast of the Sea of Galilee. It was built chiefly by Herod the tetrarch for the capital of Galilee, and named by him in honour of Tiberius Cæsar. It was celebrated for its warm baths which are still frequented, and for its Rabbinical schools. "Ruins still indicate a wall three miles long" (G. A. Smith).

24 they also took shipping. Or, "got into the boats" (R.V.): the boats mentioned ver. 23.

25 the other side of the sea. The "other side" varies according to the point of view. In 22 the phrase denotes the *eastern*, here the *western* side.

26 not because ye saw the miracles. Rather, "not because ye saw signs." To them the miracle was not a *sign*; they saw nothing of its spiritual significance. "Instead of seeing in the bread the sign, they saw in the sign nothing but the bread" (*Lange*).

27 Labour not. That is, "Do not make it your chief business"; as they were doing, by following Him from place to place.

sealed. Attested or accredited.

30 What sign, etc.? See note on Matt. xii. 38. The Jews had a tradition, founded upon a Rabbinical interpretation of Psa. lxxii. 16, that the Messiah, when He came, would repeat the miracle of the manna.

32 Moses gave you not, etc. *i.e.*, "It was not Moses that gave you," etc.. "but my Father is [now] giving you the real bread," etc. The two assertions of the Jews are denied: that *Moses* gave them the manna, and that the manna was the true heavenly bread.

true. See note on i. 9.

33 the bread of God is He. Rather, "The bread of God is *that*," etc.: see R.V.

34 evermore. The Jews, still understanding in a material sense this idea of the heavenly bread, declare themselves ready to follow Jesus if He will continue to supply them with this food. "This is the height of their carnal exultation: but this is just the moment when Jesus breaks decidedly with them" (*Godet*).

36 have seen me, and believe not. You want a sign from heaven; "you have even seen *me*," who, as I said (32), am come from heaven; "and yet you believe not." But some do and will believe; for "all that the Father giveth me shall come to me,"etc.

37 All that the Father giveth me. The form of expression seems to point to the collective universality of the gift: cp. 39, etc. The promise of reception in the second clause of 37, and of everlasting life in 40, is made to the individual believer.

him that cometh, etc. These words seem designed to obviate the impression produced by the stern manner in which Jesus might be thought to have repulsed the eager multitude (26); "Never will a heart truly labouring under a sense of spiritual need, and coming to me for relief, be sent away by me": cp. Matt. xi. 28.

40 seeth. Rather, "looketh at," with that earnest attention which leads to faith.

41 The Jews then murmured, etc. See note on i. 19. The Jews murmur at our Lord's declaration that He came down from heaven, which they deem inconsistent with His well-known humble parentage. He does not directly answer their objection, but asserts the truth more fully. This faith in me is the result of special Divine teaching; which reveals God to His children (45).

44 except the Father . . . draw him. This drawing is the gracious allurement of Divine love: cp. xii. 32. The harmony of God's influence upon the will with the free agency of man is a subject for the philosopher. It involves no practical difficulty; for there is nothing of which every man is more distinctly conscious than of freedom in action. Our Lord here presupposes this; for He is blaming His hearers for rejecting Him.

45 in the Prophets. See Isa. liv. 13 (Hebrew); Jer. xxxi. 31–34, and notes.

46 of God. Rather, "from God"; *i.e.*, He who hath come forth from God. In this verse, uniting 45 and 47, Christ emphasises Himself as the connecting link between the Father and men.

51 living bread. Possessing and giving life.

56 He that eateth, etc. "To 'eat' and to 'drink' is to take to oneself by a voluntary act that which is without, and then to assimilate it and make it part of oneself. . . . This spiritual eating and drinking brings the object of faith into the believer" (*Lightfoot*).

dwelleth. "The *believer's dwelling in Christ* comprises the renunciation of his whole life—his own merit—strength and wisdom, and the absolute resting of the soul in Christ, as alone possessing all that is requisite to fill up the void. *Christ's dwelling in the believer* denotes His complete communication of all that He has and all that He is on behalf of His people" (*Godet*). The "blood" indicates deliverance from death, the "flesh" the communication of life; the two constituting complete salvation. So in the Passover emblems.

61 knew in Himself. By His Divine knowledge (see ii. 25).

Doth this offend you? Or, "Does this cause you to stumble?" (R.V.): see note on Matt. xi. 6.

62 if ye shall see the Son of man, etc. Perhaps the meaning is as follows: You find difficulty in these teachings of mine. But if you find that I ascend corporeally to heaven, will not that both convince you that my assertions are true, and also show you that this eating my flesh is to be taken not literally, but spiritually; and that it is the reception of my words into the heart that gives life (62, 63)? But no evidence will convince the unbelieving and false (64); for there can be no faith until the heart is changed and drawn by the Father (65).

64 from the beginning. From the time when they began to follow Him.

67 the Twelve. "The Twelve" are here mentioned by John for the first time, in a manner which assumes their appointment to be well known.

69 Thou art that Christ, etc. The oldest MSS. omit "that Christ." Cp. Peter's subsequent confession (Matt. xvi. 16), before the Transfiguration.

70 Have not I chosen, etc.? This is our Saviour's reply to Peter's statement that they were not likely to leave Him, because their faith was so strong. Even the Saviour's choice did not prevent Judas from betraying Him.

a devil. The word "devil" sometimes means *adversary* (cp. Matt. xvi. 23). But, as applied to Judas here, it seems to designate him as Satan's chosen instrument: see xiii. 27.

CHAPTER VII

1 in Galilee. After the events narrated in ch. vi. our Lord remained in Galilee, probably at least six months; for the Feast of Tabernacles (2) was held in October, six months after the Passover mentioned in vi. 4, to which He appears not to have gone up. The language of His brethren in ver. 3

implies that lately He had not attended the festivals. He is now about to quit Galilee for the last time. In x. 22 He is in Jerusalem in the winter; whence He retires to Peræa, and there He probably remained until His last Passover.

the Jews. See note on i. 19.

2 feast of Tabernacles. See Lev. xxiii. 34. "The *Jews'* feast," because of Gentile readers: cp. vi. 1, 4.

3 His brethren. See note, Acts i. 14.

4 in secret. In a part of the land so obscure as Galilee. The nature of Christ's claims required that He should be "known openly." Was this the right way to secure such an end?

show. "Manifest," as R.V. (so i. 31).

5 For neither did His brethren believe in Him. They appear to have admitted the fact of His miracles: but they neither understood nor sympathised with His true character and mission.

6 My time is not yet come, etc. I have a great work to do in a hostile and ungodly world (7); and must choose my time (season) for manifesting myself, so as best to fulfil my mission. You have no such work to do, and no such enmity to meet.

8 I go not up yet. "I am not going up"; *i.e.*, not *when* and *as* you wish.

10 in secret. That is, privately, avoiding the great concourse of travellers with which the roads to Jerusalem would then be thronged: see Luke ii. 44, and note. The Twelve probably went too (see ix. 2), but perhaps not in one company.

11 sought. Jesus had become the subject of much notice at Jerusalem: partly in consequence of His former miracles there (see ii. 23; iv. 45; v.), and the fame of His miracles in Galilee.

12 murmuring. "Muttering." "The crowd disputed about him hotly" (*Moffatt*).

he deceiveth the people. "He leadeth the multitude astray," R.V.

13 no man. That is, none of those who favour Him.

15–24. These verses are placed by Moffatt at the end of ch. v., as their "original position in the Gospel."

15 letters. That is, learning; especially Scripture learning. The surprise of the Jews seems to show that Jesus had not hitherto taught publicly at Jerusalem. They wonder that one who had not been brought up in any of their schools should take upon himself the office of teacher.

16 My doctrine. That is, My teaching. On this verse see ch. v. 19, 20.

17 If any man will, etc. Rather, "If any man is willing, *i.e.*, heartily desirous, to do His will." The aspiration for moral and spiritual excellence leads to Christ, in whom the ideal is fulfilled; the *effort* to obey also guides to Him, as the soul perceives in Him the secret of strength. So the "teaching" is recognised as Divine.

18 no unrighteousness. That is, no falsehood, the opposite of the "true."

20 Thou hast a devil (demon). You speak madly, like a man possessed: see x. 20. This is said by "the people," who had come up to the feast, and were not aware of the designs of the rulers (25).

21 Jesus answered, etc. Our Lord having, in 16–18, spoken of His *teaching,* now proceeds to justify His *works;* particularly the healing of the cripple at Bethesda on the sabbath (ch. v.).

one work. A *single* act of mine, in apparent violation of your sabbath rules, astonishes you. Why, you yourselves *constantly* violate the sabbath rules, to obey a Mosaic command, in circumcising on that day! If you do this to fulfil an outward rite, surely I may do it to fulfil the law of love: see notes on Matt. xii. 6, 8.

24 according to the appearance. That is, Do not judge superficially, as you do in your ideas about sabbath-breaking.

25 them of Jerusalem. As distinguished from "the people" (20).

26 Do the rulers know, etc.? Rather, "Is it really *the opinion* of the rulers that this man is the Christ?" etc.; *i.e.*, "Have they changed their views and purpose respecting him, or why do they allow him to go on teaching thus publicly?"

27 we know, etc. Both the human ancestry and the birthplace of the Messiah were known from prophecy: see Matt. ii. 1–6, and notes. But it was a prevalent notion that He would appear in an unexpected manner, so that His origin would at first be unknown.

28 cried. He spoke out loudly and boldly.

Ye both know me, etc. You do indeed know something of me and my origin; and yet I am not come of myself, but there is a true, a real Person who sent me forth, whom you know not. This bold avowal might well lead any who were open to conviction to believe on Him (31).

32 the Pharisees and the chief priests. The acting members of the Sanhedrin.

35 the Gentiles. Lit., "the Greeks," amongst whom chiefly the Jews were dispersed: cp. 1 Pet. i. 1.

teach the Gentiles. That is, if rejected by us Jews. They could hardly believe that any Jewish teacher would instruct the Gentiles.

37 that great [day] of the feast. It is said that on the eighth day of the Feast of Tabernacles there was a solemn assembly; but that on this day the water mentioned in the note on Lev. xxiii. 34 was not brought into the sanctuary "because the eighth day marked the entrance into Canaan, the water-drawing ceased. On this day the springs of the promised land gave their waters to the people; an emblem of the spiritual blessing which Jehovah had promised to His people. To this symbolical performance the words of Jesus evidently refer" (*Lange*).

if any man thirst. Any unsatisfied soul.

drink. This figurative expression is explained by the word "believe" in the next verse (cp. iv. 10).

38 as the Scripture hath said. Our Lord appears to refer (cp. Matt. ii. 23, and note) not to one passage of Scripture, but to several; such as Isa. lviii. 11; Ezek. xlvii. 1–12; Joel iii. 18; Zech. xiv. 8, on which see notes.

out of his belly. "Out of his body." From his inmost self: see Prov. xx. 27. He who truly believes in Jesus shall possess within himself an inward spring of Divine life (see iv. 14), the fulness of which shall stream forth to bless others also.

39 the Holy Ghost was not yet [given]. That is, the manifestation of the Spirit was not yet: cp. xiv. 16, 26; xvi. 7; Acts ii. 33.

40 the Prophet. See i. 21, and note.

41 Shall Christ come, etc.? The question in the original is scornfully emphatic: "What! doth the Christ come out of Galilee?" R.V.

42 out of the town (village) **of Bethlehem.** Such was actually the fact; but these Jews were ignorant of it.

45 Then came the officers. Rather, as R.V., "The officers therefore came": *i.e.*, because no one ventured to lay hands on Him. These plain men, the constables of the Sanhedrin, whose place it was simply to obey orders, were themselves touched by the Divine words of Him whom they were bidden to apprehend. The Sanhedrin were evidently in session, waiting for their return with their Prisoner.

49 this people. "This multitude" or mob.

50 Nicodemus. See iii. 1, 2, and note. His simple appeal marks the second stage in his progress to earnest and avowed discipleship (xix. 39).

51 Doth our law judge, etc.? This just but gentle remonstrance by a member of their own body only gives occasion to fresh display of malignity, in bitter taunts and reckless assertions which they knew to be false.

52 out of Galilee ariseth no prophet. An assertion made in the heat of debate, and needing to be qualified. Jonah was of Galilee, Hosea was of the northern kingdom. Nahum and Amos, too, were possibly Galilæans; and Abel-meholah, the home of Elisha, was also in the north.

CHAPTER VIII

1–11. This passage exhibits an unusual variety of readings in the documents which contain it. Most modern editors, following the majority of the oldest MSS., omit the paragraph; but it is supposed by many to be a genuine apostolic tradition, adopted into the text about the fourth century. If this view be accepted, there is still some ground for questioning the propriety of inserting the passage here. It differs greatly from the style of John; it seems to interrupt the course of thought and remark; and it appears more suitable to the end of Luke xxi., where it is inserted in four manuscripts; while ten others place it at the end of John's Gospel.

1 the Mount of Olives. The Mount of Olives appears to have been our Lord's favourite place of retirement: see xviii. 2; Luke xxi. 37.

3 scribes. Not mentioned elsewhere in this Gospel.

5 stoned. The law provided that they should be put to death (Lev. xx. 10; Deut. xxii. 22); by stoning, in the case of a betrothed virgin (Deut. xxii. 23, 24).

6 tempting Him. "Testing Him." They thought they had placed Him in a dilemma. If He should absolve the woman, they might accuse Him of despising the law of Moses. If He condemned her, He would not only offend the people by His severe treatment of a prevailing sin, but would probably come into collision with the Roman government, which had deprived the Jews of the power to inflict capital punishment: compare the question as to the tribute money, Matt. xxii. 15–33.

wrote on the ground. The words added in italics, *as though He heard them not*, are a gloss of some ancient MSS., and probably give the meaning of the action. Our Lord thus signifies that He withdraws His attention from their questioning. *What* He wrote it is useless to conjecture. "The very strangeness of the action marks the authenticity of the detail" (*Westcott*).

7 without sin. This might mean either sin in general, or the sin of adultery, which appears to have been common among the Jews at this time. It need not be supposed that all to whom our Lord thus spoke were guilty of the actual deed; His heart-searching word appeals to the thoughts and intents of the heart. Thus His reply, without excusing the sin, or detracting from the authority of the law, gave a suitable rebuke to the hypocritical accusers.

9 went out one by one. One of the most striking and dramatic verses in the Bible.

11 Neither do I condemn thee. Rather, "Neither do I pass sentence upon thee": as if I were one of the judges: cp. Luke xii. 13, 14. But, whilst our Lord refuses to assume the functions of an ordinary magistrate, He pronounces her a sinner.

12 I am the light of the world. Having referred to the "living water" supplied to the Israelites in the wilderness (vii. 37), our Lord now applies to Himself the emblem of the fiery pillar—a guiding light, not to Israel only but to "the world." Some expositors, however, regard His words as suggested by the Temple illumination by means of two large candelabra, which took place at the Feast of Tabernacles. Both interpretations may be correct.

14 ye cannot tell. Rather, "ye know not" (R.V.).

15 I judge no man. That is, judgement is not the object of my present mission on earth (cp. iii. 17; xii. 47): but, were it so, my judgement would be true and just; for I always act in harmony with my Father.

19 Where is thy Father, etc.? Probably an expression of scorn: Let us see this other witness of yours. To this the reply is simply, The same perverseness which blinds you to my claims, blinds you to Him and His testimony. Angry as they were at His public reproof (for it was given at "the treasury," where many were passing: see Mark xii. 41, and note), they were not allowed by "the Father" to seize Him before His time (20).

21 ye shall seek me. That is, you will wish me back again (see vii. 34), but in vain; you must then perish, and be separated from me for ever: see on xiii. 33.

22 Will he kill himself? Another scoffiing remark. If he kill himself, we, sons of Abraham, certainly shall not follow him to the "darker hell" of the suicide. See Josephus, *Wars*, iii. 8, § 5. To this thought our Lord replies, To that world beneath you already belong, as your earthliness shows; and therefore, as I told you (21), you must perish: whilst I, who am come from heaven above, return thither.

25 Who art thou? Another question of cavilling "unbelief, which desires only to use the answer as a vantage ground for further opposition" (*Stier*).

Even the same that I said, etc. The phrase rendered "from the beginning" is very difficult, and has been taken in various ways; "I am *altogether* that which I speak to you"; *i.e.*, my teaching makes known who I am, as "the light by its shining bears witness to itself": cp. 14. But others take the sentence interrogatively: "How is it that I even speak to you *at all?*" That is, "The question which you ask cannot be answered" (*Lightfoot, Westcott, Moffatt, Peake*, and R.V. marg.).

26 I have many things to say, etc. That is, "I am able to speak," etc. I could expose and condemn your many sins, but my present work is rather to proclaim to the world the truth which the Fountain of Truth has sent me to declare. This is a reason for not answering more fully their captious questions.

28 When ye have lifted up, etc. He alludes to His crucifixion: see on iii. 14; xii. 32, 33. The world will first crucify me, and "then" it will know me: cp. xvi. 7–11.

32 shall make you free. Not only from the bondage of error and sin, but even from mere legal compulsion, so that your service of God shall be spontaneous and cheerful: see Rom. viii. 2, 15.

33 They answered Him, etc. Some think that this was the reply of the believing Jews (see 30); others suppose that it was spoken by some bystanders who perversely misrepresented our Lord's meaning (see 37).

were never in bondage. Politically this was not true, as they confess in xviii. 31; xix. 15. But they probably sufficiently understood our Lord's words as referring to religious freedom; and their answer may allude to their independence in religious position, which they had never resigned. The mention of Abraham as their ancestor favours this interpretation: cp. Matt. iii. 9.

34 Whosoever committeth sin, etc. Or, "Whosoever practiseth sin is a slave" (the words "of sin" being omitted by some good authorities). They boasted of being Abraham's sons; but forgot that, while Isaac, "the son of the free woman," was his heir, Ishmael, "the son of the bond woman," did not "abide in the house" (35), but was "cast out." And it is the Son, "the heir of all things," who alone can bestow this true sonship and freedom (36: cp. i. 12; Gal. iv. 19–24, and notes).

37 I know that ye are Abraham's seed, etc. True, you are his natural descendants, and included in the national covenant. But you are slaves; for instead of seeking to be made free by me (36), you "practise sin" (34), and seek to kill me (37). And, as my words show me to be the Son of God, your deeds show you, though sons of Abraham by natural descent, to be also sons of Satan (38; 44).

hath no place. Or, as R.V., "hath not free course": colloquially, "makes no way."

39 children. The important distinction to which our Lord refers here is that between natural descent and moral kinship. The Jews connect the privileges of God's covenant with the former, and assert that they are sons of God (41); Jesus binds them to the latter.

41 fornication. This word is probably used here in the sense to which the Jews had long been accustomed, suggesting affinity with idolatry: see Ezek. xvi.; Hosea ii.

43 Why do ye not understand, etc.? You misunderstand my expressions (19, 22, 27, 38, 41), because your hearts are unprepared to receive the truths I speak.

44 ye will do. "You want to do," or, "it is your will to do" (R.V.; see note on vii. 17). This refers to their efforts to put Jesus to death (40). You are proved to be Satan's by your likeness to him.

abode not in the truth, etc. The true rendering is, "doth not stand in" or "has no place in." Truth is not his element.

46 convinceth. Rather, "convicteth" (R.V.), *i.e.*, "can prove me guilty." My words are truthful, for my life is sinless.

48 Say we not well. See vii. 20, and note.

Samaritan. The Samaritans were regarded as sworn enemies of the Jews, and Jesus is charged with ranging Himself on their side by stigmatising His hearers as children of the devil.

54 It is my Father that honoureth me. If, in promising to exempt my disciples from death (51), I claim to be greater than Abraham and the prophets, this honour is given to me by my Father. You call Him your God; and yet you know Him not, you love not nor keep His truth, which I know and teach (55). You call yourselves children of Abraham; then you should rejoice to see me, for he was filled with joy by the prospect of my coming (56).

56 and he saw it. By faith; afar off. The revelation was doubtless made to the patriarch in connexion with the promise and vision granted him, or perhaps with his one hour of supreme trial in the offering of Isaac.

57 hast thou seen Abraham? Some high authorities have, "has Abraham seen you?"—a natural question on ver. 56.

58 Before Abraham was, I am. Rather, "Before Abraham was born, I am": cp. i. 1–3. The peculiar phrase, "I am," evidently refers to the name Jahveh or Jehovah (Exod. iii. 14), expressing His eternal self-existence; and it was fully understood to do so, as the people immediately prepared to treat Jesus as a blasphemer. "Before this ray of His Deity, which Christ had just set forth, it only remains for His hearers to adore or to stone Him" (*Godet*).

59 going through the midst of them, etc. Probably transcriber's addition. The words are not found in the best MSS. and the Vulgate.

CHAPTER IX

1 as [Jesus] passed by. On His way out of the Temple, viii. 59.

2 Who did sin, etc.? On the prevalent opinion that special affliction is the fruit of special sin, see Introduction to Job, and note on Luke xiii. 2. It is as if the disciples had reasoned: "May not such passages as Exod. xx. 5 involve a principle of universal application; for do we not constantly see the child suffering the ill consequences of the sins of 'his parents'? Or may there be some truth in the notion of the soul's pre-existence, which many Gentiles hold, and which the Rabbis are beginning partially to admit? Or are the man's own foreseen sins being punished by anticipation?" The questioners evidently have no definite opinion, and eagerly ask to have their doubts removed.

3 Neither hath this man sinned, etc. Do not seek the cause of this man's blindness in any of his own or his parents' sins. Think of it rather as designed to display God's power and grace, and to illustrate my office as "the Light of the World." Such cases urge me to use diligently the short time I have on earth in dispensing the blessings I came to bestow" (4, 5).

4 I must work. The lesson is for the disciples also.

the night cometh. Spoken in relation to earthly labour. These words in Greek (ἔρχεται νύξ) are on the sundial in Sir Walter Scott's garden at Abbotsford.

6 made clay. Our Lord occasionally employed outward means in working a miracle. In this case He employed more than in others. The reason for this we are not told; but it certainly served to test the man's faith, and to make the miracle more public: see note on Mark vii. 33. There was express tradition against the application of spittle to the eyes on the sabbath day.

7 Siloam. See notes on Neh. iii. 15; Isa. viii. 6; Luke xiii. 4; and Macalister (*Century of Excavation in Palestine, passim*). The Hebrew name of the pool signifies *outflow*, the water being *sent forth* (by a subterranean conduit) from the "Fountain of the Virgin." But the application which the evangelist gives to the name suggests the Divine Messenger who was *sent* into the world to give the water of life. "Christ is the true Fountain of Siloam" (*Godet*).

13 the Pharisees. The Jewish rulers, who were mostly "Pharisees." This seems to have been a formal meeting either of the Sanhedrin or of one of the inferior courts ("Synagogue Councils"), having power to summon witnesses, and to pronounce excommunication (18, 24, 34).

16 Others. These "others" were probably a few among the rulers, like Nicodemus and Joseph of Arimathæa.

17 What sayest thou, etc.? That is, What sayest thou of him, as to his opening thine eyes? They probably hoped to elicit something on which they could raise an objection. But the reply, "He is a messenger of God," is so simply natural, that they can say nothing against it; they therefore try to disprove the fact of the miracle.

22 put out of the synagogue. That is, "be excommunicated."

24 Give God the praise. Rather, "Give glory to God" (R.V.). A solemn adjuration to remember God's presence and to speak the truth (as in Josh. vii. 19). The thought is, that dishonour had been done to God, and amends must now be made. There may be also an appeal to the man to ascribe his cure to God, and not to "a sinner": cp. 1 Sam. vi. 5; Jer. xiii. 16; Luke xvii. 18.

27 Will ye also be, etc.? More exactly, as R.V., "Would ye also become," etc.? He sees that truth is not their object, and answers them ironically.

28 we are Moses' disciples. For their boast in Moses and his miracles, see v. 45-47; vi. 30-32.

30 Why herein, etc. Why truly this is "the marvel" (R.V.)—the wonderful thing in the whole matter—that you, who undertake, according to your office, to distinguish true from false prophets, should not be able to discern with whose power One has come who gives sight to a man born blind!

31 a worshipper of God. "A devout man."

32 born blind. Such blindness was universally regarded as absolutely incurable.

33 If this man were not of God, etc. If he were not commissioned by God, "he could do nothing" miraculous.

34 born in sins. See note on ver. 2. Here, as in other cases, the forcible reasoning of honesty and common sense is resented by Pharisaic arrogance, as an invasion of authority; and, as it cannot be refuted, it is met by reviling and persecution. The Pharisees subsequently resort at once to violence in place of argument: see xi. 47, 53.

cast him out. See note on ver. 22.

35 the Son of God. The weight of the best MSS. is in favour of reading "the Son of Man." If our Lord here used His customary title in speaking of Himself, "the Son of Man," the meaning would be, "Dost thou cast thyself with complete trust on Him who gathers up in Himself, who bears and who transfigures all that belongs to man?" (*Westcott*).

37 seen. Jesus does not say, "I am He"; but, referring to the new and precious power which He had conferred on the man, says, "Thou hast *seen* Him."

39 And Jesus said, etc. For "might" in this verse R.V. reads, more accurately, "may."

For judgement, etc. "Judgement" is not the great object for which Christ came (see xii. 47); but it is a necessary result: cp. Matt. x. 34; Luke ii. 34, 35. The truth which enlightens and sanctifies those who receive it, becomes the means of blinding those who reject it: see 2 Cor. ii. 16. Cp. Shakespeare:

"But when we in our viciousness grow hard
. . . . the wise gods seal our eyes;
. . . . make us
Adore our errors; laugh at us, while we strut
To our confusion" (*Antony and Cleopatra*, iii. 11).

40 Are we blind also? Lit., "Surely we also are not blind?" They adopt the figurative language of our Lord, and resent its application to themselves.

41 If ye were blind. If ye were conscious of your blindness, as in ver. 39.

CHAPTER X

1 sheepfold. The Eastern sheepfold is sometimes a space enclosed with stone walls or strong wickerwork, for the protection of the sheep at night. The "sheepfold" here represents the whole Church of God: see ver. 16.

a thief and a robber. The "thief" is one who steals; the "robber" one who steals with violence. So in ver. 8.

2 the shepherd. Or, as R.V. marg., "a shepherd." The sign by which a shepherd may be known.

sheep. The "sheep" are those who know the voice of the Good Shepherd and of every true shepherd—the true children of God, both among the Jews and the Gentiles: see ver. 16.

3 the porter. It is unnecessary to attach a symbolical meaning to every particular in the allegory. The main points of comparison designed are explained by our Lord Himself: see note on Matt. xiii. 3.

by name. Sheep are objects of much endearment in Oriental countries, having names given to them, to which they respond; and they follow the shepherd, who walks before them, instead of going after them, as in Great Britain and other countries.

4 his own sheep. "When he hath put forth all his own," R.V.

5 a stranger will they not follow. The whole picture, in its details, is a transcript of simple fact: see *The Land and the Book*, ch. xiv. The spiritual significance is equally clear. The true-hearted child of God may for a while be imposed upon by specious men; but ere long he discovers their hollowness and imposture, and refuses to follow them.

6 parable. Rather, "allegory." The word (rendered elsewhere "proverb") is different from that translated "parable" (Matt. xiii., etc.).

unto them. To the Pharisees mentioned in ix. 40.

7 of the sheep. That is, of the sheepfold; the only entrance alike for sheep and for shepherd.

8 All that [ever] came before me. This may mean, all that came before me, pretending to have Divine authority as Messiah or teacher.

did not hear them. See note on ver. 5.

9 by me, etc. Salvation is obtained by immediate access to Christ: there is no door between the soul and Him.

he shall be saved, etc. Referring, not only to shepherds, but to believers generally. The blessing is threefold: first, safety; secondly, freedom in "going in and out"; and thirdly, rich pasture, *i.e.*, Divine sustenance and support: cp. Numb. xxvii. 16, 17.

10 The thief, etc. False teachers proved themselves to be such by their selfishness and rapacity (see Ezek. xxxiv. 1–10, and notes).

more abundantly. "More" is a needless word, not in original.

12 a hireling. The "hireling" is one who serves merely for gain, without any personal interest in the flock. Such a person may seem to be better than a "thief" or "robber"; but the sheep are not safe in his care; for he will risk nothing and suffer nothing for them. He is no true shepherd; for he lacks the essential characteristic of one, that close personal intimacy which exists between Jesus and *every one* of His sheep (14), resembling that which subsists between the Father and the Son (15).

14, 15. These verses should be thus read and connected: "And I know mine own, and mine own know me; even as the Father knoweth me, and I know the Father" (R.V.).

16 one fold. Rather, "one *flock*" (R.V.). The disciples of Jesus, whether Jews or Gentiles, shall be essentially "one flock," united by their relation to the "one Shepherd." Our Lord does not say "one fold"; for their unity is not that of any mere external organisation. There are many "folds," but one "flock." Cp. note on ver. 1.

17 Therefore doth my Father, etc. Cp. Phil. ii. 6–11, and notes. This assurance not only sets before us the mutual love of the Father and the Son, but connects it most closely with their Divine compassion for mankind.

that I might take it again. It was necessary to the fulfilment of the Divine purpose of mercy that our Lord should resume His life: see Rom. iv. 25, and note.

18 of myself. My death is my own voluntary act (see xviii. 5–8), for I have the right to my own life; yet it is also an act of obedience to the "commandment" which "I have received from the Father."

21 a devil (demon). See note on vii. 20. Here are two distinct arguments, from the sayings themselves, and from the miracle.

22 Feast of the Dedication. This festival (also called the Feast of Lights) occurred in December, and lasted eight days from the 25th of Chisleu: see 1 Macc. iv. 59; 2 Macc. x. 1–8; Joseph. *Ant.* xii. 7, § 7. It was instituted by Judas Maccabeus in 164 B.C. to commemorate the rededication of the Temple after its desecration by Antiochus Epiphanes. It was a time of great rejoicing.

winter. This is mentioned as the reason why our Lord used to walk at this time under cover, in Solomon's porch, which was the eastern colonnade of the Temple; standing probably where that of Solomon formerly stood: see Acts iii. 11, and note. The whole verse betokens an eyewitness.

24 How long, etc.? Perhaps the meaning is, "How long dost thou keep us in suspense?" The object of this question appears to have been to obtain from Jesus an express declaration, upon which they might ground proceedings against Him.

26 as I said. Westcott, following high MS. authority, omits these words.

27 My sheep hear, etc. Implying, But you do not; which proves (26) that you are not of my sheep.

28 any [man]. Rather, "any one" (see R.V.); including the powers of darkness, as well as human enemies. For "pluck," R.V. reads "snatch"; so in ver. 29.

29 My Father which gave [them] me. The best reading is that of the R.V. marg., "that which the Father hath given me is greater than all." The meaning is that the Church, as the Father's gift to the Son, is mightier than all the forces that can be brought against it.

30 I and my (the) **Father are one.** The connexion appears to be as follows: "No one shall pluck them out of my hand." But does that seem too lofty a word? Should I rather say, "out of my Father's hand?" Then I say this also, and quite truly; for my hand and the hand—the power—of God are the same. I and the Father are One (*Stier*). The Jews rightly understood Him to lay claim to the possession of Divine attributes: see ver. 33.

32 Many good works, etc. To those who disbelieve His words, our Lord again adduces the evidence of His *works*, in proof of His claim to be one with the Father.

34 law. "Law" is here put for the Old Testament *generally;* the quotation being from the Psalms: cp. xii. 34; xv. 25.

gods. See note on Psa. lxxxii. 6.

35 unto whom the word of God came. That is, to whom God gave His commission (cp. Jer. i. 2; ii. 1; Ezek. i. 3; iii. 16), appointing them judges and rulers.

cannot be broken. That is, cannot be *set aside.* This passage shows that the name "God" might in some cases be given to men without blasphemy. But, if sinful mortals (Psa. lxxxii. 2, 7) were so addressed in Scripture, when appointed by Providence to judge and rule, how much more may this title be claimed by me, "the Holy One of God" sent forth with His commission to the world!

40 beyond Jordan, etc. At Bethany in Peræa (see on i. 28; xi. 1).

into the place where John at first baptised. A natural reminiscence of one of John's disciples.

41 John did no miracle, etc. Reminded by the place of John's testimony, they see its confirmation in the life and teaching of Jesus, convincing them that John was a prophet, though he wrought no miracles, and consequently that Jesus is the Messiah. And therefore they believed on Jesus. Thus the simple-minded and candid find conclusive evidence where the prejudiced find none.

CHAPTER XI

1 Lazarus. "Lazarus" is the Greek form of the Hebrew name Eleazar, "God hath helped." Bethany is now called *El-Azeriyeh;* from El-Azir' the Arabic form of Lazarus.

Bethany. See notes on Matt. xxi. 17; Luke x. 38. Bethany is here called "the village of Martha and Mary," to distinguish it from the Bethany beyond Jordan (see i. 28, and note), alluded to, though not named, in x. 40.

2 It was that Mary, etc. The allusion to this action as being well known when the evangelist wrote his Gospel is a striking illustration of the fulfilment of Matt. xxvi. 13: see notes on xii. 3–7; Mark xiv. 3–9.

4 not unto death. Death is not to be its ultimate result.

for the glory of God, etc. The Father is glorified when the Son is glorified; and the Son was glorified by the miracle to which this event gave occasion; by His own death, which was hastened by the miracle (see xii. 23; xiii. 31; xvii. 1); and doubtless also by the spiritual benefit which resulted to Lazarus and to many others.

5 Now Jesus loved Martha, etc. It was this which led the sisters to send to Him, and to give to their message in ver. 3 its peculiar form.

6 He abode two days, etc. Giving time for the burial of Lazarus, and the delay which succeeded; so that the miracle of his resurrection would more strikingly "glorify the Son." Cp. note on ver. 15.

9 Jesus answered, etc. Cp. ix. 4. Our Lord's reply is in effect as follows: I can be in no danger whilst my appointed day of labour lasts: I walk in the light of duty, and of my Father's appointment; and am therefore safe. And so it will be with every one who walks by that light, or rather, has it within him (see Matt. vi. 23).

twelve hours. See note on Matt. xx. 3.

11 Our friend. How kindly does Jesus associate His disciples with Himself in His friendships! (*Bengel*).

sleepeth. "Has fallen asleep."

12 Then said His disciples, etc. Some of them should have remembered a similar expression on a former occasion (Matt. ix. 24).

he shall do well. That is, "he will recover," as R.V.

15 for your sakes. "His absence was useful to them, because His power would have been less clearly seen, if He had at once given help to Lazarus. Therefore, that the disciples might acknowledge the resurrection of Lazarus to be a truly Divine work, it must be delayed, that it might be at the farthest remove from human remedy" (*Calvin*).

16 Didymus. See note on Matt. x. 3.

with Him. With *Jesus*. This shows at once the strength of Thomas's fears, and the greater power of his love to his Master.

17 four days. Lazarus probably died and was buried on the day on which his sisters sent their messenger. The messenger's journey would occupy one day; after that, Jesus waited two days (6); and arrived at Bethany probably on the evening of the fourth day. By this time corruption would naturally have commenced, causing the sisters to give up all hope of restoration (see note, ver. 39; and cp. Luke xxiv. 21). Jesus now came as the Lord of life and death: see Rev. i. 18.

19 and many of the Jews came, etc. Rather, as R.V., "had come to Martha and Mary." This concourse of visitors made the miracle more extensively known.

20 but Mary sat still in the house. Some think that Mary did not know of our Lord's approach. Others suppose that she did know, but they regard the difference in the conduct of the two sisters as being characteristic of the prompt activity of the one sister and the quiet reflectiveness of the other: see note on Luke x. 38.

21 If Thou hadst been here. This first expression of both the sisters (see ver. 32), when they saw Jesus, shows what had been their hope in sending to Him (3), and their leading thought ever since.

22 But I know, that even now, etc. Having, perhaps, some hope of the speedy resurrection of her brother, but hardly venturing to name it.

23–27. Jesus had referred her for comfort to the doctrine of the resurrection as held by the Jews (23). She acknowledged its truth, but in such a way as to hint that it gave her no adequate consolation (24). He now directs her to Himself, as the Author not only of the resurrection of the body, but also of that higher life (see vi. 50) beyond the reach of death, in the present possession of which every believer on earth is associated with those who have fallen asleep in Jesus. What this meant Martha may not have understood; but whatever it might mean she believed to be true, for she believed that He who said it was "the Christ," "the Son of God," "He who (according to ancient promise) was to come" (27). Martha's is a noble confession.

33 groaned. The word translated "groaned" signifies "was moved with indignation." It may here mean that our Lord was indignant against sin as the cause of all this sorrow. President Reynolds (*Pulpit Commentary*) follows Augustine, Erasmus, Luthardt, Hengstenberg and Moulton, in thinking that death itself occasioned His indignation.

was troubled. In the original, "troubled Himself"; as master of His own emotions.

35 Jesus wept. "The evangelist appears to me to express the cause of this emotion, when he says that Jesus saw Mary and the others weeping. Yet I cannot doubt that He had regard to something deeper; namely, to the universal misery of the human race" (*Calvin*). Here, as elsewhere, the human is wonderfully combined with the Divine: see Matt. viii. 24–37.

38 lay upon it. Or, "lay *against* it" (R.V.). The cave was probably horizontal; with an opening on the face of the rock, and with recesses in the sides, in which the bodies were laid. The possession of such a tomb by the family indicates that they were not of the poorer class.

39 Take ye away the stone. Why did our Lord say, "Where have ye laid him?" and, "Take ye away the stone"; and, "Loose him"? Why did He not at once raise Lazarus? Because He designed to make those to whom He gave these commands to be so many witnesses, by the eye and touch, to the reality of the miracle (*Chrysostom*).

four days. All the marks of corruption usually appear in that country within four days. The thought of this probably again overpowered Martha's faith. Her remark does not prove that the fact was so, but only that such was her impression.

40 if thou wouldest believe. Rather, as R.V., "If thou believedst."

41 hast heard me. More literally, "didst hear me." In all our Lord's work He appears to have been sustained by communion with His Father. "By thanking God for a work not yet seen He gave a crucial test of His fellowship with God" (*Westcott*).

43 He cried with a loud voice, etc. Speaking to the *dead* as He would to the *living*: cp. v. 25, 28; Rom. iv. 17.

44 he that was dead came forth. Two notable references to the raising of Lazarus occur in our English poetry. Tennyson speaks of the silence of the narrative as to where Lazarus was while his body lay in the tomb:

> "Behold a man raised up by Christ!
> The rest remaineth unreveal'd;
> He told it not; or something seal'd
> The lips of that Evangelist."
>
> (*In Memoriam*, canto XXXI.)

And Browning, in his *Epistle of Karshish, the Arab Physician*, speaks of Lazarus:

"And oft the man's soul springs into his face
As if he saw again and heard again
His sage that bade him 'Rise,' and he did rise."

a napkin. The "napkin" or "kerchief" was used probably to encircle the face and tie up the chin.

46 But some of them went their ways to the Pharisees. Evidently with a malicious intention.

47 a council. That is, a meeting of the Sanhedrin.

What do we? That is, What measures are we taking to check Him?

48 and the Romans shall come, etc. They feared, or professed to fear, lest the people should make Him king, and so bring ruin upon both the "land and people." But the course they pursued involved them in guilt which brought them these very calamities.

49 Caiaphas. See note, Matt. xxvi. 3.

that [same] year. The year of Christ's death: that notable and solemn year. There is no intimation that the office was an annual one.

51 And this spake he not of himself. God, who sometimes uses the wicked to accomplish His purposes, caused the Aaronic priesthood, just when it was about to be abolished, to speak prophetically, though unconsciously, by its unworthy representative, of the great Sin-offering then about to be presented for the sin of the world.

53 Then from that day forth they took counsel, etc. It was now agreed that Jesus should be given up to the Roman governor, to be put to death; and both parties in the council were on the watch for the best mode of doing this.

54 Ephraim. Some identify this with Ophrah of Benjamin and with the modern *Taiyibeh,* on a mountain about fourteen miles north-west of Jerusalem: perhaps the same as "Ephraim" (2 Chron. xiii. 19).

Between vers. 54 and 55 are to be placed the series of narratives and parables in Luke xiii. 22–xix. 28.

55 to purify themselves. That is, to purify themselves from any ceremonial defilement; so that they might be able to keep the Passover (2 Chron. xxx. 17).

56 That he will not come to the feast? The reason of the doubt is given in ver. 57.

CHAPTER XII

2 Martha served. Martha superintended the feast; Mary anointed the Guest in whose honour it was made. Her apparent extravagance in doing this was approved by her Lord, as the genuine expression of love and faith: see notes on Mark xiv. 3–9.

3 Then. Rather, as R.V., "Therefore"; in the spirit of the occasion.

6 bag. Or, "box"; *i.e.*, money-chest. Judas was treasurer to the company.

bare. This probably means, "carried away"; *i.e., stole.*

10 But the chief priests consulted, etc. "See the blindness of their rage; as if Christ could raise one who was dead, but not one who was killed. He did both; He who raised Lazarus raised Himself" (*Augustine*). Throughout this narrative the rulers' resolution to put Jesus to death is connected with the raising of Lazarus.

12 On the next day. This was the first day of the week. On vers. 12–15, see notes on Matt. xxi. 1–11.

13 took branches of palm trees. More precisely, "took the branches of the palm trees": words of an eye-witness. So R.V.

14 when He had found, etc. The other evangelists inform us how the colt was found.

16 These things understood not His disciples at the first. This modest confession of the evangelist is a remarkable evidence of truth. Many of our Lord's instructions were to be interpreted by the light of later events, and the teaching of the Holy Spirit (see xiv. 16).

17 when, etc. The change of a single letter (ὅτι instead of ὅτε) in some important manuscripts gives a better reading: "The multitude which was with Him bare witness that He called Lazarus out of the tomb."

20 certain Greeks. These "Greeks" (who must be distinguished from the "Hellenists" or Grecian Jews) were Gentiles, proselytes to the Jewish religion, who had come up to the Passover. They applied to Philip, perhaps in consequence of having known him in Galilee. The Greek form of his name seems to imply some family connexion with Gentiles, of whom there were many in Galilee.

21 we would see Jesus. That is, they desired a personal interview with Him. Thus the Gentiles came to "see Jesus" at the *beginning* of His ministry (Matt. ii.) and at its *close.*

22 Andrew. A fellow-townsman of Philip (i. 44), bearing also a name of Greek origin.

24 if it die, etc. The seed-corn must pass through death, in order to yield a harvest; so must I die, in order to achieve this great result. And my disciples (25) must "follow me" herein (xiii. 16); for life, if unduly loved, will be fruitless: see note on Matt. x. 39.

25 hateth. See note on Luke xiv. 26.

27 save me from this hour. A part of the question, "Shall I say this?" "The cry of nature": while the petition, *Father, glorify Thy name,* is "the voice of the Spirit" (*Godet*).

for this cause. He asks the question only to answer it in the negative. This struggle was a foretaste of the struggle of Gethsemane: see Matt. xxvi. 36–46, and notes.

28 a voice from heaven. This voice was evidently an utterance of intelligible words; and was heard, though not with equal distinctness, by all present; the greater number of whom supposed that God spoke in thunder, some that He spoke by an angel.

I have both glorified it, etc. God had glorified His own name in the life and works of His Son. He was about to do so in a still higher degree in the Saviour's death and exaltation.

31 Now is the judgement, etc. "Judgement" is the disclosure of moral condition, combined with the award of doom. In the cross, mankind is self-revealed; the death of Christ is the condemnation of the world, and in His triumph over death is justification. These are two several elements in the "judgement": and in this also is the overthrow of Satan's dominion, together with the attraction of mankind to Him by His cross. This was to begin immediately after His sufferings; and its full accomplishment, though it would be gradual, was certain.

33 what death. That is, "what manner of death" (R.V.).

34 The people answered Him, etc. It is likely that they understood Jesus not as speaking of His crucifixion, but only in general of His *removal* from earth to heaven. From the passages of the

"Law," that is, of the Old Testament, which predict the perpetuity of Messiah's reign (see Isa. ix. 7; Psa. cx. 4, lxxxix. 4, etc.), they inferred that "the Christ" would never leave the world; and they therefore ask, "Who is this Son of man" of whom thou speakest?

35 Yet a little while is the light with you. Yes: the Messiah does abide for ever; but He is with you as "the Light" only for a time. Use your day of grace by believing in Him; or the night, in which you can do nothing, will soon come upon you.

36 did hide Himself from them. From those who reject Him, Christ hides Himself. Our Lord probably went to Bethany (Luke xxi. 37). But the words signify more than simple withdrawal. He had left the Temple *finally*. His last message to Israel had been delivered.

37 so many miracles. Or, "so many signs"; referring to a much larger number than the six recorded in this book.

38 that the saying of Esaias the prophet might be fulfilled. See Isa. liii. 1, and note on Matt. i. 22.

40 He hath blinded, etc. The evangelist gives the sense, not the precise words, of the prophecy. It is part of God's *judicial* arrangement that the *self*-hardened heart shall become yet harder, and thus conversion and salvation may become an impossibility: cp. Heb. vi. 4. Every resistance to religious conviction tends to this result.

41 His glory. In Isa. vi. 1–5, this is evidently the glory of "the LORD OF HOSTS"; here it is as clearly the glory of Jesus, who is therefore identified with the Eternal whom the prophet beheld (see i. 1). The Son is "the brightness of the Father's glory" (Heb. i. 3; Col. i. 15).

42 chief rulers. Rather, simply, "rulers"; members of the Sanhedrin (see ix. 22, and note).

44 believeth not on me. That is, "not on me *only*."

45 he that seeth me, etc. See xiv. 9, and note.

47 I judge him not. See notes on iii. 17, 18: viii. 15.

CHAPTER XIII

1 before the Feast of the Passover. Lange's remarks on this narrative, as compared with those of the Synoptists, seem to express the reasonable solution of apparent discrepancies. "Since Christ desired to develop the Passover into the New Testament form of the Supper, it is quite significant that He so ordered the feast that the Passover itself took place before the beginning of the 15th Nisan and only the Supper fell into the full feast. Therefore He came early with the disciples to Jerusalem and commenced the celebration before the turning-point of the two days, *i.e.*, before six o'clock on the evening of the 14th Nisan, so early was it that the conclusion of the Paschal feast or original Agape was reached before six o'clock, or, at all events, just about that hour. This simple supposition removes all difficulties, especially when it is observed that in those days the accuracy of our measurement of time had no existence."

2 supper being ended. Rather, "when supper was come" (see ver. 26).

now. Rather, "already" (R.V.). Judas had, before this, made his compact with the Sanhedrin (Matt. xxvi. 14).

4 took a towel, and girded Himself. Coming in the dress of a menial servant, behind the couches on which the disciples were reclining (see note on Luke vii. 37).

6 dost Thou, etc.? The pronouns are emphatic, both in Peter's question and in our Lord's reply. "Surely it is not for *Thee*, the Master, thus to wait on me, the disciple, the servant." "Surely it is not for *thee*, the disciple, the servant, to understand all that I, the Master, do."

8 If I wash thee not. Our Lord, taking occasion from Peter's words, uses the word "wash" as emblematical of spiritual purification (cp. 1 Cor. vi. 11; Titus iii. 5, 6). In the *literal* washing Judas shared, yet had "no part" with Jesus.

10 He that is washed, etc. Rather, "One who has been *bathed*" (not merely "washed," as in vers. 5–8), "needs only to have his feet washed to be altogether clean." When open sandals were worn, the feet required frequent washing, even if a person had recently bathed, and therefore was otherwise clean. So the true disciple needs repeated cleansing from daily sins, although he needs not again to be cleansed "every whit" like the unrenewed sinner.

14 ye also ought to wash one another's feet. Washing the *feet*, being an office in constant requisition in Oriental countries, became a general expression for all brotherly and hospitable service: see 1 Tim. v. 10. Our Lord's design is to commend to His disciples that brotherly love which manifests itself in real self-denial and cheerful condescension to the humblest tasks.

16 The servant is not greater than his lord. A proverbial expression employed by Jesus with various applications. See xv. 20; and cp. Matt. x. 24, 25; Luke vi. 40. Here its meaning is that what the Master condescends to perform cannot be unworthy of the bondservant.

17 If ye know. etc. It is easier to admire than to practise humility.

18 I know whom I have chosen. I know [the characters of those] whom I have chosen to be apostles (see vi. 70); so that I am not surprised, though troubled (21) that one of you should be false. And I now foretell his treachery, to give you another proof that I am all that I claim to be (19), and that I have received from the Father that authority which I still delegate to those of you who are faithful (20).

that the Scripture may be fulfilled. Acting in the exercise of his own free will, he did what God's "hand and counsel had determined before to be done."

He that eateth, etc. See note on Psa. xli. 9, of which this is a free quotation.

20 He that receiveth, etc. The connexion of thought seems to be with ver. 17: "Happy" are the truly humble, in that their lot is one with that of Christ. "He had just said: *The servant is not greater than his master;* He now seems to say, *The servant is not less than his master*" (*Godet*).

21–30. See Matt. xxvi. 21–25; Luke xxii. 21–23.

22 doubting. "At a loss to know" (*Moffatt*). It was now that each asked, "Lord, is it I?" as recorded by the other evangelists. "Their consciousness of innocence was less trustworthy than the declaration of Christ."

23 leaning on Jesus' bosom. They reclined at table, each on his left side (see note on Luke vii. 37), Jesus occupying the chief place in the centre of the middle couch; the next on His right was John, who could therefore easily "lean back on Jesus' bosom," and hold a private conversation with

Him. Judas was certainly near to our Lord; possibly next to Him on the other side (see Matt. xxvi. 23, 25).

whom Jesus loved. Evidently John himself: see xix. 26; xxi. 7, 20.

26 a (the) **sop.** Probably a piece of the unleavened bread, dipped in the sauce. This action, connected with our Lord's previous words (18) and strong emotion (21), was calculated to awaken the traitor's conscience; and as if challenging our Lord's intimation, he, like the rest, demanded, "Is it I, Rabbi?" (Matt. xxvi. 25). Our Lord assents; and, probably resenting the exposure, Judas yields to Satan complete possession of his soul (27).

27 That thou doest, do quickly. Judas himself had made the decision: it only remained for him to carry it out, and to leave Jesus uninterrupted for these last precious moments of converse with His true disciples.

29 against the feast. See note, ver. 1. As the festival had only just begun, and would continue seven days longer, it is thought by many expositors that our Lord refers to the time succeeding the Paschal Supper.

30 immediately. In all probability before the institution of the Eucharist. The other evangelists do not mention the point at which Judas withdrew.

32 straightway. In the departure of the traitor Jesus not only finds relief (31), so that He can pour out all His heart to His faithful, though feeble followers; but He also sees the "immediate" hastening of that great event which is to glorify alike the Father and Himself.

33 Little children. A word indicating our Lord's tenderness towards His disciples. The same word appears six times in 1 John. It is probable that the successive acts of the "Lord's Supper" took place at intervals during these and the following remarks: see Luke xxii. 20; 1 Cor. xi. 25.

Whither I go, ye cannot come, etc. See vii. 33, 34; viii. 21, and notes. From friends and foes alike He was to be parted; but His friends shall rejoin Him (36).

34 A new commandment. The law given by Moses had long ago made our instinctive self-love the measure of our love to our fellow-men (Lev. xix. 18). But the self-sacrificing love of Jesus (see Phil. ii. 5–8) is here made both the motive and the model of our love to our fellow-Christians. This is plainly "a new commandment" (see 1 John ii. 7, 8); and is called "the law of Christ" (Gal. vi. 2).

36 thou shalt follow me afterwards. To the same home, and by a death somewhat similar: see on xxi. 18.

37 I will lay down my life, etc. Peter imagined that he would lay down his life for Jesus; whereas Jesus must first lay down His life for Peter, before Peter could be prepared to lay down his for his Lord.

CHAPTER XIV

1 Let not your heart be troubled. Although our Lord had to say of Himself at this hour, "Now is my soul troubled" (see xii. 27; xiii. 21), He addressed Himself to the comforting of His sorrowing disciples, whose distress at His approaching departure had probably been deepened by what they had just heard of Judas's treachery, Peter's denial, and the dispersion of them all (Matt. xxvi. 31).

ye believe in God, believe also in me. The word for "ye believe" and for "believe" is the same in the original, and should probably be rendered alike in both parts of the verse. R.V. marg. has, "Believe in God, and believe also in me." Your dejection shows a want of faith in both your Father and your Friend.

2 In my Father's house, etc. I am returning to my original home which is to be your home too. In that heavenly temple (Rev. iii. 12) there are dwellings (lit., "abiding-places") for you all. "Mansions" comes from the Vulgate *mansiones*, resting-places on a great road where the travellers found refreshment. "This appears to be the true meaning of the Greek word here; so that the contrasted notions of repose and progress are combined in this vision of the future" (*Westcott*).

to prepare a place for you. This our Lord did by His death, resurrection, and ascension to the right hand of God, as our Mediator and Intercessor.

3 I will come again. The view of Alford, as well as of Lange and Westcott, is that this "coming" is a continuous action, as is shown by the present tense which our Lord uses in the Greek. He comes again in His resurrection; in the spiritual life, making *them* ready for the place prepared; in the bringing of His disciples to Himself in death; and in His final coming in glory.

4 whither I go ye know. See R.V. The disciples might not clearly know "whither"; but at least they knew "the way."

5 Thomas saith, etc. The succession of questions is recorded with the vividness of an actual observer.

6 I am the way, etc. Others can *show* the way: only one can say *I am the Way.* As Jesus is the Truth (1 John v. 20) and the Life (i. 4; xi. 25), therefore He is the Way, *the only way* by which we can approach the Father. Only as He is received into the mind as the centre of all truth, and into the heart as the source of purity, strength, and joy, can God be approached, or even known (7), here on earth, or hereafter in heaven.

8 show us the Father. Philip was right in feeling that the manifestation of the Father's special presence would "suffice" to dissipate their fears; but he was wrong in desiring a repetition of the outward displays of Divine glory which had been granted to Moses (Exod. xxxiii. 19–23) and Isaiah (vi. 1–5); and in failing to learn from both the words and works of Jesus, that He who had "been so long time with" them was "the image of the invisible God" (9–11). Cp. i. 18; Col. i. 15; Heb. i. 3.

10 I am in the Father, and the Father in me. See x. 30, 38; viii. 28; xii. 49; v. 19, 20, and notes.

11 Believe me, etc. Believe it on my assertion; but, if your faith is too weak to rest on that alone, add to it the evidence of my works. He who believes on these grounds will be able to perform works more wonderful still, because works of *spiritual* power: wrought, however, through the risen Christ, and therefore His works in the highest sense. This verse should be a great encouragement and inspiration to every individual Christian.

12 because I go to the Father. These words are linked on to the next verse, "and whatsoever," etc.

13 whatsoever ye shall ask in my name, etc. "The believer asks, and the glorified Christ works from the throne of His omnipotence" (*Godet*).

14 If ye shall ask. "If ye shall ask *me* anything" is the reading of the best authorities. Prayer is not only to be made *in the name of* Christ, but *to* Him.

15 keep my commandments. Our Lord says, "Ye will keep"; *i.e.*, obedience is the certain result, and therefore the proof of love.

16 another Comforter. "Another," who will be to you all that I have been while I have been with you. The word "Paraclete" means "one called in to help," and would be best translated "Helper." It includes the idea of *Comforter*, and as in 1 John ii. 1, *Advocate*. Each of these words must be taken in its fullest sense, so as to include instruction, guidance, strength, and holy elevation of desire and purpose. The word clearly implies the *personality* of the Holy Spirit.

17 the Spirit of truth. That is, the Spirit whose office it is to reveal and apply the truth (see xvi. 13); and especially to make known Him who *is* "the Truth": see ver. 6; xv. 26; xvi. 13.

whom the world cannot receive, etc. "All that Scripture declares respecting the Holy Spirit is a dream to worldly men; for they, relying on their own reason, despise heavenly illumination." "It is the Spirit alone who, by dwelling within us, gives us the knowledge of Himself, being otherwise unknown and incomprehensible" (*Calvin*).

18 comfortless. Lit., "orphans," and so translated both in the French and German versions; persons who need a helper or guardian. Orphaned you shall not be; for I am coming to you, not indeed in bodily presence, so that the world can see me; but in "the Spirit of truth," so that I can be "seen" by you; the living Source of your life; and manifesting to your souls the Father's love and my own (18–21). The last verse is so worded as to extend this high privilege to *every* faithful disciple.

I will come. Rather, as R.V., "I come"; see note on ver. 3.

19 ye see me. Spiritually; when no longer manifest to outward vision.

22 not Iscariot. See Luke vi. 16, and note on Lebbæus, Matt. x. 3.

Lord, how is it, etc.? Judas seems to be thinking of the Messiah, as King and Judge of the nations; and inquires how this appearance of Jesus to His disciples *only* can consist with the setting up of His kingdom? cp. vii. 4. Our Lord again shows that this abiding manifestation of the invisible Father as well as of Himself must be spiritual; and can be enjoyed only by those who recognise His Divine mission, and love and obey Him (23, 24).

26 He shall teach you. Our Lord here clearly distinguishes the Holy Spirit, as a personal agent, from the Father and Himself.

27 my peace I give unto you. A striking illustration of how external circumstances or bodily suffering cannot disturb the inward peace of the soul. It was He who was reviled by His enemies and was now looking forward to the Cross, who said, "*My peace* I give unto you."

28 ye would rejoice. Rather, "you would have rejoiced"; for it is my exaltation, the resumption of that glory which I shared before the world was, of which I "emptied" myself when I took "the form of a servant" to the Father (28): cp. xvii. 5; Phil. ii. 7.

my Father is greater than I. Our Lord speaks of Himself as Mediator.

29 when it is come to pass. When I have suffered, and ascended, and sent forth the Comforter, then you will better understand and believe all this.

30 I will not talk much with you, etc. The crisis is at hand; "the prince of this world" is coming (see Luke iv. 13; xxii. 53, and notes). In me he will find nothing in common with himself. But I do and bear all in full accordance with the Father's appointment; that the world may see how entirely I love the Father, and desire to glorify Him in the salvation of man (31).

31 Arise, let us go hence. Jesus and the eleven now prepare to set out from the supper-room, to proceed to the Mount of Olives. But the discourse and prayer contained in chapters xv.–xvii. were most likely spoken before they actually quitted the house: see xviii. 1.

CHAPTER XV

1 I am the true Vine, etc. Whether our Lord's words were spoken in the upper room or as He walked along the road, a vine was pretty sure to be in sight, suggesting the parable.

2 He purgeth (cleanseth) **it.** This purifying is effected chiefly by instruction (xvii. 17; Eph. v. 26), but also by discipline (Rom. v. 3–5; Heb. xii. 11; 1 Pet. i. 7); removing what is noxious, and perfecting what is good and useful. To the disciples, this had already in part been done (3) "through the word" which Jesus had spoken; and it was to be completed through the teaching of the Spirit and the fiery trials which awaited them, and which they were to be encouraged to bear by this consideration: see Rom. viii. 28–39.

4 Abide in me, and I in you. That is, See to it that ye abide in me, and that I abide in you. This close and vital union must be carefully preserved; for, "severed from me, ye can do nothing" good (4–6).

5 without me. Or, as R.V., "apart from me": if separated from me.

9 continue. The same word as "abide" in ver. 10.

10 If ye keep my commandments, etc. The corresponding declaration to that in xiv. 15. If you love me, you will keep my commandments; and if you keep my commandments, you will abide in my love.

11 that my joy might remain in you, etc. That you may share the joy which I possess and impart, so that your joy may be perfect. See note on xiv. 27.

12 This is my commandment. Lit., "This is the commandment that is mine"; emphatically and pre-eminently.

as I have loved you, etc. See xiii. 34, and note; 1 John iii. 16. Our Lord illustrates the greatness of this love, by the unparalleled self-sacrifice which it caused Him to make (13), the close friendship to which it led Him to raise His obedient servants (14, 15), and His spontaneous choice of them to permanent fruitfulness (16).

16 Ye have not chosen me. See 1 John iv. 19. Our Lord is speaking primarily of the apostolic calling.

20 Remember the word that I said unto you, etc. See xiii. 16, and note. The proverb is there applied to the conduct of His disciples; but here it is used as in Matt. x. 24 of their treatment by the world.

21 for my name's sake. Not only as bearing the name of Christ (see Tacitus, *Ann.* xv. 44; Sueton. *Nero*, xvi.), but as representing Him by their likeness to Him: see Acts v. 41. It is Christ Himself whom the world hates in His disciples.

22 they had not had sin. That is, in rejecting my claims: cp. iii. 19.

no cloke. "No excuse."

23 He that hateth me hateth my Father also. For Jesus is the most perfect manifestation of the Father (see xiv. 9).

24 works. See note on xiv. 11.

25 in their law. Their own Scriptures: see Psa. lxix. 4; cix. 3.

26 He shall testify of me. By so enlightening your minds, that you may understand and teach these things: and by opening men's hearts to receive me and my truth.

27 ye also shall bear witness As they did (Acts i. 21, 22; Luke i. 1, 2).

CHAPTER XVI

1 these things. The warnings and promises in the preceding part of the discourse.

offended. That is, *hindered* in your Christian course: see note on Matt. xi. 6. The remembrance of this prediction would in the time of trial confirm their faith in Him who had shown that He foreknew all (4), and their confidence in His promise of the help of the Holy Spirit.

2 put you out of the synagogues. See note on ix. 22.

will think that he doeth God service. Some of the most cruel persecutions have been carried on professedly in the name and for the glory of God.

3 these things will they do, etc. See xv. 21.

4 these things I said not unto you at the beginning, etc. All our Lord's disclosures to His disciples were gradual, as occasion arose. His speedy removal would leave them to bear apparently alone the brunt of the world's enmity to Him.

5 none of you asketh me, Whither goest Thou? They had asked some questions about His departure (cp. xiii. 36; xiv. 5); but our Lord appears to mean, When you hear of my departure, you are filled with sorrow (6); for you do not consider whither, and for what purpose, I am going (*Calvin*). Why do you not ply me with eager questions as to the glory to which I am passing, and the home that I am preparing for you?

7 Nevertheless. Referring to ver. 5. Though *you* do not think so, *I* tell you the truth. The force of the assertion indicates its importance.

for if I go not away, the Comforter will not come unto you. The outward and temporary ministry of Christ was to be followed by the inward and abiding ministry of the Spirit in the hearts of the disciples; and the change thus to be effected in their spiritual condition would be obviously and immensely to their advantage.

8 when He is come, He will reprove the world, etc. Rather, as R.V., "He, when He is come, will convict the world in respect of sin, and of righteousness, and of judgement." This threefold conviction must be interpreted by our Lord's own statement of its grounds. "Sin" is brought home to the world's conscience as a result of its unbelief in Christ and rejection of Him. "Righteousness," again, is manifested in the ascension and exaltation of Christ: first *His own* righteousness, signally thus attested, with the deeper truth that He becomes righteousness to all who trust in Him. Then "judgement" is also revealed. "Now is the prince of this world cast out" (xii. 31), and in this is the final condemnation of all the power of evil. But in this is also salvation. The judgement of Satan is the deliverance of his victims. "Every sinner, snatched from Satan, and regenerated by the Spirit, is a monument of the condemnation henceforth pronounced upon him who was formerly called the prince of this world" (*Godet*).

12 many things. A few of these things our Lord Himself taught them after His resurrection (Luke xxiv. 45; Acts i. 3); but the rest were reserved till "the Spirit of truth" should "guide them into all the truth" (13: 1 John ii. 20).

ye cannot bear them now. Not only their present sorrow, but still more the slowness of their spiritual apprehension, would hinder their reception of many truths which they must learn in order to do their work: see Luke xxiv. 25; Acts x. 9–14; xi. 1–3. etc.

13 all truth. Rather, as R.V., "all the truth": collectively, of which only some portions had been hitherto revealed.

He shall not speak of Himself. This sentence shows (like v. 30) the entire oneness of purpose in the work of the Spirit and the Son with the Father, and also declares that the object of all the Spirit's teaching is to glorify the Son (14).

things to come. Lit., "the things that are coming." The things relating to the kingdom which Christ was about to establish. The whole passage (13–15) clearly teaches that "the Spirit is not coming to set up some new kingdom, but rather to confirm the glory given to Christ by the Father." "As soon as the Spirit is disunited from the word of Christ, the door is opened to all kinds of mad fancies and impostures" (*Calvin*).

14 glorify. The meaning of the original, here and elsewhere in this Gospel, is "to show forth the true character" of one, or to reveal one's greatness. The Vulgate well renders it here, "Ille me clarificabit."

receive. R.V., "take"; to show that the word is the same in this and the next verse.

15 All things that the Father hath are mine. Some commentators regard this as a direct assertion that the Son possesses all that the Father has, as being equally Divine. But others (with *Calvin*) take it to mean that all the Father's gifts are put into the Mediator's hands; so that all the blessings which the Holy Spirit confers are to be traced up to Him. Perhaps this agrees best with the preceding verses.

16 A little while, and ye shall not see me, etc. R.V., "Ye behold me no more . . . ye shall see me." Two different words in the Greek express the bodily (θεωρεῖτέ) and the spiritual vision (ὄψεσθέ). Our Lord probably refers primarily to His death, now close at hand, and His speedy resurrection and restoration to His mourning disciples. But this was itself only a prelude to another separation shortly to follow, by His ascension to the Father (see ver. 28); to be succeeded, after "a little while," by another return. This return may include the Spirit's advent and abiding with the Church; but it no doubt refers ultimately to our Lord's final coming (xiv. 3). "This is a promise to the universal Church; and, when *this little while* is past, and Christ comes again, we shall feel how short a time it has been" (*Augustine*).

18 we cannot tell what He saith. Rather, "we know not what He is talking about." They understood that He was to go away: but the speedy departure and speedy return perplexed them. This our Lord does not explain; but comforts them by the promise that their sorrow shall be turned into joy which they can never lose (20–22), and that then they shall not need to make any inquiries (23).

19 Jesus knew ("perceived," R.V.). Entering into the secret of their thoughts by virtue of His omniscience: cp. vi. 61.

20 the world shall rejoice. In the thought that they have destroyed me.

your sorrow shall be turned into joy. The joy shall not only follow, but shall spring out of the grief. It was so with the Lord Himself; His cross was the source of His glory (Phil. ii. 8, 9; Rev. v. 9, 13). And so it is still with the Christian, whose sharpest sufferings are the birth-pangs of his highest joys (2 Cor. iv. 17); and with the whole Church collectively.

21 A woman when she is in travail, etc. For a similar use of this figure, see Isa. lxvi. 7–14, and notes; which is probably referred to here; being partly quoted in ver. 22: see also Rev. xii. 2, 5.

22 your heart shall rejoice. Speedy fulfilments of this promise are found in xx. 20; Luke xxiv. 52.

23 ye shall ask me nothing, etc. Rather, "you shall not ask me *questions*": such as those of Thomas (xiv. 5), Philip (xiv. 8), Judas (xiv. 22), but you shall *pray* to the Father ("ask," in this verse, is the rendering of two different Greek words). And whatsoever ye shall pray for, He will give it you in my name. At that time you shall be taught by the Comforter, whom the Father and I will send; and instead of these questions which you desire to put to me, you shall pray for His enlightening influence. And you shall not ask in vain. By Him I will teach you concerning the Father so plainly and fully, that your joy shall be complete.

24 Hitherto have ye asked nothing in my name. Until our Lord's atonement and intercession were recognised as the ground and the means of access to the Father, the disciples could not use His name in prayer. This was one of the inestimable benefits which they and all believers were to receive from His departure to the Father: see Eph. ii. 18.

25 in proverbs. Our Lord's declarations respecing His death and resurrection, which appear plain *to us*, who have the light of subsequent events, and especially the teaching of the Holy Spirit in the Word, appeared very dark and enigmatical to the disciples.

27 I came out from God. I came forth from the Father, etc. The R.V. transposes the phrases: "I came forth from the Father: I came out from the Father." The former refers to the mission of Christ, the latter to His Sonship. The disciples (30) fasten only upon the former truth.

30 ask Thee. Or, "inquire of Thee"; for Thou knowest our thoughts. The change to which they refer seems to be rather in themselves than in our Lord's teaching, which was not yet free from enigma (see ver. 25).

31 Do ye now believe? A question not implying doubt of their faith, but rather the recognition of it (see xvii. 8), with the suggestion that their belief, ready and enthusiastic as was its expression, yet needed much to perfect it.

32 his own. That is, his own *home*.

I am not alone. See note on Matt. xxvii. 46.

33 These things. All the things contained in the preceding discourses.

ye shall have. Rather, "ye have." To the Christian, the world, with its temptations and opposition, is the source of trouble; Jesus, the Author of peace. But Jesus has "overcome the world," even when assailed by its "prince" with the strongest temptations (Matt. iv. 1–11) and the severest sufferings (Luke xxii. 53; Heb. ii. 14).

CHAPTER XVII

1 Father. Our Lord taught His disciples to say, "Our Father," but never used the phrase Himself. When praying for Himself, under the sense of His humiliation, He says, "My Father" (Matt. xxvi. 39, 42). But this simple address—"Father"—agrees with the character of the whole prayer, in which we seem to see into the very heart of Christ.

glorify Thy Son. See xii. 23, 28; xiii. 32; xvi. 14; and notes.

2 As Thou hast given Him power (authority) **over all flesh,** etc. The glorifying of the Son is sought as the means of glorifying the Father, in the giving of eternal life to believers.

that He should give eternal life, etc. Lit., "that to all that Thou hast given him, to them He should give eternal life"; *i.e.*, to the whole body of the faithful and to every individual believer.

3 and Jesus Christ, whom Thou hast sent. Rather, "and Him whom Thou didst send, [even] Jesus Christ" (R.V.).

4 I have glorified Thee, etc. See R.V., "I glorified Thee on earth, having accomplished the work," etc. This accomplishment is assigned as the method by which He glorified the Father. The work is now practically complete. He had perfectly discharged all the previous part of it, and was fully prepared for what still remained; and therefore, "as the hour of His death was now at hand, He speaks as though he had already endured it" (*Calvin*). "The verse expresses with a sublime frankness the feeling of a conscience perfectly pure. Jesus in this supreme moment of His life perceives no evil committed nor any good neglected. The duty of every day has been completely fulfilled; there has been in this human life which He now leaves behind Him neither stain nor omission" (*Godet*).

5 with Thine own self. See i. 1, 18, and notes.

the glory which I had with thee, etc. The original glory of His Godhead had been concealed by the humiliation of His manhood.

6 the world. "The world" in this chapter means man's present abode (5, 24), or its inhabitants at large (23), or the great majority who are hostile to Christ (14, 16).

they have kept Thy word. The Greek word for "keep," here used (τηρεῖν), "expresses rather the idea of intent watching than of safe guarding" (*Westcott*). It implies the careful observance of God's word and the doing of it.

8 came out (forth) **from Thee . . . and Thou didst send me.** The former phrase refers to His person; the latter to His mission. The confession of the disciples is in xvi. 30; and imperfect as it was, Jesus beholds in it the power by which salvation shall be wrought for man.

9 I pray not for the world. "I am not asking for the world." Our Lord is now interceding for His own disciples. Afterwards He does pray "that the world may believe" 21).

11 Holy Father. The Father is specially so addressed in this petition, as He is entreated to keep and sanctify the disciples.

keep through Thine own name, etc. R.V., "keep them in Thy name which Thou hast given me"; *i.e.*, preserve them in the faith and profession of that revelation of Thyself which they have received from Thee, through me. And similarly in ver. 12.

12 that the Scripture might be fulfilled. See note on xiii. 18.

13 that they might have my joy, etc. See xv. 11; xvi. 24.

16 They are not of the world, etc. These words, repeated from ver. 14, explain ver. 15, and introduce vers. 17–19. They are a plea for protection, a motive to holiness, and a ground of assurance.

17 Sanctify them, etc. That is, "Consecrate them to Thyself": see ver. 19. To "sanctify" is strictly to "set apart" from all common uses, to that which is sacred.

Thy word. This is the secret of all personal holiness and of a living and active Church.

19 I sanctify myself. Whilst praying for the "sanctification" of His disciples, our Lord speaks of His "sanctification" as His own act; reminding us that His surrender to death was perfectly spontaneous.

20 [shall] believe. "Shall," is, most probably, to be omitted. The body of believers is looked upon as actually existing.

21 that they all may be one. This unity is a deep internal oneness of will, purpose, and affection; binding the disciples of Jesus first to His Father and Himself, and then to each other; having as its *model* the unity subsisting between the Father and the Mediator (21); as its *ground*, a common faith in Jesus through the apostles' teaching (20); as the *means* of promoting it, sanctification by the truth (19); and as its *result*, the bringing of the world to believe in Jesus (21).

23 that they may be made perfect in one. Rather, as R.V., "that they may be perfected into one"; *i.e.*, that their unity may be rendered perfect. In proportion as the character of Christians grows nearer to perfection, unity becomes more possible.

that the world may know, etc. Recognising not only our Lord's Divine mission, but the fruit of it in His disciples. This is one way by which men are attracted to the Saviour, and therefore, for the sake of others, Christians should show their unity with God in likeness to Him and unity with one another.

24 I will. Here the Saviour expresses His desire for the company of His people.

that they may behold my glory. As He reveals it to those who are capable of beholding and sharing it: see 1 John iii. 2; 2 Cor. iii. 18. "His desire will not be satisfied, until they have been received into heaven" (*Calvin*).

CHAPTER XVIII

1 brook. Rather, "winter torrent." The "Cedron" (or Kedron, signifying *dark*) flowed through the Valley of Jehoshaphat, a deep ravine between the city and the Mount of Olives: see 2 Sam. xv. 23. "It is the most easterly of the three deep, steep valleys—abrupt trenches would almost be a better name to describe them—which define or cut through the plateau on which the city stands" (Macalister, *A Century of Excavation in Palestine*, 1925, p. 96).

a garden. Called "Gethsemane": see note on Matt. xxvi. 36.

2 Jesus ofttimes resorted thither. See Luke xxi. 37, and note.

3 with lanterns and torches. The moon was full; but there would be many dark recesses among the trees and rocks.

4 knowing all things that should come upon Him. Stress is laid upon the *voluntary* surrender of Jesus: see on ver. 6.

went forth. From a secluded spot in the garden: see Matt. xxvi. 39, 46. He who had fled from a crown (vi. 15) goes forth to meet the cross. John omits the record of our Lord's Agony, as given in detail by the other evangelists.

5 Judas also, which betrayed Him, stood with them. Prepared to point Jesus out by the appointed sign.

6 they went backward, and fell to the ground. Several causes, no doubt, contributed to this. Our Lord's calm courage and dignity overawed His captors. Conscience, too, had its effect, as in the cases of Mark Antony, Marius, and Coligny, where murderers recoiled, panic-stricken (*Tholuck*). In any case, the incident showed that our Lord did not yield to force. His submission was entirely voluntary: cp. Matt. xxvi. 53.

8 let these go their way. The officers seem to have been disposed to seize the disciples (Mark xiv. 51, 52).

9 that the saying might be fulfilled, etc. See xvii. 12. R.V. reads emphatically, "I lost not one."

10 Then. When Judas had given the signal (Matt. xxvi. 49).

the high priest's servant. The "high priest's servant" was probably at the head of the Jewish officials, and the foremost of those who advanced to seize Jesus. Only in John's Gospel do we find the names mentioned.

11 the cup which my Father hath given me, shall I not drink it? An evident allusion to the prayer related by the other evangelists (Matt. xxvi. 39; Mark xiv. 36; Luke xxii. 42).

12 the band and the captain. Technically, "the cohort and the chiliarch" (military tribune); the Roman soldiers placed at the service of the Sanhedrin, in addition to "the officers of the Jews." R.V. reads "seized" for "took," the word used implying violence.

13 Annas. See note on Matt. xxvi. 3. Annas was evidently a man of great influence; having been high priest, and perhaps being still regarded as such by some, though he had been deposed by the Romans. His five sons also in turn filled the office now held by his son-in-law. This examination before Annas, which is recorded only by John, was probably private. After it, Annas sends our Lord bound to Caiaphas (24), whose plans (cp. ver. 14 with xi. 49, 50) he doubtless knew. Thus "the high priest *de jure* adopts the policy of the high priest *de facto*, and makes himself responsible for it" (*Wordsworth*).

14 Now Caiaphas was he, which gave counsel, etc. See xi. 49, 50, and notes.

15 another disciple. Or, "the other disciple": the person so designated elsewhere in connexion with Peter. This is evidently John himself, who accordingly gives (19–23) the account of the private examination not recorded in the other Gospels. As to the way in which John had become "known unto the high priest" we have no information. David Smith (*In the Days of His Flesh*, p. 465) mentions the ancient tradition that John was known to the High Priest "from his fisher craft." "It may well be that he had a business connexion with the capital and supplied that wealthy mansion."

16–27. On these verses, see notes on Matt. xxvi. 57–75; Mark xiv. 53–72.

16 her that kept the door. Cp. Acts xii. 13.

17 Art not thou also? "Thou *also*" seems to imply that "the other disciple" was known to the portress as connected with Jesus.

He saith, I am not. Peter's apprehensions were no doubt increased by the remembrance of the act of violence which he had committed in the Garden.

18 And the servants and officers stood there, etc. Rather, as R.V., " Now the servants and the officer were standing [there] (having made a fire of coals [charcoal], for it was cold), and they were warming themselves ; and Peter also was with them, standing and warming himself."

19 The high priest then asked Jesus, etc. These questions were put probably in the hope of obtaining some matter of accusation before the Sanhedrin. Our Lord replies that His teaching had always been public (20), and challenges a proper legal inquiry (21).

22 struck Jesus with the palm of his hand. Rather, simply " gave Jesus a blow " ; either with his staff (3), or with the open hand.

23 Jesus answered him, If I have spoken evil, etc. Our Lord's mild answer illustrates His precepts : see Matt. v. 38–42, and notes.

24 Now Annas had sent Him. Some (as R.V.) render these words, " Annas therefore sent Him," etc. ; and suppose that vers. 19–23 relate to the hearing before Annas. If it be so, John gives no account of the hearing before Caiaphas, related Matt. xxvi. 57–68 ; Mark xiv. 53–65 ; Luke xxii. 66–71. If this view be accepted, it follows that the " court " in which Peter uttered his denials was common to the apartments occupied in the high priest's palace by Annas and Caiaphas respectively ; and that John, who had been present at the examination of Jesus by Annas, remained in the court while He was led in to Caiaphas.

26 One of the servants of the high priest . . . saith. About an hour after the former question to Peter : see Luke xxii. 59.

28–xix. 16. On these verses, see notes on Matt. xxvii. 11–26 ; Luke xxiii. 1–19.

28 the hall of judgement. Or, " the Prætorium," the residence of the Roman governor ; which was probably a part of the castle of Antonia, situated on the north-west corner of the Temple area, where the Roman soldiers were in garrison (Matt. xxvii. 27 ; Acts xxi. 31–37 ; xxiii. 10). See Robinson's *Later Researches,* p. 230, etc.

it was early. The hearing before Caiaphas had taken place before daylight.

that they might eat the passover. Respecting the use of the word " passover " here, see note on xiii. 1. This clause is interpreted by those expositors who hold that the Paschal feast had been celebrated on the previous evening, as meaning *generally,* " that they might keep the Paschal feast," which continued for a whole week. The *chagigah,* or " festive offering," eaten on the day after the Paschal Supper, was sometimes called " the Passover " (*Lightfoot*).

29 Pilate then went out unto them. They would not go further than the " judgement seat," which, according to Roman custom, was placed on a raised tessellated " pavement " (Syriac, *Gabbatha*) in a public spot near the entrance of the Prætorium. During these transactions Pilate came out, from time to time, to hear their accusations ; but he conducted the examination of Jesus within the palace, whence he brought Him forth at last to pronounce sentence publicly (see xix. 13).

30 If he were not a malefactor, etc. See note on Matt. xxvii. 1.

31 Take ye him, and judge him. " Take him yourselves," R.V. ; treating it as a trivial offence : see note on Luke xxiii. 16. Pilate appears to have made many attempts to save his prisoner. First, he declines entering on the case at all, and tells the Jews to judge it according to their law (31). Then he declares Jesus innocent of the crime charged against Him (ver. 38 ; Luke xxiii. 4). Then, upon hearing Galilee mentioned, he tries to transfer the case to Herod's jurisdiction (Luke xxiii. 7). He next hopes to get Jesus released on the ground of the festival custom of releasing a prisoner (Luke xxiii. 16, 17). And lastly, he strives to touch the hearts of the people by the pitiable condition of Jesus after He had been scourged (xix. 1–5). But the Jews, instigated by the priests, only pressed their point the more earnestly (xix. 12) ; and Pilate's courage failed. The fear of being represented as no friend to Cæsar prevailed over every other consideration ; and he weakly and wickedly sacrificed one whom he publicly pronounced innocent.

It is not lawful. When Archelaus was deposed and Judæa became a Roman province, the Jews lost the power of inflicting capital punishment. Lighter cases were decided by their own tribunals ; capital cases were reserved for the Roman governor, before whom they were brought at his visits to Jerusalem.

32 that the saying of Jesus, etc. Crucifixion was a Roman, not a Jewish punishment.

33 Then Pilate entered into the judgement hall again. To examine Jesus apart from the clamour of the accusers. Luke alone records the charge on which this question of Pilate was founded.

35 Am I a Jew, etc. ? There is contempt in the words, " What care *I* for your subtleties ? " Pilate as a Roman knew nothing of the kingly claim but in its political sense.

36 My kingdom is not of this world, etc. My kingdom is not on the same plane with human governments. Its origin is different, its methods are different, it is spiritual ; its dominion is over hearts and lives alone. Had it been otherwise, my followers would have employed force for my defence. Our Lord will not answer Pilate's question until He has defined the nature of His kingdom.

37 Art thou a king then? As in ver. 33, but with a somewhat different emphasis, as the original shows. In the former verse the tone is " *Thou* a King ! " so outwardly abject and forsaken ! Here it is " a *King !* what can be the meaning of the claim ? "

Thou sayest, etc. A Jewish form of expression meaning, " What you say is true." As the Messiah, Jesus was King of the Jews. But our Lord proceeds to show the spiritual nature of His kingdom.

38 What is truth? We find no evidence at all in the utterances of Pilate to show that this question was asked in scepticism or mockery, as suggested by Bacon in his Essay on " Truth " (" jesting Pilate ") and many commentators. Pilate's defect was a weak will, a lack of resolution and courage. (See note on ver. 31.) Here he asks the question, evidently sincere, and though he does not wait for the answer, he goes out to the Jews with the desire of releasing Jesus.

I find in him no fault [**at all**]. To Pilate's view, Jesus might be a dreamer, or a prophet, but at any rate He was no rival to Cæsar. The obvious course, therefore, for the political ruler was to release Him at once ; but Pilate feared to risk the displeasure of the Jews.

40 Now Barabbas was a robber. And yet he

was preferred to Jesus! See the contrast strongly brought out in Acts iii. 14. He was not only "a robber," but a murderer, and probably a leader of insurrectionary banditti (Mark xv. 7; Luke xxiii. 19).

CHAPTER XIX

1 scourged. See note on Matt. xxvii. 26.

3 Hail, King of the Jews! They thus insult the Jews while they deride Jesus.

smote Him with their hands. See note on xviii. 22.

5 Behold the man. That is, Look at him! Is he not a fit object for pity rather than punishment?

6 Take ye him and crucify him. The language of irony. Pilate knew that they dared not do this.

7 he made himself the Son of God. See Matt. xxvi. 63–66, and notes. In reply to Pilate's taunt, they now for the first time bring before him the charge of blasphemy.

8 he was the more afraid, etc. The accusers seem to have nearly defeated their object, by giving Pilate's fears a new direction, leading him to renew his private interrogations. His superstitious fears are excited by the message he had received from his wife (Matt. xxvii. 19); as well as by the mysterious word of Jesus.

9 Whence art thou? "What is thy real origin?" referring to the accusation which he had just heard. But He whose reply had been unheeded before (xviii. 38) now gives no answer. He has already met the charge against Him, and has explained the one fact which seemed to give it any plausibility. Now, His silence is in itself a reply.

10 I have power to crucify thee, etc. Thus Pilate condemns himself (see on xviii. 38).

11 therefore, etc. Pilate boasts of his power of life and death. Jesus makes him feel how small this is; for he is but an instrument, first of God who gave him this power, and holds him accountable for the "sin" of abusing it; and then of the high priest and his abettors, who, with better knowledge and greater strength of purpose, are making him the tool of their malicious designs, and therefore have "greater sin."

he that delivered me unto thee hath the greater sin. Unprovoked, yet unabashed, in the calmness of conscious rectitude and dignity, our Lord pronounces His sentence on the character and conduct of His accusers and His judge. Well might Pilate feel anxious "to release Him"!

12 from thenceforth. Rather, as R.V., "upon this": in consequence of our Lord's reply.

thou art not Cæsar's friend. The Jews meant Pilate to understand that, if he released Jesus, they would report him to the emperor, a severe and jealous prince (Tac. *Ann.* iii. 38). Such a charge (*læsa majestas*) involved the penalty of death. To clear himself, and at the same time to retaliate upon the Jews, Pilate takes his seat upon the place of judgement (13), and pronounces sentence upon Jesus as King of the Jews. Having thus yielded to the importunity and threats of the Jews, his only object is to make the deed as much theirs as possible.

13 Gabbatha. See note on xviii. 29.

14 the preparation, etc. Supposing the Paschal feast to have been already past, this phrase must be explained as denoting the sixth day of the week, "the preparation day" before the seventh or sabbath (see Mark xv. 42), which occurred during the Passover festival of eight days, *i.e.*, "the Friday in the Passover week." Such a sabbath was a "high day" (31): see notes on xiii. 1; xviii. 28.

about the sixth hour. That is, presuming John to have employed a different reckoning from that of the other evangelists (see i. 39; iv. 6, 52), about sunrise. This would agree with Mark xv. 25, where see note. The circumstance that it was the day of "preparation," and that the day was rapidly advancing, accounts for the extreme impatience of the accusers. They had done their utmost to finish the matter before the sabbath; having summoned their own council before daybreak, and having come early to the governor. But his unexpected delays had occupied much of the morning; and he was still shrinking from the last decisive step, and appealing to the people. Hurried on by their excitement, they make an admission which nothing else had been able to wring from them; renouncing entirely not only Jesus as their King but all national independence; and openly declaring, "We have no king but Cæsar." Pilate takes them at their word, and keeps them rigidly to it; probably being determined to humble them for the constraint they had put upon him: see vers. 21, 22, and notes.

15 We have no king but Cæsar. Thus renouncing in their enmity to Jesus their own national hope, and accepting the tyranny which in heart they all detested.

16 unto them. To the soldiers, who would work their will (Luke xxiii. 25).

16, 17. On these verses, see notes on Matt. xxvii. 32, 33.

19 And Pilate wrote a title. In this or some similar manner the crime for which a man suffered was commonly published. The evangelists probably give the sense rather than the very words of the title. The "Hebrew" (*i.e.*, Aramaic) would be understood by the Jews of Palestine; and this may have contained the contemptuous phrase, "the Nazarene." "Latin" was added, as the official language of the empire; and "Greek," as prevailing in the province. "These three languages gathered up the results of the religious, social, and intellectual, preparation for Christ, and in each witness was given to His office" (*Westcott*). The four versions of the inscription are as follows:

Matthew	THIS IS JESUS ..	THE KING OF THE JEWS.
Mark	.. ..	
Luke	.. THIS IS	
John	.. JESUS OF NAZARETH	

21 Write not, The King of the Jews, etc. The inscription suggested the idea that the King of the Jews might be crucified by a Roman officer. This galled the Jews; but it gratified Pilate's revenge, and proclaimed the humiliation of the people and the supremacy of Cæsar. But neither the priests nor Pilate thought how true was the title, in which God was pleased to proclaim to the whole world the Messiahship of Jesus and the fulfilment of prophecy.

23 took His garments. Four of the soldiers present acted as executioners, and took their usual perquisite. But they found that the large "coat" (now called *abba*), resembling a Roman *toga*, was not made of different pieces, as was often the case, but was woven throughout without seam. It was too valuable for one share, and would be spoilt by being divided; they therefore cast lots for it, and so unconsciously fulfilled the prophetic Psalm: see notes on Psa. xxii., which is here quoted from the Septuagint.

25 Cleophas. Rather, "Clopas"; who is

probably the person elsewhere called *Alphæus;* see Matt. xxvii. 56; Mark xv. 40; and note on Matt. x. 3. "Clopas" and "Alphæus" are different Greek forms of the same Hebrew name. The Cleopas named in Luke xxiv. 18 was probably another person. It must be understood that our Lord's "mother's sister" is not the same as "Mary the wife of Clopas," but Salome, the wife of Zebedee, and mother of John and James, who was certainly present (Mark xv. 40). Four women are therefore here mentioned; two by name.

26 Woman, behold thy son. See note on ii. 4. The relationship in the flesh between the Lord and His mother being about to close, He commends her to her nephew (son of Salome: see on ver. 25), who should care for and protect her, like a son. Thus, even amid His sufferings for man's redemption, He showed His human sympathy and filial love.

28 after this. For the intervening events, see Matt. xxvii. 45, 46. Some suppose that John, on receiving charge of the mother of Jesus (26), at once removed her from the dreadful scene, and afterwards returned to the cross (35). She is not mentioned among the women who were present at the close (Matt. xxvii. 56; Mark xv. 40).

that the Scripture might be fulfilled. See Psa. lxix. 21.

30 vinegar. Our Lord had previously refused the wine mingled with gall and myrrh (Matt. xxvii 34; Mark xv. 23) given to the crucified to deaden their sufferings. This vinegar was the *posca*, or common drink of the Roman soldiers; a cheap acid wine mingled with water. In Matthew and Mark the sponge is said to be put upon a reed; in John, upon hyssop (see note on 1 Kings iv. 33). *Moffatt*, following Beza and other eminent scholars, reads, "on a spear." The Greek words are very similar.

It is finished. The Greek word here used is rendered "accomplished" in ver 28; and the two verses are intimately connected.

gave up the ghost (His spirit). The word used by the evangelist imports a voluntary surrender; made with a loud cry (Matt xxvii. 50), and with the words, "Father, into Thy hands I commend my spirit" (Luke xxiii. 46).

31 The Jews, etc. These men, though very unscrupulous about the violation of the moral law (see Matt. xxvii. 6, and note), are yet very careful of the ceremonial law. They therefore apply to Pilate to hasten the lingering death of the crucified (who might otherwise possibly survive more than thirty-six hours), and to have the bodies removed: see note on Matt. xxvii. 58.

for that sabbath day was a high [day]. See note on xiii. 1; xix. 14.

34 one of the soldiers with a spear pierced his side. The soldiers were surprised to find Jesus already dead; and, to make sure of the fact, one of them with a spear pierced His heart, or at least the membrane inclosing it. This alone would have caused instant death, had He been still living; but the blood and water which flowed from the wound showed that He was really dead. On this proof of our Lord's actual death the evangelist strongly insists; first solemnly asserting that he saw it all (35), and then showing that it was a fulfilment both of type (36) and of prophecy (37). He thus takes away all excuse for doubting either that Jesus was really man, or that He actually died.

The subject of the immediate cause of the Saviour's death is very fully discussed by Dr. Stroud, *The Physical Cause of the Death of Christ,* 1871, with Preface by Sir J. Y. Simpson. He thinks that our Lord died of a broken heart, produced by intense agony of mind.

35 record. Or, "witness," as R.V.

that ye might believe. See var. read. "That ye also may believe," R.V., *i.e.*, ye who have not seen, as well as I, an actual eye-witness.

36 A bone of Him. Rather, "A bone of *it*": *i.e.*, of the Paschal lamb (see Exod. xii. 46, and note), which was a type of "Christ our Passover": see i 29, and note; and 1 Cor. v. 7.

37 They shall look on Him whom they pierced. The marginal reading of the Hebrew, and the context of Zech. xii. 10, show that John's quotation is more accurate than the present text in the Old Testament. From the scope and connexion of the original prophecy (see note on Zech. xii. 1), it is evident that "they" who "shall look on Him" are the truly penitent of all nations and all ages, who become the true Israel. The prediction is to receive a further fulfilment: see Rev. i. 7. *Westcott* remarks on the quotation of the two prophecies side by side, "It was wonderful that the legs of Christ were not broken: it was further wonderful, when He had escaped this indignity, that His side was pierced. The first fact pointed the student of Scripture to the fulfilment in Jesus of the symbolism of the Law: the second to the fulfilment in Him of the promises as to the representative of Jehovah."

38 And after this Joseph of Arimathæa, etc. See notes on Matt. xxvii. 57–61.

39 Nicodemus. John alone had mentioned Nicodemus's first visit to our Lord (iii. 1), and his timid remark in His favour (vii. 51), and now he adds his bolder avowal of reverence for the Divine Teacher, by this costly deed of honour. The courage of Nicodemus seemed to increase with the peril of the occasion.

myrrh and aloes. See note on Gen. xxxvii. 25. "Aloes" and "cassia" are aromatic woods found in the East. They were probably pulverised, and strewed in the "cloths" in which the body was wrapped. The proceeding was hurried, on account of the near approach of the sabbath.

41 a new sepulchre. Obviating all possible suspicion as to the identity of the body.

42 There laid they Jesus therefore. As the sepulchre was near, they were able to deposit the body there before the sabbath commenced. The Greek order of the words, reproduced in R.V., is very impressive: "There then because of the Jews' Preparation (for the tomb was nigh at hand), they laid Jesus."

CHAPTER XX

1 Mary Magdalene. Mary Magdalene was not alone (see parallel passages), but she is singled out by the narrator, perhaps, because she first brought the news to the apostles; or because of the subsequent narrative (11–18).

the stone. The stone mentioned in Matt. xxvii. 60; Mark xv. 46.

4 did outrun Peter. Being younger and more active. Yet when he arrives he remains outside the tomb, as if overcome with emotion or dread. Peter, more manly and practical, enters at once. These vivid and natural details are those of an actor in the scene.

6 linen clothes. See note on Luke xxiv. 12. This orderly arrangement of the grave-clothes seem to have been the first thing to make the evangelist feel that Jesus must have risen from the dead. The Greek word translated "wrapped together" (7) and its Latin equivalent "involutum," suggest the careful folding of the napkin.

8 and he saw, and believed. He believed simply because he saw these things; for he did not yet understand the predictions, and therefore did not expect their fulfilment. "Here is an incident in the author's inmost life. He initiates us into the way by which he reached faith in the resurrection first of all, and then through it, to complete faith in Christ as the Messiah and Son of God" (*Godet*).

10 their own home. Their lodging in Jerusalem (xix. 27).

11 But Mary stood without, etc. She probably arrived at the sepulchre soon after Peter and John had left it. Perhaps her tears may have blinded her to the person of her Lord (15). Conviction reached her not through the eye, but through the ear, as she recognised the voice which had bidden the demons depart from her (ver. 16: see Mark xvi. 9).

15 if thou have (hast) **borne Him hence.** Not mentioning the name. There was at that moment but One person in the world for her! An eminently characteristic touch.

17 Touch me not. Cling not to me now. Our Lord did not always refuse such tokens of attachment (see Matt. xxviii. 9). He probably means to say, You have now full proof that I am risen. This is not the time for renewing your full communion with me. I shall soon ascend to the Father, and then you will behold me in the near and higher relationship already promised (xvi. 16). But now go quickly, and carry my message to my disciples.

my brethren. A new title, indicating spiritual relationship: cp. Matt. xxviii. 10.

I ascend, etc. "I am ascending"—already on my way. These words, addressed to those who had fled in the hour of trial, must have been unspeakably cheering, conveying to them the assurance not only that they were forgiven, but that their Lord was still truly one with them in nature, and sympathy, and relation to the Father. They encourage His people in all ages to believe that, though in glory, He is still identified with them.

19 being the first [day] of the week. Rather, as R.V., "on that day, the first day of the week"; the very day of His resurrection.

when the doors were shut. It is clearly implied that He entered the room miraculously. This event is related more fully in Luke xxiv. 36–44, on which see notes.

Peace [be] unto you. This was the ordinary salutation, but it was used by our Lord, as before (see xiv. 27, and note), with peculiar meaning; and was emphatically repeated (21) before He renewed to the apostles His commission to proclaim the Gospel of peace (2 Cor. v. 18).

20 Then were the disciples glad. At first "they believed not for joy," Luke xxiv. 41; but then the conviction that they really "saw the Lord" brought to them the first-fruits of that yet deeper joy promised in xvi. 22; on which see note.

22 breathed. The same is used in Gen. ii. 7, Sept., of the first bestowal of man's natural life.

23 Whose soever sins ye remit (forgive), etc. See Matt. xvi. 19, and note.

24 Thomas, etc. Thomas, hearing that his fellow-disciples had had sensible proof of the Lord's resurrection, requires the same; though their testimony ought to have been enough for him, as it has been for so many who have been "blessed" in believing it (29). Nay, he demands the evidence not only of sight, but also of touch. In granting it, our Lord gave a fresh proof of His condescension to feeble faith, and a further evidence that He arose with the same body which had suffered.

26 after eight days. That is, on that day week. The disciples had probably met together every day in the interval. But our Lord peculiarly honoured the first day of the week, by choosing it for His second appearance to them (see Rev. i. 10).

27 Then saith He to Thomas. Showing His knowledge of the disciple's scepticism.

thrust. Rather, "put." The spear-wound was large enough to admit the hand. The Saviour's patience in dealing with doubt might well be imitated by His followers, who have sometimes repelled honest inquirers by their harshness and lack of sympathy.

be not faithless. Lit., "Do not become faithless," or "unbelieving." Do not indulge the habit of doubting and demanding fresh proof. It was undoubtedly this proof of our Lord's insight into his character, and of His evidently superhuman knowledge, as well as the proffered evidence, from sight and touch, to the reality of His resurrection, which led to Thomas's immediate confession. Cp. the case of Nathanael, i. 49.

28 My Lord and my God. Thomas, in these words, clearly addresses Jesus, recognising not only His Messiahship, but His Deity. John records this confession in harmony with the purpose of his Gospel: cp. ver. 31 and i. 1–3.

29 because thou hast seen me. This suggests that Thomas did not avail himself of our Lord's permission to touch His body.

blessed [are] they that have not seen, etc. The faith which accepts Christ on the ground of miracle actually beheld could, from the nature of the case, be possible only to a few: that resting upon testimony would characterise the Church through all time.

30 which are not written in this book. John wrote not to gratify curiosity, but to promote faith: he therefore does not profess to give a complete account of everything that Jesus said and did (which indeed would have been impossible, xxi. 25), nor even to relate all the "signs" which He wrought; but to give enough to convince those who had "not seen" (29), in order that they might be "blessed" with "eternal life," by believing in Him as "the Son of God" (i. 14, 18).

Appearances of our Lord after his Resurrection

See also notes on the several passages.

1. To the companions of Mary Magdalene (Matt. xxviii.).
2. To Mary Magdalene herself (John xx.).
   Some transpose these two.
3. To Peter (1 Cor. xv. 5; Mark xvi. 7).
4. To the two disciples on the way to Emmaus (Luke xxiv.).
5. To the apostles, excepting Thomas (1 Cor. xv. 5; John xx.).
6. To the apostles, including Thomas (John xx.).
7. To nine apostles at the Sea of Tiberias (John xxi.).
8. To above five hundred brethren at once (1 Cor. xv. 6; Matt. xxviii. 16-20).
9. To James, "the Lord's brother" (1 Cor. xv. 7).

10. To all the apostles (repeatedly) in Jerusalem (Acts i. 3–8; 1 Cor. xv. 7).

The Ascension is recorded by Luke (xxiv. 50–53; Acts i. 9; and in the last verses of Mark (xvi. 19, 20).

CHAPTER XXI

1 shewed Himself. Better, as R.V., "manifested Himself": cp. ii. 11.

at the sea of Tiberias. Resuming their former occupation (3) amidst the old scenes, in the district where the Lord had promised to meet them (Matt. xxvi. 32; xxviii. 10). They did not feel that honest work for a livelihood was inconsistent with waiting for their Lord.

3 a ship. Rather, "the boat," as R.V.—that which still belonged to their relatives.

4 when the morning was now come. Rather, as R.V., "when day was now breaking."

knew not. Perhaps from the dimness of the early dawn: or our Lord may have purposely concealed Himself for a while (Luke xxiv. 16).

5 children. Better translated "lads."

any meat. "Anything to eat." The word literally denotes anything to be eaten with bread.

7 Therefore, etc. John's mind evidently reverted to the former miraculous draught of fishes; and he concluded at once, "It is the Lord." This repetition of the "sign" would recall to their minds the lesson and encouragement then given: see Luke v. 5–10, and notes.

Now, when Simon Peter heard, etc. John, the more thoughtful, is the first to perceive; Peter, the more ardent, is the first to act.

he girt his fisher's coat unto him, etc. He put on his outer garment, which he had taken off for work; and he girt it close, so that he could swim. It was a sort of frock or blouse, reaching to the knees.

8 two hundred cubits. About one hundred yards.

11 went up. Or, "went on board," to unfasten the net and bring it ashore.

one hundred, fifty and three. Those who have watched in a fishing village the boats come in, will appreciate the reality of this. The fishermen, sharing a boat, still count "the catch."

12 Come [and] dine. Better, in modern speech, "Come and breakfast."

none of the disciples durst ask Him. The evidence was so complete, that the most incredulous "durst" not "question Him," to gain further proof.

14 This is now the third time, etc. Meaning, probably, the third appearance to the assembled disciples, recorded by John.

15 dined. "Breakfasted."

Simon, [son] of Jonas. Our Lord addresses Peter not by the name which He Himself had given him, but by his former name; perhaps to remind him of his frailty and his fall: cp. Mark xiv. 27, Luke xxii. 31.

more than these. That is, more than thy brethren do; referring to Peter's recent profession (see Matt. xxvi. 33). Peter, no longer comparing himself with them, humbly declares to the Searcher of hearts that his love is sincere, although it had sadly failed in the hour of trial. "*Thou* knowest" is emphatic.

Feed my lambs. Before re-establishing the disciple who had denied him "thrice" in the apostleship, our Lord gives him the opportunity of thrice professing his attachment. The Chief Shepherd will soon depart. Show thy love to Him by care for those whom He leaves behind. This charge was evidently in the apostle's mind when he wrote his Epistle (see 1 Pet. v. 2–4).

17 the third time. The thrice-repeated question might well grieve Peter, reminding him of his thrice-repeated denial. But it also gave our Lord opportunity for repeating the assurance that he was reinstated in his office.

lovest. In the text two different words are alike translated "lovest": the word used in the first and second questions being a word which generally implies esteem as well as love; the other, found in the third question, and in all Peter's replies, being appropriate to natural personal affection. David Smith well translates the word used here (ἀγαπᾷς) in the first and second questions by "regard"; and the word (φιλεῖς) used in the third question as "love." The Spanish (Hispano-American Version) renders the first Greek word by "amar," the second by "querer." "Simon, hijo de Juan, me amas? . . . Si, Señor, tu sabes que te quiero." Some writers suppose that, to Peter's warm and earnest feelings, the former word seemed too distant and cold; and that our Lord adopted his own expression, to show that warm feelings must be judged by their practical use. In any case this lesson is clearly taught by the narrative.

Feed. Here again there is a variation in the words rendered "feed"; the word used in vers. 15, 17, signifying more strictly to *feed*, and that which occurs in ver. 16 meaning more generally to *tend* or *shepherd*. Many take the two words to be synonymous. But some think that our Lord meant to enjoin, by the one, the "feeding" with knowledge and instruction; by the other, the "shepherding," or maintenance of discipline in the Church.

18 thou shalt stretch forth thy hands. To be bound, as a captive, or fastened as a criminal to a cross.

another shall gird thee. The particular form of this prediction, referring to common actions of daily life, would tend to keep Peter constantly in mind of his sufferings and death. It is said that he was crucified with his head downwards at Rome, in the reign of the emperor Nero, A.D. 67.

21 what shall this man do? That is, "what shall his *lot* (or his *end*) be?"

22 what [is that] to thee? Our Lord thus gently rebukes Peter's curiosity, and directs his mind to his own duties.

23 Then went this saying abroad. Better, as R.V., "This saying therefore went forth." There is here no note of time in the word *then*.

till I come. See note on Matt. xvi. 28. John not only lived to see the Lord coming in the overthrow of apostate Judaism and the establishment of His gospel kingdom; but he also had revealed to him before his death the whole further development of that coming: see Introduction to the Book of the Revelation.

24 This is the disciple, etc. Cp. xix. 35. Here the "we" probably includes the elders of Ephesus, where St. John wrote.

25 I suppose that even the world itself could not contain, etc. A popular phrase intimating the impossibility of recording all. The foregoing records of our Divine Redeemer's life have enabled us to trace Him "in infancy and in manhood; in secret and among the crowds; at work and in prayer. We have listened to His teaching; we have watched His sacrifice; we have heard the announcement of His kingdom. As man He has claimed our reverence too" (*Angus*).

THE ACTS OF THE APOSTLES

INTRODUCTION

SOME one has said that this Book might be called "The Acts of the Holy Spirit." And there is much to support this view of it. The Book opens with the Saviour's promise of the Spirit (i. 4, 8 ; cp. John xiv. 16, 26 ; xv. 26 ; xvi. 7–13), followed by the Ascension (i. 9), and the prayerful waiting of the disciples at Jerusalem (i. 14). Then comes the great manifestation of the Spirit's power at Pentecost (ii. 1–4) and the linking up of the Old Testament with the new era that had dawned upon the world (ii. 17–21). The immediate result is the transformation of character in the Apostles themselves and in the persons to whom they preached. Peter, who had denied his Master, becomes foremost in proclaiming Him as the risen and exalted Lord (ii. 32–36 ; iii. 13, 26 ; iv. 10–12) and "filled with the Holy Spirit" confronts with boldness the Jewish rulers (iv. 8–13). Upon the people of Jerusalem and the visitors there the words of Peter produce such an impression that, conscience-stricken, they repent, and three thousand of them become followers of the crucified Nazarene (ii. 37, 41). The practical consequence is a new spirit of brotherhood and unselfishness (ii. 42–46 ; iv. 32–35).

Thus the foundations of the Christian Church were laid. And when men are needed as workers, as martyrs, and as missionaries, it is men "filled with the Holy Spirit" who are chosen (vi. 3), and it is that Spirit that enables them to suffer and to die (vii. 54). When the Apostles and Evangelists began to preach among the Samaritans, then, too, the Holy Spirit accompanied them and their message (viii. 14) and directed them in their personal appeals (viii. 29). All through the new Christian communities in Judæa, Samaria, and Galilee, the Spirit's influence was felt (ix. 31), and in the great forward movement, which began in the house of Cornelius, for the evangelisation of the Gentiles, the same power was manifested (x. 44–47). When Barnabas and Saul set forth on their first missionary voyage, it is under the guidance of the Holy Spirit (xiii. 2, 4) ; and later on their plans are altered in obedience to His will (xvi. 6, 7) ; the infant Church at Ephesus is encouraged by the tokens of His presence (xix. 6), and its elders are reminded by St. Paul that their office is due to Him (xx. 28). The last utterance of that apostle recorded in the Acts is a declaration that the same Divine Spirit to whom he owed so much inspired, and spoke by, the lips of the great Old Testament prophet (xxviii. 25). Thus the Book closes, as it began (i. 16 ; ii. 17–21), by linking up the Old Testament and the New.

The Book was written by St. Luke about A.D. 80. The reader who desires to study in detail the evidences of its historical accuracy may be referred to such works as Sir William Ramsay's *The Church in the Roman Empire* and *St. Paul the Traveller and the Roman Citizen*, Paley's *Horæ Paulinæ*, Chase's *Credibility of the Book of the Acts of the Apostles*, and for its practical lessons to Dr. Charles Brown's work in *The Devotional Commentary*, and Professor G. T. Stokes's volumes in *The Expositor's Bible*.

CHAPTER I

1 Theophilus. See Luke i. 3, and note.

began both to do and teach. "A very common idiomatic expression for both did and taught." Cp. Mark v. 17, and many other passages in the Gospels. There is no emphasis on *began* (*Westcott*).

2 through the Holy Ghost. Luke is referring to our Lord's personal presence with His disciples, before the Spirit was given ; and the passage must therefore be understood as stating that the Holy Spirit in Christ instructed and commissioned the apostles.

3 after His passion. Or, "after His suffering."

infallible proofs. One word in original, rendered in R.V. simply "proofs." The Greek word means

positive (or *convincing*) *proofs.* " Infallible " is due to the Geneva (English) version.

being seen of them. Or, as R.V., " appearing unto them " : *i.e.*, from time to time. See note on Matt. xxviii. 1.

forty days. This is the only intimation of the length of the period during which the risen Saviour remained on earth.

speaking [of] the things, etc. See notes on vers. 6, 7, and on Matt. iii. 2.

4 being assembled together. In Jerusalem (Luke xxiv. 47, 49).

the promise of the Father. See notes on Luke xxiv. 49 ; John xiv. 16, 17.

5 with (" in," R.V. marg.) **the Holy Ghost.** " With water," as an outward symbol ; but " in the Holy Ghost," as the essential element of spiritual life. So in Luke iii. 16.

6 were come together. Near Bethany (Luke xxiv. 50); on a subsequent occasion to that noted in ver. 4.

wilt Thou at this time restore? etc. R.V., " Dost Thou at this time restore ? " The question refers chiefly to the time (see ver. 7); but it implies a hope that the restoration of the Hebrew monarchy would be one result of the Lord's work.

7 the times or the seasons. Rather, as R.V., " times or seasons " : a general statement. Our Lord's statement here has too often been forgotten by well-meaning Christians, who speculate and dogmatise about future events.

which the Father hath put, etc. Lit., " which the Father fixed (or settled) in [the exercise of] His own authority." He will not reveal these secrets of His government ; but He will give you " power " by " the Holy Ghost coming upon you," to fit you for your own special privilege and duty as my witnesses to the world (ver. 8). See John xv. 27. This would be the real way to help forward the coming of Christ's true kingdom, while to the apostles themselves the exchange of idle speculations for practical work would be every way beneficial.

8 ye shall be witnesses unto me (R.V., " my witnesses," according to var. read.), etc. Their work is here designated in its beginning, progress, and ultimate extent ; corresponding to the three periods of the following history.

Samaria. See note on Matt. x. 5.

9 He was taken up. Cp. Luke xxiv. 51. Our Lord did not simply *disappear*, as on former occasions (see Luke xxiv. 31, etc.) ; but " as they were looking " (R.V.), He was raised up, and a cloud (the symbol of the Divine presence, Psa. civ. (3) took Him away from their eyes, or sight.

10 looked. " Were looking intently " ; " gazing " ; a stronger word than that in vers. 9, 11.

two men. Angels in human form (cp. Luke xxiv. 4 with John xx. 12).

11 in like manner. Visibly in person as a man ; in the clouds, and with angels as His attendants.

12 Olivet. Probably from the eastern slope of the Mount of Olives, near Bethany (Luke xxiv. 50).

which is from Jerusalem, etc. Rather, as R.V., " which is nigh unto Jerusalem, a sabbath day's journey off." About a mile, the extent to which the Jews allowed themselves to go on the sabbath. It is said to have been originally fixed by the distance from the Tabernacle to the extremity of the camp in the wilderness. The village of Bethany was fifteen furlongs from Jerusalem (John xi. 18).

13 an upper room. Rather, " *the* upper room " (" upper chamber," R.V.), where they daily met together for prayer and converse.

Peter, etc. See note on Matt. x. 2. Luke here mentions the greater number of the Twelve for the *last* time.

14 with one accord. With entire harmony of feeling. The same word is used, Rom. xv. 6.

with the women. Rather, " with women " ; " with some women " (*Weymouth*).

Mary the mother of Jesus. Mary here appears for the last time in Scripture ; and is mentioned only as uniting with the disciples in prayer ; not as exercising any sort of authority, not even as giving counsel to the apostles.

His brethren. See notes on Matt. xiii. 55; John vii. 2–5 ; 1 Cor. xv. 7.

15 in those days. Between the ascension of our Lord and Pentecost.

Peter stood up. Peter appears foremost in speech and action among the apostles, both in their private counsels, and in their intercourse with the people ; but we never find him claiming or exercising any authority either over the rest, or independently of them.

the number, etc. There were doubtless many more in Galilee : see 1 Cor. xv. 6.

16 Men [and] brethren. Simply, " Brethren," as in R.V. The form, " Men, brethren " was the Greek mode of respectful address. See ii. 29, 37 ; vii. 2 ; xiii. 15 ; xv. 7 ; xxiii. 1, etc.

18 purchased. Lit., " obtained " or " acquired." The priests bought the field with the money that Judas returned to them, so that rhetorically the acquisition is said to be made by himself. From the price of his treachery " he gained " only " a field," where blood was paid for blood. Hence the name given to it : cp. Matt. xxvii. 3–8. (This and the next verse are best regarded as a parenthesis introduced by Luke : so R.V.)

falling headlong. That is, he fell forward on his face. Cp. Matt. xxvii. 5. It has been suggested that in his throwing himself from a height, or a branch of a tree, the rope broke by which he intended to strangle himself, so that he fell forward, and was dashed to pieces (*Papias*). In Matt. xxvii. 5, his own act is told, showing that he felt himself accursed (Deut. xxi. 23) ; here his additional sufferings and the actual cause of death are narrated.

19 (And it was known, etc.) The historian's own words.

their proper (their own) **tongue.** Or, " dialect." The Western Aramaic or Syriac, which was spoken by the Jews after their captivity in Babylon.

20 For it is written. This refers to ver. 16 : " the Scripture concerning Judas must be fulfilled ; for," etc.

bishopric. Rather, as R.V., " office " ; literally, " overseership " ; " his work " (*Weymouth*). The quotations are from two separate Psalms (lxix. and cix.), both referring to malignant treachery against a righteous sufferer and to its doom. Whatever the immediate historical occasions of these Psalms, their typical and prophetic reference is striking.

21 of these men, etc. A personal knowledge of what the Lord had done and taught was a necessary qualification for an apostle, as his first duty was that of a witness : see John xv. 27 ; Mark iii. 14, and notes.

22 the baptism of John. Just as it was closing, our Lord began His public work, of which His "resurrection" was the crowning act and evidence; and it was preached as such to Jews and Gentiles (ii. 32; xvii. 31).

must one be ordained to be a witness. The original is simply, "must one become a witness" (R.V.).

23 they appointed. "They (probably the whole company) set up (*i.e.*, *nominated*) two"; who may have been the only persons within reach possessing the necessary qualifications.

Barsabas . . . and Matthias. Nothing is known of either Barsabas (Barsabbas, R.V.) or Matthias. They may have belonged to "the seventy" (Luke x. 1). Joseph being a common name, his patronymic Barsabbas (son of Sabba) is added, as well as his Roman name "Justus." The Jews when among Gentiles commonly used a Gentile name bearing some resemblance to their Hebrew names: see xiii. 9. Another Barsabbas is mentioned (xv. 22) as a man of note in the church.

24 Thou, Lord. Probably addressed to the glorified Saviour, who had appointed the other eleven.

show . . . Thou hast chosen. *i.e.*, by the falling of the lot upon him (see ver. 26).

25 part. Judas, forfeiting "the position" of which he had proved himself unworthy, went to "the place" for which he had shown himself fit. The future punishment of the wicked is not of arbitrary appointment, but is suited to character.

by transgression fell. One word in original, "transgressed"; rendered in R.V., "fell away."

26 their lots. Rather, according to the best reading, "lots for them," R.V.; *i.e.*, for those who were nominated. Their names were probably written on two tablets, which were shaken in a vessel, or in the lap of a robe (see Prov. xvi. 33), and he whose lot fell out first was the person designated. This usage was very ancient (see Lev. xvi. 8; Numb. xxvi. 55, 56); but no subsequent instance of it occurs in the New Testament.

CHAPTER II

1 Pentecost. Respecting the festival of Pentecost, see Lev. xxiii. 16, and note. This day was peculiarly appropriate for this Divine interposition because of the numbers of foreign as well as native Jews who then assembled for worship. "Pentecost was the harvest festival, the feast of ingathering for the Jews; and when the type found its completion in Christ, Pentecost became the feast of ingathering for the nations" (G. T. Stokes in *Expositor's Bible*).

all. Probably all the disciples who were in Jerusalem at the time.

in one place. This was most likely the "upper room" where they had been meeting: see i. 13, and note.

2 a rushing mighty wind. Signs addressed to the ear and to the eye. Along with the sound (lit., "as of a mighty blast borne along") there was a luminous appearance, as of flames or "tongues, distributing themselves" (not *cloven*), so that one "rested upon each one of them" who were assembled (ver. 1). "The tongue of fire pointed on the Pentecostal morn to the important part in the Church's life, and in the propagation of the Gospel, which prayer, and praise, and preaching would hereafter occupy" (*G. T. Stokes*).

4 other tongues. These were clearly the vernacular languages of the nations mentioned in vers. 9–11; and the wonder was that they were spoken by illiterate Galilæans (ver. 7). The gift seems to have been possessed only in such measure, time, and manner "as the Spirit gave them to utter." The lost unity of mankind, indicated by "the confusion of tongues" (Gen. xi. 7–9), was to be spiritually restored by the gospel (1 Cor. xii. 13; Col. iii. 11). There is no indication in the history of a continuous supernatural gift of speech, enabling the early missionaries to preach in languages which they had never learned.

5 dwelling. Either as residents or as visitors.

devout men. Pious men, looking for the "consolation of Israel" (Luke ii. 25); consequently, competent and trustworthy witnesses.

out of every nation. The Jews of "the Dispersion": see John vii. 35; James i. 1; 1 Pet. i. 1.

6 when this was noised abroad. Or, as R.V., "when this sound was heard": referring to the rushing sound (ver. 2), heard throughout the city, but proceeding from the spot where the disciples were assembled.

in his own language. Spoken either by one or more of the disciples.

7 are not all these which speak Galilæans? The prominent persons being Galilæans, the rest were supposed to be so. They were all Palestinian Jews.

9–11. These verses may be regarded either as spoken by the multitude, or as a parenthetical enumeration by Luke. The list contains most of the countries in which Jews were dispersed; and it proceeds in geographical order, beginning at the north-east, and passing to the west and south: cp. Isa. xi. 11, etc.

9 Parthians, and Medes, and Elamites. The eastern part of the old Persian empire (including Parthia, Media, and Elamitis) formed the new Parthian kingdom, which became a formidable rival of the Romans in Asia.

Asia. "Asia" here, and everywhere else in the New Testament, signifies Proconsular Asia, the Roman Province, which lay along the western shore of Asia Minor, and had Ephesus for its capital.

10 in Egypt. The Jews were so numerous in Egypt that at Alexandria they occupied two out of the five districts of the city. "Libya" means here the district on the west of Egypt, including Cyrene, a large and beautiful city, near the Mediterranean. The Cyrenian Jews (Matt. xxvii. 32) had a synagogue of their own in Jerusalem (vi. 9).

strangers of Rome. The "strangers of Rome" were Roman Jews residing or sojourning at Jerusalem. The distinction between "Jews" by birth, and "proselytes," or Gentile converts to the Jewish faith, applies to the whole catalogue.

11 Cretes. Called in A.V., "Cretians" (Titus i. 12): in both places R.V. rightly, "Cretans."

13 Others mocking. The mockers may have been native Jews whose prejudices made them quick to regard these strange languages as an unintelligible jargon: cp. 1 Cor. xiv. 23.

new wine. Rather, "sweet wine"; the name given to fermented wines in which the sweetness was retained by a peculiar process, and some of which were unusually strong.

14 standing up with the eleven. The apostles came forward from the great body of believers, and Peter spoke in the name of them all (see note on i. 15). Professor G. T. Stokes (*Expositor's Bible*) thinks it probable that this and other addresses of the apostles were taken down in shorthand, supporting this view by references to Pliny.

that dwell. See note on ver. 5, where the same word is used.

15 the third hour. About nine o'clock a.m. None but the lowest revellers would be drunken so early: see Isa. v. 11.

16 spoken by the prophet Joel. See Joel ii. 28–32, and notes. The quotation agrees very nearly with the Septuagint version; but the words "the last days" appear to be supplied from Isa. ii. 2, on which see note. The prophecy began to be signally fulfilled in this miraculous display of the Holy Spirit's power; but its accomplishment is to go on throughout the Christian dispensation, until the coming of "the day of the Lord": see Matt. xxiv., and notes.

22 Jesus of Nazareth. Rather, "Jesus the Nazarene." This very name of reproach was a fulfilment of prophecy: see Matt. ii. 23, and note.

a man approved of God. Rather, "a man, from God accredited to you," etc. His miracles displayed power, excited wonder, and illustrated, as well as confirmed, His Divine mission.

23 by the determinate counsel, etc. The freedom of the human will and personal responsibility, combined with Divine foreknowledge and control, is here definitely stated. No attempt is made to explain or reconcile the apparently conflicting propositions.

by wicked hands. Lit. (and R.V.), "by the hands of lawless men" (*or*, "men without the law").

24 the pains of death. "Pains (or 'pangs') of death" is derived from the Septuagint rendering of Psa. xviii. 4; cxvi. 3.

25 For David speaketh. See notes on Psalm xvi.

I foresaw. "I saw before" me; ("beheld," R.V.) not *saw beforehand.* "I constantly fixed my eyes upon the Lord" (*Weymouth*).

29 let me freely speak. R.V., "I may say unto you freely." Peter appeals for an unprejudiced hearing from those who, being impressed with a high sense of David's greatness, might possibly take offence at what follows. He shows that the language of the Psalm could not find its accomplishment in David, the founder of the royal house, because he had not been raised from the dead. "Then" (30) it *must have* been of the Messiah that David spoke prophetically when he said that His soul was not left in Hades, etc. And (32–36) He in whom this is historically fulfilled is Jesus of Nazareth: cp. xiii. 35–37.

his sepulchre is with us. David's sepulchre on Mount Zion (see 1 Kings ii. 10; Neh. iii. 16) was well known. (Josephus, *Antiq.* vii. 15, § 3.)

31 of Christ. Rather, as R.V., "of *the* Christ," the long-promised Messiah.

32 we all are witnesses. Not only the apostles, but multitudes of others: see 1 Cor. xv. 6. In ver. 33, Peter proceeds to speak of Christ's ascension: thus explaining the outpouring of the Holy Spirit, which the people had witnessed.

34 he saith himself, etc. Peter thus reproduces the very quotation and argument which our Lord had addressed to the Scribes only a few weeks before: see Matt. xxii. 42, and notes.

36 God hath made. Or (as R.V.), more emphatically, "God hath made Him both Lord (21) and Christ (31)—this Jesus whom ye crucified.

37 pricked in their heart. "When they heard this it went straight to their hearts" (*Moffatt*). "Stung to the heart by these words" (*Weymouth*).

38 Repent, and be baptised. This is in effect what the Baptist (see Mark i. 4, and note) and our Lord (Mark i. 15) had preached; but baptism is here enjoined as the symbol of faith "upon (or in) the name of Jesus," implying acknowledgment of Him and subjection to Him as Lord and Messiah. The phrase "for the remission of sins" (R.V., "unto the remission of your sins") must be connected with both parts of the command.

39 To you and to your children. This verse is an encouragement to parents. It shows also the gradual progress of the Spirit's work and of the Gospel, beginning with the individual, extending to the family, and then spreading into all the world.

to all that are afar off. The "call" and blessings of the gospel are not confined to one age or nation. The apostles evidently believed that the Gentiles would be converted: it was their conversion *as Gentiles* which they had yet to learn: see x., xi., and notes.

41 Then they, etc. Rather, "So then, they, on accepting his word," etc. ("Gladly" seems an interpolation.) It is *implied* that most of the hearers welcomed the exhortation.

42 continued stedfastly in, etc. Lit., "were closely attending to the *teaching* of the apostles (see Matt. xxviii. 20), and to the fellowship" (*i.e.,* to the expression of brotherhood in supplying each other's temporal necessities: see ver. 45, and iv. 32–35). The same word is rendered "fellowship" here, "contribution" in Rom. xv. 26, and "to communicate" in Heb. xiii. 16.

in breaking of bread (in the breaking of the bread). Perhaps commemorating the Lord's death at the close of their daily social meals: see 46.

43 fear. Or, "awe."

44 had all things in common. The principle here exemplified is characteristic of Christianity everywhere: that property is a trust, not to be held for selfish pleasure, but for the service of others and the glory of God. In this exemplification of the principle, consequent on the first outburst of Christian love and zeal, believers followed the example of our Lord and His apostles, who evidently had all their property in common stock, out of which their expenses were defrayed. This arrangement, however, was voluntary on the part of each individual (see v. 4), and does not appear to have been adopted in any other church established by the apostles: see Gal. ii. 10; 1 Tim. vi. 8, 17–19.

46 in the Temple. Probably at the usual hours of prayer: see iii. 1. The apostles still observed the Mosaic laws and worship.

did eat their meat. Rather, "took their *food.*"

singleness of heart. That is, simplicity of purpose, aim, and motive; a peculiar characteristic of the early stages of remarkable progress, both individual and social.

47 having favour with all the people. Popular favour has generally attended the first introduction of the gospel everywhere, until men have begun to feel the contrast between its principles and precepts, and their own character and conduct.

such as should be saved. Lit., "those that were being saved," *i.e.,* that were in the way of salvation.

CHAPTER III

1 Peter and John. Peter and John, associated by our Lord among His more intimate companions, appear to have been united by a peculiar friendship. See viii. 14; Luke xxii. 8; John xx. 3; xxi. 7–20.

went. That is, "were going" (R.V.).

the ninth [**hour**]. About three o'clock p.m. The Jews were accustomed to pray three times a day: at the third (ii. 15), sixth (x. 9), and ninth hours.

2 was carried. Lit., "was being carried." Being brought daily to this public spot he had become widely known.

called Beautiful. This is supposed to be the gate described by Josephus (*Wars*, v. 5, § 3: *Antiq.* xv. 11, § 3), constructed chiefly of Corinthian brass; on the eastern side of the Temple looking towards the valley of Kedron, and opening into the Court of the Women.

6 of Nazareth. Rather, "the Nazarene." The apostolical miracles were all performed in reliance on the authority and promise of Jesus (Mark xvi. 17, 18; John xiv. 12).

7 his feet and ankle bones. Rather, "his *soles* and *ankles*."

8 leaping. This was peculiarly wonderful, as he had been lame from his birth; and we all have to learn to walk and stand.

11 the porch (portico) **that is called Solomon's.** See note on John x. 22. This porch looked towards the rising sun, and was therefore a warm and sunny spot, a usual promenade or public walk, especially in winter (*G. T. Stokes*). In the afternoon, the time here referred to, it would doubtless be somewhat cooler.

12 at this. Probably, "at this man" (R.V.), though *thing* is a possible rendering.

13 Son. Rather, "Servant" (and so in ver. 26, and iv. 27, 30); a prophetic appellation of the Messiah (see Isa. xlii. 1; lii. 13; liii. 11). Another word is used where Jesus is spoken of as the "*Son* of God."

when he was determined to let Him go. That is, "had determined" judicially and formally. See note on John xviii. 31. The circumstances which aggravated their guilt are here convincingly dwelt upon.

14 the Just. By the judgement of Pilate and your own consciences.

15 the Prince. Or, "the Author," as in Heb. xii. 2; the same word also occurs (Heb. ii. 10), "*Captain* of their salvation."

16 His name, etc. The "name" often stands for the person in all his attributes and offices. "On account of (our) faith in His name; this man, whom ye see and know, His name (He Himself) made strong." And "the faith which is by (through) Him, hath given him," etc.—faith wrought also in the mind of the cripple.

17 ignorance. Our Lord's own prayer for the Roman soldiers (Luke xxiii. 34) encourages the hope of forgiveness to those who "know not." Their sin is not like that of wilful and determined violation of their own convictions: see xiii. 27; 1 Cor. ii. 8; 1 Tim. i. 13, 14.

18 Christ. Rather, "the Christ." See Luke xxiv. 26, and note.

19 be converted. Lit. (as R.V.), "turn again"; *i.e.*, to God (Isa. vi. 10; Matt. xiii. 15).

when the times of refreshing shall come, etc. Rather, as R.V., "that so there may come seasons of refreshing from the presence of the Lord, and that He may send the Christ who hath been before appointed for you, *even* Jesus," etc. You have long looked for the divinely predicted times of revival and "restoration of all things" under your Messiah (see Deut. xviii. 15, quoted in vers. 22, 23; Isa. xxv. 1, 6; xxvi. 1, 19; Ezek. xxxvii. 1-14, etc., and notes; and cp. Luke i. 70): but they must be preceded by your personal repentance and conversion to Him (Hosea xiv.; Zech. xii. 10) who has been exalted to heaven, there to complete His restoring work. When the repentance has become general, the restoration will soon be fulfilled: see Rom. xi. 25-32.

22, 23. See Deut. xviii. 15-19; Lev. xxiii. 29; John i. 21. The quotation is not verbally exact; and in ver. 23 the more specific punishment of exclusion from God's people (see Gen. xvii. 14, and note) is substituted for the general threat.

24 Samuel. The next great prophet after Moses, and the first of a long succession who foretold the coming of Messiah.

25 children of the prophets. That is, the heirs of the promised blessings, under the old covenant. Therefore the gospel was preached "first" to the Jews (ver. 26).

in thy seed, etc. See Gen. xii. 3; Gal iii. 16, and notes.

26 His Son. Rather, "His Servant," as R.V.

from his iniquities. This last clause would preclude the fatal and favourite Jewish error, that the patriarchal promises and covenants would be fulfilled to Abraham's descendants without respect to character.

CHAPTER IV

1 captain of the Temple. See on Luke xxii. 4; and Josephus (*Wars*, vi. 5, § 3).

Sadducees. Respecting the Sadducees, see notes on Matt. iii. 7; xxii. 23. The Sadducees now became the leading opponents of the gospel, not only, perhaps, as the most powerful political party, but also because they were "sore troubled" (R.V.) that illiterate and unauthorised men should teach, and still more that they taught the doctrine of the resurrection as established "in Jesus" (cp. xxiii. 6-8). Afterwards, when the Christians were suspected of disaffection to the law of Moses (vi. 11), the Pharisees also were aroused, and Saul's persecuting zeal was excited (viii. 3; xxii. 3, 4; xxvi. 9).

3 in hold. That is, in custody.

4 was about five thousand. Rather, "had now grown to about five thousand" (*Weymouth*); this being the whole number who had avowed themselves believers.

5 rulers, and elders, and scribes. The Sanhedrin; see note on Matt. ii. 4.

6 Annas . . . Caiaphas, etc. Respecting Annas and Caiaphas, see notes on Matt. xxvi. 3 and John xviii. 13. "The kindred of the high priest": literally, "the chief-priestly race," perhaps denoting the heads of the twenty-four courses: see note, Matt. ii. 4.

7 in the centre. The Sanhedrin sat in a semicircle.

8 filled with the Holy Ghost. Another fulfilment of Matt. x. 20; Mark xiii. 11.

9 by what means. Lit., "in what," or "in whom": see R.V. marg. The reference may be either to the "power" or the "name" (ver. 7). Peter's defence is marked by boldness and pungency. Do you call us to answer for a deed of *kindness* in curing a poor sufferer?

11 This is the stone, etc. See notes on Psa. cxviii. 22 and Matt. xxi. 42; and cp. Eph. ii. 20; 1 Pet. ii. 4, 6.

12 salvation. Lit., "*the* salvation," emphatic. "Given," is literally, "that has been given."

13 boldness. Lit., "freeness of speech."

ignorant. Not educated as teachers of the law (Tyndale, *laymen*): cp. John vii. 15, and note.

they took knowledge of them. Rather, "they recognised them": recognised them by degrees, as the form of the word in the original intimates. The knowledge dawned first on one, then on another, that they had seen these men with Jesus.

14 standing. Not merely "present" (ver. 10), but *standing on his feet*, perfectly cured.

16 we cannot deny it. Lit., "we are not able to deny it," as much as to say, We would if we could.

17 straitly. That is, "strictly." The original means (as R.V.), "Let us threaten them"; some early copies (and rec. text) adding "with a threat," emphatically.

19 judge ye, etc. With manly boldness, Peter and John, appealing to the moral sense of their judges. assert the supremacy of conscience, and the paramount authority of the known will of God.

21 glorified. "Were glorifying," continuously.

22 above forty years old. A note characteristic of Luke the physician: cp. ix. 33; xiv. 8, and Luke viii. 43. The lameness had been inveterate.

24 with one accord. Perhaps, one leading, the rest audibly assenting. Luke often puts into the mouth of many what could only have been spoken by one.

Lord (Master), **Thou [art] God**, etc. Quoted from Exod. xx. 11. His servants find their support first in His omnipotence, and then in His comforting word and promise, already fulfilled in the sufferings and resurrection of Christ. Thus emboldened, they beg Him to continue to enable them, by His grace, and by proofs of His power, to brave all threats and dangers.

25 hast said. See Psa. ii. 1, 2, and notes.

Why did the heathen rage, etc.? Lit., "Why did nations rage, and peoples imagine vain things?" ("formed futile plans," *Weymouth*).

27 Child. Rather, "Servant" (see note on iii. 13), as in ver. 25; and so in ver. 30.

Herod. See Luke xxiii. 12, and note.

28 determined before, etc. See ii. 23; Isa. x. 7, and notes.

30 by stretching forth, etc. Lit., "In Thy stretching forth Thy hand for healing."

31 the place was shaken. One part of the Pentecostal sign repeated, in token of the continuance of the gift.

32 all things common. See note on ii. 44.

33 grace. Or, "favour": as in Luke ii. 52.

34 Neither. Rather, "*For* neither," etc.

laid them down, etc. Placing them at the apostles' disposal. Placing gifts at the feet is Oriental.

36 son of consolation. Or, "son of encouragement": see xi. 23, 24. The Greek word (παρακλήσεως) conveys the same idea as that of the Paraclete, "Comforter" or "Helper," applied to the Holy Spirit (John xiv. 16).

37 having land. The Levites had no part in the original division of Canaan, being specially provided for separately (Numb. xxxv. 2–8; Deut. x. 8, 9); but in later times they often acquired land (see Jer. xxxii. 7–12. The prophet was of the tribe of Levi).

CHAPTER V

1 Ananias. The Greek of this verse begins with "but," thus bringing out the contrast between the generosity and unselfishness of Barnabas, and the hypocrisy and covetousness of Ananias and Sapphira.

with Sapphira his wife. This was a deliberate sin, as "his wife was aware of it."

land. "Estate" or "property."

2 kept back. In the original an expressive word, used by the LXX for the sin of Achan (Josh. vii. 1). "Appropriated" (*Moffatt*).

laid it at the apostles' feet. Pretending that it was the whole. It was an acted lie.

3 why hath Satan, etc.? The question shows that though Satan may tempt, man may and should resist: see James iv. 7.

4 was it not in thine own power? You need not have sold your property unless you pleased; and when you had sold it, if you chose to keep the money, you were quite free to do so.

5 gave up the ghost. The sin itself deserved the punishment; and it was important that God's hatred of covetousness and hypocrisy in His Church should be shown at once. Severe punishments upon first transgressors act as a solemn and merciful warning to others: see Gen. iv. 11–15; Lev. x. 1–3; Numb. xv. 32-36; xvi. 1–35; 2 Sam. vi. 6–12.

6 wound him up. Probably in his own clothes (see Lev. x. 5). The Jews used no coffins in burial.

out. Doubtless outside the city (see note on Luke vii. 12).

8 so much. Naming the sum which Ananias had brought.

9 tempt the Spirit of the Lord. To try whether He would detect the fraud.

11 the church. The "congregation" or "assembly." The term (now used for the first time in the Acts, as it should probably be omitted in ii. 47) indicates the progress of the disciples towards permanent organisation.

12 all. Teachers and taught. On "Solomon's Porch," their stated place of meeting: see on iii. 11.

14 women. The gospel treats women as equal in privileges with men (see Gal. iii. 28). This was then somewhat new to both Jews and Gentiles.

15 beds and couches. See note on Luke v. 24. Perhaps, "beds [for the rich] and mats [for the poor]."

Peter. As the most prominent of the apostles. It is implied that the expectation of healing was not in vain. Many things may serve as links between the believing recipient and the instrument of God's blessing. The shadow, a look (Numb. xxi. 8), the hem of the robe (Matt. ix. 20), a handkerchief (xix. 11, 12), serve as well as a word or a touch.

17 indignation. "Jealousy."

19 the angel. Or, "an angel."

20 all the words of this life. The whole doctrine of *salvation* by Jesus (cp. xiii. 26); referred to especially as a revelation of life.

21 early in the morning. Rather, "about daybreak."

all the senate. Lit., "all the *eldership*."

24 the captain of the Temple. See note, iv. 1.

they doubted of them. Rather, "they were quite at a loss about them"; *i.e.*, probably, "about the apostles."

25 Professor G. T. Stokes calls attention to the accuracy of detail in St. Luke's narrative. Had the Sanhedrin been themselves meeting in the Temple, they would have known at once when they assembled that the apostles were preaching there. But only a few years before this incident, they had moved from the Temple into the city (cp. iv. 5).

26 for they feared the people. The words give the reason why they dared not put forth violence. But it would have been needless: the apostles came unresistingly.

28 bring this man's blood upon us. The tide of popular feeling was running so strongly in favour of the followers of Jesus that the rulers were afraid of becoming victims to the indignation of the people: see ver. 26; iv. 21. To this fear may have been added their own secret consciousness of wrong-doing.

30 The God of our fathers. Who gave to our fathers the covenant upon which you pride yourselves, and which is really fulfilled in Jesus.

31 with His right hand. Or, "to His right hand."

a Prince. See note on iii. 15, where the same Greek word, ἀρχηγόν, is used.

33 cut to the heart, etc. Literally, "they were sawn through (excessively irritated), and were consulting to slay them." But they were stopped by Gamaliel's prudence.

35 what ye intend to do. Rather, "what ye are about to do" (R.V.). The speaker is evidently the Gamaliel mentioned in the Talmud as the grandson of the famous Hillel, and by Josephus (*Antiq.* xx. 9, §§ 4,7). He was a Pharisee, unrivalled in that age for his knowledge of the law; a distinguished teacher (having Paul at one time among his pupils: see xxii. 3), and a man of enlarged views and tolerant spirit. His speech is a masterpiece of prudence. The advice, however prudent, was temporising. It was the duty of Gamaliel and the rest to inquire not what would succeed, but what was right.

36 Theudas. Josephus (*Antiq.* xx. 5, §§ 1) mentions a Theudas who raised an insurrection, being followed by "a very great multitude," but was put down and beheaded. This, however, was at least ten years after the speech of Gamaliel; and there are other circumstances which do not agree with his account. This must therefore have been another Theudas; the name was common, being a form of *Judas* (cp. Matt. x. 3 and Luke vi. 16); and insurrections were numerous about this time.

37 Judas of Galilee. Josephus (*Antiq.* xviii. 1, § 1) says that this Judas was a "Gaulonite of a city whose name was Gamala." Gaulonitis was a district east of Galilee, beyond the Jordan. But Josephus especially speaks of him three times as "of Galilee" (*Antiq.* xx. 5, § 2; *Wars,* ii. 8, § 1; 17, § 8). Probably he was a Gaulonite by birth and a Galilæan in the sense of his insurrection.

the taxing. Rather, "the enrolment" (R.V.): see note on Luke ii. 2. Judas excited the people to resist the census (A.D. 6) as being an introduction to slavery.

38 Refrain from these men, etc. See note, ver. 35.

40 to him they agreed. The Pharisaic element in the council prevailed over the Sadducean, but the latter secured at last the infliction of punishment on the apostles.

beaten. Scourging was a common and disgraceful punishment among the Jews (Deut. xxv. 2; Matt. x. 17; 2 Cor. xi. 24). Gamaliel, although not having advised the scourging, may have consented to it in order to prevent severer measures.

CHAPTER VI

1 was multiplied. Rather, as R.V., "was multiplying."

Grecians. The "Grecians," or Hellenists, were Jews who had been brought up in foreign countries, who generally spoke Greek and used the Septuagint version of the Old Testament. The "Hebrews" were chiefly Jews of Palestine, who spoke the vernacular Aramaic dialect, and used the Hebrew Scriptures. Between these two classes there had long been jealousy, arising from the high pretensions of the Hebrew Jews (particularly those of Jerusalem), who claimed superiority on account of their residence in the Holy Land, their use of the sacred tongue, and their stricter observance of the ritual worship.

because their widows were neglected. Rather, "that their widows were being neglected" or overlooked.

widows. Widows and fatherless children were special objects of care among the Jews and the early Christians (Exod. xxii. 22; Deut. x. 18; 1 Tim. v. 3–11).

2 It is not reason, etc. Rather, as R.V., "It is not fit" (Greek, "pleasing"). They had undertaken the task not from choice nor from a sense of fitness, but only from necessity; and it was now time to give it up. "Serving tables" may refer to the distribution either of food (as in xvi. 34) or of money (Matt. xxi. 12).

3 look ye out. "The people nominated while the apostles appointed. . . . The Church from the beginning, and in the Acts of the Apostles, clearly showed that its government was not to be an absolute clerical despotism, but a free Christian republic, where clergy and people were to take counsel together. . . . The representatives of the Emperor and other Christian princes took their seats in the Council of Trent, jointly with bishops and other ecclesiastics; and it was only at the Vatican Council of 1870 that this last lingering trace of lay rights finally disappeared" (*G. T. Stokes*).

of honest report. Lit., "attested," *i.e.*, of good repute.

5 they chose Stephen, etc. These seven men, elected by the whole company of believers, all bore Greek names: seeming to intimate that they were Hellenists, as being called to serve that particular section of the Church.

Nicolas a proselyte. As Nicolas is particularly said to be "a proselyte," it is probable that he was the only one of that class among the seven. Nowhere in Scripture are the seven called deacons; nor does the word occur at all, as a name of office, in the Acts of the Apostles. But the word *serve,* in ver. 2, is from the same root as the word *deacon,* and it is most probable that the office was founded upon this appointment: see note on 1 Tim. iii. 8. Of these seven, only Stephen and Philip are mentioned elsewhere in Scripture; Philip as "an evangelist," and "one of the seven" (xxi. 8: cp. viii. 5, 26).

6 they laid their hands on them. The imposition of hands was an ancient and well-understood practice, in pronouncing a blessing (Gen. xlviii. 14–20), in appointing to an office (Numb. xxvii. 18–21), or in transferring guilt (Lev. iii. 2). In the New Testament it is usually connected with the communication of the special gifts of the Holy Spirit: see 2 Tim. i. 6.

7 increased, etc. Lit., "was increasing . . . was multiplying . . . were becoming obedient."

8 faith. Or, "grace." Divine "grace" was the source of "power," partly shown in "signs."

9 [the synagogue] of the Libertines. There

were at Jerusalem a great number of synagogues for the use of foreign Jews. Five are here specified. "The Libertines" were families of Jews who had been slaves to Romans, and had been freed by their masters, some of them acquiring the rights of Roman citizens. Some scholars, however, with a change of two letters in the Greek, read here, for "Libertines," "Libyans," meaning "African Jews."

Cyrenians. From Upper Libya, where Jews are said to have constituted a fourth of the population.

Alexandrians. Alexandria was at that period one of the great marts of intercourse between the East and the West, and the chief seat of the Hellenistic Jews: see note on ii. 10.

Cilicia. Of this synagogue Saul of Tarsus would be a member.

Asia. Part of what is now Asia Minor; the eastern coast of the Ægean: see on ii. 9.

11 Then they suborned men. Cp. Matt. xxvi. 59–61.

12 they stirred up the people. Hitherto the people had taken part with the apostles (iv. 21; v. 13, 26). But the charge made against Stephen was peculiarly fitted to excite their anger.

13 this holy place. Probably, the Temple: cp. Matt. xxvi. 60, and note. The truth which gave some colour to this accusation appears in vii. 48–50.

15 as it had been the face of an angel. With an angelic expression: a calmness, dignity, and holy joy, arising from his consciousness of God's presence and approval.

CHAPTER VII

2 The God of glory. God who manifests His glory among us (see Exod. xiii. 21, 22; Rom. ix. 4; ver. 55) in the Shekinah. But this display of that glory was made to Abraham in Mesopotamia, before he was circumcised.

Charran. "Haran." See notes on Gen. xi. 31. This first call of Abraham is alluded to in Gen. xv. 7; Neh. ix. 7. The call (related Gen. xii. 1) was given to him in Haran.

3 the land which I shall show thee. Rather, "whatsoever land I shall show thee"; an abbreviation of the LXX of Gen. xii. 1: cp. Heb. xi. 8.

4 when his father was dead. On the dates of these events, see note on Gen. xi. 26.

6 And God spake on this wise. To Abraham (see Gen. xv. 13, 14), and to Moses (see Exod. iii. 12). Both quotations are made freely from the Septuagint.

four hundred years. See Gen. xv. 13; Exod. xii. 40; Gal. iii. 17, and notes.

8 covenant of circumcision. The covenant of which circumcision was the outward sign and confirmation (see Gen. xvii. 1–14, and notes) came after the great promise and covenant (see Gen. xii. 1–3, and notes), and therefore could not be essential to them: see a similar line of argument in Gal. iii. 6–18.

9 God was with him. "God was with him" whom our fathers hated and sold.

12 first. That is, before he himself went.

14 threescore and fifteen souls. See note on Gen. xlvi. 27, which Stephen ("as a Hellenistic Jew, naturally," *Plumptre*) quotes from the Septuagint; the variations in numbers not affecting his argument.

15 So Jacob went down into Egypt, etc. This may mean, "Jacob and our fathers (his twelve sons) died in Egypt; and they (*i.e.*, our fathers) were removed to Shechem." Jacob himself was buried at Machpelah (see Gen. l. 13). Jerome says that in his day the tombs of the twelve were shown at Shechem.

16 Emmor. Or, "Hamor." It was *Jacob* who made this purchase (see Gen. xxxiii. 19; Josh. xxiv. 32). Some suppose that Abraham had bought the land for his altar at Shechem (Gen. xii. 6, 7), and that Jacob recovered it by force (Gen. xlviii. 22), and bought more. Some regard the name "Abraham" as a mistake of an early transcriber; others suppose that Stephen followed some traditional account, which is not corrected, as the error does not affect his argument. Professor Stokes (*Expositor's Bible*) says that if there are minor inaccuracies in Stephen's speech, it is to be remembered that it was an extempore address. The very inaccuracies in the speech constitute an argument for the truthfulness of the writer of the Acts.

17 when. Rather, "as," or "in proportion as."

19 so that they cast out. Lit., as R.V., "that they should cast out." The *result* of Pharaoh's cruel oppression.

20 In which time. Just at the time of their severest oppression.

exceeding fair. Lit., "fair unto God," a Hebraism; "divinely beautiful" (*Moffatt*).

22 was learned. Rather, "was instructed," R.V. (the word *learn* being sometimes in Old English used actively, equivalent to *teach*), being brought up as the adopted son of Pharaoh's daughter. The "wisdom" of Egypt was proverbial: see 1 Kings iv. 30; Isa. xix. 11–13.

23 visit. This word almost always includes the idea of *assisting*. Cp. Gen. l. 24, 25.

25 for (and) **he supposed his brethren would have understood,** etc. They "understood" his claims, but not God's intention respecting him. So the Jews understood not our Lord's authority: see iii. 17, and note.

would deliver them. Rather, as R.V., "was giving them deliverance"; the process having actually begun.

29 Madian. Or, "Midian": see Exod. ii. 15, and note.

30–34. See Exod. iii. 1–10, and notes.

30 an angel. See Gen. xvi. 7; Isa. lxiii. 9; Mal. iii. 1, and notes.

35 This. The word here rendered "this," is emphatically repeated through vers. 35–38. "*This* Moses whom they rejected," "*this man* God commissioned," "*This man* led them out by doing wonders," etc.; "*This* is the Moses who said," etc.; "*This* it is who was in the Church in the wilderness." Stephen reminds his hearers that their fathers treated the ancient deliverer just as they have treated the Great Prophet (37) whom Moses predicted.

37 This is that Moses, which said, etc. Not Stephen, therefore, but those who rejected Jesus, dishonoured Moses: cp. John v. 46, 47.

38 the church. Or, "the congregation"; *i.e.*, of Israel; as in Deut. xviii. 16; xxiii. 1-3, LXX.

the lively oracles. Rather, "living words or utterances"; not dead letters, but living and operative; partly because the Law awakens the conscience, partly because its threatenings and promises are sure of fulfilment.

39 into Egypt. See Exod. xxxii. 4; and cp. Numb. xi. 5, 6.

42 turned. In anger: see Isa. lxiii. 10; Rom. i. 28.

and gave them up to worship the host of heaven. This is not mentioned in the Pentateuch; but see Amos v. 25–27, and notes. Stephen's quotation is from the Septuagint, excepting that in ver. 43 he substitutes "beyond Babylon," for "beyond Damascus," naturally specifying the actual place of exile.

the book of the prophets. The twelve minor prophets were regarded as one "book."

44 tabernacle of witness. See Numb. xvii. 8. They had "the tabernacle of the testimony" (R.V.), but they preferred the *tabernacle of Moloch* (43).

45 Which also our fathers that came after. Or, "Which also our fathers, receiving (it) in succession, 'in their turn' (R.V.), brought in with *Jesus*," *i.e., Joshua.*

unto the days of David. To be connected with "brought in," *i.e.*, the tabernacle was brought in by Joshua, and retained until the days of David.

46 desired to find. Rather, "asked for himself [permission] to find a habitation." The tabernacle existed already; David desired to build a temple: see Psa. cxxxii., and notes.

48 temples made with hands. The builder of the Temple himself declared at its dedication (see 1 Kings viii. 27, and note) that the Most High dwelleth not in temples made with hands; as likewise saith the prophet, "Heaven is my throne," etc.: see notes on Isa. lxvi. 1, 2, here freely quoted. The omission of the word *temples* in the original (according to best authorities), suggests that God dwells not in anything which man can construct. R.V. supplies *houses.*

51 stiffnecked and uncircumcised. In language taken from reproofs and appeals to ancient Israel by Moses (Deut. ix. 6, 13; x. 16), and the prophets (Jer. vi. 10; ix. 26), Stephen charges the council with heathenish ignorance, and obstinate disobedience.

as your fathers did. Referring, perhaps, to Isa. lxiii. 10.

52 Which of the prophets, etc.? Cp. 2 Chron. xxxvi. 16; Matt. xxiii. 31–36; Luke xiii. 31–35, and notes.

53 by the disposition of angels. Rather, "as the ordinances of angels," "as it was transmitted by angels" (*Moffatt*); not Moses only, but angels also being employed to communicate these Divine arrangements and precepts: see Deut. xxxiii. 2; Psa. lxviii. 17; Gal. iii. 19. This aggravates the guilt of those who broke them: see Heb. ii. 2, 3.

54 cut to the heart. See note on v. 33.

55 being full of the Holy Ghost. Not only at this time. The word used in original for *being,* denotes what was habitual and permanent.

standing. The word seems to imply active interposition to help, as Mediator and King, or readiness to receive His persecuted servant. Generally the representation is that of Jesus seated at the right hand of God, in calm and glorious repose (Psa. cx. 1; Matt. xxvi. 64). "To sit," says *Augustine*, "is the mark of one who reigns and judges; to stand, of a warrior, helper, and advocate."

56 Son of man. This appellation, which our Lord's disciples do not elsewhere apply to Him, is used here perhaps with reference to His own claim and prediction before the same unrighteous tribunal (Luke xxii. 69). There is a suggestion of the tenderest sympathy in this revelation of Christ in His human nature to the dying saint.

57 Then they cried out with a loud voice, etc. Stephen's concluding words, like those of our Lord (see Matt. xxvi. 65, 66, and note), gave colour to the charge of blasphemy; and upon this he was immediately (perhaps even without a formal sentence) stoned as a blasphemer, in the manner prescribed by the Law (Lev. xxiv. 10–14). See, for a full account of the process of trial and stoning, Dr. John Lightfoot's *Horæ Hebraicæ.*

58 the witnesses. See vi. 13. The witnesses were required by the law to begin the execution: see Deut. xvii. 7. To do this they threw off their loose outer garments.

Saul. See ch. xxii. 20.

59 they stoned Stephen. The punishment prescribed for blasphemy (Lev. xxiv. 16; Deut. xvii. 3). The act was illegal (John xviii. 31); but wild outbreaks of the kind were not unusual, especially in the absence of the governor. Pilate was probably in Rome at the time.

calling upon [God] and saying. Rather, "invoking and saying," etc.; for the prayer is addressed to the Lord Jesus (cp. i. 24, and note): cp. ix. 21, and note on i. 24.

receive my spirit. Cp. Luke xxiii. 46, and note. Stephen expresses the same confidence in our Lord, as our Lord had expressed in the Father.

60 Lord, lay not this sin to their charge. Cp. Luke xxiii. 34. No parallel to this prayer can be found out of Christian history. One answer to it is recorded in ch. ix. "The Church owes Paul to the prayer of Stephen" (*Augustine*).

fell asleep. This term seems to be used in touching contrast with all the outward circumstances of the occasion.

CHAPTER VIII

1 all. If literally all went, some soon returned (see ix. 26–30). Probably all the more active disciples fled, "except the apostles": see xi. 19.

except the apostles. It was plainly right that the leaders should remain at the post of danger.

3 he made havoc. Authorised by the Sanhedrin: see xxvi. 10, 11.

into every house. Rather, "into the houses"; "haling" (Old English for "hauling"), or forcibly dragging them thence. Cp. xxvi. 11, and 1 Tim. i. 13.

4 Therefore, etc. Rather, "so then"; referring to ver. 1. That which seemed to threaten the extinction of the Church only hastened the fulfilment of our Lord's command (i. 8), to carry His gospel "throughout Samaria and Galilee," and even to distant parts of the world (see xi. 19). For "went everywhere," read, as R.V., "went about," *i.e.*, from place to place.

5 Philip. Not Philip the apostle (see ver. 1); but one of the colleagues of Stephen (vi. 5; xxi. 8).

to the city of Samaria. Authorities are divided as to whether we should read "*a* city of Samaria," or "*the* city of Samaria." The extension of the gospel to Samaria was an epoch in the history of the Church, marking the transition point between its promulgation among the Jews and among the Gentiles.

6 the miracles. Rather, "the signs" (R.V.).

9 used sorcery. Or, "practised magic arts"; perhaps using superior scientific knowledge, and even tricks of legerdemain, to impose on the people. Hence his usual appellation, "Simon Magus."

bewitched. Rather, "amazed" (R.V.), and so in ver. 11.

10 the great power of God. "The Power of God, called the Great Power."

13 Then Simon himself believed also. He was convinced that the signs were real, and the doctrine consequently true. It is not said that his heart was changed.

wondered. Or, "was amazed," R.V. The same word is used that had described the feelings of the Samaritans towards Simon (9, 11). The impression made upon this skilful magician was a striking attestation to the reality of the miracles wrought by Philip.

14 Peter and John. Peter and John were sent probably to examine and confirm Philip's work, and to communicate the miraculous gifts of the Holy Spirit (15). Thus a very important step was taken (see Matt. x. 5, and note) towards abolishing the distinction between Jew and Gentile. It is observable that "the apostles," in their collective capacity, here exercise the function of rule, and thus give commission to two of their number to represent them. "Peter, then, was the messenger of the Apostles—the sent one, not the sender" (*Stokes*). "No single apostle, even though it were a Peter or a John, was *elevated above* the whole company of the apostles; but each member was *subordinate* to it. The Romish doctrine of the primacy of the apostle Peter is here decisively refuted" (*Lange*).

16 in the name. Rather, "into the name."

20 Thy money perish with thee, etc. An outburst of indignant horror at the proposal; conveying a solemn warning against attempting to make religion a means of worldly gain.

because thou hast thought, etc. Or, "didst think to purchase the gift of God with money." Simon evidently hoped to make a gain by the transaction. Hence the word "simony."

21 this matter. Lit., "this word." Either "this doctrine or gospel, which we preach"; or the gift of the Spirit.

23 the gall of bitterness. That is, malignant depravity; the poison of the serpent being supposed to be formed in the *gall*: cp. Deut. xxxii. 33; Job xx. 14; Rom. iii. 13. "The bondage of iniquity" seems to mean confirmed habits of sin.

24 Pray ye to the Lord for me, etc. Simon, like Pharaoh (Exod. viii. 28, etc.), appears only to have been anxious to avert dreaded punishment. The traditions respecting his after-life are all doubtful.

26 the angel. Rather, "*an* angel."

Gaza. The southernmost city of Palestine (Gen. x. 19), on the route between Syria and Egypt. As there were, and still are, several roads from Jerusalem to Gaza, the words, "which is desert" (or thinly peopled), may have been spoken by the angel to point out which of the routes Philip was to take. Or they may be added by Luke in order to bring the scene more vividly before the readers.

27 Ethiopia. "Ethiopia" (corresponding in part to the Hebrew *Cush*) here designates the kingdom of Meroë, in Upper Egypt or Nubia. It was governed at this period by a succession of queens, all bearing the hereditary title of "Candace" (see Pliny, *Nat. Hist.* vi. 29; and Strabo, xvii.).

28 read. Reading aloud (30), as Orientals often do even when reading only to themselves.

32 The place of the Scripture which he read was this, etc. See notes on Isa. liii. 7, 8.

35 opened his mouth. That is, he began a regular discourse, which must have included, not only the person and work, but also the commands of our Lord (36).

37 The verse is quoted by Irenæus, Cyprian, Jerome, and Augustine, but is omitted in the best MSS. "The insertion," says *Alford*, "seems to have been made to suit the formularies of the baptismal liturgies, it being considered strange that the eunuch should have been baptised without some such confession."

38 and he baptised him. The admission of this descendant of Ham to the Church of Christ, was one instance of the fulfilment of Isa. lvi. 3–6, the closing portion of that great prophecy of Messiah which he was reading (32, 33): see notes on Isa. lvi. 3–8.

39 he went on his way rejoicing. The gospel was thus carried in one direction "to the uttermost ends of the earth" (see i. 8).

40 Azotus. Or, Ashdod: see note on Isa. xx. 1.

all the cities. Including, probably, Lydda and Joppa (see ix. 32, 36).

Cæsarea. Cæsarea was a large city, built by Herod the Great, on the west coast of Palestine. Lying almost midway between Joppa and Ptolemais, and having a capacious artificial harbour, it became an important seaport. It was at this time the chief residence of the Roman governor, and contained a large number of Gentiles. Philip appears to have made it the centre of his labours, for he is found there about twenty-five years afterwards (xxi. 8, 9).

CHAPTER IX

1 yet breathing out, etc. The narrative is resumed from viii. 3. The interval was probably about a year.

2 desired of him letters to Damascus. The ecclesiastical supremacy of the high priest and Sanhedrin was acknowledged by the rulers of the synagogues in foreign countries; and the exercise of discipline over their fellow-countrymen was, to some extent, allowed by the Roman and other governments. Damascus contained a large number of Jews, and had probably just come under the rule of Aretas, king of Arabia: see 2 Cor. xi. 32.

of this way. R.V., literally, "of the Way." The term frequently recurs in this book (xix. 9, 32; xxii. 4; xxiv. 14); and describes Christianity either as a course of life, or as "the way of salvation" (xvi. 17), or as "the way of the Lord" (xviii. 25).

bound unto Jerusalem. The alleged crime being too grave for the jurisdiction of the local tribunals.

3 shined round about him (flashed around him) **a light,** etc. "Above the brightness of the sun" at "mid-day" (xxvi. 13; xxii. 6).

4 saying. In the Hebrew tongue (xxvi. 14).

why persecutest thou me? Our Lord identifies Himself with His suffering disciples: see His own declaration in Matt. xxv. 40. The appeal calls Saul to account respecting the motive of his conduct: "What injury, great or small, hast thou sustained from me that you should do these things?" (*Chrysostom*).

5 Who art thou, Lord? Saul *saw*, as well as heard, Him who spoke to him: see vers. 17, 27; xxii. 14; xxvi. 16; 1 Cor. ix. 1; xv. 8; where the context clearly relates to actual sight of the Lord's person. So that he became a witness of the Lord's resurrection.

I am Jesus. "Jesus," whom you scorn as "the Nazarene" (xxii. 8). See notes on the fuller account in xxvi. The words from "it is hard for thee" (5) to "and the Lord said unto him" (6) are not found in any ancient copies.

7 stood speechless, etc. They, like Saul, beheld the light (xxii. 9), and stood still; they also heard the sound, and fell to the earth (xxvi. 14): but they neither saw the Lord, nor distinguished the words uttered (xxii. 9). Cp. John xii. 28, and note.

8 when his eyes were opened. More correctly, "though his eyes remained open."

9 three days. Cp. 1 Sam. xxx. 12, and note.

10 a certain disciple. A man highly esteemed by the Jews (xxii. 12), and "a devout man according to the law" (cp. ii. 5; viii. 2).

11 which is called Straight. A straight street is rare in Eastern cities; but there is still at Damascus a street named "Straight," running through the whole city from east to west. The traditional "house of Judas," however, is not in this street.

Tarsus. The capital of Cilicia in Asia Minor, on the river Cydnus, and about 10 miles from the sea. It was made a city by Antony, who resided there for a time and was visited there by Cleopatra (*W. M. Ramsay*).

he prayeth. The word literally means, "he is praying"—now, in the very act.

12 hath seen in a vision. The two visions confirmed each other, like those of Cornelius and Peter: see x.

13 I have heard by many. Fugitives from Jerusalem would spread the tidings; and letters or messengers from those who remained in the holy city would have put the disciples in Damascus on their guard.

15 a chosen vessel. A chosen instrument: cp. 2 Tim. ii. 20, 21.

17 putting his hands on him. For healing (12), not for apostleship. Paul received the apostleship directly and alone from Christ (Gal. i. 1, 11, 12).

22 proving that this is very Christ. "Proving, by comparison" (συμβιβάζων) of the prophecies and types of the Messiah with the facts of the history of Jesus of Nazareth, "that He is *the Christ.*"

23 after that many days were fulfilled. Probably after "three years," including the time which he spent in Arabia: cp. vers. 19–30 with Gal. i. 16–18, and notes.

24 they watched the gates. See 2 Cor. xi. 32, 33, and note. The Jews instigated the Gentile authorities to take this measure.

25 let him down by (through) **the wall in a basket** (hamper). Through the window of a house upon the city wall (2 Cor. xi. 33: cp. Josh. ii. 15; 1 Sam. xix. 12). It is still customary in Eastern countries to build houses upon the city walls, with windows looking out upon the country.

26 to Jerusalem. He went thither partly to see Peter (Gal. i. 18), with whom he was now to be associated in the apostleship.

believed not that he was a disciple. They had doubtless heard something of his conversion, but doubted his sincerity. They may have suspected that the alleged conversion was a feint, the more easily to betray them. Barnabas, who was highly esteemed in the Church (iv. 36; xi. 22), testified to his conversion, and to his claims as one who had seen the Lord, and had been faithful in His service.

27 to the apostles. That is, to Peter and James (Gal. i. 18, 19). The others probably were absent from Jerusalem.

28 And he was with them, etc. He remained in Jerusalem fifteen days (Gal. i. 18).

29 the Grecians. The Hellenistic Jews (see note on vi. 1); the same class, and possibly some of the same persons, with whom Stephen had contended (vi. 9).

30 [Which] when the brethren knew, etc. Paul was unwilling to go; but the Lord in a vision commanded him to yield: see xxii. 17–21.

Cæsarea. From Cæsarea he might sail to Seleuceia, and from there go by land to Tarsus. At Tarsus he appears to have remained a considerable time (see xi. 25), during which he probably founded the churches in Cilicia (xv. 23, 41).

31 Then had the churches rest. "The Church" (which is the correct reading) collectively enjoyed a time of peace, partly perhaps from the check given to persecution by the conversion of Saul, partly because the attention of the Jews was called off to other subjects through the mad attempt of the Emperor Caligula to place his statue in the Temple—a design which only the entreaties of Herod Agrippa induced him to abandon (Jos. *Ant.* xviii. 8, § 6).

throughout all Judæa and Galilee and Samaria. The spread and organisation of the Christian community indicates much zealous and continued labour of which no account is given in the history.

edified. Or, "built up," *i.e.*, in faith and piety.

the comfort of the Holy Ghost. The word used for "comfort," kindred with "Paraclete," implies *exhortation* and *encouragement*, and should probably be connected with "multiplied"; lit., "was being multiplied through the comfort," etc.

32 Lydda. Lydda, anciently called *Lod* (1 Chron. viii. 12; Neh. vii. 37), was about five miles from the seaport town of Joppa. It was afterwards called Diospolis, and now *Lud.*

34 Jesus Christ maketh thee whole. An attestation to the actual presence and Divine power of Jesus; a striking proof that in His state of exaltation He is still carrying on the work of mercy that He wrought in a state of humiliation (*Lange*).

35 (the) **Saron.** In "the plain of Sharon": see 1 Chron. xxvii. 29.

36 Joppa. Respecting Joppa, see note on Jonah i. 3.

Tabitha, which by interpretation is called Dorcas. "Tabitha" and "Dorcas" are the Aramaic and Greek names of the *gazelle;* on which see Prov. v. 19, and note. On the double name, see note on i. 23.

39 made. Rather, "used to make." The "coats" and "garments" (or "cloaks") include almost the whole dress: see Matt. v. 40, and note. The widows would no doubt be wearing them.

40 put them all forth. As Elijah and Elisha, and his Divine Lord had done: see 1 Kings xvii. 19; 2 Kings iv. 33; Matt. ix. 25.

43 he tarried many days in Joppa. Joppa, being a large seaport, would afford many opportunities for spreading the gospel.

CHAPTER X

1 Cornelius. Cornelius was the name of a large Roman clan, including several noble and distinguished families.

band. Or, "cohort" (corresponding nearly to our *regiment*), composed of natives of Italy; distinguished from the rest of the troops under Roman command, which were raised in the province.

2 a devout man. There were at this time many persons who had forsaken idolatry for the worship of the one true God. To this class Cornelius, and probably most of the early Gentile converts to Christianity, belonged (see ver. 34).

which gave much alms to the people. That is, to the Jewish people: cp. Luke vii. 5. His good reputation among the Jews might help to prepare the Hebrew Christians to welcome him into the Church.

3 evidently. That is, "distinctly," or while awake (see also ver. 7): not in a dream or a trance (ver. 10; xxii. 17).

about the ninth hour of the day. At three p.m., the hour of evening prayer (iii. 1). As the mission of Peter was an answer to his prayers (31), it is probable that he had been asking Divine instruction respecting the claims of Jesus, of whom he had heard (37).

5 Joppa. A distance of thirty miles. The messengers started the same evening, and arrived at Joppa the next afternoon.

6 whose house is by the sea side. The business of a tanner was regarded by the Jews as almost unclean, and was not allowed to be carried on within the walls of cities.

7 a devout soldier. Like his master, and therefore fully informed of the purpose of his errand.

9 upon the housetop. See note on 1 Sam. ix. 25.

about the sixth hour. About noon, the second hour for prayer.

10 he fell into a trance. The form of the vision corresponded with Peter's hunger.

11 knit at the four corners. Lit., "tied by four ends," *i.e.*, or cords, reaching into the heavens above. The Spanish version (Hispano-Americana) has "bajalo por las quartas puntas" ("let down by the four corners").

13 kill, and eat. Making no distinction between clean and unclean: see Lev. xi., and notes.

16 thrice. See a reason for such a repetition in Gen. xli. 32.

17 before the gate. Or, "at the porch" or "vestibule," forming the entrance to the inner court.

20 doubting nothing, etc. Making no difficulty about visiting a Gentile; "for I have sent them."

22 the centurion. Rather, "*a* centurion"; not yet known to Peter.

24 And Cornelius waited for them. Rather, "Now, Cornelius was waiting for (*or*, expecting) them."

25 as Peter was coming in. Rather, "When Peter had come in."

worshipped. Cornelius recognises in Peter an ambassador of the true God, and, in conformity with Roman ideas, renders him Divine honour. Peter, however, makes it clear that not even a Divine commission could entitle its bearer to receive worship. Such honour must be reserved for God alone. Our Lord did not decline it.

27 talked with him. Or, "conversed with him" familiarly.

28 unlawful. The distinction between clean and unclean meats, and the prohibition of alliances and marriages between the Israelites and heathen nations (Lev. xi. 1–47; Deut. vii. 1–8), had come to be regarded as forbidding all social intercourse with Gentiles. See Josephus, *Cont. Ap.* ii. 28; Juvenal, *Sat.* xiv. 103; Tacit. *Hist.* v. 5.

30 fasting. This word is omitted by the best authorities.

34 God is no respecter of persons, etc. A new and important application of an old truth: see Deut. x. 17; Gal. ii. 6.

35 accepted with Him. Or, as R.V., "acceptable unto Him."

36 The word which [God] sent, etc. This verse is connected in sense with the preceding. God receives the pious of *every nation*; for though He first sent His "word" to the children of Israel with its glad news of peace through Jesus Christ, yet Christ is the appointed and predicted Lord of all men, not "of the Jews only, but of the Gentiles" also: see Psa. ii.; lxxii. 8–11; Isa. lv. 4, 5: Dan. ii. 44; vii. 13, 14.

37 that word. The word here rendered "word" differs from that in ver. 36. Meaning "the matter" or actual facts, as compared with "the history." Philip's preaching (viii. 40) had made the gospel well known at Cæsarea.

38 with power. His Divine goodness, working through His Divine power, to break Satan's tyranny over men's bodies (Luke xiii. 16) and souls (2 Tim. ii. 26) was the true evidence that Jesus was God's anointed (Isa. lxi. 1–3), and that God was with Him.

39 whom they slew and hanged, etc. Better as R.V., "whom also they slew, hanging Him."

on a tree. A cross, or gibbet; lit., "on a piece of wood"; the Spanish version has "en un madero."

41 not to all the people. Before His death our Lord taught and wrought His miracles in public; but when the people by rejecting Him had shown that no evidence could affect them (see Luke xvi. 31; John xii. 37), the ocular proof of His resurrection was given only to Divinely chosen and competent witnesses. See note on Matt. xxviii. 1.

42 quick and dead. That is, "the *living* and the dead": see 1 Thess. iv. 16, 17; 1 Cor. xv. 51, 52.

44 the Holy Ghost fell on all them. The gift of the Holy Spirit on this occasion ("while Peter was yet speaking") was attended by many of the same signs as at Pentecost (see ver. 46; xi. 15). This Divine interposition conclusively proves that outward rites, whether Jewish or Christian, are not essential to admission to gospel privileges.

47 Can any man forbid (the) water, etc.? It was not for men to withhold the baptism of water when God had given the baptism of the Spirit.

48 he commanded, etc. See notes on John iv. 2; 1 Cor. i. 17.

CHAPTER XI

1 in Judæa. Lit., "throughout Judæa."

2 And when Peter was come up. Accompanied by the brethren from Joppa (ver. 12) who might corroborate all his statements.

they that were of the circumcision. Jewish believers.

4 rehearsed [the matter] from the beginning. R.V., "began, and expounded [the matter] unto them in order." "It is precisely the fitting-in of single events in their history which produces so overpowering an impression, the separate parts fitting together, so that one point illustrates and confirms another, while the whole incontestably bespeaks the will of God" (*Lange*).

5–15. See notes on x. 9–44.

16 with the Holy Ghost. The gift of the Holy Spirit to believing Gentiles clearly showed that they were included in the Lord's promise here quoted from i. 5. To "forbid" the sign where God had granted the grace would have been to "forbid," or oppose, God.

18 Then, etc. Unlikely as it seemed to us

19 Phenice. Phœnicia, a district between Lebanon and the sea. It had been visited by our Lord (Matt. xv. 21–28).

Cyprus. A large island, lying off the coast of Syria. It was the birthplace of Barnabas: see iv. 36.

Antioch. Antioch on the Orontes, now *Antakia*, was the capital of Syria, and the residence of the proconsul of the province. It was one of the largest cities of the world. It contained a mixed population, including many Jews, who resided in a separate quarter, under their own governor. The Church in Antioch long retained a pre-eminence among the Eastern churches.

20 Cyrene. See note on ii. 10.

Grecians. See note on vi. 1. If this reading were retained, it would simply show that the gospel was widely extended among the Hellenic Jews through the death of the Hellenist Stephen. But most editors, on the authority of several early MSS., and on internal grounds of probability, read "Greeks" (so R.V.), which would mean "Gentiles," in distinction from the "Jews," mentioned in ver. 19. According to this reading, there is here a further extension of the gospel among the Gentiles; even more signal than the case of Cornelius. For the centurion, although not a Jew, had ceased to be an idolater. These "Greeks" in Antioch would be *heathens*.

22 Barnabas. Barnabas, as a Hellenist Jew of Cyprus, and a man of generous and candid disposition (iv. 37; ix. 27). was peculiarly fitted for this mission. On the supposition that these converts were heathen Gentiles, the mission would be one of peculiar delicacy.

23 Who, when he came, etc. Barnabas, being "a good man" (ver. 24), was anxious only to recognise the signs of the Divine working ("the grace of God"). When these appeared, he suffered no Jewish prejudices or Church traditions to stand in his way. This decision of Barnabas was, in fact, the opening of the kingdom of Christ to Gentile heathendom.

25 to seek Saul. The evangelists "from Cyprus and Cyrene" had begun a work which needed to be consolidated and continued by instruction. They were *preachers*; the Church at Antioch now needed a *teacher*. Saul of Tarsus, from his intellectual and spiritual gifts, his special commission, and his long preparation, appeared to his old comrade Barnabas the man most fitted for the task. As therefore Barnabas had introduced Saul to the apostles and to the Church in Jerusalem, so now by the same instrumentality Saul is brought into connexion with this rising Church in Antioch, henceforth the metropolis of Gentile Christianity, and the second great centre of missionary operations.

26 Christians. This name occurs only in two other passages of Scripture (xxvi. 28; 1 Pet. iv. 16), where it is applied to the disciples by unbelievers. The Jews would never have given them a name derived from that of the Messiah: cp. John xix. 21. It probably originated with the heathen population of Antioch, when the converts became a numerous and important body. At first probably the name was given in scorn, but it was afterwards adopted and gloried in by Christians themselves.

28 throughout all the world. Or, "upon the whole inhabited earth"; a phrase often used for the Roman empire (see note on Luke ii. 1, 2). During the reign of Claudius (A.D. 41–54), the different parts of the empire suffered successively from great famines, some of which were particularly severe in Judæa, about A.D. 44, 45. See Joseph. *Antiq.* xx 26.

30 elders. The office of elder (or presbyter) seems to have been adopted from the Jewish synagogue, and to have included the twofold duties of teaching and ruling; on which account, in the New Testament, elders are also called bishops or overseers.

Barnabas and Saul. This was Saul's second visit to Jerusalem after his conversion. See note xii. 25.

CHAPTER XII

1 Herod the king. This was Herod Agrippa I., an able and popular prince, son of Aristobulus and Bernice, and grandson of Herod the Great. He had been brought up at Rome, and by successive grants from Caligula and Claudius had become king of all Palestine. He courted the Jews by professing to be zealous for the law; but was unprincipled and licentious, and adopted many heathen customs. See Joseph. *Antiq.* xix. 7, § 3.

stretched forth his hands, etc. Rather, "laid hands on certain of the Church to do them ill."

2 he killed James. See Matt. iv. 21; xx. 20–23; Mark v. 37, and notes. James was the first of the apostles to suffer death; his brother appears to have survived all the rest.

3 the days of unleavened bread. See Exod. xii. 15, 16. Herod generally resided at Cæsarea, but came to Jerusalem at the great festivals.

4 four quaternions. Four soldiers for each of the four watches of the night: one at each of the doors of the prison, forming the *first* and *second* guards (10), and two chained to the prisoner (6).

after Easter. Rather, "after the *Passover*" (R.V.), here probably meaning the *whole festival*, during which the stricter Jews would not like a criminal to be executed.

5 without ceasing. Or, "earnestly" (R.V.).

6 the same night. The night preceding his intended trial or execution.

7 the angel. Rather, "an angel."

a light. Such as often attended visitants from heaven (Luke ii. 9). It might now facilitate the prisoner's escape.

in the prison. Rather, "in the cell" (R.V.).

8 garment. That is, the cloak: see note on Matt. v. 40.

10 the first and second ward. Or "guard," viz., the soldiers posted, one probably at the door of the cell, and the other at the outer gate of the prison.

12 And when he had considered [the thing]. Rather, "and having become aware of [his position], he came," etc. Recovering from his amazement, he reached Mary's house, and knocked there. This was one of the providential coincidences; for many were just then assembled there to pray (5).

13 named Rhoda. Or "Rose." The graphic narrative is that of an eye-witness. Mark must often have spoken with Paul and Barnabas of the incident; or, as they seem to have been themselves in Jerusalem at the time, they may have been among those gathered for prayer in Mary's house.

15 It is his angel. His guardian angel. The inspired writer records this simply as the opinion of the speakers.

17 James. Probably James the Just, the

"brother of the Lord," president of the Church at Jerusalem (xv. 13; xxi. 18; Gal. ii. 12).

went into another place. Peter seems to have left Jerusalem for a time; but he returned afterwards: see xv. 7.

19 put to death. Lit., "to be *led off*" to punishment; which in such a case would be death.

Cæsarea. See note on viii. 40. Josephus (*Antiq.* xix. 8, § 2) relates that Herod went down to Cæsarea to celebrate games in honour of the emperor Claudius.

20 was highly displeased. For some reason now unknown. "Desired peace" is, more accurately, "sued for peace."

because their country was nourished, etc. Cp. 2 Sam. v. 10; 1 Kings v. 9, 11, and note; Ezra iii. 7; Ezek. xxvii. and notes. The prevailing dearth made the maritime and commercial towns feel the importance of friendly relations with the agricultural districts of the interior.

22, 23. Josephus (see on ver. 19) gives a similar but more diffuse account of Herod's death, after five days of great suffering; but only the inspired historain assigns its cause—the *stroke of God,* because he had accepted the impious flattery.

23 the angel. "An angel," as ver. 7.

24 grew and multiplied. Amidst all these events, adverse or propitious, God's work continued to prosper, "growing" in influence, "multiplying" in the number of its adherents. Judæa was now again governed by a Roman procurator (Cuspius Fadus), who was not disposed to court the favour of the Jews by persecuting the Christians.

25 their ministry. That is, their ministration to the poor at Jerusalem, mentioned in xi. 29, 30. This visit to Jerusalem is not mentioned with others by Paul in Gal. i., ii.; being probably a short and private one.

CHAPTER XIII

1 prophets and teachers. Prophecy, the inspired utterance of Divine truths, is more specific than teaching. Every prophet was a teacher, not every teacher a prophet.

Niger. The *black* or dark; perhaps Symeon of Cyrene (see Matt. xxvii. 32, and note), whence Lucius came.

Manaen. The same as Menahem. He was probably "the foster-brother of Herod" Antipas; who, with his brother Archelaus, had been brought up at Rome in the house of a private person (Joseph. *Antiq.* xvii. 1, § 3). "*Foster brother or playmate of Herod.* That shows how the paths of playmates or boys brought up in the same home may afterwards diverge; and how a man by the aid of God's Spirit may get away from the evil influences which surrounded his boyhood" (Dr. Charles Brown in *The Devotional Commentary*).

2 ministered. The word is that generally employed in the LXX for the service of the sanctuary. The mention of fasting seems to intimate that the command was given on some specially solemn occasion of worship; no doubt through some of the prophets.

Separate me Barnabas and Saul. Hence, observes *Chrysostom,* we learn the personality and divinity of the Holy Spirit.

the work, etc. To carry the gospel to other regions. Saul had long been conscious of his vocation (see xxvi. 16–18); he was now publicly appointed by the Holy Ghost.

3 they sent them away. The whole Church, no doubt, united in this act of designation: cp. xv. 40. Henceforth these two "prophets and teachers" of the Church are known as "apostles"—men *sent forth.* "Missionary" is the Latin form of the Greek word "apostle."

4 Seleucia. Seleuceia was the port of Antioch, about fifteen miles from the city, near the mouth of the Orontes.

Cyprus. The island of Cyprus was near: it was the native country of Barnabas; it contained many Jews, and some of its inhabitants were already Christians; see xi. 19, 20.

5 Salamis. Salamis was on the eastern coast of Cyprus, the nearest seaport to Seleuceia, and the chief commercial city of the island.

synagogues. As the Jews scattered throughout the Roman empire were allowed the free exercise of their religion, they had at this period synagogues in all the principal cities. In these assemblies, the apostles, being Jews, not only had ready access to their own people without exciting the suspicion of the civil authorities; but they also met many of the serious and better disposed Gentiles, attracted by the moral superiority of the Old Testament, and either "proselytes" to Judaism, or "devout" worshippers of the true God. These persons, being free from the national Jewish prejudices, were the best prepared to receive the gospel.

John. *i.e.,* John Mark (see ch. xii. 12, 25).

[their] minister. Their assistant.

6 through the isle (island). About one hundred miles. Paphos on the west coast was the capital of Cyprus under the Romans, and the residence of the governor. It was notorious for the licentious worship of Venus.

a certain sorcerer. Rather, "a certain magician": see note on viii. 9. This period was remarkable for the prevalence among the educated as well as the ignorant of both scepticism and imposture. The latter was practised chiefly by adventurers from the East, many of whom were Jews: see Hor. *Sat.* i. 21; Juv. *Sat.* iii. 13–16: vi. 542–546; x. 93.

Bar-jesus. That is, "Son of Jesus," or "of Joshua."

7 deputy. Rather, "Proconsul," the title of the governors of those provinces of the Roman empire which were nominally left by the emperor under the authority of the senate and people, as distinguished from others which, requiring a military force, were governed by his legates, who were called *Proprætors.* Sir W. M. Ramsay (*St. Paul the Traveller and the Roman Citizen,* ch. iv. § 2) notes the accuracy of the title Proconsul as applied to the governor of Cyprus, and says that a Greek inscription of Soloi, on the north coast of the island, is dated "in the proconsulship of Paulus." In the same author's later book, *The Bearing of Recent Discovery on the Trustworthiness of the New Testament* (1915), he gives an account of an inscription found by him at Antioch in 1912, in honour of the son of Sergius Paulus, and of an inscription which was only fully deciphered in 1913, in honour of Sergia Paula, the sister of the proconsul. He sums up thus: "The little that we do know gives a favourable conception of the family as a whole, and is in accordance with Luke's account" (p. 163).

prudent. That is, "intelligent"; R.V., "a man of understanding."

8 sorcerer. Or, "magician." The name *Elymas* has the same meaning.

9 Then Saul, etc. Starting on his world-wide mission, the apostle is henceforth known by his Roman name. Its mention here may have been suggested by the fact that the proconsul of Cyprus happened to bear the same name.

10 child of the devil. Like him in wicked opposition to God's purposes: cp. John viii. 44.

11 a mist and a darkness. The very infliction which Paul had himself suffered, with the happiest results: see ix. 9, etc. Whether Elymas passed from the temporary visitation into the light of faith, we cannot tell.

12 the doctrine (teaching) **of the Lord.** Now confirmed by miracle.

13 Perga. Perga, the capital of Pamphylia, stood about twelve miles up the river Cestrus.

John departing from them, etc. The cause of Mark's abandonment of the work is not stated. It is supposed that he was afraid of the hardships and dangers of the journey into the interior (see note on ver. 14). Whatever it was, it was disapproved by Paul (xv. 38). It is noteworthy that Mark returned, not to Antioch, whence the missionaries had started, but to Jerusalem, where his mother lived (xii. 12). At a later period Paul is not only reconciled to Mark, but commends him, and desires the comfort of his society: Col. iv. 10; 2 Tim. iv. 11.

14 when they departed from Perga. Rather, as R.V., "passing through [the country] from Perga."

Antioch in Pisidia. "Antioch of Pisidia," near the modern *Jalobatch*, was an important town, at that time a Roman colony, situated on the great road from the Ægean Sea to Cilicia and Syria, and inhabited by many Greeks, Romans, and Jews, in addition to the native population. The route from Perga to this place was probably a rough mountain pass, crossed by dangerous torrents, and infested by wild banditti. Here the missionaries were likely to encounter "perils of rivers and perils of robbers" (2 Cor. xi. 26).

15 after the reading of the Law and the Prophets. See note on ver. 27, also on Matt. iv. 23; Luke iv. 16.

sent unto them. Distinguishing them among the congregation as strangers; or perhaps they may have become already known in the city as teachers.

16 beckoning with his hand. His customary gesture (xxi. 40; xxvi. 1).

and ye that fear God. Devout Gentiles, as well as the "men of Israel."

17 exalted the people. Or, "made the people grow"; as in Isa. i. 2. The allusions to Deut. i. and Isa. i. have led some to think that those portions of "the Law and the Prophets" were the lessons for the day in the public service. It is at least remarkable that these two chapters were the lessons for the forty-fourth Sabbath in the year (about August).

18 suffered He their manners. The difference of a single letter gives the reading preferred by many authorities, "bare them as a nursing father"; referring to Deut. i. 31: cp. Numb. xi. 12; 1 Thess. ii. 7 Weymouth has "fed them like a nurse in the desert."

19 seven nations. See Deut. vii. 1, and note.

20 He gave [unto them] judges, etc. See note on 1 Kings vi. 1. R.V. reads, "He gave [them] their land for an inheritance, for about four hundred and fifty years: and after these things He gave [them] judges," etc. This reading has the authority of the best MSS. and of the Vulgate.

21 forty years. On this number, see note on 1 Sam. xiii. 1.

22 I have found David, etc. This is the substance of various passages (1 Sam. xiii. 14; Psa. lxxxix. 20). The phrase, "after mine own heart," *i.e.*, adapted for God's purposes in respect of the government of Israel and the preparation for Messiah's kingdom.

23 Of this man's seed, etc. The order of the words is very remarkable. Every successive clause accords with the nation's highest hope, and smoothes the way for the Name which of itself would be so unwelcome to Jewish listeners.

24 before His coming. That is, before His entrance upon public life.

25 as John fulfilled, etc. Or, "as John was completing his course," etc.

26 to you. Some good authorities read "to us." Paul identifies himself with the Jews of the dispersion and the Gentile proselytes whom he addresses.

27 For, etc. The reason why the offer of salvation had been brought to Paul's present audience. The Jews of Jerusalem in their ignorance had rejected the Saviour, and this had led to the wider diffusion of the message.

read every sabbath day. The sections of the law (*Paraschioth*) were always read in the synagogues: when Antiochus Epiphanes forbade this, lessons from the prophets (*Haphtaroth*) were substituted; and when freedom of worship was again secured the two were combined.

29 they took Him down, etc. All these things are what *men* did, whether friends or foes. "But *God* raised Him from the dead": cp. ii. 23, 24. 36; iii. 14, 15, etc.

31 who are His witnesses. A better reading gives, "who are *now* His witnesses," etc. This is no tradition, but the testimony of living men, who are preaching "to the people" in Judæa what "*we*" now announce "to you" at Antioch (32).

33 He hath raised up Jesus again. Or simply, "He raised up Jesus."

Thou art my Son, etc. Psa. ii. 7.

34 I will give you, etc. Isa. lv. 3.

35 Thine Holy One. This prediction was clearly not fulfilled in David (36); but it was in the risen Jesus (37). He therefore is the Holy One, the Messiah.

36 For David, etc. Rather, as R.V., "For David, after he had in his own generation served the counsel of God," etc.

38 Be it known, etc. As Jesus is the Messiah, through Him we preach to you remission of sins. The law justified from *no* sin; but every one, Jew or Gentile, who believes in Him is justified from *all* sin: see Rom. iii. 20–26; Gal. iii. 11–14.

40 spoken of in the Prophets, etc. The words from Habakkuk i. 5 are quoted freely from the LXX as applying equally to the Jews of Paul's day.

42 And when the Jews were gone out, etc. Or, according to the best reading, "And as they were going out, they besought," etc. It was not till after the gospel had been twice offered to the Jews of this city, the second time at their own request, that Paul turned to the Gentiles (46).

45 spake against. Or, as R.V., "contradicted." "Blaspheming" forms a climax.

46 waxed bold. Rather, "spake out boldly" (R.V.).

It was necessary. According to the Divine plan (see Luke xxiv. 47, and note), as prophetically announced to the Messiah (47): see Isa. xlix. 6.

48 ordained. The Greek word here used is properly translated. (So R.V.) It means *appointed according to some plan or arrangement* of God.

50 devout and honourable women (" the devout women of honourable estate," R.V.). At this period many Gentile women of " honourable " rank had become " devout " proselytes to Judaism. Those among them who embraced the gospel were among its warmest adherents; but those who did not were easily excited to bitter hostility by the Jews, who may have acted through them upon " the chief men of the city."

coasts. Or, " borders " : see note on Exod. x. 4.

51 shook off the dust of their feet. See Matt. x. 14; Luke x. 10, 11, and note.

CHAPTER XIV

1 Iconium. Iconium was a large city, about ninety miles east of Antioch in Pisidia. It is still an important place, called *Konieh*, containing a population of about 30,000.

2 the unbelieving Jews. A better reading is, " the Jews that were disobedient."

3 therefore. Some scholars read here " however."

4 apostles. *Missionaries* or *messengers*: see note on ch. xiii. 3.

5 And when there was an assault, etc. Rather, " And when there was a hostile movement " (*Weymouth, Moffatt*). The design to assault the apostles was frustrated by their withdrawal. Paul was actually stoned only once: cp. ver. 19 with 2 Cor. xi. 25.

6 Lystra and Derbe. These two towns, which were probably small, lay south-east of Iconium, among the highlands of Mount Taurus, and were inhabited chiefly by a rough hardy race, who had been but little affected by Greek, Roman, or Jewish influences. Lystra was probably at a place now known as *Bin Bir Kilissih*, " The Thousand and One Churches," on the northern slope of *Kara Dagh*, " The Black Mountain."

11 in the speech of Lycaonia. " The use of the Lycaonian language shows that the worshippers were not the Roman *coloni*, the aristocracy of the colony, but the natives, the less educated and more superstitious part of the population (*incolæ*)," (*Ramsay*).

12 Jupiter. Zeus (or Jupiter), the chief of the gods, was probably the tutelary deity of Lystra; his temple or altar being " in front of the city." Hermes (or Mercury) was his attendant messenger and spokesman. These two gods were believed to have appeared as men in the neighbouring region. (See the well-known story of Baucis and Philemon: Ovid. *Met.* viii. 611.)

14 rent their clothes. See Gen. xxxvii. 29; Matt. xxvi. 65, and notes.

ran in. R.V., " sprang forth."

15 and saying, etc. This speech contains the thoughts more fully developed in Rom. i. 19, etc. See Rom. i. 18–21; iii. 25, and note: cp. also xvii. 22, etc.

of like passions. Having the same human nature: cp. Jas. v. 17.

vanities. " These unreal things " (*Weymouth*); " such futile ways " (*Moffatt*): see Deut. xxxii. 21.

17 rain . . . and fruitful seasons. An argument specially adapted to an agricultural people. In Rom. i. 20; ii. 15, it is further proved that God gave the heathen also an *internal moral* witness of Himself.

19 having stoned Paul, etc. They had no such scruple here as they had in Jerusalem (see vii. 58) about shedding the blood of their victim within the city.

20 disciples. Paul's labours in Lystra had not been fruitless. The youthful Timothy was probably in the group; see xvi. 1, and note. Paul reminds him of these persecutions many years afterwards (2 Tim. iii. 11).

21 had taught many. Or, as R.V., " had made many disciples " (Matt. xxviii. 19), of whom Gaius (mentioned in xx. 4) was probably one. There is no account of any open opposition at Derbe; and this place is omitted in 2 Tim. iii. 11, where Paul enumerates the scenes of his sufferings in this country.

they returned again to Lystra, etc. Instead of taking the nearest road through Tarsus to Syria, they retraced their steps through the places where they had suffered, in order to " strengthen " the new converts, who had to endure many tribulations in entering " the kingdom of God " (22).

23 ordained them. " They selected elders by show of hands " (*Weymouth*). The Greek is χειροτονήσαντες. The method of selection may perhaps have been the same as in vi. 5, 6, where the people chose, and the apostles ordained.

elders. The " elders," or " presbyters," were persons appointed in the first churches to watch over their general discipline and welfare, as well as, in many instances, to teach (1 Tim. v. 17). The term was a Jewish appellation, transferred from the synagogue. The corresponding designation in the Gentile churches, derived from Greek usage, is " bishops " or " superintendents "; which consequently is more frequently found in Paul's Epistles.

25 into Attalia. Rather, " *to* " Attalia; a seaport of Pamphylia, built by Attalus Philadelphus, king of Pergamos, in the second century B.C. It is now *Antali* or *Satalia*.

27 gathered the church together. This church in the Syrian Antioch had become the headquarters of missions to the heathen and " the mother church of Gentile Christendom ": it now accordingly receives the first of " missionary reports."

had done with them. That is, in connexion with their efforts: His grace co-operating.

opened the (a) **door of faith.** This figure is a favourite one with the Apostle Paul: see 1 Cor. xvi. 9; 2 Cor. ii. 12; Col. iv. 3. The results of this mission showed that access to the Saviour was as free and ready to Gentiles as to Jews.

28 long time. It is supposed that they had spent about two years in their missionary tour; and that they returned to Antioch about the close of the year A.D. 47, and remained there during the years 48 and 49.

CHAPTER XV

1 circumcised. As a sign of submission to the law of Moses. The persons who " taught " this dogma were " false brethren unawares brought in " (Gal. ii. 4), having no authority from the apostles or from the church (ver. 24). The *principle* assailed was the fulness and all-sufficiency of Christ. " We must beware of adding any plus to faith in Christ as essential to salvation. It is the only thing to insist upon. In all other matters men must be left to the guidance of the Holy Spirit " (*Dr. Charles Brown*).

2 to Jerusalem. See Gal. ii. 1–10, and notes. Titus, as we there learn, was in the company.

3 Phenice. That is, Phœnicia, as xi. 19.

4 received. That is, publicly and honourably received.

5 Pharisees. Who, as such, were still zealous for the law.

6 the apostles and elders. See ver. 23; Gal. ii. 2, and notes.

8 And God, which knoweth the hearts, etc. The heart-searching God has already admitted Gentile converts to Christian privileges, granting to them, equally with us, the inward purification, of which circumcision is but an emblem (ver. 9). By making salvation depend (vers. 1, 5) upon these legal requirements, you impose upon them a yoke which we ourselves have felt to be intolerable; and, more than this, you tempt God. See on ver. 10.

9 put no difference. Better, "made no distinction," as R.V.

11 But we believe, etc. Our hope, like theirs, springs entirely from the free grace of our Lord Jesus. Paul afterwards urged this very argument in controversy with Peter (Gal. ii. 15, 16).

we shall be saved. "We," the circumcised. "*Their* ground of trust is the same as *ours, ours* as *theirs*" (*Alford*).

12 miracles. Rather, "signs": see John ii. 11, and note. Their work among the Gentiles had been attested by the same Divine power as that among the Jews.

13 James. See note on xii. 17. The alleged supremacy of Peter gets no support from a passage like this. It was James's opinion, not Peter's, which was accepted as the judgement of the council (cp. vers. 19, 22).

14 Simeon (Symeon). The Hebrew form of *Simon.*

how God at the first did visit the Gentiles. Rather, "how God first visited the Gentiles" (see R.V.). The apostle refers to the first occasion of God's visiting the Gentiles, not to His visiting them before the Jews.

for His name. To bear His name, as His own people: cp. ver. 17; James ii. 7.

16 After this, etc. See notes on Amos ix. 11, 12.

17 That the residue of men, etc. This is a free quotation from the Septuagint. The variation between that and the Hebrew does not affect the object of the quotation. This "residue" signifies the Gentiles who are to be gathered into the kingdom of God equally with the Jews, and are to enter it through their own seeking.

upon whom my name is called. The gift of salvation is not conditioned by circumcision: it is through the name of the Lord being called upon them, *i.e.*, through their consecration to His service. St. James employs the same expression in his Epistle, ii. 7.

19 sentence. Or, as R.V., "judgement." James speaks as president of the assembly.

20 but that we write unto them, etc. On so important and delicate a matter, oral communication through Paul and Barnabas might be judged insufficient: see ver. 23.

pollutions of idols. Food which had been offered to idols: see 1 Cor. viii., x., and notes.

fornication. Which the Gentiles not only allowed, but even encouraged, in connexion with idolatrous worship. Its *moral* evil and guilt are insisted upon elsewhere: see Eph. v. 3; 1 Thess. iv. 3, etc.

blood. Forbidden in Gen. ix. 4, but often used in heathen feasts. This was a concession to the feelings of the Hebrews, which were founded on the law of God (see Gen. ix. 4: Lev. xvii. 13, 14; Deut. xii. 23, 24). "Things strangled" must not be eaten, because of their containing the blood. Some insist that the prohibition of blood is permanently binding on Christians; others, taking our Lord's words, Matt. xv. 11, as their guide, regard this injunction as given for the occasion, in the interest of peace.

21 of old time. Or, as R.V., "from generations of old": see xiv. 16.

22 to send chosen men, etc. Rather, as R.V., "to choose men out of their company, and send them," etc. This would preclude all suspicion of an *ex parte* statement from Paul and Barnabas, and would give them satisfactory credentials from the stricter Jewish brethren.

Barsabas (Barsabbas) **and Silas.** Of Barsabbas nothing more is known. There was a Joseph Barsabbas, i. 23. Silas (contracted from *Silvanus*) became a companion of Paul in his second journey (ver. 40; xviii. 5; 2 Cor. i. 19).

23 letters. Rather, "a letter." The important epistle contains an authoritative decision on the points in question, a condemnation of the troublers of the church, and a confirmation of the authority of Barnabas and Paul.

greeting. This form of salutation occurs James i. 1. It is used nowhere else in the apostolic writings: but is found in the letter of Claudius Lysias, xxiii. 26.

24 subverting. Lit., "unsettling."

25 being assembled with one accord. Rather, "having become unanimous."

26 hazarded their lives. Or, "given up their lives" to be spent or sacrificed for Christ.

28 it seemed good to the Holy Ghost and to us. The Holy Spirit has led us to this decision; which all are therefore bound to obey.

these necessary things. It is necessary to avoid giving offence by self-indulgence in things in themselves indifferent: see Rom. xiv. 15. On the results of this meeting, see Gal. ii. 3–9. Its effects were far-reaching, influencing as they did the whole course of apostolic missions and the history of the Gentile Church through all time.

29 ye shall do well. Rather, as R.V., "it shall be well with you."

31 the consolation. The kind and brotherly "encouragement" or help, allaying the disquietude caused by the Pharisaic demands. So in the next verse, "exhorted," really means "encouraged." It is the same Greek word as in "Paraclete" again.

32 confirmed. "Strengthened."

34 Notwithstanding, etc. It is likely that Silas returned with Judas Barsabbas to Jerusalem, and afterwards went again to Antioch, either during Paul's ministry there (35), or for the purpose of joining him on his second missionary journey (40).

35 Paul also and Barnabas. R.V., "But Paul and Barnabas."

36 some days after. How long after we know not. The circumstances related in Gal. ii. 11–13 may have taken place during the interval, and may have been connected in Paul's mind with Mark's departure from Perga: see notes on xiii. 13; Gal. ii. 11.

From this verse to xviii. 22 we have the account of St. Paul's second missionary journey, which includes his first visit to Europe.

37 determined. R.V., "was minded"; literally, "was wishing," following a slightly varied reading in original.

38 Paul thought not good, etc. The order in the original is very forcible. "Paul thought it right in regard to one who had departed from them from Pamphylia, and had not gone with them to the work—not to take this man with them." "The nature of the mission has to be remembered. It was to confirm the young converts. . . . It was a journey which would be fraught with considerable danger, and a man who had broken down once—who had put his hand to the plough and looked back—was hardly a man to go on the business of confirming others. . . . But Mark came out all right . . . Paul and he are reconciled, and Barnabas' trust in him is vindicated" (*Dr. Charles Brown*). See 2 Tim. iv. 11.

39 they departed asunder. This separation, though caused by human frailty, led to two missions instead of one. This is the last mention of Barnabas in the Book of Acts. His name occurs with indications of fraternal esteem in Paul's Epistles: 1 Cor. ix. 6; Gal. ii. 1, 9, 13; Col. iv. 10.

unto Cyprus. Barnabas was a native of this island, and had already visited it in company with Mark on the apostolic errand: ch. xiii.

40 Silas. Silas, as one of the delegates from Jerusalem (27), would best supply the absence of Barnabas, whose name was coupled with Paul's in the apostolic letter.

41 confirming. Strengthening.

CHAPTER XVI

1 Derbe. As Paul came from Cilicia (xv. 41), probably by the long pass through the range of Taurus, called the Cilician Gates, he would reach Derbe before Lystra.

there. At Lystra.

3 circumcised him, etc. Timothy's partially Jewish extraction made this a reasonable concession to Jewish feelings (see 1 Cor. ix. 20). Timothy's mixed descent would also make him peculiarly useful on a mission addressed to both Jews and Gentiles.

4 the cities. The cities in which Paul had preached before.

the decrees. The decisions of the assembly in Jerusalem, handed in written form to the custody of the disciples; the charter of the churches' freedom.

6 Phrygia. "Phrygia" here means the great central region of Asia Minor. It was a populous country, and contained many Jews. Respecting "Galatia," see the Introduction to the Epistle to the Galatians. From other notices, it appears that during this journey Paul's ministry was attested by many miracles, and crowned with great success, so that many churches were formed; and that while detained here by bodily sickness, he was treated with the greatest kindness by the Galatian converts (Gal. i. 2; iii. 2, 5, 27, 28; iv. 14–16).

and were forbidden (having been forbidden) **of the Holy Ghost,** etc. See note on xiii. 2. Paul appears to have intended to travel westward to Ephesus, the maritime capital of the Roman province of Asia, on the western coast of Asia Minor: see note on ii. 9; but on this plan failing, the missionaries made their way in a north-easterly direction to Galatia. Thence they again travelled westward. Although Paul and Silas were forbidden to preach in Asia at this time, their first convert in Europe came from this district (14); and soon afterwards "all in Asia heard the word" (xix. 10).

8 passing by Mysia. That is, passing through it, or along its borders, without stopping to preach there. Notwithstanding their own preference for work in Asia Minor, they were impelled in the direction of the sea coast ("assayed" is an old English form for *essayed*; tried. The "Spirit of Jesus" (a phrase which has high authority here in its favour) guided them in the direction of Europe, and prepared them for the vision that followed.

Troas. Alexandria Troas (now *Eski Stamboul*) was a large sea-port, and a Roman colony.

9 a man of Macedonia. As his words showed him to be. "Macedonia" was the Roman name for Northern Greece. Ramsay thinks that the "man from Macedonia" may have been Luke himself.

10 we endeavoured (sought). The pronoun "we" here indicates that the writer had now joined Paul's company.

11 came with a straight course. Or, "ran straight before the wind." On another occasion the reverse voyage, from Philippi to Troas, took five days (xx. 6).

Samothracia. An island in the northern part of the Ægean Sea; now called *Samotraki*, or *Samandrachi*. The ship appears to have anchored for the night under the lee of this lofty island, on the northern side. Neapolis was a sea-port in Thrace, near Philippi; probably the modern *Kavallo*.

12 the chief city, etc. "The first city (locally) of that district of Macedonia." It was not "*the chief*" city; for Thessalonica was the capital of the whole province, and Amphipolis of the eastern division. The R.V. has, "which is a city of Macedonia, the first of the district, a [Roman] colony."

colony. A "colony" was a city or district occupied by a colony of Roman citizens, who retained their full privileges, and were governed by their own senate and magistrates (see note on ver. 20). Philippi had been made a colony by Augustus, as a memorial of his victory over Brutus and Cassius on the neighbouring plain. For a full account of a Roman "colony," see Conybeare and Howson, *Life and Epistles of St. Paul*, ch. ix.

13 And on the sabbath, etc. There does not appear to have been any synagogue at Philippi; but Jewish worship was maintained there in some place called, after the Greek, *proseucha*.

which resorted [thither]. Rather, as R.V., "which were come together," *i.e.*, on that particular occasion. The word rendered "spake" denotes informal conversation: "we were talking." It is the same Greek word which is used of women talking in the churches (λαλεῖν; 1 Cor. xiv. 34).

14 Thyatira. A large Lydian city between Sardis and Pergamos (now *Ak-hissar*). The surrounding district has long been celebrated (see Homer, *Il.* iv. 141) for its red and purple dye, which gives employment to the women. Its "dyers" are mentioned in an ancient inscription still existing: see also Rev. ii. 18.

which worshipped God. That is, this Lydian woman was a proselyte to the Jewish faith.

heard [us]. Lit., "was listening."

15 faithful to the Lord. "A believer in the Lord."

16 as we went. Or, "as we were going." For "prayer" the preferable rendering (R.V.) is "the place of prayer": see on ver. 13.

a spirit of divination. Lit., "a Python-spirit"; the spirit which was believed to inspire the Pythia, or Priestess of Apollo. She was a demoniac (see ver. 18).

her masters. The joint owners of this slave.

17 cried, etc. Cp. Mark i. 23–25.

19 the market-place. The public meeting-place for all business.

20 the magistrates. The "duumviri" or "prætors," who governed Roman colonies.

21 being Romans. This appeal was rather to Roman prejudice against a strange and despised race than to the Roman law (which indeed was seldom enforced) against the preachers of a new religion. And it succeeded; for the mob and the magistrates disregarded all forms of law (37).

22 to beat them. Beating with rods the naked back, their garments being rent off them (see R.V.).

24 the inner prison. The prisons in those days were generally dark, damp, and pestilential, and the inner cells were the worst. Respecting "the stocks," see note on Jer. xx. 2.

26 every one's bands were loosed. The earthquake shook the prison, so that the rivets and bolts which fastened the prisoners' chains to the walls fell out.

27 would have killed himself. The gaoler was answerable for his prisoners with his life.

29 a light. Lit., "lights," probably torches, so as to explore the whole prison. The hurry and alarm of the scene are graphically indicated.

came trembling, etc. Rather, as R.V., "trembling for fear, he fell down," etc.

30 brought them out. Out of the cell into the outer prison.

31 Believe. See notes on Rom. iii.

and thy house. "The same way of salvation was open to them as to him" (*Alford*). And "all his house," receiving instruction (32), baptism (33), faith and joy (34), was saved (31) with him.

33 And he took them, etc. Kindness is the first act of the Christian man.

34 brought them. R.V., "brought them up"; the "house" being above the prison.

rejoiced, believing in God with all his house. The R.V. reads, according to the Greek order, "rejoiced greatly, with all his house, having believed in God." *Luther's version* has "rejoices with his whole household, that he had become a believer in God" ("dass er an Gott gläubig geworden war"). Similarly, *Moffatt*.

35 the serjeants. Lit., "the rod-bearers," or *lictors*, who attended the magistrates and scourged the criminals.

37 They have beaten us, etc. Every particular strengthens the complaint. A severe scourging in public, without trial, was in any case a cruel wrong; when inflicted on a Roman citizen, it was a high crime against the state (Cic. *in Verr.* v. 66).

being Romans. How Silas became a Roman citizen does not appear. Paul was so by birth: see xxii. 28, and note. They had obeyed to the letter the command in Matt. v. 39; now Paul claims his legal rights, probably as a mode of asserting his innocence, and also of protecting his converts from blind prejudice against Jewish sects: see ver. 20.

38 and they feared. They feared partly, perhaps, an inquiry at Rome (xxii. 29); and still more the national jealousy of their own citizens, which had shown itself in the recent outbreak (21, 22).

39 to depart out of the city. In order to insure both their own safety and the public peace.

40 entered into [the house of] Lydia. Deliberate in their movements, as those who had nothing to fear. They may have required rest and healing after their suffering: but in any case they would not go without leaving behind them words of consolation and cheer.

comforted. Rather, "encouraged." Luke is supposed to have remained behind to watch over the infant church (see notes on xvi. 10; xx. 6).

CHAPTER XVII

1 Amphipolis. Amphipolis (now called *Emboli*), about thirty-three miles from Philippi, was a large commercial city, the capital of the first division of Macedonia. Apollonia was about thirty, and Thessalonica about thirty-seven miles further, on the great Egnatian road, leading from Rome to the Asiatic provinces.

Thessalonica. Thessalonica (now *Saloniki*), as a great maritime city and the capital of the second district of Macedonia was well fitted to be a centre of gospel light. It was an important British base of operations in the Great War.

a synagogue. Rather, "*the* synagogue"; probably the first they reached in that country.

2 as his manner was, etc. See note on xiii. 46. These three sabbaths can hardly have embraced the whole time of Paul's stay at Thessalonica; for many of the heathen were converted (1 Thess. i. 9), and he twice received aid from Philippi, a hundred miles away, while he remained here, and worked for his support. On his ministry and success here, see the Epistles to the Thessalonians.

3 that (the) **Christ must needs have suffered.** These are almost the very words of Luke xxiv. 26; on which see note. Both the matter of Paul's discourse, and its results, were nearly the same as in ch. xiii.

and that this Jesus, etc. Rather, "and that this is the Christ, [even] Jesus whom I announce (R.V., 'proclaim') to you." He "showed" that the Scriptures had foretold one who should suffer and rise again; and he "set forth," or "affirmed" that Jesus was He.

4 consorted with. Lit., "threw in their lot with Paul and Silas." *i.e.*, as the fruits of their ministry.

devout Greeks, etc. See xvi. 13; and note on xiii. 50. Through the Gentile proselytes, Paul no doubt obtained access to the heathen population; out of which the church at Thessalonica was chiefly gathered (1 Thess. i. 9; ii. 14).

5 moved with envy, etc. Cp. xiii. 45, and note; and 1 Thess. ii. 14–16.

lewd fellows of the baser sort. Rather, "vile fellows of the rabble," R.V. The word translated "rabble" denotes literally, "frequenters of the market-place," or *idle loungers*. These people were ever ready for mischief.

Jason. Jason was Paul's host (7), and perhaps his kinsman (see Rom. xvi. 21).

the people. Thessalonica retained the rights of a free city, having its meetings of "the people," and its own "rulers."

6 drew. R.V., "dragged." The original word implies *violence*.

rulers. Lit., "politarchs." Luke's precision in the use of this term is illustrated by an inscription of about this date, on a ruined arch in the city, now in the British Museum, which gives this unusual title to the magistrates, among whom it is interesting to find names similar to those of Paul's Macedonian companions, "Sosipater," "Gaius." "Secundus" (see xx. 4).

the world. Lit., "the inhabited earth," as in Luke ii. 1.

7 saying that there is another king. This was a half-truth, ill understood, of Paul's preaching respecting the coming and kingdom of our Lord: see 1 Thess. ii. 12; 2 Thess. i. 5; and cp. Matt. xxvii. 11; John xix. 12.

8 troubled. The people and the magistrates were probably afraid that the privileges of their free city might be compromised.

9 security. As the accused persons were not present, the magistrates required security, or bail, from Jason and "the others" (*i.e.*, the "brethren" mentioned, ver. 6), to preserve the peace of the city. This end was in part gained by the departure of Paul and Silas. But the converts seem to have been afterwards maltreated: see 1 Thess. ii. 14. Paul's intention of returning to build up the church was repeatedly frustrated; but he sent Timothy to them (1 Thess. ii. 17, 18; iii. 2).

10 Berea. Beroia, now *Verria*, a large town about forty-five miles south-west of Thessalonica.

11 more noble. That is, more noble in spirit ("ingenuous"); "more amenable" (*Moffatt*). Superior to prejudice, unlike most of the Jews with whom the apostle had to deal, they listened candidly; but at the same time they freely scrutinised the message, and loyally tested it by God's written word. "Therefore many of them believed."

and searched. R.V., "examining," a different word from that in John v. 39.

12 honourable. Of good social position, as xiii. 50.

13 they came thither also, etc. Rather, "they came and stirred up the multitude there also": cp. xiv. 19, and see 1 Thess. ii. 15.

14 to go as it were to the sea. Rather, as R.V., "to go as far as to the sea." Paul probably embarked for Athens at Dium.

15 for to come to him, etc. If they did come to him quickly, they must have left him again soon: for Timothy was sent to Macedonia, and Paul was "left at Athens alone" (1 Thess. iii. 2). But Timothy may have been already directed to visit Thessalonica; and this message may have meant only that he and Silas should come "as soon as possible" after their work in Macedonia was done. They both rejoined Paul at Corinth (xviii. 5).

16 Athens. Although Athens had lost its ancient military and political greatness, it was still the metropolis of Grecian science, art, and wisdom, and was resorted to by scholars from every part of the world.

wholly given to idolatry. Lit., "full of idols" (R.V.); precisely the aspect of Athens that would strike the eye of a Jewish stranger. Petronius, a Roman satirist, declared that "it was easier to find a god than a man in Athens."

17 disputed. Rather, as R.V., "reasoned." The word in the original implies a continued course of action; "he had discussion" (*Weymouth*).

market. "Market-place"; the great place of public resort and discussion, as the Forum was at Rome.

with them that met with him. That is, "with those who happened to be there."

18 certain philosophers, etc. Better, as R.V., "Certain of the Epicurean and Stoic philosophers." Epicurus denied the creation and providential government of the world, and taught that the highest good and great end of existence was serene enjoyment: which his followers interpreted as meaning *pleasure*, and that often of the grossest kind. The Stoics derived their name from the Greek word for the Porch (*stoa*) in which their founder Zeno had taught. They professed to regard moral good as being of the highest value, and to be indifferent to pain and pleasure. They acknowledged a supreme God, but denied His personality, confounding Him with the universe; and for the conception of universal Providence substituted that of irresistible Fate.

What will (would) **this babbler say?** "Babbler" is literally, "grain-picker," a designation of a bird, contemptuously applied to a retailer of borrowed sayings; "with his scraps of learning" (*Moffatt*); a characteristic piece of Athenian slang (*Ramsay*). These persons were disposed to treat Paul with derision; others charged him with introducing "foreign gods."

19 (the) **Areopagus.** "The Council of the Areopagus" (see Ramsay: *Recent Discovery*, etc., ch. vii.). It was before this Council that Socrates had been arraigned 450 years before, for the offence of introducing strange or foreign gods. But there is no trace here of any judicial proceedings; and Paul departs unmolested at the close of his address (33).

May (can) **we know**, etc.? Probably a kind of courteous irony.

21 some new thing. Lit., "something newer": the *very latest news.* This eager appetite for news was a notorious characteristic of the Athenians: it is forcibly described by Demosthenes (*Philippic* i. 43).

22 Men of Athens. The Greek words are the same as those used by Demosthenes in his orations: ἄνδρες Ἀθηναῖοι, "Gentlemen of Athens."

ye are too superstitious. The A.V. does not here do justice either to the Greek word or to Paul's courtesy. It is rather, "ye are very religious" ("worshippers of the gods"). This was a distinction of which the Athenians were proud; and Paul avails himself of it to secure a favourable hearing. His tone is respectful; to begin by affronting his audience would have been contrary to his method.

23 I beheld your devotions. Rather, "I carefully observed the objects of your worship" (see R.V.); including temples and altars, as well as idols.

To the Unknown God. Rather, "To *an* unknown God" (R.V.); although there is considerable authority for the ordinary rendering (see R.V. marg.). Altars to unknown gods are mentioned also by two contemporary writers, Pausanias and Philostratus, as existing in Athens.

Whom therefore, etc. The best text, "*What* ye worship unknowingly, this set I forth unto you." A better English translation, however, would be: "The object of your unknowing worship I declare unto you." You rightly acknowledge that there is a Deity hitherto unknown to you: I make Him known.

24 (The) **God that made the world**, etc. The apostle proclaims the Deity, neither as an idol-being of human form, according to the Epicureans, nor as the mere soul of the world, according to the Stoics; but as an intelligent Spirit, presiding over His works.

25 neither is worshipped. Rather, "neither is *served*" (R.V.), as "one who needs something more" than he has in himself.

28 as certain also of your own poets, etc. These words are found in two poets of the third century B.C.: Aratus of Cilicia, and Cleanthes the Stoic.

29 Forasmuch then as we, etc. The Maker of rational beings cannot resemble a block of wood or stone.

the Godhead. "The Divine nature."

graven by art, etc. The device of man's genius, carved by his art. Paul uttered these words within sight of the most celebrated works of Phidias, particularly the colossal statue of Athéné (Minerva); and in the presence of an assembly who regarded these things as the highest glory of their city.

30 winked at. Rather, "overlooked"; He withheld deserved punishment: cp. xiv. 16, and Rom. iii. 25, with note.

31 [that] man. Lit., "a Man," throwing emphasis on our Lord's humanity.

hath given assurance. See John v. 19–29, and notes.

32 some mocked. The doctrine of the resurrection was repugnant alike to the Epicureans, who disbelieved a future life altogether; and to the Stoics, who held that human souls would be reabsorbed into Deity.

34 believed. It might have seemed to the credit of Christianity, had it been represented as gaining at least a few proselytes in this centre of Grecian refinement from the ranks of its scholars and philosophers. But Luke relates the case just as it was. The apostle was ridiculed, and his message was treated with contempt (*Hackett*). Only two persons of note are mentioned as believing.

Areopagite. That is, a member of the supreme court of Athens; a man, therefore, of age and consideration. Dionysius is reckoned by Eusebius as the first bishop of the church in Athens.

CHAPTER XVIII

1 Corinth. "The great city where he stayed a longer time than at any point on his previous journeys, and from which, or to which, the most important of his letters—1 and 2 Thess.; 1 and 2 Cor.; and Rom.—were written" (*Conybeare and Howson*).

2 Priscilla. Or, Prisca (2 Tim. iv. 19). On these Roman names, see note on i. 23.

had commanded, etc. This was probably the edict which Suetonius mentions, incorrectly ascribing the turbulence of the Jews to the influence of Christianity. It must have been soon revoked, or relaxed; for we find Aquila and Priscilla again at Rome (Rom. xvi. 3), and many Jews resident there (xxviii. 17).

3 the same craft. Paul, according to the custom of his nation, had been brought up to work at a trade; for it was a saying even among Jews of rank and wealth, that "the man who does not teach his son a handicraft teaches him to be a thief."

tentmakers. Tents were often made of goat's-hair cloth, the produce of Paul's native country, Cilicia. Hence it is likely that he wrought particularly in this material. For the reasons why he laboured for his support at Corinth, see 1 Cor. ix.; 2 Cor. xi. 7–12, and notes.

4 Greeks. Either "proselytes" or "devout": see note on x. 2.

5 And when Silas, etc. See xvii. 15; 1 Thess. iii. 6, and notes. After the arrival of Silas and Timothy, Paul wrote the two Epistles to the Thessalonians.

pressed (constrained) **in spirit.** Some good authorities read "constrained by the word" (R.V.), which expresses the hold that it had upon him, and his earnestness in setting it forth. He was occupied, amidst much opposition, in preaching to the Jews: cp. ver. 6 with 1 Cor. ii. 1–5. Silas and Timothy now helped him: see 2 Cor. i. 19.

6 shook his raiment. See Neh. v. 13, and note.

Your blood, etc. See Ezek. xxxiii. 4; Matt. xxvii. 25, and notes.

from henceforth. That is, whilst at Corinth (see ver. 19). Accordingly, he ceased to attend the synagogue, and held meetings of the Christian converts in the adjoining house of a Gentile proselyte (7). He did the same afterwards at Ephesus (xix. 9).

8 the [chief] ruler. Rather, simply "the ruler," as in xiii. 15. Crispus had been baptised by Paul himself (1 Cor. i. 14).

many of the Corinthians. These seem to have been Gentiles, chiefly in the middle and lower classes (1 Cor. i. 26).

10 much people. Many of the true Israel, whom I will gather amongst my "people," instead of those who reject me.

11 a year and six months. This was probably the whole period of Paul's stay at Corinth at this time. He remained there longer than usual, perhaps partly on account of the great success of his ministry, and partly in order that from Corinth the gospel might spread throughout Achaia (see 2 Cor. i. 1).

12 deputy. Rather, "proconsul": see note on xiii. 7. Tiberius had put the province of Achaia, which included all Southern Greece, under an imperial governor ("proprætor"); but Claudius had restored it to the senate. Gallio was a brother of Seneca, who describes him in his letters as a most amiable man. The language of ver. 12 seems to imply that Gallio arrived in the course of Paul's residence at Corinth.

made insurrection. Or, as R.V., simply "rose up."

13 the law. Meaning, probably, the law of Moses; which the Romans allowed the Jews to observe, but would not themselves enforce: see ver. 15.

14 If it were a matter of wrong, etc. Any *deed* of "wrong or wicked villany" (R.V.) might reasonably be brought before me; but I will entertain no "question about *words* (not *deeds*), and *names* (such as whether *Jesus* was the *Messiah*), and *your* (Jewish) law": cp. xxiii. 29; xxv. 19.

15 I will be. That is, "I am not minded to be," as R.V.

16 drave. He peremptorily dismissed them; and even allowed the mob to beat one of their leaders before his tribunal.

17 Sosthenes. See note on 1 Cor. i. 1.

Gallio cared for none of these things. Words that are constantly misapplied, as if they expressed his indifference to spiritual things. The words simply mean that the religious squabbles and the violence of the mob made no impression on him.

18 sailed. Leaving Silas, and possibly Timothy, behind him.

Cenchrea (Cenchreæ). The eastern port of Corinth. The context seems to decide that it was not Aquila (as some suppose), but Paul who "had a vow." Usually the head was shaved at Jerusalem, and the hair burned in the Temple, when the Nazirite vow was discharged (see Numb. vi. 2, etc.); but the regulations may in course of time have been relaxed or modified (*Hackett*).

Why Paul took the vow we are not told; but in doing it he seems to have carried out his principle of conforming in his own practice to the Mosaic ritual.

19 Ephesus. Ephesus was the port of Western Asia which would naturally have the most communication with Corinth.

21 this feast. This feast was probably Pentecost, as navigation was not usually commenced in the season before the Passover: cp. xx. 16.

22 up. That is, up to Jerusalem. We have no particulars of this visit.

23 after he had spent some time [there]. It is thought by some that the controversy between the Apostles Paul and Peter (Gal. ii. 11) occurred during this visit to Antioch. But see note, xv. 36.

he departed. Paul's companions on this, his third missionary journey appear to have been Timothy and Erastus (see xix. 22; 2 Cor. i. 1), Gaius and Aristarchus (see xix. 29), and perhaps Titus, whom he seems to have sent from Ephesus to Corinth.

Galatia. Respecting this visit, see the Epistle to the Galatians.

24 Alexandria. See note on vi. 9.

an eloquent man. Rather, "a man of learning."

25 fervent in the spirit. In Rom. xii. 11 the same phrase is rendered "fervent in spirit" (so R.V. here). The Greek is literally "boiling in spirit."

diligently. Rather, "accurately," as far as he knew.

the baptism of John. On this subject, see note on xix. 1.

26 the way of God. The doctrine of the gospel.

27 to pass into Achaia. His principal object probably was "to help" the converts at Corinth in the controversy with the unbelieving Jews. For this work his skill in expounding the Scriptures peculiarly fitted him; and in performing it he had great success (28; 1 Cor. iii. 5–7).

wrote. They gave him a recommendatory letter. R.V. reads, "The brethren encouraged him, and wrote to the disciples to receive him."

28 mightily convinced. The Greek words are very strong; "he powerfully, utterly confuted."

CHAPTER XIX

1 while Apollos was at Corinth. Apollos remained a considerable time at Corinth; but he returned and joined Paul at Ephesus before the First Epistle to the Corinthians was written: see 1 Cor. xvi. 12.

upper coasts (country). The upper districts are the elevated regions in the interior of Asia Minor, as Galatia and Phrygia.

certain disciples. Disciples *of Christ* (as the word always means when used alone), but imperfectly instructed. Perceiving how little they knew of the gospel, Paul asks, "Did ye receive the Holy Spirit when ye believed?" They reply, "Nay, but we did not even hear whether the Holy Ghost is," *i.e., is already given* (see John vii. 39). His existence and *future* manifestation were taught to such as received John's baptism (see Matt. iii. 11); but only those who knew the events subsequent to our Lord's ascension were aware of the actual manifestation of the Holy Spirit.

3 Unto (Into) **John's baptism.** That is, into the profession of what John's baptism indicated; repentance for the remission of sins, and faith in the coming of the Messiah.

5 in the name. Rather, "*into* the name"; *i.e.*, into the belief and acknowledgment of the Lord Jesus.

6 the Holy Ghost. See ii. 4; viii. 17; x. 44–46, and notes.

9 that way. Lit., "the Way" (R.V.): see note on ix. 2.

before the multitude. "Before the congregation," *i.e.*, in the synagogue. The violent opposition of the Jews rendering all further efforts in that place useless, Paul formally withdrew the Christian disciples, and formed a separate society (cp. xviii. 6, 7) "in the school of Tyrannus"; probably a Greek sophist or rhetorician.

10 two years. This probably means for two years after he left the synagogue. Paul remained at Ephesus three years, and formed a large church (xx. 28, 31), supporting himself, and partly also his companions, by his own manual labour (see xx. 34; 1 Cor. iv. 12). During this time he wrote his FIRST EPISTLE TO THE CORINTHIANS (see 1 Cor. xvi. 8); and possibly paid a visit to Corinth, his *second* (see 2 Cor. xii. 14; xiii. 1).

Asia. Ephesus, as the capital of the province, was a centre from which the gospel could well be carried to the inland cities. The "Seven Churches of Asia," addressed in Rev. i.–iii., were probably founded at this time.

11 special (no ordinary) **miracles.** Miracles (Greek, *powers*) performed (like those in ch. v. 15) upon great numbers, and without the apostle's personal presence. These "signs of an apostle," by which Paul's commission was attested (2 Cor. xii. 12), were particularly adapted to his position at Ephesus in the face of magicians; like that of Moses and Aaron before Pharaoh.

12 evil spirits. "Evil spirits" are here plainly distinguished from diseases.

13 vagabond Jews, exorcists. Rather, "itinerant (R.V., 'strolling') Jewish exorcists," who were very numerous at this period: see Matt. xii. 27, and note. Simon the Samaritan, and Elymas, were of the same class (viii. 9; xiii. 6). The exorcists, seeing Paul's success, used the name which they saw him employ with so great effect.

14 chief of the priests. Or, "a chief priest," R.V. (see note, Matt. ii. 4). The Aaronic priesthood must have been very degraded, when some of its leading members were travelling exorcists.

15 Jesus I know, and Paul I know. "Jesus I know, and Paul I know about."

16 overcame them. The var. read., adopted by R.V., implies that only two of the seven brothers were concerned in this attempt.

naked. See note on Mark xiv. 51.

18 that believed. Rather, "that had believed," R.V. Even after conversion some appear to have continued to be the dupes of persons who practised "occult arts" (19). They "declare" their "deeds," *i.e.*, the superstitious practices which they now see to have been inconsistent with the Christian profession.

19 books. Treatises on magic and astrology, and collections of rules or formulas of incantation. The converts showed their sincerity by burning those instruments of wickedness, instead of selling them.

fifty thousand pieces of silver. That is, 50,000 drachmas or denarii, worth altogether about £2,000; and in purchasing power, much more. All books, being in manuscript, were dear at that time, and books of this class were dearer than others.

20 So mightily grew, etc. See notes on Rom. xv. 23, 25. Respecting a supposed visit of Paul to Corinth at this time, see notes on 2 Cor. xii. 14.

22 So he sent into Macedonia, etc. Timothy was to go on, if he could, to Corinth: see 1 Cor. xvi. 10, and note. Erastus is perhaps the person who is mentioned in Rom. xvi. 23.

but he himself stayed, etc. See 1 Cor. xvi. 8, and note.

23 that Way. "The Way": see ix 2, and note.

24 shrines for Diana. Lit., "temples of Artemis," the Greek goddess corresponding most nearly to Diana of the Romans. The Ephesian Artemis, however, was an Asiatic rather than a Greek or Roman goddess. These small models of the temple and image were used for private worship, or worn on the person as charms.

26 that they be no gods, etc. Although images are employed professedly as *media* of worship, the mass of the people, and even some of the educated, soon come to regard them as the *objects* of worship. That Paul had made no open attack on the divinities of the place is evident from ver. 37; but he had doubtless spoken at Ephesus to the same effect as at Athens (xvii. 29); and those who felt or feared the diminution of their profits, by the giving up of idolatry, laid hold of such expressions.

27 our craft. A plea of self-interest cunningly associated with the appeal to religious fanaticism.

be set at nought. Lit., "be made of no account."

whom all Asia and the world worshippeth. This was no extravagant boast: for this temple had been built at the joint expense of many cities; it was accounted one of the wonders of the world, surpassing all other heathen temples in wealth and magnificence; and it was the resort of worshippers from all parts of the known world. Mr. Wood's discoveries at Ephesus "have amply vindicated the historic character" of the Acts on this point (*Stokes*).

29 Gaius and Aristarchus. Aristarchus, who was a Thessalonian, is mentioned in xx. 4; xxvii. 2; and probably in Col. iv. 10, and Philem. 24. Gaius (or Caius, a very common name) is probably different from both of those so named in xx. 4, and Rom. xvi. 23.

the theatre. The Greek theatres were large unroofed enclosures, with tiers of stone seats rising one above another; and they were used for all great assemblies. Existing ruins show that the theatre at Ephesus was a vast edifice.

31 the chief of Asia. Rather, *Asiarchs;* officers annually elected by the cities of the province from the highest and wealthiest class in the community, to preside over the religious festivals and public games, which these officers provided at their own expense. They retained the title for life. Some of these persons, without being Christians, were evidently well disposed towards the apostle.

33 And they drew Alexander, etc. Or, "And out of the crowd they drew forth Alexander, the Jews pushing him on." He seems to have been an unconverted Jew, put forward by his co-religionists to disclaim on their part any participation in Paul's proceedings. Some think that this was "Alexander the coppersmith" (1 Tim. i. 20; 2 Tim. iv. 14); but it is doubtful, as the name was very common.

34 a Jew. And therefore an enemy to all image worship.

35 the townclerk. This public officer was a magistrate of great authority, ranking next to the governor of the city. His original duty was to record and preserve the public acts and laws. He also presided over the public assemblies. He soon "stilled the mob," first soothing and flattering them, and then working upon their fears, until he had prepared them to separate quietly; when he "dissolved the meeting."

worshipper. Lit., "guardian of the temple"; a title which was deemed very honourable, and is found upon ancient Ephesian coins.

which fell down from Jupiter (Gr. *Zeus*). By such legends many other images have been similarly invested with peculiar sanctity.

37 robbers of churches. "Of temples."

38 the law is open, etc. Rather, "Court days are kept, and there are proconsuls; let them (the accusers and the accused) plead against one another."

40 in danger. The Romans jealously watched all riotous proceedings in cities which retained any of their old rights.

CHAPTER XX

1 into Macedonia. See note on xix. 22. For some particulars of this journey, and of the apostle's anxieties and consolations in Troas and Macedonia, see 2 Cor. ii. 12, 13; vii. 5, 6, and notes. He was probably accompanied by two Ephesians, Tychicus and Trophimus (see ver. 4), who frequently attended him afterwards.

2 those parts. Through Macedonia, and adjoining regions in Northern Greece, probably reaching as far as Illyricum on the Adriatic coast (see Rom. xv. 19, and note).

3 three months. During the winter (see ver. 6). This time he probably spent chiefly at Corinth, rectifying the disorders which prevailed in that church: see 2 Cor. xiii. 1–10. Here he wrote his EPISTLE TO THE ROMANS (see Rom. xvi. 1, 23).

as he was about to sail. He had intended to sail direct to Syria, as he had done before (xviii. 18), on his way to Jerusalem (xix. 21; Rom. xv. 25). But he changed his plan, and took a circuitous route by land through Macedonia.

4 into Asia. Lit., "as far as Asia" (*i.e.*, the province of Asia), where Sopater probably stopped. Luke, Trophimus, and Aristarchus went on with Paul to Jerusalem (see xxi. 29; xxvii. 2), and possibly others too.

Sopater, etc. The title is added, perhaps to distinguish him from Sosipater (Rom. xvi. 21). Respecting Aristarchus, see note on xix. 29. Of Secundus nothing more is known. Gaius (or Caius) of Derbe in Lycaonia is a different person from the Macedonian Gaius of xix. 29. Tychicus appears afterwards as Paul's messenger to the churches, and the bearer of two of his Epistles (see Eph. vi. 21; Col. iv. 7; 2 Tim. iv. 12; Tit. iii. 12). Trophimus, who became the innocent occasion of his arrest at Jerusalem (xxi. 29), is mentioned again in 2 Tim. iv. 20.

5 us. This word indicates that Luke now rejoined Paul (see note on xvi. 40). They appear to have continued together to the end of the history.

6 in five days. The wind being adverse: see xvi. 11, and note.

7 the first day of the week. See John xx. 26, and note. It is implied that the first day of the week, as being the day of our Lord's resurrection, had become the customary day of assembling of the church: cp. 1 Cor. xvi. 2.

to break bread. See note on ii. 42.

preached unto them. Or. "discoursed with

them," as R.V., implying conversation and discussion.

9 in a window. Lit., "on the window"; which was without glass, and probably projected over the street, or the interior court.

was taken up dead. This is the plain assertion of an eye-witness, who elsewhere carefully marks a case of *apparent* death by saying, "supposing him to be dead" (xiv. 19).

10 embracing. Like Elijah (1 Kings xvii. 21) and Elisha (2 Kings iv. 34, 35).

Trouble not yourselves. "Do not lament" (*Moffatt*).

his life is in him. Restored in answer to the apostle's prayer.

11 bread. Rather, "the bread," *i.e.*, of the Communion.

eaten. This was probably either the love-feast which followed the Communion, or a meal for the travellers.

13 sailed unto (set sail for) *Assos.* A small seaport, opposite to Lesbos, and about twenty miles from Troas by land.

14 Mitylene. Mitylene (now *Castro*) was the capital of Lesbos, an island near Mysia.

15 Chios. An island about five miles from the coast.

arrived (touched) **at Samos.** Samos was about fifty miles from Chios. The ship would lie-to for the night at Trogyllium, a cape and town on the continent, opposite Samos, and not far from Miletus. The reference to Trogyllium seems to have been added to the text by some transcriber acquainted with the locality.

Miletus. Now *Melos.* Miletus was formerly a great commercial port of Asia Minor. It is now some miles inland.

16 to sail by (past) **Ephesus.** Without visiting it. Paul appears to have feared to trust himself at Ephesus, lest the importunity of his friends, or the condition of the church, might detain him too long.

because he would not spend, etc. Rather, as R.V., "that he might not have to spend time in Asia."

he hasted, etc. More than three of the seven weeks between the Passover and the Pentecost were gone.

17 he sent to Ephesus. The distance being about thirty miles, he must have stayed three or four days at Miletus.

18–35. This speech is full of expressions and sentiments which peculiarly belong to the apostle, and may be traced in his Epistles. It is remarkable as being the only recorded address of the apostle on his missionary journeys which St. Luke heard; and it is no doubt reported *verbatim.*

18 Ye know, etc. More literally, "Ye yourselves know, from the first day that I set foot in Asia, how I lived among you all the time."

19 temptations. That is, trials of faith.

20 kept back. "Hesitated" or "shrank from." A nautical term, meaning to lower sail: see 27.

publicly, and from house to house. The apostle clearly regarded both public and private teaching as essential to the well-being of the church.

22 bound in the spirit. Or, "impelled by the Spirit."

25 I know. An expression of his strong conviction. For Paul's closing years, see Phil. i. 7, 12, 13; iv. 22; Eph. vi. 21; Col. i. and iv.; Philemon; 2 Tim. i. 16; ii. 9; iv. 7, 16, 17. The tradition is that he was beheaded A.D. 68.

27 I have not shunned. The same word as in ver. 20, "kept back"; "shrank not from."

to declare unto you, etc. With particular reference to God's purpose (or "counsel") of mercy to the Gentiles: see Eph. iii. 2–11.

28 over the which. Rather, "in which," that is, in the midst of which.

overseers. The word, here applied to the elders (17) of the Ephesian church, is the one which everywhere else is translated *bishops* (so here in R.V.).

to feed. Rather, "to tend, as shepherds": see note on John xxi. 17.

the church of God, etc. "Church of the Lord" is an alternative reading; see R.V. marg.

29 grievous wolves. False teachers, seeking their own private interests, would divide the believers into factions: cp. 2 Tim. ii. 17; and see the subsequent condition of the Ephesian church depicted in Rev. ii. 2–7.

30 of your own selves. For the fulfilment of this prediction in Ephesus see 1 Tim. i. 20; 2 Tim. i. 15; ii. 17.

33 apparel. See note on Matt. vi. 19.

34 these hands have ministered, etc. Cp. 1 Cor. iv. 11, 12, written from Ephesus. It is worthy of notice that Luke says nothing of this in his account of Paul's residence at Ephesus. Cp. also 1 Cor. ix. 1–18, and notes.

35 all things. Rather, "in all ways"; both by teaching and example.

the weak. The "weak" are all who need support.

the words of the Lord Jesus, how He (Himself) **said,** etc. This saying, though not preserved by any of the evangelists (see John xxi. 25, and note), was evidently cherished by the first disciples. It breathes the spirit of our Lord's life and doctrine. It teaches those who have not to labour from necessity, still to labour from benevolence, that they may be able to do more for others.

CHAPTER XXI

1 were gotten from them. "Had torn ourselves away from them" better expresses the force of the original.

came with a straight course, etc. That is, ran before the wind, as in xvi. 11. Coos (now called *Stanco*), an island forty miles south of Miletus, was celebrated for its wine, silk, and cotton; and Rhodes, about fifty miles south-east, for the huge Colossus which had stood across the harbour, but was then a ruin. Patara was a sea-port of Lycia, about sixty miles further east, where there was a remarkable oracle of Apollo. The voyage thence to Tyre, about 340 miles, would take, with a favourable wind, about forty-eight hours.

3 discovered. That is, "having sighted Cyprus"; its lofty outline lying on the left as they sailed south of it.

Tyre. Respecting Tyre, see notes on Isa. xxiii. The gospel had been brought to Phœnicia at an early period; see xi. 19; xv. 3.

4 And finding disciples. Rather, "And having found out the disciples," who needed to be sought for.

through the Spirit, etc. The Spirit revealed to them Paul's danger; from which it was *their* inference "that he should not go up to Jerusalem." But his own conviction was the contrary: see vers. 12–14; xx. 22.

5 those days. The days of their stay at Tyre

7 And when we had finished, etc. Or, "But we, having ended our voyage, arrived from Tyre at Ptolemais." Ptolemais, anciently Accho (Judges i. 31), now *Akka*, is celebrated in modern history as St. Jean d'Acre, or Acre.

8 Cæsarea. See viii. 40, and note. The journey from Ptolemais to Cæsarea seems to have been by land.

evangelist. An "evangelist" was a preacher of the gospel; particularly one who went about preaching from place to place (viii.; Eph. iv. 11; 2 Tim. iv. 5).

one of the seven. See vi. 1–7, and notes.

9 which did prophesy. Or, "preach."

10 many (several) **days.** Having travelled rapidly since he left Miletus, and being now within three days' journey of Jerusalem, Paul had a few days to spare.

11 bound his own hands and feet. For similar emblematic actions, see 1 Kings xxii. 11; Jer. xxvii. 2.

13 What mean ye, etc.? Lit., as R.V., "What do ye, weeping and breaking my heart?"

14 The will of the Lord, etc. Regarding his decision as guided by the will of God.

15 our carriages. "Our baggage" (R.V.). Sir W. Ramsay, however, translates "having equipped horses."

16 brought [with them], etc. Or the meaning may be, "they brought us to one Mnason," etc., "with whom we should lodge."

old. That is, old *as a disciple*, an early convert.

17 Jerusalem. This was Paul's fifth visit to Jerusalem since his conversion.

18 with us. That is, with Luke, and the messengers of the Gentile churches, who had come with Paul, bringing their contributions for the poor Christians in Judæa.

James. James, "the Lord's brother," chief pastor of the church in Jerusalem, mentioned in xii. 17; xv. 13.

20 thousands. Lit., "myriads"; an indefinite expression for a very large number; see 1 Cor. iv. 15; xiv. 19.

which believe. More accurately, "which have believed."

zealous of the law. In the church at Jerusalem there were many who were "zealous for the law," and who had been "carefully informed" (as the Greek word signifies, ver. 21) by the violent Judaisers, that Paul encouraged the converted Jews to neglect all the religious institutions of their nation. In fact, Paul does not appear to have discouraged the observance of these ordinances by Jewish converts, but rather the contrary. His practice in this matter may be learned from Rom. xiv.; 1 Cor. vii. 18; ix. 19–23.

24 be at charges with them. Rather, "defray their expenses." When poor persons had taken a Nazirite vow (see Numb. vi. 1–21), a devout Jew would sometimes bear the expenses of their release. This Paul was advised to do, that he might show his regard for the Mosaic institutions. The advice accorded with his own principles of action (1 Cor. ix. 20), and with his attendance at the national religious festivals (xviii. 21; xx. 16).

25 As touching the Gentiles, etc. See xv. 19–21, and notes.

26 purifying himself. So as to be ceremonially clean, and thus ready to accompany them at the completion of their vow.

to signify, etc. Rather, "giving notice [to the officiating priests] of the fulfilment of the days of purification, until the offering was presented for every one." It seems probable that seven days' notice (27) was given of the time when the appointed offering (Numb. vi. 13–17) would be presented, that they might be shaved and discharged from the vow.

27 the Jews which were of Asia. Who appear to have come chiefly from the capital of the province, Ephesus, where they had already persecuted Paul (xx. 19). They probably recognised Trophimus (29) as a fellow-townsman.

28 against the people, etc. A charge like that against Stephen (vi. 13).

Greeks. That is, "Gentiles": see Rom. i. 16.

this holy place. The inner court of the Temple, from which foreigners were strictly excluded.

29 Trophimus, an (the) **Ephesian.** See xx. 4, and note.

30 drew. R.V. "dragged"; *i.e.*, from the Court of the Israelites to the Court of the Gentiles.

31 went about. Or, "were trying to."

tidings came. Lit., "information went up," *i.e.*, to the officer in command of the Roman garrison, in the Tower of Antonia, which overlooked the Temple, communicating with it by flights of steps ("the stairs," ver. 35). The garrison was at this time a cohort ("band") of 1000 men; and the "chief captain," *i.e.*, tribune in command, was Claudius Lysias (xxiii. 26).

32 centurions. As each centurion would be accompanied by his soldiers, there would be at least 200 men. During the festivals, the garrison were constantly under arms, ready to suppress any popular outbreak: see Josephus, *Wars*, v. 5, § 8.

33 bound with two chains. Probably fastening each arm to a soldier.

34 cried. Lit., "were shouting."

castle. Or, "barracks," within the citadel.

37 Canst thou speak Greek? "Dost thou know Greek?" an exclamation of surprise; shown also by his following words, lit., "Thou art not then the Egyptian," etc.

38 that (the) **Egyptian.** An Egyptian Jew, who had lately gathered together "the four thousand of the Sicarii" (murderers or assassins), who were numerous at this time. Of these some had been slain, and the rest put to flight. Josephus gives two accounts of this man, which cannot easily be reconciled with each other: see *Wars*, ii. 13, § 5; *Antiq.* xx. 8, § 6.

40 the stairs. The stairs leading up from the Temple area to the Tower of Antonia; the crowd of people being immediately below.

CHAPTER XXII

2 kept the more silence. Being pleased as well as surprised to hear him speak their own tongue.

3 according to the perfect manner, etc. With Pharisaic "strictness": see xxvi. 5. The "law of the fathers" included the current traditional glosses on the Old Testament.

5 the high priest, etc. The high priest of that day, who was still living: see ix. 1, 2. This was probably Theophilus, son of Annas. At the time of this address, Theophilus having been deposed, Ananias held office, on the nomination of King Agrippa II. "And all the presbytery," *i.e*, the whole Sanhedrin, who commissioned Paul to their Hebrew brethren at Damascus.

6–13. Compare these verses with Luke's account of St. Paul's conversion in ix. 3–9 and St. Paul's own account in ch. xxvi.; and see notes there. The differences between the accounts are precisely such as might be looked for in two statements, on different occasions, of the same occurrence. Luke clearly regards them as perfectly harmonious.

14 The God of our fathers. Compare Stephen's language in vii. 32.

Just One. This designation of our Lord, derived from Isa. liii. 11, was used by Stephen in vii. 52: see also iii. 14.

the voice of His mouth. That is, His immediate revelations; in order that thou mayest testify what thou hast seen and heard (15).

16 wash away thy sins. Cp. ii. 38. Baptism is the outward sign of the repentance and faith which are essential to salvation.

the name of the Lord. "His name," R.V.; *i.e.*, the name of "the Just One" (14).

17 to Jerusalem. See notes on ix. 26.

in a trance. See note on x. 10.

19 And I said, etc. Paul thought that his former zeal against Christ, contrasted with his present zeal for Him, must make a deep impression on his countrymen; but his subsequent history showed that he was mistaken.

20 Thy martyr Stephen. Rather, as R.V., "Stephen Thy witness." As the early witnesses for Christ almost all suffered for their religion, the word soon came to be applied to those who suffered death for their Christian profession: see Rev. xvii. 6.

22 lifted up their voices, etc. Verifying the words of ver. 18.

it is not fit. Lit., "it was not fit"; he has deserved to die long ago.

23 cast off their clothes. Rather, they "threw their clothes into the air." A mob of exasperated Orientals still express their anger in the same way.

24 scourging. The Roman officer supposed that this new outburst of rage against Paul must be caused by some flagrant crime on his part, and determined to extort a confession by scourging. On this terrible torture, see Geikie: *Life of Christ*, ii. 547, 548.

25 as they bound, etc. Or, "as they stretched him forward with the thongs," *i.e.*, binding him to the post, that he might be scourged. He was actually bound (29), though not scourged.

stood by. To superintend the flogging.

28 this freedom. Rather, "this citizenship" (R.V.). Surely *you* could not have afforded to pay for so costly a privilege!

29 But I was [free] born. Lit., "But I was even born," *i.e.* a citizen. Paul could not have had this right simply as a native of Tarsus, a city which did not confer the right of Roman citizenship upon its inhabitants: had it been so, the Tribune, who already knew his birthplace (xxi. 39), would not have ordered the scourging. His family had acquired the privilege, probably, either by payment or by service; and he had inherited it. See note, xiii. 9. This timely assertion of his rights as a Roman citizen saved him not only from present infliction, but from many subsequent dangers at the hands of the Jews.

30 commanded the chief priests, etc. He saw that this was an affair which concerned the national religion, but wished to know whether it was necessary for him to interfere. As yet the clamour of the mob had been the only ground of procedure against Paul; the chief captain desired something official.

down. Down from the Castle of Antonia to the council room, which had formerly been in the Temple, but had been removed to a hall on Mount Zion. See note on ver. 25.

CHAPTER XXIII

1 I have lived, etc. Or, "I have conducted myself towards God" as a member of that kingdom of which He is Sovereign.

2 Ananias. See on xxii. 5. Ananias seems to have been high priest from about A.D. 48 to A.D. 59, with one interruption (A.D. 52), when his cruelty and avarice had caused him to be sent to Rome for trial.

to smite him on the mouth. An Eastern mode of silencing a speaker; intimating that what he said was false and insulting.

3 God shall smite thee. This prediction was fulfilled; for at the beginning of the great Jewish war this Ananias was assassinated.

whited wall. Fair outside, but coarse clay within. Cp. Matt. xxiii. 24–27, and note.

to judge, etc. Ananias, by his command to smite Paul, had illegally decided the case before it was heard.

5 I wist not, etc. Paul's reply has been variously explained. Lewin's explanation is that Paul had probably never seen Ananias, as he was absent from Jerusalem, except for one brief visit, during the high priesthood of the latter. The high priest was not necessarily president. Ramsay (*Recent Discovery*, etc., ch. vii.), says that it was not a formal meeting of the Council at all, but an assemblage of leading men hastily summoned as advisers by the Roman officer in command at Jerusalem, and that *he* and not the high priest, presided.

6 when Paul perceived. Rather, "Paul knowing." He knew well that the Sadducees opposed him for preaching the resurrection of the dead; and that as to this essential doctrine the belief of the Pharisees agreed to some extent with the teachings of the gospel.

8 Sadducees. See notes on Matt. iii. 7; xxii. 23.

9 let us not fight against God. The words, added by some transcriber, seem to have been a reminiscence of ch. v. 38, inserted with reference to Paul's statement xxii. 17, 18.

11 Be of good cheer, etc. This is the same Greek word, θάρσει, used by our Lord in Matt. ix. 2, 22; xiv. 27; John xvi. 33. Paul's reward was that of the faithful soldier, to be put in a place of greater responsibility and even danger.

12 a curse. "An anathema," implying the invocation of divine wrath.

14 chief priests and elders. The conspirators reckoned only too correctly upon the connivance of these professed guardians of religion.

15 signify. A legal word, meaning, "to give notice."

inquire something more perfectly, etc. Or, "ascertain more exactly the things concerning him": see R.V.

or ever. That is, before he comes near.

16 Paul's sister's son. Many conjectures have been made about this young man. We only know enough of him to show that all Paul's family were not alienated from him.

23 spearmen. "Light infantry." The strength of the escort shows that Lysias knew the desperate fanaticism of the Jews; besides which the way was infested at many points by bands of robbers.

third hour of the night. That is, at nine o'clock in the evening.

24 provide [them] beasts. "Them" is not in the Greek. The beasts were probably mules (Spanish version: *cabalgaduras*). More than one mule was needed for Paul, as the journey was long, and needed to be rapid.

Felix. Antonius Felix was brother of Pallas, a favourite of Nero, and a freedman of Antonia, the mother of the Emperor Claudius. He had been procurator of Judæa for nearly six years; his government was vigorous; but, as Tacitus says (*Hist.* v. 9, 7), "he used the power of a king with the disposition of a slave, through every kind of cruelty and licentiousness."

26 most excellent. An official title: "his Excellency"; see xxiv. 3; xxvi. 25; Luke i. 3.

27 should have been killed. Or, "was on the point of being killed by them." That Lysias claims overmuch credit to himself is an indirect proof, as *Meyer* remarks, of the genuineness of the letter.

with an army. Rather, "with the troops."

31 to Antipatris. A rapid march of about thirty-eight miles. The ruins of an ancient Roman road still indicate the route.

32 left the horsemen. The dangerous part of the journey being over.

33 Cæsarea. See note on viii. 40.

35 I will hear thee. "I will hear thy cause," R.V.: the word used implying a thorough judicial hearing. The Roman law required that when a case was sent up from an inferior to a higher tribunal, the whole should be heard anew.

Herod's judgement hall. The "prætorium," or palace; built by Herod the Great, now the governor's official residence.

CHAPTER XXIV

1 after five days. Probably on the fifth day: see note on ver. 11.

descended. That is, went down from Jerusalem to Cæsarea.

a certain orator. An advocate in the courts of law. Tertullus may have been one of the young Roman advocates who trained themselves for the forum at home by practising in the provincial courts. In accordance with the forms of Roman law, the accusers *lay information* against the defendant; he is *summoned;* and the advocate brings forward the *charges.* On the three charges brought against Paul, viz., sedition, heresy, and profanation of the Temple, the first was best suited to make the prisoner obnoxious to Felix.

3 always. "In every way and everywhere."

5 a pestilent fellow. Lit., "a pest."

the Nazarenes. The name of reproach which the Jews gave the Christians.

6 the Temple. Which the Romans had engaged to keep sacred.

would have judged according to our law. The words beginning with "and" (ver. 6) and ending with the first clause of ver. 8, are omitted by the best authorities. If the passage is genuine, it contains a false statement on the part of the Jews; the Jews were beating Paul to death when Lysias rescued him without violence.

8 whom. *i.e.*, Paul. The advocate rests his case on the examination of the prisoner himself. "He cannot deny these statements."

9 assented. Rather, "joined in the charge."

10 many years. Felix had governed Samaria under Cumanus; and had since been procurator of Judæa about six years (xxiii. 24), which was longer than the average.

11 thou mayest understand. Rather, "thou canst ascertain."

twelve days. The reckoning may be this: Arriving at Jerusalem in the evening, Paul meets the elders (first day); joins the devotees (2); on the fifth day after this he is seized (6); he appears before the Sanhedrin (7); is sent to Cæsarea (8); and makes this defence on the fifth day after he had left Jerusalem (12).

14 heresy. Rather, "sect" (R.V.), as in ver. 5. What they call "a sect" is really the proper "way" (see note on ix. 2) of carrying out the religion of our fathers.

15 which they themselves also allow (entertain). Paul takes no notice of the Sadducean minority who had forsaken the ancient faith.

16 herein. Rather, "in this," *i.e.*, in this hope.

17 alms. This book records nothing more respecting these alms; but Paul's Epistles, written just before this journey, contain many allusions to them: see Rom. xv. 25, 26, 31; 1 Cor. xvi. 1–4; 2 Cor. viii. 1–4, etc.

offerings. The "offerings" were probably those connected with the performance of the Nazirite vow, xxi. 23–26.

18 Whereupon. Rather, "In which." Whilst in these actions I was showing my devotion to the people and the Temple, I was met, not by these persons who now appear as my accusers, but by certain foreign Jews, who are the only proper witnesses against me. My accusers here can only speak to what passed when I was brought before them; and all that I said there was an avowal of my faith in the resurrection (21).

22 having more perfect knowledge, etc. Felix knew too much of Christianity (see ver. 10), and of the Jews' hatred to it, to be easily deceived by their misrepresentations; but he was unwilling to displease them or to lose his chance of a bribe (26) by at once acquitting Paul. He therefore put them off, adopting the suggestion of Tertullus (8).

23 a centurion. Rather, "*the* centurion," who had charge of Paul.

liberty ("indulgence"). As much as safe custody would allow.

his acquaintance ("friends"). Including, no doubt, Philip and his household; with Trophimus, Aristarchus, and Luke: see xxi. 8, 9, 29; xxvii. 2.

24 Drusilla. Drusilla was the daughter of Herod Agrippa (xii.), and had been married to Azizus, king of Emesa; but had been persuaded by Felix to desert her husband, and to marry him. Paul was sent for probably to gratify her. As a Jewess, she would naturally be curious to hear the famous Christian preacher.

25 righteousness. "The faith towards Christ" requires personal holiness (Rom. vi.), and sets Him forth as the future Judge (Rom. ii. 16): and Paul did not shrink from discoursing of these before the governor: referring especially to that "righteousness and self-control" which Felix so grossly outraged.

26 He hoped also, etc. Felix perceived that Paul's friends were numerous, and that they were not either too poor or too selfish to assist one another (17).

27 came into Felix' room. Felix was recalled by Nero A.D. 60, and was followed by the bitter accusations of the Jews and Samaritans. He escaped with his life, but died in obscurity and disgrace.

to show the Jews a pleasure. Or, "to gain

favour with the Jews" (R.V.), whose complaints he would have to answer at Rome. Other governors acted in a similar manner.

left Paul bound. Or, "in bonds." An increased rigour of imprisonment (see ver. 23) seems to be suggested.

CHAPTER XXV

1 Festus. Festus succeeded Felix probably about the summer or autumn of A.D. 60; and died in office, A.D. 62. He was upon the whole an upright governor.

2 high priest. Some scholars read "high priests." If "high priest" is retained, the reference is to Ismael, who succeeded Ananias.

5 Let them therefore, etc. Better perhaps, "Let those of you who can" (Gr. *οἱ δυνατοὶ ἐν ὑμῖν*).

6 more than ten days. Other authorities have "not more than eight or ten days" (so Luther's version).

7 complaints. R.V., "charges"; *i.e.*, heresy, impiety, and sedition, as xxiv. 5, 6: replied to by Paul in a different order.

8 neither against the law of the Jews, etc. This is a summary of Paul's reply, on a full hearing before Festus, to the three accusations.

9 to do the Jews a pleasure. See on xxiv. 27.

before me. Meaning probably, "in my presence"; but by the Sanhedrin, and according to Jewish law. Paul, however, seeing that Festus is inclined to yield to the Jews, and knowing that he could not expect justice at Jerusalem, insists on his right to be tried as a Roman citizen (10); and as a last resource appeals to the emperor.

11 offender. Or, "wrong-doer," R.V.

12 council. Roman governors had a council of assessors appointed to aid them in dispensing justice.

Hast thou appealed, etc.? Better, "Thou hast appealed unto Cæsar."

unto Cæsar shalt thou go. Thus fulfilling both Paul's desire (xix. 21), and the Lord's promise (xxiii. 11).

13 Agrippa. The son of Herod Agrippa I., mentioned in ch. xii. At his father's death Judæa was put under a Roman governor; but he afterwards received the kingdoms of his uncles, Herod of Chalcis, and Philip, with some additions. He was now living, it was believed, in incest with his sister Bernice; who was afterwards connected with Vespasian and Titus. He was professedly a believer in Judaism, but adhered to the Romans in the last Jewish war.

14 when they had been there many days. R.V., "as they tarried there many days": their visit being a prolonged one.

16 not the manner of the Romans. Emphatic, "of *Romans*"; implying, "whatever it may be with *Jews*."

18 such things as I supposed. See xviii. 14, and note.

19 their own superstition. Rather, of their own *religion* (R.V.) (cp. xvii. 22, and note). Festus would not be likely to speak disrespectfully of Judaism to Agrippa.

21 the hearing. R.V., "the decision."

Augustus. That is, Nero. "Augustus" and "Cæsar" had become titles of the Roman emperors.

22 I would. More precisely, "I could wish"; the form being similar to that in Rom. ix. 3.

23 chief captains. Lit., "chiliarchs," commanders of 1000 men: see on xxi. 31.

24 have dealt with me. "Made suit to me"; or "complained to me."

26 my lord. *i.e.*, to the sovereign lord. This was a title which had recently been accepted by the emperors.

CHAPTER XXVI

1 Agrippa. Presiding on this occasion, Festus, his host, courteously giving way to him, on account of his kingly rank.

answered for himself. Better, "made his defence" (R.V.). Cp. his address in ch. xxii.

2 I think myself happy, etc. I am glad now to plead before one who, being himself a Jew, knows these things so well. Rabbinical writers say that Agrippa had great knowledge of the law. The order in the original is very effective: "Touching all things whereof I am accused by Jews, O King Agrippa, I count myself happy that before thee I am this day to make my defence, because thou art especially expert," etc. (see R.V. marg.).

6 the promise. The promise of the Messiah, which still binds together our scattered tribes, and sustains us in "assiduously" attending upon our national rites (7). I am accused because I believe that this hope is fulfilled in Jesus, as demonstrated by His resurrection; which you surely do not think impossible, and which I can prove to be a fact: cp. xiii. 32, 33.

8 that God should raise. Rather, "if God raises." Paul speaks of it as a constant occurrence.

10 the saints. Or, "holy ones."

they were put to death. It appears, then, that Stephen was not the only martyr in the first persecution.

gave my voice. Lit., "a vote against them" (see viii. 1; xxii. 20). This does not prove that Paul was a member of the Sanhedrin; for the words may mean no more than hearty concurrence.

11 in every synagogue. Or, "throughout all synagogues"; *i.e.*, all that he could reach. The "punishing" was by scourging: see Matt. x. 17.

compelled. Rather, "was compelling," by all this violence. "I strove to make them blaspheme," R.V. His success, however, was probably not greater than that of Pliny, who, writing to the Emperor Trajan, says that no real Christians could be forced to blaspheme.

12–18. See notes on ix. 3–6. Our Lord's words to Saul are here more fully recorded.

14 in the Hebrew tongue. It was needless to mention this fact in Paul's Hebrew, or Aramaic address to the people (xxii. 7). He is now speaking in Greek.

to kick against the pricks ("goads"). Thy opposition injures only thyself. The metaphor is taken from animals who kick when goaded.

16 I have appeared unto thee for this purpose. Paul combines the message sent him through Ananias with the words addressed to himself personally on the way to Damascus.

17 whom. Both "the people" (the Jews) and the Gentiles.

18 to turn [them]. Rather, "that they may turn" (R.V.). We have here a clear statement of God's great object in establishing the gospel ministry, and of the way in which He accomplishes it. The mind is enlightened, so that the soul turns to God, and thus obtains, by faith in Christ, pardon, and a standing among the sanctified.

21 For these causes. For executing this Divine commission; not for any violation of the law.

22 I continue. "I have stood."

23 that Christ should suffer, etc. Lit., "since the Christ is a suffering Christ" (cp. Isa. liii.). This was and is the great stumbling-block to the Jews. The points are, a *suffering* Messiah, His *resurrection*, and a Gospel *for all mankind.*

24 thou art beside thyself. Rather, "Thou art mad" (R.V.) (25). The defence being addressed to Agrippa as a Jew, the strangeness of its topics, and the warmth of the speaker, might easily make Festus think him insane; and his appeals to the ancient Scriptures suggested a cause for his insanity. "Thy much learning" is literally in original, "the many writings."

25 most noble. An official appellation: see xxiv. 3.

26 For the king knoweth, etc. With great tact and courtesy, Paul reminds Festus that what he thought irrational was firmly believed by his royal guest, who was also cognisant of the facts alleged.

in a corner. These events occurred not in some obscure place, but in the metropolis of Judæa, and during a great public festival. This is one of the great historical evidences of the Crucifixion and Resurrection of our Lord.

28 Almost. Tyndale and Cranmer render the phrase, "somewhat." Your appeals have some force, but not enough to induce a Jewish prince to become a *Christian*, a disciple of the Nazarene. The R.V. gives a different turn to Agrippa's words: "With but little persuasion thou wouldest fain make me a Christian."

29 altogether. Lit., "both in little and in much"; that is, both in a small and large degree.

these bonds. The chains or fetters by which he was bound.

32 if he had not appealed unto Cæsar. "The procurator had now lost the control of the case; and had no more power to acquit the prisoner than to condemn him" (*Hackett*).

CHAPTER XXVII

1 we. Luke (last mentioned before in xxi. 18) was of the party.

Augustus' band. Lit., "the Augustan cohort." Several of the Roman legions bore this name; and a body-guard of veterans formed by the Emperors was named *Augustani*; but no trace can be found elsewhere of any cohort so called.

2 Adramyttium. A sea-port of Mysia (now *Endramit*) on the western coast of Asia Minor.

to sail by the coasts of Asia. Or, "to sail to the Asiatic seaports" (*Moffatt*).

Aristarchus. Aristarchus has been mentioned before: see xix. 29; xx. 4, and notes.

3 Sidon. See xii. 20, and note.

entreated. That is, "treated"; probably in part because Paul was a Roman citizen, and no doubt also by direction of the procurator, Paul's personal demeanour making also a favourable impression.

to refresh himself. Or, "to be cared for," by these friends: see xxi. 3, 4.

4 under Cyprus. That is, under the lee of Cyprus (R.V.). Their direct course would have been south of Cyprus (cp. xxi. 3); but the prevailing west wind compelled them to go north of the island ("the sea which is off Cilicia and Pamphylia," ver. 5); where they would have the land breeze in their favour, as well as a current which runs along the southern coast of Asia Minor.

5 Myra. A large city on a hill near the coast; once the metropolis of Lycia; now in ruins.

6 a ship of Alexandria. A ship sailing from Alexandria to Italy, when the west wind prevailed, would naturally stand for the north, and so reach the coast of Asia Minor.

7 scarce. Rather, "with difficulty"; for the west wind caused them to take several days in sailing about 130 geographical miles. Cnidus was a large sea-port, with a fine harbour, on a projecting peninsula between Cos and Rhodes (see xxi. 1), at the entrance of the Ægean Sea.

not (further) **suffering us.** That is, not suffering us to proceed westward. They therefore made for Crete, passed round Salmone, its eastern promontory, and kept under the lee of its southern coast, until they reached "Fair Havens," a roadstead lying a little east of Cape Matala, and sheltered by it from the prevailing wind. At this cape the land sweeps round to the north-west; so that the full force of the wind and sea from the west would be felt.

8 hardly. That is, "with difficulty (as in ver. 7) coasting along it" namely, Crete.

Lasæa. Lasæa was about five miles eastward of The Fair Havens, and was probably the nearest town. Both names are still in use.

9 the Fast. The great Jewish fast-day of Atonement occurred about the beginning of October, which was regarded as too late in the season to begin a long voyage.

10 I perceive. Already he had become familiar with the dangers of the sea: see note xxvii. 44.

11 the master. The "master" may have been the sailing-master, or pilot. The owner of the ship was usually on board, and sometimes acted as captain of the vessel.

12 not commodious, etc. "Badly placed" (Gr. ἀνευθέτου).

Phenice. Rather, "Phœnix." This harbour "looketh *down* the south-west wind and *down* the north-west wind" (literal trans.); that is, it faces the north-east and south-east (R.V.). This answers to the harbour of *Lutra*, with its two entrances formed by an island in front; one looking north-east, the other south-east.

13 supposing, etc. With a gentle south wind they might hope to pass Cape Matala, and to cross the bay to Phœnix, in a few hours, the total distance being about 38 miles.

loosing [thence], etc. More clearly in R.V., "they weighed anchor, and sailed along Crete, close inshore."

14 there arose against it. This may mean either "*struck against her,*" *i.e.*, the ship, or "*rushed down it,*" *i.e.*, the island. The R.V. adopts the latter: "there beat down from it," *i.e.*, from the shore. In that part of the Mediterranean a southerly breeze is often suddenly followed by a violent hurricane (the Greek is the same as our word "typhoon") from the north-east (*Euraquilo*).

15 And when the ship, etc. Rather, "And when the ship was seized, and could not face the wind, we gave up [the attempt to work to windward], and were borne along," *i.e.*, before the wind, to the south-west, till we neared the little island of Clauda (Cauda; now *Gozzo*), running under the lee of its southern shore (16). There, however, the sea was still so rough that "we had hard work to get the boat on board."

17 helps. Extra means to strengthen the ship. This was chiefly done by "undergirding" it, or passing cables (which ancient ships carried for the purpose) several times round the hull, so as to tighten it by outward pressure.

into the quicksands. Rather, "upon the Syrtis" (R.V.). A violent north-easter would drive them straight into the Syrtis Major, a large sandy gulf, greatly dreaded by seamen, on the north coast of Africa, near Cyrene.

strake sail. Rather, "*lowered* the gear" (R.V.), probably the heavy tackle and main-yard on the mast. To enable them to escape the Syrtis, they must have carried some sail. It is supposed that they brought the vessel to, with the right side to the wind; and that thus, with the boat secured, the ship undergirded, and the stormsails set to keep the vessel steady, they let her drift, at the rate of about a mile and a half an hour, in a leeward direction, making her course west by north.

18 lightened. They probably threw out part of the cargo. The whole narrative indicates that the ship had become leaky.

19 the tackling. "The ship's gear."

20 neither sun nor stars, etc. The sun and stars were the only guides of ancient mariners when out of sight of land.

21 after long abstinence. See note on ver. 33.

to have gained, etc. Or, "and have escaped (not have gained) this hurt and damage" (ver. 10).

23 serve. Lit., "worship."

25 I believe God. "The supernatural world was a greater reality to Paul than the natural" (*Charles Brown*).

27 fourteenth. The fourteenth since leaving Crete: see vers. 18, 19.

driven up and down. "Drifting about in." "Adria," or the Adriatic Sea, anciently comprised the whole central basin of the Mediterranean between Sicily and Greece, as well as the Venetian Gulf.

the shipmen (sailors) **deemed,** etc. Paul's intimation would quicken the sailors' attention to every sign of land. It is supposed that they were near the point of Koura, on the coast of Malta; where, though the land is too low to be seen in a dark night, the breakers can be heard at a considerable distance; the white lines of foam would also be faintly visible.

29 four anchors. Ancient vessels usually carried several anchors; and they were ordinarily anchored, like ours, by the bow. But on this occasion, by anchoring from the stern, the ship would be more easily arrested, she would be prevented from swinging round on the rocks, and would be in a better position for being run on shore in the morning.

30 under colour, etc. Pretending that they were about to "lay out anchors from the bow," carrying them in the boat as far forwards as possible.

31 Except these abide, etc. God's promises (see ver. 22) always suppose the use of proper means on our part.

32 let her fall off. The willingness of the soldiers to sacrifice the boat in such circumstances shows that the apostle had gained a wonderful ascendency over the minds of his companions.

33 meat. Rather, as elsewhere, "food."

having taken nothing. They evidently had food on board (38); but amidst the confusion and danger had been neither able nor disposed to prepare regular meals and to take adequate nourishment: see ver. 21.

34 health. "Safety."

there shall not a hair fall, etc. A proverbial expression for the slightest injury or loss: see 1 Kings i. 52; Matt. x. 30; Luke xxi. 12.

37 two hundred threescore and sixteen. The large Egyptian corn ships which brought supplies to Rome sometimes carried hundreds of passengers: see Josephus, *Life*, § 3 ("six hundred"). But the reading: "seventy-six," substituting for "two hundred" the Greek word ὡς ("about"), has considerable authority in its support.

38 the wheat. That is, probably, the ship's cargo: wheat being the chief export of Egypt to Italy. The present safety and the subsequent management of the ship made it necessary to lighten her.

39 a certain creek, etc. Rather, "a creek having a sandy beach"; on which they could run the ship, with the hope of saving their lives. The vessel appears, however, to have grounded on a shoal before they reached the point on shore at which they aimed.

40 And when, etc. Rather, "And having cut away the anchors, they let them fall into the sea; at the same time loosing the lashings of the rudders, and hoisting the foresail to the wind, they steered towards shore." The rudders were two large paddles, one on each side of the ship. These had been made fast while the ship was anchored (see 29), but were now loosed to guide her towards the shore.

41 where two seas met. That this was the Bay of St. Paul in Malta is inferred thus:—(1) A vessel lying-to, with her right side to an east-north-east wind, would drift west by north; which is the course from Clauda to Malta. (2) The rate of drift would be a mile and a half an hour, which would take her from Clauda to Malta in thirteen days. (3) The first point of land which a ship so drifting would approach is the east point of this bay. (4) The soundings and anchorage agree with those in the narrative (28, 29). (5) The channel between the island of Salmonetta and the mainland would appear "a place between two seas."

was broken. R.V., "began to break up."

42 escape. The guards being held answerable under the severest penalties, for the security of the prisoners.

44 safe to land. This was not Paul's first escape from shipwreck: see 2 Cor. xi. 25, written several years before this occasion.

CHAPTER XXVIII

1 Melita. That this was Malta is shown by the preceding notes, and also by the course of the subsequent voyage by Syracuse to Puteoli.

2 barbarous people. The Greeks, and afterwards the Romans, called all nations but themselves *barbarians;* using the term with reference to difference of language, rather than of civilisation. A parallel is the Russian name for a German—*Niemetz,* "the dumb"—because he did not speak or understand the Russian language. The ancient Maltese were of Phœnician origin.

3 out of the heat. Rather, "*on account of* the heat," which aroused the viper from its torpor. Venomous serpents are no longer found in Malta, the aboriginal forests having been all cleared away.

4 No doubt this man, etc. Seeing Paul to be a prisoner, they inferred from the attack of the viper that he had committed some atrocious crime, and that Justice (personified) exacted the penalty.

6 fallen down dead suddenly. Sudden collapse and death often ensue from the bite of serpents.

7 the chief man. Or "Governor." The title here used is found in ancient inscriptions in Malta. It was applied probably to the Deputy of the Prætor of Sicily. Publius is a Roman name.

8 fever and of a bloody flux. Lit., "attacks of fever and dysentery."

healed him. We have in vers. 3–8 two remarkable fulfilments of the Lord's promise, Mark xvi. 18.

11 three months. The three months were probably November, December, and January; after which the season may perhaps have admitted of their putting to sea earlier than usual.

whose sign was Castor and Pollux. Lit., "with the sign of Dioscuri" ("the Twin Brothers," R.V.); *i.e.*, having on the bow images of Castor and Pollux, who were the favourite gods of seamen: see Hor. *Od.* i. 3, 2.

12 Syracuse. Then the capital of Sicily, about 80 miles from Malta.

13 fetched a compass. Or, "made a circuit" (R.V.); perhaps, "tacked."

Rhegium. A sea-port on the southern coast of Italy, now called *Reggio.* From Rhegium to Puteoli, about 180 miles, they made the voyage in less than two days, the wind being favourable.

Puteoli. Now *Pozzuoli*, seven miles north-west of Naples. It was the principal port of Southern Italy, and the place where the Alexandrian corn ships were accustomed to unload. Passengers for Rome would disembark here, and finish their journey by land.

14 were desired, etc. Paul seems to have been allowed to comply with the request; and thus the Roman Christians had time to hear of his arrival and come to meet him (ver. 15).

15 Appii Forum. "The Market of Appius," R.V.; about thirty-three miles from Rome. "The Three Taverns" was a group of wine-shops or inns, ten miles nearer to the city. Some of the Roman Christians went further than others.

took courage. Paul could not but feel anxious respecting the feelings of the Roman Christians towards him.

16 the captain of the guard. Lit., "the commander of the camp": *i.e.*, of the Prætorian Camp, occupied by the Prætorian or Imperial Guard. This officer had charge of persons accused, and bound for trial. (But the best MSS. and versions omit the clause.)

Paul was suffered, etc. The letter of Festus, and still more the report of Julius, may have secured this lenient treatment. The form of imprisonment to which Paul was subjected was known as *libera custodia*: "free custody." The prisoner had his own lodgings, but was chained by one arm to "the soldiers that kept him." By the necessary changes of guards, the apostle would soon become known to many of the Prætorian soldiers: see Phil. i. 13.

17 the chief of the Jews. These were probably the rulers of the synagogue, and the influential men in the community. Respecting the Jews at Rome, see note on xviii. 2, and note on Rom. xvi. 3.

20 the hope of Israel. That is, the hope of a Messiah, which the nation cherished: see xxvi. 6, and note.

21 We neither received letters, etc. They had no official or private report about him. For this there had hardly been time.

22 this sect. Or, "heresy." The Christian sect. See note on xxiv. 14. The Jewish leaders may have adopted this conciliatory tone because they saw that Paul was favoured by the Roman officers.

25 Well spake, etc. What the prophet said is most appropriate to *you.*

26 Hearing ye shall hear, etc. This solemn passage, quoted by our Lord when He began to teach by parables (Matt. xiii. 14), and by the last evangelist in reviewing the results of the Saviour's personal ministry (John xii. 40), forms an impressive conclusion of Paul's appeal to his countrymen at this crisis. Compare the conclusion of the great Messianic prophecy, Isa. xl.–lxvi.: see Isa. lxvi. 1, and note.

THE EPISTLE OF ST. PAUL TO THE ROMANS

INTRODUCTION

THIS letter, written from Corinth probably A.D. 56–57, is a striking combination of the doctrinal and the practical. St. Paul was a theologian. The character of God—the subject of theology—was a favourite theme with him. But he thought of the character of God in relation to human life. It is true that the great doctrine of the Epistle is justification by faith. But it is true also that this is no mere academic dogma. It is a doctrine which, as the preaching of it at the Reformation, and since, has shown, has a profound influence on human life. Hence, if the theme of the earlier chapters (i.–v.) is justification, that of the later chapters (vi.; vii.; viii. 1–12; xii.–xv. and much of xvi.) is sanctification.

The letter commences with a bold declaration. The writer has never yet been to Rome, but he longs to come there (i. 10, 11). It is the time of Nero, but the apostle is not afraid. Rome is the centre of the world's thought and culture, but he is not ashamed of his Master or of His message (i. 16). And he confronts the scepticism of Rome as he had already confronted the scepticism of Athens, with his confident assertion of the resurrection of Christ (i. 4; cp. Acts xvii. 18, 31).

Righteousness is the great subject of the Epistle—the righteousness of God, producing righteousness in man. It is this that gives the Gospel the Divine power of which he speaks (i. 16, 17).

In the first chapter, St. Paul shows the need of humanity for redemption and for righteousness. He gives a terrible picture of pagan life, which is confirmed by a study of the great Latin dramatists. But his Gospel is one for Jews and Gentiles alike, and hence he shows how the Jew also needs redemption and righteousness. That the law cannot save is the theme of ii. 17–29, and of iii. and iv. "By the deeds of the law shall no flesh be justified in His sight" (iii. 20). But the righteousness of God provides a way of redemption for man (iii. 22, 25), "the redemption that is in Christ Jesus" (iii. 24). This leads up to the great doctrine of justification by faith (v. 1), in which the practical comfort and encouragement are at once shown (v. 2–5).

The climax, reasoned yet passionate, enthusiastic, convinced and convincing, is reached in the second part of the eighth chapter (18–39). Here, too, comes in the comfort for men and women who were facing death for the Gospel's sake. "Who shall separate us from the love of Christ?" (ver. 35).

And then comes the great passage which Lightfoot and Hort regard as in some sense the heart of the Epistle (ix.–xi.). It is the passage which shows that the Gospel is a message both for Jew and Gentile (ix. 8, 24, 25, 30; x. 12, 13; xi. 11, 12, 32).

Some writers of to-day contrast unfavourably the teaching of St. Paul with that of Christ, but a careful study of chapters xii.–xv. shows how very fully the apostle had imbibed the spirit and enforces the teaching of the Saviour (see especially xii. 14, 15, 17, 20; xiii. 6, 8–10; xiv. 14; xv. 3). Christ was the very heart and centre of his thought, of his life, of his teaching (xv. 18).

The closing chapter shows his deep affection and solicitude for his friends at Rome, his grateful remembrance of kindnesses shown to him, and his desire that the little company of Christians should preserve unity amongst themselves The same confidence in his message and in the final triumph of the Gospel is to be noted in the end as in the beginning of the Letter. "The God of peace shall bruise Satan under your feet shortly" (xvi. 20). "To Him that is of power to stablish you according to my Gospel, and the preaching of Jesus Christ" (xvi. 25).

CHAPTER I

1 separated unto the gospel of God. That is, set apart by God's choice and call as a preacher of the gospel (Acts ix. 15; Gal. i. 15: cp. Jer. i. 5).

2 by (*or,* through) **his prophets.** Including all (Acts iii. 22–24) who had been Divinely authorised to record God's promises and their own expectation of the Messiah, in the Old Testament. The apostle thus reminds his Roman brethren (who, though mostly Gentiles, had learned the Mosaic law before they had heard the gospel) that the gospel was the fulfilment of the hopes which the ancient Scriptures had held out.

3 concerning His Son, etc. Our Lord is here set forth as the subject of ancient promise and of "the gospel of God." As to His lower nature ("the flesh": see John i. 14, and note), He "was made" of David's royal race; and as to His higher nature, which is essentially Divine and therefore spiritual (see John iv. 24, and note), He was marked out "with power" as the Son of God. Pearson (*On the Creed,* Art. ii.) shows that the original here means more than "declared." "Thus was He defined or constituted, and appointed to be the Son of God," etc. This interpretation of "the spirit of holiness," as referring to Christ's Divine nature, rather than to the Third Person of the Trinity, seems most in accordance with the general thought of the passage. The resurrection was the proof, evidence, or seal of His Divine Sonship.

5 for obedience to the faith. R.V. reads, "unto obedience of faith," *i.e.,* "obedience springing from faith," which seems more accurately to represent the original: see xvi. 26. The words indicate the purpose of his apostleship—"to win men to obedience" (*Weymouth*).

6 the called of Jesus Christ. Or, as R.V., "called *to be* Jesus Christ's." Not merely invited, but made partakers of the blessing which Jesus Christ bestows: see 1 Cor. vii. 17, 18, 21; Heb. iii. 1.

7 called [to be] saints. Not only by external profession (see Acts ix. 32, etc.), but also by the cultivation of spirituality and holiness (see Col. i. 12, etc.).

Grace to you and peace. "Grace" is the favour of God; and "peace" all the blessedness which flows from that favour. The Lord Jesus is, equally with the Father, the source of both these blessings.

8 through Jesus Christ. Thanksgiving is acceptable only when it is prompted by the Spirit of Christ, and offered in reliance on the mediation of Christ (Eph. v. 20). Every one of Paul's Epistles, except that to the Galatians, begins with language of conciliation, if not of commendation.

throughout the whole world. "Everywhere." "Spoken of" is emphatic. R.V., "proclaimed." Cp. 1 Thess. i. 8.

9 God is my witness. Such solemn declarations, indicative of the warmth of his religious sympathies, are not infrequent in Paul's writings (see 2 Cor. i. 23; Gal. i. 20; Phil. i. 8).

whom I serve with my spirit. Rather, "whom I worship in my spirit." Paul's was no formal worship, but the spiritual service of one whose whole heart was engaged in spreading the gospel.

10 have a prosperous journey. R.V., "be prospered," *i.e.*, be favoured by the arrangements of Divine Providence, so as to be able to come. But how different the realisation of his wish from what he had anticipated! (Acts xxviii. 14).

11 some spiritual gift. The word *charisma*, "gift," applies in the apostle's writings to both the ordinary and the extraordinary effects of Divine grace. For the former see v. 15; vi. 23; for the latter, xii. 6; 1 Cor. xii. 4, 31.

12 that I may be comforted together with you, etc. Rather, as R.V., "that I with you may be comforted in you, each of us by the other's faith," *i.e.*, I by your faith, and you by mine. With the most winning modesty, and in the spirit of true sympathy, Paul refers to his own dependence on the communion of saints for instruction and comfort.

13 Now. Rather, "But."

oftentimes. See Acts xix. 21; Rom. xv. 22-24. Had these plans been fulfilled at the time, the Roman church would no doubt have been greatly edified; but the universal church would have missed a great benefit. To Paul's thwarted desire we owe, under God, this Epistle.

was let. "Let" is the old English word for "*hindered*." What were the particular hindrances we are not informed. In the course of the apostle's travels his plans were frustrated, sometimes by the various openings that offered for preaching the gospel in other countries (xv. 22), sometimes by special Divine interpositions (Acts xvi. 6, 7), once at least by opposition so malignant that it could only be attributed to Satan (1 Thess. ii. 18).

14 I am debtor, etc. He felt his personal obligation to seek the good of every man whom he could reach.

Barbarians. See note on Acts xxviii. 2; see also 1 Cor. xiv. 11. No differences in race or in mental endowment set aside this great obligation.

15 to you that are at Rome also. The Romans, now the masters of the "Greeks," were classed under this appellation. The implied thought here seems to be that Rome, with all its majesty, power, tyranny, the wonders of its art, the culture of its schools, did not deter the apostle. Hence the next verse.

16 For I am not ashamed, etc. Far from being "ashamed of the gospel," the apostle gloried (Gal. vi. 14) in its evident Divine origin and authority, displayed in forms of "power." Power was Rome's special boast: Paul seems therefore to fix on this one characteristic of the gospel, as embodying a moral and spiritual force greater than all other forms of might—a power to save, an influence adapted to all mankind; its results being secured through the exercise of simple faith. In this verse is the summary of the whole Epistle.

to the Jew first, etc. To the Jews in the first instance, and then to the Greeks, or the Gentiles in general: see Luke xxiv. 47; Acts iii. 26; xiii. 46. "Jews and Gentiles" was the Jewish, as "Greeks and Barbarians" was the Greek expression for all mankind.

17 For therein is the (*or*, a) **righteousness of God revealed.** The reason why the gospel is powerful in saving men from God's wrath (18) is, that it reveals "a righteousness of God by faith." The gospel is here spoken of as revealing "a righteousness of God." The law had made known the Divine righteousness, His holiness, His retributive justice; but the gospel further shows how this righteousness may *become ours;* in other words, God's METHOD OF JUSTIFICATION.

from faith to faith. "Depending on faith and tending to produce faith" (*Weymouth*). In faith the Christian life begins, by faith it is maintained, and faith is its consummation. "Faith" here includes not only the intellectual reception of the doctrines of the gospel, but also practical trust in the Saviour.

The just shall live by faith. Paul appeals to Hab. ii. 4 (on which see note) in proof of the importance of faith. The words, as quoted by the apostle, may mean, "The just shall live (*i.e.*, be kept safe and happy) by faith"; or, "The just by faith (*i.e.*, he that is accepted through faith) shall live." In either way the quotation shows the paramount importance of faith; but the former is more accordant with the Old Testament passage both in Heb. and LXX. It was these words of Habbakuk that helped to open the eyes of Luther. "Straightway I felt as if I were born anew," he writes.

18 the wrath of God. "The wrath of God" is His holy displeasure against sin, with His determination to punish it. These are being "revealed from heaven," *i.e.*, made known throughout the whole course of the Divine government. The statement thus stands in striking antithesis with that which closes the preceding paragraph. A "wrath of God is being revealed": as well as a "righteousness of God." The one meets the other; and to understand adequately the meaning of "salvation," it is requisite to apprehend both.

ungodliness and unrighteousness. "Ungodliness"—a wrong state of heart towards God. "Unrighteousness"—the neglect of practical virtue.

who hold the truth. Rather, "who hinder or suppress" (R.V., "hold down the truth"); not allowing what they know of it to have its due influence (21, 28). Truth repressed by sinful living is soon forgotten or perverted: cp. John vii. 17.

19 that which may be known of God. Or, "that which is known of God (by the light of nature and of human reason and consciousness, in distinction from revelation) is manifested to them," by testimony of the visible world (20), as well as from the constitution of their own nature (ii. 15).

20 the invisible things of Him, etc. God's being and perfections in themselves invisible, are yet seen, and ever have been seen since the world was created, being recognised in His works: cp. Acts xiv. 17.

21 because that, when they knew God, etc. It

is here clearly taught that it is possible for the human mind to know God. He reveals Himself, "His eternal power and Godhead" in His works. It was this that made men without excuse, that they did not "glorify Him as God."

vain in their imaginations. "Futile speculations" (*Moffatt*); "useless discussions" (*Weymouth*). Their heedless and wicked hearts lost all right apprehensions of the Divine character; and hence they became more and more degraded, worshipping even birds, beasts, and reptiles. Idols of the human form prevailed in Greece; those of the bestial in Egypt; Rome united both: see Juvenal, *Sat.* vi. 325–340.

22 Professing themselves to be wise, etc. While making high pretensions to wisdom (as did their sages and philosophers), they manifested the greatest folly.

23 changed. Instead of "changed into," this should be rendered "exchanged for"; and so in ver. 25. They exchanged "the truth of God for a lie" (see ver. 25; Jer. xvi. 19), *i.e.*, the true idea of the glorious and eternal God for images of His creatures.

24 gave them up, etc. Properly, "gave them up to uncleanness in the lusts of their own hearts." What Paul here presents as the judicial act of God in His moral government, he affirms in Eph. iv. 18, 19 to be the heathen's own act, for "they have given themselves over unto lasciviousness," etc.; see note on Matt. xiii. 14.

25 who changed. The word here rendered "who" indicates *the reason* of what has been said; as R.V., "for that they changed": see Acts xvii. 11; James iv. 14. And so in ver. 32.

more than the Creator. Better, as R.V., "rather than the Creator," implying the exclusion of God from their reverence and worship; at the thought of which Paul expresses his horror by an ascription of praise to God.

27 recompence. This sensuality, with all its physical, mental, and moral evils, is repeatedly and emphatically (24, 26, 28) declared to be an inevitable consequence, and a just penalty, of men's ("error" or) departure from God.

28 as they did not like, etc. Because they *reprobated* the knowledge of God (23–25), He gave them up to a *reprobate* mind, which showed itself in deeds not "convenient," *i.e.*, not fit or proper, including all the vices named in vers. 29–31. The writings of contemporary Greek and Latin authors show that this dark picture of the morals of the heathen world is by no means too deeply coloured. See Storrs: *The Moral Evidence of Christianity;* Leland, *On the Necessity of Divine Revelation;* Tholuck, *On Heathenism;* and Döllinger, *The Gentile and the Jew.* This is equally correct as a portraiture of the heathen in the present day.

29 whisperers. The "whisperers" are secret maligners as distinguished from "backbiters," who are rather public slanderers.

30 haters of God. Or, "hateful to God."

31 without natural affection. Self-divested of the affection naturally existing between all near relatives, whether by blood or by marriage.

32 knowing the judgement of God, etc. The climax of depravity. They know God's sentence of death—the severest punishment—for such sins, yet they commit them. And, more shamelessly still, they applaud and encourage others who commit them. Many a wicked man will condemn in others what he practises himself. To applaud it betokens a conscience utterly deadened.

CHAPTER II

1 another. Rather, "the other"; "your fellow-man."

2 we are sure. Or simply, as R.V., "we know." "Judgement *of God*"; emphatically contrasted with that of *man* (ver. 1).

3 thinkest thou this? Perhaps, "thou reckonest . . . that *thou* wilt escape the judgement of God. Or is it that thou despisest," etc.? Men will admit that others are guilty and will be condemned, yet hope that they shall themselves escape; and will make light of God's sparing mercy, not "considering" that it is intended to lead them to repent (4). Thus they incur a heavier condemnation.

4 the riches. Of His "goodness" or beneficence, shown in that long-suffering which delays deserved punishment.

5 against the day. Lit., "in the day"; wrath to be manifested in the day of wrath or judgement. God's displeasure against sin is already revealed (i. 18); but there is to be a final stage of this revelation, in which His justice will be fully vindicated.

6 who will render to every man, etc. In vers. 6–11 the strict equity of the Divine awards is set forth, to show that God will deal with the Jew as with the Gentile, according to his real character. The connexion of the "well-doing" here spoken of with the faith which justifies (see iii. 28), is shown afterwards in chapters vi. and vii.

7 immortality. Or, "incorruption" (R.V.). Men were originally crowned with "glory and honour" (Psa. viii. 5); but they were soon corrupted and destroyed. "In patient well-doing" the Christian seeks to regain them, no more liable to be corrupted, and his desire is granted in the gift of "eternal life."

8 contentious. Rather, "factious" (R.V.); *i.e.*, partisans from interested motives, and hence opponents to "the truth"; a sin of which the Jews were often guilty: see Isa. i. 2–4; Jer. v. 23; Acts vii. 51; Rom. x. 3. Such will have to endure outward inflictions and inward anguish, the dreadful consequences of Divine "wrath."

9 of the Jew first. The Jew, being "first" in privilege, is justly "first" in punishment: see i. 16; cp. Luke xii. 47, 48.

11 respect of persons. "Respect of persons," here as elsewhere means undue partiality: see 2 Chron. xix. 7; Acts x. 34.

12 without law. The Gentiles had no written law, but they had the law of nature or conscience (14, 15); and by that law they shall be judged. Their ruin will not be because they have disobeyed an unknown law, but because they have rebelled against that which they knew.

13 not the hearers of the law, etc. Law does not justify those who merely have it, like the Jews who "heard" it read constantly in their synagogues, but those who obediently keep it.

14 when the Gentiles. Rather, "when Gentiles" (R.V.), *i.e.*, if any of them, etc.

by nature. That is, following the true teachings of nature and conscience: see note on ver. 12.

15 which show. More precisely, as R.V., "in that they (the Gentiles) show," etc.

the work of the law. The law itself, here described from a practical point of view; "the conduct which the law prescribes," or "the effect of the law."

their thoughts the meanwhile accusing, etc. Rather, "one with another, their thoughts accusing, or even defending them": *i.e.*, their moral judgements and reasonings, represented as in mutual discussion, either condemned or defended their conduct.

16 in the day when, etc. This clause may be connected with the preceding verse, as referring to the anticipation of the great day of judgement, "the day" which is so often referred to by our Lord and His apostles (see Matt. vii. 22), and which is more or less in the heart and conscience of every man.

the secrets of men. The judgement will comprehend not only men's works, often done to be seen and admired, but even those hidden things in the heart and life which form the true tests of character.

my gospel. Cp. Acts xvii. 31, and Gal. i. 6–12.

17 thou. The pronoun "thou" is emphatic here, applying the argument, in the most pointed way, to the Jew.

18 approvest the things that are most excellent. Or, "triest things which differ": as one "instructed out of the law," which is "the form (or embodiment) of knowledge and truth."

21 Thou therefore, etc. If you are what you claim to be, your guilt must be the greater in sinning against all these privileges.

22 dost thou commit sacrilege? Lit., "dost thou rob temples?" So R.V. Thou that abhorrest idols, dost thou rob their temples? The reference may be to the greed of Jews, who, while professing a horror of idolatry, nevertheless made a gain out of the objects of heathen worship.

24 as it is written. As if he had said, For what is written in Ezek. xxxvi. 20–23 (on which see note) is no less true now of you. The prophet's words are equally applicable to the inconsistencies of nominal Christians.

25 For circumcision verily profiteth, etc. The apostle now puts the ceremonial distinctions, to which the Jews attributed most importance, in disparaging contrast with the "righteousness of the law" (26) or its "moral requirements"; showing that the privileges connected with these distinctions are lost by those who neglect, and enjoyed by those who observe its moral precepts.

27 And shall not (the) **uncircumcision**, etc.? Shall not the uncircumcised, if they keep God's law (see vers. 14, 15), condemn those who, while possessing the law and ordinances, only transgress them? Vers. 25–29 show that Divine ordinances do not of themselves convey grace.

29 in the spirit, etc. The circumcision of the heart is effected, not by the literal observance of mere rites, but by the spiritual truth in the law or the gospel operating in the inner nature of man, where it is seen and approved by God.

CHAPTER III

1 What advantage then hath the Jew? Having shown (cp. ver. 9) that the Jews, as well as the Gentiles, are guilty, the apostle now meets the objection that this truth robs the Jew of all his superiority. The two questions here put have substantially the same meaning; and form together the first of a series of interrogations in which a Jewish inquirer is represented as stating difficulties in the way of the apostle's conclusion (see vers. 3, 5, 7, 9).

2 chiefly. Rather, "first of all" (R.V.). Paul does not here specify the other advantages of the Jews, some of which are enumerated in ix. 4, 5.

oracles. See Acts vii. 38, and note; 1 Pet. iv. 11.

3 shall their unbelief, etc. The second question, Shall the admitted unfaithfulness of some to the covenant make God's faithful promise without effect? Nay, God is true, though all else be false.

4 God forbid. Lit., "Let it not be": and so in other places. The full sentence is found in 1 Kings xxi. 3.

as it is written, etc. The Septuagint version of Psa. li. 4 is here followed; and its difference from the Hebrew does not affect the object of the quotation. "When Thou art judged" means, "When men take account of Thy dealings."

5 if our unrighteousness, etc. The third question. To "commend" is to "give proof of," or "establish." "The righteousness of God," or "justice of God."

6 how shall God judge the world? The answer to the objection. To act upon the principle of the objector would make all moral estimates impossible.

7 why yet am I also judged, etc.? The fourth question of the supposed objector, a variation of the preceding. "If the truth of God has been more abundantly established by my unfaithfulness, why further am I, individually, also to be condemned and punished as a sinner?"

8 And not [**rather**], etc. This interrogation is best taken as the apostle's answer to the objector's plea, bringing it to an absurdity. If you claim to be exempt from punishment because your sin is overruled for God's glory, you may as well at once adopt the profoundly immoral maxim, "Let us do evil that good may come": a sentiment slanderously attributed to Christians.

whose damnation (condemnation) **is just.** Those who draw such an inference from the gospel of God's grace are to be utterly repudiated and condemned.

9 are we better than they? etc. A fifth question. Lit., "Are we before them?" The R.V. reads the question, "Are we in worse case than they?" The American Revisers (so also Moffatt and Weymouth) render the question, "Are we better than they?" In either case, the apostle's answer is applicable. No worse, no better: for all alike are guilty before God.

12 unprofitable. The Greek means "useless," "good for nothing."

18 There is no fear of God before their eyes. This last quotation indicates the source of the universal wickedness above described: cp. Psa. cxi. 10.

19 the law. The "law" here includes both the whole written word (see John x. 34, and note), as cited in vers. 10–18, and also the law written on the conscience (ii. 14, 15). Every man is "under the law" in one or both of these forms.

21 now the (a) **righteousness of God**, etc. "Now" that Christ is come, "a righteousness of God apart from the law is fully manifested."

22 the righteousness of God [**which is**] **by faith**, etc. See notes on i. 17.

unto all, etc. Intended or designed for all who believe. The best authorities omit, "and upon all."

23 come short, etc. The word *come* is in the present tense. The meaning of the phrase probably is, all men fail to secure God's *approbation*—the praise and honour which He bestows: as in John v. 44; xii. 43.

24 freely. "Gratuitously"; by no merit of their own, but by that wonderful "grace" which "ransomed" them by the "blood" of Jesus, the "propitiatory offering" now "set forth" as the great object "of faith."

redemption. "Redemption" means deliverance by the payment of a ransom, and is applied in Scripture to deliverance from sin in its guilt, power, and consequences: see Luke xxi. 28; Heb. ix. 15; xi. 35.

25 propitiation. The Greek word occurs in the New Testament only here and in Heb. ix. 5. "Mercy-seat," is its general meaning in the LXX, as Exod. xxv. 17–22. It is really an adjective: "propitiatory," and takes its meaning from the unexpressed noun that it qualifies—either "cover" (of the ark) in the Old Testament, or in the present passage, "sacrifice," the blood of which was sprinkled on the mercy-seat, in order to make atonement for sin: see Lev. xvi. 14–16.

through faith. This confirms the interpretation, "sacrifice"; effectual only through the faith of him who appropriates it.

for the remission of sins, etc. Rather (as R.V.), "because of the passing over of the sins done aforetime, in the forbearance of God" (the original word differing from that meaning *remission*). The sacrifice of Christ manifests God's judicial righteousness, which might seem to have been obscured by His forbearance in overlooking the sins of former ages. In this and other passages it should be remembered that throughout the New Testament, the words "just," and "righteous," "justify," "justification," and "righteousness," are all forms of the same Greek word.

27 boasting. Rather, "the boasting," or "glorying" (R.V.), *i.e.*, of the Jew; see ver. 29; ii. 17–20. Of course, if this boasting is excluded, so is all other; and especially that founded upon external Christian privileges.

By what law? The "law" here is the declared rule or requirement of the Divine government. "Faith," *i.e.*, the trustful acceptance of free justification (vers. 24, 25), is required, instead of works, *i.e.*, the endeavouring to merit God's favour by our own doings, as the means of obtaining salvation; and thus the glorying of the Jew is set aside.

28 conclude. Or, "reckon" (R.V.). This conclusion is the counterpart of that in ver. 20, reviving the hope which had there been destroyed.

without, etc. Or, as R.V. marg., "apart from works of law."

30 [it is] one God, which shall justify, etc. The R.V. brings out the argument more clearly: "if so be that God is one, and He shall justify," etc. As there is but one God, so there is but one way of justification for all men; for the ancient Hebrew saints (ch. iv.) were really justified "out of faith," a righteousness grounded in faith; whilst for other believers, "the faith is the means by which the benefit is secured."

CHAPTER IV

1 What shall we say then? This form of question forms henceforth in this Epistle characteristic links in the apostle's argument: see vi. 1; vii. 7; viii. 31; ix. 14, 30.

as pertaining to the flesh. The R.V. rendering seems preferable: "What has Abraham gained —our forefather according to the flesh?" The answer to the question is, Whatever the benefit might be, it was not justification; for if he were justified by works he would have ground of boasting. But he had "none before God; for what saith the Scripture?" etc. (2, 3).

2 but not before God. The connexion seems to be, Whatever glorying might be supposed to arise from works, is as nothing in sight of the all-holy God.

3 counted. It should be borne in mind that the same Greek word is rendered "counted" here and in ver. 5; "reckoned" in vers. 4, 9, 10; "imputed" in vers. 6, 8, 11, 22, 23, 24; and "conclude" in iii. 28. The means of Abraham's justification (according to Gen. xv. 6) was his faith, *i.e.*, "the believing on Him that justifieth the ungodly" (5). For the immediate purpose of the apostle's argument it was enough to contrast faith and works—promise and law; and to show that Abraham was justified by the former. Other parts of Scripture, and the subsequent statements of this chapter, clearly imply that the faith of Abraham rested upon the very truth on which that of Christians rests now: only that by him the Promised Seed (Gal. iii. 8), and the blessings which He was to bring, were "seen from afar" (John viii. 56; Heb. xi. 13).

4 Now to him that worketh, etc That is, to him who works for wages the recompense is a debt, not a favour; but to him (ver. 5) who, like Abraham, does "not work" for acceptance, but, renouncing all claim of merit, trusts only in the promise of the Justifier of the ungodly—to such an one acceptance with God must necessarily be gratuitous. David's testimony (6–8) is to the same effect. The apostle attributes Psalm xxxii. to David, whose own case gives point to the reasoning.

7 are forgiven . . . are covered. The exact rendering is "have been given" . . . "have been covered."

9 [Cometh] this blessedness, etc.? Does it relate to the Jews as circumcised, so as to exclude the Gentiles? The answer is, The case of Abraham himself shows that circumcision has nothing to do with it; for he was declared to be accepted by God some fourteen years before he was circumcised (cp. Gen. xv. 6; xvi. 16; and xvii. 24); "that he might be the father of all the faithful"; *i.e.*, the first conspicuous example, and so the leader in faith, to the Gentiles, as well as the Jews (11). The true children of "believing Abraham" are, therefore, not his natural descendants, but those who have his faith. As Abraham was justified by faith when he was in uncircumcision, so those who partake of his faith will also be justified, although they be also in uncircumcision.

11 a seal. Circumcision cannot of itself give a title to the blessings of God's righteousness; for to the father of circumcision that Divinely appointed rite was but a "sign" or token of previously existing faith—a "seal" or visible guarantee of Divine favour already conferred upon him as a believer. And therefore where that faith is wanting, that favour cannot be enjoyed, though the outward symbol may be borne.

13 For the promise, etc. The R.V. gives the true emphasis: "For not through the law (*or* through law) was the promise, . . . but through the righteousness of faith." A third reason why not circumcision, but faith, is the means of obtaining the promised blessing.

heir of the world. On this phrase, see Psa. xxv. 13; xxxvii. 9, 11; Matt. v. 3, and notes. The promises made to Abraham (Gen. xvii. 8) and to his seed (Gen. xv. 18) were like justification (ver. 4, etc.), a *gift* of *grace* (16); and therefore their fulfilment was to be obtained, not by works of law, but by faith; as indeed is shown by the fact that in the very first step towards their fulfilment (the having an heir) faith in an unusual degree was required (17–22).

17 I have made thee a father of many nations. See note on Gen. xvii. 4. As all the promises made to Abraham had an ulterior reference to spiritual blessings, of which the other fulfilment was a shadow and a pledge; so in this promise there was a reference to his spiritual posterity—true believers of every nation.

who quickeneth the dead, etc. Long before Abraham had either natural or spiritual progeny, he was regarded as father of us all, Jews and Gentiles, by God, in whom he trusted, and by whom what is dead (see ver. 19) is made alive, and what as yet exists not is spoken of as if it were actually in being.

18 against hope. That is, though everything seemed opposed to hope (19), he believed; being assured that what God had promised He could perform.

So shall thy seed be. Numerous as the stars (Gen. xv. 5; Heb. xi. 12).

19 being not weak in faith. Lit., "without being weakened in faith" (R.V.), as he might supposably have been through the apparent impossibility of the case: see ver. 20.

he considered not his own body. The negative here is omitted by the best authorities (so R.V.). The meaning is that Abraham *did* take into consideration the difficulties of the case, and yet "staggered not at the promise." For "neither yet," read simply, *and.*

20 giving glory to God. Honouring His faithfulness and power.

24 if we believe on Him. Or, "even to us who believe on Him," etc.

25 delivered. That is, delivered to death (viii. 32; Isa. liii. 12) by the Father. And yet He gave Himself (Gal. ii. 20; Eph. v. 2).

for our offences. The word *for* in both parts of the verse is the same—"on account of." "For our offences," to atone for them: "for our justification," to secure it. Both acts of Divine grace are essentially one. There is no removal of "our offences" except by "justification"; and to this our Lord's death and resurrection were both requisite. This twofold idea is seen also in the apostle's subsequent statement of the results of justification:—the destruction of the deadly fruit of sin: and the impartation of life, with the energetic working of the renewed nature (v.–vii.).

CHAPTER V

1 we have peace with God. The Revisers, following the great majority of MSS. and versions, read "let us have peace," a difference of one Greek letter. But scholars are not all agreed. Such high authorities as Scrivener, Bishop Moule (*Expositor's Bible*), and Dr. T. R. Glover support the old reading. The reading, "we have" seems better to suit the connexion, and the alteration to "let us have" (by the change of a single letter), was one which transcribers were likely to make. In fact, they often change statements into exhortations in passages where the former is certainly the correct reading. This peace with God is the result of Christ's finished work, accepted by us through faith.

2 we have access, etc. R.V., "we have had our access."

3 we glory in tribulations also, etc. We triumph not only in hope of glory, but in troubles too; for in them we gain power of "endurance"; and from this we derive further "proof" of the truth and value of our faith; by which again our "hope" is confirmed. It is a great thing to be able to endure the trials of life. But it is a still greater thing with the apostle to glory in them.

5 maketh not ashamed. R.V., "putteth not to shame," *i.e.*, by failure. "A hope which never disappoints us" (*Moffatt*).

6 when we were yet without strength. Unable to free ourselves from sin and its consequences.

in due time. See Gal. iv. 2, 4, and note.

7 yet peradventure for a good man. Lit., as R.V., "for peradventure for the good man"; *i.e.*, for that one out of the number of the "righteous," or strictly just, who was also benevolent and kind. "For the good and lovable man" (*Weymouth*).

8 commendeth. That is, proves or demonstrates His own love towards us. It is a love for the undeserving and sinful.

9 Much more then, etc. In this and the next verse, the certainty and completeness of our salvation is shown by an argument *à fortiori.* It is in threefold form. If in our state of *enmity* the Saviour would die to procure the primary blessing of Justification, "much more" in our *reconciled* state He "ever liveth" (cp. Heb. vii. 25) to complete His work in our Salvation from all the consequences of our sin and of God's displeasure.

11 And not only so, etc. *Shall* be saved, did I say? Nay, more. Our salvation is not only certain, but triumphant; not only future, but present; for "we *are* exulting in God"; "we *have already* received the reconciliation."

12 so death passed upon all men, etc. The sense appears to be: Death has passed through from Adam to all men, *because* sin has passed through to all from him. The argument is continued in ver. 18.

13 for until the law, etc. The apostle proceeds to prove the declaration made in ver. 12, that sin and death have come upon all men from their connexion with Adam. The words may be rendered, "Before the law there was sin in the world, and though sin is not put to account in the absence of law, men died," etc., *i.e.*, were treated as sinners.

14 after the similitude of Adam's transgression. Who had not sinned expressly and consciously against a known command.

figure. The point in which Adam resembled Christ appears from the context to be this: As Adam was the cause of sin and death to all who are connected with him by natural birth, so Christ is the author of righteousness and life to all who are connected with Him by spiritual birth: see 1 Cor. xv. 21, 22. But with this resemblance there are some differences (15), all showing the superiority of the work of Christ. 1. The results of the dispensation of grace are by far the richer and more abundant (15). 2. Through Adam *one* offence entails widely extended condemnation; through Christ's single work there is free justification from the guilt of *many* offences (16): and, 3. Through Adam's fall death gains universal dominion over man; through Christ man, receiving abundant grace and righteousness, regains for ever the life and dominion which he had lost (17).

16 the judgement [was] by one, etc. In the one case there was a legal judgement after one offence, pronouncing only condemnation; in the other, the free gift coming after offences, and pronouncing a sentence of acquittal.

20 Moreover the law entered, etc. "But law [revealed and enforced anew] came in beside [this representative system], in order that the trespass [the result in the *individual* of depravity in the *race*] might abound. But where sin [the depravity so brought out] abounded, grace very much exceeded." This statement meets the objection that the law of Moses was rendered useless by this representative system. The apostle shows that its place, though subordinate, was important, as it brought out the depravity of man, and so proved his need of the gospel, whilst it showed that individual responsibility was not superseded. See vii. 7–11; Gal. iii. 19; and Matt. x. 34, 35, and note.

21 unto death. Lit., "in death."

CHAPTER VI

The apostle proceeds to show that FREE JUSTIFICATION through the work of Christ ensures PERSONAL HOLINESS and FINAL SALVATION. We cannot go on in sin that grace may abound; for we are one with Christ in His baptism, death, and life (1–11). and we are subject to Him as our King (12–14).

1 What shall we say then? The reference here is to the declaration, ch. v. 20, which might be perverted into a warrant to sin: cp. iii. 7.

2 we that are dead. Lit., as R.V., "we who died"; implying also "we that are dead"—a most forcible use of a common figure for total and final separation. "The Christian's breaking with sin is undoubtedly gradual in its realisation, but absolute and conclusive in its principle" (Godet: *Commentary on the Romans*).

3 into Jesus Christ. That is, into connexion with Him, and therefore sharing His death as deliverance from sin.

4 we are buried. Rather, as R.V., "we were buried." "Just as the ceremony of interment, as a visible and public fact, attests death, so baptism, in so far as it is an outward and sensible act, attests faith, with the death to sin implicitly included in faith" (*Godet*). The baptism is that of believers. The going under the water indicated the death and burial of the old nature, and the coming up again the resurrection of the redeemed nature.

by the glory of the Father. By that power which displays God's "glory." Meyer explains the expression as "the glorious complete perfection of God."

5 if we have been planted together. Rather, "If we are grown together," like the stock and the scion. If our union to Christ is so close that we partake in His death, we shall also in His resurrection. "Baptism doth represent unto us our profession; which is, to follow the example of our Saviour Christ, and to be made like unto Him: that, as He died and rose again for us, so should we, who are baptised, die from sin, and rise again unto righteousness" (*Church of England Baptismal Service*).

6 our old man. That is, our former *self*, in its unrenewed state (see Eph. iv. 22–24): the same thing as "the body of sin"; which is represented as being crucified in Christ's death.

destroyed. The Greek word is one which St. Paul often uses. It should here be translated "rendered powerless."

serve. Better, "be in bondage to," as R.V.

7 is freed. Greek, "hath been justified." The Christian's death with Christ frees him from serving sin, and assures him of perpetual life (8, 9).

8 if we be dead with Christ. Rather, "if we died with Christ."

12 your mortal body. That is, as the word here used always means in the New Testament, "*a body in which death is already at work.*"

13 instruments. Or, as R.V. marg., "weapons"; by which the battle of life is to be maintained. The words, "unto sin" should be connected, as in R.V., with "yield."

14 ye are not under the law, etc. To free the sinner from the guilt and the control of sin is the office, not of the law, but of the gospel, which provided a gratuitous justification, constrains the sinner, by the powerful motives of love and hope, to render a grateful and cheerful obedience. This doctrine and the objections to it are discussed more at length in the next chapter.

15 What then? The inference from the fact of being "under grace" might appear to open the way to sinful living—a misuse of Christian liberty.

17 God be thanked, etc. That is, "God be thanked that whereas ye were once bond-servants of sin, ye have now obeyed," etc.

[that] form of doctrine which was delivered you. Lit., "that mould of teaching into which (like molten metal) ye were delivered." Truth is here regarded as the mould or the pattern of character.

19 I speak after the manner of men, etc. I use the phrase "*bond-servants* of righteousness," not because the Christian is really a slave, but to make my meaning plain (see John viii. 36); or (more probably) because through "the weakness of the flesh" Christ's service is sometimes hard to the imperfectly sanctified Christian.

20 ye were free from righteousness. R.V., "ye were free in regard of righteousness." It probably means, When you served sin you had nothing to do with God's righteousness. But what was the good of that freedom? What fruit but shame and death could it yield? Now your subjection to righteousness not only frees you from sin, but yields you the blessed fruit of holiness here, and eternal life hereafter. "For the wages of sin is death," etc. (23).

23 wages. The word rendered "wages" signifies properly the soldier's rations or pay: see note on the word "instruments," ver. 13. Sin recompenses its soldiers with death. God freely gives eternal life in Jesus Christ our Lord.

CHAPTER VII

1 Know ye not, etc.? The illustration is addressed both to Jews and Gentiles, and is founded upon a legal principle familiar to all, viz., that death dissolves all legal ties.

2 the law of her husband. That is, the law which bound her to her husband.

4 ye also are become dead to the law, etc. We are "made dead to the law through the death of the body (or mortal nature) of Christ"; in order that He may bring us into the new bond of love and obedience to Himself, expressed under the figure of marriage; as in Eph. v. 32.

5 the motions of sins. R.V., "the sinful passions." That is, passions that spring from and lead to sin. When we were in the flesh (*i.e.*, in our unrenewed state of enmity to God's will: see note on John iii. 6), the holy restraints and requirements of the law called forth these passions, and so led to sin and death: cp. vers. 7, 8.

6 But now we are delivered, etc. Rather, "But now having died (*i.e.*, with Christ), we are released from the law, wherein we were held fast; so that we serve" God by the free promptings of a new spiritual life, and not in the mere letter of the law: see 2 Cor. iii. 6, and note.

7 Is the law sin? If freedom from law brings freedom from sin (1–4), and if the fruit of union with law was death (5), it may be said that the law and sin are almost the same thing! By no means. The law is not sin; but it produces in us the conviction of sin, by teaching us what sin is (7), and by bringing out into greater energy the power of evil in our hearts (8).

lust. Better read, "covetousness." The Greek word is the same as that used in verb form in quoting the commandments, and the force of the words is lost by a different translation. The tenth commandment is particularly specified, probably because it explicitly refers to the desires: see note on Exod. xx. 1.

8 without the law sin [was] dead. Paul illustrates from his own experience the truth already stated in ver. 5, that the wickedness of the heart is comparatively inactive and unknown, until it is excited under a sense of the law's restraints. For men always strive for what is forbidden, and desire what is denied: cp. Prov. ix. 17.

9 I was alive, etc. The word "I" is emphatic here. All this is neither speculation nor hearsay. I have passed through it all myself.

11 Sin, taking occasion by the commandment, etc. Sin, here personified, used the law as an instrument of temptation, as the serpent did to Eve: see Gen. iii. 5, and note; and 2 Cor. xi. 3.

12 Wherefore. Or, "So that" (R.V.). Whatever may be its incidental results, the law, as a whole, and every one of its precepts, is—*holy* in its nature; *just* in its claims and sanctions; and *good* in its tendency.

13 sin, that it might appear sin, etc. By bringing such a disastrous result from that which was fitted for "good."

14 the law is spiritual. The law is a transcript of the holy will of God, requiring spiritual purity: but man is "carnal," being more or less under the influence of the "flesh," *i.e.*, of human nature apart from Divine grace.

15 I allow not. Rather, "I know not," as R.V.; either like a slave (14) who blindly does the bidding of another; or perhaps like one distracted by conflict of soul, who hardly knows what he does, and does the very thing he meant not to do. Thus the apostle is led on to the desponding cry of helplessness in ver. 24, and to the joyful announcement in ver. 28, which he amplifies in ch. viii.

19, 20, These verses repeat verses 15, 17 in very similar words.

24 the body of this death. Or, "this body of death": cp. "their body of sin" (vi. 6).

25 I thank God. That I have obtained deliverance through Jesus Christ our Lord. It was not the law, but the grace of the Saviour that brought relief and inspired hope. This leads up to the triumphant words of ch. viii.

CHAPTER VIII

1 There is therefore now no condemnation, etc. Though the conflict within us is not yet ended (vii. 25), yet the deliverance is already obtained. It was by the thought of this *present* justification that the exclamation of wretchedness was changed (vii. 24) to one of thanksgiving. The latter clause of the verse seems to have been inserted by some copyist from ver. 4.

2 the law of the Spirit of life. "The Spirit of life is that by which the spiritual life is effected in believers" (*Tholuck*).

free. In respect of condemnation, not in respect of influence.

4 the righteousness. Rather, as R.V., "the ordinance," *i.e.*, the requirement of the law "in supreme love of God and unselfish love to man."

6 to be carnally minded, etc. R.V., "The mind of the flesh . . . the mind of the Spirit," the language corresponding with that of ver. 5. So in ver. 7, "the mind of the flesh."

9 the Spirit of Christ. Belonging to, or proceeding from Christ; see John xiv. 16, 26; xvi. 7.

10 the Spirit is life, etc. The dwelling of the Spirit of Christ in the soul is a pledge of life in the fullest sense; for, although the body is doomed to die on account of sin, still the soul lives; and (11) even our mortal bodies shall be restored to life "by (or rather "because of") His Spirit that dwelleth in us."

12 we are debtors, etc. We are under obligation to the Spirit, to follow His impulses and guidance.

13 mortify. That is, "put to death." The gradual destruction of sinful inclinations is necessary to the perfecting of the Christian life.

15 to fear. Better, as R.V., "unto fear": *fear* being here the substantive.

adoption. Or, "sonship"; *i.e.*, the Spirit makes us feel and act towards God like His children, giving the spirit of sonship; so that with affection, reverence, and confidence we call Him our Father. On the word "Abba," see Mark xiv. 36, and note; Gal. iv. 6.

16 with our spirit. Rather, "to our spirits"; by His comfort, His incitement to prayer, His censure of sin, His impulse to works of love (*Olshausen*). Cp. Gal. v. 22, 23.

18 in us. Rather, "unto us," or "to us-ward" (R.V.); both as we joyfully see the creature delivered, and as we ourselves enjoy the redemption for which now "we patiently wait" (19–23). This is a new illustration of the certainty and the greatness of this glory.

19 the earnest expectation. A most expressive word in the original; lit., "the waiting with uplifted head."

20 the creature. It is the same Greek word that is rendered "creature" and "creation" throughout this passage. It appears to include all created things. Weymouth's translation appears to bring out the meaning of the clause: "For the Creation fell into subjection to failure and unreality."

vanity. "Emptiness"; superficial and unreal.

who hath subjected [the same], etc. Lit., "who subjected [it]; upon hope, that the creation itself," etc. See R.V.

21 because. Rather "that," connecting with "hope" in ver. 20.

the glorious liberty. Rather, "the liberty of the glory" (R.V.); that is, the freedom from vanity, which is part of the glory to be revealed.

23 not only [they]. Rather, as R.V., "not only so."

ourselves. Paul and his fellow-believers.

firstfruits. See Deut. xxvi. 1–11, and notes. As the firstfruits offered annually by the Israelites were an earnest of the whole harvest, the expression came to include the idea of a *pledge*, as well as of priority: see 1 Cor. xv. 20. Hence the present indwelling of the Spirit in the heart is called "the firstfruits," or "the earnest" of the Spirit, and is regarded as a pledge of the heavenly inheritance.

24–26. We are "waiting" because "we were saved in the hope" (see 18–23); *i.e.*, our complete salvation is future, beyond the reach of sight, and therefore an object of hope, to which we look forward whilst we toil and suffer here (25). And in this waiting and endurance we are sustained by the Holy Spirit (26).

26 helpeth our infirmities. Helps us on in our faltering efforts at prayer. And so, in character and life.

groanings which cannot be uttered. A few expositors think that the groanings are those of the human spirit, but the weight of opinion is that the Spirit of God is meant. It is permissible to understand both.

28 all things work together for good. Dr. Griffith Thomas (*Devotional Commentary*) gives a good illustration. "Many years ago an eminent French engineer was detained in the Mediterranean by a tedious quarantine. It was hard for one of his active temperament to endure such confinement; but as he waited on the deck of the vessel he read, and the book to which he gave extra attention, prompted him to the conception of the Suez Canal, the execution of which has made him so famous and has been of such great service to the world. Did M. de Lesseps afterwards regret those dragging days of quarantine?"

29 conformed to the image of His Son, etc. It is an essential part of "God's purpose" that those who share the glory should bear the likeness of Christ, who is to stand not alone, although pre-eminent in excellence, as the "firstborn among many brethren." St. Paul's idea of predestination was therefore predestination unto holiness. This is its practical side.

many brethren. "A multitude whom no man can number" (Rev. vii. 4, 9).

31 who [can be] against us? Or simply, "who *is* against us?" R.V., There are many against us, but God, who is for us, is infinitely greater than all (see Psa. cxxiv.), and is, as it were, pledged to "give us all things" in giving "His own Son" (32).

35 the love of Christ. That is, Christ's love toward us: cp. 34, 37, 39.

36 As it is written, etc. For we have to suffer like God's people of old: see Psa. xliv. 22.

37 more than conquerors. "All these things" not only do us no real harm, they are even made to promote our good (28): cp. v. 3.

38 For I am persuaded, etc. The apostle's eye glances over all conditions of man's existence, the mightiest of created beings, all time and all space, and he then confidently declares that no creature which he can find or conceive can separate the Christian from God's unchangeable love.

CHAPTER IX

1 my conscience, etc. My conscience, enlightened by the Holy Spirit, assures me that I am sincere in this avowal (2, 3). This burst of affectionate grief shows the strength of Paul's feelings in reference to his own people. "If the gospel brings sure salvation to God's elect (viii. 28–32), why is the chosen people Israel not found among the heirs of this salvation?" (*Speaker's Commentary*).

3 For I could wish, etc. Lit., "I was wishing," or "praying."

accursed. "Anathema": cp. 1 Cor. xvi. 22. Moses went so far as to ask that he might be "blotted out" of God's book. Paul wished himself "accursed." But Christ Himself "became sin" for us (2 Cor. v. 21).

4 to whom [pertaineth] the adoption, etc. That is, they were regarded and treated by God as His "children": see Exod. iv. 22; Jer. xxxi. 9; Hosea xi. 1. The "glory" is the *Shechinah*; the symbol of God's presence (see Exod. xiii. 21; xl. 34; 1 Kings viii. 10, and note). The "covenants" are those gracious engagements which God made and renewed at various times with their "fathers" (5) Abraham, Isaac, and Jacob, and with them as a nation. "The service" means all the symbolical rites of the national worship. The "promises" are, no doubt, those which relate especially to the Messiah: see Gal. iii. 16.

5 as concerning the flesh. That is, as respects His human nature; plainly implying that He had also another nature, which is immediately afterwards said, in the clearest and most direct language, to be that of the Supreme and ever-blessed God: see next note. It was the highest honour conferred upon the Jews that God should take upon Him human nature as one of the "seed of Abraham."

who is over all, God blessed for ever. The context favours the application of the words to Christ, according to the usual reading, the apostle contrasting our Lord's human and Divine nature.

7 In Isaac shall thy seed be called. See Gen. xxi. 12. Only the descendants of Isaac shall be called truly and properly, for the purposes of the covenant, "the seed of Abraham." Paul refers to this selection and limitation as an illustrative proof of the "election of grace" (see vers. 11, 24, and xi. 5): cp. vers. 30–33, and xi. 25. The cases of Isaac and Jacob (10–13) are adduced to show that God exercised His sovereign choice throughout His dealings with Israel.

8 the children of the promise. "Mere carnal descent establishes no claim" (*Pulpit Commentary*).

9 At this time. R.V., "According to this season," *i.e.*, this time next year.

10 And not only [this], etc. The case of Rebecca's children is still more decisive; for whereas Isaac and Ishmael were only half-brothers, Jacob and Esau were twins, and the destiny of each was announced before their birth (cp. Hosea xii. 3, and note); and therefore it could not have been on the ground of their works; but it must have been according to God's sovereign will. Moreover, the context in Gen. xxv. 23, and the quotation in Mal. i. 2, 3, show that the nations descended from the two brothers are specially intended; so that the choice affected all their posterity.

13 Jacob have I loved, but Esau have I hated. See Mal. i. 2, 3, and note.

16 So then it is not of him that willeth, etc. Not that any one who earnestly desires and strives for it will ever miss the Divine favour; but that his desires and efforts are themselves the fruit of God's spontaneous and sovereign "mercy"; for "from Him comes everything we have; from Him therefore let us learn to ask and hope everything" (*Calvin*).

17 For the Scripture saith unto Pharaoh. The case of Pharaoh shows that sovereignty may be exercised in punishment without "injustice" (14).

raised thee up. It is an instructive fact that the Divine forbearance (cp. ver. 22 with Exod. viii. 15; ix. 34, 35) particularly helped forward the fatal result: see ii. 2, 4; 2 Pet. iii. 4, 9, 15, 16. When God's patience and long-suffering are used by men to set their hearts more determinately to do evil, He may be said by His patience to give them an opportunity to do evil: cp. Eccl. viii. 11.

18 He hardeneth. See notes on Exod. iv. 21; Isa. vi. 9.

20 formed. Or, "moulded." The first of these two questions contains an allusion to Isa. xlv. 9, on which see note; the second an equally free reference to Jer. xviii. 4–6.

22 What if God, etc. God has surely a right to display His anger and His power by inflicting merited punishment, especially after long forbearance; and to glorify His grace by bestowing unmerited mercy, as He pleases. Throughout this reasoning it must be carefully observed that, in speaking of God's sovereign will, the apostle nowhere implies that He acts arbitrarily or without reasons; only that these reasons being unknown to us, the sufficient explanation of His dealings is His sovereign will.

25 As He saith also in Osee, etc. The words in Hosea i. 9, 10; ii. 23, refer primarily to the ten apostate tribes of Israel; but, like other similar prophecies, they have a far wider meaning. They are quoted here to prove that God receives even us Gentile sinners, who were once not His people, among the people of God.

26 in the place. Expositors differ as to these words, some considering they refer to Jerusalem or the Temple; others that they mean the land of exile. But a better and simpler view is that they mean any place where the people of Israel were.

27 a remnant shall be saved. That is, Even of Israel it is "the remnant" only that shall be saved.

28 the work. Rather, "the word." This verse is here quoted from the Septuagint, and may be understood thus. The Lord is rapidly fulfilling and consummating His word; overthrowing the Assyrians, and restoring a remnant of Israel. The idea is, that but few were saved: see note on Isa. x. 21-23.

29 before. That is, in an earlier passage: see Isa. i. 9, and note. In every age true believers among the Jews were only a small portion of the nation.

Sabaoth. "Sabaoth" is the Hebrew word for "hosts" or "armies"; which is retained in the Septuagint here as if it were a proper name: see note on Psa. xxiv. 10.

32 For they stumbled at that stumblingstone. The Jews, like too many of all nations, took offence at justification by faith in Jesus the Messiah, and persisted in trusting to their own works (cp. x. 3); but they fell far short even of the law of Moses, and consequently attained not to righteousness: cp. x. 5.

33 as it is written, etc. This quotation combines Isa. xxviii. 16 with viii. 14, and shows that Christ, who is the Foundation of the believer's hope, is also a Rock of offence to unbelievers: see note on Isa. viii. 12; xxviii. 16. Luther says in his *Paradoxes*, "The natural man hates the Gospel more than the Law."

CHAPTER X

1 desire. "Good will." The meaning is that his good will to Israel finds expression in this prayer.

2 zeal of God. That is, a zeal in serving God.

4 Christ is the end of the law, etc. The law itself had as its object and aim the coming and work of Christ, who is alone able to secure "righteousness" for us (cp. Gal. iii. 23, 24; Titus iii. 5) and in us.

5 the man which doeth those things shall live by them. He that obeys the law's demands shall live (*i.e.*, enjoy God's favour), on the ground of that obedience.

6 But the righteousness which is of faith, etc. Even Moses, the lawgiver (see Deut. xxx. 10–14), looking beyond the complicated ritual of the law to Him who is its "end," speaks of the blessings of justification, as being plainly brought within our reach, demanding only hearty faith and open profession. The work is done for thee; heaven has sent to thee the Divinely-anointed Deliverer; the grave has given back to thee the triumphant Redeemer: *thou* hast not to do anything in order to earn the "righteousness of God." And "the word is nigh thee," the truth is put plainly before thee, for thee cordially to accept, "believing it in thy heart," and then to avow and act out, "confessing it with thy mouth."

9 if thou shalt confess, etc. Confession here stands first because it corresponds to the "mouth" in ver. 8; but in ver. 10 the natural order is resumed.

11 For the Scripture saith, etc. The *prophets*, too, as well as *Moses*, have taught the salvation of the believer, and the rejection of the unbeliever, whether Jew or Gentile (11–21). See notes on Isa. xxviii. 16; li. 1, 9; lii. 13; liii. 1; lxv. 1, 2; Joel ii. 28, 32.

Whosoever believeth. The Scripture proof that "the word" is a "word *of faith*," vers. 8, 9. Confession is implied, ver. 13.

12 no difference. Rather, "no distinction" (R.V.). Both are alike subjects of the one "Lord over all"; and both are alike objects of His grace, for He is "rich unto all."

13 the Lord. It is evidently the Messiah, of whom it is here said, that men could not "call" upon Him unless they "believe," nor could they "believe" until they hear the "preacher" (14). He therefore is "the LORD."

14 How then shall they call, etc.? "Calling on the name of the Lord" supposes faith in a message from Him delivered by His messengers. Many, it is true, have not believed. But this fact only fulfils the prophet's words; and it proves the point in question (16, 17). For all have heard the message (18); so that unbelief on the part of any —especially of the Jews—is the result, not of ignorance, but of disobedience, of the consequences of which they had been repeatedly warned (19–21).

18 Their sound went into all the earth. See note on Psa. xix. 1, 2.

19 Did not Israel know? etc. Did not Moses "first" intimate, and have not Isaiah and others more boldly declared, to them the unwelcome truth that they would be rejected for unbelief, whilst the despised Gentiles would be admitted by faith to the privileges of God's people?

21 But to Israel. Or, "But *concerning* Israel."

CHAPTER XI

1 Hath God cast away (Did God cast off) **His people?** Am I contradicting the promise in Psa. xciv. 14? Almost the very words are quoted here.

For I also am an Israelite, etc. My own pure Hebrew descent may indicate to you that I cannot mean this. It would contradict my profession, and destroy my hopes as a Christian.

[of] the tribe of Benjamin. See Phil. iii. 5, and note.

2 Wot ye not, etc.? "Know ye not?"

of Elias. Rather, "in the history of Elijah": see 1 Kings xix. 10–18, and notes. See also Mark xii. 26, and note.

maketh intercession to God against Israel. Lit., "goes to God against Israel," *i.e.,* "pleads with" or "entreats."

4 to [the image of] Baal. Rather, simply "to Baal." Respecting Baal, see note on Numb. xxii. 41. See also note on 1 Kings xix. 18.

5 Even so then at this present time, etc. As in Elijah's time there were still some in Israel who had not rejected Jehovah, so there is still, by God's gracious choice, "a remnant" of that nation, who are Abraham's children (ver. 1) by faith, as well as by natural descent; although the great bulk of the nation are rejecting the Messiah, and are consequently rejected by God.

6 then is it no more of works. That is, the election is no longer of works. The conclusion in ver. 6 decisively opposes all attempts at compromise between the two antagonistic principles of salvation by God's free grace and salvation by man's works: cp. iv. 4. The conclusion of the verse is omitted by the best MSS.

7 that which he seeketh for. That is, righteousness before God (see ix. 31; x. 3). "The election" (8) means *the elect,* as "the circumcision" (iv. 9) means *the circumcised.*

were blinded. Rather, "were hardened" (R.V.), so that the truth and excellence of the gospel were not felt, nor its claims regarded: see notes on Isa. vi. 9; xxix. 9–24; Deut. xxix. 4; Matt. xiii. 14; and cp. Psa. lxix. 22, 23; 2 Thess. ii. 11. The quotations are not literal, but free, according to the sense.

9 Let their table be made a snare, etc. See Psa. lxix. 20. Respecting the imprecations in the Psalms, see note on Psa. v. 10.

12 if the fall of them, etc. The sense is, If the stumbling and rejection of the Jews has been the occasion of so much good to the world, how much more good may be expected from their restoration! See also ver. 15.

13 For I speak to you Gentiles, etc. Vers. 13, 14 may be thus paraphrased: It is not strange that I speak of Israel's destiny to you Gentiles (indeed, in doing so I am honouring my own peculiar ministry as *your* apostle, in order to arouse my nation, and save some of them): for great as is the blessing which you obtain in connexion with their rejection, it is but as death to life in comparison with the richer blessing resulting from their recovery, which will be to the Gentiles "life from the dead" (cp. Ezek. xxxvii. 1–14).

15 the reconciling of the world. This reconciliation is described in Eph. ii. 11–22.

16 the firstfruit. Rather, "the first part" of the *dough,* which was offered to God in order to give to the *lump* or mass the ceremonial sanctity which made it fit for the use of God's people: see Numb. xv. 20. By this illustration and that which follows Paul teaches that the piety of the *patriarchs* was a sort of dedication of the whole nation to God, and a pledge of their consecration to Him: see ver. 28; and cp. 1 Cor. vii. 14.

20 Well. "Well said." "Just so!"

22 if thou continue in [His] goodness. That is, if thou continue to exercise that faith to which His goodness is shown.

24 how much more shall these, etc.! The conversion of the Jews appeared (see note on ver. 16) a far more likely event than the introduction of the Gentiles into the Christian Church.

25 For I would not, brethren, etc. The apostle here makes known the Divine purpose respecting the Jewish people, which had been unrevealed (see note on Matt. xiii. 11); calling attention to it by his usual phrase (see 1 Cor. x. 1; xii. 1; 2 Cor. i. 8; 1 Thess. iv. 13).

blindness in part. Rather, "hardness (see ver. 7) in part," *i.e.,* extending only to a *part* of the nation, through *part* of their history; not to *all* the Jews nor to *all* time.

fulness. Or, "complement"; the full number of the Gentiles (and that evidently a large number), who were designed by the Divine purpose to be brought in before the general conversion of the Jews; for it is the conversion of the Jews which is to secure the final triumph of the gospel among the Gentiles: see vers. 12–15.

26 all Israel. The nation *as a whole.*

as it is written, etc. These quotations from Isa. lix. 20, 21; xxvii. 9, follow the Septuagint, with very slight variations. God's covenant with His ancient people looked forward to a time when their sins should be forgiven through faith, and they should enjoy the blessings of the gospel.

28 As concerning the gospel, etc. "According to the gospel," which knows no distinction except that between the believer and the unbeliever, the Jewish people are excluded from God's favour; "which is to your advantage" (*Moffatt*). But "according to God's choice" they are still lovingly cared for, and shall be restored to the enjoyment of His blessing; in order that the promises to "their fathers" may be perfectly accomplished. For god's gifts and calling cannot be retracted (29).

30 through their unbelief. That is, "by the instrumentality of their unbelief," which was the occasion of the gospel being sent to you.

32 God hath concluded them all in unbelief. Rather, "God hath shut them all up together," both Jews and Gentiles, on the same ground, as alike involved in disobedience; and hence all that shall be saved must be saved through His sovereign mercy.

33 O the depth of riches, etc.! Or, "Oh the depths of God's riches (*i.e.,* of grace: see ver. 35) and wisdom and knowledge!"

36 For of Him, etc. *From* Him, as the Creator, they spring; *by* Him, as the Governor and Disposer, they are maintained; and *to* Him, as the great End of all, they are all tending.

CHAPTER XII

1 the mercies of God. The "mercies" unfolded in iii.–viii. As a thank-offering for these (see Lev. ii. 1; iii. 1, etc., and notes), God claims not the unblemished yet lifeless bodies of irrational animals, speedily consumed, but the living bodies (once unhappily polluted by sin: i. 24; vi. 12) of the worshippers themselves, who are to be in spirit devoted to that holy worship, well-pleasing to God, which springs from the "renewing of the mind." It is important to notice the connexion between doctrine and practice. The preceding chapters have been largely theological. On this basis the apostle builds the ethical teaching of the

12th and 13th chapters. The two phases are inseparably connected.

your reasonable service. "Reasonable" here means, "pertaining to the reason"—the intellectual and moral nature: see 1 Pet. ii. 2, where the same word is used. "Service" is specially *religious* service, as in ix. 4.

2 this world. The "world" or "age," here means the whole system of society, which is not pervaded by the influence of true religion.

transformed. "Transfigured." The same Greek word which is used of our Lord's transfiguration (Matt. xvii. 2).

that ye may prove, etc. That you may ascertain and appreciate what is God's will: cp. John vii. 7.

3 faith. "Faith" here means that entire lependence upon God, and confidence in Him. This shows itself in sober judgement of our own gifts and appreciation of those of others ("according as God hath dealt to every man a measure of faith").

5 so we, [being] many. Many as we are, Christ's all-pervading life unites the whole in "one body," and makes the individual "members related to each other," having different "offices," according to their "differing gifts"; which therefore each is to use for the good of all (6–9). Cp. 1 Cor. xii.

6 prophecy. The declaring of God's will, whether for the present or the future.

the proportion of faith. The phrase corresponds with "the measure of faith" (3 and note).

7 ministry. "Ministry" (*diaconia*) means any service in the Church; but as other services are specified, it may refer here to the service described in Acts vi. 1–4. "Service in things temporal and external, such as the wants of the poor, the sick, and the stranger" (*Speaker's Commentary*).

[let us wait] on our ministering. Or, as R.V., "*let us give ourselves* to our ministry." Whole-hearted devotion is implied.

8 with simplicity. *i.e.*, without ulterior motives or calculation; therefore, as in R.V. "with liberality." The whole verse suggests active beneficence; which should be generous, energetic, and cheerful, although our errand may be sad, and the objects of our pity unpleasing. In one word, "let love be unfeigned" (9).

9 abhor. Dr. Arnold at Rugby once said, "What I want to see in the school, and what I do not find, is abhorrence of evil."

10 in honour preferring one another. Anticipating one another in the manifestation of mutual esteem.

11 not slothful in business. The Greek word means "the business of life."

fervent in spirit. The original means "boiling in spirit." Indignation against wrong, enthusiasm for the right.

13 given to hospitality. Lit., "pursuing hospitality."

14 Bless them which persecute you. This seems to be a quotation from the Sermon on the Mount, which was doubtless well known among the first Christians (cp. Matt. v. 44; Luke vi. 28).

16 condescend to men of low estate. That is, Associate and sympathise with the lowly. Many scholars, however, regard as neuter the Greek word translated "the lowly" or "men of low estate." Calvin translates it "humilibus rebus obsecundantes," which may be rendered "being true in small things."

17 Provide things honest, etc. See Prov. iii. 4. "Honest" in the English Bible always means "honourable," or "becoming."

18 If it be possible, etc. There are some with whom it is difficult, perhaps not "possible," to be at peace. But you, as God's "beloved" children, should do all that "lieth in *you*" to be at peace even with them.

19 avenge not yourselves, etc. Leave it with God to show His displeasure; for He it is to whom vengeance belongs: Deut. xxxii. 35. To "give place to the wrath" (*i.e.*, to God's wrath).

20 thou shalt heap coals of fire on his head. See note on Prov. xxv. 22.

CHAPTER XIII

1 For there is no power but of God. Magistracy, or civil government, is of Divine appointment, and therefore claims our obedience to all its lawful mandates: cp. Acts v. 29. It is supposed that Paul was led to insist upon this point by the existence of some wrong views on the part of the Roman Christians.

2 damnation. Rather, "judgement" (R.V.), and that not only from the magistrate, but from God, whose servant he is.

3 For (the) **rulers are not a terror to good works,** etc. This is the design and the proper tendency of civil government, although the actual practice has sometimes been the contrary; as it was then under the emperor Nero, who soon afterwards became a terror to all good men, and a cruel persecutor of Christians.

4 for he beareth not the sword in vain. The sword, sometimes carried by the magistrate on his own person, and sometimes borne before him by an attendant, was a symbol of the power of the civil government.

5 for (the) **wrath.** That is, for fear of the "wrath," which this minister of God executes.

6 pay ye. That is, "ye pay." As government is constituted for the benefit of society ("attending continually on this very thing"), "ye pay" the taxes for its support, as ye ought to do (7). The Jewish Christians might especially need to be reminded of this duty, as they probably felt a peculiar aversion to pay tribute to heathen rulers: see Matt. xxii. 17; Acts v. 37. "Tribute" means tax on land or persons; "custom" is tax on merchandise. "Fear" regards the power, and "honour" the rank of others.

9 if there be any other commandment. Or, "whatever other" commandment; especially the ninth, which is omitted here in the best manuscripts.

11 And that, knowing the time. The meaning is, We should do *this* (*i.e.*, fulfil every duty, and love one another); especially as remembering the flight of time and the nearness of eternity, with its full salvation.

13 honestly. Rather, "decorously." The word agrees with the figure employed, in which the habits of life are represented as a dress: see vers. 12, 14.

14 put ye on the Lord Jesus Christ, etc. "Put on as a garment." The Spanish version is, "vestios del Señor Jesucristo." Be habitually clothed in the spirit of Christ (cp. Gal. iii. 27), and do not indulge the desires of your own corrupt nature.

CHAPTER XIV

1 weak in the faith. "Holding the faith imperfectly," *i.e.*, not being able to receive the faith in its strength, so as to be above such prejudices" (*Alford*).

not to doubtful disputations. The clause may mean, " not for judging his doubts," or, " not for discussing his opinions." To do this can only disturb his mind, and confirm him in his mistake. In writing to the Christians at Corinth also, Paul touches on this subject; and decides against the rigid views of the weak brethren: see 1 Cor. x. 25–30.

2 all things. That is, *anything.*

another . . . eateth herbs. Sometimes, though not in every case, in order to avoid eating the flesh of unclean animals, and things offered to idols: see Dan. i. 8.

4 another man's servant. Rather, " Another's servant"; namely, Christ's, who alone has a right to " judge " whether one who does not abstain " stands " accepted as a Christian, and who will maintain the right of His faithful servant, although you, in your weakness, condemn him.

6–9. In all matters not essential to salvation, every one should obey his own conscience, taking care to be fully satisfied that what he does is right; but we must not seek to force the conscience of another who differs from us; for we are all subject to the same Lord.

10 the judgement seat of Christ. R.V., " of God."

11 For it is written, etc. This is a free quotation rom Isa. xlv. 23 (on which see note).

12 of himself. Emphatic: not of others.

13 occasion to fall. See Mark ix. 42, and note.

14 persuaded by (in) **the Lord Jesus.** The conviction of a mind in fellowship with Christ, guided by His teaching and His Spirit. The apostle shows that he agrees fully with the stronger brethren in disregarding the distinction of clean and unclean food: see xv. 1.

15 with [thy] meat. That is, " with what thou eatest": leading him against his conscience to imitate thee. Wilt thou gratify thyself with what grieves thy brother? Cp. 1 Cor. viii. 7–11. " Do not make more of *thy food* than Christ did of *His life* " (*Bengel*).

16 Let not then your good be evil spoken of. Be careful not to use your liberty, which is in itself a great good, in such a way as to make it the occasion of evil and reproach.

17 for the kingdom of God is not meat and drink. True religion does not consist in external observances (such as " eating and drinking "), but in the graces of the Spirit. This great principle is the effectual corrective of ritualism in all its prejudices and scruples.

18 these things. " Righteousness, peace, and joy " (17).

20 destroy not. Or, " overthrow not " (R.V.). The word used here is different from that rendered " destroy " in ver. 15; it probably refers to the word " edify " in ver. 19. Do not, for your own gratification, pull down what God is building up, whether in the soul of the weak brother, or in the church at large.

with offence. Against his conscience.

21 is made weak. Rather, " *is* weak." But the words after " stumbleth " are most probably to be omitted.

22 Hast thou faith? Have you a full persuasion that what you allow yourself is lawful? Hold it for your peace before God: he is a happy man who is not always judging himself in regard to what he can approve. But he who does what he doubts about is condemned as doing wrong (23), for whatever is done in doubt of its lawfulness must be sinful: cp. ver. 14. To do what conscience allows is not always right; to do what it questions is always wrong.

CHAPTER XV

2 Let every one of us please his neighbour, etc. The only pleasing of men here enjoined is that which has for its end their real good.

3 as it is written, etc. This quotation from Psa. lxix. 9 places in a strong light the unselfishness of Christ, who out of zeal for the Divine honour, and desire to free men from guilt, took on Himself the reproaches which the wicked cast on God.

4 through patience and comfort of the Scriptures. God gives (5) this patience and comfort through obedient attention to the Scriptures.

5 consolation. Rather, " comfort " (R.V.), as in ver. 4. Compare the three titles given to God in this chapter, with their practical and encouraging effects. " The God of patience," etc. (5); " The God of hope " (13); " The God of peace " (33). God's character is thus considered in relation to human life.

6 with one mind. The same Greek word is used in Acts i. 14.

7 to the glory of God. See John xvii. 20–23.

8 Now. Rather (as R.V.), " For." Our Lord came in the lowly character of a servant (see Matt. xx. 28), both to the Jews, to show God's truthfulness in accomplishing His promises; and also to the Gentiles, to display His mercy; so that they might both rejoice together.

9 as it is written, etc. The following quotations are from " the Law, the Prophets, and the Psalms " (Luke xxiv. 44), showing that the whole of the ancient Scripture predicts the union of Jew and Gentile in God's service: see Deut. xxxii. 1; Psa. xviii. 49; Isa. xi. 10. They are taken verbatim from the Septuagint, which sufficiently expresses the spirit of the Hebrew. In the passages quoted, the A.V. has variously, " nations," " heathen," " Gentiles "; the R.V. uniformly, " nations."

12 trust. Rather, " hope ": see ver. 13.

13 the God of (the) **hope.** God is the Author of the hope which Gentiles were encouraged (ver. 12) to place in "the root of Jesse."

15 in some sort. Rather, " in some measure."

the grace. Or, " the favour," which had conferred on him the apostolic office.

16 ministering the gospel, etc. The terms which Paul here uses describe the preaching of the gospel to the Gentiles as a priestly service rendered to Christ in bringing them to offer themselves as a living sacrifice, acceptable to God, being sanctified by the Holy Spirit: cp. xii. 1, 2.

18 For I will not dare, etc. " I will appeal only to what Christ has wrought through me in the conversion of the Gentiles."

19 so that from Jerusalem, etc. Or, " From Jerusalem and its neighbourhood even to Illyricum, I have fulfilled the gospel of Christ"; he had *fulfilled his office* as its preacher (cp. 20). The province of Illyricum lay on the north-west of Macedonia. From Acts xx. 2 it appears that Paul traversed the whole of Macedonia, on his second visit, just before he wrote this Epistle; and he would therefore be close to Illyricum. If he visited it at that time, he would naturally refer, in writing shortly afterwards, to a journey which was fresh in his thoughts.

20 so have I strived, etc. Rather, " making it my aim or ambition, to preach the gospel," etc.; *i.e.*, I determined to act in the spirit of those words

(Isa. lii. 15), which predict that the gospel shall be preached to those who have never heard it.

22 much. Rather, "many times" (R.V.): see next verse, and note on i. 13.

23 no more place, etc. That is, no opportunity for preaching the gospel in districts which it had not reached. "These parts": Greece, in the widest sense.

24 Spain. "St. Paul did not visit Spain before his first Roman imprisonment. On the hypothesis of his liberation and second imprisonment, he may have done so at a later time. The Muratorian Canon shows that his visit to Spain was an accepted tradition of the Church before the end of the second century" (*Hastings' Dict. of the Bible*).

somewhat. "In some measure." Cp. i. 13, for his desire to meet them.

25 But now I go unto Jerusalem. Respecting this intended journey to Jerusalem, cp. Acts xix. 21; xx. 22; xxiv. 17; 2 Cor. viii. 1–6; and see Paley's *Horæ Paulinæ*, ii. no. 1.

26 for the poor saints. Properly, "the poor of the saints"; or "the poor among the saints"; implying that they were not all poor, and that the community of goods (Acts iv. 32–37) had already ceased to exist in the church at Jerusalem.

27 debtors. The contribution was not merely an act of benevolence, but an acknowledgment of obligation for spiritual blessings. This remark might serve as a hint to the Roman Christians that they should follow this good example.

28 and have sealed to them this fruit. That is, when I have safely made over to them this fruit of their brethren's sympathy. Treasures and deposits were usually *sealed* for safety: see notes on 2 Kings xii. 10; Job ix. 7.

29 in the fulness of the blessing of the gospel of Christ. Rather, according to the best manuscripts, "in the fulness of the blessing of Christ"; including His personal presence, as well as the blessed teachings of His gospel. The apostle's confidence agrees with the feelings expressed in i. 11.

30 the love of the Spirit. The love which the Holy Spirit has wrought in you, one to another: cp. Phil. ii. 1; Col. i. 8.

31 that my service . . . may be accepted, etc. Paul evidently feared that the contribution he was taking might not be well received at Jerusalem, owing to the determined hostility of his unbelieving countrymen, as well as to the strong prejudices of the Hebrew Christians against him as the apostle of the Gentiles, and the defender of Christian freedom from the Mosaic law: cp. Acts xxi. 22–27.

32 be refreshed. Or, as R.V., "find rest."

CHAPTER XVI

1 Cenchrea. Properly Cenchreæ the eastern seaport of Corinth, on the Saronic Gulf, about nine miles from the city. Here was a Christian church, of which Phœbe was an active member, attending upon those of her own sex in sickness and distress. It was probably she who carried the letter to Rome.

2 succourer. Properly, a patroness or protectress; a highly honourable title.

3 Greet. The numerous salutations in this chapter show the apostle's particular and affectionate remembrance of all whom he had known as fellow-Christians, and especially as fellow-labourers and fellow-sufferers for Christ. "Besides the two household groups of 10 f., the catalogue contains twenty-six names, eight being those of women. In language, seven are Latin, one is Hebrew, the remainder Greek" (*Peake's Commentary*).

4 laid down their own necks. Risking their lives for mine. This may have happened at Corinth (Acts xviii. 6), or at Ephesus (Acts xix. 30; 2 Cor. i. 8–10).

5 the church that is in their house. Aquila and Priscilla (or Prisca, 1 Cor. xvi. 19), and some other Christian householders (Col. iv. 15; Philem. 2), received in their own houses Christian assemblies, which seem to have formed distinct bodies, here called churches. These are probably alluded to in ver. 16.

Achaia. Rather, "Asia," according to the best authorities. Epænetus, of whom nothing more is known, was probably the first convert in proconsular Asia at the time of Paul's visit (Acts xix.).

6 Mary. The other women mentioned are Phœbe, Priscilla, Tryphena, Tryphosa, Persis, and Julia, and the mother of Rufus. The circumstances mentioned in connexion with them, show the important part which women took in the labours of the primitive Church.

7 my fellow-prisoners. When or how, is not stated: see 2 Cor. vi. 5; xi. 23.

who are of note among the apostles. Highly esteemed by the apostles. "Junia" should probably be "Junias," a man's name.

9 Urbane. To be pronounced as a word of two syllables: a man's name. Better, "Urban," or "Urbanus," as R.V.

13 Rufus. Rufus was possibly the son of Simon of Cyrene (Mark xv. 21). The mother of this good man seems to have been "a mother," by kind offices, to Paul.

16 with a holy kiss. This mode of salutation was usual in that age and country as it is still, between men as well as women, in most countries of Europe. The spirit of the command is, Treat one another with all Christian affection.

17 mark. That is, keep your eye upon them. Before finally closing the Epistle, the apostle reverts to one of his great objects, and again enjoins peace and harmony among the Jewish and Gentile believers.

18 serve . . . their own belly. The teachers of error and division sought to gratify either some bodily appetite, or the love of money or power.

good words and fair speeches. R.V., "smooth and fair speech"; "plausible and pious talk" (*Moffatt*).

simple. Or, "innocent": see note on Matt. x. 16, where the same word is used.

20 shall bruise. See Gen. iii. 15. God, who is the God of peace and wants to give you His peace, will help you to defeat your greatest enemy, Satan.

The grace of our Lord, etc. The apostle apparently intended to conclude with this benediction; but other matters were suggested afterwards. The same thing occurs in other Epistles: see 1 Cor. xvi. 23, 24; Phil. iv. 20–23. The repeated benediction, ver. 24, is omitted by the best authorities.

21 Lucius. Probably Lucius of Cyrene, mentioned in Acts xiii. 1.

Jason. Probably of Thessalonica; "Sosipater" (or Sopater) of Berea: see Acts xvii. 5.

22 I Tertius, who wrote this epistle. Paul appears to have seldom written his Epistles with his own hand; but he generally added the salutation or benediction at the close in his own writing: see 1 Cor. xvi. 21; 2 Thess. iii. 17; and especially Gal. vi. 11, with note.

23 Gaius mine host. Paul had baptised Gaius, or Caius (1 Cor. i. 14); and during this second visit to Corinth had been staying at his house, where also the Christians held their meetings.

chamberlain. Or, "treasurer" of the city, *i.e.*, of Corinth.

25 the mystery which was kept secret, etc. Some intimations of this mystery had been given by the ancient prophets; but they had not been understood by the Jews, and were unknown to the Gentiles. But now by the preaching of the gospel, explaining the writings of the prophets, it was made known to all nations.

since the world began. Lit., as R.V., "through times eternal."

Written to the Romans, etc. The subscriptions to the Epistles were added at a later period (it is said by Euthalius, in the fifth century), and therefore they possess no inherent authority. Some of them are clearly correct, being confirmed by internal and other evidence; as is the case in the present instance: but others are inconsistent with the contents of the Epistles.

THE FIRST EPISTLE OF PAUL THE APOSTLE TO THE CORINTHIANS

INTRODUCTION

THREE chapters alone in this letter make it unique and memorable. The first is the 11th, containing the only account of the Lord's Supper outside the Gospels; the sacrament as Paul received it from the Lord Himself (xi. 23). The second is the 13th, that unrivalled picture of the qualities and power of love. The third is the 15th, with its noble statement of the resurrection (verses 35–54), based on the historical narrative of the resurrection of Christ (verses 3–20). It is important, in reference to the last mentioned, to note that the Epistle was written in the early part of A.D. 57, or less than thirty years after the Saviour's death and resurrection, most of the witnesses of which were still alive (xv. 6).

Though the second of St. Paul's letters in the Authorised Version, this Epistle is in reality the third, following 1 and 2 Thessalonians, and coming before the letter to the Romans. If the earlier date of Galatians be accepted (see Introduction to that Epistle), 1 Corinthians would be the fourth in order of time.

The Christian Church at Corinth was founded by St. Paul four or five years before the date of this Epistle (Acts xviii. 4, 8), and was subsequently fostered by the labours of Apollos (Acts xviii. 27, 28). But divisions had already broken out, and St. Paul devotes part of the opening chapters to dealing with these (i. 10–13; iii. 3–6, 21, 22). Even more serious was the toleration of immorality in the Church (v.). To this the surrounding licentiousness of Corinth contributed, a licentiousness notorious even among pagan writers, the background from which St. Paul wrote the first chapter of his Epistle to the Romans. From that miry pit some of the early converts had been drawn (vi. 11), and the apostle's earnest entreaties and exhortations are directed to prevent their relapse (vi. 18–20; x. 13). Such a picture is of value to us in the study of modern Christian missions and the difficulties of maintaining a high moral standard amid surrounding paganism. Laxity of manners and behaviour had crept in even to their religious gatherings and dishonoured even the Lord's Supper itself (xi. 13–17, 21, 30). The closing chapter, immediately after the glowing words about the resurrection, deals with the practical question of Christian giving and the collection for the saints at Jerusalem.

CHAPTER I

1 called [to be] an apostle. See note on Rom. i. 1. By ascribing his appointment expressly to "the will of God," Paul indicates, on the one hand, his authority (which some at Corinth slighted), and on the other, his own humble remembrance that he owed all to God's grace: cp. Gal. i. 1.

Sosthenes. It is suggested that he was "the ruler of the synagogue" at Corinth (Acts xviii. 17), having subsequently become a convert and a minister of the gospel, but this is only a conjecture.

2 sanctified. The apostle here speaks with gratitude of that holiness which characterised the church as a whole (4); not yet suggesting that some of its members were unworthy of a place in it, and that others were very imperfect: see iii. 2–4.

called [to be] saints. See notes on Rom. i. 6, 7. The addition of this phrase ("saints by calling") to the preceding epithet, "sanctified" lays stress upon this calling to holiness as the distinguishing feature of the Church of Christ.

call upon the name of Jesus Christ, etc. The great mark of Christians everywhere (Acts vii. 59, and note; ix. 14).

both theirs and ours. R.V., "their *Lord* and ours."

3 Grace be unto you, etc. See note on Rom. i. 7.

4 by. Rather, "in"; *i.e.*, by virtue of your union with Christ: see ver. 2.

5 ye are enriched. Rather, "ye were enriched" (R.V.); *i.e.*, when God's grace was bestowed on you at your conversion.

in all utterance. Lit., "in every word." *i.e.*, of the gospel revelation; "and in all knowledge," *i.e.*, in the firm hold of this Divine testimony upon their minds: see ver. 6.

7 coming. Rather, "revelation" (ἀποκάλυψιν).

8 who. That is, "our Lord Jesus Christ." The repetition of His name at the end of the verse is not sufficient reason for setting aside this reference.

blameless. "Unreproveable," R.V.; both justified and sanctified.

9 God is faithful, etc. God has taught us (see Rom. viii. 21–23) that our present "fellowship" with His Son—our union with, and conformity to Him here—is a pledge of our participation in His glory hereafter. Our confidence of complete salvation rests upon His faithfulness to His promise: cp. Phil. i. 8.

Jesus Christ our Lord. Ten times in the first ten verses the apostle expressly names the Lord Jesus Christ; speaking of Him as the object of worship, the author of grace and peace, the source of apostolic authority, the subject of the gospel testimony; with whom the Christian is now united, by whom he is sanctified, to whom he is conformed, and for whom, in "the day" of His "manifestation" in glory, he expectantly waits. In all this Paul both expresses his own reverence and love for the Saviour; and corrects those who "gloried in man," and so divided the church into parties of adherents to various religious teachers: see vers. 10–12.

10 that ye all speak the same thing. The opposite of the state described in ver. 12.

divisions. Or, "rents"; internal dissensions or "schisms"; arising from party-feeling; not conscientious differences of opinion, which must be expected in consequence of men's different capacities, education, and tempers.

11 Chloe. It is not known who Chloe was, nor what connexions of hers (children, slaves, or others in her household) had given this information to Paul at Ephesus. She is usually considered a Corinthian Christian, whose people had come to Ephesus, "but it is more in harmony with St. Paul's discretion to suppose that she was an *Ephesian*, known to the Corinthians, whose people had been in Corinth and returned to Ephesus" (*Speaker's Commentary*).

contentions. The first stage on the way to "divisions."

12 Now this I say, etc. What I mean is, that each of you says (either), I am of Paul (the founder of the church), (or) I am of Apollos (the eloquent teacher), etc. It was not so much the distinctive names, as the party spirit which appropriated them, that constituted the sin of the Corinthian factions.

Cephas. The Jewish party who claimed to be followers of Peter, "the apostle of the circumcision," probably used his Aramaic name.

I of Christ. Every true Christian can say, "I am Christ's." But these persons claimed some peculiar relation to Him which they denied to other Christians: cp. 2 Cor. x. 7. The "name which is above every name" is often profaned by being made the watchword of a party.

13 Is Christ divided? Lange well paraphrases the question: "Is there a Pauline, an Apollonian, a Petrine, a Christian Christ?" Some commentators regard the clause as an affirmation, "Christ is divided," *i.e.*, by your divisions. But the form of a question is much more in harmony with the style and character of St. Paul.

in the name of Paul. Rather, "into the name of Paul," *i.e.*, into union with and dependence on him: cp. Rom. vi. 3; and Matt. xxviii. 19, and notes.

16 besides, I know not whether I baptised any other. Paul knew that he had baptised but few; and he at once remembered Crispus as the ruler of the synagogue (Acts xviii. 8), and Gaius as his host (Rom. xvi. 23). He was reminded of Stephanas, perhaps by his presence (xvi. 17), or by an amanuensis. But the subject was not so important as to cause "any other" to be thought of or specified.

17 For Christ sent me not to baptise, etc. My business as an apostle is not baptising, but preaching. Paul and Peter (see Acts x. 48), like their Master (see John iv. 2, and note), seem to have generally left the administration of baptism to others.

not with wisdom of words. Not with philosophic or eloquent discourse, lest the mode of teaching should divert attention from the all-important lessons, and so make it "of none effect." This mention of the subject and method of Paul's preaching leads him into a digression (i. 18–ii. 16). In ch. iii. he returns to the censure of party spirit in the church at Corinth.

18 the preaching of the cross. *The Speaker's Commentary* makes clear the meaning of the original here. It is the same Greek word (λόγος) which is translated "words" in 17 and "preaching" in 18. "The nearest word in English which meets the sense in both passages is, perhaps, *argument.*" The contrast is then between "the philosophy of argument" (or philosophical argument) and "the argument of the Cross."

them that perish . . . us which are saved. Rather, as R.V., "them that are perishing . . . us which are being saved": cp. 2 Cor. ii. 15.

19 For it is written, etc. Cp. Isa. xxix. 14; xxxiii. 18.

20 Where is the wise? etc. The questions include both Jewish and Gentile reasoners. Where is the Greek philosopher? where the Jewish votary of tradition? where any and every disputant, belonging, as they do, to "this age"—the present transitory system of things.

21 For after that in the wisdom of God, etc. Since, amidst the displays of God's wisdom, human wisdom failed to recognise Him: it pleased God to save men by means of that preaching which the world deems foolishness; cp. Acts xvii. 23–29; Rom. i. 19–23.

the foolishness of preaching. Rather, "the foolishness of the preaching"; referring not to the manner but to the matter of the proclamation.

22 a sign. Rather, "signs"; probably some portents from heaven (see Matt. xii. 38, and note, also John iv. 48).

23 Christ crucified. "A crucified Messiah."

a stumblingblock. A ground of deepest offence to those who were looking for a royal and victorious Messiah.

foolishness. An absurdity to those who assumed that men's moral and intellectual needs could be met only by a system of philosophy.

27 to confound. Rather, "that He might put to shame," as R.V.

28 things which are not. Meaning, "things of no account."

30 of Him. Or, "from Him." "Redemption" seems to signify the final and entire deliverance of the body as well as the soul from all the consequences of sin: cp. Rom. viii. 23.

31 that, according as it is written. See note on Jer. ix. 23, 24, which is here quoted feeely.

CHAPTER II

1 And I . . . came not, etc. The apostle returns to his declaration in i. 17, with the view of showing that he had fully acted upon his own rule; having set before them the gospel, not with excellence of speech as an orator, or "of wisdom" as a philosopher; but in its Divine and authoritative simplicity.

2 I determined not, etc. The literal rendering (*Ellicott*) is, "I did not determine to know anything," *i.e.*, "the only thing that I made it definitely my business to know, was," etc. (*Alford*).

Jesus Christ, and Him crucified. Christ, in His person and especially in His expiatory work, was the one great theme of Paul's ministry at Corinth.

3 And I was with you, etc. The word "I" is emphatic, as in ver. 1. The "weakness" might be partly physical (cp. Gal. iv. 13; 2 Cor. xii. 7), but it was chiefly a humbling sense of his own insufficiency for the great work committed to him: see Acts xviii. 5-11, and notes.

4 enticing. Rather, "persuasive" (R.V.).

in demonstration of the Spirit. Cp. 14.

6 Howbeit we speak wisdom, etc. The apostle now sets the matter in another light. What seems folly to some is Divine wisdom to "those who are matured" in Christian knowledge, and can perceive the transcendent wisdom of the gospel as unfolded in his simple preaching; to such he taught it fully (iii. 1).

princes of this world. Or, "leaders of this age"; the wise, mighty, and noble, whose teachings accord with present systems and modes of thought. These leaders "are being brought to nought" (i. 26).

7 But we speak the wisdom of God in a mystery. We speak the wisdom so long concealed as a Divine secret (Eph. iii. 3-5), destined indeed to raise us to glory, but unknown to those (see Acts iii. 17, and note) who put to a shameful death "the Lord (the Possessor and Giver) of the glory" (see John xvii. 1-5, and notes).

9 as it is written, etc. This quotation gives only the general sense of Isa. lii. 15; lxiv. 4; lxv. 17. What God had in His mercy appointed for His people was not only unknown, but inconceivable; for the Spirit, who alone fathoms the depths of the Divine counsels, can alone teach it (10, 11). But we have the Spirit, and by His teaching we both know and speak (12-16).

11 For what man, etc.? "For who of men?" If man's inward purposes are so little known even by his fellows, how shall any less than God comprehend the Divine purposes? See Job xi. 7; and Isa. xl. 28; to which the word "searcheth" (10) may allude.

12 the things that are freely given to us of God. The treasures of wisdom and glory, which are God's free gifts in the gospel (9).

13 comparing spiritual things with spiritual. Or, "combining spiritual [truths] with spiritual [words]." Both the substance and the form of what we teach are not of "man's wisdom," but of the Holy Spirit.

14 the natural man. Both *Weymouth* and *Moffatt* translate "the unspiritual man."

discerned. Or, "judged of": see ver. 15; iv. 3, 4.

15 But he that is spiritual judgeth all things. That is, the man enlightened by God's Spirit judges of all things necessary to salvation: but no man unenlightened by Christ can rightly discern or judge the believer; for the Spirit of Christ can be known only by those who have it: cp. note on Isa. xl. 13, the passage here quoted from the Old Testament.

16 But we have the mind of Christ. These words are the apostle's comment on the prophet's question. "We," that is, "the spiritual" generally.

CHAPTER III

1 carnal. I was obliged, in my ministry among you, to treat you almost as unrenewed men, as mere infants in Christian knowledge.

2 I have fed you, etc. Rather, "I gave you milk to drink, not [solid] food, for ye were not able [to eat it]. Nay, not even now are ye able."

3 as men. Or, "according to man"; *i.e.*, as unrenewed men do.

4 Paul . . . Apollos. "Paul" and "Apollos" probably exemplify two different classes of teachers: see iv. 6, and note.

5 ministers by whom ye believed, etc. Not masters *in* whom, but "servants *through* whom ye believed, and that too as the Lord gave to each": *i.e.*, only just as the great Master allotted to each his labour and success.

6 I have planted, etc. Paul "planted" the church at Corinth; and then Apollos came and "watered" it, during Paul's journey through Upper Asia (Acts xviii.; xix. 1). In both cases it was God who made their labours effectual.

9 with God. See Acts xiv. 27; 2 Cor. vi. 1. God Himself has the work in hand. As labourers in a harvest field, or in the erection of a building, we work both *for* and *with* the Master, who will give to each his own reward according to his fidelity.

God's building. This new metaphor illustrates the different kinds of teaching; and it is appropriately used for the purpose of warning "every one" to teach only what is consistent with the fundamental truths.

10 a wise master-builder. Paul here claims to be "by God's grace" not a builder merely, but a master-builder, who has wisely laid the only true foundation, Jesus Christ (11); that which indeed "is laid" already by God Himself: see Isa. xxviii. 16; Rom. ix. 33.

12 Now if any man build upon this foundation, etc. The only foundation of a true church and of personal religion is Jesus Christ (11). But in teaching or in life and character, a man may build the abiding things, the gold, silver, and precious stones; truth, faith, love, or the perishing wood, hay, stubble, of false teaching, selfish motives, unworthy conduct.

13 it shall be revealed. Rather, "it is revealed": for every time of special Divine manifestation is a time of trial and of sifting (see Mal. iii. 1–3; Matt. iii. 11, 12, and notes); and such above all will the time of Christ's coming to judgement be: see 2 Thess. i. 8.

15 yet so as by fire. Though he himself will be saved, because he has built on the true foundation, his building will be consumed; he will lose his reward; and he will come out as one who has had a narrow escape from a burning ruin. It is plain that the apostle speaks of "fire" here only as an illustration (*so as* by fire: cp. Amos iv. 11); and that the words can give no support to the notion of purgatory.

16 Know ye not that ye are the temple of God? It is a natural transition from the thought of the work of building to the building itself. The connexion between teaching and life is also suggested. On the injury done to the Church of God by erroneous teaching or sinful life he enlarges in v., vi.

17 defile. The same word is rendered "destroy" in the other clause of this verse, and "corrupt" in 2 Cor. vii. 2; xi. 3. The word "ruin" best corresponds to its full extent of meaning (so *Conybeare and Howson*). The ruin that such a man works in God's Church God will inflict on him.

which [temple] ye are. Rather, "of which sort (*i.e.*, holy) are ye"; see R.V. marg.

18 let him become a fool. That is, a fool in the world's esteem.

19 taketh. Or "catcheth."

21 For all things are yours. Men and things which are otherwise most unlike, are yet all alike the common property of the Church. The names of apostles or teachers, instead of being a source of division, should be a cause of unity. They all lead to Christ, "ministers by whom ye believed" (5).

CHAPTER IV

1 mysteries. See note on Matt. xiii. 11. Our authority is merely ministerial, to dispense "the mysteries of God." These are not the sacraments, but the newly revealed truths of the gospel: cp. Luke viii. 10.

2 Moreover it is required, etc. The meaning of the original is best brought out in *Conybeare and Howson*: "Inquiry is made into a steward's conduct, in order that he may be proved faithful." Vers. 3–5 are added partly as a warning against over-hasty judgement of ministers, either in praise or in blame.

3 man's judgement. Lit., "a human day," *i.e.*, of judgement. "The refusal of the apostle to submit himself to human judgement was in no priestly arrogance, but in profound humility. Not because he was above judgement, or infallible, but because he was to be judged before a tribunal far more awful than that of Corinthian society. Fidelity, the chief excellence in a steward, is precisely that which men cannot judge. They can only judge of gifts" (*Robertson*).

4 For I know nothing by myself. An old English phrase, meaning, "I am conscious to myself of nothing amiss," of no unfaithfulness in my stewardship. Yet it does not follow that I am guiltless in the sight of the Lord. He is the only infallible Judge. And therefore it is not for you to judge, but to await His revelations and awards at His coming (5).

5 the hidden things of darkness. The things that are hidden in darkness.

praise. Rather, "the praise," *i.e.*, that which is his due.

6 I have in a figure transferred. Rather, simply, "I have transferred"; *i.e.*, My remarks apply to all your religious teachers; but, to avoid offence, I have used Apollos and myself to represent the whole.

that no one of you be puffed up, etc. Rather, "that ye be not puffed up, one of you on behalf of the one [teacher] against the other." If you—your teachers, your party, yourselves—were superior to others, this would be a reason, not for pride, but for gratitude to God who made you so (7).

8 Now ye are full, etc. "Ye are already (so early in your religious history) full," etc. An ironical castigation of their self-conceit.

ye have reigned as kings without us. That is, We who have trained you hoped to present you as our joy in that day: but you, it seems, have become kings already!

and I would to God ye did reign. Rather, "I would indeed that ye did reign; for then we might have some share in the glory."

9 last, as it were appointed to death, etc. Last and lowest; men condemned to death; brought out (like gladiators in the amphitheatre) to be gazed upon by all, both by sympathising angels, and by men disdainful like yourselves, who count us the fools, yourselves the wise—us the weak, yourselves the strong (10).

10 We are fools, etc. The irony here reaches its climax; but soon passes to solemn earnest.

11 naked. "Ill-clad."

12 working with our own hands. See ix. 1–18; Acts xviii. 3; xx. 34, and notes.

being reviled, we bless, etc. We not only endure, but speak kindly to those who attack us: cp. Matt. v. 44; Luke vi. 27.

13 as the filth of the earth. Lit., "as the refuse of the world." This is the climax of disgrace and contempt: cp. Lam. iii. 45.

16 followers of me. Rather, "imitators of me."

17 For this cause, etc. Timothy had already set out for Corinth (Acts xix. 22), but would not arrive until after the receipt of the Epistle (see xvi. 10).

18 as though I would not come to you. Boasting that I dare not come, and therefore send Timothy.

19 the speech. Rather, "the words," as in the next verse. I will test what they *say* by what they can *do* in God's service; for real Christianity (the reign of God established in man) is marked by spiritual energy, rather than loud profession.

CHAPTER V

1 It is reported commonly, etc. Or, perhaps, "Fornication is actually heard of among you," of so gross a kind "that one of you hath," etc.: see R.V.

his father's wife. That is, his own step-mother. The term "fornication" includes all violations of the seventh commandment.

2 And ye are puffed up. Probably a question. Instead of mourning over this scandalous sin, and excluding the offender from your fellowship, are you still elated with your fancied superiority to others ? (6).

3 For I verily, etc. Vers. 3–5 form one sentence, in which the words " such an one " (5) are inserted because of its length : " For I, present in spirit though absent in body, have already determined, as if present, that he who has thus done this thing shall, in the name of our Lord Jesus, when you are assembled and my spirit with the power of our Lord Jesus, be given over to Satan," etc.

5 to deliver such a one unto Satan, etc. " Satan is here spoken of as the instrument of physical suffering, just as in 2 Cor. xii. 7, St. Paul's own malady is described as ἄγγελος Σατανᾶ " (Lightfoot : *Notes on Epistles*).

6 Your glorying is not good (seemly). There appears here a glance backward at the high claims of the Corinthians (iv. 7–10). Such claims appeared the more unseemly in the face of this scandal.

a little leaven leaveneth the whole lump. A proverb, found also in Gal. v. 9, and implied in Matt. xiii. 33. It means that moral influence is rapidly diffusive. The sense is the same in xv. 33.

7 that ye may be a new lump, etc. That you may really be what you profess. The figure alludes to the Jewish practice of carefully removing every portion of leaven before the Passover (Exod. xii. 15).

For [even]. Rather, " For also " (R.V.) ; introducing a new and principal reason. " Christ our paschal victim was sacrificed " to ensure our exemption from the doom of the ungodly (see Exod. xii. ; John i. 29, and notes). We have therefore now to keep a perpetual festival.

9 in an epistle. Greek, " in *the* epistle." Probably referring to a letter previously sent, but not now extant.

10 yet not altogether, etc. I did not refer to casual and necessary intercourse with the ungodly, but to friendly and social recognition of immoral and avaricious professors (11).

11 But now I have written unto you, etc. That is, I now tell you that the meaning of what I wrote is, etc.

12 For what have I to do, etc. ? I am speaking only of your conduct towards those who profess faith in Christ. " For " it is not ours to judge the ungodly " without " ; God does that ; but it is ours, in the exercise of Christian discipline, to judge those " within " the Church.

CHAPTER VI

1 Dare any of you, etc. ? Dare you, instead of resorting to the arbitration of " the saints," your brethren, take your disputes before heathen and often unjust magistrates ? Is not this an offence against the dignity of the Christian character ? (2).

2 Do ye not know, etc. ? This form of question, which occurs ten times in the present Epistle (*Godet*), reminds them of truths which he had taught them. Here he calls attention to the truth that the redeemed will take a part (see Psa. xlix. 14 ; Dan. vii. 22) in the judgement of men, and even of angels (3). Surely then, he argues, even the least esteemed in the church (4) can judge between themselves in the common concerns of this life.

4 set them to judge. R.V. treats this as a question : " do ye set them," etc. ?

5 I speak to your shame. I say this (about giving over secular causes to the lowest in the church) not to exalt, but to reprove you ; for it seems there is " not even one among you " wise enough to adjust these matters " between brother " and brother.

6 before the unbelievers. More literal and emphatic in R.V., " before unbelievers."

7 Now therefore there is utterly a fault, etc. All this implies a radical defect, a prevalence of selfishness and injustice. *Lightfoot* says that the word translated " fault " includes the ideas of " loss " and " defeat."

Why do ye not rather take wrong ? In obedience to our Lord's command (Matt. v. 38–40).

8 Nay, ye do wrong. Not only is there a lack of charity, but of justice also.

9 unrighteous. The same word as in ver. 8, " wrong-doers."

10 covetous. Covetous in the widest sense ; *one who covets more than his share ;* not merely avaricious. The apostle always ranks the covetous with the most abandoned men : see vers. 10, 11 ; and cp. Col. iii. 5.

the kingdom of God. " That kingdom which, begun and established here, has its full development and consummation in the future " (*Ellicott*).

11 ye are washed. Rather, " ye washed off " these pollutions (symbolically, in baptism), " ye were sanctified," " ye were justified " (see R.V.) ; *i.e.*, when, being renewed " by the Spirit of our God " (Tit. iii. 5), ye believed unto life (John xx. 31) " in the name of the Lord Jesus."

12 All things are lawful unto me. Thus the apostle expresses his liberty as a Christian to use all God's gifts, a liberty misused by some at Corinth. Paul therefore declares that this freedom must not only be limited by expediency and by self-respect, but must on no account be applied to what is wrong in itself. The question of expediency is treated afterwards in chs. viii.–x. ; the participation in vice is shown in vers. 12–20 to be a very different matter, and is at once strongly condemned. The whole section is of great interest as showing how Christian liberty is to be kept from passing into heathen licence.

but I will not be brought under the power of any. Even my lawful desires shall not be my masters.

13 Now the body is not for fornication, etc. There are here three arguments against this vice. Meat offered to idols loses none of its natural fitness for food, and, like the bodily part, is destined to perish. But fornication (1) degrades the whole body ; (2) alienates part of the Redeemer's purchased possession : and (3) pollutes the temple of the Holy Spirit.

17 one spirit. That is, one with the Lord in spirit.

20 ye are bought. Rather, " ye *were* bought " (R.V.) ; namely, when Christ " gave His life as a ransom " from sin (1 Pet. i. 17–19). Use, then, your body (Rom. xii. 1) to His glory.

Therefore glorify, etc. Glorify *then ;* not so much a logical conclusion, as an impressive exhortation. The last clause " and in your spirit, which are God's " is omitted by the best authorities.

CHAPTER VII

1 It is good for a man not to touch a woman. The whole Bible highly commends marriage, which, as a Divine institution, founded in man's nature, must be good and conducive to individual and social well-being. The Apostle Paul elsewhere speaks of it with peculiar honour, and classes

" forbidding to marry " among the signs of a false system (1 Tim. iv. 1–3). Here he is to be understood, in answering the letter from the Corinthians, to express his own personal approval of continence.

2 Nevertheless, [to avoid] fornication, etc. Lit., " But on account of the fornications " ; lest you be drawn into the vices prevailing around you : see R.V.

let every man have his own wife. This clearly shuts out polygamy : see Mal. ii. 14–16, and notes.

6 by permission, etc. Rather, " by way of concession, not by way of command."

8 I say therefore. Rather, " *Now* I say " : see ver. 6.

10 depart. That is, be separated. You need not for this my inspired declaration ; you already have the Saviour's express command : see Mark x. 11, 12.

11 and let not the husband put away his wife. Our Lord allows divorce on the ground of conjugal unfaithfulness (see Matt. v. 32 ; xix. 9) ; but Paul does not here name the exception, which would be understood as a matter of course.

12 But to the rest, etc. That is, those who were married to heathens or Jews. Our Lord had not made a special law for such cases, and therefore the apostle gives his own decision : see ver. 40 below.

14 but now are they holy. We must remember (says *Calvin*) that Paul is not here speaking of contracting marriage, but of retaining connexions previously formed.

15 to peace. Rather, " in peace " (R.V.). The general rule is, that marriage is indissoluble ; but if your heathen partner will not stay with you, do not insist upon maintaining the connexion. For Christians are called to live in peace ; and it is only as you do so that you can hope for the conversion of your unbelieving husband or wife (16). But *you* are not to seek or to compel a separation, for every one should, as far as possible, remain in the relations which subsisted before his conversion (17) ; *e.g.*, whether circumcised or not (18–20).

16 For what knowest thou, etc. ? The connexion seems to be, that there need to be no scruple in letting the unbelieving consort depart, on the ground that remaining might lead to salvation. This, at best, would be very uncertain.

21 but if thou mayest be made free, etc. Either : " prefer to remain a slave, *if even* you can be made free " ; an extreme case illustrating the apostle's rule. Or, " yet *if also* you can be free, take advantage of the opportunity " ; the extreme case being admitted as an exception not affecting the general rule. Expositors are almost equally divided which interpretation to adopt, understanding the phrase *use it rather* in different senses : " Make use of the possibility of freedom " (*Godet*) ; " Employ thy very state of slavery as a means of spiritual profit " (*Ellicott* and others).

22 freeman. Rather, " freedman," as R.V. " Servant " is " bond-servant." So " servants " in ver. 23.

25 faithful. Or, " trustworthy." This phrase is probably adopted because the case had reference to a temporary emergency, and not to a subject of permanent command.

26 I suppose therefore, etc. Rather, " I hold then." What the existing or impending " distress" was is not clearly known ; but it was clearly so severe as to make the cares and responsibilities of the marriage state particularly undesirable.

it is good for a man so to be. " It is good for a man to be as he is " (R.V.), whether married or unmarried (27).

28 trouble in the flesh. In the midst of a community adverse to God, Christian parents especially called to suffer from the perversion or the persecution of their children.

but I spare you. I would spare you this trouble ; hence my advice.

29 the time is short, etc. " It remaineth " belongs to the preceding words, *i.e.* " what remains of it." This I would impress upon you, whether you marry or not—that God has made what remains of life short, in order that you may not be unduly affected by passing events, but be dead to the world (29–31).

31 as not abusing it. Rather, " as not using it to the full " (R.V. marg.) ; " not engrossed in it " (*Moffatt*).

fashion. Or, " form." " Passeth away," more exactly, " is passing away."

35 comely. Or, seemly ; and so in ver. 36.

36 let them marry. That is, his virgin daughter and her lover.

37 hath power over his own will. That is, can with propriety follow his own judgement as to giving his daughter in marriage.

39 only in the Lord. That is, only in accordance with the Lord's will : see 2 Cor. vi. 14 ; Eph. vi. 1. Most commentators take this to mean marrying only a Christian.

40 happier. More free from earthly cares and sorrows in troublous times (26).

if she so abide. " If she abide as she is " (R.V.). See ver. 26.

after my judgement. That is, agreeably with the judgement I have given (25).

CHAPTER VIII

1 things offered unto idols. Of an animal slain for sacrifice, part was consumed, part was reserved by the priests as their fee, part taken away by the worshippers, who might either (1) consume it at a feast within the temple precincts, or (2) take it home for the purpose, or (3) send it to the market for sale. The priests would also often sell their portion to the dealers. To all these uses the apostle's remarks apply.

we all have knowledge. Probably referring to words of the Corinthians in their letter : " We all (as you say) have knowledge." Yes, and if knowledge alone were an adequate guide, we have enough to decide the matter easily. But " knowledge [without love] puffeth up ; love [it is, that] buildeth up " in substantial practical godliness. Vers. 2, 3 are a parenthetical admonition to such as made a boast of their knowledge whilst they neglected to cultivate love : cp. xiii.

2 he knoweth nothing yet. He has not really learned what he pretends to know until he has learned to love.

3 But if any man love God, etc. He who so knows God as to love Him, is so known by God as to be loved by Him : see John xiv. 21–23 ; and especially Gal. iv. 9.

4 an idol is nothing in the world. More precisely as R.V., " no idol is [anything] in the world," *i.e.*, the beings whom the idols are designed to represent have no existence. But it is afterwards shown (x. 20) that there are other beings connected with false worship.

6 but to us there is but one God, etc. This verse shows that the doctrine of one God no more sets aside the Deity of Christ, than a belief in one Lord (Jesus Christ) sets aside the Lordship of the Father.

7 for some with conscience of the idol, etc. R.V., "being used until now to the idol." Some of the Gentile converts believed, from old habit, that an idol had real existence, although they worshipped the true God alone; so that they could not help feeling that when they ate of the idol-sacrifice they were having communion with the idol; and hence "their conscience was defiled" with the guilt of an idolatrous action: cp. note on Rom. xiv. 22.

8 meat commendeth us not to God. R.V., "Food will not commend us (*i.e.*, as acceptable) to God"; it makes us neither "better" nor "worse" in His sight. But (9) we must take care not to use our right in such a way as to injure and endanger our brethren by tempting them to act against their conscience (10, 11).

10 sit. Reclining at the meal.

be emboldened. Lit., "be built up"; as if he had said, will be edified to his ruin. "With a touch of irony" (*Speaker's Commentary*).

11 shall the weak brother perish, etc. The sentence is probably to be read affirmatively. "For he that is weak perisheth—the brother for whose sake Christ died" (R.V.: cp. Rom. xiv. 15, 16, 22, and notes).

12 wound. Properly, "strike": as one who cruelly beats a weak or sickly person.

13 meat. Rather, "food" of any kind: the particular kind here intended is denoted by "flesh," which the apostle would willingly give up altogether rather than lead a weak brother into idolatry. There is no proof that Paul habitually practised this self-denial; but his readiness to do so exhibits a characteristic regard for the good of others.

CHAPTER IX

1 have I not seen Jesus Christ our Lord? Referring to our Lord's appearance to him near Damascus (Acts ix. 17), and perhaps also to such occasions as those mentioned in Acts xviii. 9; xxii. 17, 18; see xv. 8.

2 the seal of mine apostleship, etc. Your conversion is the fruit, and therefore the evidence of my apostleship; and this is a sufficient defence (Gr. ἀπολογία) answer to all who question me (3)

4 Have we not power to eat and to drink? At the cost of the churches to which we minister.

5 as other apostles. Properly, "as the other apostles." The passage implies not only that most, if not all of them, were married; but any one of them might take his wife with him on his missionary journeys, and be regarded as being entitled to the support of the churches for both. The words translated "a sister, a wife" do not refer to two separate alternatives. The meaning really is "a sister wife," *i.e.* one of the Christian believers as a wife.

the brethren of the Lord. See Matt. xiii. 55.

Cephas. That Peter was a married man is evident from Matt. viii. 14; and his wife was proably an active Christian, if there is any truth in a tradition respecting her martyrdom, mentioned by Clem. Alex. *Strom.* b. 7.

6 Or I only and Barnabas, etc. Are Barnabas and I the only persons who have no right to be supported by the churches we serve? The apostle proceeds to defend this right (7), partly on the ground of natural justice, illustrated by the cases of soldiers, vine-dressers, and shepherds, and partly by the injunctions of the Old Testament (9).

8 as a man. Rather, "after man"; that is, according to the usages of mankind alone: is it not also a Divine principle?

9 treadeth. That is, "thresheth": see notes on Deut. xxv. 4; Isa. xxviii. 28.

10 Or saith He it altogether for our sakes? The Greek word (πάντως) translated "altogether" is in the Russian version *konetchno* ("indeed"). "Does He say it indeed for our sakes?" Blass (*Grammar of N.T. Greek*) also translates it "indeed." The idea appears to be that while the primary object of the command was care for the oxen, there was in it a higher and wider lesson.

that he that ploweth, etc. *i.e.*, all who labour ought to have a prospect of profiting by the results; and especially Christian labourers in God's field (iii. 9).

11 If we have sown unto you spiritual things, etc. If we supply the wants of your souls, is it much that you meanwhile supply our bodily wants?

12 If others be partakers of [this] power (right), etc. Your teachers, who oppose me, exact their maintenance from you (2 Cor. xi. 20); while I, your founder, "sustain all" toils and privations on your behalf (2 Cor. xi. 27), lest any appearance of selfishness should hinder the success of the gospel (18).

13 they which wait, etc. See Numb. xviii. 8–19, and note.

14 Even so (hath) the Lord ordained. The Lord *Jesus*: see Matt. x. 10; Luke x. 4, 7, and notes: cp. 1 Tim. v. 18.

15 But I have used none of these things. Whatever others have done, *I* have not used my right: nor do I write these things in order to claim my rightful support.

should make my glorying void. That is, "should deprive me of my ground of glorying." He was *bound* to preach the gospel, and therefore could not glory in doing that (16). But he was free to receive or to refuse maintenance from those to whom he preached; "and therefore his refusing to do so was a ground of glorying, that is, a proof of integrity, to which he could with confidence appeal" (*Hodge*).

17 a dispensation [of the gospel] is committed unto me. Rather, as R.V., "I have a stewardship entrusted to me" which I *must* discharge. I may do it willingly; but as the Lord's bondsman I have no option whether I will do it or not. I work, not that I may gain pay, except indeed this, that I may take no pay from you for my work, not "using my rights to the full" (18). "For when I was free to take my own course (1) I became the slave of all (19), that I might make a gain of the more," *i.e.*, of as many as possible. The gaining of many converts he regarded as his pay.

20 to them that are under the law. That is, to Jews.

21 to them that are without law. That is, to the Gentiles: see note on Rom. ii. 12.

under the law to Christ. Rather, "bound by law to Christ"; *i.e.*, the law of Christian love and obedience.

22 the weak. "The weak" are those referred to in viii. 1–13; Rom. xiv. 1. The apostle's statement here confirms that of viii. 3. "All things to all men" is no expression of flabby weakness or compromise. It is the principle of concession in non-essentials, provided the main object is kept in view.

23 And this I do. Probably (as in the best MSS.), "all things I do." This is my universal principle of action; and that not only for the sake of others, but for my own, and that I may fully share with them in gospel blessings.

24–27. Paul here illustrates his practice of self-denial and self-discipline for the gospel's sake by a reference to the Grecian games, some of which were celebrated on the Isthmus near Corinth. The chief of them were running, boxing, wrestling, leaping, and throwing the quoit and spear. The prize (25) was a crown or garland of olive, bay, pine, or parsley.

24 a race. Lit., "a race-course," which was a stadium (about a furlong) in length.

So run. R.V., "Even so run"; *i.e.*, as the successful competitor runs; "in order that ye may obtain" the prize.

25 every man that striveth for the mastery. Rather, "every one who contendeth" in the games.

26 not as uncertainly. "No want of clearness in course or direction (Phil. iii. 14), and with no uncertain or unsteady step: he knew whither and in whose presence he was running the great race of eternal life" (*Ellicott*).

so fight I. The reference is now to the contests of boxing, as though the preceding metaphor of the race had not sufficiently expressed the active and aggressive character of the struggle.

27 but I keep under my body, etc. Rather, "But I buffet (literally, 'strike under the eye,' as a boxer) my body, and lead it captive (as a vanquished adversary), lest having made proclamation [of the rules of the contest] to others, I myself [from neglect of them] should be rejected." After the contests the victors were examined by the judges; and if they were found to have contended unlawfully [or unfairly], were deprived of the prize, and were "rejected" with disgrace.

CHAPTER X

1 Moreover, brethren, etc. The apostle further illustrates the danger of negligent self-indulgence by the case of the ancient Israelites, who, though admitted, as by a baptism in the cloud and in the sea, to the privileges given through Moses, and continually sustained by miraculous provision, yet, through unbelief and sensuality, forfeited all, and perished.

3 spiritual. Or, "supernatural food," in its origin and purpose; *i.e.*, not merely to sustain life, but in doing so to foreshadow the "true bread from heaven," and the "living water" (ver. 4; John vi. 30–58; iv. 10, and notes).

4 for they drank of that spiritual Rock, etc. The exact rendering of this clause is, "for they were drinking from a spiritual following rock." The apostle seems to say that there was a rock, with its constant supplies of water, following Israel through the wilderness; not, as Jewish tradition reports, a material rock, but a "spiritual rock," "Christ," the true constant source of all the grace they had.

5 with many of them. Rather, "with the greater part of them." In fact, He was pleased only with Joshua and Caleb (see Numb. xiv. 30; xxvi. 65).

6 examples. *The Speaker's Commentary* gives the best interpretation of the original (τύποι): *Now these things come to pass for outlines or marks belonging to us* to follow or avoid, to follow the tracks of obedience and mercies, to avoid the footprints of rebellion and judgements.

8 as some of them committed. In the licentious worship of Baal-peor: see Numb. xxv. 1, 2, and note. This example was peculiarly applicable to the Corinthians, as their city was proverbially addicted to the immoral worship of Venus.

three and twenty thousand. See note on Numb. xxv. 9.

9 tempted. Gr. "tried beyond endurance." Namely, "Him," *i.e.*, "the Lord," which the best authorities regard as the correct reading instead of "Christ" in this verse.

10 the destroyer. Meaning, probably, "the destroying angel," the pestilence: see Numb xvi. 49; and cp. 2 Sam. xxiv. 13–16.

11 of the world. "Of the ages."

13 common to man. Lit., "human." "Such as man can bear," R.V.

above that ye are able. That is, to endure. Having shown the Corinthians their danger, Paul now comforts them by showing that God's faithfulness secures their safety; for "He will make with the trial the escape also"; providing suitable relief for each temptation by which He permits faith to be tested.

14 Wherefore, my dearly beloved, flee from idolatry. For your own sakes, then, as well as for the sake of others, avoid those idol-feasts (19–21), and so escape all connexion with idolatry. "God delivers only those who do their lawful utmost to deliver themselves" (*R. South*).

16 The cup of (the) **blessing.** So called, probably, because in connexion with it they blessed God for His goodness, particularly in redemption.

is it not the (a) **communion,** etc.? By partaking together of the wine and bread we signify that we partake alike in the benefits of Christ's death, and also that we are united with Him and with each other (17), forming "one loaf," "one body."

18 partakers of (in communion with) **the altar.** It follows that those who eat of idol sacrifices partake of idol-worship.

19 What say I then? In saying this do I contradict my former statement (viii. 4), that an idol has no real existence? No; but what I say is this, that idols being regarded by their worshippers as "demons" (see next note), participation in their feasts implies fellowship in idolatry, just as partaking of the Lord's Supper implies union with Christ; and it would provoke His anger (22).

20 devils. Or, "demons"; *i.e.*, [evil] spirits: see Deut. xxxii. 17; Psa. cvi. 37, and notes.

23 All things are lawful, etc. See vi. 12, and note.

24 [wealth]. That is, "weal"; *welfare* or *profit* (33).

25 Whatsoever is sold in the shambles, etc. Meat sold in the market, or served at an ordinary banquet (not an idolatrous feast), unless it were expressly stated to have been offered to an idol, might be received without question or doubt, as part of the food given to man by the bounty of the Lord of all.

for conscience sake. "Making no inquiry from regard to conscience" (*Speaker's Commentary*).

26 The earth is the Lord's. Therefore, all God's creatures and gifts in the way of food are for our use, and may properly be enjoyed, when there is no scruple in the way: see 1 Tim. iv. 4.

28 But if any man say unto you, etc. This may have special reference to a scrupulous Christian (viii. 7–11). If he say thus, then "abstain for the sake of the informant, and [particularly] of [his] conscience." The second quotation, Psa. xxiv. 1, is omitted in the most ancient manuscripts and versions.

29 for why is my liberty judged, etc. ? Why am I to be restrained of my freedom in thankfully using the bounties of God's providence, by the censoriousness and evil speaking of others ?

30 by grace. Rather, "with thankfulness" (R.V. marg.); probably referring to the giving of thanks ("saying grace"). See Luke vi. 32, etc.

31 Whether therefore ye eat, etc. All this discussion resolves itself into the great principle that we should aim to glorify God in *every* action of our lives.

33 even as I please all men, etc. See note on ix. 22.

many. Rather, "the many." The next verse (xi. 1) properly belongs to the foregoing discussion, practically summing it up.

CHAPTER XI

2 the ordinances (traditions). The apostolic injunctions.

3 the head of the woman is the man. It seems that some women in the Corinthian church claimed equality with the men (cp. Gal. iii. 28); and hence neglected the rules of propriety prevailing among the Greeks and Orientals, by appearing without their veils. "In ch. xiv. 34 *silence* is imposed on women, but *there* in the full congregation; *here* in less formal meetings for devotion, *e.g.*, in a church held in a house, xvi. 19, they are allowed to pray aloud and to utter inspirational discourses: no contradiction between the two texts" (*Speaker's Commentary*).

the head of Christ is God. Christ is subordinate to the Father both as man and as Mediator: see John xiv. 28; Phil. ii. 7. Subordination pervades the whole universe, and especially the Christian system; and it is the glory of each part to keep the place assigned to it.

4 prophesying. See note on Rom. xii. 6.

dishonoureth his head. Among the Greeks (but not the Jews) a man was required to uncover his head in worship; but a woman (5) was required, among both Greeks and Asiatics, to cover hers both in worship and in public. Hence Paul calls it a dishonouring (*i.e.*, an unseemly treatment) of the head, when either man or woman departed from the custom.

5 uncovered. "Unveiled."

shaven. A shaven head was a mark of infamy, or of mourning, both in Greece and in Judæa.

7 a man indeed ought not to cover his head. As covering the head was a sign of subjection, the woman, and not the man, should practise it; for the man is the superior, being made to be the reflection, as it were, of God's glorious image; whereas the woman is rather the reflection of the man (Gen. ii. 18–20), being made *from* him and *for* him (8, 9).

10 power. The arguments of so many commentators that this refers to the man's power or authority over the woman do not seem convincing. No clear case has been given to show that the word ἐξουσία means the power of some one else, and not one's own power. Stanley, however, who favours the former explanation, admits that to regard the veil or covering as "the sign of the power or dignity of the woman over herself" is the sense most agreeable to the usage of the word ἐξουσία. See also Ramsay (*The Cities of St. Paul*, p. 200) and Robertson, Bishop of Exeter (*International Critical Commentary*). R.V., "[a sign of] authority."

because of the angels. Holy angels, regarded as present in the assembly, and observant of the deportment of its members; perhaps also with a reference to their humility in God's presence: see Isa. vi. 2.

11 in the Lord. God, from whom all things are (12), has appointed that, as in nature, so in grace ("in the Lord"), man and woman should both have their place, and should both, in their place, be essential to the completeness of the redeemed race.

16 But if any man seem to be contentious, etc. As if he said, "I have given the reasons why women should remain covered, but if any one is not convinced, at any rate it is not our custom for women to uncover the head in worship."

17 Now in this that I declare [unto you] I praise you not. Or, as R.V., "In giving you the above charge, I praise you not"; the dispraise referring to the *following* charge, respecting the Lord's Supper. The former series of injunctions was attended with words of praise (2), not so this present one: cp. ver. 2.

18 in the church (ecclesia). Rather, "in assembly"; without any reference to the particular place or building where they met. Of recent accounts of the word "Church" and its meanings, special mention may be made of Hort's *The Christian Ecclesia* (1897), Professor Gwatkin's article "Church" in *Hastings' Dict. Bible* (9th ed., 1910), and Canon Mason's "Conceptions of the Church in Early Times," in *Essays on the Early History of the Church and Ministry*, edited by Professor H. B. Swete (1918).

I partly believe it. "The apostle excepts the innocent, and uses a gentle form of speech" (*Bengel*).

19 heresies. Rather, "factions"; not doctrinal errors, but party divisions, which seem to have exhibited themselves even at the Lord's Supper. In the present imperfect state of the church such things must occur (cp. Matt. xviii. 7), and God permits them in order that the genuine Christian may be tested and manifested (19).

20 the Lord's supper. The first Christians appear to have made the Lord's Supper part of a social meal or love-feast (like the Lord's last supper with His disciples, Luke xxii. 14–20); see Acts ii. 42–46. The communicants brought with them the supplies of the table, which were regarded as common to the whole company. But at Corinth the observance was so disorderly that it could scarcely be called "eating the Lord's Supper"; for one took the provisions before another could share (21); and the poor man who brought nothing with him got no refreshment, while the rich man with his abundant supply indulged to excess (21, 22).

21 drunken. This does not necessarily mean "intoxicated" (see John ii. 10); but at least having drunk to excess.

22 What? have ye not houses, etc.? Satisfy your appetite at home, and do not treat the church with contempt, putting the poor to shame by the display of abundance which you do not let them share. For an instructive contrast, separated by only a few years, see Acts ii. 44–46; iv. 32–35.

23 For I (have) received of the Lord, etc. These disorders were inexcusable, for Paul had taught them the original mode of celebrating this ordinance, as it had been specially revealed to him by the Lord Himself (Gal. i. 12). The striking verbal likeness between this, the earliest account, and that in Luke xxii. 19, 20, favours the supposition that the evangelist derived his narrative from the apostle.

in which He was betrayed. "In which He was being betrayed": at that very hour.

24 this is my body. That is, this *represents* my body (see note on Matt. xxvi. 26): and so in ver. 25. Cp. John x. 9; xv. 1. The word "broken," does not appear to have originally formed part of this verse: see R.V.

25 the New Testament. Which was ratified by the "blood" of Christ, here represented by the wine in the "cup": cp. Exod. xxiv. 8; and see note on Matt. xxvi. 28. It is noteworthy that Deissmann prefers the translation "the New Testament" to that of "the New Covenant." He says, "There is ample material to back me in the statement that no one in the Mediterranean world in the first century A.D. would have thought of finding in the word διαθήκη the idea of "covenant" (*Light from the Ancient East*, p. 341).

as oft as ye drink [it]. How often is not prescribed. It seems to have been observed daily in Acts ii. 46; weekly, in Acts xx. 7.

26 ye do show. Rather, as R.V., "ye proclaim": to one another and to the world.

27 Wherefore whosoever shall eat this bread, etc. As the true purpose of the observance is to commemorate and declare the Lord's death, and not to satisfy bodily appetites; so whoever partakes "unworthily," *i.e.*, without a devout remembrance of the works and claims of our crucified Redeemer, sins against His "body and blood," the only sacrifice for sin. Therefore every communicant should "test" his state of heart respecting Christ, partaking only if he can "discern the (Lord's) body," or discriminate between it and ordinary food, appreciating His death as represented in the ordinance. Otherwise he brings upon himself "judgement"; which he would have escaped had he judged himself. Of this "judgement" (the Divine disapproval of their conduct) the frequent sickness and death in the church at Corinth was a token; these afflictions being sent to "chasten" them, that they might not be "condemned."

33 tarry one for another. That ye may all partake together, and alike: see note on ver. 20.

CHAPTER XII

1 (the) spiritual [gifts]. Manifestations of the Holy Spirit (see ver. 3). "The Apostle's object is to lead his readers away from rivalry in special gifts to the one Spirit." . . . "The term 'charisma' in St. Paul's language stands for any gift of grace which enables any member of the Church to fulfil his appropriate function, however exalted or however humble that function may be" (Dean Armitage Robinson: Essay on "The Primitive Ministry" in *Essays on the Early History of the Church and Ministry*, edited by Dr. H. B. Swete, 1918).

2 even as ye were led. Blindly following from time to time the supporters of "voiceless" and senseless idols.

3 no man speaking by the Spirit of God, etc. The confession or the rejection of Jesus as Lord is the criterion of the possession of the Holy Spirit: cp. John xv. 26, 27; xvi. 14, 15; 1 John iv. 1–3, and notes. "Accursed" here is *anathema*; the negative implying a strong assertion to the contrary.

4 diversities. "Distributions" (*Lange*).

5 differences of administrations. However diverse the "gifts," they have one Divine source (4); however different the "ministries" (not *administrations*, see vers. 8–10, 28), they serve one Divine Lord (6); however various the "operations," there is but one Divine Worker (the Father, John v. 17); and they all have one great object, the "profit" of the Church (7). Therefore all should be exercised, not discordantly but in harmony.

6 all in all. "All" these various workings in "all" who exercise them.

7 to profit withal. Rather, "for the common good."

10 miracles. Other powers besides bodily cures (9).

prophecy. See note on Rom. xii. 6.

discerning (*discernings*) **of spirits.** This implies the power of knowing the secrets of another's heart: cp. Acts v. 1–10; xiii. 9–11.

[divers] kinds of tongues. See Acts ii. 4, and note. There was on the day of Pentecost a speaking in *languages of other countries*, which natives of those countries could understand; while the gift, as it displayed itself in the Corinthian church, was evidently that of *ecstatic outbursts* in no known tongue.

12 so also is Christ. The unity which pervades man's natural body and its members, pervades Christ's spiritual body, the Church, and its members.

13 by one Spirit. Lit., "in one Spirit": the Holy Spirit being, as it were, the element of this baptism: cp. Acts xi. 16.

made to drink. "Imbued with" (*Moffatt*).

14–19. The *variety* of the human frame is used to illustrate the diversity of gifts in the Church. Its *unity* is employed to show the mutual and close dependence and harmony of the several parts and their endowments.

23 bestow. Rather "put on" (as R.V. marg.): referring to clothing.

25 schism. Or, "division," of feeling or interest.

27 members in particular. Collectively, the body of Christ; individually, the members of His body. The following list of diverse and unequal gifts (not necessarily implying distinct offices) illustrates the need of mutual consideration and love, as the only effectual preventive of jealousies and bickerings (31).

28 prophets. Or, preachers, under the direct influence of the Holy Spirit: cp. xiv. 1, note.

teachers. Distinguished from preachers.

miracles. Lit., "powers": see on ver. 10.

helps. Probably the care of the poor and the sick.

governments. Or, powers of administration; a separate gift.

31 covet earnestly the best gifts, etc. Rather, "Aim at the greater gifts (such as public teaching for edification, xiv. 1–5): yea, moreover, I show you a pre-eminent way" to Christian usefulness, This is LOVE; without which they are all worthless. "The way to all higher gifts is the way of Love."

CHAPTER XIII

1 and of angels. This may mean, more than man can utter.

charity. Not almsgiving (see ver. 3), but "love," as the word is rendered in most places, and in R.V. throughout this chapter.

tinkling. Rather, "clanging" (R.V.).

2 mysteries. See note on Matt. xiii. 11. "Faith" here is the same as in xii. 9; which might exist apart from love: see Matt. vii. 21–23.

3 though I bestow all my goods, etc. "Dole out in food" (*Speaker's Commentary*). Notwithstanding this plain warning, men have confounded almsgiving with true religion, and hence have in many languages called it *charity.*

though I give my body to be burned. The highest form of self-sacrifice for one's country, friends, or religion. Such things may be done, not from love, but from ambition. An alternative reading, " that I may boast," seems on every account less probable, although sustained by many high authorities. *Nestle* (Gr. Test.) retains the old reading.

4 Is kind. The French version has " elle est douce."

charity envieth not. Love is neither envious nor jealous.

5 seeketh not her own. Love is disinterested.

is not [easily] provoked. The word *easily* has been added by the translators to the apostle's statement. It is omitted in R.V.

thinketh no evil. *i.e.*, takes no account of it, forgives it. Evil of course must be understood in the sense of *injury :* not moral evil generally.

6 In the truth. Properly, " with the truth " ; sharing the joy of its triumphs. The contrast between " iniquity " (or unrighteousness) and " truth " shows the inseparable connexion between true principles and right conduct.

7 beareth all things. The Greek means " covereth." *The Speaker's Commentary* explains : " is proof against all provocations " ; " knows how to be silent " (*Weymouth*) ; " always slow to expose " (*Moffatt*). " All things " must, of course, mean all that can be thus treated with a good conscience.

believeth all things. Love is not distrustful, but is hopeful ; looking on the brighter side of things and persons.

8 shall fail. Rather, " shall be done away," as no more needed.

it shall vanish away. Or, " be done away," as in ver. 8. Even inspired men " know " and " speak " only " in part " ; with the conceptions and utterance of " a babe." Truth is presented to them " in dark hints " ; not with open " face," but in the dimmed reflection of " a mirror " (12). This " shall be done away," superseded by perfect knowledge in heaven.

10 perfect. " Full-grown " contrasted with " babe."

12 through a glass. Rather as R.V., " in a mirror " (cp. James i. 23). " Mirrors " were generally made by the ancients of polished metal (Exod. xxxviii. 8 ; Job xxxvii. 18).

13 And now abideth. Confidence in God, and expectation of still future good, will be as permanent in heaven as love.

the greatest of these is charity. Faith and hope belong to man as a creature ; love constitutes his likeness to God (1 John iv. 7–19). Faith and hope benefit the man himself ; love diffuses its blessings to others. Faith and hope are the *results* of love (see ver. 7), which therefore as " their sentient and sustaining principle " (*Ellicott*) is greater than either.

CHAPTER XIV

1 prophesy. Here used in the sense of teaching ; " proclaiming " God's truth. It was much more adapted to edify the Church than the gift of tongues (2–5 : cp. 22–25).

2 understandeth. Lit., " heareth " ; *i.e.*, understandingly (16). He can therefore do no good, and yet perhaps " by the [power of the Holy] Spirit he speaks new revelations."

4 edifieth himself. Not always because he understands what he says, but because the correctness and sacred passion of his utterance contribute to the " building up " of his spiritual life.

6 except I shall speak to you, etc. Addressing you in your own language, and imparting " revelation " as a *prophet*, or " knowledge " as a *teacher.*

7 what is piped or harped. What tune is played on either " the flute or the harp " ; the two kinds of instrumental music used in Greece.

8 an uncertain sound. A sound whose meaning as a signal is not understood.

9 ye shall speak into the air. Futile, useless speech.

10 There are, it may be, etc. That is, However numerous the languages may be, not one of them is without meaning.

11 a barbarian. " A foreigner " ; one who speaks a language which I do not know " : see note on Acts xxviii. 2.

12 spiritual [gifts]. Lit., " spirits " · see note on xii. 1.

14 my spirit prayeth. My own spirit, under the power of the Holy Spirit, prays ; but my mind can exercise no power over the minds of others, and is " unproductive " (14) of good to them (16, 17, 19). Consequently, a man who has only this gift had better be silent in the Christian assembly ; speaking to himself and to God (28).

16 when thou shalt bless with the spirit. That is, when thou givest thanks to God in the exercise of thy spiritual gift, but in a tongue unknown to thy " unlearned " brother. The early Christians followed the ancient Jewish practice of exclaiming " Amen " (Neh. viii. 6) in token of assent to public prayer.

the unlearned. " The outsider " (*Moffatt*).

18 I thank my God, I speak with tongues, etc. I am not depreciating what I do not possess.

19 yet in the church, etc. Whatever I may do in private, in the congregation I would speak intelligibly, that I may instruct others.

20 in malice be ye children. Rather, " but in wickedness be ye babes." Join the guilelessness of infancy with the wisdom of mature age : cp. Matt. x. 16.

21 In the law. That is (as in John x. 34), in the Old Testament (Isa. xxviii. 11, 12). When of old God spoke to Israel through a foreign language, it was in judgement, not in mercy, and it brought them no benefit.

22 Wherefore tongues are for a sign, etc. Or, Accordingly the gift of tongues is not for instructing believers, but for a sign (a convincing token of God's presence) to those who do not believe ; whereas, inspired teaching is rather for believers than for unbelievers. The contrast is put absolutely ; but in vers. 24, 25 the utterance of Christian truth is shown to be the most effective upon the unbeliever too, laying bare his heart, and bringing him openly to confess God.

24 But if all prophesy. Each speaking in turn : see ver. 13.

26 How is it then, brethren? The apostle now rebukes them for their disorderly exercise of their gifts ; one being eager to sing, whilst others wished to teach, or to make new " revelations," or to speak with tongues, without regard to decorum and edification.

27 [let it be] by two, etc. Only two, or at most three, at one meeting, each in his turn.

29 the other. Rather, " the others " (R.V.).

30 let the first hold his peace. Let the first speaker stop upon being told of the new revelation.

32 the spirits of the prophets. These spiritual impulses are so far under your own control, that you can stop when you are speaking and wait for one another (30); for God, who moves you by His Spirit, loves peace and good order (33).

34 let your women keep silence in the churches. The speaking mentioned in the next clause is "chattering" (λαλεῖν) See xi. 5, 13, where teaching by women is recognised.

35 their husbands. Properly, "*their own* husbands."

36 What? came the word of God out from you, etc.? You are neither the first nor the only church, and therefore can claim no right to be singular in your practices.

37 spiritual. Spirit-inspired.

commandments of the Lord. Paul here stamps his injunctions with the authority of Christ. He adds (ver. 38) that if any one does not acknowledge this, he cannot waste time in teaching one who will not be taught; such a person must take the consequences: cp. xi. 16, and note.

CHAPTER XV

2 ye are saved. Lit., "ye are being saved"; are in the way of salvation: see on i. 18.

if ye keep in memory. Rather, "if ye hold fast."

3 first of all. Lit., "among first things"; *i.e.*, the most important. These were, in the apostle's view, Christ's atoning death (Rom. iii. 25), and His burial and resurrection, in all of which Scripture was fulfilled; see Isa. liii.; Psa. xvi. 10, etc.

that which I also received. From the Lord Himself; cp. xi. 23.

4 He rose again. Literally, and R.V., "He hath been raised," expressing the permanence of His resurrection-life.

5 that He was seen of Cephas, etc. On these evidences of our Lord's resurrection, see note on Matt. xxviii. 1.

6 of whom the greater part remain unto this present. They could therefore still be appealed to.

7 James. The Lord's brother (Gal. i. 19). This appearance may explain the fact that whereas Christ's brethren believed not on Him during His earthly life (John vii. 5), they are found as believers immediately after His resurrection (Acts i. 14). The revelation of His risen glory wrought instantaneous conviction in their minds.

then of all the apostles. This seems to refer to our Lord's ascension, when, "while they beheld, He was taken up" (Acts i. 9).

8 as of one born out of due time. Or, "as unto the untimely birth"; an allusion partly to the time and mode of his conversion (Acts ix.), but chiefly to his unworthiness (9): cp. 1 Tim. i. 12–16.

12 how say some among you, etc.? These were most probably Gentile Christians, to whom this doctrine was strange, improbable, and unwelcome, because it attached so much importance to the body (cp. Acts xvii. 18, 32). Some also objected that they could not understand how the resurrection was to be effected (35).

14 vain. Lit., "empty." *Vulg.*, "inanis."

15 false witnesses of God. Concerning God.

17 ye are yet in your sins. Having neither pardon nor life; for Christ's death as a sacrifice for sin cannot have been accepted, if He is still among the dead: see note on Rom. iv. 25.

vain. "Foolish"; idle. A different word from that in ver. 14.

19 we are of all men most miserable. Lit., "we are more pitiable than all men"; bitterly disappointed in the noblest hopes for which the greatest sacrifices have been made (see vers. 29–32).

20 the firstfruits of them that slept. That is, the forerunner and pledge of theirs: see Rom. viii. 23; and cp. 1 Thess. iv. 14. This figure was the more suitable, as our Lord rose on the morrow after the paschal sabbath, the day when the firstfruits of the harvest were presented (see Lev. xxiii. 10, 11).

22 For as in Adam all die. See note on Rom. v. 14; see also Rom. viii. 9–11.

24 Then [cometh] the end. The close of Christ's mediatorial kingdom; cp. John v. 22; vi. 39.

26 The last enemy [that] shall be destroyed [is] death. "As the last enemy, death is brought to nought" (*Ellicott*). Death is here personified as a foe, or rival king, surviving all other foes, and the one, therefore, whose destruction (Rev. xx. 14) is the last and crowning act of Messiah's reign.

27 For He (hath) put all things under His feet. See note on Psa. viii. 6.

28 then shall the Son also Himself be subject, etc. Christ's mediatorial kingdom over all things, which began when He rose from the grave, will have fulfilled its purpose when "death, the last enemy, is destroyed," and mankind have been raised and judged. "The word *Son* here designates not the Logos as such, but the Logos ['the Word'] as incarnate" (*Hodge*).

29 baptised for the dead. Many interpretations have been given of these words, which literally mean "on behalf of the dead." The suggestion appears to be that some were baptised to carry on the life and work of their departed friends.

31 I die daily. "I am daily in imminent peril of death" (2 Cor. iv. 11). Strong as this assertion may seem, I would stake all the joy which the Lord has given me in you as my converts ("that glorying in you which I have," R.V.) upon its truth.

32 after the manner of men. Under the influence of ordinary human motives, without reference to the Christian's hopes.

with beasts. Doubtless a figurative expression. Our only certain information as to what had occurred to him at Ephesus before this is in Acts xviii. 18–21; xix. 1–20. The commotion raised by Demetrius was later.

If the dead rise not. These words (connected in A.V. with the preceding) are best understood as beginning a new sentence: "If the dead are not raised, let us eat and drink," etc. (R.V.). Darkening the prospects of the future, you are thrown back into the reckless sensualism which Isaiah (xxii. 13) described. You deceive yourselves if you think that false principles will not lead to bad practices (33). They have already done so among yourselves (34).

33 Evil communications (*i.e.*, bad company) **corrupt good manners.** A proverb of universal common sense, expressed in these very words by Menander the Greek dramatist.

34 Awake to righteousness. Lit., "Awake to soberness righteously." Shake off the moral lethargy produced by the evil communications of those who question the resurrection; "not knowing the power of God": see Matt. xxii. 29, and note. These Corinthians had become "besotted with false speculation and error," and are bidden to arouse themselves "in a rightful manner, with the righteous resolve of breaking with the past, and of not continuing in the sinfulness which is the fatal associate of unbelief" (*Ellicott*).

35 with what body. "With what manner of body," R.V.

36 Thou fool. "Foolish one"; not the word used in Matt. v. 22.

that which thou sowest. The word *thou* is emphatic. Thine own act in sowing might have taught thee better; for it proceeds on the assumption that one form of life must pass away in order to the development of a very different and higher form.

except it die. Cp. John xii. 24, and note.

38 to every seed his (its) own body. All nature shows that matter is capable of the most varied organisation, fitting it for different purposes (38–41). So that no objection to the doctrine of the resurrection can be founded on the wide difference between the mortal and the immortal body.

44 natural. Rather, "animal"; *i.e.*, such as an animal needs; in distinction from "spiritual"; *i.e.*, such as is more fitted to man's spiritual nature in its celestial state.

45 a quickening spirit. "Life-giving." Adam had an animal nature derived from and suited to "the earth" (Gen. ii. 7): but Christ is [the Lord] from heaven (47; John iii. 13), having a spiritual nature and a life-giving energy: see John v. 21, 26.

48 heavenly. See Phil. iii. 20, 21, and notes.

50 Now this I say, brethren. I have something important to add. This entire change is certain, because it is necessary; for human nature in its present state, composed of "flesh and blood," and therefore "corruptible" (53), cannot enter the heavenly state of eternal glory.

51 a mystery. Cp. 1 Thess. iv. 15–17.

52 the last trump. The "trumpet" was used to summon assemblies, especially at the great Hebrew festivals: see Numb. x. 1–10, and notes; and hence the sounding of a trumpet is used to represent the gathering of a multitude.

54 then shall be brought to pass, etc. See Isa. xxv. 8. Comp. Isa. xxvi. 19, and Ezek. xxxvii. 13, and notes.

55 O grave (Hades). Another reading, supported by some of the best MSS. and adopted in R.V. and *Nestle* (Gr. Test.), gives "O death" in both clauses.

56 the strength of sin is the law. See notes on Rom. vii. 7–13.

CHAPTER XVI

1 the collection for the saints. Cp. Rom. xv. 26, 27; 2 Cor. viii.; Gal. ii. 10.

2 the first day of the week. That is, "on the first day of every week." See note on Acts xx. 7. By the hallowed associations of the day each member might be most strongly impelled to help in supplying the needs of his Lord's disciples. The offerings were to be retained by the donors until the arrival of the apostle.

3 whomsoever ye shall approve by [your] letters. Rather, "Whom ye shall approve, them I will send with letters."

4 and if it be meet that I go also. This proved to be the case: see Rom. xv. 25–27; Acts xxiv. 17.

5 when I shall pass through Macedonia. That is, on his journey to Corinth from Ephesus, where he wrote this Epistle: see ver. 8. He seems to have previously told them of another plan; on which see 2 Cor. i. 15, etc. But having changed it, he emphatically repeats the new arrangement: "I do pass," *i.e.*, such is my fixed purpose.

6 winter with you. Until the navigation was re-opened, and he could sail for Syria. See Acts xx. 3.

7 by the way. A passing visit on the way to Macedonia.

8 I will (shall) tarry at Ephesus until Pentecost. The Epistle was probably written a few weeks before Pentecost: see on ch. v. 7. Paul may have left Ephesus somewhat sooner than he intended, owing to the tumult raised by the silversmiths (Acts xx. 1).

10 if Timotheus come. Timothy had been sent to Macedonia (Acts xix. 22); whence he would probably go on to Corinth (iv. 17). Being young, and perhaps somewhat timid (see 1 Tim. iv. 12), he might be daunted by the disorderly spirit of the Corinthians. They are therefore bidden to treat him with due respect. Whether he actually reached Corinth at this time is uncertain: see on 2 Cor. i. 1.

11 the brethren. Erastus (Acts xix. 22) and others, who took charge of this Epistle. So in ver. 12.

12 [his] will was not at all to come at this time. Perhaps on account of the way in which some had used his name (see i. 12; iii. 4–6). That Paul had full confidence in his prudence and faithfulness is manifest from his great desire that he should revisit the church. Apollos might think the "convenient time" to be when they should have ceased from party strife.

13 Watch ye, etc. In this and the next verse he enforces the lesson of ch. xiii. about the supreme need of love.

15 the firstfruits of Achaia. See i. 16; and note, Rom. xvi. 5.

17 coming. Rather, "presence"; viz., in Ephesus. They may have brought the letter from Corinth (vii. 1).

that which was lacking on your part, etc. Rather, "The lack of you (*i.e.*, your absence) they have supplied" by their company, which has cheered me; and they will, when they return, cheer you by the testimony of my love (18).

19 of Asia. That is, of Proconsular Asia, of which Ephesus was the chief city: cp. Acts. xvi. 6.

Aquila and Priscilla. These two eminent Christians had removed from Corinth to Ephesus (see Acts xviii. 2, 26; Rom. xvi. 3).

20 a holy kiss. See note on Rom. xvi. 16.

21 with mine own hand. See note on Rom. xvi. 22.

22 anathema. A Greek word, signifying accursed. It should be separated by a full stop from the following word.

Maran-atha. An Aramaic phrase, meaning, "Our Lord cometh." Moffatt says it probably means, "Lord, come."

24 My love be with you, etc. My reproofs may seem severe, but be assured of the earnestness of my love.

[The first Epistle to the Corinthians, etc.] This postscript is of no authority: see note on the postscript to Romans. It appears from ver. 8, that Paul was not at Philippi, but at Ephesus, when he wrote this Epistle. Probably the postscript arose from a misunderstanding of ver. 5, "I do pass through Macedonia."

THE SECOND EPISTLE OF PAUL THE APOSTLE TO THE CORINTHIANS

INTRODUCTION

THE most notable chapter in this letter is the fourth. In this and vi. 4–10, as well as the closing verses of chap. xi. (22–33), St. Paul vindicates himself. Just as in our Lord's case, the sneers of the Pharisees and scribes led Him to tell the immortal stories of the lost sheep, the lost coin, and the lost son, so the attacks of Paul's enemies drew from him some of his most memorable passages—" persecuted, but not forsaken; cast down, but not destroyed"; "Our light affliction, which is but for a moment, worketh for us a far more exceeding and eternal weight of glory" (iv. 9, 17).

This letter was written only a few months later, in the same year as the First Epistle. The occasion of it was that the divisions mentioned in that letter had not ceased. On the contrary, the attacks on Paul himself had become more bitter and caused him much distress (i. 4; ii. 4; x. 10; xii. 20). He does not blame the Church at Corinth as a whole for this, but gratefully recognises the loyalty and stedfastness of most of its members (i. 7, 14; ii. 3; iii. 2, 3; vii. 6, 7, 15, 16; viii. 7).

In vindication of himself he asserts his devotion to Christ (iv. 5; v. 14), his sufferings on His behalf (iv. 11; vi. 5; xi. 23–27); and his unselfishness in relation to others (xi. 7–9; xii. 15, 16).

The Epistle is full of notable sayings, in addition to those above quoted, such as i. 4; iii. 17, 18; iv. 18; v. 19; viii. 9; ix. 6; xii. 9.

CHAPTER 1

1 by the will of God. See notes on Rom. i. 1 and 1 Cor. i. 1.

Timothy. Timothy had been sent to Macedonia with instructions to go on to Corinth if possible (1 Cor. iv. 17; xvi. 10). As he was now with Paul, and as no mention of any visit to Corinth is made in this Second Epistle, Waite, in *The Speaker's Commentary*, suggests that his mission had in some way miscarried. The most natural solution of the silence "is that the First Epistle had not been well received, and that, the church having declined to comply with one or more of its injunctions, Timothy had immediately gone back to the Apostle to report his ill-success."

Achaia. The Roman province of Achaia, which included all Southern Greece, contained probably several churches, at Cenchreæ (Rom. xvi. 1), and other places, besides the church at Corinth, the capital. The apostle desires this letter to be circulated among them all.

4 us. Paul sometimes speaks of himself in the plural (1 Thess. ii. 18); but here he probably includes Timothy, and other sympathising friends.

5 For as the sufferings of Christ abound in (unto) **us,** etc. We as Christ's members share His sufferings, which, as it were, overflow from Him to us: He as our Head comforts us, not for our own sakes only, but "that we may be able," by our example of "endurance," and from our experience of Divine mercy, to comfort others.

8 insomuch that we despaired even of life. The language suggests severe illness (which might be the result of persecution), the depressing effects of which would be aggravated by the apostle's intense and painful anxiety on behalf of the Corinthians as well as of the Galatian churches: cp. vii. 5.

9 but we had the sentence (answer) **of death in ourselves.** I felt that I was doomed to death; so that my deliverance was like a resurrection: cp. iv. 11; xi. 23; Acts xiv. 19, 20; 1 Cor. xv. 31.

12 For our rejoicing is this, etc. I have a right to expect your prayers, for my conscience assures me that my "conduct in the world, and especially towards you," has been "pure and guileless," free from all worldly policy ("in holiness and sincerity of God," R.V.; see on ii. 17); and now I mean just what you read in my letter and recognise in my conduct. And I hope that you will continue even to the day of judgement to acknowledge, as you have in part already, that you have cause to glory in me and I in you.

we have had our conversation. "We behaved ourselves," R.V.

14 your rejoicing. *i.e.*, cause for you to glory.

15 before. "Before going to Macedonia": see xii. 14, and note. Had he done so, the Corinthians would then have received a "second benefit" or "favour," as he would have visited them both in going and in returning (16).

16 toward Judæa. Whither he was going to convey the collection for the poor Christians (1 Cor. xvi. 3, 4).

17 did I use lightness? Or, as R.V., "did I show fickleness?" It is evident that this change of purpose had been used by Paul's enemies in disparagement of his character.

yea, yea, and nay, nay. The repetitions denote emphatic assertion. Am I a man who declares, almost in the same breath, " I will," and " I will not" ? The apostle's answer to this is that as a preacher of Him who was absolutely faithful in all His words, he too must be faithful and sincere.

18 as God is true. A solemn appeal to God as the faithful Witness and Judge: see also ver. 23. Surely God knows you have never found in my conduct and preaching any capricious changeableness or self-seeking. Our preaching was always the same, unchanged as Christ Himself and His promises (19, 20); and more than that, God has sealed it as true, by the gift of the Spirit (22).

19 the Son of God, Jesus Christ. " Word is heaped upon word to express the greatness of Him whom they preached, and so to aggravate the impossibility of His connexion with any fickleness or levity. The names of Silas and Timotheus are introduced, partly to intimate the unity with which they taught of Him, partly not to arrogate too much to himself" (*Stanley*).

20 For all the promises of God in Him are yea, etc. The R.V. translates: " for how many soever be the promises of God, in Him is the Yea, wherefore also through Him is the Amen," *i.e.* the ratification and certainty of them all. " Amen" is the " Verily" by which our Lord enforces so many of His declarations (the same word in Greek, as in John x. 1, etc.).

to the glory of God by us. We, in preaching Christ's gospel, maintain the honour of God; and this we can do only by absolute truthfulness.

21 anointed. With the Holy Spirit.

23 Moreover. Rather, " But," as R.V.

I call God for a record (witness). Having asserted his truthfulness generally, the apostle now meets the particular charge of fickleness.

to spare you. Not exerting my power to punish. Then, lest he should be charged with assumption, he adds, " Not that we are lords over your faith (for in faith you have stood firm); but we are helpers of your joy, which your disorders have impaired."

CHAPTER II

1 with myself. Or, " for myself" (R.V.). For my own sake I determined that my second visit should not be in grief; *i.e.*, I grieving you (2) and you grieving me (3). My reason for grieving you was, that I might afterwards rejoice over you. And therefore I wrote as I did in order that all cause of grief might be removed.

5 he hath not grieved me, etc. Rather, " he hath grieved not me, but in part all of you: [I say] in part, lest I should press too heavily." Dr. C. Anderson Scott (*Peake's Commentary*) questions the view so often taken that the offender here mentioned is the same as the wrong-doer of 1 Cor. v. 1–5. " It is hardly credible that Paul would refer to the same case as he does here, saying that the punishment has been sufficient, pleading for the offender's being pardoned, emphasising the fact that he, the apostle, has already forgiven him. Everything points, on the other hand, to a different offender and a different kind of offence." The latter was, he thinks, some slander or insult to Paul himself.

6 of (the) **many.** More precisely, " by the greater number." The expulsion of the offender was the act of the majority. But there was evidently some opposition. The apostle now gives his judgement.

7 lest perhaps such a one should be swallowed up, etc. Lest excessive sorrow drive him to despair.

8 confirm [your] love. By receiving the penitent offender again into your communion.

9 For to this end also did I write, etc. One of my chief objects was to test your obedience. Now that has been so well proved, you may expect that for your sakes I shall sanction, in Christ's name, whatever you do in the matter: in order that Satan, etc.

10 in the person of Christ. " In the presence of Christ" (R.V. marg.), as though Christ Himself were looking on. Luther, however, translates " an Christi Statt" (" in the place of Christ").

11 lest Satan should get an advantage of us. This might be in many ways, which the apostle leaves his readers to imagine. Perhaps the most obvious is the driving the penitent offender to despair (see ver. 7).

12 when I came to Troas. This visit to Troas is not mentioned in Luke's narrative of this journey (Acts xx. 1, 2). The apostle, although his success in preaching would otherwise have led him to remain there, was urged forward by anxiety to meet Titus (13), in order to learn from him the state of things at Corinth. Titus, no doubt, had been a bearer of the First Epistle.

14 Now thanks be unto God. The remembrance of the joy with which he received from Titus the news respecting the church at Corinth causes the apostle abruptly to break out in thankful adoration of the grace which had so removed his anxieties, and, in doing so, had given such attestation to his ministry. The triumph won at Corinth in this crisis illustrated what God was doing by His servants in the spread and power of the gospel.

causeth us to triumph. Rather, " leadeth us in triumph" (R.V.); or, " makes my life a constant pageant of triumph in Christ" (*Moffatt*). Paul here alludes to the triumphal procession of a Roman general, the most splendid spectacle then known; but the figure requires several changes in order to illustrate his thoughts. He is first a captive in the conquering Saviour's train; then a follower, sharing in the triumph, and, like the incense-bearers in a triumphal procession, scattering " sweet odour" " everywhere" in honour of the victor. He then becomes himself the " odour" of the burning incense; and finally, dropping the first figure, as he contemplates the practical results, he speaks of himself in preaching the gospel as diffusing what is deadly to some and life-giving to others, but in every case doing God's work and accomplishing His will.

15 in them that are saved, and in them that perish. More precisely, as R.V., " in them that are being saved, and in them that are perishing" : cp. 1 Cor. i. 18, and Acts ii. 47.

16 of death unto death. R.V., " from death unto death," and " from life unto life" : cp. Rom. i. 17, and note. On this *double* working of the gospel, see Matt. xxi. 44; Luke ii. 34; John ix. 39, and notes. The allusion is still to the Roman triumph, some of the conquered chieftains in the procession being destined to death, others to life. To the former, therefore, the very fragrance of the incense must be as the breath of doom, the latter the promise of life.

who is sufficient for these things? The answer to this question is intercepted by the thought of " the many" who profess to be " sufficient" for this work, though they dishonestly " adulterate" the word of God. He only can really be sufficient who " speaks" " from simplicity" of heart, with an impulse " from God," conscious that he is acting " in the sight of God," and is in union with Christ. And such an one will most feel the truth of the answer given in iii. 5, 6.

17 corrupt. "Adulterate."

sincerity. So i. 12. The Greek word is very expressive: "*transparent* purity"; used of something through which the sun's rays penetrate.

CHAPTER III

1 as some [others]. These were probably Paul's opponents at Corinth, who seem to have brought commendatory letters to the church there from Judæa. I do not (he says) "need" such, for you are yourselves my recommendation: cp. Acts xviii. 27.

2 Ye are our epistle. Privately to my own consciousness, publicly to all men; bearing no mere human testimony, but the witness of the Holy Spirit by His work on your hearts.

3 fleshy tables, etc. Better, "in tablets which are hearts of flesh" (*i.e.,* human hearts).

4 such trust. Such as springs from having this "commendation" from God, which, however, does not make me self-confident; for I feel that my "sufficiency" and success, both in comprehending and imparting saving truth, must be "from God" (5).

5 to think any thing as of ourselves. Rather, as R.V., "to account any thing as from ourselves," *i.e.,* to reckon any good thing in us as originating in ourselves ("quasi ex nobis," "as if from ourselves" (*Vulgate*)).

6 who also hath made us able ministers. "Who made us sufficient as ministers" (R.V.). The word *sufficient* refers to the previous verse and to ii. 16.

the new testament, etc. Rather, "a new covenant, not of letter, but of spirit." The contrast suggested in ver. 3 by the allusion to Jer. xxxi. 31–34 is here developed. The old covenant, here called a "writing" on "tables of stone," tended only to "condemnation" and "death" (see on Rom. iv. 14, 15; vii. 9–11); the new covenant here spoken of as the power of "the Spirit of the living God" on man's "heart," produces "righteousness" and "life." Moses administered the former "in glory": how much more must the ministry of the latter be clothed "in glory," not outwardly dazzling, but spiritually enlightening! (7–11).

7 could not stedfastly behold. "They were afraid": see Exod. xxxiv. 30.

was to be done away. Rather, as R.V., "was passing away."

8 be rather glorious. For clearness, the word *rather* should be transposed: "How shall not rather the ministration of the Spirit be with glory?"

10 in this respect. Or, "in this particular": *i.e.,* when compared with the "surpassing glory" of the gospel, which for ever "remaineth, in glory" unsurpassed.

12 as Moses, which put a vail, etc. See Exod. xxxiv. 29, 35.

13 to the end of that which is abolished. Rather, as R.V., "on (*or,* unto) the end of that which was passing away." This veiling of the Lawgiver's face, which prevented the Israelites from seeing how the glory vanished, symbolised the hiding from the Israelites of "the end," indicating the transitory nature of the dispensation (14). But meanwhile their own perception became dull, as if the veil were on their own hearts, as it now is (15) in reading the "old covenant"; it "being not made known [to them] that in Christ [the old covenant] is abolished." "But (16) whenever [the heart] shall return to the Lord the veil is taken away."

17 Now the Lord is that (the) **Spirit.** "But the Lord (to whom the heart returns) is the Spirit (spoken of before, ver. 3) who frees from the bondage of the law": see Rom. vi. 14; viii. 15, and notes.

18 But we all, etc. "All we" in whom "the Spirit of the Lord is" (instead of vainly reading the law with veiled heart), with unveiled face reflect as in a mirror the glory of the Lord (the Spirit of freedom); and are thereby transformed into His likeness, passing from one degree of glory to another, according as we receive "from the Lord the Spirit," that is, from Christ: see ver. 17.

transformed. The same Greek word is used of the transfiguration of our Lord (Matt. xvii. 2), and of the transformation of believers (Rom. xii. 2).

CHAPTER IV

2 dishonestly. Rather, "shame": *i.e.,* things which shame would make us hide; "les choses honteuses" ("shameful things") (*French version*).

by manifestation of the truth commending ourselves. This my open, straightforward preaching of Christ is another of my letters of commendation, addressed to the universal conscience of man and to the all-seeing God. It is true some cannot read it; but that is because Satan has blinded them.

3 that are lost. "That are perishing." See on ch. ii. 15.

4 the glorious gospel of Christ. Or, "the gospel the glory of Christ" (R.V.).

6 to give the light. Lit., "to give the illumination." So in ver. 4.

the glory of God in the face of Jesus Christ. A glory far transcending the brightness on the face of Moses (iii. 13).

7 treasure in earthen vessels. In vers. 8–10, Paul illustrates the meaning of the expression "earthen vessels," and the care which God takes of them, for the sake of "the treasure" which they hold, by describing the experience of himself and his fellow-labourers.

8 troubled . . . yet not distressed. More literally, "pressed . . . yet not in hopeless straits."

9 cast down. "Thrown down," a fall which does not incapacitate for further conflict.

13 the same spirit of faith. That spirit which animated the psalmist when he wrote thus (Psa. cxvi. 10).

15 For all things are for your sakes, etc. "With you," I say (14), for my sufferings are among the "all things" which God has adapted for good to you and to others; in order that His grace, through the larger number of them that receive it, may multiply the expressions of gratitude to His glory. And knowing that our suffering "is working out" all these blessed results, "we faint not" (16).

16 perish. Rather, as R.V., "is decaying," marking the process.

the inward man. The new spiritual life. Every word of these glowing verses helps to make the contrast more vivid.

17 worketh for us a far more exceeding, etc. Rather, as R.V., "worketh for us, more and more exceedingly, an eternal weight of glory." "Weight" in contrast with the "lightness" of affliction.

18 while we look, etc. Describing the state of mind which realises the lightness of the affliction and the weight of glory. This is explanatory also of verse 16.

temporal. Rather, "temporary," lasting only for a time.

CHAPTER V

1 For we know, etc. The confidence expressed in iv. 16–18 springs from the belief that though the body die, there is another and better life in heaven.

a building of God. "A building from God," *i.e.*, originating with Him: a permanent indestructible body, in contrast with the "tent-dwelling."

2 For in this we groan. "In this" earthly tent-dwelling we groan (Rom. viii. 23) with earnest longings for heaven (see 4).

3 If so be that. Or, "seeing that." The "putting off" that body in which "we groan, being pressed down," is not of itself the object of our "longing." Our hope fixes upon the assurance that we shall not remain "naked," but shall "put on over all" the glorified body, "the mortal being absorbed by life."

4 mortality. "The mortal part."

5 for the selfsame thing. That is, the change from the mortal to the immortal.

6 Therefore [we are] always confident, etc. "Emboldened" by expecting this result, we would gladly rather "be exiled from the body" by death, knowing that then we shall be "at home with the Lord" (ver. 8, R.V.). This language shows that the disembodied spirits of the saints enter into bliss immediately after death (cp. Phil. i. 23; Heb. xii. 23); although the resurrection of the body is necessary to complete their redemption: see Rom. viii. 23; 1 Cor. xv. 54–57.

7 by sight. *By what we see.* We are now absent from the Lord, and do not *see* Him; He is apprehended only by faith.

9 whether present (at home) **or absent.** That is, whether in the body or out of it.

10 appear. Rather, "be made manifest," as R.V.—shown to be exactly what we are.

in [his] body. "During his bodily lifetime" (*Speaker's Commentary*); "bei Leibes Leben" (*Luther*).

11 Knowing therefore the terror of the Lord. Better, "Therefore, knowing the fear of the Lord."

we persuade men. That is, we seek to win them.

12, 13. Paul appears to be led by the thought of the judgement day to allude to charges against him, which he afterwards more fully answers. I need not commend myself to you, in whose consciousness my uprightness is equally manifested; so that you have a good answer to those boasters (13). If I am "mad," it is a holy enthusiasm for God's glory. If I am "self-possessed," it is to serve you the better. One great motive prompts and controls all my actions—"the love of Christ," *i.e.*, Christ's love *to us*, not ours *to Him*.

14 because we thus judge, etc. Rather, "because we thus judged, that [as] one died for all, therefore all died"; *i.e.*, Christ dying in behalf of man, man *died too*, in order to live no longer to "self" and "the flesh," but to Him (cp. Rom. vi. 1–14). This takes effect in all who are "in Christ"; so that they regard men, and even the Lord Himself, not according to natural distinctions or connexions, but in their spiritual character.

15 died for them, and rose again. More precisely, "died and rose again for them."

16 after the flesh. Paul's opponents seem to have laid great stress on their own national relationship to Christ, and their personal acquaintance with Him (cp. x. 7; 1 Cor. i. 12). All this has "passed away" with me, and with all who have become "new creatures."

18 all things. That is, all these new things (17). They are all "from God" as part of His plan of mutual reconciliation; which comprises, first, the "not imputing" men's trespasses to them, and then the "beseeching" them by His servants to "be reconciled to God." And they are all "through" and "in Christ" the sinless, "the righteous" One (1 John ii. 1), whom "He made sin" for us.

20 as though God did beseech [you]. If any word is supplied here, it should be *men*, or *sinners*, not *you;* for the words "be ye reconciled to God" are part of the universal message.

in Christ's stead. "On behalf of Christ." So in the preceding part of the verse: "ambassadors on behalf of Christ," the same preposition being used.

21 For He hath made Him [to be] sin for us, etc. "He made Him who knew no sin to be sin for us," etc. Many suppose that "sin" here means a *sin-offering:* others take it to mean the *representative of sin.* That this did not involve any *personal contamination*, Scripture clearly teaches, in both history (Matt. xxvii. 4, 54) and doctrine (Heb. iv. 15; vii. 26; 1 Pet. ii. 22).

CHAPTER VI

1 [as] workers together [with Him]. See on 1 Cor. iii. 9.

2 I have heard thee, etc. These words are addressed to the "Servant of Jehovah" (Isa. xlix. 1–8, and notes); and accordingly the apostle founds upon them the cheering assurance, "*Now*, since He has been made sin for us, and has sent to you His ambassadors entreating you to be reconciled—*now* is the acceptable time of God's grace." The "day" has come to which the prophet looked forward. Do not, therefore, in your own case, nullify so great a blessing.

3 offence. Or, "stumbling-block"; an occasion to fall.

4 as the ministers of God. That is, as ministers of God should approve or commend themselves, by virtues, and services, and sufferings, such as are immediately specified.

5 imprisonments. Only one imprisonment before the date of this letter is reported in Acts (xvi. 23); but the history evidently was not designed to record all the events of the apostle's life. For many other interesting facts see xi. 23–27.

6 by pureness, by knowledge. Rather, "in pureness, in knowledge," etc.

by the Holy Ghost, etc. The meaning probably is, "in all that the Holy Spirit suggests, in all that love unfeigned prompts, in all that the word of truth teaches, in all that the power of God works."

7 by the armour of righteousness. Rather, "by means of the armour of righteousness," etc., using all the weapons which righteousness warrants: see x. 4; Eph. vi. 13–17. How this was carried out the rest of the passage shows. The armour "on the right hand" (the sword) attacks; that "on the left hand" (the shield) defends.

9 dying. Cp. note on iv. 10. On the contrast between spiritual and earthly possessions cp. 1 Cor. vii. 30.

12 ye are straitened, etc. If there is any contractedness of heart, it is in *you*, not in *us*. And I earnestly entreat you as my children to repay my strong parental affection by your filial love.

14 Be ye not unequally yoked, etc. The injunction probably includes all associations or compliances that would identify Christians with unbelievers. The expression, "incongruously yoked" was perhaps suggested by the prohibition in Lev. xix. 19; Deut. xxii. 10.

15 Belial (Greek "Beliar"). The Hebrew word "Belial" means "worthlessness," or "mischief" (see Deut. xiii. 13, and note), and is perhaps put here for Satan.

an infidel. Rather, "an *unbeliever*"; as in ver. 14.

16 ye are the temple, etc. See on 1 Cor. iii. 16; vi. 19.

as God hath said. In various Old Testament passages here grouped together, *e.g.*, Lev. xxvi. 12; Isa. lii. 11; Jer. xxxi. 1.

CHAPTER VII

1 all filthiness (R.V., "defilement"). Pollution of every kind, in thought and desire, as well as word and act.

2 Receive us. Or, "Make room for us," *i.e.*, in your hearts. (This is the reading of Nestle's Greek Test.) Paul here continues his pleading with the Corinthians from vi. 13.

3 I speak not [this] to condemn [you]. I do not say this reproachfully, but in a spirit of love; as I have told you before (iii. 2; vi. 11).

4 Great is my boldness of speech, etc. Or, "Great is my confidence," etc.

I am filled with comfort. By the arrival of Titus with good tidings from Corinth (6).

5 For when, etc. Rather, "For also when," etc., referring back to ii. 13. Not only at Troas was I anxious because Titus had not arrived; but also in Macedonia, when I had no relief till he came. In addition to "fears within" my heart for you, I had "oppositions from without."

8 a letter. Rather, "*the* letter"; *i.e.*, "my letter," the former Epistle.

I do not repent, etc. Rather (as R.V.), "I do not regret [it], though I did regret," for I had feared what might be the effect of my letter.

9 repentance. Change of mind or purpose.

10 godly sorrow. Lit., "sorrow according to God"; *i.e.*, sorrow out of regard to God, and acceptable to Him; as in ver. 9.

not to be repented of. Rather, "which bringeth no regret" (R.V.), whatever it may have cost.

death. The opposite of "salvation." Such is the sorrow of worldly men, who, regarding only the chastisement, and not the Divine love that chastens them, become only the more alienated from God.

11 carefulness. Rather, "earnestness" or "diligence."

yea, what indignation, etc.! "Indignation" against sin; "fear" and "desire" or yearning, towards the apostle; "zeal" for God's glory.

revenge. "Infliction of punishment."

this matter. Either the case of incest (1 Cor. v. 1) or, as some think, the attack on Paul himself (see v. 12, 13, and note).

12 [I did it] not for his cause, etc. It was not the private interest of individuals, but the welfare of the church that caused my interference.

14 in truth. Not deceitfully, as my enemies insinuate.

16 that I have confidence in you. Rather, "that I am encouraged in you." The word "therefore" should undoubtedly be omitted.

CHAPTER VIII

1 we do you to wit. Rather, as R.V., "we make known unto you." The churches of Macedonia included those at Philippi, Thessalonica, and Berœa. The apostle speaks of their liberality in the collection for the poor saints at Jerusalem, which he had already commended to the Corinthian church (1 Cor. xvi. 1–4).

2 the abundance of their joy, etc. The apostle strongly brings out the seemingly paradoxical nature of his assertion. Abundant joy may well overflow in abundant benevolence; but that it should exist with the deepest poverty, and that even that poverty should overflow in abundant worldly-minded people like the Corinthians; though it was happily shown to be possible by the example of the Macedonians.

4 praying us with much entreaty, etc. Rather, "with much entreaty begging of us the grace and the fellowship of the ministry (*i.e.*, that they might take their part in ministering) to the saints."

5 not as we hoped. Acting in the spirit of genuine Christian charity, they far exceeded our expectation; giving themselves as well as their alms, as those who were consecrated to the Lord, and ready to share our toils: see Acts xx. 4; Col. iv. 10; Phil. ii. 30.

6 Insomuch that. That is, encouraged by this liberality.

8 I speak not by commandment. That is, "I do not *command* this, but I *advise* it (10); for I wish to stimulate you by the example of others, and to prove the genuineness of your love; for you well (9) know, from the matchless example of our Lord Jesus, how genuine love shows itself (Phil. ii. 5–8).

10 for this is expedient for you, etc. Rather, "this *advice* [rather than *command*] is suitable for you, as you began before [those other churches] not only to act but also to will [*i.e.*, to take it up cordially] from last year." They had probably done something towards it before they received the former epistle written in the spring, but then their zeal was increased: see 1 Cor. xvi. 1, and note.

14 that their abundance also may be [a supply] for your want. If your circumstances should make it necessary.

15 as it is written, etc. Exod. xvi. 18 is adduced here, simply as an illustration of equality.

18 the brother. Unknown, but supposed by some to have been Luke, who so often appears as Paul's companion. "His praise in the gospel" means, his repute as a *preacher*. A second "brother," mentioned in ver. 22, is likewise unnamed.

19 who was also chosen of the churches, etc. He had been appointed by the churches of Macedonia to accompany Paul in making the collection and taking it to Jerusalem; the apostle having himself urged such companionship, to guard himself against any imputations of dishonesty (20, 21).

and [declaration of] your ready mind. R.V. has "[to show] our readiness"; *i.e.*, that the business may be so administered as to glorify God and to show Paul's readiness to help the Christians in Judæa (see Gal. ii. 10); and to show his uprightness by having a colleague.

21 providing for honest things. R.V., "for we take thought for things honourable." The phrase is taken from Prov. iii. 4 (LXX).

22 which [I have] in you. "He hath," should be supplied (R.V.), rather than "I have."

23 messengers. Greek, "apostles"; *i.e.*, men chosen (19) and sent by "the churches" (Phil. ii. 25); as Paul and his colleagues were by the Lord

the glory of Christ. "Whoever excels in piety is the glory of Christ, because he has nothing which is not Christ's gift" (*Calvin*).

CHAPTER IX

1 For. I boast of your readiness (viii. 24); for I know well that any urgent exhortations are unnecessary.

2 Achaia. See note on i. 1.

a year ago. See note on viii. 10.

very many. Rather, "the majority"; implying that however willing the Macedonians were of themselves "the greater part" were stirred up by the zeal of the Corinthians.

3 the brethren. The bearers of this Epistle.

4 if they of Macedonia come with me. Rather, "if [any] Macedonians should come with me." Jason, a Thessalonian, and Sopater, a Berœan, accompanied Paul: cp. Rom. xvi. 21; Acts xvii. 5; xx. 4.

5 your bounty, whereof ye had notice before. Rather, "your fore-announced blessing": cp. Gen. xxxiii. 11; Josh. xv. 19; Prov. xi. 25, 26, and notes. It is the opposite of one wrung from covetous hands: see vers. 6, 7.

7 grudgingly. Only the *cheerful* giver is acceptable to God.

8 all grace. Particularly the spirit and the means to be charitable (see viii. 1, and note); so that the words of Psa. cxii. 9 will be verified in you. For generosity is one evidence of abiding "righteousness."

10 increase the fruits of your righteousness. "Cause the fruits of your good conduct to increase" (*Lange*).

11 to all bountifulness. See note on Rom. xii. 8.

12–14. "Your discharge of this public duty not only most thoroughly supplies the need of the saints. It also abounds in many expressions of gratitude to God. [For they], by occasion of their experience of this your ministration, [first], glorify God for your obedience to the gospel of Christ, and for your liberality to them and to all; and [further, they honour Him] by their prayers for you, being drawn in love to you on account of the grace of God resting eminently upon you."

15 His unspeakable gift. "His indescribable gift": the redemption that is in Christ.

CHAPTER X

1 by the meekness and gentleness of Christ. Implying, do not force me to adopt a method of treatment so unlike His gentleness.

base. "Humble."

2 I think to be bold against some, etc. Rather, "I reckon upon being bold against some who reckon of us as walking according to the flesh." They will find that their estimate of me is false.

3 For though we walk in the flesh, etc. The weapons we mean to use against our opponents are not carnal or worldly, but God will make them mighty to bring down proud "reasonings" into obedience to Christ, and to punish all who remain disobedient, when the rest of you are completely brought to submit (6).

4 mighty through God. Lit., "mighty before God": "mighty in the strength of God" (*Conybeare and Howson*).

6 having in a readiness. Or, "being ready."

7 Do ye look on things after the outward appearance? Or, "Do you regard outward appearances?" (1). I then can appeal to external things to show you that I have as close connexion with Christ as any have.

8 For though I should boast, etc. I might, without fear of being put to shame, urge my claims further than I have ever done: but I do not, that I may not seem as if I would terrify you (9).

9 letters. The former and the present: see note on 1 Cor. v. 9.

10 say they. Rather, "saith he"; meaning, either the leader of the opposing party (11), or the "any man" (7). The language is that of a factious opponent; and it is best explained by Paul's own words in 1 Cor. ii. 3.

12 For we dare not, etc. We are not bold enough to compare ourselves with our self-commending rivals, who, however, show no wisdom in their mutual comparisons of authority and labours. But we boast only of that work which God has measured out to us; in which you are included.

13 things without [our] measure. Or, "the things not measured out" to us, by God's "rule" (*canon*), allotting various parts of service to different labourers; and so in ver. 15.

14 for we are come (we came). "We were the first to come" (R.V. marg.), in allusion to the fact that Paul was the first who preached the gospel in Corinth.

15 but having hope, etc. "But we hope, as your faith is increased among yourselves, to be enlarged according to our appointed sphere very greatly, so as to carry the gospel into the countries beyond you (see Rom. xv. 28); and not to boast as to things made ready for us in another's allotted sphere," as these men are doing.

CHAPTER XI

1 Would [to God]. The words "to God" are not in the original, and should be omitted.

and indeed bear with me. Or, "but also ye do bear."

4 For if he that cometh preacheth another Jesus, etc. If your new teacher had a new Saviour, a new Comforter, or a new and better gospel, to preach to you, you might well endure him: but it is not so, for I do not fall short of these "over-great apostles," who are, however, *false* apostles (13) in any respect, except in rhetorical display (1 Cor. ii. 1–4);—certainly not in knowledge of the only one gospel (cp. Gal. i. 7, 8), nor in openness of conduct (6), nor in toil and suffering (22–30).

7 abasing myself. Partly by labouring for my support, and partly by receiving it, as some might think, unfairly from other Christians (Phil. iv. 15–18), instead of claiming it from you. My opponents are not so self-abasing.

9 the brethren. Perhaps Silas and Timothy: see Acts xviii. 5.

12 that I may cut off occasion, etc. That I may take from them all excuse for saying that I preach for money.

that wherein they glory, etc. "I do it in order that, in the matter [of claim to support] of which they boast, they may be compelled to act as I do." Paul knew that those men would not render any disinterested services; "for (he says) they are false apostles, crafty workers," etc., pretending to seek your good, but really seeking their own unworthy ends.

14 is transformed. Rather, "transformeth (or 'fashioneth') himself." So in 13 and 15, "fashion themselves." It is the same form of the verb that is used in each of the three verses, 13, 14, 15.

15 whose end shall be according to their works. Being, not God's servants, but Satan's, and doing his work, they must receive his wages: see Rom. vi. 23; Phil. iii. 19.

16 I say again. Paul, referring to ver. 1, now says, " Even, if you do think me foolish for boasting, you can surely tolerate me, for (as such wise men should) you tolerate men who are not only foolish, but domineering, rapacious, and insolent."

17 not after the Lord. Not as a servant of Christ, but putting myself in the position of a foolish man, boasting of the doings and circumstances of his own human nature (ver. 20, etc.).

20 if a man take [of you]. Rather, as R.V., " taketh you *captive*."

21 I speak as concerning reproach. Or, " I say it (ironically) to my own disparagement, that I was weak among you " ; not boastful, arrogant, and covetous, like some others.

23 as a fool. " As if I were out of my mind " (*Weymouth*).

24–27. Only a few of the particulars referred to are related in the Book of Acts. " The five Jewish scourgings, two of the three Roman beatings (one being at Philippi), and the three shipwrecks, are unrecorded in Acts. The stoning was at Lystra. What a life of incessant adventure and peril is here disclosed to us ! " (*Conybeare*). Had Paul not been forced to defend himself against these professedly Christian enemies, the Church would have lost this wonderful record of Christian heroism and devotedness. " It is remarkable that St. Paul does not glory in what he has done, but in what he has borne " (*F. W. Robertson*).

24 forty stripes save one. See note on Deut. xxv. 3.

25 shipwreck. The shipwreck so fully related in Acts xxvii. 41–44, occurred about years after this time.

26 waters. " Rivers " ; which were probably swollen.

27 watchings often. Sleepless nights through anxiety, suffering, or business : cp. Acts xx. 7, 11, 31 ; 2 Thess. iii. 8.

28 Beside those things that are without. Rather, " Beside the things omitted, [there is] that which," etc. : implying that the list was far from being exhausted ; cp. Heb. xi. 32.

29 Who is weak, and I am not weak ? Such is my care or concern (28) for the churches, that whoever suffers, I feel it ; whoever is caused to stumble, I burn with indignation. Cp. the apostle's letter to the Galatian churches.

30 the things which concern mine infirmities. Lit., " the things of my weakness " : referring probably to those sufferings which made some think him contemptible.

32 the governor under Aretas. Damascus was at that time under Aretas, an Arabian king, who ruled it by an ethnarch, or deputy. He was the father-in-law of Herod Antipas (Josephus, *Antiq.* xviii. 5, § 1). The governor, gained perhaps by bribery, had empowered the Jews to keep the gates of the city and to kill Paul (Acts ix. 24).

33 by the wall. Rather, " *through* the wall " ; *i.e.*, through an " opening " in it.

CHAPTER XII

1 It is not expedient, etc. The best authorities read, as R.V., " I must needs glory, though it is not expedient ; but I will come," etc. If I must speak, although against my will, of things in which I may glory, I will refer to the highest.

2 I knew. Rather, " I know " (R.V.) ; and so in ver. 3. Paul is clearly speaking of himself, but he calls himself " a man in (or united to) Christ," perhaps to intimate that the vision was given to him as a " chosen vessel " of Christ, and that it helped to bind him more closely to his Lord (see ver. 9). He seems to have kept this vision a secret during the " fourteen years." So far was he from wishing to boast ! The date of the vision (unrecorded in the Acts) was about that of Paul's first missionary journey, Acts xiii.

the third heaven. " Jewish tradition generally speaks of seven heavens. . . . This third need not be regarded as the highest heaven. . . . Yet we must unquestionably make a distinction between this higher region called the third heaven and the place called Paradise, although it does not follow that the former must of course be a lower region than the latter " (*Lange*).

4 Paradise. See preceding note.

unspeakable words. " Sacred secrets " (*Moffatt*).

5 yet of myself I will not glory, etc. My boasting shall be of what the Lord did to me, not of what might be deemed my own, except my weaknesses (see vers. 7–10). Although if I chose I could reasonably boast, speaking only what is true.

6 [that] he heareth of me. *i.e.*, " from me," from my own mouth.

7 a thorn in the flesh. " Stake " is the more correct rendering of the Greek, and Weymouth best expresses it by translating : " like the agony of impalement." This " thorn (or ' stake ') in the flesh " has been variously interpreted, of some spiritual trial, of troubles from without, or, with the great majority of expositors, of some grievous bodily suffering, which might be compared to the continual piercing of the flesh with a thorn. This suffering was evidently not only most painful but both conspicuous and humiliating (Gal. iv. 14 ; x. 10 ; cp. 1 Cor. ii. 3). There are some indications in the history that the eyes of the apostle were affected by this mysterious infliction : cp. Acts ix. 9 ; xxiii. 5 ; Gal. iv. 15 ; vi. 11. But no positive conclusion on the subject can be formed. The " thorn," whatever it may have been, is called " a messenger of Satan," perhaps with reference to the trial of Job's faith (Job ii. 5, 7) when Satan " smote " or buffeted him.

8 the Lord. The Lord Christ, who possesses and imparts Divine power (9). A clear example of prayer to Christ.

9 He said unto me, etc. " Whilst in the literal sense prayer may be unavailing, in a higher sense it is heard and granted " (*Stanley*).

rest upon me. " Dwell in (or ' on ') me as a tent."

11 the very chiefest apostles. Rather, as in xi. 5, " the over-great apostles " ; or, " superlative apostles " ; an ironical reference to the false teachers.

14 the third time. So xiii. 1. The first visit is related in Acts xviii. ; a second was abandoned (see note on 1 Cor. xvi. 5) ; and now for the third time he proposes a visit, which he afterwards paid (see Acts xx. 2, 3, and notes). But some expositors think that he had already been at Corinth twice, having paid, from Ephesus, a visit unrecorded in the Acts of the Apostles. See note on xiii. 2.

15 And I will very gladly spend, etc. Rather, " But I will willingly spend, and be spent to the uttermost for your souls."

16 being crafty, I caught you with guile. He states thus the insinuation of his enemies, that though he took no money from them himself he craftily made a gain of them through others (17). This insinuation he most strongly denies.

18 I desired Titus. That is, " to go to you."

This was probably the journey from which Titus had just returned: see vii. 6.

a brother. Properly, "the brother" (R.V.); well known at Corinth, though not to us.

in the same spirit? Or, by the same Spirit? "The inward law which regulated their conduct" (*Speaker's Commentary*).

21 many which have sinned already, etc. See 1 Cor. v. 1.

CHAPTER XIII

1 the third time. See note, xii. 14, and Paley's discussion in *Horæ Paulinæ*.

In the mouth of two or three witnesses. Upon unquestionable proof: see Deut. xix. 15.

2 as if I were present the second time. The R.V. reads, "when I was present the second time." *Conybeare and Howson*, ch. xv., note 1. The same rendering is adopted by *Weymouth* and *Moffatt*.

3 which. Rather, "who"; referring to Christ. By severely punishing the offenders, Paul would prove his close connexion with Christ; sharing indeed the weakness of his Lord's crucified mortality, yet receiving from Him, and exercising towards the Church, a living Divine power (4).

4 toward you. That is, "in our dealings with you."

5 Examine (try) **yourselves.** You would test my apostleship (3); first test your own connexion with Christ. If you can prove that you are Christ's true disciples, you will then have proved that I, who taught you, am his true apostle.

reprobates. More correctly, "unapproved": unable to stand the test.

7 Now I pray to God that ye do no evil. I would rather seem "unable to give proof" of my apostolic power, than be compelled to do so in punishing you for doing evil. I am glad thus to seem weak, if only you are strong.

9 your perfection. Lit., "restoration," *i.e.*, reformation or amendment.

10 to edification, and not to destruction. R.V., "for building up, and not for casting down."

14 The grace of the Lord Jesus Christ, etc. This benediction distinctly and formally recognises the Three Persons in the Godhead, in their relations to the believer and to the Church.

communion. Or, "participation," *i.e.*, with fellow-believers.

[The second [Epistle] to the Corinthians, etc.] This Epistle was sent from Macedonia by Titus; but the other particulars are quite uncertain. See on subscription to the Epistle to the Romans.

THE EPISTLE OF PAUL THE APOSTLE TO THE GALATIANS

INTRODUCTION

The chief feature of this Epistle is its repudiation of ceremonialism and legalism in the Christian Church. Judaising teachers had come amongst the churches of Galatia, insisting upon the necessity of circumcision (i. 7; v. 10; vi. 12). In St. Paul's eyes, this was a backward movement. It was to go back to the beggarly elements. It was to be entangled again in the yoke of bondage. It was to substitute the law as a way of salvation for the free grace of God. It was "another Gospel" (i. 6; ii. 16; iii. 11; iv. 9, 31; v. 1, 4).

Over against all this, the apostle emphasises the fundamental truth that salvation is due not to any works or ceremonial observances of our own, but to the righteousness of Christ, accepted and applied through faith. "God forbid that I should glory save in the cross of our Lord Jesus Christ" (vi. 14). "If righteousness come by the law, then Christ is dead in vain" (ii. 21). The law is but the preparation for Christ, leading us to Him as the child is led to school (v. 24; see note).

In contrast with, and in opposition to, the practices of ritual, he shows what true religion is. Its motive-power is the love of Christ (ii. 20). It is "putting on Christ" as a garment (iii. 27); "taking on the character of Christ" (*Moffatt*). It is liberty, and not bondage (v. 1). It is faith working by love (v. 6). It is bringing forth the fruits of the Spirit, love, joy, peace, longsuffering, gentleness, goodness, faith, meekness, temperance (v. 22, 23). It produces sympathy and liberality (vi. 1, 2, 6). Thus it is an eminently practical thing, permeating every department of daily life and conduct. It makes a man a new creature (vi. 15).

Much of the Epistle is also taken up, as in the case of 2 Corinthians, with St. Paul's vindication of his own character and ministry against the attacks that had been made upon him. He shows how he had received the Gospel by the direct revelation of the Lord Himself (i. 12). His call was a call of God and not of man (i. 15). He had withstood even Peter himself when for a time that apostle gave way to the ritual or Judaising party (ii. 11–14). He reminds Jewish readers that Abraham was justified by faith (iii. 6), and reminds both Jew and Gentile that the Gospel is not for one nation or people only, but for all men (iii. 14, 28). He reminds them all of the sympathy and affection they had shown for him in the past (iv. 13–15), and of their early devotion to the Gospel (v. 7). And in tender words he expresses his own desire for their spiritual welfare (iv. 19; v. 16) and for their continuance in Christian life and service (vi. 9, 10).

The date of the Epistle is not later than A.D. 58, and if the "South Galatian" theory is accepted, it may even be as early as A.D. 52. The subject is fully discussed by Lightfoot (*Commentary on Galatians*), Sir William Ramsay (*Paul the Traveller and Roman Citizen*), and Rendall (*Expositor's Greek Testament*). A very fine exposition of the whole Epistle is given by Canon Girdlestone (*Devotional Commentary: Galatians*).

CHAPTER I

1 an apostle. See note on Rom. i. 1. Paul here declares, in reply to his opponents, that his commission as an apostle was not received in any sense from man (either "*from* men" as the source, or "*through* men" as the means), but "*through* (as well as *from*) Jesus Christ and God the Father," etc.: see ver. 12; Acts xxii. 17–21. The laying on of hands at Antioch (Acts xiii. 2, 3) was only an outward recognition by the church of a previous Divine call and commission; see Acts xxvi. 16–18.

who raised Him from the dead. Our Lord's resurrection was the great attestation of the truth of all His claims, especially His claim to bestow apostolic authority and gifts (Eph. iv. 8, 11).

2 all the brethren. Paul's companions and fellow-labourers at that time. The "churches" here addressed (without any honourable adjunct or description, as in other Epistles) were most likely in the leading cities of Galatia.

3 Grace, etc. See note on Rom. i. 7.

4 who gave Himself. That is, to death: see Matt. xx. 28, and note. The apostle at once makes prominent the atoning sacrifice of Christ, with its sanctifying design, and its Divine authority, in opposition to those who taught that circumcision and legal observance were essential to salvation.

God and our Father. Better, "our God and Father."

6 are so soon removed. R.V., "are so quickly removing." The verb means "to alter one's opinion"; "to fall away." So quickly, either after their conversion, or after Paul's second visit. In either case the time was comparatively short; varying from one to five years.

from Him. That is, from *God*, from whom the call proceeds: 1 Thess. ii. 12; v. 24; 2 Thess. ii. 14; 2 Tim. i. 9.

into the grace of Christ. Rather, "in the grace of Christ."

another gospel. More exactly, as R.V., "a different gospel"; the apostle immediately adding "which is not another." (Two words are rendered *another*, the former denoting difference *in kind*, the latter simply *numerical* difference). It is not another *gospel*: for in fact it is no gospel at all.

8 accursed. Or, "anathema." See note on 1 Cor xvi. 22.

10 persuade. Rather, "conciliate"; or, "seek the favour of."

11 not after man. It was not communicated to me by human teaching, but by direct revelation from Christ, and must therefore be in exact accordance with no human standard, but with His will alone.

13 conversation. Rather, "manner of life"; "career" (*Moffatt*).

in the Jews' religion. Greek, "in Judaism"; which involved obedience to the traditions of the fathers, as well as the institutions of Moses: cp. vers. 13, 14, with Acts xxii. 3, 4.

14 profited. R.V., "advanced beyond"; "outran" (*Conybeare and Howson*).

my equals. Properly, "equals in age."

15 who separated me, etc. "Who, from my birth, separated me to this service (Acts ix. 15; xiii. 2), and called me," etc.

16 to reveal His Son in me. Giving me the personal knowledge of Christ and the call to be an apostle. This began at the time of Paul's conversion on the road to Damascus (Acts ix.).

not with flesh and blood. That is, not with any human being. Paul "immediately" decided not to seek instruction from any man, not even from the apostles at Jerusalem; but he went away into Arabia (see next note), as some think, for seclusion, meditation, quiet study, and communion with God. Meyer, however, thinks that it was "a first, certainly fervent experiment of extraneous ministry." How long he remained there is uncertain: cp. Acts ix. 19–23.

17 into Arabia. This visit is not mentioned in the Acts of the Apostles. "Arabia" included the whole desert district south-east of Damascus. It has, however, been thought (see *Lightfoot*) that the apostle's sojourn was in the wilderness of Sinai, to which the after-mention of Arabia in this Epistle undoubtedly refers. "Standing on the threshold of the new covenant, he was anxious to look upon the birthplace of the old."

18 after three years. Most likely "three years" from the time of his conversion (see Acts ix. 23, "many days"; 26–30).

to see Peter. Or, "to become acquainted with Cephas."

19 save (or, "but only") **James the Lord's brother.** See notes on Matt. xiii. 55; and on Acts xii. 17.

20 before God. This solemn appeal to God refers not only to his statement of facts, but to his claim of independence of the other apostles.

21 Syria and Cilicia. See note on Acts ix. 30.

22 the churches of Judæa. Excepting the church at Jerusalem, where alone he had been since his conversion. This is also to prove his independence of the other apostles.

23 but they had heard only. Rather, " But they were hearing only " ; *i.e.*, reports about his preaching reached them from time to time.

CHAPTER II

1 fourteen years after. Fourteen years from his conversion, which is the starting-point of the whole narrative (i. 15). This visit to Jerusalem is most likely not the second (Acts xi. 30), at which nothing material to this subject occurred, Peter and others being absent, but the third (A.D. 50): see Acts xv., and notes, and *Conybeare and Howson* (Appendix I.); though *Meyer* thinks the second visit is here meant. Luke in his history relates the *public* object of this visit; here Paul speaks of its being upon himself *personally*.

Titus. An uncircumcised Gentile Christian, one of the " certain other " (Acts xv. 2).

2 by revelation. Paul had not only a commission from the church at Antioch (Acts xv. 3), but also a special revelation and commission from the Lord. This is mentioned as showing that in the subsequent discussion he was not a learner from " James, Cephas, and John," the " pillars " of the church at Jerusalem (9), but was as fully prepared and authorised to express the Holy Spirit's will as they were.

them which were of reputation. The leading men in the church at Jerusalem, of course including the apostles. Paul took care to have first a private interview with them, to prevent any such interference with his labours in the gospel as would make these efforts fruitless. But, so far from opposing him, " they gave to him the right hand of fellowship," etc. (9).

3 was compelled. Implying that the circumcision of Titus had been strongly urged by the Judaisers, as indicated in ver. 4. The apostle afterwards circumcised Timothy (Acts xvi. 3), " because of the Jews that were in those parts." But Timothy's mother was a Jewess, although his father was a Gentile. Titus was wholly a Gentile. This may have made the difference between the two cases. Or the difference may have been the *attempt to compel* in the case of Titus. Paul would do voluntarily what he would never yield to dictation.

4 and that because of false brethren, etc. This clause may be connected with ver. 5, thus: " And because of false brethren, etc., we gave not place by subjection," etc.: see note on Acts xvi. 3.

false. They were thus designated, because they did not acknowledge faith in Christ as the only method of justification. This is " the truth of the Gospel " (5); essential not only as assuring the liberty and privileges of Gentile Christians, but also as the foundation of every sinner's hope.

6 But of these. Rather, " But from those "; *i.e.*, from the leaders I received nothing. Paul makes no allusion here to the decision (Acts xv. 22–29) which confirmed the exemption of Gentile converts from the Mosaic ritual; insisting only on his own independent inspiration and authority.

whatsoever they were. " What they once were," referring to their special privilege in having been the associates of our Lord on earth.

added nothing to me. Rather, " imparted nothing to me " (R.V.).

7 the gospel of the uncircumcision. The commission to carry the glad tidings to the Gentiles. " Gospel " here, as in other places, has much the same force as our modern " evangelisation."

9 Cephas. Cp. 1 Cor. i. 12, and note.

pillars. Chief supporters of the faith. " James " is here mentioned without the adjunct " the Lord's brother," as the other James had been put to death since Paul's first visit.

10 the poor. Particularly the poor Christians *in Judœa* (Rom. xv. 26), many of whom lost all for Christ (Heb. x. 34). On the words " only that we should remember," etc., *Meyer* says: " This by no means excludes the ordinances of the apostolic council, for Paul here has in view nothing but his recognition as apostle on the part of the original apostles in the private discussions held with the latter. . . . In the face of real antagonism of doctrine, the older apostles certainly would not have tendered Paul their hands " (ver. 9).

11 But when Peter (Cephas) **was come to Antioch.** But as Barnabas was there too, it was most probably about A.D. 51: see Acts xv. 35, not so late as Paul's visit mentioned in Acts xviii. 22 (about A.D. 54). It is possible that this disagreement may have prepared the way for the subsequent dispute and separation: see note on Acts xiii. 13.

because he was to be blamed. Rather, " because he stood condemned," R.V. Peter's conduct in refusing to eat with Gentiles after the Divine lesson (Acts x. 15), which he had clearly understood, declared, and acted upon (Acts xi. 3, 17; xv. 9), brought him under the guilt of great and mischievous inconsistency. But his colleague's reproof probably led him back to right conduct, without leaving any unfriendly feeling in his heart: see 2 Pet. iii. 15.

12 came from James. Probably sent on some errand by James, as chief pastor in the church at Jerusalem.

withdrew. Or, " began to withdraw "; was so *inclined*.

he was afraid. " Here is the old enemy, timidity, which Peter no doubt thought he had conquered, but by which he was suddenly foiled " (Girdlestone: *Devotional Commentary*).

13 hypocrisy. Their practical disowning of their convictions.

14 uprightly. Or, " straightforwardly."

16 by the works of the law, etc. Cp. Psa. cxliii. 2.

17 by Christ. Rather, " in Christ " (R.V.); *i.e.*, as united with Him.

18 I make myself. Rather, " I prove myself." " If, after destroying the old ceremonial, I build it up again," I make myself out to have been guilty in destroying it.

19 I . . . am dead to the law. Properly, " I died unto the law " (R.V.). Paul seems to refer to the fact that in his conversion he became so united to Christ, as to be " crucified with Him," and consequently is no longer subject to the Mosaic law either for justification or for sanctification. He is dead to the law, but he has a new life in its place. Cp. iii. 13; Rom. vii. 4.

20 nevertheless I live, etc. Rather, " and it is no longer I that live, but Christ liveth in me " (R.V. marg.). This is fully explained in the next clause; " and the life which I now live," etc.

who loved me, and gave Himself (up) **for me.** "Paul appropriates to himself the love which belongs equally to the whole world" (*Chrysostom*).

21 I do not frustrate the grace of God. That is, I do not "set at nought" the mercy of God in Christ as if it were needless, by looking to the law for justification; see v. 4.

is dead. Rather, as A.V., "died."

CHAPTER III

1 who hath bewitched you? Or, "who fascinated you?" as with the power which the Orientals ascribe to what they call "the evil eye."

crucified [among you]. (The bracketed words "among you," are omitted by the best authorities.) "Paul represents his previous *preaching* of Christ as crucified, as a writing which he had previously *written*, προεγράφη" (*Meyer*). In the ministry and ordinances of the gospel they had so clear and affecting a representation of our Lord's death, that nothing but some strange fascination could so soon have diverted their minds from Him.

3 in the Spirit. Rather, "by the Spirit," the Author of the new life. Beginning with the spiritual, ending with the carnal!

4 Have ye suffered, etc.? Rather, "Did ye experience so many things in vain? If indeed it be in vain." Is all your Christian life, with its varied experience, its joys and trials, to have no result, or rather, perhaps worse than none? Cp. Heb. vi. 4–6.

5 among you. Perhaps rather, "in you" (R.V. marg.): see 1 Cor. xii. 6.

9 faithful. In whom faith was the prominent feature. They who share his faith shall "be blessed with" him: cp. Luke xvi. 20, and note.

10 Cursed is every one, etc. That is, all who hope to be justified by works of law must render constant and perfect obedience, or there will come upon them, not a blessing, but the curse which the Scripture expressly denounces.

11 The just shall live by faith. See note on this quotation in Rom. i. 17. Scripture says faith is essential to justification. But faith is *excluded* by law, which says only, "He who *doeth*," etc. Therefore, according to Scripture, law cannot justify a man; it can only curse him. And (13) it is Christ who alone delivers from that curse, having endured it Himself; and confers upon believing Gentiles the blessing promised to believing Abraham (14), even "the Spirit," which "we" (Jews and Gentiles alike) have received (see ver. 2).

13 being made a curse for us. "He had undergone that punishment which under the law betokened the curse of God."

15 I speak after the manner of men. Employing a human analogy, as in the case of an engagement from one man to another.

16 He saith not, "And to seeds," etc., Gen. xiii. 15 (Sept.). "The meaning of the argument is, that the recipients of God's promises are not to be looked upon as an aggregate of different individuals, or of different races, but are all one body, whereof Christ is the head. Cp. "you are the seed," ver. 29 (*Conybeare and Howson*).

17 And (Now) **this I say,** etc. Referring to what is to follow; the application of what has gone before. This promise to Abraham cannot be annulled by the *subsequent* introduction of a Law.

four hundred and thirty years after. It is not necessary to the apostle's argument that the popular computation of time which he here follows should be correct, although it probably is so: see notes on Gen. xv. 13; Exod. xii. 40; Acts vii. 6.

18 gave. Rather, "hath freely given," as that which is the fulfilment of a "promise," not a reward of "law." On the "inheritance," see Heb. xi. 8–10, 13–16.

19 Wherefore then [serveth] the law? Rather, as R.V., "What then is the law?"

added. "Superadded." This view of the Mosaic law is also presented in Rom. v. 20, where see note. This law was, so to speak, a step in the moral education of mankind, being brought in "for the sake of," or because of "the transgressions"; it instructed the people symbolically in moral distinctions, and by the expiations which it provided aroused a sense of the guilt of sin.

ordained by angels. Or, "enjoined through angels." On the ministry of angels and of Moses (the "mediator" here spoken of) at the giving of the law, see Acts vii. 38, 44, 53; Heb. ii. 2; iii. 2.

20 Now a mediator is not [a mediator] of one. The idea of mediator could not arise if there were only one party; it belongs to a contract which implies reciprocal engagements, in regard to which the two parties have a kind of equality. "But God is one," standing alone, in unapproachable supremacy. This supremacy is more prominently brought out in His sovereign promise than in a mediated covenant; so that the employment of angels and of Moses in the Hebrew economy marks it as in this respect inferior to "the promise." In the promise there are not two contracting parties.

22 the Scripture hath concluded all. Rather, "the Scripture shut up all things," as in ver. 23. It is the same Greek verb as is used in Rom. xi. 32. "Scripture" is here represented as *doing* what it *declares to be done.*

24 schoolmaster ("tutor," R.V.). The Greek word properly means the slave who had charge of the boys of a family, to conduct them to school, to watch over their morals, and to punish their faults. So the law, by its teachings and threatenings, was to convince men of their sinfulness (see Rom. vii. 7), and to train them for the salvation of Christ.

26 children. Rather, "sons," grown up; wards no longer.

27 put on. Cp. Rom. xiii. 14, and note.

28 for ye are all one (person) **in Christ Jesus.** This nullifies all earthly distinctions (28), and gives a common title to all the blessings of God's great promise (29).

CHAPTER IV

1 a child. Rather, "an infant"; *i.e.*, in a legal sense; a *minor*, who is, for a time, like a bond-servant, under the control of others, whatever his prospects may be.

2 tutors and governors. Or, "guardians," having the oversight of the person; "governors," or trustees, having the management of the property.

3 Even so we. Both Jews and Gentiles, chiefly the former.

elements. Or, "rudiments" (R.V., and so in ver. 9; Col. ii. 20); *i.e.*, an elementary state of knowledge; a ritual and ceremonial worship.

4 when the fulness of the time was come. When the time "appointed by the Father (2) was complete."

made. Or, "born." Our Lord was not only man, and so subject to the Divine law; but also a member of the Jewish nation, and so "under obligation to the law" in its fuller revelation by Moses. And His redemption is available even for those who have sinned against that fuller law (5), as well as for others.

5–7. See Rom. viii. 15–17, and notes.

8 ye did service unto. Rather, as R.V., "ye were in bondage to."

9 how turn ye again, etc. This Jewish formalism, with all its observances (10), which you are adopting, is *essentially* as much a state of "bondage" as your former Gentile condition.

beggarly elements. "The weakness and poverty of the elemental spirits" (*Moffatt*).

10 Ye observe, etc. An explanation of the foregoing. The observance of these festivals for their own sake, not as the expression of truth beyond themselves, was a fruitless ritualism.

12 be as I [**am**]. "Imitate me in rejecting Jewish observances; for I, though a Jew, have become a Gentile like you (1 Cor. ix. 21).

15 the blessedness ye spake of. "What, then, was the value of your self-congratulation ?"

your own eyes. This has been taken to confirm the view that "the thorn in the flesh" from which Paul suffered, affected his eyesight: see on 2 Cor. xii. 7. But the expression may be a general one, for the surrender of what is most precious.

16 because I tell you the truth. Dealing with you faithfully respecting your faults, and your dangers from false teachers. I have thus acted the part of a friend, not of an enemy (Prov. xxvii. 6).

17 They zealously affect you. "They make much of you" (*Moffatt*).

19 until Christ be formed in you. "His light in their minds, His love in their hearts, His law in their Conscience; His Spirit their formative impulse and power, His presence filling and assimilating their entire inner nature, and His image in visible shape and symmetry, reproducing itself in their lives" (*Eadie*).

20 I desire. More exactly, as R.V., "I could wish."

to change my voice. From tones of complaint and censure to those of satisfaction and confidence.

I stand in doubt of you. Or, "I am perplexed about you" (*Meyer*); *i.e.*, as to what is best to be done in your case.

21 the law. "The law" here means the writings of Moses. You wish to attend to their injunctions, attend then to the principles illustrated in their narratives. The history of Abraham's two sons shows the contrast between the bondage of the law and the blessed liberty of the gospel: see vers. 28–31. The apostle thus foils his adversaries with their own weapons.

23 by promise. By God's special interposition, according to His promise: cp. Rom. iv. 19–21.

24 Which things are an allegory. "As if Paul said, that it is a representation, painted for us as in a picture, of the two covenants, in Abraham's two wives, and of the two classes of people in the two sons" (*Calvin*).

these. That is, "these *women*."

which gendereth, etc. "Bringing forth children into bondage."

25 For this Agar is Mount Sinai in Arabia. The second Agar is omitted by some of the best authorities. According to the ordinary text, the sense is, "The name Agar is in Arabia [*i.e.*, is used by the Arabs for] Mount Sinai:" cp. Gen. xxi. 20, 21; 1 Chron. v. 10–20; Psa. lxxxiii. 6.

26 But Jerusalem which is above, etc. As the earthly Jerusalem (25) represents the Jewish economy, so here the heavenly one denotes the Christian dispensation, which secures freedom for all believers in Christ, whether Jews or Gentiles. This is the verse inscribed in the "Jerusalem Chamber" of Westminster Abbey, where the Westminster Assembly met during the Long Parliament.

27 For the desolate, etc. Rather, "For many are the children of the desolate, [more] than of her who has the husband."

28 children of promise. See ver. 23, and note; and compare the promise made to the Messiah in Isa. liii. 10.

29 even so it is now. The persecutions of Christians at this time arose mainly from the Jews: see Acts xiii. 49, 50; xiv. 1, 2, 19; xvii. 5, etc.; 1 Thess. ii. 14–16.

30 Cast out the bondwoman, etc. Sarah's words (Gen. xxi. 12).

31 of the bondwoman. We are children of no bondmaid, but of the free wife.

CHAPTER V

1 liberty. The best authorities connect the words with iv. 31, thus: "We are children . . . of the free with the liberty wherewith Christ makes His people free. Stand fast, therefore, and be not entangled," etc. Cp. Rom. vi. 16–20, and notes.

bondage. See iv. 9, and note; Acts xv. 10.

2 if ye be circumcised, etc. If you give yourselves up to this Judaising perversion, you do in effect reject the Saviour, and place yourselves (3) under a covenant which offers life on no other condition than perfect obedience to the whole law.

3 For I testify. Rather, "But I testify": viz., that every one who submits to be circumcised is bound, as a professed Jew, to keep all the institutions of Moses.

4 Christ is become of no effect unto you. Rather, "Ye were severed from Christ"; "your connexion with Him is annulled" (*Meyer*).

whosoever of you are justifed. Lit., "ye who are justifying yourselves"; "you who are seeking acceptance with God through the Law" (*Weymouth*).

ye are fallen (away) **from grace.** Justification by works of law necessarily excludes grace.

5 we through the Spirit, etc. "By the assistance of the Holy Spirit we are enabled to cherish the hope of being justified; and the source out of which that hope springs is faith" (*Ellicott*).

6 nor uncircumcision. Circumcision being disparaged, some might wrongly argue that the mere fact of being uncircumcised was meritorious.

8 This persuasion, etc. *i.e.*, the persuasion that circumcision is necessary. God had called you, and you were obediently following the truth; but you have suddenly stopped. It is clear that some one has "persuaded" you, and it is equally clear that whoever he be, he is not "of God." The mischief, if not checked, will soon spread through you all (9).

10 I have confidence. The *I* here is emphatic. I, who know you so well, confidently hope that you will even yet be brought to hold the truth; but the teacher, be he who he may, who disturbs you by his false reports about me, will be punished (10–12).

11 if I yet preach circumcision, etc. A slander, fully refuted by my persecutions from the Jews, to whom the doctrine, that faith in a crucified Saviour avails for salvation, without Jewish rites, is a "stumbling-block."

12 I would they were even cut off. Rather, "would mutilate themselves" (*Lightfoot; Conybeare and Howson*).

13 ye have been called unto (for) **liberty,** etc. You are brought more thoroughly under the influence of love, the higher law of the spirit of liberty: see Rom. viii.

14 fulfilled in one word. See Rom. xiii. 8. *Word* here means precept.

16 Walk in the Spirit. Probably meaning the same as Rom. viii. 4; on which see note.

17 so that ye cannot, etc. Rather, " to the end that ye do not the things that ye would"; each striving to prevent the fulfilment of the desires which the other prompts. On this conflict, see Rom. vii. 14–23.

18 not under (the) law. " But under grace"; and therefore " sin [or ' the flesh '] shall not have dominion over you " (see Rom. vi. 14, and note); and you shall produce the " fruit of the Spirit," which is in fact the fulfilling of law (23), and the crucifying of the flesh (24).

19 works of the flesh. All sin is man's *work*, and it is " fruitless " of good (Eph. v. 11). All holiness (22) is the *fruit* of the Spirit, the result of the new life which He implants.

20 witchcraft. Properly, " drugging," used for *sorcery* in general. " Strife " is rather *intriguings;* " seditions " are *factions.*

22 love. Love, as the chief, stands first (1 Cor. xiii. 13). " Faith " may here mean *fidelity* (Titus ii. 10; 1 Tim. vi. 11).

23 temperance. " Self-control"; the government of the desires.

against such (things) **there is no law.** See note on ver. 18.

24 crucified. See ii. 20; vi. 14; Rom. viii. 13, and notes.

CHAPTER VI

1 overtaken. " Detected"; " caught before he could escape " (*Ellicott*); " so that his guilt is placed beyond a doubt " (*Lightfoot*). Even in such a case, show the power of the spiritual life in you by reclaiming him, remembering your own frailty.

2 the law of Christ. To " love one another " (John xiii. 34, 35).

4 then shall he have rejoicing. R.V., " then shall he have his glorying," *i.e.*, his own special ground of glorying.

in another. Rather, " in [comparing himself with] the other," *i.e.*, with his fellow, R.V., " his neighbour." Every man's standard of self-judgement will be *absolute*, not *relative.*

5 his own burden. A different word is here used for " burden " (R.V., " load ") from that in ver. 2. There are burdens, as of trial, anxiety, sorrow, that may be shared by others in loving sympathy; there are, again, responsibilities which cannot be transferred, belonging to a man's own life and duty. The word in this verse is often applied to a soldier's pack or " kit."

6 all good things. Including means of subsistence: see 1 Cor. ix. 10. This verse appears to be a qualification or supplement of the preceding words. Each must bear his own burden, but those who are taught should help those who teach them.

7 God is not mocked. God's arrangements cannot be set aside. By His inevitable law, all our actions must develop their correspondent results. If we foster " the flesh "—the corrupt principles of our fallen state—we can have only " corruption," degradation, loathsomeness, spiritual death. If we cherish " the Spirit "—the higher principles of the Divinely renewed state—we shall certainly attain in due season, at the appointed harvest-time, " life " —purity, vigour, joy—" everlasting."

10 opportunity. Opportunity imposes obligation.

11 Ye see how large a letter. " See with how large letters " (R.V.); referring probably to the size of the writing. The Epistle up to this point had been written by an amanuensis, and now he takes the pen into his own hand, and the large bold characters indicate either (1) his defective eyesight, which compelled him to shape them thus (see on iv. 15), or (2) his great earnestness, leading him to write in this emphatic way.

12 they constrain you to be circumcised. They insist on circumcision as essential to salvation. But as they neglect much of their law (13), it is clear that they only wish to escape persecution by boasting that they have induced you to be circumcised.

14 God forbid that I should glory, etc. Far be it from me to boast in circumcision and such things; I boast only in Christ crucified. His death, making me " a new creature," has severed me for ever from all that I, like the rest of the world, once prized and pursued.

by whom. Rather, by which; *i.e.*, " the cross, by which."

16 as many as walk according to this rule. All, whether circumcised or not, who are made a " new creation," are blessed as the true " Israel of God ": cp. iii. 29; Rom. ix. 7.

17 the marks of the Lord Jesus. An allusion to the branding of a slave with the owner's mark; here referring probably to the marks of the scourgings and injuries which Paul had suffered for the sake of Christ (2 Cor. xi. 24, 25). These are perhaps put in contrast to the mark of circumcision, in which others gloried (13).

[Unto the Galatians, written from Rome.] This subscription is evidently incorrect.

THE EPISTLE OF PAUL THE APOSTLE TO THE EPHESIANS

INTRODUCTION

" STONE walls do not a prison make." This saying receives striking illustration in this letter, which was written by St. Paul in A.D. 62, during his first imprisonment at Rome (see Acts xxviii. 30). He wrote in another letter during his second imprisonment: " I suffer trouble as an evil-doer, even unto bonds; but the word of God is not bound." No chain could fetter Paul's free spirit. The bird beats its wings in futile struggles against the bars of its cage, but Paul's spirit soared far beyond even the city of Rome. Across the seas he sends his messages of encouragement and instruction to the little companies of Christians amid their pagan surroundings.

And higher still! He lives under the power of an endless life. He lifts his thoughts, and the minds of his readers, to "those shining table-lands, where God Himself is sun and moon." The outstanding expression of this Epistle, one which occurs five times in it and nowhere else in his writings, is "heavenly places." (See a fine chapter in Bishop Drury's *Prison-Ministry of St. Paul.*)

After the beautiful words of salutation, "grace" and "peace" (i. 2), this high note is at once struck in the doxology of verses 3–12. Here is praise for the enduring things of life—"all spiritual blessings in heavenly places"; "chosen in Him before the foundation of the world"; "predestinated unto the adoption of children"; "redemption through His blood"; "the riches of His grace." And here, too, as in the later chapters, he links up earth with heaven, duty with doctrine, which indeed is its motive-power—"that we should be holy and without blame before Him in love"; "that we should be to the praise of His glory."

Then comes his thanksgiving for the Christians themselves (i. 13), followed by a prayer for their wisdom and enlightenment (i. 17, 18), that they may be conscious of their hope, their glorious inheritance, the resurrection power of the living Lord; and the relation of that power to the world and to the Church (i. 18–23).

The second chapter shows how that same quickening power has been manifested in the changed lives of believers themselves (verses 1–6). Justification by faith is here expressed as being "saved by grace" (8), which is the Divine side of the same truth, and again the practical duty of "good works" is enforced (10). The wideness of God's mercy is shown in the fact that the Gentiles who were in the past regarded as "aliens" are now "brought nigh by the blood of Christ," and are "fellow-citizens with the saints," "a habitation of God through the Spirit" (11–19).

In the third chapter, the apostle speaks of his own ministry as a further evidence of God's grace to himself and to the world, especially to the Gentiles (verses 1–8). It is this that gives him confidence, and encourages him again, as in i. 18–23, in the earnest prayer that they may experience the power of the Spirit, that they may know the love of Christ, and be "filled with all the fulness of God" (12–20).

Chapter iv. is a plea for unity, not uniformity, but brotherhood amid diversity, as becomes the children of the divine Father (1–6). The apostle emphasises the truth of diversities of gifts combined with unity of spirit (11–16; cp. 1 Cor. xii. 4–11, 27, 28). The remainder of this chapter, the whole of v. and vi. 1–9, consists of an enforcement of practical duties.

And then in some of the closing verses of the Epistle (vi. 10–20) he gives an inspiring trumpet-call to vigilance and activity in the Christian warfare. The struggle is no light one. Powerful spiritual enemies have to be fought (11, 12). But God's armour is a strong defence (11, 13–17). And for those who trust not in their own strength, but look upwards to God for help (10, 18), the victory is sure (16).

CHAPTER I

1 an apostle. See notes on Rom. i. 1.

saints. See note on Rom. i. 7. Those who are consecrated as "saints" are also described as being "faithful," or endowed with faith, and so "in [union with] Christ."

at Ephesus. These words are omitted in some of the best MSS. Nestle (*Greek Test.*) puts them in brackets. Scholars are very evenly divided as to their omission or inclusion. The view of expositors such as Ellicott, Lightfoot, Howson is that the words were not in the original, and that the Epistle, while including Ephesus, was for all the churches in Asia.

3 (the) heavenly [places]. Cp. ver. 20 and ii. 6. The meaning is "the spiritual sphere." All the blessings of the Spirit bestowed on believers are given in connexion with that exalted state to which they are advanced by being "in Christ." This happy state is more fully described in ii. 1–13.

4 in love. These words may be connected with the next verse, the pause following the words "before Him": "in love having predestinated us," etc. (see R.V. marg.).

5 having predestinated us unto the adoption, etc. Cp. Rom vii. 29, and notes. God's "good pleasure" implies benevolence as well as sovereignty (cp. ver. 6).

6 His grace, wherein He hath made us accepted, etc. Lit., "His favour with which He favoured us," *i.e.*, as R.V., "which He freely bestowed on us in the Beloved." The Beloved is Christ: see Matt. iii. 17; John i. 12, 14; Col. i. 13, and notes.

7 redemption. Lit., "the (*i.e.*, our) redemption": see note on Rom. iii. 24. Here the primary idea is "remission of trespasses"; and this is obtained through the "blood," the propitiatory offering of Christ.

8 wherein He hath abounded. Rather, "which He made to abound toward us"; "qu'il a répandue sur nous abondamment" (*French version*).

9 mystery. See note on Matt. xiii. 11. "The mystery" here indicated is developed in ver. 10 and iii. 1–12.

10 that in the dispensation, etc. Rather, "in order to a dispensation of the fulness of the seasons, to gather together," or, "sum up." God's purpose with regard to the gospel dispensation was to reunite under the headship of Christ "all things," which had been, as it were, dislocated and disjointed by sin. Compare the parallel passage, Col. i. 20; see also Rom. viii. 19–22, and notes.

12 we. The word "we" here is emphatic, and contrasted with "ye" (13). It probably means "we" Hebrew believers: "who before have hoped in the Christ"; *i.e.*, we Jewish converts who hoped in Him "before" ye Gentiles "heard the word of truth."

13 In whom ye also trusted, etc. "In whom ye also, having heard, also believed," etc. The gifts of the Holy Spirit constituted the "seal" or evidence of their adoption, and "the earnest" (the pledge, or guarantee of the full possession) of their inheritance: see Acts xix. 1–6; 2 Cor. i. 22.

14 until. Or, "with a view to." This is the end in reference to *man*. The Spirit is given as a pledge of full and final redemption. "Unto the praise of His glory" is the end in reference to *God*.

the purchased possession. Believers themselves (cp. Acts xx. 28; 1 Pet. ii. 9) are the "purchased possession," being ransomed by Christ's death; and the "redemption" here spoken of is their final and complete salvation, in body as well as in soul: see notes on Rom. viii. 18–23.

15 your faith. Properly, "the faith among you"; the faith which distinguished them as communities.

16 of you. Omitted by most authorities, but understood.

17 the Father of glory. Not simply, "the glorious Father"; but the Father to whom belongs the glory so often mentioned in the context (12, 14, 18).

knowledge. That is, "full knowledge": "an experimental, living, practical knowledge" (*Stier*).

18 understanding. The best authorities read "of your heart." Only the enlightened heart can appreciate the high and noble hope to which Christians are called: see 1 John iii. 2, 3.

the hope of His calling. That eternal life which is the object of your hope, and to which God has called you.

19 the working of His mighty power. Lit., "the *energy* of the *power* of His *might*": the last word denoting inherent power; the second, power evinced in action; the first, the action itself.

22. "The fulness" is by some regarded as an epithet of the Church, *that which is filled, i.e.*, with His life and power. "The Church holds, or contains, the fulness of Christ. It is the filled-up receptacle of spiritual blessing from Him" (*Eadie*). Another rendering of the passage is, "And Him He gave to be the Head over all things to His body the Church—Him who is the fulness of that which filleth all in all" (*Speaker's Commentary*). A strong case is made out for this rendering, the Greek word for "fulness" (πλήρωμα) being the same as that used in John i. 16.

CHAPTER II

1 dead. Destitute of real spiritual life, under the power of sinful propensities and habits. To "quicken" is to bring from death to life."

2 the prince of the power (authority) **of the air.** This is clearly Satan (cp. vi. 12); but there is no exact parallel to this text elsewhere in the New Testament. It suggests an influence that is felt, but not seen, over the whole world, pervading, so to speak, its moral atmosphere: see vi. 12, and notes.

children of disobedience. (Lit., "sons"): according to Hebrew idiom, those having this character.

3 conversation. Rather, "mode of life": see note on Psa. xxxvii. 14.

others. Rather, "the rest," as R.V.

4 for His great love. "Because of that great love of His."

5 even when we were dead in sins ("through our trespasses," R.V.). To be connected with the *following* clause, "quickened," etc.

by grace ye are saved. Rather, "by grace have ye been saved" (R.V.). So also in ver. 8. The apostle here introduces the believer's actual and present salvation (see Rom. viii. 1) by God's free favour, as a subject which he could never lose sight of, and which he would have Christians always remember.

6 together. That is, together with Christ, as in 5: cp. i. 20.

heavenly [places]. See note on i. 3.

7 the ages to come. "The ages that are coming"; *i.e.*, through all the future history of the Church.

through Christ Jesus. Rather, "in Christ Jesus"; in whom the riches of Divine grace are treasured up. The repetition of His name shows emphatically that all these blessings are to be found in Him alone.

8 by grace. On the connexion between "grace" as the *source*, and "faith" as the *means* of salvation, see notes on Rom. iii. 27; iv. 4, 14.

and that not of yourselves. "And this *salvation* is not of yourselves."

10 For we are His workmanship. This is a proof that salvation must be of grace, and not of works; for our renewed nature, with all its actings, is God's own handiwork; and good works are not the cause of our new creation, but the end of it, provided for beforehand by God Himself.

11 Gentiles in the flesh. "By physical descent" (*Speaker's Commentary*).

12 covenants of (the) **promise.** See note on Rom. ix. 4.

13 sometimes. An antiquated form for "some time"; *i.e.*, "formerly."

by. Rather, "in." It is "in Christ," or more specifically in His blood, His sacrificial death, that you have reconciliation and access to God (16–18).

14 For He is our peace. Here, and in ver. 13, we have an allusion to Isa. lvii. 19 and Micah v. 5; on which see notes. Christ is "our peace" in its widest sense. In reconciling us to God, He makes both Jews and Gentiles one, having in His death put an end to the Mosaic law of rites and ordinances, which separated the Jew from the Gentile, like the partition in the Temple between the court of Israel and the court of the Gentiles.

15 the enmity. That is, the enmity between Jew and Gentile. The "twain" are reconciled to each other, because both are reconciled to God.

17 preached peace. Better, "brought glad tidings of peace." See Isa. lvii. 19.

20 prophets. A comparison with iii. 5 and iv. 11 seems to show that the "prophets" here spoken of are not those of the Old Testament, but inspired preachers of the gospel: see also Acts xiii. 1; Rom. xii. 6; 1 Cor. xii. 10. "The foundation of the apostles and prophets" may mean, either that which *they laid* in their ministry, or, that of which (like Peter, through his great confession, Matt. xvi. 16–18) they *form a part.* In either case, Jesus Christ is the "chief corner stone."

22 a habitation of God. God, who dwelt in the Temple in visible glory, now dwells in His Church "in the Spirit": cp. 2 Cor. vi. 16. There is here a marked progression: the Church is not only a *state*, but a *family* (19); not only a *family*, but a *temple* (21).

CHAPTER III

1 For this cause. Because you are thus built together in Christ: cp. 14–19 with ii. 22. The sentence beginning "I Paul the prisoner," etc., is interrupted by a long digression, extending to ver. 14, where the sentence is resumed.

2 if ye have heard, etc. Assuming, as I may, that you have heard of this. The church in Ephesus would obviously be familiar with the topic; but other churches in Asia had not possessed the advantage of Paul's direct ministrations.

3 He made known. Rather, "was made known."

as I wrote afore (*i.e.*, have just now written), etc. See i. 9, 10: see also ver. 6.

4 mystery. See vers. 9, 10; i. 19; Col. i. 26, and notes.

5 prophets. See note on ii. 20.

6 fellow-heirs. With the believing Jews in the spiritual inheritance.

7 by (according to) **the effectual working of His power.** The apostle acknowledges an act of God's omnipotence in his own change of heart, and in the qualifications bestowed on him for the service of Christ.

8 the unsearchable riches of Christ. Cp. Rom. xi. 33.

9 fellowship. Rather, the "dispensation," or carrying out of the Divine plan.

10 might be known, etc. Rather, "might be made known through the church"; God's wisdom being revealed even to the heavenly hosts by means of His redeemed people.

the manifold wisdom of God. God's "manifold wisdom" wonderfully combined and subordinated the most various agencies, institutions, and events, through many ages and dispensations, to His one great purpose; "the purpose of the ages."

13 Wherefore. On account of those glorious things (8–12). The very tribulations of the apostle were the "glory" of those on whose behalf he endured them.

14 For this cause. See note on ver. 1.

15 of whom. Referring to "the Father."

the whole family. The R.V. has "every family," but the A.V. translation is quite a possible rendering.

18 may be able to comprehend, etc. Very emphatic in original: "may be strong to apprehend," etc. (R.V.). The Greek suggests the idea of exertion.

19 with all the fulness of God. Rather, "unto all the fulness of God"; *i.e.*, approaching to God's perfection.

21 in the church. Cp. ver. 10.

CHAPTER IV

1 of the Lord. Rather, "*in* the Lord"; *i.e.*, in His cause: see iii. 1.

7 grace. Properly, "the grace"; that "gift" which Christ bestows, fitting men for the various callings and offices in the church: cp. ver. 11; Rom. xii. 6–8; 1 Cor. xii. 4–11.

8 Wherefore He (*or,* it) **saith,** etc. "The Scripture saith." See note on Psa. lxviii. 18. The main points of resemblance are in the ascent of the Divine Conqueror from the value of conflict to the "holy hill," with spoils received from conquered nations, that they may be given in royal bounty to His followers.

9 Now that He ascended, etc. The argument of the apostle is that if He who wrought this victory "ascends," He must first have "descended"; and that His deep humiliation on earth, even to the grave, was to prepare for His exaltation to the highest glory.

11 And He gave some (to be) **apostles,** etc. Cp. 1 Cor. xii. 28–30, and note. "Evangelists" were probably itinerant preachers, who had no pastoral charge.

13 till we all come in the unity of the faith, etc. "Till we all attain the same faith and knowledge of the Son of God" (*Conybeare and Howson*).

14 by the sleight of men, etc. Lit., "in the dice-playing," *i.e.*, by teachers who "deal with the Scriptures and the truth as players with dice" (*Luther*).

15 speaking the truth in love. Or, "holding truth in love"; in opposition to following error (14). R.V. marg. has "dealing truly" see also Gal. iv. 16. Cp. 2 Thess. ii. 10.

16 by that which every joint supplieth. "By every joint with which it is supplied" (*Moffatt*).

the effectual working. Of each part in due proportion.

love. Love is that in which the Church's edification and growth consist.

17 vanity. "Futility." See Rom. i. 21.

18 blindness. Rather, "hardening," as R.V.; French version has "endurcissement."

20 But ye have not so learned Christ. "Ye did not so learn Christ" (R.V.), *i.e.*, at the time of your conversion.

21 by Him. Rather, "in Him"; as part of your learning Christ.

26 Be ye angry, and sin not. See note on Psa. iv. 4.

27 place. Or, "room." Anger, or any other evil passion when cherished, makes room for Satan. "Ne donnez point accès au diable" ("do not give access to the devil") (*French version*).

28 that he may have to give. As, in dishonest indolence, he took from others, so now let him, from his honest labour, give a share to others.

29 to the use of edifying. R.V., "for edifying as the need may be."

30 whereby (in whom) **ye are** (were) **sealed.** *i.e.*, at the time of your conversion. See note on i. 13.

32 even as God for Christ's sake, etc. Lit., "as God in Christ forgave you" (or "us," var. read.): cp. 2 Cor. v. 19.

CHAPTER V

1 as dear children. Or, "as children beloved." The "beloved" should "walk in love."

2 an offering and a sacrifice, etc. Cp. Gen. viii. 21, and note.

4 not convenient. Not proper or befitting, as R.V.

5 who is an idolater. Putting the objects of his desire in the place of God. He who does this may observe outward decorum, and obtain the respect of men; but he is classed in the Scriptures with the worst of sinners.

the kingdom of Christ and of God. Properly, "the kingdom of Christ and God"; suggesting the closest connexion.

6 vain words. "Inanibus verbis" (*Vulgate*). These "empty words" are the false reasonings that are used for palliating these sins.

7 Be ye not (become not) **therefore partakers with them.** Sharing in their sins.

8 darkness. "Darkness" stands for ignorance and depravity; "light" for knowledge and purity, which are self-evidencing, diffusive, and fruitful in all good (9–13).

9 of the Spirit. R.V., "of the light." This is the reading of the best MSS.

10 proving. "Testing." Diligently examining, and, as the result, approving: see Rom. xii. 2.

13 for whatsoever doth make manifest is light. Rather, "everything that is made manifest is light." By your reproofs throw the light of truth on these deeds of darkness, and you may hope that they will become "light" or be reformed.

14 Wherefore He (*or*, it) **saith.** Perhaps Isa. lx. 1–3 is here suggested. "Shall give thee light," should rather be, as in R.V., "shall shine upon thee." Rawlinson (*Peake's Commentary*) suggests that this is part of an early hymn.

15 See then that ye walk circumspectly. Rather, "See then how strictly (or carefully) ye walk": *i.e.*, see that ye conduct yourselves as carefully as possible; the argument being, "If you are to reprove the misconduct of others, how circumspect and careful ought you to be yourselves!"

16 redeeming the time. Or, "buying up the opportunity" (R.V. marg.). "It means to make merchandise of the time, and to deal strictly with it, as men deal with goods by which they mean to make a profit" (*Letters on Church and Religion*, by W. E. Gladstone, vol. ii. p. 417).

18 but be filled with the Spirit. The contrast is between the false excitement and that which is holy and divine.

19 to yourselves. Rather, as R.V., "one to another": see Col. iii. 16. Pliny, writing to the Emperor Trajan, refers to the hymns which the early Christians used to sing among themselves to Christ as to God. Of the three words here used (*psalms* and *hymns* and spiritual *songs*), the first refers principally to those of the O.T., the second to Christian compositions on their model, the third to odes on sacred subjects generally.

21 submitting yourselves, etc. By a reasonable acquiescence in the wishes of the brethren, of whatever station they might be.

23 For the husband is the head of the wife, etc. Cp. note on 1 Cor. xi. 3. Christ's headship of His "body," the Church, results from the fact that He is its "Saviour" (cp. i. 20–23).

24 in every thing. In everything consistent with supreme allegiance to Christ.

26 that He might sanctify and cleanse it, etc. Rather, "that He may sanctify it, having cleansed [it] by the bath of water in the word." A Jewish bride, before she was "presented" to her husband was bathed in water (cp. Esth. ii. 12). So the Church, in order to its thorough consecration to Christ, is purified by the word of God (Rom. x. 8, 17): cp. John xvii. 17, and note. If baptism is here alluded to, it is represented as deriving all its efficacy from "the word."

30 of His flesh, and of His bones, etc. An allusion to Gen. ii. 23; denoting the most intimate union between Christ and His Church.

31 For this cause. Gen. ii. 24, which is here fully quoted according to the Septuagint. The allusion is to that union which makes husband and wife, as it were, one person (cp. 1 Cor. vi. 16); and which has a reference to the union of Christ and His Church.

CHAPTER VI

1 in the Lord. See notes on 1 Cor. vii. 39; Col. iii. 20.

2 first. See Exod. xx. 12 and Deut. v. 16.

4 provoke not your children to wrath. Let your government of your children be conciliatory, not irritating.

nurture. "Discipline.

5 Servants. Or, "bondmen." Dr. Charles Brown (*Devotional Commentary*) deals wisely with the question of St. Paul's attitude to slavery, and says, "Probably St. Paul felt the rank injustice of slavery as much as any man, but the way to abolish it was by evolution rather than by revolution." Of course these precepts are applicable to voluntary service.

8 the same. Properly, "this": see Col. iii. 24.

9 do the same things. In a like Christian spirit: see Col. iv. 1.

10 in the power of His might. See note on i. 19. All our spiritual strength flows from union with Christ: see John xv. 4, 5.

11 the whole armour. Both defensive and offensive armour.

12 For we wrestle not against flesh and blood. Lit., "our wrestling," indicating "the close, personal struggle" (*Lange*). These are words for the individual Christian in his struggle with temptation and opposition, as well as for the Christian Church.

the rulers of the darkness of this world. Lit., "the world-rulers of this darkness."

spiritual wickedness in high [places]. Rather, "the spiritual [hosts] of wickedness," etc. "The heavenly (not 'high') places." Weymouth translates "in the heavenly warfare."

14 truth. The word is probably used in its widest sense, including the truth of God, revealed truth, and the truth of man, truthfulness, sincerity. This, like a girdle, braces and strengthens the follower of the Captain of salvation: see Isa. xi. 5: cp. Rom. viii. 31–34; vi. 13.

the breastplate of righteousness. Worn also by the Leader of the host: see Isa. lix. 17. *Personal* righteousness is intended: the "breastplate" of the already justified; Christian integrity and loyalty.

15 preparation. Or, "readiness." The alacrity which "the good news of peace" diffuses through the Christian's service is as valuable to him as the sandals were to the warrior, who needed swiftness as well as strength: see note on 2 Sam. i. 19.

16 above all. "Over," or, "in addition to all," to complete the armour.

the shield of faith. The term here used means a large shield, covering the whole body from dangerous missiles.

the wicked. "The wicked *one*."

17 the helmet of salvation. See Isa. lix. 17, which is here referred to.

the sword of the Spirit. The Holy Spirit has furnished the sword of Divine truth; and He teaches us to wield it with success.

18 praying always, etc. "With all (every kind of) prayer and supplication, praying at all seasons in the Spirit," R.V. Prayer is not likened to any particular weapon, but is appended to the description of the Christian's panoply, perhaps as representing the attitude in which alone the armour can be successfully used.

19 mystery. See note on i. 9.

20 in bonds. Lit., "in a chain": see Acts xxviii. 16, 20.

21 that ye also may know. "That you as well as others may know," etc.

Tychicus. See Col. iv. 7. He was probably an Ephesian Christian, charged with this letter as well as with those to the Colossian church and to Philemon. His faithful companionship with the apostle to the last is shown by 2 Tim. iv. 12. The epithet, "minister" (*diaconos*, as in Col. iv. 7), refers to his work as a helper of the apostle. Cp. also Acts xx. 4; 1 Cor. xvi. 3, 4; Titus iii. 12.

22 for the same purpose. Properly, "for this very purpose."

[Written from Rome.] This note of place is doubtless correct, though the postscript itself has no authority.

THE EPISTLE OF PAUL THE APOSTLE TO THE PHILIPPIANS

INTRODUCTION

THIS letter recalls the memory of two prisons. The first was that in which its writer was imprisoned, nine or ten years before, in the very city to which he is now writing (Acts xvi. 23–39). The second is that in which the letter was written from Rome, A.D. 61 or 62. In both cases it is the same Paul, fearless, triumphant, rejoicing. In the prison at Philippi, beaten and bleeding, he and his friend Silas sang praises to God (Acts xvi. 23–25). In the prison at Rome he is not only joyful himself, but he writes letters to cheer and inspire his fellow-Christians both in Europe and in Asia.

From beginning to end this Epistle may be said to overflow with a joyous spirit. The apostle is glad at the remembrance of the loyalty of his readers to Christ and the Gospel (i. 3–5). He is glad in the thought that Christ is preached at Rome, even though some should preach in a contentious spirit (i. 15–18). In the spirit of his Master, he desires that his friends at Philippi should be partakers of his joy (i. 25, 26; cp. John xv. 11), and asks their help in contributing to his cause for rejoicing (ii. 2; 16–18). He expects them to be glad at the recovery and in the fellowship of Epaphroditus (ii. 28, 29). Enlarging on his exhortation to "rejoice in the Lord" (iii. 1), he shows that Christ is the source and centre of all the gladness of his life (iii. 3, 8) and of all his bright hopes for the life to come (iii. 20, 21). The same ideas are repeated in chapter iv. (verses 1, 4, 10, 13).

The Epistle breathes, too, the spirit of prayer. He prays constantly and with confidence (i. 4, 6). He puts love, as in 1 Cor. xiii. 13, in the first place

(i. 9), but wants their love to be discriminating ("that you may test the things that differ," Bishop Moule's rendering of the first clause of i. 10), and prays that they may be so free from doubtful motives and inconsistencies that they may be ready for the Day of Christ (i. 10, 11).

The letter is full also of practical counsels. He desires their conduct to be in harmony with the gospel they profess (i. 27); urges a spirit of humility and unselfishness (ii. 3, 4); pleads for the exercise of an active influence on the world around them (ii. 15, 16); shows the way, through prayer and thanksgiving, to a peaceful mind amid all the anxieties of life (iv. 6, 7); and sums up all that a Christian character means in the beautiful words of iv. 8.

CHAPTER I

1 bishops and deacons. It appears that the Philippian church had two kinds of officers, with a plurality of each: see 1 Tim. iii. 1–13, and notes.

3 upon every remembrance of you. "Upon all my remembrance of you" (*Lightfoot*); "my whole memory of you" (*Moule*).

5 fellowship in the gospel. Rather, "fellowship unto the gospel," *i.e.*, co-operation with the apostle for its furtherance; with some special reference to their liberality to himself (see iv. 14–16). Their generous devotedness to the service of Christ he regarded as God's work in them, and therefore as a pledge of their perseverance in their Christian calling, until their salvation should be "completed" at the time of Christ's second coming (vers. 6, 10; see also iii. 20, 21).

from the first day. That is, from the first coming of the gospel among them.

6 will perform it. Or, "will perfect it," carry it to completion.

7 to think this of you all. "Should feel like this over you all" (*Moule*).

because I have you in my heart. Their evident participation of the Divine grace, which enabled him to labour and suffer for the gospel, united him to them in the bonds of holy love; and this union of feeling assured him that they were God's children.

8 my record. That is, "my witness." For "bowels," etc., read "tender mercies of Christ Jesus," or, "the affection of Jesus Christ" (*Moffatt*).

9 judgement. Rather, "perception," or "discernment."

10 that ye may approve, etc. Or, as R.V. marg., "that ye may prove (or, 'test') the things that differ," or "are essential" (*Glover*): see Rom. ii. 18. Holy love, guided by knowledge, discerns and approves what is right.

till the day of Christ. Rather, "for," *i.e.*, in expectation of "the day of Christ."

13 the palace. "The Prætorian"; meaning, most probably, not a place, but the Prætorian guard itself, under the custody of whose Prefect the apostle was placed in Rome (Acts xxviii. 16): see R.V. Thus it had become known among all the guard, "and all the rest" at Rome, even in Cæsar's palace (iv. 22), that his imprisonment was "in Christ," *i.e.*, on account of His cause.

14 many of the brethren. Rather, "the majority of the brethren." Paul's stedfastness under persecution made them "confident in the Lord," and encouraged them boldly to "speak the word." "It indicates how absolutely consistent the Apostle's life was" (F. B. Meyer in *Devotional Commentary*).

15 Some indeed, etc. Possibly, personal opponents, belonging to the Judaising section, who, seeing the success of the apostle's ministry, endeavoured to make converts, in order to form a party against him.

16 of contention. More precisely, of "party-spirit." "Not sincerely," *i.e.*, not with pure motives.

supposing to add affliction to my bonds. Rather, "to stir up affliction to my bonds"; "to make my chains gall me" (*Lightfoot*).

20 earnest expectation. Or, "eager expectation."

22 But if I live in the flesh, etc. Rather, "But if to live in the flesh, this yields me fruit from my labour in the gospel, then I know not what I shall choose." "For myself" life and death are both blessed—life, for Christ is the source of its happiness and the object of its activity;—death, for that will bring me "gain" in respect to both enjoying and glorifying Him. But if my living in the flesh bring the more fruit of my labours, then I can hardly choose. The very construction of this passage "reflects the conflict of feeling in the apostle's mind" (*Lightfoot*).

23 having a desire. Rather, "having the desire" (R.V.); *i.e.*, my *prevailing* desire. "Far better" is very emphatic in the Greek: "very far better."

25 And having this confidence. Rather, "And being confident of this," *i.e.*, that my life is important for your "furtherance and joy in the faith." The phrase, "I know," implies strong assurance: cp. ver. 27, and Acts xx. 25.

26 for me. Lit., "in me"; *i.e.*, on my account.

27 let your conversation, etc. (Lit., behave as citizens); "do your duty as good citizens of a heavenly kingdom; act worthily of the Gospel of Christ" (*Lightfoot*). Cp. iii. 20; Acts xxiii. 1, and notes.

29 given. Or, "freely granted": see on ver. 7, and Acts v. 41.

30 which ye saw in me. When I was with you: see Acts xvi. 19–24.

CHAPTER II

1 consolation. Here, perhaps, the word παράκλησις is best rendered by "appeal." See also note on 1 Thess. ii. 3. "If your experiences in Christ appeal to you with any force, if love exerts any persuasive power upon you, if your fellowship in the Spirit is a living reality, if you have any affectionate yearnings of heart, any tender feelings of compassion, listen and obey" (*Lightfoot*).

5 this mind. The same lowly self-denying thoughts, and desire for others' good.

6 being. Rather, "subsisting"; a reference to His pre-existent and essential state. "The form of God" means the outward manifestation of His Divine perfections. Of this—not of His Divine nature—"He emptied Himself."

thought it not robbery, etc. Or, "did not account His equality with God a thing to be tenaciously grasped." All Divine glories are truly and rightfully His (see John i. 14; xvii. 5); yet He did not insist upon their manifestation, but "emptied Himself" of it; made Himself "void of the manifestation and exercise of Deity as it was His on the throne" (*Bishop Moule*).

9 a name. Properly, "the name." JESUS was the name, first, of our Lord's humiliation, and henceforth of His exaltation and glory: see vers. 10, 11.

10 at the name. Rather, "in the name." All praise and prayer offered in heaven, or on earth, must be offered to God through Him, in whom only God is fully revealed. All creation is personified, as uniting in this worship, together with the redeemed in earth and heaven: see Rev. v. 9–13, and cp. Rom. xiv. 9–11.

12 Wherefore, my beloved, etc. "Having the example of Christ's humiliation to guide you, of Christ's exaltation to encourage you, as you have always been obedient, so continue" (*Lightfoot*). "Work out . . . for it is God who worketh." The Divine and human sides of salvation are here linked together. The Divine purpose is not antagonistic to the freedom of man's will. Faith justifies and works are the fruit of faith.

15 nation. Rather, "generation": see Deut. xxxii. 5.

17 if I be offered, etc. Rather, "if I am even being poured forth [as a drink offering, Exod. xxix. 40, 41; 2 Tim. iv. 6] over the sacrifice," etc., *i.e.*, at this very time. He compares the faith of the Philippian Christians to a sacrifice, over which he will most gladly pour out his blood in martyrdom as a libation; and he believes that they sympathise with him in this feeling (18).

19 I trust. Or, "I hope"; and this, like all my hope, rests on the Lord Jesus.

Timotheus. Timothy was one of Paul's companions both in the journey in which he first visited Philippi (see Acts xvi. 1, 3, 12; xvii. 14), and when he again passed through Macedonia (2 Cor. i. 1; ii. 13; ix. 2, 4); so that the Philippians knew "his tried worth" (22).

20 naturally. Rather, "truly." He alone of all those now with me has the same "genuine" care for you as I.

23 presently. "As soon as ever I shall see how it will go with me" (*Moffatt*).

25 I supposed it necessary, etc. For the reasons assigned in vers. 26, 28.

30 not regarding his life, etc. R.V., "he came nigh unto death, hazarding his life to supply that which was lacking in your service," "and so complete your loving purposes in regard of the ministration you desired for me" (*Moule*). The illness of Epaphroditus seems to have been caused or aggravated by zealous attendance on Paul.

CHAPTER III

1 the same things. Partly, perhaps, Christian joy, so often dwelt upon in this Epistle (see i. 18; ii. 17, 18; iv. 4), but also the warning against dissensions (ii. 3, 14). "Grievous" here means *irksome*.

2 dogs. See Job xxx. 1; Psa. xxii. 16, and note. The apostle here retorts upon the Judaisers the opprobrious term that they were wont to apply to the Gentiles.

evil workers. Men whose work in regard to the gospel was deceitful and wicked: cp. 2 Cor. xi. 13.

the concision. Or, the "mutilation," not the "circumcision"; for the true circumcision is not the adherence to a mere outward rite, but the worshipping God in spirit, etc. (3): cp. Col. ii. 11. The verb corresponding to "concision" is used by the LXX to express the idolatrous mangling of the flesh, practised by the heathen, and forbidden by the Mosaic law (Lev. xxi. 5; 1 Kings xviii. 28).

4 Though I might also have, etc. This ground of "confidence," whatever its worth, was shared by the apostle with these Judaisers.

5 Benjamin. One of the two royal tribes (1 Sam. x. 20, 21), closely associated with Judah after the Captivity (Ezra iv. 1).

a Hebrew of [the] Hebrews. The Greek indicates "a Hebrew and of Hebrew ancestry."

6 in the law. Or, "in law"; in obedience to formal precepts.

blameless. Paul, before his conversion, like many young men religiously educated, seems to have lived a correct moral life, and to have observed the ritual law. But he learned the worthlessness of all this as a ground of hope and acceptance before God (8–11).

8 that I may win Christ. Or, "gain Christ"; as the very principle of my life; so that I may have the righteousness, which comes from God, and is based on faith (see Rom. i. 17, and note).

10 the power of his resurrection, etc. The thought of oneness with Christ wrought out in detail. The power of Christ's resurrection is known experimentally by all who rest upon His finished work (Rom. iv. 25; viii. 34), who receive in Him the pledge of *life* immortal (John xiv. 19), who have apprehended Him as a *living Saviour*, and have been raised through Him from the death of sin to *newness of life* (Rom. vi. 8, 9). The thought of Col. iii. 1 is in the apostle's mind.

11 if by any means, etc. The words point onward to the final redemption of the saints: cp. Rom. viii. 23. "Resurrection" here is expressed by an emphatic word not found elsewhere in the New Testament, meaning complete resurrection—not simply *of*, but *from* the dead.

12 perfect. Rather, "perfected": cp. ver. 15.

I follow after. The same word is rendered, "I press," in ver. 14.

14 toward the mark. R.V., "toward the goal."

the high calling. Rather, "my calling from above." Cp. Heb. iii. 1.

15 Let us therefore, as many as be perfect. "Perfect" here is different from the word in ver. 12. It means mature in knowledge and experience (cp. 1 Cor. ii. 6). Let such think and feel as I have just been urging.

if in any thing ye be otherwise minded. If in some minor points your opinions differ from mine, God Himself will set you right.

18 of whom I have told you often. During his personal ministry in Philippi; lit., "I was often telling you."

enemies of the cross of Christ. Either by insisting on conformity to the ritual law (the Judaisers), or by making the grace of God an excuse for sin: cp. Rom. vi. 1. The context seems to point to the latter class. *Lightfoot* points out that the abuse of the apostle's doctrine of free justification would be peculiarly painful to him. Hence his "weeping."

19 who mind earthly things. See Rom. viii. 6, and note.

20 our conversation. "The state of which we are citizens." This community is heavenly, and such should be our conduct.

21 who shall change our vile body. Rather, "who will transform (*or*, 'fashion anew') the body of our humiliation into conformity with the body of His glory": see 1 Cor. xv. 42–49 and notes.

CHAPTER IV

1 so. As imitators of the apostle, and expectants of the heavenly kingdom (iii. 17, 20).

2 Euodias. Properly, "Euodia." The two women here named had, like many others (Acts xviii. 26; Rom. xvi. 1–5), "laboured with" Paul; but their usefulness was now impeded by a disagreement, which needed for its removal not only the apostle's entreaty, but "even also" the "help" of a genuine "yokefellow." This was probably the most active of the "bishops" (i. 1).

3 those women, etc. That is, as the Greek shows, Euodia and Syntyche. R.V. has, "help these women, for they laboured."

4 Rejoice. Cp. on iii. 1.

5 moderation. That is, forbearance, or consideration for others, as in 2 Cor. x. 1.

The Lord is at hand. The expectation of the Lord's coming in judgement (see Matt. xxv. 1, and note); should lead us to considerateness in dealing with others. Cp. 1 Cor. xvi. 22.

6 Be careful for nothing. "Be anxious about nothing." Another lesson from the anticipation of the Lord's coming. Cp. Matt. vi.: see note, 1 Pet. v. 7.

prayer . . . supplication . . . thanksgiving . . . requests. "Prayer" is *general*, "supplication" *special*: "thanksgiving" is added to show that prayer should *always* be accompanied by praise; "requests" are the *several* petitions included in "supplication."

7 And the peace of God, etc. A promise dependent on the foregoing. The deep tranquillity of a soul which has thankfully referred everything in prayer to God, "shall keep," or guard the heart like a sentinel.

minds. Rather, "thoughts."

8 honest. Or, "honourable."

if there be any virtue, etc. Rather, "whatever virtue, whatever praise there is." There may be, as *Lightfoot* suggests, a reference to heathen ethics: "Whatever value may reside in your old conceptions of 'virtue,' whatever consideration is due to the 'praise' of men."

10 your care of me hath flourished again. "You have blossomed out into loving thought on my behalf" (*Moule*). See vers. 14, 15. The value of the gift at this time was probably enhanced by the apostle's condition as a prisoner, unable to labour for his support, as he had previously done.

12 I am instructed. The apostle's word is very emphatic: "I have learned the secret" (R.V.), a phrase often used of initiation into the ancient mysteries.

13 through Christ which strengtheneth me. "Through Him who strengtheneth me." The word "Christ" is not in the best MSS. There was no need to write the Name: cp. 1 Tim. i. 2.

14 that ye did communicate, etc. By sympathy and needful supplies.

15 in the beginning of the gospel. "When I left Macedonia" (and, indeed, before that, ver. 16), after introducing the gospel among you: see 2 Cor. xi. 9.

no church communicated with me, etc. Rather, "No church had fellowship with me in the matter of giving and receiving" (a technical expression like "credit and debt"), *i.e.*, supplying my bodily wants in return for the spiritual blessings they had received through me: see ver. 17, and cp. 1 Cor. ix. 11; Philem. 19.

16 even in Thessalonica. A hundred miles away: see Acts xvii. 1, note.

17 that may abound. Rather, "that aboundeth": "to your account" as to ensure a recompense in the Divine approval and blessing.

18 well-pleasing to God. Help rendered to servants of Christ is an offering peculiarly acceptable to God, and will be richly recompensed by Him (19). It was this recompense that the apostle desired for the Philippians, rather than any gifts to himself.

19 shall supply, etc. More literally, "will fully supply every need of yours."

by Christ Jesus. Rather, "*in* Christ Jesus" (Rom. viii. 32).

20 unto God and our Father. Or, "unto our God and Father" (R.V.): cp. Gal. i. 4.

21 The brethren. The brethren mentioned in i. 14; ii. 19.

22 they that are of Cæsar's household. It would be encouraging to the Philippians to learn that there were true believers among the slaves, freedmen, official functionaries, or even the domestic circle, of such a man as Nero: see note on ch. i. 13.

[It was written to the Philippians, etc.] This subscription, although absent from the best copies, and not of course authoritative, is no doubt correct.

THE EPISTLE OF PAUL THE APOSTLE TO THE COLOSSIANS

INTRODUCTION

THE similarity of this letter to the Epistle to the Ephesians has often been pointed out. How, indeed, could it be otherwise? They were both written at the same period in St. Paul's life, during his imprisonment at Rome between A.D. 59 and 62. As has been well said in *The Bible Handbook* (Angus and Green), "both Epistles being written about the same time, the same ideas, and even the same expressions, would be likely to recur."

It is noticeable, however, that the similarity is largely in the practical exhortations (cp. Col. iii. 18–22 with Eph. v. 22, 25; vi. 1–9). It was natural and inevitable that, in addressing churches which were just emerging from paganism and existing amid pagan surroundings, the apostle should lay stress on the family life, the relation between husbands and wives, parents and children, masters and servants, or that he should also give some identical exhortations about personal purity (cp. Col. iii. 5 with Eph. v. 3–7), and a forgiving spirit (cp. Col. iii. 12, 13, with Eph. iv. 31, 32).

But in the more doctrinal parts of the earlier chapters, while there are some identical expressions, as in Eph. i. 7 and Col. i. 14, there are also notable diversities. The truth is the same, but it is presented from a different point of view. The feature of the Epistle is its exaltation of Christ in His person and work. He is the image of the invisible God (i. 15). By Him all things were created (i. 16). In Him all fulness dwells (i. 19); all the fulness of the Godhead bodily (ii. 9). His cross is the sinner's hope (i. 14; ii. 14); His resurrection the believer's inspiration and strength (iii. 1–3). He "is all and in all" (iii. 11).

The Epistle was written to the Church in Colossæ, in Asia Minor, a few miles from Laodicea (see iv. 13, 15, 16). Paul had never been there, but he makes mention of several of its people (iv. 9, 12, 17).

CHAPTER I

1 Timotheus. "The brother," as in Philem. 1 (not "our").

5 for the hope. *i.e.* (the love which you have to all the brethren) "for the sake of the hope," etc.

6 in all the world. See Rom. i. 8, and note.

7 Epaphras. Epaphras appears to have been the principal teacher, if not the founder of the church at Colossæ: acting on the apostle's behalf (the best authorities reading "for us" instead of "for you" in this verse). He was now with Paul at Rome (iv. 12): a fellow-prisoner (Philem. 23).

10 increasing in the knowledge of God. Or (R.V. marg.), "increasing *by* the knowledge of God," which is the means of spiritual growth.

11 according to His glorious power. Rather, "the might of His glory"; His might being an attribute of "His glory" or perfection.

13 His dear Son. Lit., "the Son of His love": "the Beloved" (Eph. i. 6).

15 firstborn of every creature (of all creation). Rather, "the first-born before every creature."

16 thrones, etc. The apostle uses these terms doubtless as implying (cp. Rom. viii. 38; Eph. i. 21) distinctions of office and dignity among the heavenly hosts.

17 by Him all things consist. Rather, "in Him they all stand together": cp. Acts xvii. 28. "The whole universe coheres into system in Him" (Archbishop Alexander in *Speaker's Commentary*).

18 the firstborn from the dead. Not only was He the first who rose from the dead to die no more; but He is also the Lord and Author of the resurrection: cp. ver. 15, and Rev. i. 5. Referring to the latter, Archbishop Alexander says that "this verse supplies another point of contact between the Christology of St. Paul and that of St. John."

in all things. In creation, providence, and grace.

19 it pleased [the Father] that in Him, etc. Or, as R.V., "it was the good pleasure [of the Father] that in Him should all the fulness dwell" [have its permanent abode]. "The fulness" means "the totality of the Divine power and attributes" (*Lightfoot* (see ii. 9)).

23 which was preached to every creature (in all creation). This fulfilment of our Lord's commission was already begun in the wide extension of the gospel, especially through Paul's ministry: cp. ver. 6; Rom. i. 8.

24 Who now rejoice. Better, "Now I rejoice" (R.V.).

for you. "On account of you": see Acts xxi. 28–36; xxii. 21, 22, etc.

and fill up that which is behind, etc. That is, "to complete or supply what is still wanting in the sufferings of Christ"; meaning Christ's sufferings in the persons of His saints (cp. Matt. xxv. 34–40). Christ Himself suffered for the redemption of His people: His members suffer for the spiritual perfecting of the whole body, the Church. Their sufferings are in a sense His own—borne by Christ's *people,* in a Christ-like *spirit,* and for Christ's *cause.*

25 dispensation. Or, "stewardship."

to fulfil. "That I may fully deliver God's message" (*Weymouth*).

26 the mystery. See notes on Eph. i. 9, 10, and iii. 9.

27 would make known. Rather, "willed to make known."

among. Compare the next clause, "in you"; *i.e.,* among the Gentiles collectively, and in you who believe individually.

28 every man. On the triple repetition of the words "every man" Archbishop Alexander (*Speaker's Commentary*) says: "The thought of Catholicity has become passionately dear to the Apostle. The shadows lengthen in the sunset. Yet he feels that the glorious mystery, which embraces a whole fallen race, is to take in this man and that. No individual is to be neglected in the pastoral work."

in all wisdom. "Every man" is thus admitted to the full revelation: whereas other teachers reserved their mysteries for the initiated few—the perfect, or "fully instructed."

29 striving. The word implies striving *in conflict,* as in ii. 1: cp. Luke xiii. 24. The apostle's work involved not only toil, but conflict (Phil. i. 30).

mightily. Lit., "in power": cp. 1 Cor. xv. 10.

CHAPTER II

1 and for as many as have not seen my face, etc. The natural meaning, and one consistent with the context, is that the words include the Colossians and Laodiceans among those who had not seen the apostle. He assures them that his anxiety extends beyond the churches which he has founded or visited.

2 the mystery of God, etc. The R.V. has, "that they may know the mystery of God, [even] Christ": cp. 1 Tim. iii. 16, note. Christ Himself is "the mystery of God" (i. 27).

4 with enticing words. Rather, "with enticing speech": cp. 1 Cor. ii. 4. The French version has "par des raisonnements spécieux" ("by specious arguments").

5 your order. Gr. τάξις. "He uses an image, derived from the order and solidity of the soldiers of the Pretorian Guard, whom he saw so constantly during his captivity" (*Archbishop Alexander*). Perhaps the idea of discipline is suggested.

6 As ye have therefore received Christ Jesus the Lord. "Though the reference seems mainly to reception by teaching, the object is so emphatically specified, as apparently to require a more inclusive meaning; they received not merely the *doctrinam Christi*, but Christ Himself" (*Ellicott*).

7 rooted and built up in Him. Rather, "having been rooted, and being [still] built up in Him"; "marking the stable growth and organic solidity of those who truly walk in Christ" (*Ellicott*).

8 spoil you. Rather, "carry you off as spoil."

through philosophy. Respecting the "rudiments" (or elements) "of the world," see note on Gal. iv. 3; and on the "tradition of men," see Mark vii. 8.

9 For in Him dwelleth, etc. The complete perfection of the Godhead is embodied in the person of the Redeemer. Archbishop Alexander notes that "the fulness of the Godhead" corresponds to "the Word was God" (John i. 1), and "dwelleth bodily" to "the Word was made flesh" (John i. 14), again showing the agreement between St. Paul and St. John.

10 principality and power. See note on i. 16.

11 circumcised. The Judaisers insisted on circumcision as still necessary under the gospel. Therefore the apostle assures these Gentile believers that they have been already spiritually circumcised by Christ Himself in their conversion; in token of which they were baptised: cp. Rom. vi. 3–5, on which see note.

12 wherein also ye are risen. Rather, as R.V., "wherein ye were also raised."

through the faith of the operation of God. Meaning, probably, "through faith in the effectual working of God." Believing in the Divinely effected resurrection of Christ, they became subjects of a Divinely wrought spiritual resurrection.

14 handwriting. Or, "bond." When Jesus was nailed to the cross, the "handwriting of ordinances" (or bond of legal obligations) was cancelled.

15 having spoiled, etc. Lit., "having stripped off from Himself the principalities," etc. The powers of evil clung, as it were, about Him, striving to make Him their prey, but He victoriously cast them off: see R.V.

triumphing over them in it. Meaning probably, *in the cross;* for in it Christ conquered the powers of darkness: see note on Eph. vi. 12.

16 Let no man therefore, etc. As the Mosaic dispensation is entirely abrogated. Christian freedom in general is here asserted, and the particular heresies of Judaising and ascetic teachers are indicated.

holy-day. Properly, "feast" or festival. The three seasons of worship here mentioned are the *yearly, monthly,* and *weekly* celebrations, as observed by the Jews.

17 the body. The substance of reality: all that these rites signified is realised in Christ: comp. Heb. x. 1.

18 beguile you. "Rob you of the prize."

voluntary. There is now a general agreement that the word translated "voluntary" (*θέλων*) should be attached to the first part of this verse, thus: "Let no one, however he may wish it, rob you," etc.

humility. The false teachers worshipped angels on the groundless assumption that it was inconsistent with true humility towards God to offer worship directly to Him (cp. ver 23); and this is the spirit of saint-worship now.

which he hath not seen. The R.V. reading, "dwelling (or taking his stand upon) the things which he hath seen" has hardly sufficient support.

19 knit together, etc. Cp. Eph. iv. 15, 16, and notes.

20 rudiments. See note on ver. 8.

ordinances. The "ordinances" are those which follow, enjoining abstinence in various ways, from things which "are to perish in their consumption," *i.e.*, which are made to be consumed and perish: cp. Matt. xv. 1–14; Mark vii. 1–5, 14–23, and notes.

21 Touch not, taste not, handle not. The words are connected with the preceding verse: ordinances, such as "touch not," etc. "The apostle disparagingly repeats the prohibitions of the false teachers in their own words" (*Lightfoot*).

23 neglecting of the body. Or, "severity to the body." All these professed methods of overcoming evil are opposed to any true honour" and right use of the body; and though they "have the appearance of wisdom" in devotion, humility, and subjugation of the body, they do in fact only serve "to the satisfying of the flesh," the carnal element; and thus they increase the evil which they profess to overcome. Asceticism is, after all, but another form of carnality.

CHAPTER III

1 If ye then be risen. Or, "If then ye were raised" (R.V.): see note on ii. 12.

where Christ sitteth, etc. Rather, "where Christ is, being seated on," etc. He is there, and is in the place of honour there.

2 Set your affection, etc. Or, "mind the things above": see note on Rom. viii. 6.

3 For ye are dead. Rather, "For ye died"; a definite event in their experience.

your life is hid, etc. Not only securely preserved as a treasure, but also not fully revealed. "The Christian's life is hid from unbelievers who do not share it; often to a great extent from his fellow-Christians; sometimes in measure from his very self" (*Archbishop Alexander*).

5 Mortify therefore your members. As you died with Christ (ii. 20), and your true life is hidden with Him (iii. 3), "put to death your members which are upon the earth," destroy all the lusts and habits connected with them which are hostile to your heavenly destiny. It is spiritual putting to death that is meant.

fornication, uncleanness, etc. Cp. Eph. v. 3–5, and notes.

8 put off. Imperative: "put ye away," R.V.

10 which is renewed in knowledge, etc. Rather, "which is being renewed unto full knowledge after the image," etc. The renewal has God's image for its model: cp. Eph. iv. 22–24.

11 where there is neither Greek nor Jew, etc. In this renewed state the earthly distinctions of nation, customs, civilisation, and social position, become of no account; and all depends on Christ, who is the centre of all life, and is in all believers (whether Jew or Gentile, etc.), by His Spirit and likeness. On "barbarian," see note on Acts xxviii. 2. "Scythians" were regarded as the lowest savages.

13 quarrel. Rather, "complaint": cp. Eph. iv. 2, 32.

14 above. Or, "over." Love is to be the girdle that is worn over all the other graces, binding them together, and completing the spiritual attire.

15 the peace of God. The Vulgate, following the Septuagint and the best MSS., has "the peace of Christ." "St. Paul is not so much wishing for the peace of God to keep them, as enjoining them to *keep* the peace of Christ" (*Archbishop Alexander*). See John xiv. 27, etc.

16 in psalms, etc. See note on Eph. v. 19. "'Teaching' and 'admonishing' describe respectively the positive and the negative side of instruction" (*Lightfoot*). So i. 28. The phrase "speaking to yourselves" (one to another) in Eph. is thus further explained. It is sometimes forgotten in Christian churches to-day that the psalm, hymn, or anthem may be a means of teaching as well as an expression of worship.

17 [do] all in the name of the Lord Jesus. Offer all your service through Him.

18 as it is fit in the Lord. See Eph. v. 21–24, and notes.

20 in all things. All things lawful: see Eph. v. 24.

25 he that doeth wrong. That is, both the master who tyrannises over his slave, and the slave who is unfaithful to his master. "The philosophers of Greece taught, and the laws of Rome assumed, that the slave was a chattel. But a chattel could have no rights. It would be absurd to talk of treating a chattel with justice. St. Paul places their relations in a totally different light" (*Archbishop Alexander*).

shall receive for. "Shall get back the wrong," etc.

CHAPTER IV

1 Masters, give unto your servants, etc. See note on Eph. vi. 9.

2 watch in the same. Lit., "being wakeful in it"—withstanding the listlessness which is apt to creep over long-continued devotion (*Lightfoot*).

3 of utterance. Rather, "for the word."

the mystery of Christ. See notes on Eph. vi. 19, 20.

5 redeeming the time. See notes on Eph. v. 16.

6 Let your speech be alway with grace. Or, "Let your discourse be always in grace"; *i.e.*, in a kind and winning spirit, seasoned with what is pure and salutary: cp. Eph. iv. 29. "Salt" (cp. Lev. ii. 13) both preserves food from corruption and renders palatable what otherwise might be distasteful. The words have special reference to the relation to non-Christians (ver. 5).

7 my state. Or, "my affairs," as in Eph. vi. 21; on which see note.

9 Onesimus. See Epistle to Philemon, ver. 10. He had come from Colossæ, but was not yet known there as a Christian.

10 sister's son. Rather, "cousin." "This relationship is not mentioned in the history, but it accounts for Barnabas's adherence to Mark in the contest that arose concerning him (Acts xv. 37–39)" (Barrett: *Companion to the Greek Testament*). The words "receive him" seem intended to show that no ground remained for doubting his fidelity: see 2 Tim. iv. 11.

11 These only. That is, These only *of the circumcision* had proved a comfort to Paul as fellow-labourers: all the rest of the Jewish Christians in Rome having been more or less in opposition to him: cp. Phil. i. 15–17. Epaphras (12), Luke, and Demas (14) were Gentiles.

13 Hierapolis. A large city in Phrygia, near Colossæ and Laodicea. On Laodicea, see Rev. iii. 14, and note.

16 the epistle from Laodicea. This was in all probability the letter known as the "Epistle to the Ephesians"; addressed to the churches in Proconsular Asia, which letter was to be passed on from Laodicea, where Tychicus would have left a copy of it on his way from Ephesus on to Colossæ. Ellicott and Lange, however, think that the reference is to a lost Epistle from Paul to the Laodiceans.

19 Remember my bonds. The "bonds" which shackle the hand that writes this salutation: cp. 1 Cor. xvi. 21; 2 Thess. iii. 17: see Rom. xvi. 22, note. "St. Paul's bonds were providential. If he had been continually moving from place to place in missionary journeys, the Church might never have possessed this Epistle. She has therefore good cause to *remember his bonds* with thankfulness. The word of God here written is *not bound*" (*Wordsworth*).

THE FIRST EPISTLE OF PAUL THE APOSTLE TO THE THESSALONIANS

INTRODUCTION

THESSALONICA, to which two of St. Paul's letters were written, has a special interest for us to-day. It is the modern Salonika, where during the Great War many of our troops were stationed. It was there that Paul preached on his first visit to Europe, and it was there that the hostile Jews compelled him to depart from the city (Acts xvii. 1–14). A noteworthy fact about the population of Salonika to-day is that it contains a large number of Spanish-speaking Jews.

They are the descendants of Jews who were banished from Spain in the time of Ferdinand and Isabella and found a refuge under Turkish rule in Macedonia.

This letter is now generally regarded as the first of St. Paul's Epistles and was written from Corinth in A.D. 51 or 52, very soon after his visit to Thessalonica. The same persecutors who had "shamefully entreated" Paul during his visit there (ii. 2) ill-treated the Christian residents there also (ii. 14), and Paul had sent Timothy to encourage and help them (iii. 2).

Timothy had brought back a cheering account of their stedfastness in trial, their faith and Christian activity (iii. 6–9), and the opening verses of the Epistle are an expression of thanks to God for this (i. 2–6). High praise is bestowed upon them when the apostle says that they were an example to all believers in Macedonia and Achaia, and wherever the Gospel was known (i. 7, 8). This is all the more remarkable as they were converts from heathenism (i. 9).

In chapter ii. Paul vindicates himself against insinuations and attacks. He declares his sincerity and honesty (3, 5), and calls them to witness to his unselfishness, labouring as he did with his own hands that he might not be a burden to others (ii. 9). He reminds them of his faithfulness in seeking earnestly their spiritual welfare (ii. 11, 12), and assures them that they, who are the fruits of his ministry, are his joy and "crown of rejoicing" (ii. 19, 20), his very life (iii. 8).

From iii. 12 to the end the apostle gives practical exhortations—to love (iii. 12); to purity (iv. 3–8); to quietness and industry (iv. 11); to sympathy and patience (v. 14); and to the avoidance even of the appearance of evil (v. 22). The reminder that they are children of light is a favourite thought with St. Paul, combined with the exhortation to put on the armour of light (cp. v. 5–8 with Rom. xiii. 11, 12).

The most distinctive feature of the Epistle is the great passage about the Lord's second coming (iv. 13–18). It is evident that it was mainly intended to comfort those whose dear ones had died without seeing the Saviour's return (iv. 13, 18). But it is also used as motive to activity (iii. 2, 6, 8). This was apparently necessary in view of the attitude of some who thought that, as the Lord was coming soon, He would put all right and they need not make any effort.

The passage does not speak of times and seasons (v. 1). "The chief topic," says Archdeacon Buckland (*Devotional Commentary*), "is not the *when* of the Coming, but the manner. . . . The Lord's own warning as to watchfulness may not be interpreted to mean morbid speculation as to times and seasons, or constant unrest, or the dismissal of all earthly responsibilities for a state of passive waiting."

"Let us, who are of the day, be sober."

CHAPTER I

1 Silvanus. The full form of the name Silas (Acts xv. 40, etc.). The apostle joins Silvanus and Timothy with himself, as having laboured with him in founding the church at Thessalonica: see Acts xvii. 1, 4.

2 We, "We" is sometimes used for Paul alone (ii. 18); but it here probably includes Silvanus and Timothy.

3 your work of faith, etc. "The work of your faith, and the labour of your love, and the constancy of your hope, in respect of our Lord Jesus Christ"; showing the practical, operative nature of their faith in Christ, the painstaking, energetic character of their love to Him, and the unswerving constancy of their hope in Him, amid all trials and sufferings. Here is the first grouping of the "faith, hope, and love" of 1 Cor. xiii. 13.

4 knowing, brethren beloved, your election of God. Rather, "knowing, brethren beloved of God, your election." They were known to be "elect" by their reception of the gospel (6), and by the fruits of faith in their lives.

5 in much assurance. Much confidence. Referring to the use of the same Greek word in Col. ii. 2, Heb. vi. 11, and x. 2. Archdeacon Buckland (*Devotional Commentary*) says: "Thus the Apostle suggests to us hearers who were profoundly moved, were soundly convinced, and manifestly experienced the influence of the Holy Spirit."

6 in much affliction. See Acts xvii. 5–9.

7 Macedonia and Achaia. Macedonia and Achaia were the two provinces into which the whole of Greece was divided by the Romans.

8 For from you sounded out, etc. By public report, and by your missionary efforts.

9 they themselves. The people of those countries (8).

what manner of entering in we had. Cp. ii. 1.

10 which delivered us. Rather, " who delivereth us " ; *i.e.*, our Deliverer. On " the wrath to come," see ii. 16.

CHAPTER II

1 not in vain. Or, " not empty," but full of power and results.

2 but even after we had suffered before. After their recent sufferings at Philippi (Acts xvi. 19–37). God emboldened them to speak at Thessalonica ; though there again it was " amid much conflict " : see Acts xvii. 5–9.

3 exhortation. The Greek word (παράκλησις) is noteworthy. It is the same thought as that suggested in the word Paraclete or Comforter. It might be translated " our message of help and comfort." Such all preaching ought to be.

4 as we were allowed. Rather, " have been approved " ; cp. 1 Tim. i. 12. " Allowed," in Old English, means the same.

6 burdensome. Either in exercising authority, or in claiming pecuniary support (cp. ver. 9), " as Christ's apostles " might rightly do.

7 even as a nurse, etc. Rather, " As a nursing mother would cherish her own children : so we, fondly loving you," etc.

9 because we would not be chargeable, etc. Or, " not to burden any of you " (6). He therefore " laboured " at his trade : see Acts xviii. 3. See also 2 Thess.; iii. 9, for the example of it, and Acts xx. 34, for its charitable object.

13 when ye received, etc. Rather, as R.V., " when ye received . . . ye accepted it." The distinction between " received " and " accepted " appears in the original.

15 and have persecuted us. Or, " chased us out " at Thessalonica, and elsewhere (see Acts xvii. 5–14 ; xiv. 2–6, 19).

are contrary to all men. Lange quotes Juvenal and Tacitus as showing the view held by Roman writers of the antipathy of the Jews to other nationalities.

16 for the wrath is come upon them, etc. God's anger was already coming on this unbelieving nation, and reached " its end," or height, in less than twenty years after this was written, in the destruction of Jerusalem.

17 for a short time. When Paul left Thessalonica he hoped to return very soon : but owing to various causes (see next verse) he did not go there again for five years. But as meanwhile he sent Timothy, he adds, " even I Paul."

18 Satan hindered us. By arousing opposition to the gospel.

19 rejoicing. Rather, " glorying " (R.V.).

CHAPTER III

1 we. " We " here evidently means Paul himself (see ver. 5), who, finding that he could not visit them, " could no longer forbear," and therefore sent Timothy : see note on Acts xvii. 15.

3 yourselves know, etc. Both by your own experience and my forewarning (4) : cp. 2 Tim. iii. 12. " St. Paul had told them of Christ's saying (John xvi. 13) " (*Bishop Alexander*).

6 now when Timotheus came. This *now* is emphatic. Timothy had just returned to the apostle.

8 for now we live. Your stedfastness is life to me.

10 perfect that which is lacking, etc. Or, " supply the deficiencies of your faith." Paul had been compelled to leave them almost immediately after their conversion (Acts xvii. 10), without instructing them so fully as he wished.

11 direct. By the guidance of Divine Providence. In this prayer, as also at 2 Thess. ii. 16, 17, the Lord Jesus is addressed equally with the Father ; the verb which includes both being in the singular.

13 His saints. " His holy ones."

CHAPTER IV

1 [so] ye would abound, etc. Carrying out more thoroughly the directions which we gave you by the Lord's authority, and which in fact you have already observed.

4 possess. Or, " acquire," *i.e.*, gain control over. To live chastely in the married state is a safeguard against irregular indulgence of the passions. " Vessel " here probably means *body* (" son corps," *French version*).

5 the lust of concupiscence. " The passion of lust " (R.V.), as opposed to rational and Christian attachment.

6 in [any] matter. Lit., " in *the* matter " ; *i.e.*, in the matter under discussion. Reference is to the double wrong caused by adultery.

the avenger of all such. Rather, " the avenger respecting *all these things* " ; which men treat as of little consequence, but God does not. " He who rejects " (8) these admonitions, " rejects God," who " called us, not for uncleanness, but in sanctification " : and for this purpose " gave His Holy Spirit unto you."

11 study to be quiet. " Endeavour earnestly," or " make it your ambition to be."

12 honestly. That is, " becomingly."

13 which are asleep. The best authorities read, " which are falling asleep," *i.e.*, from time to time.

others. Those who are not Christians.

14 in Jesus. Rather, " *through* Jesus " ; and the words are perhaps best connected with those that follow : " God will raise them up by means of Jesus."

15 by the word of the Lord. " In *a* word of the Lord " ; probably a special revelation on this subject : cp. 1 Cor. xv. 51.

we which are alive, etc. Such of us believers as may be then alive shall not " leave behind " those that are asleep ; for these " shall rise first " (16), *i.e.*, before the living in Christ ; and " afterwards we," etc. (17) : cp. 1 Cor. xv. 52.

16 with a shout. The Greek κέλευσμα means " a word of command " : so the Vulgate translates it, " in jussu."

the archangel. Or " *an* archangel " ; a leader among the angelic hosts : cp. Jude 9.

the trump. " Trumpet." Cp. 1 Cor. xv. 52.

17 in the clouds. Rather " *in* clouds " ; *i.e.*, as Jesus Himself ascended (Acts i. 9). " And so " (*i.e.*, after the resurrection of the dead, and the change of the living) all the saved will dwell with Christ for ever (John xiv. 3).

CHAPTER V

1 the times and the seasons. Of the Lord's coming (iv. 13–17).

ye have no need that I write unto you. For you know already from Christ's own words, all that can be known on the subject (see Matt. xxiv. 42–44).

2 as a thief in the night, etc. The Lord's return to the judgement will be as unexpected and sudden as the coming of a midnight robber; and as startling as the pang of childbirth (3).

4 darkness. The darkness of ignorance and unbelief.

6 as do others. Or, "as the rest," *i.e.,* the unbelieving world: see iv. 13.

8 putting on the breastplate, etc. As soldiers, who have to keep guard, and to face danger and death: see on Eph. vi. 14–17. Note the mention of faith, hope and love; cp. 1 Cor. xiii. 13.

9 hath not appointed us. Rather, "did not appoint us."

10 wake. Better, "watch." The Greek word is the same as that used in ver. 6.

12 know them which labour among you, etc. Regard them with the respect and gratitude due to their character, office, and labours: cp. Heb. xiii. 17; Phil. ii. 30.

14 unruly. Or, "disorderly": cp. iv. 11; 2 Thess. iii. 11.

18 In every thing give thanks. For all things are for your good: see Eph. v. 20.

this is the will of God, etc. This combination of joy, prayer, and gratitude (16, 17, 18).

19 Quench not the Spirit, etc. Do not resist or neglect His influences. We may do so by want of fidelity to Christ's teaching, to the voice of conscience in daily life.

22 from all appearance. "From every form" (R.V.).

23 your whole spirit, etc. The word *whole* should be read with "preserved." R.V., "May your spirit and soul and body be preserved entire, without blame."

24 Faithful is He that calleth you, etc. Difficult as this complete sanctification may seem, it is assured by God's faithfulness.

26 with a holy kiss. See note on Rom. xvi. 16.

[The first [Epistle] unto the Thessalonians, etc.] Plainly incorrect. A comparison of i. 1; iii. 1, with Acts xviii. 1, 5, shows that Paul had left Athens and gone to Corinth.

THE SECOND EPISTLE OF PAUL THE APOSTLE TO THE THESSALONIANS

INTRODUCTION

THIS letter, written a few months later than 1 Thessalonians, and not later than A.D. 53, deals with the same subjects as the First Epistle, and especially with the coming of the Lord.

The apostle renews his expression of thankfulness for their faith, their love to one another, and their patience in suffering (i. 3, 4). And then he puts them on their guard against misunderstandings that had arisen on the immediate approach of the Lord's return (ii. 1, 2). "He had spoken rather of the unexpectedness of the event than of its nearness" (*Bible Handbook*). For the references to the "man of sin" and "that wicked One," see notes on ii. 3, 8.

He also warns them against busybodies and persons who stir up strife (iii. 6, 11, 14, 15). His advice to withdraw from them (iii. 6, 14) may be compared with 1 Tim. vi. 5 and 1 Cor. v. 11.

The closing verses of the Epistle contain a memorable advice: "Be not weary in well doing" (iii. 13), and a memorable prayer: "The Lord of peace Himself give you peace always by all means" (iii. 16).

CHAPTER I

3 the charity, etc. That is, "your mutual love."

5 [which is] a manifest token, etc. See note on Phil. i. 28. Their patience and constancy were a sign of God's faithfulness to His people. He showed that He had Himself undertaken their cause—counting them worthy of His kingdom; and also that when the time of the manifestation of that kingdom should come, He would as certainly punish the persecutors, and give the sufferers release.

7 with His mighty angels. Properly, "with angels of His power," *i.e.,* by whom He exercises His power: see Matt. xiii. 41. R.V. joins the phrase *in flaming fire* to this description: "the revelation of the Lord Jesus from heaven with the angels of His power in flaming fire."

8 taking vengeance, etc. Or, "awarding punishments to them," etc.

10 glorified in His saints. Cp. 1 Thess. iii. 13, and note.

to be admired. Or, "wondered at."

11 worthy of [this] calling. Or, "of the calling." That is, of the Divine call, with its privileges and

future: cp. 1 Thess. ii. 12. The R.V. "of your calling" weakens the force of the original.

fulfil all the good pleasure, etc. Or, "perfect in you in power (*i.e.*, powerfully), every desire of goodness, and [every] work of faith": see note on 1 Thess. i. 3.

CHAPTER II

1 by the coming. Rather, "in regard to the coming." This clause is not an adjuration, but a statement of the subject, which the apostle wishes further to clear from misconception and abuse. The "gathering together unto Him" was announced in 1 Thess. iv. 17.

2 neither by spirit, etc. Do not listen to any prediction professing to be from the Spirit, nor to any declaration, either verbal or written, said to have come from me or my colleagues, to the effect that the day of judgement "is come."

3 a falling away. Rather, "*the* falling away," or "the apostasy"; namely, that about which the apostle had already informed them (see ver. 5). The interpretation of this passage (3–12) is confessedly very difficult. But the view of the best commentators is that all past defection and corruptions are but precursors of a more awful apostasy yet to come, which shall be headed by some one person, the Man of Sin, the Antichrist: see notes on Dan. viii. 26; xi. 31; 1 John ii. 18. Some things not plain to us were known to the Thessalonians (6).

the son of perdition. According to a common Hebraism; "destined to destruction": cp. John xvii. 12.

4 showing himself that he is God. Or, "representing himself to be God."

6 And now ye know what withholdeth. That is, ye know what keeps back the manifestation of the Man of Sin, until the time appointed him by God. The Christians at Thessalonica had been told what this restraining power was; but we are not informed. Many suppose that it was the control of the Roman Empire, on the decay of which the Papacy rose into power; others think that it refers, in general, to the restraining influence of law (or "organised human society": *Buckland*).

in his time. Rather, as R.V., "in his own season."

7 the mystery of iniquity. Lit., "the mystery of lawlessness; corresponding to "the lawless one" (A.V., "that Wicked," ver. 8).

letteth. Rather, "restraineth," the same verb as in ver. 6.

8 brightness. Rather, "manifestation," as the word is elsewhere translated.

9 with all power, etc. Rather, "with all power, and signs, and wonders of falsehood"; *i.e.*, all his power, signs, and wonders are essentially false.

11 for this cause. "Because they received not the love of the truth" (10).

12 damned. Better, "judged," as R.V.

14 whereunto. That is, to salvation. "By our gospel," *i.e.*, "by means of the gospel which we preached" (1 Thess. i. 5).

15 traditions. That is, the inspired apostle's oral or written instructions: cp. 1 Cor. xi. 2, in Greek.

CHAPTER III

1 may have [free] course. Lit., "may run"; may make swift progress in Corinth, where the apostle was now preaching, as it had done in Thessalonica. Respecting the opposition alluded to in ver. 2, see Acts xviii.

2 faith. Rather, "the faith"; they do not receive, but oppose the gospel.

3 the Lord. Our Lord Jesus Christ: cp. ii. 16, and see on ver. 5.

from evil. Or, as R.V., "from the evil *one*"; see notes, Matt. vi. 13; John xvii. 15.

5 the patient waiting for Christ. Rather, "the patience of Christ," *i.e.*, such constancy as He manifested.

6 disorderly. See note on 1 Thess. v. 14. "Tradition" here means *instruction*: see note on ii. 15; and cp. ver. 10.

8 wrought with labour, etc. See Acts xviii. 3, and note.

9 power. Or, "right"; namely, to require support from those to whom we minister (1 Cor. ix. 6).

12 that with quietness they work. As opposed to the lazy and meddlesome life of the busybodies.

13 But ye, brethren. That is, ye who are free from this fault.

be not weary. "Not in the sense of physical exhaustion from over-work, but weary in the sense of losing heart in the presence of discouragement. Cp. Gal. vi. 9" (Buckland in *Devotional Commentary*).

14 have no company with him. Lit., "do not mix yourselves up with him," not absolutely prohibiting all communication (see ver. 15), but only such social intercourse as would imply connivance at his misconduct: see note on 1 Cor. v. 10.

15 Yet. Rather, "And." Let this separation be regarded as correction rather than as punishment.

16 always by all means. "At all times, in all ways," R.V.

17 which is the token, etc. To attest the genuineness of the Epistle; for Paul generally employed an amanuensis to write the letter itself: cp. on Rom. xvi. 22.

[written from Athens.] Rather, from Corinth.

THE FIRST EPISTLE OF PAUL THE APOSTLE TO TIMOTHY

INTRODUCTION

THE great value of the three "Pastoral Epistles," 1 and 2 Timothy and Titus, is that they lay down principles for the guidance of the Christian minister and for the discipline of the Christian Church. Some portions of the letters, however, are local or temporary in their immediate application.

In the first chapter of this Epistle, for instance, written as it is to Timothy at Ephesus, reference is made on the one hand to Jewish teachers who made much of the law and genealogies (i. 4–7), and on the other to the evils of surrounding paganism (i. 9, 10). In the fourth chapter, the apostle refers to early heresies, which are not yet extinct in the Christian Church (ver. 3).

Of more general application are his counsels about public worship (ii. 1–8); the behaviour and dress of women (ii. 9–12); the character and duties of bishops and deacons (iii. 1–13); the personal character of Timothy himself, as an example for all preachers and teachers (iv. 6–8, 11–16); the treatment of widows (v. 3–13); rebukes (v. 1, 20); accusations and witnesses (v. 19); masters and servants (vi. 1, 2); wealth and its temptations (vi. 9, 10); and the duty of faithful dealing with the rich (vi. 17–19). The principles here laid down are of permanent value in the Church of Christ.

And these practical counsels are enforced by an appeal to the highest ideals and motives (i. 11, 15; ii. 3–6; iv. 10) and especially by the solemn charge to Timothy to live and work as in the sight of God and as one who looks for "the appearing of our Lord Jesus Christ."

One expression which occurs three times in this Epistle (i. 15; iii. 1; iv. 9; vi. 13–16), and also occurs in 2 Tim. (ii. 11) and Titus (iii. 8), is "This is a faithful saying." T. A. Gurney, in the *Devotional Commentary*, has two chapters on "The Five *Faithful Sayings*," in which he shows the significance of the phrase, and how we find in the respective verses in which it occurs our assurance of salvation, our ideal for service, our inspiration of hope, our incentive to holiness, and our secret of fellowship.

The Epistle was written after St. Paul's first imprisonment and between A.D. 64 and 67, probably in A.D. 66. It is generally believed to have been written in Macedonia.

CHAPTER I

1 by the commandment of God. As recorded in Acts ix. 15; xiii. 2: cp. Gal. i. 1.

2 own. R.V., "my true child in faith": cp. Phil. ii. 22.

4 fables. The "fables" were probably Rabbinical legends taught by a class of Judaisers (cp. Titus i. 14): the "genealogies" family pedigrees, to which some allegorical meanings were attached (cp. Titus iii. 9).

godly edifying. The correct reading, a difference of one letter in the Greek, gives us "a dispensation (or 'stewardship') of God"; *i.e.*, "these things contribute to disputations rather than to the exercise of God's stewardship in faith."

[so do]. These words are not in the original.

5 of the commandment. Or, "of the instruction": cp. Gal. v. 6.

6 from which. That is, from a pure heart, etc. "Swerved": or, according to the literal meaning of the Greek, "missed the mark."

jangling. Idle talk.

8 lawfully. According to its nature and design: see vers. 9, 10.

9 the law. Or, "law" in general.

murderers of fathers, etc. Or, "strikers of fathers, and strikers of mothers"; not necessarily implying murder: see the command in Exod. xxi. 15. The apostle is referring to the Commandments from the fifth to the ninth.

10 menstealers. Kidnappers or slave dealers; the most flagrant violation of the eighth commandment.

(the) sound doctrine. Or, "the healthful teaching."

11 the glorious gospel, etc. Lit., "the gospel of the glory of the happy God." "The glad tidings."

12 enabled me. Or, "gave me power" for my work (Acts ix. 22). Calvin points out that the Greek word conveys the idea not of a single act, but of continuous strengthening.

putting me into the ministry. More precisely, "appointing me to His service."

13 injurious. "Ungovernable."

because I did it ignorantly in unbelief. See notes on Luke xxiii. 34; Acts iii. 17. Paul does not say this to excuse himself, but to show that he had still been within the pale of Divine mercy. "He had not sinned against his better convictions (Mark iii. 28–30); he had not deliberately set at nought the counsel of God, and defied Heaven to its face" (*P. Fairbairn*). Yet the *whole* account of God's mercy does not lie here: the latter part of the statement is essential; "and the grace," etc.

15 worthy of all acceptation. Worthy to be fully received by all without reserve or hesitation. These "faithful sayings" are characteristic of the Pastoral Epistles: see iii. 1; iv. 9; 2 Tim. ii. 11; Titus iii. 8.

of whom I am chief. This, like Eph. iii. 8, is the language of profound humility and godly sorrow.

16 that in me first. Rather, "that in me as *chief*"; as in ver. 15: implying that one of the objects for which God had shown mercy to him was that none should despair. As he thinks of this wondrous grace, Paul breaks forth in adoration of Him to whom alone, as "the Eternal King, the Incorruptible, Invisible, Only God" ("wise" should be omitted, as having no good authority), the honour and glory of salvation must be given.

18 by them. Properly, "in them": *i.e.*, clad in them, as armour for the fight. The French version gives the words a slightly different turn: "c'est que tu y répondes en combattant dans cette bonne guerre."

war a good warfare. Rather, "war *the* good warfare": see 2 Tim. iv. 7, and note.

19 put away. Or, "thrust from them" (R.V.), implying deliberateness and determination. Those who wilfully violate conscience are likely to renounce all belief of the truth.

20 Hymenæus. Hymenæus is mentioned in 2 Tim. ii. 17, as a leader in false doctrine. An "Alexander" is mentioned in Acts xix. 33; 2 Tim. iv. 14; but whether it was the same or not is unknown.

whom I have delivered. Rather, "whom I delivered" (R.V.), *i.e.*, probably when he was last at Ephesus. Respecting the nature of the act, see note on 1 Cor. v. 5.

CHAPTER II

1 for all men, etc. Rather, "I first of all exhort," etc.; *i.e.*, I begin *my directions* with this. It is not intended that the "intercession" should be the first thing in worship; especially in the public assemblies of the faithful. Not only believers, but all classes of men should be prayed for. This direction would remove any doubt as to the propriety of praying for heathen magistrates.

2 that we may lead a quiet and peaceable life, etc. Unmolested by persecution on the part of our earthly rulers. "Honesty," gravity or propriety.

3 this. Such intercession (1, 2).

4 who will have, etc. Rather, "who willeth," *i.e.*, whose will is that, etc. We should pray "for all men," because God wills "that all men should be saved, and [in order to that] should come unto the knowledge of the truth" of the gospel. Hence the proclamation (6, 7) to all mankind, that as there is one God, so there is one Mediator, who alone can intervene between our guilty souls and God, so as to obtain our pardon and peace.

5 the man. It is our Lord's manhood that connects Him with that universal human nature of which the apostle is speaking.

6 a ransom. The word here used (*antilutron*, corresponding with *lutron*, Matt. xx. 28) forcibly conveys the idea that our Lord's death was a *substitution*, "on behalf of all."

to be testified in due time. "The testimony to be borne in its own times."

8 I will. Rather, "I desire," authoritatively.

men. Rather, "the men"; as distinguished from the women (9), who were to join in the worship in silence, and in modesty of dress and behaviour.

doubting. Rather, "disputation," as in Phil. ii. 14.

9 shamefastness. An old English word for *modesty* (formed like sted*fast*ness: no reference to the *face*). So printed in original editions of A.V. "The City of Diana needed, what no priestess of the goddess learnt within her sacred precincts, the shamefastness and sobriety which are the truest grace of womanhood" (T. A. Gurney in *Devotional Commentary*).

sobriety="sobermindedness."

with broided hair. Or, "in braidings"; probably of the hair; suggesting extravagant display and waste of time. See 1 Pet. iii. 3.

12 I suffer not a woman to teach. The generally-recognised rules of womanly decorum are to be respected in the church. At Ephesus, as at Corinth (1 Cor. xiv. 34), it would be regarded as shameful for a woman to assume the office of teacher.

14 being deceived, etc. Rather, "being utterly deceived has come to be in transgression." Created last, she was the first to transgress.

15 in childbearing. Rather, she shall come "safely through childbirth" (*Moffatt*).

CHAPTER III

1 a bishop. See note, Phil. i. 1.

2 the husband of one wife. This may mean, either that an overseer or pastor of the church must not, like many Jews at that period, have more than one wife at a time; or that he must not have given way to the prevalent custom of divorce.

3 given to wine. "Violent over wine" (Wace in *Speaker's Commentary*).

4 one that ruleth well his own house, etc. This verse, like ver. 2, clearly implies that the minister of the gospel might be a family man, not bound by a vow of celibacy.

having [his] children in subjection, etc. Keeping with dignity his children in subjection.

6 not a novice. One newly converted, if raised to such a post, would be apt to be inflated with pride, and thus to fall under the condemnation which the devil brought upon himself by that sin.

7 the snare of the devil. If Satan can destroy a minister's reputation in the world, he thereby harasses his soul, spoils his usefulness, and injures the church.

8 greedy of filthy lucre. A commonly misused phrase. Money or gain is not "filthy" or evil in itself. The "filthiness" or evil is in the man using it and not in the money. The Greek word αἰσχροκερδεῖς really means "sordidly greedy of gain." See also Titus i. 11.

9 mystery. See note on Matt. xiii. 11.

10 let these also, etc. After being tested, let them serve as deacons, provided that they are irreproachable.

11 wives. Rather, "women"; meaning apparently women who acted as deaconesses (who might or might not be deacons' wives): cp. note on Rom. xvi. 1; and see Titus ii. 3, 4.

12 husbands of one wife. See above on ver. 2.

13 purchase to themselves a good degree. They "gain for themselves an honourable standing."

15 the pillar and ground of the truth. Rather, "a pillar and ground of the truth." Referring to the community of believers, which, when well disciplined according to the apostolic teaching, is a living witness and support of the truth. "The Church is the pillar and basement of the truth, because it sustains it, as Calvin says, by making it known by its preaching, by preserving it unmutilated and pure, and by transmitting it to posterity" (Wace, in *Speaker's Commentary*). Cp. Article XX. of the Thirty-Nine Articles.

16 mystery of godliness. The (revealed) secret of practical religion. The particulars that follow, setting forth the facts of redemption, appear from their terse and balanced form to have been some early creed or hymn. It may be arranged thus, so as to mark the antithetic clauses:

"who was manifested in flesh,
justified in spirit;
seen of angels:
preached among (the) nations,
believed on in the world;
received up in glory."

God. According to the reading now generally adopted by scholars, the "mystery of godliness" is itself declared to have been manifested in flesh. "Confessedly great is the mystery of godliness, *even* He who was manifested." Christ incarnate is the mystery, as in the approved reading of Col. ii. 2, where see note.

justified in the spirit. These words are very variously interpreted. No interpretation seems so satisfactory as that of Gurney (*Devotional Commentary*), or more in keeping with St. Paul's use of the word "justify." It is that the Resurrection was the Saviour's justification. He was then "declared to be the Son of God with power according to the spirit of holiness" (Rom. i. 3).

CHAPTER IV

1 doctrines of devils. Or, "teachings of demons"; *i.e.*, emanating from evil spirits, and showing themselves in the "hypocrisy of those [teachers] who speak lies, and who are branded in their own conscience," being either insensible or shameless.

3 forbidding to marry. By extolling celibacy as more holy and meritorious than the married state.

6 whereunto thou hast attained. Rather, "which thou hast closely followed."

7 old wives' fables. Silly fables: see note on i. 4.

8 bodily exercise profiteth little (for a little). Either, "in some small degree," or "for a little while." The Apostle does not condemn physical exercise. But he shows its insufficiency for the needs of the whole man. Godliness benefits both body and soul, the life of the present and that of the hereafter.

9 This is a faithful saying. The preceding statement; "godliness," etc.

10 therefore. *i.e.*, it is for the sake of this "promise" that we endure toil and reproach; because we have set our hope on God.

12 Let no man despise thy youth. Timothy must have been at this time over thirty years old, some twelve to fifteen years having passed since he became connected with the apostle (Acts xvi. 1–3).

13 reading. Properly, "the reading"; namely, of the sacred Scriptures. Till Paul's return Timothy was diligently to maintain the public reading of Scripture in the church; accompanying it with "exhortation" and "teaching."

14 the gift, etc. The supernatural endowment (see 1 Cor. xii. 4–11) which Timothy had received on his appointment to the ministry (see i. 18; 2 Tim. i. 6), and in accordance with the intimation of one or more "prophets" of the church; imparted in connexion with the act of designation by the combined body of elders.

15 thy profiting. Thy progress.

16 the doctrine. Rather, "the teaching": see on ver. 13. The faithful preacher secures his own salvation, and is made a blessing to his people: cp. Rom. x. 13–15.

CHAPTER V

1 Rebuke not an elder. That is, "Do not reprove harshly an aged man;" an elder, not in office, but in age.

intreat. Exhort or persuade.

3 Honour. Cp. ver. 16. "A widow indeed" ("left alone," ver. 5), having no relative to whom she could look for support.

4 nephews. An old word for "descendants" of any degree (*nepotes*). R.V., "grandchildren."

piety. That is, "filial piety"; which is to be shown partly by providing for the wants and comforts of the aged, the duty of supporting whom devolves in the first instance upon children and grandchildren.

requite. "To make return for" their care or love.

5 desolate. "Left alone": having none on whom she could depend; and being thus led to look to God alone in constant devotion (cp. Luke ii. 37).

6 dead. Spiritually dead.

8 the faith. Faith "is active in love, and inseparable from love; and releases none from natural duties, but imposes them on all" (*Lange*).

an infidel. Rather, an "unbeliever."

9 Let not a widow be taken, etc. Lit., "Let one be put down on the list as a widow, not under sixty years old." A widow who had been a faithful wife to one husband (see note on iii. 2), and had devoted her better days to family duties and to works of piety and charity, when she reached the age of sixty, was to be enrolled amongst those whom the church maintained in comfort and honour, while she dedicated herself to its work.

11 refuse. That is, Do not put them on the roll of church widows, for when they have become impatient of the restraint, which they have taken upon themselves as a religious obligation in joining the roll or order of widows they "desire to marry"; "having judgement" (*i.e.*, a sense of guilt) because they have broken their first faith (*i.e.*, their engagement to celibacy); and withal "they learn," etc.

14 the younger [women]. That is, the younger widows, as the context shows. "The greatest gift of Christianity to the social fabric is the development of the idea of home" (G. Matheson: *Spiritual Development of St. Paul*).

the adversary. Any opponent of the gospel.

16 If any man or woman that believeth have widows. That is, "widowed relatives": see on ver. 3.

17 doctrine. Or, "teaching." Those who excel in ruling or teaching the church, or in both, have a double claim to honour and support (see Deut. xxv. 4).

18 And the labourer, etc. A proverb, found also in Matt. x. 10 and Luke x. 7.

19 but. Or, "except." For his duties expose him to the malice of the ill-disposed.

20 Them that sin rebuke, etc. Referring to elders who transgress. These are to be reproved openly before the church, as a warning to others.

21 the elect angels. God's chosen attendants and ministers of His government. "Probably those especially selected by God as His messengers to the human race, such as Gabriel" (*Conybeare and Howson*).

without preferring. Rather, "without prejudging"; laying aside preconceived views or conclusions.

22 Lay hands, etc. In ordination to office in the church. You become responsible in part for the sins of those on whom you hastily lay hands.

23 Drink no longer water, etc. Rather, as R.V., "Be no longer a drinker of water": *i.e.*, *only;* but "use a little wine" medicinally. St. Paul feared that Timothy's abstemiousness would diminish the strength both of body and mind which the wise and energetic maintenance of discipline demanded. Paley (*Horæ Paulinæ*, ch. xii. No. 4) quotes this passage as an evidence of the genuineness of the Epistle.

24 Some men's sins are open beforehand, etc. Some sins are so evident that they go as heralds before those who commit them, as an evil report outstrips a man (*Lange*): whilst others require "after-proof." So also (ver. 25) some good deeds are evidently and unmistakeably such; whilst some are "otherwise"; *i.e.*, they are really good, but not so obvious and above suspicion. These two verses are given as a reason for the exercise of cautior hastily accepting men for the eldership.

CHAPTER VI

1 under the yoke. Slaves.

2 but rather do them service, etc. Or, "but the rather (*i.e.*, the more) serve them, because those who receive the benefit" of such service are believers and beloved. Un-Christian masters should be served with respect for the gospel's sake; believing masters, also, for their own.

4 doting. Lit., "diseased," *i.e.*, in mind; descriptive of a morbid spirit; opposed to "healthy," or "wholesome" (3).

5 destitute of the truth. Rather, as R.V., "bereft of the truth"; having possessed, and lost it.

that gain is godliness. Or, "that godliness is a source of gain"; *i.e.*, a mere trade for gain; "que la piété est un moyen de gain" (*French version*). Gain, however, it is with contentment; which looks on earthly things as soon to be left, and is satisfied with needful "food and covering."

9 they that will be rich. Rather, "they that want to be rich," etc.; making wealth the great object of pursuit.

10 the root of all evil. Rather, "a root of all kinds of evil," R.V., from which they all grow.

11 man of God. That is, one devoted not to the world, but to God.

12 a good profession. Rather, "*the* good (or noble) confession" (and so in ver. 13). "Good" refers to the truth which is "confessed" by the disciple, and has been "attested" by our Lord (13).

14 [this] commandment. Properly, "the commandment": all the moral obligations of Christian truth (i. 5).

15 which. Namely, Christ's appearing.

King of kings, and Lord of lords. This title of Divine supremacy is given to our Lord in Rev. xvii. 14; xix. 16.

17 uncertain riches. Rather, "the uncertainty of riches," both as to possession, and as to enjoyment (Prov. xxiii. 5).

to enjoy. The 18th verse shows wherein the true enjoyment of wealth consists.

19 laying up in store, etc. See Luke xvi. 9–13, and notes.

eternal life. Another reading, which is supported by the best MSS., gives the rendering: "the life which is life indeed" (R.V.). See Luke xii. 14, 15, and notes.

20 keep (guard) **that which is committed to thy trust.** "The deposit" of the pure gospel, entrusted to thee to dispense to others (2 Tim. i. 13, 14).

science. Rather, "the knowledge"; the false counterfeit of true Christian knowledge (see 1 Cor. xii. 8); in different ways opposing the gospel truths. This false teaching was already at work in the church, and afterwards became very prevalent in the form of the Gnostic heresies.

[The first to Timothy, etc.] The subscription is plainly incorrect. See note at close of Romans.

THE SECOND EPISTLE OF PAUL THE APOSTLE TO TIMOTHY

INTRODUCTION

THIS letter followed very soon upon the First Epistle, and was written about the close of A.D. 66 or early in A.D. 67.

When it was written, St. Paul was looking forward to his approaching death (iv. 6). But he meets it without fear (i. 7, 12). He is "ready to be offered" (iv. 6). His confidence is in his living Lord (iv. 18).

But he knows the grief his imprisonment and certain martyrdom are causing to Timothy (i. 4). And the Epistle is therefore one of comfort, cheerfulness and parting counsels. He recalls with thankfulness Timothy's early training and his personal faith (i. 5). He asserts his own confidence in Christ. Lest there should arise in Timothy's mind any feeling of shame that his leader is a prisoner in chains, he says, "Be not thou therefore ashamed of the testimony of our Lord or of me his prisoner" (i. 8). He is suffering hardship for the Gospel's sake (i. 12), but he is "not ashamed," showing that he is still the same in his loyalty to Christ in Rome as he was before he came there (cp. Rom. i. 16). The prison has made no difference to him except to increase his triumphant assurance (iv. 8). He may suffer bonds, but the word of God cannot be imprisoned (ii. 9). He may be put to death, but he looks to Timothy to carry on the work that he has begun (i. 14; iv. 2. 5).

He therefore counsels the younger man to be steadfast in the truth (i. 13; iii. 14), and to "hold straight onward" (Bishop Moule) in teaching it (ii. 15); to endure hardness (ii. 3); to be careful in the cultivation of his personal character (ii. 21, 22); to avoid profitless discussions and controversies (ii. 23); to be a faithful preacher and fearless pastor (iv. 2, 5).

The Epistle, therefore, is one for the constant study of every minister of the Gospel, and of every Christian congregation, that they may see the ideal that is expected of a minister of Jesus Christ. It has a double force in the fact that its glowing words came from the heart of one who had suffered, and was then suffering, trials, hardships, and persecutions for the Gospel's sake.

And the Apostle's own tender thought of others is manifest throughout, He remembers with gratitude the kindness and loyalty of Onesiphorus (i. 16–18) and the friendship of Aquila and Priscilla (iv. 19), and shows that he has forgiven Mark's one mistake and thinks only of his helpfulness (iv. 11). "He is 'Apostle of Christ Jesus' (i. 1) even to the end. . . . A serene dignity breathes in this final use of the apostolic title. It means an absolute service. It implies, in this man's case, a life which has been full of exhausting and difficult labours, and now a death violent and unjust. But it means also a relation to JESUS CHRIST profound and special; to belong to Him, to be used by Him, in life and in death. And this not only gave a divine energy to the fulness of St. Paul's prime; it infuses here a divine tranquillity into his parting hour" (Bishop Moule, in *Devotional Commentary*).

CHAPTER I

1 an apostle, etc. See notes on Rom. i. 1, and Gal. i. 1. The Greek preposition translated "according to" really means here "for the purpose of." Paul's apostleship had for its object to proclaim the promise, etc.

3 from my forefathers. As a Christian he continued to worship the God of his fathers (Acts xxiv. 14). This was what the Jews denied; but the apostle's "conscience" was "pure" in the matter.

4 being mindful of thy tears. Perhaps at their last parting.

5 thy grandmother Lois, and thy mother Eunice. Who had taught him in childhood the word of God (iii. 15): and had perhaps become Christians with him (Acts xvi. 1). On the coincidence between this Epistle and the narrative in the Acts of the Apostles, see Paley's *Horæ Paulinæ*, ch. xii. No. 2.

6 the putting (laying) **on of my hands.** The apostle taking the chief part in Timothy's ordination: see note on 1 Tim. iv. 14.

7 a sound mind. The Greek word may mean here "discipline." But the application is not very clear.

8 be thou partaker of the afflictions of the gospel. "Suffer hardship with me for the gospel."

according to the power of God. "The great things done by God in the matter of salvation are a ground and motive for something correspondent being done by us" (*P. Fairbairn*).

9 which was given . . . before the world began (lit., "from times eternal"). "Ages ago." "It was given from the beginning, it needed only time for its manifestation" (*Ellicott*).

10 who hath abolished death. Rather, "has deprived death of its power." Cp. 1 Cor. xv. 12–26, and Heb. ii. 14, 15.

immortality. Lit., "incorruption." To bring to light is not precisely the same as to "reveal." The phrase suggests rather the "throwing light upon that which was dimly shown before."

12 I know whom, etc. The emphasis is as given in the R.V., "I know *Him*, whom I," etc. Not simply, I know *who it is*, but I am acquainted with Himself. Faith is thus shown to be not mere intellectual assent, but personal trust in a living person. "I know Him whom I have trusted" would be a better rendering.

to keep that which I have committed, etc. "To guard my deposit," meaning probably himself and all his interests (cp. iv. 8).

13 form. Or, "pattern," R.V., as in 1 Tim. i. 16. Hold to this pattern in faith and love, *i.e.*, let it not be an empty dogma, but a power in your heart and life.

14 That good thing, etc., The blessed gospel: cp. 1 Tim. vi. 20. The phrase is similar to that in ver. 12, "guard the deposit" in thy hands. Let us, by the power of the Holy Spirit, do for Christ what He does for us.

15 all they which are in Asia, etc. The meaning probably is, that all the Christians from Proconsular Asia (except Onesiphorus, vers. 16, 17) who had visited Rome during Paul's imprisonment, had shunned him, being ashamed of his bonds. Their conduct is mentioned perhaps as a hint to Timothy to act a bolder and kinder part; as in ver. 8.

Phygellus and Hermogenes. Professed Christians of whom nothing more is known.

16 the house of Onesiphorus. Who himself appears to have been absent from Ephesus at the time. There is no ground for supposing, with some, that he was no longer living: cp. iv. 19.

for he oft refreshed me. By active kindness and sympathy. The prayer, ver. 18, suggests the words of our Lord (Matt. xxv. 36).

CHAPTER II

2 thou hast heard. Particularly when he was set apart to the ministry (cp. 1 Tim. i. 18), in the presence and with the sanction of "many witnesses."

3 endure hardness. Rather, "suffer hardship with me."

4 No man that warreth. More precisely, as R.V., "No soldier on service": cp. Luke iii. 4.

5 strive for masteries. Lit., "contend for a prize," *i.e.*, in the games.

lawfully. According to the rules of the public games.

6 The husbandman that laboureth, etc. It is the husbandman who labours (not the idle one) that has the first right to the fruits.

11 if we be dead with Him. Properly, "if we died with Him"; giving ourselves up to "die daily" (1 Cor. xv. 31).

13 if we believe not, etc. Rather, "if we be faithless, He remains faithful," and will fulfil His word. These words have more than once comforted those who, in times of mental or bodily trouble, thought that God had forsaken them.

15 rightly dividing. Lit., "cutting straight." Some understand this metaphor to be that of a ploughman cutting a straight furrow (so *Bishop Moule*); others take it to refer to the cutting of cloth. But the essential thought is the same, that the Christian preacher or teacher should be faithful and straightforward in his treatment and application of the Divine word.

17 a canker. Lit., "a gangrene," a mortification spreading itself.

18 saying that the resurrection is past already. It seems that these false teachers admitted the future life of the soul, but denied the resurrection of the body, and insisted that the moral renovation of believers in Christ (see Rom. vi. 3–5) was the only resurrection to be expected. They thus assailed "the foundation" of the Christian faith: see 1 Cor. xv., and notes.

19 the foundation of God standeth sure. Rather, "God's firm foundation standeth." Some men's faith may be overthrown (18); but the truth still stands as the firm basis of the church, bearing two inscriptions, which are the seal of God's authority: the first being a consolatory assurance that the Lord knows His people (see Psa. i. 6, and note); and the second a warning against all ungodliness. The first declares God's sovereignty, the second His people's responsibility.

20 But in a great house, etc. The thought of "the foundation" suggests that of "the house." While the security of the spiritual edifice is pledged, it must be remembered that, as in a house there are vessels of a baser kind, so in the visible church there will be persons and things unworthy of it.

21 from these. From "evil men and seducers," represented by vessels "to dishonour" (20); the kind of persons indicated in ver. 16 and the last clause of ver. 20.

22 Flee also youthful lusts. Timothy was yet in the prime of life (see 1 Tim. iv. 12).

24 must not strive. Must not be quarrelsome in the way in which he maintains the truth.

26 recover themselves. Or, "return to soberness"; with the idea of *escape* understood. "Wake up and escape" (*Wace*). The French version has: "Et qu'ils reviendront à eux-mêmes, en se dégageant des pièges du diable."

who are taken captive by him at ("for," or "unto") **His will.** *Him* and *His* here represent two different Greek pronouns. The probable meaning is: "having been taken captive by him (*i.e.*, by the servant of the Lord, ver. 24) for His will (*i.e.*, the will of God): see R.V., and marg. "Self-yielded, with a strange new joy, to the hands of his loving emancipator; blessing him, and rejoicing to become with him the ennobled vassal of the will of God" (Moule in *Devotional Commentary*)

CHAPTER III

1 perilous times. Lit., "difficult" or "grievous" times. The period here spoken of appears to be predicted also in 2 Thess. ii. 1–12; 1 Tim. iv. 1–3.

2 men. Professed followers of Christ (see ver. 5).

3 trucebreakers. Rather, "relentless."

incontinent. "Without self-control" generally (R.V.).

despisers of those that are good. Rather, "no lovers of good" (R.V.).

4 heady, highminded. Or, "rash, puffed up."

5 having a form of godliness. Keeping the name and profession of Christianity, but "having denied" or renounced its influence on the heart and life.

6 laden with sins. From the burden of which these designing men promise them relief. In later times this was done by auricular confession and priestly absolution, by which women are specially led captive.

8 Jannes and Jambres. These are the traditional names of two of the magicians of Egypt: see Exod. vii. 11, and note. They are often mentioned by name in Jewish writings, and Origen twice mentions an apocryphal book bearing their names. Pliny also refers to them (see *Hastings' Dictionary of the Bible*).

10 thou hast fully known. Rather, "Thou didst closely follow my teaching," etc. (see note on Luke i. 3).

11 Antioch. Antioch in Pisidia: see Acts xiii., xiv., and notes. This verse refers to Timothy's earliest observation of the apostle's career, a sample of all the rest.

12 all that will live. Properly, "who want to live." This verse contains a general truth, previously declared by our Lord (John xv. 20), and applicable more or less to all true Christians.

13 seducers. Properly, "magicians": see ver. 8, and note. R.V., "impostors."

14 knowing of whom thou hast learned [them]. If the singular pronoun for "of whom" (τίνος) is read, it would refer to Paul himself; but if the plural (τίνων), which is adopted in Nestle's Greek text, it refers to Timothy's early teachers.

15 which are able to make thee wise, etc. It is of the Old Testament that this is said: for it testifies of Christ (John v. 39). Much more must the New Testament, in which He is fully made known, be "profitable," etc. (16). It is instructive to notice that while the apostle foretells the prevalence of errors, he directs Christians, in order to be armed against them, to the study of the existing Scriptures.

16 All Scripture. Rather, as R.V., "Every Scripture."

given by inspiration of God. One word in original, *theopneustos*, "divinely-inspired." The R.V., with many of the best expositors, translates the phrase, "Every Scripture inspired of God [is] also profitable," etc. This rendering is adopted by the ancient Greek expositors (Origen, Chrysostom); by the Latin Vulgate; by Wyclif, Tyndale, and Cranmer; and in modern times by Alford, Ellicott, Wordsworth.

17 perfect. Or. "complete": in all parts and proportions.

CHAPTER IV

1 at his appearing. Rather, "by his appearing," with a comma after "dead."

2 be instant. "Keep at thy post"; be assiduous; not only embracing opportunities, but making them. "Have no definite time; let it always be time for thee" (*Chrysostom*).

3 having itching ears. Running after every new teacher whose fancies suit their corrupt inclinations.

5 make full proof of thy ministry. Or, "perform fully thy ministry" as an evangelist: see note on Eph. iv. 11.

6 I am now ready to be offered. Lit., "I am already being poured out," *i.e.*, as a drink-offering or libation; see Phil. ii. 17, and note. Paul now regarded his martyrdom as near and certain.

7 I have fought a good fight. "I have maintained the good contest," like one striving in the Grecian games: see notes on 1 Cor. ix. 26, and 2 Tim. ii. 5. The figure includes all, or any of, the contests in the games (*Wace*).

I have kept the faith. I have guarded the faith as a sacred deposit, entrusted to my care.

8 a crown. Rather, "*the* crown." Cp. 1 Cor. ix. 25; Rev. ii. 10.

that love. Should be rendered "that have loved," *i.e.*, "who shall then be found to have loved, and to be still loving" (*Alford*).

9 shortly. "Quickly"; for my martyrdom is at hand, and all my friends except Luke (11) are away.

10 Demas. Demas is honourably mentioned in Col. iv. 14, and Philem. 24; and it should be observed that what is here laid to his charge is not apostasy, but unwillingness to remain with Paul, probably at the risk of his life. Of Crescens, or of the reasons why he and Titus had left, nothing is known.

Dalmatia. A district of Illyricum, still bearing the same name, on the eastern shore of the Adriatic.

11 profitable. See Col. iv. 10.

12 have I sent. Properly, "I sent." If Timothy was at or near Ephesus, he could leave the more easily, as Tychicus would be there.

13 cloke. A warm cloak would be useful in the coming "winter" (see ver. 21). The "books" were writings on *papyrus* or some other frail material; the "parchments" were writings on prepared *skins*, and were doubtless "especially" valuable.

14 Alexander. This Alexander is perhaps the same as in Acts xix. 33. What was the nature of the "evil" we cannot tell. Some have argued from the connexion that it was connected with the apostle's trial. The phrase in Greek is plural: "many evils." *Lange* renders, "brought many evil charges against me."

the Lord reward him. R.V., "The Lord will render to him," etc. The apostle leaves his enemy in the hands of God.

16 my first answer ("defence"). Before the Emperor Nero; when some Christian friends on whom he had counted for support had been deterred from appearing, probably by Nero's fury against the Christians. But though men forsook him, his Lord did not; for He "put strength in" the apostle to declare the gospel fully before all.

17 that by me the preaching might be fully known. Or, "that through me the message might be fully proclaimed," R.V.

out of the mouth of the lion. This may mean the cruel Nero; or, generally, imminent peril of death.

18 from every evil work. From every attempt to overcome my stedfast faith in Christ. *Wace* notes that the Greek words here used are the same as those of the petition in the Lord's Prayer, "deliver us from evil."

19 Prisca. See Acts xviii. 2.

20 Trophimus (have) **I left at Miletum** (Miletus). Trophimus had accompanied Paul to Jerusalem (Acts xxi. 29). This passage, therefore, distinctly supports the supposition of a journey in Asia by the apostle after the close of the history of the Acts.

21 before winter. Before the navigation was closed for the winter (Acts xxvii. 12).

22 you. Timothy and his fellow-labourers.

[The Second Epistle unto Timotheus, etc.] This subscription is entitled to no weight: see note at the end of Romans.

THE EPISTLE OF PAUL THE APOSTLE TO TITUS

INTRODUCTION

In each of the three chapters of this letter there is a memorable saying. The three passages give distinction to it, and are keynotes of its entire message. The first is, "Unto the pure all things are pure" (i. 15). The second is, "The grace of God has appeared bringing salvation to all men, teaching us that denying ungodliness and worldly lusts, we should live soberly, righteously, and godly, in this present world; looking for that blessed hope, and the glorious appearing of our great God and Saviour Jesus Christ; who gave himself for us that he might redeem us from all inquity and purify unto himself a peculiar people, zealous of good works" (ii. 11–14). The third is, "Not by works of righteousness which we have done, but according to his mercy he saved us, by the washing of regeneration, and renewing of the Holy Ghost" (iii. 5).

In other words, the Epistle is a call to purity, and these verses supply the motive to it and the power for it. The call was necessary anywhere in that Pagan world. It was especially necessary in Crete (i. 12).

St. Paul therefore exhorts Titus, as the bishop or overseer of the church in Crete, to be himself an example of purity, in conduct, in teaching and in speech generally (ii. 7–9). The other bishops or elders are also to cultivate purity in their personal and family life, as well as in their teaching (i. 5–9). For old and young, men and women, purity of character is enjoined (ii. 2–6). So in relation to the State and its rulers, in relation to the neighbours among whom they lived, the behaviour of Christians is to be free from reproach (iii. 1–3). And the Church must safeguard its purity by enforcing discipline (iii. 10, 11).

Thus, though the Epistle has many points of similarity with 2 Timothy it has special characteristics of its own. It is most probable that it was written in A.D. 67 from Macedonia, after Paul's first imprisonment in Rome, in the journey during which he left Titus in Crete (i. 5), on his way to Nicopolis in Thrace where he expects Titus to join him (iii. 12). From 2 Tim. iv. 10, we learn that Titus, who had been with Paul during part of his second imprisonment had then gone into Dalmatia, on the Adriatic coast, where he was no doubt doing similar work to that which he had done in Crete.

CHAPTER I

1 the acknowledging of the truth, etc. The Greek word means "the *full* knowledge."

after godliness. R.V., "according to godliness."

2 before the world began. R.V., lit., "before times eternal" (*long ages ago,* Amer. Rev.). So 2 Tim. i. 9. The earliest promises of salvation (Gen. iii. 15) expressed God's eternal purpose.

3 in due times. Rather, "in His own seasons": see 1 Tim. vi. 15.

through preaching. More precisely, "in the message," or "proclamation" (R.V.); "wherewith I was entrusted."

4 mine own son. "My true child." See 1 Tim. i. 2.

5 wanting. Or, "lacking"; *i.e.,* matters that were unfinished when Paul left the island; especially the choice of elders.

as I had appointed thee. Rather, "as I ordered thee." On most of these requirements in an elder (or bishop, ver. 7), see 1 Tim. iii.

6 having faithful children ("children that believe"). A condition especially needful where the "elders" were mostly converts from heathenism.

7 a bishop. "The Greek word (*episcopos*) refers obviously to the elders already mentioned. . . The word does not imply a different office, but it describes the functions of the elder" (Canon Dawson Walker in *Devotional Commentary*).

8 a lover of good men. Properly, "lover of *good.*"

9 as he hath been taught. Rather, as R.V., "which is according to the teaching."

sound doctrine. Lit., "the healthful teaching." See note on 1 Tim. i. 10.

10 specially they of the circumcision. It appears that in Crete, as in Galatia, the disturbers of the churches were chiefly Jewish converts, who sought to pervert the gospel by Rabbinical traditions (14) and Pharisaic self-righteousness.

11 whose mouths must be stopped. By exposing their falsehood and dishonesty.

whole houses. Not individuals merely, but families.

filthy lucre. See note on 1 Tim. iii. 3.

12 One of themselves. Namely, of the Cretans. The reference is to the poet Epimenides, who lived in the sixth century before Christ, and was honoured as a prophet by his countrymen. "Slow bellies" is literal for "idle gluttons," R.V.

14 Jewish fables. See notes on 1 Tim. i. 4; iv. 3–8.

15 Unto the pure all things are pure. Moral impurity is not in question. The gospel recognises no such distinctions as these persons enjoin (14) between clean and unclean things; but teaches that outward things become to us just what the state of our own hearts makes them: see Mark vii. 1–23, and notes.

CHAPTER II

1 sound doctrine. See i. 9, note.

3 not false accusers, etc. Rather, "not slanderers, not enslaved to much wine": see i. 12.

4 that they may teach the young women, etc. Rather, "that they train the young women to love their husbands," etc.

5 keepers at home. The best authorities read "workers at home": a phrase for good housewives.

9 [Exhort] servants to be obedient. See on 1 Tim. vi. 1, 2.

not answering again. "Incessantly objecting to what is said to them, and setting up their own will in opposition to that of their masters" (*Lange*).

11 the grace of God that bringeth salvation, etc. Or, "the grace of God was manifested (*i.e.,* in Christ's coming), bringing salvation to all men, instructing us, to the intent that," etc.

12 soberly, righteously, and godly. True morality concerns ourselves ("soberly"), our fellow-men ("righteously"), and God ("godly").

13 that blessed hope, and the glorious appearing. Rather, "the blessed hope and appearing of the glory."

of the great God, etc. Or, "of our great God and Saviour Jesus Christ."

14 that He might redeem us from all iniquity, etc. His purpose in redeeming us "from the curse of the law," was to redeem us also "from all lawlessness, and to purify unto Himself a people for His own possession," etc.: cp. Exod. xix. 5, and 1 Pet. ii. 9.

15 Let no man despise thee. See 1 Tim. iv. 12, and note.

CHAPTER III

1 Put them in mind, etc. "For the Cretans, inclined as a people to rebellion, such an exhortation was necessary, especially at a time when those of Jewish proclivities were showing a disposition to resist the authority of the heathen magistrates" (*Lange*).

to obey magistrates. See Rom. xiii. 1–5, and notes.

4 But after that. Rather, "But when."

5 works of righteousness, etc. Rather, "works done in righteousness, which we ourselves did" (*we* being emphatic).

the washing of regeneration. Rather, "laver of regeneration": see note on Eph. v. 26. If there is here any allusion at all to baptism, it is as the emblem of spiritual cleansing (see Acts xxii. 16, and 1 Pet. iii. 21): for the apostle immediately names the believer's renewal by the Holy Spirit as the thing he intends.

6 which. Namely, the Holy Spirit. In this passage (4–6), the Father, the Son, and the Holy Spirit appear in their distinct offices in the great work of man's salvation.

7 justified by His grace. God "shed on us" the Holy Spirit, in order to produce in us the faith through which we are justified.

8 [This is] a faithful saying. See on 1 Tim. i. 15. The phrase is most naturally understood in reference to the preceding verses, although in general the "faithful saying" designates what follows.

9 avoid foolish questions. See note on 1 Tim. i. 4.

10 heretic. Properly, "A heretical (or schismatical) man"; *i.e.*, one who makes a division or party in the church for the sake of some notions or aims of his own (cp. Gal. iv. 17). Such a man, if found incorrigible after repeated admonition, was to be shunned as unfit for fellowship: and he would be self-condemned, as having rejected the admonition of the church, and still persisting in the course condemned (11).

12 Nicopolis. Many cities bore this name, "City of Victory"; but it is generally supposed that the one here meant was that in Epirus.

13 Bring. Or, "Set forward" (R.V.), by providing for the journey, and accompanying the travellers part of the way. Zenas may have been either a Roman or a Jewish "lawyer."

14 ours. Our brethren in Christ: cp. Rom. xii. 13.

good works for necessary uses. Rather, "honest occupations for the supply of the necessary wants."

[It was written to Titus, etc.] See Introduction to this Epistle.

THE EPISTLE OF PAUL THE APOSTLE TO PHILEMON

INTRODUCTION

THIS brief letter is noteworthy because of its bearing on the question of slavery. Onesimus was a slave who had run away from his master Philemon. St. Paul (A.D. 62) addresses the master as a brother Christian both of Philemon and of his slave Onesimus (ver. 16; cp. Col. iv. 7–9). With tactful wisdom he expresses his thankfulness to God for the love and faith shown by Philemon not only to the Lord Jesus but to all His followers (vers. 4, 5, 7), and prays that his faith may become effective in practical kindness (ver. 6). After this introduction he comes to the special object of his letter, an earnest appeal on behalf of the slave (vers. 8–12). So much did Paul value Onesimus that he would like to have kept him as his helper in the Gospel (ver. 13). But to do this would have been to break the Roman law, and he recognises that he would require the consent of the master, Philemon (ver. 14). He therefore contents himself with beseeching Philemon to receive him back, but this time not as a slave but as a brother, as if, indeed, he were so receiving Paul himself (vers. 15–19), and states his confidence that Philemon will do this, and even more (ver. 21).

Here, surely, is the germ that will one day make an end of slavery. As Bishop Lightfoot says (*Colossians and Philemon*, p. 323), "the word 'emancipation' seems to be trembling on his lips, and yet he does not once utter it. When we realise how firmly slavery was entrenched not only in the Roman Empire but throughout the whole world at that time, we can understand the reason for this. It was gradually that the overthrow of slavery was to be accomplished—by implanting a new spirit in the hearts of men, the spirit of Christ and of brotherhood. The whole subject is very fully dealt with by Storrs in his *Divine Origin of Christianity*, and is admirably summed up by Archbishop Alexander in his Introduction to Philemon in the *Speaker's Commentary*.

THE EPISTLE

1 a prisoner. A designation repeated in ver. 9, and adapted to excite Philemon's sympathy, and so to dispose him to comply with Paul's request.

2 Apphia. Or, "Appia"; probably Philemon's wife. Archippus, who was most likely their son, was a minister in the church at Colossæ (Col. iv. 17), and seems to have been a fellow-sufferer with Paul and Timothy: cp. Phil. ii. 25.

5 which thou hast toward the Lord Jesus, etc. Faith directed "towards" Christ, and evinced "to" the saints by "love" (6, 7). "Love to saints, as saints, is love to Christ Himself personally, because it is love to whatever of Christ is manifest in them" (Dr. A. H. Drysdale in *Devotional Commentary*).

6 that the communication of thy faith, etc. "That their participation in your faith may result in others fully recognising all the right affection that is in us toward Christ" (*Weymouth*). This result of faith, the practical knowledge of "every good thing" bestowed by God, would manifest itself in deeds of love.

7 the bowels of the saints are refreshed by thee, brother. Their hearts (cp. 2 Cor. vi. 12) have been comforted by thy kind ministrations. The appellation "brother" forms a touching and persuasive close to the sentence.

8 Wherefore. Because I know thy Christian love.

11 unprofitable. "Unprofitable" and "profitable," are in the Greek a play upon the words ἄχρηστον and εὔχρηστον, "useless" and "useful"; and the latter in turn has the same meaning as Onesimus, "profitable," "serviceable."

12 whom I have sent again. Whom I am sending back to thee with this letter.

16 a servant. Rather, "a bondman." His conversion had put him into a new relation to his master in earthly things ("the flesh"), as well as in religion ("the Lord"). On the principle of the law in Deut. xv. 12, this would imply a claim to his manumission.

a brother beloved. Here is the ideal that in the end shatters the chains of slavery.

17 a partner. One in Christian fellowship with thee.

18 If he hath wronged thee. By running away from his service.

19 thou owest unto me even thine own self besides. As my convert thou owest me more than thy property, thy very self.

20 let me have joy. Rather, "let me have profit": see note on ver. 11.

21 I wrote. That is, I have written what precedes.

that thou wilt also do more than I say. Hinting, probably, at Philemon giving Onesimus his freedom. "The apostle purposely refrains from being more specific, so as to admit of Philemon putting the largest construction on the marks of brotherhood and goodwill to be conferred upon Onesimus" (*Drysdale*). "So it came to pass that in this simple commonplace act of restoring a servant to his master, St. Paul was helping to lay the foundations of a new society, and was bespeaking those better relations between employer and employed which are even now slowly tending to solve some of the most pressing problems of our age" (Bishop Drury: *The Prison-Ministry of St. Paul*).

22 your prayers. The prayers of Philemon and his connexions.

23 saluteth thee. The persons here mentioned are the same as those named in the salutations to the Colossians (Col. iv. 10–14) with the exception of Justus, who is omitted here.

THE EPISTLE TO THE HEBREWS

INTRODUCTION

FOUR great topics are dealt with in this Epistle.

1. *The perfect deity and the perfect humanity of our Lord.*—He is the Creator of all things (i. 2, cp. John i. 3), the upholder of all things (i. 3), the brightness of the Father's glory and the express image of His person (i. 3), the object of worship (i. 6) and the exalted King (i. 8, 13; ii. 8). And with that perfect deity He unites perfect manhood. He became partaker of flesh and blood (ii. 14). He was tempted in all points like as we are (iv. 15). He learned obedience by the things which He suffered (v. 8).

It was in virtue of this union of the divine and human that Jesus became a perfect Saviour. It was in His human nature that He suffered and endured the agony of Gethsemane and the cross, and thus became a perfect captain of our salvation (i. 10, 14; v. 9). In His human nature He was tempted, and thus able to help us in our temptations (ii. 18; iv. 15). But if He had been merely man, He could not have offered the perfect sacrifice for sins. He must be One who is able to save to the uttermost (vii. 25–28). "He is able," says Dr. T. R. Glover, "is the refrain of the Epistle," referring to ii. 18; iv. 14; v. 2; vii. 25; v. 9; and x. 19.

2. *The contrast between the Old Testament and the New.*—Writing to the Hebrews, it was necessary that the author of this Epistle should show wherein Christianity is superior to Judaism. There are similarities between them, but there are marked differences. Moses, the great lawgiver of Israel, was but a servant, but Christ was a son over His own house (iii. 3–6). The rest into which Joshua led Israel was but a temporary and imperfect thing; there is a higher and more enduring rest (iv. 8, 9). The priesthood of Aaron and the tribe of Levi was also imperfect and temporary, but Christ is a priest for ever (v. 6; vii. 11, 24). The sacrifices of the Mosaic law were but shadows and types, and needed to be continually repeated, but Christ "offered one sacrifice for sins for ever," and "by one offering hath perfected for ever them that are sanctified" (ix. 25, 28; x. 1–14).

3. *The inspiring example of Old Testament saints.*—This is the theme of the glorious 11th chapter. It is the record of what was done and suffered by men and women of faith. They looked for a city that hath foundations (xi. 10). They confessed that they were strangers and pilgrims on the earth (xi. 13). They desired a better country, that is, an heavenly (xi. 16). They endured as seeing Him who is invisible (xi. 27). They endured terrible sufferings and hardships (xi. 35–38). Out of weakness they were made strong (xi. 34). Those were the men and women who subdued kingdoms.

4. *The practical duties of the Christian life.*—This is the subject of chapters xii. and xiii. It follows as the sequel not only on the stories of heroism, but on all that has been said of Christ as the Divine and human Saviour. "Wherefore, seeing we also are compassed about with so great a cloud of witnesses . . . let us run with patience . . . looking unto Jesus the author and finisher of our faith" (xii. 1, 2). And then follow the exhortations to patience in suffering (xii. 3–11); to peacefulness and holiness (xii. 14–16, 28, 29); to purity (xiii. 4); to a contented spirit (xiii. 5); and to deeds of kindness and generosity (xiii. 16).

The date and authorship of the Epistle are both uncertain. The internal evidence makes it fairly clear that it was written before the destruction of Jerusalem (A.D. 70) as there is no reference to the discontinuance of the Temple services. As to the authorship, there is great diversity of opinion. While some believe that St. Paul wrote it, Calvin, and in recent times Delitzsch, regarded St. Luke as the author. Luther, followed by many modern writers, attributed it to Apollos, while other eminent commentators attribute it to Barnabas. Westcott favoured either St. Luke or Barnabas, but did not dogmatise. There we must be content to leave it.

CHAPTER I

1 at sundry times and in divers manners. Or, "in many portions and many modes": denoting the gradual unfolding of God's will, through "the prophets" (in the various periods of Israel's history); in various methods, such as dreams and visions, outward appearances, and inward impressions.

by the prophets. Rather, "*in* the prophets," and "*in* a Son" (2); for God was in them, and in a higher sense in Him.

2 in these last days. The best reading has "at the end of these days"; the end of the former period of the world's history (Isa. ii. 2, and note).

heir of all things. The Lord or Possessor, *for* whom, as well as *by* whom, all things were created: cp. Col. 15–18.

the worlds (Greek, "ages"). See **xi. 3.** All things that have relation to *time.*

3 the brightness of His glory, etc. Rather, "the effulgence (*Westcott*) of His glory, and the impress of His substance." "Substance" means, properly, "essential being"; that which underlies all phenomena. It is the Son who manifests all the essential glory of the Godhead: cp. John i. 2, 17, and notes. "Impress" is in the original χαρακτήρ (character), the impression made by a die or seal.

the word of His power. The power of the Son, uttering itself in that same "word" which said, "Let there be light, and there was light"; which "spake, and it was done."

when He had [by Himself] purged [our] sins. R.V., "when He had made purification of sins." He was both Priest and Sacrifice: cp. vii. 27; ix. 12–14; Lev. xvi., and notes.

on the right hand of the Majesty on high. The dignity which He possesses as Son belongs to Him as Mediator also, by virtue of His accepted work of expiation: cp. John xvii. 1–5, and notes.

5 For unto which of the angels, etc. See notes on Psa. ii. 1–7; and comp. 2 Sam. vii. 14.

6 And again, when He bringeth in. Rather, according to the Greek order, "And when He again bringeth in." The word "again" marks not a new point in the argument, but the return of Christ to judgement. "The world" denotes the world of men (οἰκουμένην). The ancient words will receive their full meaning then. Weymouth best brings out the idea of the original: "But speaking of the time when He once more brings His firstborn into the world, he says, 'And let all God's angels worship Him' (Deut. xxxii. 43, Septuagint; Psa. xcvii. 7, Septuagint)."

first-begotten. Rather, "first-born" (R.V.), as in Rom. viii. 29, and Col. i. 15; here equivalent to "heir" or "lord" in ver. 2.

7 Who maketh His angels spirits (winds). See note on Psa. civ. 4.

8 But unto (of) **the Son [He saith].** The argument is that they are but messengers, as "winds" and "flames": Christ is Son, and Divine.

Thy throne, O God, etc. The rendering favoured by *Westcott* and *Moffatt* is "God is thy throne for ever and ever." Whether the word "God" be taken as nominative or vocative, says Westcott, "the quotation establishes the conclusion which the writer wishes to draw as to the essential difference of the Son and the angels."

10 Thou, Lord, etc. Psa. cii. clearly refers to God; and its application here to our Lord Jesus is a plain proof of His Deity: see note on Psa. cii. 25.

13 Sit on my right hand, etc. See notes on Psa. cx.; Matt. xxii. 43–45.

14 Are they not all ministering spirits, etc.? Two distinct words are here used for "ministering" and "minister"; the former denoting sanctuary (liturgic), or social service, the latter, any form of service (*diaconia*). They all render service to God in His heavenly temple, and are sent forth by Him on service for the sake of those who are to inherit salvation (Rom. viii. 17).

CHAPTER II

1 lest at any time we should let [them] slip. Rather, as R.V., "lest at any time we drift away [from them]"; carried *imperceptibly* out of our course: cp. Prov. iii. 21, where the same word occurs in the LXX.

2 spoken by (through) **angels.** See Acts vii. 53, Gal. iii. 19, and notes. If the attendance of angels at Sinai gave dignity and force to the law of Moses, how much greater are the honour and authority of the gospel, which has been communicated by the Lord of angels! (see i. 14).

3 how shall we escape, etc.? The *we* is emphatic, in contrast with the Hebrews of old.

was confirmed unto us by them that heard [Him]. The writer of the Epistle thus places himself among those who received the word from Christ's *disciples*: cp. Luke i. 2.

4 God also bearing them witness. Or, "corroborating." The adaptation of the gospel to our wants, as God's plan of salvation, is the primary evidence of its truth: but God has superadded the external evidence of miracles, as a means of arresting and fixing attention. These Divine attestations are called "signs," as illustrating spiritual truth (see John ii. 11, and note); "wonders," as exciting astonishment; "miracles" (or, rather, "powers"), as manifesting Divine power; and "distributions of the Holy Spirit," because He bestows them according to His will: cp. 1 Cor. xii. 11.

5 For unto [the] angels, etc. The meaning is, that the government of the inhabited world under the Messiah (in what the Jews called "the age to come": see vi. 5, and note on Matt. xii. 32) is not administered by angels, but by man. "Words which were used of man in himself became first true of One who being more than man took man's nature upon Him" (*Westcott*).

6 one in a certain place. See Psa. viii., and notes.

9 But we see Jesus, etc. The argument is better brought out by adhering to the arrangement of the Greek, as R.V., "But we behold Him who hath been made a little (*or*, for a little while) lower than the angels, *even* Jesus, because of the suffering of death, crowned," etc.

for the suffering of death. Christ's exaltation is the recompense of His sufferings. As the consequence of His humiliation, He is put in full possession of the dominion assigned by God to man.

10 captain. It is the same Greek word which is used in xii. 2, but in neither case does the translation, "author" or "captain" express the full meaning, which includes both ideas. Moffatt translates it "Pioneer."

11 all of (from) **one.** All alike children of God.

12 saying, I will declare, etc. See note on Psa. xxii. 22.

13 I will put my trust in Him, etc. On the two quotations in this verse, see note on Isa. viii. 16. The former (which occurs also in 2 Sam. xxii. 3; Psa. xviii. 3) expresses that confidence in God which characterises all His "children."

15 and deliver (all) **them who through fear of death**, etc. "To death itself men are still subject, but Christ has removed its terrors" (*Westcott*).

16 For verily He took not, etc. Rather, as R.V., "For verily not of angels doth He take hold, but He taketh hold on the seed of Abraham," *i.e.*, to help them.

17 Wherefore in all things, etc. In order to "help" efficiently "those who are tried," He has become able, from personal experience, to sympathise with those whom He represents before God.

reconciliation. "Expiation" or "propitiation" (R.V.).

CHAPTER III

1 the heavenly calling. The call to a heavenly life.

the Apostle. Being *sent* of God as Moses was (Exod. iii. 10–15). And as the Father sent Him, so He sent the Twelve (John xx. 21)" (*Wordsworth*). Our Lord unites in Himself the offices of both Moses (iii. 1–iv. 13) and Aaron (iv. 14–x. 22).

profession. As in iv. 14; x. 23. R.V., "confession." The meaning is, "the High Priest whom we confess or acknowledge."

2 in all His house. Or, "household." See note on Numb. xii. 7. The fidelity of Moses had respect to all the details of the management of God's house. Christ's sphere of action is the Church of God (1 Tim. iii. 15).

3 For this [man]. That is, our Lord. Moses, after all, was but part of the house *in* which he laboured. Our Lord Himself is not only the "founder of the household" *over* which He presides, but the Creator of all things: the maker must be greater than his work; and the Maker of all things must be Divine.

5 for a testimony, etc. Not only was Moses merely a servant, but his work was preparatory, to announce what should afterwards be spoken by the Son (i. 2).

6 His own house. Rather, "His house," the house of God, as ver. 2.

7 Wherefore. This seems to be connected with ver. 12. Because our Lord is superior to Moses, the warning of the Holy Spirit in Psa. xcv. should lead us to "take heed."

if ye will hear. Rather, as R.V., "if ye shall hear." It is the fact of hearing that is supposed, not willingness to hear.

8 the provocation . . . (the) **temptation.** Meribah and Massah, Exod. xvii. 7; "where your fathers," etc., ver. 9.

11 my rest. A rest, resembling that of God at the close of the six days' work; partially obtained in the possession of Canaan; which, however, was but typical of the believer's rest in Christ now, and in heaven hereafter: see ch. iv. throughout.

13 the deceitfulness of sin. Sin is deceitful both as to its nature and as to its consequences (cp. Gen. iii. 4, 13, 17, 18).

16 For some, when they had heard, etc. Rather, according to the best reading, a series of questions: "Who then, when they heard, did provoke? Nay, did not all who came out of Egypt by Moses?" Two exceptions (Caleb and Joshua) out of the hosts of Israel are too few to be mentioned.

18 that believed not. R.V., "that were disobedient."

19 So we see. Properly, "And we see"; *i.e.* from all this.

CHAPTER IV

2 For unto us was the gospel preached. Rather, "For unto us have glad tidings been proclaimed."

the words preached did not profit them, etc. Of two possible readings, *Nestle's Greek Testament* adopts, in preference to that of the R.V., the reading of the A.V., which may be translated: "the word which they heard did not benefit them, because it was not united with faith on the part of those who heard."

3 do enter into rest. Or, "are entering into rest." God speaks of this rest as *future*, "although His works were finished from the foundation of the world." This rest, again, was not reached by the generation in the wilderness; nor even did the entrance into Canaan exhaust the promise; for the exhortation is repeated "in David." A rest then still "remaineth."

if they shall enter, etc. A strong mode of asserting, "they shall not enter," etc., as the same phrase is rendered in iii. 11.

6 unbelief. Rather, "disobedience." The word in iii. 12, 19, "unbelief," is different.

7 limiteth. Or, as R.V., "defineth." "Moving forward the horizon of His invitation so as to include a later generation in it" (*Speaker's Commentary*).

saying in David, etc. Rather, "saying. To-day, in David"; *i.e.*, in the Psalter: without necessarily attributing this Psalm to David himself.

after so long a time. More than four hundred years after the former occasion.

8 Jesus. Joshua.

9 There remaineth therefore a rest (a "sabbath rest"). The word for "rest" is changed, suggesting more directly the rest of God after His works. Yet after this, after the possession of Canaan, the true fulfilment of the promise has been shown, by the Scriptures quoted, to "remain": a blessing to be attained in Christ. The Christian life possesses a higher blessedness even than the ancient heritage of God's people. The words include in their meaning the present privilege of believers.

10 For he that is entered into His rest, etc. The believer, who has entered into God's rest; ceasing to labour for salvation, but accepting it as God's free gift in Christ—a doctrine eminently Pauline.

11 labour. "giving diligence."

unbelief. See note on iii. 18.

12 the word of God. *i.e.*, in revelation.

quick. That is, "living."

14 into the heavens. Rather, "*through* the heavens," as the high priest passed through the temple courts into the Holy of Holies: see Lev. xvi. 12–15; Eph. iv. 10, "far above all the heavens."

15 a High Priest which cannot be touched, etc. See note on ii. 17.

16 boldly. Or, "with confidence": as in iii. 6. Luther has "mit Freudigkeit" (with joyfulness).

the throne of grace. An allusion to "the mercy seat": see Exod. xxv. 17, and note.

that we may obtain, etc. Or, "that we may receive mercy, and find grace." The twofold aim corresponds with the twofold necessity of life. Man needs mercy for past failure, and grace for present and future work. Mercy, again, is to be "taken" as it is extended to man in his weakness; grace is to be "sought" by man according to his necessity (*Westcott*).

CHAPTER V

1 ordained. Rather, as R.V., "appointed." See Exod. xxviii. 12, 21. Being appointed to act "on behalf of men," he must be taken from men; he must have (2) the reasonableness and patience of one who knows his own "weakness."

2 the ignorant. Sin offerings were largely for errors of ignorance and inadvertence: see Lev. iv. 2; v. 17.

5 but He that said unto Him. These words refer to our Lord's resurrection (see Rom. i. 4, and note on Psa. ii. 7); which showed that He was accepted by God as *Priest* in His offering of Himself. They thus connect His kingly and priestly offices; as is done also in the next quotation from Psa. cx.: cp. Zech. vi. 9–13, and notes.

7 and was heard in that He feared. He "was heard on account of His godly fear."

10 called of God, etc. That is, "having been addressed by God as high priest," etc. (see ver. 6). *Chadwick* translates "saluted, proclaimed, hailed"; *Moffatt* has "designated."

11 hard to be uttered, etc. Rather, "hard of interpretation, since ye have become dull of hearing."

12 for the time. "By this time."

13 unskilful. Or, "inexperienced" in the use of the deeper truths of the gospel. Such persons are liable to pervert the "solid food." The "word of righteousness" is the word which instructs in righteousness.

14 their senses exercised, etc. Trained to discriminate.

CHAPTER VI

1 Therefore leaving the principles, etc. As we ought not to remain mere children, let us leave "the word of the beginning of Christ," and press on towards the full maturity of spiritual growth. These "elements" are not indeed to be disregarded, but are pre-supposed, as essential to future advance.

the foundation of repentance, etc. The six (or seven) following particulars define " the principles " or " the foundation."

repentance from dead works. That " change of mind " which repudiates these works as a ground of acceptance with God. These works are described as " dead," being done in a state of spiritual death.

3 if God permit. Ever remembering our dependence on God's help (Phil. ii. 13).

4 For it is impossible, etc. The awful condition of apostates is a motive for advancing in the Christian life, and is also given by the writer as a reason for the character of his teaching; " not laying again the foundation." This last, he says, would be of no use; for if the foundation is once abandoned, there remains no further method of influencing the heart: see notes on 5–7.

A most important thing to remember on this much-discussed passage is that the case is hypothetical.

once. The Greek word means, not " formerly," but " once for all "; implying that there is no second enlightening.

the heavenly gift. See John iv. 10, and note.

5 and have tasted the good word of God, etc. That is, have experienced the comfort of the Divine promises. " It is significant that in the enumeration of the divine gifts received by those who are conceived as afterwards falling away there is no one which passes out of the individual. All are gifts of power, of personal endowment. There is no gift of love. Under this aspect light falls upon the passage from Matt. vii. 22 f.; 1 Cor. xiii. 1 f. " (*Westcott*).

6 if they shall fall away. Rather, as R.V., " and [then] fell away." Those who, after all this religious experience, have apostatised, cannot have the same experience a second time; their apostasy classes them with the unbelieving Jews who shouted " Crucify Him ! " (John xix. 6).

to renew them again unto repentance. All the great truths and influences of the gospel having lost their power, no other means are left of working upon the conscience: cp. Mark x. 23–27.

7 For the earth, etc. Rather, " For land," *i.e.,* any piece of ground. The difference between the fruitful and the barren professor.

by whom. Rather, " on whose account "; *i.e.,* the owners or cultivators.

9 things that accompany salvation. Rather, " things which lead up to (or involve) salvation."

10 which ye have showed toward His name. See Matt. x. 40–42; xxv. 34–40, and notes.

11 to the full assurance (or, fulness) **of hope,** That you may always enjoy a fully assured hope.

12 followers. Rather, " imitators "; *i.e.,* of their faith and patience; so as to become partakers of the same inheritance. And if, like Abraham (13), you have long to wait for the inheritance, you may well do so; for you, like him, have the oath (see vii. 20) as well as the promise of Jehovah.

15 And so. R.V., " And thus "; Abraham having the promise and the oath to assure him.

he obtained the promise. He obtained the first instalment of it in the birth of Isaac; the pledge of its complete fulfilment.

17 Wherein. Rather, " Wherefore." The " heirs of the promise" are those mentioned above in ver. 12.

willing. Rather, " desiring."

18 two immutable things. God's promise and His oath.

19 which entereth into that within the vail. The anchor of the seaman is cast *downwards* into the deep; but the anchor of the Christian is thrown *upwards,* into heaven, and finds there its firm ground and fast holding. " The stability of hope is twofold. It is undisturbed by outward influences ἀσφαλής, ' sure ') and it is firm in its inherent character (βεβαία, ' stedfast ') " (*Westcott*).

CHAPTER VII

2 king of Salem. See Gen. xiv. 18; Psa. lxxvi 2, and notes.

3 without descent. Rather, " without pedigree," *i.e., recorded* descent. We have no account of his ancestors, nor of his birth and death. So that he " continually " stands before us, simply in the fact of his unique priesthood; and thus is " likened to the Son of God," whose priesthood is a dignity purely personal; not being received by birth, or transmitted by death, like the Levitical.

4 the patriarch. The head of the whole family of Israel. Melchisedek was superior to Abraham and the priests who sprang from him. Therefore our Lord, of whom Melchisedek was a type, must also be superior to them all.

5 though they come out of the loins of Abraham. Though " the sons of Levi " and " their brethren " are all alike descended from Abraham.

7 without all contradiction, etc. " Without any dispute," R.V.

8 here. That is, in the case of the Levitical priests; " there," in the case of Melchisedek.

9 as I may so say. Rather, " And so to speak "; a phrase intended to remove any apparent strangeness in the assertion that Levi paid tithes " through Abraham." Levi shared in the consequences of Abraham's act.

13 pertaineth to another tribe. The Messiah " hath taken part in another " tribe from that of Levi. His priesthood then could not be of the order of Aaron. And from Judah it is well known that " our Lord hath sprung forth." The human nature of our Lord is here shown, as well as the Divine, which has been already emphasised.

15 And it is yet far more evident. It is still further evident that our Lord's is the superior priesthood; since it is not of a kind to be transmitted by natural succession, but is suited to one who has an endless (or " indissoluble ") life: cp. John v. 26; vi. 53–58.

for that. Rather, " if."

18 For there is verily, etc. Rather, " For there cometh, on the one hand, a setting aside of a foregoing commandment, etc.; but (19) on the other, a bringing in of a better hope."

19 For the law made nothing perfect. In the matter of human salvation: see ver. 11; cp. Gal. ii. 15; Rom. iii. 19.

by the which we draw nigh unto God. Cp. x. 19, 22; Rom. v. 1, 2, and notes.

24 hath an unchangeable priesthood. Westcott renders " unchangeable " as " inviolable," and explains " Christ's priesthood is His alone, open to no rival claim, liable to no invasion of its functions." Weymouth and Moffatt, however, translate it as " without any successor."

25 Wherefore He is able, etc. As " He ever liveth," He can and will save all, in all ages, " who draw near to God by Him," and save each of them " to the uttermost," or " to completeness."

26 harmless. More exactly, " guileless " (R.V.), or " innocent."

27 this He did once. That is, Christ offered Himself " once for all " for the sins of the people.

28 consecrated. Rather, " perfected ": see on ii. 10, and Exod. xxix. 9.

CHAPTER VIII

1 the sum. Rather, "the chief point." The writer has now come to the subject which he designates as "chief in all that is being spoken of," namely, the discharge of those functions for which our Lord was constituted High Priest.

2 the true tabernacle. The real (see note on John i. 9) tabernacle, or holy place, *i.e.*, the immediate presence of God above (see iv. 14; vi. 20); of which the ancient tabernacle was only a shadow (5).

3 ordained. See note on ch. v. 1.

this [man]. Rather supply, with R.V., "this *High Priest.*"

4 For if He were on earth, etc. Our Lord's priesthood must be exercised in heaven; for there are others "who serve [that which is] a copy and shadow of the heavenly things," *i.e.*, the tabernacle and its rites: see note on ver. 2.

7 if that first [covenant] had been faultless. See on vii. 11. The Jewish economy being only preparatory, is spoken of as not being faultless: see Jer. xxxi. 31–34, and notes.

13 In that He saith, A new [covenant], etc. Jehovah, by calling the gospel a *new* covenant, implies that the former was *old;* and thus indicates its decay and extinction.

CHAPTER IX

1 a worldly sanctuary. A sanctuary pertaining to this world, in opposition to the "heavenly" (ver. 11; viii. 2–5).

2 a tabernacle made ("prepared," or "fitted up"). Respecting the tabernacle and its contents, see Exod. xxv.–xxvii., and notes. The whole of this description refers to the tabernacle, not to the Temple, in which some of these things were wanting: see 1 Kings viii. 9.

4 which had the golden censer. The word translated "censer" has that meaning twice in the Old Testament (Sept.); 2 Chron. xxvi. 19; Ezek. viii. 11; but in Philo and Josephus it generally means the "altar of incense." So Bishop Chadwick translates it (*Devotional Commentary*). This the Holy of Holies might be said to have "had," as the two were closely connected (see Exod. xxx. 6; xi. 5). It was "the altar that belonged to the Oracle," 1 Kings vi. 22 (R.V.).

5 the cherubim. See note on Exod. xxv. 18.

6 ordained. Rather, "arranged." The verbs and participles in this paragraph have a *present* sense, and should be rendered so; as the tabernacle is regarded as "yet standing."

7 once every year. On one day in the year, the great Day of Atonement (Exod. xxx. 10). On that day he probably entered into the Holy of Holies several times (Lev. xvi. 12–16).

8 the Holy Ghost this signifying, etc. This separation of the most Holy place was a standing reminder to priests and people of a separation from God which the Jewish ritual had no power to do away.

9 a figure. Lit., "a parable." The Jewish tabernacle served for a representation of the true tabernacle (see note on viii. 2), until (10) the time of "the thorough setting to right" (the meaning of the Greek word translated "reformation") by Christ.

in which. Rather, "according to which," *i.e.*, in agreement with that old dispensation.

him that did the service. More accurately in R.V., "the worshipper": not only the officiating minister.

perfect. See note on vii. 19.

11 not of this building. Rather, "not of this creation," *i.e.*, this lower world.

12 once. That is, "once for all" (R.V.). So x. 10, where the A.V. also has the phrase.

redemption. See note on Rom. iii. 24.

13 the ashes of a heifer sprinkling the unclean. See Numb. xix., and notes.

14 dead works. See note on vi. 1.

16 testament. The word here rendered "testament" is generally translated "covenant" in Scripture, though Deissmann favours the word "testament." If it be properly rendered "testament" here, it is best to take verses 16, 17 as a parenthesis, adducing an illustrative argument, suggested partly by the mention of an "inheritence," and partly by the meaning of the word "testament," which means any valid arrangement, either by will or other disposition.

20 testament. The quotation is made freely from Exod. xxiv. 8: cp. Matt. xxvi. 28, and note.

22 almost ("I may almost say," R.V.) **all things,** etc. Some things were cleansed by water, and some by fire and water: cp. Exod. xix. 10; Numb. xxxi. 23.

without shedding of blood is no remission. Under the Mosaic law sin was supposed to be pardoned only through the shedding of a victim's blood. And this was but the representation of a universal truth.

23 patterns. Rather, "copies"; the tabernacle and its furniture: cp. viii. 5.

better sacrifices. "The plural is used for the expression of the general idea. And in point of fact the single sacrifice of Christ fulfilled perfectly the ideas presented by the different forms of the Levitical sacrifices" (*Westcott*).

24 to appear, etc. "To be manifested" as our intercessor before God.

25 with blood of others. Better, as R.V., "with blood not His own."

26 for then must He often have suffered. Like the typical atonement offered every year. The one atoning death of Christ, under the closing dispensation in the world's history, sufficed for putting away sin for all time.

27 once (for all) **to die.** Christ by once dying made atonement once for all (cp. Isa. liii. 12). So that (28) when He returns from heaven, He will be "apart from sin"; "which once He took upon Himself, but with which He needs no longer to deal" (*Chadwick*).

CHAPTER X

1 good [things]. Rather, "*the* good things," of which Christ is High Priest (ix. 11). Of these the law is the "shadow," the outline or rough, sketch, as opposed to "the image" itself, the finished picture or statue: see viii. 5.

offered. Rather, "offer"; for the word is in the present tense, and suggests that the Temple was still in existence. Cp. viii. 4; ix. 6 (R.V.).

2 then. If they could have taken away the sins of the worshippers.

3 But in those [sacrifices], etc. That is, in the yearly sacrifices on the Day of Atonement (Lev. xvi. 34). It was not in their nature or design to atone for sin (4); but only to keep in remembrance the need and the promise of the great atonement.

5 Wherefore, etc. "The writer puts into the mouth of Christ, on the ground of the typical relation of the Old and New Covenants, the words of David as His own, since they are fulfilled by Him" (*Lange*). Because those sacrifices could not

take away sin, the Messiah announces the sacrifice of Himself, which He was prepared to make by His obedience unto death. See notes on Psa. xl. 6–8.

a body hast Thou prepared me. So the LXX renders, or, as *Chadwick* suggests, paraphrases the Hebrew, " Mine ears hast Thou opened." Both clauses contain the same general idea of the spirit of obedience. " The ' body ' is the instrument for fulfilling the Divine command, just as the ' ear ' is the instrument for receiving it " (*Westcott*).

6 burnt offerings. Literally, " whole burnt offerings," emblems of complete consecration. So ver. 8.

7 In the volume of the book. Lit., " in the roll." That is, in the Pentateuch : cp. Luke xxiv. 27, 44 ; John v. 46.

8 Above when He said, etc. That is, " when He said above," " Sacrifice and offering Thou wouldest not," then He said, " Lo ! I am come," etc. ; superseding the first by the second.

10 By the which will. Rather, " In which will " ; *i.e.*, in the purpose and counsel of God, a purpose of love conceived in eternity, carried out in time by means of the free-will offering of Christ.

11 every priest. " Every priest " in his turn : see on Luke i. 5, 8.

12 for ever. To be connected with " sacrifice for sins."

on the right hand of God. Cp. i. 3, 13, and notes.

14 by one offering, etc. Our Lord's one offering is efficacious for the believer's perfect and eternal deliverance alike from the consequences and the power of sin : cp. ii. 11 ; x. 1, and notes.

them that are sanctified. Rather, " them that are being sanctified," as ii. 11.

15 after. It is difficult to determine what is here referred to as being said " after." Some think that it is only ver. 17 ; and a few ancient MSS. begin that verse with " Then saith He " (supplied in italics, R.V.). Others suppose that it is all that follows the words " saith the Lord " in ver. 16 ; and they understand this passage as first announcing the *fact* of the New Covenant, and then explaining its *nature*.

19 Having therefore, brethren, boldness, etc. Or, " having confidence in respect to entrance into the holiest," *i.e.*, into the presence of God.

20 a new (fresh) **and living way.** It is called a " new way " because it had been recently opened by Christ's death ; and " living " because it is the way of living participation in Christ's life, and active progress in Him.

21 a High Priest. Rather, " a *great* priest," superior to all others.

22 having our hearts sprinkled, etc. The sprinkling with blood (Exod. xxiv. 8), and the washing with water (Exod. xxix. 4), typify the application of our Lord's work to the soul, freeing the conscience from the sense of sin, and purifying character and conduct : cp. Titus ii. 14 ; iii. 5–7.

23 of our faith. Rather, " of the hope " ; which rests on God's faithful promises through Christ.

24 and let us consider one another. " Let us consider how to stir up one another " (*Moffatt*).

25 not forsaking the assembling of ourselves together. Some might be led to neglect the meetings for worship through indifference ; and others to absent themselves through fear of persecution.

the day. Meaning probably " the day " of Christ's coming to judge the Jewish nation : which foreshadowed the day of final judgement : see Matt. xxiv. ; 1 Cor. iii. 13, and notes.

26 if we sin wilfully, etc. He who willingly rejects (see ver. 29) Christ's atonement, after having recognised the truth of the gospel, will never find another means of salvation. Yet we cannot doubt that if he should, in penitence and faith, embrace that one atonement, he might yet be saved (1 John i. 7).

27 a certain fearful looking for, etc. Lit., " *some* fearful looking for," etc. (The phrase in R.V. is like " a certain man " in the parables—not an assertion of *certainty*.)

28 He that despised Moses' law, etc. See Deut. xvii. 2–7, and note.

29 who hath trodden under foot the Son of God, etc. The awful guilt and danger of apostasy from the faith of Christ is here set forth in the strongest language. It is an insult to the Divine Son and the Holy Spirit and a rejection of atoning " blood " and saving " grace."

30 Vengeance belongeth unto me, etc. See notes on Deut. xxxii. 35, 36, and Rom. xii. 19. It is observable that the quotation here and in Rom. is in the same words, differing slightly from the LXX.

32 illuminated. Rather, " enlightened " : see vi. 4.

34 of me in my bonds. R.V., " on them that were in bonds. This is the reading supported by Westcott and Nestle, and followed by Moffatt and Weymouth.

knowing in yourselves that ye have. Westcott's translation seems best to convey the meaning of the original : " knowing that ye had your own selves for a better possession and an enduring one."

36 patience. Or, " endurance " : so as to do " the will of God," until you obtain the fulfilment of the promise (37). It is the same Greek word which in Rom. xv. 5, is used of " the God of patience."

37 yet a little while. Lit., " a very little while." Cp. Isa. xxvi. 20.

He that shall come. Rather, " The coming One." This was a designation of our Lord : see Psa. cxviii. 26 ; Matt. xi. 3, and notes.

38 the just. The best reading gives " my righteous one." The Septuagint version of Hab. ii. 3, 4 is here quoted freely, and adapted to the form of this appeal : see notes on Hab. ii. 4 ; Rom. i. 17.

CHAPTER XI

1 faith. A practical conviction of the reality of the invisible, and of the certainty of the future, as they are revealed to us by God. R.V., " the assurance of things hoped for and the proving (or, ' test ') of things not seen." This chapter gives illustrations.

2 by it. Rather, " in this the elders had witness borne to them " ; *i.e.*, were attested as just by God.

3 the worlds. See note on i. 2. We learn the elementary fact of creation from the testimony of God's word : see Gen. i. 1, and note.

4 by it he being dead yet speaketh. By his faith, which " obtained witness " from God, Abel still speaks ; showing that God accepts and justifies those who reply upon His revealed word, and will vindicate them, even after death : see xii. 24 ; Gen. iv. 10 ; Job xix. 25.

5 By faith Enoch was translated. See note on Gen. v. 24. The phrase, " pleased God," is from the LXX.

6 and [that] He is a rewarder. Rather, " and becometh a rewarder." God always *exists*, and He *becomes* a rewarder of those who seek Him out.

Enoch, believing these truths, " walked with God," and " pleased God."

7 fear. " Godly fear," R.V., or " pious care " (*Westcott*). His provident faith condemned those who neglect God's warnings, and obtained the righteousness imputed to true believers : see Gen. vi. 9 ; Rom. i. 17.

by the which. That is, " by which *faith*."

8 Abraham, when he was called, etc. The preferable order is that of R.V., " Abraham, when he was called, obeyed to go out unto a place," etc.

9 dwelling in tabernacles. In frail shifting tents ; in contrast with " the city which hath the foundations " (10).

10 a (the) **city.** The earthly Canaan with its metropolis (cp. Psa. xlviii.) was to him but a type of the better country (14–16), and the heavenly Jerusalem (xii. 22).

13 These all, etc. " These all " were specially Abraham and the early patriarchs ; who, in believing obedience to God's command and expectation of future blessedness, lived as wanderers in this world without fixed habitations, and " died without receiving the fulfilment of the promises " which God had given to them.

embraced them. Rather, " greeted them," as the returning traveller hails from afar the distant hill of his " country " (14).

14 country. Or, " fatherland " ; which as " strangers on earth " they seek. It is a common thing now to suggest that the Old Testament saints had little, if any, idea of immortality and the hereafter. The writer of this Epistle was of a different opinion.

16 wherefore God is not ashamed, etc. He calls Himself the " God of Abraham, of Isaac, and of Jacob " : see Exod. iii. 6, and Matt. xxii. 32, and note.

He prepared for them a city. Cp. John xiv. 2, 3. It is the same Greek word for " prepare " that is used in both passages. Heaven will not be a strange place.

17 offered up. Here the first occurrence of the phrase means " hath offered up " (the sacrifice complete in *will*) ; the second, " was offering up " (the sacrifice arrested in *fact*).

19 in a figure. See note on ix. 9. Isaac's deliverance, when bound on the altar, by God's interference and the substitution of another victim, was a kind of resurrection, aptly foreshadowing that of Christ and His people.

20 concerning things to come. See Gen. xxvii. 27–40, and notes.

21 [leaning] upon the top of his staff. See note on Gen. xlvii. 31. The words are from the LXX.

22 Joseph, when he died. Lit., " when his end was nigh." See Gen. l. 24, 25, and notes.

23 because they saw he was a proper (goodly) **child.** They saw that the child was beautiful (cp. Acts vii. 20) ; they believed that the God of Israel would enable them to preserve him. Thus the great lawgiver himself owed his life to " faith."

24 refused, etc. This great renunciation is indicated in the history by the simple words, " went out unto his brethren," Exod. ii. 11.

26 the reproach of (the) **Christ.** Reproach such as Christ and His followers have to bear.

27 he forsook Egypt. Referring to his second and final departure from Egypt, when he led forth the Israelites (Exod. xii. 31–36). Each of the two principal incidents of this exodus—the keeping of she Passover (28) and the passage of the sea (29)—showed the power of faith, and the final difference that will be made between the believer and the ungodly.

31 believed not. Or, " were disobedient." Respecting Rahab, see Josh. ii. 1–21 ; Jas. ii. 25, and notes.

33 wrought righteousness. " The phrase is to be understood not only of purely individual virtues, but of the virtues of leaders. Conquerors used their success for the furtherance of right " (*Westcott*).

34 escaped the edge of the sword. As in the case of Elijah (1 Kings xix. 3) ; and Elisha (2 Kings vi. 14–20).

out of weakness were made strong. Hezekiah was restored to strength in dependence on God (2 Kings xx.).

35 raised to life again. Lit., " by a resurrection," through the intervention of Elijah and Elisha (1 Kings xvii. 19–24, and 2 Kings iv. 18–37). But as this was only a temporary restoration to life, the final resurrection is termed " better."

others were tortured. etc. As recorded in the narratives of 2 Maccabees vi., vii. ; where the sufferers are described as comforting themselves with the hope of the resurrection unto eternal life.

37 sawn asunder. See note on 2 Kings xxi. 16.

39 received not the promise. The great promise was not fulfilled until our Lord had Himself come, and had sent forth the promised Comforter ; and the Church could not be brought to a state of completeness until these great events had taken place.

CHAPTER XII

1 so great a cloud of witnesses. These witnesses are not mere spectators ; they are those who bear a testimony to the power and triumph of faith ; and in this capacity they are represented as encouraging the efforts of Christians in the heavenly race.

the sin which so easily beset us. " Sin with its clinging folds " (*Moffatt*) ; like a robe that would cling to the racer and impede his course.

patience. Rather, " endurance." For the verb, see vers. 2, 3, and 7.

2 looking unto Jesus. The Greek is " looking away." For the word translated " author," see note on ii. 10. Jesus on " the cross " and on " the throne " *is* the great Exemplar of faith's power and results.

3 contradiction. Opposition to His teaching and Himself.

4 Ye have not yet resisted unto blood. These words have been understood by many expositors to refer to physical suffering or persecution, but the second clause " striving against sin " suggests that the spiritual conflict is meant. This is borne out by vers. 1, 2.

5 speaketh unto you. More exactly, as R.V., " reasoneth with you " : see note on Prov. iii. 11, 12.

7 If ye endure chastening. The sense is : " for correction, not for punishment or in vengeance," God is dealing with you ; " as with sons."

10 after their own pleasure. Lit., " according to what seemed good to them."

11 peaceable fruit. Where righteousness is one fruit of affliction, peace will be another.

12 Wherefore lift up the hands which hang down, etc. " Hands " for conflict (ver. 4) ; " knees " for the race (ver. 1).

13 turned out of the way. Or, " put out of joint." " The word allows either rendering ; but there is no good contrast between wandering and being healed, whereas a weak limb, dislocated on a bad road, gives exactly the sense required" (*Chadwick*).

14 holiness. Rather, "the sanctification" denoting a continuous process.

15 fail of the grace of God. "Fall back from."

root of bitterness. In allusion to Deut. xxix. 18; where the insidious sin of idolatry is spoken of.

16 one morsel of meat. Rather, "for a single meal."

17 he found no place of repentance, etc. The words should be a parenthesis (as above), to show that it was the *blessing* that Esau "sought carefully."

18 [the (a) **mount].** The best reading is that rendered by *Moffatt*: "You have not come to what you can touch, to flames of fire," etc.

22 the heavenly Jerusalem. Cp. Phil. iii. 20, and note. In this description, all that the Jew gloried in with respect to the giving of the law is shown to be surpassed. The Christian believer has his holy mountain, his sacred city, his "festive gathering" of "myriads," including angels (cp. Acts vii. 53), and the "first-born" (Exod. iv. 22), enrolled, not on earth (Numb. iii. 40, 42), but in heaven; and the universal Judge, and the perfected saints, and the great Mediator, Jesus, with His efficacious blood.

23 church (ἐκκλησίᾳ, congregation) **of the first-born.** The Christian Church of the period, the earliest participant in the great salvation. For the enrolment or registration of the firstborn as representing the entire community, see Numb. iii. 42; and cp. Isa. iv. 3; Luke x. 20.

written. Or, "enrolled."

the spirits of just men made perfect. The saints who lived and died before Christ. Though their *bodies* lie in the grave their *spirits* are in blessedness with Christ: cp. Phil. i. 21, 23.

24 than [that of] Abel. Properly, "than Abel" (see note on xi. 4. The appeal for vengeance and the "plea" for pardon are here placed in contrast.

25 Him that speaketh. Offering peace by the blood of Christ (24).

26 Yet once more, etc. This is freely quoted from Hag. ii. 6; on which see notes.

27 that those things which cannot be (which are not) **shaken,** etc. The "removing" of the transitory is for the establishing of the permanent.

28 cannot be moved. Rather, "cannot be *shaken*"; repeating the word from vers. 26, 27.

let us have grace. Rather, "Let us cherish thankfulness," by which we may serve the Lord in a manner well-pleasing to Him: cp. Psa. l. 23.

29 for our God, etc. Rather, "for indeed our God," etc.; giving another reason for reverential worship, quoted from Deut. iv. 24, as applying under the gospel as well as under the law.

CHAPTER XIII

1 Let brotherly love ("love of the brethren") **continue.** The Hebrew Christians had been eminent in this grace: see vi. 10; x. 33, 34.

2 some have entertained angels unawares. See Gen. xviii. 2, and note

3 as being yourselves also in the body. "The thought is that of the body as being the home (or the prison) of the soul" (*Westcott*).

4 Marriage is honourable in all. Rather, "Let marriage be held in honour among all, and let the bed be undefiled."

but. Rather (var. read.), "for": the enforcement of the command.

5 conversation. That is, "conduct," or manner of life.

for He (Himself) **hath said,** etc. The promise quoted is found, with slight variations, in Josh. i. 5; 1 Chron. xxviii. 20.

6 So that we may boldly say. Rather, "so that we say with good courage," in the words of Psa. cxviii. 6. The Greek word translated "boldly" is from the same verb as is rendered "Be of good cheer" in Matt. ix. 2, and elsewhere.

7 Remember them which have (or, "had") **the rule over you.** Rather, "Remember your leaders." who taught you the gospel, and "imitate their faith."

their conversation. "Their activity."

8 Jesus Christ (is) **the same yesterday,** etc. A continuation of ver. 7. Jesus Christ was "the end" of their work, *i.e.*, its outcome or issue, the haven to which it all tended (ἔκβασις). Hence the exhortation not to be diverted from Him, or to be led astray by those who insist upon maintaining useless ceremonies: see Col. ii. 20–23.

10 We have an altar, etc. "That Christianity is not concerned with matters of food is clear from this, that it depends on a sacrifice of which the priests were expressly forbidden to eat" (*Peake's Commentary*). Jesus corresponds to the sacrifice on the Day of Atonement. See Lev. xvi. 27.

11 without the camp. See Lev. xvi. 27. Our Lord, as the atoning victim, was treated as if He were unclean, being led "without the gate." So His disciples must be willing to be cast out from Judaism (12).

14 For here have we no continuing city. You may well forgo your citizenship in the earthly Jerusalem, since you belong to the heavenly.

15 By Him. Or, "through Him," not through other priests or other rites, let us present a continual thank-offering of praise to God.

16 to communicate. "And do not forget to be kind and liberal" (*Weymouth*). Cp. Rom. xv. 26.

17 them which have the rule over you. Rather, "your leaders," as in ver. 7.

18 we trust we have a good conscience. A protest, probably, against the charges of Judaisers: see Acts xxiv. 16.

honestly. Rather, "honourably."

20 the God of peace. The Divine Author of the everlasting covenant of peace, which is ratified in the blood of Jesus. In this sublime benediction (20, 21) the writer sums up the leading topics of his Epistle.

that great Shepherd of the sheep. This phrase seems to allude to Isa. lxiii. 11.

24 all them that have the rule over you. "All your leaders."

They of Italy. Some render this, "those *from* Italy"; *i.e.*, now with the writer in some other place. But it may mean simply, "the Italians": cp. John xi. 1; Acts xvii. 13. The phrase does not, therefore, decide where the writer of the Epistle was at the time.

25 Grace. See on Rom. i. 7.

[Written to the Hebrews, etc.] The postscript or subscription is of no authority: see note at the end of Romans.

THE GENERAL EPISTLE OF JAMES

INTRODUCTION

THE message of this Epistle is that of Applied Christianity. It begins by applying Christian faith to the trials of life. In words that are almost identical with those of St. Paul (Rom. v. 3), the writer says, "The trying of your faith worketh patience" (i. 3). In similar agreement with St. Paul, he says that trials ought to be a source of joy (cp. i. 2 with Rom. v. 3). Beyond the trials, and as the reward of endurance, is "the crown of life" (i. 12).

He applies Christian faith to the use of speech. The Christian is to be "slow to speak" (i. 19), to bridle his tongue (i. 26). The evil produced by an unbridled tongue is pointed out. It is a little member but can do great mischief. It may be full of deadly poison (iii. 5, 6, 8).

The writer applies Christian faith to the relations between rich and poor, between employers and employed. He blames the Christian congregations for respect of persons, for favouring the rich rather than the poor (ii. 2–4). He reminds them that men may be poor in this world's goods, but rich in faith (ii. 5). In language which recalls the stern denunciations uttered by Old Testament prophets, he censures the employers who have not paid their labourers the wages they have earned (v. 4).

He applies Christian faith to all the social relationships. It should put an end to unkind and malicious gossip (iv. 11) and to envy (v. 9). It should lead us to a frank acknowledgment of our faults against others, and to prayer for one another (v. 16).

And as the motive and basis of all his practical counsels, he assumes faith. This will lead men to ask God for wisdom in their difficulties and trials (i. 5) and will produce courage and stedfastness (i. 6). It is not a substitute for good works but leads to them (i. 27; ii. 14, 17, 20, 26). It is incompatible with respect of persons (ii. 1). It produces the character which he describes as "the wisdom that is from above," peaceable, gentle, conciliatory (iii. 17). And it leads men to keep before them in all their actions the thought of the Great Judge and the Great Judgement (ii. 12; v. 4, 9).

The writer of the Epistle was not James the son of Zebedee, whose death is recorded in Acts xii. 2, but James "the Lord's brother," who is mentioned in Mark vi. 3; Acts xii. 17; xv. 13; 1 Cor. xv. 7; Gal. ii. 9. The date is uncertain, but there is much to be said in favour of as early a date as A.D. 45, in which case it is the earliest of all the Epistles. Some scholars, however, put it as late as A.D. 62.

CHAPTER I

1 to the twelve tribes, etc. Properly, "to the twelve tribes that are in the Dispersion"; *i.e.*, scattered over the Roman empire: cp. John vii. 35; 1 Pet. i. 1. The remains of the Ten Tribes are included with Judah and Benjamin: see Luke ii. 36, "of the tribe of Asher"; and cp. Acts xxvi. 7.

2 temptations. Or, "trials"; whatever might put faith and constancy to the test (3), referring especially to persecutions.

3 the trying of your faith worketh patience. "The proving of your faith (by affliction: see Rom. v. 3) worketh constancy": see Heb. xii. 1, and note. "That St. James no less than St. Paul regarded faith as the very foundation of religion, is evident from this verse as well as from ver. 6; ii. 1; v. 15" (*Mayor*).

4 wanting nothing. "Lacking nothing," the verb being the same as in ver. 5.

5 liberally, lit. "simply": that is, with pure and disinterested generosity: cp. Matt. vi. 22; Rom. xii. 8.

6 nothing wavering. Or, "nothing doubting: for (7) he that doubteth," etc. (R.V.): see Matt. xxi. 21, where the same word is used. For "a wave," the R.V., more precisely, reads, "the surge."

8 double minded. Probably (as R.V.) to be read in apposition with "that man" (omitting *is*)

"Double minded" conveys no impression of *duplicity*, but only that of indecision—"a man of two minds" ("l'homme dont le cœur est partagé" (*French version*)).

9 rejoice. Rather, "glory." The Christian brother who is poor may well glory in his elevation as a child and heir of God (see ii. 5), and the rich in having the pride of wealth taken away; for the wealth itself will pass away, as a withering flower (10, 11).

11 For the sun, etc. The literal rendering of this verse is very striking and pictorial. "For the sun arose, together with the scorching wind, and withered the grass; and the flower thereof fell off, and the beauty of its form perished."

12 when he is tried. That is, when he has stood the test; referring to the result of well-sustained trial: cp. Rom. v. 4. For "the crown of life" see 1 Cor. ix. 25; Rev. ii. 10.

14 every man. Better, as R.V., "each man," severally.

15 finished. Or, "completed" or matured (see Rom. vi. 23).

16 Do not err, etc. Lit., "Be not led astray."

17 the Father of lights, etc. There is here an allusion to heavenly bodies, in contrast with which, in their various vicissitudes, and shadows cast by their revolution (as eclipses or the shadows on a sundial), God is unfailing and unchanging, the Giver of good, and nothing but good. He shows this in the regeneration of believers (18), which, like the firstfruits at the beginning of the harvest, is to be followed by a vast ingathering of the redeemed (Rom. xi. 16).

19 Wherefore, etc. The mention of "the word of truth" leads to the thought of man's duty in respect to it, serious and careful attention, but not eagerness in entering upon the office of teachers (cp. iii. 1) or the zeal of the angry partisan. Such a caution was evidently required by those to whom the apostle wrote.

20 the righteousness of God. The character which God approves, and which is not helped by angry controversy.

21 filthiness. "Baseness." "The word was often used of counterfeit coin" (J. H. Moulton in *Peake's Commentary*).

superfluity of naughtiness. Rather, "overflowing of malice."

engrafted. Or, "implanted," R.V.

which is able to save your souls. Cp. Rom. i. 16.

23 glass. Rather, "mirror": see note on 1 Cor. xiii. 12.

24 he beholdeth himself, etc. Lit., and vividly, "he beheld himself and hath gone away; and he straightway forgot": cp. on ver. 11. Again, a vivid picture as in ver. 11.

25 looketh into. Implying close attention: see 1 Pet. i. 12.

the perfect law of liberty. The emphasis is: "the perfect law, that of liberty." The reference is to the word of gospel truth (18), which is to believers a law expressing God's will; to be obeyed, not of constraint, but willingly. Such obedience is blessed "in the doing" (Rom. viii. 2; John viii. 31). "Continueth" means "continueth looking."

26 seem to be religious. Without self-restraint no religious service can be acceptable to our Father in heaven.

27 Pure religion. The word translated "religion" denotes piety in its external aspect (Acts xxvi. 5; Col. ii. 18). This was often held to consist in ritual observances. On the contrary, says the apostle, divine service is rendered by kindness and purity.

CHAPTER II

1 have (hold) **not the faith,** etc. Let not differences of worldly rank or circumstances, which are as nothing in presence of your Lord's spiritual glory, affect your feelings towards your brethren in the faith.

2 assembly. The word here used is *synagogue* ("meeting-place").

3 have respect to. Or, "look with respect upon."

4 are ye not then partial in yourselves? Rather, as R.V., "are ye not divided in your own mind?" An illustration of the double-mindedness spoken of in i. 8: your religious theories are in contrast with your practice.

judges of (having) **evil thoughts.** Making unjust distinctions.

5 Hath not God chosen the poor, etc.? God has chosen His people chiefly from among the poor, "*to be* rich in faith" (as R.V.: cp. 1 Cor. i. 26–28), but *ye* dishonour them (6).

6 Do not rich men oppress you (lord it over you)? For "draw" read "drag," R.V.

7 that worthy name, etc. Lit., "the honourable name which has been called upon you"; the name of *Christ*: see Acts ii. 38; xi. 26; 1 Pet. iv. 16.

8 the royal law. In which the whole of the second table is summed up. Cp. Matt. xxii. 40; Gal. v. 14.

9 convinced. Or, "convicted." The whole law rests on the authority of God; and he who violates a single precept is guilty of rebellion against Him.

11 For He that said, etc. The argument is from the unity of the Divine Lawgiver to the unity of the law; to offend against one part of the law is to break it as a whole.

12 the (a) **law of liberty.** See note on i. 25. As we are to be judged by the gospel, we must manifest its spirit of universal love; for (13) mercy alone can triumph over judgement; and mercy will be shown to none but those who show it; cp. Matt. v. 7; vi. 11, 14, 15; xviii. 21–25.

13 rejoiceth against. Rather, "triumphs over."

17 being alone. Or, "in itself"; having no inward life or power.

19 that there is one God. Or (R.V.), "that God is one." The special and distinctive article of Jewish belief.

thou doest well, etc. This belief is right; but if this is all, it is no better than the belief of "demons," and it should make thee, as it makes them, to "tremble."

20 But wilt thou know, etc.? The Scripture proof that there can be no true faith which does not produce good works, is seen in the histories of Abraham and of Rahab.

21 Abraham our father. Whose example is of the highest authority to us Jews.

22 Seest thou. Or, "Thou seest." In the case of Abraham, faith co-operated with the works that sprang from it in securing his salvation; for faith cannot be perfectly developed without works.

25 Rahab. See Josh. ii. 2; Heb. xi. 31, and notes.

26 faith without works is dead. The teaching of this verse, and of ver. 24, is in perfect accordance with that of Paul in Rom. iii. 27, 28; iv. 1–8 (on which see notes); although the truth is here presented from an opposite point of view. Paul, arguing against those who, trusting in their own meritorious works, refuse to seek salvation as sinners by trusting in Christ, insists that *such works* are utterly worthless. James, opposing the notion that it is enough to hold a correct creed, without maintaining a life of practical godliness, insists that *such faith* is utterly worthless. But Paul also teaches that saving faith works by love (Gal. v. 6); and James that acceptable works are the fruit and evidence of faith (18).

CHAPTER III

1 My brethren, be not many masters, etc. Rather, "Let not many of you become teachers, my brethren, knowing that we [teachers] shall receive greater condemnation" than others, if we lead them astray.

2 For in many things we offend all. "For in many respects, all of us [even the wisest and best] stumble," and especially do we fail in the use of the tongue; so that he who thoroughly governs his tongue may be regarded as perfect master of himself.

a perfect man. One of full moral stature, indicated by this, as a test.

4 the governor. Lit., "the impulse of the steersman."

5 how great a matter. Rather, "how great a forest"; cp. Homer, *Iliad*, ii. 455; xi. 155. A spark has caused terrific conflagrations; and a word has sometimes set families and communities "in a blaze."

6 a world of iniquity. The omission of "*so*" is supported by the best MSS. and gives a different turn to the sentence. "The tongue is a fire: the world of iniquity among our members is the tongue, which defileth," etc. (R.V.). "The world of iniquity" denotes "the sum total of unrighteousness" (*Lange*). All kinds of evil result from the abuse of the tongue.

the course (wheel) **of nature.** Rather, "the whole round of life."

hell. "The Gehenna" of fire: see 2 Kings xxiii. 10; Matt. v. 22.

9 God, even the Father. The best MSS. give, "We bless the Lord and Father."

14 envying and strife. Rather, "jealousy and faction."

15 sensual. Or, "animal": see note on 1 Cor. ii. 14. The three epithets form an impressive climax: "earthly," material, opposed to that which possesses life and thought; "sensual," or animal, belonging to man's lower impulses; "devilish," or demoniacal, akin to the nature of unclean spirits.

17 without partiality. "Without wrangling."

18 the fruit of righteousness. Ambition and strife have their fruit (16); so the work of peace has righteousness for its fruit, "sown" now, to be enjoyed for ever (cp. Matt. v. 9).

CHAPTER IV

1 wars. The disruption of social and civil ties, and the prevalence of sects and parties. These evils remarkably characterised the Jewish people before the destruction of Jerusalem.

lusts. Or, "pleasures"; *i.e.*, selfish gratifications.

2 ye kill, etc. "Ye murder and envy, and cannot obtain; ye fight and war." And yet even in regard to these earthly objects of desire "ye have not," either because you seek them in this way, and not from God the Giver of all good, or because you seek them for your own selfish, sensual ends.

4 Ye adulterers and adulteresses. The best texts have "adulteresses" alone; referring either to *communities*, or to some such word as *souls* (fem.). Departure from God is represented in the Old Testament under the figure of conjugal unfaithfulness. The reference therefore is to churches, or to professors of religion, whose love of the world has made them unfaithful to God. See Isa. lvii. 3–9; and Hosea throughout; cp. Matt. xii. 39.

will be. Or, "wants to be"; having his heart set on the world. The verb is the same as in Matt. i. 19.

5 the Scripture saith. The words which immediately follow are not found elsewhere in Scripture. They may perhaps be understood as expressing the meaning of various passages. "Do ye think it is vain what the Scripture saith? The Spirit who came to dwell within us (or, see var. read., 'whom He made to dwell within us') jealously yearns for the entire devotion of the heart" (*Mayor*). See Exod. xx. 5; Deut. xxxii. 11, 12, 16–21; Isa. lxiii. 8–16; Zech. viii. 2.

6 God resisteth the proud. Prov. iii. 34 (Sept.).

8 double minded. Wavering between tendencies to good and evil: see on i. 8.

11 Speak not evil. Evil speaking is one manifestation of jealousy and party spirit. To speak evil of a brother is to condemn or slight the law which says, "Thou shalt love thy neighbour as thyself." It is also to put oneself in the position of a judge.

12 There is one lawgiver. Perhaps the best rendering is, "One is the Lawgiver and Judge, He who has power," etc. (Rom. xiv. 4). *Thou* is very emphatic in the original.

13 Go to now. Or, "Come now"; and so in v. 1. It is an expression used to arrest attention.

14 It is even a vapour. Or, "for it is a vapour," etc. With a slight change in the word translated "it is" (ἐστι), the best authorities read "ye are" (ἐστε): "Ye are a vapour."

16 But now, etc. But, as it is, you make a boast of your "proud pretensions" (*Moffatt*); in strong contrast with the humiliation expressed by, "If the Lord will."

all such rejoicing is evil. Because it proceeds from forgetfulness of God.

CHAPTER V

1 rich men. Rich men who trust in their wealth (see Luke vi. 24), and become unjust and oppressive, are here meant: see vers. 4–6.

that shall come upon you. Rather, as R.V., "that are coming upon you." The calamities which attended the destruction of Jerusalem.

3 is cankered. Properly, "has been rusted through." The rust is already in your ill-gotten gains, and will bear witness against your covetous laying up of treasure in these last days, when ye should have been preparing for the Lord's coming; see vers. 7, 8; Luke xvii. 26–30. The translation, "for the last days," is inaccurate and misses the point of the passage.

4 the hire of the labourers. The Bible has a good deal to say on the relation between employers and employed, on work and wages. Cp. on the one hand Jer. xxii. 13, Mal. iii. 5; and on the other Titus ii. 9, 10.

sabaoth. "Sabaoth" is the Hebrew word for "hosts," transliterated by the Jews into Greek; see notes on 1 Sam. i. 3; Psa. xxiv 10 Rom. ix. 29.

5 ye have nourished your hearts. You have cherished and gratified your natural desires, as in Luke xxi. 34; Acts xiv. 17. Ye are like fatted animals, feeding greedily on the very day when they are to be killed.

6 the just. " The righteous one."

he doth not resist you. His unresisting submission, like that of " the Just One," his Divine Master, aggravates your cruelty.

7 the early and latter rain. See note on Deut. xi. 14.

8 draweth nigh. Or, as in Matt. iii. 2, " is at hand."

9 Grudge not. Or, " *Sigh* not " ; *i.e.*, murmur not, " that ye be not judged."

standeth before the door. That is, He is close at hand, coming to judgement (see ver. 8).

10 Take, my brethren, the prophets, etc. Cp. Matt. v. 12; Heb. xi. 35–38.

11 we count them happy which endure. Bravely sustaining afflictions; like Job, of whose trials, and of whose endurance you have heard. Look at the happy " end " to which the Lord in His mercy brought them.

12 swear not. See Matt. v. 33, 37, and notes.

13 merry. Rather, " cheerful." Let your joy or sorrow be expressed in a Christian manner: cp. Eph. v. 19.

14 elders. See Acts xiv. 23; Phil. i. 1, and notes

anointing. See Mark vi. 13, and note.

15 the prayer of faith shall save the sick, etc. Prayer, when offered in reliance on God's promise (cp. i. 6), shall be made effectual, not only to the sick man's recovery to health (see 1 Cor. xii. 9), but " even if " he be suffering in consequence of some special sins (see 1 Cor. xi. 30), to his forgiveness also.

16 one to another. Not to the elders only, but to any believing and praying brother; for " the energetic prayer of a righteous man has much power." " People wear their hearts out in estrangements; friction is created by that native stubbornness in defending a fault rather than confess it, which is too characteristic of us all " (Charles Brown in *Devotional Commentary*).

17 he prayed earnestly. Lit., he " prayed in prayer " ; an emphatic Hebrew idiom. In 1 Kings xvii., xviii., it is not expressly said that Elijah prayed either at the beginning or the end of the drought; but the facts of the history imply that he did.

on the earth. Rather, " on the *land* " ; namely, Palestine: see 1 Kings xvii. 1, and note.

19 convert. Or, " turn him back " ; *i.e.*, restore him to the truth, from his error and ungodliness.

20 from death. That is, with an eternal salvation, such as those enjoy whose sins, however numerous, are covered or pardoned through Christ. Such is the blessedness which " any " faithful Christian may become the means, by God's grace, of conveying.

THE FIRST EPISTLE GENERAL OF PETER

INTRODUCTION

THE suffering and risen Christ is set forth in this letter as the Saviour and example for sinful and suffering men, and His resurrection as their hope and inspiration. The writer speaks of obedience and sprinkling of the blood of Jesus Christ (i. 2); of the sufferings of Christ (i. 11; ii. 21; iii. 18; iv. 1, 13); of the precious blood of Christ (i. 19); of the resurrection of Jesus Christ from the dead (i. 3, 21; iii. 18, 21); the appearing of Jesus Christ (i. 7); and the revelation of Jesus Christ (i. 13).

And all this is stated not as mere theological dogma, but as historical fact, recorded by an eyewitness, and as an encouragement and help in everyday life. St. Peter here cheers the persecuted and scattered Christians by the prospect of the incorruptible inheritance, a prospect based on the resurrection of the Lord (i. 3, 4). Here, too, we see the unity of the Apostolic teaching, when we compare his statements on suffering and trial with those of St. Paul and St. James (cp. i. 6 with Rom. v. 3 and James i. 2, 3).

The character of Christ is held up as an example to His followers. " Be ye holy " (i. 15, 16). They have been redeemed at a costly price (i. 18, 19), and therefore should put away all malice and envy, hypocrisy and evil speaking (ii. 1). As living stones they are part of God's spiritual temple, and are at the same time called as priests to offer up spiritual sacrifices (ii. 5). As citizens they are to render respect and obedience to rulers, and, when they suffer wrongfully, to keep before them the patience of Christ (ii. 13–22; iii. 14–18). Cultivating Christ's spirit of gentleness and following the purity of His character, husbands and wives are to dwell together as heirs of the grace of life (iii. 1–7). In relation to the pagan world around them, with its licentiousness and excesses, they are to arm themselves with the spirit of Christ (iv. 1–6). Amongst themselves they are above all things to cultivate love (iv. 8). And the Epistle closes with advice to the presbyters in the Churches to feed the flock of God and not to be lords but examples, and to the younger members to practise humility (v. 1–6).

The letter was written in or soon after A.D. 64, when the persecutions under Nero had begun, persecutions in which St. Peter himself was so soon to suffer martyrdom.

"If any one were tempted to doubt the historicity of the New Testament and wanted to find some solid historical footing on which to begin rebuilding his faith, it might be no bad plan for him to make a start with the Apostle Peter. . . . Peter in the Fourth Gospel is quite demonstrably the same person who makes so many characteristic appearances in the other three. . . . When one turns to the Epistle, one must beware of too easy reference of this phrase or that to suit a Gospel incident . . . yet one may claim, without straining the testimony, that the authentic Peter is recognisable here. . . . We seem to see over and over again the Peter whom we have met so often elsewhere" (J. M. E. Ross in *Devotional Commentary*).

CHAPTER I

1 to the strangers, etc. Lit., "to the elect sojourners of the Dispersion." This phrase is usually applied to the scattered Jews, but is evidently here applied also to Christians, whether Jew or Gentile, as being now the chosen people of God: see ii. 5–10; Eph. ii. 11–12; cp. note on James i. 1.

Pontus, etc. The different countries here named are the provinces of Asia Minor. Aquila was a Jewish native of Pontus (Acts xviii. 2). There were Jews from this region as well as from "Cappadocia" in Jerusalem on the day of Pentecost (Acts ii. 9). For Paul's thwarted purpose to visit "Bithynia," see Acts xvi. 7. The verse indicates many triumphs of the gospel unrecorded in the history.

Asia. Proconsular Asia: see note on Acts ii. 9.

2 through sanctification. Rather, "in sanctification." The believer's sanctification, necessarily leading "to obedience" (cp. ver. 14), and so to the enjoyment of all the privileges of the covenant which the blood of Christ has ratified, is an essential element in the Divine purpose. The union of Father, Son, and Holy Spirit in the work of salvation is here expressively indicated.

3 a lively hope. Rather, "a living hope": so called as being real, joyous, energetic, and abiding. "Hope" thus sums up the Christian life.

4 an inheritance incorruptible. The destined blessedness of God's children. This has no tendency to decay, nor any susceptibility of pollution; nor can it even lose the bloom and freshness of its joy: for it is "laid up safe in heaven"; whilst you, amidst all enemies, are "guarded as in the fortress of God's power" on earth. The Greek word for "kept" is that used in 2 Cor. xi. 32; Gal. iii. 23; Phil. iv. 7. Dr. Hort's translation suggests that the inheritance is not only future but present: "An inheritance which hath been kept in the heavens unto you who in the power of God are guarded through faith unto a salvation ready to be revealed in a season of extremity."

5 salvation ready to be revealed. This salvation is so complete that it will be found "ready to be revealed" when God's time to manifest it comes.

6 for a season. Properly, "for a little while": cp. 2 Cor. iv. 17.

manifold temptations. That is, many kinds of trials: cp. James i. 2.

7 the trial of your faith, etc. See James i. 3. "The result of the testing" is more precious than gold (not "than of gold"), which is perishable, even though it stands the test of fire; for it will be "found," etc.

praise. The reward of grace to be received at Christ's coming consists of "praise" for fidelity (Matt. xxv. 21; 1 Cor. iv. 5; Rom. ii. 7, 10; 2 Thess. i. 5); of "honour" which Christ promises to His faithful servants (John xii. 26, etc.); and of a participation in the "glory" which the Father has given to Christ (vers. 11, 21; iv. 13; v. 1; John xvii. 24).

9 the end of your faith. Salvation, the object and result of faith, is received here, to the joy of believers, and will be completed hereafter.

10 Of which salvation (the) prophets have inquired, etc. Another reason for prizing the gospel.

11 what (time) or what manner of time, etc. Desiring to know the time of Messiah's coming, and by what sort of events it would be distinguished.

when it testified beforehand. Properly, "testifying beforehand the sufferings in store for Christ, and the glories after these" sufferings: cp. Isa. liii.–lv., and notes.

12 desire to look into. The term here used means to "bend aside," in order to look at what cannot easily be seen. Angelic spirits gaze wistfully into all that concerns the great work of redemption.

13 gird up the loins of your mind, etc. If the blessings given to you excited the desires of prophets, and fix the attention of angels, surely you should vigorously lay hold of them, and "hope perfectly," without wavering, for the "grace that is to be brought unto you" at your Lord's coming.

14 obedient children. Lit., "children of obedience": cp. Eph. ii. 2, 3; v. 6, 8.

15 conversation. Rather, "manner of life": see note on Psa. xxxvii. 14.

16 Be ye holy. "Ye shall be holy" (R.V.); as in Lev. xi. 44, etc.; where ceremonial purity is enjoined, the outward type of purity of heart (Matt. v. 8, 48). "We are often surprised, in reading the New Testament, to think that it should be necessary to warn Christian people against so many of the coarser vices and the more obvious sins. Yet the very warnings remind us how great was the moral need of the world when Christianity began its work" (J. M. E. Ross in *Devotional Commentary*).

17 if ye call, etc. Meaning, "*Since* ye call on Him as Father." "The necessity of holiness is here grounded on three considerations: (1) the character of God; (2) the reality of judgement, and (3) the costliness of redemption" (Currie Martin in *Peake's Commentary*).

in fear. A child's fear of grieving a Father who has given such costly proof of love to him (18–21).

18 your vain conversation. *i.e.*, your foolish (or useless) manner of life, whether Pagan or Pharisaic.

19 precious. The order is, as R.V., "with precious blood, as of a lamb, without blemish and without spot, [even the blood] of Christ." "Precious" as compared with "silver and gold"; but chiefly in itself; for it is the blood of a spotless Victim, of God's Anointed, of Him whose manifestation in our world was purposed in eternity, and prepared for in all the preceding "times" (20)—of Him who is to us the only medium of faith and hope in God (21). All this is included in the idea of "the precious blood," and more also, when we think of its "power to save."

a lamb. See note on John i. 29. The words were spoken by the Baptist in the course of those teachings which led to Peter being brought to Jesus.

22 Seeing you have purified your souls, etc. One of the results of obeying the truth is sincere brotherly love.

with a pure heart fervently. Rather (omitting the words *a pure*), "intensely, from the heart."

23 being born again. Rather, as R.V., "having been begotten again."

which liveth and abideth (omit *for ever*). This describes "the word."

24 All flesh is as grass, etc. See notes on Isa. xl. 6–8.

25 which by the gospel is preached unto you. Or, "which was preached as good tidings unto you."

CHAPTER II

1 Wherefore. That is, in view of our redemption by Christ, and regeneration by the Spirit, as set forth in ch. i. The figure "newborn babes" carries on the thought of "begotten again" (23).

2 desire the sincere milk of the word. The word translated "sincere" means "unadulterated," and "the word" itself is described as "spiritual" or reasonable (λογικόν). The words might be paraphrased, "Desire the unadulterated milk suited to your spiritual being."

4 a living stone. Christ, the corner-stone, unlike others, has life in Himself, and imparts it to others (John v. 25, 26); so that all the stones of the building become instinct with His life, forming a spiritual temple. The reference here is peculiarly appropriate from the apostle Peter: see Matt. xvi. 18.

chosen of God [and] precious. R.V., "with God elect, precious" (or "held in honour," as ver. 6).

5 ye also, as lively stones, are built up, etc. Or, "Be ye too, as living stones, built up," etc.

a holy priesthood. Or "for (*i.e.*, to be) a holy priesthood" In virtue of their union with Christ, the true High Priest (Heb. iv. 14), the faithful (see ver. 9) are constituted a kingdom of priests unto God (Rev. i. 6).

6 Behold I lay in Sion, etc. See notes on Isa. xxviii. 16, here quoted freely.

precious. Rather, "held in honour."

shall not be confounded. Rather, "shall not be put to shame": cp. Joel ii. 26, 27; Rom. ix. 33.

7 Unto you, therefore, etc. Perhaps the most accurate rendering is, "To you then is the honour as believers." "The believer shall not be put to shame": on the contrary, he shall be "held in honour" (ver. 6), like his Lord; whom unbelievers, in their disobedience, will find to be a stone of stumbling, etc.; *i.e.*, the occasion of their fall and ruin; see notes on Psa. cxviii. 22; Matt. xxi. 42–44,

the head of the corner. That is, "chief," in the foundation of the building.

8 whereunto. *i.e.*, to the result of disobedience.

9 a chosen generation. Or, as R.V., "an elect race." The verse enumerates the privileges of believers in a series of Old Testament phrases, applying to Christians the terms describing the special honour of God's ancient people. See Exod. xix. 6; Deut. vii. 6; Isa. xliii. 21.

a peculiar people. Lit., "a people for a possession"; whom God has made His own special property.

praises. Lit., "virtues," or "excellences" (R.V.); the Divine perfections, which God's people are to imitate in their own lives.

10 which in time past were not a people. See note on Rom. ix. 25; and Hos. i. 9, 6; "Lo-ammi" and "Lo-ruhamah."

11 fleshly lusts. "Fleshly lusts" are the evil desires of our depraved nature (cp. Gal. v. 19–21; Eph. ii. 3), which, like well-armed enemies, attack our higher powers, and too often bring the judgement, imagination, and conscience under their destructive influence. "Soul" here includes the "soul and spirit" of 1 Thess. v. 23. There is a suggestion of this verse in Tennyson's poem "To the Queen" with which he concludes *The Idylls of the King*:

"... accept this old imperfect tale,
New-old, and shadowing Sense at war with Soul."

12 having your conversation honest. Rather, "having your behaviour honourable."

whereas they speak against you, etc. Heathen, in their ignorant hatred (15), imputed to the early Christians the most unseemly conduct and crimes against society and the State.

which they shall behold. Inspecting them as eyewitnesses. The Greek verb means "looking closely at."

the day of visitation. This means probably the time of God's merciful visitation in the gospel: cp. Luke xix. 44.

13 every ordinance of man. The human institutions here referred to are especially those connected with civil government. On this precept and its limitation, see Acts iv. 19; v. 29; Rom. xiii. 1–7, and notes.

14 governors. Referring specially to Roman governors sent by the emperor into the provinces, such as "Pontus, Galatia," etc. (i. 1).

for the punishment of evildoers, etc. This is the design of civil government, though all rulers may not fulfil it.

15 the ignorance of foolish men. See ver. 12, and Acts xvii. 5, etc.

16 as free, etc. Respecting Christian freedom and its abuse, see note on Gal. v. 13.

maliciousness. This means *wickedness* of any kind.

18 Servants. Rather, " domestics." The word here used, denoting household servants generally, is not that which is usually employed in the New Testament for servants or slaves.

froward. That is, perverse or unjust.

19 For this is thankworthy, etc. Lit., " grace " or " a grace," the fruit of the Divine Spirit in the heart.

conscience. Rather, consciousness or sense of God's presence.

20 acceptable. Rather, " a grace," as in ver. 19.

21 hereunto. To patient endurance of injuries.

22–25 Who did no sin, etc. In this description Peter quotes or alludes to Isa. liii. 4–7, 9, 11, 12; on which see notes.

23 committed [Himself] to Him that judgeth righteously. Or, " committed *His cause,*" etc. ; see R.V. marg. Condemned as He was, at man's tribunal, by an unjust sentence, He committed His cause to God : cp. John xii. 31 ; xvi. 11.

24 on the tree. Lit., " up to the tree." The cross was the altar on which Christ " offered up " Himself a sacrifice for " our sins."

dead to sins. Cp. Rom. vi. 2–8 ; Gal. ii. 19, and notes.

25 the Shepherd and Bishop (Guardian) **of your souls.** Perhaps alluding to Ezek. xxxiv. 11.

CHAPTER III

1 Likewise. That is, " In like manner " ; on the same principle of subjection to the obligations of social life : see ii. 13, 18. On the duties and relations of the married state, cp. Eph. v. 22–33, and notes.

if any obey not the word. Even if any should remain unconverted.

without the word. *i.e.*, by the silent eloquence of a " reverently chaste behaviour " (2).

3 let it not be that outward adorning, etc. " Whose adorning should be, not," etc. This is not a prohibition of outward adorning, but a declaration of its worthlessness if opposed to, or separated from, grace (*Speaker's Commentary*).

4 the hidden man. " But inside, in the heart " (*Moffatt*).

5 who trusted in God. Rather, " who hoped in God " (R.V.).

6 whose daughters ye are. Properly, " whose (Sarah's) children ye became " ; that is, when ye truly believed the gospel : cp. Gal. iii. 29.

as long as ye do well. Rather, " by doing well and not being afraid." " Faisant le bien et ne craignant rien de ce qui peut épouvanter " (*French version*).

7 that your prayers be not hindered. By perverted relations of any kind, especially jealousy or discord : cp. 1 Cor. vii. 5. " Two hearts shall build a family altar ; two prayers shall make a perfect strength ; and the Christian Church shall have its roots and reservoirs in the Christian home " (*J. M. E. Ross*).

8 love as brethren. Rather, " having brotherly love."

9 but contrariwise blessing. Blessing the doer or speaker of evil. Cp. Gen. xii. 1–3 ; Eph. iv. 32.

10 He that will love life. More clearly, as R.V., " He that would love life." Cp. Psa. xxxiv. 12–16.

11 eschew. Or, " avoid."

ensue. Or, " follow " : cp. Heb. xii. 14.

12 over . . . against. The same word in original, " upon."

13 who is he that will harm you, etc. ? That is, God will not suffer any real harm to befall you if you earnestly seek the good. " But if even ye suffer for righteousness' sake, happy are ye " : see Matt. v. 10.

14 be not afraid of their terror. The fear caused by persecutors ; see Isa. viii. 12, 13, and note. But honour the Lord, " the Lord Christ " (the reading of the best MSS.), etc.

15 ready always to give an answer, etc. Let not your submission show itself in unworthy silence, but be ready to maintain and defend your hope as a Christian in reply to all inquiry.

16 that falsely accuse, etc. Or, " who slander your good manner of life in Christ " : cp. ii. 12.

18 once. Rather, " once for all."

in the flesh. " The flesh " here probably means the mortal body, " flesh and blood," which was laid in the tomb ; and " the spirit," the higher part of the human nature, indissolubly united with the Divine. Read, " in the spirit " : cp. 1 Tim. iii. 16.

19 by which. Rather, " in which " ; *i.e.*, " in the spirit." Of the numerous interpretations which have been given of this most difficult passage the following are the most important :—I. That Christ preached through the instrumentality of Noah to the ungodly of his day, who perished in the Flood (2 Pet. ii. 5). Dr. C. H. H. Wright (*Biblical Essays*) translates, " Christ went and preached to the spirits in prison, disobedient aforetime, when the long-suffering of God waited in the days of Noah." II. That Christ preached personally in His disembodied state between His death and resurrection. This is the view of Dorner, Alford and Plumptre. Some consider that Christ's preaching then was either (i.) to expectant believers in Hades, or (ii.) to all the dead of former ages, or (iii.) to ancient unbelievers ; of whom those who perished in Noah's time are particularly mentioned, perhaps because of the next remark (21, 22). Whatever be the meaning of the words, there is evidently nothing in them to countenance either the notion of purgatorial suffering, or that of universal restoration.

20 saved by (through) **water.** The very water which destroyed the ungodly bore safely those who were in the ark.

21 The like figure whereunto, etc. Properly, " which (*i.e.*, water) as an antitype now saved us also, [even] baptism." As water was the means of saving those who were in the ark, so in baptism, the antitype, it is even now the means of saving us ; but only when, instead of trusting in the outward washing, we conscientiously seek after God, through faith in our risen and exalted Redeemer : cp. Rom. vi. 1–4.

the answer . . . toward God. Rather, " inquiry . . . after God."

by the resurrection. Cp. Paul's argument : Rom. vi. 4, 5.

CHAPTER IV

1 Forasmuch then as Christ hath suffered, etc. The apostle reverts to Christ's sufferings as our example (iii. 18).

arm yourselves. It is only by a severe conflict in which you must be armed with a readiness to suffer with Christ, that the power of sin over you can " be made to cease " : cp. Rom. vi. 1–7.

3 the time past of [our] life may suffice us, etc. Ironical.

abominable. Lit., "unlawful"; *i.e.*, forbidden by God: see Exod. xx. 3–5.

4 they think it strange, etc. "It is strange unto a carnal man to see the child of God disdain the pleasures of sin; he knows not the higher and purer delights and pleasures that the Christian is called to" (*Leighton*).

to the same excess of riot. Or, "into the same flood of profligacy" (*Moffatt*).

6 For this cause was the gospel preached, etc. This verse has been variously interpreted, according to the view taken of iii. 19; on which see note. It probably means: The gospel was preached to those who died, in order that, while in their mortal part they must suffer the sentence on all mankind, in their higher spiritual nature they may live a Divine life by God's power.

8 charity shall cover the multitude of sins. Rather, "Love covereth a multitude of sins": see Prov. x. 12, and note. Cp. also the πάντα στέγει of 1 Cor. xiii. 7, "covers" or "hides" the faults of others.

9 without grudging. Lit., "without murmurings": see Heb. xiii. 2.

10 hath received the gift. Lit., "received a gift."

as good stewards, etc. Extraordinary as well as ordinary gifts and graces in all their variety (Rom. xii. 4–8; 1 Cor. xii. 4–11), are a trust for the benefit of the Church.

11 [let him speak] as the oracles of God. Teaching, not his own notions, but God's revealed truth, and uttering his words with the conviction, reverence, humility, and earnestness which become so great and holy a message.

minister. See note on Rom. xii. 7.

the ability which God giveth. Lit. and more forcibly, as R.V., "the strength which God supplieth."

12 the fiery trial which is to try you. Lit., "the burning fire among you which cometh to you for trial."

13 but rejoice, etc. Those who suffer like Christ, and for Him, may rejoice in the prospect of sharing His glory: cp. Matt. v. 11, 12; Phil. iii. 10, 11; Col. i. 24, and notes.

inasmuch as. Lit., "according as," or "in so far as." In whatever degree ye partake His sufferings, rejoice.

14 for the name of Christ. Properly, "in the name of Christ"; *i.e.*, as being called by His name (16).

the [Spirit] of glory and of God, etc. The Spirit of God rests upon you (like the Shechinah upon the ark) as the Spirit of glory; shedding His glory over all your reproach, weakness, and suffering: cp. Isa. xi. 2; 2 Tim. i. 7.

on their part, etc. This contrast between the reviling and the glorifying of Christ seems to have been the comment of some transcriber. It is omitted in the best texts: so R.V.

16 as a Christian. That is, for being a Christian: then a name of scorn: see Acts xi. 26; xxvi. 28. It does not occur elsewhere in the New Testament.

on this behalf. The best MSS. have "in this name." The "name" is that of Christ, or of "Christian."

18 scarcely. Or, "with difficulty." This is the Septuagint version of Prov. xi. 31. The original idea of the Greek word is that of toil and trouble.

19 Wherefore let them that suffer, etc. See Matt. x. 28–33.

CHAPTER V

1 who am also an elder. Rather, "who am a fellow-elder."

2 feed. R.V., "Tend," the word used by our Lord in His charge to Peter (John xxi. 16). So the Saviour's words have been handed on from generation to generation: cp. 1 Cor. xi. 23.

taking the oversight. See Acts xx. 28, and note.

3 neither as being lords, etc. This may be rendered "nor as lording it over the charges allotted to you; but rather as models": living as you would wish them to live. The word "God's" is not in the original.

4 the chief Shepherd. Cp. ii. 25; John x. 11–18; Heb. xiii. 20.

that fadeth not away. One word in orig., "amaranthine," or "unwithering."

5 the elder. Rather, "the elders" (as in ver. 1); whose authority and teaching the younger persons should respect.

be clothed. The word denotes a close-knitted garment, an outer wrapper, worn by servants; hence its use in the exhortation to humility. Not elsewhere found in the New Testament.

God resisteth the proud, etc. See notes on Prov. iii. 34, and James iv. 6.

6 under the mighty hand of God. Alluding to the severe afflictions they had to pass through (iv. 12).

7 care. Rather, "anxiety": see Psa. lv. 22; Matt. vi. 25; Phil. iv. 6. The word for "careth" is different, implying loving guardianship.

8 a roaring lion. Satan instigated the persecutions to which the apostle has been referring. These imperilled not only the bodily life, but the faith and constancy of believers. Hence the need of watchfulness.

9 the same afflictions, etc. "How to pay the same tax of suffering as your brethren throughout the world" (*Moffatt*).

12 Silvanus. No doubt, the Silas or Silvanus mentioned in Acts xv. 22; 2 Cor. i. 19; 1 and 2 Thess. i. 1. He was the bearer of the letter, or perhaps Peter's amanuensis. The words "unto you" are connected in R.V. with "I have written."

as I suppose. Rather, "as I account him"; implying that Peter had carefully estimated his worth.

13 The [church that is] at Babylon, etc. Lit., "She that in Babylon is elected together with [you] salutes you"; probably meaning the church at Rome, the spiritual Babylon.

Marcus. Most likely John Mark, nephew to Barnabas, and the writer of the Gospel. From Acts xii. 12 it appears that Peter was intimate with Mark's family; and the title "son" may be expressive of the affection of an elder (cp. 1 Tim. i. 2; Titus i. 4). Or Mark may have been a convert of Peter.

14 Greet ye one another, etc. See note on Rom. xvi. 16.

Peace. This Jewish formula of salutation was appropriate from "the apostle of the circumcision," as "Grace" was from the apostle of the Gentiles; see on Heb. xiii. 25.

THE SECOND EPISTLE GENERAL OF PETER

INTRODUCTION

EACH of the three chapters of this Epistle has a distinctive message of its own.

Writing in a time of much persecution, and when various heresies had already begun to show themselves within the Christian Church, the apostle realises that the chief concern should be the character of the Christians themselves. Hence his first chapter deals with this subject. He begins by reminding them of the source of all spiritual life. Their peace comes through the knowledge of God and of Jesus Christ our Lord (i. 2). Through that same knowledge comes the assurance of Divine power in everything that relates to conduct (i. 3). The promises of God are the means of fellowship with the Divine nature and the means of deliverance from the evil that is in the world (i. 4). But the believers must not only rest in this knowledge and on these promises. They must exert themselves to activity and to make progress in Christian character (i. 5, 7). Thus the knowledge of Christ will become fruitful in spiritual results, and give them thereby the assurance of an abundant entrance into His everlasting kingdom (i. 8–11). He enforces this exhortation by an earnest appeal based on the prospect of his approaching death (vers. 13–15) and on the historical and personal certitudes on which his knowledge of Christ is founded (vers. 16–18) and the Divine origin of the Scripture revelation (vers. 19–21).

In the second chapter he enforces the need for dwelling on these primary truths by referring to false teachers (ii. 1, 2) showing their true character (vers. 3, 10, 12, 14, 17) and giving a solemn warning against the consequences of such life and teaching (vers. 12–22).

The third chapter deals with the coming of the Lord. It shall be denied by some of these false teachers (iii. 3, 4). Hence the apostle reminds his readers that one day is with the Lord as a thousand years, and a thousand years as one day, and that His delay is with a merciful purpose, to give all men opportunity for repentance (vers. 8, 9) He wants them to remember that it is the unexpectedness of the Lord's coming, and not the date of it, that is important (ver. 10), and on this point he is in full harmony with the teaching of St. Paul (1 Thess. v. 1, 2) and of our Lord Himself (Luke xii. 39, 40). The closing words of the letters are a renewed appeal to Christians to be ready for the Saviour's coming by godliness of life and character (iii. 11–14, 18).

The Epistle was written by St. Peter some time after he wrote his first Epistle (A.D. 64) and not long before his death in A.D. 68–70. For the resemblances between this letter and the Epistle of Jude, see the Introduction to the latter.

CHAPTER I

1 obtained. Lit., "obtained by lot," or by Divine appointment. The Greek word "excludes all personal agency and merit" (*Lange*). The faith of those believers who, "scattered abroad," had not seen Christ in the flesh, was "equally precious" with the faith of His immediate disciples: cp. 1 Pet. i. 8.

through the righteousness of God. etc. Rather, "in the righteousness of our God and Saviour Jesus Christ."

2 through the knowledge. Rather, "in the full knowledge." It is in personal acquaintance with our Father and our Saviour that grace and peace are multiplied to us: cp. John xvii. 3. For the benediction, cp. 1 Pet. i. 2.

3 According as, etc. Or, "Seeing that" he has given us these privileges (3, 4), "on account also of this (ver. 5, not 'beside this') giving all diligence," etc.

hath called us to glory and virtue. The best MSS. give as the reading "called us by His own glory and virtue" (R.V.). "Virtue" (see 1 Pet. ii. 9) may be, generally, excellence; or specifically and more probably, "might" or "energy."

4 whereby. That is, by God's own glory and might.

partakers of the divine nature. See Col. iii. 10; Heb. xii. 10, and notes.

5 And beside this, etc. Rather, "On account also of this very thing, contributing [on your part] all diligence," etc.

add to your faith. Lit., "supply in your faith," etc. Each of these Christian virtues is not so much to be added to its predecessor as to be infused into it or welded into it, as the link in a chain. The word rendered "add," or "supply" is taken from the Greek theatre, where it meant to supply the expenses of a chorus in a new play. It corresponds with that in 1 Pet. iv. 11, "which God *giveth*," or *supplieth*.

virtue. Energy, or might: see on ver. 3.

6 knowledge. Moral discernment in general, γνῶσις (distinguished from "full knowledge," ver. 2).

temperance. Self-control; mastery of the passions and desires.

patience. Endurance: see note on Heb. xii. 1.

godliness. See 1 Tim. iii. 16.

7 brotherly kindness. Rather, "love of the brethren": see 1 Pet. i. 22; iii. 8.

charity. Or "love"; comprehensive, universal. In this list of Christian graces, "each particular produces and facilitates the following, while it tempers and perfects that which goes before. The order is that of nature, rather than of time" (*Bengel*). An excellent treatment of the whole passage is given in a booklet, *The Gamut of Graces*, by Dr. Monro Gibson (1926). Referring to the idea mentioned in our note on ver. 5, he says, "We have the Christian graces introduced as a chorus into life, which would be dull and flat and discordant without them."

8 barren, etc. Rather, "idle."

10 the rather, brethren, give diligence. Rather, as R.V., "brethren, give the more diligence."

sure. Or, "firm." The apostle here "concludes that the only way in which we can prove ourselves to be elected by the Lord (see 1 Pet. i. 2), and called not in vain (1 Pet. ii. 21), is by having a good conscience and uprightness of life, corresponding to our profession of faith. And he says that we must use the more earnestness and diligence, because he had said before that faith should not be barren" (*Calvin*).

ye shall never fall. Rather, "ye shall never stumble."

11 for so an entrance shall be ministered, etc. Properly, "so the entrance shall be richly supplied (the same word as in ver. 5) to you."

12 the present truth. "The truth which is with you," or already known to you in the gospel, which you have learned: cp. Col. i. 6.

13 this tabernacle. Or, "tent." The body, as in 2 Cor. v. 1.

14 even as our Lord Jesus Christ (hath) showed me. As recorded in John xxi. 18, 19; and perhaps also in subsequent intimations. The apostle seems to be speaking rather of the suddenness than of the nearness of his departure.

16 power and coming. Rather, "power and appearing." Of "His majesty" they had a special glimpse in His transfiguration: see Luke ix. 28–36, and notes.

18 the holy mount. Made "holy" to Peter by the display of the Saviour's Divine glories: cp. Exod. iii. 5.

19 We have also a more sure word of prophecy. Rather, "We have the prophetic word made more firm." All ancient prophecy is, as it were, one discourse; and its fulfilment in so great part in our Lord's first coming, and in that transient glory of His (17, 18), gives us the greater certainty of its full accomplishment; until which time we should use it as a "light," or torch, to guide our steps in this dark world.

20 knowing this first, etc. As a truth essential to the knowledge of the rest.

no prophecy of the Scripture is of any private interpretation. Perhaps, meaning that it could not be explained by the prophet himself; and implying that its full meaning was hidden from the prophet's own mind (see Dan. xii. 8); so that it must be (21), not a human discovery or suggestion, but a direct communication from God; and should be received and attended to as such.

21 in old time. Rather, "at any time."

moved. Lit., "borne along," "like a ship before a strong wind" (*Lange*).

CHAPTER II

1 false prophets also. Beside the "holy men of God" (i. 21).

damnable heresies. "Destructive heresies" (R.V.). The chief of these seems to have been the rejection of the lordship and authority of our Redeemer; showing itself in "pernicious," or according to the reading of most manuscripts, "licentious practices" (2).

the Lord. The Greek word here and in Jude 4, signifies *Master*, as of bondmen, generally acquired by purchase.

3 make merchandise. Endeavouring to make gain out of their adherents: cp. 1 Tim. vi. 5; Titus i. 11.

damnation. Rather, "perdition."

4 hell. Or, "Tartarus"; the Greek name for the place of future punishment, corresponding to the Gehenna of the Jews (Matt. v. 22).

5 Noah the eighth [person]. An idiomatic phrase for "Noah with seven others": see 1 Pet. iii. 20.

7 with the filthy conversation of the wicked. Rather, "by the conduct of the lawless in licentiousness."

8 vexed. Rather, "tortured"; disturbed himself.

9 to be punished. Rather, "being tormented"; implying that the punishment has already begun.

10 government. Lit., "lordship," or authority.

12 these. Referred to in ver. 10.

13 sporting themselves, etc. Rather, "rioting in their love-feasts" (see var. read.); using their false doctrines as a cloak for sensual indulgence: cp. Jude 12; 1 Cor. xi. 20–22.

14 adultery. Properly, "an adulteress": cp. Matt. v. 28, and note.

cursed children. Lit., "children of curse": cp. Eph. ii. 3.

15 Bosor. "Bosor" is another form of "Beor," which form occurs here in many copies: see Numb. xxii. 5–30, and notes.

17 clouds. Or "mists," R.V.; promising rain, but carried away by a hurricane, and so disappointing the husbandman's hope.

18 that were clean escaped. Rather, "just escaped." The reference is to recent converts from heathenism and sin.

19 servants. Rather, "bondmen": cp. Rom. vi. 16.

20 the latter end is worse, etc. See notes on Matt. xii. 43–45, where our Lord's words here quoted are found: and cp. Heb. x. 26, 27.

21 not to have known. "Not to have *fully* known."

the holy commandment. The holy precepts of the gospel.

22 according to the true proverb, etc. This is taken in part from Prov. xxvi. 11, and in part from some popular saying. It means that these men, in returning to their evil habits, have shown that their depravity is unsubdued, and their hearts are unchanged.

CHAPTER III

1 your pure minds. Rather, as R.V., "your sincere mind." The Greek adjective means "tested by the sun" or "flawless," as of something through which the sun's rays pass.

2 spoken before by the holy prophets. Cp. i. 19–21.

and of the commandment, etc. Rather, "and of the commandment of the Lord and Saviour through us the apostles"; or according to the best authorities, "of your apostles"; *i.e.*, those who have taught you, probably referring to Paul (15) and Barnabas.

3 knowing this first. See note on i. 20; and cp. Jude, vers. 4–18.

4 Where is the promise? Implying that it has altogether failed.

5 this they willingly are ignorant of. Or, "this they wilfully forget."

and the earth, etc. Or, "and earth compacted out of water and amidst water"; by which [by *waters* from above and beneath, Gen. vii. 11] "the world that then was," etc. This is mentioned to show that all things have not continued as they were (4).

8 A thousand years. The same sentiment is implied in Psa. xc. 4.

9 longsuffering. The apparent delay of judgement, at which sinners mock, is really Divine forbearance, giving them "space to repent."

10 as a thief in the night. Cp. Matt. xxiv. 43; Luke xii. 39; 1 Thess. v. 2.

11 Seeing then that all these things shall be dissolved. Properly, "Since then all these things are being dissolved. The destiny of dissolution is already inherent in them" (*Winer*).

conversation and godliness. The Greek words, rendered "conversation" (rather, behaviour) and "godliness," are plurals, marking the various manifestations of true religion.

12 hasting unto the coming. Properly, "hastening the coming." This is expressed in R.V. by the rendering, "earnestly desiring the coming of the day of God."

wherein. Rather, "by reason of which." In order that this "day" may come, the present scene of things must pass away."

13 according to His promise. Referring to the ancient prophecies, especially to Isa. lxv. 17–25, and lxvi.; on which see notes. Here the *future* glory of the Church is particularly meant: cp. Rev. xxi. 1, 27.

14 without spot, and blameless. Cp. 1 Pet. i. 19.

15 salvation. It is not slackness, as the scoffers say (9); nor is it only space given to *them* to repent, but it is to *us* also time for the working out of our "salvation" (Phil. ii. 12, 13).

even as our beloved brother Paul . . . hath written. See Rom. ii. 4; 1 Thess. iv. 13–v. 11; 2 Thess. ii. 1–12. It is clear, however, from ver. 16, that others of his Epistles were already widely known.

16 in which. That is, in which *epistles*. The reference afterwards to "the other scriptures" is important. "The word γραφαί is used in the New Testament of the Old Testament Scriptures alone, except in this passage" (Professor Lumby, in *Speaker's Commentary*). It indicates the early formation of a New Testament canon.

17 the wicked. The false teachers and scoffers (ii. and iii.).

18 grow in grace, and in the knowledge, etc. "Diligent progress is essential to perseverance" (*Calvin*).

both now and for ever. Lit., "both now and to the day of eternity." This ascription of eternal glory to Christ clearly implies His supreme Deity. "The day of eternity" means "the day of God which marks the end of time and the beginning of eternity, or rather which is itself eternity, the endless day which shall never pass away" (Dr. Dawson-Walker in *Devotional Commentary*).

THE FIRST EPISTLE GENERAL OF JOHN

INTRODUCTION

THE very opening of this letter arrests attention. There is no greeting or salutation of any Church or individual. The writer plunges at once into his subject. It is the confident statement of an eyewitness (i. 1–3). If we had no Gospels before us, nor any other New Testament writing, we should still have evidence here as to the existence of the Lord Jesus Christ; His Divine nature (i. 3; ii. 23; iv. 9, 15; v. 1, 5); His work as Mediator for sinful men by the shedding of His blood (i. 7; ii. 1, 2; iv. 10); His victory over the power of evil (i. 8): and His gift of life eternal to them that believe on Him (ii. 24; v. 11)

If, in addition to this Epistle, we had only the Gospel by John, we should at once be struck by the identity both of ideas and expressions. The Gospel and the Epistle both begin by speaking of "the Word." "The life was the light of men," says the Gospel (i. 4); "God is light," says the Epistle (i. 5). "Love one another," says the Saviour in the Gospel (xiii. 34); "Love one another as He gave us commandment," says the Epistle (iii. 23). The words of the Epistle, "God sent His only begotten Son into the world that we might live through Him" (iv. 9), are only a slight variation of Our Lord's words in the Gospel (iii. 16). These and other similarities in Gospel and Epistle indicate that they were written by the same John, the disciple and beloved friend of Christ.

If, further, we note the references to denials of our Lord's divinity (ii. 22; iv. 3, 4) on the one hand, and to denials of His humanity on the other (iv. 2, 3; v. 6), we are able approximately to fix the date at which the Epistle was written. These heresies, of the Gnostics, Ebionites and Docetists appeared in the later years of the first century A.D., and on this and other grounds the date of the Epistle may be regarded as A.D. 90 or soon after.

Like the writings of St. Paul, the Epistle blends the practical with the doctrinal, ethics with theology. Thus we have the general call to righteousness of life (i. 6, 7), the exhortation to keep Christ's commandments (ii. 3), and to follow His example (ii. 6), to love the brethren (ii. 9–11; iii. 16–18; iv. 7, 11) and to keep from idolatry (v. 21).

"God is light" (i. 5) and "God is love" (iv. 7) are the basic truths of all Christian character and conduct.

CHAPTER I

1 our hands have handled. As Westcott points out, there is no specific mention of the Resurrection in this Epistle, yet there is here an obvious reference to the words of the risen Christ (John xx. 27).

of the Word of life. Rather, "*concerning* the Word of life." On comparing this introduction with the beginning of John's Gospel (see John i. 1–5, and notes), we obtain this meaning: We declare unto you concerning "the Word" both His eternal existence "from the beginning," and also His manifestation as the "Life" to us His apostles, giving to our very senses of hearing, sight, and touch, unquestionable evidence that He became truly man in order to become our "eternal life"; bringing us into fellowship with God and His saints.

2 for (and) **the life was manifested.** In the person of Christ the Incarnate Word: see John i. 14; 1 Tim. iii. 16.

that eternal life. The emphasis in original is brought out in R.V., "the life, the eternal life."

3 our fellowship is with the Father, etc. On this communion of the saints with the Father and the Son, and with one another, see John xvii. 20, 21, and note.

4 that your joy may be full ("complete"). Almost the very words of our Lord (John xv. 11). *Nestle's Greek Testament* (1920), however, reads "our joy."

5 of Him. That is, "from Him."

God is light. See John i. 4, and note.

(the) **darkness.** "Darkness" signifies the want of truth and purity. To "walk in the darkness" is to live in ignorance, error, or sin; to "walk in the light" is to aim at likeness to God in truth, holiness, and love.

7 if we walk in the light. The condition of what follows.

we have fellowship one with another. That is, Christian with Christian. The communion with God (3) is realised in the communion of saints.

cleanseth us from all sin. Lit., "is cleansing us," etc.: a process of purification in heart and life. This is wrought through the constant influence of that "blood of Christ," by which we have been redeemed, and so brought into the light, in which we walk. The atoning power and the continuous efficacy of the Blood are kindred truths of Scripture. In this verse the former is presupposed, the latter is declared. Both are expressed at the end of ver. 9.

9 faithful and just. He is "faithful" to His promise: "just" or righteous, because Christ has paid the price of our redemption (Eph. i. 7).

10 we make Him a liar. "God is made a liar because His entire scheme of redemption assumes the universality of sin, and the same view is set forth in His word" (Prof. A. L. Humphries in *Peake's Commentary*).

CHAPTER II

1 Advocate. The word (*Paraclete*) here used is applied to the Holy Spirit, and rendered "Comforter" in John xiv. 16; where see note: and cp. Rom. viii. 34; Heb. vii. 25. The help which our Lord thus gives us by His intercession is founded on His propitiatory work; see ver. 2; Heb. ix. 26. He therefore gives that aid as "a righteous One; appealing to *justice* as well as to *compassion*: see i. 9.

propitiation. "Atoning sacrifice" (*Weymouth*).

2 and not for ours only, etc. Not only for us who already believe in Him, but for those also who have not yet believed (iv. 14; John iii. 16; iv. 42).

3 we do know that we know Him. "Know" in the former case signifies the acquisition, in the latter the possession of knowledge. "We come to know that we know Him."

4 I know Him. Professing to be a converted man, but showing by his conduct that he is either a deceiver or self-deceived.

5 whoso keepeth His word, etc. Obedience is the test and the measure of love. When love is become perfect, obedience will be perfect too.

6 in Him. That is, in Christ: see John xv. 4–10, and notes.

7 no new commandment. Archbishop Alexander (*Speaker's Commentary*) points out that the Greek word here used for "new" refers to quality rather than to time. He translates the phrase "no fresh commandment."

8 the darkness is past. Rather, "the darkness is passing away."

10 He that loveth his brother abideth in the light, etc. Cp. John xi. 9, 10, and note.

11 he that hateth his brother, etc. See iii. 10–18, and notes.

13 little children. Three classes are here addressed—children, fathers, young men. The threefold repetition in ver. 14 makes this quite clear, and does not seem to permit of the very common interpretation that the word "children" means Christians in general, and "fathers" and "young men" two classes of them.

14 I write unto you, etc. See var. read. In vers. 12, 13 the apostle says three times, "I am writing." Now, also thrice, he says, "I have written," or "I wrote." Most of the best critics suppose that the reference is to the Gospel by John.

15 the world. "All this present order of finite and temporal existence without God" (Dr. G. S. Barrett in *Devotional Commentary*).

16 the lust of the flesh, etc. Sensuality, vanity, and pride are three of the forms in which the spirit of worldliness most frequently manifests itself.

17 the lust thereof. All worldly objects that entice to sin.

18 the last time. Lit., "the last hour."

as ye have heard that antichrist shall come. Rather, "as ye heard that antichrist (*i.e.*, the rival or opposer of Christ) cometh"; referring probably to what had been said on the subject, partly by our Lord (see Matt. xxiv. 23, 24) and partly by the apostles. The use of the present tense here, "cometh," shows, as Barrett points out, that "the coming of antichrist is not confined to one advent, though it may culminate thus, but is a series of comings." One characteristic of an antichrist is given in ver. 22 and iv. 3.

19 They went out from us, etc. These "antichrists" had been in outward fellowship with the Christians; but in heart and principle they never belonged to their number. Their defection was a proof that not all who are outwardly members of the Church are true disciples of Christ.

20 an unction (anointing) **from the Holy One.** The teaching of the Holy Spirit whom the exalted Saviour bestows, to guide His people "into all truth": see John xiv. 25, 26; xvi. 12, 13, and notes.

22 Who is a liar, etc.? The false teachers seem to have boasted of their clear views of Jesus and the Father. The apostle says that it is false and anti-Christian to deny either our Lord's incarnation, or the intimate union of the Father and the Son; for (23) there can be no more faith and love towards the Father without right views of the Son: cp. John xiv. 6.

23 he that acknowledgeth the Son, etc. This second clause, in most copies of the Authorised Version, is printed in italics, as though of doubtful genuineness, but it is now acknowledged as part of the original text, being found in the best manuscripts.

24 Let that therefore abide, etc. Lit., "As for you, let that abide," etc.

from the beginning. Since the time when you became Christians.

25 And this is the promise, etc. By abiding in Him (see John xv. 4, and note) you will attain "eternal life": see our Lord's own words in John v. 21–26; x. 10, 27, 28; xi. 25, 26; xvii. 3.

26 that seduce you. Or, "who are leading you astray." What I have now said about them is surely sufficient, without any other teaching (27); for you have the "anointing" (see note on ver. 20) of the Holy Spirit.

not be ashamed before Him. "Not shrink from Him with shame."

29 ye know. As God is the Holy One, and the only source of all holiness, every righteous man has the unspeakable privilege of being a child of God.

CHAPTER III

1 that we should be called the sons of God. The best MSS. insert after these words, "and that is what we are," or, "and we are." Our sonship is not yet manifested: but when "it is manifested," it will be seen to be a glorious likeness to our Father, or our glorified Saviour (2).

3 that hath this hope in Him (in Christ). "Who has this hope fixed on Him" (*Weymouth*). The influence of this hope is seen in continual striving after purity: "is purifying himself."

4 Whosoever committeth sin, etc. Any departure from God's law is sin. We must not sin, because all sin is opposed to God's law; so also to Christ's mission and character (5); and to union with Christ (6).

5 to take away our sins. He delivers us from the curse of sin, that He may deliver us from its dominion (John i. 29; Rom. vi. 14).

6 Whosoever abideth in Him sinneth not. Perfect union with Christ would secure absolute freedom from sin. Such is the glorious ideal, the true standard: but how far short of it do even the best saints fall in this world!

7 let no man deceive you. The reference is probably to the false teachers who held "that nothing could defile the spiritual man." This the apostle brings to a practical test: "he who doeth that which is right" shows thereby that he is partaker of Christ's nature: there is no other trustworthy evidence of this.

11 this is the message, etc. Referring to the law of brotherly love, given by Christ to His disciples: see John xiii. 34, 35, and note.

13 Marvel not, etc. See John xv. 18, 19.

15 Whosoever hateth his brother is a murderer. In the kingdom of heaven the Divine Lawgiver and Judge looks not so much at the external action as at the inward disposition and purpose—the germ from which, at any time, the deed may spring: see Matt. v. 22–32, and notes. "Murder is only hatred in action, hatred is only murder in feeling" (*Barrett*).

16 Hereby perceive we the love, etc. "Hereby know we love." The words "of God" are not in the Greek. We learn what love is, in its highest, purest, ideal: because He (*i.e.*, Christ) laid down His life for us" (John x. 15). Hatred will prompt a man to destroy another's life (15); love, to sacrifice his own. Our Lord's self-sacrifice should impel us to show love in a similar way.

19 hereby we know that we are of the truth. Brotherly love, shown in deeds of kindness, is an evidence that God's saving truth is working in us; and it will enable us to stand with confidence before Him, now and hereafter.

20 For if our heart condemn us. This clause is probably to be joined with the preceding verse, and to be rendered, "whenever our heart condemn us." The accusations of conscience will be stayed by the thought, not only of God's mercy, but of His greatness and omniscience. We may condemn ourselves; but "One is greater than our heart," and He has already both pronounced the justifying decree, and has given us the sign of it in quickening within us the love of the brethren.

22 because we keep His commandments. "Obedience is not alleged as the ground, but as the assurance of the fulfilment. The answer to prayer is given, not as a reward for meritorious action, but because the prayer itself, rightly understood, coincides with God's will" (John viii. 29; xi. 42) (*Westcott*); "the childlike obedience of him who prays, wherein God recognises him as His child" (Huther, in *Meyer's Commentary*).

23 this is His commandment, etc. Faith in Christ, and love to Christians are the primary principles of all obedience.

24 hereby we know (perceive) **that He abideth in us,** etc. The obedience (22) which is the sign of the Christian life, and the indwelling power of the Holy Spirit, are two aspects of one and the same reality.

CHAPTER IV

1 believe not every spirit. Do not acknowledge all who claim to be under the special guidance of the Holy Spirit (see 1 Thess. v. 21; 1 Cor. xii. 10; xiv. 32, and notes); but "test" them, lest you err either in receiving the false, or in rejecting the true.

2 confesseth that Jesus Christ is come in the flesh. Believing and maintaining the true humanity of Jesus Christ, the Son of God. This was the aspect of the truth which false teachers in the early Church especially denied. The Deity of Christ was incontrovertible, but it was maintained that He came only in the appearance of a man (the teaching of Docetism): see John i. 14, and note.

3 and this is that spirit of antichrist, etc. See note on ii. 18.

4 have overcome them. That is, ye have overcome the anti-Christian teachers: see ii. 13.

5 They are of the world, etc. Worldly in mind, they teach doctrines accordant with the feelings of worldly men, and are therefore eagerly followed by such; whilst, on the contrary, only those who are taught by God will listen to our spiritual teaching; and thus hearers as well as teachers are tested (6).

7 let us love one another. An inference from the preceding. If our faith truly rests in Christ incarnate, it will be proved by love: the sign of sonship and of true knowledge.

8 God is love. Love is not only an *attribute* of the Eternal, but His essential Being. His attributes and acts are but forms and revelations of Love. "No religion in the whole world outside of revealed religion, has ever attained to the knowledge of God contained in these three short and simple but unfathomable sentences: 'God is Spirit,' 'God is Light,' 'God is Love'" (*Barrett*).

9 In this was manifested the love of God toward us, etc. The gift of the only begotten Son to save us from eternal death is the great proof and manifestation of "the love of God to us": see ver. 16, and cp. John iii. 16.

10 Herein is love, etc. Love as it exists in God is self-originated and spontaneous, as well as costly in its gift.

propitiation. See Rom. iii. 25; v. 6–8, and notes.

12 No man hath seen God at any time. God is indeed invisible to the eye of sense; but in the exercise of love one toward another, we become conscious of His Spirit dwelling within us and reflect that love which constitutes His nature. "It is only through love that we can become conscious of God, and be convinced of the reality of His being and nature; love being itself the reflection and product of His nature" (*Neander*). And this love is fully developed in us only when we love all His children also (ver. 1).

13 Hereby know we that we dwell in Him, etc. The Spirit must have been imparted to every one in whom this love and faith exist: cp. iii. 24.

14 we have seen and do testify, etc. Although God is invisible (12) He has presented Himself to our sight in the person of His Son. *We* is emphatic. The testimony of the apostles as eyewitnesses is the ground of our faith in Christ, and therefore in the love of the Father who sent Him; and this again is the origin of our love.

17 Herein is our love made perfect. Rather, "Herein love with us has been perfected." Our likeness to Christ in love is the measure of our approach to Christian perfection; and it is a ground of confidence in prospect of the judgement; cp. iii. 19.

18 There is no fear in love, etc. Reverential *awe* must ever accompany true love to God; but this is quite a different thing from slavish dread, which is altogether incompatible with perfect love. For "torment," R.V. reads, more accurately, "punishment." "That which fear has to expect is regarded as inherent in it" (*Huther*).

19 We love Him. Huther, Archbishop Alexander, *Nestle's Greek Testament*, Moffatt, and Weymouth, omit "Him." Christian love of every kind has its root and origin in His.

20 he is a liar. He is shown to be so, both by the nature of the case, and by the words of Christ in John xiii. 34.

CHAPTER V

1 every one that loveth Him, etc. The true believer is a child of God (John i. 12, 13); and therefore must be an object of affection to God's children.

3 grievous. Or, "heavy": see Matt. xi. 30. God's highest commands become "not grievous," because of the new Divine life within us, manifesting itself primarily in faith; which, uniting us to Christ, makes us already participate in His victory over the world: cp. John xvi. 33; Heb. xii. 1, 2.

6 not by water only, etc. Rather, "not in the water only, but in the water and the blood." The distinction here made between the water and the blood makes it probable that the former alludes to His baptism, and the latter to His death, as the beginning and the end of His public work on earth,

His *ministry* and His *atonement*; respecting which "the Spirit of truth" testifies (John xv. 26), not only in the apostolic preaching and writing, but also in every believer's heart (10). On the contrary, the false teachers of the day (the Gnostics) asserted that He came "by water only," and that in the sacrifice His higher nature had no part. Hence the importance of asserting that HE who was baptised was in all respects the same who was crucified.

7 For there are three that bear record, etc. All Greek manuscripts for the first thirteen centuries, and the early versions and Fathers, omit parts of vers. 7, 8, and read thus: "For there are three that bear witness, the Spirit, and the water, and the blood; and these three agree in one thing," *i.e.*, in testifying that Jesus is the Son of God.

9 If we receive the witness of men, etc. Men are liable to err, yet we receive their testimony when they agree: see John viii. 17, 18. Much more then ought we to believe God, who testifies by these three witnesses (8) that His Son is truly come in the flesh.

10 hath the witness in himself. He who believes God's testimony is blessed with a new proof of the truth, in his own experience. He who disbelieves adds to his other sins the presumption of treating God as a liar; and in rejecting Christ he rejects "eternal life" (11, 12).

record. That is, witness. So in ver. 11.

13 [and that ye may believe]. The R.V. reads the whole verse. "These things have I written unto you, that ye may know that ye have eternal life, [even] unto you that believe on the name of the Son of God."

15 we know that we have, etc. See Mark xi. 24; John xiv. 13, 14; xv. 7; xvi. 23, 24, and notes.

16 He shall give him life, etc. Meaning, "And he shall give to him life (that is to say), to them who sin not unto death." The apostle is here speaking of the mutual intercessions of professed Christians, who should pray for the forgiveness of *all* one another's sins; only remembering that such a course of sin as is plainly inconsistent with the existence of spiritual life must put a person beyond the pale of this fraternal intercession.

17 All unrighteousness is sin, etc. Do not mistake me; all iniquity is sin, needing to be prayed for and pardoned, although it may not be "unto death." And (18), every real child of God, through His grace, "keepeth himself" from sin; and "the wicked one," "in [union with] whom the whole world lieth," "toucheth him not": cp. John xii. 31, and 2 Cor. iv. 4.

18 sinneth not. He does not sin habitually, as the rule of his life.

19 in wickedness. "In the evil one," *i.e.*, "in the power of the evil one."

20 that we may know Him. The sum and end of all Christian teaching is the attainment of that knowledge of the true God, the Father revealed in the Son, which results from personal union with Him, and must lead to eternal life.

THE SECOND EPISTLE OF JOHN

INTRODUCTION

ON the question whether "the elect lady" to whom the Epistle is addressed is an individual or a church, see note on ver. 1.

That "the elder" is the same as the writer of 1 John is generally agreed. The similarity of thought and expression is most marked, and it would be natural that John, as the survivor of all the apostles, should so describe himself.

The themes of this letter are the same as those of 1 John. There is the same exhortation to love (5, 6), and the same warning against false teachers (7, 10). The distinctive features of the Epistle are a more personal note (4, 12, 13), and the frequent reference to "the truth" (1, 2, 3, 4), with its unusual place in the salutation of "grace, mercy, and peace" (3).

1 the elect lady. Rather, "Kyria, the elect one." Kyria (translated "lady") may be a proper name, like Gaius in 3 John 1. Commentators, however, are almost equally divided as to whether an individual or a church is meant. Westcott, for instance, while favouring the idea that the Epistle is addressed to a church, thinks that the problem is insoluble with our present knowledge. Dr. David Smith (*Expositor's Greek Testament*), on the other hand, thinks that it is a lady that is addressed.

whom I love in (the) truth, etc. Whom I love in all Christian sincerity. The phrase "the truth," in the latter part of the verse and in vers. 2, 3, 4, denotes the Christian doctrine.

4 I found some of thy children walking in truth. John had probably seen this in the course of some apostolic tour. Whether the rest were Christians or not, he does not say; but it has been thought, from the form of the expression and the general tone of the Epistle, that some of them had been led away by prevailing errors. If so, the words contain a delicate warning.

5 that which we had from the beginning. From the Saviour's own lips: cp. on 1 John ii. 7; iii. 23.

6 ye should walk in it. A life of love is the fulfilment of God's commandments, 1 John v. 2, 3.

7 who confess not, etc. Better, as R.V., "[even] they that confess not that Jesus Christ cometh in the flesh." This is the reason for saying, in ver. 5,

"I beseech thee that we love one another." Respecting the error here specified, see on 1 John iv. 1-3.

8 that we lose not, etc. That our labours among you be not fruitless, but (see var. read.) that ye reap the full benefit of them.

9 Whosoever transgresseth. Rather (according to the best MSS.), "Whoever advanceth," *i.e.*, beyond the gospel. Such so-called "progress" is in reality departure from the truth. Some, however, prefer the meaning (R.V. marg.), "taketh the lead."

hath not God. Cp. 1 John ii. 23.

10 this doctrine. Namely, the apostolic "teachings" concerning the person and work of Christ.

neither bid him God speed. Rather, "and do not greet him," *i.e.*, as a Christian brother.

12 paper and ink. "The word 'paper' denotes papyrus, which, like parchment, was somewhat expensive. In fact, the cost of the writing material may partly account for the brevity of the Apostle's letter" (Dr. Dawson-Walker in *Devotional Commentary*).

13 thy elect sister. If the letter was addressed to a church, then "thy sister" would here mean a sister church.

THE THIRD EPISTLE OF JOHN

INTRODUCTION

In this letter also, the word "truth" has a prominent place, both in the salutation and elsewhere (1, 2, 3, 8, 12).

Diotrephes, who loved "to have the pre-eminence" has a prominence, but of an unpleasant kind (9–11). The severe language in which St. John refers to him shows that a loving and gentle disposition is compatible with indignation against wrongdoing.

The writer of the Epistle is obviously the same as the author of 2 John, and again describes himself as "the elder" (1). The personal note is found here (1–4, 13) as in the Second Epistle. Gaius, to whom the letter is addressed, is generally identified with St. Paul's host at Corinth (Rom. xvi. 23), who is also mentioned by that apostle as having been baptised by him (1 Cor. i. 14).

1 in (the) **truth.** See note on 2 John 1.

2 above all things. Rather, "*in respect to* all things." If thy temporal welfare were only equal to thy spiritual, I should be content.

3 testified of the truth. Lit., "testified to thy truth"; *i.e.*, to thy Christian sincerity and loyalty.

4 my children. His converts.

5 thou doest faithfully. "Thou doest a faithful work," R.V., *i.e.*, actest the part of a true believer.

strangers. Christians travelling in the service of the Church (7). The same persons, or others going on a similar errand, are commended to the hospitality of Gaius (6).

6 after a godly sort. Lit., "worthily of God"; *i.e.*, as becomes those who serve the Lord.

7 for His name's sake. Lit., "for the sake of the Name": with well-understood reference to Christ: cp. Acts iii. 16; iv. 12; v. 41. "There is something impressive, almost awe-inspiring in this absolute use of 'The Name' as applied to our Lord . . . tantamount to an expression by the earliest Christians of belief in their Master's divinity; for they deliberately transferred the Old Testament usage with regard to the Name of God to that of Jesus Christ" (Dr. Dawson-Walker in *Devotional Commentary*).

taking nothing of the Gentiles. They might have claimed support from their hearers (see Luke x. 4–7) and converts (see 1 Cor. ix. 13, 15, 18); but they deemed it inexpedient to do so.

8 fellow-helpers to the truth. Or, "workers together with the truth"; as though the Truth were impersonated, and the apostles were its assistants: see R.V.

9 I wrote. R.V., "I wrote somewhat"; in some previous letter to the church, referring to this missionary work. The letter may have been either suppressed or disregarded through the influence of Diotrephes.

receiveth us not. In refusing to receive those whom the apostle had sent (10), he rejected the apostle himself, and indeed his Divine Master; see Matt. xxv. 40; 1 Thess. iv. 8.

10 forbiddeth . . . casteth [them] out. Strictly, "is forbidding, and is casting out": threatening excommunication to any who should receive the apostolic messenger.

11 follow not that which is evil. Or, "imitate not." The evil example of Diotrephes, or the weakness of those who yielded to his arrogance: cp. 1 John iii. 6–9.

12 Demetrius. Demetrius was perhaps the bearer of this letter. This emphatic testimony to his Christian consistency combines general respect and esteem, the evidence of the power of gospel truth in life, and the inspired apostle's own commendation. "The truth itself" is again personified and cited as bearing joint witness to the character of this good man.

13 I will not. Rather, "I am unwilling." "Pen" was the reed then used for writing. The conclusion of this and the Second Epistle so correspond as to suggest that they were written at the same time, in anticipation of the apostle's visit to some place, now unknown.

THE GENERAL EPISTLE OF JUDE

INTRODUCTION

THERE is some uncertainty about the identity of the writer of this Epistle, but the generally accepted view among scholars now is that it was Jude or Judas, the brother of our Lord (Matt. xiii. 55). He describes himself (1) as "brother of James," who is also mentioned as one of the Lord's brethren in the passage just quoted.

The Epistle was probably written earlier than "2 Peter," to which it bears a strong resemblance, and although some authorities fix its date as late as A.D. 80, it seems more likely that it was A.D. 67 or 68. In any case it was written by one who was himself a companion of the apostles, and was written to those some of whom had heard the apostles speak and teach (17, 18).

It is a message of solemn warning. False teachers had arisen, who were men of corrupt lives (4, 8, 10, 19) and mischievous teaching (4, 8, 10, 16). Against such the writer warns them, under a strong sense of duty (ver. 2), and urges them to be on their guard, building themselves up in faith and character, continually seeking help from God in prayer (20, 21), and doing their best to save others from evil influences and their terrible consequences (22, 23). He closes by pointing them upwards, in stately language, to the only Source of all strength and of all goodness (24, 25).

1 to them that are sanctified, etc. Rather (see var. read.), "To them that are called, beloved in God the Father, and kept for Jesus Christ": cp. John xvii. 11, 17, 21; Rom. i. 6, 7, and notes.

2 be multiplied. So that you may always enjoy them abundantly.

3 the (our) common salvation. That is, common to him, to them, and to all believers. This topic was in the writer's thoughts, but he was constrained by the circumstances of the time to write about a special danger.

once. Rather, "once for all," admitting no change nor addition, see Heb. ix. 28. "He is thinking, primarily, of life and conduct" (*Dawson-Walker*).

4 crept in. Into the churches: cp. 2 Pet. ii. 1, and note.

before of old ordained to this condemnation. Lit., "written aforetime" (the phrase as in Rom. xv. 4), or "openly set forth" (as in Gal. iii. 1, the same phrase) "for this condemnation." Their sin and punishment, as teachers of anti-Christian error and licentiousness, had been already declared.

denying the only Lord God, etc. See var. read. R.V. has "denying our only Master and Lord Jesus Christ"; *i.e.*, rejecting our Saviour's Divine authority. "Master" is as in 2 Pet. ii. 1, where see note. Deissmann (*Light from the Ancient East*, p. 359) thinks that Jude's words here imply a protest against the title "Lord" being given to the Roman Cæsar.

5 I will therefore put you in remembrance, etc. Rather, "But I wish to remind *you* (emphatic), who once for all know all [these] things"; *i.e.*, you need not be taught them again, but you do need to be reminded of them: cp. 2 Pet. i. 12.

the people. Lit., "a people."

afterward. Lit., "the second time." If the first thing God did was to save His people, the next was to destroy the unbelieving: cp. 1 Cor. x. 1–12; Heb. iii. 16–19, and notes.

6 their first estate. Or, "their own domain" (*Moffatt*).

their own habitation. The Greek word, *οἰκητήριον*, is only found in one other place in the N.T., 2 Cor. v. 2, and seldom occurs in Greek literature (see Euripides, *Orestes*, 1114).

7 Even as Sodom, etc. Or, "How Sodom," etc.; that is, I wish to remind you (see ver. 5) how those wicked cities were ruined (see Gen. xviii., xix.).

in like manner. "In a manner like to these"; *i.e.*, like to Sodom and Gomorrha.

set forth for an example, etc. Or, "set forth for an example of eternal fire, suffering punishment."

8 despise dominion, etc. Cp. 2 Pet. ii. 10, and note.

9 Michael. Respecting Michael, see Dan. x. 13, and note. The brief allusion of this verse has given occasion to many ingenious but unsatisfactory conjectures. If it contains any reference to Old Testament Scripture, it must be to Zech. iii. 2, where the words are found, addressed to Satan, who, however, was contending with "Joshua the high priest." Some have thought that "the body of Moses" is a symbol for the Jewish Church, as represented by Joshua. But in any case the lesson which the passage is designed to teach is clear.

durst not. Not from fear of Satan, but because it is *wrong* to rail even at Satan. So Christians must not rail at earthly princes or dignities, even though they be instruments of Satan. "Accusation" should be "judgement," as in 2 Pet. ii. 11.

10 brute beasts. Or, "irrational animals"; led and governed only by animal instincts.

11 they have gone in the way of Cain, etc. Their

course is spoken of, in the prophetic style, as already finished. On "the way of Cain," see 1 John iii. 12. On "the error of Balaam," see 2 Pet. ii. 15. "Corè" means "Korah," whose discontent and rebellion caused his signal ruin: see Numb. xvi.

12 spots. Rather, "rocks"; meaning that these false teachers were as dangerous to Christians as sunken rocks are to mariners.

your feasts of charity. "Your love-feasts"; see 2 Pet. ii. 13.

feeding themselves without fear. Rather, as R.V., "shepherds that without fear feed themselves."

trees whose fruit withereth. Or, "trees of late autumn"; *i.e.*, completely stripped.

twice dead. They have lost leaves and fruit, as in winter; but their sap has also irretrievably gone, so that there can be no spring for them.

13 raging waves of the sea, etc. Cp. Isa. lvii. 20, and note.

wandering stars. Probably, "meteors," which, after blazing for a short time, are suddenly lost in darkness: cp. 2 Pet. ii. 17.

14 Enoch also, the seventh from Adam, etc. See Gen. v. Enoch's prophecy had probably been handed down by tradition among the Jews. The apocryphal "Book of Enoch," which contains a similar passage, is by some scholars supposed to have been founded on this and similar allusions, and seems to have been written about the second century A.D. But it is more generally attributed to the age before Christ, say 120–114.

Behold, the Lord cometh, etc. Rather, "Behold, the Lord came among His holy myriads": see Deut. xxxiii. 2. The past tense is here used in prophetic style for the future, to show the certainty of the event.

15 to convince. Rather, "to convict"; *i.e.*, to pronounce them guilty, and treat them as such.

16 having men's persons in admiration, etc. Flattering and fawning, in hope of gain. R.V., "showing respect of persons for the sake of advantage."

17 beloved, remember, etc. See note on similar passage in 2 Pet. iii. 1–3.

18 mockers. Probably ridiculing the idea of Christ's coming to judgement: see 2 Pet. iii. 4.

19 who separate themselves. That is, who separate themselves from the fellowship of the faithful: see 1 John ii. 19; "who cause divisions," or, "who make separations," as R.V.

20 building up yourselves on your most holy faith. The faith or truth of Christ, heartily embraced, is the groundwork of all Christian attainments and excellence.

praying in the Holy Ghost. Cp. Eph. vi. 18.

21 the love of God. The reciprocal affection between God and His children.

22 And of some have compassion, etc. Or, as R.V., "on some have mercy, who are in doubt." Another rendering, according to var. read., might be, "And some who are contentious rebuke."

23 pulling them out of the fire. For their peril is as great as if they were in the midst of a fire.

24 Now unto Him that is able, etc. This ascription of praise to God may be compared with Paul's words in Rom. xvi. 25–27.

to keep you from falling. R.V., "to guard you from stumbling" (2 Pet. i. 10).

25 to the only wise God our Saviour. Or, omitting "wise," as R.V., "To the only God our Saviour, through Jesus Christ our Lord [be] glory, majesty, dominion and power, before all time, and now, and for evermore. Amen."

THE REVELATION OF ST. JOHN THE DIVINE

INTRODUCTION

No book in the Bible has been the subject of such diverse interpretations. Into the discussions between the various schools, each of them including many devout and learned writers, we do not propose to enter. It may, however, be observed that too often it has been forgotten that the Book is a vision. As to the date of it, opinion is divided between the reign of Nero, before A.D. 70, or that of Domitian, between A.D. 80 and 96.

That the Book was primarily intended for the instruction, warning, and encouragement of the Seven Churches of Asia Minor appears clear from i. 11. It begins with the vision of the living Lord, given to His exiled servant, to cheer him in his loneliness and disappointments and sufferings (i. 9). For the individual and for the Church, the one hope is in the presence and power of Him who is the Alpha and Omega (i. 11), who is alive for evermore and has the keys of Hades and of death (i. 18).

Then come the direct letters to the Churches, with the Lord's praise for what is good in them (ii. 2, 3, 6, 9, 12, 19; iii. 4, 8–10); His rebuke for what is blameworthy (ii. 4, 14–16, 20–22; iii. 2, 15–17); and His encouragement to fidelity and endurance (ii. 7, 10, 17, 26, 28; iii. 4, 5, 12, 21). These letters have their searching messages for the Churches of to-day.

The keynote of the remainder of the Book is found in iv. 1, "I will show thee things which must be hereafter." Much of it deals with the majesty of God as the world's ruler (iv. 2, 9–11; vi. 16; xi. 16–18; xv. 3, 4; xvi. 7; xix. 1–6; xx. 11–13). This, too, had its message for Christians then and for Christians in all time. Earthly powers and rulers may persecute and oppress the Church, but God's throne is above all. The angels and the horsemen are the mighty messengers of His judgements (vi.; viii.; ix. 1, 13; x. 1–7; xiv. 8–11, 15–19; xvi. 1–12; xviii. 1, 2), and of His final victory (xi. 15).

The conflict at various periods between world-powers and the kingdom of Christ is depicted in chapters xii.; xiii.; xvi. 13–16; xvii. 14; xiv. 11–20; xx. 7–9; and the defeat of the powers of evil is foreshadowed in the overthrow of the dragon (xii. 9–11; xx. 1–10) and the fall of Babylon (xiv. 8; xviii. 2, 10, 15–24).

In the closing chapters (xxi. and xxii.) we have the sublime descriptions of the new heaven and the new earth, and the heavenly Jerusalem. In figurative language the heavenly city is described as something transcendently beautiful—perfect in form (xxi. 15–17) and perfect in colour (xxi. 18–21).

And the Lamb that was slain is the centre of it all (v. 6). It is He who opens the seals of the book (vi. 1–12; viii. 8); the song of the redeemed is a song of praise to Him (v. 9, 10, 12, 13; vii. 10); and it is His presence that irradiates all with a light that never fades (xxi. 23, 25).

CHAPTER I

1 Revelation. Greek, "Apocalypse." This revelation is here spoken of as being made first by God the Father to the Lord Jesus (see Mark xiii. 32; John xii. 49; Acts i. 7; Rev. v. 5), and then by Christ, through His commissioned angel, to the apostle John: who is commanded (see ver. 19) to communicate the same to the seven churches (4).

things which must shortly come to pass. "Things which must shortly" begin to be fulfilled; and in one sense will soon all "come to pass": see 2 Pet. iii. 8.

His servant John. The epithet "the divine," in the title of the Book, means "the theologian," and is found in the Vatican MS., but the mass of manuscript evidence is against its authority.

2 who bare record (witness), etc. The words apply to the present book, not, as has sometimes been supposed, to the Gospel by St. John. The "word of God" is to be understood of the *message* or contents of the Book.

3 Blessed is he that readeth, and they that hear, etc. Referring primarily to the public reading and hearing in the Christian assemblies.

4 the seven churches. The number *seven*, according to the usage of Scripture, signifies *completeness.* There were other churches in Proconsular Asia (see note on Acts ii. 9), as that of the Colossians; but these are selected, "a *representative,* not *exhaustive* list" (*Alford*), addressed as symbolising all Christian churches of every nation and age. See the call to universal attention at the end of each Epistle: ii. 7, 11, 17, 29; iii. 6, 13, 22.

Him, which is, and which was, and which is to come. The Eternal—JAHVEH (or Jehovah): cp. Exod. iii. 14.

the seven Spirits. Perhaps meaning the variety and perfection of His operation.

5 first begotten of the dead. Or, "firstborn of the dead" (R.V.); as in Col. i. 18: where see note.

that loved. The best authorities have "loveth us." So (R.V.).

washed us. Better, "loosed us." Cp. I John i. 7; Heb. ix. 22, and notes.

6 kings and priests, etc. Rather, as in R.V., "[to be] a kingdom, [to be] priests"; *i.e.*, a kingdom all whose subjects are priests: see Exod. xix. 6; 1 Pet. ii. 5.

to Him be glory, etc. Honours are here ascribed to the Saviour, and titles are given to Him in ver. 8, which it would be blasphemous to claim for any mere creature.

7 Behold, He cometh with (the) **clouds.** Cp. Dan. vii. 13; Matt. xxiv. 30; xxv. 31; xxvi. 64.

which pierced Him. See on Zech. xii. 10; cp. John xix. 37.

Even so, Amen. This means, "Yes, verily!" (see 2 Cor. i. 20). It expresses not only wish, but certainty.

8 Alpha and Omega. The first and the last letters of the Greek alphabet.

saith the Lord, etc. Cp. ver. 4 above.

Patmos. Now *Patino,* a small rocky island, about 10 miles long and 6 broad, in the Ægean Sea, nearly opposite Miletus, on the western coast of Asia Minor. Offenders were banished thither, to work in the mines or marble quarries.

10 in the Spirit. That is, the spirit of devotion and of vision; "rapt in the Spirit" (*Moffatt*).

on the Lord's day. Probably, the first day of the week, which was peculiarly honoured as the day of our Lord's resurrection: see note on John xx. 26.

11 Saying, I am Alpha and Omega, etc. The R.V., with most authorities, omits these words.

the seven churches. "Christianity, represented by these seven Churches, is the true audience to which the author addresses himself" (Godet: *Études bibliques,* 2nd series, p. 349).

unto Ephesus, etc. Ephesus is named first, probably as being the nearest to Patmos; while the others follow in geographical order; first going north, and then turning south-east.

12 to see the voice. That is, to see from whom the voice came.

candlesticks. Rather, "lamp-stands" (see Exod. xxv. 31, 32, 37; Zech. iv. 2; Heb. ix. 2). The imagery is derived from the Jewish sanctuary. The "lamp-stands" are a fit emblem of the Church (20), as "holding forth the word of life" (Matt. v. 14; Phil. ii. 15).

13 in the midst, etc. Standing as a Priest in the holy place, and clothed in a priestly dress, but somewhat different from that of the ancient priesthood.

like unto the Son of man, etc. Rather, "like unto a son of man" (R.V.); that is, a being in human form (13); but possessing superhuman knowledge, dignity, and power (14–16). He unites the eternity of God and the mortality of man; while death and the world of spirits are subject to His control (17, 18).

down to the foot. Yet leaving the feet visible (15).

a golden girdle. A symbol of princely power: see Isa. xlv. 1; Dan. x. 5.

14 white like wool, etc. Venerable and majestic: cp. Dan. vii. 9.

15 like unto fine brass, etc. "Like silver-bronze when it is white-hot in a furnace" (*Weymouth*). Perhaps suggesting endurance.

as the sound of many waters. Like the roaring of the waves: cp. Ezek. xliii. 2.

16 a sharp two-edged sword. Expressing the force of His word, whether of grace or of judgement: cp. Heb. iv. 12.

17 I fell, etc. The apostle was overpowered at such a view of Christ in His heavenly glory: cp. Dan. x. 8–12.

I am the first, etc. R.V., more literally, "I am the first and the last, and the Living One; and I was dead, and behold I am alive for evermore."

18 [Amen]. Omitted in the best texts. The word may have been introduced for public reading.

hell. Rather, "Hades," the *state of the departed*, whether righteous or wicked: see Psa. xvi. 10; Matt. xvi. 18, and notes. The "keys" express Christ's dominion over death and the unseen world. Transpose, as R.V., "Of death and of Hades."

19 the things which are. The state of things then existing in the churches as set forth in ch. ii., iii.

20 the mystery, etc. The meaning of these symbols, which can be understood only by revelation: see Matt. xiii. 11; 1 Cor. ii. 7, and notes.

the angels of the seven churches. Each one of these churches (see ii. 1) had its own "angel," *i.e.*, messenger; probably meaning a teacher or pastor, as one called and sent by the Lord: cp. Eccles. v. 6; Hag. i. 13; Mal. ii. 7; Rom. x. 15; Eph. iv. 11. Others interpret them as "a symbolical representation in which the active life of the church finds expression. To St. John every person, every thing, has its angel" (*Milligan*).

Epistles to the Seven Churches

CHAPTER II

The Church in Ephesus

1 Ephesus. See Acts xviii. 19; xix. 1, and the Epistle to the Ephesians.

He that holdeth, etc. The Greek verb means holdeth fast—preserving them.

who walketh in the midst, etc. Constantly observing the condition of the churches, and watching over their welfare.

2 thy labour. In the service of God and truth.

canst not bear . . . and hast borne. The same verb. "There are things which thou *canst not* bear, and things which thou *canst* bear" (*Trench*). The false claim to apostleship was but the culmination of the spirit against which Paul had warned the Ephesian elders (Acts xx. 30) fulfilled in the teachings of Hymenæus, Philetus, and Alexander (1 Tim. i. 20; 2 Tim. ii. 17: cp. also 2 Cor. xi. 12–15).

4 I have [somewhat] against thee, etc. Better, "I have against thee that thou hast left thy first love." Zeal for orthodoxy and moral correctness (2, 6); activity and constancy (2, 3) were there; but the early glow of love to God and man was lacking.

5 will remove thy candlestick, etc. Coldness and formality will result in darkness and decay. The Lord's gracious call to repentance seems to have been little heeded by the Ephesian church; and before very long the threatening was fulfilled. There has been no church of Ephesus for ages, and the site of the city is now a melancholy ruin. See *Modern Discoveries on the Site of Ancient Ephesus*, by J. T. Wood; Murray's *Handbook to Asia Minor;* and Sir William Ramsay's *St. Paul the Traveller and the Roman Citizen.*

6 the Nicolaitans. Nothing is now known certainly respecting the Nicolaitans except that their "deeds" and "doctrine" were most mischievous. But several of the fathers state that they were a sect of Gnostics, who taught that Christians were not under the obligations of morality—the "Antinomians" of the early Church. Nicolas, or Nicolaus, their alleged founder, is sometimes, but doubtfully, identified with the one of "the Seven" who bore that name (Acts vi. 5). See note, ver. 14.

7 To him that overcometh, etc. There is marked connexion between these promises and the blessings described in later portions of this book as belonging to the saints in the New Jerusalem: cp. 7 with xxii. 2, 14; 11 with xx. 6; iii. 4 with vii. 9; xix. 8; xx. 12–15; and iii. 21 with xx. 4; xxii. 5.

paradise. See notes on Gen. ii. 8; Luke xxiii. 43. As man, overcome by Satan, lost Paradise by his first fall; so the promise by which the "fallen" (5) are encouraged to repent and to overcome is the admission to eternal life in the heavenly Paradise.

The Church in Smyrna

8 Smyrna. Smyrna (now *Ismir*) is still a flourishing city; with a population of over 250,000. Its Christian inhabitants, Armenian and other, have at various times, and even in recent years, suffered severely at the hands of the Turks.

9 and poverty. They were poor in earthly goods, having perhaps been stripped by persecution; but they were rich in heavenly substance (Jas. ii. 5).

the blasphemy of them which say they are Jews. These unbelieving Jews, who were not true Israelites (John i. 47; Rom. ix. 6–8; Gal. iii. 7), but rather "a synagogue of Satan" (John viii. 44), railed against the Christians, and their Lord.

10 ten days. Meaning a short and definite period, in accord with the numerical symbolism of the Book.

a (the) crown of life. Life, as a crown. The allusion is to "the garland" of victory and honour. Cp. 1 Cor. ix. 5; 1 Pet. v. 4.

11 He that overcometh, etc. See xx. 14; xxi. 8.

THE CHURCH IN PERGAMOS

12 Pergamos. Pergamos (generally Pergamum), 50 miles N.E. of Smyrna, was a large city, and, as Sir William Ramsay (*Hastings' Dict. of the Bible*) has shown, for more than two centuries down to about 50 B.C., the capital of the Roman province of Asia (Asia Minor). It had many temples of the pagan gods. It is now called *Bergama*.

13 Satan's seat. Rather, "Satan's throne." Pergamum was noted for the worship of Æsculapius under the form of a serpent. This false god was entitled *Theos Soter* (God the Saviour).

14 doctrine. Or, "teaching"; *i.e.*, that of persons who, like Balaam, in confederacy with Balak, attempt to corrupt the people of God by idolatry and licentiousness. Many expositors regard the Nicolaitans and the followers of Balaam as identical. See Numb. xxii. 5, 8; xxv. 1; xxxi. 16; 1 Cor. vi. 13, 18; 2 Pet. ii. 15.

15 thou also. Thou, as well as the Ephesian church: see on ver. 6.

16 the sword of my mouth. See 12; i. 16. Christ's word of truth and justice.

17 the hidden manna. The manna laid up in the sanctuary (see Exod. xvi. 32–34); symbolising the bread which came down from heaven (John vi. 30).

a white stone. Possibly, the "white stone" of acquittal, representing the believer's justification; or perhaps an allusion to the bright stones in the high priest's breastplate, or the two onyx stones on his shoulders; bearing the names of the chosen tribes engraved on them: see Exod. xxviii. 9–12, 17–21, 29. The "new name" is probably the symbol of a new and transfigured character (*Plumptre; so also Dr. C. A. Scott*). Archdeacon Charles thinks it is the name of Christ or God, but the words "which no man knoweth" hardly bear this out.

THE CHURCH IN THYATIRA

18 Thyatira. Now *Akhissar* ("White Castle"). See note on Acts xvi. 14. It was devoted to the worship of Apollo, and was also famous for its trade-guilds, which were one of the great obstacles to Christianity (see Sir W. Ramsay in *Hastings' Dict. of the Bible*).

eyes like unto a flame of fire, etc. Having the piercing eye of Omniscience, and the tread of pure and righteous power.

19 the last [to be] more than the first. *i.e.*, "thy last works are more excellent than the first" (*Speaker's Commentary*). There had been a growth in the Christian life.

20 Jezebel. The name of Ahab's idolatrous wife (1 Kings xvi. 31) is used here, perhaps to mark the character of some woman who exerted a most disastrous influence in the church.

21 space to repent. This is the purpose of Divine delay in inflicting deserved punishment: see 2 Pet. iii. 9.

23 her children. Her disciples.

He which searcheth the reins and hearts. To "try the reins and hearts," and to "reward men according to their work," are the acts of God (see Jer. xvii. 10: Psa. lxii. 12), whose prerogative our Lord here claims as His own.

24 the depths of Satan, as they speak. The Gnostic teachers claimed an acquaintance with the deep things of God. The phrase was current among them, and is here quoted; only, instead of being depths of God they are declared to be depths "of Satan." The high spiritual claim is referred to the spirit of evil.

none other burden. No other severe duty or trial than firmly to oppose this spiritual wickedness.

27 he shall rule them with a rod of iron. Expressing the Messiah's strong and retributive government over rebellious men; and the moral power exercised by the Church in His name.

28 I will give him the morning star. Christ Himself is "the bright and Morning Star" (see xxii. 16, and note); "the sum of every spiritual blessing" (*Trench*).

CHAPTER III

THE CHURCH IN SARDIS

1 Sardis. The capital of ancient Lydia, noted in the apostle's time for wealth and voluptuousness. It was south-east of Thyatira. On its ruins now stands a miserable village called *Sart*.

He that hath the seven Spirits. And is therefore the Giver of spiritual life to the "stars," or the churches.

2 Be watchful. Rather, "become watchful."

the things which remain. The remains of true religion which still lingered in the church.

that are ready. Rather, as R.V., "that were ready"—which were going to die if I had not come and spoken to thee.

perfect. Or, as R.V., "fulfilled" or "completed."

3 as a thief. See 1 Thess. v. 2, and note.

what hour. Lit., "what kind of hour": cp. Mark xiii. 35.

4 a few names. That is, a few *persons* (as in Acts i. 15). These few had kept themselves free from the prevailing worldliness.

5 white raiment. The bright robes of purity, joy, and royalty: see iv. 4; xix. 8; and note on Song of Songs v. 14.

I will not blot out his name, etc. See Exod. xxxii. 32; Isa. iv. 3.

THE CHURCH IN PHILADELPHIA

7 Philadelphia. Philadelphia was about 30 miles south-east of Sardis. Its name is derived from Attalus II. Philadelphus, *d.* 138 B.C. "It is remarkable that the city whose noble Christian career is intimated in the message, Rev. iii. 8–14, should have had the most glorious history of all the cities of Asia Minor in the long struggle against the Turks" (Sir W. Ramsay in *Hastings' Dict. of the Bible*). It still exists under the Turkish name of *Ala Sheher*, the reddish city, and contains some churches.

the key of David. In allusion to Isa. xxii. 22; where see note. The Saviour declares that He has "all power in heaven and on earth" (Matt. xxviii. 18); controlling the whole course of events: see ver. 8.

8 an open door. Rather, "a door opened"; opportunities and facilities for spreading the gospel (as in 1 Cor. xvi. 9; 2 Cor. ii. 12; Col. iv. 3), as a reward for faithfulness.

thou hast a little strength, etc. Rather, "thou hast little strength, and [yet] hast kept my word."

9 the synagogue of Satan, etc. See note on ii. 9.

10 the word of my patience. That is, the gospel, which sets before us Christ's patient endurance.

the hour of temptation. Or, "trial"; R.V. "The great catastrophes which come upon the earth are testing-times to the world no less than to the Church" (*Trench*).

11 Behold, I come quickly. To give to the faithful a gracious reward (cp. xxii. 12), the crown of life (cp. 2 Tim. iv. 8, and Rev. ii. 10).

that no man take thy crown. That no one cause thee to lose it.

12 a pillar. Not merely a permanent part of the building (cp. 1 Pet. ii. 5), but one of its ornaments and supports (cp. Gal. ii. 9); marked by its inscriptions as belonging to God (see xiv. 1), to Christ (see ii. 17), and to the New Jerusalem (see xxi. 2); and therefore never to be removed.

THE CHURCH IN LAODICEA

14 the Laodiceans. Laodicea was a large and wealthy city about forty miles east of Ephesus and eleven miles from Colossæ. It was the capital of the Greater Phrygia, and the residence of a Roman governor. Ramsay (*Hastings' Dict. of the Bible*) shows that the references to "gold tried in the fire," and "white raiment," have their appropriateness in reference to a place which was a great centre of banking and of the wool trade. It was subject to earthquakes, and is now deserted. Its site is covered with ruins of temples, theatres, an aqueduct, etc., and is called *Eski-hissar* ("Old Fortress") by the Turks. The church in Laodicea is mentioned in Col. iv. 16, where see note.

the Amen. That is, the True or Faithful One (see note on Isa. lxv. 16); in whom also God's promises are all Yea and Amen: see on 2 Cor. i. 20.

the beginning, etc. See notes on Eph. i. 23; Col. i. 15.

15 neither cold nor hot. This lukewarm state indicates a profession of religion without the vital heat of heartfelt piety. "Tepid water provokes nausea, and a tepid Christianity is nauseous to Christ" (*Swete*).

17 I am rich, etc. The language of spiritual pride and self-satisfaction.

thou art wretched, etc. (With all thy boasting) thou art wretched; "poor" in spiritual grace, "blind" to truth and to thy own real state, "naked" as to the righteousness of the saints.

18 tried in the fire. Rather, "refined by fire." Cp. 1 Pet. i. 7.

white raiment. See ver. 5, and note.

19 As many as I love, etc. This is an allusion to Prov. iii. 11, 12. The Lord is still waiting to be gracious (20); and if you will but receive Him, He will make you happy in His friendship.

21 To him that overcometh, etc. Cp. ii. 26.

CHAPTER IV

VISION OF THE HEAVENLY TEMPLE (iv. and v.)

1 and the first voice, etc. See i. 10.

2 in the Spirit. Cp. i. 10; 2 Cor. xii. 1, 2; Ezek. xi. 1, 5.

One sat on the throne. The Eternal Father: cp. ver. 8; Dan. vii. 9.

3 sardine. "Sard," or "cornelian." The jasper and the sard, the last and the first stones in the breastplate (Exod. xxviii. 17, 20), represent the Divine splendour; but no *form* is described.

a rainbow round about the throne. The token of Divine mercy: see Gen. ix. 9–16; Ezek. i. 4, 28, and notes. It formed an arch over the throne. Cp. also x. 1.

4 seats. Rather, "thrones" (cp. i. 6; iii. 21). These "twenty-four elders" are probably representatives of the redeemed Church, in the character of a royal priesthood (see i. 6; v. 10). The most generally accepted view is that twelve represent the patriarchs, or heads of the tribes in the Old Testament Church; and twelve the apostles of the New; thus combining the Church of the past and of the present in one act of adoration.

5 the seven Spirits of God. See note on i. 4.

6 a sea of glass. An ocean-like expanse or firmament of transparent blue, before the throne; on which stood the four living creatures: cp. Exod. xxiv. 9, 10; Ezek. i. 22–26; Rev. xv. 2, and note.

four beasts. Rather, "four *living creatures*"; and so in all other places where these four beings are spoken of. The Greek word is different from that used in vi. 8; xi. 7, etc.; which denotes a *wild beast.* These living creatures closely resemble the cherubim; on which see Gen. iii. 24; Exod. xxv. 17–20; Isa. vi. 1, 2; Ezek. i. 5–11; x. 14.

full of eyes. Symbols of the highest intelligence: see note on Ezek. i. 15.

8 And the four beasts, etc. Rather, "And the four living creatures, each one of them having six wings apiece, around and within are full of eyes": cp. the description in Isa. vi. 2, 3.

9 give glory, etc. This and the following verbs are *future*—"shall give . . . shall fall . . . shall worship . . . shall cast": see R.V. The form of expression seems to denote constant repetition, through the several stages of the vision.

11 for Thy pleasure. Rather, "because of Thy will." All things owe their existence to the will of God. The elders who here praise God the *Creator,* extol in v. 8–12 God the *Redeemer;* in whose worship all created things also join (v. 13, 14).

CHAPTER V

1 in the right hand. Literally, "on the right hand," the open palm.

written within, etc. It was thoroughly filled (see Ezek. ii. 9, 10); but until every seal was broken its contents were not fully revealed. The seven seals, all visible at once, were probably in a row, securely fastening the roll, no part of which could thus be read until *all* the seals were broken. "Seven" indicates completeness.

3 no man. Properly, "no *one*"; including angels as well as men. The roll contains the record of God's secret purposes.

5 the Lion of the tribe of Judah, etc. (See Gen. xlix. 8–10; and Isa. xi. 1; iv. 2.)

hath prevailed, etc. "Hath conquered."

6 in the midst of the throne, etc. Between the throne supported by the living creatures, and the elders, representative of the Universal Church: an emblem of mediatorship.

a Lamb as it had been slain, etc. Showing that He was the victorious Lion, because He was the Lamb slain. Cp. John i. 29. The "seven horns" indicate fulness of power and dominion (see note on 1 Sam. ii. 1); and the "seven eyes" fulness of knowledge and wisdom, as connected with the work or offices of Christ.

8 vials full of odours. Rather, "bowls full of incense," R.V.

9 a new song. The song of redemption, as distinguished from the song of creation (iv. 9–11).

us. The word "us" is omitted by many good authorities. See following note.

10 and hast made us. The best authorities read "them," and, in the next clause, "they reign on the earth."

14 And the elders fell down and worshipped. "The Elders, the representatives of the Church

Universal, in silent adoration add their assent; the last tones of the hymn die away, and the opening of the Seals begins" (Archdeacon Lee in *Speaker's Commentary*).

THE SEVEN SEALS (vi. to viii. 1)

CHAPTER VI

1 Come and see. The best MSS. omit "and see." At the opening of each of the first four seals the word is "Come!" It is generally held that the summons was addressed to each of the horsemen in turn. The "horses" evidently correspond to those in Zechariah's visions.

2 a white horse. Emblem of victory: cp. Zech. i. 8–11; vi. 1–7, and notes.

4 another horse [that was] red. Emblem of carnage (Matt. x. 34).

that they should kill one another. Perhaps in civil war.

5 a black horse. Emblem of scarcity.

6 a voice in the midst of the four beasts. A voice from the throne itself.

A measure of wheat for a penny, etc. Lit., "a chœnix (two pints) of wheat for a denarius (about 20 cents); and three chœnixes of barley for a denarius." A chœnix seems to have been a man's daily allowance of wheat (*Herodotus*, vii. 187), and a denarius his daily earning (Matt. xx. 2, 9): so that after purchasing his daily food at these prices, he would have nothing left for other expenses and for his family. In other words, wheat would be about eight times its usual price. This indicates great scarcity, although not the extremity of famine: cp. Ezek. iv. 16.

[see] thou hurt not, etc. Perhaps this direction respecting the oil and wine represents a merciful alleviation of the calamity. A warning against profiteering.

8 a pale horse. Emblem of Death.

Hell. Rather, "Hades," or the state of departed spirits (cp. Isa. v. 14).

the fourth part of the earth. Each fourth part being dominated by one of the four horses and its rider.

with death. "Death," used distinctively, seems to refer to pestilence (Jer. xv. 2).

9 under the altar. That is, at the foot or lower part of the great altar, to which victims were led whose blood was shed. The scene is laid in the Temple. These no doubt are Christian martyrs.

10 How long, etc.? Cp. Luke xviii. 7, 8, and notes.

11 white robes, etc. "There was given them to each one a white robe"; denoting honour, acceptance, and triumph.

that they should rest, etc. Waiting quietly until the martyrdom of their brethren who had yet to suffer should fill up the measure of their persecutor's sins: cp. Matt. xxiii. 32; 1 Thess. ii. 16, and notes.

12 when He had opened the sixth seal, etc. The scene at the opening of the sixth seal is that of terrible natural convulsions; depicting the effects of God's wrath (17). This may refer to the utter destruction of the powers which had persecuted the martyrs (9–11): cp. Isa. xiii. 9, 10; xxxiv. 1–4; Ezek. xxii. 7, and notes.

13 the stars. Cp. Dan. viii. 10, and note; also Matt. xxiv. 29.

untimely figs. Or, "winter figs"; which seldom mature, and easily fall off in the spring of the year; "ses figues vertes" (*French version*). See Isa. xxxiv. 4; Nahum iii. 12.

16 Fall on us, etc. This is the language of consternation and despair, derived from Hosea x. 8; cp. Isa. ii. 19, 21; Luke xxiii. 30.

CHAPTER VII

1 four winds. The "four winds" (*i.e.*, winds from all quarters) appear to represent various destructive agencies (2, 3), which are to be restrained for a season. For the "angels" of the elements, see xiv. 18; xvi. 5.

3 Hurt not the earth, etc. "Earth, sea, and trees," as a combined emblem, may represent the world and its inhabitants generally.

till we have sealed. See Ezek. ix. 3–5, and note. This protection of the faithful against impending judgements resembles the protection of the Israelites in Egypt from the destroying angel (Exod. xii. 13); but with this marked difference, that there households were sealed, but here individuals: perhaps to indicate the truth that religion is a matter of personal concern (Matt. iii. 9, 10). The spiritual Israel is here plainly intended (cp. iii. 12; xxi. 10–12); preserved amid trial and finally triumphant. In the Divine purpose they are definitely numbered; to human view they are numberless (see ver. 9).

4–8. It is to be noted in this enumeration that Levi, generally omitted in the Old Testament catalogues of the tribes, is here included, that Dan, for some unexplained reason (see, however, Gen. xlix. 17) is omitted, and that *Joseph* and Manasseh appear as two distinct tribes, rather than *Ephraim* (see Judges xvii., xviii; Isa. vii. 2, 5, 9, 17; Hosea v. 3) and Manasseh, as usual.

9 white robes. See note on vi. 11.

palms. "Palm branches": tokens of victory, as among the Greeks; or of festal rejoicing, as among the Jews (see Lev. xxiii. 40; John xii. 13). The whole picture seems taken from the Feast of Tabernacles.

12 saying, Amen, etc. Angels assent and respond to the thanksgiving of the redeemed.

13 answered. "Addressed me" (*Moffatt*).

14 which came out of great tribulation. Properly, "which are coming (gradually and successively) out of the great tribulation," *i.e.*, the persecutions alluded to in vi. 9–11.

and made them white, etc. The cleansing efficacy of the blood of Christ is here strikingly set forth. Other blood pollutes, this purifies: cp. 1 John i. 7; Eph. i. 7.

15 in His temple. Not in the outer court, but (as the Greek word used for "temple" throughout this book always signifies) in the sanctuary itself; where in ancient times the priests alone could minister (Heb. ix. 2, 6).

shall dwell among them. Rather, "will spread His tent over them"; perhaps alluding to the Shechinah; or referring to John i. 14, on which see note. The Divine protection is here indicated.

16 They shall hunger no more. Referring to their sufferings while passing through the great tribulation: cp. Heb. xi. 36–38.

17 feed. Or, "tend," as a shepherd does his flock; leading them to "fountains of waters of life": cp. Psa. xxiii. 2; John iv. 10; x. 1–18, and notes.

God shall wipe away all tears from their eyes. See Isa. xxv. 8.

CHAPTER VIII

1 there was silence, etc. This silence corresponds with the interval in the worship of the Jewish sanctuary, during which the priest went in to offer incense, while the worshippers remained *silently* waiting in the court without (Luke i. 21). This function of the Jewish priests was typical of our Lord's intercession in heaven.

The Seven Trumpets

2 the seven angels. The dispensers of Divine blessings and judgements (see note on i. 4).

trumpets. Trumpets were used by the Jews to announce the appointed religious festivals, and on other great occasions: see Josh. vi. 3, 16.

3 there was given unto him much incense, etc. Cp. v. 8. The altar is the altar of incense.

all saints. Perhaps all the saints before mentioned (vi. 9; vii. 14) as coming out of the great tribulation; who now join in calling on Jehovah (as in vi. 10) to vindicate them.

the throne. The mercy-seat upon which the Divine glory rested (Exod. xxv. 20, 22).

7 the third part. Cp. Ezek. v. 12; Zech. xiii. 8. The "third part" seems to mean a considerable portion. In the midst of wrath the Lord remembers mercy (Hab. iii. 2); postponing complete destruction until these visitations have failed of their effect (see ix. 20, 21: and cp. Zech. xiii. 8, 9).

8 a great mountain burning with fire, etc. Cp. Jer. li. 25. The agitation was such as might be expected from the falling of a burning mountain into the sea: see also Exod. vii. 20, 21.

11 Wormwood. "Wormwood" represents that which poisons and embitters every source of enjoyment: see Jer. ix. 15; Lam. iii. 15, 19; Amos v. 7.

12 so as the third part of them was darkened, etc. All the luminaries both of day and night lost the third part of their usual splendour; a fit emblem of general gloom and distress; and yet a limited judgement, like the three foregoing plagues.

13 an angel. The best authorities read, "an eagle." The Divine messenger appears like a flying eagle alone in mid-heaven, uttering the eagle-like cry, *Ouai! ouai! ouai!* (cp. xiv. 8).

Woe, woe, woe. A woe from each of the three remaining trumpets.

CHAPTER IX

1 I saw a star fall (fallen) **from heaven.** Apparently Satan (cp. Luke x. 18); here employed as the executioner of Divine wrath.

the bottomless pit. Lit., "the pit of the abyss," *i.e.*, the abode of evil spirits: see xx. 1, and note on Luke viii. 31.

2 smoke. "Denotes the diffusion on earth of the diabolical spirit of cruelty and hatred. Out of this smoke come the 'locusts'" (*Dr. Vaughan*).

3 locusts. A visitation of locusts is a fearful calamity (see Exod. x. 4–15); a symbol of extensive, severe, irresistible, and continued punishments (see Joel i. 2–7; ii. 1–9, and notes). "There is much, however, here which points to an outbreak of moral evil" (Archdeacon Lee in *Speaker's Commentary*).

4 the seal of God. The seal mentioned before in vii. 2, 4.

5 five months. The term of five months may refer to the duration of the ravages of the natural locust: cp. ver. 10. It symbolises an indefinite but brief duration.

a scorpion. A symbol of merciless men (Ezek. ii. 6).

7 crowns like gold. This may refer to the horns of the locusts, which are tipped with yellow, and are here called "crowns," as emblematic of their victorious march: cp. Joel ii. 7–9.

8 And they had hair, etc. Cp. Jer. li. 27; Joel i. 4, and notes. For "teeth like lions," see Joel i. 6. The "breastplates as it were iron" (9), may refer to the hard and firm cuticle on the fore part of the locust, which serves as a shield when it moves among thorny vegetation.

11 And they had a king. etc. Moving as an organised body (see Joel ii. 7, 8), to fulfil the cruel purposes of the great Destroyer, "Abaddon": see Job xxvi. 6; xxviii. 22.

13 the golden altar. Cp. viii. 3. The judgement is proclaimed from the golden altar of incense, as if in reply to the Intercessor's prayers.

14 Loose the four angels, etc. Four ministers of Divine wrath that had hitherto been restrained, as on the outskirts of the Holy Land. Respecting the number "four," see note on vii. 1.

the great river Euphrates. "The great river is the symbolic limit which separates the Church from her enemies" (*Stern*).

Palestine had for many ages been subject to invasion by formidable hosts from the region of the Euphrates: see Gen. xiv.; Judges iii. 8; 2 Kings xv. 19, etc. Assyria and Babylon had been proverbial for the multitudes of their cavalry; and they abounded with representations of symbolical animals, to which the figures of this vision bear remarkable resemblance. And in the days of John, the Parthian horsemen from the same region were dreaded even by the legions of Rome.

15 for an hour, etc. Rather, as R.V., "For the hour and day and month and year," *i.e.*, the exact time appointed by God at which they were to lead forth their destroying army.

16 two hundred thousand thousand. "Two myriads of myriads"; an overwhelming multitude of dreadful monsters.

17 breastplates of fire, etc. Glaring and terrific.

18 By these three. The best MSS. add "plagues"; *i.e.*, the fire, smoke, and brimstone, issuing from the mouths of the horses; which are represented as performing the principal work of destruction, the riders only guiding them.

Visions Preparatory to the Seventh Trumpet

CHAPTER X

1 clothed with a cloud. The emblem of majesty (see Psa. xviii. 12; Ezek. i. 4). "The rainbow" (as iv. 3) is the emblem of mercy.

2 a little book. Cp. Ezek. iii. 1–4. This small scroll appears to have contained prophecies; perhaps some of those which John was to utter (see vers. 8–11). Godet thinks that they are contained in x. 1–13.

he set his right foot on the sea, etc. Signifying the Divine control over both land and sea.

3 seven thunders. Properly, "*the* seven thunders"; "seven peals of thunder" (*Weymouth*). Cp. Psa. xxix; John xii. 28, 29. The number seven here as elsewhere denoting *completeness*.

4 Seal up, etc. In no other instance is John forbidden to write (or publish); in i. 19 and three subsequent instances he is expressly commanded to do it (xiv. 13; xix. 9; xxi. 5); cp. Dan. xii. 4, 9.

5 lifted up his hand to heaven, and sware, etc. Cp. Dan. xii. 7, and note.

6 that there should be time no longer. Or, "that there shall be no more *delay*." The sounding of the seventh trumpet is at hand.

7 as He hath declared. Rather, "as He gave glad tidings" (εὐηγγέλισεν); referring to the blessed consummation, which had been foretold by prophets both in the Old Testament and the New, and is announced as being accomplished, in xi. 15.

9 it shall make thy belly bitter, etc. Cp. note on Ezek. iii. 3. This may mean that it is sweet to hear of the future deliverance and glory of the Church; bitter, to learn the painful path by which this happiness is to be reached.

11 before. Rather, "upon"; *i.e.,* "*concerning.*"

CHAPTER XI

1 And there was given me a reed, etc. This scene should be compared with Ezek. xl. 3–5, 17–19; and Zech. ii. 1–3.

temple. The word "temple" (see on vii. 15) denotes the principal building or sanctuary, exclusive of the open court without and around it. To "measure" the worshippers must mean to count them. Under the Christian dispensation the Temple of God is the community of all true Christians (Eph. ii. 20–22).

2 the holy city. Jerusalem was "the holy city." Here the phrase probably symbolises the great body of professed Christians at this period, as distinguished from the spiritual worshippers in the inner court of the Temple.

shall they tread under foot. Treat it with the greatest indignity: cp. Luke xxi. 24.

forty and two months. Forty-two months, of thirty days each, would be equal to 1,260 days, which would also be three and a half years (360 days in the year): see xii. 6, 14; Dan. vii. 25; xii. 7. The symbolical interpretation in the case of this number, as of others, is probably correct. Half of seven denotes the period of incompleteness, sorrow, and conflict.

3 I will give [power] unto my two witnesses. Rather, simply, "I will give unto my two witnesses"; *i.e.,* I will appoint and qualify them for their mission. "Sackcloth" was the usual clothing of the ancient prophets: see 2 Kings i. 8; Zech. xiii. 4; Matt. iii. 4. The two witnesses seem to be identified (4) with the two olive trees of Zechariah: see Zech. iv. 1–14, and notes. They are sacred to God, secured by His care, and protected by the very forces of nature (5, 6). Having finished their work, they are slain as Christ was (7); but, like Christ, they arise and ascend to heaven (11, 12). Some of their persecutors repent, and others are destroyed (13). The symbols of this vision are fulfilled whenever God's faithful witnesses come into conflict with a corrupt Church and an unbelieving world. The *two* may be the Old and New Testaments or "the Church in her function of witness-bearing" (*Swete*).

5 in this answer. That is, by fire; an evident allusion to 2 Kings i. 10. "Will" = "want to."

6 power. Or, "authority." Such as that of Elijah and Moses: cp. 1 Kings xvii. 1; Exod. vii. 17–19.

7 when they shall have finished, etc. That is, at the end of 1260 days (2).

the beast See xvii. 8.

8 the great city, etc. This "great city," the antagonist of "the holy city," is called "Sodom" for vice; and "Egypt" for tyranny and oppression of God's people; and it is further compared to the Jewish capital for its rejection of Christ, and hatred to His people.

our Lord. The best reading seems to be, "*their* Lord"; to whom in death, as in life, the witnesses are conformed.

10 and shall send gifts, etc. As on a festival: see Neh. viii. 10–12; Esther ix. 19, 22.

tormented. By their rebukes.

12 they ascended up to heaven in a cloud. Cp. Acts i. 9.

13 a great earthquake. Cp. Matt. xxvii. 50–54; xxviii. 2.

gave glory to the God of heaven. They acknowledged God's hand and power (see xiv. 7; xvi. 9).

14 the third woe. The third woe, introduced by the sounding of the seventh trumpet, is the immediate precursor of final victory. According to the declaration in x. 6, there is no further delay; the judgements of God are completed; and this awful series of visions, which commenced with the presentation of the prayers of the Church (viii. 3, 4), concludes with songs of thanksgiving and praise. The scene, like that which follows the opening of the seventh seal (viii. 1), is laid in heaven; but here, instead of silence, there is triumph and exultation.

18 the time of the dead, etc. This probably refers to the martyrs who would then be avenged, whilst all agents of evil will be punished.

19 testament. The ark in the earthly Temple was in the Most Holy Place: where the Shechinah shone forth as the symbol of Jehovah's presence. As the rending of the veil in twain indicated that the ancient dispensation had come to an end (see Matt. xxvii. 51, and note); so the throwing open of the Holy of Holies here may perhaps signify the passing away of the final earthly dispensation. "The ideal import of the holiness of the law and the truth of the redemption becomes a matter of Christian knowledge manifest to all the world" (*Lange*).

FALL OF BABYLON: PRELIMINARY VISION

CHAPTER XII

1 a woman. This is commonly thought to be an emblem of the Church of God upon earth, out of which proceeds the Messiah, the world's destined King: cp. Isa. liv. 1, 5, 6; Mic. iv. 10; Gal. iv. 26.

3 a great red dragon. Satan (see ver. 9). "Red" is the emblem of cruelty and bloodshed.

having seven heads, etc. The "heads," "horns," and royal "diadems" represent power; which the number "seven" shows to be *complete* or *universal.*

5 who was to rule all nations, etc. Cp. xix. 15; Psa. ii. 9. This clause plainly indicates that the child is the Messiah; who is delivered from Satan's assaults, and exalted to the throne of God.

6 fled into the wilderness. This may intimate that the true Church would be hidden, as well as suffering, but yet preserved by God.

a thousand two hundred and threescore days. 1,260 days make three years and a half; which many suppose to be the same as "a time, times, and half a time," in ver. 14, and Dan. vii. 25; see also xi. 2. But three and a half (being the half of seven, the number of completeness) may denote, generally, "a short time" (ver. 12).

7 there was war in heaven. The reflection in heaven of the contest of good and evil upon earth. This contest is the strife of spiritual forces: see Job i. 6–11; Zech. iii. 1–5; Rom. viii. 33.

Michael. The Guardian of God's people: see note on Dan. x. 13.

9 that old serpent, etc. That ancient Tempter, through whom the earthly Paradise was lost. See on ver. 3. The accumulated titles forcibly describe the character and influence of the evil one. The casting out of Satan the calumniator, the tempter, the adversary, represents the complete overthrow of his schemes (Luke x. 18; John xii. 31), and the deliverance of the believers through Christ Jesus from condemnation and from the power of sin.

10 Now is come salvation, etc. Rather, "Now the salvation, and the strength, and the kingdom is become our God's; and the authority, His Christ's." The meaning is as in xi. 15.

the accuser. "Accuser" is the meaning of the names "Satan" (cp. Job i. 9–11) and "devil" (1 Pet. v. 8).

11 And they overcame him, etc. "The brethren," whom he accused, overcame him "by virtue of the blood of the Lamb (cp. vii. 14), and of the word of their testimony" (*Alford*).

12 but a short time. Only a "short *season*" before his final defeat: very short compared with the future beyond.

14 two wings of a great eagle. Rather, as R.V., "the two wings of the great eagle" (cp. Exod. xix. 4; Deut. xxxii. 11, 12).

15 the flood. A "river" is a common symbol of an invading army: see Isa. viii. 7. Here widely extended persecution may be meant; from which the Church is from time to time delivered by God's overruling providence (16).

17 to make war with the remnant of her seed. The followers of Christ. The chief object of his hatred was beyond his reach (5).

The Two Beasts

CHAPTER XIII

1 I stood. R.V., following the best MSS., "he (the dragon) stood." The verse should not be separated from ch. xii. The dragon stands watching for the agencies of evil, which soon appear.

a beast. That is, a wild beast; emblem of worldly persecuting power. Cp. Dan. vii. 2–8, 17–27, and notes.

the name of blasphemy. Rather, "*names* of blasphemy" (as in xvii. 3), apparently signifying impious claims to dignity and authority belonging to God only: see ver. 6.

2 seat. Rather, "throne": cp. xvi. 10.

3 wondered after the beast. They followed him with admiration. In former visions the adversaries of the Church gained only a transient victory over Christ's faithful witnesses; but these extend their power through the world (4, 8). Many willingly submit to their dominion; and so ultimately share their doom.

4 Who is like unto the beast, etc.? The "dragon" and "the beast" are both worshipped as possessing irresistible power.

5 blasphemies. Cp. ver. 1, and Dan. vii. 8, 20. The objects of his blasphemies are God, and heaven, and its holy inhabitants (6).

forty and two months. Cp. xii. 6, and note.

8 all that dwell upon the earth, etc. Only those who are in vital union with Christ can resist this delusion: see Matt. xxiv. 24.

not written, etc. From xvii. 8 it appears that the connexion is, "not written from the foundation of the world in the book of life of the Lamb that hath been slain."

9 If any man have an ear, let him hear. See ii. 7; also Matt. xi. 15.

11 And I beheld another beast. Many think that this symbol refers to the employment of religious deception in aid of persecuting power. The two powers which have been chiefly employed by Satan in his conflict with the Church have been that of persecuting governments founded on force, and that of false priesthoods founded on delusion. Or, in a more general sense, the two evil agencies thus embodied may be described as Force and Fraud: the power that crushes and the power that deceives.

like a lamb . . . as a dragon. Fair-seeming, subtle and malicious (2 Thess. ii. 8–10).

12 all the power of the first beast. See ver. 3.

13 wonders. Or, "signs"; "false miracles: cp. Exod. vii. 8–13; Matt. xxiv. 24; Acts viii. 9–11; xiii. 6.

16 a mark. The "mark" appears to refer to the sign or token anciently borne by persons who were devoted to any particular deity, or to the branding of slaves. It has been a common mode of persecution to forbid men to "buy or sell."

18 The number of a man. Some scholars identify this number with the name of "Nero Cæsar," or "Nero Redivivus"; others with "Lateinos" (Latin; suggesting the rule of Rome); others, again, with various characters in modern history. But none of the conjectures seems convincing. "No explanation has ever been given why St. John should in this instance, and in this instance only, depart from his invariable use of the symbolism of numbers and suddenly adopt a new method" (Dr. Limmer Sheppard in *Devotional Commentary*).

CHAPTER XIV

1 a Lamb. Rather, "*the* Lamb" (see v. 6).

a hundred forty and four thousand. The Church universal, viewed as definite and complete. Cp. vii. 4, referring to the sealed on earth.

having His Father's name. The best reading is, "having His name and His Father's name": cp. vii. 3.

3 a new song. See note on v. 9.

4 virgins. "The words may imply either purity of soul, as seems pointed at in ver. 5, or spiritual loyalty to God as opposed to spiritual disloyalty" (*Speaker's Commentary*).

The Seven "Vials": Introductory Visions

6 another angel. Probably different from the "mighty angel" last seen (x. 1).

the everlasting gospel. Or, as R.V., "an eternal gospel," or "good tidings."

8 Babylon is fallen, etc. Cp. Isa. xxi. 9: Jer. li. 6–8. The order in the original is emphatic: "Fallen, fallen is Babylon the great."

9 the third angel. Rather, "a third angel."

10 with fire and brimstone. A figurative expression, derived from the doom of Sodom and Gomorrha: see Gen. xix. 24; Psa. xi. 6; Isa. xxx. 33.

11 the smoke of their torment, etc. Cp. Gen. xix. 28; Isa. xxxiv. 10; Jude 7, and notes.

12 Here is the patience of the saints. The "patience," or "endurance" of the saints is shown in stedfastly refusing to worship the beast; and its "reward," in escaping the inevitable punishment: cp. note on xiii. 10.

13 Blessed are the dead, etc. Those saints who might die (by martyrdom or otherwise) before Christ's final coming are comforted by the assurance of immediate happiness: cp. 2 Cor. v. 8: Phil. i. 23.

their works do follow them. The Greek is "follow with them," as close companions, into God's presence.

14 like unto the Son of man. Rather, as R.V., "like unto a son of man"; *i.e.*, like a human being (cp. i. 13; Dan. vii. 13). The Saviour is undoubtedly meant.

15 the harvest of the earth is ripe (over-ripe). The harvest is a frequent Scripture emblem of retribution. The grain appears to represent the righteous (cp. Matt. xiii. 38, etc.), and the grapes (18, 19) the wicked (see Joel iii. 13).

18 which had power over fire. Each of the different elements is represented as being watched over and governed by an angel: cp. vii. 1, 2; xvi. 5; xix. 17.

the vine of the earth. Cp. "the vine of Sodom" (Deut. xxxii. 32).

19 the great winepress. See notes on Isa. lxiii. 1–6; Lam. i. 15.

20 without the city. As criminals were executed outside the gates of the city: see Acts vii. 58; Heb. xiii. 11–13, and note.

a thousand and six hundred furlongs. That is, about 180 English miles.

CHAPTER XV

2 a sea of glass. See iv. 6, and note. "Repose mingled with struggle. It is peace and rest and achievement, with the power of trial and suffering yet alive and working within it. It is calmness still pervaded by the discipline through which it has been reached" (*Phillips Brooks*).

mingled with fire. "The red glow on the sea spoke of the fire through which the martyrs passed, and yet more of the wrath about to fall upon the world which had condemned them" (*Swete*).

3 the song of Moses, etc. A song of triumph celebrated the deliverance by Moses (Exod. xv. 1–21); a new song connects with this the greater salvation by the Lamb.

King of saints. The best MSS. have, "King of the ages" (as in Jer. x. 7).

4 all nations shall come, etc. This is the anticipated result of God's judgement: cp. Psa. lxxxvi. 9; Isa. xxvi. 9.

5 the temple. See note on xi. 1.

the tabernacle of the testimony. The sanctuary. "The tabernacle of testimony" is the Septuagint version of the Hebrew phrase "the tabernacle of the congregation" ("tent of meeting," R.V.): cp. Numb. xiv. 10.

6 clothed in pure and white linen, etc. The dress of priests: cp. Exod. xxviii. 27–29, 39, 40; Lev. xvi. 4; Dan. x. 5. But see var. read.

7 vials. Rather, "bowls" or vessels; such as were used in the services of the Jewish temple: see 2 Chron. iv. 8.

8 filled with smoke. Cp. Exod. xl. 34; Psa. xviii. 8; Isa. vi. 4; Heb. xii. 29. This imagery may denote not only the presence of God in unapproachable majesty, but also the exclusion of intercession; "no man was able to enter the temple," etc.

Contents of the "Vials" Poured Forth

CHAPTER XVI

1 a great voice out of the temple. Where God dwells: see xv. 8. "Vials": R.V., "bowls." See xv. 7, note.

2 upon (into) **the earth.** Rather, "into the land"; in distinction from the sea (3). There is an obvious similarity between the first four visions of this series and the first four of the preceding: in both, the land, the sea, the rivers, and the sun are presented in the same order. The plagues are, however, more extensive and more dreadful than those under the first four trumpets (cp. vers. 3, 4, 8, with viii. 8–12). They again resemble the plagues of Egypt (cp. Exod. ix. 8–11; vii. 20, 21; x. 22; ix. 18–29); and, like them, they manifest the power and the justice of God, but fail to subdue the impenitence of men.

the mark of the beast. See xiii. 16.

7 I heard another out of the altar. The best authorities omit "another out of." It is the altar itself that utters its Amen to the "true and righteous judgements" of the Almighty.

8 upon the sun. Cp. viii. 12; where the visitation is partial darkness: here it is scorching heat, occasioning blasphemous rage, yet not bringing men to repentance.

10 seat. Rather, "throne," or seat of empire, as in xiii. 2.

12 the great river Euphrates. See note on ix. 14. The ministers of God's wrath had often issued from the region of the Euphrates in ancient times. This figure seems to have reference to the fall of ancient Babylon; when Cyrus, at that time one of "the kings of the East," laid dry the bed of the Euphrates, and so obtained an entrance into the city. This drying up of the Euphrates, therefore, would seem to indicate the removal of some impediment in the way of the executioners of Divine judgement upon the spiritual Babylon.

13 frogs. Unclean creatures. Symbols of impurity.

the false prophet. "The false prophet," who is named here as if known already, is probably the same as the second beast mentioned in xiii. 11–15.

14 devils. Or, "demons": cp. ix. 20.

miracles. Or, "signs": like those anciently wrought by the Egyptian magicians.

15 Behold, I come as a thief. See Matt. xxiv. 41–44, and note.

and keepeth his garments. His "loins must be girded about" as well as his "lamps burning." See Luke xii. 35. "Think not of this as of some great battle in which you are yourself unconcerned; you are yourself, O reader, now in the midst of that conflict of which you read" (*Isaac Williams*).

16 he. This should probably be rendered "they"; *i.e.*, the spirits mentioned in ver. 14.

Armageddon. Har-Magedon, R.V. (the mount of Megiddo), is supposed to denote the high ground on which Megiddo stood; adjoining "the great plain of Esdraelon," or Jezreel; which has been the scene of many bloody battles, both in ancient times (see note on 1 Sam. xxviii. 4) and subsequently in the times of the Crusades and of Napoleon; so that it has been called "the battle-field of Palestine" (see Stanley's *Sinai and Palestine*, pp. 329–340). The great battle and its issue appear to be described in ch. xx.

18 such as was not, etc. See note on vi. 12; the greatest commotion that the earth has witnessed since the creation.

19 And the great city, etc. This scene of ruin is minutely described in ch. xviii.

divided into three parts. By the earthquake which swallowed the city.

20 every island fled away. Cp. vi. 14, where there are similar images of terrific commotions.

21 a great hail. Cp. xi. 19; and see Exod. ix. 18–29. The Jewish talent was more than a hundredweight. The futile "blasphemy" occasioned by the hail appears to be parallel to the anger of the nations (xi. 18). No earthly power can afford protection against the Divine judgements.

THE FALL OF BABYLON

CHAPTER XVII

1 talked with me, etc. Having performed his appointed work, the angel now brings before John a fuller exhibition of the chief subject of the Divine judgements. "The great harlot" is ancient Babylon (see Jer. li. 13, and note), here used symbolically (see ver. 15) "for that seductive influence or crafty policy which seeks to draw others into subjection" (*Speaker's Commentary*). The evident contrast between the woman persecuted by the dragon (xii. 1–6) and the woman supported by the beast, and between the meretricious splendour and transient prosperity of the latter, and the white raiment and everlasting blessedness of the bride of Christ, has been taken to support the view that this figure denotes antichristian empire, or more specifically, corruption and apostasy in the Church. The same figure is often used in the Old Testament: cp. Isa. i. 21; Nahum iii. 4, etc.

2 drunk with the wine of her fornication. Cp. Jer. li. 7.

3 names of blasphemy. See note on xiii. 1.

4 purple and scarlet. Symbols of royal power and magnificence.

5 Mystery. On "mystery" see note on Matt. xiii. 1. It probably means that the name which follows is symbolical; "a mystery, BABYLON THE GREAT, etc." (R.V. marg.).

6 admiration. Rather, "wonder." The angel intimates (ver. 7) that the end will explain all.

8 was, and is not. Those who accept the early date of the Apocalypse, and who understand its symbols as derived in part from contemporary events, generally apply this passage to Nero. Through a misunderstanding of John's words, the Christians of succeeding generations held that Nero would reappear in bodily form.

9 here is the mind which hath wisdom. Here is room for the exercise of a mind that has wisdom (see note on xiii. 18).

10 And there are seven kings. Rather, "And they were seven kings." The "seven mountains" evidently point in some way to Rome: and the "seven kings" appear to denote seven dynasties or forms of government, or individual rulers, in Rome. On the supposition of the earlier date of the vision, Galba, or perhaps Vespasian (acc. A.D. 69) would be the emperor that "now is." Titus followed, and held the throne "for a short space" (just two years), when Domitian succeeded, who might be called, in his relation to the Church, a re-incarnation of the spirit of Nero.

17 For God hath put in their hearts, etc. In yielding for a time their support to the patroness of evil, they only fulfil the purposes of God; and when at last they destroy her, they execute undesignedly God's sentence on her. Thus the Church in all ages is taught that both the temporary prevalence of evil, and its final destruction, will work out His wise and holy purposes.

CHAPTER XVIII

1 come. Rather, "coming." *Power, i.e.,* "authority."

2 Babylon the great is fallen, etc. The phraseology of the following denunciations and warnings is derived in great part from the prophecies of Isaiah and Jeremiah against ancient Babylon: cp. Isa. xiii.; xiv.; xlvii.; Jer. l., li.

the habitation of devils. See Isa. xiii. 21, 22, and note; see also Matt. xii. 43, where the unclean spirit is represented as wandering through "dry" or desert "places."

3 For all nations have drunk of the wine, etc. See xiv. 8.

the abundance of her delicacies. Rather, as R.V., "the power of her wantonness."

4 Come out of her, my people. The same command is found in Jer. li. 6, 45.

5 her sins have reached unto heaven. Cp. Jer. li. 9. They cry to God for vengeance.

6 Reward her, etc. Cp. Jer. l. 15, 29.

7 For she saith, etc. Cp. Isa. xlvii. 7–11, and notes.

9 Shall bewail her, etc. The following dirge resembles the lamentation over Tyre in Ezek. xxvii.

12 thyine wood. A precious, sweet-scented wood brought from Africa; perhaps citron; much used for inlaying, especially of tables. The French version has "bois odoriférant" ("odoriferous wood").

13 And horses, and chariots, etc. Rather, "And [merchandise] of horses and of chariots, and of bodies (*i.e.,* men sold as slaves), and souls of men."

14 thou shalt find them no more at all. "*They* (*i.e.,* men) shall find them no more at all.

17 and all the company in ships. Literally, "and every one sailing to a place"; *i.e.,* every *passenger.*

19 they cast dust on their heads. A common Oriental sign of grief; see Ezek. xxvii. 30.

20 ye holy apostles and prophets. R.V., "ye saints, and ye apostles, and ye prophets": see ver. 24.

21 cast it into the sea. To rise no more: cp. Jer. li. 63, 64.

22, 23. These verses contain a picture of utter desolation: cp. Jer. xxv. 10 and note.

24 And in her was found, etc. Cp. Matt. xxiii. 35. The foregoing picture of the doom of this system of evil combines the prophetic denunciations on ancient Babylon, Tyre, and Jerusalem; as if all their sins and all their punishments were here accumulated in one.

CHAPTER XIX

1 much people. Rather, "a great multitude" (as in ver. 6) of both saints and angels.

Alleluia. In Hebrew, "Hallelujah"; *i.e.,* Praise ye the Lord!

3 rose up. Rather, "*riseth* up"; always and for ever: see xiv. 11; and note on Jude 7.

8 for the fine linen is the righteousness of saints. "The righteousness" of the saints, symbolised by "fine linen," are "the fruits of righteousness": see Phil. i. 11.

9 the marriage supper. The blessed time when the Church shall be publicly avowed by her Lord, and admitted to share His heavenly glory: cp. Matt. xxv. 1–12.

11 a white horse. Cp. Zech. i. 8–11; vi. 1–7, and notes. See also vi. 2; where a crowned conqueror was beginning his victories; here the Incarnate Word is about to complete His triumphs, and to establish His universal kingdom.

Faithful and True. See i. 5; iii. 14.

12 many crowns. Or, many "diadems"; an emblem of universal dominion: see ver. 16.

a name. Cp. ii. 17, and note.

13 vesture dipped in blood. Cp. Isa. lxiii. 1-3, and notes.

The Word of God. Cp. John i. 1, and notes.

15 And out of His mouth, etc. Cp. i. 16, and note.

a rod of iron. Cp. Psa. ii. 9, and note.

17 Come [and] gather yourselves together, etc. Cp. Jer. vii. 33; Ezek. xxxix. 17-20. This imagery denotes the certainty and the completeness of the anticipated victory.

the supper of the great God. The best MSS. have "the great supper of God"; so the Vulgate and the French version.

20 a (the) **lake of fire,** etc. A description probably founded on the punishment of Sodom: see Gen. xix. 24-28; Psa. xi. 6; and cp. Isa. xxx. 3; xxxiv. 9; Dan. vii. 11.

CHAPTER XX

1 the bottomless pit (the abyss). See ix. 1, and note.

2 the dragon, etc. See xii. 3, 9. Satan is called the "old serpent" because in that form he deceived Eve: see Gen. iii. 1.

a thousand years. The phrase "a thousand years" is taken by some to mean a precise and definite period; but more probably, in accordance with the symbolical character of the book, it is a general designation of an indefinitely long time; as in 2 Pet. iii. 8, etc. Cp. Psa. xc. 4.

3 and set a seal upon him. See Dan. vi. 17; Matt. xxvii. 66, and notes.

4 And I saw thrones, etc. Cp. Dan. vii. 9; Matt. xix. 28; 1 Cor. vi. 2, 3, and notes.

the souls. Cp. vi. 9. The souls (disembodied) of the slain were then "under the altar," now they are on thrones. The spirits of the martyrs, and of all faithful adherents to the truth, are among the supreme forces of the world: 2 Tim. ii. 12; 1 Cor. vi. 2; Matt. xix. 28, etc.

and which had not worshipped the beast, etc. Lit., "and such as did not worship (or pay homage to) the beast and his image." All these are here said to live and reign with Christ the thousand years.

5 This is the first resurrection. The "clearly spiritual and not corporeal" (*Swete*).

7 his prison. The abyss, vers. 1, 3: cp. 2 Pet. ii. 4. As during our Lord's life on earth an unusual manifestation of Satan's power seems to have been permitted, especially in the form of demoniacal possession of men; so it seems to be designed that his whole power shall be let loose before the final consummation; in order that his total defeat may be the more decisive.

8 shall go out to deceive the nations, etc. Respecting "God and Magog," see Gen. x. 2-5; Ezek. xxxviii. 2, and note. "In the vision of Ezekiel, Gog of the land of Magog, and his confederates, come up against the Holy Land and people; but they are slaughtered with immense destruction, and Israel is troubled no more (Ezek. xxxviii., xxxix.). John, under imagery similar to that of Ezekiel, describes the third and last great effort of the enemies of the Church to destroy her."

of the earth. Or, "of the *land*." The scene of the battle is laid in Palestine: see xvi. 16, and note. And accordingly the object of attack is represented as Jerusalem, "the beloved city" (Psa. lxxviii. 68).

9 fire came down from God, etc. As is also predicted in Ezek. xxxviii. 22.

10 the lake. See note on xix. 20.

11 from whose face the earth and the heaven fled away. A complete passing of the world as it was.

12 [the] books were opened. See Dan. vii. 9, 10, and notes. Respecting the "book of life," see note on iii. 5. The books of death are *many*; the book of life is *one*. The record of men's works brings condemnation to all; there is one only way of salvation.

according to their works. Cp. Luke xii. 47, 48; 2 Cor. v. 10.

13 hell. Rather, "Hades," *i.e.*, the state of the departed during the separation of soul and body. Hades, together with death, is represented as giving up its subjects at the bidding of Him who has the keys of death and of Hades: see i. 18.

The New Jerusalem

CHAPTER XXI

1 a new heaven and a new earth. See xx. 11; cp. Isa. lxv. 17; 2 Pet. iii. 13, and notes. This new state is marked by the exclusion of all the wicked, and of all sin, imperfection, and suffering.

there was no more sea. In ancient times the sea was regarded as unproductive and unprofitable; a barrier to intercourse, and destructive. One can believe also that St. John's view of it was coloured by his exile on the sea-girt island.

2 New Jerusalem. The Church, in its ideal purity and blessedness, is predicted by Isaiah under the figure of a holy Jerusalem (Isa. lxvi. 20), which is more fully described by Ezekiel (Ezek. xl.-xlviii.), and is repeatedly alluded to in preceding portions of the New Testament: see Isa. lii. 1; Heb. xi. 10; xii. 22.

3 the tabernacle of God is with men. "The tent" or abode of God. Cp. Ezek. xxxvii. 25-28; John i. 14, and note.

5 Behold, I make all things new. See Isa. lxv. 17-19, and note.

6 It is done. The new creation is complete.

Alpha and Omega. See note on i. 8.

I will give unto him that is athirst. The beginning of the new creation is here connected with its completion. With the "thirsting" the "giving" begins; and it goes on increasingly; since the thirsting is the living impulse throughout the whole conflict. The correspondence between character and privilege is clearly marked in these verses, as in Matt. v. 3-12.

7 He that overcometh shall inherit all things. Cp. John i. 12; Rom. viii. 17, and notes.

8 the fearful. That is, the cowardly, who, instead of "overcoming," shrink from Christ's service, through a base fear of loss or suffering. These must share the doom of the superstitious, the impure, the cruel, and the false.

Description of the New Jerusalem

9 the bride, the Lamb's wife. This figure represents the redeemed Church in its permanent union with the Lord. Cp. ver. 2, and xix. 9.

10 the holy Jerusalem. As the ancient Jerusalem was a chosen type of the Church, the glory and blessedness of the Church in its perfection are set forth by a symbolical Jerusalem, far more magnificent. The measurements (16), the golden street (18), and the precious stones (19) signify perfection of form and of colour, something transcendently beautiful. The vision is that of the ideal Church, descending to earth and diffusing its blessings among men.

11 having the glory of God. In the ancient Holy of Holies the Shechinah or visible glory of God was the only light (23).

12 twelve. *Twelve,* the number of the tribes of Israel, is here used, with its multiples 144 (17), and 12,000 (16), probably to represent completeness. The always-open " gates " (25) fronting all points of the compass, signify ready and constant access from every quarter.

twelve angels, etc. The " twelve *angels,*" " the twelve *tribes,*" and " the twelve *apostles,*" seem to show the union of all God's faithful servants, both the unfallen and the redeemed, of every period and of all nations, in the glory of His Church.

14 in them the names of the twelve apostles. Inscriptions were often placed on foundation stones and pillars. Cp. Eph. ii. 20; 2 Tim. ii. 19, and notes. John, the beloved disciple, read his own name amongst the others there !

16 twelve thousand furlongs. Perhaps the *sum* of the four sides. Each side of the city would thus be 3,000 furlongs, little less than 400 miles; an expressive symbol of the vast *capacity* of the Church redeemed; its *security* being indicated by the loftiness of the walls, more than 200 feet in height.

17 [according] to the measure of a man. That is, the angel used human measures.

18 the building. That is, the material or structure.

22 And I saw no temple therein. No spot specially sacred, consecrated by a limited display of the Divine glory and occasional acts of worship; but the whole hallowed by God's manifest presence. See *A City without a Church*, by Henry Drummond.

24 And the nations, etc. Omit the words " of them which are saved," as not found in any good MS. The Church in its true ideal is the light of the world—a source of knowledge and purity to all mankind.

27 The Lamb's book of life. See xiii. 8 ; xx. 12, 15.

CHAPTER XXII

1 a pure river of water of life. An everflowing stream, diffusing life and beauty throughout its course. Cp. vii. 17; Gen. ii. 10; Psa. xlvi. 4; Ezek. xlvii. 1-12; John iv. 10, and notes.

proceeding out of the throne. The source of all the life and bliss of the redeemed.

2 In the midst of the street of it, etc. Or, " Between the broadway thereof and the river, on this side and on that." The idea is that of a river running through the city, with trees along its banks, and a broad street on each side of it.

the tree of life, etc. Cp. Ezek. xlvii. 12. Instead of one tree " in the midst of the garden," the tree of life is now " so multiplied that it stands on either side along the river; so fruitful, that it bears every month; so versatile, that its produce is of twelve sorts, applicable to every want and taste; and so accessible, that instead of being protected by a flaming sword, it stands in the very street, and whosoever will may freely pluck its fruit " (*Dr. Vaughan*). The contrast between the lost Paradise and the New Jerusalem—the Garden and the City—is complete. *There,* one exit at the east barred by a flaming sword (Gen. iii. 24); *here,* twelve entrances kept open by twelve angels (xxi. 12); *there,* the single tree to which the sword prohibited access; *here,* a grove with its perennial fruit: *there,* expulsion, evil, and sadness; *here,* a welcome to the rest of God.

3 there shall be no more curse. Or, " no more anything accursed."

the throne of God and of the Lamb. Christ occupies the same throne, and receives the same homage and service as the Father.

4 they shall see His face. Cp. Matt. v. 8; 1 John iii. 2. The " name on the forehead " marks them as God's servants: see vii. 3.

5 there shall be no night there. See note on xxi 24.

CONCLUSION

6 the Lord God of the holy prophets. Rather (see var. read.), " The Lord, the God of the spirits of the prophets."

7 blessed is he that keepeth, etc. See i. 3. The repeated benediction indicates the high importance of this Book, " the book with the blessing " (Dr. Limmer Sheppard in *Devotional Commentary*).

8 I fell down to worship. Cp. xix. 10.

10 Seal not, etc. Comp. x. 4, and note.

11 He that is unjust, etc. This verse is generally thought to convey the solemn truth, that after the judgement there can be no change of character and condition. But it seems rather to be an expansion of Dan. xii. 10; and to convey both a warning to the ungodly that if he continues in sin, his doom will soon be fixed; and an encouragement to the godly to persevere in the hope of speedy salvation; for " Behold, I come quickly," etc.

14 Blessed are they that do His commandments, etc. The best manuscripts and versions have, " Blessed are they who wash their robes ": cp. vii. 14.

right to the tree of life. The Vulgate, followed by Luther, gives a different turn to the meaning. The Latin of the former is " ut sit potestas eorum in ligno vitæ," and the German is " dass ihre Macht sei an dem Holz des Lebens "—both meaning " that their power may be in the tree of life." It is doubtful, however, whether the Greek bears this interpretation.

15 dogs. See Job xxx. 1; Psa. xxii. 16; Phil. iii. 2, and notes.

16 the root and the offspring of David. See ch. v. 5, and Isa. xi. 1.

the bright and morning star. See note on Isa. xiv. 12. " The Herald of the coming dawn—from Him proceeds the light of the eternal day" (*Speaker's Commentary*).

17 the Spirit and the bride say, Come. The address appears to be to Christ. " Come, Lord Jesus ! " The voice of the Spirit is heard in prophecy, that of the Bride in longing prayer. Or, in another view, the Spirit dwelling in the Church inspires her earnest entreaty.

let him that heareth. The hearer is not only to join in the petition of the Church, but is to offer it for himself.

let him that is athirst come. He who is invoked by the Church to " come " invites men to come to Him. Thus His final word repeats the most gracious invitations of the past (see Isa. lv. 1, and note).

18 If any man shall add, etc. See Deut. iv. 2, etc. The warning in its immediate application refers to " the words of the prophecy of this book," rather than to the New Testament or the Bible as a whole.

20 Amen. See note on i. 7. This is probably John's fervent response, " Come, Lord Jesus ! "

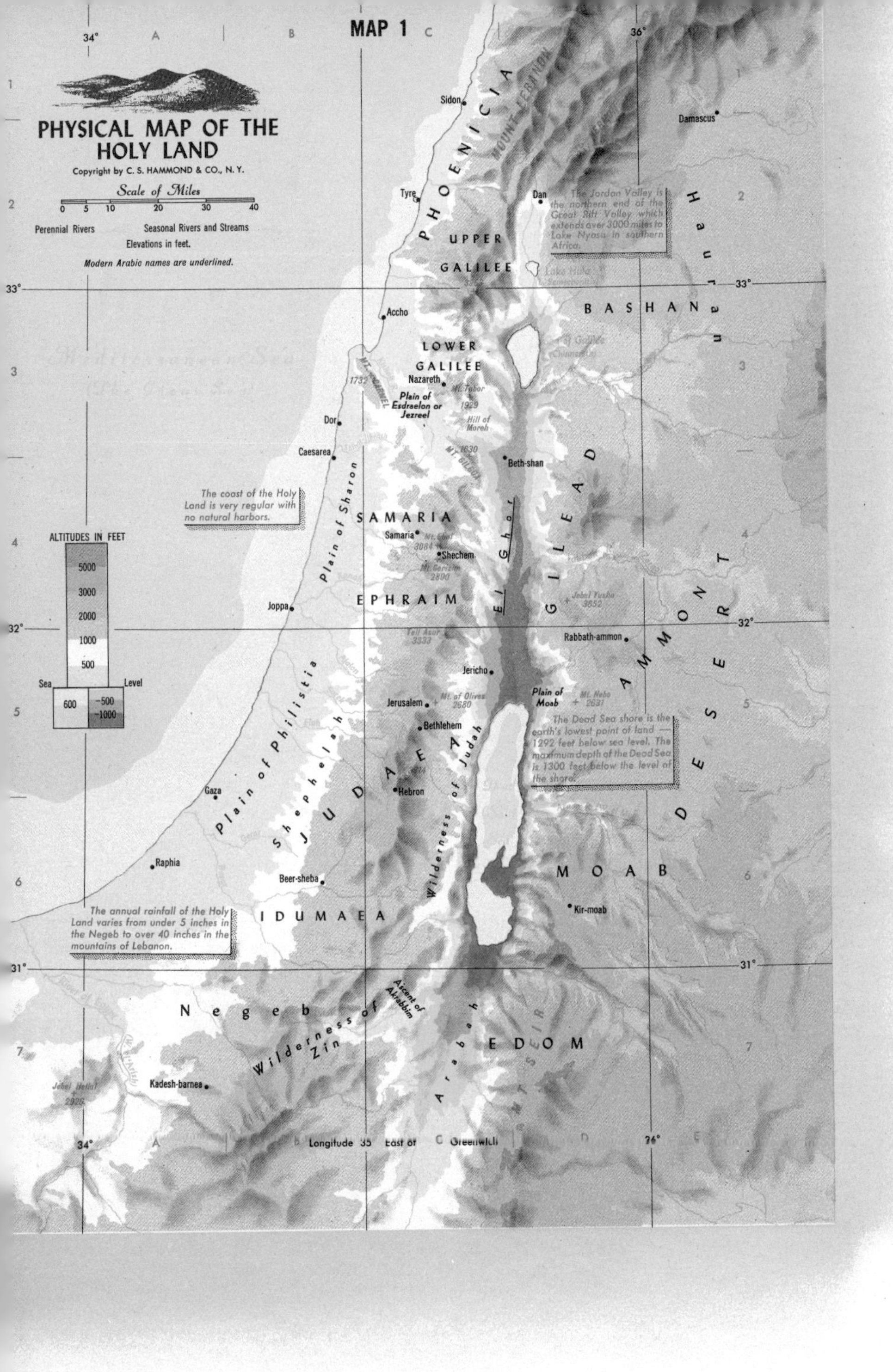

MAP 1
PHYSICAL MAP OF THE HOLY LAND
Copyright by C. S. HAMMOND & CO., N. Y.
Scale of Miles
0 5 10 20 30 40
Perennial Rivers
Seasonal Rivers and Streams
Elevations in feet.
Modern Arabic names are underlined.
ALTITUDES IN FEET
5000
3000
2000
1000
500
Sea
Level
600
-500
-1000
The coast of the Holy Land is very regular with no natural harbors.
The annual rainfall of the Holy Land varies from under 5 inches in the Negeb to over 40 inches in the mountains of Lebanon.
The Jordan Valley is the northern end of the Great Rift Valley which extends over 3000 miles to Lake Nyasa in southern Africa.
The Dead Sea shore is the earth's lowest point of land — 1292 feet below sea level. The maximum depth of the Dead Sea is 1300 feet below the level of the shore.
PHOENICIA
MOUNT LEBANON
Sidon
Damascus
Tyre
Dan
Hauran
UPPER
GALILEE
Lake Hula
BASHAN
Accho
LOWER
GALILEE
MT. CARMEL
1732
Nazareth
Mt. Tabor
1929
Plain of Esdraelon or Jezreel
Hill of Moreh
Dor
Caesarea
MT. GILBOA
1630
Beth-shan
Plain of Sharon
SAMARIA
Samaria
Mt. Ebal
3084
Shechem
Mt. Gerizim
2890
El Ghor
GILEAD
EPHRAIM
Joppa
Jebel Yusha
3652
Tell Asur
3333
Rabbath-ammon
AMMON
Jericho
Plain of Moab
Mt. Nebo
2631
Jerusalem
Mt. of Olives
2680
Bethlehem
Plain of Philistia
Shephelah
JUDAEA
Wilderness of Judah
Hebron
Gaza
DESERT
Raphia
Beer-sheba
MOAB
IDUMAEA
Kir-moab
Negeb
Ascent of Akrabbim
Wilderness of Zin
Arabah
EDOM
MT. SEIR
Kadesh-barnea
Jebel Hellal
2920
Longitude 35 East of Greenwich
34°
36°
33°
32°
31°
A
B
C
D
E
1
2
3
4
5
6
7

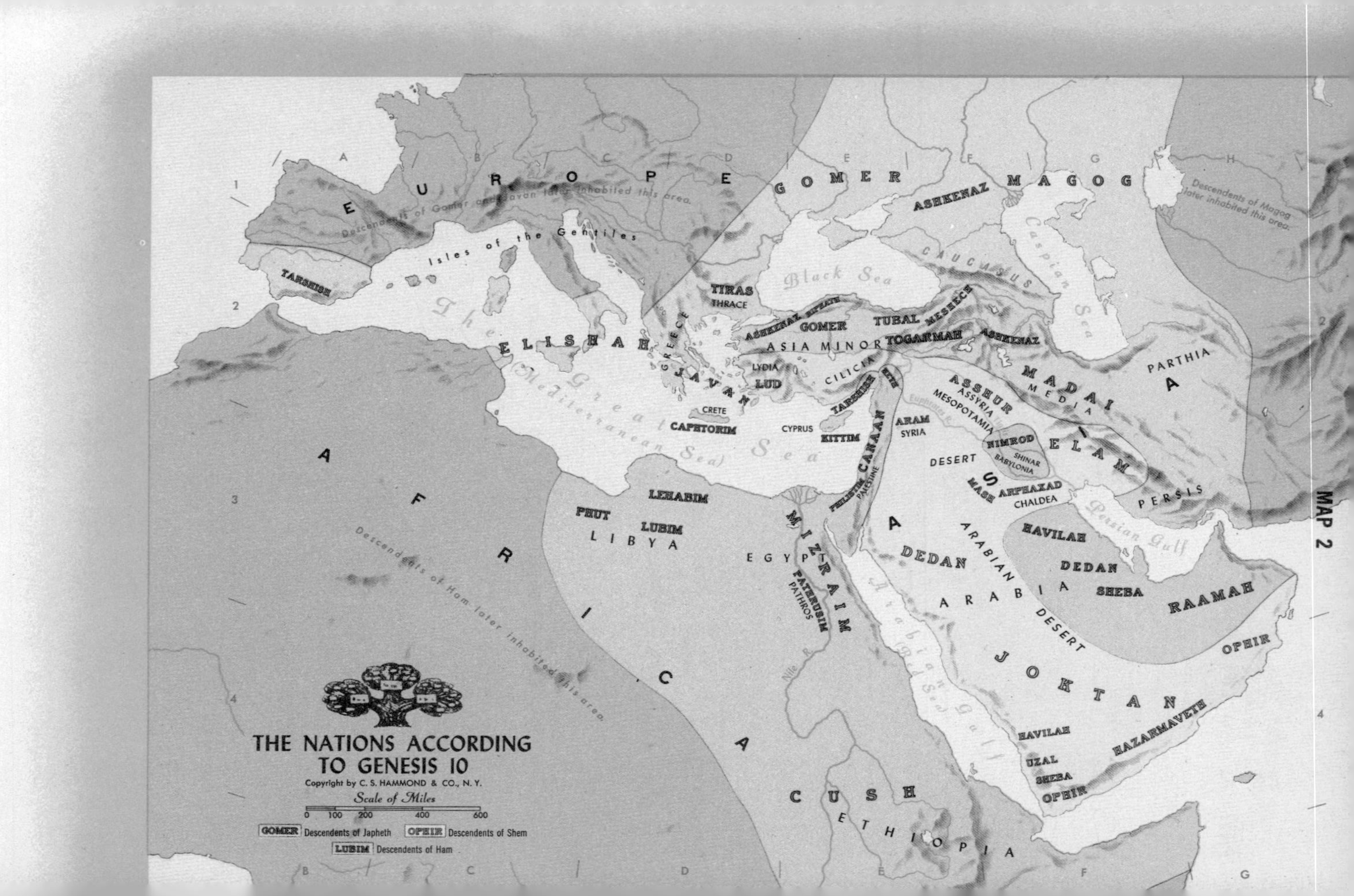
THE NATIONS ACCORDING TO GENESIS 10
Copyright by C. S. HAMMOND & CO., N. Y.
Scale of Miles
0 100 200 400 600
GOMER Descendents of Japheth
OPHIR Descendents of Shem
LUBIM Descendents of Ham
EUROPE
Descendents of Gomer and Javan later inhabited this area.
Isles of the Gentiles
TARSHISH
GOMER
MAGOG
ASHKENAZ
Descendents of Magog later inhabited this area.
Black Sea
Caspian Sea
CAUCASUS
TIRAS
THRACE
ELISHAH
GREECE
JAVAN
The Great (Mediterranean) Sea
ASHKENAZ
RIPHATH
GOMER
TUBAL
MESHECH
TOGARMAH
ASHKENAZ
ASIA MINOR
LYDIA
LUD
CILICIA
HETH
TARSHISH
CRETE
CAPHTORIM
CYPRUS
KITTIM
PARTHIA
MADAI
MEDIA
ASSHUR
ASSYRIA
MESOPOTAMIA
ARAM
SYRIA
NIMROD
SHINAR
BABYLONIA
ELAM
DESERT
MASH
ARPHAXAD
CHALDEA
PERSIS
Persian Gulf
CANAAN
PHILISTIM
PALESTINE
AFRICA
Descendents of Ham later inhabited this area.
LEHABIM
PHUT
LUBIM
LIBYA
EGYPT
MIZRAIM
PATHRUSIM
PATHROS
Nile R.
ASIA
DEDAN
ARABIAN DESERT
ARABIA
HAVILAH
DEDAN
SHEBA
RAAMAH
OPHIR
JOKTAN
HAZARMAVETH
HAVILAH
UZAL
SHEBA
OPHIR
Arabian Gulf (Red Sea)
CUSH
ETHIOPIA

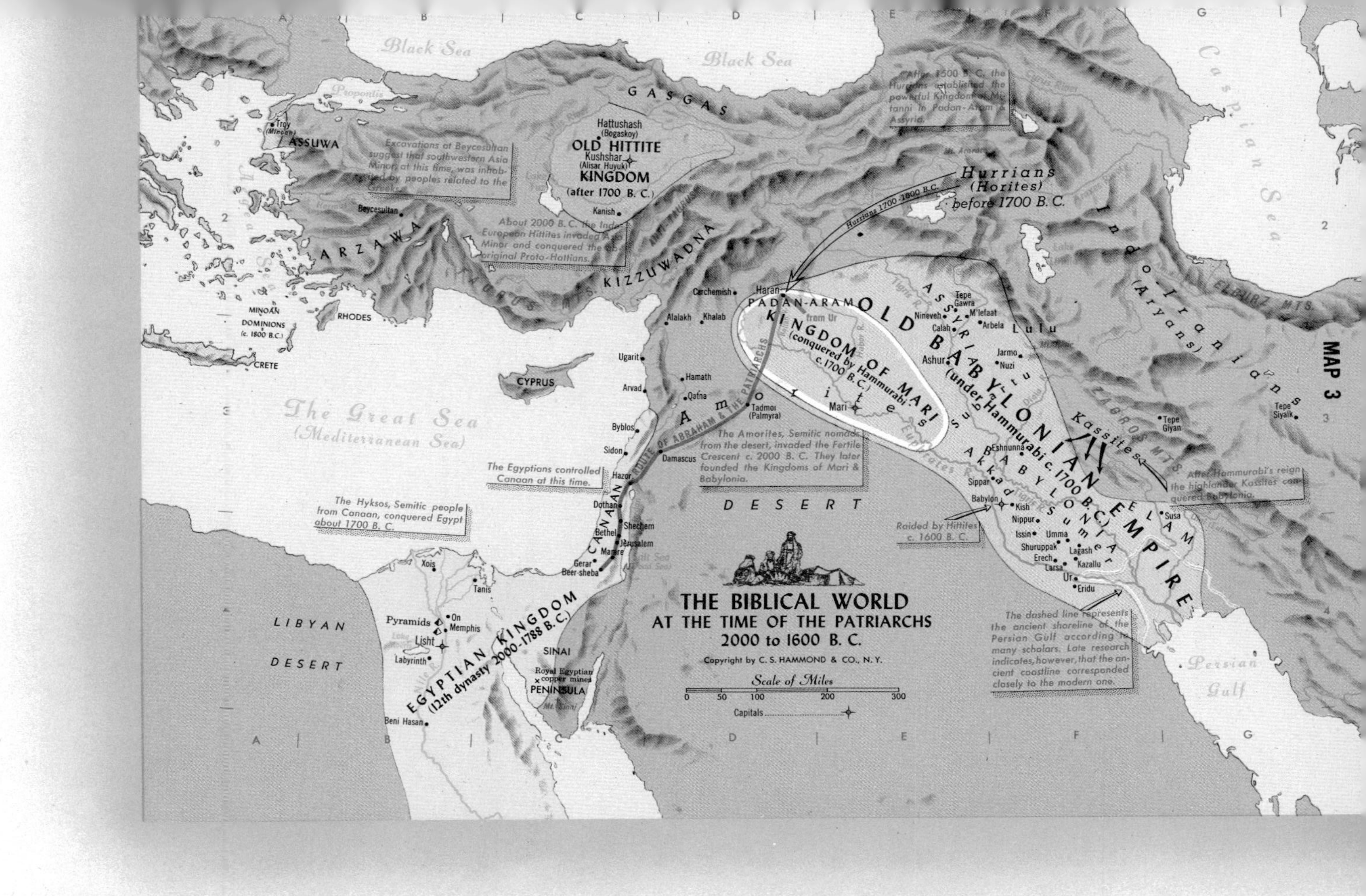
MAP 3
THE BIBLICAL WORLD
AT THE TIME OF THE PATRIARCHS
2000 to 1600 B. C.
Copyright by C. S. HAMMOND & CO., N. Y.
Scale of Miles
0 50 100 200 300
Capitals
Black Sea
Caspian Sea
Persian Gulf
The Great Sea
(Mediterranean Sea)
GASGAS
Hattushash
(Bogaskoy)
OLD HITTITE KINGDOM
Kushshar
(Alisar Huyuk)
(after 1700 B. C.)
Kanish
ASSUWA
Troy
Beycesultan
ARZAWA
KIZZUWADNA
Excavations at Beycesultan suggest that southwestern Asia Minor, at this time, was inhabited by peoples related to the Greeks.
About 2000 B. C. the Indo-European Hittites invaded Asia Minor and conquered the aboriginal Proto-Hattians.
MINOAN DOMINIONS (c. 1800 B.C.)
RHODES
CRETE
CYPRUS
After 1500 B. C. the Hurrians established the powerful Kingdom of Mitanni in Padan-Aram & Assyria.
Hurrians
(Horites)
before 1700 B. C.
Indo-Iranians
(Aryans)
ELBURZ MTS.
ZAGROS MTS.
Tepe Siyalk
Tepe Giyan
Kassites
After Hammurabi's reign the highlander Kassites conquered Babylonia.
Haran
Carchemish
PADAN-ARAM
from Ur
KINGDOM OF MARI
(conquered by Hammurabi c. 1700 B. C.)
Mari
OLD BABYLONIAN EMPIRE
(under Hammurabi c. 1700 B. C.)
ASSYRIA
Tepe Gawra
Nineveh
M'lefaat
Calah
Arbela
Lulu
Jarmo
Nuzi
Ashur
Subartu
Eshnunna
Akkad
BABYLONIA
Sumer
ELAM
Susa
Sippar
Babylon
Kish
Nippur
Issin
Umma
Shuruppak
Lagash
Erech
Kazallu
Larsa
Ur
Eridu
Raided by Hittites c. 1600 B. C.
The dashed line represents the ancient shoreline of the Persian Gulf according to many scholars. Late research indicates, however, that the ancient coastline corresponded closely to the modern one.
Alalakh
Khalab
Ugarit
Arvad
Hamath
Qatna
Tadmor
(Palmyra)
Amorites
The Amorites, Semitic nomads from the desert, invaded the Fertile Crescent c. 2000 B. C. They later founded the Kingdoms of Mari & Babylonia.
ROUTE OF ABRAHAM & THE PATRIARCHS
Byblos
Sidon
Damascus
Hazor
DESERT
The Egyptians controlled Canaan at this time.
CANAAN
Dothan
Shechem
Bethel
Jerusalem
Mamre
Gerar
Beer-sheba
The Hyksos, Semitic people from Canaan, conquered Egypt about 1700 B. C.
Xois
Tanis
Pyramids
On
Memphis
Lisht
Labyrinth
Beni Hasan
EGYPTIAN KINGDOM
(12th dynasty 2000-1788 B. C.)
SINAI
Royal Egyptian copper mines
PENINSULA
LIBYAN
DESERT

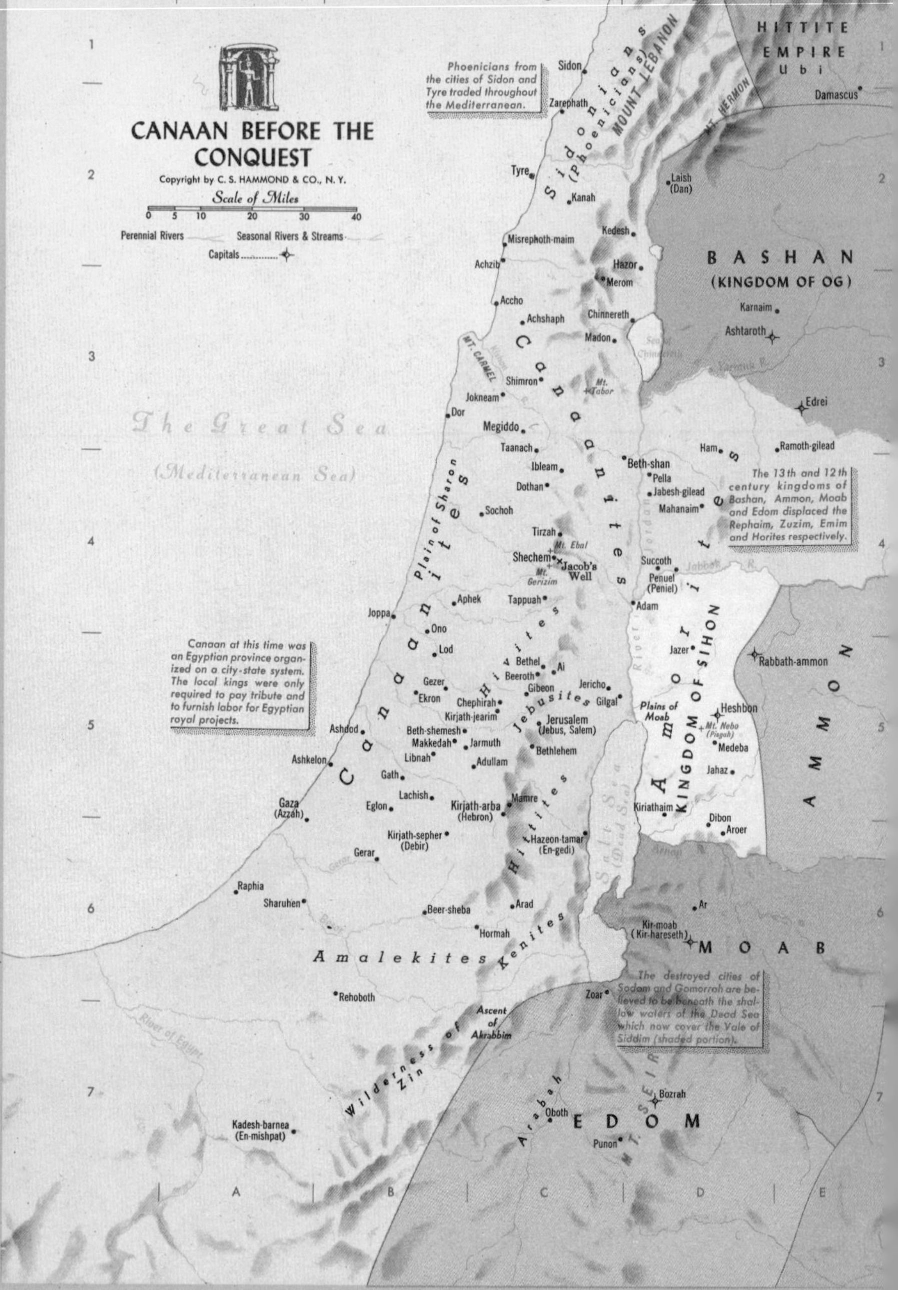

CANAAN BEFORE THE CONQUEST

Scale of Miles
0 5 10 20 30 40

Perennial Rivers
Seasonal Rivers & Streams
Capitals

Phoenicians from the cities of Sidon and Tyre traded throughout the Mediterranean.

Canaan at this time was an Egyptian province organized on a city-state system. The local kings were only required to pay tribute and to furnish labor for Egyptian royal projects.

The 13th and 12th century kingdoms of Bashan, Ammon, Moab and Edom displaced the Rephaim, Zuzim, Emim and Horites respectively.

The destroyed cities of Sodom and Gomorrah are believed to be beneath the shallow waters of the Dead Sea which now cover the Vale of Siddim (shaded portion).

HITTITE EMPIRE
Ubi
Damascus
Sidonians (Phoenicians)
MOUNT LEBANON
MT. HERMON
Sidon
Zarephath
Tyre
Kanah
Laish (Dan)
Misrephoth-maim
Kedesh
Achzib
Hazor
Merom
BASHAN (KINGDOM OF OG)
Karnaim
Ashtaroth
Accho
Achshaph
Chinnereth
Madon
Sea of Chinnereth
Yarmuk R.
MT. CARMEL
Canaanites
Shimron
Mt. Tabor
Jokneam
Edrei
Dor
The Great Sea (Mediterranean Sea)
Megiddo
Taanach
Ham
Ramoth-gilead
Ibleam
Beth-shan
Pella
Dothan
Jabesh-gilead
Mahanaim
Plain of Sharon
Sochoh
Tirzah
Mt. Ebal
Shechem
Jacob's Well
Mt. Gerizim
Succoth
Penuel (Peniel)
Jabbok R.
Jordan River
Aphek
Tappuah
Adam
Joppa
Ono
Lod
Hivites
Amorites
Jazer
Rabbath-ammon
Bethel
Ai
Beeroth
Gezer
Gibeon
Jericho
Gilgal
Ekron
Chephirah
Jebusites
Plains of Moab
Heshbon
Kirjath-jearim
Jerusalem (Jebus, Salem)
KINGDOM OF SIHON
Mt. Nebo (Pisgah)
Ashdod
Beth-shemesh
Makkedah
Jarmuth
Medeba
Libnah
Bethlehem
Ashkelon
Adullam
Jahaz
AMMON
Gath
Lachish
Mamre
Salt Sea (Dead Sea)
Kiriathaim
Gaza (Azzah)
Eglon
Kirjath-arba (Hebron)
Dibon
Aroer
Kirjath-sepher (Debir)
Hazeon-tamar (En-gedi)
Arnon R.
Gerar
Hittites
Raphia
Sharuhen
Beer-sheba
Arad
Ar
Hormah
Kir-moab (Kir-hareseth)
MOAB
Amalekites
Kenites
Rehoboth
Zoar
Ascent of Akrabbim
River of Egypt
Wilderness of Zin
MT. SEIR
Arabah
Bozrah
Kadesh-barnea (En-mishpat)
Oboth
EDOM
Punon

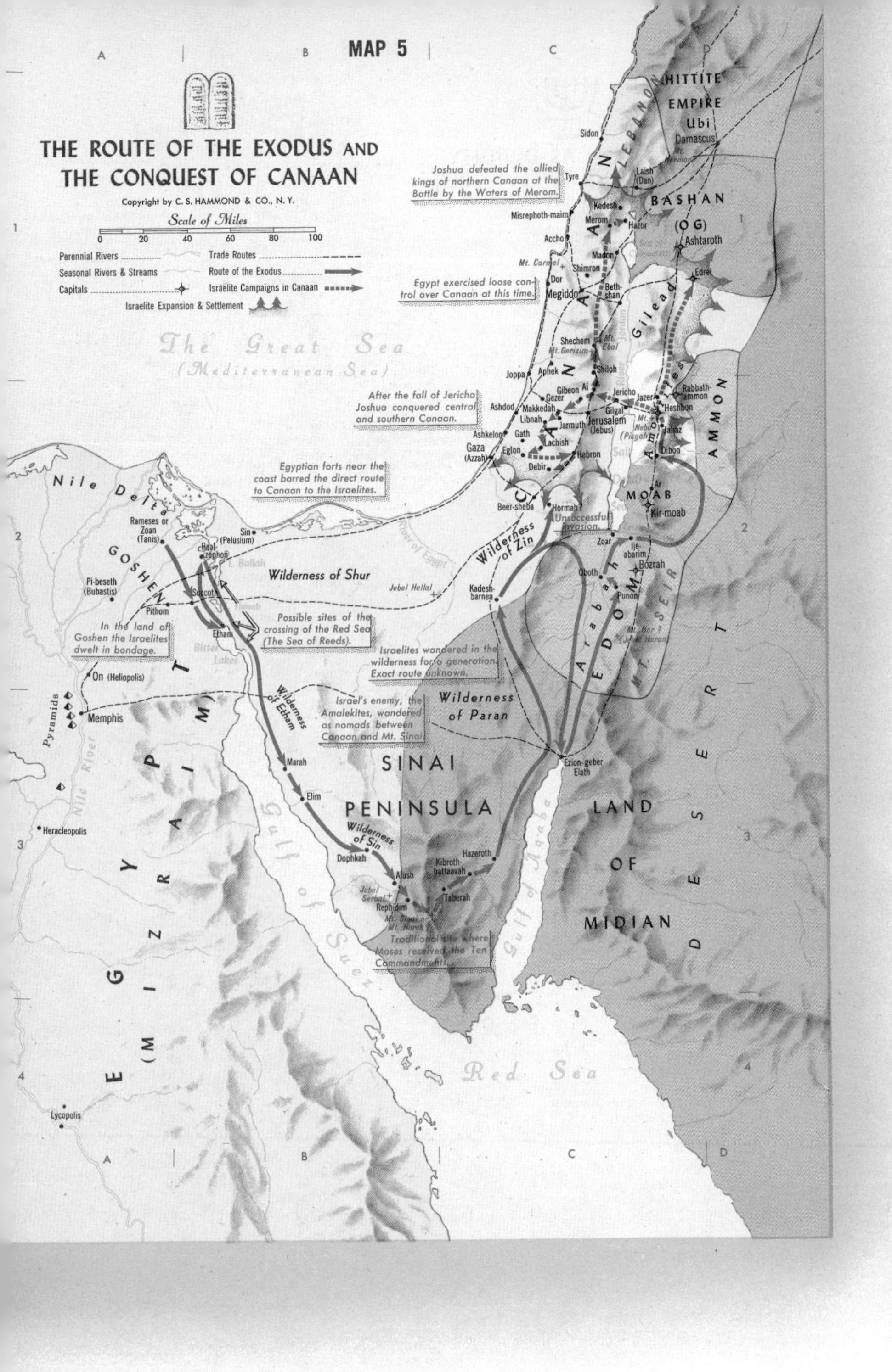
MAP 5
THE ROUTE OF THE EXODUS AND THE CONQUEST OF CANAAN
Copyright by C. S. HAMMOND & CO., N. Y.
Scale of Miles
0 20 40 60 80 100
Perennial Rivers
Seasonal Rivers & Streams
Capitals
Trade Routes
Route of the Exodus
Israelite Campaigns in Canaan
Israelite Expansion & Settlement
The Great Sea
(Mediterranean Sea)
HITTITE EMPIRE
Ubi
Damascus
LEBANON
Sidon
Tyre
Laish (Dan)
Joshua defeated the allied kings of northern Canaan at the Battle by the Waters of Merom.
BASHAN
(OG)
Ashtaroth
Edrei
Kedesh
Merom
Hazor
Misrephoth-maim
Accho
Madon
Mt. Carmel
Shimron
Dor
Megiddo
Beth-shan
Egypt exercised loose control over Canaan at this time.
Gilead
Shechem
Mt. Ebal
Mt. Gerizim
Joppa
Aphek
Shiloh
Gibeon
Ai
Gezer
Jericho
Jazer
Rabbath-ammon
Heshbon
Gilgal
Mt. Nebo (Pisgah)
Jahaz
After the fall of Jericho Joshua conquered central and southern Canaan.
Ashdod
Makkedah
Libnah
Jerusalem (Jebus)
Jarmuth
Ashkelon
Gath
Lachish
Gaza (Azzah)
Eglon
Hebron
Debir
Dibon
AMMON
AMORITES
CANAAN
Ar
MOAB
Kir-moab
Beer-sheba
Hormah
Unsuccessful invasion.
Egyptian forts near the coast barred the direct route to Canaan to the Israelites.
Nile Delta
Rameses or Zoan (Tanis)
Sin (Pelusium)
Baal-zephon
L. Ballah
GOSHEN
Wilderness of Shur
Pi-beseth (Bubastis)
Succoth
Pithom
Etham
Bitter Lakes
In the land of Goshen the Israelites dwelt in bondage.
Possible sites of the crossing of the Red Sea (The Sea of Reeds).
Jebel Hellal
River of Egypt
Wilderness of Zin
Kadesh-barnea
Zoar
Ije-abarim
Oboth
Bozrah
Punon
Arabah
EDOM
SEIR
Mt. Hor ? (Jebel Harun)
Israelites wandered in the wilderness for a generation. Exact route unknown.
On (Heliopolis)
Pyramids
Memphis
Wilderness of Etham
Israel's enemy, the Amalekites, wandered as nomads between Canaan and Mt. Sinai.
Wilderness of Paran
Ezion-geber Elath
SINAI PENINSULA
Marah
Elim
Wilderness of Sin
Dophkah
Alush
Jebel Serbal
Rephidim
Kibroth-hattaavah
Hazeroth
Taberah
Mt. Sinai or Mt. Horeb
Traditional site where Moses received the Ten Commandments.
Gulf of Suez
Gulf of Aqaba
LAND OF MIDIAN
DESERT
Nile River
Heracleopolis
EGYPT (MIZRAIM)
Red Sea
Lycopolis

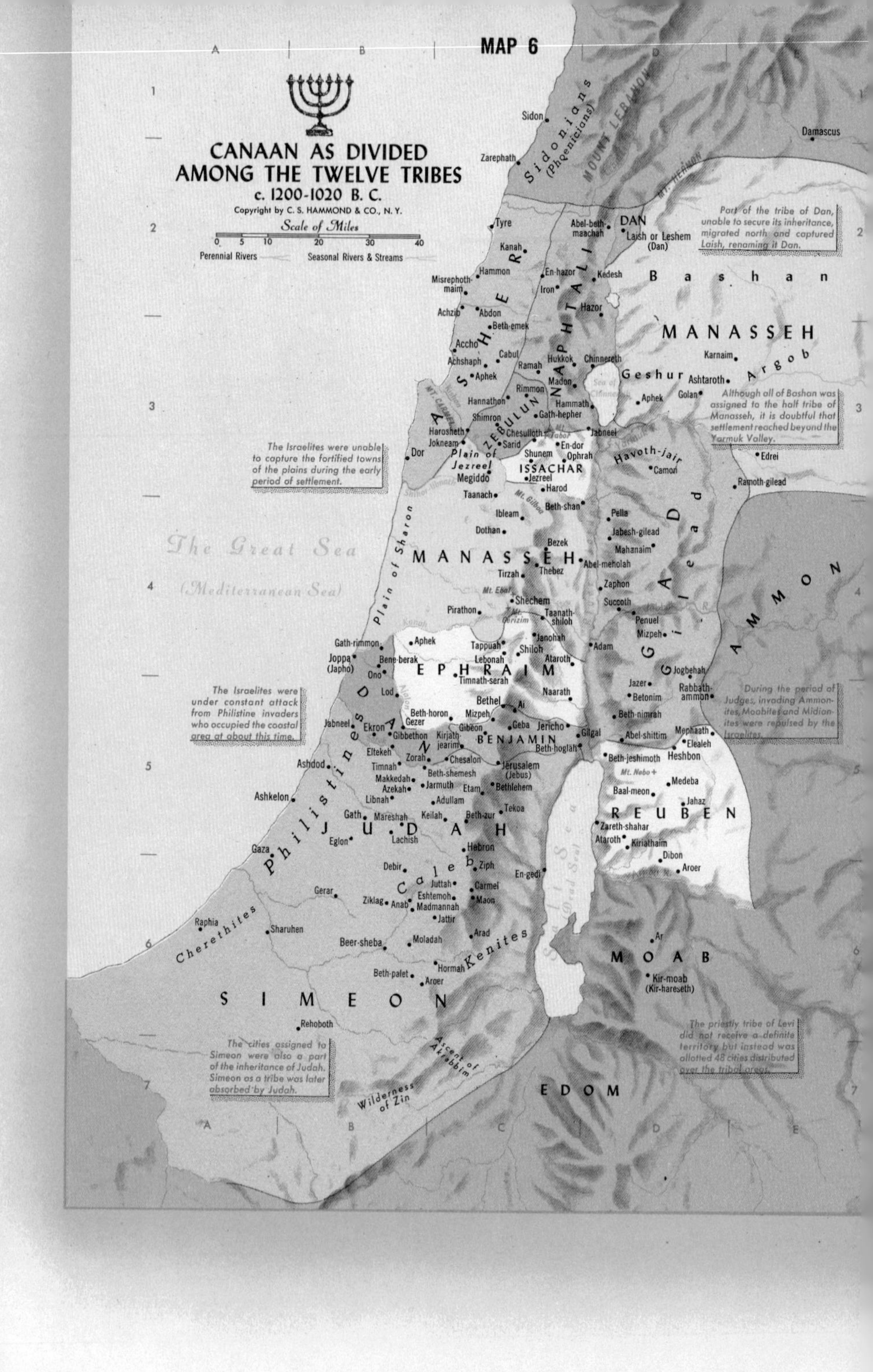

MAP 6
CANAAN AS DIVIDED
AMONG THE TWELVE TRIBES
c. 1200-1020 B. C.
Copyright by C. S. HAMMOND & CO., N. Y.
Scale of Miles
0 5 10 20 30 40
Perennial Rivers
Seasonal Rivers & Streams
The Great Sea
(Mediterranean Sea)
Sidonians (Phoenicians)
Mount Lebanon
Mt. Hermon
Sidon
Zarephath
Damascus
Tyre
Kanah
Hammon
Misrephoth-maim
Achzib
Abdon
Beth-emek
Accho
Achshaph
Cabul
Aphek
ASHER
Abel-beth-maachah
DAN
Laish or Leshem (Dan)
Part of the tribe of Dan, unable to secure its inheritance, migrated north and captured Laish, renaming it Dan.
En-hazor
Iron
Kedesh
Hazor
NAPHTALI
Bashan
MANASSEH
Karnaim
Argob
Ashtaroth
Geshur
Golan
Hukkok
Chinnereth
Ramah
Madon
Rimmon
Hammath
Sea of Chinnereth
Aphek
Although all of Bashan was assigned to the half tribe of Manasseh, it is doubtful that settlement reached beyond the Yarmuk Valley.
Mt. Carmel
Hannathon
ZEBULUN
Gath-hepher
Shimron
Chesulloth
Mt. Tabor
Jabneel
Harosheth
Jokneam
Sarid
En-dor
Shunem
Ophrah
Havoth-jair
Edrei
Camon
Dor
Plain of Jezreel
Megiddo
ISSACHAR
Jezreel
Harod
Ramoth-gilead
The Israelites were unable to capture the fortified towns of the plains during the early period of settlement.
Taanach
Mt. Gilboa
Beth-shan
Ibleam
Pella
Dothan
Jabesh-gilead
Plain of Sharon
Bezek
Mahanaim
MANASSEH
Abel-meholah
Tirzah
Thebez
GAD
Gilead
AMMON
Mt. Ebal
Zaphon
Shechem
Succoth
Pirathon
Mt. Gerizim
Taanath-shiloh
Penuel
Kanah
Janohah
Mizpeh
Gath-rimmon
Aphek
Tappuah
Shiloh
Adam
Joppa (Japho)
Bene-berak
Lebonah
Ataroth
Ono
EPHRAIM
Jogbehah
Timnath-serah
Jazer
Rabbath-ammon
Lod
Naarath
Betonim
The Israelites were under constant attack from Philistine invaders who occupied the coastal area at about this time.
Bethel
Ai
Beth-horon
Mizpeh
During the period of Judges, invading Ammonites, Moabites and Midianites were repulsed by the Israelites.
Gezer
Beth-nimrah
Jabneel
Ekron
Gibeon
Geba
Jericho
Gibbethon
Kirjath-jearim
BENJAMIN
Gilgal
Abel-shittim
Mephaath
Elealeh
Eltekeh
Beth-hoglah
DAN
Zorah
Chesalon
Beth-jeshimoth
Heshbon
Ashdod
Timnah
Jerusalem (Jebus)
Beth-shemesh
Mt. Nebo
Makkedah
Jarmuth
Azekah
Etam
Bethlehem
Medeba
Libnah
Adullam
Baal-meon
Ashkelon
Tekoa
Jahaz
Gath
Mareshah
Keilah
Beth-zur
REUBEN
Philistines
JUDAH
Zareth-shahar
Eglon
Lachish
Ataroth
Kiriathaim
Gaza
Hebron
Salt Sea (Dead Sea)
Dibon
Debir
Ziph
Aroer
Caleb
En-gedi
Juttah
Carmel
Gerar
Eshtemoh
Maon
Ziklag
Anab
Madmannah
Jattir
Raphia
Cherethites
Sharuhen
Arad
Ar
Beer-sheba
Moladah
Kenites
MOAB
Hormah
Beth-palet
Aroer
Kir-moab (Kir-hareseth)
SIMEON
Rehoboth
The priestly tribe of Levi did not receive a definite territory but instead was allotted 48 cities distributed over the tribal areas.
The cities assigned to Simeon were also a part of the inheritance of Judah. Simeon as a tribe was later absorbed by Judah.
Ascent of Akrabbim
Wilderness of Zin
EDOM

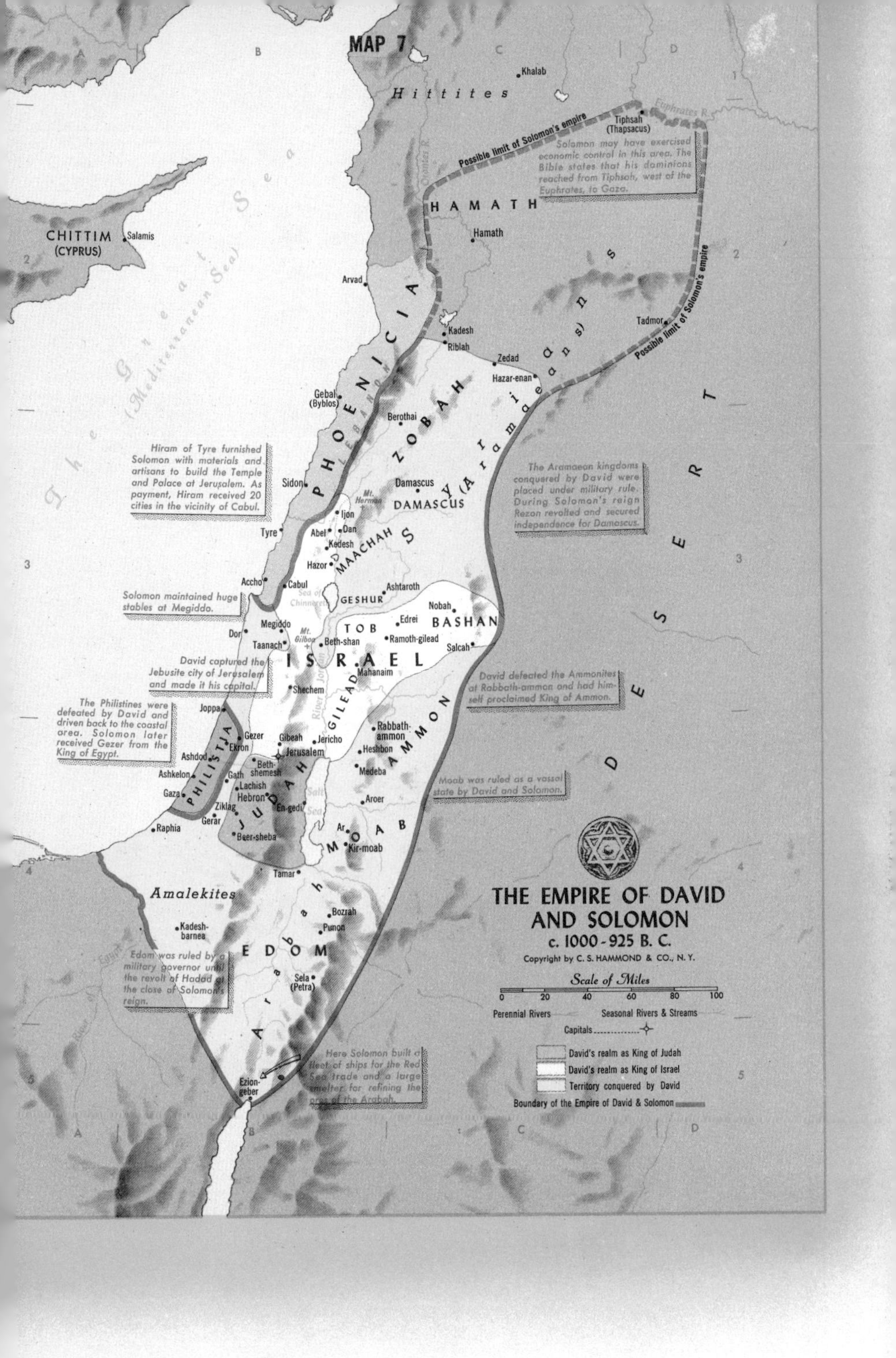
MAP 7
THE EMPIRE OF DAVID AND SOLOMON
c. 1000 - 925 B. C.
Copyright by C. S. HAMMOND & CO., N. Y.
Scale of Miles
0 20 40 60 80 100
Perennial Rivers
Seasonal Rivers & Streams
Capitals
David's realm as King of Judah
David's realm as King of Israel
Territory conquered by David
Boundary of the Empire of David & Solomon
Solomon may have exercised economic control in this area. The Bible states that his dominions reached from Tiphsah, west of the Euphrates, to Gaza.
Hiram of Tyre furnished Solomon with materials and artisans to build the Temple and Palace at Jerusalem. As payment, Hiram received 20 cities in the vicinity of Cabul.
The Aramaean kingdoms conquered by David were placed under military rule. During Solomon's reign Rezon revolted and secured independence for Damascus.
Solomon maintained huge stables at Megiddo.
David captured the Jebusite city of Jerusalem and made it his capital.
David defeated the Ammonites at Rabbath-ammon and had himself proclaimed King of Ammon.
The Philistines were defeated by David and driven back to the coastal area. Solomon later received Gezer from the King of Egypt.
Moab was ruled as a vassal state by David and Solomon.
Edom was ruled by a military governor until the revolt of Hadad at the close of Solomon's reign.
Here Solomon built a fleet of ships for the Red Sea trade and a large smelter for refining the ores of the Arabah.
Possible limit of Solomon's empire
Hittites
Khalab
Tiphsah (Thapsacus)
Euphrates R.
HAMATH
Hamath
CHITTIM (CYPRUS)
Salamis
The Great Sea (Mediterranean Sea)
Arvad
PHOENICIA
Kadesh
Riblah
Zedad
Hazar-enan
Tadmor
Syria (Aramaeans)
DESERT
ZOBAH
Gebal (Byblos)
Berothai
Sidon
Damascus
DAMASCUS
Mt. Hermon
Ijon
Dan
Abel
Kedesh
MAACHAH
Hazor
Tyre
Accho
Cabul
Sea of Chinnereth
GESHUR
Ashtaroth
Nobah
BASHAN
Edrei
TOB
Ramoth-gilead
Salcah
Dor
Megiddo
Taanach
Mt. Gilboa
Beth-shan
ISRAEL
Mahanaim
Shechem
GILEAD
River Jordan
AMMON
Joppa
Gezer
Ekron
Gibeah
Jericho
Jerusalem
Rabbath-ammon
Heshbon
Ashdod
PHILISTIA
Beth-shemesh
Medeba
Ashkelon
Gath
Lachish
Gaza
Hebron
JUDAH
En-gedi
Salt Sea
Aroer
Ziklag
Gerar
Raphia
Beer-sheba
Ar
MOAB
Kir-moab
Tamar
Amalekites
Arabah
Bozrah
Punon
Kadesh-barnea
EDOM
Sela (Petra)
River of Egypt
Ezion-geber

MAP 8

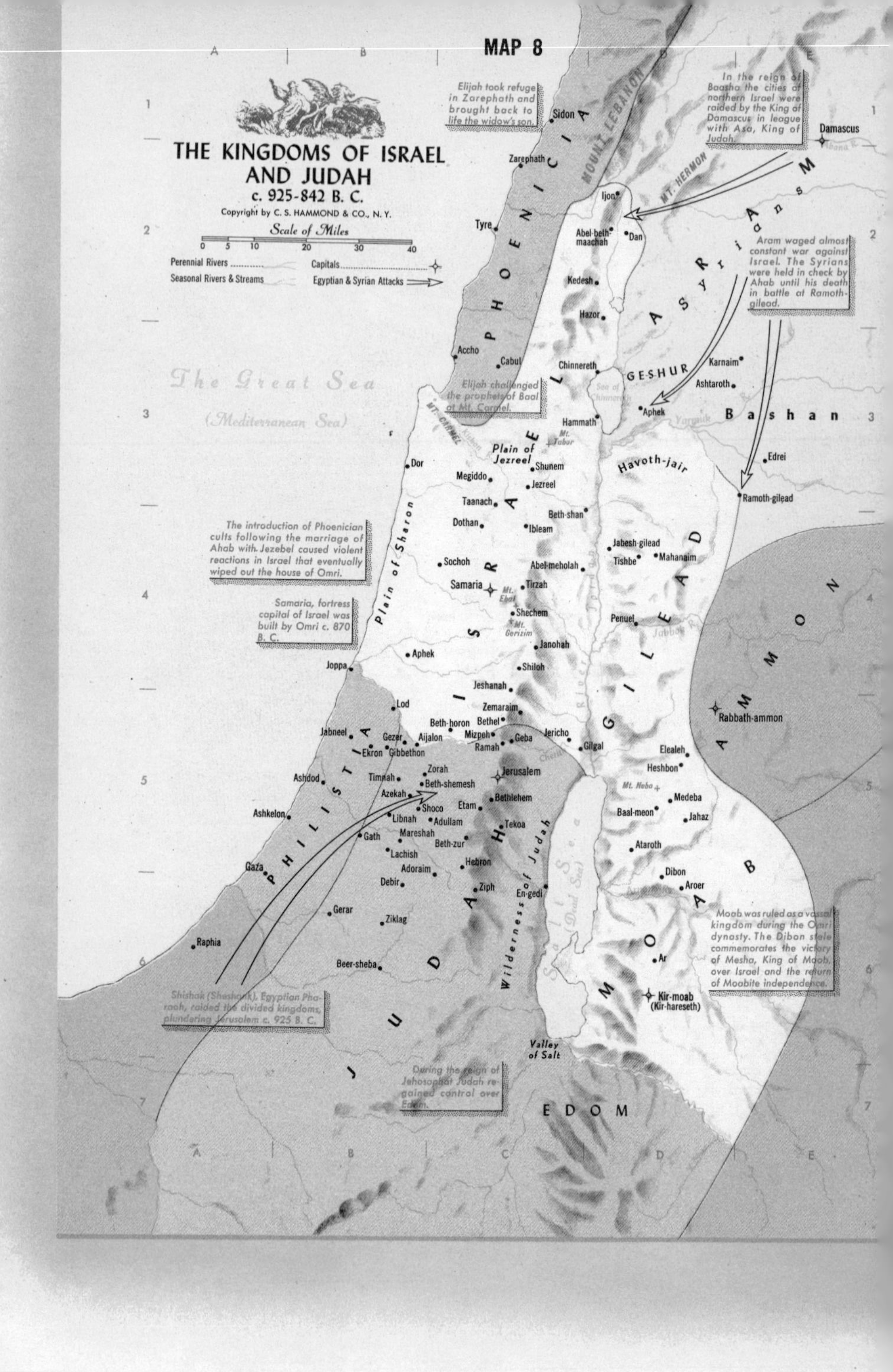
THE KINGDOMS OF ISRAEL AND JUDAH
c. 925-842 B. C.
Copyright by C. S. HAMMOND & CO., N. Y.
Scale of Miles
0 5 10 20 30 40
Perennial Rivers
Seasonal Rivers & Streams
Capitals
Egyptian & Syrian Attacks
Elijah took refuge in Zarephath and brought back to life the widow's son.
In the reign of Baasha the cities of northern Israel were raided by the King of Damascus in league with Asa, King of Judah.
Aram waged almost constant war against Israel. The Syrians were held in check by Ahab until his death in battle at Ramoth-gilead.
Elijah challenged the prophets of Baal at Mt. Carmel.
The introduction of Phoenician cults following the marriage of Ahab with Jezebel caused violent reactions in Israel that eventually wiped out the house of Omri.
Samaria, fortress capital of Israel was built by Omri c. 870 B. C.
Moab was ruled as a vassal kingdom during the Omri dynasty. The Dibon stele commemorates the victory of Mesha, King of Moab, over Israel and the return of Moabite independence.
Shishak (Sheshonk), Egyptian Pharaoh, raided the divided kingdoms, plundering Jerusalem c. 925 B. C.
During the reign of Jehoshaphat Judah regained control over Edom.
The Great Sea
(Mediterranean Sea)
PHOENICIA
MOUNT LEBANON
MT. HERMON
ARAM
Syrians
ISRAEL
GILEAD
GESHUR
Bashan
Havoth-jair
AMMON
MOAB
JUDAH
PHILISTIA
EDOM
Plain of Sharon
Plain of Jezreel
Wilderness of Judah
Valley of Salt
Sidon
Zarephath
Tyre
Damascus
Ijon
Abel-beth-maachah
Dan
Kedesh
Hazor
Accho
Cabul
Chinnereth
Karnaim
Ashtaroth
Aphek
Hammath
Mt. Tabor
Edrei
Dor
Shunem
Megiddo
Jezreel
Taanach
Ramoth-gilead
Beth-shan
Dothan
Ibleam
Jabesh-gilead
Tishbe
Mahanaim
Sochoh
Abel-meholah
Samaria
Mt. Ebal
Tirzah
Shechem
Mt. Gerizim
Penuel
Janohah
Aphek
Joppa
Shiloh
Jeshanah
Lod
Zemaraim
Rabbath-ammon
Beth-horon
Bethel
Jabneel
Gezer
Aijalon
Mizpeh
Geba
Jericho
Ramah
Ekron
Gibbethon
Gilgal
Elealeh
Heshbon
Zorah
Ashdod
Timnah
Jerusalem
Beth-shemesh
Mt. Nebo
Azekah
Medeba
Shoco
Etam
Bethlehem
Ashkelon
Libnah
Adullam
Baal-meon
Jahaz
Tekoa
Gath
Mareshah
Beth-zur
Ataroth
Lachish
Hebron
Gaza
Adoraim
Dibon
Debir
Aroer
Ziph
En-gedi
Gerar
Ziklag
Raphia
Ar
Beer-sheba
Kir-moab
(Kir-hareseth)
Salt Sea
(Dead Sea)

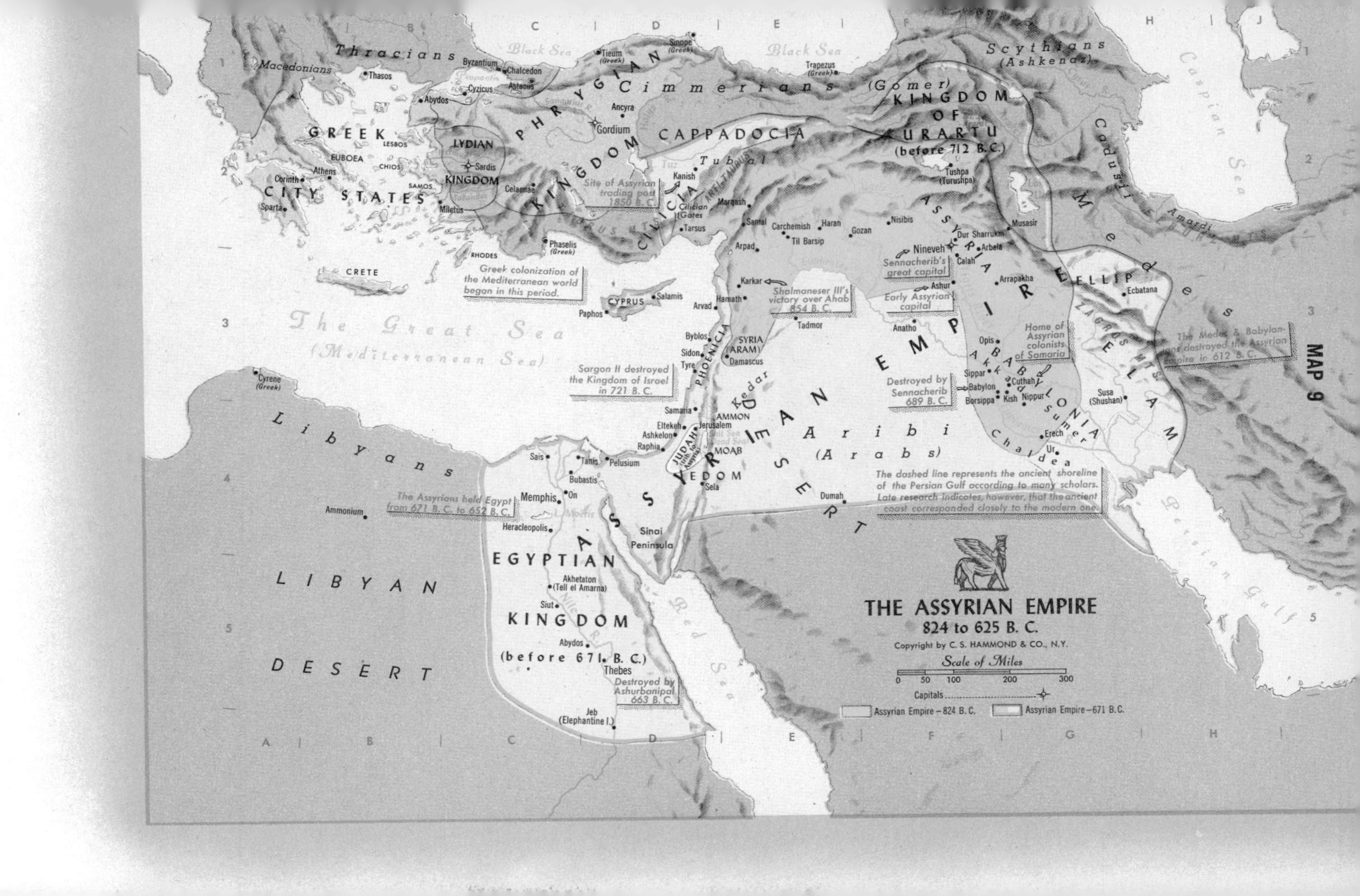
MAP 9
THE ASSYRIAN EMPIRE
824 to 625 B. C.
Copyright by C. S. HAMMOND & CO., N.Y.
Scale of Miles
0 50 100 200 300
Capitals
Assyrian Empire – 824 B. C.
Assyrian Empire – 671 B. C.
Greek colonization of the Mediterranean world began in this period.
Site of Assyrian trading post 1850 B. C.
Sargon II destroyed the Kingdom of Israel in 721 B. C.
Shalmaneser III's victory over Ahab 854 B. C.
Sennacherib's great capital
Early Assyrian capital
Destroyed by Sennacherib 689 B. C.
Home of Assyrian colonists of Samaria
The Medes & Babylonians destroyed the Assyrian Empire in 612 B. C.
The Assyrians held Egypt from 671 B. C. to 652 B. C.
Destroyed by Ashurbanipal 663 B. C.
The dashed line represents the ancient shoreline of the Persian Gulf according to many scholars. Late research indicates, however, that the ancient coast corresponded closely to the modern one.
Thracians
Macedonians
GREEK CITY STATES
LYDIAN KINGDOM
PHRYGIAN KINGDOM
Cimmerians
(Gomer)
KINGDOM OF URARTU (before 712 B.C.)
Scythians (Ashkenaz)
CAPPADOCIA
CILICIA
Tubal
ASSYRIA
ASSYRIAN EMPIRE
BABYLONIA
Akkad
Sumer
Chaldea
ELAM
ELLIP
Medes
Cadusii
Amardi
ZAGROS MTS.
SYRIA (ARAM)
PHOENICIA
JUDAH
AMMON
MOAB
EDOM
Kedar
Aribi
(Arabs)
DESERT
EGYPTIAN KINGDOM (before 671 B. C.)
Libyans
LIBYAN DESERT
Sinai Peninsula
The Great Sea (Mediterranean Sea)
Black Sea
Caspian Sea
Persian Gulf
Red Sea
CRETE
CYPRUS
RHODES
LESBOS
CHIOS
SAMOS
EUBOEA
Thasos
Athens
Corinth
Sparta
Byzantium
Chalcedon
Astacus
Cyzicus
Abydos
Tieum (Greek)
Sinope (Greek)
Trapezus (Greek)
Ancyra
Gordium
Sardis
Celaenae
Miletus
Phaselis (Greek)
Kanish
Cilician Gates
Tarsus
Marqash
Samal
Arpad
Carchemish
Til Barsip
Haran
Gozan
Nisibis
Dur Sharrukin
Musasir
Arbela
Nineveh
Calah
Ashur
Arrapakha
Tushpa (Turushpa)
Ecbatana
Anatho
Opis
Sippar
Cuthah
Babylon
Borsippa
Kish
Nippur
Erech
Ur
Susa (Shushan)
Karkar
Hamath
Arvad
Tadmor
Byblos
Sidon
Tyre
Damascus
Salamis
Paphos
Samaria
Elteke
Jerusalem
Ashkelon
Raphia
Sela
Dumah
Cyrene (Greek)
Ammonium
Sais
Tanis
Pelusium
Bubastis
On
Memphis
Heracleopolis
Akhetaton (Tell el Amarna)
Siut
Abydos
Thebes
Jeb (Elephantine I.)
Nile R.

JUDAH AFTER THE FALL OF ISRAEL

c. 700 B.C.

Scale of Miles

0 5 10 20 30

Perennial Rivers

Seasonal Rivers & Streams

Capitals

Sennacherib conquered Phoenicia, with the exception of Tyre, in 701 B.C.

With the conquest of Samaria in 721 B.C. by Sargon II, the Kingdom of Israel came to an end.

After Samaria fell, Sargon II exiled most of the influential people. The Ten Tribes were moved to various parts of Mesopotamia and disappeared forever from the pages of history.

In 701 B.C. Sennacherib captured 46 cities of Judah as he pushed down toward the Egyptians, defeating them at Eltekeh.

In 701 B.C. Jerusalem was besieged, though not taken, by Sennacherib.

Ammon, Moab and Edom fell to the Assyrian Esarhaddon in 690 B.C., but they were never held long enough to be organized as regular provinces of the empire.

Here Sargon II defeated the Egyptian army in 720 B.C.

Judah was never a province of Assyria. Throughout Assyrian domination, it preserved a nominal independence under its own king, though paying tribute regularly and homage when it was required.

The Great Sea (Mediterranean Sea)

PHOENICIA · GALILEE · SAMARIA · DU'RU · PHILISTIA · JUDAH · GILEAD · AMMON · MOAB · EDOM · DAMASCUS · QARNINI · HAURAN · Bashan · ASSYRIAN EMPIRE · EGYPTIAN KINGDOM · Arabs

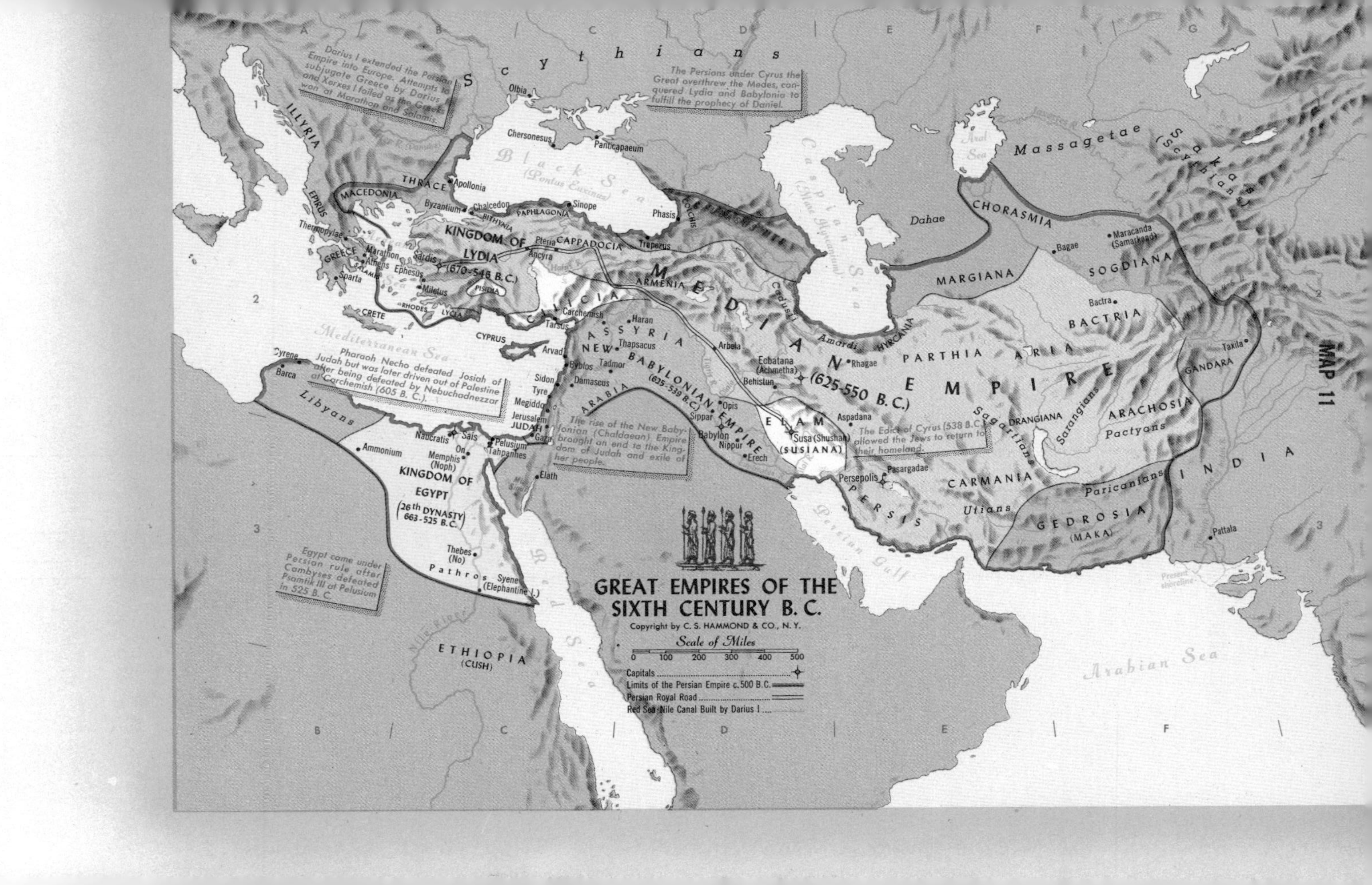
GREAT EMPIRES OF THE SIXTH CENTURY B. C.
Copyright by C. S. HAMMOND & CO., N. Y.
Scale of Miles
0 100 200 300 400 500
Capitals
Limits of the Persian Empire c. 500 B.C.
Persian Royal Road
Red Sea-Nile Canal Built by Darius I
Darius I extended the Persian Empire into Europe. Attempts to subjugate Greece by Darius and Xerxes I failed as the Greeks won at Marathon and Salamis.
The Persians under Cyrus the Great overthrew the Medes, conquered Lydia and Babylonia to fulfill the prophecy of Daniel.
Pharaoh Necho defeated Josiah of Judah but was later driven out of Palestine after being defeated by Nebuchadnezzar at Carchemish (605 B. C.).
The rise of the New Babylonian (Chaldaean) Empire brought an end to the Kingdom of Judah and exile of her people.
The Edict of Cyrus (538 B.C.) allowed the Jews to return to their homeland.
Egypt came under Persian rule after Cambyses defeated Psamtik III at Pelusium in 525 B. C.
Scythians
MEDIAN EMPIRE (625-550 B. C.)
NEW BABYLONIAN EMPIRE (625-539 B.C.)
KINGDOM OF LYDIA (670-546 B.C.)
KINGDOM OF EGYPT (26th DYNASTY 663-525 B.C.)
Black Sea (Pontus Euxinus)
Caspian Sea (Mare Hyrcanium)
Aral Sea
Mediterranean Sea
Red Sea
Persian Gulf
Arabian Sea
ILLYRIA
EPIRUS
MACEDONIA
THRACE
GREECE
Thermopylae
Marathon
Athens
Sparta
CRETE
RHODES
Miletus
Ephesus
Sardis
PISIDIA
LYCIA
Byzantium
Chalcedon
BITHYNIA
PAPHLAGONIA
Apollonia
Olbia
Chersonesus
Panticapaeum
Sinope
Pteria
Ancyra
CAPPADOCIA
Trapezus
Phasis
COLCHIS
ARMENIA
CILICIA
Tarsus
Carchemish
Haran
ASSYRIA
Thapsacus
Tadmor
CYPRUS
Arvad
Byblos
Sidon
Damascus
Tyre
Megiddo
Jerusalem
JUDAH
Gaza
ARABIA
Elath
Cyrene
Barca
Libyans
Naucratis
Sais
Pelusium
Tahpanhes
Ammonium
On
Memphis (Noph)
Thebes (No)
Pathros
Syene (Elephantine I.)
ETHIOPIA (CUSH)
Arbela
Opis
Sippar
Babylon
Nippur
Erech
ELAM
Susa (Shushan)
(SUSIANA)
Behistun
Ecbatana (Achmetha)
Cadusii
Amardi
HYRCANIA
Rhagae
Aspadana
PARTHIA
ARIA
Pasargadae
Persepolis
PERSIS
CARMANIA
Utians
Sagartians
DRANGIANA
Sarangians
ARACHOSIA
Pactyans
Paricanians
GEDROSIA (MAKA)
Dahae
CHORASMIA
MARGIANA
Massagetae
Bagae
Maracanda (Samarkand)
SOGDIANA
Saka (Scythians)
Bactra
BACTRIA
GANDARA
Taxila
INDIA
Pattala
Present shoreline

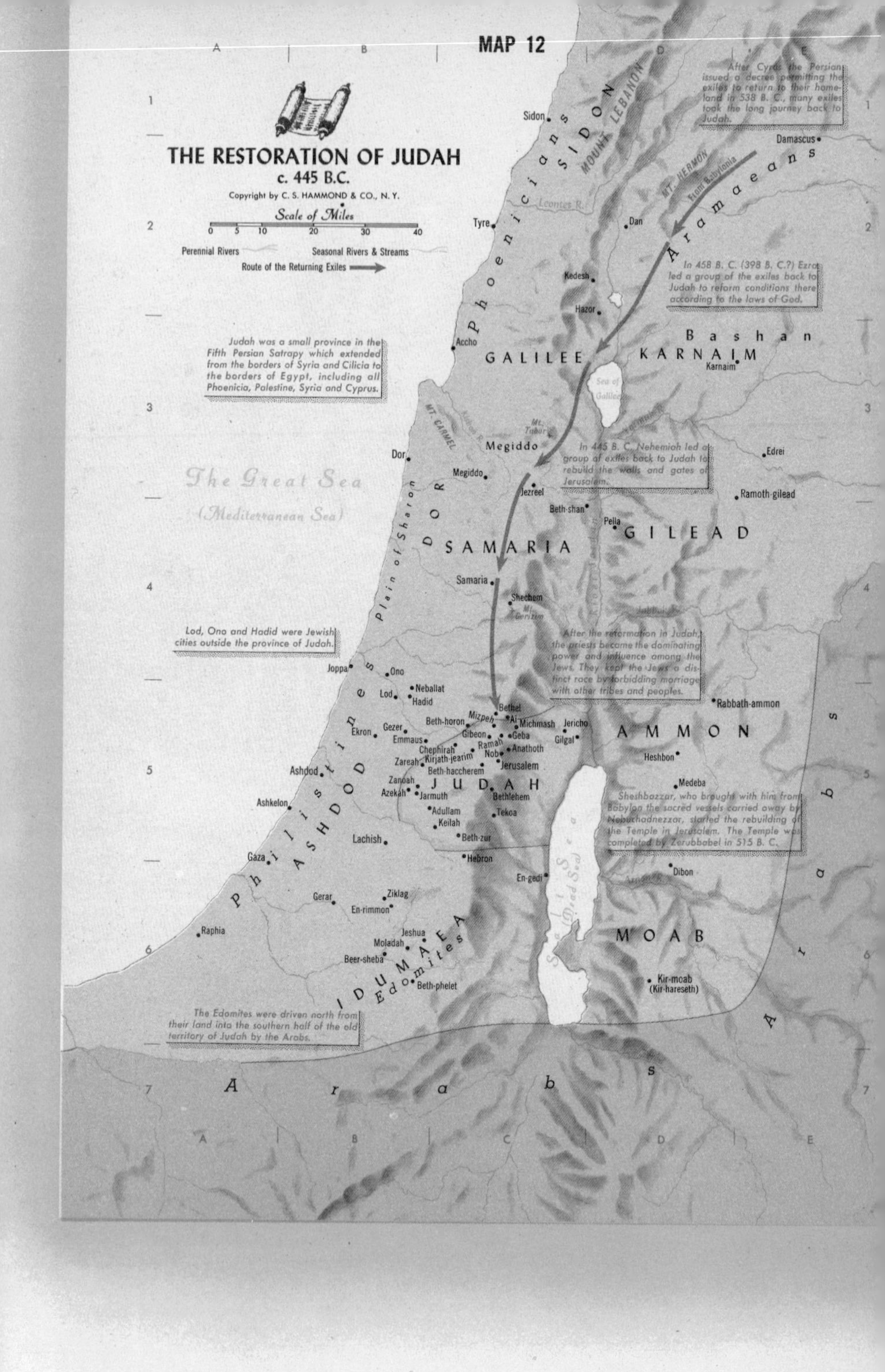
MAP 12
THE RESTORATION OF JUDAH
c. 445 B.C.
Copyright by C. S. HAMMOND & CO., N. Y.
Scale of Miles
0 5 10 20 30 40
Perennial Rivers
Seasonal Rivers & Streams
Route of the Returning Exiles
After Cyrus the Persian issued a decree permitting the exiles to return to their homeland in 538 B. C., many exiles took the long journey back to Judah.
In 458 B. C. (398 B. C.?) Ezra led a group of the exiles back to Judah to reform conditions there according to the laws of God.
Judah was a small province in the Fifth Persian Satrapy which extended from the borders of Syria and Cilicia to the borders of Egypt, including all Phoenicia, Palestine, Syria and Cyprus.
In 445 B. C. Nehemiah led a group of exiles back to Judah to rebuild the walls and gates of Jerusalem.
Lod, Ono and Hadid were Jewish cities outside the province of Judah.
After the reformation in Judah, the priests became the dominating power and influence among the Jews. They kept the Jews a distinct race by forbidding marriage with other tribes and peoples.
Sheshbazzar, who brought with him from Babylon the sacred vessels carried away by Nebuchadnezzar, started the rebuilding of the Temple in Jerusalem. The Temple was completed by Zerubbabel in 515 B. C.
The Edomites were driven north from their land into the southern half of the old territory of Judah by the Arabs.
The Great Sea
(Mediterranean Sea)
Phoenicians
SIDON
MOUNT LEBANON
MT. HERMON
From Babylonia
Aramaeans
Sidon
Damascus
Tyre
Dan
Kedesh
Hazor
Accho
GALILEE
KARNAIM
Bashan
Karnaim
Sea of Galilee
MT. CARMEL
Mt. Tabor
Megiddo
Dor
Jezreel
Edrei
Ramoth-gilead
Beth-shan
Pella
GILEAD
Plain of Sharon
DOR
SAMARIA
Samaria
Shechem
Mt. Gerizim
Joppa
Ono
Neballat
Lod
Hadid
Bethel
Ai
Michmash
Jericho
Mizpeh
Beth-horon
Gezer
Ekron
Emmaus
Gibeon
Geba
Gilgal
Chephirah
Ramah
Anathoth
Kirjath-jearim
Nob
Zareah
Jerusalem
Beth-haccherem
Rabbath-ammon
AMMON
Heshbon
Ashdod
Zanoah
JUDAH
Medeba
Azekah
Jarmuth
Bethlehem
Ashkelon
Adullam
Tekoa
Keilah
Philistines
ASHDOD
Lachish
Beth-zur
Hebron
Gaza
En-gedi
Dibon
Salt Sea (Dead Sea)
Gerar
Ziklag
En-rimmon
MOAB
Raphia
Jeshua
Moladah
Beer-sheba
IDUMAEA
Edomites
Beth-phelet
Kir-moab
(Kir-hareseth)
Arabs
A r a b s

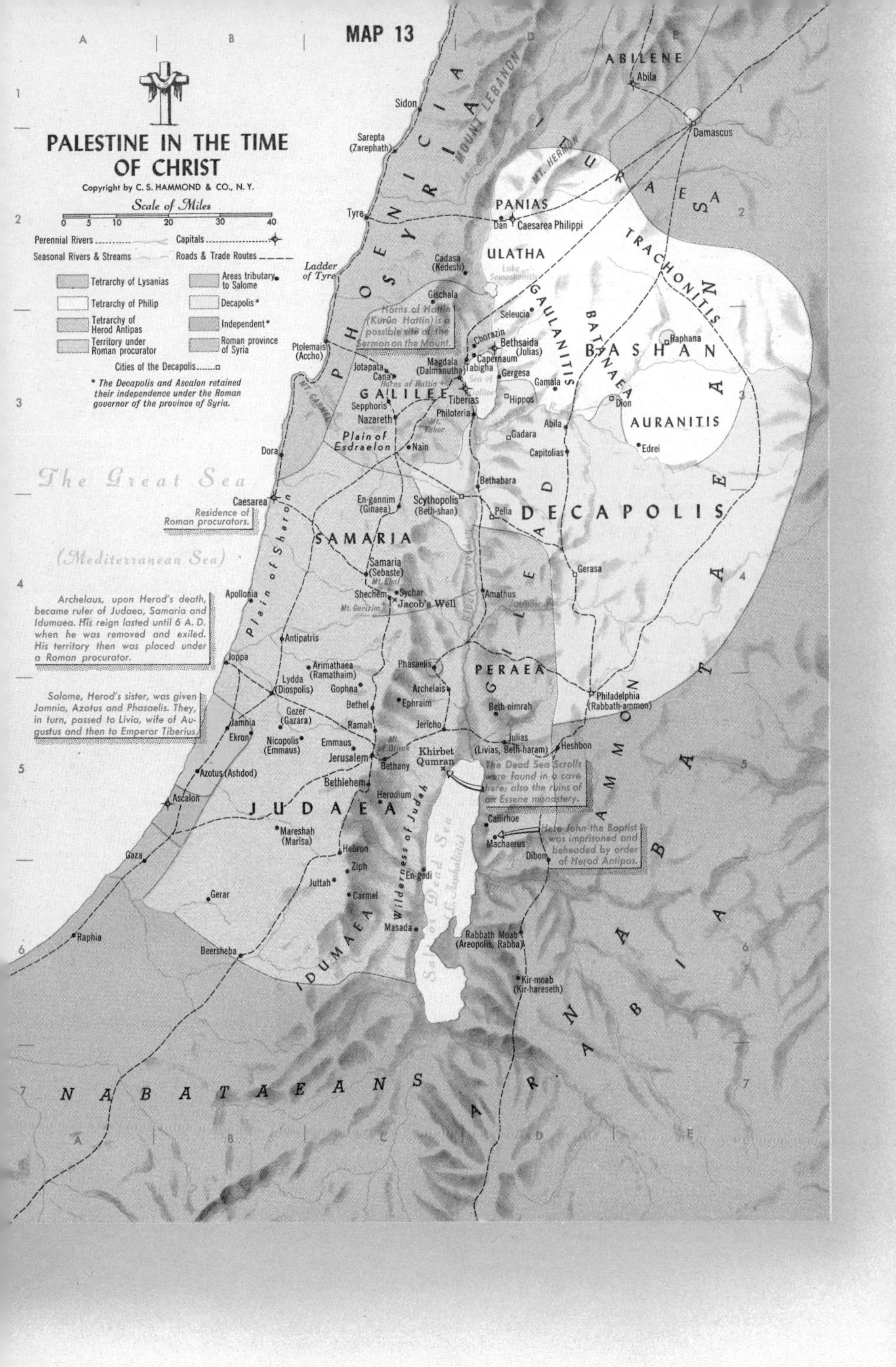
MAP 13
PALESTINE IN THE TIME OF CHRIST
Copyright by C. S. HAMMOND & CO., N. Y.
Scale of Miles
Perennial Rivers
Seasonal Rivers & Streams
Capitals
Roads & Trade Routes
Tetrarchy of Lysanias
Tetrarchy of Philip
Tetrarchy of Herod Antipas
Territory under Roman procurator
Areas tributary to Salome
Decapolis*
Independent*
Roman province of Syria
Cities of the Decapolis
* The Decapolis and Ascalon retained their independence under the Roman governor of the province of Syria.
Archelaus, upon Herod's death, became ruler of Judaea, Samaria and Idumaea. His reign lasted until 6 A. D. when he was removed and exiled. His territory then was placed under a Roman procurator.
Salome, Herod's sister, was given Jamnia, Azotus and Phasaelis. They, in turn, passed to Livia, wife of Augustus and then to Emperor Tiberius.
Residence of Roman procurators.
Horns of Hattin (Kurûn Hattin) is a possible site of the Sermon on the Mount.
The Dead Sea Scrolls were found in a cave here; also the ruins of an Essene monastery.
Here John the Baptist was imprisoned and beheaded by order of Herod Antipas.
The Great Sea
(Mediterranean Sea)
PHOENICIA
SYRIA
ITURAEA
ABILENE
PANIAS
ULATHA
TRACHONITIS
GAULANITIS
BATANAEA
BASHAN
AURANITIS
GALILEE
SAMARIA
DECAPOLIS
GILEAD
PERAEA
JUDAEA
IDUMAEA
AMMON
NABATAEANS
ARABIA
Sidon
Sarepta (Zarephath)
Tyre
Abila
Damascus
Dan
Caesarea Philippi
Cadasa (Kedesh)
Ladder of Tyre
Gischala
Seleucia
Chorazin
Bethsaida (Julias)
Capernaum
Tabigha
Magdala (Dalmanutha)
Raphana
Ptolemais (Accho)
Jotapata
Cana
Gergesa
Gamala
Hippos
Dion
Tiberias
Sepphoris
Nazareth
Philoteria
Abila
Gadara
Plain of Esdraelon
Nain
Capitolias
Edrei
Dora
Bethabara
Caesarea
En-gannim (Ginaea)
Scythopolis (Beth-shan)
Pella
Samaria (Sebaste)
Gerasa
Apollonia
Shechem
Sychar
Jacob's Well
Amathus
Plain of Sharon
Antipatris
Joppa
Arimathaea (Ramathaim)
Phasaelis
Lydda (Diospolis)
Gophna
Archelais
Ephraim
Bethel
Beth-nimrah
Philadelphia (Rabbath-ammon)
Jamnia
Gezer (Gazara)
Ramah
Jericho
Ekron
Nicopolis (Emmaus)
Emmaus
Julias (Livias, Beth-haram)
Heshbon
Jerusalem
Khirbet Qumran
Bethany
Azotus (Ashdod)
Bethlehem
Herodium
Ascalon
Callirhoe
Machaerus
Mareshah (Marisa)
Hebron
Wilderness of Judah
Dead Sea
Gaza
Ziph
Juttah
En-gedi
Dibon
Gerar
Carmel
Masada
Raphia
Rabbath Moab (Areopolis, Rabba)
Beersheba
Kir-moab (Kir-hareseth)
Salt Sea

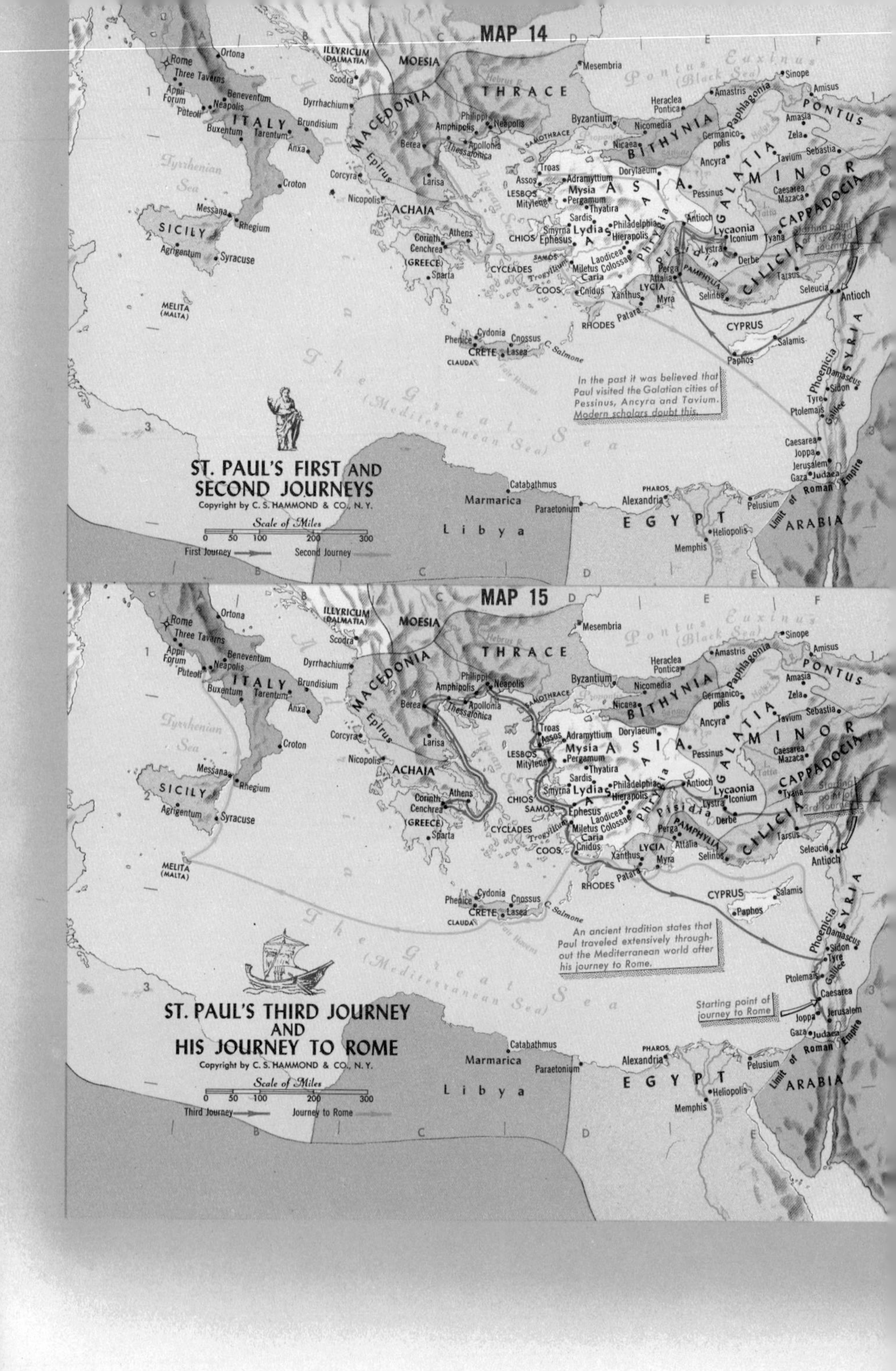

MAP 14
ST. PAUL'S FIRST AND SECOND JOURNEYS
Copyright by C. S. HAMMOND & CO., N. Y.
Scale of Miles
First Journey
Second Journey
In the past it was believed that Paul visited the Galatian cities of Pessinus, Ancyra and Tavium. Modern scholars doubt this.
MAP 15
ST. PAUL'S THIRD JOURNEY AND HIS JOURNEY TO ROME
Copyright by C. S. HAMMOND & CO., N. Y.
Scale of Miles
Third Journey
Journey to Rome
An ancient tradition states that Paul traveled extensively throughout the Mediterranean world after his journey to Rome.
Starting point of journey to Rome

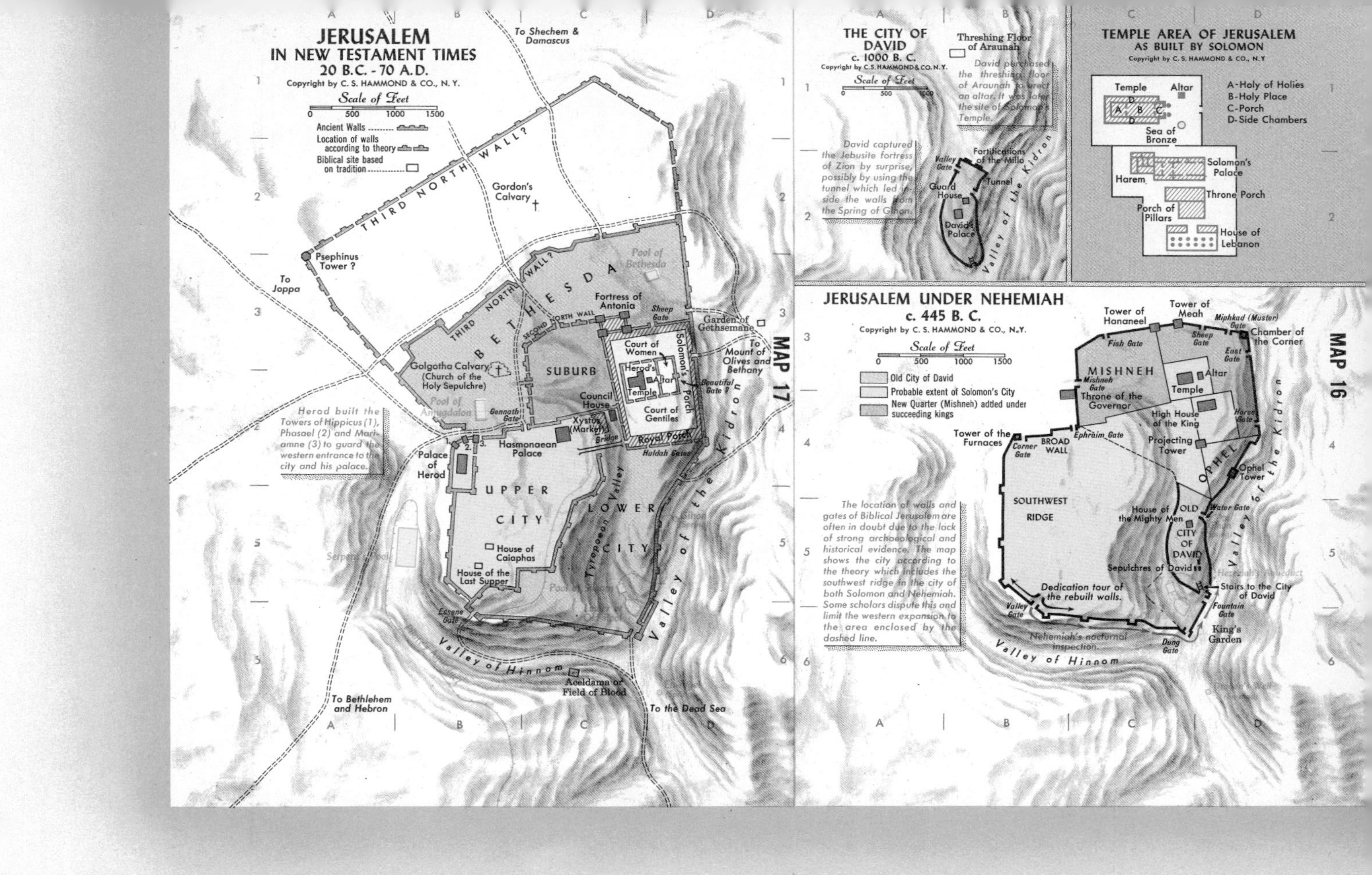
MAP 17
JERUSALEM
IN NEW TESTAMENT TIMES
20 B.C. - 70 A.D.
Copyright by C. S. HAMMOND & CO., N. Y.
Scale of Feet
0 500 1000 1500
Ancient Walls
Location of walls according to theory
Biblical site based on tradition
To Shechem & Damascus
THIRD NORTH WALL?
Gordon's Calvary
Psephinus Tower ?
To Joppa
THIRD NORTH WALL?
BETHESDA
Pool of Bethesda
Fortress of Antonia
Sheep Gate
SECOND NORTH WALL
Garden of Gethsemane
To Mount of Olives and Bethany
Golgotha Calvary (Church of the Holy Sepulchre)
SUBURB
Court of Women
Herod's Temple
Altar
Solomon's Porch
Beautiful Gate ?
Council House
Court of Gentiles
Pool of Amygdalon
Gennath Gate
Xystus (Market)
Bridge
Royal Porch
Huldah Gates
Herod built the Towers of Hippicus (1), Phasael (2) and Mariamne (3) to guard the western entrance to the city and his palace.
Palace of Herod
Hasmonaean Palace
UPPER CITY
LOWER CITY
Tyropoeon Valley
Valley of the Kidron
House of Caiaphas
House of the Last Supper
Essene Gate
Valley of Hinnom
Aceldama or Field of Blood
To Bethlehem and Hebron
To the Dead Sea
THE CITY OF DAVID
c. 1000 B. C.
Copyright by C. S. HAMMOND & CO. N.Y.
Scale of Feet
0 500 1000
Threshing Floor of Araunah
David purchased the threshing floor of Araunah to erect an altar. It was later the site of Solomon's Temple.
David captured the Jebusite fortress of Zion by surprise, possibly by using the tunnel which led inside the walls from the Spring of Gihon.
Valley Gate
Fortifications of the Millo
Tunnel
Guard House
David's Palace
Valley of the Kidron
TEMPLE AREA OF JERUSALEM
AS BUILT BY SOLOMON
Copyright by C. S. HAMMOND & CO., N.Y.
Temple
Altar
Sea of Bronze
A-Holy of Holies
B-Holy Place
C-Porch
D-Side Chambers
Harem
Solomon's Palace
Throne Porch
Porch of Pillars
House of Lebanon
MAP 16
JERUSALEM UNDER NEHEMIAH
c. 445 B. C.
Copyright by C. S. HAMMOND & CO., N.Y.
Scale of Feet
0 500 1000 1500
Old City of David
Probable extent of Solomon's City
New Quarter (Mishneh) added under succeeding kings
Tower of Hananeel
Tower of Meah
Miphkad (Muster) Gate
Chamber of the Corner
Fish Gate
Sheep Gate
East Gate
MISHNEH
Mishneh Gate
Throne of the Governor
Altar
Temple
High House of the King
Horse Gate
Tower of the Furnaces
Corner Gate
BROAD WALL
Ephraim Gate
Projecting Tower
OPHEL
Ophel Tower
Valley of the Kidron
SOUTHWEST RIDGE
House of the Mighty Men
OLD CITY OF DAVID
Water Gate
Sepulchres of David
Hezekiah's Aqueduct
Stairs to the City of David
Fountain Gate
King's Garden
Dedication tour of the rebuilt walls.
Valley Gate
Dung Gate
Nehemiah's nocturnal inspection.
Valley of Hinnom
The location of walls and gates of Biblical Jerusalem are often in doubt due to the lack of strong archaeological and historical evidence. The map shows the city according to the theory which includes the southwest ridge in the city of both Solomon and Nehemiah. Some scholars dispute this and limit the western expansion to the area enclosed by the dashed line.

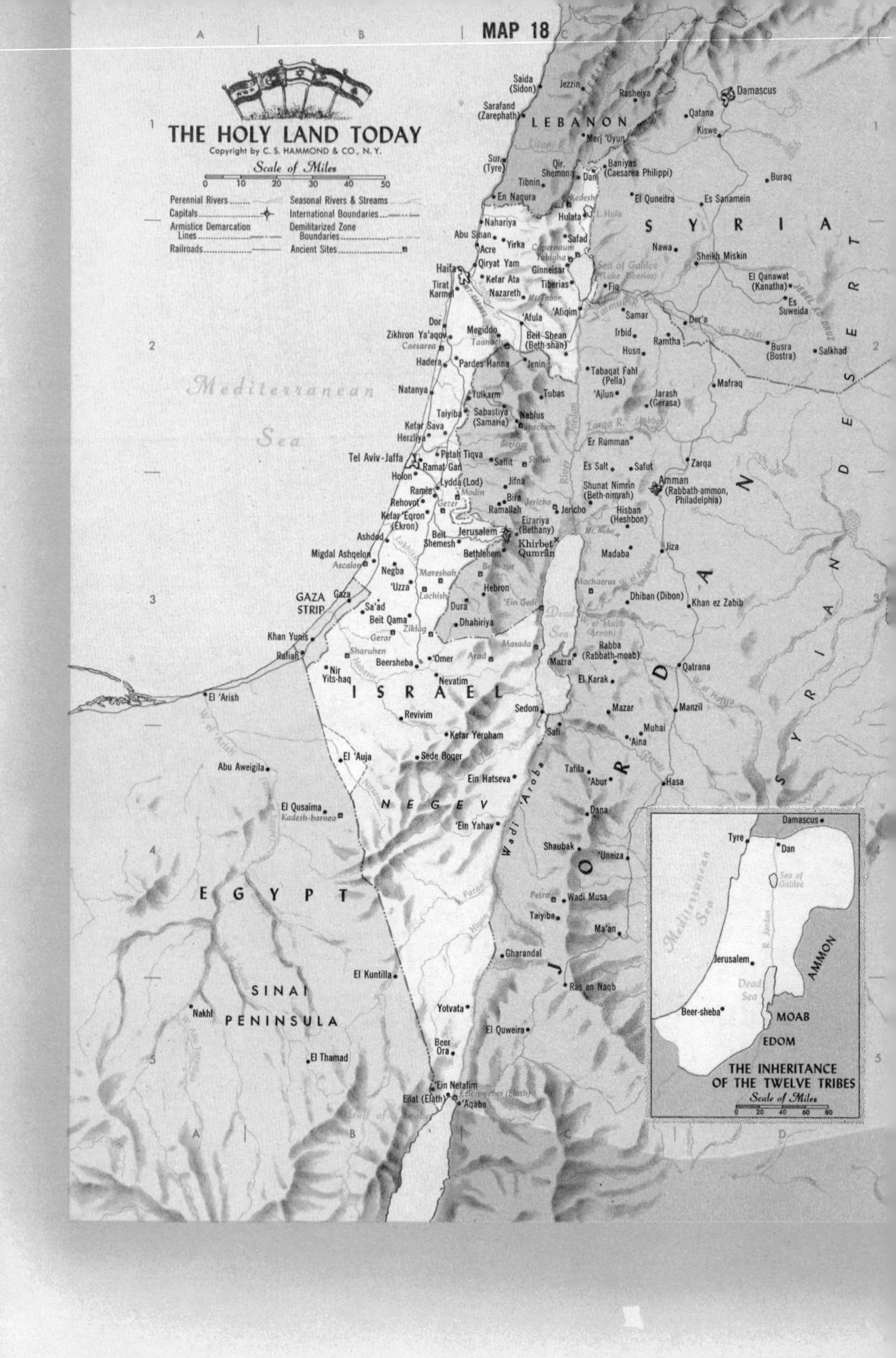

MAP 18
THE HOLY LAND TODAY
Copyright by C. S. HAMMOND & CO., N. Y.
Scale of Miles
0 10 20 30 40 50
Perennial Rivers
Seasonal Rivers & Streams
Capitals
International Boundaries
Armistice Demarcation Lines
Demilitarized Zone Boundaries
Railroads
Ancient Sites
A
B
C
D
1
2
3
4
5
Mediterranean Sea
LEBANON
SYRIA
ISRAEL
JORDAN
EGYPT
SINAI PENINSULA
NEGEV
SYRIAN DESERT
GAZA STRIP
Saida (Sidon)
Jezzin
Rasheiya
Damascus
Sarafand (Zarephath)
Qatana
Kiswe
Merj 'Uyun
Sur (Tyre)
Qir. Shemona
Dan
Baniyas (Caesarea Philippi)
Tibnin
Buraq
En Naqura
Kedesh
El Quneitra
Es Sanamein
Nahariya
Hulata
Abu Sinan
Yirka
Safad
Acre
Nawa
Sheikh Miskin
Haifa
Qiryat Yam
Ginneisar
Sea of Galilee (Lake Tiberias)
Tiberias
Fiq
El Qanawat (Kanatha)
Es Suweida
Tirat Karmel
Kefar Ata
Nazareth
Mt. Tabor
'Afula
'Afiqim
Samar
Der'a
Dor
Megiddo
Beit Shean (Beth-shan)
Irbid
Zikhron Ya'aqov
Caesarea
Ramtha
Husn
Busra (Bostra)
Salkhad
Hadera
Pardes Hanna
Jenin
Tabaqat Fahl (Pella)
Mafraq
Natanya
Tulkarm
Tubas
'Ajlun
Jarash (Gerasa)
Taiyiba
Sabastiya (Samaria)
Nablus
Shechem
Kefar Sava
Herzliya
Zarqa R.
Er Rumman
Tel Aviv-Jaffa
Petah Tiqva
Ramat Gan
Salfit
Shiloh
Es Salt
Safut
Zarqa
Holon
Lydda (Lod)
Jifna
Shunat Nimrin (Beth-nimrah)
Amman (Rabbath-ammon, Philadelphia)
Ramle
Modin
Rehovot
Gezer
Bira
Ramallah
Jericho
Hisban (Heshbon)
Kefar 'Eqron (Ekron)
Eizariya (Bethany)
Jerusalem
Mt. Nebo
Ashdod
Beit Shemesh
Bethlehem
Khirbet Qumrân
Madaba
Jiza
Migdal Ashqelon
Ascalon
Negba
Mareshah
Beth-zur
Machaerus
'Uzza
Lachish
Hebron
Gaza
Dura
'Ein Gedi
Dhiban (Dibon)
Khan ez Zabib
Sa'ad
Beit Qama
Dhahiriya
Dead Sea
Khan Yunis
Ziklag
Gerar
Arnon
Masada
Rabba (Rabbath-moab)
Rafiah
Sharuhen
Beersheba
'Omer
Arad
Mazra'
Qatrana
Nir Yits-haq
Nevatim
El Karak
El 'Arish
Sedom
Mazar
Manzil
Revivim
Muhai
Safi
'Aina
Kefar Yeroham
El 'Auja
Sede Boqer
Tafila
Abu Aweigila
Ein Hatseva
'Abur
Hasa
El Qusaima
Kadesh-barnea
Dana
'Ein Yahav
Wadi 'Araba
Shaubak
'Uneiza
Petra
Wadi Musa
Paran
Taiyiba
Ma'an
Gharandal
El Kuntilla
Ras en Naqb
Nakhl
Yotvata
El Quweira
Beer Ora
El Thamad
'Ein Netafim
Eilat (Elath)
Ezion-geber (Elath)
'Aqaba
Damascus
Tyre
Dan
Sea of Galilee
Mediterranean Sea
R. Jordan
Jerusalem
AMMON
Dead Sea
Beer-sheba
MOAB
EDOM
THE INHERITANCE OF THE TWELVE TRIBES
Scale of Miles
0 20 40 60 80